AA

THE HOTEL GUIDE

Published by AA Publishing, a trading name of AA Media Limited, whose registered office is Fanum House, Basing View, Basingstoke, Hampshire RG21 4EA. Registered number 06112600

First published by the Automobile Association as the Hotel and Restaurant Guide, 1967
© AA Media Limited 2017
51st edition 2017

The contents of this publication are believed correct at the time of printing. Nevertheless, the publishers cannot be held responsible for any errors or omissions or for any changes in the details given in this guide or for the consequences of any reliance on the information provided by the same. This does not affect your statutory rights.

Assessments of AA inspected establishments are based on the experience of the Hotel and Restaurant inspectors on the occasion(s) of their visit(s) and therefore descriptions given in this guide necessarily contain an element of subjective opinion which may not reflect or dictate a reader's own opinion on another occasion. See 'AA Star Classification' in the preliminary section for a clear explanation of how, based on our inspectors' inspection experiences, establishments are graded. If the meal or meals experienced by an inspector or inspectors during an inspection fall between award levels the restaurant concerned may be awarded the lower of any award levels considered applicable.

AA Media Limited strives to ensure accuracy of the information in this guide at the time of printing. Due to the constantly evolving nature of the subject matter the information is subject to change. AA Media Limited will gratefully receive any advice from our readers of any necessary updated information.

For queries relating to the guide, please contact: lifestyleguides@theAA.com

Website addresses are included in entries and specified by the respective establishment. Such websites are not under the control of AA Media Limited and as such AA Media Limited will not accept any responsibility or liability in respect of any and all matters whatsoever relating to such web sites including access, content, material and functionality. By including the addresses of third party websites the AA does not intend to solicit business or offer any security to any person in any country, directly or indirectly.

Image credits:
The Automobile Association wishes to thank the following photographers and organisations for their assistance in the preparation of this book. Abbreviations for the picture credits are as follows – (t) top; (b) bottom; (l) left; (r) right; (c) centre; (AA) AA World Travel Library.
3 Courtesy of The London Bridge Hotel, London SE1; 4 Courtesy of The Aviator, Farnborough; 7 Courtesy of The Corinthia Hotel London, SW1A; 9 Courtesy of Dormy House Hotel, Broadway; 10 Courtesy of The Northcote Hotel, Blackburn; 12 Courtesy of The Beach Hotel, Bude; 14 Courtesy of Fawsley Hall Hotel & Spa, Daventry; 15 Courtesy of Best Western Plus The Connaught Hotel, Bournemouth; 16-19 BG AA/C Sawyer; 16 Courtesy of The Gainsborough Bath Spa, Bath; 17l Courtesy of The Goring, London SW1; 17r Courtesy of Douneside House, Aboyne; 18l Courtesy of Twr Y Felin Hotel, St Davids; 18r Courtesy of The Old Inn, Crawfordsburn; 19 All images Courtesy of Andrew Brownsword Hotels; 28-29 AA/D Clapp; 199, AA/D Clapp; 200-201, 218 AA/J Tims; 412 AA/W Voysey; 422-423 & 465 AA/J Henderson; 468-469 AA/S Lewis; 479 AA/S Lewis; 493 AA/M Bauer; 494 AA/S Hill; 526 AA/P Wilson; 528 AA/J Love
Every effort has been made to trace the copyright holders, and we apologise in advance for any unintentional omissions or errors. We would be pleased to apply any corrections in a following edition of this publication.

Photographs in the gazetteer are provided by the establishments.

This guide was compiled by the AA Lifestyle Guides team.

Maps prepared by the Mapping Services Department of AA Publishing.

Maps © AA Media Limited 2017.

Contains Ordnance Survey data © Crown copyright and database rights 2017.

This is based upon Crown Copyright and is reproduced with the permission of Land & Property Services under delegated authority from the Controller of Her Majesty's Stationery Office.
© Crown copyright and database rights 2017 PMLPA No. 100497

Republic of Ireland mapping based on © Ordnance Survey Ireland/Government of Ireland Copyright Permit No. MP000717

A CIP catalogue record for this book is available from the British Library.

Printed in Italy by Printer Trento SRL, Trento

ISBN: 978-0-7495-7888-6

A05518

Visit theaa.com/hotels

Contents

Welcome to the AA Hotel Guide

For more than 50 years our readers have been using the AA Hotel Guide to find different types of accommodation, for a huge variety of reasons. As the AA inspects such a wide range of establishments, we hope that this guide will prove an invaluable asset in helping you to find the right place to stay.

Who's in the guide?

From the most opulent and sophisticated of London's elite hotels to personally-run small hotels in the British countryside; from the practical and convenient budget hotel aimed at business or air travellers, to the luxurious country house hotel catering for leisure and sporting guests, The AA Hotel Guide has it all.

All year round, our specially-trained team of expert inspectors are visiting, grading and advising the hotels that appear in this guide. Each one is judged on presentation, quality of accommodation, leisure and sporting facilities, food operation, service, hospitality, conference facilities and cleanliness. It is then rated according to our classification system (pages 12–13).

Any hotel applying for AA recognition receives a regular unannounced visit to check standards. If the hotel changes hands, the new owners must reapply for classification, as AA recognition is not transferable.

Our inspectors have also chosen their Hotels of the Year, for England, London, Scotland, Wales, and Northern Ireland, as well as Hotel Group of the Year (see pages 16–19).

Red Stars and Inspector's Choice

All of the hotels in this guide should be of a high standard, but some are a cut above, and these are specially selected by our inspectors. At these establishments you can expect a little more of everything: more comfort, more facilities, more extras and more attention. From two Red Stars to five Red Stars, these are the best of British hotels. Every Red Star hotel is highlighted as an INSPECTOR'S CHOICE, but these are not the only places that are singled out.

Silver Stars and Highly Recommended

Hotels with Silver Stars ★ have been selected for their superior levels of quality, high standards of hotel keeping and for the quality of food within their star rating. These are highlighted as HIGHLY RECOMMENDED.

Rosettes

Most of the hotels in this guide have their own restaurants, and a large proportion of them serve food that has attained an AA Rosette award; including some that have reached the four and five Rosette level, making them among the finest restaurants in the world. These are regularly visited by the AA inspectorate and awarded Rosettes strictly on the basis of the inspector's experience alone.

Dine & Stay: Restaurants with Rooms

This edition includes a special section (pages 528–61) dedicated to Restaurants with Rooms, which are rated under our Guest Accommodation scheme. Most will have been awarded AA Rosettes for their food. So, if you're looking for accommodation with excellent dining options, then this is the section for you.

Anonymous inspection

All hotel and restaurant inspections are made anonymously. After taking a meal or staying overnight at the hotel, the inspector will announce to a member of staff and ask to speak to the manager, or the chef in the case of a Rosette visit.

Tell us what you think

We welcome your feedback about the hotels included in this guide, and about the guide itself. Please write in, or email us at: **lifestyleguides@theaa.com**.

The hotels are visited throughout the year by our team of inspectors. For the very latest updates, you can search for the hotel of your choice at www.theaa.com/hotels

How to use the guide

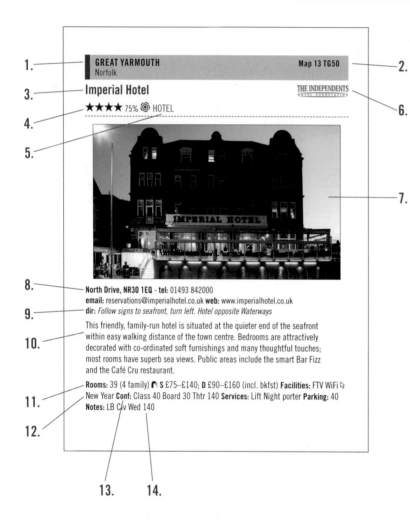

1.

GREAT YARMOUTH
Norfolk

Map 13 TG50

2.

3.

Imperial Hotel

THE INDEPENDENTS
HOTEL ASSOCIATION

6.

4.

★★★★ 75% ◉ HOTEL

5.

7.

8.

North Drive, NR30 1EQ - tel: 01493 842000
email: reservations@imperialhotel.co.uk **web:** www.imperialhotel.co.uk

9.

dir: *Follow signs to seafront, turn left. Hotel opposite Waterways*

10.

This friendly, family-run hotel is situated at the quieter end of the seafront within easy walking distance of the town centre. Bedrooms are attractively decorated with co-ordinated soft furnishings and many thoughtful touches; most rooms have superb sea views. Public areas include the smart Bar Fizz and the Café Cru restaurant.

11.

Rooms: 39 (4 family) ◐ **S** £75–£140; **D** £90–£160 (incl. bkfst) **Facilities:** FTV WiFi ⬆
New Year **Conf:** Class 40 Board 30 Thtr 140 **Services:** Lift Night porter **Parking:** 40

12.

Notes: LB Civ Wed 140

13.   14.

1. Location
Towns are listed alphabetically within each country (the county name appears under the town name).

2. Map reference
Map page number followed by a National Grid reference (see page 9).

3. Hotel name

4. Grading
Hotels are listed in star rating and merit score order (see page 8) within each location (for full explanation of ratings and awards see page 12-13).
★ Star rating
% Merit score
◉ Rosette award
⬒ Breakfast award

5. Type of hotel
See page 10.

6. Hotel logo
If a symbol appears here it represents a hotel group or consortium (see pages 21–26).

7. Picture
Optional photograph supplied by the establishment.

8. Address and contact details

9. Directions
Brief details of how to find the hotel.

10. Description
Written by the AA inspector at the time of the last inspection.

11. Rooms
Number of rooms and prices
(see page 8).

12. Facilities
Additional facilities including those for children, and leisure activities

13. Conference
Conference facilities as available (see page 8).

14. Notes
Additional information (see pages 14–15).

Key to symbols and abbreviations

★	Black stars	HL	Hearing loop installed
★	Red stars – indicate AA Inspector's Choice	Air con	Air conditioning
★	Silver stars – indicate superior level of quality – Highly Recommended	⟨⟩	Heated indoor swimming pool
		⟨⟩	Outdoor swimming pool
◉	AA Rosettes – indicate an AA award for food	⟨⟩	Heated outdoor swimming pool
		♫	Entertainment
⟨⟩	Breakfast Award	**Child facilities**	
%	Inspectors' Merit score (see page 8)		Children's facilities (see page 8)
A	Associate Hotels (see page 10)	**Xmas/New Year**	
○	Hotel due to open during the currency of the guide (see page 10)		Special programme for Christmas/New Year
U	Star rating not confirmed (see page 10)	⟨⟩	Tennis court
		⟨⟩	Croquet lawn
Fmly	Number of family rooms available	⟨⟩	Golf course
GF	Ground floors rooms available	Conf	Conference facilities
⟨⟩	Bedrooms with walk-in showers available	Thtr	Number of theatre style seats
		Class	Number of classroom style seats
Smoking	Number of bedrooms allocated for smokers	Board	Number of boardroom style seats
		No children	
S	Single room		Children cannot be accommodated (a number followed by 'yrs' indicate that children below that age are not accommodated)
D	Double room		
∗	2017 prices		
fr	From	RS	Restricted opening time
incl. bkfst	Breakfast included in the price	Civ Wed	Establishment licensed for civil weddings (+ maximum number of guests at ceremony)
incl. dinner	Dinner included in the price		
FTV	Freeview television		
STV	Satellite television	LB	Special leisure breaks available
WiFi	Wireless network connection	Spa	Hotel has its own spa
⟨⟩	High speed internet connection (bedrooms)		

How to use the guide *continued*

Merit Score (%)

AA inspectors supplement their reports with an additional quality assessment of everything the hotel provides – including hospitality – based on their findings as a 'mystery guest'. This wider ranging quality assessment results in an overall Merit Score which is shown as a percentage beside the hotel name. When making your selection of hotel accommodation this enables you to see at a glance that a three star hotel with a Merit Score of 79% offers a higher standard overall than one in the same star classification but with a Merit Score of 69%. To gain AA recognition, a hotel must achieve a minimum score of 50%.

AA Awards

Every year the AA presents a range of awards to the finest AA-inspected and rated hotels from England, London, Scotland, Wales, and Northern Ireland. The Hotel of the Year is our ultimate accolade and is awarded to those hotels that are recognised as outstanding examples in their field. Often innovative, the winning hotels always set high standards in hotel keeping. The winners for all the 2017–18 awards are listed on pages 16–19.

Rooms

Where the information has been provided by the hotelier, each entry shows the total number of en suite rooms available (this total will include any annexe rooms). The total number may be followed by a breakdown of the type of rooms available, i.e. the number of annexe rooms; number of family rooms (fmly); number of ground-floor rooms (GF); and number of rooms available for smokers.

Bedrooms in an annexe or extension are only noted if they are at least equivalent in quality to those in the main building, but facilities and prices may differ. In some hotels all bedrooms are in an annexe or extension.

If the hotel has highspeed or broadband internet access in the bedrooms, this may be chargeable.

Prices

Prices are per room per night and are provided by the hoteliers in good faith. These prices are indications and not firm quotations. An asterisk (*) indicates 2017 prices. Many hotels have special rates, so it is worth looking at their websites for the latest information.

Payment

Credit cards may be subject to a surcharge. Check when booking if this is how you intend to pay.

Children

Child facilities may include baby intercom, baby-sitting service, playroom, playground, laundry, drying/ironing facilities, cots, high chairs or special meals. In some hotels children can sleep in parents' rooms at no extra cost – check when booking.

If 'No children' is indicated, a minimum age will also given e.g. No children 4yrs indicates that no children under 4 years of age would be accepted.

Some hotels, although accepting children, may not have any special facilities for them.

Leisure breaks (LB)

Some hotels offer special leisure breaks. The cost of these may differ from those quoted in this guide and availability may vary through the year.

Parking

We indicate the number of parking spaces available for guests. This may include covered parking. Please note that some hotels make a charge for the use of their car park.

Civil weddings (Civ Wed)

Indicates that the establishment holds a civil wedding licence, and we indicate the number of guests that can be accommodated at the ceremony.

Conference facilities

We include three types of meeting layouts – Theatre, Classroom and Boardroom style – and state the maximum number of delegates for each. The price shown is the 24-hour rate per delegate. Please note that as arrangements vary between a hotel and a business client, VAT may or may not be included in the price quoted in the guide. We also show if WiFi connectivity is available, but please check with the hotel that this is suitable for your requirements.

Dogs

Although many hotels allow dogs, they may be excluded from some areas of the hotel and some breeds, particularly those requiring an exceptional licence, may not be acceptable at all. Under the Equality Act 2010 access should be allowed for guide dogs and assistance dogs. Please check the hotel's policy when making your booking.

Entertainment (♫)

This indicates that live entertainment will be available at least once a week all year. Some hotels provide live entertainment only in summer or on special occasions.

Hotel logos

If an establishment belongs to a hotel group or consortium their logo is included in their entry (see pages 21–26).

Map references

Each town is given a map reference – the map page number and a map reference based on the National Grid. For example: **Map 05 SU48**:

05 refers to the page number of the map section at back of the guide

SU is the National Grid lettered square (representing 100,000sq metres) in which the location will be found

4 is the figure reading across the top or bottom of the map page

8 is the figure reading down at each side of the map page

Restricted service

Some hotels have restricted service (RS) during quieter months – usually during the winter – and at this time some of the listed facilities will not be available. If your booking is out-of-season, check with the hotel and enquire specifically.

Smoking regulations

If a bedroom has been allocated for smokers, the hotel is obliged to clearly indicate that this is the case. If either the freedom to smoke, or to be in a non-smoking environment is important to you, please check with the hotel when you book.

Spa

For the purposes of this guide the word 'Spa' in an entry indicates that the hotel has its own spa which is either managed by themselves or outsourced to an external management company. Facilities will vary but will include a minimum of two treatment rooms. Any specific details are also given, and these are as provided to us by the establishment (i.e. steam room, beauty therapy etc).

Types of hotel

The majority of establishments in this guide fall under the category of Hotel; other categories are listed below.

Town House Hotel A small, individual city or town centre property, which provides a high degree of personal service and privacy.

Country House Hotel These are quietly located in a rural area.

Small Hotel Has fewer than 20 bedrooms and is owner-managed.

Metro Hotel A hotel in an urban location that does not offer an evening meal.

Budget Hotel These are usually purpose-built modern properties offering inexpensive accommodation. Often located near motorways and in town or city centres.

Restaurant with Rooms This category of accommodation is assessed under the AA's Guest Accommodation Scheme. They appear in a dedicated section starting on page 528. They all have star ratings, but these are Guest Accommodation Scheme ratings, details of which can be found at the start of the section or in the latest edition of *The AA Bed and Breakfast Guide.*

A These are establishments that have not been inspected by the AA, but by one of the national tourist boards in Britain and Northern Ireland. An establishment marked as 'Associate' has paid to belong to the AA Associate Hotel Scheme and therefore receives a limited entry in the guide.

U A small number of hotels in the guide have this symbol because their star classification was not confirmed at the time of going to press. This may be due to a change of ownership or because the hotel has only recently joined the AA rating scheme. If you want to find out more about these places, you should check our website for updates.

AA Advertised
These establishments are not rated or inspected by the AA, but are displayed for advertising purposes only.

O These hotels were not open at the time of going to press, but will open in late 2017, or in 2018.

AA classifications and awards

AA assessment

Since 2006, Common Quality Standards for inspecting and rating accommodation have been applied throughout the British Isles in association with VisitBritain, VisitScotland and VisitWales.

Any hotel applying for AA recognition receives an unannounced visit from an AA inspector to check standards. Although AA inspectors do not stay overnight at Budget Hotels, they do carry out regular visits to verify standards and procedures.

A guide to some of the general expectations for each star classification is as follows:

★ One Star

Polite, courteous staff providing a relatively informal yet competent style of service, available during the day and evening to receive guests
• At least one designated eating area open to residents for breakfast
• If dinner is offered it should be on at least five days a week, with last orders no earlier than 6.30pm
• Television in bedroom
• All rooms en suite, or private facilities with bath or shower room available at all times

★★ Two Star

As for one star, plus
• At least one restaurant or dining room open to residents for breakfast (and for dinner at least five days a week)
• Last orders for dinner no earlier than 7pm
• Easy access to both sides of beds for double occupancy

★★★ Three Star

• Management and staff smartly and professionally presented and usually uniformed
• A dedicated receptionist on duty at peak times
• At least one restaurant or dining room open to residents and non-residents for breakfast and dinner whenever the hotel is open
• Last orders for dinner no earlier than 8pm
• Remote-control television, direct-dial telephone
• En suite bath or shower and WC

★★★★ Four Star

- A formal, professional staffing structure with smartly presented, uniformed staff, anticipating and responding to your needs or requests. Usually spacious, well-appointed public areas
- Reception staffed 24 hours by well-trained staff
- Express checkout facilities where appropriate
- Porterage available on request
- Night porter available
- At least one restaurant open to residents and non-residents for breakfast and dinner seven days per week, and lunch to be available in a designated eating area
- Last orders for dinner no earlier than 9pm
- En suite bath with fixed overhead shower and WC

★★★★★ Five Star

- Luxurious accommodation and public areas with a range of extra facilities
- First time guests shown to their bedroom
- Multilingual service
- Guest accounts well explained and presented
- Porterage offered
- Guests greeted at hotel entrance, full concierge service provided
- At least one restaurant open to residents and non-residents for all meals seven days per week
- Last orders for dinner no earlier than 10pm
- High-quality menu and wine list
- Evening service to turn down the beds. Remote-control television, direct-dial telephone at bedside and desk, a range of luxury toiletries, bath sheets and robes. En suite bathroom incorporating fixed overhead shower and WC

★ Inspector's Choice

Each year we select the best hotels in each rating. These hotels stand out as the very best in the British Isles, regardless of style. Red Star hotels appear in highlighted panels throughout the guide. Inspector's Choice Restaurants with Rooms have been chosen to represent the best offerings of both dining and accommodation.

★ Highly Recommended

Hotels with Silver Stars ★ have been selected for their superior levels of quality, high standards of hotel keeping and for the quality of food within their star rating.

AA Rosette awards

Out of the many thousands of restaurants in the UK, the AA identifies over 2,000 as the best. The following is an outline of what to expect from restaurants with AA Rosette awards.

◉ Excellent local restaurants serving food prepared with care, understanding and skill, using good quality ingredients.

◉◉ The best local restaurants, which aim for and achieve higher standards, and better consistency; where a greater precision is apparent in the cooking. There will be obvious attention to the selection of quality ingredients.

◉◉◉ Outstanding restaurants that demand recognition well beyond their local area.

◉◉◉◉ Among the very best restaurants in the British Isles, where the cooking demands national recognition.

◉◉◉◉◉ The finest restaurants in the British Isles, where the cooking stands comparison with the best in the world.

Additional information

Hints on booking your stay

It's always worth booking as early as possible, particularly for the peak holiday period from the beginning of June to the end of September. Bear in mind that Easter and other public holidays may be busy too and in some parts of Scotland, the ski season is a peak holiday period.

Some hotels will ask for a deposit or full payment in advance, especially for one-night bookings. Some hotels charge half-board (bed, breakfast and dinner) whether you require the meals or not, while others may only accept full-board bookings. Not all hotels will accept advance bookings for bed and breakfast, overnight or short stays. Some will not take reservations from mid week.

Once a booking is confirmed, let the hotel know at once if you are unable to keep your reservation. If the hotel cannot re-let your room you may be liable to pay about two-thirds of the room price (a deposit will count towards this payment). In Britain a legally binding contract is made when you accept an offer of accommodation, either in writing or by telephone, and illness is not accepted as a release from this contract. You are advised to take out insurance against possible cancellation, for example AA Single Trip Insurance (telephone 0800 912 5002).

AA Hotels online

Locating and booking somewhere to stay can be a time-consuming process, but all the hotels inspected and rated by the AA are searchable online at: www.theaa.com/hotels

Facilities for disabled guests

The Equality Act 2010 provides legal rights for disabled people including access to goods, services and facilities, and means that service providers may have to consider making adjustments to their premises. For more information about the Act see: www.gov.uk/rights-disabled-person/the-equality-act-2010-and-un-convention or www.gov.uk/definition-of-disability-under-equality-act-2010

The establishments in this guide should be aware of their obligations under the Act. We recommend that you always telephone in advance to ensure that the establishment you have chosen has appropriate facilities.

Please note: AA inspectors are not accredited to make inspections under the National Accessible Scheme. We indicate in entries if an establishment has ground floor rooms, walk-in showers and whether the hotel has a hearing loop system; and if a hotel tells us that they have disabled facilities this is included in the description.

Food allergies

Since December 2014, when a new EU regulation came into force, it has been easier for those with food allergies to make safer food choices when eating out. There are 14 allergens listed in the regulation, and pubs and restaurants are required to list any of these that are used in the dishes they offer. These may be highlighted on the menus or customers can ask staff for full information. Remember, if you are allergic to a food and are in any doubt speak to a member of the hotel's staff. For further information see: www.food.gov.uk/science/allergy-intolerance/label/labelling-changes

Licensing laws

Licensing laws differ in England, Wales, Scotland, the Republic of Ireland, the Isle of Man, the Isles of Scilly and the Channel Islands. Public houses are generally open from mid morning to early afternoon, and from about 6 or 7pm until 11pm, although closing times may be earlier or later and some pubs are open all afternoon. Unless otherwise stated, establishments listed are licensed to serve alcohol. Hotel residents can obtain alcoholic drinks at all times, if the licensee is prepared to serve them. Non-residents eating at the hotel restaurant can have drinks with meals. Children under 14 may be excluded from bars where no food is served. Those under 18 may not purchase or consume alcoholic drinks.

Club licence means that drinks are served to club members only, 48 hours must lapse between joining and ordering.

The Fire Safety Order 2005 does not apply to the Channel Islands or the Republic of Ireland which have their own rules. As far as we are aware, all hotels listed in Great Britain have applied for and not been refused a fire certificate.

For information on Ireland see page 495.

Bank and Public Holidays 2018

New Year's Day	1st January	Spring Bank Holiday	28th May
2nd January (Scotland)	2nd January	Orangemen's Day (NI)	12th July
St Patrick's Day (NI & ROI)		Summer Bank Holiday (Scotland)	6th August
(Substitute Day)	19th March	Summer Bank Holiday	27th August
Good Friday	30th March	St Andrew's Day (Scotland)	30th November
Easter Monday	2nd April	Christmas Day	25th December
Early May Bank Holiday	7th May	Boxing Day	26th December

AA Hotels of the Year

Each year the AA celebrates the best among those Hotels that are part of the AA Hotel rating scheme. Our inspectors nominate those places that they feel to be a cut above the rest, and award-winners are chosen from these nominations. Held this year at Grosvenor House, a JW Marriott Hotel, London, the AA Hospitality Awards 2017–18 recognised and rewarded the best that the British hospitality industry has to offer. Awards are given for the Hotel of the Year for England, London, Scotland, Wales and Northern Ireland, as well as an overall Hotel Group of the Year. Find out more about the winners of these awards over the next four pages. The AA Hospitality Awards website features information about current and previous AA awards. Awards are also given for B&Bs, Caravan & Camping, and Restaurants, along with many more:

www.theaa.com/hospitality-awards

BATH page 48

ENGLAND

THE GAINSBOROUGH BATH SPA ★★★★★ 88% ⊛⊛⊛

Built in the 19th century, The Gainsborough Bath Spa occupies two Grade II listed buildings with distinguished Georgian and Victorian façades in the heart of this wonderful World Heritage Site. Named after the artist, Sir Thomas Gainsborough (1727–88), this luxury hotel is centred around Spa Village Bath and, uniquely in the UK, has the exclusive privilege of access to the natural thermal, mineral-rich waters. Its style is understated, with smart, well-equipped bedrooms and public areas. If you were to arrive unaware it might seem that you were in a top London establishment with service to match. Service, style and décor slick yet not intrusive; good value but nowhere near cheap. Spa facilities themselves are top of the range, but this place does not just live off the accolade of private thermal waters alone. The Gainsborough Restaurant offers British cuisine based on the very best ingredients. Sourcing is key here, letting the ingredients do the shouting, be it with a little expert help from the kitchen. Head Chef Daniel Moon heads up the kitchen and is causing some great ripples in the Bath eating scene. Overall facilities are impressive and include a smart lounge and a sophisticated and buzzing cocktail bar.

LONDON

THE GORING ★★★★★ ❀❀❀
LONDON SW1 page 228

The Goring has been an icon of luxurious yet intimate British hospitality since it was completed in 1910, just a few months before the death of Edward VII, making it one of the last hotels that can call itself truly Edwardian. In keeping with the innovation of the new century it was a truly modern establishment – believed to be the first hotel in the world to have central heating in every room. Its location, less than half a mile from Buckingham Palace, gives it a strong royal connection; The Queen Mother was a regular guest, and the Duchess of Cambridge stayed in the newly created Royal Suite on the night before her wedding in 2011. Essentially, The Goring is a family business. Opened by Otto Goring, it is now overseen by his great-grandson Jeremy, who took over as CEO in 2005. Other top members of the team include Managing Director, David Morgan-Hewitt, who has been at the hotel since 1990; and Hotel Manager, Stuart Geddes, who has done much to increase The Goring's share of awards and accolades.

SCOTLAND

DOUNESIDE HOUSE ★★★★ 86% ❀❀❀
TARLAND page 462

Set in the grounds of the MacRobert Estate, this hotel has only recently come on the scene; its recent transformation has provided a range of accommodation, now rich with a wealth of rooms and cottages that are both stylish and luxurious. The public rooms are a contemporary blend of original features with art and antiques. The extensive grounds and estate farms are a source of excellent produce for the kitchen. The estate gardens have been set up as a Royal Horticultural Society (RHS) apprenticeship training scheme for kitchen gardens. Here a team of eight RHS apprentices work hand-in-hand with David Butters and the kitchen team to produce a true marriage of cuisine and horticulture. Along with the hotel, the health club is a shining new feature, with gym, pool and fitness classes. Importantly, the proprietors here have invested in the team, not just the physical aspects. Management are not some back office 'never seen lot', but genuinely there to host and ensure guests are well cared for. The staff are a skilled friendly lot too, and hail from a number of well-recognised, high-quality backgrounds.

AA Hotels of the Year *continued*

WALES

TWR Y FELIN HOTEL ★★★★ 86% ◉◉ ♀
ST DAVIDS page 489

Twr Y Felin is the vision of one of the leading architects and designers in the world, Keith Griffiths. As a Pembrokeshire boy, Keith grew up in this area and his heart is firmly set in Wales. With his pedigree it would be easy to build the ideal hotel, so why pick a windmill dating back to 1806? Setting up the Griffiths Roch Foundation, the remit was to buy and restore historic buildings to help reinvigorate the local economy. With limitations on building in the national park, Keith was able to use his knowledge to convert the existing building into a luxury hotel, five years in planning, design and construction. Commissioning over 100 works of art from 33 internationally renowned artists, this is Wales' first true Art Hotel. The original windmill tower is now part of a luxurious two-storey suite and has unrivalled 360 degree views from its observatory over the peninsula. Blas Restaurant focusses on local sourcing and showcasing the best welsh produce and has been awarded two AA Rosettes in its first year of opening. Keith is still very much involved with the project and is a regular visitor to the Hotel even though he's based in Japan; his right-hand woman is Paula Ellis, a dedicated hospitality professional, renowned throughout Wales.

NORTHERN IRELAND

THE OLD INN ★★★★ 81% ◉◉
CRAWFORDSBURN page 497

Dating from around 1600, with a rich history that takes in figures from the worlds of literature, music and politics, The Old Inn is a family-run hotel which has grown and transformed year after year. In fact, over the last six years a complete remodelling of the hotel has taken place with projects still ongoing. All bedrooms were refurbished with additional bedrooms also added to the portfolio. A few years ago the kitchen was ripped out and a bespoke kitchen built from scratch, creating a state-of-the-art space to service the restaurant, the thriving bar operation and a busy conference and wedding market. The restaurant is named Lewis, after the author C. S. Lewis, who used to meet friends here, and stayed here for his honeymoon in 1958. The bar is typical of an old-world Irish pub complete with open wood and turf-burning fires; locals from the surrounding area come for morning coffee and the long-serving staff know them all by name and also what their regular tipple is. This is a smart, friendly, well-run hotel, which makes the most of its fascinating and intriguing past, but also has a bright and hospitable future.

AA Hotel Group of the Year

Andrew Brownsword Hotels

![BROWNSWORD THE HOTELS logo] The Andrew Brownsword Hotels Collection consists of thirteen properties in both countryside settings and city centre locations. Andrew Brownsword Hotels is owned by Christina and Andrew Brownsword CBE DL, who strive to create very special places that truly embody their own ethos of great hospitality.

The collection includes the following award-winning hotels:

Gidleigh Park, Chagford, Devon - ★★★★★ ⊚⊚⊚⊚⊚ 🍷
The Bath Priory Hotel, Restaurant & Spa, Bath,
  Somerset - ★★★★★ ⊚⊚⊚
Amberley Castle, Amberley, West Sussex - ★★★★ ⊚⊚⊚ 🍷
The Slaughters Manor House,
  Lower Slaughter, Gloucs - ★★★★ ⊚⊚⊚
Buckland Manor, Buckland, Gloucs - ★★★★ ⊚⊚⊚ 🍷

An award-winning team of chefs and a number of long-serving general managers are key to the operation; the newly-created senior management team includes CEO Stephanie Hocking, and Associate Director Alan Swinson. The owners also naturally have a strong input. Excellent country houses are the standard here; truly the best of British, with eccentricity of design in some places but above all, classical refinement offering an impressive market mix with two brands under the Brownsword Collection umbrella.

"We have chosen to acquire each property on the basis that we not only love the location but also have a real desire to provide the highest of standards in comfort and care. Every hotel is situated in some of the most beautiful areas of our English countryside or in the centre of our more historic cities. Indeed, as we travel between them on a regular basis we feel we have created a journey filled with the pleasures of discovery. And through our travels here and abroad we have come to appreciate great service and this too has become an ethos of our operations across the collection. Our dedicated teams care about the the service they give, proven time and time again when our guests return. You will also find a part of our personal style across our hotels including our passion for the comforts of good interior design and our collection of 20th century art. Whatever the reason for your journey to us, our hope is that you find a warmth of welcome and an experience to enjoy on every level – good food, fine wines, comfortable rooms and a feeling that you have 'come home'. We truly want you to enjoy our houses as we do."

- Andrew & Christina Brownsword

Buckland Manor

Gidleigh Park

The Bath Priory

discover award winning hotels

Discover our eleven luxury hotels and three wonderful restaurants, all in unique locations throughout Devon and Cornwall including staggeringly beautiful golden beaches and historic market towns.

AA Hotel Group of the Year 2015-2016.

brendhotels.com

Taw Buildings, Taw Vale, Barnstaple, Devon EX32 9AE | 08455 760 760

Carlyon Bay Hotel St Austell ★★★★ | Royal Duchy Hotel Falmouth ★★★★
Saunton Sands Hotel Saunton ★★★★ | Imperial Hotel Barnstaple ★★★★
Victoria Hotel Sidmouth ★★★★ | Belmont Hotel Sidmouth ★★★★
Devon Hotel Exeter ★★★ | Barnstaple Hotel Barnstaple ★★★ | Park Hotel Barnstaple ★★★
Royal & Fortescue Hotel Barnstaple ★★★ | Royal Hotel Bideford ★★★

Hotel groups information

ÆBode HOTELS	**Abode Hotels** A contemporary collection of three city centre hotels in Canterbury, Chester and Manchester that have a wide variety of dining outlets and are well geared to both corporate and leisure markets. Part of Andrew Brownsword Hotels.	www.abodehotels.co.uk
Best Western.	**Best Western** Britain's largest consortia group - over 280 independently owned and managed hotels, modern and traditional, in the two-, three- and four-star range. Many have leisure facilities and AA Rosettes.	0845 767676 *(Calls cost 7p per minute plus your phone company's access charge)* www.bestwestern.co.uk
Best Western PLUS	**Best Western Plus** 30 independently owned and managed hotels that offer that little something extra in the three- and four-star range. Some of these hotels have AA Rosette awards.	0845 767676 *(Calls cost 7p per minute plus your phone company's access charge)* www.bestwestern.co.uk
PREMIER | BEST WESTERN	**Best Western Premier** These hotels are selected for their beautiful settings, range of facilities and enhanced levels of service. There are currently ten Best Western Great Britain hotels that have achieved Premier status. These join over 45 Best Western Premier accredited hotels across Europe and Asia.	0845 767676 *(Calls cost 7p per minute plus your phone company's access charge)* www.bestwestern.co.uk
Brend Hotels	**Brend** A privately owned group of eleven three- and four-star hotels in Devon and Cornwall.	01271 344496 www.brend-hotels.co.uk
Andrew BROWNSWORD THE HOTELS	**Brownsword Hotels** A small group of country hotels each with unique qualities, personalised service, memorable locations and a strong focus on food and wine.	www.brownswordhotels.co.uk
CHOICE HOTELS EUROPE	**Choice Hotels** Choice has four different brands in the UK: Clarion and Quality Hotels are three- and four-star hotels, Comfort Inns are two- and three-star hotels, and Sleep Inns are budget hotels.	0800 444444 www.choicehotelseurope.com
CLASSIC BRITISH HOTELS	**Classic British Hotels** An exclusive upmarket collection of four-star and quality three-star independent hotels throughout the UK, noted for its comfort, fine dining, spas, golf and event facilities.	0845 070 7090 *(Calls cost 7p per minute plus your phone company's access charge)* www.classicbritishhotels.com
COACHING INN GROUP	**The Coaching Inn Group** is a small selection of historic coaching inns based in market towns within the UK. All sites are filled with character and offer a great quality in food, drink and rooms.	01858 438300 www.coachinginngroup.co.uk
COTSWOLD INNS & HOTELS	**Cotswold Inns & Hotels** Charming three- and four-star small hotels located in the Cotswolds.	www.cotswold-inns-hotels.co.uk
CROWNE PLAZA HOTELS & RESORTS	**Crowne Plaza** Four-star hotels predominantly found in key city centre locations.	0871 423 4876 *(Calls cost 13p per minute plus your phone company's access charge)* www.crowneplaza.co.uk
DAYS INN	**Days Inn** Good quality modern budget hotels with good coverage across the UK.	0800 028 0400 www.daysinn.com

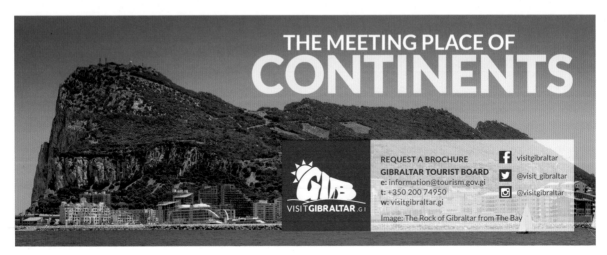

Hotel groups information *continued*

	Eden Hotel Collection A privately owned collection of individual hotels, featuring award-winning dining in quality surroundings.	0845 351 0980 *(Calls cost 7p per minute plus your phone company's access charge)* *www.edenhotelcollection.com*
English Lakes Hotels Resorts & Venues	**English Lakes Hotels** A collection of individually styled four-star hotels located in and around the Lake District.	*015394 33773 www.englishlakes.co.uk*
EXCLUSIVE HOTELS and VENUES	**Exclusive Hotels** A small privately owned group of luxury five-star hotels, all located in the south of England.	*01276 471774 www.exclusive.co.uk*
FBD Hotels & Resorts	**FBD Hotels & Resorts** An Irish owned and operated group offering quality hotels in convenient locations.	*00 353 1 428 2400 www.fdbhotels.com*
fOCUS hotels	**Focus Hotels** A group of three- and four-star hotels in both city and country locations across England. All offer WiFi and a number have spa facilities.	0844 225 1625 *(Calls cost 7p per minute plus your phone company's access charge)* *www.focushotels.co.uk*
hallmark	**Hallmark Hotels** A collection of nine hotels that provide comfortable accommodation; some have leisure facilities.	*0113 307 6760 www.hallmarkhotels.co.uk*
Hand PICKED HOTELS	**Hand Picked Hotels** A collection of predominantly four-star, high quality country house hotels, with a real emphasis on quality food and service. Some have stylish spa facilities.	*01642 706606 www.handpickedhotels.co.uk*
Hillbrooke QUIRKYLUXURY	**Hillbrooke Hotels** A growing portfolio of hotels and inns under the banner 'Quirky Luxury'. Excellent locations, comfortable surroundings, relaxed informal service.	*www.hillbrookehotels.co.uk*
Holiday Inn	**Holiday Inn** A major international group with many hotels across the UK.	0871 423 4896 *(Calls cost 10p per minute plus your phone company's access charge)* *www.holidayinn.co.uk*
Holiday Inn **Express**	**Holiday Inn Express** A major international hotel brand with over 100 hotels in the UK.	*www.hiexpress.co.uk*
Hotel du Vin & Bistro	**Hotel du Vin** A small expanding group of high quality four-star hotels, with a strong emphasis on its destination restaurant concept and appealing menus.	0871 943 0345 *(Calls cost 10p per minute plus your phone company's access charge)* *www.hotelduvin.com*

Hotel groups information *continued*

THE INDEPENDENTS HOTEL ASSOCIATION	**The Independents** A consortium of independently owned, mainly two-, three- and four-star hotels across Britain.	*0844 800 9965* *(Calls cost 7p per minute plus your phone company's access charge)* *www.theindependents.co.uk*
IRELAND'S BLUE BOOK	**Ireland's Blue Book** A collection of country houses, historic hotels, castles and restaurants throughout Ireland.	*00 353 1 676 9914* *www.irelands-blue-book.ie*
IRISH COUNTRY HOTELS	**Irish Country Hotels** A collection of family-run hotels, all across Ireland.	*00 353 1 295 8900 (local) 0818 281 281* *www.irishcountryhotels.com*
LAKE DISTRICT HOTELS	**Lake District Hotels** A small collection of hotels situated in some beautiful parts of Lake District countryside and in some Lakeland towns.	*0800 840 1240 www.lakedistricthotels.net*
LEGACY HOTELS	**Legacy Hotels** A small group of three- and four-star hotels growing its coverage across the UK.	*0844 411 9011* *(Calls cost 7p per minute plus your phone company's access charge)* *www.legacy-hotels.co.uk*
Leisureplex HOLIDAY HOTELS	**Leisureplex** A group of 21 three-star hotels located in many popular seaside resorts.	*01257 248000 www.leisureplex.co.uk*
MACDONALD HOTELS & RESORTS	**Macdonald** A large group of predominantly four-star hotels, both traditional and modern in style and located across the UK. Many hotels enjoy rural settings and state-of-the-art spa facilities.	*0844 879 9000* *(Calls cost 7p per minute plus your phone company's access charge)* *www.macdonaldhotels.co.uk*
Malmaison	**Malmaison** A growing brand of modern, luxurious city centre hotels that provide deeply comfortable bedrooms, exciting restaurants and carefully selected wine lists.	*0871 943 0350* *(Calls cost 10p per minute plus your phone company's access charge)* *www.malmaison.com*
MANOR HOUSE HOTELS	**Manor House** Located throughout Ireland, this group offers a selection of independent, high quality country and manor house hotels.	*00 353 1 295 8900 (local) 0818 281 281* *www.manorhousehotels.com*
Marriott	**Marriott** This international brand has four- and five-star hotels in primary locations. Most are modern and have leisure facilities with a focus on activities such as golf.	*00800 1927 1927 www.marriott.co.uk*
MAYBOURNE HOTEL GROUP	**Maybourne Hotels** A hotel group representing the prestigious London five-star hotels – The Berkeley, Claridge's and The Connaught.	*020 7107 8800 (Head Office)* *www.maybourne.com*
Mercure HOTELS	**Mercure Hotels** A large group of three- and four-star hotels throughout England, Scotland and Wales.	*0871 663 0627* *(Calls cost 10p per minute plus your phone company's access charge)* *www.mercure.com*
	MGallery A series of upmarket, leisure-based and individually presented hotels. Part of the Accor brand.	*0871 663 0624* *(Calls cost 10p per minute plus your phone company's access charge)* *www.mgallery.com*

Millennium & Copthorne Group with ten high-quality, four-star hotels, and one five-star, mainly in central London.	*0800 414741 www.millenniumhotels.com*
Moran Hotels A privately owned group with two four-star Moran Hotels, and one three-star Bewley's Hotel. All have strategic locations in the UK and Ireland.	*00 353 1 459 3650 www.moranhotels.com*
New Forest Hotels A collection of properties situated in the New Forest National Park, each with its own distinct character. All have an AA Rosette award for culinary excellence.	*0800 444441 www.newforesthotels.co.uk*
Novotel Part of French group Accor, Novotel provides mainly modern three-star hotels and a new generation of four-star hotels in key locations throughout the UK.	*0871 663 0626* *(Calls cost 10p per minute plus your phone company's access charge)* *www.novotel.com*
Park Plaza Hotels A European based group increasing its presence in the UK with quality four-star hotels in primary locations.	*0800 169 6128 www.parkplaza.com*
Peel Hotels A group of mainly three- and four-star hotels located across the UK.	*0845 601 7335* *(Calls cost 7p per minute plus your phone company's access charge)* *www.peelhotels.co.uk*
Premier Inns The largest and fastest growing budget hotel group with over 700 hotels offering quality, modern accommodation in key locations throughout the UK and Ireland. Each hotel is located adjacent to a family restaurant and bar.	*0871 527 8000* *(Calls cost 13p per minute plus your phone company's access charge)* *www.premierinn.com*
Pride of Britain A consortium of privately owned high quality British hotels, often in the country house style, many of which have been awarded Red Stars and AA Rosettes.	*0800 089 3929* *www.prideofbritainhotels.com*
Principal Hotel Company A collection of luxury properties from Victorian grandeur to iconic city centre hotels.	*0844 854 2910* *(Calls cost 7p per minute plus your phone company's access charge)* *www.phcompany.com*
QHotels A hotel group with individually styled 4 star establishments located across the UK, in city locations and countryside retreats.	*0845 074 0060* *(Calls cost 7p per minute plus your phone company's access charge)* *www.qhotels.co.uk*
Ramada A large hotel group with many properties throughout the UK in three brands – Ramada, Ramada Hotel & Resort, and Ramada Plaza.	*0808 100 0783 www.ramada.co.uk*
Red Carnation A unique collection of prestigious four and five star hotels in Dorset, the Channel Islands. London and Ireland providing luxurious surroundings and attentive service.	*www.redcarnationhotels.com*
Relais et Chateaux An international consortium of rural, privately owned hotels, mainly in the country house style.	*00800 2000 0002 www.relaischateaux.com*

Hotel groups information *continued*

RENAISSANCE. HOTELS & RESORTS	**Renaissance** One of the Marriott brands, Renaissance is a collection of individual hotels offering comfortable guest rooms, quality cuisine and good levels of service.	*00800 1927 1927 www.marriott.co.uk*
RICHARDSON HOTELS	**Richardson Hotels** A group of five hotels located in Cornwall and Devon, all rated three or four star.	*www.richardsonhotels.co.uk*
ROCCO FORTE HOTELS	**Rocco Forte Hotels** A small group of luxury hotels spread across Europe. Owned by Sir Rocco Forte, with two hotels in the UK, situated in major city locations.	*00800 7666 6667 www.roccofortehotels.com*
	Scotland's Hotels of Distinction A consortium of independent Scottish hotels in the three- and four-star range.	*www.hotels-of-distinction.com*
Sheraton Grand	**Sheraton** Represented in the UK by a small number of four- and five-star hotels in London and Scotland.	*www.starwoodhotels.com*
	Small Luxury Hotels of the World Part of an international consortium of mainly privately-owned hotels, often in the country-house style.	*0800 037 1888 www.slh.com*
SURYA	**Surya Hotels** A privately owned group of six three- and four-star hotels in East Anglia and the South East of England	*www.suryahotels.co.uk*
T|A|HOTEL COLLECTION	**TA Hotel Collection** A privately owned collection of three- and four-star hotels across Suffolk	*01728 452176 www.tahotelcollection.co.uk*
THE CIRCLE	**The Circle** A consortium of independently owned, mainly two- and three-star hotels, across Britain.	*01865 875888 www.circlehotels.co.uk*
THWAITES	**Thwaites** A small group of four-star hotels which feature spa facilities and well-equipped bedrooms ideal for both business and leisure guests.	*www.thwaites.co.uk*
WARNER LEISURE HOTELS	**Warner Leisure Hotels** A collection of three- and four-star country hotels and villages, exclusively for adults. Renowned for their restaurants, daytime activities and live entertainment.	*0330 100 9774 www.warnerleisurehotels.co.uk*
WELCOMEBREAK	**Welcome Break** Good quality, modern, budget accommodation at motorway services.	*01908 299700 www.welcomebreak.co.uk*
Z HOTELS	**Z Hotels** Modern hotels in city centre locations with out-of-town prices	*www.thezhotels.com*

AA WALKING GUIDES

The 50 Best Walks of 2–10 Miles by Region and City

- Easy-to-follow directions with clear waypointed maps
- Colour-coded routes – pick from easy strolls through to more challenging walks
- Fascinating background reading for every walk
- Advice for dog owners
- Great for a full day out with recommended sights and attractions plus places to eat and drink

AA
50 Walks in
BRECON BEACONS
& SOUTH WALES
50 Walks of 2–10 Miles

AA
50 Walks in
HAMPSHIRE &
THE ISLE OF WIGHT
50 Walks of 2–10 Miles

AA
50 Walks in
THE LAKE DISTRICT
50 Walks of 2–10 Miles

AA
50 Walks in
BERKSHIRE &
BUCKINGHAMSHIRE
50 Walks of 2–10 Miles

AA
50 Walks in
KENT
50 Walks of 2–10 Miles

AA
50 Walks in
DERBYSHIRE
50 Walks of 2–10 Miles

AA
50 Walks in
SOMERSET
50 Walks of 2–10 Miles

AA
50 Walks in
THE COTSWOLDS
50 Walks of 2–10 Miles

AA
50 Walks in
DURHAM &
NORTHUMBERLAND
50 Walks of 2–10 Miles

AA
50 Walks in
CORNWALL
50 Walks of 2–10 Miles

AA
50 Walks in
NORFOLK
50 Walks of 2–10 Miles

AA
50 Walks in
SUSSEX &
SOUTH DOWNS
50 Walks of 2–10 Miles

AA
50 Walks in
OXFORDSHIRE
50 Walks of 2–10 Miles

AA
50 Walks in
THE PEAK DISTRICT
50 Walks of 2–10 Miles

AA
50 Walks in
WARWICKSHIRE &
WEST MIDLANDS
50 Walks of 2–10 Miles

AA
50 Walks in
DORSET
50 Walks of 2–10 Miles

AA
50 Walks in
THE YORKSHIRE
DALES
50 Walks of 2–10 Miles

AA
50 Walks in
SNOWDONIA &
NORTH WALES
50 Walks of 2–10 Miles

Follow @TheAA_Lifestyle

Available now at shop.theAA.com

England

A

ABINGDON-ON-THAMES
Oxfordshire
Map 5 SU49

Premier Inn Abingdon

BUDGET HOTEL

Marcham Road, OX14 1AD - **tel:** 0871 527 8014 (Calls cost 13p per minute plus your phone company's access charge) **web:** www.premierinn.com
dir: *On A415. Approx 0.5m from A34 at Abingdon South junct Marcham Interchange*

High quality, budget accommodation ideal for both families and business travellers. Spacious, en suite bedrooms feature tea and coffee making facilities, Freeview TV in most hotels and free WiFi. The adjacent family restaurant features a wide and varied menu.

Rooms: 27

ACCRINGTON
Lancashire
Map 18 SD72

Mercure Blackburn Dunkenhalgh Hotel & Spa

★★★★ 74% HOTEL

Blackburn Road, Clayton-le-Moors, BB5 5JP - **tel:** 01254 398021
email: H6617@accor.com **web:** www.mercure.com
dir: *M65 junct 7, left at rdbt, left at lights, hotel 100yds on left*

Set in delightfully tended grounds yet only a stone's throw from the M65, this fine mansion has conference and banqueting facilities that attract the wedding and corporate markets. The state-of-the-art thermal suite allows guests to relax and take life easy. Bedrooms come in a variety of styles, sizes and standards; some are located away from the main hotel building.

Rooms: 175 (119 annexe) (36 family) (43 GF) ☁ **S** £65–£125; **D** £80–£145*
Facilities: Spa STV WiFi HL ⓢ Gym Thermal suite Aerobics studio Xmas New Year **Conf:** Class 200 Board 100 Thtr 400 Del from £125 **Services:** Lift Night porter **Parking:** 400 **Notes:** LB Civ Wed 300

ALCESTER
Warwickshire
Map 10 SP05

Kings Court Hotel

★★★ 78% HOTEL

Kings Coughton, B49 5QQ - **tel:** 01789 763111
email: info@kingscourthotel.co.uk **web:** www.kingscourthotel.co.uk
dir: *1m N on A435*

This privately-owned hotel dates back to Tudor times and the bedrooms in the original house have oak beams. Most guests are accommodated in the well-appointed modern wings. The bar and restaurant offer very good dishes from interesting menus. The hotel is licensed to hold civil ceremonies, and the pretty garden is ideal for summer weddings.

Rooms: 61 (58 annexe) (2 family) (30 GF) ☁ **S** £99; **D** £109 (incl. bkfst)*
Facilities: FTV WiFi ⓭ Gym Xmas New Year **Conf:** Class 60 Board 40 Thtr 100 Del £125 **Parking:** 100 **Notes:** Civ Wed 100

ALDEBURGH
Suffolk
Map 13 TM45

HIGHLY RECOMMENDED

Brudenell Hotel

★★★★ 85% ◉◉ HOTEL

T|A|HOTEL COLLECTION

The Parade, IP15 5BU - **tel:** 01728 452071
email: info@brudenellhotel.co.uk **web:** www.brudenellhotel.co.uk
dir: *A12, A1094. In town, right into High St. Hotel on seafront adjoining Fort Green car park*

Situated at the far end of the town centre just a step away from the beach, this hotel has a contemporary appearance, enhanced by subtle lighting and quality soft furnishings. Many of the bedrooms have superb sea views; they include deluxe rooms with king-sized beds and superior rooms suitable for families. The informal restaurant showcases skilfully prepared dishes that use fresh, seasonal produce, especially local fish, seafood and game.

Rooms: 44 (17 family) ☁ **Facilities:** STV WiFi Xmas New Year **Conf:** Class 20 Board 20 Thtr 20 **Services:** Lift Night porter **Parking:** 18

HIGHLY RECOMMENDED

The White Lion Hotel

★★★ 88% ◉ HOTEL

T|A|HOTEL COLLECTION

Market Cross Place, IP15 5BJ - **tel:** 01728 452720
email: info@whitelion.co.uk **web:** www.whitelion.co.uk
dir: *A12 onto A1094, follow signs to Aldeburgh at junct on left. Hotel on right*

A popular 15th-century hotel situated at the quiet end of town overlooking the sea. Bedrooms are pleasantly decorated and thoughtfully equipped, many rooms have lovely sea views. Public areas include two lounges and an elegant restaurant, where locally-caught fish and seafood are served. There is also a modern brasserie.

Rooms: 38 **Facilities:** STV WiFi ⓭ Xmas New Year **Conf:** Class 50 Board 30 Thtr 80 **Services:** Night porter **Parking:** 10 **Notes:** Civ Wed 90

Find out more
about the AA's Hotel rating scheme on pages 12–13

A

Alderley Edge Hotel

★★★★ 78% ®®® HOTEL

Macclesfield Road, SK9 7BJ - tel: 01625 583033
email: reservations@alderleyedgehotel.com **web:** www.alderleyedgehotel.com
dir: *From A34 in Alderley Edge onto B5087 towards Macclesfield.*
Hotel 200yds on right

This well-furnished hotel, with its charming grounds, was originally a country house built for one of the region's 'cotton kings'. The bedrooms and suites are attractively furnished, offering excellent quality and comfort. The welcoming bar and adjacent lounge lead into the conservatory restaurant where imaginative, memorable food and friendly, attentive service are highlights of any visit.

Rooms: 50 (4 family) (6 GF) ♠ **Facilities:** STV WiFi � **Conf:** Class 40 Board 30 Thtr 120 **Services:** Lift Night porter **Parking:** 90 **Notes:** Closed 1 Jan RS 25-26 Dec Closed for dinner Civ Wed 114

INSPECTOR'S CHOICE

Ettington Park Hotel

★★★★ ®® COUNTRY HOUSE HOTEL

CV37 8BU - tel: 01789 450123 & 0845 072 7454 (Calls cost 5p per minute plus your phone company's access charge)
email: ettingtonpark@handpicked.co.uk
web: www.handpickedhotels.co.uk/ettingtonpark
dir: *Off A3400 5m S of Stratford, just outside Alderminster. M40 junct 15/A46 towards Stratford-Upon-Avon, A439 in town centre, A3400 to Shipston, 0.5m on left*

Set in 40 acres of grounds in the picturesque Stour Valley, Ettington Park offers the best of both worlds – the peace of the countryside and easy access to main roads and motorway networks. Bedrooms are spacious and individually decorated; views include the delightful grounds and gardens, or the historic chapel. Luxurious day rooms extend to the period drawing room, the oak-panelled dining room with inlays of family crests, a range of contemporary meeting rooms and an indoor leisure centre.

Rooms: 48 (20 annexe) (5 family) (10 GF) ♠ **Facilities:** STV WiFi HL ⌂ ♨ ⌥ Clay pigeon shooting Archery Sauna Steam room Xmas New Year **Conf:** Class 48 Board 48 Thtr 90 **Services:** Lift Night porter **Parking:** 100 **Notes:** Civ Wed 96

Potters International Hotel

★★★ 72% HOTEL

1 Fleet Road, GU11 2ET - tel: 01252 344000
email: reservations@pottersinthotel.com **web:** www.pottersinthotel.com
dir: *Access via A325 & A321 towards Fleet*

This modern hotel is located within easy reach of Aldershot. Extensive air-conditioned public areas include ample lounge areas, a pub and a more formal restaurant; there are also conference rooms and a very good leisure club. Bedrooms, mostly spacious, are well equipped and have been attractively decorated and furnished.

Rooms: 103 (9 family) (9 GF) **Facilities:** STV WiFi ⌂ Gym Beauty treatment room **Conf:** Class 250 Board 100 Thtr 400 **Services:** Lift Night porter **Parking:** 120

ALDERSHOT *continued*

Premier Inn Aldershot

BUDGET HOTEL

7 Wellington Avenue, GU11 1SQ - **tel:** 0871 527 8018 (Calls cost 13p per minute plus your phone company's access charge) **web:** www.premierinn.com
dir: *M3 junct 4, A331. A325 through Farnborough. Pass Barons BMW then Queens Rdbt. Adjacent to Willems Park Brewers Fayre*

High quality, budget accommodation ideal for both families and business travellers. Spacious, en suite bedrooms feature tea and coffee making facilities, and Freeview TV in most hotels. Internet access and WiFi are available for a small fee. The adjacent family restaurant features a wide and varied menu.

Rooms: 84

ALDWARK	Map 19 SE46
North Yorkshire	

Aldwark Manor Golf & Spa Hotel

★★★★ 79% ⚜ HOTEL

INSPIRED BY YOU

Y061 1UF - **tel:** 01347 838146
email: aldwarkmanor@qhotels.co.uk **web:** www.qhotels.co.uk
dir: *A1/A59 towards Green Hammerton, then B6265 Little Ouseburn. Follow signs for Aldwark Bridge/Manor. A19 through Linton-on-Ouse*

Mature parkland forms the impressive backdrop for this rambling 19th-century mansion, with the River Ure flowing gently through the hotel's own 18-hole golf course. Bedrooms vary - the rooms in the main house are traditional and those in the extension are modern in design. Impressive conference and banqueting facilities and a stylish, very well equipped leisure club are available.

Rooms: 53 (6 family) 🐾 **Facilities:** Spa FTV WiFi 🏊 ⚓ 18 Putting green Gym Sauna Steam room Xmas New Year **Conf:** Class 100 Board 80 Thtr 240 **Services:** Lift Night porter **Parking:** 150 **Notes:** LB Civ Wed 140

ALFRISTON	Map 6 TQ50
East Sussex	

Deans Place

★★★ 85% ⚜⚜ HOTEL

Seaford Road, BN26 5TW - **tel:** 01323 870248
email: mail@deansplacehotel.co.uk **web:** www.deansplacehotel.co.uk
dir: *Exit A27 between Eastbourne & Brighton, signed Alfriston & Drusillas Zoo Park. S through village towards Seaford*

Situated on the southern fringe of the village, this friendly hotel is set in attractive gardens. Bedrooms vary in size and are well appointed with good facilities. A wide range of food is offered, including an extensive bar menu and a fine dining option in The Dining Room restaurant.

Deans Place

Rooms: 36 (4 family) (8 GF) 🐾 **S** fr £67.50; **D** £75–£135* **Facilities:** FTV WiFi 🏊 🎯 Putting green ⛳ Boules Xmas New Year **Conf:** Class 100 Board 60 Thtr 200 **Services:** Night porter **Parking:** 100 **Notes:** LB Civ Wed 150

ALMONDSBURY	Map 4 ST68
Gloucestershire	

Aztec Hotel & Spa

★★★★ 81% ⚜ HOTEL

THWAITES

Aztec West, BS32 4TS - **tel:** 01454 201090
email: reservations@aztechotelbristol.co.uk **web:** www.aztechotelbristol.co.uk

(for full entry see Bristol)

ALNWICK

See Embleton

ALSAGER	Map 15 SJ75
Cheshire	

Best Western Plus Manor House Hotel

★★★ 82% HOTEL

BW Best Western PLUS

Audley Road, ST7 2QQ - **tel:** 01270 884000
email: res@manorhousealsager.com **web:** www.manorhousealsager.co.uk
dir: *M6 junct 16, A500 towards Stoke-on-Trent. 1st junct signed Audley, left to Alsager, hotel 2m on left*

Manor House Hotel is peacefully located in the village of Alsager, with easy links to the M6 and major road networks. Modern refurbishment and period architecture sit comfortably together to create a stylish interior. Bedrooms are decorated in attractive colour schemes and are well equipped for both business and leisure guests. Complimentary WiFi is available throughout. Public areas include Stables bar, a large lobby lounge, and Ostler's restaurant, which is set in the oldest part of the property.

Rooms: 57 (4 family) (8 GF) 🐾 **S** £69–£109; **D** £69–£109* **Facilities:** FTV WiFi 🏊 🎯 **Conf:** Class 108 Board 82 Thtr 200 Del from £125 **Services:** Lift Night porter **Parking:** 150 **Notes:** Civ Wed 150

ALTRINCHAM	Map 15 SJ78
Greater Manchester	

Mercure Altrincham Bowden Hotel

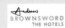

★★★ 75% HOTEL

Langham Road, Bowdon, WA14 2HT - tel: 0161 928 7121
email: enquiries@hotels-altrincham.com **web:** www.hotels-altrincham.com
dir: A556 towards Manchester, into Park Rd at lights, hotel 1m on right

Situated within easy access of Manchester and the Airport, this hotel offers comfortable and well equipped bedrooms. Public areas include the Café Bar and The Restaurant, both serving a good choice of dishes. A well-equipped leisure centre has an indoor heated pool, spa, sauna and comprehensive air-conditioned gym. There is free WiFi throughout.

Rooms: 87 (8 family) (13 GF) **Facilities:** FTV WiFi ⊛ Gym Sauna Steam room Xmas New Year **Conf:** Class 48 Board 50 Thtr 120 **Services:** Night porter **Parking:** 125 **Notes:** Civ Wed 120

Premier Inn Manchester Altrincham

BUDGET HOTEL

Manchester Road, WA14 4PH - tel: 0871 527 8738 (Calls cost 13p per minute plus your phone company's access charge) **web:** www.premierinn.com
dir: From N: M60 junct 7, A56 towards Altrincham. From S: M6 junct 19, A556 then A56 towards Sale

High quality, budget accommodation ideal for both families and business travellers. Spacious, en suite bedrooms feature tea and coffee making facilities, Freeview TV in most hotels and free WiFi. The adjacent family restaurant features a wide and varied menu.

Rooms: 43

ALVESTON	Map 4 ST68
Gloucestershire	

Alveston House Hotel

★★★ 84% ⊛ HOTEL

Davids Lane, BS35 2LA - tel: 01454 415050
email: info@alvestonhousehotel.co.uk **web:** www.alvestonhousehotel.co.uk
dir: M5 junct 14 from N or junct 16 from S, on A38

In a quiet area with easy access to the city and a short drive from both the M4 and M5, this smartly presented hotel provides an impressive combination of good service, friendly hospitality and a relaxed atmosphere. The comfortable bedrooms are well equipped for both business and leisure guests. The restaurant offers carefully prepared fresh food, and the pleasant bar and conservatory area is perfect for enjoying a pre-dinner drink.

Rooms: 29 (1 family) (6 GF) ⌒ **S** £85–£110; **D** £100–£140* **Facilities:** FTV WiFi ⅃ Beauty treatments Xmas New Year **Conf:** Class 48 Board 50 Thtr 85 Del from £130 **Parking:** 75 **Notes:** Civ Wed 75

AMBERLEY	Map 6 TQ01
West Sussex	

Amberley Castle

★★★★ ⊛⊛⊛ 🏆 COUNTRY HOUSE HOTEL

BN18 9LT - tel: 01798 831992
email: info@amberleycastle.co.uk **web:** www.amberleycastle.co.uk
dir: On B2139, off A29 between Bury & Storrington

The delightful castle hotel is idyllically set in the Sussex countryside, and boasts 900 years of history. The battlements (complete with mighty portcullis; one of the few in Europe that still works) enclose the hotel. Beyond these walls are acres of stunning parkland that feature formal gardens, koi ponds and a thatched treehouse accessed by a rope bridge. Guests can enjoy the magnificent restaurant where pre-booking is essential. Named after castles in Sussex, each of the sumptuously furnished bedrooms and suites is unique in design. Luxury amenities are provided in all rooms. Andrew Brownsword Hotels is the AA Hotel Group of the Year 2017-2018.

Rooms: 19 (5 annexe) (5 family) (5 GF) ⌒ **D** £175–£395 (incl. bkfst)*
Facilities: FTV WiFi ⅃ Putting green ⊛ ⅃ Xmas New Year **Conf:** Class 30 Board 30 Thtr 56 Del from £365 **Services:** Night porter **Parking:** 40 **Notes:** LB No children 8yrs Civ Wed 56

AMBLESIDE	Map 18 NY30
Cumbria	

See also **Elterwater**

Waterhead Hotel

English Lakes
Hotels Resorts & Venues

★★★★ 79% ⊛ TOWN HOUSE HOTEL

Lake Road, LA22 0ER - tel: 015394 32566
email: waterhead@englishlakes.co.uk **web:** www.englishlakes.co.uk
dir: A591 to Ambleside. Hotel opposite Waterhead Pier

With an enviable location opposite the bay, this well-established hotel offers contemporary and comfortable accommodation with CD/DVD players, plasma screens and internet access. There is a bar with a garden terrace overlooking the lake and a stylish restaurant serving classical cuisine with a modern twist. Staff are very attentive and friendly. Guests can enjoy full use of the leisure facilities at a nearby hotel.

Rooms: 41 (3 family) (7 GF) **Facilities:** FTV WiFi ⅃ Free use of leisure facilities at sister hotel (1m) Xmas New Year **Conf:** Class 30 Board 26 Thtr 40 **Services:** Night porter **Parking:** 43 **Notes:** Civ Wed 80

Rothay Manor

★★★★ 76% ⊛⊛ HOTEL

Rothay Bridge, LA22 0EH - tel: 015394 33605
email: hotel@rothaymanor.co.uk **web:** www.rothaymanor.co.uk
dir: Phone for directions

Originally built in 1823 for a wealthy Liverpool merchant, Rothay Manor exists today as a welcoming hotel. Perfectly located for touring the Lakes and set in its own stunning grounds, the hotel features 19 individual bedrooms. Public areas include a range of comfortable lounges and the popular restaurant where a range of imaginative dishes are provided. There are a number of dog friendly and accessible bedrooms available.

Rooms: 19 (2 family) (2 GF) ⌒ **S** £110–£130; **D** £150–£230 (incl. bkfst)*
Facilities: STV FTV WiFi ⅃ ⅃ Xmas New Year **Conf:** Board 18 Thtr 22 **Services:** Night porter **Parking:** 30 **Notes:** Closed 3-21 Jan Civ Wed 40

A

AMBLESIDE *continued*

Ambleside Salutation Hotel

PREMIER | BEST WESTERN

★★★★ 76% HOTEL

Lake Road, LA22 9BX - **tel:** 015394 32244
email: ambleside@hotelslakedistrict.com **web:** www.hotelslakedistrict.com
dir: *A591 to Ambleside, onto one-way system, Wansfell Rd into Compston Rd.*
Right at lights into village

A former coaching inn, this hotel lies squarely in the centre of Ambleside. Bedrooms are tastefully appointed and thoughtfully equipped; many boast balconies, fine views and hot tubs. Inviting public areas include an attractive restaurant and a choice of comfortable lounges for relaxing. For the more energetic there is a swimming pool and small gym, and for relaxation a spa and treatment rooms.

Ambleside Salutation Hotel

Rooms: 54 (12 annexe) (4 family) (1 GF) ✆ **S** £79–£104; **D** £132–£178 (incl. bkfst)*
Facilities: Spa WiFi ⓢ Gym Sauna Steam room Fountain spa Xmas New Year
Conf: Class 36 Board 26 Thtr 80 Del from £152 **Services:** Lift **Parking:** 54
Notes: Closed 17-18 Dec LB

See advert below

Regent Hotel

★★★ 86% HOTEL

Waterhead Bay, LA22 0ES - **tel:** 015394 32254
email: info@regentlakes.co.uk **web:** www.regentlakes.co.uk
dir: *M6 junct 36, 13m S on A591*

This attractive holiday hotel, situated close to Waterhead Bay, offers a warm welcome. Bedrooms come in a variety of styles, including three suites and five bedrooms in the garden wing. Public areas are contemporary and comfortable; the light, airy restaurant is the setting for hearty, enjoyable meals.

Rooms: 32 (2 family) (9 GF) ✆ **S** £67–£169; **D** £81–£189 (incl. bkfst) **Facilities:** FTV
WiFi ⚲ New Year **Parking:** 38

ANDOVER
Hampshire

Map 5 SU34

Esseborne Manor

★★★ 81% HOTEL

Hurstbourne Tarrant, SP11 0ER - **tel:** 01264 736444
email: info@esseborne-manor.co.uk **web:** www.esseborne-manor.co.uk
dir: *Halfway between Andover & Newbury on A343, 1m N of Hurstbourne Tarrant*

Set in two acres of well-tended gardens, this attractive manor house is surrounded by the open countryside of the North Wessex Downs. Bedrooms are delightfully individual and are split between the main house, an adjoining courtyard and separate garden cottage. There's a wonderfully relaxed atmosphere throughout, and public rooms combine elegance with comfort.

Rooms: 18 (7 annexe) (5 family) (4 GF) S £85–£112; D £112–£165 (incl. bkfst)*
Facilities: STV FTV WiFi New Year **Conf:** Class 40 Board 30 Thtr 60 Del from £150
Parking: 50 **Notes:** LB Civ Wed 100

Premier Inn Andover

BUDGET HOTEL

West Portway Industrial Estate, Joule Road, SP10 3UX - **tel:** 0871 527 8020 (Calls cost 13p per minute plus your phone company's access charge) **web:** www.premierinn.com
dir: *From A303 follow A342/A343 signs. Hotel at rdbt junct of A342 & A343 adjacent to Portway Inn Brewers Fayre*

High quality, budget accommodation ideal for both families and business travellers. Spacious, en suite bedrooms feature tea and coffee making facilities, Freeview TV in most hotels and free WiFi. The adjacent family restaurant features a wide and varied menu.

Rooms: 81

ANSTY
Warwickshire

Map 11 SP48

Macdonald Ansty Hall

★★★★ 76% HOTEL   MACDONALD HOTELS & RESORTS

Main Road, CV7 9HZ - **tel:** 0344 879 9031
email: general.ansty@macdonald-hotels.co.uk
web: www.macdonald-hotels.co.uk/anstyhall
dir: *M6 junct 2 onto B4065 signed Ansty. Hotel 1.5m on left*

Dating back to 1678, this Grade II listed Georgian house is set in eight acres of attractive grounds and woodland. The hotel enjoys a central yet tranquil location. Spacious bedrooms feature a traditional decorative style and a range of extras. Rooms are divided between the main house and the newer annexe.

Rooms: 62 (39 annexe) (4 family) (22 GF) S £59–£149; D £69–£159 (incl. bkfst)*
Facilities: FTV WiFi Xmas New Year **Conf:** Class 60 Board 60 Thtr 150 Del from £129 **Services:** Lift Night porter **Parking:** 100 **Notes:** LB Civ Wed 100

APPLEBY-IN-WESTMORLAND
Cumbria

Map 18 NY62

HIGHLY RECOMMENDED

Appleby Manor Hotel & Garden Spa

★★★★ 83% COUNTRY HOUSE HOTEL

Roman Road, CA16 6JB - **tel:** 017683 51571
email: reception@applebymanor.co.uk **web:** www.applebymanor.co.uk
dir: *M6 junct 40, A66 towards Brough. Take Appleby turn, immediately right. 0.5m to hotel*

Appleby Manor Hotel and Garden Spa is an imposing country mansion, set in extensive grounds amid stunning Cumbrian scenery. The Dunbobbin family and their experienced staff ensure a warm welcome and attentive service. Comfortable and well-presented bedrooms vary in style, but all cater well for the modern guest; some rooms benefit from having patio areas. The bar offers a wide range of malt whiskies, with the restaurant and bistro offering high-quality, award-winning food. A recent addition is the luxury Garden Spa boasting treatment rooms, hydrotherapy pool, outdoor hot tubs and thermal rooms.

Rooms: 30 (7 annexe) (9 family) (10 GF) D £129–£260 (incl. bkfst)*
Facilities: Spa FTV WiFi Putting green Steam room Sauna Salt room Experience shower Hydrotherapy pool Outdoor spa bath New Year Child facilities **Conf:** Class 25 Board 28 Thtr 38 Del from £45 **Parking:** 51 **Notes:** LB Closed 24-26 Dec Civ Wed 60

ARUNDEL
West Sussex

Map 6 TQ00

Premier Inn Arundel

BUDGET HOTEL

Crossbush Lane, BN18 9PQ - **tel:** 0871 527 8022 (Calls cost 13p per minute plus your phone company's access charge) **web:** www.premierinn.com
dir: *At junct of A27 & A284, 1m E of Arundel*

High quality, budget accommodation ideal for both families and business travellers. Spacious, en suite bedrooms feature tea and coffee making facilities, Freeview TV in most hotels and free WiFi. The adjacent family restaurant features a wide and varied menu.

Rooms: 31

Follow us on twitter
@TheAA_Lifestyle

ASCOT	Map 6 SU96
Berkshire	

INSPECTOR'S CHOICE

Coworth Park

★★★★★ ◉◉◉ COUNTRY HOUSE HOTEL

Blacknest Road, SL5 7SE - **tel:** 01344 876600 & 756784
email: reservations.CPA@dorchestercollection.com **web:** www.coworthpark.com
dir: M25 junct 13 S onto A30 Egham/Bagshot. Past Wentworth Golf Club turn right at lights onto Blacknest Rd (A329) hotel on left

Set in 240 acres of stunning parkland, Coworth Park is part of the luxury Dorchester Collection, sister to The Dorchester in London. The hotel offers luxurious guest rooms and suites, polo grounds, stables and a spa. Children are well cared for too, with a 'Kids Concierge' who can arrange a wide variety of activities for them. The hotel maintains a strong 'green' policy, as does the kitchen team where local quality suppliers are a priority. Casual dining is available in the popular Barn restaurant, which is located in a converted stable block.

Rooms: 70 (40 family) (27 GF) **D** £295–£5950 (incl. bkfst)* **Facilities:** Spa STV FTV WiFi Gym Polo Equestrian centre Archery Laser clays Falconry Duck herding Xmas New Year Child facilities **Conf:** Class 54 Board 40 Thtr 100 **Services:** Lift Night porter Air con **Parking:** 100 **Notes:** LB Civ Wed 250

Macdonald Berystede Hotel & Spa

★★★★ 80% HOTEL

Bagshot Road, Sunninghill, SL5 9JH - **tel:** 01344 623311
email: general.berystede@macdonald-hotels.co.uk
web: www.macdonald-hotels.co.uk/berystede
dir: A30, B3020 (Windmill Pub). 1.25m to hotel on left just before junct with A330

This impressive Victorian mansion, close to Ascot Racecourse, offers executive bedrooms that are spacious, comfortable and particularly well equipped. Public rooms include a cosy bar and an elegant restaurant which serves creative dishes. The impressive self-contained conference centre and spa facility appeal to both conference and leisure guests.

Rooms: 126 (61 family) (33 GF) **Facilities:** Spa STV WiFi Gym Leisure complex (thermal & beauty treatments) Outdoor garden spa Xmas New Year **Conf:** Class 220 Board 150 Thtr 330 **Services:** Lift Night porter **Parking:** 200 **Notes:** Civ Wed 300

ASHBY-DE-LA-ZOUCH	Map 11 SK31
Leicestershire	

Premier Inn Ashby De La Zouch

BUDGET HOTEL

Flagstaff Island, LE65 1DS - **tel:** 0871 527 8026 (Calls cost 13p per minute plus your phone company's access charge) **web:** www.premierinn.com
dir: M1 junct 23a, follow A42 (M42), Tamworth & Birmingham signs. Hotel at rdbt at A42 junct 13. NB for Sat Nav use LE65 1JP

High quality, budget accommodation ideal for both families and business travellers. Spacious, en suite bedrooms feature tea and coffee making facilities, Freeview TV in most hotels and free WiFi. The adjacent family restaurant features a wide and varied menu.

Rooms: 76

ASHFORD	Map 7 TR04
Kent	

Ashford International Hotel

★★★★ 80% HOTEL

Simone Weil Avenue, TN24 8UX - **tel:** 01233 219988
email: ashford@qhotels.co.uk **web:** www.qhotels.co.uk
dir: M20 junct 9, exit for Ashford/Canterbury. Left at 1st rdbt, hotel 200mtrs on left

Situated just off the M20 and with easy links to the Eurotunnel, Eurostar and ferry terminals, this hotel has been stunningly appointed. The slick, stylishly presented bedrooms are equipped with the latest amenities. Public areas include the spacious Horizons Wine Bar and Restaurant serving a competitively priced menu, and Quench Sports Bar for relaxing drinks. The Reflections leisure club boasts a pool, fully-equipped gym, spa facilities and treatment rooms.

Rooms: 179 (29 family) (57 GF) **S** £91–£141; **D** £103–£153 (incl. bkfst)* **Facilities:** Spa WiFi Gym Aroma steam room Rock sauna Feature shower Ice fountain Xmas New Year **Conf:** Class 180 Board 26 Thtr 400 Del from £135 **Services:** Lift Night porter Air con **Parking:** 400 **Notes:** Civ Wed 400

Premier Inn Ashford Central

BUDGET HOTEL

Hall Avenue, Orbital Park, TN24 0GN - **tel:** 0871 527 8030 (Calls cost 13p per minute plus your phone company's access charge) **web:** www.premierinn.com
dir: M20 junct 10 S'bound: 4th exit at rdbt. N'bound: 1st exit onto A2070 signed Brenzett. Hotel on right at next rdbt

High quality, budget accommodation ideal for both families and business travellers. Spacious, en suite bedrooms feature tea and coffee making facilities, Freeview TV in most hotels and free WiFi. The adjacent family restaurant features a wide and varied menu.

Rooms: 60

Premier Inn Ashford (Eureka Leisure Park)

BUDGET HOTEL

Eureka Leisure Park, TN25 4BN - **tel:** 0871 527 8028 (Calls cost 13p per minute plus your phone company's access charge) **web:** www.premierinn.com
dir: M20 junct 9, take 1st exit on left

Rooms: 74

Premier Inn Ashford North

BUDGET HOTEL

Maidstone Road (A20), Hothfield Common, TN26 1AP - **tel:** 0871 527 8032 (Calls cost 13p per minute plus your phone company's access charge) **web:** www.premierinn.com
dir: M20 junct 9, A20 follow Lenham signs. Hotel between Ashford & Charing

Rooms: 60

A

ASHINGTON
Northumberland — Map 21 NZ28

Premier Inn Ashington

BUDGET HOTEL

Queen Elizabeth Country Park, Woodhorn, NE63 9AT - tel: 0871 527 8034 (Calls cost 13p per minute plus your phone company's access charge) **web:** www.premierinn.com
dir: *From A1 follow signs to Morpeth then Woodhorn Colliery Museum/Ashington. Through Ashington. Hotel in Queen Elizabeth II Country Park*

High quality, budget accommodation ideal for both families and business travellers. Spacious, en suite bedrooms feature tea and coffee making facilities, Freeview TV in most hotels and free WiFi. The adjacent family restaurant features a wide and varied menu.

Rooms: 61

ATTLEBOROUGH
Norfolk — Map 13 TM09

Sherbourne House Hotel

★★★ 77% METRO HOTEL

8 Attleborough Road, NR17 2JX - tel: 01953 454363
email: stay@sherbourne-house.co.uk **web:** www.sherbourne-house.co.uk
dir: *A11 from London/Thetford towards Attleborough, through town centre, pass church on right, next left, hotel on right after 500mtrs*

Built in 1740, this fine manor house is set among beautifully landscaped gardens and is a short walk from the historic market town of Attleborough. Much of the house has been refurbished and many of the original features sympathetically restored. Bedrooms are spacious and comfortable, and there is a light-filled conservatory lounge for guests. An extensive dinner menu is available in the evenings and freshly prepared breakfasts are served in the charming breakfast room overlooking the gardens. WiFi is available throughout the property, and the hotel is ideally placed for visitors to Snetterton motor racing circuit.

Rooms: 9 (1 family) (1 GF) ☏ **S** fr £50; **D** fr £90 (incl. bkfst)* **Facilities:** FTV WiFi **Conf:** Class 18 Board 22 Thtr 30 Del from £150 **Parking:** 20

AXMINSTER
Devon — Map 4 SY29

Fairwater Head Hotel

★★★ 79% ⊛ HOTEL

Hawkchurch, EX13 5TX - tel: 01297 678349
email: stay@fairwaterheadhotel.co.uk **web:** www.fairwaterheadhotel.co.uk
dir: *From B3165 Crewkerne to Lyme Regis road, follow Hawkchurch signs*

This elegant Edwardian country house provides a perfect location for anyone looking for a peaceful break. Surrounded by extensive gardens and rolling countryside, the setting guarantees relaxation. Bedrooms are located both within the main house and the garden wing, and all provide good levels of comfort. Public areas are very appealing and include lounge areas, a bar and an elegant restaurant. Food is a highlight, with excellent local produce prepared with care and skill.

Rooms: 16 (4 annexe) (8 GF) ☏ **D** £110–£180 (incl. bkfst)* **Facilities:** FTV WiFi Library **Conf:** Class 25 Board 20 Thtr 35 Del from £125 **Parking:** 30 **Notes:** Closed Jan LB

AYLESBURY
Buckinghamshire — Map 11 SP81

Hartwell House Hotel, Restaurant & Spa
★★★★ ⊛⊛ HOTEL

Lower Hartwell, HP17 8NR - tel: 01296 747444
email: info@hartwell-house.com **web:** www.hartwell-house.com
dir: *From S: M40 junct 7, A329 to Thame, then A418 towards Aylesbury. After 6m, through Stone, hotel on left. From N: M40 junct 9 for Bicester. A41 to Aylesbury, A418 to Oxford for 2m. Hotel on right*

This beautiful, historic house is set in 90 acres of unspoilt parkland. The grand public rooms are truly magnificent, and feature many fine works of art. The service standards are very high; guests will find that the staff offer attentive and traditional hospitality without stuffiness. There is an elegant, award-winning restaurant where carefully prepared dishes use the best local produce. Bedrooms are spacious, elegant and very comfortable. Most are in the main house, but some, including suites, are in the nearby, renovated coach house, which also houses an excellent spa.

Rooms: 46 (16 annexe) (3 family) (10 GF) ☏ **S** £190–£550; **D** £300–£700 (incl. bkfst)* **Facilities:** Spa STV WiFi ⃝ ⃝ supervised ⃝ ⃝ Gym Sauna Steam rooms ♫ Xmas New Year **Conf:** Class 40 Board 40 Thtr 100 **Services:** Lift Night porter **Parking:** 91 **Notes:** No children 6yrs LB RS Xmas/New Year Residential guests only Civ Wed 120

Premier Inn Aylesbury

BUDGET HOTEL

Buckingham Road, HP19 9QL - tel: 0871 527 8036 (Calls cost 13p per minute plus your phone company's access charge) **web:** www.premierinn.com
dir: *From Aylesbury on A413 towards Buckingham. Hotel in 1m on left adjacent to lights*

High quality, budget accommodation ideal for both families and business travellers. Spacious, en suite bedrooms feature tea and coffee making facilities, Freeview TV in most hotels and free WiFi. The adjacent family restaurant features a wide and varied menu.

Rooms: 64

A

AYNHO
Northamptonshire   Map 11 SP53

Cartwright Hotel

★★★ 80% HOTEL

1-5 Croughton Road, OX17 3BE - **tel:** 01869 811885
email: cartwright@oxfordshire-hotels.co.uk **web:** www.oxfordshire-hotels.co.uk
dir: M40 junct 10, A43, B4100 to Aynho

This former coaching inn is between Banbury and Oxford, making it ideally located for visiting the many tourist attractions the area has to offer, including Blenheim Palace and the circuit at Silverstone. The hotel features individually designed bedrooms which range from double to executive, and premiere standards with flat-screen digital TVs and complimentary WiFi. Secure parking is available.

Rooms: 21 (12 annexe) (2 family) (12 GF) 🛏 **S** £95–£125; **D** £105–£150 (incl. bkfst)* **Facilities:** FTV WiFi ↘ Xmas New Year **Conf:** Class 40 Board 20 Thtr 45 Del from £125 **Parking:** 15 **Notes:** LB

BABBACOMBE

See **Torquay**

BAGSHOT
Surrey   Map 6 SU96

INSPECTOR'S CHOICE

Pennyhill Park, an Exclusive Hotel & Spa

★★★★★ @@@@ COUNTRY HOUSE HOTEL

London Road, GU19 5EU - **tel:** 01276 471774 **email:** enquiries@pennyhillpark.co.uk **web:** www.exclusive.co.uk
dir: M3 junct 3, follow signs to Camberley. On A30 between Bagshot & Camberley

This delightful country-house hotel, set in 120 acres of grounds, provides every modern comfort. The stylish bedrooms are individually designed and have impressive bathrooms. Leisure facilities include a jogging trail, a golf course and a state-of-the-art spa with a thermal sequencing experience, ozone treated swimming and hydrotherapy pools, along with a comprehensive range of therapies and treatments. In addition there is a choice of eating options, lounges and bars to relax in.

Rooms: 123 (97 annexe) (6 family) (26 GF) 🛏 **D** fr £255* **Facilities:** Spa STV WiFi ↘ 🐾 ✈ ♨ 🏊 Fishing Gym Archery Clay shooting Plunge pool Turkish steam room Rugby pitch Bike hire 🎵 Xmas New Year Child facilities **Conf:** Class 144 Board 72 Thtr 200 Del from £300 **Services:** Lift Night porter **Parking:** 500 **Notes:** LB Civ Wed 140

Premier Inn Bagshot

BUDGET HOTEL

1 London Road, GU19 5HR - **tel:** 0871 527 8040 (Calls cost 13p per minute plus your phone company's access charge) **web:** www.premierinn.com
dir: On A30 (London Rd) just before junct with A322 (Bracknell Rd). Adjacent to Cricketers Beefeater

High quality, budget accommodation ideal for both families and business travellers. Spacious, en suite bedrooms feature tea and coffee making facilities, Freeview TV in most hotels and free WiFi. The adjacent family restaurant features a wide and varied menu.

Rooms: 53

BALDOCK
Hertfordshire   Map 12 TL23

Days Inn Stevenage North - A1

AA Advertised

Baldock Extra Motorways, A1(M) Junction 10, SG7 5TR - **tel:** 01462 730598
email: stevenage.hotel@welcomebreak.co.uk **web:** www.welcomebreak.co.uk
dir: A1(M) junct 10 Baldock Extra Services

This modern, purpose built accommodation offers smartly appointed, well-equipped bedrooms, with good power showers. There is a choice of adjacent food outlets where guests may enjoy breakfast, snacks and meals.

Rooms: 62 (14 family) (30 GF) (8 smoking) **Facilities:** STV FTV WiFi ↘ **Services:** Air con **Parking:** 120

BALSALL COMMON
West Midlands   Map 10 SP27

Nailcote Hall

★★★★ 79% @ HOTEL

Nailcote Lane, Berkswell, CV7 7DE - **tel:** 024 7646 6174 **email:** info@nailcotehall.co.uk **web:** www.nailcotehall.co.uk
dir: On B4101

This 17th-century house, set in 15 acres of grounds, boasts a 9-hole championship golf course and Roman bath-style swimming pool amongst its many facilities. The bedrooms are spacious and elegantly furnished. The eating options are the fine dining restaurant where smart casual dress is required, or The Piano Bar where more informal meals are served.

Rooms: 40 (19 annexe) (2 family) (15 GF) **Facilities:** STV FTV WiFi 🏊 supervised ♨ 9 Putting green 🐾 ⛳ Gym 🎵 Xmas New Year **Conf:** Class 80 Board 44 Thtr 140 **Services:** Lift Night porter **Parking:** 200 **Notes:** Civ Wed 120

Premier Inn Balsall Common (Near NEC)

BUDGET HOTEL

Kenilworth Road, CV7 7EX - **tel:** 0871 527 8042 (Calls cost 13p per minute plus your phone company's access charge) **web:** www.premierinn.com
dir: M42 junct 6, A45 towards Coventry for 0.5m. A452 signed Leamington/Kenilworth. In 3m hotel on right

High quality, budget accommodation ideal for both families and business travellers. Spacious, en suite bedrooms feature tea and coffee making facilities, Freeview TV in most hotels and free WiFi. The adjacent family restaurant features a wide and varied menu.

Rooms: 66

B

BAMBURGH
Northumberland

Map 21 NU13

Waren House Hotel

★★★ 84% ⊛⊛ COUNTRY HOUSE HOTEL

Waren Mill, NE70 7EE - **tel:** 01668 214581 **email:** enquiries@warenhousehotel.co.uk
web: www.warenhousehotel.co.uk
dir: *2m E of A1 turn onto B1342 to Waren Mill, at T-junct turn right, hotel 100yds on right*

This delightful Georgian mansion is set in six acres of woodland and offers a welcoming atmosphere and views of the coast. The individually themed bedrooms and suites include many with large bathrooms. Good, home-cooked, AA Rosette-worthy food is served in the elegant dining room. A comfortable lounge and library are also available.

Rooms: 13 (4 annexe) (3 GF) ⌣ **Facilities:** FTV WiFi Xmas New Year **Parking:** 20
Notes: No children 14yrs

BANBURY
Oxfordshire

Map 11 SP44

HIGHLY RECOMMENDED

Best Western Plus Wroxton House Hotel

★★★ 87% ⊛⊛ HOTEL

Wroxton St Mary, OX15 6QB - **tel:** 01295 730777
email: reservations@wroxtonhousehotel.com
web: www.wroxtonhousehotel.com
dir: *M40 junct 11, A422 signed Banbury & Wroxton. Approx 3m, hotel on right on entering Wroxton*

Dating in part from 1649, this partially thatched hotel is set just off the main road. Bedrooms, either created from cottages or situated in a contemporary wing, are comfortable and well equipped with WiFi and LCD TVs. The public areas are open plan and the low-beamed Restaurant 1649 has a peaceful atmosphere for dining.

Rooms: 32 (3 annexe) (5 family) (8 GF) ⌣ S £78–£108; D £98–£128* **Facilities:** FTV WiFi ⌐ New Year **Conf:** Class 40 Board 40 Thtr 90 Del £142
Services: Night porter **Parking:** 60 **Notes:** LB Civ Wed 90

Mercure Banbury Whately Hall Hotel

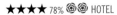

★★★ 78% HOTEL

Banbury Cross, OX16 0AN - **tel:** 01295 253261 **email:** h6633@accor.com
web: www.mercure.com
dir: *M40 junct 11, straight over 2 rdbts, left at 3rd, 0.25m to Banbury Cross, hotel on right*

Dating back to 1677, this historic inn boasts many original features such as stone passages, priests' holes and a fine wooden staircase. Spacious public areas include the oak-panelled restaurant, which overlooks the attractive well-tended gardens, a choice of lounges and a traditional bar. Smartly appointed bedrooms vary in size and style but all are thoughtfully equipped.

Rooms: 69 (6 family) (2 GF) **Facilities:** FTV WiFi Xmas New Year **Conf:** Class 40 Board 40 Thtr 120 **Services:** Lift Night porter **Parking:** 52 **Notes:** Civ Wed 120

Premier Inn Banbury (M40 Jct 11)

BUDGET HOTEL

Stroud Park, Ermont Way, OX16 4AE - **tel:** 0871 527 9458 (Calls cost 13p per minute plus your phone company's access charge) **web:** www.premierinn.com
dir: *M40 junct 11, follow Banbury signs. Keep in left lane, take slip road on left. Hotel in Stroud Park Estate on left*

High quality, budget accommodation ideal for both families and business travellers. Spacious, en suite bedrooms feature tea and coffee making facilities, Freeview TV in most hotels and free WiFi. The adjacent family restaurant features a wide and varied menu.

Rooms: 128

BARKING
Greater London

Map 6 TQ48

Premier Inn Barking

BUDGET HOTEL

Highbridge Road, IG11 7BA - **tel:** 0871 527 8048 (Calls cost 13p per minute plus your phone company's access charge) **web:** www.premierinn.com
dir: *A13 onto A406 signed Barking/Ilford. At Barking, exit at Tesco/A406 slip road. Hotel on left*

High quality, budget accommodation ideal for both families and business travellers. Spacious, en suite bedrooms feature tea and coffee making facilities, Freeview TV in most hotels and free WiFi. The adjacent family restaurant features a wide and varied menu.

Rooms: 88

BARNARD CASTLE
County Durham

Map 19 NZ01

The Morritt Country House Hotel & Spa

★★★★ 78% ⊛⊛ HOTEL

Greta Bridge, DL12 9SE - **tel:** 01833 627232 **email:** relax@themorritt.co.uk
web: www.themorritt.co.uk
dir: *From M1 (east) exit at junct 57 onto A66 westbound. From M6 (west) exit at junct 40 onto A66 eastbound. Follow signs to Greta Bridge*

In the heart of beautiful Teesdale, this 17th-century former coaching house, with connections to Dickens, is full of character and is a popular meeting place. The bar area has two amazing Dickens murals - one created in 2012 to commemorate Dickens' 200th birthday. The hotel prides itself on its traditional values, apparent in the quality of its service, locally-sourced food and individually styled rooms. Guests can enjoy pampering and treatments in the adjoining new spa.

Rooms: 26 (6 annexe) **Facilities: Conf:** Class 60 Board 40 Thtr 120

B

Ye Olde Bell Hotel & Spa

★★★★ 80% @ HOTEL

DN22 8QS - tel: 01777 705121
email: enquiries@yeoldebell-hotel.co.uk web: www.yeoldebell-hotel.co.uk
dir: A1(M) south near junct 34, exit Barnby Moor or A1(M) north exit A620 Retford. Hotel on A638 between Retford & Bawtry

This beautifully refurbished 17th-century hotel is conveniently located just off the A1 between Retford and Doncaster in the rural village of Barnby Moor. Public rooms have a wealth of original character such as traditional log fires and ornate plaster work, and there is an outside terrace also available at the front of the main bar. Restaurant 1650 features elegant wood panelling as well as a striking contemporary bar. The tastefully appointed bedrooms are furnished to a high standard and are attractively co-ordinated. All benefit from modern bathrooms. A brand new multi-million pound luxury Spa opened in 2017 with indoor/outdoor vitality pool and 10 thermal experiences including the unique 'Snowstorm'. There are also beauty treatment rooms and a hair salon. The gardens are a feature – perfect for weddings or outside entertaining in warmer weather.

Ye Olde Bell Hotel & Spa

Rooms: 59 (10 annexe) (5 family) (8 GF) ⌒ **S** £69–£130; **D** £99–£190 (incl. bkfst)*
Facilities: Spa FTV WiFi ⬙ ⬙ ⬙ Gym Hair salon Xmas New Year **Conf:** Class 100 Board 50 Thtr 250 Del from £99 **Services:** Night porter **Parking:** 200 **Notes:** LB Civ Wed 250

Tankersley Manor

★★★★ 75% HOTEL

QHOTELS
INSPIRED
BY YOU

Church Lane, S75 3DQ - tel: 01226 744700
email: tankersleymanor@qhotels.co.uk web: www.qhotels.co.uk

(for full entry see Tankersley)

B

Premier Inn Barnsley Central M1 Jct 37

BUDGET HOTEL

Gateway Plaza, Sackville Street, S70 2RD - tel: 0871 527 9204 (Calls cost 13p per minute plus your phone company's access charge) **web:** www.premierinn.com
dir: *M1 junct 37, A628 (Dodworth Rd) signed Barnsley. In approx 1m 2nd exit at rdbt into Shambles St, car park entrance on left*

High quality, budget accommodation ideal for both families and business travellers. Spacious, en suite bedrooms feature tea and coffee making facilities, Freeview TV in most hotels and free WiFi. The adjacent family restaurant features a wide and varied menu.

Rooms: 110

BARNSTAPLE	Map 3 SS53
Devon	

The Imperial Hotel

★★★★ 76% HOTEL

Taw Vale Parade, EX32 8NB - tel: 01271 345861
email: reservations@brend-imperial.co.uk **web:** www.brend-imperial.co.uk
dir: *M5 junct 27/A361 to Barnstaple. Follow town centre signs, passing Tesco. Straight on at next 2 rdbts. Hotel on right*

This smart and attractive hotel is pleasantly located at the centre of Barnstaple and overlooks the River Taw. Staff are friendly and offer attentive service. The comfortable bedrooms are of various sizes; some have balconies and many enjoy

Find out more about AA Rosettes
– page 13

river views. Afternoon tea is available in the lounge, and the appetising cuisine is freshly prepared.

The Imperial Hotel

Rooms: 63 (8 annexe) (9 family) (4 GF) ★ **S** £90–£105; **D** £110–£270*
Facilities: FTV WiFi ♭ Leisure facilities at sister hotel Xmas New Year **Conf:** Class 40 Board 30 Thtr 60 **Services:** Lift Night porter **Parking:** 80 **Notes:** LB Civ Wed 50

See advert opposite

The Royal & Fortescue Hotel

★★★ 84% HOTEL

Boutport Street, EX31 1HG - tel: 01271 342289
email: reservations@royalfortescue.co.uk **web:** www.royalfortescue.co.uk
dir: *From A361 onto Barbican Rd signed town centre, right into Queen St, left into Boutport St, hotel on left*

Formerly a coaching inn, this friendly and convivial hotel is conveniently located in the centre of town. Bedrooms vary in size and all are decorated and furnished to a consistently high standard. In addition to the formal restaurant, guests can take snacks in the popular coffee shop or dine more informally in The Bank, a bistro and café bar.

Rooms: 48 (4 family) (4 GF) ★ **S** £65–£85; **D** £80–£160* **Facilities:** FTV WiFi ♭ Leisure facilities available at sister hotel Xmas New Year **Conf:** Class 25 Board 25 Thtr 25 **Services:** Lift Night porter **Parking:** 40 **Notes:** LB

B

BARNSTAPLE *continued*

The Barnstaple Hotel

★★★ 82% HOTEL

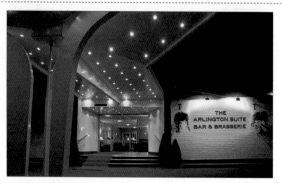

Braunton Road, EX31 1LE - **tel:** 01271 376221
email: reservations@barnstaplehotel.co.uk **web:** www.barnstaplehotel.co.uk
dir: *Outskirts of Barnstaple on A361*

This well-established hotel enjoys a convenient location on the edge of town.
Bedrooms are spacious and well equipped, many with access to a balcony
overlooking the outdoor pool and garden. A wide choice is offered from various
menus based on local produce, served in the Brasserie Restaurant. There is an
extensive range of leisure and conference facilities.

Rooms: 60 (4 family) (17 GF) **S** £72–£122; **D** £79–£139* **Facilities:** FTV WiFi ⌨ ⏱
✈ Gym Beauty treatment room Saunas Chill out sanctuary Xmas New Year Child
facilities **Conf:** Class 100 Board 50 Thtr 250 **Services:** Night porter **Parking:** 250
Notes: LB Civ Wed 150

The Park Hotel

★★★ 78% HOTEL

Taw Vale, EX32 9AE - **tel:** 01271 372166
email: reservations@parkhotel.co.uk **web:** www.parkhotel.co.uk
dir: *A361 to Barnstaple, 0.5m from town centre. Opposite Rock Park*

Enjoying views across the park and within easy walking distance of the town centre,
this modern hotel offers a choice of bedrooms in both the main building and the

Garden Court, just across the car park. Public rooms are open-plan in style and the friendly staff offer attentive service in a relaxed atmosphere.

The Park Hotel

Rooms: 49 (16 annexe) (3 family) (10 GF) ⚓ **S** £55–£155; **D** £75–£165*
Facilities: FTV WiFi ⌂ Leisure facilities available at sister hotel Xmas New Year
Conf: Class 50 Board 30 Thtr 80 **Services:** Lift Night porter **Parking:** 80 **Notes:** LB Civ Wed 100

See advert opposite

Premier Inn Barnstaple

BUDGET HOTEL

Whiddon Drive, off Eastern Avenue, EX32 8RY - tel: 0871 527 8052 (Calls cost 13p per minute plus your phone company's access charge) **web:** www.premierinn.com
dir: *Exit A361 (North Devon Link Rd) towards Barnstaple. Right at Portmore rdbt*

High quality, budget accommodation ideal for both families and business travellers. Spacious, en suite bedrooms feature tea and coffee making facilities, Freeview TV in most hotels and free WiFi. The adjacent family restaurant features a wide and varied menu.

Rooms: 71

BARROW-IN-FURNESS	Map 18 SD26
Cumbria	

Abbey House Hotel & Gardens

★★★★ 80% ⊛ HOTEL

Abbey Road, LA13 0PA - tel: 01229 838282
email: enquiries@abbeyhousehotel.com **web:** www.abbeyhousehotel.com
dir: *From A590 follow signs for Furness General Hospital & Furness Abbey. Hotel approx 100yds on left*

Set in 14 acres of private gardens and woodland, this red stone building is a local landmark. A redevelopment project has seen striking results; a sharp and contemporary style sits well with the original architectural features and charm of the building. Bedrooms are stylish and well equipped. Service is personal and food is a highlight of any stay. Business and function facilities also impress.

Rooms: 61 (4 annexe) (6 family) (2 GF) ⚓ **S** £56–£125; **D** £56–£125 (incl. bkfst)*
Facilities: STV FTV WiFi ⌂ Beauty treatment room Xmas New Year **Conf:** Class 120 Board 80 Thtr 300 Del from £135 **Services:** Lift Night porter **Parking:** 100 **Notes:** Civ Wed 120

Premier Inn Barrow-in-Furness

BUDGET HOTEL

North Road, LA14 2PW - tel: 0871 527 9470 (Calls cost 13p per minute plus your phone company's access charge) **web:** www.premierinn.com
dir: *M6 junct 36, A590. In 3m take slip road signed Barrow-in-Furness. Follow signs for Barrow-In-Furness & A590. At rdbt 2nd exit signed Walney Island & A590. Approx 0.5m, hotel on right*

High quality, budget accommodation ideal for both families and business travellers. Spacious, en suite bedrooms feature tea and coffee making facilities, Freeview TV in most hotels and free WiFi. The adjacent family restaurant features a wide and varied menu.

Rooms: 80

BARTON	Map 18 SD53
Lancashire	

Barton Grange Hotel

★★★★ 78% HOTEL

Garstang Road, PR3 5AA - tel: 01772 862551
email: stay@bartongrangehotel.com **web:** www.bartongrangehotel.co.uk
dir: *M6 junct 32, follow Garstang (A6) signs for 2.5m. Hotel on right*

Situated close to the M6, this modern, stylish hotel benefits from extensive public areas that include leisure facilities with a swimming pool, sauna and gym. Comfortable, well-appointed bedrooms include executive rooms and family rooms, as well as attractive accommodation in an adjacent cottage. The unique Walled Garden Bistro offers all-day eating.

Rooms: 51 (8 annexe) (8 family) (4 GF) ⚓ **S** £81–£136; **D** £92–£147 (incl. bkfst)*
Facilities: STV WiFi ⌂ ⊛ Gym Sauna ♫ Xmas New Year **Conf:** Class 100 Board 80 Thtr 300 **Services:** Lift Night porter **Parking:** 250 **Notes:** LB Civ Wed 300

BASILDON	Map 6 TQ78
Essex	

Premier Inn Basildon (East Mayne)

BUDGET HOTEL

Felmores, East Mayne, SS13 1BW - tel: 0871 527 8054 (Calls cost 13p per minute plus your phone company's access charge) **web:** www.premierinn.com
dir: *M25 junct 29 , A127 towards Southend, take A132 S signed Basildon & Wickford at Neverdon exit. Hotel on left*

High quality, budget accommodation ideal for both families and business travellers. Spacious, en suite bedrooms feature tea and coffee making facilities, Freeview TV in most hotels and free WiFi. The adjacent family restaurant features a wide and varied menu.

Rooms: 74

Premier Inn Basildon (Festival Park)

BUDGET HOTEL

Festival Leisure Park, Pipps Hill Road South, SS14 3WB - tel: 0871 527 8056 (Calls cost 13p per minute plus your phone company's access charge) **web:** www.premierinn.com
dir: *M25 junct 9, A217 towards Basildon. Take A17. Hotel just off A1235 adjacent to David Lloyd Leisure Club*

Rooms: 82

B

BASILDON *continued*

Premier Inn Basildon South

BUDGET HOTEL

High Road, Fobbing, SS17 9NR - tel: 0871 527 8060 (Calls cost 13p per minute plus your phone company's access charge) **web:** www.premierinn.com
dir: M2 junct 30/31, A13 towards Southend. 10m to Five Bells Rdbt junct with A176. Right into Fobbing High Rd. Hotel on left

Rooms: 61

BASINGSTOKE
Hampshire   **Map 5 SU65**

INSPECTOR'S CHOICE

Tylney Hall Hotel

★★★★ ◉◉ ♡ HOTEL

Ridge Lane, RG27 9AZ - tel: 01256 764881
email: sales@tylneyhall.com **web:** www.tylneyhall.com

(for full entry see Rotherwick)

HIGHLY RECOMMENDED

Oakley Hall Hotel

★★★★ 90% ◉◉ COUNTRY HOUSE HOTEL

Rectory Road, Oakley, RG23 7EL - tel: 01256 783350
email: enquiries@oakleyhall-park.com **web:** www.oakleyhall-park.com
dir: M3 junct 7, follow Basingstoke signs. In 500 yrds before lights turn left onto A30 towards Oakley, immediately right onto unclass road towards Oakley. In 3m left at T-junct into Rectory Road. Left onto B3400. Hotel signed first on left

An impressive drive leads to this country house which benefits from delightful country views across north Hampshire. Built in 1795, it was once owned by the Bramston family who were friends of Jane Austen. An ideal wedding venue, Oakley Hall also has an excellent range of conference facilities, and is a great place to spend a relaxing leisure break. The bedrooms are spacious; many are located in the impressively restored courtyard and are particularly well equipped; there is also the delightful Garden Cottage. The stylish 1795 Bar & Lounge and the Glasshouse Restaurant offer contemporary surroundings in which to relax and enjoy the excellent food and friendly service.

Rooms: 47 (18 annexe) (14 family) (23 GF) ⬧ **S** fr £179; **D** fr £179 (incl. bkfst)*
Facilities: FTV WiFi ⬧ ⬧ Clay pigeon shooting Archery In room pamper treatments Xmas New Year **Conf:** Class 82 Board 50 Thtr 300 Del from £199 **Services:** Lift Night porter Air con **Parking:** 100 **Notes:** LB Civ Wed 100

Find out more
about the AA's Hotel rating scheme on pages 12–13

Audleys Wood Hotel

★★★★ 81% ◉◉ HOTEL

Alton Road, RG25 2JT - tel: 01256 817555 & 0845 072 7405 (Calls cost 5p per minute plus your phone company's access charge)
email: audleyswood@handpicked.co.uk
web: www.handpickedhotels.co.uk/hotels/audleys-wood-hotel-basingstoke
dir: M3 junct 6. From Basingstoke take A339 towards Alton, hotel on right

A long sweeping drive leads to what was once a Victorian hunting lodge. This traditional country-house hotel offers bedrooms with flat-screen TVs and MP3 player connections. Smart and traditional public areas have log fires, and the dining options include the award-winning Simonds Room and a contemporary conservatory with a small minstrels' gallery.

Rooms: 72 (23 family) (34 GF) **Facilities:** STV FTV WiFi ⬧ HL ⬧ Xmas New Year **Conf:** Class 80 Board 60 Thtr 200 **Services:** Night porter **Parking:** 100 **Notes:** Civ Wed 100

The Hampshire Court Hotel

★★★★ 79% HOTEL

Centre Drive, Chineham, RG24 8FY - tel: 01256 319700
email: hampshirecourt@qhotels.co.uk **web:** www.qhotels.co.uk
dir: Off A33 Reading Rd, behind Chineham Shopping Centre, via Great Binfields Rd

This hotel boasts a range of smart, comfortable and stylish bedrooms, and leisure facilities that are unrivalled locally. Facilities include indoor and outdoor tennis courts, two swimming pools, a gym and a number of treatment rooms.

Rooms: 90 (6 family) ⬧ **Facilities:** Spa STV WiFi ⬧ HL ⬧ ⬧ Gym Steam room Sauna Exercise studios Xmas New Year **Conf:** Class 800 Board 60 Thtr 1500 **Services:** Lift Night porter **Parking:** 220 **Notes:** Civ Wed 1500

Apollo Hotel

★★★★ 78% HOTEL

Aldermaston Roundabout, RG24 9NU - tel: 01256 796700
email: enquiries@apollohotels.com **web:** www.apollohotels.com
dir: M3 junct 6. Follow ring road N towards Newbury. Follow A340 Aldermaston signs. Hotel on rdbt, 5th exit into Popley Way for access

This modern hotel provides well-equipped accommodation and spacious public areas, appealing to both the leisure and business guest. Facilities include a smartly appointed leisure club, a business centre, along with a good choice of formal and informal eating in two restaurants; Vespers is the fine dining option.

Rooms: 125 (49 GF) ⬧ **S** £79–£189; **D** £89–£199 (incl. bkfst)* **Facilities:** Spa FTV WiFi ⬧ ⬧ Gym Sauna Steam room Spa pool New Year **Conf:** Class 196 Board 30 Thtr 255 Del from £125 **Services:** Lift Night porter **Parking:** 200 **Notes:** LB Civ Wed 150

Premier Inn Basingstoke Central

BUDGET HOTEL

Basingstoke Leisure Park, Worting Road, RG22 6PG - tel: 0871 527 8062 (Calls cost 13p per minute plus your phone company's access charge) **web:** www.premierinn.com
dir: M3 junct 6, A339 towards Newbury. A340 follow brown Leisure Park signs. At next rdbt right onto B3400 (Churchill Way West). Right on next rdbt into Leisure Park. Hotel adjacent to Spruce Goose Beefeater

High quality, budget accommodation ideal for both families and business travellers. Spacious, en suite bedrooms feature tea and coffee making facilities, Freeview TV in most hotels and free WiFi. The adjacent family restaurant features a wide and varied menu.

Rooms: 99

B

Premier Inn Basingstoke Town Centre Hotel

BUDGET HOTEL

Victoria Street, RG21 3BT - tel: 0871 527 9518 (Calls cost 13p per minute plus your phone company's access charge) **web:** www.premierinn.com
dir: *M3 junct 6 signed Basingstoke. Then follow A30 & Alton signs. At next rdbt take 3rd exit to Fairfield, left into New Road. Hotel on left after Caston's car park*

Rooms: 81

BASLOW	Map 16 SK27
Derbyshire	

Cavendish Hotel

★★★★ 80% ◉◉ HOTEL

Church Lane, DE45 1SP - tel: 01246 582311
email: info@cavendish-hotel.net **web:** www.cavendish-hotel.net
dir: *M1 junct 29/A617 W to Chesterfield & A619 to Baslow. Hotel in village centre, off main road*

This stylish property, dating back to the 18th century, is delightfully situated on the outskirts of the Chatsworth Estate. All rooms enjoy far-reaching views across the estate and benefit from the slightly elevated position. Bedrooms are elegantly appointed and offer a host of thoughtful amenities, while bathrooms have been refurbished and have Temple Spa toiletries. Comfortable public areas are furnished with period pieces and paintings from the Duke's extensive art collection. Guests have a choice of dining in either the informal conservatory Garden Room or the elegant Gallery Restaurant. A sun terrace overlookings the croquet lawn and estate beyond.

Rooms: 24 (3 family) (2 GF) ☎ S £165–£340; D £215–£340* **Facilities:** FTV WiFi Putting green Fishing offsite can be arranged Xmas New Year **Conf:** Class 8 Board 18 Thtr 25 **Services:** Night porter **Parking:** 50 **Notes:** LB RS 25 Dec evening Restaurant closed to non residents Civ Wed 50

Fischer's Baslow Hall

★★★ ◉◉◉ HOTEL

Calver Road, DE45 1RR - tel: 01246 583259
email: reservations@fischers-baslowhall.co.uk **web:** www.fischers-baslowhall.co.uk
dir: *On A623 between Baslow & Calver*

Located at the end of a chestnut tree-lined drive on the edge of the Chatsworth Estate, in marvellous gardens, this beautiful Derbyshire manor house offers sumptuous accommodation and facilities. Staff provide very friendly and personally attentive service. There are two styles of bedroom available - traditional, individually-themed rooms in the main house, and spacious, more contemporary-styled rooms with Italian marble bathrooms in the Garden House. The cuisine is excellent and may prove the highlight of any stay.

Rooms: 11 (5 annexe) (4 GF) ☎ S £155–£195; D £230–£295 (incl. bkfst)*
Facilities: FTV WiFi ⅃ **Conf:** Board 15 Thtr 20 Del from £255 **Parking:** 40
Notes: No children 8yrs LB Closed 25-26 Dec RS 24 & 31 Dec Closed in evening Civ Wed 38

B

INSPECTOR'S CHOICE

Armathwaite Hall Hotel and Spa
★★★★ ◉◉ COUNTRY HOUSE HOTEL

CA12 4RE - tel: 017687 76551
email: reservations@armathwaite-hall.com **web:** www.armathwaite-hall.com
dir: M6 junct 40/A66 to Keswick rdbt then A591 signed Carlisle. 8m to Castle Inn
junct, turn left. Hotel 300yds

Enjoying fine views over Bassenthwaite Lake, this impressive mansion, dating
from the 17th century, is situated amid 400 acres of deer park. The comfortably
furnished bedrooms and well-appointed bathrooms are complemented by a
choice of public rooms that have many original features. The spa is an
outstanding asset to the leisure facilities; it offers an infinity pool, thermal
suite, sauna, state-of-the-art gym, treatments, exercise classes and a hot tub
overlooking the landscaped gardens.

Rooms: 46 (8 family) (8 GF) ✿ **Facilities:** Spa STV WiFi ⓩ supervised ⌇ Fishing
⌇ Gym Archery Clay shooting Quad & mountain bikes Falconry Xmas New Year
Conf: Class 50 Board 60 Thtr 200 **Services:** Lift Night porter **Parking:** 100
Notes: Civ Wed 150

Best Western Plus Castle Inn
★★★★ 76% HOTEL

Best Western **PLUS**

CA12 4RG - tel: 017687 76401
email: reservations@castleinncumbria.co.uk **web:** www.castleinncumbria.co.uk
dir: A591 to Carlisle, pass Bassenthwaite village on right. Hotel on left of T-junct

Overlooking some of England's highest fells and Bassenthwaite Lake, this fine hotel
is ideally situated for exploring Bassenthwaite, Keswick and the Lake District.
The accommodation, extensive leisure facilities, and friendly service are certainly
strong points here. Ritson's Restaurant and Laker's Lounge offer a range of dishes
using locally sourced meats from the fells; managed, sustainable fish stocks; and
international and seasonal ingredients.

Rooms: 42 (4 family) (9 GF) ✿ **Facilities:** FTV WiFi ⓩ Putting green ⌇ Gym Sauna
Steam room Xmas New Year **Conf:** Class 108 Board 60 Thtr 200 **Services:** Night
porter **Parking:** 120 **Notes:** Civ Wed 180

HIGHLY RECOMMENDED

The Pheasant
★★★ 87% ◉◉ HOTEL

CA13 9YE - tel: 017687 76234
email: info@the-pheasant.co.uk **web:** www.the-pheasant.co.uk
dir: Midway between Keswick & Cockermouth, signed from A66

Enjoying a rural setting, within well-tended gardens, on the western side of
Bassenthwaite Lake, this friendly 500-year-old inn is steeped in tradition.
The attractive oak-panelled bar has seen few changes over the years, and
features log fires and a great selection of malt whiskies. The individually
decorated bedrooms are stylish and thoughtfully equipped.

Rooms: 15 (2 annexe) (2 GF) ✿ **Facilities:** FTV WiFi ⌇ New Year **Parking:** 40
Notes: No children 12yrs Closed 25 Dec

Ravenstone Lodge Country House Hotel
★★★ 84% ◉ COUNTRY HOUSE HOTEL

CA12 4QG - tel: 01768 776629
email: enquiries@ravenstonelodge.co.uk **web:** www.ravenstonelodge.co.uk
dir: 5m N of Keswick on A591

Close to both Keswick and Bassenthwaite, set in rolling countryside, this small
country house hotel offers warm, genuine hospitality along with high quality food.
Bedrooms are well equipped and appointed, benefitting from a rolling
refurbishment programme. Outside garden seating or the large conservatory offer
unrestricted views of the picture postcard location.

Rooms: 9 (1 family) (2 GF) ✿ **D** £60–£180 (incl. bkfst)* **Facilities:** FTV WiFi ⌇
Parking: 15

B

BATH
Somerset   Map 4 ST76

See also **Colerne & Hinton Charterhouse**

INSPECTOR'S CHOICE

The Bath Priory Hotel, Restaurant & Spa
★★★★★ ◎◎◎ HOTEL

BROWNSWORD
THE HOTELS

Weston Road, BA1 2XT - **tel:** 01225 331922
email: info@thebathpriory.co.uk **web:** www.thebathpriory.co.uk
dir: *Adjacent to Victoria Park*

The Bath Priory Hotel is a country house set in four acres of beautiful grounds. It features a luxury spa, and the Priory Restaurant that delivers food derived from modern European cuisine; created from the very finest local produce and seasonal fruit, vegetable and herbs from the property's own garden. Opening onto the leafy gardens, the Mediterranean-style spa features an indoor heated swimming pool with a pool-side sauna and modern steam pod. Luxury beauty treatments are also available by appointment. Luxurious bedrooms have elegant decor and free WiFi access. All rooms feature period furniture and spacious en suite bathrooms with fluffy bathrobes and designer toiletries. Andrew Brownsword Hotels is the AA Hotel Group of the Year 2017-2018.

Rooms: 33 (6 annexe) (2 family) (1 GF) ⚑ D £215–£915* **Facilities:** Spa STV FTV WiFi ⊗ ✴ Steam pod Sauna Xmas New Year **Conf:** Class 24 Board 16 Thtr 24 **Services:** Night porter **Parking:** 40 **Notes:** LB Civ Wed 70

INSPECTOR'S CHOICE

The Royal Crescent Hotel & Spa
★★★★★ ◎◎◎ HOTEL

RELAIS & CHATEAUX

6 Royal Crescent, BA1 2LS - **tel:** 01225 823333
email: info@royalcrescent.co.uk **web:** www.royalcrescent.co.uk
dir: *From A4 at junction of London Rd and George St turn up Lansdowne Hill. 2nd left into Bennett St, into The Circus, 2nd exit into Brock St, merge into Royal Crescent*

The Royal Crescent Hotel is set in a number of houses in Bath's famous Royal Crescent, and is one of the country's most interesting and historic places to stay. Bedrooms offer a range of suites and sizes, all with individual style and character; many have views across the city, and all are most comfortably appointed. Public rooms make the most of the character of the houses and are styled in keeping with the elegance of the period. The hotel has a superb spa and range of leisure facilities, as well as a number of meeting rooms and private dining venues. The bar and Dower House restaurant offer the very best of contemporary dining and are not to be missed. Ingredients are sourced locally where possible, and elegantly presented by Head Chef David Campbell and his team.

Rooms: 45 (8 family) (8 GF) ⚑ D £295–£1410 (incl. bkfst)* **Facilities:** Spa STV FTV WiFi ⊳ ⊗ ✴ Gym Xmas New Year **Conf:** Class 18 Board 30 Thtr 60 Del from £365 **Services:** Lift Night porter Air con **Parking:** 41 **Notes:** Civ Wed 50

Silver Stars
The AA Silver Star rating denotes a Hotel that we highly recommend. They have a superior level of quality within their star rating, high standards of hospitality, service and cleanliness.

B

BATH *continued*

The Gainsborough Bath Spa

★★★★★ 88% @@@ HOTEL

Beau Street, BA1 1QY - **tel:** 01225 358888 **web:** www.thegainsboroughbathspa.co.uk
dir: *From St James Parade into Lower Borough Walls, left into Bilbury Lane*

The latest 5-star hotel in this grand city, The Gainsborough Bath Spa offers guests, whether on business or pleasure, a full range of facilities including a world class thermae Bath House Spa Village utilising natural Bath spa waters. Public areas, bed and bathrooms are luxuriously furnished with high quality decor, furniture and fittings throughout. The friendly and attentive team do all they can to accommodate guest requirements. Meals are served in the smart and stylish Dan Moon at The Gainsborough Restaurant. Valet parking is available though pre-booking is advised.

Rooms: 99 (10 family) (2 GF) ⮡ **D** fr £285* **Facilities:** Spa STV FTV WiFi ⏲ Gym Xmas New Year **Conf:** Board 24 Thtr 60 Del from £395 **Services:** Night porter **Parking:** 20 **Notes:** Civ Wed 60

Macdonald Bath Spa

★★★★★ 80% @@ HOTEL

Sydney Road, BA2 6JF - **tel:** 0344 879 9106
mail: sales.bathspa@macdonald-hotels.co.uk **web:** www.macdonaldhotels.co.uk/bathspa
dir: *A4, left onto A36 at 1st lights. Right at lights after pedestrian crossing left into Sydney Place. Hotel 200yds on right*

A delightful Georgian mansion set in seven acres of pretty landscaped grounds, just a short walk from the many and varied delights of the city centre. A timeless elegance pervades the gracious public areas and bedrooms. Facilities include a popular leisure club, The Vellore Restaurant, and a number of meeting rooms. Ample parking on site.

Rooms: 131 (3 family) (17 GF) ⮡ **Facilities:** Spa STV FTV WiFi ⏲ HL ⏲ ⏲ ⮡ Gym Thermal suite Outdoor hydro pool Whirlpool Xmas New Year **Conf:** Class 100 Board 50 Thtr 130 **Services:** Lift Night porter Air con **Parking:** 160 **Notes:** Civ Wed 130

Bailbrook House Hotel

★★★★ 83% @@ HOTEL

Eveleigh Avenue, London Road West, BA1 7JD - **tel:** 01225 855100 & 0845 072 7515
(Calls cost 7p per minute plus your phone company's access charge)
email: reception.bailbrook@handpicked.co.uk **web:** www.bailbrookhouse.co.uk
dir: *M4 junct 18/A46, at bottom of long hill take slip road to city centre. At rdbt take 1st exit, London Rd. Hotel 200mtrs on left*

Over the last few years, Bailbrook House Hotel has seen a dramatic rebuilding programme, and offers superior accommodation, ideally situated on the edge of Bath, set in attractive grounds with ample parking. It is perfectly placed to avoid parking and driving in the city, but close enough to allow ease of access. Bedrooms are spacious and extremely well appointed. There are two dining options and a range of meeting and conference facilities.

Rooms: 94 (81 annexe) (2 family) (27 GF) ⮡ **S** £99–£464; **D** £109–£474 (incl. bkfst) **Facilities:** STV FTV WiFi ⮡ Gym New Year **Conf:** Class 72 Board 40 Thtr 160 Del from £145 **Services:** Lift Night porter Air con **Parking:** 120 **Notes:** Civ Wed 120

Francis Hotel Bath – MGallery

★★★★ 76% HOTEL

Queen Square, BA1 2HH - **tel:** 01225 424105
email: h6636@accor.com **web:** www.francishotel.com
dir: *M4 junct 18/A46 to Bath junct. 3rd exit onto A4, right into George St, left into Gay St then into Queen Sq. Hotel on left*

This unique and distinctive hotel occupies seven of the original 18th-century townhouses that make up the south side of the centrally located Queen Square, with all of Bath's main attractions within walking distance. In each bedroom, guests can expect a comfortable bed with Egyptian cotton linen, a bathrobe, luxury toiletries, flat screen TV, air-conditioning, a safe, and complimentary WiFi. The Regency-inspired No. 10 Bar and Emily's Tea Room offer welcoming settings for the enjoyment of the hotel's signature cocktails and menus (including an extensive selection of afternoon teas). A short stroll through the hotel takes guests into Raymond Blanc's 'Brasserie Blanc'. There are a number of meeting rooms and private dining venues for any special occasion or gathering.

Rooms: 98 (3 GF) ⮡ **Facilities:** STV WiFi ⮡ HL Xmas **Conf:** Class 40 Board 30 Thtr 80 **Services:** Lift Night porter Air con **Parking:** 40 **Notes:** LB Civ Wed 100

Abbey Hotel

★★★★ 75% HOTEL

1 North Parade, BA1 1LF - **tel:** 01225 461603
email: katiesimmonds@kaleidescope.co.uk **web:** www.abbeyhotelbath.co.uk
dir: *M4 junct 18/A46 for approx 8m. At rdbt right onto A4 for 2m. Once past Morrissons stay in left lane & turn left at lights. Over bridge & right at lights. Over rdbt & right at lights. Hotel at end of road*

Perfectly located in the heart of Bath, just a two minute stroll from the famous Abbey, this popular hotel offers a relaxing welcome with professional, helpful service in contemporary surroundings. The impressive Brasserie offers an excellent range of the highest quality dishes with something to suit all tastes. In the warmer months, outdoor seating on the front terrace is the ideal location for coffee or lunch.

Rooms: 62 (7 family) (3 GF) ⮡ **S** fr £89; **D** fr £99* **Facilities:** WiFi ⮡ Xmas New Year **Conf:** Class 10 Board 16 Thtr 30 Del from £185 **Services:** Lift Night porter **Notes:** LB Civ Wed 60

B

The Queensberry Hotel

★★★ ◉◉◉ ⚘ HOTEL

Russell Street, BA1 2QF - tel: 01225 447928
email: reservations@thequeensberry.co.uk **web:** www.thequeensberry.co.uk
dir: *100mtrs from the Assembly Rooms*

This charming family-run hotel, situated in a quiet residential street near the city centre, consists of four delightful townhouses. The spacious bedrooms offer deep armchairs, marble bathrooms and a range of modern comforts. Sumptuously furnished sitting rooms add to The Queensberry's appeal and allow access to the very attractive and peaceful walled gardens. The Olive Tree is a stylish restaurant that combines Georgian opulence with contemporary simplicity. Innovative menus are based on best quality ingredients and outstanding cooking. Valet parking proves a useful service.

Rooms: 29 (2 family) (4 GF) ⚘ **D** £99–£420 **Facilities:** FTV WiFi ⓘ **Conf:** Class 12 Board 25 Thtr 35 Del from £225 **Services:** Lift Night porter **Parking:** 6

Haringtons Hotel

★★★ 81% METRO HOTEL

8-10 Queen Street, BA1 1HE - tel: 01225 461728
email: post@haringtonshotel.co.uk **web:** www.haringtonshotel.co.uk
dir: *A4 into George St, into Milsom St. 1st right into Quiet St, 1st left into Queen St*

Dating back to the 18th century, this hotel is situated in the heart of the city and provides all the expected modern facilities and comforts. Although a full dinner in a restaurant is not offered, the comfortably furnished lounge is light and airy and open throughout the day for light snacks and refreshments. A warm welcome is assured from the proprietors and staff, making this a delightful place to stay.

Rooms: 13 (3 family) ⚘ **S** £85–£125; **D** £89–£205 (incl. bkfst)* **Facilities:** STV FTV WiFi **Conf:** Class 10 Board 12 Thtr 18 **Services:** Night porter **Parking:** 11

Premier Inn Bath

BUDGET HOTEL

James Street West, BA1 2BX - tel: 0871 527 9454 (Calls cost 13p per minute plus your phone company's access charge) **web:** www.premierinn.com
dir: *M4 junct 18, A46 towards city centre. In approx 7m 3rd exit A4 towards city centre. 1.5m left into Gay St, through Queen Sq, straight ahead into Charles St. At 2nd lights left into James St West. Hotel 200mtrs on right*

High quality, budget accommodation ideal for both families and business travellers. Spacious, en suite bedrooms feature tea and coffee making facilities, Freeview TV in most hotels and free WiFi. The adjacent family restaurant features a wide and varied menu.

Rooms: 108

BATTLE Map 7 TQ71
East Sussex

The Powder Mills Hotel

★★★ 82% ◉◉ HOTEL

Powdermill Lane, TN33 0SP - tel: 01424 775511
email: reservations@thepowdermills.com **web:** www.powdermillshotel.com
dir: *M25 junct 5, A21 towards Hastings. At Johns Cross take A2100 to Battle. Pass Abbey on right, 1st right into Powdermill Ln. 1m, hotel on right*

A delightful 18th-century country-house hotel set amidst 150 acres of landscaped grounds with lakes and woodland. The individually decorated bedrooms are tastefully furnished and thoughtfully equipped; some rooms have sun terraces with lovely views over the lake. Public rooms include a cosy lounge bar, music room, drawing room, library, restaurant and conservatory.

Rooms: 48 (18 annexe) (5 GF) ⚘ **S** £95–£120; **D** £140–£350 (incl. bkfst)*
Facilities: FTV WiFi ⓘ ⚘ ⚘ Fishing Jogging trails Woodland walks Clay pigeon shooting Archery Xmas New Year **Conf:** Class 50 Board 16 Thtr 250 Del from £155 **Services:** Night porter **Parking:** 101 **Notes:** LB Civ Wed 100

Brickwall Hotel

★★★ 80% HOTEL

The Green, TN33 0QA - tel: 01424 870253
email: info@brickwallhotel.com **web:** www.brickwallhotel.com
dir: *A21 on B2244 at top of Sedlescombe Green*

This is a well-maintained Tudor house, which is situated in the heart of a pretty village overlooking the green. The spacious public rooms feature a lovely wood-panelled restaurant with a wealth of oak beams, a choice of lounges and a smart bar. Bedrooms are pleasantly decorated and some have garden views.

Rooms: 24 (2 family) (17 GF) ⚘ **S** £65–£90; **D** £100–£140 (incl. bkfst)*
Facilities: FTV WiFi ⓘ ⚘ Xmas New Year **Conf:** Class 40 Board 30 Thtr 30 **Parking:** 40 **Notes:** LB

B

BEAMINSTER
Dorset   Map 4 ST40

BridgeHouse
★★★ 82% ◎◎ HOTEL

3 Prout Bridge, DT8 3AY - tel: 01308 862200
email: enquiries@bridge-house.co.uk **web:** www.bridge-house.co.uk
dir: *A3066 to Beaminster, hotel 100yds from town square*

Dating back to the 13th century, Bridge House offers friendly and attentive service. The stylish bedrooms feature finest Italian cotton linens, flat-screen TVs and WiFi. There are five types of room to choose from, including four-poster and coach house rooms. Smartly presented public areas include the Georgian dining room and medieval lounge with inglenook fireplace and bar. There's also additional dining in The Sun Room, which backs onto the alfresco eating area under a canopy overlooking the ancient walled garden.

Rooms: 13 (4 annexe) (2 family) (4 GF) ⌕ **S** £95–£150; **D** £119–£250 (incl. bkfst) **Facilities:** FTV WiFi ⌕ Xmas New Year **Conf:** Class 14 Board 10 Thtr 24 Del from £185 **Services:** Night porter **Parking:** 20 **Notes:** Civ Wed 100

BEANACRE
Wiltshire   Map 4 ST96

INSPECTOR'S CHOICE

Beechfield House
★★★★ ◎◎ COUNTRY HOUSE HOTEL

SN12 7PU - tel: 01225 703700
email: reception@beechfieldhouse.co.uk **web:** www.beechfieldhouse.co.uk
dir: *M4 junct 17, A350 S, bypass Chippenham, towards Melksham. Hotel on left in Beanacre*

This is a charming, privately-owned hotel set within eight acres of beautiful grounds that has its own arboretum. Bedrooms are individually styled and include four-poster rooms, and ground-floor rooms in the coach house. Relaxing public areas are comfortably furnished and there is a beauty salon with a range

of pampering treatments available. At dinner there is a very good selection of carefully prepared dishes with an emphasis on seasonal and local produce.

Beechfield House

Rooms: 24 (7 family) (4 GF) **S** fr £100; **D** fr £125 (incl. bkfst)* **Facilities:** FTV WiFi ⌕ ⌕ ⌕ Beauty treatment room Xmas New Year **Conf:** Class 60 Board 36 Thtr 80 **Services:** Night porter **Parking:** 70 **Notes:** LB Civ Wed 70

BEAULIEU
Hampshire   Map 5 SU30

HIGHLY RECOMMENDED

The Montagu Arms Hotel
★★★★ 85% ◎◎◎ ⌕ HOTEL

(PRIDE OF BRITAIN HOTELS logo)

Palace Lane, SO42 7ZL - tel: 01590 612324
email: reservations@montaguarmshotel.co.uk **web:** www.montaguarmshotel.co.uk
dir: *M27 junct 2, follow signs for Beaulieu. In Dibden Purlieu right at rdbt. Hotel on left in Beaulieu*

Situated at the heart of this charming village and surrounded by glorious New Forest scenery, the Montagu Arms dates back to 1742, and still retains the character of a traditional country house. The individually designed bedrooms include some with four-posters. Public rooms include a choice of two dining options: the informal Monty's brasserie serving home-cooked classics, and the stylish, award-winning Terrace Restaurant. Much produce comes from the kitchen garden project which saw a derelict piece of land to the rear transformed to produce organic fruit, vegetables and herbs plus free-range eggs from the hens. In warmer weather there is a sheltered alfresco eating area overlooking the pretty terraced garden. Complimentary use of leisure and spa facilities is available to guests at a sister hotel six miles away.

Rooms: 22 (3 family) ⌕ **S** £139–£159; **D** £159–£199 (incl. bkfst)* **Facilities:** FTV WiFi ⌕ Complimentary use of spa in Brockenhurst Xmas New Year **Conf:** Class 45 Board 30 Thtr 60 Del from £186 **Services:** Night porter **Parking:** 86 **Notes:** LB Civ Wed 100

B

Beaulieu Hotel

 NEW FOREST HOTELS

★★★ 82% ⊛ HOTEL

Beaulieu Road, SO42 7YQ - **tel:** 023 8029 3344
email: beaulieu@newforesthotels.co.uk **web:** www.newforesthotels.co.uk
dir: M27 junct 1, A337 towards Lyndhurst. Left at lights, through Lyndhurst, right onto B3056, hotel in 3m

Located in the heart of the beautiful New Forest National Park and close to Beaulieu Road railway station, this popular, small hotel provides an ideal base for exploring the area. Once a coaching inn, the hotel now particularly welcomes families. Bedrooms, all with free WiFi and flat-screen TVs, range from cosy Keeper rooms to Crown rooms which also have four-posters and iPod docking stations. The relaxing Exbury Restaurant has doors that lead out onto the patio area and the landscaped gardens, and alfresco eating is possible in the summer.

Rooms: 35 (14 annexe) (5 family) (4 GF) ⟡ **S** £50–£119; **D** £99–£179 (incl. bkfst)*
Facilities: FTV WiFi ⟲ HL ⊛ Steam room Xmas New Year Child facilities **Conf:** Class 100 Board 100 Thtr 250 Del from £132 **Services:** Lift **Parking:** 60 **Notes:** LB Civ Wed 200

The Master Builder's at Buckler's Hard

 Hillbrooke QUIRKY LUXURY

★★★ 81% ⊛ HOTEL

Buckler's Hard, SO42 7XB - **tel:** 01590 616253
email: enquiries@themasterbuilders.co.uk **web:** www.themasterbuilders.co.uk
dir: M27 junct 2, follow Beaulieu signs. At T-junct left onto B3056, 1st left to Buckler's Hard. Hotel 2m on left before village

A tranquil historic riverside is the backdrop for this delightful property. The main house bedrooms are full of historical features and are of individual design, and in addition there are some bedrooms in the newer wing. Public areas include a popular bar and guest lounge, while the grounds are ideal for alfresco dining in the summer months. Award-winning cuisine is served in the stylish dining room.

Rooms: 26 (18 annexe) (4 family) (8 GF) **Facilities:** FTV WiFi ⟲ Xmas New Year **Conf:** Class 30 Board 20 Thtr 40 **Services:** Night porter **Parking:** 40 **Notes:** LB Civ Wed 100

BECCLES	Map 13 TM48
Suffolk	

Waveney House Hotel

★★★ 81% HOTEL

Puddingmoor, NR34 9PL - **tel:** 01502 712270
email: enquiries@waveneyhousehotel.co.uk **web:** www.waveneyhousehotel.co.uk
dir: From A146 onto Common Lane North, left into Pound Rd, left into Ravensmere, right onto Smallgate, right onto Old Market, continue to Puddingmoor

Waveney House is an exceptionally well presented, privately-owned hotel situated by the River Waveney on the edge of this busy little market town. The stylish public rooms include a smart lounge bar and a contemporary-style restaurant with views over the river. All of the rooms have individual decor, and second-floor rooms include vaulted oak-beamed rafters. Some also enjoy picturesque River Waveney and Waveney Marsh views, and two bridal suites are available. The bar menu is sure to include something for everyone, and meals can be taken on the Riverside Terrace.

Rooms: 12 (3 family) ⟡ **Facilities:** FTV WiFi Xmas New Year **Conf:** Class 100 Board 50 Thtr 160 **Services:** Night porter **Parking:** 45 **Notes:** Civ Wed 80

BEDFORD	Map 12 TL04
Bedfordshire	

Barns Hotel

 CLASSIC BRITISH HOTELS

★★★★ 74% HOTEL

Cardington Rd, MK44 3SA - **tel:** 01234 270044
email: reservations@barnshotelbedford.co.uk **web:** www.barnshotelbedford.co.uk
dir: M1 junct 13, A421, approx 10m to A603 Sandy/Bedford exit, hotel on right at 2nd rdbt

A tranquil location on the outskirts of Bedford, friendly staff and well-equipped bedrooms all combine to make this a good choice. Cosy day rooms and two informal bars add to the hotel's appeal, while large windows in the restaurant make the most of the view over the river. The original barn houses the conference and function suite.

Rooms: 49 (18 GF) ⟡ **Facilities:** WiFi Free use of local leisure centre (1m) Xmas New Year **Conf:** Class 40 Board 40 Thtr 120 **Services:** Night porter **Parking:** 90 **Notes:** Civ Wed 90

The Bedford Swan Hotel

★★★★ 72% HOTEL

The Embankment, MK40 1RW - **tel:** 01234 346565
email: info@bedfordswanhotel.co.uk **web:** www.bedfordswanhotel.co.uk
dir: Towards Bedford - A421 or A1M/A428

This historic hotel successfully combines original features with modern comforts. The bedrooms ooze style and quality, and the needs of the modern traveller are well catered for. The River Room Restaurant offers a varied choice of freshly prepared dishes. The hotel also offers meeting and function rooms, spa facilities and secure parking.

Rooms: 113 (10 family) (12 smoking) **Facilities:** Spa STV FTV WiFi ⟲ ⊛ Xmas New Year **Conf:** Class 40 Board 60 Thtr 250 **Services:** Lift Night porter Air con **Parking:** 80 **Notes:** Civ Wed 250

Premier Inn Bedford (Priory Marina)

 Premier Inn

BUDGET HOTEL

Priory Country Park, Barkers Lane, MK41 9DJ - **tel:** 0871 527 8066 (Calls cost 13p per minute plus your phone company's access charge) **web:** www.premierinn.com
dir: M1 junct 13, A421, A6, A428 signed Cambridge. Cross River Ouse, right at next rdbt into Barkers Lane. Follow Priory Country Park signs. Hotel adjacent to Priory Marina Beefeater

High quality, budget accommodation ideal for both families and business travellers. Spacious, en suite bedrooms feature tea and coffee making facilities, Freeview TV in most hotels and free WiFi. The adjacent family restaurant features a wide and varied menu.

Rooms: 57

Premier Inn Bedford South (A421)

BUDGET HOTEL

Marsh Leys, Kempston, MK42 7DN - **tel:** 0871 527 9410 (Calls cost 13p per minute plus your phone company's access charge) **web:** www.premierinn.com
dir: See website for detailed directions

Rooms: 60

B

BELTON
Lincolnshire
Map 11 SK93

Belton Woods
★★★★ 77% HOTEL

QHOTELS
INSPIRED BY YOU

NG32 2LN - tel: 01476 593200
email: beltonreception@qhotels.co.uk **web:** www.qhotels.co.uk
dir: A1 to Gonerby Moor Services. B1174 towards Great Gonerby. At top of hill turn left towards Manthorpe/Belton. At T-junct turn left onto A607. Hotel 0.25m on left

Beautifully located amidst 475 acres of picturesque countryside, this is a destination venue for lovers of sport, especially golf, as well as a relaxing executive retreat for seminars. Comfortable and well-equipped accommodation complements the elegant and spacious public areas, which provide a good choice of drinking, dining and relaxing options.

Rooms: 136 (136 family) (68 GF) ☎ **S** £85–£175; **D** £99–£189 (incl. bkfst)*
Facilities: Spa FTV WiFi ⌨ HL ✆ supervised ⚓ 45 Putting green ☁ ⛳ Gym Squash Outdoor activity centre ♪ Xmas New Year **Conf:** Class 160 Board 80 Thtr 270 Del from £139 **Services:** Lift Night porter **Parking:** 350 **Notes:** LB Civ Wed 100

BEMBRIDGE
Isle of Wight
Map 5 SZ68

Bembridge Coast Hotel
★★★ 80% HOTEL

WARNERLEISUREHOTELS
We're all grown up

Fishermans Walk, PO35 5TH - tel: 01983 873931 **web:** www.warnerleisurehotels.co.uk
dir: A3055 Ryde to Sandown, approx 1.5m, left at lights into Carpenter's Rd to St Helens. At mini-rdb 2nd exit onto A3395 signed Bembridge. In Bembridge follow one-way system to right, left after bakery into Forelands Rd. 1m, left into Lane End Rd. Follow to end, right to hotel entrance

This hotel occupies a delightfully peaceful location on the east coast of the Isle of Wight in 23-acre grounds. The accommodation is comfortable, and there are a number of rooms with sea views for which a small supplementary charge applies. A full activities itinerary ensures that guests can make the most of what the hotel, and this beautiful island, has to offer. The helpful reservations team can also arrange ferry bookings from the UK mainland. Please note that this is an adults-only (over 21 years) hotel.

Rooms: 258 (30 annexe) (76 GF) ☎ **S** £50–£125; **D** £100–£250 (incl. bkfst & dinner)* **Facilities:** Spa FTV WiFi HL ✆ supervised Putting green ⛳ Gym Tropicarium Archery Rifle shooting Crossbow Indoor & outdoor bowls ♪ Xmas New Year **Services:** Lift Night porter **Parking:** 154

BERWICK-UPON-TWEED
Northumberland
Map 21 NT95

Queens Head
★★★ 86% ◉ SMALL HOTEL

Sandgate, TD15 1EP - tel: 01289 307852
email: info@queensheadberwick.co.uk **web:** www.queensheadberwick.co.uk
dir: A1 towards centre & town hall, into High St. Right at bottom to Hide Hill

The Queens Head is a small hotel situated in the town centre, close to the old walls of this former garrison town. Bedrooms provide many thoughtful extras as

standard. Dining remains a strong aspect with a carte menu that offers an impressive choice of tasty, freshly prepared dishes served in the comfortable lounge or dining room.

Rooms: 6 (1 family) ☎ **Facilities:** STV FTV WiFi ⌨ **Services:** Night porter
Notes: Closed 26 Dec & 1 Jan

BEVERLEY
East Riding of Yorkshire
Map 17 TA03

Best Western Lairgate Hotel
★★★ 72% HOTEL

 Best Western.

30/32 Lairgate, HU17 8EP - tel: 01482 882141
email: lairgate@bestwestern.co.uk **web:** www.bestwestern.co.uk
dir: A63 towards town centre. Hotel 220yds on left, follow one-way system

Located just off the market square, this pleasing Georgian hotel has been appointed to offer stylish accommodation. Bedrooms are elegant and well equipped, and public rooms include a comfortable lounge, a lounge bar, and restaurant with a popular sun terrace.

Rooms: 30 (1 family) (8 GF) ☎ **Facilities:** FTV WiFi ♪ New Year **Conf:** Class 40 Board 30 Thtr 80 **Services:** Night porter **Parking:** 18 **Notes:** Closed 26 Dec & 1 Jan RS 25 Dec No accommodation

Premier Inn Beverley Town Centre
BUDGET HOTEL

Premier Inn

Flemingate Centre, HU17 0NQ - tel: 0871 527 9490 (Calls cost 13p per minute plus your phone company's access charge) **web:** www.premierinn.com
dir: From N: From York on A1079, at rdbt onto A1174, follow Flemingate Centre Car Park signs. From S: M62 junct 38, B1230. 7m, left into Wold Rd. 1m, right into Walkington. Left into Coppleflat Ln, to Killingwoldgraves. At rdbt 3rd exit onto A1174, follow Flemingate Centre Car Park signs

High quality, budget accommodation ideal for both families and business travellers. Spacious, en suite bedrooms feature tea and coffee making facilities, Freeview TV in most hotels and free WiFi. The adjacent family restaurant features a wide and varied menu.

Rooms: 80

BEWDLEY
Worcestershire
Map 20 SO77

Mercure Kidderminster Hotel
★★★★ 69% HOTEL

Mercure
HOTELS

Habberley Road, DY12 1LA - tel: 01299 406402 & 0844 815 9033 (Calls cost 7p per minute plus your phone company's access charge)
email: info@mercurekidderminster.co.uk **web:** www.mercurekidderminster.co.uk
dir: A456 towards Kidderminster to ring road, follow signs to Bewdley. Pass Safari Park then exit A456/Town Centre, take sharp right after 200yds onto B4190, hotel 400yds on right

This 19th-century property is set in 20 acres of neat landscaped grounds in the Worcestershire countryside, close to West Midland Safari Park. The bedrooms are modern and well equipped; some rooms have great views of the grounds.
Public rooms include a choice of lounges and the brasserie restaurant; the property also boasts great leisure facilities that include a coffee shop, hairdressers and a 25 metre swimming pool.

Rooms: 44 (9 family) (17 GF) ☎ **Facilities:** FTV WiFi ⌨ ✆ supervised ☁ Gym Beauty treatment room Sauna Steam room Spa bath **Conf:** Class 150 Board 80 Thtr 450 **Services:** Night porter **Parking:** 150 **Notes:** Civ Wed 350

B

BEXHILL
East Sussex
Map 6 TQ70

The Cooden Beach Hotel

★★★ 81% HOTEL

Cooden Beach, TN39 4TT - **tel:** 01424 842281
email: rooms@thecoodenbeachhotel.co.uk **web:** www.thecoodenbeachhotel.co.uk
dir: A259 towards Bexhill. Signed at rdbt in Little Common Village. Hotel at end of road in Cooden, just past railway station

This privately owned hotel is situated in private gardens which have direct access to the beach. With a train station within walking distance the location is perfectly suited for both business and leisure guests. Bedrooms are comfortably appointed, and public areas include a spacious restaurant, lounge, bar and leisure centre with swimming pool.

Rooms: 41 (8 annexe) (10 family) (4 GF) **Facilities:** FTV WiFi ⏃ Gym Sauna Steam room Spa bath Beauty treatment room Xmas New Year **Conf:** Class 40 Board 40 Thtr 150 **Services:** Night porter **Parking:** 60 **Notes:** Civ Wed 160

BEXLEYHEATH
Greater London
Map 6 TQ47

Premier Inn London Bexleyheath

BUDGET HOTEL

51 Albion Road, DA6 7AR - **tel:** 0871 527 9562 (Calls cost 13p per minute plus your phone company's access charge) **web:** www.premierinn.com
dir: From M25 follow sings for M1 & M11. Take A2(W) exit towards London (SE & C)/Bexleyheath). Merge onto A2, take A223 signed Bexley/Bexleyheath Town Centre/A220. At rdbt take 1st exit into Bourne Rd, left into Albion Rd (A207). At rdbt 3rd exit, hotel on left

High quality, budget accommodation ideal for both families and business travellers. Spacious, en suite bedrooms feature tea and coffee making facilities, Freeview TV in most hotels and free WiFi. The adjacent family restaurant features a wide and varied menu.

Rooms: 92

BIBURY
Gloucestershire
Map 5 SP10

Swan Hotel

★★★★ 77% HOTEL

COTSWOLD
INNS & HOTELS

GL7 5NW - **tel:** 01285 740695
email: info@swanhotel.co.uk **web:** www.cotswold-inns-hotels.co.uk
dir: 9m S of Burford A40 onto B4425. 6m N of Cirencester A4179 onto B4425

This hotel, built in the 17th century as a coaching inn, is set in peaceful and picturesque surroundings. It provides well-equipped and smartly presented accommodation, including four luxury cottage suites set just outside the main hotel. The elegant public areas are comfortable and have feature fireplaces. There is a choice of dining options to suit all tastes.

Rooms: 22 (4 annexe) (1 family) **D** fr £99 (incl. bkfst)* **Facilities:** FTV WiFi ⏃ Xmas New Year **Conf:** Class 50 Board 32 Thtr 80 **Services:** Lift Night porter **Parking:** 22 **Notes:** Civ Wed 100

BICESTER
Oxfordshire
Map 11 SP52

Premier Inn Bicester

BUDGET HOTEL

Oxford Road, OX26 1BT - **tel:** 0871 527 9394 (Calls cost 13p per minute plus your phone company's access charge) **web:** www.premierinn.com
dir: M40 junct 9, A41 towards Bicester. 1.5m, hotel on left adjacent to Brewers Fayre

High quality, budget accommodation ideal for both families and business travellers. Spacious, en suite bedrooms feature tea and coffee making facilities, Freeview TV in most hotels and free WiFi. The adjacent family restaurant features a wide and varied menu.

Rooms: 84

BIDEFORD
Devon
Map 3 SS42

The Royal Hotel

Brend Hotels

★★★ 75% HOTEL

Barnstaple Street, EX39 4AE - **tel:** 01237 472005
email: reservations@royalbideford.co.uk **web:** www.royalbideford.co.uk
dir: At eastern end of old Bideford Bridge

A quiet and relaxing hotel, The Royal is set near the river within a five-minute walk of the busy town centre and the quay. The bright, well maintained public areas retain much of the charm and style of the hotel's 17th-century origins, particularly in the wood-panelled Kingsley Suite. Bedrooms are well equipped and comfortable. Meals and lounge snacks are delicious.

Rooms: 32 (2 family) (2 GF) **S** £60–£150; **D** £80–£170* **Facilities:** FTV WiFi ⏃ Xmas New Year **Conf:** Class 100 Board 100 Thtr 100 **Services:** Lift Night porter **Parking:** 70 **Notes:** LB Civ Wed 130

BIDEFORD *continued*

Durrant House Hotel

★★★ Ⓐ HOTEL

Heywood Road, Northam, EX39 3QB - **tel:** 01237 472361
email: info@durranthousehotel.com **web:** www.durranthousehotel.com
dir: *A39 to Bideford, over New Torridge Bridge, right at rdbt, hotel 500yds on right*

This large hotel offers bedrooms with Italian-marble bathrooms, and all include a hospitality tray, hairdryer, TV, clock radio and an iron with ironing board; superior rooms have wonderful views of the Torridge estuary and Taw Valley, plus rain showers, sofas and luxury toiletries. The fine dining, oak-panelled Olive Tree Restaurant offers dishes based on locally sourced produce.

Rooms: 125 (20 family) ↖ **S** fr £45; **D** fr £70 (incl. bkfst)* **Facilities:** Spa FTV WiFi ⮱ Gym Sauna Sun shower Pool table 🎵 Xmas New Year **Conf:** Class 100 Board 80 Thtr 350 **Services:** Lift Night porter **Parking:** 100 **Notes:** Civ Wed 200

Find out more

about the AA's Hotel rating scheme on pages 12–13

BILDESTON
Suffolk
Map 13 TL94

HIGHLY RECOMMENDED

The Bildeston Crown

★★★ 88% ◉◉ HOTEL

104-106 High Street, IP7 7EB - **tel:** 01449 740510
email: reception@thebildestoncrown.co.uk **web:** www.thebildestoncrown.co.uk
dir: *A12 junct 31, B1070 towards Hadleigh. At T-junct left onto A1141, right onto B1115. Hotel 0.5m*

The Bildeston Crown is a delightful Grade II former coaching inn situated in a peaceful village location just a short drive from the historic town of Lavenham. The public areas feature beams, exposed brickwork and oak floors, with contemporary style decor. There is a choice of bars, a lounge and a restaurant. The individually designed bedrooms, including a romantic four-poster room, have well co-ordinated fabrics and modern facilities including internet access.

Rooms: 12 ↖ **S** £70–£100; **D** £80–£150 (incl. bkfst)* **Facilities:** STV FTV WiFi Xmas New Year **Conf:** Class 25 Board 16 Thtr 40 **Services:** Lift Night porter **Parking:** 30 **Notes:** LB

BILLINGHAM
County Durham
Map 19 NZ47

INSPECTOR'S CHOICE

Wynyard Hall Hotel

★★★★ ◉◉ HOTEL

Wynyard, TS22 5NF - **tel:** 01740 644811
email: reception@wynyardhall.co.uk **web:** www.wynyardhall.co.uk
dir: *A19, A1027 towards Stockton. At rdbt take B1274 (Junction Rd). At next rdbt take A177 (Durham Rd). Right onto Wynyard Rd signed Wolviston. Left into estate*

Drive through the gates, over the lion bridge, and Wynyard Hall will immediately impress with its grandeur and elegance. The opulent public areas are as much a feature of the property as are the grounds and gardens. The individually designed bedrooms and suites are stunning, with a combination of modern and period style furniture. The elegant, award-winning Duke of Wellington restaurant is also impressive. The Essential Time Treatment Suite offers relaxing therapies and beauty treatments. As a wedding venue the hall has options for a civil ceremony, or a religious service in the chapel, followed by a memorable reception.

Rooms: 24 (5 annexe) (1 family) (3 GF) ↖ **D** £195–£260 (incl. bkfst)*
Facilities: Spa FTV WiFi ⮱ Clay pigeon shooting Archery Hawk walk Boot camp Walled garden Farmshop Xmas New Year **Conf:** Class 680 Board 100 Thtr 1000 Del from £135 **Services:** Lift Night porter **Parking:** 500 **Notes:** LB Civ Wed 150

BILSBORROW
Lancashire
Map 18 SD53

Premier Inn Preston North

BUDGET HOTEL

Garstang Road, PR3 0RN - **tel:** 0871 527 8912 (Calls cost 13p per minute plus your phone company's access charge) **web:** www.premierinn.com
dir: *4m from M6 junct 32 on A6 towards Garstang. 7m from Preston*

High quality, budget accommodation ideal for both families and business travellers. Spacious, en suite bedrooms feature tea and coffee making facilities, Freeview TV in most hotels and free WiFi. The adjacent family restaurant features a wide and varied menu.

Rooms: 42

B

Mercure Bradford, Bankfield Hotel

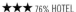

★★★ 76% HOTEL

Bradford Road, BD16 1TU - tel: 01274 519300 & 0844 815 9004 (Calls cost 7p per minute plus your phone company's access charge)
email: info@mercurebradford.co.uk web: www.mercurebradford.co.uk
dir: *From M62 junct 26 onto M606, at rdbt follow signs for A650 Skipton/Keighley, hotel 2m from Shipley*

This striking gothic-style mansion house is set in landscaped gardens and is a short walk from the River Aire. The rural setting is peaceful, yet the hotel is also convenient for Bradford and Leeds. The hotel is understandably a popular wedding venue and also caters well for corporate guests, with extensive meeting facilities available in a designated conference centre. Free WiFi access is provided throughout the hotel.

Rooms: 103 (8 family) Facilities: FTV WiFi Conf: Class 200 Board 80 Thtr 350 Services: Lift Night porter Parking: 350 Notes: Civ Wed 350

Days Inn London Stansted Airport - M11

AA Advertised

Birchanger Services, M11 Motorway, CM23 5QZ - tel: 01279 656477
email: daysinnlsa@welcomebreak.co.uk web: www.welcomebreak.co.uk
dir: *M11 junct 8*

This modern building offers accommodation in smart, spacious and well-equipped bedrooms, suitable for families and business travellers, and all with en suite bathrooms. Continental breakfast is available and other refreshments may be taken at the nearby family restaurant.

Rooms: 60 (12 family) (29 GF) (8 smoking) Facilities: FTV WiFi Services: Night porter Parking: 60

Premier Inn Birkenhead Town Centre

BUDGET HOTEL

Conway Street, CH41 5AP - tel: 0871 527 9630 (Calls cost 13p per minute plus your phone company's access charge)
dir: *M53 junct 5, follow Birkenhead, A41 & New Chester Rd signs. Straight on at 3 rdbts. Keep left towards A41/New Ferry Bypass. Keep right, follow signs for Wallasey/All Docks. Under flyover, left into Market St. 1st left into Hamilton St. Hotel on right*

High quality, budget accommodation ideal for both families and business travellers. Spacious, en suite bedrooms feature tea and coffee making facilities, Freeview TV in most hotels and free WiFi. The adjacent family restaurant features a wide and varied menu.

Rooms: 67

Premier Inn Wirral (Greasby)

BUDGET HOTEL

Greasby Road, Greasby, CH49 2PP - tel: 0871 527 9176 (Calls cost 13p per minute plus your phone company's access charge) web: www.premierinn.com
dir: *9m from Liverpool city centre. 2m from M53 junct 2. Just off B5139*

Rooms: 30

See also **Bromsgrove, Lea Marston, Oldbury & Sutton Coldfield (Royal)**

Hotel du Vin & Bistro Birmingham

★★★★ 81% TOWN HOUSE HOTEL

Church Street, B3 2NR - tel: 0121 794 3005 & 0844 736 4250 (Calls cost 5p per minute plus your phone company's access charge)
email: info@birmingham.hotelduvin.com web: www.hotelduvin.com
dir: *M6 junct 6/A38(M) to city centre, over flyover. Keep left & exit at St Chads Circus signed Jewellery Quarter. At lights & rdbt take 1st exit, follow signs for Colmore Row, opposite cathedral. Right into Church St, across Barwick St. Hotel on right*

The former Birmingham Eye Hospital has become a chic and sophisticated hotel. The stylish, high-ceilinged rooms, all with a wine theme, are luxuriously appointed and feature stunning bathrooms, sumptuous duvets and Egyptian cotton sheets. The Bistro offers relaxed dining and a top-notch wine list, while other attractions include a champagne bar, a wine boutique and a health club.

Rooms: 66 S £89–£189; D £99–£199 (incl. bkfst)* Facilities: Spa STV FTV WiFi Gym Steam room Sauna Plunge shower Xmas New Year Conf: Class 40 Board 40 Thtr 84 Del from £143 Services: Lift Night porter Air con Notes: LB Civ Wed 84

Macdonald Burlington Hotel

★★★★ 75% HOTEL

Burlington Arcade, 126 New Street, B2 4JQ - tel: 0344 879 9019
email: events.burlington@macdonald-hotels.co.uk
web: www.macdonaldhotels.co.uk/our-hotels/macdonald-burlington-hotel/
dir: *M6 junct 6, A38, follow city centre signs*

The Burlington's original Victorian grandeur - the marble and iron staircases and the high ceilings - blend seamlessly with modern facilities. Bedrooms are equipped to a good standard and public areas include a stylish bar and coffee lounge. The Berlioz Restaurant specialises in innovative dishes using fresh produce.

Rooms: 114 (6 family) Facilities: FTV WiFi HL New Year Conf: Class 200 Board 80 Thtr 500 Services: Lift Night porter Air con Notes: Closed 24–26 Dec Civ Wed 400

Novotel Birmingham Centre

NOVOTEL
HOTELS & RESORTS

★★★★ 75% HOTEL

70 Broad Street, B1 2HT - tel: 0121 643 2000
email: h1077@accor.com web: www.novotel.com
dir: *M6 junct 6, A38(M) Aston Expressway, A456 towards Kidderminster*

This large, modern, purpose-built hotel benefits from an excellent city centre location, with the bonus of secure parking. Bedrooms are spacious, modern and well equipped especially for business users; four rooms have facilities for less able guests. Public areas include the Garden Brasserie, function rooms and a fitness suite with sauna and steam room.

Rooms: 148 (148 family) Facilities: WiFi Gym Fitness room Cardiovascular equipment Sauna Steam room New Year Conf: Class 120 Board 90 Thtr 300 Services: Lift Parking: 53

B

BIRMINGHAM *continued*

Malmaison Birmingham
★★★★ 73% @ HOTEL

1 Wharfside Street, The Mailbox, B1 1RD - **tel:** 0121 246 5000
email: birmingham@malmaison.com **web:** www.malmaison.com
dir: *M6 junct 6, A38 towards Birmingham. Hotel within The Mailbox, signed from A38*

The 'Mailbox' development, of which this stylish and contemporary hotel is a part, incorporates the very best in fashionable shopping outlets, an array of restaurants and ample parking. The air-conditioned bedrooms are stylishly decorated and feature comprehensive facilities. Public rooms include a contemporary bar and brasserie which prove a hit with guests and locals alike. Gymtonic, and a Petit Spa offering rejuvenating treatments are also available.

Rooms: 192 ⬥ **Facilities:** Spa STV FTV WiFi ⬥ Gym Sauna Steam room ♫
Conf: Class 40 Board 24 Thtr 150 **Services:** Lift Night porter Air con
Notes: LB Civ Wed 120

Hallmark Hotel Birmingham Strathallan
★★★★ 72% HOTEL

225 Hagley Road, Edgbaston, B16 9RY - **tel:** 0330 028 3410
email: strathallan@hallmarkhotels.co.uk **web:** www.hallmarkhotels.co.uk
dir: *From A38 follow signs for ICC into Broad St, towards Five Ways island, take underpass to Hagley Rd. Hotel 0.5m*

Located just a few minutes from the city's central attractions and with the benefit of excellent parking, this hotel provides a range of comfortable and well-equipped bedrooms. A modern lounge bar and contemporary restaurant offer a good range of dining options.

Rooms: 135 (36 family) ⬥ **Facilities:** STV FTV WiFi ⬥ Gym Xmas New Year
Conf: Class 90 Board 50 Thtr 170 **Services:** Lift Night porter **Parking:** 120

Best Western Westley Hotel
★★★ 81% HOTEL

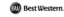 Best Western.

80-90 Westley Road, B27 7UJ - **tel:** 0121 706 4312
email: reservations@westley-hotel.co.uk **web:** www.westley-hotel.co.uk
dir: *A41 signed Birmingham on Solihull by-pass, to Acocks Green. At rdbt, 2nd exit B4146 Westley Rd. Hotel 200yds on left*

Situated in the city suburbs and conveniently located for the N.E.C. and the airport, this friendly hotel provides well-equipped, smartly presented bedrooms. In addition to the main restaurant, there is also a lively bar and brasserie together with a large function room.

Rooms: 37 (11 annexe) (3 family) (3 GF) **S** £39–£109; **D** £49–£139* **Facilities:** STV FTV WiFi ⬥ New Year **Conf:** Class 80 Board 50 Thtr 200 Del from £145
Services: Night porter **Parking:** 150 **Notes:** LB Civ Wed 180

Edgbaston Palace Hotel
★★★ 75% HOTEL

198-200 Hagley Road, Edgbaston, B16 9PQ - **tel:** 0121 452 1577
email: enquiries@edgbastonpalacehotel.com **web:** www.edgbastonpalacehotel.com
dir: *M5 junct 3 N, A456 for 4.3m. Hotel on right*

Dating back to the 19th century, this Grade II listed Victorian property has bedrooms that are modern, well appointed and offer good comfort levels.

The hospitality is warm, personal and refreshing. Supervised children under 18 are welcome.

Rooms: 48 (21 annexe) (3 family) (16 GF) **Facilities:** FTV WiFi **Conf:** Class 70 Board 60 Thtr 200 **Services:** Night porter **Parking:** 70 **Notes:** Civ Wed

Great Barr Hotel & Conference Centre
★★★ 68% HOTEL

Pear Tree Drive, Newton Road, B43 6HS - **tel:** 0121 357 1141
email: sales@thegreatbarrhotel.com **web:** www.thegreatbarrhotel.com
dir: *M6 junct 7, at Scott Arms x-rds right towards West Bromwich (A4010) Newton Rd. Hotel 1m on right*

This busy hotel, situated in a leafy residential area, is particularly popular with business clients; the hotel has excellent, state-of-the-art training and seminar facilities. There is a traditional oak-panelled bar and formal restaurant, and bedrooms are appointed to a good standard with the expected amenities.

Rooms: 92 (6 family) ⬥ **S** £49–£75; **D** £79–£95 **Facilities:** STV WiFi ⬥ **Conf:** Class 90 Board 60 Thtr 200 Del from £95 **Services:** Night porter **Parking:** 200 **Notes:** RS BH (restaurant may close, continental breakfast only may apply) Civ Wed 200

Holiday Inn Express Birmingham - South A45
BUDGET HOTEL

1270 Coventry Road, Yardley, B25 8BS - **tel:** 0121 289 3333
email: reservations@hiex-birmingham.co.uk **web:** www.hiexpressbirminghamsouth.co.uk
dir: *A45 Coventry*

A modern hotel ideal for families and business travellers. Fresh and uncomplicated, the spacious rooms include Sky TV, power shower and tea and coffee-making facilities. Continental buffet breakfast is included in the room rate; other meals may be taken at the nearby family pub or restaurant.

Rooms: 83 ⬥ **Conf:** Board 16 Thtr 24

Premier Inn Birmingham Broad St Canal Side
BUDGET HOTEL

20 Bridge Street, B1 2JH - **tel:** 0871 527 8078 (Calls cost 13p per minute plus your phone company's access charge) **web:** www.premierinn.com
dir: *M6 junct 6, A38(M) towards city centre. Follow signs for city centre/ICC/A456 (Broad St). Left at Hyatt Hotel, hotel on right at bottom of Bridge St*

High quality, budget accommodation ideal for both families and business travellers. Spacious, en suite bedrooms feature tea and coffee making facilities, Freeview TV in most hotels and free WiFi. The adjacent family restaurant features a wide and varied menu.

Rooms: 85

Premier Inn Birmingham Broad Street (Brindley Place)
BUDGET HOTEL

80 Broad Street, B15 1AU - **tel:** 0871 527 8076 (Calls cost 13p per minute plus your phone company's access charge) **web:** www.premierinn.com
dir: *M6 junct 6, A38(M) (Aston Expressway). Follow City Centre, ICC & NIA signs into Broad St. Right into Sheepcote St. 2nd left at rdbt into Essington St. Hotel on left. NB Sat Nav use B16 8AL*

Rooms: 58

Premier Inn Birmingham Central East

BUDGET HOTEL

Richard Street, Aston, B7 4AA - **tel:** 0871 527 8080 (Calls cost 13p per minute plus your phone company's access charge) **web:** www.premierinn.com
dir: M6 junct 6, signed city centre. A38(M) signed A4540 (ring road). At rdbt 1st exit 50mtrs left into Richard St, hotel on left, barrier access to car park

Rooms: 100

Premier Inn Birmingham Central (Hagley Road)

BUDGET HOTEL

Hagley Road, B16 9NY - **tel:** 0871 527 8082 (Calls cost 13p per minute plus your phone company's access charge) **web:** www.premierinn.com
dir: M6 junct 6, A38(M) (Aston Express Way). Follow city centre, ICC & NIA signs, into Broad St. From M5 junct 3, A456 for approx 3m, hotel on left

Rooms: 65

Premier Inn Birmingham City Centre New Street

BUDGET HOTEL

Birmingham Exchange Buildings, Stephenson Place, B2 4NH - **tel:** 0871 527 9442 (Calls cost 13p per minute plus your phone company's access charge) **web:** www.premierinn.com
dir: M6 junct 6, A38 (Corporation St) keep right at fork. Exit towards New St, merge into Suffolk St Queensway. At rdbt 1st exit into Smallbrook Queensway, left into Hill St, right into Queen's Drive. Multi-storey parking at New St Station, The Pallasades or Bull Ring

Rooms: 140

Premier Inn Birmingham City Centre (Waterloo St)

BUDGET HOTEL

3-6 Waterloo Street, B2 5PG - **tel:** 0871 527 8074 (Calls cost 13p per minute plus your phone company's access charge) **web:** www.premierinn.com
dir: M6 junct 6, A38 (Corporation St). Follow West Bromwich/A41 signs. Merge into St Chad's Queensway. 2nd exit for Great Charles St Queensway, becomes Livery St. Left into Waterloo St

Rooms: 152

Premier Inn Birmingham (Great Barr/M6 Jct 7)

BUDGET HOTEL

Birmingham Road, Great Barr, B43 7AG - **tel:** 0871 527 8072 (Calls cost 13p per minute plus your phone company's access charge) **web:** www.premierinn.com
dir: M6 junct 7, A34 towards Walsall. Hotel on left behind Beacon Harvester

Rooms: 33

Premier Inn Birmingham South (Hall Green)

BUDGET HOTEL

Stratford Road, Hall Green, B28 9ES - **tel:** 0871 527 8092 (Calls cost 13p per minute plus your phone company's access charge) **web:** www.premierinn.com
dir: M42 junct 4, A34 towards Shirley signed Birmingham. Straight on at 6 rdbts. At 7th rdbt 4th exit. Hotel on left

Rooms: 52

Premier Inn Birmingham South (Longbridge St)

BUDGET HOTEL

2 College Street, Longbridge, B31 2US - **tel:** 0871 527 9434 (Calls cost 13p per minute plus your phone company's access charge) **web:** www.premierinn.com
dir: M5 junct 4, A38 towards Birmingham. 3m (pass Morrisons & McDonald's) to rdbt. 1st exit towards A38 (B'ham). Right at 1st lights signed Longbridge train station. 1st right at Sainsburys, hotel on right. NB for Sat Nav use B31 2TW

Rooms: 75

BIRMINGHAM AIRPORT   Map 10 SP18
West Midlands

Novotel Birmingham Airport

★★★★ 74% HOTEL

B26 3QL - **tel:** 0121 782 7000 **email:** H1158@accor.com **web:** www.novotel.com
dir: M42 junct 6, A45 to Birmingham, signed to airport. Hotel opposite main terminal

This smartly decorated hotel with air conditioning throughout its public areas and bedrooms benefits from being less than a minute's walk from the main terminal of Birmingham International Airport. Spacious bedrooms are comfortable, and modern bathrooms are stylish with powerful showers. The Elements bar and restaurant provides a great atmosphere for meals and a fitness room is available on site. Long-stay car parking packages can be arranged.

Rooms: 195 (24 family) **Facilities:** FTV WiFi Gym Fitness room **Conf:** Class 10 Board 20 Thtr 35 **Services:** Lift Night porter Air con

---

BIRMINGHAM [NATIONAL EXHIBITION CENTRE]   Map 10 SP18
West Midlands

Moor Hall Hotel & Spa

★★★★ 80% ⚜⚜ HOTEL - **tel:** 0121 308 3751 **Moor Hall Dr, Four Oaks B75 6LN**

email: mail@moorhallhotel.co.uk **web:** www.moorhallhotel.co.uk

(For full entry see Sutton Coldfield (Royal))

Nailcote Hall

★★★★ 79% ⚜ HOTEL - **tel:** 024 7646 6174 **Nailcote Ln, Berkswell CV7 7DE**

email: info@nailcotehall.co.uk **web:** www.nailcotehall.co.uk

(For full entry see Balsall Common)

Arden Hotel & Leisure Club

★★★ 76% HOTEL

Coventry Road, Bickenhill, B92 0EH - **tel:** 01675 443221
email: enquiries@ardenhotel.co.uk **web:** www.ardenhotel.co.uk
dir: M42 junct 6, A45 towards Birmingham. Hotel 0.25m on right, just off Birmingham International railway island

This smart hotel neighbouring the NEC and Birmingham Airport, offers modern rooms and well-equipped leisure facilities. After dinner in the formal restaurant, the place to relax is the spacious lounge area, or the large snooker room available to resident guests. A buffet breakfast is served in the bright and airy Meeting Place. Free WiFi and on-site parking are also available.

Rooms: 216 (6 family) (6 GF) (4 smoking) **S** fr £40; **D** fr £40* **Facilities:** Spa FTV WiFi Gym Xmas New Year **Conf:** Class 40 Board 60 Thtr 200 **Services:** Lift Night porter **Parking:** 300 **Notes:** Civ Wed 100

B

BIRMINGHAM [NATIONAL EXHIBITION CENTRE] *continued*

Premier Inn Birmingham NEC/Airport

BUDGET HOTEL

Off Bickenhill Parkway, National Exhibition Centre, B40 1QA - **tel:** 0871 527 8086
(Calls cost 13p per minute plus your phone company's access charge)
web: www.premierinn.com
dir: *M42 junct 6 signed NEC. Turn right towards North Way. Follow Premier Inn signs.*
Hotel on left at 5th rdbt

High quality, budget accommodation ideal for both families and business
travellers. Spacious, en suite bedrooms feature tea and coffee making facilities,
Freeview TV in most hotels and free WiFi. The adjacent family restaurant features a
wide and varied menu.

Rooms: 247

BISHOP AUCKLAND
County Durham   Map 19 NZ22

Premier Inn Bishop Auckland

BUDGET HOTEL

West Auckland Road, DL14 9AP - **tel:** 0871 527 8096 (Calls cost 13p per minute plus
your phone company's access charge) **web:** www.premierinn.com
dir: *From S: A1 junct 58, left onto A68 signed Corbridge/Bishop Auckland. At 1st rdbt 2nd*
exit onto A6072 signed Shildon. Straight on at 4 rdbts, follow Shildon/Bishop Auckland
signs. Hotel approx 1m on left

High quality, budget accommodation ideal for both families and business
travellers. Spacious, en suite bedrooms feature tea and coffee making facilities,
Freeview TV in most hotels and free WiFi. The adjacent family restaurant features a
wide and varied menu.

Rooms: 60

Silver Stars

The AA Silver Star rating
denotes a Hotel that
we highly recommend.
They have a superior level of
quality within their star rating,
high standards of hospitality,
service and cleanliness.

BISHOP'S STORTFORD   Map 6 TL42
Hertfordshire

HIGHLY RECOMMENDED

Down Hall Country House Hotel

★★★★ 87% ⊛ HOTEL

Hatfield Heath, CM22 7AS - **tel:** 01279 731441 **email:** info@downhall.co.uk
web: www.downhall.co.uk
dir: *A1060, at Hatfield Heath keep left. Right into lane opposite Hunters Meet*
restaurant, left at end, follow signs

This imposing country house hotel is set in 100 acres of mature grounds in a
peaceful location just a short drive from Stansted Airport. Bedrooms are
generally quite spacious; each one is pleasantly decorated, tastefully furnished
and equipped with modern facilities. Public rooms include a choice of
restaurants, a cocktail bar, two lounges and leisure facilities.

Rooms: 100 (20 GF) 🐾 **S** £109–£149; **D** £119–£159* **Facilities:** Spa FTV WiFi
🌊 ⛳ Gym Giant chess Sauna Steam room Hydrotherapy pool Xmas New Year
Conf: Class 140 Board 68 Thtr 200 Del from £229 **Services:** Lift Night porter
Parking: 150 **Notes:** Civ Wed 150

The Great Hallingbury Manor Hotel

★★★ 82% HOTEL

Tilekiln Green, Great Hallingbury, CM22 7TJ - **tel:** 01279 506475
email: info@greathallingburymanor.co.uk **web:** www.greathallingburymanor.co.uk
dir: *M11 junct 8 rdbt take exit to B1256, turn immediately right at petrol station. Under*
bridge, sharp left bend, continue for 500yds. Hotel on left

This Tudor-style manor is set in lovely landscaped grounds and is surrounded by
open countryside. The property is situated close to Stansted Airport, and the major
road networks are within easy reach. The interior has a very contemporary feel, and
bedrooms are smartly appointed with a range of thoughtful touches; public areas
include a choice of lounges, a bar and an open-plan restaurant.

Rooms: 45 (22 annexe) (3 family) (16 GF) 🐾 **S** £40–£95; **D** £80–£140*
Facilities: FTV WiFi ⇂ Xmas New Year **Conf:** Class 80 Board 30 Thtr 170 Del
from £165 **Services:** Night porter **Parking:** 50 **Notes:** LB Civ Wed 170

Ramada London Stansted Airport - M11

AA Advertised

Birchanger Services, M11 Motorway, CM23 5QZ - **tel:** 01279 213900
email: ramadalsa@welcomebreak.co.uk **web:** www.welcomebreak.co.uk
dir: *M11 junct 8*

This modern building offers accommodation in smart, spacious and well-equipped
bedrooms, suitable for families and business travellers, and all with en suite

B

bathrooms. There is an attractive lounge area and a dining room where breakfast is served and other refreshments may be taken.

Rooms: 76 (15 family) (16 GF) (8 smoking) **Facilities:** FTV WiFi **Services:** Lift Air con **Parking:** 100

BLACKBURN
Lancashire   Map 18 SD62

See also **Langho**

Premier Inn Blackburn South (M65 Jct 4)

BUDGET HOTEL

Off Eccleshill Road, Riversway Drive, BB3 0SN - tel: 0871 527 8100 (Calls cost 13p per minute plus your phone company's access charge) **web:** www.premierinn.com
dir: *At M65 junct 4*

High quality, budget accommodation ideal for both families and business travellers. Spacious, en suite bedrooms feature tea and coffee making facilities, Freeview TV in most hotels and free WiFi. The adjacent family restaurant features a wide and varied menu.

Rooms: 62

Premier Inn Blackburn Town Centre Hotel

BUDGET HOTEL

3 Cathedral Square, BB1 1FB - tel: 0871 527 9622 (Calls cost 13p per minute plus your phone company's access charge) **email:** blackburntowncentre.pi@premierinn.com **web:** www.premierinn.com
dir: *M6 junct 29, M65 (West) towards Blackburn. At junct 4 follow signs for A666/ Blackburn Town Centre, then follow signs for Blackburn Railway Station. On Jubilee St the car park is adjacent to railway station, hotel opposite*

Rooms: 60

BLACKPOOL
Lancashire   Map 18 SD33

Best Western Carlton Hotel Blackpool

★★★ 76% HOTEL

282 North Promenade, FY1 2EZ - tel: 01253 628966
email: mail@carltonhotelblackpool.co.uk **web:** www.bw-carltonhotel.co.uk
dir: *M6 junct 32/M55 - follow signs for North Shore. Between Blackpool Tower & Gynn Sq*

Enjoying a prime seafront location, this hotel offers bedrooms that are attractively furnished in modern style. Refreshed public areas, including a choice of bar lounge and seaview lounge, are bright and reflect the seaside location. Well cooked meals are served in the elegant restaurant; extensive function facilities are available.

Rooms: 58 (7 family) **Facilities:** FTV WiFi Xmas New Year **Conf:** Class 40 Board 40 Thtr 90 **Services:** Lift Night porter **Parking:** 40 **Notes:** LB Civ Wed 90

Carousel Hotel
★★★ 72% HOTEL

663-671 New South Prom, FY4 1RN - tel: 01253 402642
email: carousel.reservations@sleepwellhotels.com **web:** www.sleepwellhotels.com
dir: *From M55 follow signs to airport, pass airport to lights. Turn right, hotel 100yds on right*

This friendly seafront hotel, close to the Pleasure Beach, offers smart, contemporary accommodation. Bedrooms are comfortably appointed and have a modern, stylish feel to them. An airy restaurant and a spacious bar/lounge

both overlook the Promenade. The hotel has good conference and meeting facilities and its own car park.

Rooms: 92 (22 family) **S** £50–£90; **D** £60–£100 (incl. bkfst)* **Facilities:** FTV WiFi Xmas New Year **Conf:** Class 30 Board 40 Thtr 100 Del from £85 **Services:** Lift Night porter **Parking:** 28 **Notes:** Civ Wed 150

Queens Hotel
Leisureplex HOLIDAY HOTELS
★★★ 66% HOTEL

469-471 South Promenade, FY4 1AY - tel: 01253 342015
email: queens.blackpool@leisureplex.co.uk **web:** www.leisureplex.co.uk
dir: *Phone for details*

Queens Hotel is situated on the South Promenade overlooking the Irish Sea, close to the South Pier and Pleasure Beach. The bedrooms are well equipped and some rooms have lovely sea views. The spacious public areas include a choice of lounges, a range of bars, a conservatory and a large dining room as well as a refurbished 300-seat theatre bar.

Rooms: 117 (9 family) **Facilities:** FTV WiFi HL supervised Xmas New Year **Conf:** Class 60 Board 60 Thtr 80 **Services:** Lift Night porter **Parking:** 55 **Notes:** Closed Jan-Feb

New Guilderoy Hotel
★★ 77% SMALL HOTEL

57-59 Holmfield Road, North Shore, FY2 9RU - tel: 01253 351547
email: simon_connelly@yahoo.com **web:** www.new-guilderoy-hotel-blackpool.co.uk
dir: *M55 Blackpool. Follow signs North Shore. Located behind The Cliffs Hotel, Queens Promenade*

This pleasant, personally-run hotel caters for a wide market and sits in a quiet location, away from the hubbub of the town, yet conveniently close to attractions and the famous north promenade (very handy for Illuminations season). There is a relaxing lounge and a cosy bar with a very good wine list to choose from. Home cooked food is a feature here and menus at both dinner and breakfast offer a good choice.

Rooms: 15 (4 family) **S** £25–£40; **D** £30–£75 (incl. bkfst)* **Facilities:** FTV WiFi Xmas New Year **Notes:** LB Closed 10 Nov–22 Dec RS 2 Jan-28 Feb limited availability

The Viking Hotel
★★ 77% HOTEL

479 South Promenade, FY4 1AX - tel: 01253 348411 & 0844 811 5570 (Calls cost 5p per minute plus your phone company's access charge)
email: reservations@choice-hotels.co.uk **web:** www.choicehotels.co.uk
dir: *M55 junct 3, follow Pleasure Beach signs*

In a prime location at the centre of the South Promenade, this hotel offers comfortable accommodation and a warm welcome. Meals are served in the attractive sea view restaurant and entertainment is available nightly in the renowned 'Talk of the Coast' night club. Secure on-site parking is a boon and leisure facilities at sister hotels are also available free of charge.

Rooms: 100 (10 GF) **S** £42–£100; **D** £72–£140 (incl. bkfst & dinner)
Facilities: FTV WiFi Cabaret club Xmas New Year **Services:** Lift Night porter **Parking:** 50 **Notes:** LB No children 18yrs

B

BLACKPOOL *continued*

The Claremont Hotel

★★ 74% HOTEL

270 North Promenade, FY1 1SA - tel: 01253 293122 & 0844 811 5570 (Calls cost 5p per minute plus your phone company's access charge)
email: reservations@choice-hotels.co.uk **web:** www.choicehotels.co.uk
dir: *M55 junct 3 follow sign for promenade. Hotel beyond North Pier*

Conveniently situated, the Claremont is a popular family holiday hotel. Bedrooms are bright and attractively decorated, and extensive public areas include a spacious air-conditioned restaurant which offers a good choice of dishes. There is a well equipped, supervised children's play room, and entertainment is provided during the season.

Rooms: 143 (50 family) S £46–£79; **D** £80–£144 (incl. bkfst & dinner)
Facilities: FTV WiFi Xmas New Year **Services:** Lift Night porter **Parking:** 40
Notes: LB

The Cliffs Hotel

★★ 74% HOTEL

Queens Promenade, FY2 9SG - tel: 01253 595559 & 0844 811 5570 (Calls cost 5p per minute plus your phone company's access charge)
email: reservations@choice-hotels.co.uk **web:** www.choicehotels.co.uk
dir: *M55 junct 3, follow Promenade signs. Hotel just after Gynn rdbt*

This large, privately owned and extremely popular promenade hotel is within easy reach of the town centre. The well equipped bedrooms, including spacious family rooms, vary in size. Public areas offer an all-day coffee shop, a smart restaurant and a suite of games rooms where kids of all ages are entertained. A modern gym and leisure pool complete the experience.

Rooms: 163 (47 family) S £38–£72; **D** £74–£142 (incl. bkfst & dinner)
Facilities: FTV WiFi supervised Gym Xmas New Year **Conf:** Class 210 Board 50 Thtr 475 Del from £105 **Services:** Lift Night porter **Parking:** 30 **Notes:** LB Civ Wed 100

The Craig-y-Don Hotel

★★ 71% HOTEL

211-213 Central Promenade, FY1 5DL - tel: 01253 624249
email: craig-y-donhotel@btconnect.com **web:** www.craig-y-don.com
dir: *On promenade, 2/3m past Blackpool Pleasure Beach*

The Craig-y-Don Hotel has a prime promenade position, and many rooms enjoy sea views. This is very much a holiday hotel which offers great value packages throughout the year. Freshly cooked dinner is available in the spacious dining room. Bedrooms are available in a range of sizes all equipped to a modern standard. The busy bar features cabaret and entertainment most nights.

Rooms: 62 (33 family) (11 GF) **Facilities:** FTV WiFi Xmas New Year **Services:** Lift Night porter **Notes:** RS Nov-May wknds only

Lyndene Hotel

★★ Ⓐ HOTEL

303/315 Promenade, FY1 6AN - tel: 01253 346779
email: enquiries@lyndenehotel.com **web:** www.lyndenehotel.com
dir: *Phone for directions*

Family run for over 20 years, this hotel is on the promenade and offers bedrooms with LCD flat-screen TVs, safes and hospitality trays; some rooms are on the ground floor. Public rooms include two air-conditioned lounges, two restaurants and an outside seating area and sun terrace. Entertainment is offered every evening.

Rooms: 140 (60 family) (12 GF) (140 smoking) **Facilities:** FTV WiFi Xmas New Year **Services:** Lift Night porter **Parking:** 70 **Notes:** No children 5yrs

Hotel Ibis Styles Blackpool

fOCUS hotels
management limited

BUDGET HOTEL

Talbot Square, FY1 1ND - tel: 01253 752478
email: H9148@accor.com **web:** www.focushotels.co.uk/hotels
dir: *M55 junct 4, follow signs for A583 Blackpool North Shore, approx 4m to seafront. Property on right opposite North Pier entrance*

Modern, budget hotel offering comfortable accommodation in bright and practical bedrooms. Breakfast is self-service and dinner is available in the restaurant.

Rooms: 90 (4 family) S £49–£99; **D** £54–£104 (incl. bkfst) *

Premier Inn Blackpool Airport

BUDGET HOTEL

Squire Gate Lane, FY4 2QS - **tel:** 0871 527 8106 (Calls cost 13p per minute plus your phone company's access charge) **web:** www.premierinn.com
dir: M55 junct 4, A5230, left at 1st rdbt towards airport. Hotel just before Squires Gate rail station

High quality, budget accommodation ideal for both families and business travellers. Spacious, en suite bedrooms feature tea and coffee making facilities, Freeview TV in most hotels and free WiFi. The adjacent family restaurant features a wide and varied menu.

Rooms: 39

Premier Inn Blackpool (Bispham)

BUDGET HOTEL

Devonshire Road, Bispham, FY2 0AR - **tel:** 0871 527 8102 (Calls cost 13p per minute plus your phone company's access charge) **web:** www.premierinn.com
dir: M55 junct 4, A583. At 5th lights turn right (Whitegate Drive). Approx. 4.5m onto A587 Devonshire Rd

Rooms: 67

Premier Inn Blackpool Central

BUDGET HOTEL

Yeadon Way, South Shore, FY1 6BF - **tel:** 0871 527 8108 (Calls cost 13p per minute plus your phone company's access charge) **web:** www.premierinn.com
dir: M55 junct 4 to Blackpool, straight on at last island onto Yeaden Way. Follow signs for Central Car Park/Coach Area. Left at Total garage

Rooms: 103

Premier Inn Blackpool East (M55 Jct 4)

BUDGET HOTEL

Whitehills Park, Preston New Road, FY4 5NZ - **tel:** 0871 527 8110 (Calls cost 13p per minute plus your phone company's access charge) **web:** www.premierinn.com
dir: Just off M55 junct 4. 1st left off rdbt. Hotel on right

Rooms: 81

Discover more places to stay
www.theaa.com/travel

BLAKENEY
Norfolk — Map 13 TG04

B

INSPECTOR'S CHOICE

Morston Hall
★★★★ ◎◎◎◎ SMALL HOTEL

Morston, Holt, NR25 7AA - **tel:** 01263 741041
email: reception@morstonhall.com **web:** www.morstonhall.com
dir: 1m W of Blakeney on A149 - King's Lynn to Cromer road

This delightful 17th-century country house hotel enjoys a tranquil setting amid well-tended gardens. The comfortable public rooms offer a choice of attractive lounges and a sunny conservatory, while the elegant dining room is the perfect setting to enjoy Galton Blackiston's award-winning cuisine. The spacious bedrooms are individually decorated and stylishly furnished with modern opulence.

Rooms: 13 (6 annexe) (7 GF) D £390–£410 (incl. bkfst & dinner)*
Facilities: STV FTV WiFi New Year **Conf:** Class 20 Board 16 **Parking:** 40
Notes: LB Closed 1 Jan-last Fri in Jan & 2 days Xmas Civ Wed 55

HIGHLY RECOMMENDED

The Blakeney Hotel
★★★★ 83% ◎ HOTEL

The Quay, NR25 7NE - **tel:** 01263 740797
email: reception@blakeneyhotel.co.uk **web:** www.blakeneyhotel.co.uk
dir: From A148 between Fakenham & Holt, take B1156 to Langham & Blakeney

A traditional, privately-owned hotel situated on the quayside with superb views across the estuary and the salt marshes to Blakeney Point. Public rooms feature an elegant restaurant, ground-floor lounge, a bar and a first-floor sun lounge overlooking the harbour. Bedrooms are smartly decorated and equipped with modern facilities. The leisure area is a real feature with pool, sauna, steam room and mini-gym.

Rooms: 64 (16 annexe) (20 family) (17 GF) S £102–£171; D £240–£386 (incl. bkfst & dinner)* **Facilities:** FTV WiFi HL Gym Billiards Snooker Table tennis Sauna Steam room Spa bath Xmas New Year **Conf:** Class 100 Board 100 Thtr 150 **Services:** Lift Night porter **Parking:** 60 **Notes:** LB

B

BLANCHLAND
Northumberland

Map 18 NY95

The Lord Crewe Arms Blanchland

★★★ ⊛ COUNTRY HOUSE HOTEL

The Square, DH8 9SP - **tel:** 01434 675469
email: enquiries@lordcrewearmsblanchland.co.uk
web: www.lordcrewearmsblanchland.co.uk
dir: 10m S of Hexham via B6306

Set in the tranquil and picturesque Northumbrian countryside, "The Crewe" dates back to the 12th century, and was built as the Abbot's Priory. The building has plenty of character from the vaulted crypt bar to the numerous large open log fires. Bedrooms come in three styles: Cosy, Canny, and Champion. The team are naturally friendly with two dining options serving "proper, unpretentious country grub".

Rooms: 21 (17 annexe) (6 GF) ♠ **Facilities:** FTV WiFi ⇲ Fishing ⥅ Xmas New Year **Conf:** Class 60 Board 30 Thtr 60 **Parking:** 25 **Notes:** Civ Wed 60

BLEADON
Somerset

Map 4 ST35

Premier Inn Weston-Super-Mare (Lympsham)

BUDGET HOTEL

Bridgwater Road, Lympsham, BS24 0BP - **tel:** 0871 527 9154 (Calls cost 13p per minute plus your phone company's access charge) **web:** www.premierinn.com
dir: M5 junct 22, A38 (Bristol Rd) signed Weston-Super-Mare. At 1st rdbt take 1st exit into Bridgewater Rd (A370). Approx 2m to hotel

High quality, budget accommodation ideal for both families and business travellers. Spacious, en suite bedrooms feature tea and coffee making facilities, Freeview TV in most hotels and free WiFi. The adjacent family restaurant features a wide and varied menu.

Rooms: 45

BODMIN
Cornwall & Isles of Scilly

Map 2 SX06

Trehellas House Hotel & Restaurant

★★★ 77% ⊛ SMALL HOTEL

Washaway, PL30 3AD - **tel:** 01208 72700
email: enquiries@trehellashouse.co.uk **web:** www.trehellashouse.co.uk
dir: A389 from Bodmin towards Wadebridge. Hotel on right 0.5m beyond road to Camelford

This 18th-century former posting inn retains many original features and provides comfortable accommodation. Bedrooms are located in both the main house and adjacent coach house - all provide the same high standards. An interesting choice of cuisine, with an emphasis on locally-sourced ingredients, is offered in the impressive slate-floored restaurant.

Rooms: 12 (7 annexe) (2 family) (5 GF) **S** £50–£75; **D** £75–£150 (incl. bkfst)*
Facilities: FTV WiFi ⥲ Xmas New Year **Conf:** Board 20 Thtr 20 **Parking:** 32 **Notes:** LB No children 13yrs

Premier Inn Bodmin

BUDGET HOTEL

Launceston Road, PL31 2AR - **tel:** 0871 527 8112 (Calls cost 13p per minute plus your phone company's access charge) **web:** www.premierinn.com
dir: From A30 S'bound exit onto A389, hotel 0.5m on right. N'bound exit onto A38, follow A389 signs. Left at T-junct

High quality, budget accommodation ideal for both families and business travellers. Spacious, en suite bedrooms feature tea and coffee making facilities, Freeview TV in most hotels and free WiFi. The adjacent family restaurant features a wide and varied menu.

Rooms: 44

BOGNOR REGIS
West Sussex

Map 6 SZ99

The Inglenook

★★★ 73% SMALL HOTEL

255 Pagham Road, Nyetimber, PO21 3QB - **tel:** 01243 262495
email: reception@the-inglenook.com **web:** www.the-inglenook.com
dir: A27 into Vinnetrow Rd, left at Walnut Tree, hotel 2.5m on right

This 16th-century inn retains much of its original character, including exposed beams throughout. Bedrooms are individually decorated and vary in size. There is a cosy lounge, a well-kept garden and a bar that offers a popular evening menu and convivial atmosphere. The restaurant, overlooking the garden, also serves enjoyable cuisine.

Rooms: 18 (1 family) (2 GF) ♠ **S** £60; **D** £100–£215 (incl. bkfst) **Facilities:** STV FTV WiFi Xmas New Year **Conf:** Class 50 Board 50 Thtr 100 Del from £125 **Parking:** 35 **Notes:** LB Civ Wed 80

The Royal Norfolk Hotel

Leisureplex
HOLIDAY HOTELS

★★★ 72% HOTEL

The Esplanade, PO21 2LH - **tel:** 01243 826222
email: royalnorfolk@leisureplex.co.uk **web:** www.leisureplex.co.uk
dir: From A259 follow Longford Rd through lights to Canada Grove to T-junct. Right, take 2nd exit at rdbt. Hotel on right

Located on the seafront, but set back behind well-tended lawns and gardens, is this fine Regency hotel. The bedrooms are traditionally furnished and provide guests with modern comforts. There are sea views from the bar and restaurant, as well as the lounges.

Rooms: 60 (4 family) (7 GF) ☾ **S** £40–£93; **D** £64–£130 (incl. bkfst)*
Facilities: FTV WiFi ♬ Xmas New Year **Services:** Lift Night porter **Parking:** 40
Notes: LB Closed 2 Jan-14 Feb

Premier Inn Bognor Regis

BUDGET HOTEL

Shripney Road, PO22 9PA - **tel:** 0871 527 8114 (Calls cost 13p per minute plus your phone company's access charge) **web:** www.premierinn.com
dir: From A27 & A29 rdbt junct follow Bognor Regis signs. Approx 4m, hotel on left

High quality, budget accommodation ideal for both families and business travellers. Spacious, en suite bedrooms feature tea and coffee making facilities, Freeview TV in most hotels and free WiFi. The adjacent family restaurant features a wide and varied menu.

Rooms: 46

BOLTON
Greater Manchester — Map 15 SD70

Mercure Bolton Georgian House Hotel

★★★ 75% HOTEL

Manchester Road, Blackrod, BL6 5RU - **tel:** 01942 850900 & 0844 815 9029 (Calls cost 7p per minute plus your phone company's access charge)
email: info@mercurebolton.co.uk **web:** www.mercurebolton.co.uk
dir: M61 junct 6, follow Blackrod A6027 signs. 200mtrs turn right onto A6 signed Chorley. Hotel 0.5m on right

This hotel has a pleasant location and very good parking, convenient for corporate or leisure guests alike. Bedrooms are pleasantly appointed, and beds very comfortable. There is a range of meeting rooms and the hotel is popular for weddings. There is a choice of dining venues and a pleasant bar.

Rooms: 91 (6 family) **Facilities:** FTV WiFi ❄ Gym Sauna Beauty treatments Dance studio **Conf:** Class 100 Board 40 Thtr 275 **Services:** Night porter **Parking:** 250
Notes: Civ Wed 275

Premier Inn Bolton (Reebok Stadium)

BUDGET HOTEL

Arena Approach 3, Horwich, BL6 6LB - **tel:** 0871 527 8116 (Calls cost 13p per minute plus your phone company's access charge) **web:** www.premierinn.com
dir: M61 junct 6, right at rdbt, left at 2nd rdbt

High quality, budget accommodation ideal for both families and business travellers. Spacious, en suite bedrooms feature tea and coffee making facilities, Freeview TV in most hotels and free WiFi. The adjacent family restaurant features a wide and varied menu.

Rooms: 126

Premier Inn Bolton West

BUDGET HOTEL

991 Chorley New Road, Horwich, BL6 4BA - **tel:** 0871 527 8118 (Calls cost 13p per minute plus your phone company's access charge) **web:** www.premierinn.com
dir: M61 junct 6, follow dual carriageway signed Bolton/Horwich (Reebok Stadium on left). Hotel at 2nd rdbt

Rooms: 60

BOLTON ABBEY
North Yorkshire — Map 19 SE05

The Devonshire Arms Hotel & Spa

★★★★ ☕ HOTEL

BD23 6AJ - **tel:** 01756 718100 & 718111
email: res@devonshirehotels.co.uk **web:** www.thedevonshirearms.co.uk
dir: On B6160, 250yds N of junct with A59

With stunning views of the Wharfedale countryside this beautiful hotel, owned by the Duke and Duchess of Devonshire, dates back to the 17th century. A long tradition of fine hospitality continues to this day, as guests' needs are accommodated in fine style, with attention to detail and friendly, personalised service. Bedrooms are elegantly furnished; those in the old part of the house are particularly spacious and have four-posters and fine antiques. The rest of the hotel is equally elegant, and it is a pleasure to spend time in one of the cosy sitting rooms. The Burlington Restaurant offers accomplished cuisine, while the Brasserie provides a lighter alternative. Both serve fresh and seasonal produce, largely from neighbouring farms, fields and rivers of the estate, as well as from the hotel's own kitchen garden.

Rooms: 40 (1 family) (17 GF) ☾ **S** £117.50–£400; **D** £135–£420 (incl. bkfst)*
Facilities: Spa STV FTV WiFi ❄ 🏊 supervised ⚓ Fishing ⛳ Gym Classic cars Falconry Laser pigeon shooting Fly fishing Cricket Xmas New Year **Conf:** Class 40 Board 30 Thtr 120 Del from £225 **Services:** Night porter **Parking:** 150 **Notes:** LB Civ Wed 90

BOREHAMWOOD
Hertfordshire — Map 6 TQ19

Premier Inn London Elstree/Borehamwood

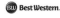

BUDGET HOTEL

Warwick Road, WD6 1US - **tel:** 0871 527 8654 (Calls cost 13p per minute plus your phone company's access charge) **web:** www.premierinn.com
dir: Exit A1 signed Borehamwood onto A5135 (Elstree Way). Pass BP Garage, left into Warwick Rd

High quality, budget accommodation ideal for both families and business travellers. Spacious, en suite bedrooms feature tea and coffee making facilities, Freeview TV in most hotels and free WiFi. The adjacent family restaurant features a wide and varied menu.

Rooms: 124

BOROUGHBRIDGE
North Yorkshire — Map 19 SE36

Best Western Crown Hotel

★★★ 77% HOTEL

Horsefair, YO51 9LB - **tel:** 01423 322328
email: sales@crownboroughbridge.co.uk **web:** www.crownboroughbridge.co.uk
dir: A1(M) junct 48 towards Boroughbridge. Hotel 1m

Situated in the centre of town but convenient for the A1(M), The Crown provides a full leisure complex, conference rooms and a secure car park. Bedrooms are well appointed. A wide range of well-prepared dishes can be enjoyed in both the restaurant and bar.

Rooms: 37 (3 family) (2 GF) **Facilities:** FTV WiFi ❄ HL ❄ supervised Gym Xmas New Year **Conf:** Class 80 Board 80 Thtr 150 **Services:** Night porter **Parking:** 60 **Notes:** Civ Wed 120

B

See also **Keswick & Rosthwaite**

Lodore Falls Hotel

★★★★ 81% HOTEL

LAKE DISTRICT HOTELS

CA12 5UX - **tel:** 017687 77285
email: lodorefalls@lakedistricthotels.net **web:** www.lakedistricthotels.net/lodorefalls
dir: *M6 junct 40, A66 to Keswick, B5289 to Borrowdale. Hotel on left*

Please note: 2017 saw a number of major improvements at the Lodore Falls Hotel. The ground floor of the hotel was completely renovated at the start of the year, and re-opened in mid-February. The leisure club and beauty salon will remain closed until Summer 2018, when a brand new luxury spa, and a brasserie restaurant with an outdoor terrace, as well as 18 new exclusive bedroom suites will be opened. While this carefully planned development is underway the hotel will be open and the management have promised to do everything in their power to ensure these works do not impact on guest experience. This impressive hotel has an enviable location overlooking Derwentwater. The bedrooms, many with lake or fell views, are comfortably equipped; family rooms and suites are also available. The dining room, bar and lounge areas are appointed to a very high standard.

Rooms: 69 (11 family) **Facilities:** Spa STV FTV WiFi Fishing Gym Sauna Xmas New Year **Conf:** Class 90 Board 45 Thtr 200 **Services:** Lift Night porter **Parking:** 103 **Notes:** Civ Wed 130

Borrowdale Gates Hotel

★★★★ 80% COUNTRY HOUSE HOTEL

CA12 5UQ - **tel:** 017687 77204
email: hotel@borrowdale-gates.com **web:** www.borrowdale-gates.com
dir: *From A66 follow B5289 for approx 4m. Turn right over bridge, hotel 0.25m beyond village*

This friendly hotel is peacefully located in the Borrowdale Valley, close to the village but in its own three acres of wooded grounds. Public rooms include comfortable lounges and a restaurant with picture postcard views.

Rooms: 25 (2 family) (9 GF) **D** £194–£276 (incl. bkfst & dinner)* **Facilities:** FTV WiFi Xmas New Year **Services:** Lift Air con **Parking:** 25 **Notes:** Closed 5-25 Jan

Borrowdale Hotel

★★★★ 77% HOTEL

LAKE DISTRICT HOTELS

CA12 5UY - **tel:** 017687 77224
email: borrowdale@lakedistricthotels.net
web: www.lakedistricthotels.net/borrowdalehotel
dir: *3m from Keswick, on B5289 at S end of Lake Derwentwater*

Situated in the beautiful Borrowdale Valley overlooking Derwentwater, this traditionally styled hotel guarantees a friendly welcome. Extensive public areas include a choice of lounges, traditional dining room, lounge bar and popular conservatory which serves more informal meals. Bedrooms vary in style and size, including two that are suitable for less able guests.

Rooms: 40 (2 family) (4 GF) **Facilities:** STV FTV WiFi Leisure facilities available at nearby sister hotel Xmas New Year **Conf:** Class 30 Board 24 Thtr 80 **Services:** Night porter **Parking:** 30

HIGHLY RECOMMENDED

Leathes Head Hotel

★★★ 87% HOTEL

CA12 5UY - **tel:** 017687 77247
email: reservations@leatheshead.co.uk **web:** www.leatheshead.co.uk
dir: *3.5m from Keswick on B5289 (Borrowdale road). Hotel on left 0.25m before Grange Bridge*

Leathes Head Hotel is a fine Edwardian building, with lovely gardens, set in the heart of the unspoilt Borrowdale Valley. The hospitality and customer care are really outstanding here. The bedrooms have commanding views and the award-winning food, including a wonderful Cumbrian breakfast, will not disappoint.

Rooms: 11 (2 family) (3 GF) **D** £140–£250 (incl. bkfst)* **Facilities:** FTV WiFi **Parking:** 16 **Notes:** LB No children 15yrs Closed late Nov-mid Feb

The Wellington Hotel

★★★ 80% HOTEL

The Harbour, PL35 0AQ - **tel:** 01840 250202
email: info@wellingtonhotelboscastle.com **web:** www.wellingtonhotelboscastle.com
dir: *A30/A395 at Davidstowe follow Boscastle signs. B3266 to village. Right into Old Rd*

This 16th-century coaching inn is very much a landmark in Boscastle and has been providing rest and relaxation for weary travellers for many years. There is character in abundance which adds to its engaging charm and personality. The Long Bar is popular with visitors and locals alike and features a delightful galleried area. The stylish bedrooms come in varying sizes, including the spacious Tower Rooms; all provide contemporary comforts and the expected necessities. In addition to the bar menus, The Waterloo Restaurant is the elegant setting for accomplished cuisine.

Rooms: 17 (3 annexe) (3 family) **S** £60–£70; **D** £125–£140 (incl. bkfst)* **Facilities:** FTV WiFi Xmas New Year **Conf:** Class 40 Board 24 Thtr 50 Del from £120 **Parking:** 14 **Notes:** LB

BOSHAM
West Sussex

Map 5 SU80

HIGHLY RECOMMENDED

The Millstream Hotel & Restaurant

★★★ 86% ◉◉ HOTEL

Bosham Lane, PO18 8HL - **tel:** 01243 573234
email: info@millstreamhotel.com **web:** www.millstreamhotel.com
dir: *4m W of Chichester on A259, left at Bosham rdbt. After 0.5m right at T-junct signed to church & quay. Hotel 0.5m on right*

Located in the idyllic village of Bosham, this attractive hotel provides comfortable, well-equipped and tastefully decorated bedrooms. Many guests regularly return here for the relaxed atmosphere created by the notably efficient and friendly staff. Public rooms include a cocktail bar that opens onto the garden, and a pleasant award-winning restaurant where varied and freshly prepared cuisine can be enjoyed. Markwick's Brasserie Restaurant is open all day for coffee, snacks, light lunches and dinners.

Rooms: 35 (2 annexe) (2 family) (9 GF) ↻ **S** fr £79; **D** fr £135 (incl. bkfst)*
Facilities: FTV WiFi Painting & Bridge breaks ♫ Xmas New Year **Conf:** Class 20 Board 20 Thtr 45 Del from £150 **Services:** Night porter **Parking:** 44 **Notes:** LB Civ Wed 75

BOSTON
Lincolnshire

Map 12 TF34

Supreme Inns Boston

★★★ 77% HOTEL

Donnington Road, Bicker Bar Roundabout, PE20 3AN - **tel:** 01205 822804
email: enquiries@supremeinns.co.uk **web:** www.supremeinns.co.uk
dir: *At rdbt junct of A52 & A17*

Situated south west of Boston and surrounded by the Lincolnshire Fens, this modern, purpose-built hotel offers well equipped bedrooms that have flat-screen TVs and internet access. Food is available in the restaurant or all day in the relaxing bar area. Private dining and conference facilities are available.

Rooms: 55 (27 GF) **S** £59; **D** £59* **Facilities:** FTV WiFi ↻ Xmas New Year **Conf:** Board 30 Thtr 50 **Services:** Night porter **Parking:** 65 **Notes:** LB

White Hart Hotel and Eatery

★★★ 77% HOTEL

1-5 High Street, PE21 8SH - **tel:** 01205 311900
email: whitehartboston@innmail.co.uk **web:** www.whitehartboston.com
dir: *In town centre*

The White Hart Hotel is well appointed and attractive, and is conveniently located in the centre of this market town with great views of the 700-year-old St Botolph's Church, known as the Boston Stump, from its riverside location. The hotel has spacious public areas including the Riverside Restaurant for evening meals, and the lively Courtyard Bar which is open for brunch, lunch and afternoon tea. There is a wonderful outside area for relaxing, eating and drinking. Conferences and weddings are catered for, and off-street parking in a private car park is also available. Rooms are comfortable and come complete with Sky TV.

Rooms: 26 ↻ **S** £79–£99; **D** £89–£119 (incl. bkfst)* **Facilities:** FTV WiFi ↻ HL Xmas New Year **Conf:** Class 26 Board 26 Thtr 80 **Services:** Night porter **Parking:** 45 **Notes:** Civ Wed 80

Premier Inn Boston

BUDGET HOTEL

Wainfleet Road, PE21 9RW - **tel:** 0871 527 8120 (Calls cost 13p per minute plus your phone company's access charge) **web:** www.premierinn.com
dir: *A52, 300yds E of junct with A16 Boston/Grimsby road*

High quality, budget accommodation ideal for both families and business travellers. Spacious, en suite bedrooms feature tea and coffee making facilities, Freeview TV in most hotels and free WiFi. The adjacent family restaurant features a wide and varied menu.

Rooms: 73

BOTLEY
Hampshire

Map 5 SU51

Macdonald Botley Park Hotel & Spa

★★★★ 75% HOTEL

Winchester Road, Boorley Green, SO32 2UA - **tel:** 01489 780888
email: general.botleypark@macdonald-hotels.co.uk **web:** www.macdonald-hotels.co.uk/botleypark
dir: *M27 junct 7, A334 towards Botley. At 1st rdbt left, pass M&S store, over at next 5 mini rdbts. At 6th mini rdbt turn right. In 0.5m hotel on left*

This modern and spacious hotel has bedrooms which are comfortably appointed with a good range of extras, and extensive leisure facilities are on offer. Attractive public areas include the relaxing Winchester restaurant and the more informal Sports Bar.

Rooms: 130 (30 family) (34 GF) ↻ **S** £70–£140; **D** £80–£150 **Facilities:** Spa STV FTV WiFi ⊗ Gym Squash Dance studio Sauna Steam Room Relaxation lounge Xmas New Year **Conf:** Class 180 Board 140 Thtr 450 Del from £145 **Services:** Night porter Air con **Parking:** 310 **Notes:** LB Civ Wed 400

Red Stars

The AA Red Star rating denotes an Inspector's Choice hotel. They stand out as the very best in the British Isles and appear in highlighted panels throughout the guide.

B

BOURNEMOUTH
Dorset

Map 5 SZ19

See also **Christchurch**

Cumberland Hotel

★★★★ 80% ◎◎ HOTEL

27 East Overcliffe Drive, BH1 3AF - **tel:** 01202 290722 & 298350
email: kwood@oceanahotels.co.uk **web:** www.cumberlandbournemouth.co.uk
dir: *A35 towards East Cliff & beaches, right onto Holdenhurst Rd, straight over 2 rdbts, left at junct to East Overcliff Drive, hotel on seafront*

An art deco hotel where many of the bedrooms are appointed in keeping with the hotel's original character whilst offering all that the modern traveler would need.

Front-facing bedrooms have balconies with superb sea views. The well appointed public areas are spacious and striking in their design. The Ventana Grand Café and Mirabelle Restaurant offer cuisine with local produce at its heart.

Cumberland Hotel

Rooms: 107 (16 family) 🐾 **S** £35–£89; **D** £69–£299 **Facilities:** Spa FTV WiFi ⓣ 🐝 ✈
Gym Squash Xmas New Year **Conf:** Class 80 Board 50 Thtr 120 Del from £79
Services: Lift Night porter **Parking:** 55 **Notes:** LB Civ Wed 120

See advert below

The Green House

★★★★ 80% ◎◎ TOWN HOUSE HOTEL

4 Grove Road, BH1 3AX - **tel:** 01202 498900
email: reception@thegreenhousehotel.com **web:** www.thegreenhousehotel.com
dir: *Phone for directions*

This hotel has a clear commitment to the environment which goes beyond just energy efficient lighting; everything has been designed and built to be sympathetic to the environment. The beautifully appointed bedrooms and bathrooms demonstrate the 'green' principle from the locally-made 100% wool carpets and solid wood furniture, to the wallpapers and paint that have been used. The ingredients used for the menus are locally sourced and organic.

Rooms: 32 (3 family) (6 GF) 🐾 **S** £99–£139; **D** £109–£179 (incl. bkfst) **Facilities:** FTV
WiFi ⓣ In room beauty treatments Xmas New Year **Conf:** Class 40 Board 40 Thtr 100
Del from £160 **Services:** Lift Night porter **Parking:** 32 **Notes:** LB Civ Wed 100

Park Central Hotel

★★★★ 77% ❀❀ HOTEL

Exeter Road, BH2 5AJ - tel: 01202 203600
email: reception@parkcentralhotel.co.uk **web:** www.parkcentralhotel.co.uk
dir: *A338, A35 (St Pauls Rd). At rdbt 3rd exit onto B3066 (Holdenburst Rd). Straight on at 3 rdbts, hotel on right opposite Bournemouth International Centre*

Located opposite Bournemouth International Centre, this modern, contemporary hotel is in a good location and has sea views; bedrooms are comfortable and attractively furnished. The menu features creative modern ideas based on intuitive combinations of well-sourced raw materials featuring, of course a great deal of seafood. A pre-theatre menu is also available, but be sure to book as this can prove very popular.

Rooms: 48 (6 family) (7 GF) 🐾 **S** £59–£175; **D** £69–£210 (incl. bkfst)* **Facilities:** FTV WiFi ↝ In room spa New Year **Services:** Lift Night porter **Parking:** 29 **Notes:** LB

Hotel Miramar

★★★★ 77% HOTEL

East Overcliff Drive, East Cliff, BH1 3AL - tel: 01202 556581
email: sales@miramar-bournemouth.com **web:** www.miramar-bournemouth.com
dir: *From Wessex Way rdbt into St Pauls Rd, right at next rdbt. 3rd exit at next rdbt, 2nd exit at next rdbt into Grove Rd. Hotel car park on right*

Conveniently located on the East Cliff, this Edwardian hotel enjoys glorious sea views. The Miramar was a favoured destination of famed author J.R.R. Tolkien, who often stayed here. The bedrooms are comfortable and well equipped, and there are spacious public areas and a choice of lounges. The friendly staff and relaxing environment are also noteworthy.

Rooms: 43 (6 family) 🐾 **S** £51.50–£115; **D** £103–£230 (incl. bkfst & dinner)* **Facilities:** FTV WiFi ↝ HL 🎵 Xmas New Year **Conf:** Class 50 Board 50 Thtr 200 Del from £120 **Services:** Lift Night porter **Parking:** 90 **Notes:** LB Civ Wed 110

Best Western Plus The Connaught Hotel

★★★★ 76% ❀❀ HOTEL   Best Western PLUS

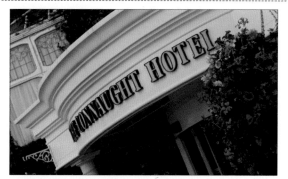

30 West Hill Road, West Cliff, BH2 5PH - tel: 01202 298020
email: reception@theconnaught.co.uk **web:** www.theconnaught.co.uk
dir: *Follow Town Centre West & BIC signs*

Conveniently located on the West Cliff, close to the BIC, beaches and town centre, this privately-owned hotel offers well equipped, neatly decorated rooms, some

with balconies. The hotel boasts a very well-equipped leisure complex with a large pool and gym. Breakfast and dinner offer imaginative dishes made with quality local ingredients.

Best Western Plus The Connaught Hotel

Rooms: 81 (28 annexe) 🐾 **S** £60–£75; **D** £110–£160 (incl. bkfst)* **Facilities:** Spa FTV WiFi ↝ ⊛ supervised Gym Beauty treatments Sauna room Steam room 🎵 Xmas New Year **Conf:** Class 60 Board 35 Thtr 180 Del from £165 **Services:** Lift Night porter **Parking:** 66 **Notes:** Civ Wed 130

See advert on following page

Hermitage Hotel

★★★★ 76% ❀ HOTEL

Exeter Road, BH2 5AH - tel: 01202 557363
email: info@hermitage-hotel.co.uk **web:** www.hermitage-hotel.co.uk
dir: *A338 Ringwood, follow signs for BIC & pier. Hotel directly opposite*

Occupying an impressive location overlooking the seafront, at the heart of the town centre, the Hermitage offers friendly and attentive service. The majority of the smart bedrooms are comfortably appointed and all are very well equipped; many rooms have sea views. The wood-panelled lounge provides an elegant and tranquil area, as does the restaurant where well-prepared and interesting dishes are served.

Rooms: 74 (11 annexe) (9 family) (7 GF) 🐾 **Facilities:** FTV WiFi ↝ Xmas New Year **Conf:** Class 60 Board 60 Thtr 180 Del from £106.90 **Services:** Lift Night porter **Parking:** 58

The Norfolk Royale Hotel

★★★★ 74% HOTEL   PEEL HOTELS PLC

Richmond Hill, BH2 6EN - tel: 01202 551521
email: rooms@norfolkroyale-hotel-bournemouth.com **web:** www.peelhotels.co.uk
dir: *A338 into Bournemouth take Richmond Hill exit to A347 Wimborne, turn left at top into Richmond Hill. Hotel on right*

Easily recognisable by its wrought iron balconies, this Edwardian hotel is conveniently located for the centre of the town. Most of the bedrooms are contained in a modern wing at the side of the building, overlooking the pretty landscaped gardens. There is a car park at the rear of the hotel.

Rooms: 95 (23 family) (9 GF) 🐾 **S** £99–£168; **D** £138–£213 (incl. bkfst)* **Facilities:** STV FTV WiFi ↝ HL⊛ Membership of nearby health club Xmas New Year **Conf:** Class 50 Board 40 Thtr 150 Del from £140 **Services:** Lift Night porter **Parking:** 95 **Notes:** LB Civ Wed 150

B

BOURNEMOUTH *continued*

Hallmark Hotel Bournemouth Carlton

★★★★ 73% HOTEL

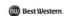

East Overcliff, BH1 3DN - **tel:** 0330 028 3411
email: carlton@hallmarkhotels.co.uk **web:** www.hallmarkhotels.co.uk
dir: *From M3, M27 towards Bournemouth on A338, follow signs to East Cliff, hotel on seafront*

Enjoying a prime location on the East Cliff, and with views of the Isle of Wight and Dorset coastline, the Carlton has attractive gardens and pool area. Most of the spacious bedrooms enjoy sea views. Leisure facilities include an indoor and outdoor pool as well as a gym. Guests can enjoy an interesting range of carefully prepared dishes in Frederick's restaurant. The conference and banqueting facilities are varied.

Rooms: 76 (17 family) (8 GF) **Facilities:** Spa FTV WiFi Gym Hair & beauty salon Xmas New Year **Conf:** Class 110 Board 50 Thtr 200 **Services:** Lift Night porter **Parking:** 87 **Notes:** Civ Wed 200

Hallmark Hotel Bournemouth East Cliff

★★★★ 73% HOTEL

East Overcliff Drive, BH1 3AN - **tel:** 01202 554545
email: eastcliff@hallmarkhotels.co.uk
web: www.hallmarkhotels.co.uk
dir: *From M3, M27 towards Bournemouth on A33 follow signs to East Cliff, hotel on seafront*

Enjoying panoramic views across the bay, this popular hotel offers bedrooms that are modern and contemporary in style; they are appointed to a very high standard, and many have the benefit of balconies and sea views. Stylish public areas include a range of inviting lounges, a spacious restaurant and a selection of conference rooms.

Rooms: 67 (15 family) (2 GF) (5 smoking) **Facilities:** FTV WiFi Full leisure facilities at adjacent Hallmark Carlton Xmas New Year **Conf:** Class 60 Board 40 Thtr 150 **Services:** Lift Night porter **Parking:** 45 **Notes:** Civ Wed 250

Hallmark Hotel Bournemouth West Cliff

★★★★ 71% HOTEL

Durley Chine Road, West Cliff, BH2 5JS - **tel:** 0330 028 3413
email: westcliff@hallmarkhotels.co.uk **web:** www.hallmarkhotels.co.uk
dir: *A338 follow signs to West Cliff & BIC, hotel on right*

This property is conveniently located and offers a friendly atmosphere and attentive service. The comfortable bedrooms are tastefully appointed and are suitable for both business and leisure guests. The restaurant and bar serve a good choice of dishes, and the well-appointed leisure area is popular with both residents and locals alike. There is also a good range of conference facilities and meeting rooms.

Rooms: 83 (5 GF) **Facilities:** Spa FTV WiFi Gym Sauna Steam room Aromatherapy cave Relaxation room Xmas New Year **Conf:** Class 80 Board 40 Thtr 250 **Services:** Lift Night porter **Parking:** 80 **Notes:** LB Civ Wed 200

Best Western Hotel Royale

★★★ 82% HOTEL

16 Gervis Road, BH1 3EQ - **tel:** 01202 554794
email: patgreen@oceanahotels.com **web:** www.thehotelroyale.com
dir: *M27 junct 1, A31 onto A338 to Bournemouth, follow signs for East Cliff & seafront. Over 2 rdbts into Gervis Rd. Hotel on right*

Located on the East Cliff, just a short walk from the seafront and local shops and amenities, is this privately-owned hotel. Public areas are contemporary in style, and

---

facilities include a small health club and spacious function rooms. Bedrooms are comfortable and well furnished.

Best Western Hotel Royale

Rooms: 64 (8 annexe) (22 family) (8 GF) 🐾 **S** fr £50; **D** fr £80 (incl. bkfst)*
Facilities: STV FTV WiFi ⚡ ☒ Xmas New Year **Conf:** Class 60 Board 40 Thtr 100
Services: Lift Night porter **Parking:** 80 **Notes:** LB Civ Wed 100

The Riviera Hotel

★★★ 81% 🏵 HOTEL

Burnaby Road, Alum Chine, BH4 8JF - tel: 01202 763653
email: info@rivierabournemouth.co.uk **web:** www.rivierabournemouth.co.uk
dir: *A338, follow signs to Alum Chine*

The Riviera offers a range of comfortable, well-furnished bedrooms and bathrooms. Welcoming staff provide efficient service delivered in a friendly manner. In addition to a spacious lounge with regular entertainment, there are indoor and outdoor pools, all just a short walk from the beach. Accomplished cuisine is not to be missed.

Rooms: 70 (4 annexe) (24 family) (7 GF) 🐾 **S** £35–£85; **D** £55–£120 **Facilities:** Spa
FTV WiFi ☒ 🏊 Gym Games room Spa bath Treatments available in the Coast Spa
🎵 Xmas New Year **Conf:** Class 120 Board 50 Thtr 180 Del from £65 **Services:** Lift
Night porter **Parking:** 45 **Notes:** LB Civ Wed 160

Elstead Hotel

★★★ 78% HOTEL

Knyveton Road, BH1 3QP - tel: 01202 293071
email: info@the-elstead.co.uk **web:** www.the-elstead.co.uk
dir: *A338 (Wessex Way) to St Pauls rdbt, left & left again*

Ideal as a base for business and leisure travellers, Elstead Hotel is conveniently located for the town centre, seafront and BIC. An impressive range of facilities is offered, including meeting rooms, an indoor leisure centre and comfortable lounges.

Rooms: 50 (15 family) 🐾 **Facilities:** Spa FTV WiFi ☒ supervised Gym Sauna Steam
room Pool & snooker tables Xmas New Year **Conf:** Class 70 Board 35 Thtr 80
Services: Lift Night porter **Parking:** 40 **Notes:** Civ Wed 60

Mayfair Hotel

★★★ 78% HOTEL

27 Bath Road, BH1 2NW - tel: 01202 551983
email: info@themayfair.com **web:** www.themayfair.com
dir: *Exit A338 at St Pauls Rd (Asda rdbt), right into Holdenhurst Rd, 3rd exit from Lansdowne rdbt*

Occupying a central location in the heart of Bournemouth and within walking distance of both the town centre and the seafront, this hotel offers guests comfortable, modern accommodation. There is a spacious restaurant and bar area, plus a pleasant outdoor patio and function room.

Rooms: 40 (8 family) (1 GF) 🐾 **S** £50–£80; **D** £90–£120 (incl. bkfst)* **Facilities:** WiFi
Ballroom dancing programme on request Xmas New Year **Conf:** Class 40 Board 30
Thtr 60 Del from £75 **Services:** Lift Night porter **Parking:** 30 **Notes:** LB Civ Wed 80

Royal Exeter Hotel

★★★ 78% HOTEL

Exeter Road, BH2 5AG - tel: 01202 438000
email: enquiries@royalexeterhotel.com **web:** www.royalexeterhotel.com
dir: *Opposite Bournemouth International Centre*

Ideally located opposite the Bournemouth International Centre, and convenient for the beach and town centre, this busy hotel caters for both business and leisure guests. Public areas are smart, and there's a modern open-plan lounge bar and restaurant, together with an exciting adjoining bar complex.

Rooms: 54 (13 family) (12 smoking) 🐾 **S** £50–£90; **D** £70–£140* **Facilities:** FTV WiFi
Gym 🎵 **Conf:** Class 40 Board 40 Thtr 100 **Services:** Lift Night porter **Parking:** 50
Notes: LB

See advert on following page

B

BOURNEMOUTH *continued*

Durley Dean Hotel

★★★ 77% HOTEL

West Cliff Road, BH2 5HE - **tel:** 01202 557711
email: reservations@durleydean.co.uk **web:** www.durleydean.co.uk
dir: *Into Bournemouth, follow signs for Westcliff. Onto Durley Chine Rd South to next rdbt, hotel at 2nd exit on left*

Situated close to the seafront on the West Cliff, Durley Dean is a modern hotel with bedrooms that vary in size and style. The hotel has a restaurant, a comfortable bar and several meeting rooms. Parking is also a bonus. Additional facilities include a spa with indoor pool, gym, and treatment rooms for a touch of pampering.

Rooms: 115 (36 family) (6 GF) **S** £40–£80; **D** £50–£180* **Facilities:** Spa FTV WiFi ⓨ ⓣ Gym Sauna Steam room ♫ Xmas New Year **Conf:** Class 40 Board 45 Thtr 150 Del from £115 **Services:** Lift Night porter **Parking:** 30 **Notes:** LB Civ Wed 120

Hotel Collingwood

★★★ 76% HOTEL

11 Priory Road, West Cliff, BH2 5DF - **tel:** 01202 557575
email: info@hotelcollingwood.co.uk **web:** www.hotelcollingwood.co.uk
dir: *A338 left at West Cliff sign, over 1st rdbt, left at 2nd rdbt. Hotel 500yds on left*

This privately owned and managed hotel is situated close to the BIC. The bedrooms are airy, with an emphasis on guest comfort. An excellent range of leisure facilities is available, and the public areas are spacious and welcoming. Pinks Restaurant offers carefully prepared cuisine and a fixed-price, five-course dinner.

Rooms: 53 (16 family) (6 GF) ⓝ **S** £34–£90; **D** £68–£180 (incl. bkfst & dinner)* **Facilities:** FTV WiFi ⓨ ⓣ Gym Steam room Sauna Games room Snooker room ♫ Xmas New Year **Conf:** Class 40 Board 20 Thtr 80 **Services:** Lift Night porter **Parking:** 55 **Notes:** LB

Marsham Court Hotel

★★★ 76% HOTEL

Russell Cotes Road, East Cliff, BH1 3AB - **tel:** 01202 552111
email: reservations@marshamcourthotel.co.uk **web:** www.marshamcourthotel.co.uk
dir: *A338, at St Pauls rdbt follow signs to East Cliff, Pier & Beaches. 3rd exit Holdenhurst Rd, at next rdbt 3rd exit Bath Rd, at next rdbt 2nd exit, hotel car park immediately on right*

This hotel, in a quiet location, is set in attractive gardens with splendid views over the bay; it is just a short stroll from the town, beach and BIC. Bedrooms vary in size but all are comfortably appointed, and some have sea views. The bar and lounge areas lead onto the south-facing terrace, which has an outdoor pool. Impressive conference and banqueting facilities are available.

Rooms: 87 (25 family) ⓝ **S** £71–£116; **D** £71–£116* **Facilities:** FTV WiFi ⓨ ⓣ Indoor games room Xmas New Year **Conf:** Class 120 Board 80 Thtr 230 Del from £99 **Services:** Lift Night porter **Parking:** 99 **Notes:** LB Civ Wed 180

Trouville Hotel

★★★ 75% HOTEL

Priory Road, BH2 5DH - **tel:** 01202 552262
email: reception@trouvillehotel.com **web:** www.trouvillehotel.com
dir: *Follow Town Centre West signs. Exit at rdbt signed BIC/West Cliff/Beaches. 2nd exit at next rdbt, left at next rdbt. Hotel on left near end of Priory Rd*

Located near Bournemouth International Centre, the seafront and the shops, this hotel has the advantage of indoor leisure facilities and a large car park. Bedrooms are generally a good size with comfortable furnishings, and there are plenty of family rooms. The air-conditioned restaurant offers a daily changing menu.

Rooms: 99 (19 annexe) (21 family) (2 GF) ⓝ **S** £40–£65; **D** £80–£130 (incl. bkfst)* **Facilities:** FTV WiFi ⓨ ⓣ Gym Sauna Beauty treatment room ♫ Xmas New Year **Conf:** Class 100 Board 80 Thtr 250 **Services:** Lift Night porter **Parking:** 70 **Notes:** LB Civ Wed 130

B

Devon Towers Hotel

Leisureplex
HOLIDAY HOTELS

★★★ 71% HOTEL

58-62 St Michael's Road, West Cliff, BH2 5ED - tel: 01202 553863
email: devontowers@leisureplex.co.uk **web:** www.leisureplex.co.uk
dir: A338 into Bournemouth, follow signs for BIC. Left into St Michaels Rd at top of hill. Hotel 100mtrs on left

Located in a quiet road within walking distance of the West Cliff and shops, this hotel appeals to the budget leisure market. The four-course menus offer plenty of choice and entertainment is featured most evenings. The bar and lobby area provide plenty of space for relaxing.

Rooms: 60 (8 GF) ↻ **S** £38–£54; **D** £60–£92 (incl. bkfst)* **Facilities:** FTV WiFi ♫ Xmas New Year **Services:** Lift Night porter **Parking:** 2 **Notes:** LB Closed Jan-mid Feb (ex Xmas) RS mid-end Feb, Mar & Nov Mon-Fri only

Tower House Hotel

★★ 80% HOTEL

West Cliff Gardens, BH2 5HP - tel: 01202 290742
email: towerhouse.hotel@btconnect.com **web:** www.towerhousehotelbournemouth.com
dir: Phone for directions

Tower House Hotel is a popular family-owned and run hotel on the West Cliff. The owners and their staff are friendly and helpful. The bedrooms are comfortable and well maintained, and the hotel provides good off-road parking.

Rooms: 32 (12 family) (3 GF) ↻ **S** £35–£60; **D** £70–£120 (incl. bkfst)* **Facilities:** FTV WiFi Xmas New Year **Services:** Lift **Parking:** 30 **Notes:** Closed 2-31 Jan

Bourne Hall Hotel

★★ 69% METRO HOTEL

14 Priory Road, BH2 5DN - tel: 01202 299715
email: info@bournehall.co.uk **web:** www.bournehall.co.uk
dir: Phone for directions

Situated on the West Cliff, this welcoming family-run establishment is ideally located for a relaxing break in Bournemouth. Just a short stroll from the wonderful stretch of golden sands, there is much to explore. Bedrooms are simply furnished and some have the benefit of sea views, while public areas include a spacious bar and lounge with outside terrace area. Breakfast is served in the elegant dining room.

Rooms: 47 (7 family) (5 GF) ↻ **Facilities:** FTV WiFi Xmas New Year **Services:** Lift Night porter **Parking:** 37 **Notes:** Closed some weekends, phone for details

Premier Inn Bournemouth Central

Premier Inn

BUDGET HOTEL

Westover Road, BH1 2BZ - tel: 0871 527 8124 (Calls cost 13p per minute plus your phone company's access charge) **web:** www.premierinn.com
dir: M27 junct 1, A31. Left at Ashley Heath junct. A338 towards Bournemouth. At rdbt 1st exit. At next rdbt 3rd exit (Holdenhurst Rd). At next rdbt 3rd exit (Bath Rd). At next rdbt 3rd exit onto Bath Hill. At next rdbt into Westover Rd, right into Hinton Rd, hotel on right

High quality, budget accommodation ideal for both families and business travellers. Spacious, en suite bedrooms feature tea and coffee making facilities, Freeview TV in most hotels and free WiFi. The adjacent family restaurant features a wide and varied menu.

Rooms: 120

Premier Inn Bournemouth East (Lynton Court)

Premier Inn

BUDGET HOTEL

47 Christchurch Road, Boscombe, BH1 3PA - tel: 0871 527 8126 (Calls cost 13p per minute plus your phone company's access charge) **web:** www.premierinn.com
dir: M27 junct 1, A31, 9m, left at Ashley Heath junct, take A338 signed Bournemouth. At 1st rdbt take 1st exit into Saint Paul's Rd. At 2nd rdbt 1st exit onto Christchurch Rd. Hotel on right

Rooms: 20

Premier Inn Bournemouth Westcliffe

BUDGET HOTEL

Poole Road, BH2 5QU - tel: 0871 527 8128 (Calls cost 13p per minute plus your phone company's access charge) **web:** www.premierinn.com
dir: M27 junct 1, A31. At Ashley Heath junction, left. Take A338 signed Bournemouth. At Bournemouth West rdbt 1st exit signed Ring Road, West Cliff. At next rdbt (St Michael's) 3rd exit (signed Westbourne) into Poole Rd. Hotel on right

Rooms: 168

BOURTON-ON-THE-WATER Map 10 SP12
Gloucestershire

Chester House Hotel

★★★ 80% SMALL HOTEL

Victoria Street, GL54 2BU - tel: 01451 820286
email: info@chesterhousehotel.com **web:** www.chesterhousehotel.com
dir: On A429 between Northleach & Stow-on-the-Wold

Chester House Hotel occupies a secluded but central location in this delightful Cotswold village. Bedrooms, some at ground floor level, are situated in the main house and adjoining coach house. The public areas are stylish, light and airy. Breakfast is taken in the main building whereas dinner is served in the attractive restaurant just a few yards away.

Rooms: 22 (10 annexe) (3 family) (8 GF) ↻ **Facilities:** FTV WiFi ♦ Beauty therapist New Year **Parking:** 18 **Notes:** Closed 2 Jan-10 Feb

BOWNESS-ON-WINDERMERE
See **Windermere**

BRACKNELL Map 5 SU86
Berkshire

Coppid Beech

★★★★ 74% HOTEL

John Nike Way, RG12 8TF - tel: 01344 303333
email: sales@coppidbeech.com **web:** www.coppidbeech.com
dir: M4 junct 10 take Wokingham/Bracknell onto A329. In 2m take B3408 to Binfield, at lights turn right. Hotel 200yds on right

This chalet designed hotel offers extensive facilities and includes a ski-slope, ice rink, nightclub, health club and Bier Keller. Bedrooms range from suites to standard rooms - all are impressively equipped. A choice of dining is offered; there's a full bistro menu available in the Keller, and for more formal dining, Rowan's restaurant provides award-winning cuisine.

Rooms: 205 (6 family) (16 GF) **Facilities:** STV WiFi ⊛ Gym Beauty treatment room Ice rink Dry ski slope Snow boarding Freestyle park ♫ New Year **Conf:** Class 161 Board 24 Thtr 350 **Services:** Lift Night porter Air con **Parking:** 350 **Notes:** Civ Wed 200

B

BRACKNELL *continued*

Stirrups Country House Hotel

★★★ 82% HOTEL

Maidens Green, RG42 6LD - tel: 01344 882284
email: reception@stirrupshotel.co.uk **web:** www.stirrupshotel.co.uk
dir: *3m N on B3022 towards Windsor*

Situated in a peaceful location between Maidenhead, Bracknell and Windsor, this hotel has high standards of comfort particularly in the bedrooms; some rooms have a small sitting room area. There is a popular bar, a restaurant, function rooms and delightful grounds.

Rooms: 36 (5 annexe) (6 family) (5 GF) ⌁ **S** £92.50–£127.50; **D** £105–£140 (incl. bkfst)* **Facilities:** FTV WiFi ⚑ HL New Year **Conf:** Class 50 Board 40 Thtr 100 **Services:** Lift Night porter **Parking:** 100 **Notes:** Civ Wed 100

Premier Inn Bracknell Central

BUDGET HOTEL

Wokingham Road, RG42 1NA - tel: 0871 527 8132 (Calls cost 13p per minute plus your phone company's access charge) **web:** www.premierinn.com
dir: *M4 junct 10, A329(M) (Bracknell) to lights. 1st left, 3rd exit rdbt by Morrisons to town centre. Left at rdbt, left at next rdbt. Hotel on left*

High quality, budget accommodation ideal for both families and business travellers. Spacious, en suite bedrooms feature tea and coffee making facilities, Freeview TV in most hotels and free WiFi. The adjacent family restaurant features a wide and varied menu.

Rooms: 80

Premier Inn Bracknell (Twin Bridges)

BUDGET HOTEL

Downshire Way, RG12 7AA - tel: 0871 527 8130 (Calls cost 13p per minute plus your phone company's access charge) **web:** www.premierinn.com
dir: *M4 junct 10, A329(M) towards Bracknell. Straight on at mini rdbt. At Twin Bridges rdbt take 2nd exit. Hotel on right adjacent to Downshire Arms Beefeater*

Rooms: 28

BRADFORD	Map 19 SE13
West Yorkshire	

See also **Gomersal**

Midland Hotel

★★★ 78% HOTEL

Forster Square, BD1 4HU - tel: 01274 735735
email: info@midland-hotel-bradford.com **web:** www.peelhotels.co.uk
dir: *M62 junct 26, M606, past ASDA, left at rdbt onto A650. Through 2 rdbts & 2 lights. Follow A6181/Haworth signs. Up hill, next left into Manor Row. Hotel 400mtrs*

Ideally situated in the heart of the city, this grand Victorian hotel provides modern, very well equipped accommodation and comfortable, spacious day rooms. Ample parking is available in what was once the city's railway station, and a Victorian walkway linking the hotel to the old platform can still be used today.

Rooms: 90 (5 family) (4 smoking) ⌁ **Facilities:** STV FTV WiFi ⚑ HL New Year **Conf:** Class 150 Board 100 Thtr 450 Del from £115 **Services:** Lift Night porter **Parking:** 60 **Notes:** Civ Wed 450

Best Western Bradford Guide Post Hotel

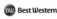

★★★ 75% HOTEL

Common Road, Low Moor, BD12 0ST - tel: 01274 607866
email: sue.barnes@guideposthotel.net **web:** www.guideposthotel.net
dir: *From M606 rdbt take 2nd exit. At next rdbt take 1st exit (Cleckheaton Rd). 0.5m, turn right at bollard into Common Rd*

Situated south of the city, this hotel offers attractively styled, modern, comfortable bedrooms. The restaurant offers an extensive range of food using fresh, local produce; lighter snack meals are served in the bar. There is also a choice of well-equipped meeting and function rooms. There is disabled access to the hotel, restaurant and one function room.

Rooms: 42 (10 family) (13 GF) ⌁ **S** £50–£70; **D** £50–£70* **Facilities:** FTV WiFi ⚑ Complimentary use of nearby swimming & gym facilities **Conf:** Class 80 Board 60 Thtr 120 Del from £108.50 **Services:** Night porter **Parking:** 100 **Notes:** LB Civ Wed 120

Premier Inn Bradford Central

BUDGET HOTEL

Vicar Lane, BD1 5LD - tel: 0871 527 9306 (Calls cost 13p per minute plus your phone company's access charge) **web:** www.premierinn.com
dir: *M62 junct 24, M606, at junct 3 take 4th exit into Rooley Ln (A6177) towards Ring Rd/ A650/Leeds/A647. In 1m 1st exit into Wakefield Rd towards City Centre. Follow Wakefield Rd/A650 signs. Straight on at 2 rdbts, right into Vicar Ln*

High quality, budget accommodation ideal for both families and business travellers. Spacious, en suite bedrooms feature tea and coffee making facilities, Freeview TV in most hotels and free WiFi. The adjacent family restaurant features a wide and varied menu.

Rooms: 118

BRADFORD-ON-AVON	Map 4 ST86
Wiltshire	

Widbrook Grange

★★★ 80% COUNTRY HOUSE HOTEL

Trowbridge Road, BA15 1UH - tel: 01225 864750
email: stay@widbrookgrange.com **web:** www.widbrookgrange.co.uk
dir: *1m SE from Bradford on A363, hotel diagonally opposite Bradford Marina & Arabian Stud*

Widbrook Grange is an impressive Bath-stone country house, offering a quiet retreat a short drive from the bustle of Bath. Spacious bedrooms are located either in the main house or in the converted farm buildings, with some rooms having four-poster beds. Leisure facilities include a small gym and indoor swimming pool with beauty treatments available on request. The brasserie focuses on local seasonal produce at breakfast and dinner.

Rooms: 19 (15 annexe) (6 family) (13 GF) ⌁ **D** £90–£185 (incl. bkfst)* **Facilities:** FTV WiFi ⚑ ⊛ Gym Children's weekend play room Beauty treatments Xmas New Year **Conf:** Class 35 Board 25 Thtr 50 Del from £145 **Parking:** 50 **Notes:** LB Civ Wed 50

BRAINTREE
Essex Map 7 TL72

Premier Inn Braintree (A120)

BUDGET HOTEL

Cressing Road, Galley's Corner, CM77 8GG - **tel:** 0871 527 8138 (Calls cost 13p per minute plus your phone company's access charge) **web:** www.premierinn.com
dir: On A120 (Stansted to Braintree link road). Adjacent to Mulberry Tree Brewers Fayre

High quality, budget accommodation ideal for both families and business travellers. Spacious, en suite bedrooms feature tea and coffee making facilities, Freeview TV in most hotels and free WiFi. The adjacent family restaurant features a wide and varied menu.

Rooms: 78

Premier Inn Braintree (Freeport Village)

BUDGET HOTEL

Fowlers Farm, Cressing Road, CM77 8DH - **tel:** 0871 527 8140 (Calls cost 13p per minute plus your phone company's access charge) **web:** www.premierinn.com
dir: M11 junct 8, follow signs to A120 Colchester & Freeport Shopping Village. At Galley's Corner rdbt, 4th exit, left into Wyevale Garden Centre. Hotel adjacent

Rooms: 48

BRAMPTON
Cumbria Map 21 NY56

INSPECTOR'S CHOICE

Farlam Hall Hotel
★★★ HOTEL

Hallbankgate, CA8 2NG - **tel:** 016977 46234
email: farlam@relaischateaux.com **web:** www.farlamhall.co.uk
dir: On A689 (Brampton to Alston). Hotel 2m on left - not in Farlam village

This delightful country house has a history dating back to 1428, although the building today is very much the result of alterations carried out in the mid-19th century. The hotel is run by a friendly family team and their enthusiastic staff, and is set in beautifully landscaped Victorian gardens complete with an ornamental lake and stream. Lovingly restored over many years, it provides very high standards of comfort and hospitality. Gracious public rooms are very

relaxing, and a lot of thought has gone into the beautiful bedrooms, many of which are simply stunning. Nearby are Hadrian's Wall and the Northern Pennines Area of Outstanding Natural Beauty, which both provide endless opportunities for walking and sightseeing.

Rooms: 12 (1 annexe) (2 GF) ⋒ **S** £165–£195; **D** £310–£370 (incl. bkfst & dinner)* **Facilities:** FTV WiFi ♨ ⛵ New Year **Conf:** Class 24 Board 12 Thtr 24 **Parking:** 25 **Notes:** LB No children 5yrs Closed 24-30 Dec & 4-21 Jan Civ Wed 45

BRANCASTER STAITHE
Norfolk Map 13 TF74

The White Horse
★★★ 84% ⊛⊛ HOTEL

PE31 8BY - **tel:** 01485 210262
email: reception@whitehorsebrancaster.co.uk **web:** www.whitehorsebrancaster.co.uk
dir: On A149 (coast road) midway between Hunstanton & Wells-next-the-Sea

The White Horse is a charming hotel situated on the north Norfolk coast with contemporary bedrooms in two wings, some featuring an interesting cobbled fascia. Each room is attractively decorated and thoughtfully equipped. There is a large bar and a lounge area leading through to the conservatory restaurant, with stunning tidal marshland views across to Scolt Head Island.

Rooms: 15 (8 annexe) (5 family) (8 GF) ⋒ **S** £110–£150; **D** £110–£190 (incl. bkfst)* **Facilities:** FTV WiFi ♨ Holistic therapies in room Xmas New Year **Parking:** 30 **Notes:** LB

BRANDON
Warwickshire Map 11 SP47

Mercure Coventry Brandon Hall Hotel & Spa
★★★★ 70% HOTEL

Mercure
HOTELS

Main Street, CV8 3FW - **tel:** 024 7654 6000
email: h6625@accor.com **web:** www.mercure.com
dir: A45 towards Coventry S. After Peugeot-Citroen garage on left, at island take 5th exit to M1 South/London (back onto A45). After 200yds, immediately after Texaco garage, left into Brandon Ln, hotel after 2.5m

An impressive tree-lined avenue leads to this 17th-century property which sits in 17 acres of grounds. The hotel provides a peaceful and friendly sanctuary away from the hustle and bustle. Bedrooms provide comfortable facilities and a good range of extras for guest comfort. There is a Spa Naturel with health, beauty and fitness facilities in a separate building.

Rooms: 120 (30 annexe) (10 family) (50 GF) ⋒ **Facilities:** Spa STV WiFi ♨ Gym Steam room Sauna Xmas New Year **Conf:** Class 120 Board 112 Thtr 280 **Services:** Lift Night porter **Parking:** 200 **Notes:** Civ Wed 280

BRANKSOME

See **Poole**

B

BRANSCOMBE
Devon

Map 4 SY18

The Bulstone Hotel
★★ 75% HOTEL

High Bulstone, EX12 3BL - tel: 01297 680446
email: bulstone@aol.com web: www.childfriendlyhotels.com
dir: A3052 (Exeter to Lyme Regis road) at Branscombe Cross follow brown hotel sign

Situated in a peaceful location close to the beautiful east Devon coast, this family-friendly hotel is ideally placed for a relaxing break with plenty of attractions within easy reach. All bedrooms consist of a main bedroom and separate children's room, each being practically furnished and equipped. Additional facilities include a playroom, a snug lounge, and the dining room where enjoyable home-cooked meals are offered. There is no charge for children under ten, and children's tea is at 5pm.

Rooms: 7 (7 family) (4 GF) **Facilities:** FTV WiFi Children's playroom Xmas New Year **Conf:** Class 25 Board 25 **Services:** Night porter **Parking:** 25 **Notes:** LB

BRANSFORD
Worcestershire

Map 10 SO75

Bank House Hotel, Spa & Golf Club
[U]

WR6 5JD - tel: 01886 833551
email: reception@bankhouseworcester.com web: www.bankhouseworcester.com

Currently the rating for this establishment is not confirmed. This may be due to a change of ownership or because it has only recently joined the AA rating scheme.

Rooms: 50 **S** £67.50-£140; **D** £120-£162 (incl bkfst)

BRENTFORD
Greater London

Novotel London Brentford
★★★★ 80% HOTEL PLAN 1 C3

NOVOTEL
HOTELS & RESORTS

Great West Road, TW8 0GP - tel: 020 3693 1800
email: H6995@accor.com web: www.novotel.com
dir: Please call for directions

Located just 20 minutes from Heathrow with Richmond and Twickenham Stadium just a couple of minutes away, Novotel London Brentford offers stylish public areas throughout, and comfortably appointed rooms ideal for both corporate and leisure guests. There are conference facilities on site and a leisure suite on the lower ground. Parking is available on site and South Ealing and Brentford station is less than one mile from the hotel.

Rooms: 202 (90 family) **Facilities:** FTV WiFi HL Gym **Conf:** Class 50 Board 30 Thtr 90 **Services:** Lift Night porter Air con **Parking:** 100

Premier Inn London Kew
BUDGET HOTEL PLAN 1 C3

52 High Street, TW8 0BB - tel: 0871 527 8670 (Calls cost 13p per minute plus your phone company's access charge) web: www.premierinn.com
dir: At junct of A4 (M4), A205 & A406, Chiswick rdbt, take A205 towards Kew & Brentford. 200yds right fork onto A315 (High St), for 0.5m. Hotel on left

High quality, budget accommodation ideal for both families and business travellers. Spacious, en suite bedrooms feature tea and coffee making facilities, Freeview TV in most hotels and free WiFi. The adjacent family restaurant features a wide and varied menu.

Rooms: 141

BRENTWOOD
Essex

Map 6 TQ59

Marygreen Manor Hotel
★★★★ 75% ◉◉ HOTEL

London Road, CM14 4NR - tel: 01277 225252
email: info@marygreenmanor.co.uk web: www.marygreenmanor.co.uk
dir: M25 junct 28, onto A1023 over 2 sets of lights, hotel on right

This 16th-century house was built by Robert Wright, who named the house 'Manor of Mary Green' after his young bride. Public rooms exude character and have a wealth of original features that include exposed beams, carved panelling and the impressive Tudors Restaurant. Bedrooms are tastefully decorated and thoughtfully equipped.

Rooms: 44 (40 annexe) (35 GF) **S** £97-£160; **D** £97-£160* **Facilities:** STV FTV WiFi **Conf:** Class 20 Board 25 Thtr 50 Del from £125 **Services:** Night porter **Parking:** 100 **Notes:** Civ Wed 60

De Rougemont Manor
★★★★ 72% HOTEL

Great Warley Street, CM13 3JP - tel: 01277 226418
email: info@derougemontmanor.co.uk web: www.derougemontmanor.co.uk
dir: M25 junct 29, A127 to Southend then B186 towards Great Warley

Expect a warm welcome at this family-owned and managed hotel, situated on the outskirts of Brentwood just off the M25. The stylish bedrooms are divided between the main hotel and a bedroom wing; each one is tastefully appointed and well equipped. Public rooms include a smart lounge bar, restaurant and a choice of seating areas.

Rooms: 75 (9 annexe) (6 family) (16 GF) **Facilities:** FTV WiFi Gym Beauty treatment rooms 3-acre nature reserve Xmas New Year **Conf:** Class 66 Board 42 Thtr 260 **Services:** Lift Night porter Air con **Parking:** 200 **Notes:** Civ Wed 90

Premier Inn Brentwood
BUDGET HOTEL

Brentwood House, 169 Kings Road, CM14 4EG - tel: 0871 527 8142 (Calls cost 13p per minute plus your phone company's access charge) web: www.premierinn.com
dir: From S: M25 junct 28 take A1023 (or from N: at Brook Street rdbt 2nd exit onto A1023). Right at lights into Kings Rd, at rdbt 2nd exit into Kings Rd

High quality, budget accommodation ideal for both families and business travellers. Spacious, en suite bedrooms feature tea and coffee making facilities, Freeview TV in most hotels and free WiFi. The adjacent family restaurant features a wide and varied menu.

Rooms: 122

BRIDGWATER
Somerset

Map 4 ST23

Walnut Tree Hotel
★★★ 77% ◉ HOTEL

North Petherton, TA6 6QA - tel: 01278 662255
email: reservations@walnuttreehotel.com web: www.walnuttreehotel.com
dir: M5 junct 24. Follow North Petherton signs. 1.3m. Hotel in village centre

Popular with both business and leisure guests, this 18th-century former coaching inn is conveniently located within easy reach of the M5. The spacious and smartly decorated bedrooms are well furnished to ensure a comfortable and relaxing stay.

An extensive selection of dishes is offered in either the restaurant, or the more informal setting of the bistro.

Rooms: 30 (3 family) (3 GF) **Facilities:** FTV WiFi ♨ Xmas New Year **Conf:** Class 60 Board 50 Thtr 100 **Services:** Night porter **Parking:** 70 **Notes:** Civ Wed 100

Apple Tree Hotel

★★★ 73% HOTEL

Keenthorne, TA5 1HZ - **tel:** 01278 733238
email: reservations@appletreehotel.com **web:** www.appletreehotel.com
dir: *A39 from Bridgwater towards Minehead. Hotel on left, 2m past Cannington*

Once a farm cottage, dating back over 300 years, this popular hotel now provides a perfect base from which to explore the many and varied places of interest in the locale, including the unspoilt beauty of the Quantock Hills. Whether choosing to stay for business or leisure, the warmth of welcome is always the same, with the owners ensuring guests are well looked after. Bedrooms provide all the expected contemporary comforts, with rooms offered in both the main building and adjacent garden rooms. Dinner is served in the conservatory restaurant, perhaps preceded by a relaxing drink in the bar or library lounge.

Rooms: 16 (2 family) (7 GF) **S** £75–£97; **D** £118–£145 (incl. bkfst)*
Facilities: FTV WiFi ♨ **Conf:** Class 12 Board 12 Thtr 20 **Parking:** 30

Premier Inn Bridgwater

BUDGET HOTEL

Express Park, Bristol Road, TA6 4RR - **tel:** 0871 527 8148 (Calls cost 13p per minute plus your phone company's access charge) **web:** www.premierinn.com
dir: *M5 junct 23, A38 to Bridgwater. Hotel on right in 2m*

High quality, budget accommodation ideal for both families and business travellers. Spacious, en suite bedrooms feature tea and coffee making facilities, Freeview TV in most hotels and free WiFi. The adjacent family restaurant features a wide and varied menu.

Rooms: 67

BRIDLINGTON
East Riding of Yorkshire   Map 17 TA16

Expanse Hotel

★★★ 78% HOTEL

North Marine Drive, YO15 2LS - **tel:** 01262 675347
email: reservations@expanse.co.uk **web:** www.expanse.co.uk
dir: *Follow North Beach signs, pass under railway arch for North Marine Drive. Hotel at bottom of hill*

This traditional seaside hotel overlooks the bay and has been in the same family's ownership for many years. Service is relaxed and friendly and the modern bedrooms

are well equipped. Comfortable public areas include a conference suite, a choice of bars and an inviting lounge. Complimentary WiFi is available.

Rooms: 45 (2 family) **S** £37.95–£72; **D** £104–£162 (incl. bkfst)* **Facilities:** FTV WiFi ♨ 🎵 Xmas New Year **Conf:** Class 50 Board 50 Thtr 180 **Services:** Lift Night porter **Parking:** 17 **Notes:** LB Civ Wed 140

BRIGHOUSE
West Yorkshire   Map 16 SE12

Premier Inn Huddersfield North

BUDGET HOTEL

Wakefield Road, HD6 4HA - **tel:** 0871 527 8530 (Calls cost 13p per minute plus your phone company's access charge) **web:** www.premierinn.com
dir: *M62 junct 25, A644 signed Huddersfield, Dewsbury & Wakefield. Hotel 500mtrs up hill on right*

High quality, budget accommodation ideal for both families and business travellers. Spacious, en suite bedrooms feature tea and coffee making facilities, Freeview TV in most hotels and free WiFi. The adjacent family restaurant features a wide and varied menu.

Rooms: 99

BRIGHTON & HOVE
East Sussex   Map 6 TQ30

See also **Steyning**

Hotel du Vin Brighton

★★★★ 77% ◎ TOWN HOUSE HOTEL

2-6 Ship Street, BN1 1AD - **tel:** 01273 718588
email: info@brighton.hotelduvin.com **web:** www.hotelduvin.com
dir: *From A23 follow seafront/city centre signs. Right at seafront, right into Middle St. Follow to end bear right into Ship St. Hotel on right*

This tastefully converted mock-Tudor building occupies a convenient location in a quiet side street close to the seafront. The individually designed bedrooms have a wine theme, and all are comprehensively equipped. Public areas offer a spacious split-level bar, an atmospheric and locally popular restaurant, and useful private dining and meeting facilities.

Rooms: 49 (2 family) (4 GF) **Facilities:** STV WiFi 🎵 Xmas New Year **Conf:** Class 50 Board 60 Thtr 80 **Services:** Night porter Air con **Notes:** Civ Wed 120

The Old Ship Hotel

★★★★ 74% HOTEL

King's Road, BN1 1NR - **tel:** 01273 329001
email: oldship@thehotelcollection.co.uk **web:** www.thehotelcollection.co.uk
dir: *A23 to seafront, right at rdbt along Kings Rd. Hotel 200yds on right*

This historic hotel enjoys a stunning seafront location and offers guests elegant surroundings to relax in. Bedrooms are well designed, with modern facilities ensuring comfort. Many original features have been retained, including the Paganini Ballroom. Facilities include a sleek bar, alfresco dining and a variety of conference rooms.

Rooms: 154 **Facilities:** FTV WiFi HL Gym Xmas New Year **Conf:** Class 100 Board 35 Thtr 250 **Services:** Lift Night porter **Parking:** 40 **Notes:** LB Civ Wed 150

BRIGHTON & HOVE *continued*

Blanch House

★★★ 82% TOWN HOUSE HOTEL

17 Atlingworth Sreet, BN2 1PL - tel: 01273 603504
email: info@blanchhouse.co.uk **web:** www.blanchhouse.co.uk
dir: *Take A23 to A259, left at the pier/seafront*

Blanch House is located in the heart of Kemp Town with the seafront and town centre just a couple of minutes walk away. Bedrooms are individual in their design and style, yet all are comfortable and of a very good quality. The spacious function suite is ideal for private meetings, dinners or weddings. There is a bar (open daily) where guests can enjoy cocktails, champagne and afternoon tea.

Rooms: 12 ☎ **S** £99–£235; **D** £109–£245 (incl. bkfst)* **Facilities:** FTV WiFi ⌂
Conf: Class 16 Board 20 Thtr 40 Del £185 **Notes:** No children 15yrs Civ Wed 40

Best Western Princes Marine

★★★ 79% HOTEL

153 Kingsway, BN3 4GR - tel: 01273 207660
email: princesmarine@bestwestern.co.uk **web:** www.princesmarinehotel.co.uk
dir: *Right at Brighton Pier, follow seafront for 2m. Hotel 200yds from King Alfred leisure centre*

This friendly hotel enjoys a seafront location and offers spacious, comfortable bedrooms equipped with a good range of facilities including free WiFi. Ten newly created rooms on the top floor, some with private balconies, offer incredible sea views and tranquillity. There is a stylish restaurant, modern bar and a flexible meeting room. Limited and secure parking is available at the rear.

Rooms: 57 (4 family) ☎ **S** £50–£200; **D** £60–£220 (incl. bkfst)* **Facilities:** STV FTV WiFi ⌂ **Conf:** Class 40 Board 40 Thtr 60 Del from £125 **Services:** Lift Night porter **Parking:** 25

Mercure Brighton Seafront Hotel

★★★ 75% HOTEL

149 Kings Road, BN1 2PP - tel: 0844 815 9061 (Calls cost 5p per minute plus your company's access charge)
email: info@mercurebrighton.co.uk **web:** www.mercurebrighton.co.uk
dir: *A23 follow signs for seafront. Right at Brighton Pier rdbt. Hotel on right, just after West Pier*

Located right on the seafront in the heart of Brighton, this hotel offers uninterrupted sea views from all seafront-facing rooms and public areas. Brighton Pier, the Lanes and Town Centre are just a couple of minutes walk. The Hotel is spacious and offers comfortably appointed accommodation, all with complimentary WiFi access. Plenty of secure off-road parking is available.

Rooms: 116 (11 family) **Facilities:** FTV WiFi ⌂ **Conf:** Class 80 Board 60 Thtr 180 **Services:** Night porter **Parking:** 36 **Notes:** Civ Wed 180

Queens Hotel

★★★ 75% HOTEL

1-3 King's Road, BN1 1NS - tel: 01273 321222 & 0800 970 7570
email: info@queenshotelbrighton.com **web:** www.queenshotelbrighton.com
dir: *A23 to Brighton town centre, follow signs for seafront. At Brighton Pier right onto seafront, hotel 500mtrs on right*

This hotel has a fantastic location with views of the beach and pier. The modern bedrooms and bathrooms are spacious, and many benefit from uninterrupted sea

views. All bedrooms have LCD TVs and free WiFi. There is a spacious bar and restaurant area plus fully equipped spa, gym and swimming pool.

Rooms: 94 (28 family) **S** £59–£350; **D** £59–£400 (incl. bkfst) **Facilities:** Spa FTV WiFi ⌂ HL ⊛ supervised Gym Beauty salon **Conf:** Class 50 Board 50 Thtr 150 Del from £140 **Services:** Lift Night porter

The Kings Hotel

★★★ 72% METRO HOTEL

139-141 Kings Road, BN1 2NA - tel: 01273 820854
email: info@kingshotelbrighton.co.uk **web:** www.kingshotelbrighton.com
dir: *Follow signs to seafront. At Brighton Pier rdbt take 3rd exit & drive west (seafront on left). Hotel adjacent to West Pier*

Located on the seafront adjacent to West Pier, this Grade II listed, Regency building has been restored to offer contemporary accommodation. Although the hotel does not provide a full dinner service, light snacks are available throughout the day and evening in the public areas and also in the guests' bedrooms. There is limited parking space which is a bonus in Brighton.

Rooms: 96 (5 family) (9 GF) ☎ **Facilities:** FTV WiFi ⌂ **Services:** Lift Night porter **Parking:** 11

Ambassador Brighton

★★ 68% METRO HOTEL

22-23 New Steine, Marine Parade, BN2 1PD - tel: 01273 676869
email: reservations@ambassadorbrighton.co.uk **web:** www.ambassadorbrighton.co.uk
dir: *Phone for directions*

At the heart of bustling Kemp Town, overlooking the attractive garden square next to the seaside, this well-established property has a friendly and relaxing atmosphere. Bedrooms are well equipped and vary in size, with the largest having the best views. A small lounge with a separate bar is available.

Rooms: 24 (9 family) (3 GF) (2 smoking) **S** £55–£95; **D** £59–£155 (incl. bkfst)* **Facilities:** FTV WiFi ⌂ HL **Notes:** LB

Premier Inn Brighton City Centre

BUDGET HOTEL

144 North Street, BN1 1RE - tel: 0871 527 8150 (Calls cost 13p per minute plus your phone company's access charge) **web:** www.premierinn.com
dir: *From A23 follow signs for city centre. Right at lights near Royal Pavilion, take road ahead on left (runs adjacent to Pavilion) into Church St, 1st left into New Rd leading to North St*

High quality, budget accommodation ideal for both families and business travellers. Spacious, en suite bedrooms feature tea and coffee making facilities, Freeview TV in most hotels and free WiFi. The adjacent family restaurant features a wide and varied menu.

Rooms: 160

The Grand Brighton

AA Advertised ⊛⊛

97-99 King's Road, BN1 2FW - tel: 01273 224300
email: reservations@grandbrighton.co.uk **web:** www.grandbrighton.co.uk
dir: *On A259 adjacent to Brighton Centre*

Dating back to the mid-19th century, this landmark seafront hotel, with its eye-catching white façade and intricate balconies, is as grand as the name suggests. Bedrooms include a number of deluxe sea view rooms, some with balconies, and suites, also with sea views. The hotel is perhaps best known for its extensive conference and banqueting facilities; there is also an impressive conservatory adjoining the bar.

Rooms: 201 (60 family) ✆ **S** £87–£320; **D** £117–£350 (incl. bkfst)* **Facilities:** Spa FTV WiFi Gym Thermal suite 🎵 Xmas New Year **Conf:** Class 450 Board 60 Thtr 800 Del from £204 **Services:** Lift Night porter **Parking:** 50 **Notes:** Civ Wed 800

BRISTOL
Bristol

Map 4 ST57

Aztec Hotel & Spa
★★★★ 81% ⊛ HOTEL

Aztec West, BS32 4TS - **tel:** 01454 201090
email: reservations@aztechotelbristol.co.uk **web:** www.aztechotelbristol.co.uk
dir: Access via M5 junct 16 & M4

Situated close to Cribbs Causeway shopping centre and major motorway links, this stylish hotel offers comfortable, very well-equipped bedrooms and suites. Built in a Nordic style, public rooms boast log fires and vaulted ceilings. Leisure facilities include a popular gym and good size pool. The Quarter Jacks Restaurant Bar & Lounge offers relaxed informal dining with a focus on simply prepared, quality regional foods. The hotel has a spa with a gym, pool, children's pool, whirlpool, sauna, steam room and a range of treatments.

Rooms: 128 (8 family) (29 GF) **D** £100–£200* **Facilities:** Spa STV WiFi ⬦ HL ⟳ Gym Steam room Sauna Children's splash pool Activity studio New Year **Conf:** Class 120 Board 36 Thtr 200 Del from £120 **Services:** Lift Night porter **Parking:** 240 **Notes:** LB Civ Wed 120

DoubleTree by Hilton Bristol City Centre
★★★★ 79% HOTEL

fOCUShotels
management limited

Redcliffe Way, BS1 6NL - **tel:** 0117 926 0041
email: sales@focusbristol.co.uk **web:** www.doubletree3.hilton.com
dir: 1m from M32. 400yds from Temple Meads BR station, before church

This large modern hotel is situated in the heart of the city centre and offers spacious public areas and ample parking. Bedrooms are well equipped for both business and leisure guests. Dining options include a relaxed bar and a unique kiln restaurant where a good selection of freshly prepared dishes is available.

Rooms: 206 ✆ **S** £79–£209; **D** £79–£209* **Facilities:** FTV WiFi ⬦ Gym **Conf:** Class 120 Board 75 Thtr 300 Del from £127 **Services:** Lift Night porter Air con **Parking:** 150 **Notes:** LB Civ Wed 250

Hotel du Vin Bristol
★★★★ 78% ⊛ TOWN HOUSE HOTEL

Hotel du Vin & Bistro

The Sugar House, Narrow Lewins Mead, BS1 2NU - **tel:** 0117 925 5577 & 0844 736 4252 (Calls cost 5p per minute plus your phone company's access charge)
email: info.bristol@hotelduvin.com **web:** www.hotelduvin.com
dir: From A4 follow city centre signs. After 400yds pass Rupert St NCP on right. Hotel on opposite carriageway

This hotel is part of one of Britain's most innovative hotel groups, offering high standards of hospitality and accommodation. Housed in a Grade II listed, converted 18th-century sugar refinery, it provides great facilities with a modern, minimalist design. The bedrooms are exceptionally well designed and the bistro offers an excellent menu and wine list.

Rooms: 40 (10 family) ✆ **Facilities:** STV FTV WiFi ⬦ 🎵 New Year **Conf:** Class 36 Board 34 Thtr 72 **Services:** Lift Night porter **Parking:** 9 **Notes:** Civ Wed 65

Mercure Bristol Holland House Hotel & Spa
★★★★ 77% HOTEL

Mercure
HOTELS

Redcliffe Hill, BS1 6SQ - **tel:** 0117 968 9900
email: h6698@accor.com **web:** www.mercure.com
dir: M4 junct 19 towards city centre, follow signs A4 then A370, take A38 Redcliffe Hill. Hotel opposite St Mary Redcliffe Church

This modern hotel, just a ten-minute walk from Bristol Temple Meads, has striking, contemporary style throughout, and offers some impressive facilities including a spa, a fitness suite and meeting rooms. The hotel has a green-bicycle service for guests. Bedrooms are stylishly designed with large plasma-screen TVs, comfortable beds and free internet access. An impressive new dining area offers a wide range of dishes with a menu to suit all tastes.

Rooms: 275 (59 family) (44 GF) ✆ **S** fr £99; **D** fr £129* **Facilities:** Spa FTV WiFi ⬦ HL ⟳ Gym Xmas New Year **Conf:** Class 150 Board 80 Thtr 220 Del from £140 **Services:** Lift Night porter Air con **Parking:** 140 **Notes:** LB Civ Wed 220

Mercure Bristol North The Grange
★★★★ 76% ⊛ COUNTRY HOUSE HOTEL

Northwoods, Winterbourne, BS36 1RP - **tel:** 01454 777333 & 0844 815 9063 (Calls cost 7p per minute plus your phone company's access charge)
email: gm.mercurebristolnorthgrange@jupiterhotels.co.uk
web: www.mercurebristol.co.uk
dir: A38 towards Filton/Bristol. At rdbt 1st exit into Bradley Stoke Way, at lights 1st left into Woodlands Ln, at 2nd rdbt left into Tench Ln. In 1m left at T-junct, hotel 200yds on left

Built in the 19th century and surrounded by 18 acres of attractive grounds, this is a pleasant hotel situated only a short drive from the city centre. The bedrooms are spacious and well equipped with a range of meeting facilities also available. The conservatory bar has a terrace which makes a delightful place to enjoy a drink under the shade of a 200-year-old cedar tree. The hotel is popular as a wedding venue.

Rooms: 68 (6 annexe) (4 family) (22 GF) ✆ **S** £99–£199; **D** £99–£199 (incl. bkfst)* **Facilities:** STV FTV WiFi ⬦ Xmas New Year **Conf:** Class 60 Board 76 Thtr 180 Del from £130 **Services:** Night porter **Parking:** 150 **Notes:** LB Civ Wed 150

Novotel Bristol Centre
★★★★ 75% HOTEL

NOVOTEL
HOTELS & RESORTS

Victoria Street, BS1 6HY - **tel:** 0117 976 9988
email: H5622@accor.com **web:** www.novotel.com
dir: At end of M32 follow signs for Temple Meads station to rdbt. Final exit, hotel immediately on right

This city centre hotel provides smart, contemporary style accommodation. Most of the bedrooms demonstrate the Novotel 'Novation' style with unique swivel desk, internet access, air-conditioning and a host of extras. The hotel is convenient for the mainline railway station and also has its own car park.

Rooms: 131 (34 family) ✆ **S** £65–£265; **D** £65–£265* **Facilities:** STV FTV WiFi ⬦ HL Gym Sauna Steam room **Conf:** Class 70 Board 35 Thtr 210 **Services:** Lift Night porter Air con **Parking:** 100 **Notes:** LB Civ Wed 100

B

BRISTOL *continued*

Mercure Brigstow Bristol

★★★★ 74% HOTEL

5-7 Welsh Back, BS1 4SP - **tel:** 0117 929 1030
email: H6548@accor.com **web:** www.mercure.com
dir: *From the centre follow Baldwin St then right into Queen Charlotte St*

In a prime position on the river, this handsome, purpose-built hotel is designed and finished with care. The shopping centre and theatres are within easy walking distance. Bedrooms are stylish and extremely well equipped, including plasma TV screens in the bathrooms. There is an integrated state-of-the-art conference and meeting centre, and a smart restaurant and bar overlooking the harbour. Guests have free use of a squash and health club, plus free internet access.

Rooms: 116 ♦ **Facilities:** STV FTV WiFi Gym Free access to nearby gym & squash courts New Year **Conf:** Class 40 Board 30 Thtr 85 **Services:** Lift Night porter Air con **Notes:** Civ Wed 80

Rodney Hotel

★★★ 68% HOTEL

4 Rodney Place, Clifton, BS8 4HY - **tel:** 0117 973 5422
email: rodney@cliftonhotels.com **web:** www.cliftonhotels.com/bristolhotels/rodney
dir: *Off Clifton Down Rd*

With easy access from the M5, this attractive, listed building in Clifton is conveniently close to the city centre. The individually decorated bedrooms provide a useful range of extra facilities for the business traveller; the public areas include a smart bar, and a small restaurant offering enjoyable and carefully prepared dishes. A pleasant rear garden provides additional seating in the summer months.

Rooms: 31 (1 family) (2 GF) ♦ **S** £66–£112; **D** £80–£122* **Facilities:** FTV WiFi **Conf:** Class 20 Board 20 Thtr 30 **Services:** Night porter **Parking:** 7 **Notes:** LB Closed 22 Dec-3 Jan RS Sun Restaurant open 6pm-10pm Civ Wed 40

Clifton Hotel

★★ 72% HOTEL

St Pauls Road, Clifton, BS8 1LX - **tel:** 0117 973 6882
email: clifton@cliftonhotels.com **web:** www.cliftonhotels.com/bristolhotels/clifton
dir: *M32 follow Bristol/Clifton signs, along Park St. Left at lights into St Pauls Rd*

This popular hotel offers a relaxed, friendly service and very well equipped bedrooms. There is a welcoming lounge by the reception, and in summer months drinks and meals can be enjoyed on the terrace. Racks Bar and Restaurant offers an interesting selection of modern dishes in informal surroundings. There is some street parking, but for a small charge, secure garage parking is available.

Rooms: 59 (2 family) (12 GF) ♦ **Facilities:** STV FTV WiFi **Services:** Lift Night porter **Parking:** 12

Premier Inn Bristol Airport (Sidcot)

BUDGET HOTEL

Bridgwater Road, Winscombe, BS25 1NN - **tel:** 0871 527 8154 (Calls cost 13p per minute plus your phone company's access charge) **web:** www.premierinn.com
dir: *Between M5 junct 21 & 22 (9m from Bristol Airport), onto A371 towards Banwell, Winscombe to A38. Right at lights, hotel 300yds on left*

High quality, budget accommodation ideal for both families and business travellers. Spacious, en suite bedrooms feature tea and coffee making facilities, Freeview TV in most hotels and free WiFi. The adjacent family restaurant features a wide and varied menu.

Rooms: 31

Premier Inn Bristol (Alveston)

BUDGET HOTEL

Thornbury Road, Alveston, BS35 3LL - **tel:** 0871 527 8152 (Calls cost 13p per minute plus your phone company's access charge) **web:** www.premierinn.com
dir: *Just off M5. From N: exit at junct 14 onto A38 towards Bristol. From S: exit at junct 16 onto A38 towards Gloucester*

Rooms: 75

Premier Inn Bristol City Centre (Haymarket)

BUDGET HOTEL

The Haymarket, BS1 3LR - **tel:** 0871 527 8156 (Calls cost 13p per minute plus your phone company's access charge) **web:** www.premierinn.com
dir: *M4 junct 19, M32 towards city centre. Through 2 sets of lights, at 3rd lights turn right, to rdbt, take 2nd exit. Hotel on left*

Rooms: 224

Premier Inn Bristol City Centre King St

BUDGET HOTEL

Llandoger Trow, King Street, BS1 4ER - **tel:** 0871 527 8158 (Calls cost 13p per minute plus your phone company's access charge) **web:** www.premierinn.com
dir: *A38 into city centre. Left onto B4053 Baldwin St. Right into Queen Charlotte St, follow one-way system, bear right at river. Hotel on right*

Rooms: 60

Premier Inn Bristol City Centre (Lewins Mead)

BUDGET HOTEL

Lewins Mead, BS1 2PY - **tel:** 0871 527 9594 (Calls cost 13p per minute plus your phone company's access charge) **web:** www.premierinn.com
dir: *From N: M4 junct 19, M32 (city centre/Clifton/bus station). 3rd exit at rdbt. 4th left into Lower Moulden St, hotel on right. From S: M5 junct 19, A369. Keep right, at rdbt 1st exit, merge onto A370. Right into Hotwell Rd. At rdbt 3rd exit to next rdbt. Keep right, left onto A38. Hotel on left*

Rooms: 167

Premier Inn Bristol Cribbs Causeway

BUDGET HOTEL

Cribbs Causeway, Catbrain Lane, BS10 7TQ - **tel:** 0871 527 8160 (Calls cost 13p per minute plus your phone company's access charge) **web:** www.premierinn.com
dir: *M5 junct 17, A4018. 1st left at rdbt into Lysander Rd. Right into Catbrain Hill, leads to Catbrain Lane*

Rooms: 177

Premier Inn Bristol East (Emersons Green)

BUDGET HOTEL

200/202 Westerleigh Road, Emersons Green, BS16 7AN - **tel:** 0871 527 8162 (Calls cost 13p per minute plus your phone company's access charge) **web:** www.premierinn.com
dir: *M4 junct 19 onto M32 junct 1, left onto A4174 (Avon Ring Rd). Hotel at 3rd rdbt*

Rooms: 83

Premier Inn Bristol Filton

BUDGET HOTEL

Shield Retail Park, Gloucester Road North, BS34 7BR - **tel:** 0871 527 8164 (Calls cost 13p per minute plus your phone company's access charge) **web:** www.premierinn.com
dir: *M5 junct 16, A38 signed Filton/Patchway. Pass airport & Royal Mail on right. Left at 2nd rdbt, 1st left into retail park*

Rooms: 62

Premier Inn Bristol South

BUDGET HOTEL

Hengrove Leisure Park, Hengrove Way, BS14 0HR - **tel:** 0871 527 8166 (Calls cost 13p per minute plus your phone company's access charge) **web:** www.premierinn.com
dir: *From city centre take A37 to Wells & Shepton Mallet. Right onto A4174. Hotel at 3rd lights*

Rooms: 88

BRIXHAM
Devon   Map 3 SX95

Berry Head Hotel

★★★ 81% HOTEL

Berry Head Road, TQ5 9AJ - **tel:** 01803 853225
email: stay@berryheadhotel.com **web:** www.berryheadhotel.com
dir: *From marina 1m, hotel on left*

Set in a stunning cliff-top location, this imposing property dates back to 1809, and has spectacular views across Torbay. Public areas include two comfortable lounges, an outdoor terrace, and a swimming pool, together with a bar serving a range of popular dishes. Many of the bedrooms have the benefit of splendid sea views.

Rooms: 32 (7 family) ✚ **S** £68–£83; **D** £136–£166 (incl. bkfst)* **Facilities:** FTV WiFi ♨ 🎯 🚤 Petanque Sailing Deep sea fishing Yacht charter 🎵 Xmas New Year **Conf:** Class 250 Board 40 Thtr 300 Del from £100 **Services:** Lift Night porter **Parking:** 100 **Notes:** Civ Wed 200

Quayside Hotel

★★★ 78% 🏆 HOTEL

41-49 King Street, TQ5 9TJ - **tel:** 01803 855751
email: reservations@quaysidehotel.co.uk **web:** www.quaysidehotel.co.uk
dir: *On A380 continue towards Brixham taking the A3022*

With views over the harbour and bay, this hotel was formerly six cottages, and the public rooms retain a certain cosiness and intimacy. These include the lounge,

residents' bar and Ernie Lister's public bar. Freshly-landed fish features on the menus, alongside a number of creative and skilfully prepared dishes, served in the well-appointed restaurant. Good food is also available in the public bar. The owners and their team of local staff provide friendly and attentive service.

Rooms: 29 (2 family) ✚ **S** £70–£175; **D** £98–£185 (incl. bkfst)* **Facilities:** FTV WiFi ♨ 🎵 Xmas New Year **Conf:** Class 18 Board 18 Thtr 25 **Services:** Night porter **Parking:** 30 **Notes:** LB

BROADWAY
Worcestershire   Map 10 SP03

Foxhill Manor

★★★★★ 85% SMALL HOTEL

Farncombe Estate, WR12 7LJ - **tel:** 01386 852711 **email:** reservations@foxhillmanor.com **web:** www.foxhillmanor.com
dir: *Off A44 between Broadway & Moreton-in-Marsh on Fish hill. 1m outside Broadway village*

Located within the sprawling Farncombe estate, this intimate country house offers excellent accommodation with a truly personalised service experience. The team of house managers and butlers will ensure your stay is designed for you, from start to finish. Chef will meet you to discuss the very best of seasonal produce from the estate and surrounding areas. Technology is embraced with touch-screen tablets connecting you to the amenities throughout the estate.

Rooms: 8 (1 family) (2 GF) ✚ **Facilities:** STV FTV WiFi ♨ 🎯 🚴 Gym In room treatments 🎵 **Conf:** Class 40 Board 28 Thtr 70 **Services:** Night porter Air con **Parking:** 30 **Notes:** No children 12yrs Civ Wed 70

B

BROADWAY *continued*

Dormy House Hotel

★★★★ ◉◉ HOTEL

Willersey Hill, WR12 7LF - **tel:** 01386 852711
email: reservations@dormyhouse.co.uk. **web:** www.dormyhouse.co.uk
dir: *2m E of Broadway off A44, at top of Fish Hill turn for Saintbury/Picnic area. In 0.5m turn left, hotel on left*

Dormy House is a converted 17th-century farmhouse set in 400-acre grounds on the Farncombe Estate, with stunning views over Broadway. Not long ago the hotel underwent a multi-million pound refurbishment, part of which was a luxury spa offering a wide range of treatments, a swimming pool, a Veuve Clicquot Champagne nail bar, gym and thermal suite. The best traditions are retained - customer care, real fires, comfortable sofas and afternoon teas. Dinner features an interesting choice of dishes created by a skilled kitchen brigade.

Rooms: 38 (19 annexe) (8 family) (19 GF) **Facilities:** Spa STV FTV WiFi
Gym Nature & jogging trail Circular walks Champagne nail bar Xmas New Year
Conf: Class 16 Board 16 Thtr 16 **Services:** Night porter **Parking:** 70 **Notes:** LB Civ Wed 80

See advert opposite

The Fish

★★★ 86% ◉ HOTEL

Farncombe Estate, WR12 7LJ - **tel:** 01386 858000
email: reception@thefishhotel.co.uk **web:** www.thefishhotel.co.uk
dir: *Follow A44 to Moreton-in-Marsh then follow signs to Evesham & Broadway. Take Saintbury turn by Broadway Tower, estate on the left*

Part of the 400-acre Farncombe Estate, The Fish enjoys far-reaching views across the Worcestershire countryside. Smartly appointed bedrooms are located on the hillside in former farm houses and converted buildings, within easy reach of The Lodge, where all the hotel's main facilities can be found. Outdoor activities can be arranged in addition to the on-site tennis court and gym.

Rooms: 47 (44 GF) **Facilities:** FTV WiFi HL Gym Xmas New Year
Conf: Class 70 Board 50 Thtr 120 **Services:** Night porter Air con **Parking:** 200

The Broadway Hotel

★★★ 85% ◉◉ HOTEL

The Green, High Street, WR12 7AA - **tel:** 01386 852401
email: info@broadwayhotel.info **web:** www.cotswold-inns-hotels.co.uk
dir: *Follow signs to Evesham, then Broadway. Left onto Leamington Rd, hotel just off village green*

The Broadway Hotel is a half-timbered Cotswold stone property, built in the 15th century as a retreat for the Abbots of Pershore. It combines modern, attractive decor with original charm and character. Bedrooms are tastefully furnished and well equipped while public rooms include a relaxing lounge, cosy bar and charming restaurant; alfresco all-day dining in summer months proves popular.

Rooms: 19 (1 family) (3 GF) **D** fr £99 (incl. bkfst)* **Facilities:** FTV WiFi Xmas New Year **Parking:** 20

BROCKENHURST
Hampshire

Map 5 SU30

Rhinefield House Hotel

★★★★ HOTEL

the making) that is worth taking time to admire. If the weather permits, the delightful terrace is just the place for enjoying alfresco eating.

Rhinefield House Hotel

Rooms: 50 (10 family) (16 GF) **S** £165–£350; **D** £165–£350 (incl. bkfst)*
Facilities: Spa STV WiFi ⏸ HL ⏱ ↙ ♨ ⛱ Gym Hydrotherapy pool Plunge pool Steam room Sauna Xmas New Year **Conf:** Class 72 Board 56 Thtr 160 Del from £175 **Services:** Lift Night porter **Parking:** 100 **Notes:** LB Civ Wed 130

See advert on following page

Rhinefield Road, SO42 7QB - tel: 01590 622922 & 0845 072 7516 (Calls cost 5p per minute plus your phone company's access charge)
email: rhinefieldhouse@handpicked.co.uk
web: www.handpickedhotels.co.uk/rhinefieldhouse
dir: *A35 towards Christchurch. 3m from Lyndhurst turn left to Rhinefield, 1.5m to hotel*

This stunning 19th-century, mock-Elizabethan mansion is set in 40 acres of beautifully landscaped gardens and forest. Bedrooms are spacious and great consideration is given to guest comfort. The elegant and award-winning Armada Restaurant is richly furnished, and features a fireplace carving (nine years in

BROCKENHURST *continued*

HIGHLY RECOMMENDED

Careys Manor Hotel & Senspa

★★★★ 84% ⚜⚜⚜ HOTEL

Lyndhurst Road, SO42 7RH - tel: 01590 624467 **email:** stay@careysmanor.com
web: www.careysmanor.com
dir: *M27 junct 3, M271, A35 to Lyndhurst. A337 towards Brockenhurst. Hotel on left after Beaulieu sign*

This smart property offers a host of facilities that include an Oriental-style spa and leisure suite with an excellent range of unusual treatments, as well as three contrasting restaurants that offer a choice of Thai, French or modern British cuisine. Many of the spacious and well-appointed bedrooms have balconies overlooking the gardens. Function and conference facilities are also available.

Rooms: 79 (61 annexe) (31 GF) ⌕ **S** £159–£239; **D** £199–£359 (incl. bkfst)*
Facilities: Spa FTV WiFi ⓢ HL ⓢ ⤳ Gym Steam room Hydrotherapy pool Sauna Herbal sauna Crystal steam room Laconicum Tepidarium Experience showers Xmas New Year **Conf:** Class 70 Board 40 Thtr 120 **Services:** Lift Night porter **Parking:** 180 **Notes:** Civ Wed 100

The Balmer Lawn Hotel

★★★★ 81% ⚜⚜ HOTEL

Lyndhurst Road, SO42 7ZB - tel: 01590 623116
email: info@blh.co.uk **web:** www.balmerlawnhotel.com
dir: *Just off A337 from Brockenhurst towards Lymington*

Situated in the heart of the New Forest, this peacefully located hotel provides comfortable public rooms and a wide range of bedrooms. A selection of carefully prepared and enjoyable dishes is offered in the spacious restaurant. The extensive function and leisure facilities make this popular with both families and conference delegates.

Rooms: 53 (10 family) ⌕ **S** £129; **D** £129–£189 (incl. bkfst)* **Facilities:** Spa FTV WiFi ⓢ ⤳ ⤳ Gym Squash Indoor leisure suite Sauna ♫ Xmas New Year **Conf:** Class 76 Board 48 Thtr 150 Del from £135 **Services:** Lift Night porter **Parking:** 100 **Notes:** Civ Wed 120

THE PIG

★★★ ⚜⚜ 🍴 COUNTRY HOUSE HOTEL

Beaulieu Road, SO42 7QL - tel: 01590 622354
email: info@thepighotel.com **web:** www.thepighotel.co.uk
dir: *At Brockenhurst onto B3055 Beaulieu Road. 1m on left up private road*

A delightful country house where the focus is very much on the food, with the chef, gardener and forager working as a team to create menus of seasonal, locally sourced produce; all ingredients are found within a 15-mile radius. The result of such a policy is that menus change daily, and sometimes even more frequently. The stylish dining room is an authentically reproduced Victorian greenhouse, and alfresco eating is possible as there is a wood-fired oven in the courtyard. The bedrooms have eclectic furnishings, good beds and views of either the forest or the garden; two suites with private courtyards are available.

Rooms: 31 (15 annexe) (4 family) (15 GF) ⌕ **S** £155–£420; **D** £155–£420*
Facilities: STV FTV WiFi ⓢ ⤳ Massage treatment rooms Xmas New Year
Conf: Board 14 Del from £255 **Services:** Night porter **Parking:** 30
Notes: Civ Wed 60

B

Cloud Hotel

★★★ 80% SMALL HOTEL

Meerut Road, SO42 7TD - tel: 01590 622165
email: enquiries@cloudhotel.co.uk web: www.cloudhotel.co.uk
dir: M27 junct 1 signed New Forest, A337 through Lyndhurst to Brockenhurst. On entering Brockenhurst 1st right. Hotel 300mtrs

This charming hotel enjoys a peaceful location on the edge of the village. The bedrooms are bright and comfortable with pine furnishings and smart en suite facilities. Public rooms include a selection of cosy lounges, a delightful rear garden with outdoor seating and a restaurant specialising in home-cooked, wholesome English food.

Rooms: 18 (1 family) (2 GF) 🐾 Facilities: FTV WiFi ᗷ Conf: Class 12 Board 12 Thtr 40 Parking: 20 Notes: No children 14yrs Closed 27 Dec–11 Jan

Forest Park Hotel

★★★ 73% HOTEL

Rhinefield Road, SO42 7ZG - tel: 01590 622844
email: reservations@forestpark-hotel.co.uk web: www.forestpark-hotel.co.uk
dir: M27 junct 1, follow signs for A337 Lyndhurst. Follow road for 3m, left at lights onto A35, A337 Lymington Brockenhurst, right into Meerut Road, right at T-junct

Located in the heart of the beautiful New Forest National Park this popular hotel provides an ideal base for exploring this remarkable area. Accommodation offers bedrooms with garden or forest views, and free WiFi available throughout. The hotel is child friendly; children will delight in seeing the ponies on the doorstep. The refurbished restaurant has views of the lovely landscaped gardens, with delicious food to match. The bar offers a more relaxed atmosphere and food is served from midday to nine in the evening.

Rooms: 38 (6 family) (7 GF) 🐾 S £65–£350;* Facilities: FTV WiFi HL 🎵 Conf: Class 15 Board 20 Thtr 40 Del from £115 Services: Night porter Parking: 38 Notes: Civ Wed 70

The Cottage Hotel

★★ 72% HOTEL

Sway Road, SO42 7SH - tel: 01590 622296
email: enquiries@cottagelodge.co.uk web: www.cottagelodge.co.uk
dir: Exit A337 opposite Careys Manor Hotel into Grigg Ln, 0.25m over x-rds, cottage next to war memorial

Parts of this attractive small hotel date back over 300 years, and it has been skilfully modernised by the resident owners, to provide a choice of well furnished, bright bedrooms. There is a low-beamed lounge and a licensed restaurant which offers both table d'hôte and a varied à la carte menu. Light refreshments and cream teas are served on the terrace tea garden between Easter and October.

Rooms: 15 (3 family) (7 GF) 🐾 S £50–£120; D £60–£170 (incl. bkfst)* Facilities: FTV WiFi ᗷ Conf: Class 8 Board 8 Thtr 8 Parking: 15 Notes: LB Closed 1 week at Xmas

BROMBOROUGH
Merseyside

Map 15 SJ38

Premier Inn Wirral (Bromborough)

BUDGET HOTEL

High Street, Bromborough Cross, CH62 7EZ - tel: 0871 527 9172 (Calls cost 13p per minute plus your phone company's access charge) web: www.premierinn.com
dir: On A41 (New Chester Rd), 2m from M53 junct 5

High quality, budget accommodation ideal for both families and business travellers. Spacious, en suite bedrooms feature tea and coffee making facilities,

Freeview TV in most hotels and free WiFi. The adjacent family restaurant features a wide and varied menu.

Rooms: 32

BROME
Suffolk

Map 13 TM17

HIGHLY RECOMMENDED

Best Western Brome Grange Hotel

★★★ 86% ⚫⚫ HOTEL

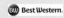

Norwich Road, Nr Diss, IP23 8AP - tel: 01379 870456
email: info@bromegrangehotel.co.uk web: www.bromegrange.co.uk
dir: Located on the A140 between Ipswich & Norwich in the village of Brome

Conveniently located between Ipswich and Norfolk the Best Western Brome Hotel offers bedrooms that are spacious, well equipped and attractively presented. The charming cosy bar has lots of character and the restaurant is very popular with locals and residents. A warm welcome is assured and ample secure parking is available for guests.

Rooms: 42 (24 annexe) (2 family) (24 GF) 🐾 S £69–£129; D £79–£139* Facilities: Spa FTV WiFi ᗷ Gym Xmas New Year Conf: Class 60 Board 40 Thtr 150 Del from £95 Services: Lift Night porter Parking: 100 Notes: Civ Wed 110

BROMLEY
Greater London

Bromley Court Hotel

★★★ 80% HOTEL PLAN 1 H1

Bromley Hill, BR1 4JD - tel: 020 8461 8600
email: enquiries@bromleycourthotel.co.uk web: www.bromleycourthotel.co.uk
dir: N of town centre, off A21. Private drive opposite Volkswagen garage on Bromley Hill

Set amid three acres of grounds, this smart hotel enjoys a peaceful location, in a residential area on the outskirts of town. Well maintained bedrooms are smartly appointed and thoughtfully equipped. The contemporary-style restaurant offers a good choice of meals in comfortable surroundings. Extensive facilities include a leisure club and a good range of meeting rooms.

Rooms: 117 (4 family) 🐾 S fr £60; D fr £70* Facilities: STV FTV WiFi ᗷ Gym Steam room 🎵 Xmas New Year Conf: Class 70 Board 40 Thtr 150 Del from £100 Services: Lift Night porter Air con Parking: 86 Notes: Civ Wed 180

BROMSGROVE
Worcestershire

Map 10 SO97

Premier Inn Bromsgrove Central

BUDGET HOTEL

Birmingham Road, B61 0BA - tel: 0871 527 8168 (Calls cost 13p per minute plus your phone company's access charge) web: www.premierinn.com
dir: M42 junct 1 (S'bound access only) or M5 junct 4 S'bound or M5 junct 5 N'bound onto A38 towards Bromsgrove. Hotel adjacent to Guild Brewers Fayre. NB for Sat Nav use B60 1GJ

High quality, budget accommodation ideal for both families and business travellers. Spacious, en suite bedrooms feature tea and coffee making facilities, Freeview TV in most hotels and free WiFi. The adjacent family restaurant features a wide and varied menu.

Rooms: 78

BROMSGROVE *continued*

Premier Inn Bromsgrove South (Worcester Road)

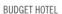

BUDGET HOTEL

Worcester Road, Upton Warren, B61 7ET - **tel:** 0871 527 8170 (Calls cost 13p per minute plus your phone company's access charge) **web:** www.premierinn.com
dir: *M5 junct 5, A38 towards Bromsgrove, 1.2m. Or M42 junct 1, A38 S, cross over A448*
Rooms: 27

BROXTON	Map 15 SJ45
Cheshire	

Carden Park Hotel, Golf Resort & Spa

★★★★ 82% HOTEL

Carden Park, CH3 9DQ - **tel:** 01829 731000
email: reservations@cardenpark.co.uk **web:** www.cardenpark.co.uk
dir: *M56 junct 15, M53 Chester. Take A41 signed Whitchurch. 8m. At Broxton rdbt right onto A534 (signed Wrexham). Hotel 1.5m on left*

This impressive Cheshire estate dates back to the 17th century and consists of 1,000 acres of mature parkland. The hotel offers a choice of dining options along with superb leisure facilities that include golf courses, a fully equipped gym, a swimming pool and popular spa. Spacious, thoughtfully equipped bedrooms have excellent business and in-room entertainment facilities.

Rooms: 196 (83 annexe) (24 family) (68 GF) **Facilities:** Spa STV FTV WiFi 36 Putting green Gym Archery Mountain bike Laser clay shooting Sauna Steam room Segway Quad bikes Xmas New Year **Conf:** Class 240 Board 125 Thtr 350 **Services:** Lift Night porter **Parking:** 700 **Notes:** Civ Wed 350

BRYHER	Map 2 SV81
Cornwall (Isles of Scilly)	

HIGHLY RECOMMENDED

Hell Bay

★★★★ 86% HOTEL

TR23 0PR - **tel:** 01720 422947
email: contactus@hellbay.co.uk **web:** www.hellbay.co.uk
dir: *Access by boat from Penzance, plane from Exeter, Newquay or Land's End*

Located on the smallest of the inhabited islands of the Scilly Isles on the edge of the Atlantic, this hotel makes a really special destination. The owners have filled the hotel with original works of art by artists who have connections with the islands, and the interior is decorated in cool blues and greens creating an extremely restful environment. The contemporary bedrooms are equally stylish, and many have garden access and stunning sea views. Eating here is a delight, and naturally, seafood features strongly on the award-winning, daily-changing menus.

Rooms: 25 (25 annexe) (4 family) (15 GF) **S** £135–£437.50; **D** £285–£700 (incl. bkfst & dinner)* **Facilities:** Spa FTV WiFi 7 Gym **Conf:** Class 36 Board 20 **Notes:** LB Closed Nov–Feb

BUCKHURST HILL	Map 6 TQ49
Essex	

Premier Inn Loughton/Buckhurst Hill

BUDGET HOTEL

High Road, IG9 5HT - **tel:** 0871 527 8686 (Calls cost 13p per minute plus your phone company's access charge) **web:** www.premierinn.com
dir: *M25 junct 26 towards Loughton. A121 into Buckhurst Hill (approx 5m), hotel on left*

High quality, budget accommodation ideal for both families and business travellers. Spacious, en suite bedrooms feature tea and coffee making facilities, Freeview TV in most hotels and free WiFi. The adjacent family restaurant features a wide and varied menu.

Rooms: 50

BUCKINGHAM	Map 11 SP63
Buckinghamshire	

Buckingham Villiers Hotel

★★★★ 75% HOTEL

3 Castle Street, MK18 1BS - **tel:** 01280 822444 **email:** villiers@oxfordshire-hotels.co.uk **web:** www.villiers-hotel.co.uk
dir: *M1 junct 13 N or junct 15 S follow signs to Buckingham. Castle St by Old Town Hall*

Guests can enjoy a town centre location with a high degree of comfort at this 400-year-old former coaching inn. Relaxing public areas feature flagstone floors, oak panelling and real fires, while bedrooms are modern, spacious and equipped to a high level. Diners can unwind in the atmospheric bar before taking dinner in the award-winning restaurant.

Rooms: 49 (4 family) (3 GF) **S** £95–£140; **D** £110–£180 (incl. bkfst)* **Facilities:** STV FTV WiFi Xmas New Year **Conf:** Class 120 Board 80 Thtr 250 Del from £135 **Services:** Lift Night porter **Parking:** 52 **Notes:** LB Civ Wed 180

Best Western Buckingham Hotel

★★★ 72% HOTEL

Buckingham Ring Road, MK18 1RY - **tel:** 01280 822622
email: info@thebuckinghamhotel.co.uk **web:** www.thebuckinghamhotel.co.uk
dir: *A421 to Buckingham, take ring road S towards Brackley & Bicester. Hotel on left*

A purpose-built hotel, which offers comfortable and spacious rooms with well designed working spaces for business travellers. There are also extensive conference facilities. The open-plan restaurant and bar offer a good range of dishes, and the well-equipped leisure suite is popular with guests.

Rooms: 70 (6 family) (31 GF) **Facilities:** STV FTV WiFi supervised Gym Sauna Steam room Xmas New Year **Conf:** Class 60 Board 60 Thtr 200 **Services:** Night porter **Parking:** 200 **Notes:** Civ Wed 120

BUCKLAND (NEAR BROADWAY)
Gloucestershire

Map 10 SP03

INSPECTOR'S CHOICE

Buckland Manor

★★★★ ◉◉◉ ≜ COUNTRY HOUSE HOTEL

Andrew
BROWNSWORD
THE HOTELS

WR12 7LY - **tel:** 01386 852626
email: info@bucklandmanor.co.uk **web:** www.bucklandmanor.co.uk
dir: *2m S of Broadway, off B4632*

Buckland Manor is a grand 13th-century manor house, surrounded by well-kept and beautiful gardens that feature a stream and waterfall. Everything at this hotel is geared to encourage rest and relaxation. Spacious bedrooms and public areas are furnished with high quality pieces and decorated in keeping with the style of the manor; crackling log fires warm the wonderful lounges. The elegant dining room, with views over the rolling hills, is the perfect place to enjoy dishes that use excellent local produce. Andrew Brownsword Hotels is the AA Hotel Group of the Year 2017-2018.

Rooms: 15 (1 family) (4 GF) ☏ **S** £175–£580; **D** £195–£600 (incl. bkfst)*
Facilities: FTV WiFi Putting green ☺ ⚓ Xmas New Year **Conf:** Board 25 Thtr 30
Services: Night porter **Parking:** 20 **Notes:** LB No children 10yrs Civ Wed 40

BUDE
Cornwall & Isles of Scilly

Map 2 SS20

The Beach Hotel

★★★★ 78% ◉◉ SMALL HOTEL

Summerleaze Crescent, EX23 8HJ - **tel:** 01288 389800
email: enquiries@thebeachatbude.co.uk **web:** www.thebeachatbude.co.uk
dir: *M5 to Exeter, then A30 to Launceston. B3254 to Red Post Cross, turn left on to A3072 & follow to Bude. Through town, 1st left after the Post Office*

The Beach Hotel is a contemporary operation which naturally enjoys very good views of the beach below. In the restaurant are plain wooden tables; the only linen is the napkins. The ethos is Modern British cuisine meets seaside chic. This is reflected in the restaurant and throughout the hotel. The terrace offers great seating for the warmer months.

Rooms: 16 (1 GF) ☏ **S** £137.50–£237.50; **D** £150–£250 (incl. bkfst)* **Facilities:** FTV WiFi � ♫ New Year **Conf:** Class 10 Board 20 Thtr 25 **Services:** Lift Night porter **Parking:** 8 **Notes:** Closed 24–26 Dec

Red Stars The AA Red Star rating denotes an Inspector's Choice hotel. They stand out as the very best in the British Isles and appear in highlighted panels throughout the guide.

BURFORD
Oxfordshire

Map 5 SP21

The Bay Tree Hotel
★★★★ 79% HOTEL

COTSWOLD INNS & HOTELS

Sheep Street, OX18 4LW - tel: 01993 822791
email: info@baytreehotel.info **web:** www.cotswold-inns-hotels.co.uk
dir: *A40 or A361 to Burford. From High St turn into Sheep St, next to old market square. Hotel on right*

The Bay Tree's modern decorative style combines seamlessly with features from this delightful inn's long history. Bedrooms are tastefully furnished and some have four-poster or half-tester beds. Public areas consist of a character bar, a sophisticated airy restaurant, a selection of meeting rooms and an attractive walled garden.

Rooms: 21 (13 annexe) (2 family) (3 GF) **D** fr £105 (incl. bkfst)* **Facilities:** FTV WiFi ↳ ⍾ Xmas New Year **Conf:** Class 12 Board 25 Thtr 40 **Parking:** 50 **Notes:** Civ Wed 90

HIGHLY RECOMMENDED

The Lamb Inn
★★★ 87% SMALL HOTEL

COTSWOLD INNS & HOTELS

Sheep Street, OX18 4LR - tel: 01993 823155
email: info@lambinn-burford.co.uk
web: www.cotswold-inns-hotels.co.uk/the-lamb-inn
dir: *A40 into Burford, downhill, 1st left into Sheep St, hotel last on right*

The Lamb is an enchanting old inn, just a short walk from the centre of this delightful Cotswold village. An abundance of character and charm is found in the cosy lounge with log fire, and intimate bar with flagged floors. An elegant restaurant offers locally sourced produce in carefully prepared dishes. Bedrooms, some with original features, are comfortable and well appointed.

Rooms: 17 (1 family) (4 GF) ⌁ **D** fr £110 (incl. bkfst)* **Facilities:** FTV WiFi ↳ Xmas New Year **Services:** Night porter

BURGESS HILL
West Sussex

Map 6 TQ31

Premier Inn Burgess Hill
BUDGET HOTEL

Charles Avenue, RH15 9AG - tel: 0871 527 8172 (Calls cost 13p per minute plus your phone company's access charge) **web:** www.premierinn.com
dir: *M25 junct 7, M23, A23. Left at Burgess Hill follow A2300 signs. At rdbt 2nd exit onto A2300. At next rdbt 4th exit onto A273, straight on at next 2 rdbts, at 3rd rdbt (Tesco) 1st left. Hotel 2nd left*

High quality, budget accommodation ideal for both families and business travellers. Spacious, en suite bedrooms feature tea and coffee making facilities, Freeview TV in most hotels and free WiFi. The adjacent family restaurant features a wide and varied menu.

Rooms: 60

BURLEY
Hampshire

Map 5 SU20

Burley Manor
★★★★ 80% HOTEL

NEW FOREST HOTELS

Ringwood Road, BH24 4BS - tel: 01425 403522
email: burley.manor@newforesthotels.co.uk **web:** www.burleymanor.com
dir: *From E - M27 end to A31 for 7m take Burley slip road. follow signs to hotel. From W - A31, 2nd slip road after Ringwood to Burley. Follow signs to hotel.*

Burley Manor is located in the New Forest and enjoys beautiful parkland views. Bedrooms are located in the main manor house as well as the stables, and all have been refurbished to a high standard with quality furnishings and bold use of colours. Drinks can be enjoyed in the comfortable, elegantly furnished lounge and bar; and when weather permits, on the garden patio. In the restaurant, the menu has Mediterranean influences, and some dishes are cooked in the wood-fired oven. There is also the chef's pantry for small private dinners; while the barn is ideal for larger celebrations.

Rooms: 40 **Facilities:** WiFi ⌁ **Conf:** Class 24 Board 40 Thtr 70 **Notes:** No children 13yrs

Moorhill House Hotel
★★★ 79% COUNTRY HOUSE HOTEL

NEW FOREST HOTELS

BH24 4AG - tel: 01425 403285
email: moorhill@newforesthotels.co.uk **web:** www.newforesthotels.co.uk
dir: *M27, A31, follow signs to Burley, through village, up hill, right opposite school & cricket grounds*

Situated deep in the heart of the New Forest and formerly a grand gentleman's residence, this charming hotel offers a relaxed and friendly environment. Bedrooms, which come in varying sizes, are smartly decorated. A range of facilities is provided and guests can relax by walking around the extensive grounds. Both dinner and breakfast offer a choice of interesting and freshly prepared dishes.

Rooms: 31 (13 family) (3 GF) ⌁ **S** £50–£99; **D** £89–£169 (incl. bkfst)* **Facilities:** FTV WiFi ↳ HL ⍾ ⍾ Badminton (Apr-Sep) Sauna Xmas New Year Child facilities **Conf:** Class 60 Board 65 Thtr 120 **Parking:** 50 **Notes:** LB Civ Wed 90

BURNHAM
Buckinghamshire

Map 6 SU98

Burnham Beeches Hotel
★★★★ 75% HOTEL

corus hotels

Grove Road, SL1 8DP - tel: 01628 429955
email: burnhambeeches@corushotels.com **web:** www.corushotels.com/burnham-beeches
dir: *M40 junct 2, A355 towards Slough, right at 2nd rdbt, 1st right to Grove Rd*

Set in attractive mature grounds on the fringes of woodland, this extended Georgian manor house has spacious, comfortable and well-equipped bedrooms. Public rooms include a cosy lounge/bar offering all-day snacks and an elegant wood-panelled restaurant that serves interesting cuisine; there are also conference facilities, a fitness centre and pool.

Rooms: 82 (22 family) (12 GF) ⌁ **S** fr £75; **D** fr £94* **Facilities:** FTV WiFi ↳ ⍾ Gym Beauty treatment room Xmas New Year **Conf:** Class 80 Board 60 Thtr 150 Del from £179 **Services:** Lift Night porter **Parking:** 150 **Notes:** Civ Wed 120

B

BURNLEY
Lancashire Map 18 SD83

Premier Inn Burnley

BUDGET HOTEL

Queen Victoria Road, BB10 3EF - **tel:** 0871 527 8174 (Calls cost 13p per minute plus your phone company's access charge) **web:** www.premierinn.com
dir: *M65 junct 12, 5th exit at rdbt, 1st exit at rdbt, keep in right lane at lights, 2nd exit at next rdbt, 3rd at next rdbt, under bridge, left before football ground*

High quality, budget accommodation ideal for both families and business travellers. Spacious, en suite bedrooms feature tea and coffee making facilities, Freeview TV in most hotels and free WiFi. The adjacent family restaurant features a wide and varied menu.

Rooms: 67

BURRINGTON (NEAR PORTSMOUTH ARMS STATION)
Devon Map 3 SS61

INSPECTOR'S CHOICE

Northcote Manor
★★★ ◎◎ COUNTRY HOUSE HOTEL

EX37 9LZ - **tel:** 01769 560501
email: rest@northcotemanor.co.uk **web:** www.northcotemanor.co.uk
dir: *From A377 opposite Portsmouth Arms, into hotel drive. NB do not enter Burrington village*

A warm and friendly welcome is assured at this beautiful country house hotel, built in 1716 and surrounded by 20 acres of grounds and woodlands. Guests can enjoy wonderful views over the Taw River Valley while relaxing in the delightful environment created by the attentive staff. A meal in either the intimate, more formal Manor House Restaurant or the Walled Garden Restaurant will prove a highlight; both offer menus of the finest local produce used in well-prepared dishes. Bedrooms, including some suites, are individually styled, spacious and well appointed.

Rooms: 16 (2 family) (3 GF) ❦ **S** £120–£215; **D** £170–£340 (incl. bkfst & dinner) **Facilities:** FTV WiFi ☺ ☃ Xmas New Year **Conf:** Class 50 Board 30 Thtr 80 **Parking:** 50 **Notes:** Civ Wed 100

BURTON UPON TRENT
Staffordshire Map 10 SK22

Mercure Burton Upon Trent Newton Park

★★★★ 72% COUNTRY HOUSE HOTEL

Newton Solney, DE15 0SS - **tel:** 01283 703568
email: info@mercureburton.co.uk **web:** www.mercureburton.co.uk
dir: *On B5008 past Repton to Newton Solney. Hotel on left*

Standing in eight acres of grounds, this Grade II listed 18th-century Italian-style country manor provides comfort in elegant surroundings. The well-equipped bedrooms are suitable for both business and leisure guests. The oak-panelled restaurant serves a good choice of dishes and overlooks the landscaped gardens. Eight fully-equipped meeting rooms are available.

Rooms: 50 (3 family) (5 GF) ❦ **Facilities:** STV FTV WiFi ↕ **Conf:** Class 70 Board 60 Thtr 100 **Services:** Lift Night porter **Parking:** 100 **Notes:** Civ Wed 100

Holiday Inn Express Burton upon Trent

BUDGET HOTEL

2nd Avenue, Centrum 100, DE14 2WF - **tel:** 01283 504300
email: reservations@exhiburton.co.uk **web:** www.exhiburton.co.uk
dir: *From A38 Branston exit take A5121 signed Town Centre. At McDonalds rdbt, turn left into 2nd Avenue. Hotel on left*

A modern hotel ideal for families and business travellers. Fresh and uncomplicated, the spacious rooms include Sky TV, power shower and tea and coffee-making facilities. Continental buffet breakfast is included in the room rate; other meals may be taken at the nearby family pub or restaurant.

Rooms: 82 (47 family) (14 GF) ❦ **S** £50–£150; **D** £50–£150 (incl. bkfst) **Conf:** Class 30 Board 25 Thtr 60 Del from £90

Premier Inn Burton upon Trent Central
BUDGET HOTEL

Wellington Road, DE14 2WD - **tel:** 0871 527 9280 (Calls cost 13p per minute plus your phone company's access charge) **web:** www.premierinn.com
dir: *Exit A38 at Branston junction onto A5121 to Burton on Trent. Straight on at lights. At rdbt take 3rd exit, hotel on left*

High quality, budget accommodation ideal for both families and business travellers. Spacious, en suite bedrooms feature tea and coffee making facilities, Freeview TV in most hotels and free WiFi. The adjacent family restaurant features a wide and varied menu.

Rooms: 64

Premier Inn Burton upon Trent East
BUDGET HOTEL

Ashby Road East, DE15 0PU - **tel:** 0871 527 8176 (Calls cost 13p per minute plus your phone company's access charge) **web:** www.premierinn.com
dir: *2m E of Burton upon Trent on A50*

Rooms: 32

B

BURY
Greater Manchester — Map 15 SD81

Red Hall Hotel
★★★ 83% HOTEL

Manchester Road, Walmersley, BL9 5NA - tel: 01706 822476
email: info@red-hall.co.uk web: www.red-hall.co.uk
dir: M66 junct 1, A56. Over motorway bridge, hotel approx 300mtrs on right

Originally a farmhouse, this now much enlarged hotel is located in the picturesque village of Warmersley just off the M66, making it ideal for business and leisure guests alike. Bright bedrooms are comfortable, contemporary, and equipped to a modern standard. The newly revamped 'Oscars' restaurant serves a wide-ranging menu. Meeting and event facilities complete the package.

Rooms: 37 (2 family) (18 GF) ☞ S £55–£85; D £75–£105 (incl. bkfst)*
Facilities: STV FTV WiFi ☆ Xmas New Year Conf: Class 60 Board 30 Thtr 140 Del from £105 Services: Lift Night porter Parking: 100 Notes: LB Civ Wed 80

Premier Inn Manchester Bury
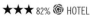
BUDGET HOTEL

5 Knowsley Place, Duke Street, BL9 0EJ - tel: 0871 527 9294 (Calls cost 13p per minute plus your phone company's access charge) web: www.premierinn.com
dir: M66 junct 2, A58 towards Bolton & Bury. At rdbt in Bury centre follow A58 (Angouleme Way). Left in Knowsley St, hotel on left

High quality, budget accommodation ideal for both families and business travellers. Spacious, en suite bedrooms feature tea and coffee making facilities, Freeview TV in most hotels and free WiFi. The adjacent family restaurant features a wide and varied menu.

Rooms: 115

BURY ST EDMUNDS
Suffolk — Map 13 TL86

HIGHLY RECOMMENDED

The Angel Hotel
★★★★ 85% TOWN HOUSE HOTEL

Angel Hill, IP33 1LT - tel: 01284 714000
email: staying@theangel.co.uk web: www.theangel.co.uk
dir: From A134, left at rdbt into Northgate St. Continue to lights, right into Mustow St, left into Angel Hill. Hotel on right

The Angel Hotel is an impressive building situated just a short walk from the town centre. One of the hotel's more notable guests over the last 400 years was Charles Dickens, who is reputed to have written part of The Pickwick Papers while in residence. The hotel offers a range of individually designed bedrooms that include a selection of four-poster rooms and a suite.

Rooms: 78 (5 family) (22 GF) ☞ Facilities: FTV WiFi Conf: Class 16 Board 16 Thtr 22 Services: Lift Night porter Parking: 20 Notes: LB

Best Western Priory Hotel
★★★ 82% HOTEL

Mildenhall Road, IP32 6EH - tel: 01284 766181
email: reservations@prioryhotel.co.uk web: www.prioryhotel.co.uk
dir: From A14 (junct 43) take Bury St Edmunds W slip road. Follow signs to Brandon. At mini-rdbt turn right. Hotel 0.5m on left

Priory Hotel is an 18th-century Grade II listed building set in landscaped grounds on the outskirts of town. The attractively decorated, tastefully furnished and thoughtfully equipped bedrooms are split between the main house and garden wings, which have their own sun terraces. Public rooms feature a smart restaurant, a conservatory dining room and a lounge bar.

Rooms: 36 (29 annexe) (1 family) (30 GF) ☞ Facilities: FTV WiFi Xmas New Year Conf: Class 24 Board 30 Thtr 75 Services: Night porter Parking: 60 Notes: Civ Wed 75

The Grange Hotel
★★★ 77% COUNTRY HOUSE HOTEL

Barton Road, Thurston, IP31 3PQ - tel: 01359 231260
email: info@grangecountryhousehotel.com
web: www.grangecountryhousehotel.com
dir: A14 junct 45 towards Gt Barton, right at T-junct. At x-rds left into Barton Rd to Thurston. At rdbt, left after 0.5m, hotel on right

The Grange Hotel is a Tudor-style country house hotel situated on the outskirts of town. The individually decorated bedrooms have co-ordinated fabrics and many thoughtful touches; some rooms have nice views of the gardens. Public areas include a smart lounge bar, two private dining rooms, the Garden Restaurant and banqueting facilities.

Rooms: 18 (5 annexe) (1 family) (3 GF) ☞ S £45.92–£82.50; D £45.92–£145*
Facilities: FTV WiFi Beauty treatment room ♫ Xmas New Year Conf: Class 40 Board 30 Thtr 135 Del from £101.50 Parking: 100 Notes: Civ Wed 150

Premier Inn Bury St Edmunds Town Centre
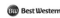
BUDGET HOTEL

Raingate Street, IP33 2AR - tel: 0871 527 9512 (Calls cost 13p per minute plus your phone company's access charge) web: www.premierinn.com
dir: A14 junct 44 signed Bury St Edmunds East/Sudbury A134. At rdbt 3rd exit towards Bury St Edmunds. At next rdbt 2nd exit (Town Centre/A1302). At next rdbt 3rd exit (town centre). At mini rdbt 3rd exit onto Westgate St. At Greene King Brewery (one-way system) into Crown St. Hotel at bottom of hill

High quality, budget accommodation ideal for both families and business travellers. Spacious, en suite bedrooms feature tea and coffee making facilities, Freeview TV in most hotels and free WiFi. The adjacent family restaurant features a wide and varied menu.

Rooms: 75

BUXTON
Derbyshire — Map 16 SK07

Best Western Lee Wood Hotel
★★★★ 76% HOTEL

The Park, SK17 6TQ - tel: 01298 23002
email: reservations@leewoodhotel.co.uk web: www.leewoodhotel.co.uk
dir: From town centre take A5004 NE, hotel 150mtrs beyond University of Derby - Buxton Campus

This elegant Georgian hotel offers high standards of comfort and hospitality. The individually furnished bedrooms are generally spacious, with all of the expected modern conveniences. There is a choice of two comfortable lounges and a conservatory restaurant. The quality cooking, good service and fine hospitality are noteworthy.

Rooms: 39 (5 annexe) (4 family) **Facilities:** STV FTV WiFi ⌨ Gym Serenity beauty & wellbeing New Year **Conf:** Class 65 Board 40 Thtr 120 **Services:** Lift Night porter **Parking:** 50 **Notes:** Civ Wed 120

CADNAM	Map 5 SU31
Hampshire	

HIGHLY RECOMMENDED

Bartley Lodge Hotel

★★★ 87% HOTEL

 NEW FOREST HOTELS

Lyndhurst Road, SO40 2NR - tel: 023 8081 2248
email: bartley@newforesthotels.co.uk **web:** www.newforesthotels.co.uk
dir: M27 junct 1, at 1st rdbt 1st exit, at 2nd rdbt 3rd exit onto A337. Hotel sign on left

This 18th-century former hunting lodge is very quietly situated, yet is just minutes from the M27. Bedrooms vary in size but all are well equipped. There is a selection of small lounge areas, a cosy bar and an indoor pool, together with a small fitness suite. The Crystal dining room offers a tempting choice of well prepared dishes.

Rooms: 40 (15 family) (4 GF) ✆ **S** £50–£129; **D** £99–£189 (incl. bkfst)*
Facilities: FTV WiFi ⌨ HL ⏧ ♨ Sauna Xmas New Year **Conf:** Class 60 Board 60 Thtr 120 **Services:** Lift **Parking:** 60 **Notes:** LB Civ Wed 100

CAMBERLEY	Map 6 SU86
Surrey	

See also Yateley

Macdonald Frimley Hall Hotel & Spa

★★★★ 80% ⏧ HOTEL

MACDONALD HOTELS & RESORTS

Lime Avenue, GU15 2BG - tel: 01276 413100
email: sales.frimleyhall@macdonald-hotels.co.uk
web: www.macdonaldhotels.co.uk/frimleyhall
dir: M3 junct 3, A321 follow Bagshot signs. Through lights, left onto A30 signed Camberley & Basingstoke. To rdbt, 2nd exit onto A325, take 5th right

The epitome of classic English elegance, Macdonald Frimley Hall Hotel is an ivy-clad Victorian manor house set in two acres of immaculate grounds in the heart of Surrey. The bedrooms and public areas are smart and have a modern decorative theme. The hotel boasts an impressive health club and spa with treatment rooms, a fully equipped gym and heated indoor swimming pool.

Rooms: 98 (15 family) ✆ **Facilities:** Spa FTV WiFi ⌨ HL ⏧ Gym Technogym Sauna Steam room Relaxation room Xmas New Year **Conf:** Class 100 Board 60 Thtr 250 **Services:** Night porter **Parking:** 150 **Notes:** Civ Wed 220

Lakeside International

★★★ 73% HOTEL

Wharf Road, Frimley Green, GU16 6JR - tel: 01252 838000
email: info@lakesideinthotel.com **web:** www.lakesideinternationalhotel.com
dir: Exit A321 at mini-rdbt turn into Wharf Rd. Lakeside complex on right

This hotel, geared towards the business market, enjoys a lakeside location with noteworthy views. Bedrooms are modern, comfortable and with a range of facilities. Public areas are spacious and include a residents' lounge, bar, games room, a smart restaurant and an established health and leisure club.

Rooms: 98 (1 family) (31 GF) ✆ **S** £79–£119; **D** £89–£149 (incl. bkfst)*
Facilities: FTV WiFi ⏧ Gym Squash Sauna Steam room **Conf:** Class 100 Board 40 Thtr 120 **Services:** Lift Night porter **Parking:** 250 **Notes:** Civ Wed 100

Premier Inn Camberley

BUDGET HOTEL

 Premier Inn

Park Street, GU15 3SG - tel: 0871 527 9322 (Calls cost 13p per minute plus your phone company's access charge) **web:** www.premierinn.com
dir: M3 junct 4, A331 towards Camberley. In 2m, at major junct into right lane, 4th exit signed A30. For parking, in 1m, right into Southern Rd for Atrium Car Park

High quality, budget accommodation ideal for both families and business travellers. Spacious, en suite bedrooms feature tea and coffee making facilities, Freeview TV in most hotels and free WiFi. The adjacent family restaurant features a wide and varied menu.

Rooms: 95

Premier Inn Sandhurst

BUDGET HOTEL

221 Yorktown Road, College Town, GU47 0RT - tel: 0871 527 8958 (Calls cost 13p per minute plus your phone company's access charge) **web:** www.premierinn.com
dir: M3 junct 4, A331 to Camberley. At large rdbt take A321 towards Bracknell. At 3rd lights, hotel on left

Rooms: 54

CAMBORNE	Map 2 SW63
Cornwall & Isles of Scilly	

Premier Inn Camborne

BUDGET HOTEL

 Premier Inn

Treswithian Road, TR14 7NF - tel: 0871 527 9308 (Calls cost 13p per minute plus your phone company's access charge) **web:** www.premierinn.com
dir: From M5 (S) junct 31, A30 to Bodmin, then to Redruth, follow signs to Camborne. Left onto A3047, to rdbt, 1st exit to hotel

High quality, budget accommodation ideal for both families and business travellers. Spacious, en suite bedrooms feature tea and coffee making facilities, Freeview TV in most hotels and free WiFi. The adjacent family restaurant features a wide and varied menu.

Rooms: 110

CAMBOURNE	Map 12 TL35
Cambridgeshire	

The Cambridge Belfry

★★★★ 79% HOTEL

QHOTELS
INSPIRED BY YOU

Back Street, CB23 6BW - tel: 01954 714600
email: cambridgebelfry@qhotels.co.uk **web:** www.qhotels.co.uk
dir: M11 junct 13, A428 towards Bedford, follow signs to Cambourne. Exit at Cambourne, keep left. Left at rdbt, hotel on left

This exciting hotel, built beside the water, is located at the gateway to Cambourne Village and Business Park. The hotel boasts excellent leisure facilities, including Reflections Spa offering a range of therapies and treatments, and extensive conference and banqueting rooms. Meals are served in the Bridge Restaurant, and original artwork is displayed throughout the hotel.

Rooms: 120 (30 GF) ✆ **S** £85–£160; **D** £97–£172 (incl. bkfst)* **Facilities:** Spa FTV WiFi ⌨ HL ⏧ ♨ Gym Beauty treatments Fitness classes Xmas New Year **Conf:** Class 70 Board 70 Thtr 250 Del from £130 **Services:** Lift Night porter **Parking:** 200 **Notes:** LB Civ Wed 130

 C

CAMBRIDGE
Cambridgeshire

Map 12 TL45

HIGHLY RECOMMENDED

Quy Mill Hotel & Spa, Cambridge
★★★★ 83% ❀❀ HOTEL

Church Road, Stow Cum Quy, CB25 9AF - **tel:** 01223 293383
email: info@cambridgequymill.co.uk **web:** www.cambridgequymill.co.uk
dir: Exit A14 at junct 35, E of Cambridge, onto B1102 for 50yds. Entrance opposite church

Set in open countryside, this 19th-century former watermill is conveniently situated for access to Cambridge. Bedroom styles differ, yet each room is smartly appointed and brightly decorated; superior, spacious courtyard rooms are noteworthy. Well-designed public areas include several spacious bar/lounges, with a choice of casual and formal eating areas; service is both friendly and helpful. There is a smart leisure club with state-of-the-art equipment, as well as a health spa.

Rooms: 51 (30 annexe) (4 family) (24 GF) 🐾 **Facilities:** Spa FTV WiFi ᐅ HL 🐾 Gym Sauna Steam room Wellness suite New Year **Conf:** Class 30 Board 24 Thtr 80 **Services:** Night porter **Parking:** 90 **Notes:** Civ Wed 80

Hotel Felix
★★★★ 81% ❀❀ HOTEL

Whitehouse Lane, Huntingdon Road, CB3 0LX - **tel:** 01223 277977
email: help@hotelfelix.co.uk **web:** www.hotelfelix.co.uk
dir: M11 junct 13. From A1 N, take A14 onto A1307. At 'City of Cambridge' sign left into Whitehouse Ln

A beautiful Victorian mansion set amidst three acres of landscaped gardens, this property was originally built in 1852 for a surgeon from the famous Addenbrookes Hospital. The contemporary-style bedrooms have carefully chosen furniture and many thoughtful touches, while public rooms feature an open-plan bar, the adjacent Graffiti restaurant and a small quiet lounge.

Rooms: 52 (5 family) (26 GF) 🐾 **Facilities:** STV WiFi ᐅ Xmas New Year **Conf:** Class 36 Board 34 Thtr 60 **Services:** Lift Night porter **Parking:** 90 **Notes:** LB Civ Wed 60

The Varsity Hotel & Spa
★★★★ 81% HOTEL

Thompson's Lane, CB5 8AQ - **tel:** 01223 306030
email: info@thevarsityhotel.co.uk **web:** www.thevarsityhotel.co.uk
dir: M11 junct 13, pass Park & Ride, next rdbt 1st left, right at next junct into Bridge St, right into Thompou's Lane

Situated close to the River Cam and occupying a central location, The Varsity Hotel is a stylish property. The bedrooms are smartly decorated and have all the expected facilities including power showers, CD players and free internet access. The River Bar, to the side of the hotel, has a buzzing atmosphere and offers a range of popular dishes, while on the 6th floor there is another restaurant with stunning views of the city. The hotel has a health club and spa, and a roof top bar.

Rooms: 44 (2 family) 🐾 **D** £115–£700 (incl. bkfst)* **Facilities:** Spa FTV WiFi ᐅ Gym Sauna Steam room Valet parking New Year **Conf:** Class 40 Board 30 Thtr 60 **Services:** Lift Night porter Air con **Notes:** Civ Wed 60

The Gonville Hotel
★★★★ 80% HOTEL

Gonville Place, CB1 1LY - **tel:** 01223 366611
email: info@gonvillehotel.co.uk **web:** www.gonvillehotel.co.uk
dir: M11 junct 11, on A1309 follow city centre signs. At 2nd mini rdbt right into Lensfield Rd, over junct with lights. Hotel 25yds on right

This is a well-established hotel situated on the inner ring road, a short walk across the green from the city centre. The air-conditioned public areas are cheerfully furnished, and include a lounge bar and brasserie. Bedrooms are well appointed and appealing, offering a good range of facilities for both corporate and leisure guests.

Rooms: 84 (2 family) (8 GF) 🐾 **S** £99–£150; **D** £150–£300 (incl. bkfst)*
Facilities: FTV WiFi ᐅ HL 🎵 New Year **Conf:** Class 30 Board 30 Thtr 50 **Services:** Lift Night porter Air con **Parking:** 70 **Notes:** RS 24-29 Dec B&B only

Hotel du Vin Cambridge
★★★★ 78% ❀ TOWN HOUSE HOTEL

15-19 Trumpington Street, CB2 1QA - **tel:** 01223 227330 & 0844 736 4253 (Calls cost 5p per minute plus your phone company's access charge)
email: info.cambridge@hotelduvin.com **web:** www.hotelduvin.com
dir: M11 junct 11 Cambridge S, pass Trumpington Park & Ride on left. Hotel 2m on right after double rdbt

This beautiful building, which dates back in part to medieval times, has been transformed to enhance its many quirky architectural features. The bedrooms and suites, some with private terraces, have the company's trademark monsoon showers and Egyptian linen. The French-style bistro has an open kitchen and the bar is set in the unusual labyrinth of vaulted cellar rooms. Other parts of the hotel include a library, a specialist wine-tasting room and a private dining room.

Rooms: 41 (3 annexe) (6 GF) 🐾 **S** £150–£495* **Facilities:** STV WiFi Xmas New Year **Conf:** Class 18 Board 18 Thtr 30 **Services:** Lift Night porter Air con **Parking:** 24

Hallmark Hotel Cambridge
★★★★ 73% HOTEL

Bar Hill, CB23 8EU - **tel:** 0330 028 3400
email: cambridge@hallmarkhotels.co.uk **web:** www.hallmarkhotels.co.uk
dir: M11 junct 13, A14, follow signs for Huntingdon. Take B1050 Bar Hill, hotel 1st exit on rdbt

The Hallmark Hotel Cambridge is ideally situated in 200 acres of open countryside, just five miles from the university city of Cambridge. Public rooms include a brasserie restaurant and the popular Gallery Bar. The contemporary-style bedrooms are smartly decorated and equipped with a good range of useful facilities. The hotel also has a leisure club, swimming pool and golf course.

Rooms: 136 (35 family) (68 GF) **S** fr £69; **D** fr £79* **Facilities:** Spa STV FTV WiFi ᐅ HL 🐾 🏌 18 Putting green 🐾 Gym Hair & beauty salon Steam room Sauna Xmas New Year **Conf:** Class 90 Board 45 Thtr 220 Del from £109 **Services:** Lift Night porter **Parking:** 200 **Notes:** LB Civ Wed 200

C

The Lensfield Hotel

★★★ 80% METRO HOTEL

53-57 Lensfield Road, CB2 1EN - **tel:** 01223 355017
email: reservations@lensfieldhotel.co.uk **web:** www.lensfieldhotel.co.uk
dir: *M11 juncts 11, 12 or 13, follow signs to city centre. Access via Silver St, Trumpington St, left into Lensfield Rd*

Located close to all the city's attractions, this constantly improving hotel provides a range of attractive bedrooms, equipped with thoughtful extras. Comprehensive breakfasts are taken in an elegant dining room, and a comfortable bar and cosy foyer lounge are also available.

Rooms: 40 (3 family) (4 GF) **S** fr £77; **D** fr £118 (incl. bkfst)* **Facilities:** Spa STV FTV WiFi ☇ HL Gym Thermal suite Fitness suite **Services:** Night porter Air con **Parking:** 5 **Notes:** Closed last 2 weeks in Dec-4 Jan

Arundel House Hotel

★★★ 78% HOTEL

Chesterton Road, CB4 3AN - **tel:** 01223 367701
email: info@arundelhousehotels.co.uk **web:** www.arundelhousehotels.co.uk
dir: *In city centre on A1303*

Overlooking the River Cam and enjoying views of open parkland, this popular and smart hotel was originally a row of townhouses dating from Victorian times. Bedrooms are attractive and have a special character. The smart public areas feature a conservatory for informal snacks, a spacious bar and an elegant restaurant for more serious dining.

Rooms: 103 (22 annexe) (7 family) (14 GF) **Facilities:** FTV WiFi ☇ New Year **Conf:** Class 24 Board 22 Thtr 50 **Services:** Night porter **Parking:** 70 **Notes:** LB Closed 25-26 Dec

Centennial Hotel

★★★ 76% HOTEL

63-71 Hills Road, CB2 1PG - **tel:** 01223 314652
email: reception@centennialhotel.co.uk **web:** www.centennialhotel.co.uk
dir: *M11 junct 11, A1309 to Cambridge. Right Into Brooklands Ave to end. Left, hotel 100yds on right*

This friendly hotel is convenient for the railway station and town centre. Well-presented public areas include a welcoming lounge, a relaxing bar and restaurant on the lower-ground level. Bedrooms are generally spacious, well maintained and thoughtfully equipped with a good range of facilities; several rooms are available on the ground floor.

Rooms: 39 (1 family) (7 GF) ☏ **S** £85–£105; **D** £100–£135 (incl. bkfst) **Facilities:** FTV WiFi ☇ **Conf:** Class 22 Board 22 Thtr 25 **Services:** Night porter **Parking:** 28 **Notes:** Closed 23 Dec-1 Jan

Ashley Hotel

★★ 76% METRO HOTEL

74-76 Chesterton Road, CB4 1ER - **tel:** 01223 350059
email: info@arundelhousehotels.co.uk **web:** www.arundelhousehotels.co.uk
dir: *On city centre ring road*

Expect a warm welcome at this delightful Victorian property situated just a short walk from the River Cam. The smartly decorated bedrooms are generally quite spacious and equipped with a good range of useful extras. Breakfast is served at individual tables in the smart lower ground floor dining room.

Rooms: 16 (5 family) (5 GF) **Facilities:** FTV WiFi ☇ **Services:** Night porter **Parking:** 12 **Notes:** Closed 24-26 Dec

Premier Inn Cambridge (A14 Jct 32)

BUDGET HOTEL

Ring Fort Road, CB4 2GW - **tel:** 0871 527 8186 (Calls cost 13p per minute plus your phone company's access charge) **web:** www.premierinn.com
dir: *A14 junct 32, follow B1049/city centre signs. At 1st lights left into Kings Hedges Rd, 2nd left into Ring Fort Rd*

High quality, budget accommodation ideal for both families and business travellers. Spacious, en suite bedrooms feature tea and coffee making facilities, Freeview TV in most hotels and free WiFi. The adjacent family restaurant features a wide and varied menu.

Rooms: 154

Premier Inn Cambridge City Centre

BUDGET HOTEL

Newmarket Road, CB1 3EP - **tel:** 0871 527 9396 (Calls cost 13p per minute plus your phone company's access charge) **web:** www.premierinn.com
dir: *M11 junct 12, A603, left at mini rdbt then take 2nd exit at next rdbt (continue on A603). Through lights, at rdbt take 3rd exit onto A1134 signed Ring Road, Newmarket & Airport. Hotel on right*

Rooms: 120

C

CAMBRIDGE SERVICES
Cambridgeshire   Map 12 TL36

Days Inn Cambridge - A1

AA Advertised

Cambridge Extra Services, Junction A14/M11, CB23 4WU - tel: 01954 267176
email: cambridge.hotel@welcomebreak.co.uk **web:** www.welcomebreak.co.uk
dir: *A14/M11 Cambridge Extra Services*

This modern, purpose built accommodation offers smartly appointed, well-equipped bedrooms, with good power showers. There is a choice of adjacent food outlets where guests may enjoy breakfast, snacks and meals.

Rooms: 82 (14 family) (40 GF) (19 smoking) **Facilities:** FTV WiFi ↘ **Services:** Air con
Parking: 120

CANNOCK
Staffordshire   Map 10 SJ91

Premier Inn Cannock (Orbital)

BUDGET HOTEL

Eastern Way, WS11 8XR - tel: 0871 527 8190 (Calls cost 13p per minute plus your phone company's access charge) **web:** www.premierinn.com
dir: *N'bound: M6 (Toll) junct 7, A5. At rdbt 1st exit (A5), 4th exit onto A460, 1st exit. S'bound: (no access from M6 Toll). M6 junct 11, A460 signed Cannock. At next 2 rdbts take 3rd exit. At next rdbt 1st exit onto service road. Hotel adjacent to Orbital Brewers Fayre*

High quality, budget accommodation ideal for both families and business travellers. Spacious, en suite bedrooms feature tea and coffee making facilities, Freeview TV in most hotels and free WiFi. The adjacent family restaurant features a wide and varied menu.

Rooms: 21

Premier Inn Cannock South

BUDGET HOTEL

Watling Street, WS11 1SJ - tel: 0871 527 8192 (Calls cost 13p per minute plus your phone company's access charge) **web:** www.premierinn.com
dir: *At junct of A5 & A460, 2m from M6 juncts 11 & 12*

Rooms: 60

CANTERBURY
Kent   Map 7 TR15

ABode Canterbury

★★★★ 82% ⚘⚘ HOTEL   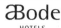

High Street, CT1 2RX - tel: 01227 766266
email: reservations@abodecanterbury.co.uk **web:** www.abodecanterbury.co.uk
dir: *M2 junct 7. Follow Canterbury signs onto ring road. At Wincheap rdbt turn into city. Left into Rosemary Ln, into Stour St. Hotel at end*

ABode Canterbury is a stylish hotel set on Canterbury's main street. A range of well appointed bedrooms and suites are available, many retaining original features, all boasting modern facilities and smart en suites. A choice of dining options and bars include The County Restaurant, a smart Champagne Bar, and the more relaxed and hip Old Brewery Tavern.

Rooms: 72 (10 family) ↘ **S** £90–£350; **D** £100–£400* **Facilities:** FTV WiFi ↘ Gym Xmas New Year **Conf:** Class 48 Board 20 Thtr 140 **Services:** Lift Night porter Air con
Parking: 44 **Notes:** Civ Wed 100

Best Western Abbots Barton Hotel

★★★ 79% ⚘ HOTEL

New Dover Road, CT1 3DU - tel: 01227 760341
email: info@abbotsbartonhotel.com **web:** www.abbotsbartonhotel.com
dir: *Phone for directions*

Abbots Barton Hotel is in a central location, just a 10-minute walk from the city centre, and benefits from two acres of gardens and on-site parking. Bedrooms are comfortably appointed throughout, traditional in style yet with all modern amenities including free WiFi and digital TV. The bar and restaurant are open daily, and there are good function facilities with a private bar and patio - ideal for conferences and weddings.

Rooms: 53 (3 family) (6 GF) **S** £75–£110; **D** £75–£160* **Facilities:** FTV WiFi ↘ Xmas New Year **Conf:** Class 60 Board 60 Thtr 130 **Services:** Lift Night porter **Parking:** 40
Notes: Civ Wed 80

Castle House

★★★ 73% METRO HOTEL

28 Castle Street, CT1 2PT - tel: 01227 761897
email: info@castlehousehotel.co.uk **web:** www.castlehousehotel.co.uk
dir: *Next to Canterbury Castle*

Conveniently located in the city centre opposite the imposing ruins of the ancient Norman castle; part of the building dates back to the 1730s. Bedrooms are spacious, all with en suite facilities and many useful extras, such as WiFi. There is a walled garden in which to relax during the warmer months.

Rooms: 15

Premier Inn Canterbury City Centre

BUDGET HOTEL

New Dover Road, CT1 1UP - tel: 0871 527 9408 (Calls cost 13p per minute plus your phone company's access charge) **web:** www.premierinn.com
dir: *M2 junct 7. At Brenley Corner rdbt 4th exit onto A2. Left then merge onto A2050. At London Rd rdbt 2nd exit (A2050). At St Peters rdbt 3rd exit onto A290. At Wincheap rdbt 2nd exit onto A28. At St Georges rdbt 2nd exit onto A257. At lights right (A257). At lights right onto A2050. Hotel in view*

High quality, budget accommodation ideal for both families and business travellers. Spacious, en suite bedrooms feature tea and coffee making facilities, Freeview TV in most hotels and free WiFi. The adjacent family restaurant features a wide and varied menu.

Rooms: 120

CARBIS BAY

See **St Ives (Cornwall)**

C

CARLISLE
Cumbria
Map 18 NY35

Crown Hotel

★★★★ 76% ⊛ HOTEL

Station Road, Wetheral, CA4 8ES - tel: 01228 561888
email: info@crownhotelwetheral.co.uk web: www.crownhotelwetheral.co.uk
dir: M6 junct 42, B6263 to Wetheral, right at village shop, car park at rear of hotel

Set in the attractive village of Wetheral, with landscaped gardens to the rear, this hotel is well suited for both business and leisure guests, as well as families. There are more than fifty bedrooms in a variety of sizes and styles, and include two apartments in an adjacent house, ideal for longer stays. A choice of dining options is available, with the popular Waltons Bar as an informal alternative to the main Conservatory Restaurant. Weddings and conferences can be catered for, and there are also leisure club facilities which include a swimming pool, jacuzzi, squash court, two gyms, and a sauna.

Rooms: 51 (2 annexe) (10 family) (3 GF) ⌕ Facilities: Spa STV WiFi HL ⓑ supervised Gym Squash Children's splash pool Steam room Beauty room Sauna Dance studio Xmas New Year Conf: Class 60 Board 65 Thtr 140 Services: Night porter Parking: 55 Notes: Civ Wed 120

Hallmark Hotel Carlisle

★★★★ 75% HOTEL

Court Square, CA1 1QY - tel: 0330 028 3401 email: carlisle@hallmarkhotels.co.uk
web: www.hallmarkhotels.co.uk
dir: M6 junct 43, to city centre, then follow road to left & railway station

This hotel is at the heart of the town, opposite the railway station. Most of the bedrooms have benefited from an investment programme, and the smart ground-floor areas include a popular bar and restaurant. A number of meeting rooms are available and at the rear of the hotel is a small car park.

Rooms: 70 (3 family) ⌕ S £58–£179; D £68–£269* Facilities: FTV WiFi Xmas New Year Conf: Class 100 Board 30 Thtr 240 Del from £110 Services: Lift Night porter Parking: 26 Notes: Civ Wed 200

The Crown & Mitre

★★★ 78% HOTEL

4 English Street, CA3 8HZ - tel: 01228 525491
email: info@crownandmitre-hotel-carlisle.com
web: www.crownandmitre-hotel-carlisle.com
dir: A6 to city centre, pass station on left. Turn left at end of English St, then immediate right onto Blackfriars St

Located in the heart of the city, this Edwardian hotel is close to the cathedral and a few minutes' walk from the castle. Bedrooms vary in size and style, from smart executive rooms to more functional standard rooms. Public rooms include a comfortable lounge area and the lovely bar with its feature stained-glass windows.

Rooms: 90 (20 annexe) (3 family) ⌕ S £65–£75; D £87–£107* Facilities: STV FTV WiFi ⓑ ⓑ Xmas New Year Conf: Class 250 Board 50 Thtr 400 Services: Lift Night porter Parking: 42 Notes: LB Civ Wed 200

Premier Inn Carlisle Central

BUDGET HOTEL

Warwick Road, CA1 2WF - tel: 0871 527 8210 (Calls cost 13p per minute plus your phone company's access charge) web: www.premierinn.com
dir: M6 junct 43, on A69

High quality, budget accommodation ideal for both families and business travellers. Spacious, en suite bedrooms feature tea and coffee making facilities, Freeview TV in most hotels and free WiFi. The adjacent family restaurant features a wide and varied menu.

Rooms: 65

Premier Inn Carlisle Central North

BUDGET HOTEL

Kingstown Road, CA3 0AT - tel: 0871 527 8212 (Calls cost 13p per minute plus your phone company's access charge) web: www.premierinn.com
dir: M6 junct 44, A7 towards Carlisle, hotel 1m on left

Rooms: 49

Premier Inn Carlisle (M6 Jct 42)

BUDGET HOTEL

Carleton, CA4 0AD - tel: 0871 527 8206 (Calls cost 13p per minute plus your phone company's access charge) web: www.premierinn.com
dir: Just off M6 junct 42, S of Carlisle

Rooms: 80

Premier Inn Carlisle (M6 Jct 44)

BUDGET HOTEL

Parkhouse Road, CA3 0JR - tel: 0871 527 8208 (Calls cost 13p per minute plus your phone company's access charge) web: www.premierinn.com
dir: M6 junct 44, A7 signed Carlisle. Hotel on right at 1st set of lights

Rooms: 127

Find out more
about the AA's Hotel rating scheme on pages 12–13

C

CARTMEL
Cumbria
Map 18 SD37

HIGHLY RECOMMENDED

Aynsome Manor Hotel

★★★ 86% COUNTRY HOUSE HOTEL

LA11 6HH - **tel:** 015395 36653
email: aynsomemanor@btconnect.com **web:** www.aynsomemanorhotel.co.uk
dir: *M6 junct 36, A590 signed Barrow-in-Furness towards Cartmel. Left at end of road, hotel before village*

A warm and genuine welcome is guaranteed at this well-situated Lake District country house. Dating back, in part, to the early 16th century, the manor overlooks the Fells and the nearby Cartmel priory. Spacious bedrooms, including some courtyard rooms, are comfortably furnished. Dinner in the elegant restaurant features local produce and there is a choice of deeply comfortable lounges to relax in beside open fires.

Rooms: 12 (2 annexe) (2 family) **S** £70–£125; **D** £85–£125 (incl. bkfst)
Facilities: FTV WiFi New Year **Parking:** 20 **Notes:** LB Closed 2-31 Jan

CASTLE BROMWICH
West Midlands
Map 10 SP18

Castle Bromwich Hall Hotel

[U]

Chester Road, B36 9DE - **tel:** 0121 748 0030 **email:** info@cbhh.co.uk
web: www.castlebromwichhallhotel.co.uk
dir: *Just off M6 junct 5*

Currently the rating for this establishment is not confirmed. This may be due to a change of ownership or because it has only recently joined the AA rating scheme.

Rooms: 42 (23 annexe) (5 family) (1 GF) **D** £72–£100; **D** £89–£150*
Facilities: Xmas New Year **Conf:** Class 100 Board 60 Thtr 120 Del from £140*
Services: Night porter **Notes:** Civ wed 90

CASTLE COMBE
Wiltshire
Map 4 ST87

The Manor House, an Exclusive Hotel & Golf Club

★★★★★ 84% COUNTRY HOUSE HOTEL

SN14 7HR - **tel:** 01249 782206
email: enquiries@manorhouse.co.uk **web:** www.exclusive.co.uk
dir: *M4 junct 17 follow Chippenham signs onto A420 Bristol, then right onto B4039. Through village, right after bridge. Follow brown tourist signs to Castle Combe Racing Circuit*

This delightful hotel is situated in a secluded valley adjacent to a picturesque village, where there have been no new buildings for 300 years. There are 365 acres of grounds to enjoy, complete with an Italian garden and an 18-hole golf course. Bedrooms, some in the main house and some in a row of stone cottages, have been superbly furnished, and public rooms include a number of cosy lounges with roaring fires. Service is a pleasing blend of professionalism and friendliness. The award-winning food utilises top quality local produce.

Rooms: 48 (27 annexe) (8 family) (13 GF) **D** fr £162 (incl. bkfst)* **Facilities:** STV WiFi 18 Putting green Fishing Beauty treatment room Jogging track Giant games on lawns Xmas New Year Child facilities **Conf:** Class 50 Board 34 Thtr 100 **Services:** Night porter **Parking:** 100 **Notes:** LB Civ Wed 110

CASTLE DONINGTON
See **East Midlands Airport**

CASTLEFORD
West Yorkshire
Map 16 SE42

Premier Inn Castleford M62 Jct 31

BUDGET HOTEL

Pioneer Way, WF10 5TG - **tel:** 0871 527 8216 (Calls cost 13p per minute plus your phone company's access charge) **web:** www.premierinn.com
dir: *M62 junct 31, A655 towards Castleford, right at 1st lights, then left*

High quality, budget accommodation ideal for both families and business travellers. Spacious, en suite bedrooms feature tea and coffee making facilities, Freeview TV in most hotels and free WiFi. The adjacent family restaurant features a wide and varied menu.

Rooms: 62

Premier Inn Castleford (Xscape, M62 Jct 32)

BUDGET HOTEL

Colarado Way, WF10 4TA - **tel:** 0871 527 8218 (Calls cost 13p per minute plus your phone company's access charge) **web:** www.premierinn.com
dir: *M62 junct 32, follow signs for Xscape. Hotel adjacent to Xscape complex*

Rooms: 119

CATTERICK
North Yorkshire
Map 19 SE29

Premier Inn Catterick Garrison

BUDGET HOTEL

Princes Gate, DL9 3BA - **tel:** 0871 527 9568 (Calls cost 13p per minute plus your phone company's access charge) **web:** www.premierinn.com
dir: *A1 towards Wetherby, right onto A6136 (Catterick Garrison). At 1st rdbt take 1st exit (A6136/Richmond), straight on at 4 mini rdbts. At 5th rdbt 3rd exit, hotel on left*

High quality, budget accommodation ideal for both families and business travellers. Spacious, en suite bedrooms feature tea and coffee making facilities, Freeview TV in most hotels and free WiFi. The adjacent family restaurant features a wide and varied menu.

Rooms: 60

Symbols and abbreviations
explained on pages 6–7

CHADDESLEY CORBETT	Map 10 SO87
Worcestershire	

Brockencote Hall Country House Hotel

★★★★ ◉◉◉ 🏠 COUNTRY HOUSE HOTEL

DY10 4PY - tel: 01562 777876
email: info@brockencotehall.com **web:** www.brockencotehall.com
dir: *A38 to Bromsgrove, off A448 towards Kidderminster*

Brockencote Hall Hotel is a Victorian country manor house hotel set in 70 acres of stunning parkland, complete with a scenic lake, tennis courts and dovecote. A fountain adorns the approach, the terrace and gardens are beautifully landscaped, and the private dining rooms, restaurant and public areas are classically decorated in gentle greys, lavenders and damson velvets. The kitchen brigade create inspired dishes that revolve around the seasons and local suppliers, with a focus on the purity of flavours.

Rooms: 21 (4 family) (5 GF) 🐾 **S** £105–£285; **D** £135–£365 (incl. bkfst)
Facilities: FTV WiFi 🏌 🎣 Fishing 🛶 Xmas New Year **Conf:** Class 35 Board 35 Thtr 80 Del from £195 **Services:** Night porter **Parking:** 60 **Notes:** LB Civ Wed 90

Find out more about
the AA Hotel Group
of the Year – see page 19

CHAGFORD	Map 3 SX78
Devon	

Gidleigh Park

★★★★★ ◉◉◉◉◉ 🏠 COUNTRY HOUSE HOTEL

ANDREW BROWNSWORD THE HOTELS

TQ13 8HH - tel: 01647 432367
email: info@gidleigh.co.uk **web:** www.gidleigh.co.uk
dir: *From Chagford, right at Lloyds Bank into Mill St. After 150yds fork right. 2m to end*

Built in 1928 as a private residence for an Australian shipping magnate and set in 107 acres of lovingly tended grounds, this world-renowned hotel retains a timeless charm and a very endearing, homely atmosphere. The individually styled bedrooms are sumptuously furnished; some with separate seating areas, some with balconies and many enjoying panoramic views. There are spa suites, a loft suite which is ideal for families, and the stunning thatched Pavilion in the grounds. The latter has two bedrooms, two bathrooms, a lounge and kitchen diner. The spacious public areas feature antique furniture, beautiful flower arrangements and magnificent artwork. All of this is topped off with accomplished cuisine to complete the Gidleigh experience. Andrew Brownsword Hotels is the AA Hotel Group of the Year 2017-2018.

Rooms: 24 (3 annexe) (4 family) (3 GF) 🐾 **D** £350–£1085 (incl. bkfst)*
Facilities: STV FTV WiFi 🏌 Putting green 🎣 Fishing 🛶 Bowls Xmas New Year
Services: Night porter **Parking:** 45 **Notes:** Civ Wed 50

Mill End Hotel

★★★ 82% ◉◉ COUNTRY HOUSE HOTEL

Dartmoor National Park, TQ13 8JN - tel: 01647 432282
email: info@millendhotel.com **web:** www.millendhotel.com
dir: *From A30 at Whiddon Down take A382 to Moretonhampstead. In 3.5m hump back bridge at Sandy Park, hotel on right*

A Dartmoor hotel on the banks of Devon's majestic River Teign, Mill End Hotel is a secluded country house hideaway. There are 20 individually-styled bedrooms, comfy lounges, log fires and beautiful riverside gardens. The hotel restaurant is open for breakfast, lunch, and dinner; and non-residents are very welcome too. After a day on the moors or a trip to the coast, one can simply relax in front of an open fire or be tempted by the cream tea on offer. This hotel is dog friendly.

Rooms: 20 🐾 **S** £85–£150; **D** £120–£300 (incl. bkfst)* **Conf:** Class 20 Board 30 Thtr 30 Del from £100 **Notes:** LB Civ Wed 60

C

CHANDLER'S CROSS
Hertfordshire
Map TQ09

The Grove
★★★★★ ◉◉◉ HOTEL

WD3 4TG - **tel:** 01923 807807
email: info@thegrove.co.uk **web:** www.thegrove.co.uk
dir: M25 junct 19, A411 towards Watford. Hotel on right

Set amid 300 acres of rolling countryside, much of which is golf course, The Grove combines historic features with cutting-edge, modern design. The spacious bedrooms have the latest in temperature control, lighting technology and flat-screen TVs; many have balconies. Suites in the original mansion are particularly stunning. Championship golf, a world-class spa and three dining options are just a few of the treasures to sample here. Those dining options are Collette's with 3 AA Rosettes that offers fine dining, and a more relaxed style in the Glasshouse and Stables restaurants. The walled garden is also well worth exploring. The hotel also has extensive crèche facilities.

Rooms: 215 (69 family) (23 GF) 🐾 **D** fr £280* **Facilities:** Spa STV FTV WiFi ⓘ ⓘ supervised ⓘ supervised ⓘ 18 Putting green ⓘ ⓘ Gym Walk & cycle trails Giant chess Driving range Kids club Games room Xmas New Year **Conf:** Class 300 Board 78 Thtr 450 **Services:** Lift Night porter Air con **Parking:** 400 **Notes:** Civ Wed 450

CHARD
Somerset
Map 4 ST30

Cricket St Thomas Hotel
★★★★ 75% COUNTRY HOUSE HOTEL

WARNERLEISUREHOTELS

TA20 4DD - **tel:** 01460 30111
email: cricket.sales@bourne-leisure.co.uk **web:** www.warnerleisurehotels.co.uk
dir: M5 junct 25, A358 towards Chard, A30 to Crewkerne. Hotel 3m from Chard

This Grade II listed house has an interesting history, including the fact that Lord Nelson and Lady Hamilton were frequent visitors. The hotel is set in splendid parkland, with colourful gardens, lakes, and a unique woodland area. Various holiday packages are available, and there are extensive leisure facilities, as well as live entertainment and various dining venues, including Fenocchi's, with an Italian-themed menu. The bedrooms are spacious and well appointed. Please note that this is an adults-only (over 21 years) hotel.

Rooms: 239 (84 GF) 🐾 **Facilities:** Spa FTV WiFi HL ⓘ Putting green ⓘ ⓘ Gym Rifle shooting Archery ⓘ Xmas New Year **Conf:** Class 50 Board 25 Thtr 80 **Services:** Lift Night porter **Parking:** 351 **Notes:** Civ Wed 80

Lordleaze Hotel
★★★ 77% HOTEL

THE INDEPENDENTS
HOTEL ASSOCIATION

Henderson Drive, Forton Road, TA20 2HW - **tel:** 01460 61066
email: info@lordleazehotel.com **web:** www.lordleazehotel.com
dir: A358 from Chard, left at St Mary's Church to Forton & Winsham on B3162. Follow signs to hotel

Conveniently and quietly located, this hotel is close to the Devon, Dorset and Somerset borders, and only minutes from Chard. All bedrooms are well equipped and comfortable. The friendly lounge bar has a wood-burning stove and serves tempting bar meals. The conservatory restaurant offers more formal dining.

Rooms: 25 (2 family) (7 GF) 🐾 **S** £79–£90; **D** £125–£135 (incl. bkfst)* **Facilities:** FTV WiFi Xmas New Year **Conf:** Class 60 Board 40 Thtr 180 Del £126 **Parking:** 55 **Notes:** LB Civ Wed 100

CHARMOUTH
Dorset
Map 4 SY39

Fernhill Hotel
★★★ 82% HOTEL

Fernhill, DT6 6BX - **tel:** 01297 560492
email: mail@fernhill-hotel.co.uk **web:** www.fernhill-hotel.co.uk
dir: A35 onto A3052 to Lyme Regis. Hotel 0.25m on left

Fernhill is a small, friendly hotel in well-tended grounds on top of a hill. It boasts an outdoor pool and treatment rooms, together with elegant public areas. Each of the comfortable bedrooms is individually styled and many have views of the Char Valley and beyond. The menus are based on seasonal, locally sourced produce.

Rooms: 10 (1 family) 🐾 **Facilities:** FTV WiFi ⓘ ⓘ Fishing Holistic treatment centre Massage baths Xmas **Conf:** Class 20 Board 24 Thtr 100 **Parking:** 48 **Notes:** LB Closed 31 Dec-30 Jan Civ Wed 100

C

CHARNOCK RICHARD MOTORWAY SERVICE AREA (M6)
Lancashire   Map 15 SD51

Days Inn Charnock Richard - M6
WELCOMEBREAK

AA Advertised

Welcome Break Service Area, PR7 5LR - tel: 01257 791746
email: charnockhotel@welcomebreak.co.uk **web:** www.welcomebreak.co.uk
dir: *Between junct 27 & 28 of M6 N'bound. 500yds from Camelot Theme Park via Mill Lane*

This modern building offers accommodation in smart, spacious and well-equipped bedrooms, suitable for families and business travellers, and all with en suite bathrooms. Continental breakfast is available and other refreshments may be taken at the nearby family restaurant.

Rooms: 100 (68 family) (32 GF) (20 smoking) **Facilities:** FTV WiFi ⟐ **Conf:** Class 16 Board 24 Thtr 40 **Services:** Night porter **Parking:** 100

CHATHAM
Kent   Map 7 TQ76

Bridgewood Manor
QHOTELS
INSPIRED BY YOU

★★★★ 80% HOTEL

Bridgewood Roundabout, Walderslade Woods, ME5 9AX - tel: 01634 201333
email: bridgewoodmanor@qhotels.co.uk **web:** www.qhotels.co.uk
dir: *Adjacent to Bridgewood rdbt on A229. Take 3rd exit signed Walderslade & Lordswood. Hotel 50mtrs on left*

Bridgewood Manor is a modern, purpose-built hotel situated on the outskirts of Rochester. Bedrooms are pleasantly decorated, comfortably furnished and equipped with many thoughtful touches. The hotel has an excellent range of leisure and conference facilities. Guests can dine in the informal Terrace Bistro or experience fine dining in the more formal Squires restaurant, where the service is both attentive and friendly.

Rooms: 100 (12 family) (26 GF) **S** fr £81; **D** fr £93 (incl. bkfst)* **Facilities:** Spa FTV WiFi ⟐ supervised ⟐ Gym Beauty treatments Xmas New Year **Conf:** Class 110 Board 80 Thtr 200 Del from £116 **Services:** Lift Night porter **Parking:** 170 **Notes:** Civ Wed 130

Find out more
about the AA Hotel of the Year
for England on page 16

CHATHILL
Northumberland   Map 21 NU12

Doxford Hall Hotel & Spa
★★★★ ◉◎ COUNTRY HOUSE HOTEL

NE67 5DN - tel: 01665 589700
email: info@doxfordhall.com **web:** www.doxfordhall.com
dir: *8m N of Alnwick just off A1, signed Christon Bank & Seahouses. Take B6347 follow signs for hotel*

A beautiful country-house hotel set in a private estate, surrounded by countryside and convenient for visiting nearby historic towns and attractions. Bedrooms are spacious and luxuriously furnished, each named after Northumbrian Castles. The dining room and lounges are very attractive. There is an impressive grand staircase and beautiful wood throughout the hotel. The spa adds to the range of facilities.

Rooms: 34 (3 annexe) (1 family) (11 GF) ⟐ **S** £75–£300; **D** £99–£315 (incl. bkfst)* **Facilities:** Spa FTV WiFi ⟐ HL ⟐ supervised Gym Sauna Steam room Xmas New Year **Conf:** Class 100 Board 22 Thtr 250 **Services:** Lift Night porter **Parking:** 100 **Notes:** LB Civ Wed 250

CHEADLE
Greater Manchester   Map 16 SJ88

Premier Inn Manchester (Cheadle)

BUDGET HOTEL

Royal Crescent, SK8 3FE - tel: 0871 527 8728 (Calls cost 13p per minute plus your phone company's access charge) **web:** www.premierinn.com
dir: *Exit A34 at Cheadle Royal rdbt behind TGI Friday's*

High quality, budget accommodation ideal for both families and business travellers. Spacious, en suite bedrooms feature tea and coffee making facilities, Freeview TV in most hotels and free WiFi. The adjacent family restaurant features a wide and varied menu.

Rooms: 65

C

CHELMSFORD
Essex

Map 6 TL70

County Hotel

★★★★ 72% HOTEL

29 Rainsford Road, CM1 2PZ - **tel:** 01245 455700
email: sales@countyhotelgroup.co.uk **web:** www.countyhotelgroup.co.uk
dir: *From city centre, past rail & bus station. Hotel 300yds left beyond lights*

This popular hotel is ideally situated within easy walking distance of the railway station, bus depot and town centre. Stylish bedrooms offer spacious comfort and plentiful extras including free WiFi. There is a smart restaurant, a bar and a lounge as well as sunny outdoor terraces for making the most of warm weather. The hotel also has a range of meeting rooms and banqueting facilities.

Rooms: 50 (2 family) ⟡ **S** £50–£190; **D** £60–£200* **Facilities:** FTV WiFi ⟩ HL Xmas New Year **Conf:** Class 54 Board 40 Thtr 150 Del from £165 **Services:** Lift Night porter **Parking:** 80 **Notes:** LB Closed 27-30 Dec Civ Wed 80

Best Western Ivy Hill

★★★ 81% HOTEL

Writtle Road, Margaretting, CM4 0EH - **tel:** 01277 353040
email: sales@ivyhillhotel.co.uk **web:** www.heritageleisure.co.uk
dir: *Just off A12 junct 14. Hotel on left at top of slip road*

A smartly appointed hotel conveniently situated just off the A12. The spacious bedrooms are tastefully decorated, have co-ordinated fabrics and all the expected facilities. Public rooms include a choice of lounges, a cosy bar, a smart conservatory and restaurant, as well as a range of conference and banqueting facilities.

Rooms: 31 (5 family) (9 GF) **D** fr £130* **Facilities:** FTV WiFi ⟩ **Conf:** Class 80 Board 40 Thtr 180 **Services:** Night porter **Parking:** 200 **Notes:** Closed 24-26 Dec Civ Wed 100

Pontlands Park

★★★ 81% HOTEL

West Hanningfield Road, Great Baddow, CM2 8HR - **tel:** 01245 476444
email: sales@pontlandsparkhotel.co.uk **web:** www.heritageleisure.co.uk
dir: *A12, A130 , A1114 to Chelmsford. 1st exit at rdbt, 1st slip road on left. Left towards Great Baddow, 1st left into West Hanningfield Rd. Hotel 400yds on left*

A Victorian country-house hotel situated in a peaceful rural location amid attractive landscaped grounds. The stylishly furnished bedrooms are generally quite spacious; each is individually decorated and equipped with modern facilities. The elegant public rooms include a tastefully furnished sitting room, a cosy lounge bar, smart conservatory restaurant and an intimate dining room.

Rooms: 35 (10 family) (11 GF) **D** fr £140 (incl. bkfst)* **Facilities:** FTV WiFi ⟨s⟩ ⟨ Gym Beauty room **Conf:** Class 40 Board 40 Thtr 100 **Services:** Night porter **Parking:** 100 **Notes:** LB Closed 24-26 Dec Civ Wed 100

Best Western Atlantic Hotel

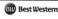

★★★ 79% HOTEL

New Street, CM1 1PP - **tel:** 01245 268168
email: info@atlantichotel.co.uk **web:** www.atlantichotel.co.uk
dir: *From Chelmsford rail station, left into Victoria Rd, left at lights into New St, hotel on right*

Ideally situated just a short walk from the railway station with its quick links to London, this modern, purpose-built hotel has contemporary-style bedrooms equipped with modern facilities. The open-plan public areas include the Italian Sapori Ristorante, a lounge bar and a conservatory.

Rooms: 59 (3 family) (27 GF) ⟡ **S** £75–£200; **D** £85–£200* **Facilities:** STV WiFi Gym Complimentary use of facilities at Absalute Gym **Conf:** Class 40 Board 10 Thtr 15 Del from £150 **Services:** Night porter Air con **Parking:** 60 **Notes:** LB Closed 23 Dec-3 Jan

Premier Inn Chelmsford (Boreham)

BUDGET HOTEL

Main Road, Boreham, CM3 3HJ - **tel:** 0871 527 8220 (Calls cost 13p per minute plus your phone company's access charge) **web:** www.premierinn.com
dir: *M25 junct 28, A12 to Colchester, B1137 to Boreham*

High quality, budget accommodation ideal for both families and business travellers. Spacious, en suite bedrooms feature tea and coffee making facilities, Freeview TV in most hotels and free WiFi. The adjacent family restaurant features a wide and varied menu.

Rooms: 80

Premier Inn Chelmsford City Centre

BUDGET HOTEL

Victoria Road, CM1 1NY - **tel:** 0871 527 9534 (Calls cost 13p per minute plus your phone company's access charge) **web:** www.premierinn.com
dir: *A12 junct 15 (Harlow,Chelmsford/A414). At rdbt take A414 (3 Mile Hill). At next rdbt take A41114. 1st exit at next rdbt (Moulsham St/B1007), continue into New London Rd. Left into Parkway. At rdbt 2nd exit into Victoria St. At next rdbt 1st exit into Duke St. At next rdbt 1st exit into Victoria Rd*

Rooms: 99

Premier Inn Chelmsford (Springfield)

BUDGET HOTEL

Chelmsford Service Area, Colchester Rd, CM2 5PY - **tel:** 0871 527 8222 (Calls cost 13p per minute plus your phone company's access charge) **web:** www.premierinn.com
dir: *At A12 junct 19, Chelmsford bypass, signed Chelmsford Service Area*

Rooms: 91

C

CHELTENHAM
Gloucestershire

Map 10 S092

Ellenborough Park

★★★★★ 86% COUNTRY HOUSE HOTEL

Southam Road, GL52 3NH - **tel:** 01242 545454
email: info@ellenboroughpark.com **web:** www.ellenboroughpark.com
dir: *A46 right after 3m onto B4079, merges with A435, 4m, over 3 rdbts, left onto Southam Lane, right onto Old Road, right onto B4632, hotel on right*

Set on the original Cheltenham Racecourse estate, this impressive hotel dates in part from the 16th century and has been beautifully restored. The Nina Campbell-designed bedrooms and suites are spread across the main house and adjacent buildings, and all feature superb beds, a great range of modern amenities, and luxurious bathrooms. The stylish Indian-themed spa has a gym and outdoor heated pool. There are two dining options; the modern Brasserie offers a country house menu, while the elegant, oak-panelled Beaufort dining room is more formal and offers a high standard of classic cuisine.

Rooms: 61 (44 annexe) (16 family) (19 GF) ↑ **Facilities:** Spa STV FTV WiFi ↘ HL ↗ ⤵ Gym Xmas New Year **Conf:** Class 70 Board 40 Thtr 120 **Services:** Lift Night porter Air con **Parking:** 130 **Notes:** LB Civ Wed 120

The Greenway Hotel & Spa

★★★★ 82% ⊛⊛ COUNTRY HOUSE HOTEL

Shurdington, GL51 4UG - **tel:** 01242 862352
email: info@thegreenway.co.uk **web:** www.thegreenwayhotelandspa.com
dir: *From Cheltenham centre 2.5m S on A46*

This hotel, with a wealth of history, is peacefully located in a delightful setting within easy reach of the many attractions of the Cotswolds and also the M5. The Manor House bedrooms are luxuriously appointed - traditional in style yet with plasma TVs and internet access. The tranquil Coach House rooms, in the converted stable block, have direct access to the beautiful grounds. The attractive dining room overlooks the sunken garden and is the venue for excellent food, proudly served by dedicated and attentive staff.

Rooms: 21 (8 annexe) (1 family) ↑ **S** £139–£209; **D** £209–£409 (incl. bkfst)* **Facilities:** Spa FTV WiFi ⏰ ⤵ Gym Xmas New Year **Conf:** Board 18 Thtr 50 Del from £175 **Services:** Night porter **Parking:** 30 **Notes:** LB Civ Wed 60

The Cheltenham Chase Hotel

★★★★ 80% HOTEL

Shurdington Road, Brockworth, GL3 4PB - **tel:** 01452 519988
email: cheltenhamreservations@qhotels.co.uk **web:** www.qhotels.co.uk
dir: *M5 junct 11a onto A417 Cirencester. 1st exit A46 to Stroud, hotel 500yds on left.*

Conveniently positioned for Cheltenham, Gloucester, and the M5, this hotel is set in landscaped grounds with ample parking. Bedrooms are spacious with attractive colour schemes and excellent facilities; executive rooms and suites benefit from air conditioning. Public areas include an open-plan bar/lounge, Hardy's restaurant, extensive meeting and functions rooms and a well-equipped leisure club.

Rooms: 122 (19 family) (44 GF) ↑ **S** £89–£164; **D** £99–£174 (incl. bkfst)* **Facilities:** Spa STV FTV WiFi ↘ HL ⏰ Gym Steam room Sauna Sun beds Spa bath Xmas New Year **Conf:** Class 160 Board 80 Thtr 350 Del from £130 **Services:** Lift Night porter Air con **Parking:** 240 **Notes:** LB Civ Wed 344

Hotel du Vin Cheltenham

★★★★ 78% ⊛ HOTEL

Parabola Road, GL50 3AQ - **tel:** 01242 588450 & 0844 736 4254 (Calls cost 5p per minute plus your phone company's access charge)
email: info@cheltenham.hotelduvin.com **web:** www.hotelduvin.com
dir: *M5 junct 11, follow signs for city centre. At rdbt opposite Morgan Estate Agents take 2nd left, 200mtrs to Parabola Rd*

This hotel, in the Montpellier area of the town, has spacious public areas that are packed with stylish features. The pewter-topped bar has comfortable seating and the spacious restaurant has the Hotel du Vin trademark design; alfresco dining is possible on the extensive terrace area. Bedrooms are very comfortable, with Egyptian linen, deep baths and power showers. The spa is the ideal place to relax and unwind. Although parking is limited, it is a definite bonus. Service is friendly and attentive.

Rooms: 49 (2 family) (5 GF) ↑ **D** £99–£350* **Facilities:** Spa STV WiFi Steam room **Conf:** Class 24 Board 24 Thtr 30 **Services:** Lift Night porter Air con **Parking:** 26 **Notes:** Civ Wed 60

The Cheltenham Park

★★★★ 78% HOTEL

Cirencester Road, Charlton Kings, GL53 8EA - **tel:** 01242 229280
email: cphreservations@cheltenhampark-hotel.co.uk
web: www.cheltenhampark-hotel.co.uk
dir: *On A435, 2m SE of Cheltenham near Lilley Brook Golf Course*

Located south of Cheltenham, this attractive Georgian property is set in its own landscaped gardens, adjacent to Lilley Brook Golf Course. All the bedrooms, whether premium or standard, are spacious and well equipped for both business and leisure guests. The hotel has an impressive health and leisure club with the latest gym equipment, plus a pool, steam room and beauty salon; extensive meeting facilities are also available.

Rooms: 148 (111 annexe) ↑ **D** £79–£699* **Facilities:** Spa WiFi ⏰ supervised Gym Beauty treatment rooms Sauna Steam room Xmas New Year **Conf:** Class 120 Board 60 Thtr 250 Del from £129 **Services:** Night porter **Parking:** 170 **Notes:** Civ Wed 250

CHELTENHAM *continued*

Queen's Hotel Cheltenham-MGallery by Sofitel

★★★★ 78% HOTEL

The Promenade, GL50 1NN - **tel:** 01242 514754
email: h6632@accor.com **web:** www.mgallery.com
dir: *Follow town centre signs. Left at Montpellier Walk rdbt. Entrance 500mtrs right*

With its spectacular position at the top of the main promenade, this landmark hotel is an ideal base from which to explore the charms of this Regency spa town and also the Cotswolds. Bedrooms are very comfortable and include two beautiful four-poster rooms. Smart public rooms include the popular Gold Cup bar and a choice of dining options, including the Napier Restaurant.

Rooms: 84 📞 **D** fr £105* **Facilities:** FTV WiFi HL Xmas New Year **Conf:** Class 60 Board 40 Thtr 120 Del from £170 **Services:** Lift Night porter **Parking:** 70 **Notes:** Civ Wed 100

George Hotel

★★★ 80% 🏆🏆 HOTEL

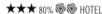
COTSWOLD INNS & HOTELS

St Georges Road, GL50 3DZ - **tel:** 01242 235751
email: hotel@stayatthegeorge.co.uk **web:** www.stayatthegeorge.co.uk
dir: *M5 junct 11 follow town centre signs. At 2nd lights left into Gloucester Rd, past rail station over mini-rdbt. At lights right into St Georges Rd. Hotel 0.75m on left*

The George Hotel is a genuinely friendly, privately-owned hotel occupying part of a Regency terrace, just two-minutes walk from the town centre. The contemporary interior is elegant and stylish, and the well-equipped, modern bedrooms offer a relaxing haven; individually designed junior suites and deluxe double rooms are available. Lunch or dinner can be enjoyed in the lively atmosphere of Monty's Brasserie, perhaps followed by an evening in the vibrant cocktail bar which hosts live entertainment on Friday and Saturday evenings.

Rooms: 31 (1 GF) 📞 **D** fr £70* **Facilities:** STV FTV WiFi Live music at wknds 🎵 **Conf:** Class 18 Board 24 Thtr 30 **Services:** Night porter **Parking:** 30 **Notes:** Closed 25-26 Dec RS 24 Dec Closed after dinner

Cotswold Grange Hotel

★★★ 78% 🏆 HOTEL

Pittville Circus Road, GL52 2QH - **tel:** 01242 515119
email: info@cotswoldgrange.co.uk **web:** www.cotswoldgrangehotel.co.uk
dir: *From town centre, follow Prestbury signs. Right at 1st rdbt, next rdbt straight over, hotel 100yds on left*

This beautifully restored Georgian property is in a quiet leafy street less than half a mile from the centre of Cheltenham. There is a range of bedroom types on offer, and all have been recently refurbished to offer high levels of comfort and facilities. Original features are cleverly blended with a more contemporary feel. Bathrooms are well equipped, many with both bath and separate shower facilities. Dining is not to be missed, with a range of interesting dishes, prepared by the talented chef and his team, using the best local produce.

Rooms: 20 (4 family) 📞 **S** fr £80; **D** fr £90 (incl. bkfst)* **Facilities:** FTV WiFi 🛏 **Conf:** Class 24 Board 28 Thtr 35 Del from £115 **Parking:** 19

Premier Inn Cheltenham Central

BUDGET HOTEL

Premier Inn

374 Gloucester Road, GL51 7AY - **tel:** 0871 527 8224 (Calls cost 13p per minute plus your phone company's access charge) **web:** www.premierinn.com
dir: *M5 junct 11, A40 (Cheltenham). Follow dual carriageway to end, straight on at 1st rdbt, right at 2nd rdbt*

High quality, budget accommodation ideal for both families and business travellers. Spacious, en suite bedrooms feature tea and coffee making facilities, Freeview TV in most hotels and free WiFi. The adjacent family restaurant features a wide and varied menu.

Rooms: 67

Premier Inn Cheltenham Town Centre

BUDGET HOTEL

Premier Inn

The Brewery, GL50 4FA - **tel:** 0871 527 9668 (Calls cost 13p per minute plus your phone company's access charge)
dir: *Phone for details*

Rooms: 104

Premier Inn Cheltenham West

BUDGET HOTEL

Premier Inn

Tewkesbury Road, Uckington, GL51 9SL - **tel:** 0871 527 8226 (Calls cost 13p per minute plus your phone company's access charge) **web:** www.premierinn.com
dir: *M5 junct 10 (S'bound exit only), A4019, hotel in 2m. Or M5 junct 11, A40 towards Cheltenham. At Benhall Rdbt left onto A4103 (Princess Elizabeth Way) follow racecourse signs. At rdbt left onto A4019 signed Tewkesbury/M5 North. Hotel opposite Sainsburys*

Rooms: 58

CHESSINGTON
Greater London
Map 6 TQ16

Premier Inn Chessington

BUDGET HOTEL

Premier Inn

Leatherhead Road, KT9 2NE - **tel:** 0871 527 8228 (Calls cost 13p per minute plus your phone company's access charge) **web:** www.premierinn.com
dir: *M25 junct 9, A243 towards Kingston-upon-Thames for approx 2m. Hotel adjacent to Chessington World of Adventures*

High quality, budget accommodation ideal for both families and business travellers. Spacious, en suite bedrooms feature tea and coffee making facilities, Freeview TV in most hotels and free WiFi. The adjacent family restaurant features a wide and varied menu.

Rooms: 62

C

See also **Puddington**

INSPECTOR'S CHOICE

The Chester Grosvenor
★★★★★ HOTEL

Eastgate, CH1 1LT - tel: 01244 324024
email: reservations@chestergrosvenor.com **web:** www.chestergrosvenor.com
dir: *A56 follow signs for city centre hotels. On Eastgate St next to the Eastgate clock*

Located within the Roman walls of the city, this Grade II listed, half-timbered building is the essence of Englishness. Furnished with fine fabrics and queen or king-size beds, the suites and bedrooms are of the highest standard, each designed with guest comfort as a priority. The eating options are the art deco La Brasserie, a bustling venue awarded two AA Rosettes; the Arkle Bar and Lounge for morning coffee, light lunches, afternoon tea and drinks; plus the fine dining restaurant, Simon Radley at The Chester Grosvenor, which offers creative cuisine with flair and style, and has been awarded four AA Rosettes. The hotel has a luxury spa and small fitness centre.

Rooms: 80 **Facilities:** Spa STV FTV WiFi ⅃ HL Gym Thermal suite Relaxation room ♫ New Year **Conf:** Class 100 Board 50 Thtr 250 **Services:** Lift Night porter Air con **Notes:** Closed 25 Dec RS Sun & Mon Simon Radley Restaurant closed Civ Wed 250

Hallmark Hotel Chester The Queen
★★★★ 79% HOTEL

City Road, CH1 3AH - tel: 0330 028 3402
email: queen@hallmarkhotels.co.uk **web:** www.hallmarkhotels.co.uk
dir: *Follow signs for railway station, hotel opposite*

This hotel is ideally located opposite the railway station and just a couple of minutes' walk from the city. Public areas include a restaurant, small gym, waiting room bar, separate lounge and Roman-themed gardens. Bedrooms are generally spacious and reflect the hotel's Victorian heritage.

Rooms: 218 (11 family) (12 GF) **Facilities:** STV FTV WiFi ⅃ HL Gym Beauty treatment room Table tennis ♫ Xmas New Year **Conf:** Class 150 Board 60 Thtr 400 **Services:** Lift Night porter **Parking:** 150 **Notes:** Civ Wed 400

Grosvenor Pulford Hotel & Spa
★★★★ 78% HOTEL

Wrexham Road, Pulford, CH4 9DG - tel: 01244 570560
email: reservations@grosvenorpulfordhotel.co.uk **web:** www.grosvenorpulfordhotel.co.uk
dir: *M53, A55 at junct signed A483 Chester/Wrexham & North Wales. Left onto B5445, hotel 2m on right*

Set in a rural location, this modern, stylish hotel features a magnificent spa with a large Roman-style swimming pool. Among the range of bedrooms are several executive suites, and others that have spiral staircases leading to the bedroom sections. A smart brasserie restaurant and bar provides a wide range of imaginative dishes in a relaxed atmosphere.

Rooms: 73 (10 family) (19 GF) **S** £115–£219; **D** £125–£229 (incl. bkfst)
Facilities: Spa STV FTV WiFi ⅃ HL Gym Steam room Sauna Xmas New Year **Conf:** Class 100 Board 60 Thtr 220 **Services:** Lift Night porter **Parking:** 200 **Notes:** Civ Wed 200

ABode Chester
★★★★ 77% HOTEL

ABode
HOTELS

Grosvenor Road, CH1 2DJ - tel: 01244 347000
email: generalmanager@abodechester.co.uk **web:** www.abodechester.co.uk
dir: *Phone for details*

This modern, glass-fronted property sits prominently in the centre of Chester overlooking the Castle and adjacent to the racecourse. Bedrooms are well designed and equipped for the modern traveller with a range of large spacious suites also available. Food is a highlight here, with a range of dining options and bars. The restaurant, on the fifth floor, crowns the top of the building with far-reaching views over Chester Racecourse and beyond. Additional facilities include secure parking and a gym.

Rooms: 84 (7 family) **S** £85–£339; **D** £100–£354 (incl. bkfst)* **Facilities:** FTV WiFi ⅃ Gym ♫ Xmas New Year **Conf:** Class 24 Board 36 Thtr 90 **Services:** Lift Night porter Air con **Parking:** 39 **Notes:** LB Civ Wed 60

C

CHESTER *continued*

Macdonald New Blossoms Hotel

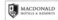

★★★★ 75% HOTEL

St John Street, CH1 1HL - tel: 01244 323186
email: events.blossoms@macdonald-hotels.co.uk
web: www.macdonaldhotels.co.uk/blossoms
dir: *M53 junct 12 follow city centre signs for Eastgate, through pedestrian zone, hotel on left*

Ideally located to explore the historic city of Chester, this is a modern and contemporary hotel. Bedrooms range from executive to feature four-poster rooms, with many retaining the charm of the original Victorian building. A stylish brasserie restaurant and bar offer an informal dining experience.

Rooms: 67 (1 family) ⟡ **S** £94–£260; **D** £94–£260* **Facilities:** FTV WiFi ⟡ Xmas New Year **Conf:** Class 50 Board 40 Thtr 90 Del from £115 **Services:** Lift Night porter Air con **Notes:** LB Civ Wed 80

Mercure Chester Abbots Well Hotel

★★★★ 74% HOTEL

Whitchurch Road, Christleton, CH3 5QL - tel: 0844 815 9001 (Calls cost 7p per minute plus your phone company's access charge)
email: gm.mercurechester@jupiterhotels.co.uk **web:** www.mercurechester.co.uk
dir: *A41 Whitchurch, hotel on right in 200mtrs*

This smart, modern hotel is located just a short drive from the city centre; with extensive meeting and function facilities, a well-equipped leisure club and ample parking, it is a popular conference venue. Bedrooms vary in size and style but all are well equipped for both business and leisure guests. Food is served in the airy restaurant and also in the large open-plan bar lounge.

Rooms: 126 (9 family) (58 GF) ⟡ **S** fr £75; **D** fr £75* **Facilities:** STV WiFi ⟡ ⟳ Gym Treatment room Xmas New Year **Conf:** Class 140 Board 100 Thtr 230 Del from £129 **Services:** Lift Night porter **Parking:** 280 **Notes:** LB Civ Wed 180

Mill Hotel & Spa Destination

★★★ 78% HOTEL

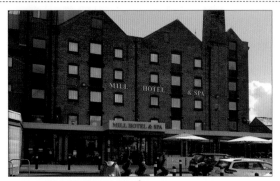

Milton Street, CH1 3NF - tel: 01244 350035
email: reservations@millhotel.com **web:** www.millhotel.com
dir: *M53 junct 12, A56, left at 2nd rdbt A5268, 1st left, 2nd left*

There have been constant improvements at this stylish conversion of an old corn mill which enjoys an idyllic canalside location close to the city centre. The bedrooms come in a variety of styles, some accessed over the enclosed canal bridge. There are several dining and bar options, and meals are even served on a broad-beam boat that cruises Chester's canal system, to and from the hotel. A well-equipped leisure centre and spa treatments are also provided.

Mill Hotel & Spa Destination

Rooms: 132 (49 annexe) (57 family) ⟡ **Facilities:** Spa STV FTV WiFi HL ⟳ supervised Gym Aerobic studio Hairdresser Sauna Steam room Kinesis studio ♪ Xmas New Year **Conf:** Class 36 Board 30 Thtr 100 **Services:** Lift Night porter **Parking:** 120

Hallmark Hotel Chester Westminster

★★★ 77% METRO HOTEL

City Road, CH1 3AF - tel: 0330 028 3424
email: westminster@hallmarkhotels.co.uk **web:** www.hallmarkhotels.co.uk
dir: *A56, 3m to city centre, left signed rail station. Hotel opposite station, on right*

Situated next to the railway station and close to the city centre, the Westminster is an established hotel catering for a wide market. It has an attractive Tudor-style exterior, but bedrooms are modern and well equipped with a few luxurious touches; family rooms are also available. There is a choice of bars and lounges, and the dining room serves a broad range of dishes.

Rooms: 75 (5 family) (5 GF) **Facilities:** FTV WiFi Free gym facilities at sister hotel Xmas New Year **Conf:** Class 60 Board 40 Thtr 150 **Services:** Lift Night porter **Notes:** Civ Wed 100

Brookside Hotel

★★★ 75% HOTEL

Brook Lane, CH2 2AN - tel: 01244 381943
email: info@brookside-hotel.co.uk **web:** www.brookside-hotel.co.uk
dir: *M53 junct 12, A56 towards Chester, A41. 0.5m left signed Newton (Plas Newton Ln). 0.5m right into Brook Ln. Hotel 0.5m. Or from Chester inner ring road follow A5116/ Ellesmere Port/Hospital signs (keep in right lane to take right fork). Immediately left. At mini-rdbt 2nd right*

This hotel is conveniently located in a residential area just north of the city centre. The attractive public areas consist of a foyer lounge, a small bar and a split-level restaurant. The homely bedrooms are thoughtfully furnished and some feature four-poster beds.

Rooms: 26 (9 family) (4 GF) **Facilities:** WiFi **Conf:** Class 20 Board 12 **Parking:** 20 **Notes:** Closed 20 Dec-3 Jan

C

Premier Inn Chester Central (North)

BUDGET HOTEL

76 Liverpool Road, CH2 1AU - tel: 0871 527 8230 (Calls cost 13p per minute plus your phone company's access charge) **web:** www.premierinn.com
dir: M53 junct 12, A56. At 2nd rdbt right signed A41 to Chester Zoo. At 1st lights left into Heath Rd, leads into Mill Ln. Under small rail bridge. Hotel at end on right

High quality, budget accommodation ideal for both families and business travellers. Spacious, en suite bedrooms feature tea and coffee making facilities, Freeview TV in most hotels and free WiFi. The adjacent family restaurant features a wide and varied menu.

Rooms: 31

Premier Inn Chester Central (South East)

BUDGET HOTEL

Caldy Valley Road, Boughton, CH3 5PR - tel: 0871 527 8232 (Calls cost 13p per minute plus your phone company's access charge) **web:** www.premierinn.com
dir: M53 junct 12, A56 to Chester. At 1st lights onto A41 (Whitchurch). At 2nd rdbt exit into Caldy Valley Rd (Huntington). Hotel on right

Rooms: 93

Premier Inn Chester City Centre

BUDGET HOTEL

20-24 City Road, CH1 3AE - tel: 0871 527 8234 (Calls cost 13p per minute plus your phone company's access charge) **web:** www.premierinn.com
dir: M53 junct 12, follow A56/Chester City Centre signs. At rdbt 1st exit onto A5268 (St Oswalds Way) follow railway station signs. At Bar's Rdbt 1st exit. Hotel on right

Rooms: 120

CHESTERFIELD	Map 16 SK37
Derbyshire	

HIGHLY RECOMMENDED

Casa Hotel

★★★★★ 83% ◉◉ HOTEL

Lockoford Lane, S41 7JB - tel: 01246 245999
email: enquiries@casahotels.co.uk **web:** www.casahotels.co.uk
dir: M1 junct 29 to A617 Chesterfield/A61 Sheffield, 1st exit at rdbt, hotel on left

Casa Hotel is a luxurious building with a contemporary Spanish theme throughout. The stylish bedrooms feature air conditioning, Hypnos beds and

bathrooms with rain showers. Four suites are equipped with their own jacuzzi hot tubs on the balconies, and two also have private saunas. Cocina Restaurant offers appealing menus featuring locally sourced produce direct from the owner's farm. The conference and event facilities are excellent and offer complimentary WiFi throughout.

Casa Hotel

Rooms: 100 (6 family) ☕ **S** £99–£150; **D** £114–£165 (incl. bkfst)* **Facilities:** STV FTV WiFi ⓑ HL Gym **Conf:** Class 140 Board 50 Thtr 280 **Services:** Lift Night porter Air con **Parking:** 200 **Notes:** LB Civ Wed 280

Peak Edge Hotel at the Red Lion

★★★★ 82% ◉◉ HOTEL

Darley Road, Stone Edge, S45 0LW - tel: 01246 566142
email: sleep@peakedgehotel.co.uk **web:** www.peakedgehotel.co.uk
dir: M1 junct 29, A617 to Chesterfield. At rdbt take 1st exit onto A61, at next rdbt 2nd exit onto Whitecotes Ln, continue onto Matlock Rd (A632) then Darley Rd (B5057)

The Peak Edge Hotel is set in the heart of the Derbyshire countryside and surrounded by great views on all sides. The modern rooms are spacious, comfortable, and all benefit from high quality bathrooms. The inn has a rustic, 17th-century feel, with stone walls and wooden flooring. The staff are very friendly and well informed. Food is a highlight of any stay, with locally sourced produce put to good use.

Rooms: 27 (2 family) (15 GF) ☕ **S** £80–£150 (incl. bkfst)* **Facilities:** Spa FTV WiFi ⓑ ♫ Xmas New Year **Conf:** Class 120 Board 40 Thtr 140 **Services:** Lift Night porter Air con **Parking:** 70 **Notes:** LB Civ Wed 140

Ringwood Hall Hotel

★★★ 86% HOTEL

Brimington, S43 1DQ - tel: 01246 280077
email: reception@ringwoodhallhotel.com **web:** www.ringwoodhallhotel.com
dir: M1 junct 30, A619 to Chesterfield through Staveley. Hotel on left

Ringwood Hall is a beautifully presented Georgian manor house set in 29 acres of peaceful grounds, between the M1 and Chesterfield. The stylish bedrooms include 'Feature Rooms' and three apartments within the grounds. Public areas include comfortable lounges, the Markham Bar and a cocktail lounge. The health and fitness club has a pool, sauna, steam room and gym.

Rooms: 74 (10 annexe) (32 family) (32 GF) ☕ **D** £138–£158 (incl. bkfst)* **Facilities:** Spa FTV WiFi ⓢ Gym Steam room Sauna Xmas New Year **Conf:** Class 80 Board 60 Thtr 250 Del from £126.50 **Services:** Night porter **Parking:** 150 **Notes:** LB Civ Wed 250

C

CHESTERFIELD *continued*

Premier Inn Chesterfield North

BUDGET HOTEL

Tapton Lock Hill, off Rotherway, S41 7NJ - **tel:** 0871 527 8238 (Calls cost 13p per minute plus your phone company's access charge) **web:** www.premierinn.com
dir: *Adjacent to Tesco, at A61 & A619 rdbt, 1m N of city centre*

High quality, budget accommodation ideal for both families and business travellers. Spacious, en suite bedrooms feature tea and coffee making facilities, Freeview TV in most hotels and free WiFi. The adjacent family restaurant features a wide and varied menu.

Rooms: 88

Premier Inn Chesterfield West

BUDGET HOTEL

Baslow Road, Eastmoor, S42 7DA - **tel:** 0871 527 8240 (Calls cost 13p per minute plus your phone company's access charge) **web:** www.premierinn.com
dir: *M1 junct 29, A617. At next rdbt 2nd exit. At next rdbt 1st exit into Markham Rd. At next rdbt 2nd exit into Wheatbridge Rd, left into Chatsworth Rd. 2.5m to hotel*

Rooms: 25

CHESTER-LE-STREET	**Map 19 NZ25**
County Durham	

Lumley Castle Hotel

★★★★ 77% HOTEL

DH3 4NX - **tel:** 0191 389 1111
email: reservations@lumleycastle.com **web:** www.lumleycastle.com
dir: *A1(M) junct 63, follow Chester-le-Street signs. Follow signs for Riverside then Lumley Castle*

Dominating the Country Durham landscape for the past 600 years, Lumley Castle cannot help but impress. The place has a real sense of theatre and as a guest you are left in no doubt that you are in a proper castle. The magnificent state rooms, along with other public areas, are very well presented in accord with all expectations. Bedrooms differ in style, size and type and make good use of all available space. The staff are warm and welcoming, and quality food is served throughout.

Rooms: 73 (47 annexe) (9 family) (27 GF) ♠ **S** £69–£109; **D** £89–£440*
Facilities: FTV WiFi ♨ HL Xmas New Year **Conf:** Class 60 Board 50 Thtr 150 Del from £145 **Services:** Lift Night porter **Parking:** 150 **Notes:** LB Closed 24–26 Dec & 1–2 Jan Civ Wed 144

CHICHESTER	**Map 5 SU80**
West Sussex	

The Goodwood Hotel

★★★★ 80% @@ HOTEL - **tel:** 01243 775537 PO18 0QB

email: reservations@goodwood.com **web:** www.goodwood.com/estate/the-goodwood-hotel

(For full entry see Goodwood)

Chichester Harbour Hotel

★★★★ 77% @ HOTEL

57 North Street, PO19 1NH - **tel:** 01243 778000
email: chichester@harbourhotels.co.uk **web:** www.chichester-harbour-hotel.co.uk
dir: *From A27, onto inner ring road to Northgate. At Northgate rdbt left into North St, hotel on left*

This well-presented Grade II listed, Georgian property occupies a prime position at the top of North Street. The stylish bedrooms have flat-screen TVs, Egyptian cotton linen and high-speed WiFi access. The bar and restaurant are contemporary venues for enjoying meals and refreshments, which are served all day. The hotel is just a few minutes' away from the famous Festival Theatre; and Goodwood, for motorsport and horse racing, is also close by.

Rooms: 37 (1 annexe) (2 family) **Facilities:** FTV WiFi ♨ Xmas New Year **Conf:** Class 50 Board 30 Thtr 50 **Services:** Lift Night porter **Parking:** 35 **Notes:** LB Civ Wed 70

Crouchers Restaurant & Hotel

★★★ 86% @@ HOTEL

Birdham Road, PO20 7EH - **tel:** 01243 784995
email: crouchers@btconnect.com **web:** www.crouchershotel.co.uk
dir: *From A27 (Chichester bypass) onto A286 towards West Wittering, 2m, hotel on left between Chichester Marina & Dell Quay*

This friendly, family-run hotel, situated in open countryside, is just a short drive from the harbour. The stylish and well-equipped bedrooms are situated in a separate barn, coach house and stable block, and include four-poster rooms and rooms with patios that overlook the fields. The modern oak-beamed restaurant, with country views, serves award-winning cuisine.

Rooms: 26 (23 annexe) (2 family) (15 GF) ♠ **S** £85–£165; **D** £130–£205 (incl. bkfst)* **Facilities:** STV FTV WiFi Xmas New Year **Conf:** Class 80 Board 30 Thtr 80 **Parking:** 80 **Notes:** LB Civ Wed 75

Premier Inn Chichester

BUDGET HOTEL

Chichester Gate Leisure Park, Terminus Road, PO19 8EL - **tel:** 0871 527 8242 (Calls cost 13p per minute plus your phone company's access charge)
web: www.premierinn.com
dir: *A27 towards city centre. Follow Terminus Road Industrial Estate signs. Left at 1st lights, left at next lights into Chichester Gate Leisure Park. Hotel on right*

High quality, budget accommodation ideal for both families and business travellers. Spacious, en suite bedrooms feature tea and coffee making facilities, Freeview TV in most hotels and free WiFi. The adjacent family restaurant features a wide and varied menu.

Rooms: 83

CHILDER THORNTON	**Map 15 SJ37**
Cheshire	

Premier Inn Wirral (Childer Thornton)

BUDGET HOTEL

New Chester Road, CH66 1QW - **tel:** 0871 527 9174 (Calls cost 13p per minute plus your phone company's access charge) **web:** www.premierinn.com
dir: *M53 junct 5, A41 towards Chester. Hotel on right, same entrance as Burleydam Garden Centre*

High quality, budget accommodation ideal for both families and business travellers. Spacious, en suite bedrooms feature tea and coffee making facilities,

C

Freeview TV in most hotels and free WiFi. The adjacent family restaurant features a wide and varied menu.

Rooms: 68

CHIPPENHAM
Wiltshire — Map ST97

Best Western Plus Angel Hotel

★★★ 82% HOTEL

Market Place, SN15 3HD - **tel:** 01249 652615
email: reception@angelhotelchippenham.co.uk **web:** www.angelhotelchippenham.co.uk
dir: Follow tourist signs for Bowood House. Under railway arch, follow 'Borough Parade Parking' signs. Hotel adjacent to car park

Several impressive buildings combine to make this smart and comfortable hotel. The well-equipped bedrooms vary from those in the main house where character is the key, to the smart executive-style, courtyard rooms. The lounge and restaurant are bright and modern, and offer an imaginative carte and an all-day menu.

Rooms: 50 (35 annexe) (3 family) (12 GF) **D** fr £80 (incl. bkfst)* **Facilities:** FTV WiFi ⓘ ⓒ Gym **Conf:** Class 50 Board 50 Thtr 100 **Services:** Night porter **Parking:** 50 **Notes:** LB

Premier Inn Chippenham

BUDGET HOTEL

Cepen Park, West Cepen Way, SN14 6UZ - **tel:** 0871 527 8244 (Calls cost 13p per minute plus your phone company's access charge) **web:** www.premierinn.com
dir: M4 junct 17, A350 towards Chippenham. Hotel at 1st main rdbt

High quality, budget accommodation ideal for both families and business travellers. Spacious, en suite bedrooms feature tea and coffee making facilities, Freeview TV in most hotels and free WiFi. The adjacent family restaurant features a wide and varied menu.

Rooms: 130

CHIPPING CAMPDEN
Gloucestershire — Map 10 SP13

Cotswold House Hotel & Spa

★★★★ 79% ⓦⓦ HOTEL

Upper High Street, The Square, GL55 6AN - **tel:** 01386 840330 & 848928
email: reservations@cotswoldhouse.com **web:** www.bespokehotels.com/cotswoldhouse
dir: A44 take B4081 to Chipping Campden. Right at T-junct into High St. Hotel in The Square behind town hall

Following substantial refurbishment under new management, this hotel offers contemporary style within a classic townhouse set in the heart of idyllic Chipping Campden. The hotel boasts a spa and two dining outlets: The Brasserie for a relaxed casual experience, and 'Fig', a new fine dining destination. Gardens to the rear of the property offer a tranquil retreat.

Rooms: 28 (6 annexe) (4 family) (5 GF) **S** fr £110; **D** fr £120 (incl. bkfst)* **Facilities:** Spa STV FTV WiFi ⓘ ⓒ ⓓ Steam room Hydrotherapy pool Xmas New Year **Conf:** Class 60 Board 40 Thtr 100 Del from £165 **Services:** Night porter Air con **Parking:** 27 **Notes:** LB Civ Wed 100

HIGHLY RECOMMENDED

Three Ways House

★★★ 86% ⓦ HOTEL

Chapel Lane, Mickleton, GL55 6SB - **tel:** 01386 438429
email: reception@puddingclub.com **web:** www.threewayshousehotel.com
dir: In Mickleton centre, on B4632 Stratford-upon-Avon to Broadway road

Built in 1870, this charming hotel has welcomed guests for over 100 years and is home to the world famous Pudding Club, formed in 1985 to promote traditional English puddings. Individuality is a hallmark here, as reflected in a number of the bedrooms that have been designed around a pudding theme. Public areas are stylish and include the air-conditioned restaurant, lounges and meeting rooms.

Rooms: 48 (7 family) (14 GF) ⓝ **S** £88–£130; **D** £155–£260 (incl. bkfst)* **Facilities:** FTV WiFi ⓘ Xmas New Year **Conf:** Class 40 Board 35 Thtr 100 **Services:** Lift Night porter **Parking:** 37 **Notes:** LB Civ Wed 100

CHIPPING NORTON
Oxfordshire — Map 10 SP32

Premier Inn Chipping Norton

BUDGET HOTEL

Spring Street, OX7 5LM - **tel:** 0871 527 9688 (Calls cost 13p per minute plus your phone company's access charge) **web:** www.premierinn.com
dir: Phone for details

High quality, budget accommodation ideal for both families and business travellers. Spacious, en suite bedrooms feature tea and coffee making facilities, Freeview TV in most hotels and free WiFi. The adjacent family restaurant features a wide and varied menu.

Rooms: 72

CHITTLEHAMHOLT
Devon — Map 3 SS62

Highbullen Hotel, Golf & Country Club

★★★★ 79% ⓦⓦ HOTEL

EX37 9HD - **tel:** 01769 540561
email: welcome@highbullen.co.uk **web:** www.highbullen.co.uk
dir: M5 junct 27/A361/B3227 towards South Molton. Near end of High St bear left onto B3226. Follow road along Mole Valley for 5m then follow brown tourist signs

Highbullen Hotel offers luxury accommodation in an idyllic North Devon setting. In The Manor House, the rooms have been individually designed, with colour schemes, furniture and fittings designed to match the atmosphere of each room. These rooms offer a luxurious stay with many individual stylish touches. The Estate Rooms have all seen a significant modernisation and offer comfort and elegance in the peaceful surroundings around the Estate. All the rooms have smart TVs and internet access throughout. Also on offer is a well equipped leisure centre and spa on site. The food and drink offering is extensive, with dinner and breakfast served in the elegant Devon View Restaurant daily.

Rooms: 42 (7 family) (15 GF) **S** £79–£119; **D** £109–£129 (incl. bkfst)* **Facilities:** FTV WiFi ⓘ ⓒ ⓣ ⓛ 18 Putting green ⓢ Fishing ⓖ Gym Sauna Steam room Shooting Pilates classes Fitness classes Xmas New Year **Conf:** Class 180 Board 50 Thtr 400 Del from £145 **Services:** Night porter **Parking:** 100 **Notes:** LB Civ Wed 200

C

CHORLEY
Lancashire   Map 15 SD51

Premier Inn Chorley North

BUDGET HOTEL

Malthouse Farm, Moss Lane, PR6 8AB - tel: 0871 527 8246 (Calls cost 13p per minute plus your phone company's access charge) **web:** www.premierinn.com
dir: *M61 junct 8 onto A674 (Wheelton), 400yds on left into Moss Ln*

High quality, budget accommodation ideal for both families and business travellers. Spacious, en suite bedrooms feature tea and coffee making facilities, Freeview TV in most hotels and free WiFi. The adjacent family restaurant features a wide and varied menu.

Rooms: 80

Premier Inn Chorley South

BUDGET HOTEL

Bolton Road, PR7 4AB - tel: 0871 527 8248 (Calls cost 13p per minute plus your phone company's access charge) **web:** www.premierinn.com
dir: *From N: M61 junct 8, A6 to Chorley. From S: M6 junct 27 follow Standish signs. Left onto A5106 to Chorley, A6 towards Preston. Hotel 0.5m on right*

Rooms: 29

CHRISTCHURCH
Dorset   Map 5 SZ19

HIGHLY RECOMMENDED

Captain's Club Hotel & Spa

★★★★ 83% ◉◉ HOTEL

Wick Ferry, Wick Lane, BH23 1HU - tel: 01202 475111
email: reservations@captainsclubhotel.com **web:** www.captainsclubhotel.com
dir: *B3073 to Christchurch. On Fountain rdbt take 5th exit (Sopers Ln) 2nd left (St Margarets Ave) 1st right onto Wick Ln*

The Captain's Club Hotel is situated in the heart of the town on the banks of the River Stour at Christchurch Quay, and only ten minutes from Bournemouth. All bedrooms, including the suites and apartments, have views overlooking the river. Guests can relax in the hydrotherapy pool, enjoy a spa treatment or sample the cuisine in Tides Restaurant.

Captain's Club Hotel & Spa

Rooms: 29 (12 family) 🛈 **S** £189–£289; **D** £189–£289 (incl. bkfst)*
Facilities: Spa STV FTV WiFi ⇘ Hydrotherapy pool Sauna Dry flotation ♫
Conf: Class 72 Board 64 Thtr 140 Del £214 **Services:** Lift Night porter Air con
Parking: 41 **Notes:** LB Civ Wed 100

See advert opposite

HIGHLY RECOMMENDED

Christchurch Harbour Hotel

★★★★ 82% ◉◉ HOTEL

95 Mudeford, BH23 3NT - tel: 01202 483434
email: christchurch@harbourhotels.co.uk **web:** www.christchurch-harbour-hotel.co.uk
dir: *On A35 to Christchurch onto A337 to Highcliffe. Right at rdbt, hotel 1.5m on left*

Delightfully situated on the side of Mudeford Quay close to sandy beaches, and conveniently located for Bournemouth Airport and the BIC, this hotel boasts an impressive spa and leisure facility. The bedrooms are particularly well appointed and stylishly finished; many have excellent views, and some have balconies. Guests can eat in the award-winning Jetty Restaurant, or the Upper Deck Bar and Restaurant.

Rooms: 64 (2 family) (14 GF) 🛈 **Facilities:** Spa FTV WiFi ⇘ ⓣ Gym Steam room Sauna Exercise classes Hydrotherapy pool Xmas New Year **Conf:** Class 20 Board 30 Thtr 100 **Services:** Lift Night porter **Parking:** 55 **Notes:** Civ Wed 100

Premier Inn Christchurch East

BUDGET HOTEL

Somerford Road, BH23 3QG - tel: 0871 527 8250 (Calls cost 13p per minute plus your phone company's access charge) **web:** www.premierinn.com
dir: *In Christchurch from A35 & B3059 rdbt junct take B3059 Somerford Rd*

High quality, budget accommodation ideal for both families and business travellers. Spacious, en suite bedrooms feature tea and coffee making facilities, Freeview TV in most hotels and free WiFi. The adjacent family restaurant features a wide and varied menu.

Rooms: 124

Premier Inn Christchurch West

BUDGET HOTEL

Barrack Road, BH23 2BN - tel: 0871 527 8252 (Calls cost 13p per minute plus your phone company's access charge) **web:** www.premierinn.com
dir: *From A338 take A3060 towards Christchurch. Left onto A35. Hotel on right*

Rooms: 61

C

CHURT
Surrey
Map 5 SU83

Best Western Frensham Pond Hotel

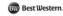 **Best Western.**

★★★★ 78% HOTEL

Bacon Lane, GU10 2QB - **tel:** 01252 795161
email: info@frenshampondhotel.co.uk **web:** www.bw-frenshampondhotel.co.uk
dir: A3 onto A287. 4m left at 'Beware Horses' sign. Hotel 0.25m

This 15th-century house occupies a superb location on the edge of Frensham Pond. Bedrooms offer style, comfort and a host of amenities including air conditioning. The annexe rooms have their own patio and private entrance. The contemporary bar and lounge offers a range of snacks while the restaurant offers a more formal menu for both lunch and dinner. Flexible meeting rooms are well equipped to host a range of functions from business meetings to wedding celebrations and private dining. There is a well-equipped fitness room and secure parking.

Rooms: 53 (12 annexe) (16 family) (27 GF) **S** fr £85; **D** fr £85 **Facilities:** STV FTV WiFi Gym Xmas New Year **Conf:** Class 45 Board 40 Thtr 120 **Services:** Night porter Air con LB **Parking:** 120 **Notes:** Civ Wed 130

CIRENCESTER
Gloucestershire
Map 5 SP00

Barnsley House

★★★★ ⊛⊛ ≋ COUNTRY HOUSE HOTEL

GL7 5EE - **tel:** 01285 740000
email: info@barnsleyhouse.com **web:** www.barnsleyhouse.com
dir: 4m NE of Cirencester on B4425

This delightful Cotswold country house has been appointed to provide the highest levels of quality, comfort and relaxation. Individually styled bedrooms come in a range of shapes and sizes, from the large character rooms in the main house to the more contemporary-style stable rooms; all rooms have garden views and are packed with guest extras and little luxuries, including plasma TVs in the bathrooms. The delightful gardens, originally designed in the late 1950s by previous owner and award-winning gardener Rosemary Verey and her husband, include a fruit and vegetable area which is the home of much of the produce used in the delicious cuisine on offer in Potager Restaurant. In the grounds is the Garden Spa with treatment rooms, sauna, steam room and an outdoor hydrotherapy pool. The hotel also has a cinema.

Rooms: 18 (12 annexe) (10 GF) **S** £201–£601; **D** £219–£619 (incl. bkfst)*
Facilities: Spa STV FTV WiFi Cinema Bicycles Hydrotherapy pool Relaxation rooms Xmas New Year **Conf:** Class 20 Board 18 Thtr 30
Services: Night porter **Parking:** 30 **Notes:** LB No children 14yrs Civ Wed 120

C

CIRENCESTER *continued*

Corinium Hotel & Restaurant

★★★ A SMALL HOTEL

12 Gloucester Street, GL7 2DG - tel: 01285 659711
email: info@coriniumhotel.co.uk web: www.coriniumhotel.co.uk
dir: *From A417/A419/A429 towards Cirencester. A435 at rdbt. After 500mtrs turn left at lights, then 1st right, car park on left*

This delightful 16th-century small hotel is quietly situated just five minutes walk from town, and is an ideal base from which to explore the Cotswolds. The Corinium has a locally renowned restaurant offering Modern British cuisine, as well as a cosy bar full of Cotswold charm. Other benefits include free WiFi throughout the hotel, an attractive secluded garden for alfresco dining, and ample free parking.

Rooms: 15 (2 family) (2 GF) S £70–£90; D £105–£130 (incl. bkfst)* Facilities: FTV WiFi ⓥ Conf: Class 30 Board 34 Thtr 70 Parking: 30 Notes: LB

Premier Inn Cirencester Town Centre

BUDGET HOTEL

Kings Meadow, GL7 1NP - tel: 0871 527 9674 (Calls cost 13p per minute plus your phone company's access charge) web: www.premierinn.com
dir: *NW on Cirencester Rd/A419. At rdbt, take 1st exit onto Cricklade Rd. At next rdbt hotel on right*

High quality, budget accommodation ideal for both families and business travellers. Spacious, en suite bedrooms feature tea and coffee making facilities, Freeview TV in most hotels and free WiFi. The adjacent family restaurant features a wide and varied menu.

Rooms: 62

CLACTON-ON-SEA	Map 7 TM11
Essex	

The Kingscliff Hotel

★★★ 78% HOTEL

55 King's Parade, Holland on Sea, CO15 5JB - tel: 01255 812343
email: info@thekingscliffhotel.com web: www.thekingscliffhotel.co.uk
dir: *A12 junct 29 onto A120, then A133, at Weeley rdbt take 3rd exit, turn onto Marine Parade East & continue onto Kings Parade*

The Kingscliff Hotel enjoys a prominent position along the seafront. Bedrooms are all attractively presented, comfortable and very well equipped; some front-facing rooms enjoy wonderful sea views. There is a popular restaurant along with a stylish lounge bar for guests. Secure parking is available and free WiFi is offered throughout the hotel. This is also a very popular wedding and conference venue.

Rooms: 30 (2 family) (7 GF) ☞ Facilities: FTV WiFi ⓥ Xmas New Year Conf: Class 50 Board 30 Thtr 90 Services: Night porter Parking: 50 Notes: Civ Wed 100

Premier Inn Clacton-on-Sea

BUDGET HOTEL

Crown Green Roundabout, Colchester Road, CO16 9AA - tel: 0871 527 8254 (Calls cost 13p per minute plus your phone company's access charge) web: www.premierinn.com
dir: *A12, A120 towards Harwich. In 4m take A133 to Clacton-on-Sea. Hotel off Weeley Rdbt*

High quality, budget accommodation ideal for both families and business travellers. Spacious, en suite bedrooms feature tea and coffee making facilities, Freeview TV in most hotels and free WiFi. The adjacent family restaurant features a wide and varied menu.

Rooms: 66

Premier Inn Clacton-on-Sea (Seafront) Hotel

BUDGET HOTEL

8 Marine Parade West, CO15 1RD - tel: 0871 527 8254 (Calls cost 13p per minute plus your phone company's access charge) web: www.premierinn.com
dir: *From A12 take A120 towards Harwich. 4m, take A133 to Clacton-on-Sea. Hotel accessed from rdbt at Weeley. Adjacent to bowling green*

Rooms: 66

CLAVERDON	Map 10 SP16
Warwickshire	

Ardencote

★★★★ 76% ⚜ HOTEL

The Cumsey, Lye Green Road, CV35 8LT - tel: 01926 843111
email: hotel@ardencote.com web: www.ardencote.com
dir: *Phone or see website for directions*

Originally built as a gentleman's residence around 1860, this hotel is set in 83 acres of landscaped grounds. Public rooms include a choice of lounge areas, a cocktail bar and conservatory breakfast room. Main meals are served in the modern Brasserie with lighter meals in the Brasserie Bar. Sunday lunch is served in the Lodge Restaurant, a separate building with a light contemporary style which sits beside a small lake. An extensive range of leisure, golf and conference facilities are provided and bedrooms are smartly decorated and tastefully furnished.

Rooms: 110 (10 family) (30 GF) ☞ S £95–£115; D £115–£165 (incl. bkfst)* Facilities: Spa STV FTV WiFi ⓥ HL ⓢ ⟩ ⌁ 18 Putting green ☞ ☞ Gym Squash Sauna Steam room Dance studio Relaxation rooms Xmas New Year Conf: Class 70 Board 50 Thtr 175 Del from £135 Services: Lift Night porter Air con Parking: 350 Notes: LB Civ Wed 150

CLEARWELL
Gloucestershire

Map 4 SO50

Tudor Farmhouse Hotel & Restaurant
★★★ ◉◉ ﹍ HOTEL

High Street, GL16 8JS - tel: 01594 833046
email: info@tudorfarmhousehotel.co.uk **web:** www.tudorfarmhousehotel.co.uk
dir: A4136 onto B4228, through Coleford, right into Clearwell, hotel on right just before War Memorial Cross

Dating from the 13th century, this idyllic former farmhouse retains a host of original features including exposed stonework, oak beams, wall panelling and wonderful inglenook fireplaces. Bedrooms have great individuality and style and are located either in the main house or in converted buildings in the grounds. Creative menus offer quality cuisine, served in the intimate, candlelit restaurant.

Rooms: 23 (18 annexe) (3 family) (10 GF) ﹍ **Facilities:** STV FTV WiFi ﹍ HL Xmas New Year **Conf:** Class 20 Board 12 Thtr 30 **Parking:** 30 **Notes:** Closed 2-5 Jan

CLECKHEATON
West Yorkshire

Map 19 SE12

Premier Inn Bradford South
BUDGET HOTEL

Whitehall Road, Dye House Drive, BD19 6HG - tel: 0871 527 8136 (Calls cost 13p per minute plus your phone company's access charge) **web:** www.premierinn.com
dir: On A58 at intersection with M62 & M606

High quality, budget accommodation ideal for both families and business travellers. Spacious, en suite bedrooms feature tea and coffee making facilities, Freeview TV in most hotels and free WiFi. The adjacent family restaurant features a wide and varied menu.

Rooms: 60

CLEETHORPES
Lincolnshire

Map 17 TA30

Kingsway Hotel
★★★ 80% HOTEL

C

Kingsway, DN35 0AE - tel: 01472 601122
email: reception@kingsway-hotel.com **web:** www.kingsway-hotel.com
dir: Exit A180 at Grimsby, to Cleethorpes seafront. Hotel at Kingsway & Queen Parade junct - A1098

This seafront hotel has been in the same family for four generations and continues to provide traditional comfort and friendly service. The lounges are comfortable, and good food is served in the pleasant dining room. The bedrooms are bright and nicely furnished - most are comfortably proportioned.

Rooms: 46 ﹍ **S** £68–£94; **D** £89–£112 (incl. bkfst)* **Facilities:** STV FTV WiFi
Conf: Board 18 Thtr 22 Del from £120 **Services:** Lift Night porter **Parking:** 50
Notes: No children 5yrs Closed 25-26 Dec

Premier Inn Cleethorpes
BUDGET HOTEL

Meridian Point, DN35 0PN - tel: 0871 527 9470 (Calls cost 13p per minute plus your phone company's access charge) **web:** www.premierinn.com
dir: A180 through Grimsby to Cleethorpes. At 4th rdbt take 2nd exit into Isaac's Hill (A1098). In 0.5m take 2nd exit at rdbt into Alexandra Rd (A1098). At next rdbt take 1st exit into Kingsway. Hotel 1m on right

High quality, budget accommodation ideal for both families and business travellers. Spacious, en suite bedrooms feature tea and coffee making facilities, Freeview TV in most hotels and free WiFi. The adjacent family restaurant features a wide and varied menu.

Rooms: 60

CLOWNE
Derbyshire

Map 16 SK47

Hotel Van Dyk
★★★★ 76% ◉ SMALL HOTEL

Worksop Road, S43 4TD - tel: 01246 387386
email: info@hotelvandyk.co.uk **web:** www.vandykhotel.co.uk
dir: M1 junct 30, 2nd right towards Worksop, 2nd rdbt 1st exit, 3rd rdbt straight over. Through lights, hotel 100yds on right

A sympathetic renovation has resulted in a small vibrant boutique-style hotel where staff are always on hand to offer friendly and welcoming service. Accommodation is luxurious and equipped with many thoughtful extras. Bowdens Restaurant offers fine dining and makes the ideal setting for a memorable evening; alternatively there's Southgate Grill for those looking for a more casual eating option.

Rooms: 15 (4 family) ﹍ **S** £99; **D** £149 (incl. bkfst)* **Facilities:** FTV WiFi Xmas New Year **Conf:** Class 50 Board 60 Thtr 150 **Services:** Night porter **Parking:** 120 **Notes:** Civ Wed 120

COBHAM
Surrey

Map 6 TQ16

Premier Inn Cobham

BUDGET HOTEL

Portsmouth Road, Fairmile, KT11 1BW - **tel:** 0871 527 8256 (Calls cost 13p per minute plus your phone company's access charge) **web:** www.premierinn.com
dir: M25 junct 10, A3 towards London, A245 towards Cobham. In Cobham town centre left onto A307 (Portsmouth Rd). Hotel on left

High quality, budget accommodation ideal for both families and business travellers. Spacious, en suite bedrooms feature tea and coffee making facilities, Freeview TV in most hotels and free WiFi. The adjacent family restaurant features a wide and varied menu.

Rooms: 48

Days Inn Cobham - M25

WELCOMEBREAK

AA Advertised

Cobham Services, M25 J9/10 Downside, KT11 3DB - **tel:** 01932 868958
email: cobham.hotel@welcomebreak.co.uk **web:** www.welcomebreak.co.uk
dir: Between junct 9 & 10 at Extra Cobham services on M25. Accessible from both sides of motorway

This modern building offers accommodation in smart, spacious and well-equipped bedrooms, suitable for families and business travellers, and all with en suite bathrooms. Continental breakfast is available and other refreshments may be taken at the nearby family restaurant.

Rooms: 75 (18 family) (35 GF) ⋒ **Facilities:** FTV WiFi ↳ HL **Services:** Lift Night porter Air con **Parking:** 200

COCKERMOUTH
Cumbria

Map 18 NY13

HIGHLY RECOMMENDED

The Trout Hotel

★★★★ 84% ◉ HOTEL

Crown Street, CA13 0EJ - **tel:** 01900 823591
email: reservations@trouthotel.co.uk **web:** www.trouthotel.co.uk
dir: Adjacent to Wordsworth House

Dating back to 1670, this privately owned hotel has an enviable setting on the banks of the River Derwent. The well-equipped bedrooms, some contained in a wing overlooking the river, are comfortable and mostly spacious. The Terrace Bar & Bistro, serving food all day, has a sheltered patio area. There is also a cosy bar, a choice of lounge areas and an attractive, traditional-style dining room that offers a good choice of set-price dishes.

Rooms: 49 (4 family) (15 GF) ⋒ **S** £105–£120; **D** £135–£240 (incl. bkfst)*
Facilities: STV FTV WiFi ↳ Fishing Xmas New Year **Conf:** Class 20 Board 20 Thtr 25 **Services:** Night porter **Parking:** 40 **Notes:** LB Civ Wed 60

COLCHESTER
Essex

Map 13 TL92

Wivenhoe House Hotel

★★★★ 83% HOTEL

Wivenhoe Park, CO4 3SQ - **tel:** 01206 863666
email: info@wivenhoehouse.co.uk **web:** www.wivenhoehouse.co.uk
dir: From A12 take exit signed Colchester. Follow A133 towards Clacton. Take B1027 for Wivenhoe, right on Boundry Rd, right on Park Rd, signed

A superb building which forms part of Essex University, the property has been totally refurbished. The bedrooms are split between the main building and the more contemporary extension; each one has been individually decorated, furnished to a very high standard and has modern technology. Public rooms include the Signatures fine dining restaurant and a modern brasserie; there is also a choice of lounges with plush furnishings.

Rooms: 40 (6 family) ⋒ **S** £105–£245; **D** £105–£245 (incl. bkfst)* **Facilities:** FTV WiFi ↳ Xmas New Year **Conf:** Class 70 Board 22 Thtr 180 **Services:** Lift Night porter **Parking:** 150 **Notes:** LB Civ Wed 180

Stoke by Nayland Hotel, Golf & Spa

★★★★ 78% ◉◉ HOTEL

Keepers Lane, Leavenheath, CO6 4PZ - **tel:** 01206 262836
email: reservations@stokebynayland.com **web:** www.stokebynayland.com
dir: Exit A134 at Leavenheath onto B1068, hotel 0.75m on right

This hotel is situated on the edge of Dedham Vale, an Area of Outstanding Natural Beauty, in 300 acres of undulating countryside with lakes and two golf courses. The spacious bedrooms are attractively decorated and equipped with modern facilities, such as free WiFi available throughout. Public rooms include the Spikes bar, a conservatory, a lounge, a smart restaurant, conference and banqueting suites, and the superb Peake Spa and Fitness Centre that offers extensive facilities including health and beauty treatments. There's even a shop that provides all the essentials, plus an array of hand-made gifts. Conveniently located for Ipswich, Bury St Edmunds and Colchester.

Rooms: 80 (6 family) (26 GF) **S** £66–£126; **D** £76–£196* **Facilities:** Spa STV FTV WiFi ↳ ☺ supervised ⌛ 36 Putting green Fishing Gym Squash Driving range Pro golf tuition ♫ Xmas New Year **Conf:** Class 300 Board 60 Thtr 450 **Services:** Lift Night porter **Parking:** 400 **Notes:** Civ Wed 200

Crowne Plaza Resort Colchester - Five Lakes

★★★★ 76% HOTEL - **tel:** 01621 868888 **Colchester Rd CM9 8HX**

email: enquiries@cpcolchester.co.uk **web:** www.cpcolchester.co.uk

(For full entry see Tolleshunt Knights)

C

The North Hill Hotel

★★★ 82% HOTEL

51 North Hill, CO1 1PY - **tel:** 01206 574001
email: info@northhillhotel.com **web:** www.northhillhotel.com
dir: *Follow directions for town centre, down North Hill, hotel on left*

The North Hill Hotel is situated in the centre of this historic town. The contemporary open-plan public areas include a small lounge bar and the Green Room restaurant. The smartly appointed bedrooms are modern and well equipped with large flat-screen TVs and many thoughtful touches.

Rooms: 24 (7 annexe) (3 family) (4 GF) 🐾 **Facilities:** FTV WiFi New Year **Conf:** Class 25 Board 20 Thtr 30 **Services:** Night porter

Best Western The Rose & Crown Hotel

★★★ 79% HOTEL

East Street, CO1 2TZ - **tel:** 01206 866677
email: info@rose-and-crown.com **web:** www.rose-and-crown.com
dir: *From A12 follow Rollerworld signs, hotel by level crossing*

This delightful 14th-century coaching inn is situated close to the shops and is full of charm and character. Public areas feature a wealth of exposed beams and timbered walls, and include the contemporary East St Grill. Although the bedrooms vary in size, all are stylishly decorated and equipped with many thoughtful extras suitable for both business and leisure guests; luxury executive rooms are available.

Rooms: 39 (3 family) (12 GF) **S** £65–£125; **D** £75–£145* **Facilities:** FTV WiFi **Conf:** Class 50 Board 45 Thtr 100 Del from £135 **Services:** Lift Night porter **Parking:** 50 **Notes:** Civ Wed 80

Premier Inn Colchester (A12)

BUDGET HOTEL

Ipswich Road, CO4 9WP - **tel:** 0871 527 8260 (Calls cost 13p per minute plus your phone company's access charge) **web:** www.premierinn.com
dir: *From A12 exit at Colchester North/A1232 junct off towards Colchester. Hotel on right, 200yds from rdbt. NB for Sat Nav use CO4 9TD*

High quality, budget accommodation ideal for both families and business travellers. Spacious, en suite bedrooms feature tea and coffee making facilities, Freeview TV in most hotels and free WiFi. The adjacent family restaurant features a wide and varied menu.

Rooms: 104

Premier Inn Colchester Central

BUDGET HOTEL

Cowdray Avenue, CO1 1UT - **tel:** 0871 527 8258 (Calls cost 13p per minute plus your phone company's access charge) **web:** www.premierinn.com
dir: *From Ipswich A12 junct 29. At rdbt onto A1232 (Ipswich road). At 2nd rdbt 2nd exit onto A133 (Cowdray Ave). Hotel approx 0.5m on right*

Rooms: 20

Premier Inn Colchester Town Centre

BUDGET HOTEL

St Peter's Street, CO1 1HY - **tel:** 0871 527 9506 (Calls cost 13p per minute plus your phone company's access charge) **web:** www.premierinn.com
dir: *A12 to Colchester. Follow Colchester & A133 signs. At rdbt onto A133. At next rdbt 3rd exit signed Westway & A134. At next rdbt 2nd exit onto Middleborough, continue to St Peter's St, hotel on left*

Rooms: 85

COLEFORD
Gloucestershire
Map 4 SO51

Bells Hotel & The Forest of Dean Golf Club

★★★ 71% HOTEL

Lords Hill, GL16 8BE - **tel:** 01594 832583
email: enquiries@bells-hotel.co.uk **web:** www.bells-hotel.co.uk
dir: *0.25m from Coleford. Off B4228*

Set in its own grounds, with an 18-hole golf course, this purpose-built establishment offers a range of facilities. Bedrooms vary in style and space, and a number are on the ground floor. There is a small gym, and a comfortable bar and lounge which is available until late. The hotel's club house, just yards away, has a bar with all-day meals and snacks, a restaurant, a games/TV room and conference and function rooms.

Rooms: 53 (12 family) (36 GF) (5 smoking) 🐾 **Facilities:** FTV WiFi ⌁ 18 Putting green Bowling green Short mat bowling room 🎵 Xmas New Year **Conf:** Class 250 Board 100 Thtr 350 **Services:** Night porter **Parking:** 100 **Notes:** Civ Wed 150

COLERNE
Wiltshire
Map 4 ST87

INSPECTOR'S CHOICE

Lucknam Park Hotel & Spa

★★★★★ ◉◉◉ ⌂ COUNTRY HOUSE HOTEL

SN14 8AZ - **tel:** 01225 742777
email: reservations@lucknampark.co.uk **web:** www.lucknampark.co.uk
dir: *M4 junct 17, A350 towards Chippenham, then A420 towards Bristol for 3m. At Ford left to Colerne, 3m, right at x-rds, entrance on right*

Approaching this Palladian mansion along a magnificent mile-long avenue of beech and lime trees, builds a wonderful sense of anticipation. Surrounded by 500 acres of parkland and beautiful gardens, the hotel offers a wealth of choices ranging from pampered relaxation within the indulgent spa, complete with an innovative Well-Being centre; to more energetic equestrian pursuits. Elegant bedrooms and suites are split between the main building and adjacent courtyard, all of which exude quality, individuality and comfort. Dining options range from the informal Brasserie (awarded two AA Rosettes), to the formal and very accomplished main restaurant, The Park (with three AA Rosettes), where skilled, sincere and engaging staff contribute to a memorable experience. For anyone with a passion for food, the Cookery School is also worth investigating.

Rooms: 42 (18 annexe) (16 GF) 🐾 **D** £360–£1425* **Facilities:** Spa STV FTV WiFi ⌁ 🔄 ♨ 💆 🏊 Gym Cross country course Mountain bikes Equestrian centre Cookery school Xmas New Year **Conf:** Class 24 Board 24 Thtr 60 Del from £378 **Services:** Night porter **Parking:** 80 **Notes:** Civ Wed 110

C

COLTISHALL
Norfolk
Map 13 TG21

Norfolk Mead Hotel

★★★★ 83% ◉◉ COUNTRY HOUSE HOTEL

Church Loke, NR12 7DN - tel: 01603 737531
email: info@norfolkmead.co.uk **web:** www.norfolkmead.co.uk
dir: *Coltishall village, go right with petrol station on left, 200 yds church on right, go down driveway*

This beautiful hotel enjoys a peaceful location and is set in its own extensive grounds, while still being a short walk to the pretty village of Coltishall. Bedrooms are all beautifully designed, and the public areas are very well appointed. Afternoon tea can be enjoyed in the walled garden on finer days and the cosy bar is very comfortable. There is an award-winning restaurant, which benefits from garden and river views.

Rooms: 15 (4 annexe) (4 family) (3 GF) ⬩ **D** £135–£210 (incl. bkfst)
Facilities: Spa FTV WiFi ⬩ ⬩ Beauty treatment rooms Xmas New Year
Conf: Class 150 Board 150 Thtr 200 Del from £177.50 **Parking:** 40
Notes: Civ Wed 40

CONSETT
County Durham
Map 19 NZ15

Best Western Derwent Manor Hotel

★★★ 82% HOTEL

BW Best Western.

Hole Row, Allensford, DH8 9BB - tel: 01207 592000
email: reservations@bw-derwentmanor.co.uk **web:** www.bw-derwentmanor-hotel.co.uk
dir: *Phone for details*

The Best Western Derwent Manor Hotel enjoys an elevated position overlooking the Derwent Valley. Set in 20 acres, the hotel is ideally located within easy distance of both Newcastle and Durham with a wealth of visitor attractions close by. Bedrooms are generous in size and comfortable, and guests have use of a well-appointed gym and pool area as well as a welcoming bar serving food throughout the day. The main restaurant offers a full-on dining experience with local produce used to create a balanced menu.

Rooms: 48 (15 family) (24 GF) ⬩ **Facilities:** FTV WiFi ⬩ ⬩ supervised Gym Xmas New Year **Conf:** Class 170 Board 80 Thtr 350 **Services:** Lift Night porter **Parking:** 100
Notes: LB Civ Wed 300

COPTHORNE
See Gatwick Airport

CORBY
Northamptonshire
Map 11 SP88

Premier Inn Corby

BUDGET HOTEL

1 Little Colliers Field, NN18 8TJ - tel: 0871 527 8264 (Calls cost 13p per minute plus your phone company's access charge) **web:** www.premierinn.com
dir: *M1 junct 19, A14 E'bound. Exit at junct 7, left at rdbt onto A43. At next rdbt left onto A6003. Hotel at next rdbt. NB for Sat Nav use NN18 9EX*

High quality, budget accommodation ideal for both families and business travellers. Spacious, en suite bedrooms feature tea and coffee making facilities, Freeview TV in most hotels and free WiFi. The adjacent family restaurant features a wide and varied menu.

Rooms: 71

CORFE CASTLE
Dorset
Map 4 SY98

Mortons House Hotel

★★★ 86% ◉◉ HOTEL

49 East Street, BH20 5EE - tel: 01929 480988
email: stay@mortonshouse.co.uk **web:** www.mortonshouse.co.uk
dir: *On A351 between Wareham & Swanage*

Set in delightful gardens and grounds with excellent views of Corfe Castle, this impressive building dates back to Tudor times. The oak-panelled drawing room has a roaring log fire in cooler months, and an interesting range of enjoyable cuisine is available in the well-appointed dining room. Bedrooms, many with views of the castle, are comfortable and well equipped.

Rooms: 21 (7 annexe) (2 family) (4 GF) ⬩ **S** £95–£130; **D** £160 (incl. bkfst)*
Facilities: FTV WiFi HL Xmas New Year **Conf:** Class 45 Board 20 Thtr 45 Del from £135 **Parking:** 40 **Notes:** LB Civ Wed 60

CORLEY MOTORWAY SERVICE AREA (M6)
Warwickshire
Map 10 SP38

Days Inn Corley - NEC - M6

WELCOMEBREAK

AA Advertised

Junction 3-4, M6 North, Corley, CV7 8NR - tel: 01676 543800
email: corley.hotel@welcomebreak.co.uk **web:** www.welcomebreak.co.uk
dir: *On M6 between juncts 3 & 4 N'bound*

This modern building offers accommodation in smart, spacious and well-equipped bedrooms, suitable for families and business travellers, and all with en suite bathrooms. Continental breakfast is available and other refreshments may be taken at the nearby family restaurant.

Rooms: 50 (13 family) (24 GF) (8 smoking) ⬩ **Facilities:** FTV WiFi ⬩ **Parking:** 120

CORNHILL-ON-TWEED
Northumberland
Map 21 NT83

Tillmouth Park Country House Hotel

★★★ 88% ◉ COUNTRY HOUSE HOTEL

TD12 4UU - tel: 01890 882255
email: reception@tillmouthpark.f9.co.uk **web:** www.tillmouthpark.co.uk
dir: *Exit A1(M) at East Ord rdbt at Berwick-upon-Tweed. Take A698 signed Cornhill & Coldstream. Hotel 9m on left*

Tillmouth Park is an imposing mansion set in landscaped grounds by the River Till. Gracious public rooms include a stunning galleried lounge with a drawing room adjacent. The quiet, elegant dining room overlooks the gardens, while lunches and early dinners are available in the bistro. Bedrooms retain much traditional character and include several magnificent master rooms.

Rooms: 14 (2 annexe) (2 family) (2 GF) (4 smoking) **S** fr £72; **D** fr £175 (incl. bkfst)* **Facilities:** FTV WiFi Game shooting Fishing **Conf:** Class 20 Board 20 Thtr 50 Del from £200 **Parking:** 50 **Notes:** LB Closed 26 Dec-1 Apr

C

CORSE LAWN
Gloucestershire

Map 10 SO83

Corse Lawn House Hotel

★★★ 80% HOTEL

GL19 4LZ - **tel:** 01452 780771
email: enquiries@corselawn.com **web:** www.corselawn.com
dir: On B4211 5m SW of Tewkesbury

This gracious Grade II-listed Queen Anne house, in twelve acres of grounds, has been home to the Hine family for more than thirty years. Aided by an enthusiastic and committed team, the family continues to preside over all aspects of the hotel, creating a wonderfully relaxed environment. Bedrooms offer a reassuring mix of comfort and quality, and include four-poster rooms. In both The Restaurant and The Bistro the impressive cuisine is based on excellent produce, much of it locally sourced.

Rooms: 18 (3 family) (5 GF) S £70–£100; D £120–£180 (incl. bkfst)*
Facilities: STV FTV WiFi Badminton Table tennis New Year **Conf:** Class 30 Board 25 Thtr 50 Del from £135 **Parking:** 62 **Notes:** LB Closed 24-26 Dec Civ Wed 70

CORSHAM
Wiltshire

Map 4 ST87

Guyers House Hotel

★★★★ 76% COUNTRY HOUSE HOTEL

Pickwick, SN13 0PS - **tel:** 01249 713399
email: enquiries@guyershouse.com **web:** www.guyershouse.com
dir: A4 between Pickwick & Corsham

This privately owned hotel retains the charm and ambience of a country house. The bedrooms are well appointed in keeping with the style of the house, and equipped with all modern amenities. The award-winning restaurant is the ideal place for an intimate dinner or a family gathering; alfresco dining is possible when the weather is favourable. The gardens are a feature and are open to the public on certain days under the National Garden Scheme. The hotel is conveniently located for easy access to Bath.

Rooms: 37 (13 GF) S £105–£190; D £160–£249 (incl. bkfst & dinner)*
Facilities: FTV WiFi Gym Xmas **Conf:** Class 34 Board 24 Thtr 75 Del from £139.50 **Services:** Night porter **Parking:** 70 **Notes:** LB Closed 30 Dec-3 Jan Civ Wed 100

COVENTRY
West Midlands

Map 10 SP37

See also **Meriden** & **Nuneaton**

Best Western Plus Windmill Village Hotel, Golf Club & Spa

★★★★ 75% HOTEL

Birmingham Road, Allesley, CV5 9AL - **tel:** 024 7640 4040
email: reservations@windmillvillagehotel.co.uk **web:** www.windmillvillagehotel.co.uk
dir: A45, close to Coventry City Centre

This modern hotel is conveniently located on the outskirts of Coventry and is a short drive from Birmingham and the NEC. Bedrooms are all very attractively presented and most rooms have views over the hotel's challenging golf course. The leisure facilities are first rate and include a very well-equipped gym and a swimming pool.

Business guests are well catered for with a range of conference facilities including business suites, and free WiFi is available throughout the hotel.

Rooms: 105 (35 annexe) (10 family) (39 GF) S £59–£199; D £69–£209*
Facilities: Spa FTV WiFi supervised 18 Putting green Gym Xmas New Year **Conf:** Class 140 Board 60 Thtr 400 Del from £125 **Services:** Lift Night porter **Parking:** 400 **Notes:** LB Civ Wed 100

Novotel Coventry

★★★ 78% HOTEL

Wilsons Lane, CV6 6HL - **tel:** 024 7636 5000
email: h0506@accor-hotels.com **web:** www.novotel.com
dir: M6 junct 3. Follow signs for B4113 towards Longford & Bedworth. 3rd exit on large rdbt

Novotel Coventry is a modern hotel convenient for Birmingham, Coventry and the motorway network, offering spacious, well-equipped accommodation. The bright brasserie has extended dining hours, alternatively there is an extensive room-service menu. Family rooms and a play area make this a child-friendly hotel, and for adults, there is also a mini-gym and a selection of meeting rooms.

Rooms: 98 (25 GF) **Facilities:** STV WiFi Mini gym **Conf:** Class 100 Board 40 Thtr 200 **Services:** Lift Night porter **Parking:** 120 **Notes:** Civ Wed 50

The Chace Hotel

★★★ 71% HOTEL

Toll Bar End, London Road, CV3 4EQ - **tel:** 024 7630 3398
email: thechace@corushotels.com **web:** www.corushotels.com/coventry
dir: A45 or A46 follow to Toll Bar Rdbt/Coventry Airport, take B4116 to Willenhall, over mini-rdbt, hotel on left

Conveniently located for ease of access to the motorway network and Coventry Airport, The Chace Hotel has a long history as an important residence in Willenhall, and was once the home of a local surgeon. Rooms vary in style across the property; all are furnished to a good standard. Public areas boast many original and period features including portraits of the doctor and his wife. A popular restaurant and number of function rooms along with ample free parking are also available.

Rooms: 66 (49 annexe) (2 family) (24 GF) **Facilities:** FTV WiFi Xmas New Year **Conf:** Class 40 Board 56 Thtr 100 **Services:** Night porter **Parking:** 100 **Notes:** Civ Wed 100

Premier Inn Coventry City Centre

BUDGET HOTEL

Belgrade Plaza, Bond Street, CV1 4AH - **tel:** 0871 527 8272 (Calls cost 13p per minute plus your phone company's access charge) **web:** www.premierinn.com
dir: A4053 (ring road) junct 9, follow Belgrade Plaza car park signs. Hotel in same complex

High quality, budget accommodation ideal for both families and business travellers. Spacious, en suite bedrooms feature tea and coffee making facilities, Freeview TV in most hotels and free WiFi. The adjacent family restaurant features a wide and varied menu.

Rooms: 120

Premier Inn Coventry City Centre (Earlsdon Park)

BUDGET HOTEL

Earlsdon Park, CV1 3BH - **tel:** 0871 527 9318 (Calls cost 13p per minute plus your phone company's access charge) **web:** www.premierinn.com
dir: From Coventry ring road follow Ikea signs. Hotel adjacent to Coventry RFC on Butts Rd. Parking in multi storey adjacent

Rooms: 100

C

COVENTRY *continued*

Premier Inn Coventry East (Ansty)

BUDGET HOTEL

Coombe Fields Road, Ansty, CV7 9JP - **tel:** 0871 527 8274 (Calls cost 13p per minute plus your phone company's access charge) **web:** www.premierinn.com
dir: M6 junct 2, B4065 towards Ansty. After village right onto B4029 signed Brinklow. Right into Coombe Fields Rd, hotel on right

Rooms: 28

Premier Inn Coventry East (Binley/A46)

BUDGET HOTEL

Rugby Road, Binley Woods, CV3 2TA - **tel:** 0871 527 8268 (Calls cost 13p per minute plus your phone company's access charge) **web:** www.premierinn.com
dir: M6 junct 2 follow Warwick, A46 & M40 signs. Follow 'All traffic' signs, under bridge onto A46. Left at 1st rdbt to Binley. Hotel on right at next rdbt

Rooms: 96

Premier Inn Coventry East (M6 Jct 2)

BUDGET HOTEL

Gielgud Way, Cross Point Business Park, CV2 2SZ - **tel:** 0871 527 8266 (Calls cost 13p per minute plus your phone company's access charge) **web:** www.premierinn.com
dir: M6 junct 2 towards Coventry onto A4600 (Hinckley road). At rdbt 1st exit into Parkway, left at next rdbt into Olivier Way. At next rdbt straight on into retail park towards cinema, hotel on right

Rooms: 48

Premier Inn Coventry South (A45)

BUDGET HOTEL

Kenpas Highway, CV3 6PB - **tel:** 0871 527 8270 (Calls cost 13p per minute plus your phone company's access charge) **web:** www.premierinn.com
dir: M6 junct 2, A46. Follow A45 towards Birmingham

Rooms: 38

COWES
Isle of Wight — Map 5 SZ49

Best Western New Holmwood Hotel

★★★ 79% HOTEL

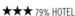 Best Western.

Queens Road, Egypt Point, PO31 8BW - **tel:** 01983 292508
email: reception@newholmwoodhotel.co.uk **web:** www.newholmwoodhotel.co.uk
dir: From A3020 at Northwood Garage lights, left & follow to rdbt. 1st left then sharp right into Baring Rd, 4th left into Egypt Hill. At bottom turn right, hotel on right

Just by the Esplanade, this hotel has an enviable outlook. Bedrooms are comfortable and very well equipped, and the light and airy, glass-fronted restaurant looks out to sea and serves a range of interesting meals. The sun terrace is delightful in the summer and there is a choice of meeting rooms for all occasions. Parking is available on a first-come, first-serve basis.

Rooms: 26 (1 family) (9 GF) ☂ **Facilities:** STV FTV WiFi ⓦ Xmas New Year **Conf:** Class 60 Board 50 Thtr 100 **Services:** Night porter **Parking:** 20 **Notes:** Civ Wed 60

CRAMLINGTON
Northumberland — Map 21 NZ27

Premier Inn Newcastle Gosforth/Cramlington

BUDGET HOTEL

Moor Farm Roundabout, Off Front Street, NE23 7QA - **tel:** 0871 527 8788 (Calls cost 13p per minute plus your phone company's access charge) **web:** www.premierinn.com
dir: At rdbt junct of A19 & A189, S of Cramlington

High quality, budget accommodation ideal for both families and business travellers. Spacious, en suite bedrooms feature tea and coffee making facilities, Freeview TV in most hotels and free WiFi. The adjacent family restaurant features a wide and varied menu.

Rooms: 79

CRAWLEY

See **Gatwick Airport**

CREWE
Cheshire — Map 15 SJ75

Crewe Hall

★★★★ 81% ⍟ HOTEL

QHOTELS
INSPIRED BY YOU

Weston Road, CW1 6UZ - **tel:** 01270 253333
email: crewehall@qhotels.co.uk **web:** www.qhotels.co.uk
dir: M6 junct 16, A500 to Crewe. Take A5020. 1st exit at next rdbt to Crewe. Hotel 150yds on right

Standing in 500 acres of mature grounds, this historic hall dates back to the 17th century, yet retains an elaborate interior with Victorian-style architecture. Bedrooms are spacious, well equipped and comfortable with traditionally styled suites in the main hall and modern rooms in the west wing. Afternoon tea is served in The Sheridan Lounge, while The Brasserie Restaurant and Bar is contemporary and has a relaxed atmosphere. The health and beauty spa ensure that the hotel is a popular choice with both corporate and leisure guests.

Rooms: 117 (91 annexe) (5 family) (35 GF) ☂ **S** £89–£199; **D** £99–£215 (incl. bkfst)* **Facilities:** Spa STV WiFi ⓦ ⓣ ⌘ Gym Enclosed events field **Conf:** Class 172 Board 96 Thtr 364 Del from £145 **Services:** Lift Night porter **Parking:** 500 **Notes:** LB Civ Wed 180

Hunters Lodge Hotel

★★★ 67% HOTEL

Sydney Road, Sydney, CW1 5LU - **tel:** 01270 539100
email: info@hunterslodge.co.uk **web:** www.hunterslodge.co.uk
dir: M6 junct 16. 1m from Crewe station, off A534

Dating back to the 18th century, the hotel has been extended and modernised over the years. Accommodation, mainly located in adjacent well-equipped bedroom wings, includes family and four-poster rooms. Imaginative dishes are served in the popular bar which also offers open fires and friendly and efficient service.

Rooms: 57 (52 annexe) (4 family) (31 GF) ☂ **S** £68; **D** £75.50–£89.50 (incl. bkfst)* **Facilities:** STV FTV WiFi ⓦ Gym **Conf:** Class 100 Board 80 Thtr 160 Del from £133.05 **Services:** Night porter **Parking:** 240 **Notes:** RS Sun eve Restaurant closed - bar food available Civ Wed 130

Premier Inn Crewe Central

BUDGET HOTEL

Weston Road, CW1 6FX - tel: 0871 527 8276 (Calls cost 13p per minute plus your phone company's access charge) **web:** www.premierinn.com
dir: *M6 junct 16, A500, at rdbt 3rd exit onto A5020 (Old Park Rd). At next rdbt 2nd exit into Western Rd, at next rdbt 3rd exit, hotel on left*

High quality, budget accommodation ideal for both families and business travellers. Spacious, en suite bedrooms feature tea and coffee making facilities, Freeview TV in most hotels and free WiFi. The adjacent family restaurant features a wide and varied menu.

Rooms: 34

Premier Inn Crewe West

BUDGET HOTEL

Coppenhall Lane, Woolstanwood, CW2 8SD - tel: 0871 527 8278 (Calls cost 13p per minute plus your phone company's access charge) **web:** www.premierinn.com
dir: *At junct of A530 & A532, 9m from M6 junct 16 N'bound*

Rooms: 80

CROMER Norfolk — Map 13 TG24

Sea Marge Hotel

★★★★ 75% ◉◉ HOTEL

16 High Street, Overstrand, NR27 0AB - tel: 01263 579579
email: seamarge@mackenziehotels.com **web:** www.mackenziehotels.com
dir: *A140 from Norwich then A149 to Cromer, B1159 to Overstrand. Hotel in village centre*

An elegant Grade II listed Edwardian mansion perched on the clifftop amidst pretty landscaped gardens which lead down to the beach. Bedrooms are tastefully decorated and thoughtfully equipped; many have superb sea views. Public rooms offer a wide choice of areas in which to relax, including Frazer's restaurant and a smart lounge bar.

Rooms: 25 (6 annexe) (6 family) (3 GF) **Facilities:** FTV WiFi Xmas New Year **Conf:** Class 55 Board 30 Thtr 70 **Services:** Lift **Parking:** 50 **Notes:** LB

The Cliftonville Hotel
★★★ 78% HOTEL

Seafront, NR27 9AS - tel: 01263 512543
email: reservations@cliftonvillehotel.co.uk **web:** www.cliftonvillehotel.co.uk
dir: *From A149 (coast road) 500yds from town centre, N'bound on clifftop by sunken gardens*

The Cliftonville Hotel is an imposing Edwardian hotel situated on the main coast road with stunning views of the sea. Public areas feature a magnificent staircase, minstrels' gallery, coffee shop, lounge bar, a further residents' lounge, Boltons Bistro and an additional restaurant. The pleasantly decorated bedrooms are generally quite spacious and have lovely sea views.

Rooms: 30 (3 family) S £65–£100; D £130–£210 (incl. bkfst)* **Facilities:** FTV WiFi Xmas New Year **Conf:** Class 100 Board 60 Thtr 150 Del from £115 **Services:** Lift Night porter **Parking:** 20 **Notes:** LB

Hotel de Paris

★★★ 71% HOTEL

High Street, NR27 9HG - tel: 01263 513141
email: deparis.cromer@alfatravel.co.uk **web:** www.leisureplex.co.uk
dir: *Enter Church St (one way) after lights left straight into Jetty St, car park at end on left*

An imposing, traditional-style resort hotel, situated in a prominent position overlooking the pier and beach. The bedrooms are pleasantly decorated and equipped with a good range of useful extras; many rooms have lovely sea views. The spacious public areas include a large lounge bar, restaurant, games room and a further lounge.

Rooms: 67 (8 family) (4 GF) **Facilities:** FTV WiFi Xmas New Year **Services:** Lift Night porter **Parking:** 14 **Notes:** Closed Jan–Feb RS Mar & Nov–Dec closed some weekends

CROOKLANDS Cumbria — Map 18 SD58

Crooklands Hotel
★★★ 79% HOTEL

LA7 7NW - tel: 015395 67432
email: reception@crooklands.com **web:** www.crooklands.com
dir: *M6 junct 36 onto A65. Left at rdbt. Hotel 1.5m on right past garage*

Although only a stone's throw from the M6, this hotel enjoys a peaceful rural location. Housed in a converted 200-year-old farmhouse, the restaurant retains many original features such as the beams and stone walls. Bedrooms are a mix of modern and traditional and vary in size. The hotel is a popular stop-over for both leisure and corporate guests travelling between England and Scotland.

Rooms: 30 (1 family) (14 GF) S £75–£95; D £110–£125 (incl. bkfst)* **Facilities:** FTV WiFi New Year **Conf:** Class 50 Board 40 Thtr 80 Del from £135 **Services:** Lift **Parking:** 80 **Notes:** LB Closed 24-28 Feb

CROYDON Greater London — Map 6 TQ36

Hallmark Hotel London Croydon Aerodrome
★★★★ 74% HOTEL

Purley Way, CR9 4LT - tel: 0330 028 3403
email: admin@hallmarkhotels.co.uk **web:** www.hallmarkhotels.co.uk
dir: *Follow A23 & Central London signs. Hotel on left adjacent to Airport House*

This hotel (formerly the Aerodrome Hotel) sits in a prime location and offers comfortably appointed bedrooms, all with LCD TVs and free WiFi throughout. Public areas are stylish and modern in their design and include a spacious open-plan bar and brasserie. Ideal for both the leisure and corporate market, there are a number of fully-equipped meeting and conference facilities.

Rooms: 110 (10 family) **Facilities:** FTV WiFi **Conf:** Class 60 Board 36 Thtr 170 **Services:** Lift Night porter Air con **Parking:** 79 **Notes:** Civ Wed 150

CROYDON *continued*

De Vere Selsdon Estate

PRINCIPAL EST. 1898 HOTEL COMPANY LTD

★★★★ 73% HOTEL

Addington Road, Sanderstead, CR2 8YA - **tel:** 020 8657 8811
email: SelsdonReservations@devere.com
web: www.phcompany.com/de-vere/selsdon-estate
dir: *3m SE of Croydon, off A2022*

Surrounded by 200 acres of mature parkland with its own 18-hole golf course, this imposing Jacobean mansion is less than 20 minutes from central London. The hotel's impressive range of conference rooms along with the spectacular views of the North Downs countryside, make this a popular venue for both weddings and meetings. The leisure facilities are impressive.

Rooms: 199 (19 family) (33 GF) ✿ **Facilities:** Spa FTV WiFi ☼ HL ☺ ⚡ 18 Putting green ☺ ☜ Gym Squash Xmas **Conf:** Class 250 Board 100 Thtr 350 **Services:** Lift Night porter **Parking:** 300 **Notes:** Civ Wed 350

Croydon Park Hotel

★★★★ 71% HOTEL

7 Altyre Road, CR9 5AA - **tel:** 020 8680 9200
email: info@croydonparkhotel.com **web:** www.croydonparkhotel.com
dir: *3 min walk from East Croydon Station*

This hotel is located in the heart of the town centre, a 3-minute walk from East Croydon train station and with easy access to both Gatwick Airport and central London. Bedrooms vary in style, but all are comfortably appointed. The two dining options are Whistlers Bar with a menu available throughout the day, and Oscars Brasserie with a daily buffet and carte menu. Conference and leisure facilities are available.

Rooms: 211 (36 family) (6 GF) **S** £59–£259; **D** £59–£259* **Facilities:** FTV WiFi ☼ ☺ Gym Squash Sauna Xmas New Year **Conf:** Class 100 Board 30 Thtr 220 **Services:** Lift Night porter Air con **Parking:** 91 **Notes:** Civ Wed 220

Holiday Inn Express London - Croydon

BUDGET HOTEL

1 Priddys Yard, Off Frith Road, CR0 1TS - **tel:** 020 8253 1200
email: gm@exhicroydon.com **web:** www.hiexpress.com/london-croydon
dir: *From A235 into Lower Coombe St, at rdbt 1st exit, at next rdbt 2nd exit onto dual carriageway, right to Centrale Shopping Centre, under car park, follow to right, 1st left*

A modern hotel ideal for families and business travellers. Fresh and uncomplicated, the spacious rooms include Sky TV, power shower and tea and coffee-making facilities. Continental buffet breakfast is included in the room rate; other meals may be taken at the nearby family pub or restaurant.

Rooms: 156 (62 family) ✿ **Conf:** Class 30 Board 30 Thtr 60

Premier Inn Croydon (Purley A23)

BUDGET HOTEL

The Colonnades Leisure Park, 619 Purley Way, CR0 4RQ - **tel:** 0871 527 8282 (Calls cost 13p per minute plus your phone company's access charge)
web: www.premierinn.com
dir: *From N: M1, M25, A23 towards Croydon. From S: M25 junct 7, A23 towards Purley Way, 8m, hotel close to junct with Waddon Way*

High quality, budget accommodation ideal for both families and business travellers. Spacious, en suite bedrooms feature tea and coffee making facilities, Freeview TV in most hotels and free WiFi. The adjacent family restaurant features a wide and varied menu.

Rooms: 84

Premier Inn Croydon South (A212)

BUDGET HOTEL

104 Coombe Road, CR0 5RB - **tel:** 0871 527 8280 (Calls cost 13p per minute plus your phone company's access charge) **web:** www.premierinn.com
dir: *M25 junct 7, A23 to Purley, A235 to Croydon. Pass Tree House pub on left. Right at lights onto A212*

Rooms: 39

Premier Inn London Croydon Town Centre Hotel

BUDGET HOTEL

Philips House, Lansdowne Road, CR0 2BX - **tel:** 0871 527 9438 (Calls cost 13p per minute plus your phone company's access charge) **web:** www.premierinn.com
dir: *Phone for directions*

Rooms: 168

CULLOMPTON	Map 3 ST00
Devon	

Padbrook Park

★★★ 79% HOTEL

EX15 1RU - **tel:** 01884 836100
email: info@padbrookpark.co.uk **web:** www.padbrookpark.co.uk
dir: *1m from M5 junct 28, follow brown signs*

This purpose-built hotel and leisure complex is located in the Culm Valley, just one mile from the M5. Set within acres of rolling parkland with a popular FootGolf course for those looking to try out this new and expanding sport. Padbrook Park has a friendly, relaxed atmosphere and a contemporary feel. A variety of room types is available, including family, inter-connecting, superior and deluxe rooms.

Rooms: 40 (4 family) (11 GF) ✿ **S** £65–£95; **D** £85–£120 **Facilities:** STV FTV WiFi ☼ HL Putting green Fishing Gym 3 rink bowling centre Crazy golf Beauty treatment room Hairdressing salon ♫ Xmas New Year **Conf:** Class 150 Board 50 Thtr 200 **Services:** Lift Night porter **Parking:** 250 **Notes:** LB Civ Wed 200

D

DAGENHAM
Greater London
Map 6 TQ48

Premier Inn London Dagenham

BUDGET HOTEL

Chequers Corner, 2 New Road, RM9 6YS - **tel:** 0871 527 9364 (Calls cost 13p per minute plus your phone company's access charge) **web:** www.premierinn.com
dir: *M25 junct 30/A13 signed Barking. Continue on A13 through underpass then flyover, following directions to Central London, Barking & Docklands. Left off A13 - Dagenham East. At rdbt 4th exit, then left at traffic signals onto A1306 Dagenham. Continue at traffic signals. Inn on left*

High quality, budget accommodation ideal for both families and business travellers. Spacious, en suite bedrooms feature tea and coffee making facilities, Freeview TV in most hotels and free WiFi. The adjacent family restaurant features a wide and varied menu.

Rooms: 80

DARLINGTON
County Durham
Map 19 NZ21

INSPECTOR'S CHOICE

Rockliffe Hall
★★★★★ ◉◉◉◉ HOTEL

Rockliffe Park, Hurworth-on-Tees, DL2 2DU - **tel:** 01325 729999
email: enquiries@rockliffehall.com **web:** www.rockliffehall.com
dir: *A66 towards Darlington, A167, through Hurworth-on-Tees. In Croft-on-Tees left into Hurworth Rd*

This impressive hotel enjoys a peaceful setting on a restored 18th-century estate by the banks of the River Tees. Luxurious, spacious bedrooms, contemporary in style, are split between the original old hall, the new hall and Tiplady Lodge. Dining options include The Orangery, The Clubhouse and The Brasserie. A state-of-the-art spa and championship golf course, with a first-class club house, complete the picture.

Rooms: 61 (5 family) (17 GF) ❦ **S** £165–£515; **D** £205–£550 (incl. bkfst)
Facilities: Spa STV FTV WiFi ⊹ ⊛ ➘ ⅃ 18 Putting green ⚲ Fishing ⛳ Gym Nordic walking Maze ♫ Xmas New Year Child facilities **Conf:** Class 100 Board 30 Thtr 180 Del from £270 **Services:** Lift Night porter Air con **Parking:** 200 **Notes:** LB Civ Wed 180

Headlam Hall
★★★★ 82% ◉◉ HOTEL

Headlam, Gainford, DL2 3HA - **tel:** 01325 730238
email: admin@headlamhall.co.uk **web:** www.headlamhall.co.uk
dir: *2m N of A67 between Piercebridge & Gainford*

This impressive Jacobean hall lies in farmland north-east of Piercebridge and has its own 9-hole golf course. The main house retains many historical features, including flagstone floors and a pillared hall. Bedrooms are well proportioned and traditionally styled; a converted coach house contains the more modern rooms. There are extensive conference facilities, and the hotel is popular as a wedding venue. Further facilities include a stunning spa complex with a 14-metre pool, an outdoor hot spa, drench shower, sauna and steam room, as well as a gym with the latest cardio and resistance equipment, and five treatment rooms offering a range of therapies and beauty treatments.

Rooms: 38 (22 annexe) (4 family) (9 GF) ❦ **S** £110–£200; **D** £140–£230 (incl. bkfst)* **Facilities:** Spa STV FTV WiFi ⊹ ⊛ ⅃ 9 Putting green ⚲ Fishing ⛳ Gym New Year **Conf:** Class 40 Board 40 Thtr 120 Del from £145 **Services:** Lift Night porter **Parking:** 80 **Notes:** LB Closed 24-26 Dec Civ Wed 150

Hall Garth Hotel, Golf and Country Club
★★★ 81% HOTEL

Coatham Mundeville, DL1 3LU - **tel:** 01325 300400
email: gm@hallgarthdarlington.co.uk **web:** www.hallgarthdarlington.co.uk
dir: *A1(M) junct 59, A167 towards Darlington. After 600yds left at top of hill, hotel on right*

Peacefully situated in grounds that feature a golf course, this hotel is just a few minutes from the motorway network. The well-equipped bedrooms come in various styles - it's worth asking for one of the modern rooms. Public rooms include relaxing lounges, a fine-dining restaurant and a separate pub. The extensive leisure and conference facilities are an important focus here.

Rooms: 56 (16 annexe) (3 family) (1 GF) **S** £55–£149; **D** £65–£159 (incl. bkfst)*
Facilities: Spa STV FTV WiFi ⊹ ⊛ supervised ⅃ 9 Putting green Gym Steam room Beauty salon Sauna Xmas New Year **Conf:** Class 160 Board 80 Thtr 250 Del from £115 **Services:** Night porter **Parking:** 150 **Notes:** LB Civ Wed 170

Best Western Walworth Castle Hotel
★★★ 75% HOTEL

Best Western.

Walworth, DL2 2LY - **tel:** 01325 485470
email: enquiries@walworthcastle.co.uk **web:** www.bw-walworthcastle.co.uk
dir: *A1(M) junct 58 follow signs to Corbridge. Left at The Dog pub. Hotel on left after 2m*

This 12th-century castle is privately owned and has been tastefully converted. Accommodation is offered in a range of styles, including an impressive suite and more compact rooms in an adjoining wing. Dinner can be taken in the fine dining Hansards Restaurant or the more relaxed Farmer's Bar. This is a popular venue for conferences and weddings, and there is also a falconry in the grounds.

Rooms: 32 (14 annexe) (4 family) (8 GF) ❦ **Facilities:** FTV WiFi ⊹ ⛳ Falconry centre Xmas New Year **Conf:** Class 60 Board 40 Thtr 120 **Services:** Night porter **Parking:** 100 **Notes:** Civ Wed 100

DARLINGTON *continued*

Premier Inn Darlington

BUDGET HOTEL

Morton Park Way, Morton Park, DL1 4PJ - **tel:** 0871 527 8286 (Calls cost 13p per minute plus your phone company's access charge) **web:** www.premierinn.com
dir: *A1(M) junct 57, A66(M), A66 towards Teeside. At 3rd rdbt left onto B6280. Hotel on right. From N: A1(M) junct 57 onto A167, A1150, A66 towards Darlington, right onto B6280. Hotel on right*

High quality, budget accommodation ideal for both families and business travellers. Spacious, en suite bedrooms feature tea and coffee making facilities, Freeview TV in most hotels and free WiFi. The adjacent family restaurant features a wide and varied menu.

Rooms: 79

Premier Inn Darlington Town Centre

BUDGET HOTEL

Unit 3, Feethams Leisure, Feethams, DL1 5AD - **tel:** 0871 527 9650 (Calls cost 13p per minute plus your phone company's access charge) **web:** www.premierinn.com
dir: *Phone for directions*

Rooms: 80

DARTFORD	Map 6 TQ57
Kent	

HIGHLY RECOMMENDED

Rowhill Grange Hotel & Utopia Spa

★★★★ 83% ◎◎ HOTEL

Wilmington, DA2 7QH - **tel:** 01322 615136
email: admin@rowhillgrange.co.uk **web:** www.rowhillgrange.co.uk
dir: *M25 junct 3 take B2173 to Swanley, then B258 to Hextable*

Set in nine acres of mature woodland this hotel enjoys a tranquil setting, yet is still easily accessible to road networks. Bedrooms are stylishly and individually decorated; many have four-poster or sleigh beds. The elegant lounge is popular for afternoon teas, and the leisure and conference facilities are impressive. There is a smart, conservatory restaurant and also a more informal brasserie.

Rooms: 38 (8 annexe) (4 family) (3 GF) ✆ **S** fr £115; **D** fr £115* **Facilities:** Spa STV FTV WiFi ▷ ✿ Gym Beauty treatment Hair salon Aerobic studio Japanese therapy pool Xmas New Year **Conf:** Class 64 Board 34 Thtr 160 Del from £165 **Services:** Lift Night porter **Parking:** 150 **Notes:** Civ Wed 150

Premier Inn Dartford

BUDGET HOTEL

Halcrow Avenue, DA1 5FX - **tel:** 0871 527 9328 (Calls cost 13p per minute plus your phone company's access charge) **web:** www.premierinn.com
dir: *M25 junct 1A , A206 towards Erith. At next rdbt right to Bridge Business Park. At next rdbt left towards Power Station. Hotel 300yds on left*

High quality, budget accommodation ideal for both families and business travellers. Spacious, en suite bedrooms feature tea and coffee making facilities, Freeview TV in most hotels and free WiFi. The adjacent family restaurant features a wide and varied menu.

Rooms: 120

DARTMOUTH	Map3 SX85
Devon	

The Dart Marina Hotel

★★★★ 80% ◎ HOTEL

Sandquay Road, TQ6 9PH - **tel:** 01803 832580
email: reservations@dartmarina.com **web:** www.dartmarina.com
dir: *A3122 from Totnes to Dartmouth. Follow road which becomes College Way, before Higher Ferry. Hotel sharp left in Sandquay Road*

Boasting a stunning riverside location with its own marina, this is a very special place to stay. Bedrooms vary in style, all have wonderful views, and some have private balconies where you can sit and soak up the atmosphere. The stylish public areas take full advantage of the waterside setting with opportunities to dine alfresco. The River Restaurant is the venue for accomplished cooking.

Rooms: 49 (4 annexe) (4 family) (4 GF) ✆ **S** £115–£155; **D** £180–£450 (incl. bkfst)* **Facilities:** Spa FTV WiFi ✿ Gym Xmas New Year **Services:** Lift Night porter **Parking:** 50 **Notes:** LB

Royal Castle Hotel

★★★ 82% ◎ HOTEL

11 The Quay, TQ6 9PS - **tel:** 01803 833033
email: enquiry@royalcastle.co.uk **web:** www.royalcastle.co.uk
dir: *In centre of town, overlooking Inner Harbour*

At the edge of the harbour, this imposing 17th-century former coaching inn is filled with charm and character. Bedrooms are well equipped and comfortable, and many have harbour views. A choice of quiet seating areas is offered in addition to both the traditional and contemporary bars. A variety of eating options is available, including the main restaurant which has lovely views.

Rooms: 24 (3 family) ✆ **S** £95–£130; **D** £125–£245 (incl. bkfst)* **Facilities:** FTV WiFi ▷ ♫ Xmas New Year **Conf:** Class 30 Board 20 Thtr 50 **Services:** Night porter **Parking:** 15 **Notes:** Civ Wed 80

D

DAVENTRY
Northamptonshire · Map 11 SP56

Fawsley Hall Hotel & Spa
★★★★ ◉◉ 🅢 HOTEL

Fawsley, NN11 3BA - tel: 01327 892000 & 0845 072 7482 (Calls cost 5p per minute plus your phone company's access charge)
email: reservations.fawsley@handpicked.co.uk
web: www.handpickedhotels.co.uk/fawsleyhall
dir: A361 south of Daventry, between Badby and Charwelton, hotel signed single track lane

Dating back to the 15th century, this delightful hotel is peacefully located in beautiful parkland designed by 'Capability' Brown. Spacious, individually designed bedrooms and stylish public areas are beautifully furnished with antique and period pieces. The different wings of the house - Tudor, Georgian and Victorian - all have their distinct identity. For a true sense of the past, why not stay in the Queen's Suite, where Elizabeth I slept in 1575. Afternoon tea is served in the impressive Great Hall, Tudor Bar and Lounge and dinner is available in the award-winning Cedar Restaurant, with its original beams and stonework, an impressive inglenook fireplace, and candlelit tables dressed in fine white linen. The hotel has its own cinema and The Grayshot Spa features an ozone pool, treatment rooms and fitness studio.

Rooms: 60 (14 annexe) (3 family) (2 GF) 🌰 **Facilities:** Spa STV WiFi HL 🔁 🌲 ⛲ Gym Health and beauty treatment rooms Fitness studio 29-seat cinema Xmas New Year **Conf:** Class 64 Board 40 Thtr 120 Del from £174 **Services:** Night porter **Parking:** 140 **Notes:** Civ Wed 120

Mercure Daventry Court Hotel
★★★★ 75% HOTEL

Sedgemoor Way, NN11 0SG - tel: 01327 307000
email: HA010@accor.com **web:** www.themercure.com/Daventrycourt
dir: M1 junct 16, A45 to Daventry, at 1st rdbt turn right signed Kilsby/M1(N). Hotel on right in 1m

This modern, striking hotel overlooking Drayton Water boasts spacious public areas that include a good range of banqueting, meeting and leisure facilities. It is a popular venue for conferences. Bedrooms are suitable for both business and leisure guests.

Rooms: 155 (17 family) 🌰 **Facilities:** Spa FTV WiFi HL 🔁 supervised Gym Steam room Sauna Health & beauty salon New Year **Conf:** Class 200 Board 100 Thtr 600 **Services:** Lift Night porter **Parking:** 350 **Notes:** Civ Wed 280

DAWLISH
Devon · Map 3 SX97

Langstone Cliff Hotel
★★★ 81% HOTEL

Dawlish Warren, EX7 0NA - tel: 01626 868000
email: reception@langstone-hotel.co.uk **web:** www.langstone-hotel.co.uk
dir: 1.5m NE off A379 – Exeter Road to Dawlish Warren

A family-owned and run hotel, the Langstone Cliff Hotel offers a range of leisure, conference and function facilities. Bedrooms, many with sea views and balconies, are spacious, comfortable and well equipped. The hotel has a number of attractive lounges and a well-stocked bar. Dinner is served, often carvery style, in the restaurant.

Rooms: 64 (2 annexe) (19 family) (1 GF) 🌰 **S** fr £29; **D** fr £65 (incl. bkfst)*
Facilities: STV FTV WiFi ⚐ HL 🔁 🌲 Putting green ⛲ Gym Table tennis Golf practice area Hair and beauty salon Treatment room Therapy room Ballroom Xmas New Year Child facilities **Conf:** Class 200 Board 80 Thtr 400 Del from £80 **Services:** Lift Night porter **Parking:** 200 **Notes:** LB Civ Wed 400

DEAL
Kent · Map 7 TR35

Dunkerleys Hotel & Restaurant
★★★ 78% ◉◉ HOTEL

19 Beach Street, CT14 7AH - tel: 01304 375016
email: info@dunkerleys.co.uk **web:** www.dunkerleys.co.uk
dir: From M20 or M2 follow signs for A258 Deal. Hotel close to Pier

Dunkersley Hotel is centrally located and is also on the seafront. Bedrooms are furnished to a high standard with a good range of amenities. The restaurant and bar offer a comfortable and attractive environment in which to relax and to enjoy the cuisine that makes the best use of local ingredients. Service throughout is friendly and attentive.

Rooms: 16 (2 family) **S** £50–£110; **D** £80–£150 (incl. bkfst)* **Facilities:** FTV WiFi Xmas New Year **Services:** Night porter **Notes:** LB RS Sun eve & Mon A la carte restaurant closed

D

DEDDINGTON
Oxfordshire — Map 11 SP43

Deddington Arms
★★★ 77% HOTEL

Horsefair, OX15 0SH - **tel:** 01869 338364
email: deddarms@oxfordshire-hotels.co.uk **web:** www.oxfordshire-hotels.co.uk
dir: *From S: M40 junct 10/A43. 1st rdbt left to Aynho B4100 & left to Deddington B4031. From N: M40 junct 11 to hospital & Adderbury on A4260, then to Deddington*

This charming and friendly old inn is conveniently located off the market square. The well-equipped bedrooms are comfortably appointed and situated either in the main building or a purpose-built courtyard wing. The bar is full of character, and the delightful restaurant enjoys a well-deserved reputation locally.

Rooms: 27 (4 family) (10 GF) **S** £70–£120; **D** £75–£180 (incl. bkfst)* **Facilities:** FTV WiFi ♬ Xmas New Year **Conf:** Class 20 Board 25 Thtr 40 Del from £135 **Parking:** 36 **Notes:** LB

DEDHAM
Essex — Map 13 TM03

INSPECTOR'S CHOICE

Maison Talbooth
★★★ ❀❀ COUNTRY HOUSE HOTEL

Stratford Road, CO7 6HN - **tel:** 01206 322367
email: maison@milsomhotels.co.uk **web:** www.milsomhotels.com/maisontalbooth
dir: *A12 towards Ipswich, 1st turn signed Dedham, follow to left bend, turn right. Hotel 1m on right*

Warm hospitality and quality service are to be expected at this Victorian country house hotel, situated in a peaceful rural location amid pretty landscaped grounds overlooking the Stour River Valley. Public areas include a comfortable drawing room where guests may take afternoon tea or snacks. Residents are chauffeured to the popular Le Talbooth Restaurant just a mile away for dinner.

The spacious bedrooms are individually decorated and tastefully furnished with lovely co-ordinated fabrics and many thoughtful touches.

Maison Talbooth

Rooms: 12 (1 family) (5 GF) ♞ **D** £260–£475 (incl. bkfst)* **Facilities:** Spa STV WiFi ⚘ ☻ ⛳ Xmas **Conf:** Class 20 Board 16 Thtr 30 **Parking:** 40 **Notes:** LB Civ Wed 50

milsoms
★★★ 83% ❀ SMALL HOTEL

Stratford Road, CO7 6HN - **tel:** 01206 322795
email: milsoms@milsomhotels.com **web:** www.milsomhotels.com/milsoms
dir: *6m N of Colchester off A12, follow Stratford St Mary/Dedham signs. Turn right over A12, hotel on left*

Situated in the Dedham Vale, an Area of Outstanding Natural Beauty, milsoms is the perfect base to explore the countryside on the Essex/Suffolk border. This small hotel is styled along the lines of a contemporary 'gastro bar' combining good food served in an informal atmosphere, with stylish and well-appointed accommodation.

Rooms: 15 (3 family) (4 GF) **D** £125–£160 (incl. bkfst)* **Facilities:** STV WiFi Use of spa at nearby sister hotel Maison Talbooth Xmas **Conf:** Board 24 **Services:** Night porter **Parking:** 90

DELPH
Greater Manchester   Map 16 SD90

The Saddleworth Hotel
★★★★ 82% @ COUNTRY HOUSE HOTEL

Huddersfield Road, OL3 5LX - **tel:** 01457 871888
email: enquiries@thesaddleworthhotel.co.uk **web:** www.thesaddleworthhotel.co.uk
dir: *M62 junct 21, A640 towards Huddersfield. At Junction Inn take A6052 towards Delph; at White Lion left onto unclassified road; in 0.5m left on A62 towards Huddersfield. Hotel 0.5m on right*

Situated in nine acres of landscaped gardens and woodlands in the Castleshaw Valley, this lovingly restored 17th-century building, once a coaching station, has stunning views. The hotel offers comfort and opulence together with a team of staff who provide delightful customer care. Antique pieces have been acquired from far and wide, and no expense has been spared to provide guests with the latest up-to-date facilities. The restaurant, with black table linen and crystal glassware, offers an award-winning, fashionably understated, modern European menu.

Rooms: 16 (8 annexe) (4 family) (4 GF) **S** £80–£110; **D** £150–£170* **Facilities:** FTV WiFi ₰ ⚲ Gym Xmas New Year **Conf:** Class 40 Board 40 Thtr 150 **Parking:** 140
Notes: LB Civ Wed 250

DERBY
Derbyshire   Map 11 SK33
See also **Morley**

Hallmark Hotel Derby Mickleover Court
★★★★ 76% HOTEL

Etwall Road, Mickleover, DE3 0XX - **tel:** 0330 028 3404
email: mickleover@hallmarkhotels.co.uk **web:** www.hallmarkhotels.co.uk
dir: *A50 towards Derby, exit at junction 5. A516 towards Derby, take exit signed Mickleover*

Located close to Derby, this modern hotel is well suited to both the conference and leisure markets. Bedrooms are spacious, air conditioned, well equipped and include some smart executive rooms and suites. The well presented leisure facilities are amongst the best in the region.

Rooms: 99 (20 family) (5 smoking) ₰ **D** £49–£180* **Facilities:** STV FTV WiFi ₰ ⊛ Gym Beauty salon Steam room Xmas New Year **Conf:** Class 106 Board 45 Thtr 200 **Services:** Lift Night porter Air con **Parking:** 225 **Notes:** LB Civ Wed 200

Hallmark Hotel Derby Midland
★★★★ 74% HOTEL

Midland Road, DE1 2SQ - **tel:** 0330 028 3405
email: derby@hallmarkhotels.co.uk **web:** www.hallmarkhotels.co.uk
dir: *Opposite rail station*

This early Victorian hotel situated opposite Derby Midland Station provides very comfortable accommodation. The executive rooms are ideal for business travellers as they are equipped with writing desks and high speed internet access. Public rooms include a comfortable lounge and a popular restaurant. Service is skilled, attentive and friendly. There is also a walled garden and private parking.

Rooms: 102 (6 family) **Facilities:** FTV WiFi ♫ Xmas New Year **Conf:** Class 50 Board 35 Thtr 150 **Services:** Lift Night porter **Parking:** 70 **Notes:** Civ Wed 150

Hallmark Inn Derby
★★★ 66% METRO HOTEL

Midland Road, DE1 2SL - **tel:** 0330 028 3405
email: derbyinn@hallmarkhotels.co.uk **web:** www.hallmarkhotels.co.uk
dir: *City centre, adjacent to railway station*

This is a contemporary hotel, offering quality accommodation plus a lounge bar, free WiFi and free parking. Situated just 100 metres from the railway station and not far from the city centre.

Rooms: 87 (24 family) **S** £55–£100; **D** £65–£150* **Facilities:** FTV WiFi **Conf:** Class 20 Board 30 Thtr 60 Del from £99 **Services:** Lift Night porter **Parking:** 90

Premier Inn Derby City Centre
BUDGET HOTEL

Cathedral Quarter, Full Street, DE1 3AF - **tel:** 0871 527 9638 (Calls cost 13p per minute plus your phone company's access charge) **web:** www.premierinn.com
dir: *From N: M1 junct 25, A52. 10m, 2nd exit at rdbt into Eastgate. In 0.6m, exit for Irongate, left into Queens St, left into Full St. From S: From A38 onto A516 (M1 South/Nottingham). 2nd exit at rdbt into Uttoxeter New Rd. 1.4m, 2nd exit at rdbt into Stafford St, right into Cathedral Rd, then Full St*

High quality, budget accommodation ideal for both families and business travellers. Spacious, en suite bedrooms feature free WiFi and tea and coffee making facilities, and in most hotels, Freeview TV is also available. The adjacent family restaurant features a wide and varied menu.

Rooms: 118

Premier Inn Derby East
BUDGET HOTEL

The Wyvern, Stanier Way, DE21 6BF - **tel:** 0871 527 8292 (Calls cost 13p per minute plus your phone company's access charge) **web:** www.premierinn.com
dir: *M1 junct 25, A52 towards Derby. After 6.5m exit for Wyvern/Pride Park. 1st exit at rdbt (A52 Nottingham), straight on at next rdbt. Hotel on left*

Rooms: 108

Premier Inn Derby North West
BUDGET HOTEL

95 Ashbourne Road, Mackworth, DE22 4LZ - **tel:** 0871 527 8294 (Calls cost 13p per minute plus your phone company's access charge) **web:** www.premierinn.com
dir: *Exit M1 junct 25 onto A52 towards Derby. At Pentagon Island straight ahead towards city centre. Follow A52/Ashbourne signs into Mackworth*

Rooms: 22

Premier Inn Derby South
BUDGET HOTEL

Foresters Leisure Park, Osmaston Park Road, DE23 8AG - **tel:** 0871 527 8296 (Calls cost 13p per minute plus your phone company's access charge) **web:** www.premierinn.com
dir: *M1 junct 24, A6 towards Derby. Left onto A5111 (ring road), hotel in 2m*

Rooms: 51

DERBY *continued*

Premier Inn Derby West

BUDGET HOTEL

Manor Park Way, Uttoxeter New Road, DE22 3HN - **tel:** 0871 527 8298 (Calls cost 13p per minute plus your phone company's access charge) **web:** www.premierinn.com
dir: *M1 junct 25, A38 W towards Burton upon Trent (approx 15m). Left at island (city hospital), right at lights, 3rd exit at city hospital island*

Rooms: 86

DERBY SERVICE AREA (A50)	Map 11 SK42
Derbyshire	

Days Inn Donington - A50

AA Advertised

Welcome Break Services, A50 Westbound, DE72 2WA - **tel:** 01332 799666
email: derby.hotel@welcomebreak.co.uk **web:** www.welcomebreak.co.uk
dir: *M1 junct 24/24a, onto A50 towards Stoke/Derby. Hotel between juncts 1 & 2*

This modern building offers accommodation in smart, spacious and well-equipped bedrooms, suitable for families and business travellers, and all with en suite bathrooms. Continental breakfast is available and other refreshments may be taken at the nearby family restaurant.

Rooms: 47 (38 family) (17 GF) (9 smoking) **Facilities:** FTV WiFi ⌨ **Conf:** Class 20 Board 40 Thtr 40 **Parking:** 80

DIDCOT	Map 5 SU59
Oxfordshire	

Premier Inn Oxford South (Didcot)

BUDGET HOTEL

Milton Heights, Milton, OX14 4TX - **tel:** 0871 527 8868 (Calls cost 13p per minute plus your phone company's access charge) **web:** www.premierinn.com
dir: *On A4130. Just off A34 at Milton interchange, between Oxford & Newbury*

High quality, budget accommodation ideal for both families and business travellers. Spacious, en suite bedrooms feature free WiFi and tea and coffee making facilities, and in most hotels, Freeview TV is also available. The adjacent family restaurant features a wide and varied menu.

Rooms: 135

DONCASTER	Map 16 SE50
South Yorkshire	

Best Western Premier Mount Pleasant Hotel

★★★★ 78% HOTEL

Great North Rd DN11 0HW - **tel:** 01302 868696
email: reception@mountpleasant.co.uk **web:** www.mountpleasant.co.uk

(For full entry see Rossington)

Premier Inn Doncaster Central East

BUDGET HOTEL

Doncaster Leisure Park, Herten Way, DN4 7NW - **tel:** 0871 527 8304 (Calls cost 13p per minute plus your phone company's access charge) **web:** www.premierinn.com
dir: *M18 junct 3, signed Doncaster racecourse. Left into Whiterose Way (B&Q on left). Straight on at rdbt into Wilmington Dr, right at next rdbt into Lakeside Boulevard. At next rdbt 2nd exit. Straight on at next rdbt, hotel ahead*

High quality, budget accommodation ideal for both families and business travellers. Spacious, en suite bedrooms feature free WiFi and tea and coffee making facilities, and in most hotels, Freeview TV is also available. The adjacent family restaurant features a wide and varied menu.

Rooms: 80

Premier Inn Doncaster Central (High Fishergate)

BUDGET HOTEL

High Fishergate, DN1 1QZ - **tel:** 0871 527 8302 (Calls cost 13p per minute plus your phone company's access charge) **web:** www.premierinn.com
dir: *Off A630 Church Way*

Rooms: 138

Premier Inn Doncaster (Lakeside)

BUDGET HOTEL

Wilmington Drive, Doncaster Carr, DN4 5PJ - **tel:** 0871 527 8300 (Calls cost 13p per minute plus your phone company's access charge) **web:** www.premierinn.com
dir: *M18 junct 3, A6182. Hotel near junct with access road*

Rooms: 66

DORCHESTER	Map 4 SY69
Dorset	

Best Western Wessex Royale Hotel

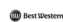

★★★ 79% HOTEL

High West Street, DT1 1UP - **tel:** 01305 262660
email: info@wessexroyalehotel.co.uk **web:** www.wessexroyalehotel.co.uk
dir: *From A35 follow town centre signs. Straight on, hotel at top of hill on left*

This centrally situated Georgian townhouse dates from 1756 and successfully combines historic charm with modern comforts. The restaurant is a relaxed venue for enjoying innovative food, and the hotel offers the benefit of a smart conservatory, ideal for functions. Limited courtyard parking is available.

Rooms: 27 (2 annexe) (3 family) (2 GF) ⌂ **S** £89–£99; **D** £99–£159 (incl. bkfst)*
Facilities: STV FTV WiFi ⌨ **Conf:** Class 40 Board 40 Thtr 80 **Services:** Night porter **Parking:** 11 **Notes:** LB Closed 23 Dec-2 Jan

Premier Inn Dorchester

BUDGET HOTEL

21 Weymouth Avene, DT1 1GA - **tel:** 0871 527 9376 (Calls cost 13p per minute plus your phone company's access charge) **web:** www.premierinn.com
dir: *On A35 follow Dorchester & Weymouth signs. At rdbt take B3150 (Stinsford Hill) left into Kings Rd. At rdbt 2nd exit into Prince of Wales Rd (B3144). Left into Weymouth Ave. Left into Brewery Sq*

High quality, budget accommodation ideal for both families and business travellers. Spacious, en suite bedrooms feature free WiFi and tea and coffee making facilities, and in most hotels, Freeview TV is also available. The adjacent family restaurant features a wide and varied menu.

Rooms: 76

DORCHESTER (ON THAMES)
Oxfordshire

Map 5 SU59

White Hart Hotel

★★★ 74% HOTEL

High Street, OX10 7HN - **tel:** 01865 340074
email: whitehart@oxfordshire-hotels.co.uk **web:** www.oxfordshire-hotels.co.uk
dir: *M40 junct 6, take B4009 through Watlington & Benson to A4074. Follow signs to Dorchester. Hotel on right*

Period charm and character are plentiful throughout this centuries old coaching inn, which is situated in the heart of a picturesque village. The spacious bedrooms are individually decorated and thoughtfully equipped. Public rooms include a cosy bar, a choice of lounges and an atmospheric restaurant, complete with vaulted timber ceiling.

Rooms: 28 (4 annexe) (2 family) (9 GF) **Facilities:** FTV WiFi Xmas New Year **Conf:** Class 20 Board 18 Thtr 30 **Parking:** 36

DORKING
Surrey

Map 6 TQ14

Mercure Boxhill Burford Bridge Hotel

★★★★ 80% HOTEL

Burford Bridge, Box Hill, RH5 6BX - **tel:** 01306 884561
email: h6635@accor.com **web:** www.mercure.com
dir: *M25 junct 9, A245 towards Dorking. Hotel approx 5m on A24*

Steeped in history, this hotel was reputedly where Lord Nelson and Lady Hamilton met for the last time, and it is said that the landscape around the hotel has inspired many poets. The hotel has a contemporary feel throughout. The grounds, running down to the River Mole, are extensive, and there are good transport links to major centres, including London. The elegant Emlyn Restaurant offers a modern award-winning menu.

Rooms: 57 (22 family) (3 GF) **S** £95–£216; **D** £95–£216* **Facilities:** STV FTV WiFi supervised Xmas New Year **Conf:** Class 80 Board 60 Thtr 200 Del from £185 **Services:** Night porter Air con **Parking:** 130 **Notes:** LB Civ Wed 200

DORRIDGE
West Midlands

Map 10 SP17

Hogarths Hotel

★★★★ 84% HOTEL

Four Ashes Road, B93 8QE - **tel:** 01564 779988
email: reception@hogarths.co.uk **web:** www.hogarths.co.uk
dir: *M42 junct 4, 1st exit to A3400. Left to Gate Ln. Left onto Four Ashes Rd. Hotel 300mtrs on left*

Hogarths Hotel, with its contemporary interior design and panoramic views of the gardens from the open-plan and airy Brasserie, is a stunning property. The relaxed style of service is in keeping and effective. Bedrooms meet all modern requirements, and many have their own balcony or outside area. The young team deliver high quality and friendly service throughout. The lake area for weddings and conference events is a stunning attraction in the well-kept and managed gardens.

Rooms: 49 (5 annexe) (9 family) (15 GF) **S** £95–£120; **D** £140–£260 (incl. bkfst)* **Facilities:** FTV WiFi Putting green Gym Xmas New Year **Conf:** Class 200 Board 60 Thtr 400 **Services:** Lift Night porter **Parking:** 120 **Notes:** LB Civ Wed 270

DOVER
Kent

Map 7 TR34

Ramada Hotel Dover

★★★★ 76% HOTEL

Singledge Lane, Whitfield, CT16 3EL - **tel:** 01304 821230
email: reservations@ramadadover.co.uk **web:** www.ramadadover.co.uk
dir: *From M20 follow signs to A2 towards Canterbury. Turn right after Whitfield rdbt. From A2 towards Dover, turn left before Whitfield rdbt*

Ramada Hotel Dover is a modern purpose-built hotel situated in a quiet location between Dover and Canterbury, close to the ferry port and seaside. The open-plan public areas are contemporary in style and include a lounge, a bar and The Olive Tree Restaurant. The stylish bedrooms are simply decorated with co-ordinated soft furnishings and many thoughtful extras.

Rooms: 68 (19 family) (68 GF) **Facilities:** FTV WiFi HL Gym Xmas New Year **Conf:** Class 150 Board 40 Thtr 400 **Services:** Night porter **Parking:** 110 **Notes:** Civ Wed 80

D

DOVER continued

Best Western Plus Dover Marina Hotel & Spa

★★★★ 75% HOTEL

Dover Waterfront, CT17 9BP - tel: 01304 203633
email: reservations@dovermarinahotel.co.uk web: www.dovermarinahotel.co.uk
dir: M20 junct 13, A20 to Dover, straight on at 2 rdbts, at 3rd take 2nd exit
into Union St. Cross swing bridge, next left into Marine Pde/Waterloo Cres.
Hotel 200yds on left

An attractive terraced waterfront hotel overlooking the harbour, offering a wide
range of facilities including meeting rooms, health club, hairdresser and beauty
treatments. Some of the tastefully decorated bedrooms have balconies, some have
broadband access and many have superb sea views. Public rooms include a large,
open-plan lounge bar and a smart bistro restaurant.

Rooms: 81 (5 family) Facilities: Spa STV FTV WiFi HL Gym Sauna Xmas
New Year Conf: Class 60 Board 50 Thtr 110 Services: Lift Night porter Notes:
Civ Wed 100

Premier Inn Dover (A20)

BUDGET HOTEL

Folkestone Road, CT15 7AB - tel: 0871 527 8310 (Calls cost 13p per minute plus your
phone company's access charge) web: www.premierinn.com
dir: A20 to Dover. Through tunnel, take 2nd exit onto B2011. 1st left at rdbt.
In 1m hotel on left

High quality, budget accommodation ideal for both families and business
travellers. Spacious, en suite bedrooms feature free WiFi and tea and coffee making
facilities, and in most hotels, Freeview TV is also available. The adjacent family
restaurant features a wide and varied menu.

Rooms: 64

Premier Inn Dover Central (Eastern Ferry Terminal)

BUDGET HOTEL

Marine Court, Marine Parade, CT16 1LW - tel: 0871 527 8306 (Calls cost 13p per minute
plus your phone company's access charge) web: www.premierinn.com
dir: In town centre adjacent to ferry terminal. M20 junct 13 onto A20 for 8.2m

Rooms: 100

Premier Inn Dover East

BUDGET HOTEL

Jubilee Way, Guston Wood, CT15 5FD - tel: 0871 527 8308 (Calls cost 13p per minute
plus your phone company's access charge) web: www.premierinn.com
dir: At rdbt junct of A2 & A258

Rooms: 40

DRIFFIELD (GREAT)
East Riding of Yorkshire
Map 17 TA05

Best Western Bell Hotel

★★★ 81% HOTEL

46 Market Place, YO25 6AN - tel: 01377 256661
email: bell@bestwestern.co.uk web: www.bw-bellhotel.co.uk
dir: From A164, right at lights. Car park 50yds on left behind black railings

This 250-year-old hotel incorporates the old corn exchange and town hall. It is
furnished with antique and period pieces, and contains many items of local
historical interest. The bedrooms vary in size, but all offer modern facilities and
some have their own sitting rooms. The hotel has a relaxed and very friendly
atmosphere. In the separate leisure club there is an impressive range of facilities
including a pool, a gym, and a spa which boasts a wide range of treatments and
features a hydrotherapy pool, a saunarium, a Rasul chamber and a flotation
chamber. Spa packages and pamper days are available.

Rooms: 16 (3 GF) S £67–£92; D £77–£112* Facilities: Spa FTV WiFi Gym
Squash Elemis treatments Snooker room New Year Conf: Class 100 Board 40
Thtr 150 Services: Lift Night porter Parking: 18 Notes: LB No children 16yrs
Closed 25 Dec & 1 Jan RS 24 & 26 Dec No accommodation Civ Wed 120

DROITWICH
Worcestershire
Map 10 SO86

St Andrews Town Hotel

★★★ 80% HOTEL

St Andrews Drive, WR9 8AL - tel: 01905 779677
email: enquiries@st-andrewshotel.com web: www.st-andrewshotel.com
dir: From N: M5 junct 5, right onto A38, left onto B4065 Bromsgrove Rd, Queen St, B4090
Worcester Rd, right into St Andrews Drive. From S: M5 junct 6, left onto A4538, right onto
A38, B4090 Worcester Rd, left into St Andrews Drive after Methodist Church

Ideally located in the heart of Droitwich and only minutes from both the town
centre and motorway links, this elegant Georgian hotel is the ideal place to enjoy
a comfortable stay in attractively designed bedrooms. Classic British dishes
are served in the restaurant, with good use made of locally sourced, seasonal
ingredients. The tranquil gardens make an ideal location for weddings and
special occasions.

Rooms: 31 (4 family) (6 GF) S fr £59; D fr £79 (incl. bkfst)* Facilities: FTV WiFi
Conf: Class 50 Board 30 Thtr 150 Del from £135 Services: Night porter Parking: 60
Notes: Civ Wed 100

D

DUDLEY
West Midlands   Map 10 SO99

Premier Inn Dudley Town Centre

BUDGET HOTEL

Castlegate Business Park, Castlegate Way, DY1 4TA - tel: 0871 527 9420 (Calls cost 13p per minute plus your phone company's access charge) web: www.premierinn.com
dir: *From N: M5 junct 2, A4123 signed Dudley. At rdbt onto A4123. 4th exit into Wolverhampton Rd (A4123). Left into Birmingham Rd (A461). At rdbt 4th exit into Castlegate Way. At next rdbt 3rd exit*

High quality, budget accommodation ideal for both families and business travellers. Spacious, en suite bedrooms feature free WiFi and tea and coffee making facilities, and in most hotels, Freeview TV is also available. The adjacent family restaurant features a wide and varied menu.

Rooms: 63

DUMBLETON
Gloucestershire   Map 10 SP03

Dumbleton Hall Hotel

★★★ 79% COUNTRY HOUSE HOTEL

WR11 7TS - tel: 01386 881240 email: dh@pofr.co.uk web: www.dumbletonhall.co.uk
dir: *M5 junct 9/A46. 2nd exit at rdbt signed Evesham. Through Beckford for 1m, turn right signed Dumbleton. Hotel at S end of village*

Standing on the site of a 16th-century building also known as Dumbleton Hall, the current mansion, surrounded by 19 acres of landscaped gardens and parkland, was built in the mid-18th century. Panoramic views of the Vale of Evesham can be seen from every window, and the spacious public rooms make this an ideal venue for weddings, conferences or just as a hideaway retreat. The individually designed bedrooms vary in size and layout; one room is adapted for less able guests.

Rooms: 34 (9 family) Facilities: WiFi � Xmas New Year Conf: Class 60 Board 60 Thtr 100 Services: Lift Night porter Parking: 60 Notes: Civ Wed 100

DUNSTABLE
Bedfordshire   Map 11 TL02

Premier Inn Dunstable South (A5)

BUDGET HOTEL

Watling Street, Kensworth, LU6 3QP - tel: 0871 527 8332 (Calls cost 13p per minute plus your phone company's access charge) web: www.premierinn.com
dir: *M1 junct 9 towards Dunstable on A5, hotel on right after Packhorse pub*

High quality, budget accommodation ideal for both families and business travellers. Spacious, en suite bedrooms feature free WiFi and tea and coffee making facilities, and in most hotels, Freeview TV is also available. The adjacent family restaurant features a wide and varied menu.

Rooms: 40

Premier Inn Dunstable/Luton

BUDGET HOTEL

350 Luton Road, LU5 4LL - tel: 0871 527 8330 (Calls cost 13p per minute plus your phone company's access charge) web: www.premierinn.com
dir: *M1 junct 11, follow Dunstable signs. At 1st rdbt turn right. Hotel on left on A505*

Rooms: 42

DUNSTER
Somerset   Map 3 SS94

The Luttrell Arms Hotel

★★★ 81% ⊛ HOTEL

Exmoor National Park, TA24 6SG - tel: 01643 821555
email: enquiry@luttrellarms.co.uk web: www.luttrellarms.co.uk
dir: *M5 junct 24, A38 then A39 towards Minehead. Left at Dunster junct onto A396. Hotel at top of high street*

This charming and privately-owned hotel is located in the heart of the picturesque village of Dunster - right next to the famous Yarn Market. With parts dating back to the 15th century, the hotel offers plenty of character and quality throughout. Bedrooms and bathrooms offer a range of shapes and sizes including some with four-poster beds. Guests can enjoy a drink with the locals in the friendly bar or, in warmer weather, enjoy the pleasant garden to the rear. Dinner and breakfast are highlights offering a range of carefully prepared dishes utilising much local produce.

Rooms: (2 family) (4 GF) D £150-£220 (incl. bkfst)* Facilities: FTV WiFi ⎎ Xmas New Year Conf: Class 40 Board 30 Thtr 60 Services: Night porter Notes: Civ Wed 60

DURHAM
County Durham   Map 19 NZ24

HIGHLY RECOMMENDED

Ramside Hall Hotel Golf & Spa

★★★★ 84% ⊛ HOTEL

Carrville, DH1 1TD - tel: 0191 386 5282
email: mail@ramsidehallhotel.co.uk web: www.ramsidehallhotel.co.uk
dir: *A1(M) junct 62, A690 to Sunderland. Straight on at lights. 200mtrs after rail bridge turn right*

With its proximity to the motorway and delightful parkland setting, this establishment combines the best of both worlds - convenience and tranquillity. The hotel boasts two championship golf courses, a choice of lounges, several eating options including the Rib Room, specialising in steaks, and Fusion, their Asian-inspired concept. Bedrooms are furnished and decorated to a very high standard and include some stunning suites. There is also an excellent spa and leisure facility.

Rooms: 128 (10 family) (28 GF) Facilities: Spa STV FTV WiFi ⎎ ⚲ supervised ⚲ supervised ⌇ 36 Putting green Gym Steam room Sauna Hydro pool Golf academy Driving range ⎌ Xmas New Year Conf: Class 160 Board 40 Thtr 500 Services: Lift Night porter Parking: 750 Notes: Civ Wed 500

Premier Inn Durham City Centre

BUDGET HOTEL

Freemans Place, Walkergate, DH1 1SQ - tel: 0871 527 8338 (Calls cost 13p per minute plus your phone company's access charge) web: www.premierinn.com
dir: *A1(M) junct 62, A690 (Leazes Rd) towards city centre. In Durham follow Watergate signs, under bridge immediately left into Walkergate (one way). Back under A690, hotel on right*

High quality, budget accommodation ideal for both families and business travellers. Spacious, en suite bedrooms feature free WiFi and tea and coffee making facilities, and in most hotels, Freeview TV is also available. The adjacent family restaurant features a wide and varied menu.

Rooms: 103

DURHAM *continued*

Premier Inn Durham East

BUDGET HOTEL

Broomside Park, Belmont Industrial Estate, DH1 1GG - tel: 0871 527 8340 (Calls cost 13p per minute plus your phone company's access charge) **web:** www.premierinn.com
dir: *A1(M) junct 62, A690 W towards Durham. In 1m left. Hotel on left*
Rooms: 62

Premier Inn Durham North

BUDGET HOTEL

adj. Arnison Retail Centre, Pity Me, DH1 5GB - tel: 0871 527 8342 (Calls cost 13p per minute plus your phone company's access charge) **web:** www.premierinn.com
dir: *A1 junct 63, A167 to Durham. Straight on at 5 rbts, left at 6th rbt. Hotel on right after 200yds*
Rooms: 77

EAST GRINSTEAD   Map 6 TQ33
West Sussex

Premier Inn East Grinstead

BUDGET HOTEL

London Road, Felbridge, RH19 2QR - tel: 0871 527 8348 (Calls cost 13p per minute plus your phone company's access charge) **web:** www.premierinn.com
dir: *M25 junct 6. Hotel at junction of A22 & A264*

High quality, budget accommodation ideal for both families and business travellers. Spacious, en suite bedrooms feature free WiFi and tea and coffee making facilities, and in most hotels, Freeview TV is also available. The adjacent family restaurant features a wide and varied menu.

Rooms: 41

EAST HORSLEY   Map 6 TQ05
Surrey

The Thatcher's Hotel

★★★ 73% HOTEL

Guildford Road, KT24 6TB - tel: 01483 284291
email: reception@thatchershotel.co.uk **web:** www.thatchershotel.co.uk
dir: *M25 junct 10/A3 exit to London/Guildford/Kingston. At rdbt take 3rd exit onto A3 for 0.5m, turn left onto Old Lane, 2.3m turn right onto Hirsham Road, at end turn left*

This Tudor-style property sits within its own garden in the tranquil Surrey countryside, and is the ideal base for visiting Thorpe Park. The hotel offers a choice of comfortable accommodation, meeting rooms for all occasions, free parking and a well-appointed restaurant overlooking the garden. Traditional afternoon tea is served in the Club Bar, together with a range of beverages. Free WiFi is offered throughout the hotel.

Rooms: 87 (12 family) (20 GF) **Facilities:** FTV WiFi Xmas New Year **Conf:** Class 70 Board 66 Thtr 170 **Services:** Lift Night porter **Parking:** 140 **Notes:** Civ Wed 140

EAST MIDLANDS AIRPORT   Map 11 SK42
Leicestershire

Best Western Premier Yew Lodge Hotel & Spa

★★★★ 80% HOTEL

Packington Hill, DE74 2DF - tel: 01509 672518
email: info@yewlodgehotel.co.uk **web:** www.yewlodgehotel.co.uk
dir: *M1 junct 24. Follow signs to Loughborough & Kegworth on A6. On entering village, right 1st lights, hotel 400yds on right*

This smart, family-owned hotel is close to both the motorway and airport, yet is peacefully located. Modern, stylish bedrooms and public areas are thoughtfully appointed and smartly presented. The restaurant serves interesting dishes, while lounge service and extensive conference facilities are available. A very well equipped spa and leisure centre complete the picture.

Rooms: 114 (22 family) **Facilities:** Spa STV FTV WiFi HL Gym Beauty therapy suite Steam room Sauna Power plate Xmas New Year **Conf:** Class 150 Board 84 Thtr 330 **Services:** Lift Night porter **Parking:** 180 **Notes:** Civ Wed 260

Premier Inn East Midlands Airport

BUDGET HOTEL

Pegasus Business Park, Herald Way, DE74 2TQ - tel: 0871 527 8350 (Calls cost 13p per minute plus your phone company's access charge) **web:** www.premierinn.com
dir: *From S: M1 junct 23a, A453 signed to airport. From N: M1 junct 24, A456 signed to airport. Hotel on Pegasus Business Park*

High quality, budget accommodation ideal for both families and business travellers. Spacious, en suite bedrooms feature free WiFi and tea and coffee making facilities, and in most hotels, Freeview TV is also available. The adjacent family restaurant features a wide and varied menu.

Rooms: 80

EASTBOURNE   Map 6 TV69
East Sussex

The Grand Hotel

★★★★★ 86% HOTEL

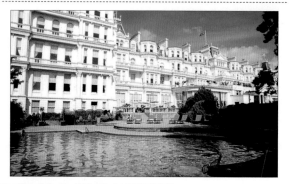

King Edwards Parade, BN21 4EQ - tel: 01323 412345
email: reservations@grandeastbourne.com
web: www.grandeastbourne.com
dir: *On seafront W of Eastbourne, 1m from railway station*

This famous Victorian hotel offers high standards of service and hospitality, and is in close proximity to both the beach and the South Downs National Park. The extensive public rooms feature a magnificent Great Hall, with marble columns

E,

and high ceilings, where guests can relax and enjoy afternoon tea. The spacious bedrooms provide high levels of comfort; many with stunning sea views and a number with private balconies. Guests can choose fine dining in The Mirabelle, or the Garden Restaurant, and there are bars as well as superb spa and leisure facilities.

The Grand Hotel

Rooms: 152 (20 family) (4 GF) ✆ **S** £120–£220; **D** £150–£250 (incl. bkfst)*
Facilities: Spa STV FTV WiFi ↳ HL ⊕ supervised ⚲ supervised Putting green Gym Snooker table ♫ Xmas New Year Child facilities **Conf:** Class 200 Board 40 Thtr 350 Del from £200 **Services:** Lift Night porter **Parking:** 80 **Notes:** LB Civ Wed 300

Langham Hotel

★★★★ 77% ⊛ HOTEL

43-49 Royal Parade, BN22 7AH - tel: 01323 731451
email: simon.brown@langhamhotel.co.uk **web:** www.langhamhotel.co.uk
dir: *Follow seafront signs. Hotel 0.5m E of pier*

This popular hotel is situated in a prominent position with superb views of the sea and pier. Bedrooms are pleasantly decorated, and equipped with modern facilities. Superior rooms, some with four-poster beds, are stylish and offer sea views. The spacious public rooms include the Grand Parade bar, a lounge and a fine dining conservatory restaurant. The hotel has 40 additional secure, charged-for parking spaces within 350 yards on Fridays, Saturdays and Sundays.

Rooms: 77 (2 family) ✆ **S** £55–£79; **D** £80–£125 (incl. bkfst)* **Facilities:** STV FTV WiFi ↳ ♫ Xmas New Year **Conf:** Class 40 Board 30 Thtr 80 Del from £100 **Services:** Lift Night porter **Parking:** 9 **Notes:** Civ Wed 120

Hydro Hotel

★★★ 83% HOTEL

Mount Road, BN20 7HZ - tel: 01323 720643
email: sales@hydrohotel.com **web:** www.hydrohotel.com
dir: *From pier/seafront, right along Grand Parade. At Grand Hotel follow Hydro Hotel sign. Into South Cliff, 200mtrs*

This well-managed and popular hotel enjoys an elevated position with views of attractive gardens and the sea beyond. The spacious bedrooms are attractive and well equipped. In addition to the comfortable lounges, guests also have access to fitness facilities and a hairdressing salon. Service is both professional and efficient throughout.

Rooms: 82 (3 family) (3 GF) ✆ **S** £80–£115; **D** £150–£250 (incl. bkfst)*
Facilities: FTV WiFi ⚲ Putting green ⚑ Beauty room Hair salon Xmas New Year **Conf:** Class 90 Board 40 Thtr 140 Del from £110 **Services:** Lift Night porter **Parking:** 40 **Notes:** LB RS 24-28 & 30-31 Dec Restricted opening to non-residents Civ Wed 120

Best Western Lansdowne Hotel

★★★ 81% HOTEL

Ⓑⓦ Best Western.

King Edward's Parade, BN21 4EE - tel: 01323 725174
email: enquiries@lansdowne-hotel.co.uk **web:** www.bw-lansdownehotel.co.uk
dir: *At W end of seafront opposite Western Lawns, 1m from railway station*

Enjoying an enviable position at the quieter end of the parade, this hotel overlooks the Western Lawns and Wish Tower, and is just a few minutes' walk from many of the town's attractions. Public rooms include a variety of lounges, a range of meeting rooms, and games rooms. Bedrooms are attractively decorated and many offer sea views. The hotel has a wheelchair lift near the front entrance that operates between the pavement and one of the ground-floor public rooms.

Rooms: 102 (10 family) ✆ **S** £75–£95; **D** £124–£184 (incl. bkfst) **Facilities:** FTV WiFi ↳ HL Table tennis Pool table 2 Snooker tables Xmas New Year **Conf:** Class 40 Board 40 Thtr 80 Del from £110 **Services:** Lift Night porter **Parking:** 22 **Notes:** LB Civ Wed 60

The Devonshire Park Hotel

★★★ 79% HOTEL

27-29 Carlisle Road, BN21 4JR - tel: 01323 728144
email: info@devonshire-park-hotel.co.uk **web:** www.devonshire-park-hotel.co.uk
dir: *Follow signs to seafront, exit at Wish Tower. Hotel opposite Congress Theatre*

A handsome family-run hotel handily placed for the seafront and theatres. Attractively furnished rooms are spacious and comfortable; many boast king-size beds and all are equipped with WiFi and satellite TV. Guests can relax in the well presented lounges, the cosy bar or, when the weather's fine, on the garden terrace.

Rooms: 35 (8 GF) ✆ **Facilities:** STV WiFi Xmas New Year **Services:** Lift Night porter **Parking:** 25 **Notes:** LB No children 12yrs

E

EASTBOURNE *continued*

New Wilmington Hotel

★★★ 79% HOTEL

25-27 Compton Street, BN21 4DU - **tel:** 01323 721219
email: info@new-wilmington-hotel.co.uk **web:** www.new-wilmington-hotel.co.uk
dir: *A22 to Eastbourne seafront. Right along promenade to Wish Tower. Right,
then left at end of road, hotel 2nd on left*

This friendly, family-run hotel is conveniently located close to the seafront,
the Congress Theatre and Winter Gardens. Public rooms are well presented and
include a cosy bar, a small comfortable lounge and a spacious restaurant.
Bedrooms are comfortably appointed and tastefully decorated; family and superior
bedrooms are available.

Rooms: 40 (14 family) (3 GF) ⬥ **Facilities:** STV FTV WiFi ⬥ ♬ Xmas New Year
Conf: Class 20 Board 20 Thtr 40 **Services:** Lift Night porter **Parking:** 3 **Notes:** LB
Closed 3 Jan-mid Feb

Queens Hotel

Leisureplex
HOLIDAY HOTELS

★★★ 72% HOTEL

Marine Parade, BN21 3DY - **tel:** 01323 722822
email: queens.eastbourne@alfatravel.co.uk **web:** www.leisureplex.co.uk
dir: *Follow signs for seafront, hotel opposite pier*

Popular with tour groups, this long-established hotel enjoys a central, prominent
seafront location overlooking the pier. Spacious public areas include a choice of
lounges, and regular entertainment is also provided. Bedrooms are suitably
appointed and equipped.

Rooms: 127 (5 family) ⬥ S £40–£67; D £64–£118 (incl. bkfst)* **Facilities:** FTV WiFi
Snooker ♬ Xmas New Year **Services:** Lift Night porter **Parking:** 50 **Notes:** LB Closed
Jan (ex New Year) RS Nov, Feb-Mar Mon-Fri

The Palm Court

★★★ 71% HOTEL

15 Burlington Place, BN21 4AR - **tel:** 01323 725811
email: thepalmcourt@btconnect.com **web:** www.thepalmcourthotel.co.uk
dir: *From pier, W along seafront, Burlington Place 5th right*

This family-run hotel is ideally situated close to the seafront and local theatres.
The well appointed public areas include the lounge, spacious bar and stylish

restaurant. Bedrooms vary in size but all offer plenty of handy accessories,
comfortable furnishings and bright modern bathrooms. Good mobility facilities
are provided.

Rooms: 38 (5 GF) ⬥ S £42–£50; D £84–£120 (incl. bkfst)* **Facilities:** FTV WiFi
Xmas New Year **Services:** Lift Night porter **Notes:** LB

Imperial Hotel

★★★ 68% HOTEL

16–32 Devonshire Place, BN21 4AH - **tel:** 01323 411043
email: info@holdsworthhotels.co.uk **web:** www.holdsworthhotels.co.uk/imperial.php
dir: *Phone for details*

The Imperial is an impressive Victorian hotel situated at the seaward end of
Devonshire Place, an imposing tree-lined boulevard, less than fifteen minutes'
walk from the facilities and amenities in the town centre, and just across the road
from the promenade and the bandstand. The hotel offers a good standard of
accommodation, spacious lounge areas, and a large restaurant offering hearty,
home-cooked food.

Rooms: 113 (1 family) (5 GF) ⬥ S fr £45; D fr £90 (incl. bkfst)* **Facilities:** FTV WiFi
♬ Xmas New Year **Services:** Lift Night porter **Notes:** LB Closed 3 Jan-8 Feb

The Big Sleep Hotel

★★★ 64% METRO HOTEL

Landsdown Terrace, King Edward Parade, BN21 4EB - **tel:** 01323 722676
email: bookings.eastbourne@thebigsleephotel.com **web:** www.thebigsleephotel.com
dir: *Phone for details*

Located on the seafront with front rooms offering relaxing views, The Big Sleep is a
new breed of establishment whose ethos is design, comfort and value for money.
There is a range of stylish rooms to choose from, and rates include a continental
buffet breakfast, with a cooked breakfast available at an extra cost. Free WiFi is
available in the recreation room, together with a pool table and other games. Sky
Sports is available in all rooms. The lounge offers a limited and well-priced menu.
The hotel also offers two contemporary meeting rooms for business meetings. Sister
properties can be found in Cheltenham and Cardiff.

Rooms: 50 (4 family) (4 GF) ⬥ S £29–£69; D £45–£125 (incl. bkfst)* **Facilities:** STV
FTV WiFi **Conf:** Class 24 Board 26 Thtr 40 **Services:** Lift Night porter

Premier Inn Eastbourne

BUDGET HOTEL

Willingdon Drive, BN23 8AL - **tel:** 0871 527 8352 (Calls cost 13p per minute plus your
phone company's access charge) **web:** www.premierinn.com
dir: *From A22 or A27 at Polegate, take bypass signed Eastbourne (A22).
Continue to Shinewater rdbt. Left towards Langney. Hotel 0.25m on left*

High quality, budget accommodation ideal for both families and business
travellers. Spacious, en suite bedrooms feature free WiFi and tea and coffee making
facilities, and in most hotels, Freeview TV is also available. The adjacent family
restaurant features a wide and varied menu.

Rooms: 47

Premier Inn Eastbourne (Polegate)

BUDGET HOTEL

Hailsham Road, Polegate, BN26 6QL - **tel:** 0871 527 8354 (Calls cost 13p per minute plus your phone company's access charge) **web:** www.premierinn.com
dir: *At rdbt junct of A22 & A27*

Rooms: 56

Premier Inn Eastbourne Town Centre

BUDGET HOTEL

Terminus Road, BN21 3DF - **tel:** 0871 527 9448 (Calls cost 13p per minute plus your phone company's access charge) **web:** www.premierinn.com
dir: *From Lewis on A27, A2270, right at lights (Polegate). At next rdbt 1st exit onto A2021 (E'bourne). At rdbt 2nd exit (All other routes). At rdbt 2nd exit onto A2040. At rdbt 1st exit (Upper Ave). At end left into Cavendish Pl (Seafront). At pier right into Grand Parade, next right into Terminus Rd*

Rooms: 65

EASTLEIGH	Map 5 SU41
Hampshire	

Premier Inn Southampton (Eastleigh)

BUDGET HOTEL

Leigh Road, SO50 9YX - **tel:** 0871 527 8994 (Calls cost 13p per minute plus your phone company's access charge) **web:** www.premierinn.com
dir: *M3 junct 13, A335 towards Eastleigh. Hotel on right*

High quality, budget accommodation ideal for both families and business travellers. Spacious, en suite bedrooms feature free WiFi and tea and coffee making facilities, and in most hotels, Freeview TV is also available. The adjacent family restaurant features a wide and varied menu.

Rooms: 80

EDENBRIDGE	Map 6 TQ44
Kent	

Best Western Plus Hever Hotel

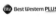

★★★ 79% HOTEL

Hever Road, TN8 7NP - **tel:** 01732 700700
email: reception@heverhotel.co.uk **web:** www.heverhotel.co.uk
dir: *Exit M25 junct 5/6, follow tourist signs for Hever Castle. Hotel 1m north*

Convenient for Gatwick and the M5, located in the vicinity of Hever Golf Club, and next door to the historic Hever Castle, this hotel is in an ideal spot for both leisure and business guests. The hotel has a comfortable bar and restaurant facility, as well as a games room. All bedrooms are annexed in the original stable blocks for Hever Castle, and have been tastefully decorated throughout. Dinner, lunch and a hearty breakfast are served daily in the main restaurant.

Rooms: 81 (3 family) (59 GF) **Facilities:** STV FTV WiFi Gym New Year
Conf: Class 60 Board 40 Thtr 130 Del from £144 **Services:** Night porter **Parking:** 70
Notes: Civ Wed 100

EDGWARE	Map 6 TQ19
Greater London	

Premier Inn London Edgware

BUDGET HOTEL

435 Burnt Oak Broadway, HA8 5AQ - **tel:** 0871 527 8652 (Calls cost 13p per minute plus your phone company's access charge) **web:** www.premierinn.com
dir: *M1 junct 4, A41, A5 towards Edgware. 3m to hotel*

High quality, budget accommodation ideal for both families and business travellers. Spacious, en suite bedrooms feature free WiFi and tea and coffee making facilities, and in most hotels, Freeview TV is also available. The adjacent family restaurant features a wide and varied menu.

Rooms: 114

EDMONTON	Map 6 TQ39
Greater London	

Premier Inn London Edmonton

BUDGET HOTEL

Advent Way, Edmonton, N18 3AF - **tel:** 0871 527 9404 (Calls cost 13p per minute plus your phone company's access charge) **web:** www.premierinn.com
dir: *From A406 exit at Cooks Ferry rdbt. 1st exit into Advent Way. Left (remain on Advent Way). Right into Eley Rd. Left into Nobel Rd. 2nd left into Advent Way*

High quality, budget accommodation ideal for both families and business travellers. Spacious, en suite bedrooms feature free WiFi and tea and coffee making facilities, and in most hotels, Freeview TV is also available. The adjacent family restaurant features a wide and varied menu.

Rooms: 96

E

EGHAM
Surrey   Map 6 TQ07

INSPECTOR'S CHOICE

Great Fosters
★★★★ ◉◉◉ HOTEL

Stroude Road, TW20 9UR - tel: 01784 433822
email: reception@greatfosters.co.uk **web:** www.greatfosters.co.uk
dir: From A30 Bagshot to Staines, right at lights by Wheatsheaf pub into Christchurch Rd. Straight on at rdbt. Left at lights into Stroude Rd. Hotel 0.75m on right

This Grade II listed mansion dates back to the 16th century. The main house rooms are very much in keeping with the house's original style but are, of course, up-to-date with modern amenities. The stables and cloisters provide particularly stylish and luxurious accommodation. A stimulating range of award-winning cuisine can be enjoyed in The Estate Grill. The beautiful public rooms, including the Terrace during the summer months, provide the perfect setting for afternoon tea and cocktails. A host of meeting and event facilities provide the setting for a range of individual events.

Rooms: 43 (22 annexe) (1 family) (13 GF) ⚓ **S** £180–£225; **D** £225–£575 (incl. bkfst) **Facilities:** STV WiFi ⦂ ↜ ♨ ✗ Xmas New Year **Conf:** Class 72 Board 50 Thtr 150 Del from £275 **Services:** Night porter **Parking:** 200 **Notes:** LB Civ Wed 180

HIGHLY RECOMMENDED

The Runnymede on Thames
★★★★ 83% ◉ HOTEL

Windsor Road, TW20 0AG - tel: 01784 220600
email: info@therunnymede.co.uk **web:** www.therunnymede.co.uk
dir: M25 junct 13, onto A308 towards Windsor

Enjoying a peaceful location beside the River Thames, this large modern hotel, with its excellent range of facilities, balances both leisure and corporate business. The extensive function suites, with spacious lounges and stylish, well laid-out bedrooms, make a good impression. Superb spa facilities are available, and the good food and beverage venues offer wonderful river views.

Rooms: 180 (19 family) ⚓ **S** £140–£278; **D** £175–£386 (incl. bkfst)* **Facilities:** Spa STV WiFi ⦂ HL ⟳ supervised ↜ supervised ♨ Gym Dance studio Boat hire Sauna Steam room Outdoor pool available summer only ♫ **Conf:** Class 180 Board 80 Thtr 300 Del from £249 **Services:** Lift Night porter Air con **Parking:** 300 **Notes:** LB Closed 27-28 Dec, 1-2 Jan Civ Wed 142

ELSTREE
Hertfordshire   Map 6 TQ19

HIGHLY RECOMMENDED

Laura Ashley The Manor
★★★★ 83% ◉◉ HOTEL

Barnet Lane, WD6 3RE - tel: 020 8327 4700 **email:** elstree@lauraashleyhotels.com
web: www.lauraashleyhotels.com/themanorelstree
dir: Phone for directions

This old Tudor house, built circa 1540, is set in ten acres of grounds, and was purchased by Laura Ashley in 2012. It was then refurbished throughout to reflect the rich design heritage of the company. Public rooms include a smart bar with original features, and the panelled Cavendish restaurant. Bedrooms are tastefully decorated and furnished in Laura Ashley-style, and have modern facilities.

Rooms: 49 (36 annexe) **Facilities:** FTV WiFi Gym Xmas New Year **Conf:** Class 30 Board 36 Thtr 80 **Services:** Night porter **Parking:** 100 **Notes:** LB Civ Wed 86

ELTERWATER
Cumbria   Map 18 NY30

HIGHLY RECOMMENDED

Langdale Hotel & Spa
★★★★ 82% ◉ COUNTRY HOUSE HOTEL

The Langdale Estate, LA22 9JD - tel: 015394 38014 & 37302
email: info@langdale.co.uk **web:** www.langdale.co.uk
dir: In Langdale Valley W of Ambleside

Built on the site of an abandoned 19th-century gunpowder works, this thoroughly modern hotel and resort is set in 35 acres of woodland and waterways. Comfortable bedrooms, many with spa baths, vary in size. Extensive public areas include the exceptional new Stove restaurant and bar. The ever-improving, luxurious spa and leisure facilities are on hand, and there is also a traditional pub, run by the hotel, just along the main road.

Rooms: 52 (47 annexe) (4 family) (25 GF) ⚓ **S** £125–£280; **D** £125–£280 (incl. bkfst)* **Facilities:** Spa STV FTV WiFi ⟳ supervised ♨ Fishing Gym Steam room Solarium Aerobics studio Health & beauty salon Cycle hire Xmas New Year **Conf:** Class 20 Board 18 Thtr 40 Del from £140 **Services:** Night porter **Parking:** 65 **Notes:** Civ Wed 34

E

ELY
Cambridgeshire   Map 12 TL58

HIGHLY RECOMMENDED

Poets House
★★★★ 83% ◉ HOTEL

40-44 St Mary's Street, CB7 4EY - **tel:** 01353 887777
email: reception@poetshouse.uk.com **web:** www.poetshouse.uk.com
dir: *Follow A10 into Ely, cathedral on right, hotel on left*

Poets House is a Grade II listed building situated in the heart of Ely just a few minutes' walk from the historic Cathedral and town centre. The property has been totally refurbished and features stylish, individually designed, well equipped bedrooms; the public rooms include a smart restaurant (The Dining Room) and a bar (The Study) as well as a smart outside garden/terrace.

Rooms: (4 GF) ⚘ **S** fr £150; **D** fr £170 (incl. bkfst)* **Facilities:** FTV WiFi
Conf: Class 30 Board 25 Thtr 60 Del from £225 **Services:** Lift Night porter
Notes: Civ Wed 65

EMBLETON
Northumberland   Map 21 NU22

Dunstanburgh Castle Hotel
★★ 85% HOTEL

NE66 3UN - **tel:** 01665 576111 **email:** stay@dunstanburghcastlehotel.co.uk
web: www.dunstanburghcastlehotel.co.uk
dir: *From A1 take B1340 to Denwick through Rennington. Right signed Embleton, over level crossing, left at x-rds, 2m to Embleton, hotel on right.*

The focal point of the village, this friendly, family-run hotel has a dining room and grill room that offer different menus, plus a cosy bar and two lounges. In addition to the main bedrooms, a barn conversion houses three stunning suites, each with a lounge and gallery bedroom above.

Rooms: 18 (6 family) ⚘ **S** £75; **D** £130 (incl. bkfst) **Facilities:** WiFi **Parking:** 26
Notes: LB Closed Dec–Jan

EMSWORTH
Hampshire   Map 5 SU70

Brookfield Hotel
★★★ 82% HOTEL

Havant Road, PO10 7LF - **tel:** 01243 373363
email: bookings@brookfieldhotel.co.uk **web:** www.brookfieldhotel.co.uk
dir: *From A27 onto A259 towards Emsworth. Hotel 0.5m on left*

This well-established family-run hotel has spacious public areas with popular conference and banqueting facilities. Bedrooms are in a modern style, and comfortably furnished. The popular Hermitage Restaurant offers a seasonally changing menu and an interesting wine list.

Rooms: 39 (6 family) (12 GF) ⚘ **S** £65–£100; **D** £120–£190 (incl. bkfst)*
Facilities: FTV WiFi ♨ Xmas New Year **Conf:** Class 50 Board 50 Thtr 100
Services: Night porter **Parking:** 80 **Notes:** LB Civ Wed 100

ENFIELD
Greater London   Map 6 TQ39

Royal Chace Hotel
★★★★ 79% HOTEL

162 The Ridgeway, EN2 8AR - **tel:** 020 8884 8181
email: reservations@royalchacehotel.co.uk **web:** www.royal-chace.com
dir: *M25 junct 24, A1005 towards Enfield. Hotel 3m on right*

This professionally-run, privately owned hotel enjoys a peaceful location with open fields to the rear. Public rooms are smartly appointed; the ground-floor Kings Restaurant is particularly appealing with its warm colour schemes and friendly service. Bedrooms are well presented and thoughtfully equipped.

Rooms: 92 (5 family) (32 GF) ⚘ **Facilities:** FTV WiFi ⚘ Gym New Year **Conf:** Class 100 Board 40 Thtr 250 **Services:** Night porter **Parking:** 200 **Notes:** RS Sun eve Restaurant closed Civ Wed 220

Premier Inn Enfield
BUDGET HOTEL

Innova Park, Corner of Solar Way, EN3 7XY - **tel:** 0871 527 8374 (Calls cost 13p per minute plus your phone company's access charge) **web:** www.premierinn.com
dir: *M25 junct 25, A10 towards London, left into Bullsmoor Lane & Mollison Ave. Over rdbt, right at lights into Innova Science Park*

High quality, budget accommodation ideal for both families and business travellers. Spacious, en suite bedrooms feature free WiFi and tea and coffee making facilities, and in most hotels, Freeview TV is also available. The adjacent family restaurant features a wide and varied menu.

Rooms: 202

EPSOM
Surrey   Map 6 TQ26

Premier Inn Epsom Central
BUDGET HOTEL

2-4 St Margarets Drive, off Dorking Road, KT18 7LB - **tel:** 0871 527 8376 (Calls cost 13p per minute plus your phone company's access charge) **web:** www.premierinn.com
dir: *M25 junct 9, A24 towards Epsom, hotel on left, just before town centre*

High quality, budget accommodation ideal for both families and business travellers. Spacious, en suite bedrooms feature free WiFi and tea and coffee making facilities, and in most hotels, Freeview TV is also available. The adjacent family restaurant features a wide and varied menu.

Rooms: 58

Premier Inn Epsom North
BUDGET HOTEL

272 Kingston Road, Ewell, KT19 0SH - **tel:** 0871 527 8380 (Calls cost 13p per minute plus your phone company's access charge) **web:** www.premierinn.com
dir: *M25 junct 8, A217 towards Sutton. A240 towards Ewell. At Beggars Hill rdbt 2nd exit into Kingston Rd*

Rooms: 29

E

ESCRICK
North Yorkshire   Map 16 SE64

HIGHLY RECOMMENDED

The Parsonage Country House Hotel

★★★ 85% ⊛ COUNTRY HOUSE HOTEL

York Road, YO19 6LF - tel: 01904 728111
email: reservations@parsonagehotel.co.uk **web:** www.parsonagehotel.co.uk
dir: A64 onto A19 Selby, Follow to Escrick. Hotel by St Helens Church

This 19th-century, former parsonage has been carefully restored and extended, and is situated in six acres of gardens. Bedrooms are smartly appointed and well equipped for both business and leisure guests. Public areas include an elegant restaurant, conference facilities and a choice of attractive lounges. Cloisters Spa is located in the formal gardens and includes a swimming pool, jacuzzi, sauna, steam room, aromatherapy salt room and an excellent gym. Please note that the Spa and Health Club is for adults aged 18+ only. The Fat Abbot is the newly refurbished gastro pub also located in the grounds offering a more relaxed dining experience.

Rooms: 53 (16 annexe) (4 family) (9 GF) ☏ **S** £79–£105; **D** £85–£140 (incl. bkfst)* **Facilities:** Spa FTV WiFi ⊠ ⊗ Gym Sauna Steam room Aromatherapy room Salt room Xmas New Year **Conf:** Class 80 Board 50 Thtr 150 **Services:** Lift Night porter **Parking:** 120 **Notes:** LB Civ Wed 100

EVERSHOT
Dorset   Map 4 ST50

Summer Lodge Country House Hotel, Restaurant & Spa

RED CARNATION
HOTEL COLLECTION

★★★★★ 84% ⊛ ⊛ ⊛ ⌇ COUNTRY HOUSE HOTEL

Fore Street, DT2 0JR - tel: 01935 482000
email: summer@relaischateaux.com **web:** www.summerlodgehotel.co.uk
dir: 1m W of A37 halfway between Dorchester & Yeovil

This picturesque hotel is situated in the heart of Dorset and is the ideal retreat; it's worth arriving in time for the excellent afternoon tea. Bedrooms are appointed to a very high standard; each is individually designed, with upholstered walls and a wealth of luxurious facilities. Expect plasma screen TVs, DVD players, radios, air conditioning and WiFi access, plus little touches such as homemade shortbread, fresh fruit and scented candles. The delightful public areas include a sumptuous lounge complete with an open fire, and the elegant restaurant where the cuisine continues to be the high point of any stay.

Rooms: 24 (14 annexe) (6 family) (3 GF) ☏ **S** £215–£760; **D** £215–£760 (incl. bkfst)* **Facilities:** Spa STV FTV WiFi ⊠ ⊗ ⊕ ⊱ Gym Sauna Xmas New Year **Conf:** Board 12 Thtr 20 Del £375 **Services:** Night porter Air con **Parking:** 41 **Notes:** No children 7yrs Closed 2-25 Jan Civ Wed 30

George Albert Hotel

★★★ 82% ⊛ HOTEL

Wardon Hill, DT2 9PW - tel: 01935 483430
email: enquiries@gahotel.co.uk **web:** www.gahotel.co.uk
dir: On A37 - between Yeovil & Dorchester. Adjacent to Southern Counties Kart Track

Situated mid-way between Dorchester and Yeovil, this hotel has much to offer for both business and leisure guests. The bedrooms offer impressive levels of comfort and many also have wonderful views across the Dorset countryside. Stylish public areas include extensive function rooms, a relaxing lounge, and a choice of dining options. Additional facilities include a karting track and clay-pigeon shooting.

Rooms: 39 (3 family) ☏ **S** £65–£110; **D** £75–£130 (incl. bkfst)* **Facilities:** FTV WiFi ⊠ Clay pigeon Kart track Xmas New Year **Conf:** Class 60 Board 90 Thtr 250 **Services:** Lift Night porter Air con **Parking:** 200 **Notes:** Civ Wed 405

EVESHAM
Worcestershire   Map 10 SP04

Wood Norton Hotel

★★★★ 79% ⊛ ⊛ HOTEL

Worcester Road, WR11 4YB - tel: 01386 765611
email: info@thewoodnorton.com **web:** www.thewoodnorton.com
dir: 2m from Evesham on A44, after Chadbury

Equidistant from Worcester, Stratford-Upon-Avon and Cheltenham, this 19th-century former hunting lodge, originally built for European royalty, is ideally located for exploring the Cotswolds. Modern refurbishment and period architecture sit comfortably together, creating a stylish interior. Bedrooms are well equipped for both business and leisure guests, and complimentary WiFi is available throughout. Public areas encompass a stylish bar, guest lounges and an oak-panelled dining room overlooking the gardens.

Rooms: 50 (30 annexe) (6 family) (12 GF) ☏ **Facilities:** FTV WiFi Xmas New Year **Conf:** Class 60 Board 40 Thtr 200 **Services:** Lift Night porter **Notes:** LB Civ Wed

Dumbleton Hall Hotel

★★★ 79% COUNTRY HOUSE HOTEL

WR11 7TS - tel: 01386 881240 **email:** dh@pofr.co.uk **web:** www.dumbletonhall.co.uk

(For full entry see Dumbleton)

Premier Inn Evesham

BUDGET HOTEL

Evesham Country Park, A46 Trunk Road, WR11 4TP - tel: 0871 527 8384 (Calls cost 13p per minute plus your phone company's access charge) **web:** www.premierinn.com
dir: At rdbt junct of A46(T) & A4184 at N end of Evesham bypass. Adjacent to Evesham Country Park

High quality, budget accommodation ideal for both families and business travellers. Spacious, en suite bedrooms feature free WiFi and tea and coffee making facilities, and in most hotels, Freeview TV is also available. The adjacent family restaurant features a wide and varied menu.

Rooms: 108

E

EXETER
Devon

Map 3 SX99

Hotel du Vin Exeter

★★★★ 75% HOTEL

Magdalen Street, EX2 4HY - **tel:** 01392 790120 & 288165
email: reception.exeter@hotelduvin.com **web:** www.hotelduvin.com/location/exeter
dir: *M5 junct 29 from north & junct 30 from south. See website for detailed directions*

Once an eye infirmary, this statuesque building in the heart of the city is now home to Hotel du Vin Exeter. The fusion of traditional and contemporary provides a fascinating environment in which to relax and enjoy the genuine hospitality from the committed team. Stylish bedrooms come in a variety of shapes and sizes with a host of thoughtful extras and wonderfully snuggly beds. Cosseting towels, fluffy robes and REN toiletries also contribute to equally impressive bathrooms. The bistro is the venue for flavoursome, French-inspired cuisine, complemented by a cosmopolitan wine list. Public areas provide a number of options in which to sink back into a sofa and soak up the unique atmosphere. A spa and swimming pool are also available, housed within the secluded walled garden.

Rooms: 59 (6 family) (3 GF) S £89–£249; **D** £135–£369* **Facilities:** Spa FTV WiFi Gym Xmas New Year **Conf:** Class 30 Board 16 Thtr 100 Del from £140 **Services:** Lift Night porter Air con **Parking:** 12 **Notes:** LB Civ Wed 100

Mercure Exeter Southgate Hotel & Spa

★★★★ 74% HOTEL

Southernhay East, EX1 1QF - **tel:** 01392 412812
email: h6624@accor.com **web:** www.mercure.com
dir: *M5 junct 30, 3rd exit (Exeter), 2nd left towards city centre, 3rd exit at next rdbt, hotel 2m on right*

Centrally located and with excellent parking, The Southgate offers a diverse range of leisure and business facilities. Public areas are pleasantly spacious with comfortable seating in the bar and lounge; there is also a terrace. The bedrooms, in differing sizes, are well equipped and have modern facilities.

Rooms: 156 (21 family) (23 GF) S £68–£265; **D** £68–£265* **Facilities:** FTV WiFi Gym Sauna Spa bath Xmas New Year **Conf:** Class 90 Board 60 Thtr 180 Del from £135 **Services:** Lift Night porter **Parking:** 101 **Notes:** Civ Wed 100

The Devon Hotel

★★★ 80% HOTEL

Exeter Bypass, Matford, EX2 8XU - **tel:** 01392 259268
email: reservations@devonhotel.co.uk **web:** www.devonhotel.co.uk
dir: *M5 junct 30 follow Marsh Barton Ind Est signs on A379. Hotel on Marsh Barton rdbt*

Within easy access of the city centre, the M5 and the city's business parks, this smart Georgian hotel offers modern, comfortable accommodation. The Carriages

Bar and Brasserie is popular with guests and locals alike, offering a wide range of dishes as well as a carvery at both lunch and dinner. Service is friendly and attentive, and extensive meeting and business facilities are available.

Rooms: 60 (60 annexe) (17 family) (21 GF) S £65–£125; **D** £75–£125* **Facilities:** FTV WiFi Gym Xmas New Year **Conf:** Class 80 Board 40 Thtr 150 **Services:** Night porter **Parking:** 150 **Notes:** LB Civ Wed 100

Best Western Lord Haldon Country Hotel

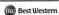

★★★ 79% HOTEL

Dunchideock, EX6 7YF - **tel:** 01392 832483
email: enquiries@lordhaldonhotel.co.uk **web:** www.lordhaldonhotel.co.uk
dir: *M5 junct 31, A30, 1st exit, follow signs through Ide to Dunchideock*

Set in rural tranquillity, this is an attractive country house where guests are assured of a warm welcome from the professional team of staff. The well-equipped bedrooms are comfortable, and many have stunning views. The daily-changing menu features skilfully cooked dishes, with most of the produce sourced locally.

Rooms: 25 (3 family) S fr £55; **Facilities:** FTV WiFi Xmas New Year **Conf:** Class 100 Board 40 Thtr 250 Del from £100 **Parking:** 120 **Notes:** Civ Wed 120

Queens Court Hotel

★★★ 77% HOTEL

6-8 Bystock Terrace, EX4 4HY - **tel:** 01392 272709
email: enquiries@queenscourt-hotel.co.uk **web:** www.queenscourt-hotel.co.uk
dir: *Exit dual carriageway at junct 30 onto B5132 Topsham Rd, towards city centre. Hotel 200yds from Central Station*

Quietly located within walking distance of the city centre, this privately owned hotel is a listed, early Victorian property that provides friendly hospitality. The smart public areas and contemporary bedrooms are tastefully furnished, and the stylish and attractive Olive Tree restaurant offers an award-winning selection of dishes. Rooms are available for conferences, meetings, weddings and parties. Complimentary parking is available in a public car park directly opposite the hotel entrance.

Rooms: 19 (1 family) (1 GF) S fr £75; **D** fr £85* **Facilities:** FTV WiFi **Conf:** Class 30 Board 35 Thtr 60 **Services:** Lift **Notes:** Closed Xmas & New Year RS 23 Dec-1 Jan Civ Wed 60

Gipsy Hill Hotel

THE INDEPENDENTS
HOTEL ASSOCIATION

★★★ 77% HOTEL

Gipsy Hill Lane, Monkerton, EX1 3RN - **tel:** 01392 465252
email: stay@gipsyhillhotel.co.uk **web:** www.gipsyhillhotel.co.uk
dir: *M5 junct 29 towards Exeter. Right at 1st rdbt, right again at next rdbt, turn left onto Pinn Lane, right onto Gipsy Hill Lane*

Located on the edge of the city, with easy access to the M5 and the airport, this popular hotel is set in attractive, well-tended gardens and boasts far-reaching country views. The hotel offers a range of conference and function rooms, comfortable bedrooms and modern facilities including free WiFi. An intimate bar and lounge are adjacent to the elegant restaurant. Secure indoor cycle storage is also provided.

Rooms: 37 (17 annexe) (4 family) (12 GF) **Facilities:** FTV WiFi Xmas New Year **Conf:** Class 80 Board 80 Thtr 300 **Services:** Night porter **Parking:** 74 **Notes:** Civ Wed 160

EXETER *continued*

Mercure Exeter Rougemont Hotel

[U]

Queen Street, EX4 3SP - tel: 01392 254982 **email:** ha0h6@accor.com
web: www.mercure.com
dir: *Phone for directions*

Currently the rating for this establishment is not confirmed. This may be due to a change of ownership or because it has only recently joined the AA rating scheme.

Rooms: 98 (13 family) ⌇ **S** £69–£300; **D** £79–£355* **Facilities:** STV FTV WiFi ↷ HL ♫ Xmas New Year **Conf:** Class 120 Board 84 Thtr 250 Del from £102 **Services:** Lift Night porter **Parking:** 26 **Notes:** Civ Wed 120

Premier Inn Exeter Central St Davids

BUDGET HOTEL

Bonhay Road, EX4 4BG - tel: 0871 527 9278 (Calls cost 13p per minute plus your phone company's access charge) **web:** www.premierinn.com
dir: *M5 junct 31, A30 towards Bodmin & Oakehampton. Exit onto A377 towards Exeter & Crediton. Hotel on left*

High quality, budget accommodation ideal for both families and business travellers. Spacious, en suite bedrooms feature free WiFi and tea and coffee making facilities, and in most hotels, Freeview TV is also available. The adjacent family restaurant features a wide and varied menu.

Rooms: 102

Premier Inn Exeter City Centre

BUDGET HOTEL

2 Southernhay Gardens, EX1 1SG - tel: 0871 527 9570 (Calls cost 13p per minute plus your phone company's access charge) **web:** www.premierinn.com
dir: *M5 junct 29, A3015. Right at lights into Honiton Rd. At Moor Lane rdbt 2nd exit (A3015) then B3183. At next rdbt 1st exit into Western Way (B3212). Right into Barnfield Rd, left then left again into Southernhay Gardens*

Rooms: 120

Premier Inn Exeter (Countess Wear)

BUDGET HOTEL

398 Topsham Road, EX2 6HE - tel: 0871 527 8386 (Calls cost 13p per minute plus your phone company's access charge) **web:** www.premierinn.com
dir: *2m from M5 junct 30/A30 junct 29. Follow signs for Exeter & Dawlish (A379). On dual carriageway take 2nd slip road on left at Countess Wear rdbt. Hotel adjacent to Beefeater*

Rooms: 44

Premier Inn Exeter M5 Jct 29

BUDGET HOTEL

Fitzroy Road, EX1 3LJ - tel: 0871 527 9468 (Calls cost 13p per minute plus your phone company's access charge) **web:** www.premierinn.com
dir: *M5 junct 29, A3015 towards city centre. Straight on at 1st rdbt. 2nd right (at lights) into Fitzroy Rd*

Rooms: 102

EXMOUTH
Devon

Map 3 SY08

Cavendish Hotel

★★★ 70% HOTEL

11 Morton Crescent, The Esplanade, EX8 1BE - tel: 01395 272528
email: cavendish.exmouth@alfatravel.co.uk **web:** www.leisureplex.co.uk
dir: *Follow seafront signs, hotel in centre of large crescent*

Situated on the seafront, this terraced hotel attracts many groups from around the country, and is within walking distance of the town centre. The bedrooms are neatly presented, and front-facing rooms are always popular. Entertainment is provided on most evenings during the summer.

Rooms: 78 (3 family) (21 GF) ⌇ **S** £40–£56; **D** £64–£96 (incl. bkfst)* **Facilities:** FTV WiFi Snooker ♫ Xmas New Year **Services:** Lift Night porter **Parking:** 25 **Notes:** LB Closed Dec-Jan (ex Xmas) RS Nov & Feb-Mar Mon-Fri

Premier Inn Exmouth Seafront

BUDGET HOTEL

The Esplanade, EX8 2AZ - tel: 0871 527 9400 (Calls cost 13p per minute plus your phone company's access charge) **web:** www.premierinn.com
dir: *M5 junct 30, A376 signed Exeter/Exmouth. At rdbt take A376. At 4th rdbt take 2nd exit into Imperial Rd. After next rdbt, right onto Alexandra Terr. 1st left into Morton Rd, left onto Esplanade. Hotel on left*

High quality, budget accommodation ideal for both families and business travellers. Spacious, en suite bedrooms feature free WiFi and tea and coffee making facilities, and in most hotels, Freeview TV is also available. The adjacent family restaurant features a wide and varied menu.

Rooms: 60

FALFIELD
Gloucestershire

Map 4 ST69

Best Western The Gables Hotel

★★★ 77% HOTEL

Bristol Road, GL12 8DL - tel: 01454 260502
email: mail@thegablesbristol.co.uk **web:** www.thegablesbristol.co.uk
dir: *M5 junct 14 N'bound. Left at end of sliproad. Right onto A38, hotel 300yds on right*

Conveniently located just a few minutes from the motorway, this establishment is ideally suited to both business and leisure guests, with easy access to Cheltenham, Gloucester, Bristol and Bath. Bedrooms are spacious and well equipped. Relaxing public areas consist of a light and airy bar, and a restaurant where meals and all-day snacks are available; a more formal restaurant is open for dinner. There is also a range of meeting rooms.

Rooms: 46 (4 family) (18 GF) **S** £49–£109; **D** £59–£249 (incl. bkfst) **Facilities:** FTV WiFi ↷ New Year **Conf:** Class 90 Board 50 Thtr 200 Del from £115 **Services:** Night porter **Parking:** 104 **Notes:** LB Civ Wed 150

FALMOUTH
Cornwall & Isles of Scilly

Map 2 SW83

See also **Mawnan Smith**

The Royal Duchy Hotel
★★★★ 81% @@ HOTEL

Brend Hotels

Cliff Road, TR11 4NX - tel: 01326 313042
email: reservations@royalduchy.com **web:** www.royalduchy.com
dir: *On Cliff Rd, along Falmouth seafront*

Staff at this hotel, which looks out over the sea and towards Pendennis Castle, create a very friendly environment. The comfortable lounge and cocktail bar are well appointed and just the place for a light lunch. Leisure facilities include a beauty salon, and meeting rooms are also available. The award-winning Terrace Restaurant serves carefully prepared dishes, and guests can sit on the sea-facing terrace in warmer weather. The bedrooms vary in size and aspect, and many have sea views. Babysitting is happily arranged for families with small children and babies.

Rooms: 45 (6 family) (1 GF) ☎ **S** £55–£127; **D** £168–£360 (incl. bkfst)*
Facilities: Spa FTV WiFi ☕ Games room Sauna Hot stone therapy beds ♪
Xmas New Year Child facilities **Conf:** Thtr 50 **Services:** Lift Night porter **Parking:** 50
Notes: LB Civ Wed 100

See advert on following page

St Michael's Hotel and Spa
★★★★ 78% @@ HOTEL

Gyllyngvase Beach, Seafront, TR11 4NB - tel: 01326 312707
email: greghenry@stmichaelshotel.co.uk **web:** www.stmichaelshotel.co.uk
dir: *A39 into Falmouth, follow beach signs, at 2nd mini-rdbt into Pennance Rd.
Take 2nd left & 2nd left again*

Overlooking the bay, this hotel is in an excellent position and commands lovely views. It is appointed in a fresh, contemporary style that reflects its location by the sea. The Flying Fish restaurant has a great atmosphere and a real buzz about it. The light and bright bedrooms, some with balconies, are well equipped. There are excellent leisure facilities including a fitness and health club together with a spa offering many treatments. The attractive gardens also provide a place to relax and unwind.

Rooms: 93 (40 annexe) (7 family) (12 GF) ☎ **S** fr £50; **D** fr £100 (incl. bkfst)*
Facilities: Spa FTV WiFi ☕ ☕ Gym Sauna Steam room Aqua aerobics Fitness classes Xmas New Year **Conf:** Class 40 Board 30 Thtr 80 **Services:** Lift Night porter **Parking:** 60 **Notes:** LB Civ Wed 80

Merchants Manor
★★★★ 76% @@ HOTEL

1 Weston Manor, TR11 4AJ - tel: 01326 312734
email: info@merchantsmanor.com **web:** www.merchantsmanor.com
dir: *Phone for directions*

Merchants Manor is an historical country house situated within walking distance of the busy Falmouth town centre and pretty beaches. Beautiful original features have been sympathetically mixed with modern and contemporary style and design. Newly renovated rooms are trendy and comfortable with a keen eye on quality and standards. It's ideal for that special wedding or family celebration with the added benefit of leisure facilities for families, including a good size gym. There is also generous seating in the lounge, perfect for a morning coffee or afternoon tea.

Rooms: 39 (2 family) (11 GF) ☎ **S** £75–£87; **D** £150–£165* **Facilities:** Spa FTV WiFi ☕ HL ☕ Gym Sauna In room treatments Xmas New Year **Conf:** Class 140 Board 60 Thtr 180 **Services:** Night porter **Parking:** 126 **Notes:** Civ Wed 120

The Greenbank Hotel
★★★★ 75% @@ HOTEL

Harbourside, TR11 2SR - tel: 01326 312440
email: reception@greenbank-hotel.co.uk **web:** www.greenbank-hotel.co.uk
dir: *A39 to Falmouth, left at Ponsharden rdbt onto North Parade. 500yds past Falmouth Marina on the Harbourfront*

Located by the marina, and with its own private quay dating from the 17th century, The Greenbank Hotel has a strong maritime theme throughout. Set at the water's edge, the lounge, restaurant and many bedrooms all benefit from harbour views. The restaurant provides a choice of interesting and enjoyable dishes.

Rooms: 60 (6 family) ☎ **S** fr £99; **D** fr £109 (incl. bkfst)* **Facilities:** FTV WiFi ☕ Private beach, quay & pontoons Beauty treatment room Xmas New Year **Conf:** Class 30 Board 50 Thtr 120 Del from £159 **Services:** Lift Night porter **Parking:** 68 **Notes:** LB Civ Wed 120

F

FALMOUTH *continued*

Falmouth Hotel

★★★ 81% HOTEL

Castle Beach, TR11 4NZ - tel: 01326 312671
email: reservations@falmouthhotel.com **web:** www.falmouthhotel.com
dir: *A30 to Truro then A390 to Falmouth. Follow signs for beaches,
hotel on seafront near Pendennis Castle*

This spectacular beach-front Victorian property affords wonderful sea views from
many of its comfortable bedrooms, some of which have their own balconies.
Spacious public areas include a number of inviting lounges, a choice of dining
options and an impressive range of leisure facilities.

Rooms: 71 (16 family) Facilities: Spa FTV WiFi Gym Elemis Spa treatment
rooms Xmas New Year **Conf:** Class 150 Board 100 Thtr 250 **Services:** Lift Night
porter **Parking:** 120 **Notes:** Civ Wed 250

R RICHARDSON HOTELS
Where Memories are Made

Penmorvah Manor

★★★ 80% HOTEL

Budock Water, TR11 5ED - tel: 01326 250277
email: reception@penmorvah.co.uk **web:** www.penmorvah.co.uk
dir: *A39 to Hillhead rdbt, take 2nd exit. 2nd exit at next rdbt, right at Falmouth Football
Club, through Budock. Hotel opposite Penjerrick Gardens*

Situated within two miles of central Falmouth, this extended Victorian manor
house is a peaceful hideaway, set in six acres of private woodland and gardens.
Penmorvah is well positioned for visiting the local gardens, and offers many
garden-tour breaks. Dinner features locally sourced, quality ingredients such as
Cornish cheeses, meat, fish and game.

Rooms: 27 (1 family) (10 GF) **S** £75–£115; **D** £115–£179 (incl. bkfst)*
Facilities: FTV WiFi Xmas New Year **Conf:** Class 100 Board 40 Thtr 120
Del from £99 **Parking:** 100 **Notes:** LB Civ Wed 120

Penmere Manor Hotel

★★★ 80% HOTEL

Mongleath Road, TR11 4PN - tel: 01326 211411
email: reservations@penmere.co.uk **web:** www.penmere.co.uk
dir: *Take 2nd exit at Hillhead rdbt, over next rdbt to Union Rd. Follow road
and turn left onto Mongleath Rd*

Set in five acres on the outskirts of town, this Georgian manor house was originally
built for a ship's captain. Now a family-owned hotel it provides friendly service and
a good range of facilities. Bedrooms vary in size and are located in the manor house
and the garden wing. Various menus are available in the bar and the smart
restaurant. There is a leisure club with an indoor heated pool, jacuzzi, sauna and
a well-equipped small gymnasium. The water in the pool is UV filtered.

Rooms: 37 (12 family) (13 GF) **S** £75–£85; **D** £140–£160 (incl. bkfst)*
Facilities: FTV WiFi Gym Sauna New Year **Conf:** Class 20 Board 30 Thtr 60
Del from £144.50 **Parking:** 50 **Notes:** LB Closed 22-27 Dec

Membly Hall Hotel

★★ 75% HOTEL

Sea Front, Cliff Road, TR11 4NT - tel: 01326 312869
email: memblyhallhotel@tiscali.co.uk **web:** www.memblyhallhotel.co.uk
dir: *A39 to Falmouth. Follow seafront & beaches signs*

Located conveniently on the seafront and enjoying splendid views, this family-run
hotel offers friendly service. Bedrooms are pleasantly spacious and well equipped.
Carefully prepared and enjoyable meals are served in the spacious dining room.
Live entertainment is provided on some evenings and there is also a sauna and
spa pool.

Rooms: 35 (3 family) (6 GF) **S** £35–£70; **D** £70–£140 (incl. bkfst)* **Facilities:** FTV
WiFi Gym Indoor short bowls Table tennis Pool table Sauna Spa pool New Year
Conf: Class 130 Board 60 Thtr 150 Del from £75 **Services:** Lift **Parking:** 30 **Notes:**
Closed Xmas week RS Dec–Jan Advance bookings only

F

FAREHAM
Hampshire   Map 5 SU50

Solent Hotel & Spa
★★★★ 82% HOTEL

Rookery Avenue, Whiteley, PO15 7AJ - tel: 01489 880000
email: reservations@solenthotel.co.uk **web:** www.solenthotel.co.uk
dir: M27 junct 9, hotel on Solent Business Park

Close to the M27 with easy access to Portsmouth, the New Forest and other attractions, this smart, purpose-built hotel enjoys a peaceful location. Bedrooms are spacious and very well appointed and there is a well-equipped spa with health and beauty facilities.

Rooms: 115 (9 family) (39 GF) **D** £100–£200* **Facilities:** Spa STV WiFi ↘ HL 🄫 ⚐
Gym Steam room Sauna Children's splash pool Activity studio Xmas New Year
Conf: Class 100 Board 80 Thtr 200 Del from £120 **Services:** Lift Night porter
Parking: 200 **Notes:** LB Civ Wed 160

Lysses House Hotel
★★★ 75% HOTEL

51 High Street, PO16 7BQ - tel: 01329 822622
email: lysses@lysses.co.uk **web:** www.lysses.co.uk
dir: M27 junct 11 follow Fareham signs, stay in left lane to Delme rdbt.
At rdbt 3rd exit into East St, follow into High St. Hotel at top on right

This attractive Georgian hotel is situated on the edge of the town in a quiet location and provides spacious and well-equipped accommodation. There are conference facilities, and a lounge bar serving a range of snacks together with the Richmond Restaurant that offers imaginative cuisine.

Rooms: 21 (2 family) (7 GF) 🅔 **S** £70–£75; **D** £102.50 (incl. bkfst)* **Facilities:** FTV WiFi Free entry to gym/pool 5mins walk away **Conf:** Class 42 Board 28 Thtr 95 Del from £117 **Services:** Lift Night porter **Parking:** 30 **Notes:** Closed 25 Dec–1 Jan RS 24 Dec & BHs Restaurant closed BHs, hotel closed PM 24 Dec Civ Wed 100

Premier Inn Fareham
BUDGET HOTEL

Southampton Road, Park Gate, SO31 6AF - tel: 0871 527 8396 (Calls cost 13p per minute plus your phone company's access charge) **web:** www.premierinn.com
dir: M27 junct 9, follow Fareham West, A27 signs. NB for Sat Nav use SO31 6BZ

High quality, budget accommodation ideal for both families and business travellers. Spacious, en suite bedrooms feature free WiFi and tea and coffee making facilities, and in most hotels, Freeview TV is also available. The adjacent family restaurant features a wide and varied menu.

Rooms: 61

FARINGDON
Oxfordshire   Map 5 SU29

HIGHLY RECOMMENDED

Sudbury House
★★★★ 83% HOTEL

56 London Street, SN7 7AA - tel: 01367 241272
email: gm@sudburyhouse.co.uk **web:** www.sudburyhouse.co.uk
dir: M40 junct 9, A34. A420, London St 0.5m on left

Set in nine acres of well-tended grounds and located on the edge of the Cotswolds, Sudbury House is a great place to relax and unwind. Restaurant 56

offers fine dining while the brasserie, with its open-plan kitchen is more relaxed. Accommodation has a contemporary design and offers great comfort.

Rooms: 50 (2 family) (10 GF) 🅔 **Facilities:** FTV WiFi ↘ Xmas New Year
Conf: Class 16 Board 30 Thtr 100 **Services:** Lift Night porter **Parking:** 60
Notes: LB Civ Wed 180

FARNBOROUGH
Hampshire   Map 5 SU85

INSPECTOR'S CHOICE

Aviator
★★★★ ◉◉ HOTEL

Farnborough Road, GU14 6EL - tel: 01252 555890
email: enquiries@aviatorbytag.com **web:** www.aviatorbytag.com
dir: A325 to Aldershot, 3m, hotel on right

Aviator is a striking property with a modern, sleek interior overlooking Farnborough airfield, located close to the main transport networks. This hotel is suitable for both business and leisure travellers. The bedrooms are well designed and provide complimentary WiFi. Both the Brasserie and the One Eleven source local ingredients for their menus.

Rooms: 169 🅔 **S** £125–£250; **D** £125–£250* **Facilities:** Spa STV WiFi ↘ Gym Exercise studio Theraputic, holistic & beauty treatments Xmas New Year
Conf: Class 48 Board 40 Thtr 110 Del from £245 **Services:** Lift Night porter Air con **Parking:** 169 **Notes:** LB Civ Wed 150

Premier Inn Farnborough
BUDGET HOTEL

Ively Road, Southwood, GU14 0JP - tel: 0871 527 8398 (Calls cost 13p per minute plus your phone company's access charge) **web:** www.premierinn.com
dir: M3 junct 4a, A327 to Farnborough. Hotel on left at 5th rdbt, Monkey Puzzle Rdbt

High quality, budget accommodation ideal for both families and business travellers. Spacious, en suite bedrooms feature free WiFi and tea and coffee making facilities, and in most hotels, Freeview TV is also available. The adjacent family restaurant features a wide and varied menu.

Rooms: 82

F

FARNBOROUGH *continued*

Premier Inn Farnborough Town Centre

BUDGET HOTEL

3 Kingsmead, GU14 7NY - **tel:** 0871 527 9628 (Calls cost 13p per minute plus your phone company's access charge) **web:** www.premierinn.com
dir: *Phone for directions*
Rooms: 80

FARNHAM
Surrey
Map 5 SU84

Best Western Frensham Pond Hotel

★★★★ 78% HOTEL

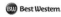

Bacon Lane, GU10 2QB - **tel:** 01252 795161 **email:** info@frenshampondhotel.co.uk
web: www.bw-frenshampondhotel.co.uk

(For full entry see Churt)

Mercure Farnham Bush Hotel

★★★ 79% HOTEL

The Borough, GU9 7NN - **tel:** 01252 234800
email: H6621@accor.com **web:** www.mercure.com
dir: *M3 junct 4, A31, follow town centre signs. At East Street lights turn left, hotel on right*

Dating back to the 17th century, this extended former coaching inn is attractively presented and has a courtyard and a lawned garden. The bedrooms are well appointed, with quality fabrics and good facilities. The public areas include the panelled Oak Lounge, a smart cocktail bar and a conference facility in an adjoining building.

Rooms: 94 (3 family) (27 GF) **Facilities:** FTV WiFi Xmas **Conf:** Class 80 Board 30 Thtr 140 **Services:** Night porter **Parking:** 70 **Notes:** Civ Wed 100

The Farnham Hog's Back Hotel

★★★ 77% HOTEL

Hog's Back, Seale, GU10 1EX - **tel:** 01252 782345
email: res@farnhamhogsbackhotel.co.uk **web:** www.farnhamhogsbackhotel.co.uk
dir: *On A31 Hogs Back Road 15 mins from Farnham & Guildford*

The Farnham Hog's Back Hotel offers a convenient location, plenty of free parking, comfortable rooms with all the required amenities, including free WiFi, and the extensive Active Life Health Club. There is also a choice of two event suites, one of which has its own exclusive entrance, designed to host a range of different occasions such as business meetings, weddings or civil partnerships.

Rooms: 96 (17 family) (24 GF) **Facilities:** Spa WiFi HL Gym Steam room Sauna Xmas New Year **Conf:** Class 120 Board 40 Thtr 180 **Services:** Night porter **Parking:** 150 **Notes:** Civ Wed 150

FAWKHAM GREEN
Kent
Map 6 TQ56

Brandshatch Place Hotel & Spa

★★★★ 77% @@ HOTEL

Brands Hatch Road, Fawkham Green, DA3 8NQ - **tel:** 01474 875000 & 0845 072 7395 (Calls cost 5p per minute plus your phone company's access charge)
email: brandshatchplace@handpicked.co.uk
web: www.handpickedhotels.co.uk/brandshatchplace
dir: *M25 junct 3, A20 West Kingsdown. Left at paddock entrance/Fawkham Green sign. 3rd left signed Fawkham Rd. Hotel 500mtrs on right*

This charming 18th-century Georgian country house close to the famous racing circuit offers stylish and elegant rooms. Bedrooms are appointed to a very high standard, offering impressive facilities and excellent levels of comfort and quality. The hotel also features a comprehensive leisure club with substantial crèche facilities.

Rooms: 38 (12 annexe) (1 family) (6 GF) **Facilities:** Spa STV FTV WiFi Gym Aerobic dance studio Sauna Steam room Spin studio Xmas New Year **Conf:** Class 60 Board 50 Thtr 160 Del from £99 **Services:** Lift Night porter **Parking:** 100 **Notes:** Civ Wed 110

FELIXSTOWE
Suffolk
Map 13 TM33

Best Western Brook Hotel

★★★ 77% HOTEL

Orwell Road, IP11 7PF - **tel:** 01394 278441
email: welcome@brookhotel.com **web:** www.brookhotel.com
dir: *Phone for details*

The Brook Hotel is a modern, well furnished building ideally situated in a residential area close to the town centre and the sea. Public areas include a lounge bar, a large open-plan restaurant with a bar area and a residents' lounge. Bedrooms are generally quite spacious; each one is pleasantly decorated and equipped with modern facilities.

Rooms: 25 (5 family) (3 GF) **Facilities:** FTV WiFi Xmas New Year **Conf:** Class 60 Board 60 Thtr 100 **Parking:** 20 **Notes:** Civ Wed 150

Marlborough Hotel

★★ 69% HOTEL

Sea Front, IP11 2BJ - **tel:** 01394 285621 **email:** hsm@marlborough-hotel-felix.com
web: www.marlborough-hotel-felix.com
dir: *From A14 follow 'Docks' signs. Over Dock rdbt, rail crossing & lights. Left at T-junct. Hotel 400mtrs on left*

Situated on the seafront, overlooking the beach and just a short stroll from the pier and town centre, this traditional resort hotel offers a good range of facilities including the smart Rattan Restaurant, Flying Boat Bar and L'Aperitif lounge. The pleasantly decorated bedrooms come in a variety of styles; some have lovely sea views.

Rooms: 48 (1 family) **Facilities:** STV WiFi Pool table Xmas New Year **Conf:** Class 60 Board 40 Thtr 80 **Services:** Lift Night porter **Parking:** 16

Premier Inn Felixstowe Town Centre

BUDGET HOTEL

Undercliffe Rd West, IP11 2AN - tel: 0871 527 9536 (Calls cost 13p per minute plus your phone company's access charge) **web:** www.premierinn.com
dir: *A14 towards Felixstowe. At rdbt (Trimley St Mary on right) follow Town Centre (A154) signs. At next rdbt right into Garrison Ln. Hotel on left before Undercliffe Rd*

High quality, budget accommodation ideal for both families and business travellers. Spacious, en suite bedrooms feature free WiFi and tea and coffee making facilities, and in most hotels, Freeview TV is also available. The adjacent family restaurant features a wide and varied menu.

Rooms: 60

FERNDOWN
Dorset   Map 5 SU00

Premier Inn Bournemouth/Ferndown

BUDGET HOTEL

Ringwood Road, Tricketts Cross, BH22 9BB - tel: 0871 527 8122 (Calls cost 13p per minute plus your phone company's access charge) **web:** www.premierinn.com
dir: *Off A348 just before Tricketts Cross rdbt*

High quality, budget accommodation ideal for both families and business travellers. Spacious, en suite bedrooms feature free WiFi and tea and coffee making facilities, and in most hotels, Freeview TV is also available. The adjacent family restaurant features a wide and varied menu.

Rooms: 32

FLAMBOROUGH
East Riding of Yorkshire   Map 17 TA27

North Star Hotel

★★ 85% SMALL HOTEL

North Marine Drive, YO15 1BL - tel: 01262 850379
email: thenorthstarhotel@live.co.uk **web:** www.thenorthstarhotel.co.uk
dir: *B1229 or B1255 to Flamborough. Follow signs for North Landing along North Marine Dr. Hotel 100yds from sea*

Standing close to the North Landing of Flamborough Head, this family-run hotel overlooks delightful countryside, and provides excellent accommodation and caring hospitality. A good range of fresh local food, especially fish, is available in both the bar and the dining room.

Rooms: 9 (2 GF) ⬧ **S** fr £65; **D** £90–£100 (incl. bkfst)* **Facilities:** FTV **Parking:** 60
Notes: LB Closed Xmas RS Nov-Etr Closed Sun night for accommodation

---

FLEET
Hampshire   Map 5 SU85

Premier Inn Fleet

BUDGET HOTEL

Waterfront Business Park, 7-11 Fleet Road, GU51 3QT - tel: 0871 527 9446 (Calls cost 13p per minute plus your phone company's access charge)
web: www.premierinn.com
dir: *On A3013*

High quality, budget accommodation ideal for both families and business travellers. Spacious, en suite bedrooms feature free WiFi and tea and coffee making facilities, and in most hotels, Freeview TV is also available. The adjacent family restaurant features a wide and varied menu.

Rooms: 70

FLEET MOTORWAY SERVICE AREA (M3)
Hampshire   Map 5 SU75

Days Inn Fleet - M3

WELCOMEBREAK

AA Advertised

Fleet Services, GU51 1AA - tel: 01252 815587
email: fleet.hotel@welcomebreak.co.uk **web:** www.welcomebreak.co.uk
dir: *Between junct 4a & 5 southbound on M3*

This modern building offers accommodation in smart, spacious and well-equipped bedrooms, suitable for families and business travellers, and all with en suite bathrooms. Continental breakfast is available and other refreshments may be taken at the nearby family restaurant.

Rooms: 59 (46 family) (5 smoking) **Facilities:** STV FTV WiFi **Services:** Night porter **Parking:** 60

FLITWICK
Bedfordshire   Map 11 TL03

Hallmark Hotel Flitwick Manor

★★★★ 77% ◉◉ COUNTRY HOUSE HOTEL

Church Road, MK45 1AE - tel: 0330 028 3406
email: flitwick@hallmarkhotels.co.uk **web:** www.hallmarkhotels.co.uk
dir: *M1 junct 12, follow signs for Flitwick, turn left into Church Rd, hotel on left*

With its picturesque setting in acres of gardens and parkland, yet only minutes from the motorway, this lovely Georgian house combines the best of both worlds, being both accessible and peaceful. Bedrooms are individually decorated and furnished with period pieces; some are air conditioned. Cosy and intimate, the lounge and restaurant give the hotel a home-from-home feel.

Rooms: 18 (1 family) (5 GF) (1 smoking) ⬧ **Facilities:** STV FTV WiFi ⬧ Putting green ⬧ ⬧ Xmas New Year **Conf:** Class 30 Board 22 Thtr 50 **Services:** Night porter **Parking:** 18 **Notes:** LB Civ Wed 58

F

F

FOLKESTONE
Kent

Map 7 TR23

The Southcliff Hotel

★★ 71% METRO HOTEL

22-26 The Leas, CT20 2DY - tel: 01303 850075
email: sales@thesouthcliff.co.uk **web:** www.thesouthcliff.co.uk
dir: *M20 junct 13, follow signs for The Leas. Left at rdbt onto Sandgate Rd,*
right onto Shakespeare Terrace, right at end of road, hotel on right

Located on the town's panoramic promenade with a bird's eye view of the sea, this
Victorian hotel is perfectly located for cross channel connections and is only
minutes from the town centre. Bedrooms are spacious and airy and some have
balconies and sea views. Enjoy a freshly prepared breakfast in the spacious
breakfast room on the lower ground floor or relax in the bar. There's a guest lounge
and plenty of street parking available.

Rooms: 68 **Facilities:** FTV WiFi **Conf:** Class 120 Board 50 Thtr 200 **Services:** Lift
Night porter

Premier Inn Folkestone (Channel Tunnel)

BUDGET HOTEL

Cherry Garden Lane, CT19 4AP - tel: 0871 527 8400 (Calls cost 13p per minute plus your
phone company's access charge) **web:** www.premierinn.com
dir: *M20 junct 13. Follow Folkestone, A20 signs. At lights turn right, hotel on right*

High quality, budget accommodation ideal for both families and business
travellers. Spacious, en suite bedrooms feature free WiFi and tea and coffee making
facilities, and in most hotels, Freeview TV is also available. The adjacent family
restaurant features a wide and varied menu.

Rooms: 81

FOREST ROW
East Sussex

Map 6 TQ43

Ashdown Park Hotel & Country Club

★★★★ ⊛⊛ 🍷 HOTEL

Wych Cross, RH18 5JR - tel: 01342 824988
email: reservations@ashdownpark.com **web:** www.ashdownpark.com
dir: *A264 to East Grinstead, then A22 to Eastbourne. 3m S of Forest Row*
at Wych Cross lights. Left to Hartfield, hotel on right 0.75m

Situated in 186 acres of landscaped gardens and parkland, this impressive
country house enjoys a peaceful countryside setting in the heart of the Ashdown
Forest. Bedrooms are individually styled and decorated. Public rooms include a
restored 18th-century chapel, ideal for exclusive meetings and wedding parties,
plus three drawing rooms, a cocktail bar and the award-winning Anderida
Restaurant. The extensive indoor and outdoor leisure facilities include the
Country Club and Spa plus an 18-hole, par 3 golf course and driving range.

Rooms: 106 (12 family) (16 GF) **Facilities:** Spa FTV WiFi HL 🏊 ♨ 18 Putting
green 🏌 🚴 Gym Aerobics Snooker Clay pigeon Archery Falconry Cycling Xmas
New Year **Conf:** Class 100 Board 40 Thtr 160 **Services:** Night porter **Parking:** 200
Notes: Civ Wed 150

FOWEY
Cornwall & Isles of Scilly   Map 2 SX15

The Fowey Hotel
RICHARDSON HOTELS
Where Memories are Made

★★★★ 78% ◉◉ HOTEL

The Esplanade, PL23 1HX - tel: 01726 832551
email: reservations@thefoweyhotel.co.uk **web:** www.thefoweyhotel.co.uk
dir: *A30 to Okehampton, continue to Bodmin. Then B3269 to Fowey for 1m,
on right bend left junct then right into Dagands Rd. Hotel 200mtrs*

This attractive hotel stands proudly above the estuary, with marvellous views of the
river from the public areas and the majority of the bedrooms. High standards are
evident throughout, augmented by a relaxed and welcoming atmosphere. There is a
spacious bar, an elegant restaurant and a smart drawing room. Imaginative
dinners make good use of quality local ingredients.

Rooms: 37 (2 family) ⚓ **Facilities:** FTV WiFi Xmas New Year **Conf:** Class 60 Board 20
Thtr 100 **Services:** Lift Night porter **Parking:** 17 **Notes:** Civ Wed 120

Fowey Hall

AA Advertised ◉◉

Hanson Drive, PL23 1ET - tel: 01726 833866
email: info@foweyhallhotel.co.uk **web:** www.foweyhallhotel.co.uk
dir: *M5, A30 turn off at Bodmin, follow signs to Lostwithiel & Fowey*

Built in 1899, this listed mansion looks out on to the English Channel. The
imaginatively designed bedrooms offer charm, individuality and sumptuous
comfort; the Garden Wing rooms add an extra dimension to a stay here. The
beautifully appointed public rooms include the wood-panelled dining room where
accomplished cuisine is served. This is a very family friendly hotel with a crèche,
baby sitting and listening services, plus many other facilities for children. The
luxury spa includes a swimming pool, treatment rooms and a sun deck with a
glorious view.

Rooms: 36 (8 annexe) (30 family) (10 GF) **D** £140–£690 (incl. bkfst)*
Facilities: Spa FTV WiFi ⓘ Free crèche for children of 0-8 yrs Xmas New Year
Conf: Class 20 Board 20 Thtr 40 **Services:** Night porter **Parking:** 40 **Notes:** Civ
Wed 120

FRADDON
Cornwall & Isles of Scilly   Map 2 SW95

Premier Inn Newquay (A30/Fraddon)

BUDGET HOTEL

Penhale Round, TR9 6NA - tel: 0871 527 8816 (Calls cost 13p per minute plus your
phone company's access charge) **web:** www.premierinn.com
dir: *On A30, 2m S of Indian Queens*

High quality, budget accommodation ideal for both families and business
travellers. Spacious, en suite bedrooms feature free WiFi and tea and coffee making
facilities, and in most hotels, Freeview TV is also available. The adjacent family
restaurant features a wide and varied menu.

Rooms: 65

FRANKBY
Merseyside   Map 15 SJ28

Hillbark Hotel & Spa

★★★★★ 86% ◉◉ HOTEL

Royden Park, CH48 1NP - tel: 0151 625 2400
email: enquiries@hillbarkhotel.co.uk **web:** www.hillbarkhotel.co.uk
dir: *M53 junct 3, A552 Upton, right onto A551 Arrowe Park Rd. 0.6m at lights
left into Arrowe Brook Rd. 0.5m on left*

Originally built in 1891 on Bidston Hill, this Elizabethan-style mansion was actually
moved, brick by brick, to its current site in 1931. The house now sits in a 250-acre
woodland estate and enjoys delightful views towards the River Dee and to hills in
North Wales. Bedrooms are luxuriously furnished and well equipped, while elegant
day rooms are richly styled. There is a choice of eating options, including a fine
dining restaurant, and guests also have use of a spa.

Rooms: 18 (1 family) ⚓ **S** £170–£715; **D** £190–£735 (incl. bkfst)* **Facilities:** Spa
STV FTV WiFi ⓘ Gym Cinema Library Games room Children's play area Xmas
New Year **Conf:** Class 300 Board 60 Thtr 750 Del from £204 **Services:** Lift Night
porter **Parking:** 160 **Notes:** LB Civ Wed 500

FRESHWATER
Isle of Wight   Map 5 SZ38

Albion Hotel

★★★ 73% HOTEL

PO40 9RA - tel: 01983 755755 **email:** enquiries@albionhotel.info
web: www.sandringhamhotel.co.uk/albion
dir: *Phone for directions*

In an idyllic location on the island's southern heritage coast, the Albion Hotel is
right on the seafront with stunning views of Freshwater Bay. The bedrooms and
bathrooms are spacious and offer guests modern, comfortable accommodation;
many rooms have balconies. Breakfast and dinner are served in the traditionally
styled restaurant that also enjoys the lovely views.

Rooms: 40 **Facilities:** ⓘ Xmas **Conf:** Class 30 Board 40 Thtr 60 **Parking:** 30

FROME
Somerset   Map 4 ST74

Premier Inn Frome

BUDGET HOTEL

Commerce Park, Jenson Avenue, BA11 2LD - tel: 0871 527 8404 (Calls cost 13p per
minute plus your phone company's access charge) **web:** www.premierinn.com
dir: *M4 junct 18, A46 follow Warminster & Frome signs. Hotel off A361 (Frome bypass)
in Commerce Park*

High quality, budget accommodation ideal for both families and business
travellers. Spacious, en suite bedrooms feature free WiFi and tea and coffee making
facilities, and in most hotels, Freeview TV is also available. The adjacent family
restaurant features a wide and varied menu.

Rooms: 119

F

GARSTANG
Lancashire   Map 18 SD44

Best Western Garstang Country Hotel & Golf Centre

★★★ 77% HOTEL

Garstang Road, Bowgreave, PR3 1YE - tel: 01995 600100
email: reception@garstanghotelandgolf.com **web:** www.garstanghotelandgolf.com
dir: *M6 junct 32 take 1st right after Shell garage on A6 onto B6430. 1m, hotel on left*

This smart, purpose-built hotel enjoys a peaceful location alongside its own 18-hole golf course. Comfortable and spacious bedrooms are well equipped for both business and leisure guests, while inviting public areas include quiet lounges, the Kingfisher restaurant and the more informal Brad Beer Brasserie.

Rooms: 33 (17 GF) ⌂ **S** £60–£85; **D** £75–£100* **Facilities:** STV FTV WiFi ⌂ ⌘ 18 Putting green Golf driving range Xmas New Year **Conf:** Class 150 Board 80 Thtr 250 Del from £75 **Services:** Lift Night porter **Parking:** 172 **Notes:** LB Civ Wed 200

GATESHEAD
Tyne & Wear   Map 21 NZ26

HIGHLY RECOMMENDED

Eslington Villa Hotel
★★★ 84% HOTEL

8 Station Road, Low Fell, NE9 6DR - tel: 0191 487 6017
email: home@eslingtonvilla.co.uk **web:** www.eslingtonvilla.co.uk
dir: *From A1(M) exit for Team Valley Trading Estate. Right at 2nd rdbt along Eastern Avenue. Left at car show room, hotel 100 yds on left*

Set in a residential area, this smart hotel combines a bright, contemporary atmosphere with the period style of a fine Victorian villa. The overall ambience is relaxed and inviting. Chunky sofas grace the cocktail lounge, while tempting dishes can be enjoyed in either the classical dining room or modern conservatory overlooking the Team Valley.

Rooms: 17 (2 family) (3 GF) ⌂ **S** £74.50–£89.50; **D** £94.50–£125 (incl. bkfst)* **Facilities:** FTV WiFi **Conf:** Class 30 Board 25 Thtr 36 Del from £130 **Services:** Night porter **Parking:** 28 **Notes:** LB Closed 25–26 Dec, 1 Jan

Ramada Encore Newcastle - Gateshead
★★★ 79% HOTEL

Hawks Road, Gateshead Quays, NE8 3AD - tel: 0191 481 3600
email: enquiries@encorenewcastlegateshead.co.uk
web: www.encorenewcastlegateshead.co.uk
dir: *Located Gateshead Quays*

This modern, purpose-built hotel is located at the Gateshead Quays. Bedrooms are well appointed and comfortable, with well-presented en suites. Public areas are open-plan with a relaxed all-day menu serving food in all locations. A small gym and off-road parking are added benefits.

Rooms: 200 (75 family) ⌂ **Facilities:** FTV WiFi ⌂ HL Gym **Conf:** Class 14 Board 18 Thtr 20 **Services:** Lift Night porter **Parking:** 70

Premier Inn Newcastle (Metro Centre)

BUDGET HOTEL

Derwent Haugh Road, Swalwell, NE16 3BL - tel: 0871 527 8792 (Calls cost 13p per minute plus your phone company's access charge) **web:** www.premierinn.com
dir: *From A1 & A694 junct into Derwent Haugh Rd. 1m N of Metro Centre*

High quality, budget accommodation ideal for both families and business travellers. Spacious, en suite bedrooms feature free WiFi and tea and coffee making facilities, and in most hotels, Freeview TV is also available. The adjacent family restaurant features a wide and varied menu.

Rooms: 72

Premier Inn Newcastle South
BUDGET HOTEL

Lobley Hill Road, NE11 9NA - tel: 0871 527 8806 (Calls cost 13p per minute plus your phone company's access charge) **web:** www.premierinn.com
dir: *A1 onto A692*

Rooms: 42

Premier Inn Newcastle (Team Valley)
BUDGET HOTEL

Maingate, Kingsway North, NE11 0BE - tel: 0871 527 8794 (Calls cost 13p per minute plus your phone company's access charge) **web:** www.premierinn.com
dir: *A1 onto B1426 signed Team Valley (S'bound) or Teams/Consett (N'bound). Take Gateshead exit at rdbt. At bottom of hill straight on at rdbt. Hotel opposite*

Rooms: 115

GATWICK AIRPORT
West Sussex   Map 6 TQ24

See also **Dorking, East Grinstead & Reigate**

INSPECTOR'S CHOICE

Langshott Manor
★★★★ COUNTRY HOUSE HOTEL

Langshott Lane, RH6 9LN - tel: 01293 786680
email: admin@langshottmanor.com **web:** www.langshottmanor.com
dir: *From A23 take Ladbroke Rd, off rdbt to Langshott, after 0.75m hotel on right*

On the outskirts of Horley, this charming timber-framed Tudor manor house is set amidst beautifully landscaped grounds with an ancient moat. The stylish public areas feature a choice of inviting lounges with polished oak panelling, exposed beams and crackling log fires. Each bedroom - whether in the manor itself or in one of three mews buildings in the grounds - has been designed with flair and imagination. Expect sumptuous furnishings, Egyptian linens, flat-screen TVs and bathrooms with deep baths and power showers. The Mulberry restaurant overlooks a picturesque pond and offers an imaginative menu.

Rooms: 22 (15 annexe) (2 family) (8 GF) ☞ **S** £99–£119; **D** £129–£259* **Facilities:** FTV WiFi ↴ ⛄ Xmas New Year **Conf:** Class 20 Board 22 Thtr 40 **Services:** Night porter **Parking:** 25 **Notes:** Civ Wed 60

Holiday Inn London Gatwick Worth

★★★★ 79% HOTEL

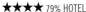

Crabbet Park, Turners Hill Road, RH10 4SS - **tel:** 01293 884806 **email:** info@ higatwickworth.co.uk **web:** www.higatwickworth.co.uk **dir:** M23 junct 10/A264 Copthorne Way at rdbt last exit towards Three Bridges. 1st left along Old Hollow, right at end of lane then 1st right into Crabbet Park

This purpose-built hotel is ideally placed for access to Gatwick Airport. The bedrooms are spacious and suitably appointed with good facilities. Public areas consist of a light and airy bar area and a brasserie-style restaurant offering good value meals. Guests have use of the superb leisure club next door.

Rooms: 118 (39 family) (56 GF) ☞ **Facilities:** FTV WiFi ↴ HL Use of gym & pool next door (chargeable) Xmas New Year **Conf:** Class 80 Board 80 Thtr 250 **Services:** Lift Night porter Air con **Parking:** 150 **Notes:** Civ Wed 60

Sofitel London Gatwick

★★★★ 78% ⬤⬤ HOTEL

North Terminal, RH6 0PH - **tel:** 01293 567070 **email:** slg@sofitelgatwick.com **web:** www.sofitelgatwick.com **dir:** M23 junct 9, follow to 2nd rdbt. Hotel straight ahead

One of the closest hotels to the airport, this modern, purpose-built hotel is located only minutes from the terminals. Bedrooms are contemporary and all are air conditioned. Guests have a choice of eating options including a French-style café, a brasserie and an oriental restaurant.

Rooms: 518 (19 family) **S** £234; **D** £234* **Facilities:** FTV WiFi ↴ Gym **Conf:** Class 150 Board 90 Thtr 300 **Services:** Lift Night porter Air con **Parking:** 565

Hilton London Gatwick Airport Hotel

★★★★ 74% HOTEL

South Terminal, RH6 0LL - **tel:** 01293 518080 **email:** london.gatwick@hilton.com **web:** www.hilton.com **dir:** M23 junct 9 towards Gatwick Airport, then 1st exit at junct 9a & follow the road. Right after 600yds

In an excellent location at Gatwick Airport with a direct covered link from the main hotel to the Gatwick South Terminal, this hotel offers a range of facilities including two restaurants, bars, fitness facilities and onsite parking. Bedrooms are modern and comfortably appointed, very quiet rooms offering a good overnight stay for corporate and leisure guests alike.

Rooms: 821 (31 family) (47 GF) (22 smoking) ☞ **Facilities:** FTV HL Gym **Conf:** Class 225 Board 80 Thtr 450 **Services:** Lift Night porter Air con **Notes:** LB

Stanhill Court Hotel

★★★ 81% HOTEL

Stanhill Road, Charlwood, RH6 0EP - **tel:** 01293 862166 **email:** enquiries@stanhillcourthotel.co.uk **web:** www.stanhillcourthotel.co.uk **dir:** N of Charlwood towards Newdigate

This hotel dates back to 1881 and enjoys a secluded location of 35 acres of well-tended grounds with views over the Downs. Bedrooms are individually furnished and decorated, and many have four-poster beds. Public areas include a library, a bright Spanish-style bar and a traditional wood-panelled restaurant. Extensive and varied function facilities make this a popular wedding venue.

Rooms: 34 (2 family) (1 GF) ☞ **Facilities:** FTV WiFi ↴ ⛄ Xmas New Year **Conf:** Class 100 Board 70 Thtr 300 **Parking:** 150 **Notes:** Civ Wed 300

Premier Inn Gatwick Airport North

BUDGET HOTEL

Crossway, Gatwick North Terminal, RH6 0PH - **tel:** 0871 527 9354 (Calls cost 13p per minute plus your phone company's access charge) **web:** www.premierinn.com **dir:** M23 junct 9. Follow signs for Gatwick North Terminal, at North Terminal rdbt enter at Arrivals Road (2nd exit), turn right onto Northway (Drop Off point), hotel is on right

High quality, budget accommodation ideal for both families and business travellers. Spacious, en suite bedrooms feature free WiFi and tea and coffee making facilities, and in most hotels, Freeview TV is also available. The adjacent family restaurant features a wide and varied menu.

Rooms: 701

Premier Inn Gatwick Airport South

BUDGET HOTEL

London Road, Lowfield Heath, RH10 9ST - **tel:** 0871 527 8408 (Calls cost 13p per minute plus your phone company's access charge) **web:** www.premierinn.com **dir:** M23 junct 9a towards North Terminal rdbt. Follow A23 & Crawley signs. Hotel in 2m

Rooms: 105

Premier Inn Gatwick Crawley Town (Goffs Park)

BUDGET HOTEL

45 Goffs Park Road, RH11 8AX - **tel:** 0871 527 8414 (Calls cost 13p per minute plus your phone company's access charge) **web:** www.premierinn.com **dir:** M23 junct 11, A23 towards Crawley. At 2nd rdbt take 3rd exit for town centre, then 2nd right into Goffs Park Rd

Rooms: 48

Premier Inn Gatwick Crawley Town West

BUDGET HOTEL

Crawley Avenue, Gossops Green, RH10 8BA - **tel:** 0871 527 8412 (Calls cost 13p per minute plus your phone company's access charge) **web:** www.premierinn.com **dir:** M23 junct 11, A23 towards Crawley & Gatwick Airport

Rooms: 83

GATWICK AIRPORT *continued*

Premier Inn London Gatwick Airport A23

BUDGET HOTEL

Longbridge Way, North Terminal, RH6 0NX - tel: 0871 527 8406 (Calls cost 13p per minute plus your phone company's access charge) **web:** www.premierinn.com **dir:** *M23 junct 9/9A towards North Terminal, at rdbt take 3rd exit, hotel on right*

Rooms: 220

Premier Inn London Gatwick Airport East

BUDGET HOTEL

Balcombe Road, Worth, RH10 3NL - tel: 0871 527 8410 (Calls cost 13p per minute plus your phone company's access charge) **web:** www.premierinn.com **dir:** *M23 junct 10, B2036 S towards Crawley*

Rooms: 42

Premier Inn London Gatwick Manor Royal

BUDGET HOTEL

Crawley Business Quarter, Fleming Way, RH10 9DF - tel: 0871 527 9214 (Calls cost 13p per minute plus your phone company's access charge) **web:** www.premierinn.com **dir:** *M23 junct 10, A2011 (Crawley Ave). At rdbt 4th exit onto A23 (London Rd), at rdbt right into Fleming Way. Hotel 300yds on left*

Rooms: 204

Arora Hotel Gatwick

AA Advertised

Southgate Avenue, Southgate, RH10 6LW - tel: 01293 597701 & 530000 **email:** gatwick@arorahotels.com **web:** www.arorahotels.com **dir:** *M23 junct 10 then A2011 to Crawley. At 1st rdbt take 2nd exit towards town centre, at 2nd rdbt take 1st exit towards the County Mall. At both sets of lights proceed straight over; the County Mall on right, go straight under railway bridge, hotel on right*

The Arora Hotel Gatwick/Crawley is situated in the heart of Crawley town centre, perfectly placed for easy access to M23/A23 and M25 motorways, direct access to Crawley train station, and a short journey from Gatwick Airport by direct bus transfer. Accommodation is stylish and there are excellent meeting, conference, training and banqueting facilities. Meals and drinks can be taken in the Grill restaurant, a traditional pub or the bar. There is also an internet café, a luxurious health and fitness club and on-site car parking facilities.

Rooms: 432 (120 annexe) (15 family) (24 GF) ⬥ **S** £65–£160; **D** £65–£185 **Facilities:** FTV WiFi ↕ HL Gym Treatment room Xmas **Conf:** Class 150 Board 60 Thtr 270 Del from £125 **Services:** Lift Night porter Air con **Parking:** 245 **Notes:** Civ Wed 270

GERRARDS CROSS	Map 6 TQ08
Buckinghamshire	

The Bull Hotel

★★★★ 78% ◉ HOTEL

Oxford Road, SL9 7PA - tel: 01753 885995 **email:** bull@sarova.com **web:** www.sarova.com **dir:** *M40 junct 2 follow Beaconsfield on A355. After 0.5m 2nd exit at rdbt signed A40 Gerrards Cross for 2m. The Bull is on right*

Dating from the 17th-century, this former inn has been extensively refurbished to provide smart, well-equipped bedrooms. Public areas include the popular bar and

Beeches Restaurant, serving a wide variety of dishes to suit all tastes. In addition there is the informal Jack Shrimpton bar offering snacks and bar meals. Attractive gardens and a good range of function rooms make this a popular wedding and events venue.

Rooms: 150 (15 family) (19 GF) ⬥ **S** £80–£240; **D** £90–£250* **Facilities:** FTV WiFi ↕ Use of private leisure facilities Xmas New Year **Conf:** Class 108 Board 40 Thtr 180 Del from £180 **Services:** Lift Night porter **Parking:** 150 **Notes:** Civ Wed 114

GILLINGHAM	Map 7 TQ76
Kent	

Premier Inn Chatham/Gillingham (Victory Pier)

BUDGET HOTEL

Blake Avenue, ME7 1GB - tel: 0871 527 9510 (Calls cost 13p per minute plus your phone company's access charge) **web:** www.premierinn.com **dir:** *From A289 (Pier Rd) in Gillingham, at lights, into Pegasus Way. 1st left*

High quality, budget accommodation ideal for both families and business travellers. Spacious, en suite bedrooms feature free WiFi and tea and coffee making facilities, and in most hotels, Freeview TV is also available. The adjacent family restaurant features a wide and varied menu.

Rooms: 80

Premier Inn Gillingham Business Park

BUDGET HOTEL

Will Adams Way, ME8 6BY - tel: 0871 527 8416 (Calls cost 13p per minute plus your phone company's access charge) **web:** www.premierinn.com **dir:** *M2 junct 44, A278 to A2. Left at Tesco. Hotel at next rdbt*

Rooms: 76

Premier Inn Gillingham/Rainham

BUDGET HOTEL

High Street, Rainham, ME8 7JE - tel: 0871 527 9268 (Calls cost 13p per minute plus your phone company's access charge) **web:** www.premierinn.com **dir:** *M25 junct 2 (Canterbury/Dover/A2), A2 to M2 (Dover). Exit at junct 4 (Rainham/Medway Tunnel), straight on at 2 rdbts. At 3rd rdbt take 3rd exit (Rainham High St). Hotel on right at 3rd lights*

Rooms: 26

GIRTON	Map 12 TL46
Cambridgeshire	

Premier Inn Cambridge North (Girton)

BUDGET HOTEL

Huntingdon Road, CB3 0DR - tel: 0871 527 8188 (Calls cost 13p per minute plus your phone company's access charge) **web:** www.premierinn.com **dir:** *A14 junct 31 follow signs towards Cambridge. Pass BP garage, next right. Hotel adjacent to Traveller's Rest Beefeater*

High quality, budget accommodation ideal for both families and business travellers. Spacious, en suite bedrooms feature free WiFi and tea and coffee making facilities, and in most hotels, Freeview TV is also available. The adjacent family restaurant features a wide and varied menu.

Rooms: 20

GLASTONBURY
Somerset

Map 4 ST53

Premier Inn Glastonbury

BUDGET HOTEL

Morland Road, BA6 9FW - **tel:** 0871 527 9398 (Calls cost 13p per minute plus your phone company's access charge) **web:** www.premierinn.com
dir: *From A361 & A39 rdbt junct (SW of Glastonbury) take A39 towards Street. Right at lights into Morlands Enterprise Park. Left at 1st rdbt*

High quality, budget accommodation ideal for both families and business travellers. Spacious, en suite bedrooms feature free WiFi and tea and coffee making facilities, and in most hotels, Freeview TV is also available. The adjacent family restaurant features a wide and varied menu.

Rooms: 78

GLENRIDDING
Cumbria

Map 18 NY31

HIGHLY RECOMMENDED

Inn on the Lake

★★★★ 83% HOTEL

Lake Ullswater, CA11 0PE - **tel:** 017684 82444
email: innonthelake@lakedistricthotels.net
web: www.lakedistricthotels.net/innonthelake
dir: *M6 junct 40, A66 to Keswick. At rdbt take A592 to Ullswater Lake. Along lake to Glenridding. Hotel on left on entering village*

In a picturesque lakeside setting, this restored Victorian hotel is a popular leisure destination as well as catering for weddings and conferences. Superb views can be enjoyed from the bedrooms and from the garden terrace where afternoon teas are served during warmer months. There is a popular pub in the grounds, and moorings for yachts are available to guests. Sailing tuition can be arranged.

Rooms: 47 (20 family) (1 GF) **Facilities:** FTV WiFi Putting green Gym Sauna 9 hole pitch & putt course Xmas New Year **Conf:** Class 42 Board 30 Thtr 100 **Services:** Lift Night porter **Parking:** 100 **Notes:** Civ Wed 110

Best Western Glenridding Hotel
BW Best Western.

★★★ 79% HOTEL

CA11 0PB - **tel:** 01768 482289
email: glenridding@bestwestern.co.uk **web:** www.bw-glenriddinghotel.co.uk
dir: *N'bound M6 junct 36, A591 Windermere then A592 for 14m. S'bound M6 junct 40, A592 for 13m*

Like a phoenix rising from the ashes, The Best Western Glenridding Hotel has reopened after a massive refurbishment programme which shows great results. This friendly hotel benefits from a picturesque location in the village centre, and many rooms have fine views of the lake and fells. Public areas are extensive, and include a choice of dining options: the Garden Room Restaurant, Let it Brew café and the fantastic Beckside Bar with great outside seating by the bubbling beck. Leisure facilities are available along with a conference room and a garden function room.

Rooms: 36 (7 family) (8 GF) **Facilities:** STV WiFi Spa bath Sauna Snooker Table tennis Xmas New Year **Conf:** Class 30 Board 24 Thtr 30 **Services:** Lift **Parking:** 30 **Notes:** Civ Wed 120

GLOSSOP
Derbyshire

Map 16 SK09

Wind in the Willows Hotel
★★ 85% COUNTRY HOUSE HOTEL

Derbyshire Level, SK13 7PT - **tel:** 01457 868001
email: info@windinthewillows.co.uk **web:** www.windinthewillows.co.uk
dir: *1m E of Glossop on A57, turn right opposite Royal Oak, hotel 400yds on right*

This impressive house sits in peaceful grounds with lovely views of the Peak District National Park. Individually furnished bedrooms are in keeping with the Victorian style of the house. Beautiful original oak panelling and crackling log fires add to the charm of the lounges and dining room. There is also a conference suite that is perfect for meetings, private dining or special occasions.

Rooms: 12 **Facilities:** FTV WiFi Xmas New Year **Conf:** Class 12 Board 16 Thtr 40 **Parking:** 16 **Notes:** LB No children 10yrs

G

GLOUCESTER
Gloucestershire

Map 10 SO81

Hatherley Manor

★★★★ 76% HOTEL

Down Hatherley Lane, GL2 9QA - **tel:** 01452 730217
email: reservations@hatherleymanor.com **web:** www.hatherleymanor.com
dir: *A38 into Down Hatherley Lane, signed. Hotel 600yds on left*

Within easy striking distance of the M5, Gloucester, Cheltenham and the Cotswolds, this stylish 17th-century manor, set in attractive grounds, remains popular with both business and leisure guests. Bedrooms are well appointed and offer contemporary comforts. A particularly impressive range of meeting and function rooms is available.

Rooms: 50 (5 family) (18 GF) **Facilities:** FTV WiFi Xmas New Year **Conf:** Class 90 Board 75 Thtr 400 **Services:** Night porter **Parking:** 250 **Notes:** Civ Wed 300

Hatton Court
★★★★ 76% COUNTRY HOUSE HOTEL

Upton Hill, Upton St Leonards, GL4 8DE - **tel:** 01452 617412
email: res@hatton-court.co.uk **web:** www.hatton-court.co.uk
dir: *From Gloucester on B4073 Painswick Rd. Hotel at top of hill on right*

Built in the style of a 17th-century Cotswold manor house and set in seven acres of well-kept gardens, this hotel is popular with both business and leisure guests. It stands at the top of Upton Hill and commands truly spectacular views of the Severn Valley. The bedrooms, including a four-poster room, are comfortable and tastefully furnished with many extra facilities. The elegant Tara Restaurant offers varied menus, and outdoor seating in summer; there is also a bar and foyer lounge.

Rooms: 45 (28 annexe) (6 family) **Facilities:** FTV WiFi HL Gym Xmas New Year **Conf:** Class 100 Board 60 Thtr 200 **Services:** Night porter **Parking:** 80 **Notes:** LB Civ Wed 120

GLOUCESTER *continued*

Hallmark Hotel Gloucester

★★★★ 74% HOTEL

Matson Lane, Robinswood Hill, GL4 6EA - **tel:** 0330 028 3408
email: gloucester@hallmarkhotels.co.uk **web:** www.hallmarkhotels.co.uk
dir: *A40 towards Gloucester onto A38. 1st exit at 4th rdbt (Painswick Rd).
Right onto Matson Lane*

Ideally located for exploring the Cotswolds and Gloucester, this hotel offers
well-appointed bedrooms and relaxing public areas. The large leisure club has
a well-equipped gym, squash courts and pool. Complimentary WiFi is available
throughout.

Rooms: 95 (6 family) (21 GF) ⌖ **S** fr £55; **D** fr £55* **Facilities:** Spa FTV WiFi ⌖ ⌖
supervised Gym Squash Beauty salon Xmas New Year **Conf:** Class 150 Board 18
Thtr 220 Del from £125 **Services:** Night porter **Parking:** 200 **Notes:** Civ Wed 120

Mercure Gloucester, Bowden Hall Hotel

★★★★ 74% HOTEL

Bondend Lane, Upton St Leonards, GL4 8ED - **tel:** 01452 614121 & 0844 815 9077
(Calls cost 7p per minute plus your phone company's access charge) **email:** info@
mercuregloucester.co.uk **web:** www.mercuregloucester.co.uk
dir: *A417/A38/Gloucester. At rdbt take 2nd exit. At 2nd lights left onto Abbeymead Ave/
Metz Way. 1.5m, 3rd left onto Upton Lane, left into Bondend Rd, then left into Bondend
Lane. Hotel at end*

Conveniently located a short distance from the M5, the hotel is set in delightful
grounds and is an ideal venue for weddings, banquets and meetings, or for a quiet
break. Bedrooms are spacious and nicely appointed and many have lovely views of
the grounds. Guests can choose to dine in the restaurant or bar.

Rooms: 72 (15 family) ⌖ **Facilities:** FTV WiFi ⌖ HL ⌖ Xmas New Year **Conf:** Class 70
Board 35 Thtr 180 **Parking:** 180 **Notes:** Civ Wed 200

Premier Inn Gloucester (Barnwood)

BUDGET HOTEL

Barnwood, GL4 3HR - **tel:** 0871 527 8456 (Calls cost 13p per minute plus your phone
company's access charge) **web:** www.premierinn.com
dir: *M5 junct 11, A40 towards Gloucester. At 1st rdbt A417 towards Cirencester,
at next rdbt take 4th exit*

High quality, budget accommodation ideal for both families and business
travellers. Spacious, en suite bedrooms feature free WiFi and tea and coffee making
facilities, and in most hotels, Freeview TV is also available. The adjacent family
restaurant features a wide and varied menu.

Rooms: 83

Premier Inn Gloucester Business Park

BUDGET HOTEL

Gloucester Business Park, Brockworth, GL3 4AJ - **tel:** 0871 527 8462 (Calls cost 13p
per minute plus your phone company's access charge) **web:** www.premierinn.com
dir: *M5 junct 11a, A417 towards Cirencester. At Brockworth Rdbt follow Gloucester
Business Park signs, onto dual carriageway (Valiant Way). At next rdbt left into Delta Way.
Hotel adjacent to Tesco*

Rooms: 48

Premier Inn Gloucester (Little Witcombe)

BUDGET HOTEL

Witcombe, GL3 4SS - **tel:** 0871 527 8458 (Calls cost 13p per minute plus your phone
company's access charge) **web:** www.premierinn.com
dir: *M5 junct 11a, A417 signed Cirencester. At 1st exit turn right onto A46 towards Stroud
& Witcombe. Left at next rdbt by Crosshands pub*

Rooms: 59

Premier Inn Gloucester (Longford)

BUDGET HOTEL

Tewkesbury Road, Longford, GL2 9BE - **tel:** 0871 527 8460 (Calls cost 13p per minute
plus your phone company's access charge) **web:** www.premierinn.com
dir: *M5 junct 11, A40 towards Gloucester & Ross-on-Wye. Hotel on A38
towards Gloucester*

Rooms: 60

Premier Inn Gloucester (Twigworth)

BUDGET HOTEL

Tewkesbury Road, Twigworth, GL2 9PG - **tel:** 0871 527 8464 (Calls cost 13p per minute
plus your phone company's access charge) **web:** www.premierinn.com
dir: *On A38, 1m N from junct with A40*

Rooms: 50

GOATHLAND	Map 19 NZ80
North Yorkshire	

HIGHLY RECOMMENDED

Mallyan Spout Hotel

★★★ 86% ⌖ COUNTRY HOUSE HOTEL

YO22 5AN - **tel:** 01947 896486
email: info@mallyanspout.co.uk **web:** www.mallyanspout.co.uk
dir: *A169 Pickering to Whitby. Take Goathland turn, hotel opp St Mary's Church*

This Grade II listed building is set in the charming village of Goathland, which is
best known as the setting of the fictional village of Aidensfield in the popular TV
series *Heartbeat*. The popular seaside resort of Whitby is just a short driving
distance away. The hotel is privately owned and is full of character and charm.
The bedrooms provide comfortable accommodation and the public areas house
three lounges, some with open fires, and a bar boasting a selection of real ales.
The restaurant serves a good mix of modern and traditional dishes.

Rooms: 20 (4 family) ⌖ **S** £75; **D** £120–£165 (incl. bkfst)* **Facilities:** FTV WiFi
New Year **Conf:** Class 50 Board 35 Thtr 50 Del from £145 **Services:** Night porter
Parking: 24 **Notes:** Closed 23-27 Dec Civ Wed 65

G

GODALMING
Surrey   Map 6 SU94

Premier Inn Godalming

BUDGET HOTEL

Guildford Road, GU7 3BX - **tel:** 0871 527 8466 (Calls cost 13p per minute plus your phone company's access charge) **web:** www.premierinn.com
dir: *Exit A3 onto A3000 signed Godalming. 1m to rdbt, turn right into Guildford Rd towards Godalming. Hotel on left in 500yds*

High quality, budget accommodation ideal for both families and business travellers. Spacious, en suite bedrooms feature free WiFi and tea and coffee making facilities, and in most hotels, Freeview TV is also available. The adjacent family restaurant features a wide and varied menu.

Rooms: 16

GOLANT
Cornwall & Isles of Scilly   Map 2 SX15

Cormorant Hotel & Restaurant

★★★ 82% ◉◉ HOTEL

PL23 1LL - **tel:** 01726 833426
email: relax@cormoranthotel.co.uk **web:** www.cormoranthotel.co.uk
dir: *A390 onto B3269 signed Fowey. In 3m left to Golant, through village to end of road, hotel on right*

This hotel focuses on traditional hospitality, attentive service and good food. All the bedrooms enjoy views of the river, and guests can expect goose down duvets, flat-screen digital TVs and free WiFi access. Breakfast and lunch may be taken on the terrace which overlooks the river.

Rooms: 14 (4 GF) ☏ **S** £75–£235; **D** £100–£235 (incl. bkfst)* **Facilities:** FTV WiFi ⅛ Xmas New Year **Parking:** 20 **Notes:** LB No children 16yrs

GOMERSAL
West Yorkshire   Map 19 SE22

Gomersal Park Hotel

★★★ 79% HOTEL

Moor Lane, BD19 4LJ - **tel:** 01274 869386
email: enquiries@gomersalparkhotel.com **web:** www.gomersalparkhotel.com
dir: *A62 to Huddersfield. At junct with A65, by Greyhound Pub right, after 1m take 1st right after Oakwell Hall*

Constructed around a 19th-century house, this stylish, modern hotel enjoys a peaceful location and pleasant grounds. Deep sofas ensure comfort in the open-plan lounge, and the Massimo Italian Restaurant offers a wide choice of freshly prepared meals. The well-equipped bedrooms are contemporary and comfortable. Extensive public areas include a fantastic, newly built leisure spa and a wide variety of air-conditioned conference and function suites.

Rooms: 86 (3 family) (32 GF) ☏ **S** £89–£109; **D** £89–£109 **Facilities:** Spa FTV WiFi ⅛ ⓧ supervised Gym Sauna **Conf:** Class 130 Board 60 Thtr 250 **Services:** Lift Night porter **Parking:** 150 **Notes:** Civ Wed 200

GOODRINGTON
See **Paignton**

GOODWOOD
West Sussex   Map 6 SU81

The Goodwood Hotel

★★★★ 80% ◉◉ HOTEL

PO18 0QB - **tel:** 01243 775537
email: reservations@goodwood.com **web:** www.goodwood.com/estate/the-goodwood-hotel
dir: *Off A285, 3m NE of Chichester*

Set at the centre of the 12,000-acre Goodwood Estate, this attractive hotel boasts extensive indoor and outdoor leisure facilities, along with a range of meeting rooms plus conference and banqueting facilities. Bedrooms are furnished to a consistently high standard, including individually decorated character rooms located in the old coaching inn; and garden rooms, each with a patio. Eating options include The Richmond Arms which sources produce extensively from the Estate's very own farm; The Richmond Arms Bar, and The Goodwood Bar and Grill. Overnight guests can also choose to dine in The Kennels, a private members' clubhouse.

Rooms: 91 (15 family) (31 GF) ☏ **S** £105–£170; **D** £115–£180 (incl. bkfst)* **Facilities:** Spa STV FTV WiFi ⅛ ⓧ ⅃ 18 Putting green ⌣ Gym Golf driving range Sauna Steam room Fitness studio Xmas New Year **Conf:** Class 60 Board 40 Thtr 150 Del from £192 **Services:** Night porter **Parking:** 150 **Notes:** LB Civ Wed 120

GOOLE
East Riding of Yorkshire   Map 17 SE72

Premier Inn Goole

BUDGET HOTEL

Rawcliffe Road, Airmyn, DN14 8JS - **tel:** 0871 527 8468 (Calls cost 13p per minute plus your phone company's access charge) **web:** www.premierinn.com
dir: *M62 junct 36, A614 signed Rawcliffe. Hotel immediately on left*

High quality, budget accommodation ideal for both families and business travellers. Spacious, en suite bedrooms feature free WiFi and tea and coffee making facilities, and in most hotels, Freeview TV is also available. The adjacent family restaurant features a wide and varied menu.

Rooms: 73

GORDANO SERVICE AREA (M5)
Somerset   Map 4 ST57

Days Inn Bristol West - M5

AA Advertised

BS20 7XG - **tel:** 01275 373709
email: gordano.hotel@welcomebreak.co.uk **web:** www.welcomebreak.co.uk
dir: *M5 junct 19, follow signs for Gordano Services*

This modern building offers accommodation in smart, spacious and well-equipped bedrooms, suitable for families and business travellers, and all with en suite bathrooms. Continental breakfast is available and other refreshments may be taken at the nearby family restaurant.

Rooms: 60 (52 family) (29 GF) (8 smoking) **Facilities:** FTV WiFi ⅛ **Conf:** Board 10 **Parking:** 60

GORLESTON ON SEA
Norfolk   Map 13 TG50

The Pier Hotel
★★★ 86% HOTEL

Harbourmouth, South Pier, NR31 6PL - tel: 01493 662631
email: bookings@pierhotelgorleston.co.uk **web:** www.pierhotelgorleston.co.uk
dir: *From A47 W of Great Yarmouth take A12 signed Lowestoft. At 3rd rdbt 1st left Beccles Rd, signed Gorleston. At rdbt 2nd left Church Rd. Next rdbt 1st left Baker St. Right into Pier Plain, then Pier Walk to Pier Gdns*

Ideally situated on the seafront this hotel offers smartly appointed bedrooms that are thoughtfully equipped and have a good range of useful extras; some rooms have superb sea views. The public areas include a large restaurant and a conservatory, which leads to a terrace and bar.

Rooms: 21 (1 family) 🕭 **S** £55–£75; **D** £70–£160 (incl. bkfst)* **Facilities:** STV FTV WiFi ⌦ New Year **Services:** Night porter **Parking:** 25 **Notes:** LB

GOSFORTH
Cumbria   Map 18 NY00

Westlakes Hotel
★★★ 87% HOTEL

CA20 1HP - tel: 019467 25221
email: info@westlakeshotel.co.uk **web:** www.westlakeshotel.co.uk
dir: *From A595 take B5344 signed Seascale. Hotel entrance 1st right*

Located amid the stunning scenery of the western lakes and within easy striking distance of a whole array of visitor attractions, Westlakes Hotel offers accommodation of a high standard, with many thoughtful extras provided. High quality food is served in the restaurant with relaxed and friendly service led by the hands-on owners and their team. There are excellent walking opportunities from this hotel.

Rooms: 10 (4 annexe) (1 GF) 🕭 **S** £91–£115; **D** £96.67–£125 (incl. bkfst)*
Facilities: FTV WiFi **Conf:** Class 30 Board 30 Thtr 50 Del from £135.50 **Parking:** 50
Notes: LB

GOSPORT
Hampshire   Map 5 SZ69

Premier Inn Gosport

BUDGET HOTEL

Fareham Road, PO13 0ZX - tel: 0871 527 9436 (Calls cost 13p per minute plus your phone company's access charge) **web:** www.premierinn.com
dir: *M27 junct 11 (W'bound exit), at Wallington rdbt 1st exit onto A27 (Fareham Central Gosport & A32). At Quay St rdbt left onto A32. At rdbt 2nd exit onto A32. Left at one-way system signed Gosport. Right at lights into Forrest Way, left into Holbrook, & Gosport Leisure Centre*

High quality, budget accommodation ideal for both families and business travellers. Spacious, en suite bedrooms feature free WiFi and tea and coffee making facilities, and in most hotels, Freeview TV is also available. The adjacent family restaurant features a wide and varied menu.

Rooms: 63

GRANGE-OVER-SANDS
Cumbria   Map 18 SD47

Netherwood Hotel
★★★ 77% HOTEL

Lindale Road, LA11 6ET - tel: 015395 32552
email: enquiries@netherwood-hotel.co.uk **web:** www.netherwood-hotel.co.uk
dir: *On B5277 before station*

This imposing hotel stands in terraced grounds, enjoys fine views of Morecambe Bay and is also popular as a conference and wedding venue. Good levels of hospitality and service ensure all guests are well looked after. Bedrooms vary in size with newly refurbished rooms that are bright and modern. Magnificent woodwork is a feature of the public areas.

Rooms: 34 (5 family) 🕭 **Facilities:** FTV WiFi ⌦ supervised ⅙ Gym Steam room Fitness centre Xmas New Year **Conf:** Class 150 Board 60 Thtr 150 **Services:** Lift Night porter **Parking:** 100 **Notes:** LB Civ Wed 200

Cumbria Grand Hotel
★★★ 73% HOTEL

LA11 6EN - tel: 015395 32331
email: salescumbria@strathmorehotels.com **web:** www.strathmorehotels.com
dir: *M6 junct 36, A590 & follow Grange-over-Sands signs*

Set within extensive grounds, this ever-improving, grand hotel offers fine views over Morecambe Bay. Public areas are pure nostalgia, and include comfortable lounges, a magnificent dining room, a fine ballroom and conference suites. Bedrooms are comfortably equipped and some have views of the bay.

Rooms: 122 (10 family) (25 GF) 🕭 **S** £35–£85; **D** £80–£130 (incl. bkfst)*
Facilities: STV WiFi Putting green ♟ Snooker & pool table Table tennis 🎵 Xmas New Year **Conf:** Class 80 Board 36 Thtr 160 Del from £65 **Services:** Lift Night porter **Parking:** 75 **Notes:** LB Civ Wed 100

INSPECTOR'S CHOICE

Clare House
★★ ◉ HOTEL

Park Road, LA11 7HQ - tel: 015395 33026
email: info@clarehousehotel.co.uk **web:** www.clarehousehotel.co.uk
dir: *A590 onto B5277, through Lindale into Grange, keep left, hotel 0.5m on left past Crown Hill & St Paul's Church*

A warm, genuine welcome awaits guests at this delightful hotel, proudly run by the Read family for over 40 years. Situated in its own secluded gardens, it provides a relaxed haven in which to enjoy the panoramic views across Morecambe Bay. The stylish bedrooms and public areas are comfortable and attractively furnished. Skilfully prepared dinners and hearty breakfasts are served in the elegant dining room.

Rooms: 18 (4 GF) ❀ **S** £96–£104; **D** £192–£208 (incl. bkfst & dinner)*
Facilities: FTV WiFi ☙ **Parking:** 18 **Notes:** Closed mid Dec-late Mar

GRANTHAM	Map 11 SK93
Lincolnshire	

Premier Inn Grantham
BUDGET HOTEL

A1/607 Junction, Harlaxton Road, NG31 7UA - tel: 0871 527 8470 (Calls cost 13p per minute plus your phone company's access charge) **web:** www.premierinn.com
dir: *A1 onto A607. N'bound: hotel on right. S'bound: under A1, hotel on left*

High quality, budget accommodation ideal for both families and business travellers. Spacious, en suite bedrooms feature free WiFi and tea and coffee making facilities, and in most hotels, Freeview TV is also available. The adjacent family restaurant features a wide and varied menu.

Rooms: 95

GRASMERE	Map 18 NY30
Cumbria	

HIGHLY RECOMMENDED

Forest Side
★★★★ 85% ◉◉◉◉ 🍷 HOTEL

Keswick Road, LA22 9RN - tel: 015394 35250
email: info@theforestside.com **web:** www.theforestside.com
dir: *M6 junct 36, 1st exit at rdbt onto A590 to Grasmere. 2nd exit at mini-rdbt. Hotel 0.5m on right*

Located on the edge of Grasmere village this former mansion house has been lovingly converted into a charming and relaxing hotel. Dinner is a must, with the team working closely with local suppliers and also growing much of their own produce in the walled garden, or foraging the local area. Twenty bedrooms provide stunning views of the hills and countryside beyond.

Rooms: 20 (5 family) (2 GF) ❀ **D** £189–£329 (incl. bkfst)* **Facilities:** FTV WiFi ☙ ♨ Xmas New Year **Parking:** 42 **Notes:** Civ Wed 60

HIGHLY RECOMMENDED

Rothay Garden Hotel
★★★★ 84% ◉◉ HOTEL

Broadgate, LA22 9RJ - tel: 015394 35334
email: stay@rothaygarden.com **web:** www.rothaygarden.com
dir: *A591, opposite Swan Hotel, into Grasmere, 300yds on left*

Situated just on the edge of Grasmere Village in two acres of riverside gardens, this stylishly designed hotel offers comfort and luxury. Bedrooms include five loft suites which are named after the fells they overlook, while upper floors have their own balconies. The Garden Spa is the perfect place to relax with steam room, sauna and heated relaxing beds. The chic bar and lounges provide somewhere to unwind before dinner which is served in the Garden Restaurant.

Rooms: 30 (3 family) (8 GF) ❀ **S** £115.50–£170; **D** £151–£281 (incl. bkfst)*
Facilities: Spa FTV WiFi ☙ HL Sauna Aromatherapy room Infra red loungers Spa pool Xmas New Year **Parking:** 35 **Notes:** LB No children 12yrs

HIGHLY RECOMMENDED

The Daffodil Hotel & Spa
★★★★ 83% ◉ HOTEL

Keswick Road, LA22 9PR - tel: 015394 63550
email: stay@daffodilhotel.com **web:** www.daffodilhotel.com
dir: *M6 junct 36 then A591, past Windermere & Ambleside. Hotel on left on entering Grasmere*

Recently reopened after Cumbrian flooding, the Daffodil Hotel provides very high levels of service, comfort and luxury in a spectacular location on the edge of Grasmere. It's an easy walk both into the village and onto the local Wordsworth trail, and it is of course set in a hill-walker's paradise. Most rooms have either a lake or a valley view, several with private balconies, and are equipped to high standards.

Rooms: 78 (11 family) ❀ **S** £103–£213; **D** £111–£223 (incl. bkfst)*
Facilities: Spa FTV WiFi ☙ HL Sauna Steam room Tepidarium Thermal pool Mud rasul room Xmas New Year **Conf:** Class 150 Board 32 Thtr 400 Del from £169 **Services:** Lift Night porter Air con **Parking:** 96 **Notes:** Civ Wed 200

GRASMERE *continued*

HIGHLY RECOMMENDED

The Wordsworth Hotel & Spa

★★★★ 80% ⊛ HOTEL

Stock Lane, LA22 9SW - tel: 015394 35592
email: enquiry@thewordsworthhotel.co.uk **web:** www.thewordsworthhotel.co.uk
dir: *Off A591. In centre of village adjacent to St Oswald's Church*

This historic hotel ideally situated in the heart of Grasmere provides high levels of style and luxury. The bedrooms are equipped with smart furnishings, comfortable beds with Egyptian cotton linens and quality accessories. Guests can enjoy fine dining in the modernised Signature Restaurant which boasts stylish and elegant decor and for a less formal dining experience, light meals and fine ales are offered in the Dove Bistro. The hotel has a heated swimming pool and the sauna and spa make the ideal place for relaxation.

Rooms: 38 (4 family) (3 GF) ⋒ **Facilities:** Spa FTV WiFi ⋈ ⓧ ⤳ Sauna Xmas New Year **Conf:** Class 80 Board 40 Thtr 120 Del from £167 **Services:** Lift Night porter **Parking:** 40 **Notes:** LB Civ Wed 100

HIGHLY RECOMMENDED

Oak Bank Hotel

★★★ 86% ⊛⊛ SMALL HOTEL

Broadgate, LA22 9TA - tel: 015394 35217
email: info@lakedistricthotel.co.uk **web:** www.lakedistricthotel.co.uk
dir: *N'bound: M6 junct 36 onto A591 to Windermere, Ambleside, then Grasmere. S'bound: M6 junct 40 onto A66 to Keswick, A591 to Grasmere*

Privately owned and personally-run by friendly proprietors, Oak Bank is a Victorian house in the very heart of the English lakes. Bedrooms are well-equipped and include one suite with a jacuzzi. The four superior view rooms have fantastic views of the surrounding fells. In colder weather, welcoming log fires burn in the comfortable lounges. The dining room is the focus for food, serving technically accomplished cooking in a stylish conservatory setting overlooking the garden.

Rooms: 13 (1 GF) ⋒ **S** £54–£135; **D** £70–£180 (incl. bkfst) **Facilities:** STV FTV WiFi New Year **Parking:** 13 **Notes:** LB Closed 2-19 Jan, 29 Jul-9 Aug, 17-26 Dec

Macdonald Swan Hotel

★★★ 80% HOTEL

LA22 9RF - tel: 01539 435742
email: sales/oldengland@macdonald-hotels.co.uk **web:** www.macdonaldhotels.co.uk
dir: *M6 junct 36, A591 towards Kendal, A590 to Keswick through Ambleside. Hotel on right on entering village*

Close to Dove Cottage and occupying a prominent position on the edge of the village, this 300-year-old inn is mentioned in Wordsworth's poem, *The Waggoner*. Attractive public areas are spacious and comfortable, and bedrooms are equally stylish. A modern bar and grill menu is available, while the elegant restaurant offers more formal dining.

Rooms: 37 (2 family) (21 GF) ⋒ **Facilities:** FTV WiFi HL Xmas New Year **Conf:** Class 20 Board 30 Thtr 40 **Services:** Night porter **Parking:** 45 **Notes:** Civ Wed 60

GRAVESEND Map 6 TQ67
Kent

Premier Inn Gravesend (A2/Singlewell)

BUDGET HOTEL

Hevercourt Road, Singlewell, DA12 5UQ - tel: 0871 527 8472 (Calls cost 13p per minute plus your phone company's access charge) **web:** www.premierinn.com
dir: *At Gravesend East exit on A2*

High quality, budget accommodation ideal for both families and business travellers. Spacious, en suite bedrooms feature free WiFi and tea and coffee making facilities, and in most hotels, Freeview TV is also available. The adjacent family restaurant features a wide and varied menu.

Rooms: 31

Premier Inn Gravesend Central

BUDGET HOTEL

Wrotham Road, DA11 7LF - tel: 0871 527 8474 (Calls cost 13p per minute plus your phone company's access charge) **web:** www.premierinn.com
dir: *A2 onto A227 towards town centre, 1m to hotel*

Rooms: 55

GREAT CHESTERFORD Map 12 TL54
Essex

The Crown House

★★★ 79% HOTEL

CB10 1NY - tel: 01799 530515
email: reservations@crownhousehotel.com **web:** www.crownhousehotel.com
dir: *From N: M11 at junct 9 (from S junct 10) follow signs for Saffron Walden, then Great Chesterford B1383*

This Georgian coaching inn, situated in a peaceful village close to the M11, has been sympathetically restored and retains much original character. The bedrooms are well equipped and individually decorated; some rooms have delightful four-poster beds. Public rooms include an attractive lounge bar, an elegant oak-panelled restaurant and an airy conservatory.

G

Imperial Hotel

★★★★ 75% ⊛ HOTEL

THE INDEPENDENTS
HOTEL ASSOCIATION

North Drive, NR30 1EQ - tel: 01493 842000
email: reservations@imperialhotel.co.uk **web:** www.imperialhotel.co.uk
dir: *Follow signs to seafront, turn left. Hotel opposite Waterways*

This friendly, family-run hotel is situated at the quieter end of the seafront within easy walking distance of the town centre. Bedrooms are attractively decorated with co-ordinated soft furnishings and many thoughtful touches; most rooms have superb sea views. Public areas include the smart Bar Fizz and the Café Cru restaurant.

Rooms: 39 (4 family) ⋒ **S** £75–£140; **D** £90–£160 (incl. bkfst) **Facilities:** FTV WiFi ⇘ New Year **Conf:** Class 40 Board 30 Thtr 140 **Services:** Lift Night porter **Parking:** 40 **Notes:** LB Civ Wed 140

Andover House

★★★ 81% ⊛⊛ SMALL HOTEL

28-30 Camperdown, NR30 3JB - tel: 01493 843490
email: bookings@andoverhouse.co.uk **web:** www.andoverhouse.co.uk
dir: *Opposite Wellington Pier turn into Shadingfield Close, right into Kimberley Terrace, follow into Camperdown. Hotel on left*

This charming Victorian building enjoys a peaceful location on a tree-lined avenue close to the town centre and the beach, making it an ideal base from which to explore the Norfolk Broads. Andover House offers a range of individually styled comfortable bedrooms along with a modern bar and well-appointed lounge areas. The award-winning brasserie-style restaurant offers an extensive choice of imaginative dishes and there is a smart sun terrace available for guests.

Rooms: 27 (1 GF) ⋒ **S** fr £69; **D** fr £89 (incl. bkfst)* **Facilities:** STV WiFi ⇘ **Conf:** Class 18 Board 18 Thtr 18 **Services:** Night porter **Notes:** No children 13yrs

Rooms: 18 (10 annexe) (1 family) (5 GF) ⋒ **Facilities:** FTV WiFi ⇘ New Year **Conf:** Class 14 Board 12 Thtr 30 **Parking:** 30 **Notes:** Closed 27–30 Dec Civ Wed 60

The Crown House

INSPECTOR'S CHOICE

Belmond Le Manoir aux Quat'Saisons

★★★★★ ⊛⊛⊛⊛⊛ HOTEL

RELAIS &
CHATEAUX

Church Road, OX44 7PD - tel: 01844 278881
email: manoir.mqs@belmond.com **web:** www.belmond.com/lemanoir
dir: *From A329 2nd right to Great Milton Manor, hotel 200yds on right*

Even though Le Manoir is now very much part of the British scene, its iconic chef patron, Raymond Blanc, still fizzes with new ideas and projects. His first loves are his kitchen and his garden and the vital link between them. The fascinating grounds feature a Japanese tea garden and two acres of vegetables and herbs that supply the kitchen with an almost never-ending supply of top-notch produce. Even the car park has a stunning artichoke sculpture. The kitchen is the epicentre, with outstanding cooking highlighting freshness and seasonality. Bedrooms in this idyllic 'grand house on a small scale' are either in the main house or around an outside courtyard; all offer the highest levels of comfort and quality, have magnificent marble bathrooms and are equipped with a host of thoughtful extra touches. For something really special there is the 15th-century dovecot with a stunning upper-floor bedroom and a bathroom below. La Belle Epoque is the private dining room, ideal for weddings, celebrations and corporate events.

Rooms: 32 (23 annexe) (13 GF) ⋒ **Facilities:** STV FTV WiFi ⇘ ⏛ Cookery school Water gardens Bikes Spa treatment Xmas New Year **Conf:** Class 30 Board 24 Thtr 80 **Services:** Night porter **Parking:** 60 **Notes:** Civ Wed 50

GREAT YARMOUTH *continued*

The Prom Hotel

★★★ 81% 🏵 HOTEL

77 Marine Parade, NR30 2DH - tel: 01493 842308
email: info@promhotel.co.uk **web:** www.promhotel.co.uk
dir: *Phone for details*

The Prom Hotel is ideally situated on the seafront close to the bright lights and attractions of Marine Parade. The open-plan public areas include a smart lounge bar with views of the sea, and a relaxed restaurant; guests also have the use of a further quieter lounge bar with plush seating. The modern contemporary bedrooms are smartly appointed and have many thoughtful touches; many rooms have lovely sea views..

Rooms: 42 (1 family) ❦ **S** £75–£90; **D** £80–£130* **Facilities:** STV FTV WiFi ⌕ Xmas New Year **Conf:** Class 40 Board 30 Thtr 50 Del from £109 **Services:** Lift Night porter **Parking:** 30 **Notes:** Civ Wed 60

The Cliff Hotel

★★★ 79% HOTEL

Cliff Hill, Gorleston, NR31 6DH - tel: 01493 662179
email: reception@thecliffhotel.co.uk **web:** www.thecliffhotel.co.uk
dir: *A47 Acle new road rdbt 3rd exit, continue A12 3rd rdbt, 1st exit onto Victoria Rd, 3rd right onto Avondale Rd, follow round*

The Cliff Hotel offers an extensive choice of stylish, very well appointed bedrooms. Overlooking the harbour and Gorleston Beach, the hotel enjoys a prominent position in the town. Ample secure parking is available, and the modern terrace, along with the contemporary lounge, is very popular with guests.

Rooms: 37 (4 family) ❦ **S** fr £94; **D** fr £109 (incl. bkfst)* **Facilities:** FTV WiFi Children's play area ♫ Xmas New Year **Conf:** Class 60 Board 45 Thtr 160 Del from £110 **Services:** Night porter **Parking:** 30 **Notes:** Civ Wed 80

Furzedown Hotel

★★★ 79% HOTEL

19-20 North Drive, NR30 4EW - tel: 01493 844138
email: paul@furzedownhotel.co.uk **web:** www.furzedownhotel.co.uk
dir: *At end of A47 or A12, towards seafront, left, hotel opposite Waterways*

Expect a warm welcome at this family-run hotel situated at the northern end of the seafront overlooking the town's Venetian Waterways. Bedrooms are pleasantly decorated and thoughtfully equipped; many rooms have superb sea views. The stylish public areas include a comfortable lounge bar, a smartly appointed restaurant and a cosy TV room.

Rooms: 20 (11 family) **S** £68–£72; **D** £87–£98 (incl. bkfst)* **Facilities:** FTV WiFi New Year **Conf:** Class 80 Board 40 Thtr 75 Del from £106.50 **Parking:** 30

New Beach Hotel

★★★ 78% HOTEL

Leisureplex
HOLIDAY HOTELS

67 Marine Parade, NR30 2EJ - tel: 01493 332300
email: newbeach.gtyarmouth@alfatravel.co.uk **web:** www.leisureplex.co.uk
dir: *Follow signs to seafront. Hotel facing Britannia Pier*

This Victorian building is centrally located on the seafront, overlooking Britannia Pier and the sandy beach. Bedrooms are pleasantly decorated and equipped with modern facilities; many have lovely sea views. Dinner is taken in the restaurant which doubles as the ballroom, and guests can also relax in the bar or sunny lounge.

Rooms: 95 (8 family) ❦ **S** £37–£51; **D** £58–£88 (incl. bkfst)* **Facilities:** FTV WiFi ♫ Xmas New Year **Services:** Lift Night porter **Notes:** LB Closed Jan-Feb RS Mar

Knights Court Hotel

★★★ 73% HOTEL

22 North Drive, NR30 4EW - tel: 01493 843089
email: enquiries@knights-court.co.uk **web:** www.knights-court.co.uk
dir: *Within close proximity of A12/A47, Great Yarmouth*

Knights Court Hotel is situated on the sea front at Great Yarmouth and is a small privately-owned hotel. Expect friendly service from Malcolm and the team, who will ensure all guests are welcomed. Bedrooms are comfortable and some offer good views of the sea. High quality ingredients are used at dinner, which is served in the stylish dining room. There is also a cosy lounge bar with thoughtful extras such a library of books and magazines.

Rooms: 20 (6 annexe) (5 family) (6 GF) (6 smoking) **S** £50–£90; **D** £50–£90 (incl. bkfst) **Facilities:** FTV WiFi ⌕ **Conf:** Class 24 Board 24 Thtr 24 **Services:** Night porter **Parking:** 15 **Notes:** Closed 10 Dec-5 Jan

The Nelson Hotel

★★★ 69% HOTEL

1 Marine Parade, NR30 3AG - tel: 01493 855551
email: johnrushworth@theukholidaygroup.com **web:** www.grandukhotels.co.uk
dir: *On right of Marine Parade, opposite Sealife Centre*

The Nelson Hotel is ideally situated overlooking the sea, close to the pier and just a short stroll from the town centre and local amenities. It is ideal for both business and leisure guests, and all of the bedrooms are well equipped, while some rooms have lovely sea views. Public areas include a lounge with plush sofas, a bar and a separate dining room.

Rooms: 50 (10 family) ❦ **S** £25–£55; **D** £50–£80 (incl. bkfst)* **Facilities:** FTV WiFi ♫ Xmas New Year **Conf:** Class 60 Board 60 Thtr 100 **Services:** Lift Night porter **Notes:** LB

Burlington Palm Hotel

★★★ Ⓐ HOTEL

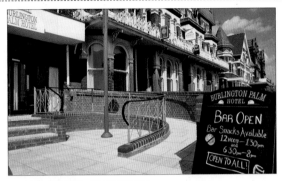

11 North Drive, NR30 1EG - **tel:** 01493 844568
email: enquiries@burlington-hotel.co.uk **web:** www.burlington-hotel.co.uk
dir: *A12 to seafront, left at Marine Lodge. Hotel near tennis courts*

This privately owned hotel is situated at the quiet end of the resort, overlooking the sea. Bedrooms come in a variety of sizes and styles; they are pleasantly decorated and well equipped, and many have lovely sea views. The spacious public rooms include a range of seating areas, a choice of dining rooms, two bars and a heated indoor swimming pool.

Rooms: 69 (9 family) (1 GF) ⚓ **Facilities:** FTV WiFi ⊕ Xmas **Conf:** Class 60 Board 30 Thtr 120 **Services:** Lift **Parking:** 70 **Notes:** LB Closed 28 Dec-2 Jan

See advert on page 155

The Waverley Hotel

★★ 76% HOTEL

32-34 Princes Road, NR30 2DG - **tel:** 01493 853388
email: thewaverleyhotel.gy@gmail.com **web:** www.thewaverleyhotelgy.com
dir: *Follow A47 from London to Great Yarmouth or A143 from Haverhill. Hotel opposite Britannia Pier at Princes Rd*

The Waverley is situated in a side road adjacent to the seafront and close to the local amenities. The property has been totally refurbished by the current owner to a very good standard. Public rooms include a large lounge bar, foyer and spacious restaurant. Bedrooms are contemporary in style and have a good range of extra facilities.

Rooms: 47 (2 family) ⚓ **Facilities:** FTV WiFi Library ♫ Xmas New Year **Conf:** Class 60 Board 60 Thtr 60 **Services:** Lift Night porter

Premier Inn Great Yarmouth

BUDGET HOTEL

Runham Road, NR30 1SH - **tel:** 0871 527 9494 (Calls cost 13p per minute plus your phone company's access charge) **web:** www.premierinn.com
dir: *A12 onto A149, at rdbt left into Runham Rd*

High quality, budget accommodation ideal for both families and business travellers. Spacious, en suite bedrooms feature free WiFi and tea and coffee making facilities, and in most hotels, Freeview TV is also available. The adjacent family restaurant features a wide and varied menu.

Rooms: 80

GREENFORD
Greater London

G

Premier Inn London Greenford

BUDGET HOTEL PLAN 1 C4

Western Avenue, UB6 8TE - **tel:** 0871 527 8658 (Calls cost 13p per minute plus your phone company's access charge) **web:** www.premierinn.com
dir: *From A40 (Western Avenue) E'bound, exit at Perivale. Right, left at 2nd lights. Hotel opposite Hoover Building*

High quality, budget accommodation ideal for both families and business travellers. Spacious, en suite bedrooms feature free WiFi and tea and coffee making facilities, and in most hotels, Freeview TV is also available. The adjacent family restaurant features a wide and varied menu.

Rooms: 39

GRIMSBY
Lincolnshire
Map 17 TA21

Millfields Hotel

★★★ Ⓐ HOTEL

THE INDEPENDENTS
HOTEL ASSOCIATION

53 Bargate, DN34 5AD - **tel:** 01472 356068
email: info@millfieldshotel.co.uk **web:** www.millfieldshotel.co.uk
dir: *A180, right at KFC rdbt then left at next rdbt. Right at 2nd lights & right onto Bargate, hotel 0.5m on left after Wheatsheaf pub*

Dating from 1879 this hotel is surrounded by its own grounds and caters for both leisure and business guests. The bedrooms are individually designed and there is a four-poster room. The contemporary Orangery Restaurant offers both carte and traditional bar menus. The hotel has extensive leisure facilities.

Rooms: 27 (4 annexe) (7 family) (13 GF) ⚓ **S** fr £65; **D** fr £65* **Facilities:** FTV WiFi Gym Squash Sauna Steam room Hairdresser Beauty salon Aromatherapist **Conf:** Class 25 Board 25 Thtr 50 **Services:** Night porter **Parking:** 75 **Notes:** LB Civ Wed 50

Premier Inn Grimsby

BUDGET HOTEL

Europa Park, Appian Way, DN31 2UT - **tel:** 0871 527 8478 (Calls cost 13p per minute plus your phone company's access charge) **web:** www.premierinn.com
dir: *M180 junct 5, A180 towards town centre. At 1st rdbt take 2nd exit. 1st left, left at mini rdbt into Appian Way*

High quality, budget accommodation ideal for both families and business travellers. Spacious, en suite bedrooms feature free WiFi and tea and coffee making facilities, and in most hotels, Freeview TV is also available. The adjacent family restaurant features a wide and varied menu.

Rooms: 58

GRIMSTON	Map 12 TF72
Norfolk	

Congham Hall Country House Hotel

★★★ @@ COUNTRY HOUSE HOTEL

Lynn Road, PE32 1AH - tel: 01485 600250
email: info@conghamhallhotel.co.uk **web:** www.conghamhallhotel.co.uk
dir: *At A149/A148 junct NE of King's Lynn, take A148 towards Fakenham for 100yds. Right to Grimston, hotel 2.5m on left*

Congham Hall is an elegant 18th-century Georgian manor set amid 30 acres of mature landscaped grounds and surrounded by parkland. The inviting public rooms provide a range of tastefully furnished areas in which to sit and relax. Imaginative cuisine is served in the Orangery Restaurant which has an intimate atmosphere and panoramic views of the gardens. The bedrooms, tastefully furnished with period pieces, have modern facilities and many thoughtful touches.

Rooms: 26 (6 annexe) (12 GF) 🐾 **Facilities:** Spa WiFi ⊗ Putting green ⛳ Xmas New Year **Conf:** Class 12 Board 28 Thtr 50 **Services:** Night porter **Parking:** 50 **Notes:** LB Civ Wed 100

GRINDLEFORD	Map 16 SK27
Derbyshire	

The Maynard

★★★ 84% @@ HOTEL

Main Road, S32 2HE - tel: 01433 630321
email: info@themaynard.co.uk **web:** www.themaynard.co.uk
dir: *A625 from Sheffield to Castleton. Left into Grindleford on B6521. Hotel on left after Fox House Hotel*

This building, dating back over 100 years, is situated in a beautiful and tranquil location yet within easy reach of Sheffield and the M1. The bedrooms are contemporary in style and offer a wealth of accessories. The Peak District views from the restaurant and garden are stunning.

Rooms: 10 (1 family) 🐾 **Facilities:** FTV WiFi **Conf:** Class 60 Board 40 Thtr 120 **Parking:** 60 **Notes:** Civ Wed 120

GUILDFORD	Map 6 SU94
Surrey	

The Mandolay Hotel

★★★★ 83% @@ HOTEL

36-40 London Road, GU1 2AE - tel: 01483 303030
email: info@guildford.com **web:** www.guildford.com
dir: *M25 junct 10, follow A3(S) for 7m. Take 3rd exit at 1st rdbt onto London Rd for 1m*

Situated close to the centre of Guildford, The Mandolay Hotel offers 72 comfortable bedrooms. Extensive meeting facilities provide for business visitors with off-street parking available. Free unrestricted WiFi is available throughout the hotel and there are over 900 international TV channels free of charge. A range of dining options, from coffee shop and bar menu to full restaurant service, are on offer.

Rooms: 72 (4 family) (13 GF) 🐾 **S** £95–£145; **D** £110–£165 **Facilities:** STV FTV WiFi ↘ Xmas New Year **Conf:** Class 200 Board 100 Thtr 700 **Services:** Lift Night porter **Parking:** 41 **Notes:** Civ Wed 500

Premier Inn Guildford Central

BUDGET HOTEL

Parkway, GU1 1UP - tel: 0871 527 8482 (Calls cost 13p per minute plus your phone company's access charge) **web:** www.premierinn.com
dir: *M25 junct 10, follow Portsmouth (A3) signs. Exit for Guildford Centre/Leisure Complex (A322/A320/A25). Turn left, hotel on left*

High quality, budget accommodation ideal for both families and business travellers. Spacious, en suite bedrooms feature free WiFi and tea and coffee making

facilities, and in most hotels, Freeview TV is also available. The adjacent family restaurant features a wide and varied menu.

Rooms: 109

GUISBOROUGH
North Yorkshire   **Map 19 NZ61**

HIGHLY RECOMMENDED

Gisborough Hall
★★★★ 83% HOTEL

Whitby Lane, TS14 6PT - **tel:** 01287 611500 **web:** www.gisborough-hall.com
dir: *A171, follow signs for Whitby to Waterfall rdbt, 3rd exit into Whitby Ln, hotel 500yds on right*

Dating back to the mid-19th century, this elegant country house provides a pleasing combination of original features and modern facilities. Bedrooms, including four-poster and family rooms, are richly furnished. The elegant Drawing Room is welcoming and has an open fire, while the opulent G Bar & Bistro provides a contemporary alternative. Excellent food is served in Chaloner's Restaurant.

Rooms: 71 (2 family) (12 GF) ↑ **S** fr £99; **D** fr £99* **Facilities:** Spa WiFi ↓ HL ⚘
⚘ Sauna Xmas New Year **Conf:** Class 150 Board 32 Thtr 400 Del from £155
Services: Lift Night porter **Parking:** 180 **Notes:** Civ Wed 250

HADLEY WOOD
Greater London   **Map 6 TQ29**

West Lodge Park Hotel
★★★★ 82% HOTEL

Cockfosters Road, EN4 0PY - **tel:** 020 8216 3900
email: westlodgepark@bealeshotels.co.uk **web:** www.bealeshotels.co.uk
dir: *On A111, 1m S of M25 junct 24*

West Lodge Park Hotel is a stylish country house set in stunning parkland and gardens, yet only 12 miles from central London and a few miles from the M25. Bedrooms are individually decorated in traditional style and offer excellent facilities. Annexe rooms feature air-conditioning and have access to an outdoor

patio area. Public rooms include the award-winning Cedar Restaurant, cosy bar area and separate lounge.

Rooms: 59 (13 annexe) (4 family) (11 GF) ↑ **Facilities:** STV FTV WiFi ↓ Putting green
⚘ Free use of nearby leisure club ♫ Xmas New Year **Conf:** Class 30 Board 30 Thtr 64 **Services:** Lift Night porter **Parking:** 200 **Notes:** Civ Wed 72

HADLOW
Kent   **Map 6 TQ65**

Hadlow Manor Hotel
★★★ 75% HOTEL

Goose Green, TN11 0JH - **tel:** 01732 851442
email: hotel@hadlowmanor.co.uk **web:** www.hadlowmanor.co.uk
dir: *On A26 Maidstone to Tonbridge rd. 1m E of Hadlow*

This is a friendly, independently owned country-house hotel, ideally situated between Maidstone and Tonbridge. Traditionally styled bedrooms are spacious and attractively furnished with many amenities. Public areas include a sunny restaurant, bar and lounge. The gardens are delightful and there's a seated area ideal for relaxation in warmer weather. Meeting and banqueting facilities are available.

Rooms: 29 (2 family) (8 GF) **Facilities:** STV FTV WiFi Xmas New Year **Conf:** Class 90 Board 103 Thtr 200 **Parking:** 120 **Notes:** Civ Wed 200

HAGLEY
Worcestershire   **Map 10 SO98**

Premier Inn Hagley
BUDGET HOTEL

Birmingham Road, DY9 9JS - **tel:** 0871 527 8484 (Calls cost 13p per minute plus your phone company's access charge) **web:** www.premierinn.com
dir: *M5 junct 3, A456 towards Kidderminster (dual carriageway). Hotel visible on opposite side of road. At next rdbt double back follow A456 Birmingham signs. Hotel on left*

High quality, budget accommodation ideal for both families and business travellers. Spacious, en suite bedrooms feature free WiFi and tea and coffee making facilities, and in most hotels, Freeview TV is also available. The adjacent family restaurant features a wide and varied menu.

Rooms: 40

H

HALIFAX
West Yorkshire

Map 19 SE02

Holdsworth House Hotel
★★★★ 76% HOTEL

Holdsworth Rd, Holmfield, HX2 9TG - tel: 01422 240024
email: info@holdsworthhouse.co.uk **web:** www.holdsworthhouse.co.uk
dir: *From town centre take A629 towards Keighley. 1.5m right at garage,
into Shay Ln. Hotel on right after 1m*

This delightful 17th-century Jacobean manor house, set in well-tended gardens,
offers individually decorated, thoughtfully equipped bedrooms. Public rooms,
adorned with beautiful paintings and antique pieces, include a choice of inviting
lounges and superb conference and function facilities. Dinner provides the
highlight of any stay and is served in the elegant restaurant by friendly,
attentive staff.

Rooms: 38 (9 family) (20 GF) **Facilities:** FTV WiFi New Year **Conf:** Class 75 Board
50 Thtr 150 **Services:** Night porter **Parking:** 60 **Notes:** Civ Wed 120

Premier Inn Halifax South
BUDGET HOTEL

Salterhebble Hill, Huddersfield Road, HX3 0QT - tel: 0871 527 8486 (Calls cost 13p per
minute plus your phone company's access charge) **web:** www.premierinn.com
dir: *Just off M62 junct 24 on A629 towards Halifax*

High quality, budget accommodation ideal for both families and business
travellers. Spacious, en suite bedrooms feature free WiFi and tea and coffee making
facilities, and in most hotels, Freeview TV is also available. The adjacent family
restaurant features a wide and varied menu.

Rooms: 31

Premier Inn Halifax Town Centre
BUDGET HOTEL

Broad Street Plaza, HX1 1YA - tel: 0871 527 9348 (Calls cost 13p per minute plus your
phone company's access charge) **web:** www.premierinn.com
dir: *Phone for directions*

Rooms: 100

HANDFORTH
See **Manchester Airport**

HARROGATE
North Yorkshire

Map 19 SE35

INSPECTOR'S CHOICE

Rudding Park Hotel, Spa & Golf
★★★★ HOTEL

Rudding Park, Follifoot, HG3 1JH - tel: 01423 871350
email: reservations@ruddingpark.com **web:** www.ruddingpark.co.uk
dir: *From A61 at rdbt with A658 take York exit, follow signs to Rudding Park*

Set in beautiful parkland, Rudding Park dates from the early 19th century.
Interiors are stylishly contemporary and elegant, with luxurious bedrooms;
the Follifoot wing features stunning suites and bedrooms with spas. Carefully
prepared meals and Yorkshire tapas are served in the Clocktower, which has a
striking pink chandelier and relaxed feel. The stylish bar and conservatory lead
to a generous terrace which is perfect for eating alfresco. The latest dining
option here is "Horto" (Latin for garden) which showcases produce and
innovation from the hotel's own kitchen garden; Spa café by day and fine dining
by night. The grandeur of the mansion house and grounds make this a popular
wedding venue. The hotel has a newly built impressive spa and treatment
rooms, gym, private cinema and extensive conference facilities, plus an
adjoining 18-hole, par 72 golf course and driving range.

Rooms: 90 (15 family) (35 GF) **S** fr £161; **D** fr £189 (incl. bkfst)*
Facilities: Spa STV FTV WiFi HL 18 Putting green Gym Driving range
Jogging trail Roof top spa and garden Xmas New Year **Conf:** Class 150 Board
40 Thtr 300 Del from £185 **Services:** Lift Night porter **Parking:** 350 **Notes:**
Civ Wed 300

West Park Hotel
★★★★ 81% HOTEL

West Park, HG1 1BJ - tel: 01423 524471
email: enquiries@thewestparkhotel.com **web:** www.thewestparkhotel.com
dir: *A1(M) junct 47, A59 to Harrogate. 2m straight on A658, 3rd exit at rdbt
onto A661 for 2.5m. 1st exit at rdbt onto A6040, 3rd exit next rdbt onto West Park.
Hotel 500mtrs on right*

Perfectly situated within a busy area of the popular town of Harrogate, West Park
Hotel is perfect for the modern day traveller. Bedrooms are equipped with plentiful
amounts of accessories and gadgets such as climate control, smart televisions,
and Nespresso machines as well as well-stocked hospitality trays. Many bathrooms
have separate shower and bath facilities, and luxurious toiletries are provided.
Meals can be enjoyed in the bustling restaurant and bar area, and outdoor seating
is provided for alfresco dining in the summer months.

Rooms: 25 (8 family) **D** fr £125 (incl. bkfst)* **Facilities:** FTV WiFi Xmas
New Year **Conf:** Class 24 Board 30 Thtr 60 Del from £285 **Services:** Lift Night porter
Air con **Notes:** LB

H

Nidd Hall Hotel

WARNER LEISURE HOTELS

★★★★ 77% ◎◎ COUNTRY HOUSE HOTEL

Nidd, HG3 3BN - tel: 01423 771598 **web:** www.warnerleisurehotels.co.uk
dir: *A59 through Knaresborough, follow signs for Ripley. Hotel on right*

This fine hotel is set in 45 acres of Victorian and Edwardian gardens. Bedrooms are spacious and appointed to a high standard, while public areas are delightful and retain many original features. Leisure and spa facilities are available along with a variety of outdoor activities. This is an adults-only (above 21 years old) hotel.

Rooms: 193 (57 GF) ↟ **S** fr £68; **D** fr £136 (incl. bkfst & dinner)* **Facilities:** Spa FTV WiFi HL ⊛ supervised Putting green ≈ Fishing ✦ Gym ♬ Xmas New Year **Conf:** Class 40 Board 30 Thtr 60 **Services:** Lift Night porter **Parking:** 200 **Notes:** LB

Studley Hotel

★★★★ 77% ◎◎ HOTEL

28 Swan Road, HG1 2SE - tel: 01423 560425
email: info@studleyhotel.co.uk **web:** www.studleyhotel.co.uk
dir: *Adjacent to Valley Gardens, opposite Mercer Gallery*

This friendly, well-established hotel, close to the town centre and Valley Gardens, is well known for its Orchid Restaurant, which provides a dynamic and authentic approach to Pacific Rim and Asian cuisine. Bedrooms are modern and come in a variety of styles and sizes, while the stylish bar lounge provides an excellent place for relaxing. A PC is available for guests' use.

Rooms: 28 (1 family) ↟ **S** fr £108; **D** fr £128 (incl. bkfst)* **Facilities:** FTV WiFi ➘ Free use of facilities at local Health Club **Conf:** Class 15 Board 12 Thtr 15 **Services:** Lift Night porter **Parking:** 14 **Notes:** LB Closed 22-30 Dec

White Hart Hotel

★★★★ 76% ◎◎ HOTEL

2 Cold Bath Road, HG2 0NF - tel: 01423 505681
email: reception@whiteharthotelharrogate.com **web:** www.whiteharthotelharrogate.com
dir: *A59 to Harrogate. A661 3rd exit on rdbt to Harrogate. Left at rdbt onto A6040 for 1m. Right onto A61. Bear left down Montpellier Hill*

Set in the heart of Harrogate's antiques quarter, this fine Georgian hotel has free WiFi and luxurious bedrooms, just a few minutes stroll from the town centre, Harrogate International Centre and the famous Valley Gardens. The newly refurbished 'Deluxe' bedrooms have been fully modernised with USB ports and soft tartan furnishings, while the 'Classic' bedrooms retain their older shabby-chic style and antique furniture. All rooms feature flat-screen TVs with Freeview, and en suite bathroom with H2K toiletries. Guests can choose to relax in the residents' lounge or enjoy the atmosphere of The Fat Badger, an adjoining, traditional English pub. The on-site restaurant, The Fat Badger Grill, is the place for breakfast, lunch and dinner. The White Hart Hotel also offers parking for over 80 vehicles.

Rooms: 82 (18 annexe) ↟ **S** £45–£139; **D** £49–£189* **Facilities:** FTV WiFi ➘ Gym Xmas New Year **Conf:** Class 40 Board 25 Thtr 80 £153.50 **Services:** Lift Night porter **Parking:** 80 **Notes:** Civ Wed 80

Hotel du Vin & Bistro Harrogate

Hotel du Vin & Bistro

★★★★ 76% ◎ TOWN HOUSE HOTEL

Prospect Place, HG1 1LB - tel: 01423 856800 & 0844 736 4257 (Calls cost 5p per minute plus your phone company's access charge)
email: info@harrogate.hotelduvin.com **web:** www.hotelduvin.com
dir: *A1(M) junct 47, A59 to Harrogate, follow town centre signs to Prince of Wales rdbt, 3rd exit, remain in right lane. Right at lights into Albert St, right into Prospect Place*

This town house was created from eight Georgian-style properties and overlooks The Stray, a large expanse of parkland set aside for public use. The spacious, open-plan lobby has seating, a bar and the reception desk. Hidden downstairs is a cosy snug cellar. The French-influenced bistro offers high quality cooking and a great choice of wines. Bedrooms face front and back, and are smart and modern, with excellent 'deluge' showers.

Rooms: 48 (4 GF) ↟ **Facilities:** Spa STV FTV WiFi ➘ New Year **Conf:** Class 20 Board 30 Thtr 60 **Services:** Lift Night porter **Parking:** 30 **Notes:** Civ Wed 90

The Majestic Hotel

★★★★ 74% HOTEL

Ripon Road, HG1 2HU - tel: 01423 700300
email: majestic@majestichotelharrogate.co.uk **web:** www.majestichotelharrogate.co.uk
dir: *M1 onto A1(M) at Wetherby. Take A661 to Harrogate. Hotel in town centre adjacent to Royal Hall & next to Harrogate International Centre*

Popular for conferences and functions, this grand Victorian hotel is set in 12 acres of landscaped grounds that is within walking distance of the town centre. It benefits from spacious public areas, and the comfortable bedrooms, including some spacious suites, come in a variety of sizes.

Rooms: 170 (8 family) ↟ **S** fr £60; **D** fr £70* **Facilities:** Spa FTV WiFi ➘ HL ⊛ Gym Saunas Xmas New Year **Conf:** Class 260 Board 70 Thtr 500 Del from £115 **Services:** Lift Night porter **Parking:** 250 **Notes:** Civ Wed 200

Cairn Hotel

★★★ 70% HOTEL

HG1 2JD - tel: 01423 504005
email: salescairn@strathmorehotels.com **web:** www.strathmorehotels.com
dir: *Phone for details*

This large Victorian hotel is just a short walk from the town centre and also benefits from free on-site parking. Many of the original features have been retained and the spacious foyer lounge and bar areas are perfect for relaxing. Bedrooms are comfortable, with Club Packages offering extra accessories and luxury touches. Complimentary WiFi is also provided in public areas and there is a fitness room with a mini gym.

Rooms: 135 (7 family) ↟ **S** fr £35; **D** fr £70 (incl. bkfst)* **Facilities:** WiFi Gym Xmas New Year **Conf:** Class 170 Board 100 Thtr 400 **Services:** Lift Night porter **Parking:** 150 **Notes:** LB Civ Wed 150

HARROGATE *continued*

Premier Inn Harrogate

BUDGET HOTEL

Hornbeam Park Avenue, HG2 8RA - **tel:** 0871 527 8490 (Calls cost 13p per minute plus your phone company's access charge) **web:** www.premierinn.com
dir: *A1(M) junct 46 W, A661 to Harrogate. In 2m left at The Woodlands lights. 1.5m left into Hornbeam Park Ave*

High quality, budget accommodation ideal for both families and business travellers. Spacious, en suite bedrooms feature free WiFi and tea and coffee making facilities, and in most hotels, Freeview TV is also available. The adjacent family restaurant features a wide and varied menu.

Rooms: 68

Premier Inn Harrogate Town Centre

BUDGET HOTEL

Springfield Avenue, HG1 2HY - **tel:** 0871 527 9432 (Calls cost 13p per minute plus your phone company's access charge) **web:** www.premierinn.com
dir: *A1 junct 47, follow Ripon/A61 signs. After Ripton follow Harrogate signs. After Cairn Hotel (on right) turn left into Springfield Ave. Hotel on right. Parking at hotel (chargeable)*

Rooms: 107

HARTINGTON	Map 16 SK16
Derbyshire	

Biggin Hall Hotel

★★ 80% HOTEL

Biggin-by-Hartington, SK17 0DH - **tel:** 01298 84451
email: enquiries@bigginhall.co.uk **web:** www.bigginhall.co.uk
dir: *0.5m off A515, midway between Ashbourne & Buxton*

Dating back to the 17th century Biggin Hall is peacefully situated; surrounded by open countryside in the heart of the Peak District. Its location makes it ideal for exploring the local area with the Tissington trail virtually on the doorstep. There are a host of historical market towns all within easy reach. Bedrooms are arranged across three main buildings and offer a mix of styles; all are comfortably furnished with a number benefiting from luxury bathrooms.

Rooms: 21 (13 annexe) (2 family) (5 GF) ♠ **S** £85–£130; **D** £95–£140 (incl. bkfst)*
Facilities: FTV WiFi Xmas New Year **Parking:** 25 **Notes:** LB No children 12yrs Civ Wed 40

HARTLEPOOL	Map 19 NZ53
County Durham	

Premier Inn Hartlepool Marina

BUDGET HOTEL

Maritime Avenue, Hartlepool Marina, TS24 0XZ - **tel:** 0871 527 8492 (Calls cost 13p per minute plus your phone company's access charge) **web:** www.premierinn.com
dir: *Approx 1m from A689/A179 junct. On marina*

High quality, budget accommodation ideal for both families and business travellers. Spacious, en suite bedrooms feature free WiFi and tea and coffee making facilities, and in most hotels, Freeview TV is also available. The adjacent family restaurant features a wide and varied menu.

Rooms: 98

HARTSHEAD MOOR MOTORWAY SERVICE AREA (M62)	Map 19 SE12
West Yorkshire	

Days Inn Bradford - M62

AA Advertised

Hartshead Moor Service Area, Clifton, HD6 4JX - **tel:** 01274 851706
email: hartshead.hotel@welcomebreak.co.uk **web:** www.welcomebreak.co.uk
dir: *M62 between junct 25 & 26*

This modern building offers accommodation in smart, spacious and well-equipped bedrooms, suitable for families and business travellers, and all with en suite bathrooms. Continental breakfast is available and other refreshments may be taken at the nearby family restaurant.

Rooms: 38 (33 family) (17 GF) **Facilities:** FTV WiFi ♨ **Conf:** Board 10 **Parking:** 100

HARWICH	Map 13 TM23
Essex	

The Pier at Harwich

★★★★ 80% ⊛⊛ SMALL HOTEL

The Quay, CO12 3HH - **tel:** 01255 241212
email: pier@milsomhotels.com **web:** www.milsomhotels.com/thepier
dir: *From A12 take A120 to Quay. Hotel opposite lifeboat station*

The Pier is situated on the quay, overlooking the ports of Harwich and Felixstowe. The bedrooms are tastefully decorated, thoughtfully equipped, and furnished in a contemporary style; many rooms have superb sea views. The public rooms include the restaurant which is influenced by the best in European cooking, the NAVYARD bar and terrace, and a plush residents' lounge.

Rooms: 14 (7 annexe) (5 family) (1 GF) ♠ **D** £125–£205 (incl. bkfst)* **Facilities:** STV WiFi Day cruises on yachts Golf breaks arranged with nearby course Sea bass fishing Xmas **Conf:** Board 16 **Services:** Lift Night porter **Parking:** 12 **Notes:** LB Civ Wed 50

Tower Hotel

★★★ 78% HOTEL

Dovercourt, CO12 3PJ - tel: 01255 504952
email: reception@tower-hotel-harwich.co.uk **web:** www.tower-hotel-harwich.co.uk
dir: *Follow main road into Harwich. Past BP garage on left*

The Tower Hotel is an impressive late 17th-century Italian-style building, with a wealth of ornamental ceiling cornices, beautiful architraves and an impressive balustrade. Bedrooms, many named after prominent people from Harwich's past, are spacious and furnished to a very high standard. Evening meals and breakfast are served in the decorative dining rooms, and Rigby's bar offers tempting meals and a wide range of refreshments.

Rooms: 13 (2 family) (2 GF) S fr £55; **D** £68–£120* **Facilities:** WiFi **Conf:** Class 30 Board 30 Thtr 30 **Services:** Night porter **Parking:** 30 **Notes:** Closed 25-26 Dec Civ Wed 70

Premier Inn Harwich

BUDGET HOTEL

Parkstone Road, Dovercourt, CO12 4NX - tel: 0871 527 8494 (Calls cost 13p per minute plus your phone company's access charge) **web:** www.premierinn.com
dir: *A120 to Harwich, hotel opposite Morrisons. Right at rdbt. Hotel entrance through Lidl car park*

High quality, budget accommodation ideal for both families and business travellers. Spacious, en suite bedrooms feature free WiFi and tea and coffee making facilities, and in most hotels, Freeview TV is also available. The adjacent family restaurant features a wide and varied menu.

Rooms: 45

| **HASSOCKS**
West Sussex | Map 6 TV31 |

Wickwoods Country Club Hotel & Spa

★★★ 82% HOTEL

Shaveswood Lane, Aubourne, BN6 9DY - tel: 01273 857567
email: reception@wickwoods.co.uk **web:** www.wickwoods.co.uk
dir: *On B2117 just off A23. From the N take Sayerscommon exit; from the S take Henfield turning*

Wickwoods Country Club Hotel & Spa offers guests and members accommodation, leisure, spa facilities and dining set in 22 acres of landscaped gardens and woodland within the South Downs National Park. The Glass House restaurant serves good quality meals and is a popular venue for weddings and functions. Bedrooms are individually decorated and provide a comfortable night's sleep.

Rooms: (2 family) S £65–£95; **D** £75–£120 (incl. bkfst)* **Facilities:** Spa FTV WiFi Gym Sauna Steam room Exercise classes **Parking:** 140 **Notes:** LB Civ Wed 80

| **HASTINGS & ST LEONARDS**
East Sussex | Map 7 TQ80 |

Bannatyne Spa Hotel Hastings

★★★★ 78% HOTEL

Battle Road, TN38 8EA - tel: 01424 851222 & 0844 248 3836 (Calls cost 7p per minute plus your phone company's access charge)
email: enquiries.hastingshotel@bannatyne.co.uk **web:** www.bannatyne.co.uk
dir: *M25 junct 5, A21 Hastings. At 5th rdbt take 2nd exit Hastings/Filwell. After 2 rdbts turn right Folkestone/A259/Battle/A2100. Left at A2100/The Ridge Way. At 2nd rdbt right to hotel*

This hotel offers a range of facilities that will appeal to both leisure and business travellers. The well-appointed accommodation is available in a range of types and sizes from small doubles to superior rooms, while the public areas are a tasteful blend of contemporary design and period features. The Conservatory Restaurant has attractive views over the formal garden. There is a spa and health club plus meeting facilities. Free WiFi is available.

Rooms: 38 (7 family) (4 GF) **Facilities:** Spa FTV WiFi supervised Gym Xmas New Year **Conf:** Class 300 Board 50 Thtr 425 **Services:** Lift Night porter **Parking:** 150 **Notes:** Civ Wed 300

Best Western Royal Victoria Hotel

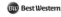

★★★ 73% HOTEL

Marina, St Leonards-on-Sea, TN38 0BD - tel: 01424 445544
email: reception@royalvichotel.co.uk **web:** www.royalvichotel.co.uk
dir: *On A259 (seafront road) 1m W of Hastings pier*

This imposing 18th-century property is situated in a prominent position overlooking the sea. A superb marble staircase leads up from the lobby to the main public areas on the first floor which has panoramic views of the sea. The spacious bedrooms are pleasantly decorated and well equipped, and include duplex and family suites.

Rooms: 50 (15 family) S £55–£115; **D** £60–£120 **Facilities:** STV WiFi Xmas New Year **Conf:** Class 40 Board 40 Thtr 100 Del from £125 **Services:** Lift Night porter **Parking:** 6 **Notes:** LB Civ Wed 100

Premier Inn Hastings

BUDGET HOTEL

1 John Macadam Way, St Leonards on Sea, TN37 7DB - tel: 0871 527 8496 (Calls cost 13p per minute plus your phone company's access charge) **web:** www.premierinn.com
dir: *A21 into Hastings. Hotel on right after junct with A2100 - Battle road*

High quality, budget accommodation ideal for both families and business travellers. Spacious, en suite bedrooms feature free WiFi and tea and coffee making facilities, and in most hotels, Freeview TV is also available. The adjacent family restaurant features a wide and varied menu.

Rooms: 73

H

HATFIELD
Hertfordshire

Map 6 TL20

Beales Hotel

★★★★ 82% HOTEL

Comet Way, AL10 9NG - tel: 01707 288500
email: hatfield@bealeshotels.co.uk **web:** www.bealeshotels.co.uk
dir: *On A1001 opposite Galleria Shopping Mall - follow signs for Galleria*

Beales Hotel is a stunning contemporary property. Within easy access of the M25, its striking exterior incorporates giant glass panels and cedar wood slats. Bedrooms have luxurious beds, flat-screen TVs and smart bathrooms. Public areas include a small bar and attractive restaurant, which opens throughout the day. The hotel is fully air-conditioned and free wired broadband is available in bedrooms, conference and banqueting rooms.

Rooms: 53 (3 family) (21 GF) ⬡ **S** £79–£129; **D** £79–£129* **Facilities:** STV FTV WiFi ⬡ Free use of nearby leisure club Xmas New Year **Conf:** Class 124 Board 64 Thtr 300 **Services:** Lift Night porter Air con **Parking:** 126 **Notes:** LB RS 27-30 Dec breakfast & dinner only served in restaurant Civ Wed 300

Mercure Hatfield Oak Hotel

focushotels management limited

★★★ 75% HOTEL

Roehyde Way, AL10 9AF - tel: 01707 275701
email: enquiries@hotels-hatfield.com **web:** www.hotels-hatfield.com
dir: *M25 junct 23 between juncts 2 & 3 of A1(M). Roehyde Way runs parallel to A1(M))*

This hotel enjoys an enviable location for both leisure and business guests, as it is within easy reach of major roads and central London. In addition, the University of Hertfordshire is situated nearby. The accommodation has been appointed to a good standard with flat-screen TVs and WiFi, among other facilities. The hotel also caters for conferences and banqueting.

Rooms: 85 (14 family) (37 GF) ⬡ **S** £60–£170; **D** £60–£170* **Facilities:** FTV WiFi ⬡ Xmas New Year **Conf:** Class 60 Board 40 Thtr 100 Del from £128 **Services:** Night porter **Parking:** 85 **Notes:** Civ Wed 100

Premier Inn Hatfield

BUDGET HOTEL

Lemsford Road, AL10 0DZ - tel: 0871 527 8498 (Calls cost 13p per minute plus your phone company's access charge) **web:** www.premierinn.com
dir: *From A1(M) junct 4, A1001 towards Hatfield. At rdbt take 2nd exit, 1st right*

High quality, budget accommodation ideal for both families and business travellers. Spacious, en suite bedrooms feature free WiFi and tea and coffee making facilities, and in most hotels, Freeview TV is also available. The adjacent family restaurant features a wide and varied menu.

Rooms: 40

HAVANT
Hampshire

Map 5 SU70

Premier Inn Portsmouth (Havant)

BUDGET HOTEL

65 Bedhampton Hill, Bedhampton, PO9 3JN - tel: 0871 527 8900 (Calls cost 13p per minute plus your phone company's access charge) **web:** www.premierinn.com
dir: *At rdbt just off A3(M) junct 5 towards Bedhampton*

High quality, budget accommodation ideal for both families and business travellers. Spacious, en suite bedrooms feature free WiFi and tea and coffee making facilities, and in most hotels, Freeview TV is also available. The adjacent family restaurant features a wide and varied menu.

Rooms: 59

HAVERHILL
Suffolk

Map 12 TL64

Days Inn Haverhill

DAYS INN

BUDGET HOTEL

Phoenix Road & Bumpstead Road, Haverhill Business Park, CB9 7AE - tel: 01440 716950 **email:** info@daysinnhaverhill.co.uk
web: www.haverhilldaysinn.co.uk
dir: *A1017 (Haverhill bypass). Hotel on 5th rdbt*

This modern building offers accommodation in smart, spacious and well-equipped bedrooms, suitable for families and business travellers, and all with en suite bathrooms. Continental breakfast is available and other refreshments may be taken at the nearby family restaurant.

Rooms: 80 (8 family) (14 GF) ⬡ **Conf:** Class 28 Board 24 Thtr 60

Red Stars

The AA Red Star rating denotes an Inspector's Choice hotel. They stand out as the very best in the British Isles and appear in highlighted panels throughout the guide.

HAWES
North Yorkshire   Map 18 SD88

Simonstone Hall Hotel

★★★ 80% ⊛ COUNTRY HOUSE HOTEL

Simonstone, DL8 3LY - tel: 01969 667255
email: enquiries@simonstonehall.com **web:** www.simonstonehall.com
dir: *1.5m N of Hawes on road signed Muker & Buttertubs*

This former hunting lodge provides professional, friendly service and a relaxed atmosphere. Public areas include an inviting drawing room, a bar and a conservatory. For dining there is the Garden Room Brasserie, which offers a lunchtime and extended afternoon menu as well as the evening à la carte menu. Afternoon tea is also available if pre-booked. The generally spacious bedrooms are elegantly designed to reflect the style of the house, and many offer spectacular views of the countryside.

Rooms: 18 (10 family) (2 GF) 🐾 **S** £65–£120; **D** £80–£185 (incl. bkfst)*
Facilities: FTV WiFi Xmas New Year **Conf:** Class 20 Board 20 Thtr 50 **Parking:** 40
Notes: Civ Wed 100

HAYDOCK
Merseyside   Map 15 SJ59

Premier Inn Haydock

BUDGET HOTEL

Yew Tree Way, Golbourne, WA3 3JD - tel: 0871 527 8500 (Calls cost 13p per minute plus your phone company's access charge) **web:** www.premierinn.com
dir: *M6 junct 23, A580 towards Manchester. Approx 2m. Straight on at major rdbt. Hotel on left*

High quality, budget accommodation ideal for both families and business travellers. Spacious, en suite bedrooms feature free WiFi and tea and coffee making facilities, and in most hotels, Freeview TV is also available. The adjacent family restaurant features a wide and varied menu.

Rooms: 60

HAYES
See **Heathrow Airport**

HAYLE
Cornwall & Isles of Scilly   Map 2 SW53

Premier Inn Hayle

BUDGET HOTEL

Carwin Rise, Loggans, TR27 4PN - tel: 0871 527 8506 (Calls cost 13p per minute plus your phone company's access charge) **web:** www.premierinn.com
dir: *On A30 at Loggans Moor rdbt exit into Carwin Rise. Hotel on right*

High quality, budget accommodation ideal for both families and business travellers. Spacious, en suite bedrooms feature free WiFi and tea and coffee making facilities, and in most hotels, Freeview TV is also available. The adjacent family restaurant features a wide and varied menu.

Rooms: 57

HAYLING ISLAND
Hampshire   Map 5 SU70

Langstone Hotel

★★★★ 77% ⊛⊛ HOTEL

Northney Road, PO11 0NQ - tel: 023 9246 5011
email: info@langstonehotel.co.uk **web:** www.langstonehotel.co.uk
dir: *From A27 take A3023 signed Havant/Hayling Island. Over bridge onto Hayling Island, sharp left after bridge*

This hotel is located on the north shore of Hayling Island, yet is only minutes from the M27 with easy access to Fareham, Havant and Chichester. All the smartly designed bedrooms, including 45 superior rooms, have views over Langstone harbour. The Brasserie offers a good choice of dishes and overlooks the harbour. A gym, indoor pool, sauna, steam, beauty salon and fitness club are also available.

Rooms: 148 (25 family) (60 GF) (3 smoking) 🐾 **D** £69.95–£299.95 (incl. bkfst)*
Facilities: Spa FTV WiFi ⇣ HL ⊛ supervised Gym Sauna Steam room Jacuzzi Fitness classes Xmas New Year **Conf:** Class 80 Board 50 Thtr 160 **Services:** Lift Night porter **Parking:** 220 **Notes:** Civ Wed 150

Sinah Warren Hotel

WARNER LEISURE HOTELS

★★★ 82% HOTEL

Ferry Road, PO11 0BZ - tel: 023 9246 6421
email: sinahwarren2@bourne-leisure.co.uk **web:** www.warnerleisurehotels.co.uk
dir: *A27 at Havant junct, take A3023 to Hayling Island, 2nd exit at rdbt towards Manor Rd, 3rd exit at next rdbt into Ferry Rd. Hotel 1.5m on right*

Located in a beautiful part of Hampshire, this hotel offers a great range of leisure facilities and numerous daily in-house and external activities catering for all. The accommodation is spacious, and some rooms have sea views. The packages range from a minimum two-night, half-board stay. Please note that this is an adults-only (over 21 years) hotel.

Rooms: 280 (34 annexe) (116 GF) 🐾 **S** £199–£450; **D** £398–£900 (incl. bkfst & dinner)* **Facilities:** Spa FTV WiFi HL ⊛ ⚘ supervised ⚑ ⚑ Gym ♫ Xmas New Year **Conf:** Class 300 Board 250 Thtr 500 **Services:** Lift Night porter **Parking:** 260
Notes: LB

H

HEACHAM
Norfolk

Map 12 TF63

See also **Slough & Staines-upon-Thames**

HIGHLY RECOMMENDED

Heacham Manor Hotel

★★★ 87% ● HOTEL

Hunstanton Road, PE31 7JX - **tel:** 01485 536030
email: info@heacham-manor.co.uk **web:** www.heacham-manor.co.uk
dir: *On A149 between Heacham & Hunstanton. Near Hunstanton rdbt with water tower*

This delightful 16th-century, Grade II listed house has been beautifully restored. The property is approached via a winding driveway through landscaped grounds to the front of the hotel. Public areas include a smart dining room, a sunny conservatory and a cosy bar which leads out onto a terrace. The bedrooms are very stylish and have modern facilities such as free WiFi. Dogs are very welcome at Heacham Manor. There is a selection of dog-friendly family suites; these are limited and subject to availability, so please contact the hotel if you need one. An extra charge applies to each dog that visits.

Rooms: 45 (32 annexe) (10 family) (12 GF) **Facilities:** FTV WiFi ⌖ 18 Spa, swimming pools & leisure facilities available at sister resort Xmas New Year **Conf:** Class 35 Board 20 Thtr 40 **Services:** Night porter **Parking:** 55 **Notes:** LB Civ Wed 100

HIGHLY RECOMMENDED

Hilton London Heathrow Airport Terminal 5

★★★★ 85% ●● HOTEL PLAN 1 A3

Poyle Road, Colnbrook, SL3 0FF - **tel:** 01753 686860
email: heathrowairportterminal5.info@hilton.com **web:** www.hilton.com/heathrowt5
dir: *Please phone for directions*

Hilton London Heathrow Airport Terminal 5, is located just one mile from Terminal 5 with easy access to the M25. Bedrooms offer practical and modern amenities such as soundproof windows and high quality comfortable beds. A complimentary shuttle service is available to businesses in Stockley Park and Bedfont Lakes. It is an ideal venue for conferences, meetings and banqueting events for up to 1,000 guests. There are two restaurants; The Gallery offering traditional British dishes, or Mr Todiwala's which offers Pan-Indian cuisine. Guests can relax in the luxury onsite Spa and 24 Fitness Centre.

Rooms: 350 (4 family) ⌁ **S** £115–£315; **D** £115–£315 **Facilities:** Spa STV FTV WiFi ⌖ Gym **Conf:** Class 430 Board 78 Thtr 1400 Del from £169 **Services:** Lift Night porter Air con **Parking:** 486 **Notes:** Civ Wed 1170

Novotel London Heathrow Airport

NOVOTEL
HOTELS & RESORTS

★★★★ 77% HOTEL PLAN 1 A3

Cherry Lane, UB7 9HB - **tel:** 01895 431431
email: H1551-gm@accor.com **web:** www.novotel.com
dir: *M4 junct 4, follow Uxbridge signs on A408. Keep left, take 2nd exit off traffic island into Cherry Ln signed West Drayton. Hotel on left*

Conveniently located for Heathrow Airport and the motorway network, this modern hotel provides comfortable accommodation. The large, airy indoor atrium creates a sense of space in the public areas, which include an all-day restaurant and bar, meeting rooms, fitness centre and swimming pool. Ample secure parking is available.

Rooms: 178 (178 family) (10 GF) **S** £55–£300; **D** £65–£310* **Facilities:** FTV WiFi ⌖ HL ⌖ Gym Xmas **Conf:** Class 100 Board 90 Thtr 250 Del from £130 **Services:** Lift Night porter Air con **Parking:** 100 **Notes:** LB Civ Wed 160

DoubleTree by Hilton London Heathrow Airport

fOCUShotels
management limited

★★★★ 75% HOTEL PLAN 1 A3

Bath Road, Cranford, TW5 9QE - **tel:** 020 8564 4450
email: reservations@doubletree-heathrow.com **web:** www.doubletree3.hilton.com
dir: *M4 junct 3 follow signs to Heathrow Terminals 1, 2 & 3. Hotel on right of A4 Bath Rd*

This well presented hotel is conveniently situated just three miles from Heathrow Airport. Bedrooms are located in a smart block and all are well appointed for both business and leisure guests; each has a flat-screen TV, climate control and good lighting. Arts Bar and Brasserie lead from a contemporary open-plan reception area. Chargeable car park on site.

Rooms: 200 (21 family) (38 GF) ⌁ **S** £59–£255; **D** £59–£255* **Facilities:** FTV WiFi ⌖ Gym **Conf:** Class 35 Board 30 Thtr 70 Del from £145 **Services:** Lift Night porter Air con **Parking:** 72 **Notes:** LB

Leonardo Heathrow Airport Hotel

★★★★ 74% HOTEL PLAN 1 A3

Bath Road, UB7 0DP - **tel:** 020 8990 0000
email: res.heathrow@leonardo-hotels.com **web:** www.leonardo-hotels.com
dir: *Please phone for directions*

The Leonardo Heathrow Hotel is conveniently located on Bath Road just a couple of minutes from the Heathrow Terminals and only 15 minutes by express from Central London. This hotel offers modern accommodation, a good range of meeting and event rooms, a large open-plan bar and restaurant and plenty of parking on site. Free WiFi is available throughout the hotel.

Rooms: 230 (58 GF) 🐾 **S** fr £54; **D** fr £64* **Facilities:** Spa STV FTV WiFi ⬭ HL Gym Xmas New Year **Conf:** Class 60 Board 80 Thtr 120 Del from £110 **Services:** Lift Night porter Air con **Parking:** 90

Best Western Plus Park Grand London Heathrow

★★★★ 73% HOTEL PLAN 1 B3

449 Great West Road, TW5 0BY - **tel:** 020 7479 2266
email: john@montcalm.co.uk **web:** www.parkgrandheathrow.co.uk
dir: *From A4 Great Western Rd, turn into Jersey Rd, 3rd exit at rdbt, turn left. Hotel on the left*

This modern hotel is in a convenient location just five miles from London Heathrow Airport and with easy access to Central London. The hotel is modern in style with spacious open-plan public areas including a stylish bar and restaurant. Bedrooms are also modern in style and are very comfortable; all fully air-conditioned and benefiting from digital TV and complimentary WiFi. Parking is available on site.

Rooms: 124 (14 family) 🐾 **Facilities:** STV FTV WiFi ⬭ HL Gym New Year **Conf:** Class 60 Board 40 Thtr 70 **Services:** Lift Night porter Air con **Parking:** 38 **Notes:** Civ Wed 80

Ramada Hounslow - Heathrow East

★★★ 76% HOTEL PLAN 1 B2

8-10 Lampton Road, TW3 1JL - **tel:** 020 8538 1230
email: gm@ramadahounslow.co.uk **web:** www.ramada.co.uk/hounslow
dir: *A4 Bath Rd, A3006, into Lampton Rd A3005*

A purpose-built hotel situated in the centre of Hounslow, within walking distance of the tube station and with easy access to the motorway network. The accommodation is comfortable and offers a range of amenities. The public areas are light and airy, and parking is available.

Rooms: 96 (11 family) (4 GF) **S** £89–£120; **D** £89–£145 **Facilities:** FTV WiFi 🎵 Xmas New Year **Conf:** Class 50 Board 60 Thtr 100 Del from £145 **Services:** Lift Night porter Air con **Parking:** 20

Premier Inn Hayes Heathrow

BUDGET HOTEL PLAN 1 A4

362 Uxbridge Road, UB4 0HF - **tel:** 0871 527 8504 (Calls cost 13p per minute plus your phone company's access charge) **web:** www.premierinn.com
dir: *M4 junct 3, A312 N straight across next rdbt onto dual carriageway, at A4020 junct turn left, hotel 100yds on right*

High quality, budget accommodation ideal for both families and business travellers. Spacious, en suite bedrooms feature free WiFi and tea and coffee making facilities, and in most hotels, Freeview TV is also available. The adjacent family restaurant features a wide and varied menu.

Rooms: 86

Premier Inn Heathrow Airport (Bath Road)

BUDGET HOTEL PLAN 1 A3

15 Bath Road, TW6 2AB - **tel:** 0871 527 8508 (Calls cost 13p per minute plus your phone company's access charge) **web:** www.premierinn.com
dir: *M4 junct 4, follow signs for Heathrow Terminals 1, 2 & 3. Left onto Bath Rd signed A4/London. Hotel on right after 0.5m*

Rooms: 594

Premier Inn Heathrow Airport (M4 Jct 4)

BUDGET HOTEL PLAN 1 A3

Shepiston Lane, Heathrow Airport, UB3 1RW - **tel:** 0871 527 8510 (Calls cost 13p per minute plus your phone company's access charge) **web:** www.premierinn.com
dir: *M4 junct 4 take 3rd exit off rdbt. Hotel on right*

Rooms: 134

Premier Inn Heathrow Airport Terminal 5

BUDGET HOTEL PLAN 1 A3

Bath Road, Hillingdon, UB7 0EB - **tel:** 0871 527 9344 (Calls cost 13p per minute plus your phone company's access charge) **web:** www.premierinn.com
dir: *M25 junct 14, follow A3113/Heathrow T4 & Cargo signs. At rdbt 1st left onto A3044, at next rdbt 3rd exit signed Longford. Hotel approx 250yds on left*

Rooms: 400

Premier Inn London Brentford

BUDGET HOTEL PLAN 1 C3

Alfa Laval, Great West Road, TW8 9AD - **tel:** 0871 527 9560 (Calls cost 13p per minute plus your phone company's access charge) **web:** www.premierinn.com
dir: *M4 junct 2, to Chiswick Rdbt. Take 5th exit onto A4 (keep right to next rdbt). Take 1st exit, hotel on right*

Rooms: 124

Sofitel London Heathrow

AA Advertised ⓐⓐⓐ PLAN 1 A3

Terminal 5, Wentworth Drive, TW6 2GD - **tel:** 020 8757 7777
email: slh@sofitelheathrow.com **web:** www.sofitelheathrow.com
dir: *M25 junct 14. At rdbt take 2nd exit, after 80mtrs turn left. Hotel on right*

This is the only Heathrow Airport hotel with direct access to Terminal 5 via a covered walkway and Terminals 1, 2, 3 and 4 via the Heathrow Express/Connect rail connection. It is only 21 minutes from Central London by train. Sofitel London Heathrow boasts 605 non-smoking bedrooms including 27 suites, 45 meeting rooms, 2 restaurants, 2 bars and a tea salon as well as private dining options. The hotel also offers a hair salon, a state-of-the-art health spa and gym, as well as an on-site car park.

Rooms: 605 (38 GF) 🐾 **S** £229–£329; **D** £229–£329* **Facilities:** Spa STV FTV WiFi Gym **Conf:** Class 820 Board 80 Thtr 1200 **Services:** Lift Night porter Air con **Parking:** 360 **Notes:** Civ Wed 220

HEATHROW AIRPORT *continued*

Renaissance London Heathrow Hotel

RENAISSANCE
LONDON HEATHROW HOTEL

AA Advertised PLAN 1 A3

Bath Road, TW6 2AQ - **tel:** 020 8897 6363 **email:** re3@renaissanceheathrow.co.uk
web: www.renaissancelondonheathrow.co.uk
dir: *M4 junct 4 take spur road towards airport, then 2nd left. At rdbt, 2nd exit signed 'Renaissance Hotel'. Hotel adjacent to Customs House*

This spacious hotel is located on the perimeter of Heathrow Airport with spectacular views of the main runway, and is within easy reach of Windsor, and motorway and rail networks to London. The hotel has excellent conference and leisure facilities.

Rooms: 710 (87 GF) ⮡ **D** £99–£313* **Facilities:** Spa STV WiFi ⮡ Gym Steam room Solarium Fitness studio Beauty & massage treatments Personal trainer **Conf:** Class 300 Board 80 Thtr 450 Del from £159 **Services:** Lift Night porter Air con **Parking:** 560 **Notes:** LB Civ Wed 360

HELLIDON
Northamptonshire
Map 11 SP55

Hellidon Lakes Golf & Spa Hotel

★★★★ 76% HOTEL

QHOTELS
INSPIRED
BY YOU

NN11 6GG - **tel:** 01327 262550
email: hellidonlakes@qhotels.co.uk **web:** www.qhotels.co.uk
dir: *Off A361 between Daventry & Banbury, signed*

Some 220 acres of beautiful countryside, which include 27 holes of golf and 12 lakes, combine to form a rather spectacular backdrop to this impressive hotel. Bedroom styles vary, from ultra smart, modern rooms through to those in the original wing that offer superb views. There is an extensive range of facilities available, from meeting rooms to a swimming pool, gym and ten-pin bowling. Golfers of all levels can try some of the world's most challenging courses on the indoor golf simulator.

Rooms: 110 (5 family) ⮡ **S** £89–£121; **D** £101–£133 (incl. bkfst)* **Facilities:** Spa FTV WiFi ⮡ HL ⮡ ⮡ 27 Putting green ⮡ Fishing ⮡ Gym Beauty therapist Indoor smart golf 10-pin bowling Steam room Coarse fishing lake Xmas New Year **Conf:** Class 110 Board 50 Thtr 300 Del from £132 **Services:** Lift Night porter **Parking:** 200 **Notes:** LB Civ Wed 176

HELMSLEY
North Yorkshire
Map 19 SE68

Feversham Arms Hotel & Verbena Spa

★★★★ ◉◎ HOTEL

PRIDE OF BRITAIN HOTELS

1-8 High Street, YO62 5AG - **tel:** 01439 770766
email: info@fevershamarmshotel.com **web:** www.fevershamarmshotel.com
dir: *A168 signed Thirsk A1, A170 or A64 signed York from A1 to York North, B1363 to Helmsley. Hotel 125mtrs from Market Place*

This long established hotel lies just round the corner from the main square, and under caring ownership proves to be a refined operation, yet without airs and graces. There are several lounge areas and a high-ceilinged conservatory restaurant where menus are created with skill and minimal fuss from good local ingredients. The bedrooms, including four air-conditioned poolside suites (some with wood-burners) and spa suites with balconies or French balconies, all have their own individual character and decor. Expect Egyptian cotton sheets, duck down duvets and Bang and Olufsen TVs with DVD and CD player. The spa offers a comprehensive range of pampering treatments.

Rooms: 33 (9 family) (8 GF) ⮡ **S** £110–£420; **D** £120–£430 (incl. bkfst)* **Facilities:** Spa STV FTV WiFi ⮡ ⮡ Sauna Saunarium Aromethery room Monsoon showers Relaxation lounge Xmas New Year **Conf:** Class 20 Board 24 Thtr 35 **Services:** Lift Night porter **Parking:** 50 **Notes:** Civ Wed 50

Red Stars The AA Red Star rating denotes an Inspector's Choice hotel. They stand out as the very best in the British Isles and appear in highlighted panels throughout the guide.

Black Swan Hotel

★★★★ 80% ◉◉◉ HOTEL

Market Place, YO62 5BJ - **tel:** 01439 770466
email: enquiries@blackswan-helmsley.co.uk **web:** www.blackswan-helmsley.co.uk
dir: A1 junct 49, A168, A170 east, hotel 14m from Thirsk

People have been visiting this establishment for over 200 years and it has become
a landmark that dominates the market square. The hotel is renowned for its
hospitality and friendliness; many of the staff are long-serving and dedicated.
The bedrooms are stylish and include a junior suite and feature rooms. Dinner in
the award-winning restaurant is the highlight of any stay. The hotel has a Tearoom
and Patisserie that is open daily.

Rooms: 45 (4 family) ✿ **S** fr £140; **D** fr £155 (incl. bkfst)* **Facilities:** STV FTV WiFi
Xmas New Year **Conf:** Class 30 Board 26 Thtr 50 **Services:** Night porter **Parking:** 40
Notes: Civ Wed 90

INSPECTOR'S CHOICE

The Pheasant Hotel

★★★ ◉◉ ♨ COUNTRY HOUSE HOTEL

Mill Street, Harome, YO62 5JG - **tel:** 01439 771241
email: reservations@thepheasanthotel.com **web:** www.thepheasanthotel.com
dir: Leave A1(M) at Thirsk, follow A170 E towards Helmsley/Scarborough & then
through Helmsley. Right after 0.5m to Harome, follow road for 2.5m

The Pheasant Hotel sits in a delightful small North Yorkshire village, overlooking
the village pond. The public areas are delightful in a very country house style,
with ample outside seating areas that are ideal for a delightful afternoon tea.
The rooms are spacious, very well appointed and have a luxury feel to them.

The small heated pool is easily accessible and the hotel has ample parking.
Food is the highlight of the stay with the menu boasting local produce and
inventive cooking.

Rooms: 16 (2 family) (3 GF) ✿ **S** fr £90; **D** fr £170 (incl. bkfst)* **Facilities:** FTV
WiFi ♨ ⊗ Xmas New Year **Conf:** Class 30 Board 20 Thtr 30 Del from £250
Parking: 10 **Notes:** LB Civ Wed 60

HELSTON   **Map 2 SW62**
Cornwall & Isles of Scilly

Premier Inn Helston

BUDGET HOTEL

Clodgey Lane, TR13 8FZ - **tel:** 0871 527 8512 (Calls cost 13p per minute plus
your phone company's access charge) **web:** www.premierinn.com
dir: A39 towards Falmouth. Right onto A394 towards Helston, 8m. At rdbt 1st exit
(Helston bypass) signed Penzance (A394)/Lizard. Hotel at next rdbt on left.
NB for Sat Nav use TR13 0QD

High quality, budget accommodation ideal for both families and business
travellers. Spacious, en suite bedrooms feature free WiFi and tea and coffee making
facilities, and in most hotels, Freeview TV is also available. The adjacent family
restaurant features a wide and varied menu.

Rooms: 50

HEMEL HEMPSTEAD   **Map 6 TL00**
Hertfordshire

Aubrey Park Hotel

★★★★ 80% ◉ HOTEL

Hemel Hempstead Road, Redbourn, AL3 7AF - **tel:** 01582 792105
email: reception@aubreypark.co.uk **web:** www.aubreypark.co.uk
dir: M1 junct 9 follow Hemel Hempstead & St Albans signs for 3m,
straight across 2 rdbts onto B487 signed Hemel Hempstead. Hotel on right

The hotel is conveniently located a short drive from the historic Roman city of St
Albans, close to the M1 and the M25, and is an ideal venue for both corporate and
leisure guests. Recently refurbished, the hotel is modern with attentive staff, good
food, ample parking and extensive, well-equipped meeting areas.

Rooms: 137 (10 family) (65 GF) ✿ **Facilities:** FTV WiFi ♨ Xmas New Year **Conf:** Class
96 Board 65 Thtr 200 **Services:** Lift Night porter **Parking:** 129 **Notes:** LB Civ Wed 85

The Watermill

★★★ 73% HOTEL

London Road, Bourne End, HP1 2RJ - **tel:** 01442 349955
email: info@hotelwatermill.co.uk **web:** www.hotelwatermill.co.uk
dir: From M25 & M1 follow signs to Aylesbury on A41, A4251 to Bourne End.
Hotel 0.25m on right

In the heart of the county this modern hotel has been built around an old flour mill
on the banks of the River Bulbourne with water meadows adjacent. The thoughtfully
equipped, contemporary bedrooms are located in three annexes situated around the
complex. A good range of air-conditioned conference and meeting rooms
complement the lounge bar and restaurant.

Rooms: 71 (71 annexe) (10 family) (35 GF) (8 smoking) ✿ **Facilities:** STV FTV WiFi
Fishing Xmas New Year **Conf:** Class 150 Board 125 Thtr 200 **Services:** Night porter
Parking: 100 **Notes:** Civ Wed 180

H

HEMEL HEMPSTEAD *continued*

Premier Inn Hemel Hempstead Central

BUDGET HOTEL

Moor End Road, HP1 1BT - tel: 0871 527 8514 (Calls cost 13p per minute plus your phone company's access charge) **web:** www.premierinn.com
dir: *M1 junct 8, A414, follow town centre signs. Right at 1st mini rdbt, right at 2nd mini rdbt into Seldon Hill Rd, follow Riverside car park signs (footbridge to hotel from floor 3).*

High quality, budget accommodation ideal for both families and business travellers. Spacious, en suite bedrooms feature free WiFi and tea and coffee making facilities, and in most hotels, Freeview TV is also available. The adjacent family restaurant features a wide and varied menu.

Rooms: 114

Premier Inn Hemel Hempstead West

BUDGET HOTEL

A41 Service Area, Bourne End, HP1 2SB - tel: 0871 527 8516 (Calls cost 13p per minute plus your phone company's access charge) **web:** www.premierinn.com
dir: *M25 junct 20, A41 exit at services. Or from M1 junct 8, A414, A41, exit at services*

Rooms: 62

HENLEY-ON-THAMES	Map 5 SU78
Oxfordshire	

Hotel du Vin Henley-on-Thames

★★★★ 76% ◉ TOWN HOUSE HOTEL

New Street, RG9 2BP - tel: 01491 848400 & 0844 736 4258 (Calls cost 5p per minute plus your phone company's access charge)
email: info.henley@hotelduvin.com **web:** www.hotelduvin.com
dir: *M4 junct 8/9 signed High Wycombe, 2nd exit onto A404 in 2m. A4130 to Henley, over bridge, through lights, into Hart St, right into Bell St, right into New St, hotel on right*

Situated just 50 yards from the water's edge, this hotel retains the character and much of the architecture of its former life as a brewery. Food, and naturally wine, take on a strong focus here and guests will find an interesting mix of dishes to choose from; there are three private dining rooms where the fermentation room and old malt house once were; alfresco dining is popular when the weather permits. Bedrooms provide comfort, style and a good range of facilities including power showers. Parking is available and there is a drop-off point in the courtyard.

Rooms: 43 (4 family) (4 GF) ⚲ **Facilities:** STV FTV WiFi ☇ Xmas New Year **Conf:** Class 20 Board 36 Thtr 56 **Services:** Night porter Air con **Parking:** 46 **Notes:** Civ Wed 60

HEREFORD	Map 10 SO54
Herefordshire	

See also **Leominster**

Holme Lacy House Hotel

★★★★ 73% COUNTRY HOUSE HOTEL

Holme Lacy, HR2 6LP - tel: 01432 870870
email: kellie.appleyard@bourne-leisure.co.uk **web:** www.warnerleisurehotels.co.uk
dir: *B4399 at Holme Lacy, take lane opposite college. Hotel 500mtrs on right*

This is a grand Grade I listed mansion with a rich history, just a short drive from Hereford, set in twenty acres of superb parkland in the heart of the Wye Valley. The well-appointed bedrooms are comfortable and vary in size and style. There's plenty to do here, with a full daily entertainment programme, an indoor pool, and health and beauty treatments. The three restaurants provide carefully selected menus of quality cuisine. Exclusively for adults (above 21 years old).

Rooms: 181 (150 annexe) (53 GF) ⚲ **S** £180–£280; **D** £230–£450 (incl. bkfst & dinner)* **Facilities:** Spa FTV WiFi HL ⊛ Putting green ⚲ Fishing ⚲ Gym Archery Rifle shooting Aquafit Yoga ♫ Xmas New Year **Services:** Lift Night porter **Parking:** 200 **Notes:** LB

Castle House

★★★ 88% ◉◉ HOTEL

Castle Street, HR1 2NW - tel: 01432 356321
email: info@castlehse.co.uk **web:** www.castlehse.co.uk
dir: *Follow signs to City Centre East. At junct of Commercial Rd & Union St follow brown hotel signs*

Enjoying a prime city centre location, with a terraced garden leading to the castle moat, this delightful Grade II-listed Georgian mansion is the epitome of elegance and sophistication. The character bedrooms are equipped with every luxury to ensure a memorable stay and are complemented perfectly by the well-proportioned and restful lounge and bar. The elegant topiary-themed restaurant is the setting for award-winning modern British cuisine.

Rooms: 24 (8 annexe) (1 family) (4 GF) ⚲ **Facilities:** STV FTV WiFi ☇ Xmas New Year **Services:** Lift Night porter **Parking:** 12 **Notes:** LB Civ Wed 50

Three Counties Hotel

★★★ 77% HOTEL

Belmont Road, HR2 7BP - tel: 01432 299955
email: enquiries@threecountieshotel.co.uk **web:** www.threecountieshotel.co.uk
dir: *On A465 Abergavenny road*

Just a mile west of the city centre, this large, privately owned, modern complex has well-equipped, spacious bedrooms; many are located in separate single-storey buildings around the extensive car park. There is a spacious, comfortable lounge, a traditional bar and an attractive restaurant.

Rooms: 60 (32 annexe) (4 family) (46 GF) **S** £77–£97; **D** £86–£106 (incl. bkfst)*
Facilities: STV FTV WiFi **Conf:** Class 200 Board 120 Thtr 450 Del from £128
Services: Night porter **Parking:** 250 **Notes:** Civ Wed 350

Premier Inn Hereford

BUDGET HOTEL

Holmer Road, Holmer, HR4 9RS - tel: 0871 527 8518 (Calls cost 13p per minute plus your phone company's access charge) **web:** www.premierinn.com
dir: *From N: M5 junct 7, A4103 to Worcester. M50 junct 4, A49 (Leominster road). Hotel 800yds on left*

High quality, budget accommodation ideal for both families and business travellers. Spacious, en suite bedrooms feature free WiFi and tea and coffee making facilities, and in most hotels, Freeview TV is also available. The adjacent family restaurant features a wide and varied menu.

Rooms: 101

HERNE BAY	Map 7 TR16
Kent	

Premier Inn Canterbury North/Herne Bay

BUDGET HOTEL

Blacksole Farm, Margate Road, CT6 6LA - tel: 0871 527 8520 (Calls cost 13p per minute plus your phone company's access charge) **web:** www.premierinn.com
dir: *From M2 junct 7 follow Canterbury signs, A299 signed Ramsgate/Margate. Exit at Broomfield & Beltinge. Hotel just off rdbt*

High quality, budget accommodation ideal for both families and business travellers. Spacious, en suite bedrooms feature free WiFi and tea and coffee making facilities, and in most hotels, Freeview TV is also available. The adjacent family restaurant features a wide and varied menu.

Rooms: 50

HESWALL	Map 15 SJ28
Merseyside	

Premier Inn Wirral (Heswall)

BUDGET HOTEL

Chester Road, Gayton, CH60 3SD - tel: 0871 527 9178 (Calls cost 13p per minute plus your phone company's access charge) **web:** www.premierinn.com
dir: *M53 junct 4, A5137 signed Heswall. In 3m left at next rdbt, hotel on left*

High quality, budget accommodation ideal for both families and business travellers. Spacious, en suite bedrooms feature free WiFi and tea and coffee making facilities, and in most hotels, Freeview TV is also available.

Rooms: 87

HETHERSETT	Map 13 TG10
Norfolk	

Park Farm Hotel

★★★★ 77% ◎ HOTEL

NR9 3DL - tel: 01603 810264
email: enq@parkfarm-hotel.co.uk **web:** www.parkfarm-hotel.co.uk
dir: *5m S of Norwich, exit A11 onto B1172*

Park Farm is an elegant Georgian farmhouse set in landscaped grounds surrounded by open countryside. The property has been owned and run by the Gowing family since 1958. Bedrooms are pleasantly decorated and tastefully furnished; some rooms have patio doors with a sun terrace. Public rooms include a stylish conservatory, a lounge bar, a smart restaurant and superb leisure facilities.

Rooms: 53 (16 annexe) (15 family) (26 GF) **Facilities:** Spa FTV WiFi supervised Gym Beauty salon Hairdressing Xmas New Year **Conf:** Class 50 Board 50 Thtr 120 **Services:** Night porter **Parking:** 150 **Notes:** LB Civ Wed 100

HEXHAM	Map 21 NY96
Northumberland	

HIGHLY RECOMMENDED

Langley Castle Hotel

★★★★ 83% ◎◎ HOTEL

Langley, NE47 5LU - tel: 01434 688888
email: manager@langleycastle.com **web:** www.langleycastle.com
dir: *From A69 S on A686 for 2m. Hotel on right*

Langley is a magnificent 14th-century fortified castle, with its own chapel, set in ten acres of parkland. There is an award-winning restaurant, a comfortable drawing room and a cosy bar. Bedrooms are furnished with period pieces and most feature window seats. Restored buildings in the grounds have been converted into very stylish Castle view bedrooms.

Rooms: 27 (18 annexe) (8 family) (9 GF) S £99.50–£219.50; D £159–£279 (incl. bkfst) **Facilities:** STV WiFi HL Xmas **Conf:** Class 60 Board 40 Thtr 120 Del from £220 **Services:** Lift Night porter Air con **Parking:** 70 **Notes:** LB Civ Wed 120

H

HEXHAM *continued*

Slaley Hall

★★★★ 80% HOTEL

QHOTELS
INSPIRED
BY YOU

Slaley, NE47 0BX - **tel:** 01434 673350 & 0871 222 4688 (Calls cost 10p per minute plus your phone company's access charge)
email: Slaleyreception@qhotels.co.uk **web:** www.qhotels.co.uk
dir: *A1 from S to A68 link road follow signs for Slaley Hall*

One thousand acres of Northumbrian forest and parkland, two championship golf courses and indoor leisure facilities can all be found here. Spacious bedrooms are fully air conditioned, equipped with a range of extras and the deluxe rooms offer excellent standards. Public rooms include a number of lounges and dining options, including the fine-dining Dukes Grill, informal Claret Jug and the impressive main restaurant that overlooks the golf course.

Rooms: 141 (5 family) (45 GF) S £99–£180; **D** £99–£200 (incl. bkfst)*
Facilities: Spa FTV WiFi 36 Putting green Gym Quad bikes Archery Clay pigeon shooting 4x4 driving Xmas New Year **Conf:** Class 220 Board 150 Thtr 350 Del from £132 **Services:** Lift Night porter Air con **Parking:** 500 **Notes:** LB Civ Wed 250

Battlesteads

★★★ 85% HOTEL

Wark On Tyne, NE48 3LS - **tel:** 01434 230209
email: info@battlesteads.com **web:** www.battlesteads.com
dir: *Phone for details*

Battlesteads has been described as one of the greenest hotels in the country with many different eco-systems in place, but it is much more than this. Boasting an observatory to make the best of the area's Dark Skies status, and an award-winning kitchen team sourcing local produce, and even growing their own items for use in the kitchen. Bedrooms are well appointed and presented with quality beds, décor and flooring as standard. The team are warm and friendly, and really do strive to go that extra mile for guests. The log-burning stove in the bar makes it the place to sit while sampling one of a host of real ales available.

Rooms: 22 (5 annexe) (2 family) (4 GF) S £60–£85; **D** £100–£170 (incl. bkfst)*
Facilities: FTV WiFi **Parking:** 30 **Notes:** Closed 25 Dec Civ Wed 70

Find out more
about the AA Hotel of the Year
for England on page 16

Santo's Higham Farm Hotel

★★★ 77% HOTEL

Main Road, DE55 6EH - **tel:** 01773 833812
email: reception@santoshighamfarm.co.uk **web:** www.santoshighamfarm.co.uk
dir: *M1 junct 28, A38 towards Derby, then A61 towards Chesterfield. Onto B6013 towards Belper, hotel 300yds on right*

With panoramic views across the rolling Amber Valley, this 15th-century crook barn and farmhouse has been expertly restored and extended. There's an Italian wing and an international wing of themed bedrooms and mini suites. Freshly prepared dishes, especially fish, are available in Guiseppe's restaurant. This hotel makes an ideal romantic hideaway.

Rooms: 31 (3 family) (7 GF) S £55–£225; **D** £70–£266 (incl. bkfst)*
Facilities: FTV WiFi Xmas New Year **Conf:** Class 40 Board 34 Thtr 100 Del from £105 **Services:** Night porter **Parking:** 100 **Notes:** LB Civ Wed 100

Laburnum House Lodge Hotel

★★ 62% HOTEL

Sloway Lane, West Huntspill, TA9 3RJ - **tel:** 01278 781830
email: laburnumhh@aol.com **web:** www.laburnumhousehotel.co.uk
dir: *M5 junct 22. W on A38 approx 5m, right at Crossways Inn. 300yds & left into Sloway Ln, 300yds to hotel*

This hotel is in an excellent rural location, set in its own grounds, and offers an impressive range of facilities. The spacious bedrooms are all in individual lodges with their own access, and many are suitable for families. The hotel also offers a range of meeting rooms and leisure facilities. Dogs are welcome here.

Rooms: 68 (9 family) (68 GF) S £50–£80; **D** £60–£90* **Facilities:** FTV WiFi HL Gym **Conf:** Class 60 Board 40 Thtr 100 Del from £90 **Services:** Night porter **Parking:** 100 **Notes:** LB Civ Wed 100

HIGHCLIFFE
Dorset

Map 5 SZ29

Premier Inn Christchurch/Highcliffe

BUDGET HOTEL

266 Lymington Road, BH23 5ET - **tel:** 0871 527 9276 (Calls cost 13p per minute plus your phone company's access charge) **web:** www.premierinn.com
dir: From A35 (Christchurch rdbt) onto A337 towards New Milton & Lymington. Approx 2m hotel on left

High quality, budget accommodation ideal for both families and business travellers. Spacious, en suite bedrooms feature free WiFi and tea and coffee making facilities, and in most hotels, Freeview TV is also available. The adjacent family restaurant features a wide and varied menu.

Rooms: 62

HIGH WYCOMBE
Buckinghamshire

Map 5 SU89

Premier Inn High Wycombe/Beaconsfield

BUDGET HOTEL

Thanstead Farm, London Road, HP10 9YL - **tel:** 0871 527 8522 (Calls cost 13p per minute plus your phone company's access charge) **web:** www.premierinn.com
dir: M40 junct 3, A40 towards High Wycombe

High quality, budget accommodation ideal for both families and business travellers. Spacious, en suite bedrooms feature free WiFi and tea and coffee making facilities, and in most hotels, Freeview TV is also available. The adjacent family restaurant features a wide and varied menu.

Rooms: 135

Premier Inn High Wycombe Central

BUDGET HOTEL

Arch Way, HP13 5HL - **tel:** 0871 527 9326 (Calls cost 13p per minute plus your phone company's access charge) **web:** www.premierinn.com
dir: M4, junct 8/9, A404(M) signed Marlow & Wycombe. Exit for High Wycombe, right at rdbt (town centre) via Marlow Hill. Left at 1st mini rdbt, right at next rdbt, left signed Dovecot. Right at next junct into Arch Way, (Sainsburys on left) 1st left, left to hotel. NB for Sat Nav use HP11 2DN

Rooms: 120

HINCKLEY
Leicestershire

Map 11 SP49

Sketchley Grange Hotel

★★★★ 80% HOTEL

Sketchley Lane, Burbage, LE10 3HU - **tel:** 01455 251133
email: info@sketchleygrangehotel.co.uk **web:** www.sketchleygrangehotel.co.uk
dir: M69 junct 1, B4109 towards Hinkley. Left at 2nd rdbt. Into Sketchley Ln, 1st right, also Sketchley Ln

Close to motorway connections, this hotel is peacefully set in its own grounds, and enjoys open country views. Extensive leisure facilities include a stylish health and leisure spa. There are modern meeting facilities, a choice of bars, and two dining options, together with comfortable bedrooms furnished with many extras.

Rooms: 102 (7 family) (11 GF) ✎ **S** £69–£179; **D** £79–£189 **Facilities:** Spa FTV WiFi ⬦ ⊛ Gym Steam room Sauna Xmas New Year **Conf:** Class 150 Board 50 Thtr 280 Del from £115 **Services:** Lift Night porter **Parking:** 300 **Notes:** Civ Wed 220

Premier Inn Hinckley

BUDGET HOTEL

Coventry Road, LE10 0NB - **tel:** 0871 527 8524 (Calls cost 13p per minute plus your phone company's access charge) **web:** www.premierinn.com
dir: M69 junct 1, A5 towards Nuneaton. In 2.5m right at rdbt onto B4666 signed Hinckley Town Centre. Hotel on right, entrance via Total petrol station

High quality, budget accommodation ideal for both families and business travellers. Spacious, en suite bedrooms feature free WiFi and tea and coffee making facilities, and in most hotels, Freeview TV is also available. The adjacent family restaurant features a wide and varied menu.

Rooms: 91

H

H

HINTLESHAM
Suffolk

Map 13 TM04

Hintlesham Hall Hotel

★★★★ ◎◎ HOTEL

George Street, IP8 3NS - **tel:** 01473 652334
email: reservations@hintleshamhall.com **web:** www.hintleshamhall.com
dir: *4m W of Ipswich on A1071 to Hadleigh & Sudbury*

Hospitality and service are key features at this imposing Grade I listed country house hotel, situated in 175 acres of grounds and landscaped gardens. Originally a manor house dating from the Elizabethan era, the building was extended in the 17th and 18th centuries. It was a Red Cross hospital in World War II and has been a hotel for nearly 40 years. Individually decorated bedrooms offer a high degree of comfort; each one is tastefully furnished and equipped with many thoughtful touches. The Hintlesham Spa has three treatment rooms (including one for couples), a sumptuous relaxation area, nail bar, and enclosed outdoor area with hot tub. The spacious public rooms include a series of comfortable lounges, and an elegant restaurant which serves fine classical cuisine based on top-notch and where practical, local ingredients. WiFi is available throughout. A helicopter landing area is also available.

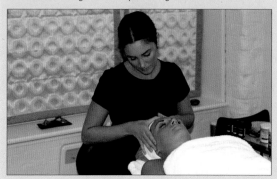

Rooms: 32 (10 annexe) (9 GF) 🐾 **S** £65–£120; **D** £85–£390* **Facilities:** Spa FTV WiFi HL 🏊 💆 Health & beauty services Clay pigeon shooting 🎵 Xmas New Year **Conf:** Class 50 Board 32 Thtr 80 Del from £150 **Services:** Night porter **Parking:** 60 **Notes:** Civ Wed 110

HINTON CHARTERHOUSE
Somerset

Map 4 ST75

Homewood Park Hotel & Spa

★★★★ 83% ◎◎ HOTEL

Abbey Lane, BA2 7TB - **tel:** 01225 723731
email: info@homewoodpark.co.uk **web:** www.homewoodpark.co.uk
dir: *6m SE of Bath on A36, left at 2nd sign for Freshford*

This hotel has a delightful location in attractive parkland, close to Bath and the Longleat estate. Bedrooms are stylishly and comfortably appointed, and many enjoy splendid countryside views. The spa and leisure facilities are notable, and a meal in the restaurant should not be missed.

Rooms: 21 (2 annexe) (3 family) (2 GF) 🐾 **Facilities:** Spa FTV WiFi ✈ 💆 Sauna Steam room Nail bar Hydrotherapy pool Xmas New Year **Conf:** Class 30 Board 25 Thtr 40 **Services:** Night porter **Parking:** 40 **Notes:** LB Civ Wed 120

HITCHIN
Hertfordshire

Map 12 TL12

Needham House Hotel

★★★★ 80% ◎◎ HOTEL

Blakemore End Road, Little Wymondley, SG4 7JJ - **tel:** 01462 417240
email: reservations@needhamhouse.co.uk **web:** www.needhamhouse.co.uk
dir: *3m from both Hitchin & Stevenage*

Ideally situated just a short drive from the A1(M) the property is set in well-presented grounds and features a spa, gym, open-plan lounge bar, a range of meeting rooms, and a function suite. The hotel was totally refurbished and reopened in early 2016; the bedrooms are modern and well equipped, some rooms have private terraces.

Rooms: 80 🐾 **S** fr £60; **D** fr £70* **Facilities:** Spa WiFi Sauna Steam room Relaxation lounge Turkish Hammam Xmas New Year **Conf:** Class 80 Board 60 Thtr 200 Del from £140 **Services:** Night porter **Parking:** 80 **Notes:** LB Civ Wed 200

Premier Inn Hitchin Town Centre

BUDGET HOTEL

Portmill Lane, SG5 1DJ - **tel:** 0871 527 9578 (Calls cost 13p per minute plus your phone company's access charge) **web:** www.premierinn.com
dir: *A1(M) junct 8, A602 (Hitchin). At 1st rdbt take 4th exit into St Johns Rd, left into Hitchin Hill. At next rdbt 2nd exit into Queen St. 4th left turn into Portmill Ln, hotel on right*

High quality, budget accommodation ideal for both families and business travellers. Spacious, en suite bedrooms feature free WiFi and tea and coffee making facilities, and in most hotels, Freeview TV is also available. The adjacent family restaurant features a wide and varied menu.

Rooms: 60

H

HOCKLEY HEATH
West Midlands   Map 10 SP17

Nuthurst Grange Hotel
★★★★ 79% ◎◎ HOTEL

Nuthurst Grange Lane, B94 5NL - tel: 01564 783972
email: info@nuthurst-grange.co.uk **web:** www.nuthurst-grange.co.uk
dir: Exit A3400, 0.5m south of Hockley Heath. Turn at sign into Nuthurst Grange Lane

A stunning avenue is the approach to this country house hotel, set amid several acres of well-tended gardens and mature grounds, with views over rolling countryside. The spacious bedrooms and bathrooms offer considerable luxury and comfort, and public areas include restful lounges, meeting rooms and a sunny restaurant. The kitchen brigade produces highly imaginative British and French cuisine, complemented by very attentive, professional restaurant service.

Rooms: 19 (7 family) (2 GF) **S** fr £130; **D** fr £140 (incl. bkfst)* **Facilities:** STV FTV WiFi **Conf:** Class 50 Board 35 Thtr 100 **Parking:** 80 **Notes:** Civ Wed 100

HOLLINGBOURNE
Kent   Map 7 TQ85

Mercure Maidstone, Great Danes Hotel
★★★★ 73% HOTEL

ME17 1RE - tel: 0844 815 9045 (Calls cost 7p per minute plus your phone company's access charge) **email:** info@mercuremaidstone.co.uk **web:** www.mercuremaidstone.co.uk
dir: M20 junct 8, follow Leeds Castle signs, at 2nd rdbt turn right

The property is set within 26 acres of private grounds just a few minutes from junction 8 of the M20 and close to the channel ports and Eurotunnel. The smartly appointed bedrooms are well equipped and suitable for business and leisure guests. Public rooms include Art's Bar and Grill as well as an indoor pool, fitness centre and a 9-hole golf course.

Rooms: 126 (15 family) **Facilities:** FTV WiFi Gym Squash Steam room Beauty treatments **Conf:** Class 220 Board 90 Thtr 650 **Services:** Night porter **Parking:** 500 **Notes:** Civ Wed 650

HOLT
Norfolk   Map 13 TG03

The Pheasant Hotel & Restaurant
★★★★ 81% ◎ HOTEL

Coast Road, Kelling, NR25 7EG - tel: 01263 588382
email: enquiries@pheasanthotelnorfolk.co.uk **web:** www.pheasanthotelnorfolk.co.uk
dir: On A149 coast road, mid-way between Sheringham & Blakeney

The Pheasant is a charming country house hotel set in its own extensive grounds, enjoying a peaceful rural location in the small village of Kelling, making it an ideal base from which to explore the beautiful North Norfolk coast and the surrounding villages of Cley and Blakeney. All bedrooms are beautifully presented and most comfortable. Afternoon tea is served on the terrace on warmer days and the lounge bar is cosy.

Rooms: 32 (1 family) (24 GF) (incl. bkfst) **Facilities:** FTV WiFi Xmas New Year **Conf:** Class 50 Thtr 100 **Notes:** LB Civ Wed 200

HONITON
Devon   Map 4 ST10

The Deer Park Country House Hotel
★★★★ 79% ◎◎ COUNTRY HOUSE HOTEL

Weston, EX14 3PG - tel: 01404 41266
email: admin@deerpark.co.uk **web:** www.deerparkcountryhotel.co.uk
dir: A30, take slip road into Honiton signed Turks Head. Next right then next left into Heathpark Industrial Estate. Hotel approx 1.6m

This country manor hotel is set in 80 acres of gardens, which includes an alfresco dining area with wood-burning oven and a walled kitchen garden. The hotel is just a short drive from Honiton and has easy access to the A30. The spacious accommodation is located in both the main house and separate garden rooms; there is even a luxurious treehouse with stunning views across the countryside. Deer Park is ideal for both business and leisure guests, and its picturesque setting makes it ideal for weddings and events. The hotel also boasts the Priory Collection, the largest collection of sporting memorabilia in the country.

Rooms: 33 (18 annexe) (2 family) (10 GF) **S** £65–£195; **D** £90–£325 (incl. bkfst)* **Facilities:** STV FTV WiFi Putting green Fishing Clay shooting Archery Quad Bikes Segways Xmas New Year **Conf:** Class 32 Board 22 Thtr 250 Del from £175 **Services:** Night porter **Parking:** 70 **Notes:** LB Civ Wed 170

THE PIG at Combe
Ⓤ

Gittisham, EX14 3AD - tel: 01404 540400 & 0345 225 9494
email: info@thepigatcombe.com **web:** www.thepighotel.com/at-combe
dir: M5 junct 29, left onto Honiton Road/A3015, at rdbt take 2nd exit & stay on Honiton Road/A3015. Take exit towards B3177/Fenton/Fairmile, turn right then left. Continue on B3177, slight right then left then right again

Currently the rating for this establishment is not confirmed. This may be due to a change of ownership or because it has only recently joined the AA rating scheme.

Rooms: 30 (13 annexe) (5 family) (6 GF) **S** £145–£490; **D** £145–£490* **Facilities:** FTV WiFi Two treatment rooms **Conf:** Class 14 Board 14 Thtr 14 Del from £255 **Services:** Night porter **Parking:** 50 **Notes:** Civ Wed 20

Premier Inn Honiton
BUDGET HOTEL

Turks Head Lane, EX14 1BQ - tel: 0871 527 9508 (Calls cost 13p per minute plus your phone company's access charge) **web:** www.premierinn.com
dir: From A30 S'bound, exit at 'Turks Head' junction signed Sidmouth & Cullompton. Turn left, hotel on left. Or from A30 N'bound, follow Honiton & Heathpark signs. Hotel on left

High quality, budget accommodation ideal for both families and business travellers. Spacious, en suite bedrooms feature free WiFi and tea and coffee making facilities, and in most hotels, Freeview TV is also available. The adjacent family restaurant features a wide and varied menu.

Rooms: 66

H

HOPE
Derbyshire   Map 16 SK18

Losehill House Hotel & Spa

★★★★ 78% ◎◎ HOTEL

Losehill Lane, Edale Road, S33 6AF - tel: 01433 621219
email: info@losehillhouse.co.uk web: www.losehillhouse.co.uk
dir: A6187 into Hope. Into Edale Rd opposite church. 1m, left & follow signs to hotel

Situated down a quiet leafy lane, this hotel occupies a secluded spot in the Peak District National Park. Bedrooms are comfortable and beautifully appointed. The outdoor hot tub, with stunning views over the valley, is a real indulgence; a heated swimming pool, sauna and spa treatments are also on offer. The views from the Orangery Restaurant are a real delight.

Rooms: 24 (3 annexe) (4 family) (3 GF) ⚑ S £125–£180; D £195–£235 (incl. bkfst)*
Facilities: Spa FTV WiFi 🕯 ♫ Xmas New Year Conf: Class 20 Board 15 Thtr 30
Services: Lift Night porter Parking: 30 Notes: Civ Wed 100

HORLEY

Hotels are listed under Gatwick Airport

HORNCASTLE
Lincolnshire   Map 17 TF26

Admiral Rodney Hotel

★★★ 79% HOTEL

North Street, LN9 5DX - tel: 01507 523131
email: admiralrodney@innmail.co.uk web: www.admiralrodney.com
dir: Phone for directions

The Admiral Rodney, a former coaching inn, is located in the picturesque town of Horncastle. Public areas are mostly open plan with a large lounge and bar area to relax in. The spacious bedrooms are well appointed and feature up-to-date technology including Sky TV; free WiFi is also available throughout the hotel. A brasserie-style menu is served throughout the day and evening, and guests can eat in either the Courtyard Restaurant or alfresco when the weather's warmer. Large function rooms and extensive parking are all available. The staff are very welcoming.

Rooms: 31 (4 family) (7 GF) S £79–£99; D £89–£119 (incl. bkfst)* Facilities: STV FTV WiFi 🕯 HL Conf: Class 60 Board 40 Thtr 140 Services: Lift Night porter Parking: 60 Notes: Civ Wed 100

HORRINGER
Suffolk   Map 13 TL86

The Ickworth

AA Advertised ◎◎

IP29 5QE - tel: 01284 735350
email: info@ickworthhotel.co.uk web: www.ickworthhotel.co.uk
dir: A14 exit for Bury St Edmunds, follow brown signs for Ickworth House, 4th exit at rdbt, cross staggered x-rds. Then onto T-junct, right into village, almost immediately right into Ickworth Estate

The Ickworth is set in 1,800 acres of Suffolk parkland with opportunities for spotting deer, walking, geo-caching, cycling and just generally relaxing. The hotel interior is full of period and contemporary furnishings, marble flooring and modern chandeliers, creating a luxurious and memorable impression. The hotel is also very family-friendly, offering free childcare, a cinema room, adventure playground, lawn games, flexible mealtimes, children's menus, swimming pools, wendy houses, a fairy garden and lots more. The ideal setting for a satisfying family break.

Rooms: 51 (23 annexe) (49 family) (5 GF) ⚑ Facilities: Spa FTV WiFi 🕯 🕯 🍃 ⚶ 1800 Acres of grounds and up to 60 Bikes Xmas New Year Child facilities
Conf: Class 30 Board 24 Thtr 45 Services: Lift Night porter Parking: 75 Notes: LB Civ Wed 50

HORSHAM
West Sussex   Map 6 TQ13

Premier Inn Horsham

BUDGET HOTEL

57 North Street, RH12 1RB - tel: 0871 527 8526 (Calls cost 13p per minute plus your phone company's access charge) web: www.premierinn.com
dir: Opposite railway station, 5m from M23 junct 11

High quality, budget accommodation ideal for both families and business travellers. Spacious, en suite bedrooms feature free WiFi and tea and coffee making facilities, and in most hotels, Freeview TV is also available. The adjacent family restaurant features a wide and varied menu.

Rooms: 64

HORSLEY
Derbyshire   Map 11 SK34

Horsley Lodge Hotel & Golf Club

★★★ 84% HOTEL

Smalley Mill Road, DE21 5BL - tel: 01332 780838
email: reception@horsleylodge.co.uk web: www.horsleylodge.co.uk
dir: M1 junct 25 from the S or junct 28 from the N. Off A38 Coxbench/Little Eaton exit

This family-run hotel is full of character. Situated equidistant from Derby and Nottingham, it is ideal for exploring the Peak District. Bedrooms and bathrooms have stylish decor, beautiful fabrics and quality furnishings. Barn Cottage offers even greater luxury and is tucked away not far from the main building. The Brasserie overlooks the 18-hole golf course.

Rooms: 14 (3 annexe) (2 family) (1 GF) ⚑ Facilities: FTV WiFi 🕯 ⚶ 18 Putting green Fishing Golf driving range Xmas New Year Conf: Class 70 Board 50 Thtr 100 Parking: 100 Notes: Civ Wed 100

HOUGHTON-LE-SPRING
Tyne & Wear   Map 19 NZ34

Chilton Country Pub & Hotel

★★★ 75% HOTEL

Black Boy Road, Chilton Moor, DH4 6PY - tel: 0191 385 2694
email: reception@chiltoncountrypub.co.uk web: www.chiltoncountrypubandhotel.co.uk
dir: A1(M) junct 62, onto A690 towards Sunderland. Left at Rainton Bridge & Fencehouses sign, right at rdbt, next rdbt straight over, next left. At next junct left, hotel on right

This country pub and hotel has been extended from the original farm cottages. Bedrooms are modern and comfortable and some rooms are particularly spacious. This hotel is popular for weddings and functions; there is also a well stocked bar, and a wide range of dishes is served in the Orangery and restaurant.

Rooms: 25 (7 family) (11 GF) ⚑ Facilities: STV FTV WiFi 🕯 ♫ Xmas New Year Conf: Class 50 Board 30 Thtr 150 Services: Night porter Parking: 200 Notes: LB Civ Wed 100

HOVE

See Brighton & Hove

HOVINGHAM
North Yorkshire   Map 19 SE67

The Worsley Arms Hotel

★★★ 79% ◉◉ SMALL HOTEL

High Street, YO62 4LA - **tel:** 01653 628130 & 628130
email: enquiries@worsleyarms.co.uk **web:** www.worsleyarms.co.uk
dir: On B1257 between Malton & Helmsley

This proprietor-run hotel offers a truly gastronomic experience. Food and wine are taken seriously here, and there is a strong commitment to local provenance. Guests can take the restaurant menu in either the restaurant or in the less formal Cricket bar. The hotel has some very attractive gardens, and the village is a delightfully tranquil location, close to many of North Yorkshire's tourist offerings. Rooms are located in the main house, or cottages across the road; all are pleasantly appointed and comfortable.

Rooms: 20 **S** £75–£105; **D** £135–£150 (incl. bkfst)*

HOYLAKE
Merseyside   Map 15 SJ28

Holiday Inn Express Liverpool - Hoylake

BUDGET HOTEL

The Kings Gap, CH47 1HE - **tel:** 0151 632 2073
email: info@hiexpresshoylake.com **web:** www.hiexpresshoylake.co.uk
dir: M53 towards Liverpool junct 2, then A551 towards Hoylake, at rdbt turn right onto The King's Gap. Hotel on right

A modern hotel ideal for families and business travellers. Fresh and uncomplicated, the spacious rooms include Sky TV, power shower and tea and coffee-making facilities. Continental buffet breakfast is included in the room rate; other meals may be taken at the nearby family pub or restaurant.

Rooms: 56 (24 family) (10 GF) ⌂ **Conf:** Class 40 Board 40 Thtr 100

HUCKNALL
Nottinghamshire   Map 16 SK54

Premier Inn Nottingham North West (Hucknall)

BUDGET HOTEL

Nottingham Road, NG15 7PY - **tel:** 0871 527 8852 (Calls cost 13p per minute plus your phone company's access charge) **web:** www.premierinn.com
dir: A611, A6002, straight on at 2 rdbts. Hotel 500yds on right

High quality, budget accommodation ideal for both families and business travellers. Spacious, en suite bedrooms feature free WiFi and tea and coffee making facilities, and in most hotels, Freeview TV is also available. The adjacent family restaurant features a wide and varied menu.

Rooms: 34

HUDDERSFIELD
West Yorkshire   Map 16 SE11

The Huddersfield Central Lodge

★★★ 75% METRO HOTEL

11/15 Beast Market, HD1 1QF - **tel:** 01484 515551
email: joe@centrallodge.com **web:** www.centrallodge.com
dir: Off main town centre ring road, take turning for Kirkgate, town centre, 1st right & 1st right again. Hotel on left

This friendly, family-run Metro Hotel offers smart, spacious bedrooms, all en suite. Across a private courtyard from the main building are more rooms, many with kitchenettes. Public rooms include a fully licensed bar and lounge, a 40 square metre conservatory and an outdoor covered and heated smoking area. Large screen TVs are in all of these areas. Many recommended restaurants with a wide variety of cuisine are within a 5 to 10 minute walk from the Central Lodge. On site secure free parking is available to all guests along with free WiFi throughout.

Rooms: 23 (4 family) (6 smoking) ⌂ **Facilities:** FTV WiFi ⌖ **Services:** Night porter **Parking:** 50 **Notes:** LB

Premier Inn Huddersfield Central

BUDGET HOTEL

St Andrews Way, HD1 3AQ - **tel:** 0871 527 8528 (Calls cost 13p per minute plus your phone company's access charge) **web:** www.premierinn.com
dir: Phone or see website for detailed directions

High quality, budget accommodation ideal for both families and business travellers. Spacious, en suite bedrooms feature free WiFi and tea and coffee making facilities, and in most hotels, Freeview TV is also available. The adjacent family restaurant features a wide and varied menu.

Rooms: 52

Premier Inn Huddersfield West

BUDGET HOTEL

New Hey Road, Ainley Top, HD2 2EA - **tel:** 0871 527 8532 (Calls cost 13p per minute plus your phone company's access charge) **web:** www.premierinn.com
dir: Just off M62 junct 24. From M62 take Brighouse exit from rdbt (A643). 1st left into Grimescar Rd, right into New Hey Rd

Rooms: 42

HUNGERFORD
Berkshire   Map 5 SU36

Littlecote House Hotel

WARNER LEISURE HOTELS
We're all grown up

★★★★ 78% ◉◉ COUNTRY HOUSE HOTEL

Chilton Foliat, RG17 0SU - **tel:** 01488 682509
email: phil.howden@bourne-leisure.co.uk **web:** www.warnerleisurehotels.co.uk
dir: M4 junct 14, A338, right onto A4, right onto B4192, left into Littlecote Road, hotel 0.5m on right at top of hill

This hotel provides comfortable, spacious accommodation and is located in stunning grounds close to the Cotswolds, only a 10-minute drive from Hungerford. There are traditional-style bedrooms in the ornate Grade I listed Tudor building and more contemporary rooms in the main building. Facilities include a regular programme of entertainment, beauty treatments and a choice of dining locations in either Oliver's Bistro or Pophams Restaurant. This is an adults-only (over 21 years) hotel.

Rooms: 208 (19 annexe) (57 GF) ⌂ **S** £199–£309; **D** £398–£618 (incl. bkfst & dinner)* **Facilities:** Spa FTV WiFi HL ⌖ supervised Putting green ⌫ ⌫ Gym Bowling Table tennis Snooker Archery Rifle shooting ♫ Xmas New Year **Services:** Lift Night porter **Notes:** LB

H

HUNGERFORD *continued*

Three Swans Hotel

★★★ 71% HOTEL

117 High Street, RG17 0LZ - **tel:** 01488 682721
email: swans.hungerford@innmail.co.uk **web:** www.threeswans.net
dir: *M4 junct 14 follow signs to Hungerford. Hotel in High St on left*

Centrally located in the bustling market town of Hungerford, this charming former inn, dating back some 700 years, has undergone a major refurb, which sees a new outside area and a coffee shop. Visitors will still see the original arch under which the horse-drawn carriages once passed. There is a wood-panelled bar, a spacious lounge and attractive rear garden to relax in. The informal restaurant is decorated with artwork by local artists. Bedrooms are well appointed and comfortable.

Rooms: 26 (10 annexe) (2 family) (5 GF) (3 smoking) **Facilities:** FTV WiFi Access to local private gym Xmas New Year **Conf:** Class 40 Board 30 Thtr 55 **Services:** Night porter **Parking:** 30 **Notes:** LB

HUNSTANTON	Map 12 TF64
Norfolk	

Best Western Le Strange Arms Hotel

BW Best Western.

★★★★ 74% HOTEL

Golf Course Road, Old Hunstanton, PE36 6JJ - **tel:** 01485 534411
email: reception@lestrangearms.co.uk **web:** www.abacushotels.co.uk
dir: *Off A149 1m N of Hunstanton. Left at sharp right bend by pitch & putt course*

Le Strange Arms is an impressive hotel with superb views from the wide lawns down to the sandy beach and across The Wash. Bedrooms in the main house are individually decorated. Public rooms include the comfortable Oak House and lounge, open for meals from midday, and a conference and banqueting suite. There is a choice of dining options - The Le Strange Bistro, or the Ancient Mariner, a traditional inn adjacent to the hotel, serving good food and real ales.

Rooms: 43 (7 annexe) (2 family) **S** £85–£195; **D** £95–£205* **Facilities:** FTV WiFi Xmas New Year **Conf:** Class 150 Board 50 Thtr 180 **Services:** Lift Night porter **Parking:** 80 **Notes:** Civ Wed 70

Caley Hall Hotel

★★★ 85% HOTEL

Old Hunstanton Road, PE36 6HH - **tel:** 01485 533486
email: mail@caleyhallhotel.co.uk **web:** www.caleyhallhotel.co.uk
dir: *1m from Hunstanton, on A149*

Situated within easy walking distance of the seafront, Caley Hall Hotel offers tastefully decorated bedrooms in a series of converted outbuildings. Each is smartly furnished and thoughtfully equipped. Public rooms feature a large open-plan

lounge/bar with plush leather seating, and a restaurant offering an interesting choice of dishes.

Rooms: 39 (20 family) (30 GF) **S** £75–£150; **D** £85–£195 (incl. bkfst)* **Facilities:** STV FTV WiFi New Year **Parking:** 50 **Notes:** Closed 18-26 Dec & 8-19 Jan

HUNSTRETE	Map 4 ST66
Somerset	

THE PIG near Bath

★★★ ◉◉ HOTEL

Hunstrete House, Pensford, BS39 4NS - **tel:** 01761 490490
email: info@thepignearbath.com **web:** www.thepighotel.com
dir: *From Bath take A4 to Bristol. At Globe Inn rdbt 2nd left onto A368 to Wells. 1m after Marksbury turn right for Hunstrete. Hotel next left*

A beautiful country house set in delightful grounds with its own deer park, livestock and walled garden, the latter providing the kitchen with much of its excellent produce. Alfresco eating is possible in the warmer months as there is a wood-fired oven in the courtyard. Bedrooms come in an array of shapes and sizes; some located in the main house, some around the courtyard, and others in beautifully converted garden sheds. All are spacious, have high quality fixtures, and come with their own larders and Nespresso machines. There are plenty of comfortable lounges where guests can make themselves at home too. The old dining room can accommodate meetings, and treatments can be taken in the potting shed.

Rooms: 29 (5 annexe) (10 GF) **Facilities:** FTV WiFi Treatment rooms Xmas New Year **Conf:** Board 22 **Services:** Night porter **Parking:** 100 **Notes:** Civ Wed

HUNTINGDON	Map 12 TL27
Cambridgeshire	

The Old Bridge Hotel

★★★ 88% ◉ HOTEL

1 High Street, PE29 3TQ - **tel:** 01480 424300
email: oldbridge@huntsbridge.co.uk **web:** www.huntsbridge.com
dir: *From A14 or A1 follow Huntingdon signs. Hotel visible from inner ring road*

The Old Bridge Hotel is an imposing 18th-century building prominently situated close to shops and amenities. On offer is superb accommodation in stylish and individually decorated bedrooms that include many useful extras. Guests can choose from the same menu whether dining in the recently refurbished restaurant or on the terrace in favourable weather. There is also an excellent business centre.

Rooms: 24 (2 family) (2 GF) ☾ **S** £95–£160; **D** £148–£230 (incl. bkfst)*
Facilities: STV FTV WiFi ☼ Fishing Private mooring for boats Xmas New Year
Conf: Class 50 Board 30 Thtr 60 **Services:** Night porter Air con **Parking:** 50
Notes: LB Civ Wed 100

Premier Inn Huntingdon (A1/A14)

BUDGET HOTEL

Great North Road, Brampton, PE28 4NQ - **tel:** 0871 527 8540 (Calls cost 13p per minute plus your phone company's access charge) **web:** www.premierinn.com
dir: *At junct of A1 & A14. (NB from N do not use junct 14. Take exit for Huntingdon & Brampton). Access to hotel via Services*

High quality, budget accommodation ideal for both families and business travellers. Spacious, en suite bedrooms feature free WiFi and tea and coffee making facilities, and in most hotels, Freeview TV is also available. The adjacent family restaurant features a wide and varied menu.

Rooms: 104

HYDE
Greater Manchester

Map 16 SJ99

Premier Inn Manchester (Hyde)

BUDGET HOTEL

Stockport Road, Mottram, SK14 3AU - **tel:** 0871 527 8712 (Calls cost 13p per minute plus your phone company's access charge) **web:** www.premierinn.com
dir: *At end of M67 between A57 & A560*

High quality, budget accommodation ideal for both families and business travellers. Spacious, en suite bedrooms feature free WiFi and tea and coffee making facilities, and in most hotels, Freeview TV is also available. The adjacent family restaurant features a wide and varied menu.

Rooms: 83

HYTHE
Kent

Map 7 TR13

Hythe Imperial

CLASSIC BRITISH HOTELS

★★★★ 77% ◉ HOTEL

Princes Parade, CT21 6AE - **tel:** 01303 267441
email: reception@hytheimperialhotel.com **web:** www.hytheimperial.co.uk
dir: *M20, junct 11 onto A261. In Hythe follow Folkestone signs. Right into Twiss Rd to hotel*

This imposing seafront hotel is enhanced by impressive grounds including a 13-green golf course and pleasing gardens. The majority of bedrooms have been refurbished and offer modern facilities with pleasing interiors; many also enjoy stunning sea views. Award-winning cuisine is served in Coast Restaurant while a varied afternoon tea menu is offered in the Afternoon Tea Parlour. The new Champagne Bar is the latest addition, while the leisure club includes a gym, a squash court, an indoor pool, and a spa offering a range of luxury treatments.

Rooms: 92 (11 family) (6 GF) ☾ **Facilities:** Spa FTV WiFi ☼ ☀ ♨ 9 Putting green Gym Aerobic studio Sauna Steam room Xmas New Year **Conf:** Class 120 Board 80 Thtr 220 **Services:** Lift Night porter **Parking:** 207 **Notes:** Civ Wed 120

Stade Court

★★★ 72% HOTEL

Stade Street, West Parade, CT21 6DT - **tel:** 01303 268263
email: stadecourt@bestwestern.co.uk **web:** www.stadecourthotel.co.uk
dir: *M20 junct 11 follow signs for Hythe town centre. Follow brown tourist sign for hotel*

Stade Court is situated right on the seafront with many bedrooms having the benefit of uninterrupted views of the English Channel. The comfortable bedrooms are tastefully decorated and provide free WiFi and in-room beverage-making facilities. Guests can enjoy traditional English or Indian cuisine in the sea-facing restaurant.

Rooms: 41 (5 family) ☾ **Facilities:** STV FTV WiFi ☼ Xmas New Year **Conf:** Class 20 Board 30 Thtr 40 **Services:** Lift Night porter **Parking:** 11 **Notes:** LB Civ Wed 100

ILFORD
Greater London

Premier Inn Ilford

BUDGET HOTEL PLAN 1 H5

Redbridge Lane East, IG4 5BG - **tel:** 0871 527 8542 (Calls cost 13p per minute plus your phone company's access charge) **web:** www.premierinn.com
dir: *At end of M11 follow London East, A12 & Chelmsford signs onto A12, hotel on left at bottom of slip road*

High quality, budget accommodation ideal for both families and business travellers. Spacious, en suite bedrooms feature free WiFi and tea and coffee making facilities, and in most hotels, Freeview TV is also available. The adjacent family restaurant features a wide and varied menu.

Rooms: 44

ILFRACOMBE
Devon

Map 3 SS54

Sandy Cove Hotel

★★★ 79% ◉◉ HOTEL

Old Coast Road, Combe Martin Bay, EX34 9SR - **tel:** 01271 882 243
email: info@sandycove-hotel.co.uk **web:** www.sandycove-hotel.co.uk
dir: *A339 to Combe Martin, through village towards Ilfracombe for approx 1m. Turn right just over brow of hill marked Sandy Cove*

This hotel enjoys a truly spectacular position, with front-facing bedrooms that benefit from uninterrupted views of the north Devon coastline. In addition, guests can relax on the sea decks or in the terraced garden, and really appreciate the peace and tranquillity. Locally sourced produce is a feature of the menus offered in the dining room, which makes the perfect setting for a romantic dinner or a family gathering.

Rooms: 36 (15 family) (7 GF) ☾ **S** £50–£85; **D** £100–£250 (incl. bkfst & dinner)*
Facilities: Spa WiFi ☼ ♨ Sauna Steam room Heated relaxation loungers Xmas New Year **Conf:** Class 20 Board 30 Thtr 30 **Parking:** 45 **Notes:** Civ Wed 150

ILFRACOMBE *continued*

Imperial Hotel

Leisureplex
HOLIDAY HOTELS

★★★ 70% HOTEL

Wilder Road, EX34 9AL - tel: 01271 862536
email: imperial.ilfracombe@alfatravel.co.uk **web:** www.leisureplex.co.uk
dir: *Opposite Landmark Theatre*

This popular hotel is just a short walk from the shops and harbour, overlooking gardens and the sea. Public areas include the spacious sun lounge, where guests can relax and enjoy the excellent views. Comfortable bedrooms are well equipped, with several having the added bonus of sea views.

Rooms: 104 (6 family) **Facilities:** FTV WiFi 🎵 Xmas New Year **Services:** Lift Night porter **Parking:** 7 **Notes:** Closed Dec–Feb (ex Xmas/New Year) RS Mar & Nov Mon–Fri

---

ILKLEY
West Yorkshire
Map 19 SE14

Best Western Plus Craiglands Hotel

Best Western PLUS

★★★ 73% HOTEL

Cowpasture Road, LS29 8RQ - tel: 01943 430001
email: reservations@craiglands.co.uk **web:** www.craiglands.co.uk
dir: *A65 into Ilkley. Left at T-junct. Past rail station, fork right into Cowpasture Rd. Hotel opposite school*

This grand Victorian hotel is situated close to the town centre. Spacious public areas and a good range of services are ideal for business or leisure. Extensive conference facilities are available along with an elegant restaurant and traditionally styled bar and lounge. Bedrooms, varying in size and style, are comfortably furnished and well equipped.

Rooms: 63 (5 family) **D** £79–£109 (incl. bkfst)* **Facilities:** FTV WiFi 🐾 Xmas New Year **Conf:** Class 200 Board 100 Thtr 500 Del from £109 **Services:** Lift Night porter **Parking:** 100 **Notes:** Civ Wed 500

ILSINGTON
Devon
Map 3 SX77

HIGHLY RECOMMENDED

Ilsington Country House Hotel

CLASSIC BRITISH HOTELS

★★★ 88% COUNTRY HOUSE HOTEL

Ilsington Village, TQ13 9RR - tel: 01364 661452
email: hotel@ilsington.co.uk **web:** www.ilsington.co.uk
dir: *M5 onto A38 to Plymouth. Exit at Bovey Tracey. 3rd exit from rdbt to Ilsington, then 1st right. Hotel in 5m by Post Office*

This friendly, family-owned hotel, offers tranquillity and far-reaching views from its elevated position on the southern slopes of Dartmoor. The stylish suites and bedrooms, some on the ground floor, are individually furnished. The restaurant provides a stunning backdrop for the innovative, daily-changing menus which feature local fish, meat and game. Additional facilities include an indoor pool and the Blue Tiger Inn, where a pint, a bite to eat and convivial conversation can all be enjoyed.

Rooms: 25 (4 family) (6 GF) **S** £95–£125; **D** £125–£250 (incl. bkfst)*
Facilities: Spa FTV WiFi 🏊 🏋 Gym Steam room Sauna Beauty treatment rooms Hydrotherapy pool Xmas New Year **Conf:** Class 60 Board 40 Thtr 100
Services: Lift **Parking:** 70 **Notes:** LB Civ Wed 100

INSTOW
Devon
Map 3 SS43

Commodore Hotel

★★★ 85% HOTEL

Marine Parade, EX39 4JN - tel: 01271 860347
email: admin@commodore-instow.co.uk **web:** www.commodore-instow.co.uk
dir: *M5 junct 27 follow N Devon link road to Bideford. Right before bridge, hotel in 3m*

Maintaining its links with the local maritime and rural communities, The Commodore provides an interesting place to stay. Situated at the mouth of the Taw and Torridge rivers and overlooking a sandy beach, it offers well-equipped bedrooms, many with balconies. There are five ground-floor suites. Eating options include the restaurant, the Quarterdeck bar, or the terrace in the warmer months.

Rooms: 25 (1 family) (5 GF) **S** £95–£130; (incl. bkfst & dinner)* **Facilities:** FTV WiFi 🐾 Xmas New Year **Services:** Night porter **Parking:** 200
Notes: LB No children 3yrs

IPSWICH
Suffolk
Map 13 TM14

INSPECTOR'S CHOICE

Hintlesham Hall Hotel

★★★★ @@ HOTEL

George Street, IP8 3NS - tel: 01473 652334
email: reservations@hintleshamhall.com **web:** www.hintleshamhall.com

(For full entry see Hintlesham)

INSPECTOR'S CHOICE

Salthouse Harbour Hotel

★★★★ @@ TOWN HOUSE HOTEL

No 1 Neptune Quay, IP4 1AX - tel: 01473 226789
email: frontdesk@salthouseharbour.co.uk **web:** www.salthouseharbour.co.uk
dir: *From A14 junct 56 follow signs for town centre, then Salthouse signs*

Situated just a short walk from the town centre, this waterfront warehouse conversion is a clever mix of contemporary styles and original features. The hotel is stylishly designed throughout with modern art, sculptures, interesting artefacts and striking colours. The spacious bedrooms provide luxurious comfort;

some have feature bathrooms and some have balconies. Two air-conditioned penthouse suites, with stunning views, have extras such as state-of-the-art sound systems and telescopes. Award-winning food is served in the busy, ground-floor brasserie, and alfresco eating is possible in warmer weather.

Rooms: 70 (6 family) **Facilities:** STV FTV WiFi **Services:** Lift Night porter **Parking:** 30 **Notes:** LB

milsoms Kesgrave Hall

★★★★ 82% ⦿ HOTEL

Hall Road, Kesgrave, IP5 2PU - **tel:** 01473 333741
email: reception@kesgravehall.com **web:** www.milsomhotels.com/kesgravehall
dir: A12 N of Ipswich, left at Ipswich/Woodbridge rdbt onto A1214. Right after 0.5m into Hall Rd. Hotel 200yds on left

Kesgrave Hall is a superb 18th-century, Grade II listed Georgian mansion set amidst 38 acres of mature grounds. Appointed in a contemporary style, the large open-plan public areas include a smart bar, a lounge with plush sofas, and a restaurant where guests can watch the chefs in action. Bedrooms are tastefully appointed and thoughtfully equipped.

Rooms: 23 (9 annexe) (3 family) (8 GF) **S** £145–£175; **D** £145–£325 (incl. bkfst)* **Facilities:** STV FTV WiFi **Xmas Conf:** Class 200 Board 24 Thtr 600 Del from £204 **Services:** Night porter **Parking:** 100 **Notes:** LB Civ Wed 300

Best Western Ipswich Hotel

BW Best Western.

★★★★ 77% HOTEL

Old London Road, Copdock, IP8 3JD - **tel:** 01473 209988
email: reception@hotelipswich.co.uk **web:** www.hotelipswich.co.uk
dir: Phone for directions

Ideally situated on the outskirts of Ipswich within easy access to the town centre and major routes via the Copdock interchange. The bedrooms are contemporary and well equipped with modern facilities; the public areas include a large open-plan lounge/bar area and a restaurant overlooking the neat garden to the rear; a range of meeting rooms are also available.

Rooms: 76 (29 annexe) (23 GF) **S** £60–£95; **D** £65–£100 (incl. bkfst)* **Facilities:** FTV WiFi ⚄ supervised ♫ Xmas New Year **Conf:** Class 120 Board 90 Thtr 450 Del from £95 **Services:** Lift Night porter **Parking:** 350 **Notes:** LB Civ Wed 85

Novotel Ipswich Centre

NOVOTEL
HOTELS & RESORTS

★★★★ 75% HOTEL

Greyfriars Road, IP1 1UP - **tel:** 01473 232400
email: h0995@accor.com **web:** www.novotel.com
dir: From A14 towards Felixstowe. Left onto A137, 2m into town centre. Hotel on double rdbt by Stoke Bridge

This modern, red brick hotel is perfectly placed in the centre of town close to shops, bars and restaurants. The open-plan public areas include a Mediterranean-style restaurant and a bar with a small games area. The bedrooms are smartly appointed and have many thoughtful touches; three rooms are suitable for less mobile guests.

Rooms: 101 (8 family) **S** £47–£165; **D** £47–£165* **Facilities:** STV FTV WiFi HL Gym Xmas New Year **Conf:** Class 100 Board 45 Thtr 180 **Services:** Lift Night porter Air con **Parking:** 53 **Notes:** Civ Wed 150

Best Western Claydon Hotel

BW Best Western.

★★★ 78% HOTEL

16-18 Ipswich Road, Claydon, IP6 0AR - **tel:** 01473 830382
email: enquiries@hotelsipswich.com **web:** www.hotelsipswich.com
dir: From A14, NW of Ipswich. After 4m take Great Blakenham Rd B1113 to Claydon, hotel on left

A delightful hotel situated just off the A14, within easy driving distance of the town centre. The pleasantly decorated bedrooms are thoughtfully equipped and one room has a lovely four-poster bed. An interesting choice of freshly prepared dishes is available in the smart restaurant, and guests have the use of a relaxing lounge bar.

Rooms: 36 (12 GF) **Facilities:** FTV WiFi New Year **Conf:** Class 50 Board 40 Thtr 80 **Services:** Night porter Air con **Parking:** 85 **Notes:** Civ Wed 65

Best Western Gatehouse Hotel

BW Best Western.

★★★ 77% HOTEL

799 Old Norwich Road, IP1 6LH - **tel:** 01473 741897
email: enquiries@gatehousehotel.com **web:** www.gatehousehotel.com
dir: A14 junct 53, A1156 signed Ipswich, left at lights into Norwich Rd, hotel on left

A Regency-style property set amidst three acres of landscaped grounds, on the outskirts of town in a quiet road just a short drive from the A14. The spacious bedrooms have co-ordinated soft furnishings and many thoughtful touches. Public rooms include a smart lounge bar, an intimate restaurant and a cosy drawing room with plush leather sofas.

Rooms: 15 (4 annexe) (1 family) (6 GF) **Facilities:** FTV WiFi **Parking:** 25

IPSWICH *continued*

Premier Inn Ipswich (Chantry Park)

BUDGET HOTEL

Old Hadleigh Road, IP8 3AR - **tel:** 0871 527 8548 (Calls cost 13p per minute plus your phone company's access charge) **web:** www.premierinn.com
dir: *From A12/A14 junct take A1214 to Ipswich town centre. Left at lights by Holiday Inn, left onto A1071. At mini rdbt turn right. Hotel on right*

High quality, budget accommodation ideal for both families and business travellers. Spacious, en suite bedrooms feature free WiFi and tea and coffee making facilities, and in most hotels, Freeview TV is also available. The adjacent family restaurant features a wide and varied menu.

Rooms: 74

Premier Inn Ipswich North

BUDGET HOTEL

Paper Mill Lane, Claydon, IP6 0BE - **tel:** 0871 527 8550 (Calls cost 13p per minute plus your phone company's access charge) **web:** www.premierinn.com
dir: *A14 junct 52. At rdbt exit onto Paper Mill Lane. Hotel 1st left*

Rooms: 90

Premier Inn Ipswich South

BUDGET HOTEL

Bourne Hill, Wherstead, IP2 8ND - **tel:** 0871 527 8552 (Calls cost 13p per minute plus your phone company's access charge) **web:** www.premierinn.com
dir: *From A14 follow Ipswich Central A137 signs, then Ipswich Central & Docks signs. At bottom of hill at rdbt 2nd exit. Hotel on right*

Rooms: 40

Premier Inn Ipswich South East

BUDGET HOTEL

Augusta Close, Ransomes Euro Park, IP3 9SS - **tel:** 0871 527 8554 (Calls cost 13p per minute plus your phone company's access charge) **web:** www.premierinn.com
dir: *A14 junct 57, stay in right lane. At rdbt 2nd exit, then 1st left. Hotel adjacent to Swallow Restaurant*

Rooms: 36

Premier Inn Ipswich Town Centre (Quayside)

BUDGET HOTEL

33 Key Street, IP4 1BZ - **tel:** 0871 527 9388 (Calls cost 13p per minute plus your phone company's access charge) **web:** www.premierinn.com
dir: *Phone for directions*

Rooms: 85

KEGWORTH

See **East Midlands Airport**

KEIGHLEY
West Yorkshire   Map 19 SE04

Dalesgate Hotel

★★ 72% HOTEL

406 Skipton Road, Utley, BD20 6HP - **tel:** 01535 664930
email: info@dalesgate.co.uk **web:** www.dalesgate.co.uk
dir: *In town centre follow A629 over rdbt onto B6265. Right after 0.75m into St John's Rd. 1st right into hotel car park*

Originally the residence of a local chapel minister, this modern, well-established hotel provides well-equipped, comfortable bedrooms. It also boasts a cosy bar and pleasant restaurant, serving an imaginative range of dishes. A large car park is provided to the rear.

Rooms: 20 (2 family) (3 GF) **S** fr £54.50; **D** fr £70 (incl. bkfst) **Parking:** 25

Premier Inn Bradford North (Bingley)

BUDGET HOTEL

502 Bradford Road, Sandbeds, BD20 5NG - **tel:** 0871 527 8134 (Calls cost 13p per minute plus your phone company's access charge) **web:** www.premierinn.com
dir: *M62 juncts 26 or 27 follow A650/Keighley & Skipton signs. From Bingley Bypass (A650 Cottingley) right at 1st rdbt signed Crossflatts & Micklethwaite. Hotel 50yds on left. NB for Sat Nav use BD20 5NH*

High quality, budget accommodation ideal for both families and business travellers. Spacious, en suite bedrooms feature free WiFi and tea and coffee making facilities, and in most hotels, Freeview TV is also available. The adjacent family restaurant features a wide and varied menu.

Rooms: 61

KENDAL
Cumbria   Map 18 SD59

See also **Crooklands**

Castle Green Hotel in Kendal

★★★★ 80% ◉◉ HOTEL

Castle Green Lane, LA9 6RG - **tel:** 01539 734000
email: reception@castlegreen.co.uk **web:** www.castlegreen.co.uk
dir: *M6 junct 37, A684 towards Kendal. Hotel on right in 5m*

This smart, modern hotel enjoys a peaceful location and is conveniently situated for access to both the town centre and the M6. Stylish bedrooms are thoughtfully equipped for both the business and leisure guest. The Greenhouse Restaurant

I

provides imaginative dishes and boasts a theatre kitchen; alternatively Alexander's Pub serves food all day. The hotel has a fully equipped business centre and leisure club.

Rooms: 99 (3 family) (25 GF) **S** £90–£190; **D** £110–£240 (incl. bkfst)* **Facilities:** Spa FTV WiFi ⓈⒷ Gym Steam room Aerobics Yoga Beauty salon Xmas New Year **Conf:** Class 120 Board 100 Thtr 300 Del from £125 **Services:** Lift Night porter **Parking:** 200 **Notes:** LB Civ Wed 250

Premier Inn Kendal Central

BUDGET HOTEL

Maude Street, LA9 4QD - tel: 0871 527 8562 (Calls cost 13p per minute plus your phone company's access charge) **web:** www.premierinn.com
dir: *M6 junct 36, A591 to Kendal. (NB ignore exit for Kendal South). At Plumbgarm Rdbt take 3rd exit, 0.5m to Kendal. Hotel on right*

High quality, budget accommodation ideal for both families and business travellers. Spacious, en suite bedrooms feature free WiFi and tea and coffee making facilities, and in most hotels, Freeview TV is also available. The adjacent family restaurant features a wide and varied menu.

Rooms: 92

KENILWORTH
Warwickshire   Map 10 SP27

Chesford Grange

★★★★ 79% HOTEL

INSPIRED BY YOU

Chesford Bridge, CV8 2LD - tel: 01926 859331
email: chesfordreservations@qhotels.co.uk **web:** www.qhotels.co.uk
dir: *0.5m SE of junct A46/A452. At rdbt turn right signed Leamington Spa, follow signs to hotel*

This much-extended hotel set in 17 acres of private grounds is well situated for Birmingham International Airport, the NEC and major routes. Bedrooms range from traditional style to contemporary rooms featuring state-of-the-art technology. Public areas include a leisure club and extensive conference and banqueting facilities.

Rooms: 205 (20 family) (43 GF) **Facilities:** Spa STV WiFi ⓈⒷ supervised Gym Steam room Solarium Xmas New Year **Conf:** Class 350 Board 50 Thtr 710 **Services:** Lift Night porter **Parking:** 650 **Notes:** Civ Wed 700

Symbols and abbreviations
explained on pages 6–7

KENTISBURY
Devon   Map 3 SS64

HIGHLY RECOMMENDED

Kentisbury Grange

★★★★ 84% ◉◉◉ HOTEL

EX31 4NL - tel: 01271 882295
email: reception@kentisburygrange.co.uk **web:** www.kentisburygrange.com
dir: *From Barnstaple take A3125. At rdbt take 2nd exit onto A39 to Burrington through Shirwell and Arlington. After Kentisbury Ford, follow sign for hotel for approx 0.75m.*

High quality and comfort are in generous supply at this Victorian country house. It is an impressive blend of traditional elegance and contemporary luxury. Bedrooms and bathrooms offer those pampering touches which make all the difference, thus ensuring a relaxing and rewarding stay. The Coach House restaurant is the venue for dining, where a skilled kitchen team maximise the benefits of excellent local produce. Surrounded by the stunning North Devon countryside and a short drive from superb beaches, this is a great base from which to explore all the area has to offer.

Rooms: 16 (5 annexe) (9 GF) **D** £125–£260 (incl. bkfst)* **Facilities:** FTV WiFi ⓈⒷ Xmas New Year **Conf:** Class 12 Board 20 Thtr 30 **Services:** Night porter **Parking:** 50 **Notes:** LB Civ Wed 50

KENTON
Greater London

Premier Inn London Harrow

BUDGET HOTEL PLAN 1 C5

Kenton Road, HA3 8AT - tel: 0871 527 8664 (Calls cost 13p per minute plus your phone company's access charge) **web:** www.premierinn.com
dir: *M1 junct 5, follow Harrow & Kenton signs. Hotel between Harrow & Wembley on A4006 opposite Kenton railway station*

High quality, budget accommodation ideal for both families and business travellers. Spacious, en suite bedrooms feature free WiFi and tea and coffee making facilities, and in most hotels, Freeview TV is also available. The adjacent family restaurant features a wide and varied menu.

Rooms: 119

K

KESWICK
Cumbria

Map 18 NY22

Inn on the Square
★★★★ 81% ⊛ HOTEL

LAKE DISTRICT
■■■■■ HOTELS

Main Street, CA12 5JF - tel: 017687 73333
email: innonthesquare@lakedistricthotels.net **web:** www.innonthesquare.co.uk
dir: *A66 to Keswick centre then follow signs to Bell Close car park. Rear entrance to hotel can be accessed from the car park.*

This luxury hotel opened in 2015 and enjoys a fantastic location as you may expect; on the square in the centre of Keswick. Modern, contemporary and funky design is matched by high levels of comfort. Public areas include the Brossen Steak House and a choice of bars; simply named the Front and Back Bars. Bedrooms are impressive; deeply luxurious beds and furniture feature. Bathrooms are a stunning companion to these. Friendly staff ensure a warm Lakes welcome.

Rooms: 34 (1 family) ⬥ **Facilities:** STV FTV WiFi ⬥ ♫ Xmas New Year
Services: Lift Night porter **Parking:** 7

Skiddaw Hotel
★★★ 82% HOTEL

LAKE DISTRICT
■■■■■ HOTELS

Main Street, CA12 5BN - tel: 017687 72071
email: skiddawhotel@lakedistricthotels.net **web:** www.lakedistricthotels.net/skiddawhotel
dir: *A66 to Keswick, follow town centre signs. Hotel in market square*

Occupying a central position overlooking the market square, this hotel provides smartly furnished bedrooms that include several family suites and a room with a four-poster bed. In addition to the restaurant, food is served all day in the bar and in the conservatory. There is also a quiet residents' lounge and two conference rooms.

Rooms: 43 (7 family) ⬥ **Facilities:** STV WiFi Use of leisure facilities at sister hotels (3m) ♫ Xmas New Year **Conf:** Class 60 Board 40 Thtr 90 **Services:** Lift Night porter **Parking:** 35 **Notes:** Civ Wed 90

Dale Head Hall Lakeside Hotel
★★★ 81% COUNTRY HOUSE HOTEL

Lake Thirlmere, CA12 4TN - tel: 017687 72478
email: onthelakeside@daleheadhall.co.uk **web:** www.daleheadhall.co.uk
dir: *Between Keswick & Grasmere. Exit A591 onto private drive*

Set in attractive, private grounds on the shores of Lake Thirlmere, this historic lakeside residence dates from the 16th century. Comfortable and inviting public areas include a choice of lounges and a traditionally furnished restaurant featuring a daily-changing menu. Bedrooms have views of the lake or surrounding mountains and are undergoing refurbishment this year.

Rooms: 12 (1 family) (2 GF) ⬥ **S** £90–£200; **D** £100–£300 **Facilities:** STV FTV WiFi ⬥ Fishing ⬥ Fishing permits Boating Xmas New Year **Conf:** Class 20 Board 20 Thtr 20 Del from £150 **Parking:** 34 **Notes:** Closed 3-30 Jan Civ Wed 60

Keswick Country House Hotel
★★★ 79% HOTEL

Station Road, CA12 4NQ - tel: 0844 811 5580 (Calls cost 5p per minute plus your phone company's access charge) **email:** reservations@choicehotels.co.uk
web: www.thekeswickhotel.co.uk
dir: *M6 junct 40, A66, 1st slip road into Keswick, then follow signs for leisure pool*

This impressive Victorian hotel is set amid attractive gardens close to the town centre. Eight superior bedrooms are available in the Station Wing, which is accessed through a conservatory. The attractively appointed main house rooms

are modern in style and offer a good range of amenities. Public areas include a well-stocked bar, a spacious and relaxing lounge, and a restaurant serving interesting dinners.

Rooms: 70 (6 family) (4 GF) ⬥ **S** £58–£134; **D** £99–£206 (incl. bkfst & dinner) **Facilities:** FTV WiFi Putting green ⬥ Xmas New Year **Conf:** Class 70 Board 60 Thtr 110 Del from £125 **Services:** Lift Night porter **Parking:** 70 **Notes:** LB Civ Wed 100

Kings Arms Hotel
★★★ 79% HOTEL

LAKE DISTRICT
■■■■■ HOTELS

27 Main Street, CA12 5BL - tel: 017687 72083
email: kingsarms@lakedistricthotels.net **web:** www.lakedistricthotels.net/kingsarms
dir: *M6 junct 40, follow A66 to Keswick then follow signs to town centre*

Located in the heart of Keswick, the Kings Arms Hotel offers modern, tastefully refurbished bedrooms and en suites, alongside intimate public areas and a choice of two restaurants. The bar offers some great local real ales and changing guest beers. The small hands-on team offer friendly and relaxed service.

Rooms: 13 ⬥ **Facilities:** FTV WiFi Complimentary leisure club membership at sister hotel Xmas **Parking:** 13

KETTERING
Northamptonshire

Map 11 SP87

INSPECTOR'S CHOICE

Rushton Hall Hotel and Spa
★★★★ ⊛⊛⊛ COUNTRY HOUSE HOTEL

Rushton, NN14 1RR - tel: 01536 713001
email: enquiries@rushtonhall.com **web:** www.rushtonhall.com
dir: *A14 junct 7, A43 to Corby then A6003 to Rushton, turn after bridge*

Ruston Hall is an elegant country house hotel set amidst 30 acres of parkland and surrounded by open countryside. The stylish public rooms include a library, a superb open-plan lounge bar with a magnificent vaulted ceiling and plush sofas, and an oak-panelled dining hall, where Adrian Coulthard oversees a very high quality operation. The tastefully appointed bedrooms have co-ordinated fabrics and many thoughtful touches.

Rushton Hall Hotel and Spa

Rooms: 46 (5 family) (2 GF) **Facilities:** Spa FTV WiFi ⓈⒷⒷⒷ Gym Billiard table Sauna Steam room Xmas New Year **Conf:** Class 100 Board 40 Thtr 200 **Services:** Lift Night porter **Parking:** 140 **Notes:** Civ Wed 160

Kettering Park Hotel & Spa

★★★★ 81% ⓖ HOTEL

THWAITES

Kettering Parkway, NN15 6XT - **tel:** 01536 416666
email: reseravtions@ketteringparkhotel.co.uk **web:** www.ketteringparkhotel.co.uk
dir: *Exit A14 junct 9 (M1 to A1 link road), hotel in Kettering Venture Park*

Expect a warm welcome at this stylish hotel situated just off the A14. The spacious, smartly decorated bedrooms are well equipped and meticulously maintained. Guests can choose from classical or contemporary dishes in the restaurant and lighter meals that are served in the bar. The extensive leisure facilities are impressive.

Rooms: 119 (29 family) (35 GF) **D** £100–£200* **Facilities:** Spa STV FTV WiFi ⓈⒷ HL Ⓢ Gym Steam room Sauna Children's splash pool Activity studio New Year **Conf:** Class 120 Board 40 Thtr 260 Del from £120 **Services:** Lift Night porter Air con **Parking:** 200 **Notes:** LB Civ Wed 120

Barton Hall Hotel

★★★ 85% ⓖⓖ HOTEL

Barton Road, Barton Seagrave, NN15 6SG - **tel:** 01536 515505
email: enquiries@bartonhall.com **web:** www.bartonhall.com
dir: *From A14 junct 10 onto Barton Rd. Hotel on right, approx 0.5m*

Barton Hall Hotel offers modern and comfortable accommodation to suit both business and leisure guests. All of the rooms include 40" smart TVs, with

complementary WiFi throughout. Dinner can be enjoyed in Vines Brasserie, which serves a traditional menu in a relaxing and friendly environment.

Barton Hall Hotel

Rooms: 29 (3 family) (8 GF) **D** £90–£240 (incl. bkfst) **Facilities:** FTV WiFi Ⓢ **Conf:** Class 150 Board 60 Thtr 300 Del from £145 **Services:** Night porter **Parking:** 150 **Notes:** Civ Wed 160

Premier Inn Kettering

BUDGET HOTEL

Premier Inn

Rothwell Road, NN16 8XF - **tel:** 0871 527 8564 (Calls cost 13p per minute plus your phone company's access charge) **web:** www.premierinn.com
dir: *Off A14 junct 7*

High quality, budget accommodation ideal for both families and business travellers. Spacious, en suite bedrooms feature free WiFi and tea and coffee making facilities, and in most hotels, Freeview TV is also available. The adjacent family restaurant features a wide and varied menu.

Rooms: 83

| KIDDERMINSTER | Map 10 SO87 |
| Worcestershire | |

Stone Manor Hotel

★★★★ 72% ⓖ HOTEL

Stone, DY10 4PJ - **tel:** 01562 777555 **email:** enquiries@stonemanorhotel.co.uk
web: www.hogarths.co.uk/hogarths-stone-manor
dir: *2.5m from Kidderminster on A448, on right*

This converted and much-extended former manor house set in 25 acres has a history that dates back as far as the Domesday Book. Rooms are comfortably furnished and equipped with modern day essentials, and many of them benefit from far-reaching views across the Worcestershire countryside. This property is well placed for the Midlands motorway network and local attractions, making it a popular venue for both corporate and leisure guests.

Rooms: 56 (5 annexe) (2 family) (6 GF) **Facilities:** STV WiFi Ⓢ Xmas New Year **Conf:** Class 40 Board 50 Thtr 100 **Services:** Night porter **Parking:** 400 **Notes:** LB Civ Wed 170

KIDDERMINSTER *continued*

The Granary Hotel & Restaurant

★★★ 80% ◉◉ HOTEL

Heath Lane, Shenstone, DY10 4BS - tel: 01562 777535
email: info@granary-hotel.co.uk **web:** www.granary-hotel.co.uk
dir: *On A450 between Stourbridge & Worcester, 1m from Kidderminster*

This modern hotel offers spacious, well-equipped accommodation with many rooms enjoying views towards Great Witley and the Amberley Hills. Public areas include a bar and a residents' lounge. The attractive, modern restaurant serves dishes created from locally sourced produce that is cooked with flair and imagination. There are also extensive conference facilities, and the hotel is popular as a wedding venue.

Rooms: 18 (1 family) (18 GF) ⟲ **S** £50–£85; **D** £60–£150 (incl. bkfst)*
Facilities: FTV WiFi ⓑ **Conf:** Class 80 Board 70 Thtr 200 Del from £115
Services: Night porter **Parking:** 96 **Notes:** LB Closed 2-8 Jan Civ Wed 120

Gainsborough House Hotel

THE INDEPENDENTS
HOTEL ASSOCIATION

★★★ 79% HOTEL

Bewdley Hill, DY11 6BS - tel: 01562 820041
email: reservations@gainsboroughhousehotel.com
web: www.gainsboroughhousehotel.com
dir: *Follow A456 to Kidderminster (West Midlands Safari Park) pass hospital, hotel 500yds on left*

This listed Georgian hotel provides a wide range of thoughtfully furnished bedrooms that have smart modern bathrooms. The contemporary decor and furnishing throughout the public areas highlights the many retained period features. A large function suite and several meeting rooms are available.

Rooms: 42 (16 family) (12 GF) **S** £61–£94; **D** £61–£94* **Facilities:** STV FTV WiFi ⓑ Xmas New Year **Conf:** Class 70 Board 60 Thtr 250 Del from £95 **Services:** Night porter Air con **Parking:** 90 **Notes:** LB Civ Wed 250

Premier Inn Kidderminster

BUDGET HOTEL

Slingfield Mill, Weavers Wharf, DY10 1AA - tel: 0871 527 9350 (Calls cost 13p per minute plus your phone company's access charge) **web:** www.premierinn.com
dir: *M5 junct 3, A456 towards Kidderminster, 5.5m. Straight on at 1st rdbt, left into Lower Mill St. Straight on into Crown Ln*

High quality, budget accommodation ideal for both families and business travellers. Spacious, en suite bedrooms feature free WiFi and tea and coffee making facilities, and in most hotels, Freeview TV is also available. The adjacent family restaurant features a wide and varied menu.

Rooms: 56

KINGSBRIDGE   Map 3 SX74
Devon

Buckland-Tout-Saints

LUXURY HOTEL COLLECTION
Unique in character · Individual in style

★★★ 84% ◉◉ COUNTRY HOUSE HOTEL

Goveton, TQ7 2DS - tel: 01548 853055
email: info@bucklandtoutsaints.co.uk **web:** www.tout-saints.co.uk
dir: *Turn off A381 to Goveton. Follow brown tourist signs to St Peter's Church. Hotel 2nd right after church*

It is well worth navigating the winding country lanes to dine at this delightful Queen Anne manor house that has been host to many famous guests over the years.

Set in over four acres of gardens the hotel is a peaceful retreat. Bedrooms are tastefully furnished and attractively decorated; the majority are very spacious. Local produce is used with care and imagination to create the dishes offered. This is a popular choice for weddings.

Rooms: 16 (6 family) ⟲ **Facilities:** STV WiFi ⓑ ⛵ Xmas New Year **Conf:** Class 40 Board 26 Thtr 80 **Services:** Night porter **Parking:** 16 **Notes:** Civ Wed 120

KINGSCLERE   Map 5 SU55
Hampshire

Sandford Springs Hotel and Golf Club

★★★★ 78% HOTEL

RG26 5RT - tel: 01635 291500 & 296800
email: info@sandfordsprings.co.uk **web:** www.sandfordsprings.co.uk
dir: *M3 junct 6, A339 for 9m, hotel on right; M4 junct 13, A34 to Newbury then A339 for 11m, hotel on left*

This modern hotel is located in a lovely country location and offers a super range of facilities with three 9-hole golf courses; the parks, woods and lakes. In addition there are also conference and meeting rooms. The bedrooms are spacious and have good facilities. There is a choice of restaurants, the Dining Room in the hotel and the Kingsclere, which overlooks the golf course, providing all-day dining.

Rooms: 40 (4 family) (21 GF) ⟲ **S** fr £89; **D** fr £99 (incl. bkfst) **Facilities:** FTV WiFi ⓑ ⛳ 27 Putting green New Year **Conf:** Class 80 Board 40 Thtr 180 Del from £140 **Services:** Lift Night porter Air con **Parking:** 150 **Notes:** LB Civ Wed 100

KINGS LANGLEY   Map 6 TL00
Hertfordshire

Premier Inn Kings Langley

BUDGET HOTEL

Hempstead Road, WD4 8BR - tel: 0871 527 8568 (Calls cost 13p per minute plus your phone company's access charge) **web:** www.premierinn.com
dir: *1m from M25 junct 20 on A4251 after King's Langley*

High quality, budget accommodation ideal for both families and business travellers. Spacious, en suite bedrooms feature free WiFi and tea and coffee making facilities, and in most hotels, Freeview TV is also available. The adjacent family restaurant features a wide and varied menu.

Rooms: 63

KING'S LYNN   Map 12 TF62
Norfolk

HIGHLY RECOMMENDED

The Duke's Head Hotel

SURYA
Stay · Explore · Discover

★★★★ 83% ◉ HOTEL

5-6 Tuesday Market Place, PE30 1JS - tel: 01553 774996 & 0844 411 9484 (Calls cost 7p per minute plus your phone company's access charge)
email: reception@dukeshotel.com **web:** www.dukesheadhotel.com
dir: *From A10/A47/A17 enter King's Lynn via South Gates rdbt. Hotel opposite Corn Exchange.*

Occupying a central location and overlooking the market square, this hotel is a beautiful property. The bedrooms are smartly decorated, and include wide-screen TVs, free WiFi and bathrooms with walk-in showers. Parking is also available.

Rooms: 78 (6 family) ⟲ **Facilities:** FTV WiFi ⓑ Xmas New Year **Conf:** Class 80 Board 100 Thtr 220 **Services:** Lift Night porter **Parking:** 40 **Notes:** Civ Wed 200

Best Western Plus Knights Hill Hotel and Spa

★★★★ 75% HOTEL

Knights Hill Village, South Wootton, PE30 3HQ - tel: 01553 675566
email: reception@knightshill.co.uk **web:** www.abacushotels.co.uk
dir: *At junct A148 & A149*

This hotel village complex is set on a 16th-century site on the outskirts of King's Lynn. The smartly decorated, well-equipped bedrooms are situated in extensions of the original hunting lodge. Public areas have a wealth of historic charm including the Garden Bistro & Bar and the Farmers Arms Inn, which serves good food and real ales. The hotel also has conference and leisure facilities, including the Imagine Spa.

Rooms: 79 (12 annexe) (1 family) (38 GF) ✒ **S** £70–£125; **D** £80–£135*
Facilities: Spa STV WiFi ⌁ ⌂ ⌘ ⌇ Gym Xmas New Year **Conf:** Class 150 Board 30 Thtr 200 **Services:** Night porter **Parking:** 350 **Notes:** LB Civ Wed 90

INSPECTOR'S CHOICE

Congham Hall Country House Hotel

★★★ ◍◉ COUNTRY HOUSE HOTEL

Lynn Road, PE32 1AH - tel: 01485 600250
email: info@conghamhallhotel.co.uk **web:** www.conghamhallhotel.co.uk

(for full entry see Grimston)

Bank House

★★★ 84% ◉ HOTEL

King's Staithe Square, PE30 1RD - tel: 01553 660492
email: info@thebankhouse.co.uk **web:** www.thebankhouse.co.uk
dir: *In King's Lynn Old Town follow quay, through floodgates, hotel on right opposite Custom House*

This Grade II listed, 18th-century town house is situated on the quay side in the heart of King's Lynn's historical quarter. Bedrooms are individually decorated and have high quality fabrics and furnishings along with a range of useful facilities. Public rooms include the Counting House coffee shop, a wine bar and brasserie restaurant, as well as a residents' lounge.

Rooms: 12 (5 family) ✒ **S** £85–£120; **D** £115–£275 (incl. bkfst)*
Facilities: FTV WiFi ⌁ Xmas New Year **Conf:** Class 20 Board 15 Thtr 30
Notes: LB

Grange Hotel

★★ 75% HOTEL

Willow Park, South Wootton Lane, PE30 3BP - tel: 01553 673777
email: info@thegrangehotelkingslynn.co.uk **web:** www.thegrangehotelkingslynn.co.uk
dir: *A148 towards King's Lynn for 1.5m. At lights left into Wootton Rd, 400yds, on right into South Wootton Ln. Hotel 1st on left*

Expect a warm welcome at this Edwardian house which is situated in a quiet residential area in its own grounds. Public rooms include a smart lounge bar and a cosy restaurant. The spacious bedrooms are pleasantly decorated and equipped with many thoughtful touches; some are located in an adjacent wing.

Rooms: 9 (4 annexe) (2 family) (4 GF) **Facilities:** WiFi Xmas **Conf:** Class 15 Board 12 Thtr 20 **Parking:** 15

Premier Inn King's Lynn

BUDGET HOTEL

Clenchwarton Road, West Lynn, PE34 3LJ - tel: 0871 527 8570 (Calls cost 13p per minute plus your phone company's access charge) **web:** www.premierinn.com
dir: *At junct of A47 & A17*

High quality, budget accommodation ideal for both families and business travellers. Spacious, en suite bedrooms feature free WiFi and tea and coffee making facilities, and in most hotels, Freeview TV is also available. The adjacent family restaurant features a wide and varied menu.

Rooms: 149

KINGSTON UPON HULL
East Riding of Yorkshire

Map 17 TA02

Best Western Willerby Manor Hotel

★★★ 82% HOTEL

Well Lane, HU10 6ER - tel: 01482 652616
email: willerbymanor@bestwestern.co.uk **web:** www.willerbymanor.co.uk

(For full entry see Willerby)

Premier Inn Hull City Centre

BUDGET HOTEL

Tower Street, HU9 1TQ - tel: 0871 527 8534 (Calls cost 13p per minute plus your phone company's access charge) **web:** www.premierinn.com
dir: *M62, A63 into Hull city centre. At rdbt left onto A1165 (Great Union St), left into Citadel Way. Hotel at end on right*

High quality, budget accommodation ideal for both families and business travellers. Spacious, en suite bedrooms feature free WiFi and tea and coffee making facilities, and in most hotels, Freeview TV is also available. The adjacent family restaurant features a wide and varied menu.

Rooms: 136

Premier Inn Hull North

BUDGET HOTEL

Ashcombe Road, Kingswood Park, HU7 3DD - tel: 0871 527 8536 (Calls cost 13p per minute plus your phone company's access charge) **web:** www.premierinn.com
dir: *A63 to town centre, take A1079 N for approx 5m. Right at rdbt onto A1033. Hotel at 2nd rdbt in New Kingswood Park*
Rooms: 65

Premier Inn Hull West

BUDGET HOTEL

Ferriby Road, Hessle, HU13 0JA - tel: 0871 527 8538 (Calls cost 13p per minute plus your phone company's access charge) **web:** www.premierinn.com
dir: *A63 onto A15 to Humber Bridge (Beverley & Hessle Viewpoint). Hotel at 1st rdbt*
Rooms: 83

K

KINGSTON UPON THAMES
Greater London

Premier Inn London Kingston upon Thames

BUDGET HOTEL PLAN 1 C1

Combined House, 15 Wheatfield Way, KT1 2PA - **tel:** 0871 527 9586 (Calls cost 13p per minute plus your phone company's access charge) **web:** www.premierinn.com
dir: *M25 junct 13, A30 (signed Staines), A308 towards Kingston upon Thames. Pass Bentalls shopping centre, stay in right lane, left at Odeon cinema. On one-way system pass Cattle Market car park on left. Right after car park, left into Eden St. Left into Lady Booth Rd*

High quality, budget accommodation ideal for both families and business travellers. Spacious, en suite bedrooms feature free WiFi and tea and coffee making facilities, and in most hotels, Freeview TV is also available. The adjacent family restaurant features a wide and varied menu.

Rooms: 160

KINGSWINFORD
West Midlands   Map 10 SO88

Premier Inn Dudley (Kingswinford)

BUDGET HOTEL

Dudley Road, DY6 8WT - **tel:** 0871 527 8314 (Calls cost 13p per minute plus your phone company's access charge) **web:** www.premierinn.com
dir: *A4123 to Dudley, A461 follow signs for Russell's Hall Hospital. On A4101 to Kingswinford, hotel opposite Pennsett Trading Estate*

High quality, budget accommodation ideal for both families and business travellers. Spacious, en suite bedrooms feature free WiFi and tea and coffee making facilities, and in most hotels, Freeview TV is also available. The adjacent family restaurant features a wide and varied menu.

Rooms: 60

KNUTSFORD
Cheshire   Map 15 SJ77

The Mere Golf Resort & Spa

★★★★ 81% HOTEL

Chester Road, Mere, WA16 6LJ - **tel:** 01565 830155 **web:** www.themereresort.co.uk
dir: *M6 junct 19 or M56 junct 7*

This hotel sits alongside Mere Lake and is close to the picturesque town of Knutsford; there are excellent transport links with Manchester International Airport being only ten minutes away. The resort's historic main Victorian building conveys the classic charm of that era, and offers stylish, luxury accommodation. The championship golf course designed by James Braid is both beautiful and challenging. The spa features an extensive range of treatments and facilities including a Thermal Zone. The staff are professional and very friendly, offering personal service.

Rooms: 81 **Facilities: Conf:** Class 350 Board 40 Thtr 700

Cottons Hotel & Spa

★★★★ 80% HOTEL

Manchester Road, WA16 0SU - **tel:** 01565 650333
email: reservations@cottonshotel.co.uk **web:** www.cottonshotel.co.uk
dir: *On A50, 1m from M6 junct 19*

The superb leisure facilities and quiet location are great attractions at this hotel, which is just a short distance from Manchester Airport. Bedrooms are smartly appointed in various styles, and executive rooms have very good working areas. The hotel has spacious lounges and an excellent leisure centre.

Rooms: 139 (14 family) (48 GF) **D** £100–£200* **Facilities:** Spa STV WiFi Gym Steam room Activity studio for exercise classes Sauna Children's splash pool Xmas New Year **Conf:** Class 100 Board 36 Thtr 200 Del from £120 **Services:** Lift Night porter Air con **Parking:** 180 **Notes:** LB Civ Wed 120

Mere Court Hotel & Conference Centre

★★★★ 77% HOTEL

Warrington Road, Mere, WA16 0RW - **tel:** 01565 831000
email: sales@merecourt.co.uk **web:** www.merecourt.co.uk
dir: *A50, 1m W of junct with A556, on right*

This is a smart and attractive hotel, set in extensive, well-tended gardens. The elegant and spacious bedrooms are individually styled and offer a host of thoughtful extras. Conference facilities are particularly impressive and there is a large, self contained, conservatory function suite. Dining is available in the fine dining Arboreum Restaurant.

Rooms: 34 (24 family) (12 GF) **Facilities:** STV FTV WiFi Xmas New Year **Conf:** Class 75 Board 50 Thtr 200 **Services:** Lift Night porter **Parking:** 150 **Notes:** Civ Wed 150

The Longview Hotel

★★ 80% HOTEL

55 Manchester Road, WA16 0LX - **tel:** 01565 632119
email: enquiries@longviewhotel.com **web:** www.longviewhotel.com
dir: *M6 junct 19 take A556 W towards Chester. Left at lights onto A5033, 1.5m to rdbt then left. Hotel 200yds on right*

This friendly, personally-run hotel is within a Victorian terrace near the centre of Knutsford, offering high standards of hospitality and attractive public areas including a cellar bar. The restaurant serves a range of dishes. Bedrooms, located either in a superb renovation of a nearby house or within the main building, are individually styled and offer comfortable, modern appointment.

Rooms: 32 (19 annexe) (1 family) (5 GF) **Facilities:** FTV WiFi **Conf:** Class 20 Board 20 **Services:** Night porter **Parking:** 20 **Notes:** Closed 21 Dec-6 Jan

Premier Inn Knutsford (Bucklow Hill)

BUDGET HOTEL

Bucklow Hill, WA16 6RD - **tel:** 0871 527 8572 (Calls cost 13p per minute plus your phone company's access charge) **web:** www.premierinn.com
dir: *M6 junct 19, A556 towards Manchester Airport & Stockport*

High quality, budget accommodation ideal for both families and business travellers. Spacious, en suite bedrooms feature free WiFi and tea and coffee making facilities, and in most hotels, Freeview TV is also available. The adjacent family restaurant features a wide and varied menu.

Rooms: 68

Premier Inn Knutsford (Mere)

BUDGET HOTEL

Warrington Road, Hoo Green, WA16 0PZ - **tel:** 0871 527 8574 (Calls cost 13p per minute plus your phone company's access charge) **web:** www.premierinn.com

dir: *M6 junct 19, A556, follow Manchester signs. At 1st lights left onto A50 towards Warrington. Hotel 1m on right*

Rooms: 28

LACEBY
Lincolnshire   **Map 17 TA20**

Best Western Oaklands Hall Hotel

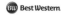

★★★ 81% ◉◉ HOTEL

Barton Street, DN37 7LF - **tel:** 01472 872248
email: reception@oaklandshallhotel.co.uk **web:** www.oaklandshallhotel.co.uk
dir: *At junct of A46 & A18 at Laceby, on edge of Grimsby*

This attractive 19th-century property is located on a private estate in five acres of parkland. It has been refurbished with a contemporary style while retaining beautiful period features. The Comfy Duck restaurant is stylish, and food is a highlight of any stay, with a strong emphasis on local produce. Bedrooms are comfortable and complimentary WiFi is provided.

Rooms: 46 (5 family) (10 GF) ⌇ **D** £69–£175* **Facilities:** FTV WiFi ⬆ 🎵 New Year **Conf:** Class 150 Board 50 Thtr 180 **Services:** Night porter **Parking:** 80
Notes: Civ Wed 150

LANCASTER
Lancashire   **Map 18 SD46**

Lancaster House

English Lakes
Hotels Resorts & Venues

★★★★ 78% ◉ HOTEL

Green Lane, Ellel, LA1 4GJ - **tel:** 01524 844822
email: lancasterhouse@englishlakes.co.uk **web:** www.englishlakes.co.uk
dir: *M6 junct 33 N towards Lancaster. Through Galgate into Green Ln. Hotel before university on right*

This modern hotel enjoys a rural setting south of the city and close to the university. The attractive open-plan reception and lounge boast a roaring log fire in colder months. Bedrooms are spacious, and include 19 rooms that are particularly well equipped for business guests. There are leisure facilities with a hot tub and a function suite.

Rooms: 99 (29 family) (44 GF) ⌇ **S** £94–£194; **D** £104–£204 (incl. bkfst)*
Facilities: Spa STV WiFi ⬆ HL 🏊 supervised Gym Beauty salon Xmas New Year
Conf: Class 60 Board 48 Thtr 250 **Services:** Night porter **Parking:** 120
Notes: Civ Wed 140

Premier Inn Lancaster

BUDGET HOTEL

Lancaster Business Park, Caton Road, LA1 3PE - **tel:** 0871 527 8576 (Calls cost 13p per minute plus your phone company's access charge) **web:** www.premierinn.com
dir: *M6 junct 34, A683 towards Lancaster. Hotel 0.25m on left at entrance to Business Park*

High quality, budget accommodation ideal for both families and business travellers. Spacious, en suite bedrooms feature free WiFi and tea and coffee making facilities, and in most hotels, Freeview TV is also available. The adjacent family restaurant features a wide and varied menu.

Rooms: 85

LAND'S END   **Map 2 SW32**
Cornwall & Isles of Scilly

The Land's End Hotel

★★★ 79% HOTEL

TR19 7AA - **tel:** 01736 871844
email: reservations@landsendhotel.co.uk **web:** www.landsendhotel.co.uk
dir: *From Penzance take A30, follow Land's End signs. After Sennen 1m to Land's End*

This famous location provides a memorable setting for The Land's End Hotel. Bedrooms, many with stunning views of the Atlantic, are pleasantly decorated and comfortable. Refurbished public areas provide plenty of style and comfort with a relaxing lounge and convivial bar. The restaurant is equally impressive with accomplished cuisine complementing the amazing views out to sea.

Rooms: 30 (4 family) **Facilities:** FTV WiFi Free entry to Land's End Visitor Centre & Attractions Xmas **Conf:** Class 50 Board 30 Thtr 100 **Services:** Night porter **Parking:** 100 **Notes:** Civ Wed 120

L

Silver Stars

The AA Silver Star rating denotes a Hotel that we highly recommend. They have a superior level of quality within their star rating, high standards of hospitality, service and cleanliness.

L

LANGHO
Lancashire

Map 18 SD73

INSPECTOR'S CHOICE

Northcote
★★★★ ⊛⊛⊛⊛ 🍽 SMALL HOTEL

Northcote Road, BB6 8BE - tel: 01254 240555
email: reception@northcote.com **web:** www.northcote.com
dir: M6 junct 31, 9m to Northcote. Follow Clitheroe A59 signs, Hotel on left before rdbt

This is a gastronomic haven where guests return to sample the delights of its famous kitchen. The outstanding cooking includes Lancashire's finest fare, and fruit and herbs from the hotel's own beautifully laid-out organic gardens. Drinks can be enjoyed in the comfortable, elegantly furnished lounges and bar. Each of the luxury bedrooms has its own identity with sumptuous fabrics and soft furnishings, sophisticated lighting and ultra modern bathrooms; some have a garden patio. New annexe rooms are particularly impressive.

Rooms: 26 (8 annexe) (3 family) (8 GF) ⟁ **Facilities:** STV FTV WiFi 🦢 Xmas New Year **Conf:** Class 40 Board 20 Thtr 40 **Services:** Lift Night porter **Parking:** 50 **Notes:** Civ Wed 60

Best Western Mytton Fold Hotel and Golf Club
★★★ ⓐ HOTEL

Whalley Road, BB6 8AB - tel: 01254 240662
email: reception@myttonfold.co.uk **web:** www.myttonfold.co.uk
dir: At large rdbt on A59, follow signs for Whalley, exit into Whalley Road. Hotel on right

Set in pretty and well maintained grounds that are a riot of colour in the summer, this hotel has views over the golf course to Pendle Hill beyond. The bedrooms are smart and include two with four-posters. This is a popular wedding venue.

Rooms: 43 (12 family) (10 GF) ⟁ **S** fr £59; **D** fr £79* **Facilities:** FTV WiFi ⤓ ♨ 18 Putting green Xmas **Conf:** Class 60 Board 40 Thtr 290 Del from £95 **Services:** Lift Night porter **Parking:** 300 **Notes:** LB Closed 1 Jan Civ Wed 250

LASTINGHAM
North Yorkshire

Map 19 SE79

Lastingham Grange Hotel
★★★ 79% HOTEL

YO62 6TH - tel: 01751 417345 **email:** reservations@lastinghamgrange.com
web: www.lastinghamgrange.com
dir: From A170 follow signs for Appleton-le-Moors, continue into Lastingham, pass church on left, right, then left up hill. Hotel on right

A warm welcome and sincere hospitality have been the hallmarks of this hotel for over 60 years. Antique furniture is plentiful, and the lounge and the dining room both look out onto the terrace and sunken rose garden below. There is a large play area for older children and the moorland views are breathtaking

Rooms: 12 (2 family) **S** £120–£150; **D** £150–£210 (incl. bkfst)* **Facilities:** FTV WiFi 🦢 Large adventure playground **Parking:** 30 **Notes:** LB Closed Dec-Feb

LAVENHAM
Suffolk

Map 13 TL94

INSPECTOR'S CHOICE

The Swan at Lavenham Hotel and Spa
★★★★ ⊛⊛ HOTEL

High Street, CO10 9QA - tel: 01787 247477
email: info@theswanatlavenham.co.uk **web:** www.theswanatlavenham.co.uk
dir: From Bury St Edmunds take A134 S, then A1141 to Lavenham

The Swan Hotel and Spa is a delightful collection of listed buildings, dating back to the 14th century, lovingly restored to retain their original charm. Public rooms include comfortable lounge areas, a charming rustic bar, an informal brasserie and a fine-dining restaurant. Bedrooms are tastefully furnished and equipped with many thoughtful touches. The friendly staff are helpful, attentive and offer professional service. Facilities in the award-winning spa, Weavers' House Spa include six treatment rooms offering over 30 treatments, a hot stone sauna, steam room, manicure and pedicure area, a beautiful spa boutique, outdoor terrace and a vitality pool.

Rooms: 45 (7 family) (9 GF) ⟁ **S** £97; **D** £120–£360 (incl. bkfst)* **Facilities:** Spa FTV WiFi ⤓ Steam room Sauna Vitality pool Xmas New Year **Conf:** Class 36 Board 30 Thtr 50 Del from £188 **Services:** Night porter **Parking:** 30 **Notes:** Civ Wed 100

LEA MARSTON
Warwickshire   Map 10 SP29

Lea Marston Hotel & Spa
★★★★ 78% ◉◉ HOTEL

Haunch Lane, B76 0BY - tel: 01675 470468
email: info@leamarstonhotel.co.uk **web:** www.leamarstonhotel.co.uk
dir: *M42 junct 9, A4097 to Kingsbury. Hotel signed 1.5m on right*

Excellent access to the motorway network and a good range of sports facilities make this hotel a popular choice for conferences and leisure breaks. Bedrooms are mostly set around an attractive quadrangle and are generously equipped. Diners can choose between the popular Sportsman's Lounge Bar and the elegant Adderley Restaurant.

Rooms: 118 (16 family) (66 GF) ☛ **Facilities:** Spa STV FTV WiFi ⓦ ⑤ ⚓ 9 Putting green Gym Golf driving range Golf simulator Sauna Steam room Rasul Xmas New Year **Conf:** Class 50 Board 30 Thtr 140 **Services:** Lift Night porter **Parking:** 220 **Notes:** Civ Wed 100

LEAMINGTON SPA (ROYAL)
Warwickshire   Map 10 SP36

INSPECTOR'S CHOICE

Mallory Court Country House Hotel & Spa
★★★★ ◉◉ ⓦ HOTEL

Harbury Lane, Bishop's Tachbrook, CV33 9QB - tel: 01926 330214
email: info@mallory.co.uk **web:** www.mallory.co.uk
dir: *M40 junct 13 N'bound left, left again towards Bishops Tachbrook, right into Harbury Ln after 0.5m. M40 junct 14 S'bound A452 to Leamington, at 2nd rdbt left into Harbury Ln*

Mallory Court Hotel is part of the Eden Hotel Collection and with its tranquil rural setting, this elegant Lutyens-style country house is an idyllic retreat, set in ten acres of landscaped gardens with immaculate lawns and an orchard. Relaxation is easy in the two sumptuous lounges, drawing room or conservatory. Dining is a treat in either the elegant restaurant or the brasserie. Bedrooms in the main house are luxuriously decorated and most have wonderful views. Those in the Knights Suite are more contemporary and have their own access via a smart conference and banqueting facility. A brand new spa opened in 2017.

Rooms: 43 (23 annexe) (2 family) (5 GF) ☛ **S** £125–£395; **D** £159–£550 (incl. bkfst)* **Facilities:** Spa FTV WiFi ⑤ ☺ ⚓ Gym Xmas New Year **Conf:** Class 160 Board 50 Thtr 200 Del from £199 **Services:** Lift Night porter **Parking:** 120 **Notes:** LB Civ Wed 160

Falstaff Hotel
★★★ 71% HOTEL

16-20 Warwick New Road, CV32 5JQ - tel: 01926 312044
email: sales@falstaffhotel.com **web:** www.falstaffhotel.com
dir: *M40 junct 13 or 14, follow Leamington Spa signs. Over 4 rdbts, under bridge. Left into Princes Dr, right at mini-rdbt*

Bedrooms at this hotel come in a variety of sizes and styles and are well equipped, with many thoughtful extras. Snacks can be taken in the relaxing lounge bar, and an interesting selection of English and continental dishes is offered in the restaurant; 24-hour room service is also available. Conference and banqueting facilities are extensive.

Rooms: 59 (3 family) (16 GF) ☛ **S** £45–£75; **D** £60–£110 (incl. bkfst)*
Facilities: FTV WiFi ⓦ Arrangement with local health club Xmas New Year **Conf:** Class 30 Board 30 Thtr 70 Del from £100 **Services:** Night porter **Parking:** 40

Premier Inn Leamington Spa Town Centre
BUDGET HOTEL

Regency Arcade, The Parade, CV32 4BQ - tel: 0871 527 9380 (Calls cost 13p per minute plus your phone company's access charge) **web:** www.premierinn.com
dir: *From N: M40 junct 15/A452. Through 4 rdbts. At next rdbt take 4th exit, at final rdbt, take 1st exit A452 (Adelaide Rd). Right onto Dormer Place & left onto St Peters Rd into St Peters car park. Follow directional signage to Premier Inn. From S: M40 junct 13 then follow directions as above*

High quality, budget accommodation ideal for both families and business travellers. Spacious, en suite bedrooms feature free WiFi and tea and coffee making facilities, and in most hotels, Freeview TV is also available. The adjacent family restaurant features a wide and varied menu.

Rooms: 82

LEDBURY
Herefordshire   Map 10 SO73

Feathers Hotel
★★★ 84% ◉ HOTEL

High Street, HR8 1DS - tel: 01531 635266
email: mary@feathers-ledbury.co.uk **web:** www.feathers-ledbury.co.uk
dir: *S from Worcester on A449, E from Hereford on A438, N from Gloucester on A417. Hotel in town centre*

A wealth of authentic features can be found at this historic timber-framed hotel, situated in the middle of town. The comfortably equipped bedrooms are tastefully decorated; there is also Eve's Cottage, in the grounds, and Lanark House, a two-bedroom apartment that is ideal for families and self-catering use. Well-prepared meals can be taken in Fuggles Brasserie with its adjoining bar, and breakfast is served in Quills Restaurant. A swimming pool and gym are available for use by guests.

Rooms: 22 (3 annexe) (2 family) ☛ **S** £99–£130; **D** £155–£240 (incl. bkfst)*
Facilities: STV FTV WiFi ⓦ ⑤ Gym Steam room New Year **Conf:** Class 80 Board 40 Thtr 140 **Services:** Night porter **Parking:** 30 **Notes:** Civ Wed 100

L

LEDBURY *continued*

Leadon House Hotel

★★ A SMALL HOTEL

Ross Road, HR8 2LP - tel: 01531 631199
email: leadon.house@btconnect.com **web:** www.leadonhouse.com
dir: *M5 junct 8/M50/A417 exit Ledbury. Left at 1st rdbt then take A449.
Hotel 400yds on right by Ledbury Rugby Club*

Enjoy a relaxing break at this family-run hotel, which has been tastefully
refurbished in an Edwardian style, offering an idyllic environment and a peaceful
night's stay. Many interesting architectural features add to the unique charm and
elegance. All rooms are en suite and finished to a high standard, with plenty of
attention paid to detail. Also available is the Coach House two bedroom apartment.

Rooms: 8 (2 annexe) (1 family) (1 GF) **Facilities:** FTV WiFi **Parking:** 10 **Notes:**
No children 16yrs

LEEDS	Map 19 SE23
West Yorkshire	

See also **Gomersal & Wakefield**

Thorpe Park Hotel & Spa

THWAITES

★★★★ 84% ⊛ HOTEL

Century Way, Thorpe Park, LS15 8ZB - tel: 0113 264 1000
email: reservations@thorpeparkhotel.co.uk **web:** www.thorpeparkhotel.co.uk
dir: *M1 junct 46, follow signs for Thorpe Park*

Conveniently close to the M1, this hotel offers bedrooms that are modern in both
style and facilities. The Terrace and courtyard offer all-day casual dining and

refreshments, and the restaurant features a Mediterranean-themed menu.
There is also a state-of-the-art spa and leisure facilities.

Thorpe Park Hotel & Spa

Rooms: 117 (13 family) (25 GF) ⚓ **D** £100–£200* **Facilities:** Spa STV WiFi ⌕ HL
☯ Gym Activity studio Steam room Sauna New Year **Conf:** Class 100 Board 50
Thtr 200 Del from £120 **Services:** Lift Night porter Air con **Parking:** 200 **Notes:** LB Civ
Wed 150

Oulton Hall

QHOTELS
INSPIRED
BY YOU

★★★★ 81% HOTEL

Rothwell Lane, Oulton, LS26 8HN - tel: 0113 282 1000 & 0845 034 5777
(Calls cost 2p per minute plus your phone company's access charge)
email: oultonreception@qhotels.co.uk **web:** www.qhotels.co.uk/oultonhall
dir: *2m from M62 junct 30, follow Rothwell signs, then 'Oulton 1m' sign.
1st exit at next 2 rdbts. Hotel on left. Or 1m from M1 junct 44, follow Castleford
& Pontefract sign on A639*

Surrounded by the beautiful Yorkshire Dales, yet only 15 minutes from the city
centre, this elegant 19th-century house offers the best of both worlds. Impressive
features include stylish, opulent day rooms and delightful formal gardens, which
have been restored to their original design. The hotel boasts a choice of dining
options, and extensive leisure facilities. Golfers can book preferential tee times at
the adjacent golf club.

Rooms: 152 **D** £99–£259 (incl. bkfst)* **Facilities:** Spa STV FTV WiFi HL ☯ ⚷ 27
Putting green ⚐ Gym Beauty therapy Sauna Steam room Juice bar Xmas New Year
Conf: Class 160 Board 40 Thtr 350 Del from £130 **Services:** Lift Night porter Air con
Parking: 300 **Notes:** Civ Wed 250

The New Ellington

★★★★ 80% TOWN HOUSE HOTEL

23-25 York Place, LS1 2EY - tel: 0113 204 2150
email: info@thenewellington.com **web:** www.thenewellington.com
dir: *Phone for details*

Near the central railway station and the civic and business quarters, this hotel,
with an art deco and a musical theme in part, offers guests modern amenities.
Bedrooms are air-conditioned, and come with free WiFi, high-quality bed linen and
Nespresso coffee machines; some have quiet balconies too. The ground-floor atrium
Gin Bar lounge leads to the lower ground floor restaurant that serves a range of
interesting dishes. Limited on-site chargeable parking is available on a first-come
first-served basis.

Rooms: 34 (3 GF) ⚓ **Facilities:** FTV WiFi ⌕ **Services:** Lift Night porter Air con
Notes: Closed 24-27 Dec

The Queens

★★★★ 80% HOTEL

City Square, LS1 1PJ - **tel:** 0113 243 1323
email: queensreservations@qhotels.co.uk **web:** www.qhotels.co.uk
dir: *M621, M1 & M62 follow signs for city centre & rail station,*
along Neville St towards City Square. Under rail bridge, at lights left into slip road in front of hotel

A legacy from the golden age of railways and located in the heart of Leeds, overlooking City Square, this grand Victorian hotel retains much of its original splendour. Public rooms include the spacious lounge bar, a range of conference and function rooms along with the grand ballroom. Bedrooms vary in size but all are very well equipped, and there is a choice of suites available.

Rooms: 215 (16 family) **Facilities:** STV WiFi New Year **Conf:** Class 200 Board 80 Thtr 500 **Services:** Lift Night porter Air con **Parking:** 55 **Notes:** Civ Wed 500

Malmaison Leeds

★★★★ 76% HOTEL

1 Swinegate, LS1 4AG - **tel:** 0113 398 1000 & 0844 693 0654
(Calls cost 7p per minute plus your phone company's access charge)
email: leeds@malmaison.com **web:** www.malmaison.com
dir: *M621/M1 junct 3, follow city centre signs. At KPMG building,*
right into Sovereign Street. Hotel at end on right

Close to the waterfront, this stylish property offers striking bedrooms with CD players and air conditioning. The popular bar and brasserie feature vaulted ceilings and intimate lighting, and offer a choice of a full three-course meal or a substantial snack. Service is both willing and friendly. A small fitness centre and impressive meeting rooms complete the package.

Rooms: 100 (4 family) **Facilities:** STV WiFi Xmas New Year **Conf:** Class 30 Board 30 Thtr 80 **Services:** Lift Night porter Air con **Notes:** Civ Wed 70

The Met Hotel, Leeds

★★★★ 75% HOTEL

King Street, LS1 2HQ - **tel:** 0113 245 0841
email: metropole.sales@principal-hotels.com **web:** www.phcompany.com
dir: *From M1, M62 & M621 follow city centre signs. A65 into Wellington St.*
At 1st traffic island right into King St, hotel on right

Said to be the best example of this type of building in the city, this splendid terracotta-fronted hotel is centrally located and convenient for the railway station. All bedrooms are appointed to suit the business traveller, with hi-speed internet access and a working area. The Restaurant and the Tempest Bar make convenient dining options. There are also impressive conference and banqueting facilities. Some parking space is available.

Rooms: 120 (5 family) **S** fr £69; **D** fr £79 **Facilities:** STV FTV WiFi Gym Mini gym **Conf:** Class 120 Board 100 Thtr 250 Del from £129 **Services:** Lift Night porter **Parking:** 30 **Notes:** Civ Wed 200

Park Plaza Leeds

★★★★ 75% HOTEL

Park Plaza
Hotels & Resorts

Boar Lane, LS1 5NS - **tel:** 0113 380 4000 & 0844 415 6720
(Calls cost 7p per minute plus your phone company's access charge)
email: pplinfo@pphe.com **web:** www.parkplaza.com
dir: *Follow signs for city centre*

Chic, stylish, ultra modern, city-centre hotel located just opposite City Square. Chino Latino, located on the first floor, is a fusion Far East and modern Japanese restaurant with a Latino bar. Stylish, air-conditioned bedrooms are spacious and have a range of modern facilities, including high-speed internet connection.

Rooms: 187 **Facilities:** FTV WiFi Gym Xmas New Year **Conf:** Class 70 Board 60 Thtr 220 **Services:** Lift Night porter Air con **Parking:** 6 **Notes:** Civ Wed 120

Novotel Leeds Centre

★★★★ 74% HOTEL

NOVOTEL
HOTELS & RESORTS

4 Whitehall, Whitehall Quay, LS1 4HR - **tel:** 0113 242 6446
email: H3270@accor.com **web:** www.novotel.com
dir: *M621 junct 3, follow signs to rail station. Into Aire St & left at lights*

With a minimalist style, this contemporary hotel provides a quality experience close to the city centre and within walking distance of the train station. Spacious, climate-controlled bedrooms are provided, while public areas are smartly presented. The bar is modern and airy, and Elements Restaurant offers an informal brasserie style. Facilities also include a fitness suite and a sauna. There is complimentary WiFi throughout the hotel.

Rooms: 196 (50 family) **Facilities:** STV FTV WiFi HL Gym Steam room Sauna **Conf:** Class 50 Board 50 Thtr 100 **Services:** Lift Night porter **Parking:** 80

The Cosmopolitan

★★★ 80% HOTEL

PEEL HOTELS PLC

2 Lower Briggate, LS1 4AE - **tel:** 0113 243 6454
email: info@cosmopolitan-hotel-leeds.com **web:** www.cosmopolitan-hotel-leeds.com
dir: *M621 junct 3. Keep in right lane. Follow until road splits into 4 lanes. Keep right, right at lights. (ASDA House on left). Left at lights. Over bridge, left, hotel opposite. Parking in 150mtrs*

This smartly presented, Victorian building is located on the south side of the city. The well-equipped bedrooms offer a choice of standard or executive grades. Staff are friendly and helpful ensuring a warm and welcoming atmosphere. Discounted overnight parking is provided in the adjacent 24-hour car park.

Rooms: 89 (5 family) (14 smoking) **S** £69–£110; **D** £89–£140* **Facilities:** STV FTV WiFi Xmas New Year **Conf:** Class 45 Board 40 Thtr 120 Del from £99 **Services:** Lift Night porter

Chevin Country Park Hotel & Spa

★★★ 78% HOTEL

Yorkgate, LS21 3NU - **tel:** 01943 467818
email: chevin@crerarhotels.com **web:** www.crerarhotels.com

(For full entry see Otley)

LEEDS *continued*

Mercure Leeds Parkway Hotel

★★★ 76% HOTEL

Otley Road, LS16 8AG - tel: 0844 815 9020 (Calls cost 7p per minute plus your phone company's access charge) & 0113 269 9000
email: sales.mercureleedsparkway@jupiterhotels.co.uk **web:** www.mercureleeds.co.uk
dir: From A1 take A58 towards Leeds, then right onto A6120. At A660 turn right towards Airport/Skipton. Hotel 2m on right

This hotel is conveniently located and caters well for both business and leisure guests. It is close to Leeds yet has a quiet spot near to the Yorkshire Dales. The lovely gardens lead on to wildlife walks that can be followed directly into Golden Acre Park (a beautiful 179 acre park and wildlife sanctuary). The hotel is a popular wedding venue and also has extensive conference facilities in the adjacent Summit Centre. A leisure club with indoor pool and fitness centre is also available and the hotel offers complimentary WiFi.

Rooms: 118 (4 family) (18 GF) **Facilities:** Spa STV FTV WiFi ♨ Gym Beauty facilities Hair salon Physiotherapy Xmas New Year **Conf:** Class 100 Board 65 Thtr 280 **Services:** Lift Night porter **Parking:** 250 **Notes:** Civ Wed 200

Holiday Inn Express Leeds - East

BUDGET HOTEL

Aberford Road, Oulton, LS26 8EJ - tel: 0113 288 0574
email: reservations@hiexpressleedseast.co.uk **web:** www.hiexpressleedseast.co.uk
dir: M62 junct 29, E towards Pontefract. Exit at junct 30, A642 signed Rothwell. Hotel opposite at 1st rdbt

A modern hotel ideal for families and business travellers. Fresh and uncomplicated, the spacious rooms include Sky TV, power shower and tea and coffee-making facilities. Continental buffet breakfast is included in the room rate; other meals may be taken at the nearby family pub or restaurant.

Rooms: 77 (50 family) (32 GF) **S** £49–£115; **D** £49–£115 (incl. bkfst)*
Conf: Class 20 Board 20 Thtr 25

Premier Inn Leeds/Bradford Airport

BUDGET HOTEL

Victoria Avenue, Yeadon, LS19 7AW - tel: 0871 527 8578 (Calls cost 13p per minute plus your phone company's access charge) **web:** www.premierinn.com
dir: On A658, near Leeds/Bradford Airport

High quality, budget accommodation ideal for both families and business travellers. Spacious, en suite bedrooms feature free WiFi and tea and coffee making facilities, and in most hotels, Freeview TV is also available. The adjacent family restaurant features a wide and varied menu.

Rooms: 76

Premier Inn Leeds City Centre

BUDGET HOTEL

Citygate, Wellington Street, LS3 1LW - tel: 0871 527 8582 (Calls cost 13p per minute plus your phone company's access charge) **web:** www.premierinn.com
dir: At A65 & A58 junct

Rooms: 140

Premier Inn Leeds City Centre (Leeds Arena)

BUDGET HOTEL

Hepworth Point, Claypit Lane, LS2 8BQ - tel: 0871 527 9356 (Calls cost 13p per minute plus your phone company's access charge) **web:** www.premierinn.com
dir: On foot from Leeds rail station cross road into Park Row, continue into Cookridge St to Clay Pit Ln. Hotel on left at top of lane

Rooms: 131

Premier Inn Leeds City Centre (Whitehall Road)

BUDGET HOTEL

1 Whitehall Riverside, Lower Wortley, LS1 4EQ - tel: 0871 622 2412
web: www.premierinn.com
dir: Exit M621 at J2. 1st exit at rdbt, onto A643, keep left. Left onto road just before CEF and Arco. Left onto Gelderd Rd. 1st exit at rdbt onto Domestic Rd. At next rdbt, 1st exit onto A58. 2nd exit at following rdbt and follow rd to right onto Whitehall Rd E. Right onto Riverside Way.

Rooms: 136

Premier Inn Leeds City West

BUDGET HOTEL

City West One Office Park, Gelderd Road, LS12 6LX - tel: 0871 527 8584 (Calls cost 13p per minute plus your phone company's access charge) **web:** www.premierinn.com
dir: M621 junct 1 take ring road towards Leeds. At 1st lights right into Gelderd Rd, right at rdbt

Rooms: 126

Premier Inn Leeds East

BUDGET HOTEL

Selby Road, Whitkirk, LS15 7AY - tel: 0871 527 8586 (Calls cost 13p per minute plus your phone company's access charge) **web:** www.premierinn.com
dir: M1 junct 46 towards Leeds. At 2nd rdbt follow Temple Newsam signs. Hotel 500mtrs on right

Rooms: 88

Premier Inn Leeds South (Birstall)

BUDGET HOTEL

Wakefield Road, Drighlington, BD11 1EA - tel: 0871 527 8580 (Calls cost 13p per minute plus your phone company's access charge) **web:** www.premierinn.com
dir: On Drighlington bypass, adjacent to M62 junct 27. Take A650, right to Drighlington, right, hotel on left

Rooms: 60

LEEK
Staffordshire   Map 16 SJ95

Premier Inn Leek Town Centre

BUDGET HOTEL

Ashbourne Road, ST13 5AS - **tel:** 0871 527 9330 (Calls cost 13p per minute plus your phone company's access charge) **web:** www.premierinn.com
dir: *M6 junct 16, A500. In 6m left at Eturia junction onto A53 signed Leek to the town centre. At lights in town centre turn right onto A523 (Ashbourne Rd). Hotel adjacent to war memorial on left*

High quality, budget accommodation ideal for both families and business travellers. Spacious, en suite bedrooms feature free WiFi and tea and coffee making facilities, and in most hotels, Freeview TV is also available. The adjacent family restaurant features a wide and varied menu.

Rooms: 63

LEEK WOOTTON
Warwickshire   Map 10 SP26

The Warwickshire Hotel & Country Club
★★★★ 74% HOTEL

CV35 7QT - **tel:** 01926 409409 & 622550
email: g.rayner@theclubcompany.com **web:** www.thewarwickshire.com
dir: *M40 junct 15 towards Coventry A46, then B4115 towards Leek Wootton. At rdbt 1st exit towards Leek Wootton, at next rdbt 1st exit to hotel*

This well-established golf and leisure facility has recently seen a full refurbishment which means it now also boasts a brand new 56 bedroom hotel. Bedrooms offers a very high level of quality and comfort for both leisure and corporate guests. The dining operation offers a casual café/lounge area or the club lounge for a quieter meal.

Rooms: 56 (12 family) (28 GF) 🐾 **Facilities:** Spa FTV WiFi ↻ 🎦 supervised ⚓ 45 Putting green Gym Sauna Solarium Steam room New Year **Conf:** Class 100 Board 80 Thtr 200 Del from £149 **Services:** Lift Night porter Air con **Parking:** 264 **Notes:** Civ Wed 173

LEICESTER
Leicestershire   Map 11 SK50

Belmont Hotel
★★★★ 77% ◉◉ HOTEL

De Montfort Street, LE1 7GR - **tel:** 0116 254 4773
email: info@belmonthotel.co.uk **web:** www.belmonthotel.co.uk
dir: *From A6 take 1st right after rail station. Hotel 200yds on left*

This well-established hotel, under the same family ownership, has been welcoming guests for over 70 years. It is conveniently situated within easy walking distance of the railway station and city centre though it sits in a quiet leafy residential area. Extensive public rooms are smartly appointed and include the informal Bowie's Bistro, Jamie's Bar with its relaxed atmosphere, and the more formal Cherry Restaurant.

Rooms: 74 (7 family) (8 GF) (2 smoking) 🐾 **S** £70–£99; **D** £80–£120 (incl. bkfst)*
Facilities: FTV WiFi ↻ Gym **Conf:** Class 75 Board 65 Thtr 175 Del from £125 **Services:** Lift Night porter **Parking:** 70 **Notes:** LB Civ Wed 100

Mercure Leicester The Grand Hotel

★★★★ 73% HOTEL

Granby Street, LE1 6ES - **tel:** 0844 815 9012 (Calls cost 7p per minute plus your phone company's access charge)
email: info@mercureleicester.co.uk **web:** www.mercureleicester.co.uk
dir: *A5460 into city. Follow Leicester Central Station signs. Left off St Georges Way, A594 onto Charles St. 1st left onto Northampton St, right onto Granby St. Hotel on left*

Located in the heart of Leicester city centre, this hotel offers well appointed bedrooms and spacious public areas. Conferences and weddings are catered for. On site parking is a plus. Free WiFi is available throughout.

Rooms: 104 🐾 **Facilities:** FTV WiFi ↻ Xmas New Year **Conf:** Class 200 Board 90 Thtr 350 **Services:** Lift Night porter **Parking:** 120 **Notes:** Civ Wed 200

Premier Inn Leicester (Braunstone)

BUDGET HOTEL

Meridian Business Park, Thorpe Astley, LE19 1LU - **tel:** 0871 527 8590 (Calls cost 13p per minute plus your phone company's access charge) **web:** www.premierinn.com
dir: *M1 junct 21, follow A563 (outer ring road) signs W to Thorpe Astley. At slip road after Texaco garage. Hotel on left*

High quality, budget accommodation ideal for both families and business travellers. Spacious, en suite bedrooms feature free WiFi and tea and coffee making facilities, and in most hotels, Freeview TV is also available. The adjacent family restaurant features a wide and varied menu.

Rooms: 75

Premier Inn Leicester Central (A50)

BUDGET HOTEL

Heathley Park, Groby Road, LE3 9QE - **tel:** 0871 527 8594 (Calls cost 13p per minute plus your phone company's access charge) **web:** www.premierinn.com
dir: *Off A50, city centre side of County Hall & Glenfield General Hospital*

Rooms: 76

Premier Inn Leicester City Centre

BUDGET HOTEL

1 St Georges Way, LE1 1AA - **tel:** 0871 527 8596 (Calls cost 13p per minute plus your phone company's access charge) **web:** www.premierinn.com
dir: *Phone for detailed directions*

Rooms: 135

Premier Inn Leicester (Forest East)

BUDGET HOTEL

Hinckley Road, Leicester Forest East, LE3 3GD - **tel:** 0871 527 8592 (Calls cost 13p per minute plus your phone company's access charge) **web:** www.premierinn.com
dir: *M1 junct 21, A5460. At major junct (Holiday Inn on right), left into Braunstone Lane. In 2m left onto A47 towards Hinkley. Hotel 400yds on left*

Rooms: 60

L

LEICESTER *continued*

Premier Inn Leicester Fosse Park

BUDGET HOTEL

Braunstone Lane East, LE3 2FW - **tel:** 0871 527 8588 (Calls cost 13p per minute plus your phone company's access charge) **web:** www.premierinn.com
dir: *M1 junct 21, at M69 junct take A5460 towards city. After 1m right at lights to hotel*
Rooms: 176

Premier Inn Leicester North West

BUDGET HOTEL

Leicester Road, Glenfield, LE3 8HB - **tel:** 0871 527 8598 (Calls cost 13p per minute plus your phone company's access charge) **web:** www.premierinn.com
dir: *M1 junct 21a N'bound, A46. Onto A50 for Glenfield & County Hall. Or M1 junct 22 S'bound onto A50 towards Glenfield. Into County Hall. Hotel on left adjacent to Gynsills*
Rooms: 45

Premier Inn Leicester South (Oadby)

BUDGET HOTEL

Glen Rise, Oadby, LE2 4RG - **tel:** 0871 527 8600 (Calls cost 13p per minute plus your phone company's access charge) **web:** www.premierinn.com
dir: *M1 junct 21, A563 signed South. Right at Leicester racecourse. Follow Market Harborough signs. Dual carriageway, straight on at rdbt. Into single lane, hotel on right*
Rooms: 30

LEICESTER FOREST MOTORWAY SERVICE AREA | Map 11 SK50
Leicestershire

Days Inn Leicester Forest East - M1

AA Advertised

Leicester Forest East, M1 Junct 21, LE3 3GB - **tel:** 0116 239 0534
email: leicester.hotel@welcomebreak.co.uk **web:** www.welcomebreak.co.uk
dir: *On M1 N'bound between junct 21 & 21A*

This modern building offers accommodation in smart, spacious and well-equipped bedrooms, suitable for families and business travellers, and all with en suite bathrooms. Continental breakfast is available, and other refreshments may be taken at the nearby family restaurant.

Rooms: 86 (71 family) (10 smoking) **Facilities:** FTV WiFi **Conf:** Board 10
Services: Lift **Parking:** 100

LENHAM | Map 7 TQ85
Kent

INSPECTOR'S CHOICE

Chilston Park Hotel

★★★★ ⊛ ⊛ HOTEL

Sandway, ME17 2BE - **tel:** 01622 859803 & 0845 072 7426 (Calls cost 5p per minute plus your phone company's access charge) **email:** chilstonpark@handpicked.co.uk
web: www.handpickedhotels.co.uk/chilstonpark
dir: *Exit A20 to Lenham, right into High St, pass station on right, 1st left, over x-rds, hotel 0.25m on left*

This elegant Grade I listed country house is set in 23 acres of immaculately landscaped gardens and parkland. An impressive collection of original paintings and antiques creates a unique environment. The sunken Venetian-style restaurant serves modern British food with French influences. Bedrooms are individual in design, some have four-poster beds and many have garden views.

Rooms: 53 (23 annexe) (2 family) (3 GF) S £99–£350; D £109–£350 (incl. bkfst)* **Facilities:** STV FTV WiFi HL Fishing Xmas New Year **Conf:** Class 60 Board 50 Thtr 100 Del from £135 **Services:** Lift Night porter **Parking:** 100
Notes: LB Civ Wed 90

LEOMINSTER | Map 10 SO45
Herefordshire

Talbot Hotel

★★★ 72% HOTEL

West Street, HR6 8EP - **tel:** 01568 616347
email: info@talbothotelleominster.com **web:** www.talbothotelleominster.com
dir: *From A49, A44 or A4112, hotel in town centre*

This charming former coaching inn is located in the town centre and makes an ideal base for exploring the area. Public areas feature original beams and antique furniture, and include an atmospheric bar and elegant restaurant. The bedrooms vary in size, but all are comfortably furnished and equipped. Facilities are available for private functions and conferences.

Rooms: 28 (3 family) (2 GF) S £49–£68; D £79–£91.50 **Facilities:** FTV WiFi
Conf: Class 60 Board 30 Thtr 130 **Parking:** 26 **Notes:** LB

LETCHWORTH GARDEN CITY
Map 12 TL23
Hertfordshire

Mercure Letchworth Hall Hotel
★★★★ 72% HOTEL

Mercure
HOTELS

Letchworth Lane, SG6 3NP - **tel:** 01462 683747
email: mlreservations@mercureletchworth.com **web:** www.fairviewhotels.com
dir: *Phone for details*

This hotel has an interesting history, and retains much of its country house style and tranquility. It also has plenty of leisure facilities and a host of meeting and function rooms. Bedrooms are spacious and well equipped. Cuisine is a feature, and menus feature local suppliers and interesting choices.

Rooms: (10 GF) ☎ **S** £59–£159; **D** £79–£179* **Facilities:** Spa FTV WiFi ⊗ supervised Gym Xmas New Year **Conf:** Class 100 Board 60 Thtr 200 Del from £79 **Services:** Lift Night porter Air con **Parking:** 200 **Notes:** LB Civ Wed 80

LEVENS
Map 18 SD48
Cumbria

The Villa Levens
★★★★ 79% ⊛ HOTEL

Brettargh Holt, LA8 8EA - **tel:** 01539 980980
email: reception@thevillalevens.co.uk **web:** www.thevillalevens.co.uk
dir: *M6 junct 36, A590 signed Barrow. At next rdbt (Brettargh Holt Roundabout), 1st left signed Barrow, hotel 200yds on left*

This former family home and convent, is now a charming hotel on the edge of the Lake District, making it a great base for exploring the area. Bedrooms are spacious, with the feature room having a copper bath in the bedroom. Two dining options are available; the brasserie is open throughout the day while the restaurant offers a more formal dining option to guests at lunch and dinner. Conference facilities are also available.

Rooms: 22 (3 family) (4 GF) ☎ **S** £55–£250; **D** £65–£250 (incl. bkfst)* **Facilities:** FTV WiFi ᐅ ⚓ Xmas New Year **Conf:** Class 250 Board 100 Thtr 300 **Services:** Night porter **Parking:** 130 **Notes:** LB Civ Wed 300

LEWES
Map 6 TQ41
East Sussex

Premier Inn Lewes Town Centre
BUDGET HOTEL

Premier Inn

BN7 2FT - **tel:** 0871 527 9524 (Calls cost 13p per minute plus your phone company's access charge) **web:** www.premierinn.com
dir: *From A27 take Lewes, East Grinstead, Tunbridge Wells exit onto A26 at Southerham Rdbt. Through Cuilfail Tunnel, take 1st exit left at rdbt after tunnel onto Malling Street/ A2029. Continue over next rdbt onto Phoenix Causeway, at lights continue onto Friars Walk B2193. Hotel on left*

High quality, budget accommodation ideal for both families and business travellers. Spacious, en suite bedrooms feature free WiFi and tea and coffee making facilities, and in most hotels, Freeview TV is also available. The adjacent family restaurant features a wide and varied menu.

Rooms: 61

LEYLAND
Map 15 SD52
Lancashire

Hallmark Hotel Preston Leyland
★★★★ 72% ⊛ HOTEL

Leyland Way, PR25 4JX - **tel:** 0330 028 3420
email: leyland@hallmarkhotels.co.uk **web:** www.hallmarkhotels.co.uk
dir: *M6 junct 28, left at end of slip road, hotel 100mtrs on left*

This purpose-built hotel enjoys a convenient location, just off the M6, within easy reach of Preston and Blackpool. Spacious public areas include extensive conference and banqueting facilities as well as a smart leisure club.

Rooms: 93 (4 family) (31 GF) ☎ **Facilities:** FTV WiFi ᐅ HL ⊗ supervised Xmas New Year **Conf:** Class 100 Board 40 Thtr 220 **Services:** Night porter **Parking:** 150 **Notes:** LB Civ Wed 200

L

L

LICHFIELD
Staffordshire   Map 10 SK10

INSPECTOR'S CHOICE

Swinfen Hall Hotel
★★★★ ◉◉◉ HOTEL

Swinfen, WS14 9RE - **tel:** 01543 481494
email: info@swinfenhallhotel.co.uk **web:** www.swinfenhallhotel.co.uk
dir: Set back from A38, 2.5m outside Lichfield, towards Birmingham

Dating from 1757, this lavishly decorated mansion has been painstakingly restored by the present owners. It is set in 100 acres of parkland which includes a deer park. Public rooms are particularly stylish, with intricately carved ceilings and impressive oil portraits. Bedrooms on the first floor boast period features and tall sash windows; those on the second floor (the former servants' quarters) are smaller and more contemporary by comparison. Service in the award-winning restaurant is both professional and attentive.

Rooms: 17 (5 family) ⬧ **S** £125–£330; **D** £155–£350 (incl. bkfst)*
Facilities: STV FTV WiFi ⬧ ⬧ Fishing ⬧ Jogging trail 100 acre park New Year
Conf: Class 50 Board 50 Thtr 160 Del £190 **Services:** Night porter **Parking:** 80
Notes: Civ Wed 120

Best Western The George Hotel
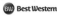 Best Western.
★★★ 80% HOTEL

12-14 Bird Street, WS13 6PR - **tel:** 01543 414822
email: mail@thegeorgelichfield.co.uk **web:** www.thegeorgelichfield.co.uk
dir: From Bowling Green Island on A461 take Lichfield exit. Left at next island into Swan Rd, as road bears left, turn right into Bird St for hotel car park

Situated in the city centre, this privately-owned hotel provides good quality, well-equipped accommodation which includes a room with a four-poster bed. Facilities here include a large ballroom, plus several other rooms for meetings and functions.

Rooms: 45 (5 family) **S** £50–£109; **D** £60–£130 (incl. bkfst)* **Facilities:** FTV WiFi ⬧
HL Gym **Conf:** Class 60 Board 40 Thtr 110 Del from £130 **Services:** Lift Night porter
Parking: 45 **Notes:** LB Civ Wed 110

Premier Inn Lichfield City Centre

BUDGET HOTEL

Swan Road, WS13 6QZ - **tel:** 0871 527 9440 (Calls cost 13p per minute plus your phone company's access charge) **web:** www.premierinn.com
dir: From M6 Toll junct T5 take A5148. Take A5206 ramp to Lichfield. At rdbt 1st exit (London Rd/A5206) into Upper St John Street (A51). Left into The Friary. 3rd exit at rdbt (Swan Rd). Hotel on right

High quality, budget accommodation ideal for both families and business travellers. Spacious, en suite bedrooms feature free WiFi and tea and coffee making facilities, and in most hotels, Freeview TV is also available. The adjacent family restaurant features a wide and varied menu.

Rooms: 79

Premier Inn Lichfield North East (A38)

BUDGET HOTEL

Fine Lane, Fradley, WS13 8RD - **tel:** 0871 527 8602 (Calls cost 13p per minute plus your phone company's access charge) **web:** www.premierinn.com
dir: On A38, 3 NE of Lichfield

Rooms: 30

LIFTON
Devon   Map 3 SX38

Arundell Arms
★★★ 86% ◉◉ HOTEL

Fore Street, PL16 0AA - **tel:** 01566 784666
email: reservations@arundellarms.co.uk **web:** www.arundellarms.co.uk
dir: 1m off A30, 3m E of Launceston

This former coaching inn, boasting a long history, sits in the heart of a quiet Devon village, and is internationally famous for its country pursuits such as winter shooting and angling. The bedrooms offer individual style and comfort. Public areas are full of character with a relaxed atmosphere, particularly around the open log fire during colder evenings. Award-winning cuisine is a celebration of local produce.

Rooms: 27 (6 annexe) (3 family) (4 GF) ⬧ **S** £89–£125; **D** £140–£160 (incl. bkfst)*
Facilities: FTV WiFi ⬧ Fishing ⬧ Game shooting (in winter) Fly fishing school Riding
Xmas New Year **Conf:** Class 30 Board 40 Thtr 100 **Services:** Night porter **Parking:** 70
Notes: Closed 24-27 Dec

LINCOLN	**Map 17 SK97**
Lincolnshire	

Washingborough Hall Hotel

★★★ 87% ◎◎◉ COUNTRY HOUSE HOTEL

Church Hill, Washingborough, LN4 1BE - tel: 01522 790340
email: enquiries@washingboroughhall.com **web:** www.washingboroughhall.com
dir: *B1190 into Washingborough. Right at rdbt, hotel 500yds on left*

This Georgian manor stands on the edge of the quiet village of Washingborough and is set in attractive gardens. Public rooms are pleasantly furnished and comfortable, while the restaurant offers interesting menus. Bedrooms are individually designed and most have views out over the grounds to the countryside beyond.

Rooms: 20 (6 annexe) (2 family) (3 GF) ♙ **S** fr £65; **D** fr £95* **Facilities:** FTV WiFi ↕ ♨ **Conf:** Class 70 Board 30 Thtr 100 Del from £175 **Parking:** 40
Notes: Civ Wed 100

The White Hart

★★★ 81% ◉ HOTEL

Bailgate, LN1 3AR - tel: 01522 526222
email: info@whitehart-lincoln.co.uk **web:** www.whitehart-lincoln.co.uk
dir: *A46 onto B1226, through Newport Arch. Hotel 0.5m on left as road bends left*

Lying in the shadow of Lincoln's magnificent cathedral, this hotel is perfectly positioned for exploring the shops and sights of this medieval city. The attractive bedrooms are furnished and decorated in a traditional style and many have views of the cathedral. Given the hotel's central location, parking is a real benefit.

Rooms: 50 (3 family) **S** fr £60; **D** fr £80 (incl. bkfst) **Facilities:** FTV WiFi ↕ ♫ **Conf:** Class 70 Board 50 Thtr 160 **Services:** Lift Night porter **Parking:** 50
Notes: Civ Wed 120

Best Western Plus Bentley Hotel & Spa

BW Best Western PLUS

★★★ 81% HOTEL

Newark Road, South Hykeham, LN6 9NH - tel: 01522 878000
email: info@bentleyhotellincoln.co.uk **web:** www.bentleyhotellincoln.co.uk
dir: *A1 onto A46 E towards Lincoln for 10m. Over 1st rdbt on Lincoln Bypass to hotel 50yds on left*

This conveniently located hotel is perfect for business and leisure guests alike. Staff are friendly and adapt a personal approach to hospitality, a warm welcome is guaranteed. Bedrooms and bathrooms are comfortably appointed and modern accessories such as complimentary WiFi is provided. Leisure facilities including swimming pool, sauna, steam room and gym are included for residential guests. Ample amounts of car parking also available. A good range of meal options are available in both the bar and the restaurant.

Rooms: 80 (5 family) (23 GF) (4 smoking) ♙ **S** £56–£99; **D** £63–£104 (incl. bkfst)*
Facilities: Spa STV FTV WiFi ↕ HL ☟ Gym Steam room Sauna New Year **Conf:** Class 150 Board 30 Thtr 300 Del from £132 **Services:** Lift Night porter Air con **Parking:** 170 **Notes:** LB Civ Wed 120

The Lincoln Hotel

★★★ 80% ◉ HOTEL

Eastgate, LN2 1PN - tel: 01522 520348
email: reservations@thelincolnhotel.com **web:** www.thelincolnhotel.com
dir: *Adjacent to cathedral*

This privately-owned modern hotel enjoys superb uninterrupted views of Lincoln Cathedral. There are ruins of the Roman wall and Eastgate in the grounds. Bedrooms are contemporary with up-to-the-minute facilities. An airy restaurant and bar, a cellar bar, plus a comfortable lounge are provided. There are substantial conference and meeting facilities.

Rooms: 71 (4 family) (10 GF) ♙ **S** fr £75; **D** fr £90 (incl. bkfst)* **Facilities:** FTV WiFi Gym **Conf:** Class 50 Board 40 Thtr 100 **Services:** Lift Night porter **Parking:** 54
Notes: Civ Wed 150

Tower Hotel

★★★ 76% ◉ HOTEL

38 Westgate, LN1 3BD - tel: 01522 529999
email: tower.hotel@btclick.com **web:** www.lincolntowerhotel.com
dir: *From A46 follow signs to Lincoln N then to Bailgate area. Through arch, 2nd right*

This hotel faces the Norman castle wall and is in a very convenient location for the city. The relaxed and friendly atmosphere is very noticeable here. There's a modern conservatory bar and a stylish restaurant where contemporary dishes are available throughout the day.

Rooms: 15 (1 family) ♙ **Facilities:** STV FTV WiFi **Conf:** Class 24 Board 16 Thtr 24 **Services:** Night porter **Notes:** Closed 24-27 Dec & 1 Jan

Branston Hall Hotel

★★★ 75% ◉ COUNTRY HOUSE HOTEL

Branston Park, Branston, LN4 1PD - tel: 01522 793305
email: info@branstonhall.com **web:** www.branstonhall.com
dir: *On B1188, 3m SE of Lincoln*

Dating back to 1885, this country house sits in 88 acres of beautiful grounds complete with a lake. There is an elegant restaurant, a spacious bar and a beautiful lounge in addition to impressive conference and leisure facilities. Individually styled bedrooms vary in size and include several with four-poster beds. The hotel is a popular wedding venue.

Rooms: 50 (7 annexe) (3 family) (4 GF) **Facilities:** Spa STV FTV WiFi ☟ Gym Jogging circuit Xmas New Year **Conf:** Class 54 Board 40 Thtr 200 **Services:** Lift Night porter **Parking:** 100 **Notes:** Civ Wed 160

L

LINCOLN *continued*

Premier Inn Lincoln (Canwick)

BUDGET HOTEL

Lincoln Road, Canwick Hill, LN4 2RF - tel: 0871 527 8604 (Calls cost 13p per minute plus your phone company's access charge) **web:** www.premierinn.com
dir: Approx 1m S of city centre at junction of B1188 & B1131

High quality, budget accommodation ideal for both families and business travellers. Spacious, en suite bedrooms feature free WiFi and tea and coffee making facilities, and in most hotels, Freeview TV is also available. The adjacent family restaurant features a wide and varied menu.

Rooms: 98

Premier Inn Lincoln City Centre

BUDGET HOTEL

Broadgate, LN2 5AQ - tel: 0871 527 9418 (Calls cost 13p per minute plus your phone company's access charge) **web:** www.premierinn.com
dir: From N: from A57 left into Mint St B1003. Right into Broadgate A15. From S: on A46 to A1434/Newark Rd rdbt. Straight on next rdbt into St Catherines A15, straight on at next rdbt. Left into St Swithins Sq. Right into Silver St B1003. Right into Broadgate A15

Rooms: 131

LIPHOOK	Map 5 SU83
Hampshire	

Old Thorns Manor Hotel Golf & Country Estate

★★★★ 78% HOTEL

Griggs Green, GU30 7PE - tel: 01428 724555
email: reservations@oldthorns.com **web:** www.oldthorns.com
dir: At Griggs Green exit A3, hotel 0.5m

Old Thorns is a modern, relaxed and welcoming hotel, set in 400 acres of peaceful Hampshire countryside. The bedrooms are spacious and stylish and offer high levels of comfort. The leisure facilities are extensive and include a health club, wellness centre and spa; in addition there is also a sports bar, champagne and cocktail bar, Kings Restaurant and all-day dining is also available.

Rooms: 175 (2 family) (64 GF) 🐾 **Facilities:** Spa STV FTV WiFi ↔ 🕃 ⚓ 18 Putting green 🏌 Gym Xmas New Year **Conf:** Class 100 Board 30 Thtr 300 **Services:** Lift Night porter **Parking:** 278 **Notes:** Civ Wed 250

LISKEARD	Map 2 SX26
Cornwall & Isles of Scilly	

Premier Inn Liskeard

BUDGET HOTEL

Liskeard Retail Park, Haviland Road, PL14 3PR - tel: 0871 527 8608 (Calls cost 13p per minute plus your phone company's access charge) **web:** www.premierinn.com
dir: Off A38, on A390 SW of Liskeard

High quality, budget accommodation ideal for both families and business travellers. Spacious, en suite bedrooms feature free WiFi and tea and coffee making facilities, and in most hotels, Freeview TV is also available. The adjacent family restaurant features a wide and varied menu.

Rooms: 51

LITTLEHAMPTON	Map 6 TQ00
West Sussex	

Premier Inn Littlehampton

BUDGET HOTEL

Roundstone Lane, East Preston, BN16 1EB - tel: 0871 527 8610 (Calls cost 13p per minute plus your phone company's access charge) **web:** www.premierinn.com
dir: A27 onto A280 signed Littlehampton/Rustington & Angmering. At next rdbt follow Littlehampton, Rustington/A259 signs. At next rdbt 1st exit signed East Preston. Hotel on left

High quality, budget accommodation ideal for both families and business travellers. Spacious, en suite bedrooms feature free WiFi and tea and coffee making facilities, and in most hotels, Freeview TV is also available. The adjacent family restaurant features a wide and varied menu.

Rooms: 39

LIVERPOOL	Map 15 SJ39
Merseyside	

Thornton Hall Hotel and Spa

★★★★ 81% ⧓⧓⧓ HOTEL

Neston Road, CH63 1JF - tel: 0151 336 3938
email: reservations@thorntonhallhotel.com **web:** www.thorntonhallhotel.com

(For full entry see Thornton Hough)

Hope Street Hotel

★★★★ 77% ⧓⧓ HOTEL

40 Hope Street, L1 9DA - tel: 0151 709 3000
email: sleep@hopestreethotel.co.uk **web:** www.hopestreethotel.co.uk
dir: Follow Cathedral & University signs on entering city. Telephone for detailed directions

This stylish property is located in the Georgian quarter and is within easy walking distance of the city's cathedrals, theatres, major shops and attractions. Stylish bedrooms and suites, many of which benefit from far reaching views across the city's skyline, are appointed with flat-screen TVs, DVD players, internet access and comfy beds with Egyptian cotton sheets; the bathrooms have rain showers and deep tubs. The London Carriage Works Restaurant specialises in local, seasonal produce and the adjacent lounge bar offers lighter all-day dining and wonderful cocktails.

Hope Street Hotel

Rooms: 89 (16 family) (5 GF) 🐾 **S** £89–£295; **D** £89–£295* **Facilities:** STV FTV WiFi
⌁ Gym Massage & beauty therapists Xmas New Year **Conf:** Class 40 Board 30 Thtr
Del £ 165 70 **Services:** Lift Night porter Air con **Parking:** 10 **Notes:** LB Civ Wed 70

Malmaison Liverpool
★★★★ 76% 🅖 HOTEL

7 William Jessop Way, Princes Dock, L3 1QZ - **tel:** 0151 229 5000 & 0844 693 0655
(Calls cost 5p per minute plus your phone company's access charge)
email: reception.liverpool@malmaison.com **web:** www.malmaison.com
dir: *A5080 follow signs for Pier Head/Southport/Bootle. Into Baln St to rdbt,
1st exit at rdbt, immediately left onto William Jessop Way*

This is a purpose-built hotel with cutting edge and contemporary style. 'Mal'
Liverpool, as its known, has a stunning location, alongside the river and docks, and
in the heart of the city's regeneration. Bedrooms are stylish and comfortable and
are provided with lots of extra facilities. The public areas are packed with fun and
style, and there are a number of meeting rooms as well as private dining, including
a chef's table.

Rooms: 130 🐾 **S** £79–£300; **D** £79–£350* **Facilities:** STV FTV WiFi ⌁ Gym 🎵 Xmas
New Year **Conf:** Class 85 Board 80 Thtr 100 Del from £129 **Services:** Lift Night porter
Air con **Notes:** LB Civ Wed 120

Novotel Liverpool Centre
★★★★ 76% HOTEL

NOVOTEL
HOTELS & RESORTS

40 Hanover Street, L1 4LN - **tel:** 0151 702 5100
email: h6495@accor.com **web:** www.novotel.com
dir: *Phone for directions*

This attractive and stylish city centre hotel is convenient for Liverpool Echo Arena,
Liverpool One shopping centre and the Albert Dock; it is also adjacent to a town
centre car park. Novotel Liverpool Centre has a range of conference and leisure
facilities which include an indoor heated pool and fitness suite. Rope Walks
restaurant offers a contemporary-style menu and relaxed lounge bar concept -
taking influences from Liverpool's industrial and shipping history. The open-plan
bar has many seating options, from high stools to button-backed benches, soft
sofas and armchairs. The bedrooms are comfortable and stylishly designed.

Rooms: 209 (127 family) 🐾 **D** £89–£329 **Facilities:** FTV WiFi ⌁ 🅢 Gym Steam room
🎵 **Conf:** Class 60 Board 50 Thtr 90 **Services:** Lift Night porter

Hard Days Night Hotel
★★★★ 74% HOTEL

MILLENNIUM
HOTELS AND RESORTS

Central Buildings, North John Street, L2 6RR - **tel:** 0151 236 1964
email: info@harddaysnighthotel.com **web:** www.harddaysnighthotel.com
dir: *Phone for directions*

In the heart of Liverpool; close to Liverpool One (a shoppers delight) and less than a
stone's throw from the iconic Cavern Club, Hard Days Night Hotel is a very tasteful
celebration of Beatle Mania. Guests travel from far and wide to stay at this hotel,
each attractively furnished modern room is very well equipped, and all benefit from
a Beatles-inspired, specially commissioned piece of artwork. Blakes restaurant
provides a relaxed and informal dining venue, cocktails are served nightly in the
'Fab Four' bar.

Rooms: 110 🐾 **Facilities:** STV WiFi ⌁ HL 🎵 **Conf:** Class 40 Board 20 Thtr 120
Services: Lift Night porter Air con **Notes:** Civ Wed 60

Hallmark Hotel Liverpool Alicia
★★★ 76% HOTEL

3 Aigburth Drive, Sefton Park, L17 3AA - **tel:** 0330 028 3416 & 0151 727 4411
email: alicia@hallmarkhotels.co.uk **web:** www.hallmarkhotels.co.uk
dir: *From end of M62 take A5058 to Sefton Park, then left, follow park around*

This stylish and friendly hotel overlooks Sefton Park and is just a few minutes' drive
from both the city centre and John Lennon Airport. Bedrooms are well equipped and
comfortable. Day rooms include a striking modern restaurant and bar. Extensive,
stylish function facilities make this a popular wedding venue.

Rooms: 41 (8 family) 🐾 **Facilities:** STV WiFi HL Xmas New Year **Conf:** Class 80
Board 40 Thtr 120 Del from £124 **Services:** Lift Night porter **Parking:** 40 **Notes:** Civ
Wed 120

Jurys Inn Liverpool
★★★ 76% HOTEL

No 31 Keel Wharf, L3 4FN - **tel:** 0151 244 3777
email: jurysinnliverpool@jurysinns.com **web:** www.jurysinns.com
dir: *Follow City Centre & Albert Dock signs. Hotel at Kings Waterfront
adjacent to Albert Dock, opposite BT Convention Centre & Echo Arena*

Located on the Kings Waterfront adjacent to the BT Convention Centre, Echo Arena,
Albert Dock complex and a short walk from the very popular shopping district of
Liverpool One, this hotel offers contemporary and spacious bedrooms. Guests have
a choice of dining options - the Innfusion restaurant and the Inntro bar. There are
10 dedicated meeting rooms and WiFi is available throughout. There is ample
secure parking nearby.

Rooms: 310 (58 family) 🐾 **Facilities:** FTV WiFi ⌁ HL **Conf:** Class 50 Board 40
Thtr 100 **Services:** Lift Night porter Air con **Notes:** Civ Wed 100

L

LIVERPOOL *continued*

Hallmark Hotel Liverpool Feathers

★★★ 73% METRO HOTEL

115-125 Mount Pleasant, L3 5TF - **tel:** 0330 028 3426
email: feathers@hallmarkhotels.co.uk **web:** www.hallmarkhotels.co.uk
dir: *Located in the city centre*

This stylish and friendly metro hotel has a prime city centre location close to both cathedrals, universities, and handy for trendy local eateries. Bedrooms come in a variety of distinctive styles and are well equipped and comfortable. Limited secure parking is available on a first come, first served basis.

Rooms: 81 🐾 **Facilities:** FTV WiFi Xmas New Year **Conf:** Board 12 **Parking:** 24
Notes: Civ Wed 80

Premier Inn Liverpool (Aintree)

BUDGET HOTEL

Ormskirk Road, Aintree, L9 5AS - **tel:** 0871 527 8612 (Calls cost 13p per minute plus your phone company's access charge) **web:** www.premierinn.com
dir: *M58, A57, A59 towards Liverpool. Pass Aintree Retail Park, left at lights into Aintree Racecourse. Hotel on left*

High quality, budget accommodation ideal for both families and business travellers. Spacious, en suite bedrooms feature free WiFi and tea and coffee making facilities, and in most hotels, Freeview TV is also available. The adjacent family restaurant features a wide and varied menu.

Rooms: 40

Premier Inn Liverpool Albert Dock

BUDGET HOTEL

East Britannia Building, Albert Dock, L3 4AD - **tel:** 0871 527 8622 (Calls cost 13p per minute plus your phone company's access charge) **web:** www.premierinn.com
dir: *Follow signs for Liverpool City Centre & Albert Dock*

Rooms: 186

Premier Inn Liverpool City Centre

BUDGET HOTEL

Vernon Street, L2 2AY - **tel:** 0871 527 8624 (Calls cost 13p per minute plus your phone company's access charge) **web:** www.premierinn.com
dir: *From M62 follow Liverpool City Centre & Birkenhead Tunnel signs. At rdbt 3rd exit into Dale St, right into Vernon St. Hotel on left*

Rooms: 165

Premier Inn Liverpool City Centre (Liverpool 1)

BUDGET HOTEL

48 Hanover Street, L1 4AF - **tel:** 0871 527 9382 (Calls cost 13p per minute plus your phone company's access charge) **web:** www.premierinn.com
dir: *A5047 follow signs for city centre. At lights left onto A5048, at next lights right onto A5047. A5038 signed Toxteth, Airport. Right into Renshaw St & right onto Ranelagh St. Hotel on left opposite BBC Radio Merseyside*

Rooms: 183

Premier Inn Liverpool John Lennon Airport

BUDGET HOTEL

57 Speke Hall Avenue, L24 1YQ - **tel:** 0871 527 8626 (Calls cost 13p per minute plus your phone company's access charge) **web:** www.premierinn.com
dir: *A561 towards Liverpool follow 'Liverpool John Lennon Airport' signs into Seake Hall Ave, at 1st rdbt take 2nd left. Hotel 300mtrs on left*

Rooms: 101

Premier Inn Liverpool North

BUDGET HOTEL

Northern Perimeter Road, L30 7PT - **tel:** 0871 527 8628 (Calls cost 13p per minute plus your phone company's access charge) **web:** www.premierinn.com
dir: *0.25m from end of M58/M5, on A5207*

Rooms: 83

Premier Inn Liverpool (Roby)

BUDGET HOTEL

Roby Road, Huyton, L36 4HD - **tel:** 0871 527 8616 (Calls cost 13p per minute plus your phone company's access charge) **web:** www.premierinn.com
dir: *Just off M62 junct 5 on A5080*

Rooms: 56

Premier Inn Liverpool (Tarbock)

BUDGET HOTEL

Wilson Road, Tarbock, L36 6AD - **tel:** 0871 527 8618 (Calls cost 13p per minute plus your phone company's access charge) **web:** www.premierinn.com
dir: *At M62 & M57 junct. M62 junct 6, take A5080 (Huyton).1st right into Wilson Rd*

Rooms: 41

Premier Inn Liverpool (West Derby)

BUDGET HOTEL

Queens Drive, West Derby, L13 0DL - **tel:** 0871 527 8620 (Calls cost 13p per minute plus your phone company's access charge) **web:** www.premierinn.com
dir: *At end of M62 right under flyover onto A5058 (follow football stadium signs). Hotel 1.5m on left, just past Esso garage*

Rooms: 85

The Z Hotel Liverpool

AA Advertised

2 North John Street, L2 4SA - tel: 0151 556 1770
email: liverpool@thezhotels.com **web:** www.thezhotels.com
dir: *M62 junct 7, continue onto Bowring Park Road/A5080, then Edge Lane/A5047. Right onto Low Hill, continue onto Erskine Street, then Churchill Way/A57. Left onto North John St, hotel on right*

Z Liverpool has 92 rooms predominantly over the top three floors, with stunning views over the city. This budget boutique hotel is perfectly located for all the city has to offer. Bedrooms all have en suite wet room, crisp bed linen, 40" TV with Sky channels, and complimentary WiFi. Key local attractions include Albert Dock (home to Tate Liverpool and the Maritime Museum), Pier Head, Mann Island, and the Echo arena.

Rooms: 92 ⌁ **Facilities:** STV FTV WiFi ⌁ **Services:** Lift Night porter Air con

LIVERSEDGE
West Yorkshire   Map 16 SE12

Healds Hall Hotel & Restaurant

★★★ 79% ⊛ HOTEL

THE INDEPENDENTS
HOTEL ASSOCIATION

Leeds Road, WF15 6JA - tel: 01924 409112
email: enquire@healdshall.co.uk **web:** www.healdshall.co.uk
dir: *On A62 between Leeds & Huddersfield. 50yds on left after lights at Swan Pub*

This 18th-century house, in the heart of West Yorkshire, provides comfortable and well-equipped accommodation and excellent hospitality. The hotel has earned a good local reputation for the quality of its food and offers a choice of casual or more formal dining styles, and a wide range of dishes on the various menus.

Rooms: 24 (3 family) (3 GF) ⌁ **S** £60–£100; **D** £75–£130 (incl. bkfst) **Facilities:** FTV WiFi ⌁ **Conf:** Class 60 Board 45 Thtr 100 Del from £130 **Services:** Night porter **Parking:** 90 **Notes:** LB Closed 1 Jan & BH Mon RS Sun evening limited service Civ Wed 100

LIZARD
Cornwall & Isles of Scilly   Map 2 SW71

Housel Bay Hotel

★★★ 75% ⊛ HOTEL

Housel Cove, TR12 7PG - tel: 01326 290417 **email:** info@houselbay.com
web: www.houselbay.com
dir: *A39 or A394 to Helston, then A3083. At Lizard sign turn left, left at school, down lane to hotel*

This long-established hotel has stunning views across the Western Approaches, equally enjoyable from the lounge and many of the bedrooms. Good cuisine is available in the stylish dining room, from where guests might enjoy a stroll to the end of the garden, which leads directly onto the Cornwall coastal path.

Rooms: 20 (1 family) ⌁ **Facilities:** FTV WiFi ⌁ Xmas New Year **Services:** Lift **Parking:** 35 **Notes:** LB Closed 2 Jan-1 Feb

The Three Graces, Liverpool

London

Index of London hotels

This index shows hotels in London in alphabetical order, followed by their postal district or location and plan or map references. Page numbers precede each entry.

London Plan 5

London Plan 9

LONDON

Greater London Plans 1-9, pages 206-218. (Small scale maps 6 & 7 at back of book.) Hotels are listed below in postal district order, commencing East, then North, South and West. Detailed plans 2-9 show the locations of AA-appointed hotels within the Central London postal districts. If you do not know the postal district of the hotel you want, please refer to the index preceding the street plans for the entry and map pages. The plan reference for each AA-appointed hotel also appears within its directory entry.

LONDON E1

hub by Premier Inn London Spitalfields

BUDGET HOTEL PLAN 3 J3

86 Brick Lane, Spitalfields, E1 6RL - tel: 0333 321 3104
email: Spitalfields.hub@whitbread.com web: www.premierinn.com
dir: Nearest tube stations Aldgate East & Liverpool Street

This modern hotel offers self-check-in kiosks, superfast free WiFi, and cleverly designed and compact bedrooms with all the entertainment and comfort you need: 40" flat-screen smart TV, temperature and lighting controlled by a special Premier Inn app, Hypnos bed, and monsoon shower. The Deli+Bar is open for grab-and-go breakfast boxes, pastries, grilled sandwiches, Costa Coffee, beer, wine and more.

Rooms: 189

Premier Inn London City (Aldgate)

BUDGET HOTEL PLAN 3 K2

66 Alie Street, Aldgate, E1 8PX - tel: 0871 527 9526 (Calls cost 13p per minute plus your phone company's access charge) web: www.premierinn.com
dir: Exit Aldgate East tube station, S along Leman St. Left into Alie St, hotel on right

High quality, budget accommodation ideal for both families and business travellers. Spacious, en suite bedrooms feature free WiFi and tea and coffee making facilities, and in most hotels, Freeview TV is also available. The adjacent family restaurant features a wide and varied menu.

Rooms: 250

Premier Inn London City (Tower Hill)

BUDGET HOTEL PLAN 3 J1

22-24 Prescott Street, Tower Hill, E1 8BB - tel: 0871 527 8646 (Calls cost 13p per minute plus your phone company's access charge) web: www.premierinn.com
dir: Nearest tube: Tower Hill. 3 mins walk from Docklands Light Rail DLR

Rooms: 165

LONDON E4   Map 6 TQ39

Premier Inn Chingford

BUDGET HOTEL

Rangers Road, Chingford, E4 7QH - tel: 0871 527 9836 (Calls cost 13p per minute plus your phone company's access charge) web: www.premierinn.com
dir: M25 junct 26, A121 (Loughton) At next rdbt 1st exit (A121). At Wake Arms rdbt 2nd exit onto A104 (Woodford). Right onto A1069 (Rangers Rd). 1m, hotel on right

High quality, budget accommodation ideal for both families and business travellers. Spacious, en suite bedrooms feature free WiFi and tea and coffee making facilities, and in most hotels, Freeview TV is also available. The adjacent family restaurant features a wide and varied menu.

Rooms: 24

LONDON E6

Premier Inn London Beckton

BUDGET HOTEL PLAN 3 K2

1 Woolwich Manor Way, Beckton, E6 5NT - tel: 0871 527 8644 (Calls cost 13p per minute plus your phone company's access charge) web: www.premierinn.com
dir: A13 onto A117 (Woolwich Manor Way) towards City Airport, hotel on left after 1st rdbt

High quality, budget accommodation ideal for both families and business travellers. Spacious, en suite bedrooms feature free WiFi and tea and coffee making facilities, and in most hotels, Freeview TV is also available. The adjacent family restaurant features a wide and varied menu.

Rooms: 124

LONDON E8

Premier Inn London Hackney

BUDGET HOTEL PLAN 1 F4

27 Dalston Lane, E8 3DF - tel: 0871 527 9582 (Calls cost 13p per minute plus your phone company's access charge) web: www.premierinn.com
dir: A406, A10 onto Kingsland High St, left onto A104, hotel approx 200yds on left

High quality, budget accommodation ideal for both families and business travellers. Spacious, en suite bedrooms feature free WiFi and tea and coffee making facilities, and in most hotels, Freeview TV is also available. The adjacent family restaurant features a wide and varied menu.

Rooms: 90

LONDON E14

Canary Riverside Plaza

★★★★★ 85% ◉ HOTEL PLAN 6 A3

46 Westferry Circus, Canary Wharf, E14 8RS - tel: 020 7510 1999
web: www.canaryriversideplaza.com
dir: Phone for directions

Located in Canary Wharf and positioned by the river, this modern and elegant hotel has a popular bar and restaurant, small 24-hour gym and an open-air terrace. Bedrooms and bathrooms are very spacious, some with stunning riverside views, all equipped to a very high standard. There is also a business centre and meeting/banquet facilities.

Rooms: 142 ⬦ S £280–£1700; D £280–£1700* Facilities: Spa STV FTV WiFi ⬥ ⬦ supervised ⬦ Gym Xmas New Year Conf: Class 135 Board 50 Thtr 220 Del from £300 Services: Lift Night porter Air con Notes: LB Civ Wed 220

LONDON E15

Premier Inn London Stratford

BUDGET HOTEL PLAN 9 B3

International Square, Westfield Stratfield City, E15 1AZ - tel: 0871 527 9286 (Calls cost 13p per minute plus your phone company's access charge) web: www.premierinn.com
dir: From A11 or A12 follow signs for Westfield Shopping City & Stratford International & Car Park A

High quality, budget accommodation ideal for both families and business travellers. Spacious, en suite bedrooms feature free WiFi and tea and coffee making facilities, and in most hotels, Freeview TV is also available. The adjacent family restaurant features a wide and varied menu.

Rooms: 267

LONDON

LONDON E16

DoubleTree by Hilton Hotel London ExCel

★★★★ 78% HOTEL PLAN 7 E1

Excel 2 Festoon Way, Royal Victoria Dock, E16 1RH - tel: 020 7540 4820
email: reservations@ramadadocklands.co.uk **web:** www.ramadadocklands.co.uk
dir: *Follow signs for ExCeL East & London City Airport. Over Connaught Bridge then immediately left at rdbt*

This hotel benefits from a stunning waterfront location and is close to the events venue, ExCeL, the O2 Arena, Canary Wharf and London City Airport. The accommodation comprises a mix of spacious bedrooms and suites. The relaxed public areas consist of a modern restaurant and informal lounge area. Parking, a fitness room and meeting rooms are available on site. Free WiFi is available.

Rooms: 224 (71 family) (23 smoking) **Facilities:** FTV WiFi Gym **Conf:** Class 20 Board 25 Thtr 30 **Services:** Lift Night porter Air con **Parking:** 60 **Notes:** LB Civ Wed 120

Novotel London ExCeL

★★★★ 78% HOTEL PLAN 7 C1

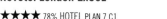

7 Western Gateway, Royal Victoria Docks, E16 1AA - tel: 020 7540 9700
email: H3656@accor.com **web:** www.novotel.com/3656
dir: *M25 junct 30, A13 follow City signs, exit at Canning Town. Follow ExCeL West signs. Hotel adjacent*

This hotel is situated adjacent to the ExCeL exhibition centre and overlooks the Royal Victoria Dock. Design throughout the hotel is contemporary and stylish. Public rooms include a range of meeting rooms, a modern coffee station, indoor leisure facilities and a smart bar and restaurant, both with a terrace overlooking the dock. Bedrooms feature modern decor, a bathroom with separate bath and shower, and an extensive range of extras.

Rooms: 257 (176 family) **Facilities:** STV FTV WiFi ☼ HL Gym Sauna Steam room Relaxation room with massage bed **Conf:** Class 55 Board 30 Thtr 70 **Services:** Lift Night porter Air con **Parking:** 72

Crowne Plaza London Docklands

PLAN 7 B1

Western Gateway, E16 1AL - tel: 020 7055 2100
email: sales@cpdocklands.co.uk **web:** www.cpdocklands.co.uk
dir: *30 seconds from Royal Victoria DLR, 30 seconds from Emerates Cable Car*

Currently the rating for this establishment is not confirmed. This may be due to a change of ownership or because it has only recently joined the AA rating scheme.

Rooms: 210 (65 family) (3 smoking) **S** £125–£525; **D** £135–£535 (incl. bkfst)*
Facilities: Spa STV FTV WiFi ☼ HL ☼ Gym Xmas New Year **Conf:** Class 126 Board 40 Thtr 250 Del from £205 **Services:** Lift Night porter Air con **Parking:** 75 **Notes:** LB Civ Wed 250

Premier Inn London Docklands (ExCeL)

BUDGET HOTEL PLAN 7 B1

Excel East, E16 1SJ - tel: 0871 527 8650 (Calls cost 13p per minute plus your phone company's access charge) **web:** www.premierinn.com
dir: *A13 onto A1020. At Connaught rdbt take 2nd exit into Connaught Rd. Hotel on right*

High quality, budget accommodation ideal for both families and business travellers. Spacious, en suite bedrooms feature free WiFi and tea and coffee making facilities, and in most hotels, Freeview TV is also available. The adjacent family restaurant features a wide and varied menu.

Rooms: 203

LONDON EC1

Malmaison Charterhouse Square

★★★★ 79% ⓦ HOTEL PLAN 3 E3

18-21 Charterhouse Square, Clerkenwell, EC1M 6AH - tel: 020 70123700
email: reception@malmaison.com **web:** www.malmaison.com
dir: *Exit Barbican Station turn left, take 1st left. Hotel on far left corner of Charterhouse Square*

Situated in a leafy and peaceful square, Malmaison Charterhouse maintains the same focus on quality service and food as the other hotels in the group. The bedrooms, stylishly decorated in calming tones, have all the expected facilities including power showers, CD players and free internet access. The brasserie and bar at the hotel's centre has a buzzing atmosphere and offers traditional French cuisine.

Rooms: 97 (5 GF) **S** £139–£259; **D** £169–£339* **Facilities:** STV FTV WiFi ☼ HL Gym Xmas **Conf:** Board 20 Thtr 45 **Services:** Lift Night porter Air con **Parking:** 5 **Notes:** LB

The Montcalm London City at The Brewery

AA Advertised ⓦ PLAN 3 F3

52 Chiswell Street, EC1Y 4SB - tel: 020 7614 0100
email: info@themontcalmlondoncity.co.uk **web:** www.themontcalmlondoncity.co.uk
dir: *From Gatwick M23 N to M25 signed Heathrow Airport/Central London to M4. From Heathrow M4 E 9m*

Situated in the heart of The City is The Montcalm London City at The Brewery. This Grade II listed building has been converted into a luxury hotel, while maintaining many original features. As the name implies, this was formerly the site of Whitbread & Co, Britain's first purpose-built mass production brewery. The last beer brewed here was in 1976, when the site was turned into Whitbread PLC's Head Office. With luxurious suites, deluxe studios and City or Club rooms, The Montcalm London City at The Brewery is ideal for business or leisure.

Rooms: 236 **Facilities:** STV FTV WiFi ☼ HL Gym Xmas New Year **Conf:** Class 40 Board 40 Thtr 60 **Services:** Lift Night porter Air con **Notes:** Civ Wed

The Z Hotel Shoreditch

AA Advertised PLAN 3 G5

136-144 City Road, EC1V 2RL - tel: 020 3551 3700
email: shoreditch@thezhotels.com **web:** www.thezhotels.com
dir: *Phone for details*

Z Shoreditch is a converted former office building, with over one hundred bedrooms. Z Shoreditch is part of The Bower, a new landmark quarter for Old Street comprising offices, restaurants and retail units. As with the others in the Z Hotels chain, bedrooms have en suite wet rooms, crisp bed linen, 40" TV with Sky, and complimentary WiFi.

Rooms: 111 **S** fr £59; **D** fr £70* **Facilities:** STV FTV WiFi ☼ HL **Services:** Lift Night porter Air con

LONDON EC2

ANdAZ Liverpool Street

★★★★★ 86% ⓦ HOTEL PLAN 3 H3

40 Liverpool Street, EC2M 7QN - tel: 020 7961 1234
email: guestservices.londonliv@andaz.com **web:** www.london.liverpoolstreet.andaz.com
dir: *On corner of Liverpool St & Bishopsgate, attached to Liverpool St station*

ANdAZ is an exciting and contemporary place to stay - no reception desk here so guests are checked-in by staff with laptops. Bedrooms are stylish, and designed very much with the executive in mind, with iPods and WiFi as well as a mini bar stocked with healthy choices. The dining options are varied and many; Japanese cuisine in Miyako, 1901 Restaurant and Wine Bar, light snacks available in Catch and Champagne bar and the Eastway brasserie. There are also rooms for private dining and other events.

Rooms: 267 **Facilities:** Spa STV FTV WiFi Gym Steam room Beauty treatment rooms New Year **Conf:** Class 120 Board 60 Thtr 250 **Services:** Lift Night porter Air con **Notes:** Civ Wed 230

LONDON EC3

Novotel London Tower Bridge

★★★★ 79% HOTEL PLAN 3 J1

10 Pepys Street, EC3N 2NR - tel: 020 7265 6000
email: H3107@accor.com **web:** www.novotel.com
dir: *Phone for directions*

Located near the Tower of London, this smart hotel is convenient for Docklands, the City, Heathrow and London City airports. Air-conditioned bedrooms are spacious, modern, and offer a great range of facilities. There is a smart bar and restaurant, a small gym, children's play area and extensive meeting and conference facilities.

Rooms: 203 (130 family) **Facilities:** STV FTV WiFi Gym Steam room Sauna Fitness room Xmas New Year **Conf:** Class 56 Board 25 Thtr 100 **Services:** Lift Night porter

hub by Premier Inn London Tower Bridge

BUDGET HOTEL PLAN 3 H1

28 Great Tower Street, EC3R 5AT - tel: 0333 321 3104 (Calls cost 13p per minute plus your phone company's access charge)
email: opsmgr.towerbridge.hub@whitbread.com **web:** www.premierinn.com
dir: *Nearest tube stations: Tower Hill & Monument*

This modern hotel offers self-check-in kiosks, superfast free WiFi, and cleverly designed and compact bedrooms with all the entertainment and comfort you need: 40" flat-screen smart TV, temperature and lighting controlled by a special Premier Inn app, Hypnos bed, and monsoon shower. The Deli+Bar is open for grab-and-go breakfast boxes, pastries, grilled sandwiches, Costa Coffee, beer, wine and more.

Rooms: 112

Premier Inn London City (Monument)

BUDGET HOTEL PLAN 3 H1

20 St Mary at Hill, EC3R 8EE - tel: 0871 527 9452 (Calls cost 13p per minute plus your phone company's access charge) **web:** www.premierinn.com
dir: *Nearest tube stations: Monument & Bank*

High quality, budget accommodation ideal for both families and business travellers. Spacious, en suite bedrooms feature free WiFi and tea and coffee making facilities, and in most hotels, Freeview TV is also available. The adjacent family restaurant features a wide and varied menu.

Rooms: 184

LONDON EC4

Crowne Plaza London - The City

★★★★ 84% HOTEL PLAN 3 E1

19 New Bridge Street, EC4V 6DB - tel: 020 7438 8000
email: loncy.info@ihg.com **web:** www.cplondoncityhotel.co.uk
dir: *Opposite Blackfriars station*

With a 1919 façade, and a modern, stylish interior, Crowne Plaza London-The City is located in London's historic Square Mile, near Blackfriars station, minutes away

from some of London's most famous attractions such as The London Eye, St Paul's Cathedral and Covent Garden. At the hotel, guests can enjoy great dining in two destination restaurants: the celebrated Italian Diciannove or the Chinese Cricket Club, offering a mouth-watering range of Sichuan and dim sum specialities with a modern twist. In addition, you can enjoy all-day dining in the comfortable City Lounge, or relax in the stylish champagne bar and cigar terrace, Voltaire.

Rooms: 204 (60 family) (7 smoking) **Facilities:** STV WiFi HL Gym Xmas New Year **Conf:** Class 100 Board 50 Thtr 160 **Services:** Lift Night porter Air con **Notes:** Civ Wed 160

Premier Inn London Blackfriars

BUDGET HOTEL PLAN 3 E2

1-2 Dorset Rise, EC4Y 8EN - tel: 0871 527 9362 (Calls cost 13p per minute plus your phone company's access charge) **web:** www.premierinn.com
dir: *Phone for detailed directions*

High quality, budget accommodation ideal for both families and business travellers. Spacious, en suite bedrooms feature free WiFi and tea and coffee making facilities, and in most hotels, Freeview TV is also available. The adjacent family restaurant features a wide and varied menu.

Rooms: 310

The Z Hotel City

AA Advertised PLAN 3 D2

24-28 Fleet Street, EC4Y 1AA - tel: 020 3551 3718
email: city@thezhotels.com **web:** www.thezhotels.com/z-city
dir: *Within Temple between Aldwych & Ludgate Circus*

Z City is situated in the Temple area, nestled between Aldwych and Ludgate Circus. Immediately behind the hotel is Temple Church, built by the Knights Templar, while opposite is the Royal Courts of Justice. Z City is a designer conversion of a former office building, with 109 bedrooms arranged over lower ground, ground and three upper floors. The bedrooms are functional rather than attractive, yet are carefully considered. Each offers an en suite wet room, crisp bed linen, 48" TV with a full selection of Sky channels, and complimentary WiFi. Some rooms are internal, and therefore windowless.

Rooms: 109 (10 family) (7 GF) **Facilities:** STV FTV WiFi HL **Services:** Lift Air con

LONDON N1

Premier Inn London Angel Islington

BUDGET HOTEL PLAN 1 F4

Parkfield Street, Islington, N1 0PS - tel: 0871 527 8558 (Calls cost 13p per minute plus your phone company's access charge) **web:** www.premierinn.com
dir: *From A1 (Islington High St) into Berners Rd bear left into Parkfield St. N1 car park opposite hotel*

High quality, budget accommodation ideal for both families and business travellers. Spacious, en suite bedrooms feature free WiFi and tea and coffee making facilities, and in most hotels, Freeview TV is also available. The adjacent family restaurant features a wide and varied menu.

Rooms: 95

LONDON N1 *continued*

Premier Inn London City (Old Street)

BUDGET HOTEL PLAN 3 G5

1 Silicon Way, N1 6AT - **tel:** 0871 527 9312 (Calls cost 13p per minute plus your phone company's access charge) **web:** www.premierinn.com
dir: *From Old Street tube station exit 1 (on foot) onto A501 (City Rd). Right into East St. 2nd right into Brunswick Place (Three Crowns pub on corner), 1st left into Corsham St*

Rooms: 251

Premier Inn London Kings Cross

BUDGET HOTEL PLAN 3 B6

26-30 York Way, N1 9AA - **tel:** 0871 527 8672 (Calls cost 13p per minute plus your phone company's access charge) **web:** www.premierinn.com
dir: *M25 junct 16 onto M40 (becomes A40). Follow City signs, exit at Euston Rd, follow one-way system to York Way*

Rooms: 281

LONDON N17

Premier Inn London Tottenham Hale hotel

BUDGET HOTEL PLAN 1 G5

N17 9LR - **tel:** 0871 527 9614 (Calls cost 13p per minute plus your phone company's access charge) **web:** www.premierinn.com
dir: *From the A10, turn onto Monument Way/A503. Stay in right lane to stay on Monument Way. Continue onto The Hale. Turn left onto Station Road, hotel on left*

High quality, budget accommodation ideal for both families and business travellers. Spacious, en suite bedrooms feature free WiFi and tea and coffee making facilities, and in most hotels, Freeview TV is also available. The adjacent family restaurant features a wide and varied menu.

Rooms: 96

LONDON N19

Premier Inn London Archway

BUDGET HOTEL PLAN 1 E5

Hamlyn House, Highgate Hill, N19 5PA - **tel:** 0871 527 9598 (Calls cost 13p per minute plus your phone company's access charge) **web:** www.premierinn.com
dir: *M1 junct 2, follow Barnet Bypass/Great N Way/A1 signs towards central London. From A406 to A1 junction. Follow Archway Rd until it becomes MacDonald Rd. Hotel on left*

High quality, budget accommodation ideal for both families and business travellers. Spacious, en suite bedrooms feature free WiFi and tea and coffee making facilities, and in most hotels, Freeview TV is also available. The adjacent family restaurant features a wide and varied menu.

Rooms: 163

LONDON NW1

INSPECTOR'S CHOICE

The Landmark London

★★★★★ ◉◉ ☕ HOTEL PLAN 2 F3

222 Marylebone Road, NW1 6JQ - **tel:** 020 7631 8000
email: reservations@thelandmark.co.uk **web:** www.landmarklondon.co.uk
dir: *Adjacent to Marylebone Station. Hotel on Marylebone Rd*

Once one of the last truly grand railway hotels, The Landmark London boasts a number of stunning features, the most spectacular being the naturally lit central atrium forming the hotel's focal point. When it comes to eating and drinking there are a number of choices, including the Mirror Bar for expertly crafted cocktails and the Gazebo - ideal for a business meeting or a quick snack. The Winter Garden Restaurant has the centre stage in the atrium and is a great place to watch the world go by; and the twotwentytwo restaurant and bar is a relaxing place to meet, eat and drink. The air-conditioned bedrooms are luxurious and have large, stylish bathrooms. There is also a health club that offers a complete wellbeing experience.

Rooms: 300 (77 family) (52 smoking) **Facilities:** Spa STV FTV WiFi ⇘ ⌖ Gym Beauty treatments & massages ♬ Xmas New Year **Conf:** Class 266 Board 50 Thtr 512 **Services:** Lift Night porter Air con **Parking:** 25 **Notes:** Civ Wed 300

Meliã White House

★★★★ 82% ◉◉ HOTEL PLAN 2 H4

Albany Street, Regents Park, NW1 3UP - **tel:** 020 7391 3000
email: melia.white.house@melia.com **web:** www.melia-whitehouse.com
dir: *Opposite Gt Portland St underground station & next to Regents Park/Warren Street underground*

Owned by the Spanish Solmelia company, this impressive art deco property is located opposite Great Portland Street tube station. Spacious public areas offer a high degree of comfort and include the cocktail bar 'Dry Martini by Javier de las Muelas', where guests can enjoy classic cocktails alongside Javier de las Muelas' signature cocktails; the award-winning fine dining Spanish restaurant, L' Albufera; and The Place Restaurant, where tapas-style dishes are served in an informal setting. Stylish bedrooms come in a variety of sizes and styles, but all offer high levels of comfort and are thoughtfully equipped. For longer stays, "The Apartments" are the obvious choice.

Rooms: 580 (28 family) **S** £120–£435; **D** £120–£435* **Facilities:** STV FTV WiFi ⇘ Gym Beauty treatment room ♬ Xmas New Year **Conf:** Class 80 Board 60 Thtr 140 **Services:** Lift Night porter Air con **Notes:** LB

Pullman London St Pancras

★★★★ 80% HOTEL PLAN 3 A5

100-110 Euston Road, NW1 2AJ - **tel:** 020 7666 9000
email: H5309@accor.com **web:** www.accorhotels.com/5309
dir: *Between St Pancras & Euston stations, entrance opposite British Library*

This hotel enjoys a central location adjacent to the British Library and close to some of London's main transport hubs. The style is modern and contemporary throughout. Bedrooms vary in size but are all very well equipped and many have views over the city. Open-plan public areas include a leisure suite and extensive conference facilities including the Shaw Theatre. Free WiFi is available.

Rooms: 312 ☏ **D** fr £165* **Facilities:** STV FTV WiFi ⬧ HL Gym Sauna ♫ Xmas New Year **Conf:** Class 220 Board 80 Thtr 446 Del from £298 **Services:** Lift Night porter Air con

Premier Inn London St Pancras

BUDGET HOTEL PLAN 3 B5

Euston House, 81-103 Euston Street, NW1 2EZ - **tel:** 0871 527 9492 (Calls cost 13p per minute plus your phone company's access charge) **web:** www.premierinn.com
dir: *Nearest tube: London Euston, King's Cross St Pancras*

High quality, budget accommodation ideal for both families and business travellers. Spacious, en suite bedrooms feature free WiFi and tea and coffee making facilities, and in most hotels, Freeview TV is also available. The adjacent family restaurant features a wide and varied menu.

Rooms: 266

LONDON NW2

Clayton Crown Hotel

★★★★ 77% HOTEL PLAN 1 D5

MORAN HOTELS

142-152 Cricklewood Broadway, Cricklewood, NW2 3ED - **tel:** 020 8452 4175
email: info.crown@claytonhotels.com **web:** www.claytonhotels.com
dir: *M1 junct 1 follow signs onto North Circular W A406. Junct with A5 Staples Corner. At rdbt take 1st exit onto A5 to Cricklewood*

This striking hotel is connected by an impressive glass atrium to the popular Crown Pub. Features include excellent function and conference facilities, a leisure club, a choice of stylish lounges and bars and a contemporary restaurant. The air-conditioned bedrooms are appointed to a high standard and include a number of trendy suites.

Rooms: 152 (63 family) (35 GF) ☏ **Facilities:** STV WiFi ⬧ ⊕ Gym ♫ Xmas New Year **Conf:** Class 150 Board 80 Thtr 300 **Services:** Lift Night porter Air con **Parking:** 39 **Notes:** Civ Wed 300

LONDON NW3

Premier Inn London Hampstead

BUDGET HOTEL PLAN 1 E4

215 Haverstock Hill, Hampstead, NW3 4RB - **tel:** 0871 527 8662 (Calls cost 13p per minute plus your phone company's access charge) **web:** www.premierinn.com
dir: *A41 to Swiss Cottage. Before junct take feeder road left into Buckland Cresent into Belsize Ave. Left into Haverstock Hill*

High quality, budget accommodation ideal for both families and business travellers. Spacious, en suite bedrooms feature free WiFi and tea and coffee making facilities, and in most hotels, Freeview TV is also available. The adjacent family restaurant features a wide and varied menu.

Rooms: 143

LONDON NW9

Premier Inn London Hendon The Hyde

BUDGET HOTEL PLAN 1 D5

Hyde House, NW9 6LH - **tel:** 0871 527 9450 (Calls cost 13p per minute plus your phone company's access charge) **web:** www.premierinn.com
dir: *M1 junct 4, A41, A5 towards Edgware. Hotel opposite junct of A4006 & Kingsbury*

High quality, budget accommodation ideal for both families and business travellers. Spacious, en suite bedrooms feature free WiFi and tea and coffee making facilities, and in most hotels, Freeview TV is also available. The adjacent family restaurant features a wide and varied menu.

Rooms: 99

LONDON SE1

Shangri-La Hotel at The Shard

★★★★★ 86% HOTEL PLAN 5 G6

31 St Thomas Street, SE1 9QU - **tel:** 020 7234 8000
email: info.slln@shangri-la.com **web:** www.shangri-la.com/london
dir: *Phone for details*

This hotel in the iconic London Shard is the first foray of the upmarket global brand into the UK and the second into Europe. It won't come as a surprise that every room has a stupendous view, as does the 52nd floor bar, sky pool and, slightly lower down on floor 35, Ting Restaurant. Rooms are fully equipped for business and leisure travellers - free WiFi, air conditioning and ample work space. There are luxurious toiletries in the well-proportioned bathrooms; many with double wash hand basins and heated toilet seats. Full automatic black-out blinds prevent those with vertigo from suffering too much.

Rooms: 202 (202 family) ☏ **S** £350–£10000; **D** £350–£10000* **Facilities:** STV WiFi ⬧ ⊕ Gym Spa treatments available in room or spa residences **Conf:** Class 60 Board 50 Thtr 120 **Services:** Lift Night porter Air con **Parking:** 15 **Notes:** Civ Wed 120

Plaza on the River London

★★★★★ 83% TOWN HOUSE HOTEL PLAN 5 B2

Park Plaza
Hotels & Resorts

18 Albert Embankment, SE1 7TJ - **tel:** 020 7620 8656 & 0844 854 5295 (Calls cost 7p per minute plus your phone company's access charge)
email: guestrelations@plazaontheriver.co.uk **web:** www.plazaontheriver.co.uk
dir: *From Houses of Parliament turn into Millbank, at rdbt left into Lambeth Bridge. At rdbt 3rd exit into Albert Embankment*

This is a superb modern townhouse overlooking London from the south bank of the Thames, with outstanding views of the capital's landmarks. The bedrooms are large and many are full suites with state-of-the-art technology and kitchen facilities; all are decorated in an elegant modern style. Service includes a full range of in-room dining options; additionally, the bar and restaurant in the adjacent Park Plaza are available to guests.

Rooms: 127 (127 family) (65 smoking) ☏ **S** £179–£600; **D** £185–£630* **Facilities:** WiFi ⬧ HL Gym ♫ Xmas New Year **Conf:** Class 450 Board 40 Thtr 650 **Services:** Lift Night porter Air con **Notes:** Civ Wed 540

LONDON SE1 *continued*

London Bridge Hotel

★★★★ 83% HOTEL PLAN 5 G6

8-18 London Bridge Street, SE1 9SG - **tel:** 020 7855 2200
email: sales@londonbridgehotel.com **web:** www.londonbridgehotel.com
dir: *Access through London Bridge Station, past taxi rank, towards Shard into London Bridge St (one way). Hotel on left*

This elegant, independently owned hotel enjoys a prime location on the edge of the City, adjacent to London Bridge station. Smartly appointed, well-equipped bedrooms include a number of spacious deluxe rooms and suites. Free WiFi is available throughout. The Quarter Bar & Lounge is the ideal place for light bites, old favourites and cocktails. The Londinium restaurant offers a seasonal British menu.

Rooms: 138 (10 family) (5 smoking) **Facilities:** STV FTV WiFi ♦ Gym **Conf:** Class 36 Board 36 Thtr 80 **Services:** Lift Night porter Air con

Park Plaza Westminster Bridge London

★★★★ 81% ⊛⊛ HOTEL PLAN 5 C5

SE1 7UT - **tel:** 020 7620 1110 & 0844 415 6790 (Calls cost 7p per minute plus your phone company's access charge)
email: ppwlres@pphe.com **web:** www.parkplaza.com
dir: *Phone for details*

A very smart hotel located in The City, close to Waterloo Station, featuring eye-catching, contemporary decor, a state-of-the-art indoor leisure facility and extensive conference and banqueting facilities. There is the awarding-wining

Joel brasserie as well as Ichi, the popular sushi bar. The bedrooms are also up-to-the-minute in style and feature a host of extras including a mini bar, a safe and modem points.

Rooms: 1019 (575 family) ♦ **S** fr £149; **D** fr £159* **Facilities:** Spa STV FTV WiFi ♦ HL ⊛ Gym ♫ Xmas New Year **Conf:** Class 800 Board 50 Thtr 2000 Del from £240 **Services:** Lift Night porter Air con **Notes:** LB Civ Wed 1400

Novotel London City South

★★★★ 79% HOTEL PLAN 5 F6

NOVOTEL
HOTELS & RESORTS

Southwark Bridge Road, SE1 9HH - **tel:** 020 7660 0676
email: H3269@accor.com **web:** www.novotel.com
dir: *At junct at Thrale St, off Southwark St*

Conveniently located for both business and leisure guests, with The City just across the Thames; other major attractions are also easily accessible. The hotel is contemporary in design with smart, modern bedrooms and spacious public rooms. There are a gym, sauna and steam room on the 6th floor, and limited parking is available at the rear of the hotel.

Rooms: 182 (164 family) ♦ **S** fr £99; **D** fr £119* **Facilities:** STV FTV WiFi ♦ HL Gym Steam room Sauna **Conf:** Class 45 Board 40 Thtr 100 **Services:** Lift Night porter Air con **Parking:** 50

H10 London Waterloo Hotel

★★★★ 78% ⊛ HOTEL PLAN 5 E5

284-302 Waterloo Road, SE1 8RQ - **tel:** 020 7928 4062
email: h10.london.waterloo@h10hotels.com **web:** www.h10hotels.com
dir: *450mtrs from Waterloo Station, 300mtrs from Lambeth North*

This hotel, conveniently situated for the South Bank and Waterloo Station, has a host of features. Bedrooms are stylish and designed with the international traveller in mind. The bar provides a useful internet facility and the stylish restaurant offers fresh and interesting dishes. The staff are friendly and efficient.

Rooms: 177 ♦ **S** fr £99; **D** fr £119* **Facilities:** STV FTV WiFi ♦ Gym Beauty treatment room Xmas New Year **Conf:** Class 45 Board 24 Thtr 70 **Services:** Lift Night porter Air con

Mercure London Bridge

★★★★ 78% HOTEL PLAN 5 E6

Mercure
HOTELS

71-79 Southwark Street, SE1 0JA - **tel:** 020 7660 0683
email: H2814@accor.com **web:** www.mercure.com
dir: *A200 to London Bridge. Left into Southwark St*

This smart, contemporary hotel forms part of the rejuvenation of the South Bank. With the City of London just over the river and a number of tourist attractions within easy reach, the hotel is well located for business and leisure visitors alike. Facilities include spacious air-cooled bedrooms, a modern bar and the stylish Loft Restaurant.

Rooms: 144 (15 family) (5 GF) **Facilities:** STV FTV WiFi ♦ HL Gym Xmas **Conf:** Class 40 Board 30 Thtr 60 **Services:** Lift Night porter Air con

LONDON

Park Plaza London Riverbank

★★★★ 77% HOTEL PLAN 5 C3

18 Albert Embankment, SE1 7SP - tel: 020 7958 8000 & 0844 854 5290
(Calls cost 7p per minute plus your phone company's access charge)
email: rppres@pphe.com **web:** www.parkplazariverbank.com
dir: *From Houses of Parliament turn onto Millbank, at rdbt left onto Lambeth Bridge. At rdbt take 3rd exit onto Albert Embankment*

Situated on the south side of the River Thames, this hotel offers guests the convenience of a central London location and high levels of comfort. Contemporary design coupled with a host of up-to-date facilities, the hotel is home to the Chino Latino brasserie. The air-conditioned bedrooms have TVs and large work desks; some rooms and suites have stunning views of the Houses of Parliament. Other facilities include WiFi throughout, high-tech conference rooms, a business centre, and a fitness centre with cardiovascular equipment.

Rooms: 521 **Facilities:** STV FTV WiFi HL Gym **Conf:** Class 405 Board 40 Thtr 700
Services: Lift Night porter Air con **Notes:** Civ Wed 400

Park Plaza County Hall London

★★★★ 77% HOTEL PLAN 5 C5

1 Addington Street, SE1 7RY - tel: 020 7021 1800 & 0844 415 6760
(Calls cost 7p per minute plus your phone company's access charge)
email: ppchinfo@pphe.com **web:** www.parkplazacountyhall.com
dir: *From Houses of Parliament cross Westminster Bridge A302. At rdbt take 4th right at dedicated lights*

This hotel is located just south of Westminster Bridge near Waterloo International Rail Station. A contemporary design-led, air-conditioned establishment, Park Plaza County Hall London features studios and suites, most with kitchenettes and seating areas with a TV. There are six meeting rooms, an executive lounge, a restaurant and bar, plus a fully-equipped gym with sauna and steam room. WiFi is available.

Rooms: 399 (304 family) **Facilities:** Spa STV FTV WiFi HL Gym Sauna Steam room Beauty therapy room Xmas New Year **Conf:** Class 60 Board 40 Thtr 100
Services: Lift Night porter Air con **Notes:** LB

Novotel London Waterloo

★★★★ 77% HOTEL PLAN 5 C3

113 Lambeth Road, SE1 7LS - tel: 020 7793 1010
email: h1785@accor.com **web:** www.novotel.com/1785
dir: *Opposite Houses of Parliament on S bank of River Thames*

This hotel is in an excellent location, with Lambeth Palace, the Houses of Parliament and Waterloo Station all within a short walk. The bedrooms are spacious and benefit from air conditioning. Open-plan public areas include the Elements bar and restaurant, and also a children's play area. There's also a fitness room, well-equipped conference facilities and secure parking.

Rooms: 187 (80 family) **Facilities:** STV WiFi HL Gym Steam room Sauna
Conf: Class 24 Board 24 Thtr 40 **Services:** Lift Air con **Parking:** 40

Novotel London Blackfriars

★★★★ 76% HOTEL PLAN 5 E6

46 Blackfriars Road, SE1 8NZ - tel: 020 7660 0834
email: H7942@accor.com **web:** www.novotel.com
dir: *Phone for details*

This latest generation Novotel is just south of the Thames and was opened in late 2012, utilising the latest in hotel and bedroom technology. There are media hubs in each bedroom, as well as air conditioning and glass walls to the bathroom that

"steam-over" in an instant for privacy if desired. There are also a swimming pool, gym and sauna in the basement, and a bar and restaurant on the ground floor.

Rooms: 182 (39 family) **Facilities:** FTV WiFi HL Gym Saunarium
Conf: Class 50 Board 40 Thtr 90 **Services:** Lift Air con

Days Hotel London Waterloo

BUDGET HOTEL PLAN 5 D4

54 Kennington Road, SE1 7BJ - tel: 020 7922 1331
email: book@hotelwaterloo.com **web:** www.hotelwaterloo.com
dir: *On corner of Kennington Rd & Lambeth Rd. Opposite Imperial War Museum*

This modern building offers accommodation in smart, spacious and well-equipped bedrooms, suitable for families and business travellers, and all with en suite bathrooms. Continental breakfast is available and other refreshments may be taken at the nearby family restaurant.

Rooms: 162 (15 family) (13 GF) **S** £99–£299; **D** £99–£299*

Premier Inn London Bridge hotel

BUDGET HOTEL PLAN 5 G6

135 Borough High Street, SE1 1NP - tel: 0871 527 9690 (Calls cost 13p per minute plus your phone company's access charge) **web:** www.premierinn.com
dir: *Phone for details*

High quality, budget accommodation ideal for both families and business travellers. Spacious, en suite bedrooms feature free WiFi and tea and coffee making facilities, and in most hotels, Freeview TV is also available. The adjacent family restaurant features a wide and varied menu.

Rooms: 99

Premier Inn London County Hall

BUDGET HOTEL PLAN 5 C5

Belvedere Road, SE1 7PB - tel: 0871 527 8648 (Calls cost 13p per minute plus your phone company's access charge) **web:** www.premierinn.com
dir: *In County Hall building. Nearest tube: Waterloo*

Rooms: 316

Premier Inn London Southwark (Borough Market)

BUDGET HOTEL PLAN 5 F6

Bankside, 34 Park Street, SE1 9EF - tel: 0871 527 8676 (Calls cost 13p per minute plus your phone company's access charge) **web:** www.premierinn.com
dir: *A3200 onto A300 (Southwark Bridge Rd), 1st left into Sumner St, right into Park St. From S: M3, A3 follow Central London signs*

Rooms: 59

Premier Inn London Southwark (Tate Modern)

BUDGET HOTEL PLAN 5 E6

15A Great Suffolk Street, Southwark, SE1 0FL - tel: 0871 527 9332 (Calls cost 13p per minute plus your phone company's access charge) **web:** www.premierinn.com
dir: *Phone for detailed directions*

Rooms: 122

LONDON

LONDON SE1 *continued*

Premier Inn London Tower Bridge

BUDGET HOTEL PLAN 5 H5

159 Tower Bridge Road, SE1 3LP - tel: 0871 527 8678 (Calls cost 13p per minute plus your phone company's access charge) **web:** www.premierinn.com
dir: *S of Tower Bridge on A100*

Rooms: 196

Premier Inn London Waterloo

BUDGET HOTEL PLAN 5 C5

York Road, Waterloo, SE1 7NJ - tel: 0871 527 9412 (Calls cost 13p per minute plus your phone company's access charge) **web:** www.premierinn.com
dir: *Nearest station: Waterloo*

Rooms: 234

citizenM London Bankside

AA Advertised PLAN 5 E6

20 Lavington Street, SE1 0NZ - tel: 020 3519 1680
email: supportlba@citizenm.com **web:** www.citizenm.com
dir: *Phone for details*

Just a short walk from Tate Modern and Shakespeare's Globe, citizenM London Bankside is the height of urban, stylish, business-and-pleasure, boutique accommodation. From the '1 minute check in/out' to the new-media friendly meeting rooms and lobby, this is something different. The bedrooms are stylishly economical, making the most of limited space, with super-sized beds, blackout blinds, free WiFi, ambient mood lighting, a rain shower and a wall-to-wall window above the bed. CanteenM serves breakfast, lunch and dinner, and also has as a 24-hour bar.

Rooms: 192 **Facilities:** STV FTV WiFi **Services:** Lift

LONDON SE9

Premier Inn London Eltham hotel

BUDGET HOTEL PLAN 1 H2

SE9 3NS - tel: 0871 527 9604 (Calls cost 13p per minute plus your phone company's access charge) **web:** www.premierinn.com
dir: *Phone for details*

High quality, budget accommodation ideal for both families and business travellers. Spacious, en suite bedrooms feature free WiFi and tea and coffee making facilities, and in most hotels, Freeview TV is also available. The adjacent family restaurant features a wide and varied menu.

Rooms: 91

LONDON SE10

Novotel London Greenwich

★★★★ 77% HOTEL PLAN 8 A2

173-185 Greenwich High Road, Greenwich, SE10 8JA - tel: 020 8312 6800
email: H3476@accor.com **web:** www.novotel.com
dir: *Adjacent to Greenwich Station*

This purpose-built hotel is conveniently located for rail and DLR stations, as well as major attractions such as the Royal Maritime Museum and the Royal Observatory.

Air-conditioned bedrooms are spacious and equipped with a host of extras, and public areas include a small gym, contemporary lounge bar and restaurant.

Rooms: 151 (34 family) **Facilities:** STV FTV WiFi HL Gym Steam room Xmas
Conf: Class 40 Board 32 Thtr 92 **Services:** Lift Night porter Air con **Parking:** 30

Premier Inn London Greenwich

BUDGET HOTEL PLAN 8 A1

43-81 Greenwich High Road, Greenwich, SE10 8JL - tel: 0871 527 9208 (Calls cost 13p per minute plus your phone company's access charge) **web:** www.premierinn.com
dir: *Phone for detailed directions*

High quality, budget accommodation ideal for both families and business travellers. Spacious, en suite bedrooms feature free WiFi and tea and coffee making facilities, and in most hotels, Freeview TV is also available. The adjacent family restaurant features a wide and varied menu.

Rooms: 156

InterContinental London – The O2

AA Advertised ◉◉◉ PLAN 6 E3

1 Waterview Drive, SE10 0TW - tel: 020 8463 6868
email: tim.reynolds@iclondon.theo2.com **web:** www.iclondon-the02.com
dir: *Greenwich Peninsular, 5 min walk from North Greenwich tube station*

Situated between the O2 Arena and the Thames, the InterContinental London - The O2 offers the perfect location for those attending any kind of event at the Arena; it is actually physically connected to the former Millennium Dome by the means of a direct walkway. The views are impressive in any direction, while the rooms themselves are spacious, contemporary and luxurious. There is also a top-of-the-range spa, an exclusive club lounge, and a range of eating and drinking options including a roof-top bar.

Rooms: 453 (57 family) **Facilities:** Spa FTV WiFi HL Gym Xmas New Year
Conf: Class 1800 Thtr 3000 **Services:** Lift Night porter Air con **Parking:** 220

LONDON SE13

Premier Inn London Lewisham

BUDGET HOTEL PLAN 1 G2

1-13 Lewisham High Street, SE13 5AF - tel: 0871 527 9480 (Calls cost 13p per minute plus your phone company's access charge) **web:** www.premierinn.com
dir: *From A2 at lights into Lewisham Rd, under rail bridge, inn on left. Or from Lewisham Station (walking), left into Station Rd. At road end, left into Lewisham Rd (A2211). 1st right into Lewisham High St, 1st left into Kings Hall Mews*

High quality, budget accommodation ideal for both families and business travellers. Spacious, en suite bedrooms feature free WiFi and tea and coffee making facilities, and in most hotels, Freeview TV is also available. The adjacent family restaurant features a wide and varied menu.

Rooms: 60

LONDON SE15

Best Western London Peckham Hotel

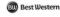

★★★ 75% HOTEL PLAN 1 F3

110 Peckham Road, Peckham, SE15 5EU - tel: 020 7701 4222
email: peckham@eurohotelsgroup.co.uk **web:** www.thelondonpeckhamhotel.co.uk
dir: *Phone for directions*

Located just a couple of miles south of central London, this newly refurbished hotel offers stylish and contemporary accommodation. All rooms are well equipped and have air conditioning, digital TVs and WiFi; a new restaurant is to be launched shortly. There's easy access into central London, with a bus stop right outside the hotel, and the over-ground rail line is just a short walk away.

Rooms: 215 ⓕ **S** £49–£125; **D** £55–£159* **Facilities:** FTV WiFi ⓦ **Services:** Lift Air con **Parking:** 6 **Notes:** LB No children 18yrs

---

LONDON SW1

INSPECTOR'S CHOICE

The Berkeley

MAYBOURNE
HOTEL GROUP

★★★★★ ⓐⓐⓐⓐⓐ 🍴 HOTEL PLAN 4 G5

Wilton Place, Knightsbridge, SW1X 7RL - **tel:** 020 7235 6000
email: info@the-berkeley.co.uk **web:** www.the-berkeley.co.uk
dir: *300mtrs from Hyde Park Corner along Knightsbridge*

This stylish hotel, just off Knightsbridge, boasts an excellent range of bedrooms, each furnished with care and a host of thoughtful extras. Newer rooms feature trendy, spacious, glass and marble bathrooms, and some of the private suites have their own roof terrace. The striking Blue Bar enhances the reception rooms, all of which are adorned with magnificent flower arrangements. Various eating options include the Collins Room which offers breakfast, all-day dining, and a wonderful afternoon tea. Marcus Wareing at The Berkeley has attained five AA Rosettes for stunning French cuisine, and a chef's table is available. The health spa offers a range of treatment rooms and includes a stunning open-air, roof-top pool.

Rooms: 190 (33 smoking) ⓕ **S** £315–£819; **D** £378–£945* **Facilities:** Spa STV FTV WiFi ⓦ ⓦ Gym Beauty/therapy treatments Personal training Xmas New Year **Conf:** Class 120 Board 54 Thtr 250 **Services:** Lift Night porter Air con **Parking:** 8 **Notes:** Civ Wed 250

INSPECTOR'S CHOICE

St James's Hotel and Club

★★★★★ ⓐⓐⓐⓐ TOWN HOUSE HOTEL PLAN 4 J6

7-8 Park Place, SW1A 1LP ⓕ - **tel:** 020 7316 1600
email: info@stjameshotelandclub.com **web:** www.stjameshotelandclub.com
dir: *On A4 near Picadilly Circus & St James's St*

Dating back to 1857, this elegant property with its distinctive neo-Gothic exterior is discreetly set in the heart of St James. Inside there is impressive decor created by interior designer Anne Maria Jagdfeld. Air-conditioned bedrooms are appointed to a very high standard and feature luxurious beds alongside a range of modern facilities. Stylish open-plan public areas offer a smart bar/lounge and the fine dining restaurant, Seven Park Place by William Drabble, which serves modern French dishes based on primarily British ingredients.

Rooms: 60 (8 family) (15 GF) ⓕ **Facilities:** STV FTV WiFi **Conf:** Class 30 Board 25 Thtr 40 **Services:** Lift Night porter Air con **Notes:** LB Civ Wed 40

Find out more
about the AA Hotel of the Year
for London on page 17

LONDON

LONDON SW1 *continued*

INSPECTOR'S CHOICE

COMO The Halkin

★★★★★ ◉◉◉ ⌷ TOWN HOUSE HOTEL PLAN 4 G5

Halkin Street, Belgravia, SW1X 7DJ - tel: 020 7333 1000
email: res.thehalkin@comohotel.com **web:** www.comohotels.com/thehalkin
dir: *Between Belgrave Sq & Grosvenor Place. Via Chapel St into Headfort Place,
left into Halkin St*

Set in an enviable and peaceful position just a short stroll from both Hyde Park
and the designer shops of Knightsbridge, COMO The Halkin can claim pride of
place in Belgravia, and combines the timeless with the contemporary.
The hotel's Georgian-styled façade of weathered bricks, Portland stone and
arching windows blends comfortably into its surroundings. Inside, the Milan-
based architecture studio Laboratorio Associati have created a scheme imbued
with a warm, contemporary spirit. For dining, Ametsa with Arzak Instruction
offers award-winning Basque cuisine, while The Halkin Bar offers all-day eating
including an Ametsa afternoon tea menu.

Rooms: 41 ⌁ **D** £565–£1825* **Facilities:** STV FTV WiFi ↳ Gym Complimentary use
of spa at sister hotel **Conf:** Class 20 Board 26 Thtr 40 **Services:** Lift Night porter
Air con **Notes:** LB

INSPECTOR'S CHOICE

AA HOTEL OF THE YEAR
FOR LONDON 2017–18

The Goring

★★★★★ ◉◉◉ ⌷ HOTEL PLAN 4 H4

Beeston Place, SW1W 0JW - tel: 020 7396 9000
email: reception@thegoring.com **web:** www.thegoring.com
dir: *Off Lower Grosvenor Place, just prior to Royal Mews*

This icon of British hospitality for over 100 years is centrally located and within
walking distance of the Royal Parks and principal shopping areas. Spacious
bedrooms and suites - some contemporary in style with state-of-the-art
technology, and others more classically furnished - all boast high levels of
comfort and quality. The Duchess of Cambridge stayed in the newly created
Royal Suite on the night before her wedding in 2011. Elegant day rooms include
the Garden Bar and the drawing room, both popular for afternoon tea and
cocktails. The stylish airy restaurant offers a popular menu of contemporary
British cuisine, and delightful private dining rooms are available. Guests will
experience a personalised service from the attentive and friendly team.

Rooms: 69 (9 family) ⌁ **S** £360–£615; **D** £410–£710* **Facilities:** STV WiFi ↳ 🏊
Gym Free membership of nearby health club Xmas New Year **Conf:** Board 20 Thtr
50 **Services:** Lift Night porter Air con **Parking:** 16 **Notes:** LB Civ Wed 50

INSPECTOR'S CHOICE

Jumeirah Carlton Tower

★★★★★ ⌷ HOTEL PLAN 4 F4

Cadogan Place, SW1X 9PY - tel: 020 7235 1234
email: jctinfo@jumeirah.com **web:** www.jumeirah.com
dir: *A4 towards Knightsbridge, right onto Sloane St. Hotel on left
before Cadogan Place*

This impressive hotel enjoys an enviable position in the heart of Knightsbridge,
overlooking Cadogan Gardens. The stunningly designed bedrooms, including a
number of suites, vary in size and style. Many have wonderful city views and all
have free WiFi. Leisure facilities include a glass-roofed swimming pool, a well-
equipped gym and a number of treatment rooms. The Rib Room Bar will soon be
replaced by a Tom Kerridge restaurant. Other options include the Club Room and
Chinoiserie.

Rooms: 216 (76 smoking) ⌁ **Facilities:** Spa STV FTV WiFi ↳ 🏌 Gym Golf
simulator (50 courses) 🎵 **Conf:** Class 250 Board 90 Thtr 400 **Services:** Lift
Night porter Air con **Parking:** 30 **Notes:** Civ Wed 400

Find out more about
the AA Hotel Group
of the Year – see page 19

LONDON

The Lanesborough

★★★★★ ◉◉◉ 🛏 HOTEL PLAN 4 G5

Hyde Park Corner, SW1X 7TA - **tel:** 020 7259 5599
email: mryan@lanesborough.com **web:** www.lanesborough.com
dir: *At Hyde Park corner*

The Lanesborough has recently benefited from a huge multi-million pound refurbishment; no detail too small and no luxury spared. Set in prestigious Knightsbridge, with panoramic views of Hyde Park, this elegant and luxurious hotel offers nearly a hundred rooms, including almost fifty suites, with a personal butler service for all guests 24 hours a day. Public areas include Céleste Restaurant, The Library Bar and the Withdrawing room. The Garden Room (a lounge for cigar connoisseurs), and the Spa Studio complete these first-class facilities.

Rooms: 93 (7 family) (6 GF) (38 smoking) 🐾 **S** £490–£4200; **D** £490–£4200*
Facilities: Spa STV FTV WiFi ♿ Gym Hydropool Rasul 🎵 Xmas New Year
Conf: Class 60 Board 45 Thtr 100 **Services:** Lift Night porter Air con **Parking:** 48
Notes: LB Civ Wed 100

Mandarin Oriental Hyde Park, London

★★★★★ ◉◉◉ 🛏 HOTEL PLAN 4 F5

66 Knightsbridge, SW1X 7LA - **tel:** 020 7235 2000
email: molon-reservations@mohg.com **web:** www.mandarinoriental.com/london
dir: *Harrods 400mtrs on right & Harvey Nichols directly opposite hotel*

Situated in fashionable Knightsbridge and overlooking Hyde Park, this iconic venue is a popular destination for highfliers, celebrities and the young and fashionable. Bedrooms, many with park views, are appointed to the highest standards with luxurious features such as the finest Irish linen and goose down pillows. Guests have a choice of dining options - Bar Boulud (with 2 AA Rosettes) offering a contemporary bistro menu of seasonal, rustic French dishes; and Dinner by Heston Blumenthal where the dishes are based on recipes that date back as far as the 14th century, but with Heston's legendary modern twist. The Mandarin Bar serves light snacks and cocktails. The stylish spa is a destination in its own right and offers a range of innovative treatments.

Rooms: 181 (30 smoking) 🐾 **S** £540–£1100; **D** £540–£1100* **Facilities:** Spa STV FTV WiFi ♿ ⚲ Gym Sanarium Steam room Vitality pool Zen colour therapy Relaxation area Xmas New Year **Conf:** Class 140 Board 70 Thtr 300 **Services:** Lift Night porter Air con **Parking:** 25 **Notes:** LB Civ Wed 250

Corinthia Hotel London

★★★★★ ◉◉ HOTEL PLAN 5 B6

Whitehall Place, SW1A 2BD - **tel:** 020 7930 8181
email: london@corinthia.com **web:** www.corinthia.com/london
dir: *M4 onto A4, follow Central London signs. Pass Green Park, right into Coventry St, 1st right into Haymarket, left into Pall Mall East, right into Trafalgar Sq, 3rd exit into Whitehall Place*

Steeped in history, this elegant hotel is reputed to be one of London's earliest, having opened in 1885. The team are welcoming and friendly and all requests are skilfully dealt with. Bedrooms, including suites and penthouses, are equipped to very high standards and offer all modern amenities. Eating options are The Northall with British cuisine and The Massimo Restaurant offering Mediterranean seafood. The Bassoon Bar is the place for cocktails and it's worth noting the counter which is actually an elongated piano. Afternoon tea is another highlight served in the stunning lobby lounge. The Espa Spa offers world-class facilities. Valet parking is available.

Rooms: 294 (10 family) (46 smoking) 🐾 **D** £438–£21600* **Facilities:** Spa STV WiFi ♿ ⚲ Gym Vitality pool Nail studio Hair salon Relaxation sleep pod Xmas New Year **Conf:** Class 120 Board 50 Thtr 250 **Services:** Lift Night porter Air con **Notes:** Civ Wed 250

LONDON SW1 *continued*

The Stafford London

★★★★★ ◎◎ ⊛ HOTEL PLAN 4 J6

16–18 St James's Place, SW1A 1NJ - tel: 020 7493 0111
email: reservations@thestaffordlondon.com **web:** www.thestaffordlondon.com
dir: *Exit Pall Mall into St James's St. 2nd left into St James's Place*

Tucked away in a quiet corner of St James's, this classically styled boutique hotel has an air of understated luxury. While much is unchanged here, there is a new restaurant – 'Game Bird' – which serves wonderful modern British food. The American Bar is a fabulous venue in its own right, festooned with an eccentric array of celebrity photos, caps and ties. Also, afternoon tea is a long established tradition here. From the pristine, tastefully decorated and air-conditioned bedrooms, to the highly professional, yet friendly service, this exclusive hotel maintains the highest standards. 26 stunning mews suites are also available.

Rooms: 105 (38 annexe) (8 GF) (2 smoking) ⊛ **S** fr £350; **D** fr £350*
Facilities: STV WiFi ↘ Gym Use of fitness club Xmas New Year **Conf:** Class 20 Board 24 Thtr 60 **Services:** Lift Night porter Air con **Notes:** Civ Wed 44

Taj 51 Buckingham Gate, Suites and Residences

★★★★★ ◎◎ ⊛ TOWN HOUSE HOTEL PLAN 4 J4

SW1E 6AF - tel: 020 7769 7766
email: info.london@tajhotels.com **web:** www.taj51buckinghamgate.co.uk
dir: *From Buckingham Palace into Spur Road. Right into Birdcage Walk, 1st left into Buckingham Gate, 100mtrs, hotel on right*

This all-suites hotel is a favourite with those who desire a quiet, sophisticated environment. Each of the suites has its own butler on hand plus a kitchen, and most have large lounge areas furnished in a contemporary style with modern accessories. There are one, two, three and four bedroom suites to choose from, which include the stunning Jaguar Suite and the spectacular Cinema Suite. The hotel has a spa and a well-equipped gym.

Rooms: 85 (85 family) (3 GF) ⊛ **D** £300–£700* **Facilities:** Spa STV FTV WiFi ↘ HL Gym Sauna Steam room Xmas New Year **Conf:** Class 90 Board 60 Thtr 180 **Services:** Lift Night porter Air con **Notes:** Civ Wed 150

41

★★★★★ ⊛ TOWN HOUSE HOTEL PLAN 4 H4

41 Buckingham Palace Road, SW1W 0PS - tel: 020 7300 0041
email: book41@rchmail.com **web:** www.41hotel.com
dir: *Opposite Buckingham Palace Mews entrance*

Small, intimate and very private, this stunning town house is located opposite the Royal Mews. Decorated in stylish black and white, bedrooms successfully combine comfort with state-of-the-art technology such as iPod docking stations, interactive TV and free high-speed internet access. Thoughtful touches such as fresh fruit, flowers and scented candles add to the very welcoming atmosphere. The large lounge is the focal point; food and drinks are available as are magazines and newspapers from around the world plus internet access. Attentive personal service and a host of thoughtful extra touches make 41 really special.

Rooms: 30 (2 family) ⊛ **S** £329–£499; **D** £369–£599* **Facilities:** STV WiFi ↘ Local health club Beauty treatments In-room spa **Conf:** Board 8 Del from £400 **Services:** Lift Night porter Air con

DUKES London

★★★★★ ⊛ HOTEL PLAN 4 J6

35 St James's Place, SW1A 1NY - tel: 020 7491 4840
email: bookings@dukeshotel.com **web:** www.dukeshotel.com
dir: *From Pall Mall into St James's St. 2nd left into St James's Place. Hotel in courtyard on left*

Discreetly tucked away in St James's, Dukes is over 100 years old. Its style is understated, with smart, well-equipped bedrooms and public areas. The

Penthouse Suite has its own balcony with views over Green Park. Facilities include a gym, marble steam room and body-care treatments. GBR (Great British Restaurant) is the new, all-day dining concept here, offering many British classics using the very best ingredients. A smart lounge and a sophisticated and buzzing cocktail bar add to guests' enjoyment, and Martinis are a must.

Rooms: 90 (40 family) (4 GF) ☎ **D** £356–£526* **Facilities:** STV FTV WiFi ⚡ Gym Steam room Health club Personal training Beauty treatment room Xmas New Year **Conf:** Class 30 Board 30 Thtr 70 **Services:** Lift Night porter Air con **Notes:** Civ Wed 60

The Park Tower Knightsbridge

★★★★★ 88% ⚜⚜⚜ HOTEL PLAN 4 F5

101 Knightsbridge, SW1X 7RN - tel: 020 7235 8050
email: theparktowerknightsbridge@reservestarwood.com
web: www.theparktowerknightsbridge.com
dir: *Adjacent to Harvey Nichols*

The hotel sits just a short walk from leafy Hyde Park and some of the most distinguished shops of Knightsbridge. The interiors are luxurious, with handcrafted pieces and marble bathrooms, while the iconic design of the building allows all guests views over Knightsbridge or the park. Relax in the Lounge, where an idyllic tea parlour with afternoon tea is served under magnolia blossom. Dining in Pascal Proyart's One-O-One restaurant is a must for fish lovers.

Rooms: 280 ☎ **Facilities:** STV FTV WiFi ⚡ Gym ♫ **Conf:** Class 60 Board 26 Thtr 120 **Services:** Lift Night porter Air con

Sofitel London St James

★★★★★ 88% ⚜⚜ HOTEL PLAN 4 K6

SOFITEL

6 Waterloo Place, SW1Y 4AN - tel: 020 7747 2200
email: H3144@sofitel.com **web:** www.sofitelstjames.com
dir: *3 mins walk from Piccadilly Circus & Trafalgar Square*

Located moments away from Trafalgar Square, Sofitel London St James offers a sophisticated yet relaxed welcome, enhanced by a spa; The Balcon, an all-day dining restaurant; and the Rose Lounge, ideal for afternoon tea. With 12 meeting rooms and a private dining room, the hotel can also cater for all manners of functions.

Rooms: 183 (102 family) ☎ **Facilities:** Spa STV WiFi ⚡ Gym So FIT So SPA Xmas New Year **Conf:** Class 120 Board 44 Thtr 170 **Services:** Lift Night porter Air con **Notes:** Civ Wed 140

The Royal Horseguards

★★★★★ 82% ⚜ HOTEL PLAN 5 B6

2 Whitehall Court, SW1A 2EJ - tel: 0871 376 9033 (Calls cost 7p per minute plus your phone company's access charge)
email: royalhorseguards@guoman.co.uk **web:** www.theroyalhorseguards.com
dir: *Trafalgar Sq to Whitehall, left to Whitehall Pl, turn right*

This majestic hotel in the heart of Whitehall sits beside the Thames and enjoys unrivalled views of the London Eye and the city skyline. Bedrooms, appointed to a high standard, are well equipped and some of the luxurious bathrooms are finished in marble. Impressive public areas and outstanding meeting facilities are also available.

Rooms: 282 (7 family) ☎ **Facilities:** STV WiFi Gym ♫ Xmas New Year **Conf:** Class 180 Board 84 Thtr 240 **Services:** Lift Night porter Air con **Notes:** Civ Wed 228

St Ermins Hotel

★★★★ 87% ⚜ HOTEL PLAN 4 K4

2 Caxton Street, St James Park, SW1H 0QW - tel: 020 7222 7888
email: reservations@sterminshotel.co.uk **web:** www.sterminshotel.co.uk
dir: *Just off Victoria St, directly opposite New Scotland Yard*

Located in an enviable London location, the delightful courtyard offers a sanctuary from the hustle and bustle of the city. St Ermins' day rooms are fresh, modern and innovative, with a respectful nod to the hotel's former character. No detail has been overlooked. Food is served in the popular Caxton Grill. Limited valet parking is available by arrangement.

Rooms: 331 (18 family) (12 GF) ☎ **Facilities:** STV FTV WiFi ⚡ HL Gym Xmas New Year **Conf:** Class 80 Board 60 Thtr 160 **Services:** Lift Night porter Air con **Parking:** 5 **Notes:** Civ Wed 160

The Rubens at the Palace

★★★★ 85% ⚜⚜ HOTEL PLAN 4 H4

THE RED CARNATION HOTEL COLLECTION

39 Buckingham Palace Road, SW1W 0PS - tel: 020 7834 6600
email: bookrb@rchmail.com **web:** www.rubenshotel.com
dir: *Opposite Royal Mews, 100mtrs from Buckingham Palace*

This hotel enjoys an enviable location close to Buckingham Palace. Stylish, air-conditioned bedrooms include the pinstripe-walled Savile Row rooms, which follow a tailoring theme, and the opulent Royal rooms, named after different monarchs. Public rooms include The Library fine dining restaurant, and a comfortable stylish cocktail bar and lounge. The team here pride themselves on their warmth and friendliness.

Rooms: 161 (25 family) ☎ **S** £239–£407; **D** £275–£479* **Facilities:** STV WiFi ⚡ Health club & beauty treatment available nearby ♫ Xmas New Year **Conf:** Class 50 Board 30 Thtr 90 Del from £299 **Services:** Lift Night porter Air con **Notes:** Civ Wed 80

Cavendish London

★★★★ 82% ⚜⚜ HOTEL PLAN 4 J6

81 Jermyn Street, SW1Y 6JF - tel: 020 7930 2111
email: info@thecavendishlondon.com **web:** www.thecavendish-london.co.uk
dir: *From Piccadilly, pass The Ritz, 1st right into Dukes St before Fortnum & Mason*

This smart, stylish hotel enjoys an enviable location in the prestigious St James's area, just a short walk from Green Park and Piccadilly. Bedrooms have a fresh, contemporary feel, and there are a number of spacious executive rooms, studios and suites. Elegant public areas include a spacious first-floor lounge and well-appointed conference and function facilities. The popular Petrichor restaurant is committed to sourcing sustainable ingredients, especially from British producers. A good value, pre-theatre menu is available.

Rooms: 230 (7 family) ☎ **Facilities:** STV WiFi HL **Conf:** Class 50 Board 40 Thtr 80 **Services:** Lift Night porter Air con **Parking:** 50

LONDON SW1 *continued*

Park Plaza Victoria London

★★★★ 79% ◎◎ HOTEL PLAN 4 J3

239 Vauxhall Bridge Road, SW1V 1EQ - tel: 020 7769 9999
email: ppvlinfo@pphe.com **web:** www.parkplaza.com
dir: *Turn right from Victoria Station*

This smart modern hotel close to Victoria station is well located for all of central London's major attractions. Air-conditioned bedrooms are tastefully appointed and thoughtfully equipped for both business and leisure guests. Airy, stylish public areas include an elegant and popular lounge bar and extensive conference facilities complete with a business centre. The exciting and buzzing Tozi dining space provides small 'cicchetti' dishes highlighting the best Italian produce.

Rooms: 299 ⬧ **S** £139–£409; **D** £139–£409* **Facilities:** STV FTV WiFi ⬧ HL Gym Sauna Steam room Xmas **Conf:** Class 260 Board 63 Thtr 550 **Services:** Lift Night porter Air con **Parking:** 36 **Notes:** Civ Wed 550

Millennium Hotel London Knightsbridge

★★★★ 78% ◎ HOTEL PLAN 4 F4

17 Sloane Street, Knightsbridge, SW1X 9NU - tel: 020 7235 4377
email: reservations.knightsbridge@millenniumhotels.co.uk
web: www.millenniumhotels.co.uk
dir: *From Knightsbridge tube station towards Sloane St. Hotel 70mtrs on right*

This fashionable hotel boasts an enviable location in Knightsbridge's chic shopping district. Air-conditioned, thoughtfully equipped bedrooms are complemented by a popular lobby lounge and the Tangerine Café Bar that serves food throughout the day. Le Chinois restaurant offers modern Chinese cuisine. Valet parking is available if pre-booked.

Rooms: 222 (41 family) **Facilities:** STV FTV WiFi ⬧ Xmas **Conf:** Class 80 Board 50 Thtr 120 **Services:** Lift Night porter Air con **Parking:** 11

hub by Premier Inn London Westminster

BUDGET HOTEL PLAN 4 K4

St James's Park, 15 Dacre Street, SW1H 0DJ - tel: 0871 5279608 (Calls cost 13p per minute plus your phone company's access charge) **web:** www.premierinn.com
dir: *Phone for directions.*

This modern hotel offers self-check-in kiosks, superfast free WiFi, and cleverly designed and compact bedrooms with all the entertainment and comfort you need: 40" TV, temperature and lighting controlled by a special Premier Inn app, Hypnos bed, and monsoon shower. The Deli+Bar is open for grab-and-go breakfast boxes, pastries, grilled sandwiches, Costa Coffee, beer, wine and more.

Rooms: 137

Premier Inn London Victoria

BUDGET HOTEL PLAN 4 J3

82-83 Eccleston Square, SW1V 1PS - tel: 0871 527 8680 (Calls cost 13p per minute plus your phone company's access charge) **web:** www.premierinn.com
dir: *From Victoria Station, right into Wilton Rd, 3rd right into Gillingham St, hotel 150mtrs*

High quality, budget accommodation ideal for both families and business travellers. Spacious, en suite bedrooms feature free WiFi and tea and coffee making facilities, and in most hotels, Freeview TV is also available. The adjacent family restaurant features a wide and varied menu.

Rooms: 110

Jumeirah Lowndes Hotel

AA Advertised PLAN 4 F4

21 Lowndes Street, SW1X 9ES - tel: 020 7823 1234
email: jlhinfo@jumeirah.com **web:** www.jumeirah.com
dir: *M4 onto A4 into London. Left from Brompton Rd into Sloane St. Left into Pont St, Lowndes St next left. Hotel on right*

This chic, contemporary hotel is a smart modern townhouse set in timelessly stylish Belgravia. Guests can enjoy a meal in the international bistro Lowndes Bar & Kitchen, or relax outside on The Terrace with an open-air barbeque. Bedrooms and suites all have a contemporary style with high-spec facilities such as iPads and WiFi. There are also extensive leisure facilities at the nearby Jumeirah Carlton Tower, which includes access to The Peak Health Club & Spa.

Rooms: 88 (12 family) ⬧ **D** £216–£450* **Facilities:** Spa STV FTV WiFi ⬧ ⬧ supervised Gym **Conf:** Class 15 Board 16 Thtr 25 **Services:** Lift Night porter Air con **Notes:** LB

The Z Hotel Victoria

AA Advertised PLAN 4 H4

5 Lower Belgrave Street, SW1W 0NR - tel: 020 3589 3990
email: victoria@thezhotels.com **web:** www.thezhotels.com
dir: *Near Victoria Station, via Buckingham Palace Rd/A3214*

Z Victoria is the ideal location for Victoria Station, one of the UK's busiest transport interchanges, as well as the Apollo Victoria Theatre, Belgrave Square, Sloane Square and Knightsbridge. The building is a designer conversion of a Victorian townhouse, set in a block of mixed architectural styles. Inside there are just over a hundred rooms, set over eight floors. Each room has an en suite wet room, crisp bed linen, 40" TV with Sky, and complimentary WiFi.

Rooms: 106 (8 GF) ⬧ **Facilities:** STV WiFi **Services:** Lift Air con

LONDON SW3

The Capital

★★★★★ ⚫⚫⚫ TOWN HOUSE HOTEL PLAN 4 F5

Basil Street, Knightsbridge, SW3 1AT - tel: 020 7589 5171
email: reservations@capitalhotel.co.uk **web:** www.capitalhotel.co.uk
dir: *20yds from Harrods, & Knightsbridge tube station*

Personal service is assured at this small, family-owned hotel set in the heart of Knightsbridge. Beautifully designed bedrooms come in a number of styles, but all rooms feature antique furniture, a marble bathroom and a thoughtful range of extras. Cocktails are a speciality in the delightful, stylish bar, while afternoon tea in the elegant, bijou lounge is a must. The signature restaurant 'Outlaw's at The Capital' provides stunning dishes, featuring the best in British seafood from Nathan Outlaw.

Rooms: 49 (4 family) ☎ S £295–£425; D £315–£495* **Facilities:** STV FTV WiFi ☼ Xmas New Year **Conf:** Class 24 Board 24 Thtr 30 **Services:** Lift Night porter Air con **Parking:** 7

The Egerton House Hotel

★★★★★ ⚫ TOWN HOUSE HOTEL PLAN 4 E4

THE RED CARNATION HOTEL COLLECTION

17 Egerton Terrace, Knightsbridge, SW3 2BX - tel: 020 7589 2412
email: bookeg@rchmail.com **web:** www.egertonhousehotel.com
dir: *Just off Brompton Rd, between Harrods & Victoria & Albert Museum, opposite Brompton Oratory*

This delightful town house enjoys a prestigious Knightsbridge location, a short walk from Harrods and close to the Victoria & Albert Museum. Air-conditioned

bedrooms and public rooms are appointed to the highest standards, with luxurious furnishings and quality antique pieces; an exceptional range of facilities include iPods, safes, mini bars and flat-screen TVs. Staff offer the highest levels of personalised, attentive service.

Rooms: 28 (5 family) (2 GF) ☎ S £295–£1600; D £295–£1600 **Facilities:** STV WiFi Xmas New Year **Conf:** Class 12 Board 10 Thtr 14 **Services:** Lift Night porter Air con

The Draycott Hotel

★★★★★ 80% TOWN HOUSE HOTEL PLAN 4 F3

26 Cadogan Gardens, SW3 2RP - tel: 020 7730 6466
email: reservations@draycotthotel.com **web:** www.draycotthotel.com
dir: *From Sloane Sq station towards Peter Jones, keep to left. At Kings Rd take 1st right into Cadogan Gdns, 2nd right, hotel on left corner*

Enjoying a prime location just yards from Sloane Square, this town house provides an ideal base in one of the most fashionable areas of London. Many regular guests regard this as their London residence and staff pride themselves on their hospitality. Beautifully appointed bedrooms include a number of very spacious suites and all are equipped to a high standard. Attractive day rooms, furnished with antique and period pieces, include a choice of lounges, one with access to a lovely sheltered garden.

Rooms: 35 (9 family) (2 GF) ☎ **Facilities:** STV FTV WiFi Beauty treatments Massage **Services:** Lift Night porter Air con

Find out more about AA Rosettes
– page 13

LONDON SW3 *continued*

The Levin

★★★★ TOWN HOUSE HOTEL PLAN 4 F4

28 Basil Street, Knightsbridge, SW3 1AS - tel: 020 7589 6286
email: reservations@thelevinhotel.co.uk **web:** www.thelevinhotel.co.uk
dir: *20yds from Harrods, & Knightsbridge tube station*

This sophisticated town house is the sister property to the adjacent Capital Hotel and enjoys a prime location on the doorstep of Knightsbridge's stylish department and designer stores. Bedrooms and en suites offer timeless elegance alongside a host of up-to-date modern comforts; extra touches include champagne bars, state-of-the-art audio-visual systems, and complimentary WiFi. Guests can enjoy all-day dining in the stylish, popular, lower ground-floor Metro Restaurant.

Rooms: 12 (1 GF) **D** £245–£379* **Facilities:** STV FTV WiFi ⇗ Xmas New Year
Services: Lift Night porter Air con **Parking:** 7

The Beaufort

★★★★ 80% TOWN HOUSE HOTEL PLAN 4 F4

33 Beaufort Gardens, SW3 1PP - tel: 020 7584 5252
email: reservations@thebeaufort.co.uk **web:** www.thebeaufort.co.uk
dir: *100yds past Harrods on left of Brompton Rd*

This friendly, attractive town house enjoys a peaceful location in a tree-lined cul-de-sac just a few minutes' walk from Knightsbridge. Air-conditioned bedrooms are thoughtfully furnished and equipped with CD player, movie channel access, safe, and free WiFi. Guests are offered complimentary drinks and afternoon cream tea with home-made scones and clotted cream. A good continental breakfast is served in bedrooms.

Rooms: 29 (3 GF) **S** £150–£228; **D** £216–£358* **Facilities:** STV FTV WiFi **Conf:** Thtr 10 Del from £150 **Services:** Lift Night porter Air con

Best Western Burns Hotel

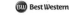

★★★ 75% METRO HOTEL PLAN 4 B3

18-26 Barkston Gardens, Kensington, SW5 0EN - tel: 020 7373 3151
email: info@burnshotel.co.uk **web:** www.burnshotel.co.uk
dir: *From A4, right to Earls Court Rd (A3220), 2nd left*

This friendly Victorian hotel overlooks a leafy garden in a quiet residential area not far from the Earls Court tube station. Bedrooms are attractively appointed, with modern facilities. Public areas, although not extensive, are stylish.

Rooms: 105 (10 family) **S** £50–£120; **D** £80–£165* **Facilities:** STV WiFi ⇗
Services: Lift Night porter

Premier Inn London Kensington (Earl's Court)

BUDGET HOTEL PLAN 4 B3

11 Knaresborough Place, SW5 0TJ - tel: 0871 527 8666 (Calls cost 13p per minute plus your phone company's access charge) **web:** www.premierinn.com
dir: *Just off A4 (Cromwell Rd). Nearest tube: Earls Court*

High quality, budget accommodation ideal for both families and business travellers. Spacious, en suite bedrooms feature free WiFi and tea and coffee making facilities, and in most hotels, Freeview TV is also available. The adjacent family restaurant features a wide and varied menu.

Rooms: 184

Premier Inn London Kensington (Olympia)

BUDGET HOTEL PLAN 4 A3

22-32 West Cromwell Road, SW5 9QJ - tel: 0871 527 8668 (Calls cost 13p per minute plus your phone company's access charge) **web:** www.premierinn.com
dir: *On N side of West Cromwell Rd, between juncts of Cromwell Rd, Earls Court Rd & Warwick Rd*

Rooms: 90

Millennium & Copthorne Hotels at Chelsea FC

★★★★ 78% HOTEL PLAN 1 E3

Stamford Bridge, Fulham Road, SW6 1HS - tel: 020 7565 1400
email: reservations@chelseafc.com **web:** www.millenniumhotels.co.uk
dir: *4 mins walk from Fulham Broadway tube station*

A unique destination in a fashionable area of the city. Situated at Chelsea's famous Stamford Bridge ground, the accommodation offered here is very up-to-the-minute. Bedroom facilities include flat-screen LCD TVs, video-on-demand, broadband, WiFi and good-sized desk space; larger Club rooms have additional features. For eating and drinking there's Frankie's, Marco Grill, 55 Bar and lounge, and for corporate guests a flexible arrangement of meeting and event rooms is available.

Rooms: 281 (64 family) **↖ S** £127.50–£300;* **Facilities:** STV WiFi ⇗ Stadium & museum tours **Conf:** Class 20 Board 25 Thtr 55 **Services:** Lift Night porter Air con

LONDON

Ibis London Earls Court

★★★ 72% HOTEL PLAN 4 A1

47 Lillie Road, SW6 1UD - **tel:** 020 7610 0880
email: h5623@accor.com **web:** www.ibishotel.com
dir: *From Hammersmith flyover towards London, keep in right lane, right at Kings pub on Talgarth Rd to join North End Rd. At mini-rdbt turn right. Hotel on left*

Ideally located for access to the Olympia Exhibition Centre, the London Underground, and fashionable Kensington, the Ibis London Earls Court offers a range of well-appointed rooms with superb beds and all modern amenities, including free WiFi. There are also extensive and flexible conference facilities, as well as a choice of dining options: La Table Restaurant with its daily changing self-service buffet and à la carte menu; plus The George & Dragon, a traditional English pub for a more relaxing and authentic experience. Secure, underground parking is also available.

Rooms: 504 (20 family) **Facilities:** FTV WiFi ⌕ **Conf:** Class 750 Board 25 Thtr 1200 **Services:** Lift **Parking:** 114

Premier Inn London Putney Bridge

BUDGET HOTEL PLAN 1 D2

3 Putney Bridge Approach, SW6 3JD - **tel:** 0871 527 8674 (Calls cost 13p per minute plus your phone company's access charge) **web:** www.premierinn.com
dir: *Nearest tube: Putney Bridge. Hotel on A219, N of River Thames*

High quality, budget accommodation ideal for both families and business travellers. Spacious, en suite bedrooms feature free WiFi and tea and coffee making facilities, and in most hotels, Freeview TV is also available. The adjacent family restaurant features a wide and varied menu.

Rooms: 179

LONDON SW7

INSPECTOR'S CHOICE

Bulgari Hotel, London

★★★★★ ⊛⊛⊛ HOTEL PLAN 4 F5

171 Knightsbridge, SW7 1DW - **tel:** 020 7151 1010
email: london@bulgarihotels.co.uk **web:** www.bulgarihotels.com/london
dir: *Almost opposite Hyde Park Knightsbridge*

This striking, contemporary hotel is in the heart of Knightsbridge and becomes the third Bulgari property, after Milan and Bali. Luxury accommodation is stylish and deeply comfortable, complete with Bulgari trunks mini-bar and beverage facility. Bathrooms are equally lavish with deep baths and rain showers. Spacious public areas include a stunning spa complete with a 25 metre swimming pool, separate vitality pool and range of treatment rooms. A unique,

hammered silver, oval bar provides the focal point of the bar with a sweeping staircase taking guests down to the Rivea London restaurant which is overseen by Alain Ducasse and his protégé Alexandre Nicolas. Immaculately attired staff offer high standards of service and hospitality.

Rooms: 85 (17 smoking) ⌕ **Facilities:** Spa STV WiFi ⌕ HL ⓣ Gym The Screening Room cinema Xmas New Year **Conf:** Class 80 Board 40 Thtr 100 **Services:** Lift Night porter Air con **Parking:** 6

INSPECTOR'S CHOICE

Baglioni Hotel London

★★★★★ ⊛ ⍟ HOTEL PLAN 4 C5

60 Hyde Park Gate, Kensington Road, SW7 5BB - **tel:** 020 7368 5700
email: info.london@baglionihotels.com **web:** www.baglionihotels.com
dir: *On corner of Hyde Park Gate & De Vere Gardens*

Located in the heart of Kensington and overlooking Hyde Park, this small hotel buzzes with Italian style and chic. Bedrooms, mostly suites, are generously sized and designed in bold dark colours; they have Illy espresso machines, interactive flat-screen TVs and a host of other excellent touches. Service is both professional and friendly. Public areas include the main open-plan space with bar, lounge and Brunello restaurant, all merging together with great elan; there is a spa with four treatment rooms and a techno-gym, and a fashionable private club bar downstairs.

Rooms: 67 (7 family) (30 smoking) ⌕ **S** £212–£6500; **D** £232–£6500* **Facilities:** Spa STV FTV WiFi ⌕ Gym Steam room ♫ Xmas New Year **Conf:** Class 48 Board 34 Thtr 65 **Services:** Lift Night porter Air con **Parking:** 2 **Notes:** LB Civ Wed 60

Crowne Plaza London - Kensington

★★★★ 79% HOTEL PLAN 4 C3

100 Cromwell Road, SW7 4ER - **tel:** 020 7373 2222
email: lonke.reservations@ihg.com **web:** www.cplondonkensingtonhotel.co.uk
dir: *Opposite Gloucester Road tube station. From M4 follow Central London signs. At Cromwell Rd hotel is visible on left*

A contemporary hotel with a grand Victorian townhouse façade offering accommodation that meets the needs of both leisure and business traveller. The spilt-level Superior Suites are ideal for families and long stays. Facilities include complimentary high-speed WiFi, a state-of-the-art fitness suite and sauna, to name but a few. A one-acre landscaped private garden is an oasis of peace and tranquillity. The ground-floor Umami Restaurant offers a real taste of Pan-Asian cooking and a relaxed atmosphere. There are two public car parks in the vicinity.

Rooms: 162 (74 family) ⌕ **Facilities:** STV FTV WiFi ⌕ Gym **Conf:** Class 64 Board 60 Thtr 150 **Services:** Lift Night porter Air con

LONDON SW7 *continued*

The Gore

★★★★ 78% TOWN HOUSE HOTEL PLAN 4 C4

190 Queen's Gate, SW7 5EX - tel: 020 7584 6601
email: reservations.thegore@starhotels.com **web:** www.gorehotel.com
dir: *Adjacent to Royal Albert Hall*

Convenient for many of London's attractions including the Royal Albert Hall and close to Gloucester Rd tube station stands this characterful townhouse. The lounge serves afternoon tea and 190 Queens Gate restaurant and Bar is popular with diners and guests wanting a pre-theatre meal/cocktail. The bedrooms are varied in size from the cosy classics to the more spacious suites, but all are well equipped and are high in quality.

Rooms: 50 **S** £160–£280; **D** £180–£380* **Facilities:** WiFi ⟑ Child facilities
Conf: Class 30 Board 30 Thtr 80 **Services:** Night porter Air con **Notes:** LB Civ Wed 80

The Rembrandt Hotel

★★★★ 78% HOTEL PLAN 4 E4

11 Thurloe Place, Knightsbridge, SW7 2RS - tel: 020 7589 8100
email: rembrandt@sarova.com **web:** www.sarova.com
dir: *M4 onto A4 Cromwell Rd into central London. Hotel opposite Victoria & Albert Museum*

In the heart of South Kensington and Knightsbridge, this attractive hotel has free WiFi and elegant Edwardian architecture. It is opposite the V&A Museum, while tube stations and Harrods are nearby. All of the smartly designed rooms feature a TV, a work desk, tea and coffee making facilities and a mini bar. Enjoy fine dining in the sophisticated Palette restaurant, or relax with a drink in the glamorous 1606 lounge bar. Guests at The Rembrandt have reduced-rate access to Aquilla Health and Fitness, a private health club adjacent to the hotel. This neighbourhood is a great choice for those interested in museums, parks and culture.

Rooms: 194 ⟑ **S** £159–£450; **D** £179–£495 (incl. bkfst) **Facilities:** Spa STV FTV WiFi ⟑ ⟑ Gym **Conf:** Class 84 Board 80 Thtr 200 Del from £230 **Services:** Lift Night porter Air con **Notes:** Civ Wed 200

Millennium Bailey's Hotel London Kensington

★★★★ 77% ⟑ HOTEL PLAN 4 C3

140 Gloucester Road, SW7 4QH - tel: 020 7373 6000
email: reservations.baileys@millenniumhotels.co.uk **web:** www.thebaileyshotel.co.uk
dir: *From A4, at Cromwell Hospital, into Knaresborough Place, to Courtfield Rd to corner of Gloucester Rd, hotel opposite tube station*

This elegant hotel has a town house feel and enjoys a prime location. The newly refurbished bedrooms and bathrooms have been completed to a high standard; each floor has a different theme reflecting the history of the building and national heritage. All rooms have been very well equipped and include large TVs, minibars and air-conditioning amongst other things. The public areas include a stylish, contemporary, and award-winning restaurant. Alfresco dining is available during the warmer months. Guests may also use the facilities at the larger sister hotel which is adjacent.

Rooms: 212 (27 family) ⟑ **Facilities:** FTV WiFi ⟑ HL Xmas New Year **Services:** Lift Night porter Air con **Parking:** 60

Millennium Gloucester Hotel London Kensington

★★★★ 76% HOTEL PLAN 4 C3

4-18 Harrington Gardens, SW7 4LH - tel: 020 7373 6030
email: reservations.gloucester@millenniumhotels.co.uk
web: www.millenniumhotels.co.uk
dir: *Opposite Gloucester Road underground station*

This spacious, stylish hotel is centrally located, close to The Victoria & Albert Museum and Gloucester Road tube station. Air-conditioned bedrooms are furnished in a variety of contemporary styles, and Clubrooms benefit from a dedicated club lounge with complimentary breakfast and snacks. A wide range of eating options includes Singaporean and Mediterranean cuisine.

Rooms: 610 (10 family) ⟑ **Facilities:** STV WiFi ⟑ HL Gym **Conf:** Class 300 Board 100 Thtr 500 **Services:** Lift Night porter Air con **Parking:** 110 **Notes:** Civ Wed 500

Holiday Inn London - Kensington Forum

★★★★ 75% HOTEL PLAN 4 C3

97 Cromwell Road, SW7 4DN - tel: 020 7370 6815 & 0871 942 9100
(Calls cost 10p per minute plus your phone company's access charge)
email: reservations@hikensington.co.uk **web:** www.hikensingtonforumhotel.co.uk
dir: *From S Circular onto N Circular at Chiswick Flyover. Onto A4 Cromwell Rd to Gloucester Rd*

This hotel is ideally situated within a few minutes' walk of the Gloucester Road underground station and close to many of London's attractions, such as the Natural History Museum, Science Museum, Kensington High Street and the West End. The bedrooms and bathrooms are well appointed and vary in size. The ground-floor areas include a gym and a stylish business lounge.

Rooms: 906 (26 family) **S** £119–£299; **D** £129–£329* **Facilities:** STV FTV WiFi ⟑ HL Gym Fitness room Xmas New Year **Conf:** Class 150 Board 50 Thtr 330 Del from £180 **Services:** Lift Night porter Air con **Parking:** 76 **Notes:** Civ Wed 250

LONDON SW8

Premier Inn London Clapham hotel

BUDGET HOTEL PLAN 1 E2

638-640 Wandsworth Road, Clapham, SW8 3JW - tel: 0871 527 9678 (Calls cost 13p per minute plus your phone company's access charge) **web:** www.premierinn.com
dir: *Phone for detailed directions*

High quality, budget accommodation ideal for both families and business travellers. Spacious, en suite bedrooms feature free WiFi and tea and coffee making facilities, and in most hotels, Freeview TV is also available. The adjacent family restaurant features a wide and varied menu.

Rooms: 92

LONDON SW9

Premier Inn London Brixton

BUDGET HOTEL PLAN 1 F2

457-461 Brixton Road, SW9 8HH - **tel:** 0871 527 9530 (Calls cost 13p per minute plus your phone company's access charge) **web:** www.premierinn.com
dir: *From South Circular Road, turn onto Brixton Hill/A23. Slight right onto Coldharbour Lane/A2217, hotel on left*

High quality, budget accommodation ideal for both families and business travellers. Spacious, en suite bedrooms feature free WiFi and tea and coffee making facilities, and in most hotels, Freeview TV is also available. The adjacent family restaurant features a wide and varied menu.

Rooms: 736

LONDON SW10

The Chelsea Harbour Hotel

★★★★★ 83% HOTEL PLAN 1 E3

Chelsea Harbour, SW10 0XG - **tel:** 020 7823 3000
email: reservations.chelseaharbour@millenniumhotels.com
web: www.thechelseaharbourhotel.co.uk
dir: *A4 to Earls Court Rd S towards river. Right into Kings Rd, left into Lots Rd*

Against the picturesque backdrop of Chelsea Harbour's small marina, this modern hotel offers spacious, comfortable accommodation. All rooms are suites, which are superbly equipped; many enjoy splendid views of the marina. In addition, there are also several luxurious penthouse suites. Public areas include a modern bar and restaurant, excellent leisure facilities (including a spa) and extensive meeting and function rooms.

Rooms: 158 (158 family) S £300–£450; D £325–£475 **Facilities:** Spa STV FTV WiFi ⌕ ⊗ Gym Sauna Steam room Relaxation lounge Hair salon Xmas New Year **Conf:** Class 250 Board 50 Thtr 500 **Services:** Lift Night porter Air con **Parking:** 2000 **Notes:** Civ Wed 450

LONDON SW18

Premier Inn London Wandsworth

BUDGET HOTEL PLAN 1 E2

45 Garratt Lane, SW18 4AD - **tel:** 0871 527 9486 (Calls cost 13p per minute plus your phone company's access charge) **web:** www.premierinn.com
dir: *From A3 (Wandsworth High St) at lights into Garratt Ln. Hotel on left*

High quality, budget accommodation ideal for both families and business travellers. Spacious, en suite bedrooms feature free WiFi and tea and coffee making facilities, and in most hotels, Freeview TV is also available. The adjacent family restaurant features a wide and varied menu.

Rooms: 120

LONDON SW19

Hotel du Vin Wimbledon

★★★★ 80% ⊛⊛ COUNTRY HOUSE HOTEL PLAN 1 D2

Cannizaro House, West Side, SW19 4UE - **tel:** 020 8879 1464
email: reservations@hotelduvin.com **web:** www.hotelduvin.com
dir: *From A3 follow A219 signed Wimbledon into Parkside, right into Cannizaro Rd, sharp right into West Side*

This unique, 18th-century house located opposite Wimbledon Common and set within 34 acres of Cannizaro Park, offers a tranquil setting, just a short distance from Central London. The hotel has a large stylish bar and dining options including the main restaurant, and the Orangery which enjoys excellent views of the terrace and common. Bedrooms are spacious and stylish with feature walls, high quality furnishings and a good range of amenities including coffee machines, WiFi and Sky TV. Function facilities are available and there is complimentary parking.

Rooms: 48 (5 family) (5 GF) S £124–£285; D £135–£305* **Facilities:** STV FTV WiFi ⌕ ⊘ **Conf:** Class 50 Board 40 Thtr 120 **Services:** Lift Night porter Air con **Parking:** 95 **Notes:** LB Civ Wed 200

Holiday Inn Express Wimbledon South

BUDGET HOTEL PLAN 1 E1

Miller's Meadhouse, 200 High Street, SW19 2BH - **tel:** 020 8545 7300
email: reservations@exhiwimbledon.co.uk **web:** www.exhiwimbledon.co.uk
dir: *A238 Kingston Rd, at lights into Merton High St, signed Colliers Wood. Hotel directly opposite Colliers Wood underground station*

A modern hotel ideal for families and business travellers. Fresh and uncomplicated, the spacious rooms include Sky TV, power shower and tea and coffee-making facilities. Continental buffet breakfast is included in the room rate; other meals may be taken at the nearby family pub or restaurant.

Rooms: 139 (92 family) (12 GF) **Conf:** Class 12 Board 12 Thtr 20

Premier Inn London Wimbledon South

BUDGET HOTEL PLAN 1 E1

27 Chapter Way, Off Merantun Way, SW19 2RF - **tel:** 0871 527 8684 (Calls cost 13p per minute plus your phone company's access charge) **web:** www.premierinn.com
dir: *M25 junct 10, A3 towards London. Exit A298 (Wimbledon) onto A238. Right onto A219, left onto A24 (Merantun Way). At rdbt 3rd exit signed Merton Abbey Mills*

High quality, budget accommodation ideal for both families and business travellers. Spacious, en suite bedrooms feature free WiFi and tea and coffee making facilities, and in most hotels, Freeview TV is also available. The adjacent family restaurant features a wide and varied menu.

Rooms: 134

LONDON

LONDON W1

INSPECTOR'S CHOICE

The Connaught

★★★★★ ◉◉◉◉◉ ⬢ HOTEL PLAN 2 G1

MAYBOURNE
HOTEL GROUP

Carlos Place, W1K 2AL - tel: 020 7499 7070
email: info@the-connaught.co.uk **web:** www.the-connaught.com
dir: *Between Grosvenor Sq & Berkeley Sq*

This iconic hotel is truly spectacular, with stunning interior design. There are sumptuous day rooms and stylish bedrooms with state-of-the-art facilities and marble en suites with deep tubs, TV screens and power showers. Butlers are available at the touch of a button and guests are pampered by friendly, attentive staff offering intuitive service. There is a choice of bars and restaurants including the Espelette bistro, and the award-winning cuisine of Hélène Darroze which is imaginative, inspired and truly memorable. The excellent Aman Spa at the hotel offers health and beauty treatments, a swimming pool and fitness centre.

Rooms: 121 (17 smoking) **Facilities:** Spa STV FTV WiFi Gym **Conf:** Class 70 Board 60 Thtr 120 **Services:** Lift Night porter Air con **Notes:** Civ Wed 200

INSPECTOR'S CHOICE

45 Park Lane

★★★★★ ◉◉◉ HOTEL PLAN 4 G6

45 Park Lane, W1K 1PN - tel: 020 7493 4545
email: reservations.45L@dorchestercollection.com **web:** www.45parklane.com
dir: *Park Lane, near The Dorchester*

This hotel offers luxurious and contemporary interiors. The bedrooms, including ten suites, all have a view of Hyde Park; the Penthouse Suite has its own roof terrace. A striking central staircase leads to a mezzanine featuring Bar 45, a library and a private media room. Other public areas include a lounge area and CUT at 45 Park Lane, a modern American steak restaurant.

Rooms: 46 **Facilities:** STV WiFi HL Gym **Services:** Lift Night porter Air con **Parking:** 12

INSPECTOR'S CHOICE

The Ritz London

★★★★★ ◉◉◉ ⬢ HOTEL PLAN 4 J6

150 Piccadilly, W1J 9BR - tel: 020 7493 8181
email: enquire@theritzlondon.com **web:** www.theritzlondon.com
dir: *From Hyde Park Corner E on Piccadilly. Hotel on right after Green Park*

This renowned, stylish hotel offers guests the ultimate in sophistication while still managing to retain all its former historic glory. Bedrooms and suites are exquisitely furnished in Louis XVI style, with fine marble bathrooms and every imaginable comfort. The Ritz London offers complimentary high-speed WiFi. Elegant reception rooms include the Palm Court with its legendary afternoon teas, the beautiful fashionable Rivoli Bar and the sumptuous Ritz Restaurant, complete with gold chandeliers and extraordinary trompe-l'oeil decoration.

Rooms: 136 (65 family) (24 smoking) **S** £430–£1130; **D** £430–£1130*
Facilities: STV FTV WiFi Gym The Ritz Club & Casino The Ritz Salon Xmas New Year **Conf:** Class 40 Board 30 Thtr 70 **Services:** Lift Night porter Air con **Parking:** 10 **Notes:** Civ Wed 60

Red Stars

The AA Red Star rating denotes an Inspector's Choice hotel. They stand out as the very best and appear in highlighted panels throughout the guide.

INSPECTOR'S CHOICE

The Athenaeum Hotel

★★★★★ ◉◉ HOTEL PLAN 4 H6

116 Piccadilly, W1J 7BJ - tel: 020 7499 3464
email: info@athenaeumhotel.com **web:** www.athenaeumhotel.com
dir: *On Piccadilly, overlooking Green Park*

With a discreet address in Mayfair, this well-loved hotel offers bedrooms appointed to the highest levels of comfort; all include Bose iPod speakers, a pillow menu and WiFi, and several boast views over Green Park. The hotel also has suites, and for the ultimate luxury there's a roof-top suite with a private balcony. The hotel bar is renowned for its range of whisky and cocktails created by Italian cocktail maker Giancarlo Mancino. Galvins at the Athenaeum offers wonderful French-inspired dishes with a British slant. A range of spacious and well-appointed apartments can be found in a row of Edwardian townhouses adjacent to the hotel. There is an extensive range of beauty treatments available along with conference and meeting facilities.

Rooms: 164 (18 family) (12 GF) ☏ **S** £292.80–£3000; **D** £292.80–£3000*
Facilities: Spa STV FTV WiFi Gym Beauty treatment room Steam rooms Sauna Free bike hire Xmas New Year **Conf:** Class 35 Board 36 Thtr 70 **Services:** Lift Night porter Air con **Notes:** LB Civ Wed 80

INSPECTOR'S CHOICE

Brown's Hotel

★★★★★ ◉◉ ◉ HOTEL PLAN 2 J1

ROCCO FORTE HOTELS

RF

Albemarle Street, Mayfair, W1S 4BP - tel: 020 7493 6020
email: reservations.browns@roccofortehotels.com **web:** www.roccofortehotels.com
dir: *A short walk from Green Park, Bond St, Piccadilly & Buckingham Palace*

Brown's is a London hospitality icon that maintains its charm through the

successful balance of traditional and contemporary. Bedrooms are luxurious, furnished to the highest standard and come with all the modern comforts expected of such a grand Mayfair hotel. The hotel has 29 suites including two Royal Suites and two Presidential Suites. The elegant, yet informal, HIX Mayfair serves a traditional selection of popular British dishes that are created with great skill, and it is also home to a collection of works by leading British artists. The English Tea Room proves a great meeting place for afternoon tea.

Rooms: 115 (33 family) ☏ **D** £475–£6500* **Facilities:** Spa STV WiFi ☈ Gym ♫ Xmas New Year Child facilities **Conf:** Class 30 Board 30 Thtr 70 Del from £110 **Services:** Lift Night porter Air con **Parking:** 4 **Notes:** Civ Wed 70

INSPECTOR'S CHOICE

The Dorchester

★★★★★ ◉◉◉◉ ◉ HOTEL PLAN 4 G6

Park Lane, W1K 1QA - tel: 020 7629 8888
email: reservations.TDL@dorchestercollection.com **web:** www.thedorchester.com
dir: *Halfway along Park Ln between Hyde Park Corner & Marble Arch*

One of London's finest, The Dorchester remains one of the best-loved hotels in the country and always delivers. The spacious bedrooms and suites are beautifully appointed and feature fabulous marble bathrooms. Leading off from the foyer, The Promenade is the perfect setting for afternoon tea or drinks. In the evening guests can relax to the sound of live jazz, while enjoying a cocktail in the stylish bar. Dining options include the sophisticated Chinese restaurant, China Tang; Alain Ducasse at The Dorchester from the world-renowned French chef of the same name; and of course, The Grill.

Rooms: 250 ☏ **S** £425–£1000; **D** fr £500* **Facilities:** Spa STV FTV WiFi ☈ HL Gym Steam rooms Fitness suite ♫ Xmas New Year **Conf:** Class 300 Board 42 Thtr 400 **Services:** Lift Night porter Air con **Notes:** LB Civ Wed 432

LONDON W1 *continued*

Four Seasons Hotel London at Park Lane

★★★★★ ◉◉ 🍽 HOTEL PLAN 4 G6

Hamilton Place, Park Lane, W1J 7DR - tel: 020 7499 0888
email: reservations@fourseasons.com **web:** www.fourseasons.com/london
dir: *From Piccadilly into Old Park Ln, into Hamilton Place*

This long-established popular hotel is discreetly located near Hyde Park Corner, in the heart of Mayfair. It successfully combines modern efficiencies with traditional luxury. Guest care is consistently of the highest order, even down to the smallest detail of the personalised wake-up call. The bedrooms are elegant and spacious, and the unique conservatory rooms are particularly special. Spacious public areas include extensive conference and banqueting facilities, Lane's bar and fine-dining restaurant, and an elegant lounge where wonderful afternoon teas are served.

Rooms: 193 (49 smoking) ✆ **D** fr £480* **Facilities:** Spa STV FTV WiFi ⚑
Gym Fitness Centre 🎵 Xmas New Year **Conf:** Class 174 Board 108 Thtr 375
Services: Lift Night porter Air con **Parking:** 10 **Notes:** Civ Wed 350

Claridge's

★★★★★ 🍽 HOTEL PLAN 2 H1

MAYBOURNE
HOTEL GROUP

Brook Street, W1K 4HR - tel: 020 7629 8860
email: info@claridges.co.uk **web:** www.claridges.co.uk
dir: *1st turn after Green Park tube station to Berkeley Sq & 4th exit into Davies St. 3rd right into Brook St*

Once renowned as the resort of kings and princes, Claridge's today continues to set the standards by which other hotels are judged. The sumptuous, air-

conditioned bedrooms are elegantly themed to reflect the Victorian or art deco architecture of the building. Fera at Claridge's, is now well established, and like the stylish cocktail bar, is a hit with residents and non-residents alike. Service throughout is meticulous and thoroughly professional.

Rooms: 190 (144 family) ✆ **S** £900; **D** £1020* **Facilities:** Spa STV WiFi Gym Beauty & health treatments Use of sister hotel's swimming pool 🎵 Xmas New Year **Conf:** Class 130 Board 60 Thtr 250 **Services:** Lift Night porter Air con **Notes:** Civ Wed 200

Hyatt Regency London – The Churchill

★★★★★ 87% ◉◉◉ HOTEL PLAN 2 F2

30 Portman Square, W1H 7BH - tel: 020 7486 5800
email: london.churchill@hyatt.com **web:** www.londonchurchill.regency.hyatt.com
dir: *From Marble Arch rdbt, follow signs for Oxford Circus into Oxford St. Left after 2nd lights into Portman St. Hotel on left*

This smart hotel enjoys a central location overlooking Portman Square. Excellent conference and in-room facilities, plus a fitness room make this the ideal choice for both corporate and leisure guests. To set the style, guests are greeted by stunning floral displays in the sophisticated lobby. The Montagu restaurant offers contemporary dining, plus the option to sit at the Chef's Table for a front row seat to watch all the action in the kitchen.

Rooms: 440 ✆ **S** fr £279; **Facilities:** STV FTV WiFi ⚑ 🛳 Gym Jogging track 🎵 Xmas New Year **Conf:** Class 160 Board 68 Thtr 250 **Services:** Lift Night porter Air con **Parking:** 48 **Notes:** Civ Wed 250

COMO Metropolitan London

★★★★★ 87% ◉◉ HOTEL PLAN 4 G6

Old Park Lane, W1K 1LB - tel: 020 7447 1000
email: res.met.lon@comohotels.com **web:** www.comohotels.com/metropolitanlondon
dir: *On corner of Old Park Ln & Hertford St*

Overlooking Hyde Park this hotel is located within easy reach of the fashionable stores of Knightsbridge and Mayfair. The hotel's contemporary style allows freedom and space to relax. Understated luxury is the key here with bedrooms enjoying great natural light. There is also a Shambhala Spa, steam room and fully equipped gym. For those seeking a culinary experience, Nobu offers innovative Japanese cuisine with an upbeat atmosphere.

Rooms: 144 (23 smoking) ✆ **S** fr £310; **D** fr £340* **Facilities:** Spa STV FTV WiFi ⚑ Gym Steam rooms **Conf:** Class 25 Board 30 Thtr 80 **Services:** Lift Night porter Air con **Parking:** 8 **Notes:** LB Civ Wed 80

The Langham, London

★★★★★ 87% ◉◉ HOTEL PLAN 2 H3

Portland Place, W1B 1JA - tel: 020 7636 1000 & 7965 0187
email: tllon.info@langhamhotels.com **web:** www.langhamhotels.com/london
dir: *N of Regent St, left opposite All Soul's Church*

This hotel has a grand entrance which leads into restored interior elegance. Dating back to 1865 the building displays a contemporary, luxurious style. Situated near Regent Street it is ideally located for both theatreland and the principal shopping areas. Bedrooms are delightfully appointed and many have excellent views. The Landau restaurant and Artesian bar offer high standards of service, delivered by a friendly team. Palm Court is a great place for afternoon tea or a glass of champagne. There is also an extensive health club complete with a 16-metre pool.

Rooms: 380 (5 family) **S** £360–£720; **D** £360–£720* **Facilities:** Spa STV WiFi HL supervised Gym Health club Sauna Steam room Xmas New Year **Conf:** Class 144 Board 80 Thtr 250 **Services:** Lift Night porter Air con **Notes:** Civ Wed 250

The Beaumont

★★★★★ 87% HOTEL PLAN 2 G1

8 Balderton Street, Mayfair, W1K 6TF - **tel:** 020 7499 1001
email: info@thebeaumont.com **web:** www.thebeaumont.com
dir: M1 junct 1/A41/A501, Oxford St onto North Audley St. 1st left onto North Row, 1st right onto Balderton St

The Beaumont is a beautifully renovated hotel in the Mayfair area, just a stone's throw from Oxford Street and many of London's attractions. This is the first hotel of restaurateurs, Chris Corbin and Jeremy King. The Art décor-style bedrooms vary in size and are deeply comfortable, with marble bathrooms and up-to-the-minute technology. The Art décor theme is continued into the public areas, which include the popular Colony Grill Room restaurant, American bar and residents' club lounge. A unique aspect of the hotel is ROOM, a monumental mixture of installation space, sculpture, and architecture by Antony Gormley. From the outside, ROOM looks like a crouching figure, perched on one part of the original building; inside is an unusual suite of rooms. Sculpture you can sleep in. The hotel also has a small spa, meeting room, gym and hair salon. A courtesy car is available subject to availability. The Beaumont was the AA Hotel of the Year for London 2016-2017.

Rooms: 73 (25 family) **D** fr £395 (incl. bkfst)* **Facilities:** Spa STV FTV WiFi HL Gym Sauna Steam room Xmas New Year **Conf:** Board 18 Thtr 40 **Services:** Lift Night porter Air con **Parking:** 3 **Notes:** LB

The Westbury Mayfair, A Luxury Collection Hotel, London

★★★★★ 85% HOTEL PLAN 2 H1

37 Conduit Street, Mayfair, W1S 2YF - **tel:** 020 7629 7755
email: reservations@westburymayfair.com **web:** www.westburymayfair.com
dir: From Oxford Circus S down Regent St, right onto Conduit St, hotel at junct of Conduit St & Bond St

A well-known London favourite with an international clientele, The Westbury Hotel is located in the heart of the Capital's finest shopping district, neighbour to the world's most exclusive fashion brands, restaurants and nightlife destinations. The standards of accommodation are very high throughout with newly renovated bedrooms and suites offering stunning panoramic views of picturesque Mayfair.

Foodies and cocktail fanatics will find plenty to enjoy in-house at Four AA Rosetted restaurant Alyn Williams at The Westbury, Tsukiji Sushi Restaurant, and the award-winning Polo Bar. Private dining is also available.

The Westbury Mayfair, A Luxury Collection Hotel, London

Rooms: 225 **Facilities:** STV FTV WiFi Gym Fitness centre Steam room Sauna Xmas New Year **Conf:** Class 45 Board 35 Thtr 100 **Services:** Lift Night porter Air con **Parking:** 10 **Notes:** Civ Wed 90

Grosvenor House, A JW Marriott Hotel

★★★★★ 85% HOTEL PLAN 2 G1

GROSVENOR HOUSE
A JW MARRIOTT HOTEL
LONDON

Park Lane, W1K 7TN - **tel:** 020 7499 6363
email: grosvenor.house@marriotthotels.com **web:** www.londongrosvenorhouse.co.uk
dir: Centrally located on Park Ln, between Hyde Park Corner & Oxford St

This quintessentially British hotel, overlooking Hyde Park, offers luxurious accommodation, warm hospitality and exemplary service that epitomises the fine hotel culture of London. The property boasts the largest ballroom in Europe, and there is a steakhouse and a cocktail bar. The Park Room and The Library make perfect settings for afternoon tea.

Rooms: 496 (10 family) (65 smoking) **Facilities:** STV WiFi Gym Fitness centre Xmas New Year **Conf:** Class 800 Board 140 Thtr 1500 **Services:** Lift Night porter Air con **Parking:** 48 **Notes:** Civ Wed 1500

LONDON W1 *continued*

The London EDITION

★★★★★ 84% ◉◉ HOTEL PLAN 2 J2

10 Berners Street, W1T 3NP - tel: 020 7781 0000
email: reservations.london@editionhotels.com **web:** www.editionhotels.com/london
dir: *Located in Fitzrovia on the edges of London's Soho neighbourhood, Central London*

The London EDITION is the latest from the EDITION portfolio, transforming this landmark building with innovation and truly great design. Excellent dining is provided in the Berners Tavern, under direction of award-winning chef Jason Atherton. The reservations-only Punch Room is a great place to unwind, with a traditional punch bowl. Service is personal and friendly with a modern twist, ensuring a flawless and memorable guest experience. A dynamic fusion of past and present makes the best use of space with stunning public areas and artwork. Bedrooms are finished in either light oak or dark walnut creating a cosy, cabin like feel; akin to that of a private yacht.

Rooms: 173 (12 family) ☎ **S** £285–£5995; **D** £285–£5995* **Facilities:** STV FTV WiFi ⇘ Gym ♬ **Conf:** Class 36 Board 14 Thtr 60 Del from £495 **Services:** Lift Night porter Air con

Hotel Café Royal

★★★★★ 83% ◉◉ HOTEL PLAN 2 J1

68 Regent Street, W1B 4DY - tel: 020 7406 3333
email: enquiries@hotelcaferoyal.com **web:** www.hotelcaferoyal.com
dir: *Please phone for directions*

This impressive and imposing hotel has an enviable location in Piccadilly. Public rooms are impressive and successfully blend modern and classic styles well. There is the popular café, the opulent Oscar Wilde bar for that traditional afternoon tea, and the Ten Room for all day dining. The Green bar specialises in cocktails and there is even a members club. The contemporary bedrooms are appointed to an extremely high standard, have marble bathrooms and are amply proportioned. The spa has a luxurious feel where guests can swim, use the gym or enjoy a range of treatments.

Rooms: 160 (111 family) ☎ **Facilities:** Spa STV FTV WiFi ⇘ HL ⊕ Gym ♬ Xmas New Year **Conf:** Class 60 Board 57 Thtr 160 **Services:** Lift Night porter Air con **Notes:** Civ Wed 120

The Arch London

★★★★★ 83% ◉ HOTEL PLAN 2 F2

50 Great Cumberland Place, W1H 7FD - tel: 020 7724 4700
email: info@thearchlondon.com **web:** www.thearchlondon.com
dir: *200yds from Marble Arch*

Convenient for many of London's attractions and close to Marble Arch Tube station, stands this luxurious hotel. The Martini Library serves afternoon tea, along with light-bites all day, and Hunter 486 offers relaxed dining for both lunch and dinner. Cocktails can be taken in Le Salon de Champagne. Bedrooms are varied in size from the cosy standards to the more spacious suites, but all are well equipped and are high in quality. There is also a well equipped gym for guest use.

Rooms: 82 (29 family) (8 GF) ☎ **S** £198–£570; **D** £228–£600* **Facilities:** STV FTV WiFi ⇘ Gym Xmas New Year **Conf:** Class 30 Board 20 Thtr 30 **Services:** Lift Night porter Air con **Notes:** LB

The Montcalm

★★★★★ 83% HOTEL PLAN 2 F2

Great Cumberland Place, W1H 7TW - tel: 020 7402 4288
email: reservations@montcalm.co.uk **web:** www.montcalm.co.uk
dir: *2 mins' walk N from Marble Arch station*

The Montcalm is ideally situated in the heart of London, just a short walk from Marble Arch, Oxford Street, Park Lane, Mayfair, Hyde Park and Theatreland. The elegantly decorated bedrooms are tastefully appointed and have many thoughtful touches. Public areas include a contemporary lounge bar and The Crescent restaurant which serves modern European cuisine. The hotel has a range of private rooms and conference suites, as well as spa, sauna, steam room, gym and exercise pool.

Rooms: 143 (17 family) (7 GF) ☎ **Facilities:** Spa STV WiFi ⊕ Gym **Conf:** Class 250 Board 250 Thtr 500 **Services:** Lift Night porter Air con **Notes:** Civ Wed 60

London Hilton on Park Lane

★★★★★ 81% ◉◉◉ HOTEL PLAN 4 G6

22 Park Lane, W1K 1BE - tel: 020 7493 8000
email: reservations.parklane@hilton.com **web:** www.parklanehilton.com
dir: *From N: M1/A41 towards central London & West End. W along Oxford St, into Park Lane. From S: A23 for central London & West End, cross Vauxhall Bridge (A202) & into Park Lane*

Located in the heart of Park Lane, this landmark hotel offers a luxury environment overlooking Hyde Park and the City. A dedicated team of staff is available to meet their guests' every need. Bedrooms are designed with quality appointments and luxury fabrics. Several eating options are available - from the renowned Galvin at Windows to the all-day dining of Podium, which also serves a splendid afternoon tea.

Rooms: 453 (52 smoking) ☎ **Facilities:** Spa STV FTV WiFi ⇘ Gym ♬ Xmas New Year **Conf:** Class 600 Board 60 Thtr 1100 **Services:** Lift Night porter Air con **Parking:** 242 **Notes:** Civ Wed 1000

Le Meridien Piccadilly

★★★★★ 80% ◉ HOTEL PLAN 2 J1

21 Piccadilly, W1J 0BH - tel: 020 7734 8000
email: reservations.piccadilly@lemeridien.com **web:** www.lemeridien.com/piccadilly
dir: *100mtrs from Piccadilly Circus*

Situated in the heart of Piccadilly, this well established hotel is ideally located for the West End and Theatreland. The well-equipped, air-conditioned bedrooms, varying in shape and size, are modern and contemporary in style. Public areas include extensive leisure facilities, with a state-of-the-art gym, pool and sauna, the trendy Longitude 0° 8' cocktail bar, and the popular Terrace Restaurant which overlooks Piccadilly.

Rooms: 283 (11 family) ☎ **S** £250–£500; **D** £270–£520* **Facilities:** Spa STV WiFi ⇘ ⊕ supervised Gym Squash ♬ Xmas New Year **Conf:** Class 160 Board 80 Thtr 250 Del from £300 **Services:** Lift Night porter Air con **Notes:** LB Civ Wed 200

INSPECTOR'S CHOICE

The Chesterfield Mayfair

★★★★ @@ HOTEL PLAN 4 H6

THE RED CARNATION HOTEL COLLECTION

35 Charles Street, Mayfair, W1J 5EB - tel: 020 7491 2622
email: bookch@rchmail.com **web:** www.chesterfieldmayfair.com
dir: *Hyde Park Corner along Piccadilly, left into Half Moon St.
At end left & 1st right into Queens St, then right into Charles St*

Quiet elegance and an atmosphere of exclusivity characterise this stylish Mayfair hotel where attentive, friendly service is paramount. The bedrooms, each with a marble-clad bathroom, have contemporary styles - perhaps with floral fabric walls, an African theme or with Savile Row stripes. In addition to these deluxe bedrooms there are 13 individually designed suites; some with four-poster beds and some with Jacuzzis. The Butler's Restaurant is the fine dining option, and The Conservatory, with views over the garden, is just the place for cocktails, light lunches and afternoon teas. The hotel is air-conditioned throughout.

Rooms: 107 📞 **S** £195–£390; **D** £220–£1470* **Facilities:** STV FTV WiFi ♨ ♫
Conf: Class 45 Board 45 Thtr 100 Del from £275 **Services:** Lift Night porter
Air con **Notes:** LB Civ Wed 120

The Mandeville Hotel

★★★★ 83% @ HOTEL PLAN 2 G2

Mandeville Place, W1U 2BE - tel: 020 7935 5599
email: sales@mandeville.co.uk **web:** www.mandeville.co.uk
dir: *3 mins walk from Bond St tube station*

This is a stylish and attractive boutique-style hotel with a very contemporary feel. Bedrooms are high in quality, are air conditioned and large, and have very comfortable beds. One of the suites, The Penthouse, has a patio with views over

London. The Reform Social & Grill Restaurant offers award-winning modern British cuisine, and the cocktail bar is always popular.

Rooms: 142 (6 family) 📞 **Facilities:** STV FTV WiFi ♨ Xmas New Year **Conf:** Class 20 Board 20 Thtr 40 **Services:** Lift Night porter Air con

Millennium Hotel London Mayfair

★★★★ 80% @@@ HOTEL PLAN 2 G1

MILLENNIUM HOTELS AND RESORTS

Grosvenor Square, W1K 2HP - tel: 020 7629 9400
email: reservations@millenniumhotels.co.uk **web:** www.millenniumhotels.co.uk
dir: *S side of Grosvenor Square, 5 mins walk from Oxford St & Bond St stations*

This hotel benefits from a prestigious location in the heart of Mayfair, close to Bond Street. Smart bedrooms are generally spacious and club-floor rooms have exclusive use of their own lounge with complimentary refreshments. A choice of bars and dining options is available along with conference facilities and a fitness room.

Rooms: 336 📞 **S** £216–£540; **D** £216–£540* **Facilities:** STV FTV WiFi ♨ HL Gym Fitness suite ♫ Xmas New Year **Conf:** Class 250 Board 70 Thtr 500 Del from £307
Services: Lift Night porter Air con **Notes:** LB Civ Wed 250

DoubleTree by Hilton Hotel, Marble Arch

★★★★ 78% HOTEL PLAN 2 F2

4 Bryanston Street, W1H 7BY - tel: 020 7935 2361
email: lonma.res@hilton.com **web:** www.londonmarblearch.doubletreebyhilton.com
dir: *Walking distance from Oxford St, Marble Arch & Hyde Park*

This hotel is a well located, historic property. The bedrooms, including executive and deluxe club floor rooms, vary in size but all are smartly equipped, boast bright trendy soft furnishings and are air conditioned; the en suites are equally modern and stylish. The public areas include the Indigo Bar & Lounge, and Fire & Spice Bar & Kitchen. The hotel offers free WiFi throughout.

Rooms: 122 (12 family) (5 GF) 📞 **S** £169–£269; **D** £199–£309 (incl. bkfst)*
Facilities: STV FTV WiFi ♨ HL Gym **Conf:** Class 45 Board 34 Thtr 90 Del from £300
Services: Lift Night porter Air con

Park Plaza Sherlock Holmes

★★★★ 71% HOTEL PLAN 2 F3

Park Plaza Hotels & Resorts

108 Baker Street, W1U 6LJ - tel: 020 7486 6161 & 0844 415 6740 (Calls cost 7p per minute plus your phone company's access charge)
email: info@sherlockholmeshotel.com **web:** www.sherlockholmeshotel.com
dir: *From Marylebone Flyover into Marylebone Rd. At Baker St turn right for hotel on left*

Chic and modern, this boutique-style hotel is near a number of London underground and rail stations. Public rooms include a popular bar, sited just inside the main entrance, and Sherlock's Grill, where the mesquite-wood burning stove is a feature of the cooking. The hotel also features an indoor health suite and a relaxing lounge.

Rooms: 119 (20 family) 📞 **Facilities:** STV WiFi ♨ Gym Beauty treatment room
Xmas **Conf:** Class 35 Board 30 Thtr 80 **Services:** Lift Night porter Air con
Notes: Civ Wed 80

LONDON W1 *continued*

Z at Gloucester Place

AA Advertised PLAN 2 F3

23 Gloucester Place, W1U 8JF - **tel:** 020 3551 3719
email: gloucesterplace@thezhotels.com **web:** www.thezhotels.com
dir: *Phone for details*

Z Hotels at Gloucester Place is a designer conversion of two individual townhouses, 23 and 33 Gloucester Place, ideally located between Portman Square and Marylebone Road. 23 Gloucester Place offers a comprehensive breakfast buffet and a 24/7 full alcohol license.

Rooms: 114

The Z Hotel Soho

AA Advertised PLAN 3 A2

17 Moor Street, W1D 5AP - **tel:** 020 3551 3701
email: soho@thezhotels.com **web:** www.thezhotels.com
dir: *Phone for directions*

Z Soho offers a Central London stay for an out-of-town price. This designer conversion of twelve Georgian townhouses combines classic architectural proportions with contemporary style. The rooms are gathered around a central courtyard, set between Charing Cross Road and Old Compton Street. Bedrooms have an en suite wet room, crisp bed linen, 40" TV with Sky, and complimentary WiFi.

Rooms: 85 🌫 **S** fr £95; **D** fr £120* **Facilities:** STV FTV WiFi ⮧ HL **Services:** Lift Air con

LONDON W2

HIGHLY RECOMMENDED

The Royal Park Hotel

★★★★ 85% ◉ TOWN HOUSE HOTEL PLAN 2 D2

3 Westbourne Terrace, W2 3UL - **tel:** 020 7479 6600
dir: *Phone for directions*

The Royal Park Hotel was once private residences in Westbourne Terrace, now converted into an quintessential townhouse hotel within walking distance of Hyde Park and all major attractions and fashionable restaurants. The elegant public areas have been refurbished in a classic yet contemporary style, while the bedrooms offer comfort and a reassuring homely feel. The award-winning restaurant offers a tapas-style menu for all dining occasions. Afternoon teas are served in bespoke china, and cocktails are expertly prepared in the evening. The rear terrace is a haven of tranquility. Limited parking available.

Rooms: 48 **S** £129–£299; **D** £129–£299*

Hotel Indigo

★★★★ 76% HOTEL PLAN 2 D2

16 London Street, Paddington, W2 1HL - **tel:** 020 7706 4444
email: malcolm@lth-hotels.com **web:** www.indigopaddington.com
dir: *Phone for directions*

This smart hotel is located within a stone's throw of Paddington Station. Contemporary and stylish, bedrooms vary in size but are equipped with all modern extras; they boast high quality comfy beds and en suites with power showers and quality toiletries. Delightful public areas include a restaurant, bar and a coffee shop offering tempting cakes. The cosy and tranquil seating area at the back of the property can be accessed from the first-floor's corridor. Parking is available at the nearby public car park.

Rooms: 64 🌫 **Facilities:** STV FTV WiFi HL Gym **Services:** Lift Night porter Air con

Novotel London Paddington

★★★★ 76% HOTEL PLAN 2 C3

3 Kingdom Street, Paddington, W2 6BD - **tel:** 020 7266 6000
email: h6455@accor.com **web:** www.novotel.com
dir: *Easy access from Westway A40 & Bishops Bridge Rd A4206*

Located in the Paddington Central area, this hotel is easily accessible by road, and is only a few minutes walk from Paddington Station. Ideal for business or leisure guests. The facilities include the Elements Restaurant, a bar, conference facilities, a swimming pool, sauna, plus steam and fitness rooms. An NCP car park is a 5-minute walk away.

Rooms: 206 (24 family) **Facilities:** STV WiFi ⮧ ⊛ Gym Steam room Sauna **Conf:** Class 70 Board 40 Thtr 150 **Services:** Lift Night porter

Lancaster Gate Hotel

★★★ 78% HOTEL PLAN 2 C1

66 Lancaster Gate, W2 3NA - **tel:** 020 7479 2500
email: info@lghhydepark.co.uk **web:** www.lancastergatehotelhydepark.co.uk
dir: *Just off Bayswater Rd*

This hotel offers a convenient location between Oxford Street and Knightsbridge and is also close to Hyde Park and Kensington Gardens. Bedrooms are well equipped with broadband and safes, as well as TVs with a wide range of channels. There is a comfortable bar and stylish restaurant, and the hotel also has a range of meeting rooms.

Rooms: 188 (7 family) (13 GF) (5 smoking) **S** £69–£229; **D** £74–£234*
Facilities: STV FTV WiFi Off site leisure facilities available **Conf:** Class 24 Board 28 Thtr 50 Del from £150 **Services:** Lift Night porter Air con **Notes:** LB No children 18yrs

Mitre House Hotel

★★ 76% METRO HOTEL PLAN 2 D2

178-184 Sussex Gardens, Hyde Park, W2 1TU - **tel:** 020 7723 8040
email: reservations@mitrehousehotel.com **web:** www.mitrehousehotel.com
dir: *Parallel to Bayswater Rd & one block from Paddington Station*

This family-run hotel continues to offers a warm welcome and attentive service. It is ideally located, close to Paddington station and near the West End and major attractions. Bedrooms include a number of family suites and there is a lounge bar. Limited parking is available.

Rooms: 69 (7 family) (7 GF) (69 smoking) **S** £80–£110; **D** £100–£145 (incl. bkfst)*
Facilities: STV WiFi ⮧ **Services:** Lift Night porter **Parking:** 20

Lancaster London

AA Advertised ◉◉ PLAN 2 D1

Lancaster Terrace, W2 2TY - **tel:** 020 7551 6000
email: book@lancasterlondon.com **web:** www.lancasterlondon.com
dir: *Adjacent to Lancaster Gate tube station, 1m from Paddington Heathrow Express, 1m from A40, opposite Hyde Park*

Located adjacent to Hyde Park, this large hotel offers a wide range of facilities. There are many room types; higher floors have excellent panoramic views of the city and park, and the suites are truly impressive. The hotel also offers two contrasting award-winning restaurants - the contemporary Island Restaurant & Bar, and Nipa restaurant with authentic Thai cuisine. There are spacious state-of-the-art, flexible conference and banqueting facilities, a 24-hour business centre and secure parking. This is an environmentally conscious hotel which has instigated many initiatives including a honey farm on the roof.

Rooms: 416 (40 family) (28 smoking) 🐾 **Facilities:** STV FTV WiFi ⌨ Gym Xmas New Year **Conf:** Class 550 Board 46 Thtr 1000 **Services:** Lift Night porter Air con **Parking:** 12 **Notes:** LB Civ Wed 1000

LONDON W4

Clayton Hotel Chiswick

★★★★ 78% HOTEL PLAN 1 C3

626 Chiswick High Road, W4 5RY - tel: 020 8996 5200
email: info.chiswick@claytonhotels.com **web:** www.claytonhotelchiswick.com
dir: Located 0.2m from Chiswick rbdt/London M4

This stylish, modern hotel is conveniently located for Heathrow and central London, with Gunnersby tube station just a few minutes' walk away. Airy, spacious public areas include a modern restaurant, a popular bar and excellent meeting facilities. Fully air-conditioned bedrooms are stylish and extremely well appointed with broadband, laptop safes and flat-screen TVs. All boast spacious, modern bathrooms, many with walk-in rain showers.

Rooms: 227 (10 family) (9 GF) 🐾 **Facilities:** STV FTV WiFi ⌨ Gym Xmas New Year **Conf:** Class 45 Board 40 Thtr 300 **Services:** Lift Night porter Air con **Parking:** 100 **Notes:** LB Civ Wed 300

Premier Inn London Chiswick

BUDGET HOTEL PLAN 1 D3

Hogarth Roundabout, Great West Road, W4 2TH - tel: 0871 527 9728 (Calls cost 13p per minute plus your phone company's access charge) **web:** www.premierinn.com
dir: Phone for directions

High quality, budget accommodation ideal for both families and business travellers. Spacious, en suite bedrooms feature free WiFi and tea and coffee making facilities, and in most hotels, Freeview TV is also available. The adjacent family restaurant features a wide and varied menu.

Rooms: 167

LONDON W5

Premier Inn London Ealing

BUDGET HOTEL PLAN 1 C3

22-24 Uxbridge Road, Ealing, W5 2SR - tel: 0871 527 9368 (Calls cost 13p per minute plus your phone company's access charge) **web:** www.premierinn.com
dir: M4 junct 1, A406 (signed North Circular & M1). Left onto A4020 (signed Ealing & Southall). Hotel on right after Ealing Broadway tube station

High quality, budget accommodation ideal for both families and business travellers. Spacious, en suite bedrooms feature free WiFi and tea and coffee making facilities, and in most hotels, Freeview TV is also available. The adjacent family restaurant features a wide and varied menu.

Rooms: 165

Premier Inn London Hanger Lane

BUDGET HOTEL PLAN 1 C4

1-6 Ritz Parade, Ealing, W5 3RA - tel: 0871 527 8346 (Calls cost 13p per minute plus your phone company's access charge) **web:** www.premierinn.com
dir: M4 junct 2, A4 follow North Circular/A406 signs, for 0.5m. Take A406 for approx 2.5m. Right into Ashbourne Rd, immediately left into Ashbourne Parade, right into Ritz Parade. Hotel on right

Rooms: 167

LONDON W6

Novotel London West

★★★★ 76% 🌐 HOTEL PLAN 1 D3

1 Shortlands, W6 8DR - tel: 020 8741 1555
email: H0737@accor.com **web:** www.novotellondonwest.co.uk
dir: M4 (A4) & A316 junct at Hogarth rdbt. Along Great West Rd, left for Hammersmith before flyover. On Hammersmith Bridge Rd to rdbt, take 5th exit. 1st left into Shortlands, 1st left to hotel main entrance

A Hammersmith landmark, this substantial hotel is a popular base for both business and leisure travellers. Spacious, air-conditioned bedrooms have a good range of extras and many have additional beds, making them suitable for families. The comfort of the bedrooms is complemented by a choice of dining options; the Aroma Restaurant offers a daily changing buffet style cuisine, the award-winning Artisan Grill with its à la carte menu of the highest quality meats and fish simply prepared, or the Lounge Bar for a more informal experience with a menu showcasing old favourites and light dishes. The hotel also has its own car park, business centre and shop, and boasts one of the largest convention centres in Europe.

Rooms: 630 (148 family) **D** fr £109 (incl. bkfst)* **Facilities:** STV WiFi Gym **Conf:** Class 540 Board 75 Thtr 1000 **Services:** Lift Night porter Air con **Parking:** 240 **Notes:** Civ Wed 1000

Premier Inn London Hammersmith

BUDGET HOTEL PLAN 1 D3

255 King Street, Hammersmith, W6 9LU - tel: 0871 527 8660 (Calls cost 13p per minute plus your phone company's access charge) **web:** www.premierinn.com
dir: From central London on A4 to Hammersmith, follow A315 towards Chiswick

High quality, budget accommodation ideal for both families and business travellers. Spacious, en suite bedrooms feature free WiFi and tea and coffee making facilities, and in most hotels, Freeview TV is also available. The adjacent family restaurant features a wide and varied menu.

Rooms: 119

LONDON W8

INSPECTOR'S CHOICE

Royal Garden Hotel

★★★★★ ◉◉◉ HOTEL PLAN 4 B5

2-24 Kensington High Street, W8 4PT - tel: 020 7937 8000
email: reservations@royalgardenhotel.co.uk **web:** www.royalgardenhotel.co.uk
dir: *Adjacent to Kensington Palace*

This landmark hotel, just a short walk from the Royal Albert Hall, has airy, stylish public rooms that include the Park Terrace Restaurant, Lounge and Bar; Bertie's cocktail bar and the contemporary 10th-floor Min Jiang Restaurant. The latter offers authentic Chinese cuisine and enjoys breathtaking views of the city.

The stylish and contemporary bedrooms are equipped with up-to-date facilities and include a number of spacious, air-conditioned rooms and suites with super views over Kensington Gardens. All rooms have iPod docking stations, flat-screen TVs and triple-glazed windows as standard.

Royal Garden Hotel

Rooms: 394 (59 family) (35 smoking) ✆ **S** £190–£440; **D** £230–£490*
Facilities: Spa STV FTV WiFi ⚓ HL Gym Health club Therapy Suites 🎵 Xmas New Year **Conf:** Class 320 Board 100 Thtr 550 **Services:** Lift Night porter Air con **Parking:** 200 **Notes:** Civ Wed 400

See advert below

The Milestone Hotel

★★★★★ ⊛⊛ 🍴 HOTEL PLAN 4 B5

1 Kensington Court, W8 5DL - **tel:** 020 7917 1000
email: bookms@rchmail.com **web:** www.milestonehotel.com
dir: *From Warwick Rd right into Kensington High St. Hotel 400yds past Kensington tube station. Adjacent to Kensington Palace*

This delightful town house enjoys a wonderful location opposite Kensington Palace and is near some seriously elegant shops. The individually themed bedrooms include a selection of stunning suites that are equipped with every conceivable extra - fruit, cookies, chocolates, complimentary newspapers and even the next day's weather forecast. Up-to-the-minute technology includes high speed WiFi and interactive TV. Public areas include the luxurious Park Lounge where afternoon tea is served, the delightful split-level Stables Bar, a conservatory, the sumptuous Cheneston's restaurant and a fully equipped small gym, resistance pool and spa treatment room.

Rooms: 62 (12 family) (1 GF) 🐾 **S** £360–£710; **D** £400–£760* **Facilities:** STV FTV WiFi ☆ HL 🏊 Gym Beauty treatment room Sauna Yoga 🎵 Xmas New Year **Conf:** Class 20 Board 20 Thtr 50 Del from £479 **Services:** Lift Night porter Air con **Parking:** 1 **Notes:** LB

See advert below

Copthorne Tara Hotel London Kensington

MILLENNIUM
HOTELS AND RESORTS

★★★★ 77% HOTEL PLAN 4 B4

Scarsdale Place, Wrights Lane, W8 5SR - **tel:** 020 7937 7211
email: reservations.tara@millenniumhotels.co.uk **web:** www.millenniumhotels.com
dir: *From Kensington High St into Wrights Ln. NB for Sat Nav use W8 5SY*

This expansive hotel is ideally placed for Kensington High Street shops and tube station. Smart public areas include a trendy coffee shop, a gym, a stylish brasserie and bar, plus extensive conference facilities. Bedrooms include several well-equipped rooms for less mobile guests, in addition to a number of Connoisseur rooms that have the use of a club lounge as one of its many complimentary facilities.

Rooms: 833 (3 family) 🐾 **Facilities:** FTV WiFi ☆ HL Fitness room Xmas New Year **Conf:** Class 160 Board 90 Thtr 280 **Services:** Lift Night porter Air con **Parking:** 126 **Notes:** Civ Wed 280

London Lodge Hotel

★★★ 78% TOWN HOUSE HOTEL PLAN 4 A3

134-136 Lexham Gardens, Kensington, W8 6JE - **tel:** 020 7244 8444
email: info@londonlodgehotel.com **web:** www.londonlodgehotel.com
dir: *Located in the heart of Kensington, close to Olympia exhibition centre. At junct of A4 & Cromwell Rd*

The London Lodge Hotel is made out of two beautiful Victorian town houses; sympathetically converted to form a home away from home. The hotel is located in a quiet residential area of Kensington, close to public transport and within walking distance of major attractions. All rooms are nicely appointed and offer all modern facilities.

Rooms: 28 (1 family) (6 GF) **S** £50–£250; **D** £70–£350 (incl. bkfst)* **Facilities:** FTV WiFi ☆ **Conf:** Class 15 Board 10 Thtr 25 Del from £100 **Services:** Lift Night porter Air con

LONDON

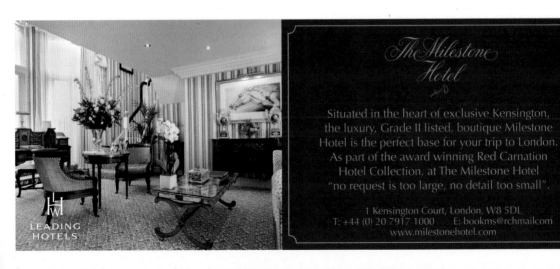

LONDON W14

K West Hotel & Spa

★★★★ 80% HOTEL PLAN 1 D3

Richmond Way, W14 0AX - tel: 020 8008 6600
email: info@k-west.co.uk **web:** www.k-west.co.uk
dir: *From A40(M) take Shepherd's Bush exit. At Holland Park rdbt 3rd exit. 1st left & left again. Hotel straight ahead*

This stylish, contemporary hotel is conveniently located for Notting Hill, the exhibition halls and the BBC; Bond Street is only a 10-minute tube journey away. Funky, minimalist public areas include a trendy lobby bar and mezzanine-style restaurant. Spacious bedrooms and suites are extremely well appointed and offer luxurious bedding and a host of thoughtful extras such as CD and DVD players. WiFi is available throughout. The spa offers a comprehensive range of health, beauty and relaxation treatments.

Rooms: 219 (31 GF) ☞ **S** £109–£259; **D** £119–£269* **Facilities:** Spa STV FTV WiFi ☝ Gym Hydrotherapy pool Sauna Steam room Snow room Solarium ♬ Xmas New Year **Conf:** Class 20 Board 25 Thtr 55 **Services:** Lift Night porter Air con **Parking:** 50

LONDON WC1

INSPECTOR'S CHOICE

Rosewood London

★★★★★ ◎◎ HOTEL PLAN 3 C3

252 High Holborn, WC1V 7EN - tel: 020 7781 8888
email: london@rosewoodhotels.com **web:** www.rosewoodhotels.com/london
dir: *200mtrs E from Holborn underground station*

Situated in the heart of Holborn, this impressive hotel was originally built in 1912, and designed by H. Percy Monckton in a flamboyant Edwardian style. Interior design by Tony Chi is striking, stylish, and unconventional in parts, and so combines a London residential feel which is wholly sympathetic to its many heritage features. Spacious public areas include the very popular Scarfes Bar, Holborn Dining Room and the elegant Mirror Room salon, complete with stunning flower displays, where afternoon tea is served. Modern contemporary accommodation is luxurious with many super touches, and includes an impressive range of suites.

Rooms: 306 (24 family) (10 smoking) ☞ **Facilities:** Spa STV FTV WiFi ☝ Gym Amethyst steam rooms Sauna Relaxation lounge ♬ Xmas New Year **Conf:** Class 255 Board 82 Thtr 370 **Services:** Lift Night porter Air con **Parking:** 10 **Notes:** Civ Wed 340

HIGHLY RECOMMENDED

The Montague on the Gardens

★★★★ 87% ◎ HOTEL PLAN 3 B3

15 Montague Street, Bloomsbury, WC1B 5BJ - tel: 020 7637 1001
email: bookmt@rchmail.com **web:** www.montaguehotel.com
dir: *Just off Russell Square, adjacent to British Museum*

This stylish hotel is situated right next to the British Museum. A special feature is the alfresco terrace overlooking a delightful garden. Other public rooms include the Blue Door Bistro and Chef's Table, a bar, a lounge and a conservatory where traditional afternoon teas are served. The bedrooms are beautifully appointed and range from split-level suites to more compact rooms.

Rooms: 100 (10 family) (19 GF) ☞ **S** £186–£354; **D** £210–£378* **Facilities:** STV FTV WiFi ☝ HL Gym ♬ Xmas New Year **Conf:** Class 50 Board 50 Thtr 120 Del from £270 **Services:** Lift Night porter Air con **Notes:** LB Civ Wed 90

The Principal London

★★★★ 76% HOTEL PLAN 3 B4

EST. 1898
PRINCIPAL
HOTEL COMPANY LTD

Russell Square, WC1B 5BE - tel: 020 7123 5000
email: londonreservations@theprincipalhotel.com
dir: *From A501 into Woburn Place. Hotel 500mtrs on left*

This landmark Grade II, Victorian hotel is located on Russell Square, within walking distance of the West End and theatre district. Many bedrooms are stylish and state-of-the-art in design, while others are more traditional. Spacious public areas include the impressive foyer with a restored mosaic floor, a choice of lounges and an elegant restaurant. As we went to press, we learnt that this hotel would re-open after a refurbishment in the autumn of 2017.

Rooms: 334 (2 family) ☞ **S** £175–£300; **D** £249–£500 **Facilities:** STV FTV WiFi HL Gym **Conf:** Class 200 Board 75 Thtr 450 **Services:** Lift Night porter Air con **Notes:** Civ Wed 300

Crowne Plaza London – Kings Cross

★★★★ 74% HOTEL PLAN 3 C5

CROWNE PLAZA
HOTELS & RESORTS

1 Kings Cross Road, WC1X 9HX - tel: 020 7833 3900
email: reservations@cplondon.co.uk **web:** www.ihg.com/crowneplaza/hotels
dir: *On corner of King Cross Rd & Calthorpe St*

Conveniently located for Kings Cross station and The City, this modern hotel offers smart, spacious air-conditioned accommodation with a wide range of facilities. There are versatile meeting rooms, a bar, a well-equipped fitness centre and a choice of restaurants including one serving Indian cuisine.

Rooms: 405 (163 family) (126 smoking) ☞ **Facilities:** Spa STV FTV WiFi HL ☝ Gym **Conf:** Class 120 Board 30 Thtr 220 **Services:** Lift Night porter Air con **Parking:** 14

Premier Inn London Euston

BUDGET HOTEL PLAN 3 A5

1 Duke's Road, Euston, WC1H 9PJ - tel: 0871 527 8656 (Calls cost 13p per minute plus your phone company's access charge) **web:** www.premierinn.com
dir: *On corner of Euston Road & Duke's Road, between Kings Cross/St Pancras & Euston stations*

High quality, budget accommodation ideal for both families and business travellers. Spacious, en suite bedrooms feature free WiFi and tea and coffee making facilities, and in most hotels, Freeview TV is also available. The adjacent family restaurant features a wide and varied menu.

Rooms: 265

Premier Inn London Holborn

BUDGET HOTEL PLAN 3 C3

27 Red Lion Street, WC1R 4PS - tel: 0871 527 9496 (Calls cost 13p per minute plus your phone company's access charge) web: www.premierinn.com
dir: *Nearest tube: Holborn & Chancery Lane*

Rooms: 150

LONDON WC2

INSPECTOR'S CHOICE

The Savoy

★★★★★ ◉◉◉ ⓢ HOTEL PLAN 3 C1

Strand, WC2R 0EU - tel: 020 7836 4343
email: savoy@fairmont.com web: www.fairmont.com/savoy
dir: *Halfway along The Strand between Trafalgar Sq & Aldwych & steps from Covent Garden*

The Savoy has been at the forefront of the London hotel scene since it opened in 1889. The hotel was lovingly restored in 2010, with much of its art deco and Edwardian heritage kept intact. The bedrooms, including an extensive range of stunning suites, vary in style and size, and many overlook the River Thames. The Savoy Grill and American Bar remain as well-loved favourites; Kaspar's offers informal yet luxury all-day dining; the Thames Foyer is renowned for its afternoon teas; and the Beaufort Bar offers cocktails that push the boundaries of mixology. Immaculately presented staff offer excellent standards of hospitality and service.

Rooms: 267 (5 family) (10 smoking) ⓡ Facilities: Spa STV FTV WiFi ⓑ ⓧ supervised Gym Fitness gallery Health & beauty treatments Personal training ♫ Xmas New Year Conf: Class 300 Board 60 Thtr 500 Services: Lift Night porter Air con Parking: 20 Notes: Civ Wed 300

Premier Inn London Leicester Square

BUDGET HOTEL PLAN 3 A1

1 Leicester Place, Leicester Square, WC2H 7BP - tel: 0871 527 9334 (Calls cost 13p per minute plus your phone company's access charge) web: www.premierinn.com
dir: *Nearest tube station: Leicester Sq. From Cranbourne St into Leicester Sq. Hotel on right (Leicester Pl). Car parks: China Town & Witcombe St, approx 10 mins walk*

High quality, budget accommodation ideal for both families and business travellers. Spacious, en suite bedrooms feature free WiFi and tea and coffee making facilities, and in most hotels, Freeview TV is also available. The adjacent family restaurant features a wide and varied menu.

Rooms: 83

The Z Hotel Piccadilly

Z HOTELS

AA Advertised PLAN 3 A1

2 Orange Street, WC2H 7DF - tel: 020 3551 3720
email: piccadilly@thezhotels.com web: www.thezhotels.com
dir: *Phone for directions*

Z Piccadilly is just a short walk from Piccadilly Circus, and offers a West End location for an out-of-town price. This is a converted office building, with 112 bedrooms arranged over lower ground, ground and five upper floors. Each room has an en suite wet room, crisp bed linen, 48" TV with Sky, and complimentary WiFi.

Rooms: 112 (10 GF) ⓡ Facilities: STV FTV WiFi Services: Lift Night porter Air con

LONDON GATEWAY MOTORWAY SERVICE AREA (M1) Map 6 TQ19
Greater London

Ramada London North - M1

AA Advertised

Welcome Break Services Area, M1 junct 2-4, NW7 3HU - tel: 020 8906 7000
email: ramadaln@welcomebreak.co.uk web: www.welcomebreak.co.uk
dir: *On M1 between junct 2/4 N'bound & S'bound*

This modern building offers accommodation in smart, spacious and well-equipped bedrooms, suitable for families and business travellers, and all with en suite bathrooms. Continental breakfast is available and other refreshments may be taken at the nearby family restaurant.

Rooms: 200 (190 family) (80 GF) (20 smoking) Facilities: FTV WiFi ⓑ Gym Conf: Class 30 Board 50 Thtr 70 Services: Lift Night porter Air con Parking: 160 Notes: Civ Wed 80

LONGHORSLEY Map 21 NZ19
Northumberland

Macdonald Linden Hall, Golf & Country Club

MACDONALD HOTELS & RESORTS

★★★★ 79% ◉◉ HOTEL

NE65 8XF - tel: 01670 500000 email: lindenhall@macdonald-hotels.co.uk
web: www.macdonaldhotels.co.uk
dir: *N'bound on A1 take A697 towards Coldstream. Hotel 1m N of Longhorsley*

This impressive Georgian mansion lies in 400 acres of parkland and offers extensive indoor and outdoor leisure facilities including a golf course. The Dobson Restaurant provides a fine dining experience, or guests can eat in the more informal Linden Tree pub. The good-sized bedrooms have a restrained modern style. The team of staff are enthusiastic and professional.

Rooms: 50 (3 family) (16 GF) ⓡ Facilities: Spa STV FTV WiFi ⓑ supervised ♨ 18 Putting green ⚘ ⚘ Gym Steam room Sauna Xmas New Year Conf: Class 120 Board 50 Thtr 300 Services: Lift Night porter Parking: 300 Notes: Civ Wed 120

L

L

LOOE
Cornwall & Isles of Scilly

Map 2 SX25

Trelaske Hotel & Restaurant

★★★ 83% ◎◎ HOTEL

Polperro Road, PL13 2JS - **tel:** 01503 262159
email: info@trelaske.co.uk **web:** www.trelaske.co.uk
dir: B252 signed Looe. Over Looe bridge signed Polperro. 1.9m, hotel signed on
left, turn right

This small and welcoming hotel offers comfortable accommodation, professional
and friendly service plus award-winning food. Set in its own very well-tended and
pretty grounds, it is only two miles from Polperro and Looe.

Rooms: 7 (4 annexe) (2 family) (2 GF) ✆ **S** £90–£100; **D** £110–£125 (incl. bkfst)*
Facilities: FTV WiFi **Conf:** Class 30 Board 40 Thtr 100 Del from £140 **Parking:** 50
Notes: LB Closed 17 Oct-1 Mar

Hannafore Point Hotel

★★★ 75% HOTEL

THE INDEPENDENTS
HOTEL ASSOCIATION

Marine Drive, West Looe, PL13 2DG - **tel:** 01503 263273
email: stay@hannaforepointhotel.com **web:** www.hannaforepointhotel.com
dir: A38, left onto A385 to Looe. Over bridge turn left. Hotel 0.5m on left

With panoramic coastal views of St George's Island around to Rame Head,
this popular hotel provides a warm welcome. The wonderful view is certainly a
feature of the spacious restaurant and bar, creating a scenic backdrop for both
dinners and breakfasts. Additional facilities include a heated indoor pool and
a gym.

Rooms: 37 (5 family) ✆ **S** £35–£80; **D** £70–£186 (incl. bkfst)* **Facilities:** Spa
FTV WiFi Gym Steam room Sauna Hydro pool & shower Xmas New Year
Conf: Class 80 Board 40 Thtr 120 Del from £60 **Services:** Lift Night porter
Parking: 32 **Notes:** LB Civ Wed 150

LOUGHBOROUGH
Leicestershire

Map 11 SK51

Burleigh Court Hotel and Conference Centre

★★★★ ⊞ HOTEL

Off Ashby Road, LE11 3TD - **tel:** 01509 211515
email: info@welcometoimago.com **web:** www.burleigh-court.co.uk
dir: M1 junct 23 then A512 Ashby Road to Loughborough. At 1st rdbt right into Holywell
Way, signed Burleigh Court & Holywell Park. Obtain visitors badge from gatehouse then
turn left at next rdbt & enter Loughborough University Campus using West Entrance. Hotel
car park on 2nd right

Set in the grounds of Loughborough University, with modern design, clean lines,
and bright, airy public areas, Burleigh Court is an ideal choice for anyone planning
a conference in the East Midlands, or visiting the Uni. Accommodation ranges from
luxury suites and executive rooms to high quality economy lodge rooms. The
restaurant and bar provide a wide choice of cuisine, made with locally-sourced
produce. Guests can enjoy extensive spa facilities, with a well-equipped gym, a
swimming pool, a whirlpool spa, a steam room, and a sauna. Conference facilities
are also extensive, and offer a wide range of packages and options.

Rooms: 225 (40 annexe) (8 family) (79 GF) ✆ **S** £88–£113; **D** £98–£123 (incl.
bkfst)* **Facilities:** Spa FTV WiFi HL Gym **Conf:** Class 90 Board 56 Thtr 200
Del from £133 **Services:** Lift Night porter **Parking:** 189 **Notes:** Closed 25-30 Dec Civ
Wed 200

Link Hotel

★★★ 78% HOTEL

New Ashby Road, LE11 4EX - **tel:** 01509 211800
email: info@linkhotel.co.uk **web:** www.linkhotelloughborough.co.uk
dir: M1 junct 23, follow A512 signed Loughborough. Continue on A512, turn left onto
slip road to reach hotel

Ideally located, close to Loughborough University, and only half a mile away from
junction 23 on the M1, this hotel offers modern and stylish accommodation, with
warm hospitality at the forefront. A modern restaurant, bar and lounge area are
available. A small gym is also on site.

Rooms: 94 (12 family) (47 GF) ✆ **S** £101; **D** £111 (incl. bkfst)* **Facilities:** FTV WiFi
Gym Xmas New Year **Conf:** Class 40 Board 30 Thtr 180 **Services:** Night porter Air con
Parking: 164 **Notes:** Civ Wed 154

Premier Inn Loughborough

BUDGET HOTEL

Premier Inn

Southfields Road, LE11 9SA - **tel:** 0871 527 9314 (Calls cost 13p per minute plus your
phone company's access charge) **web:** www.premierinn.com
dir: M1 junct 23, A512 towards Loughborough. Left into Greenclose Ln. Right onto A6,
Right into Southfield Rd, hotel on left

High quality, budget accommodation ideal for both families and business
travellers. Spacious, en suite bedrooms feature free WiFi and tea and coffee making
facilities, and in most hotels, Freeview TV is also available. The adjacent family
restaurant features a wide and varied menu.

Rooms: 112

LOUTH
Lincolnshire

Map 17 TF38

HIGHLY RECOMMENDED

Brackenborough Hotel

★★★ 88% ◎ HOTEL

Cordeaux Corner, Brackenborough, LN11 0SZ - **tel:** 01507 609169
email: reception@brackenborough.co.uk **web:** www.oakridgehotels.co.uk
dir: On A16, Louth to Grimsby road, 1m from Louth

In an idyllic setting amid well-tended gardens, this hotel offers attractive
bedrooms, each individually decorated with co-ordinated furnishings and many
extras. The award-winning bistro offers informal dining and the menu is based
on locally sourced produce. The hotel specialises in weddings, events and
private functions and has excellent conference facilities. Free WiFi is available.
Guests have free access to state-of-the-art leisure facilities (less than half a
mile away) that includes a swimming pool, tennis courts and a gym.

Rooms: 24 (2 family) (6 GF) ✆ **Facilities:** FTV WiFi Gym Xmas New Year
Conf: Class 150 Board 50 Thtr 300 **Services:** Night porter Air con **Parking:** 90
Notes: Civ Wed 220

Best Western Plus Kenwick Park Hotel

Best Western PLUS

★★★ 79% HOTEL

Kenwick Park Estate, LN11 8NR - **tel:** 01507 608806
email: enquiries@kenwick-park.co.uk **web:** www.kenwick-park.co.uk
dir: A16 from Grimsby, then A157 Mablethorpe/Manby Rd. Hotel 400mtrs
down hill on right

This elegant Georgian house is situated on the 320-acre Kenwick Park estate,
overlooking its own golf course. Bedrooms are spacious and comfortable, and

provide modern facilities. Public areas include a restaurant and a conservatory bar that overlook the grounds. There is also an extensive leisure centre and state-of-the-art conference and banqueting facilities.

Rooms: 34 (5 annexe) (10 family) (11 GF) **S** £85–£120; **D** £90–£140 (incl. bkfst) **Facilities:** Spa FTV WiFi 🕸 supervised 🏊 supervised ⛳ 18 Putting green 🏋 Gym Health & beauty centre Xmas New Year **Conf:** Class 40 Board 90 Thtr 250 Del from £130 **Services:** Night porter **Parking:** 100 **Notes:** LB Civ Wed 200

LOWER BARTLE
Lancashire — Map 18 SD43

Bartle Hall Hotel
★★★★ 78% ⍟ HOTEL

Lea Lane, PR4 0HA - **tel:** 01772 690506
email: info@bartlehall.co.uk **web:** www.bartlehall.co.uk
dir: *M6 junct 32 into Tom Benson Way, follow signs for Woodplumpton/Bartle Hall*

Ideally situated between Preston and Blackpool, Bartle Hall is within easy access of the M6 and the Lake District. Set in its own extensive grounds the hotel offers comfortable, well-equipped and renovated accommodation. The restaurant cuisine uses local produce and there is a large comfortable bar and lounge. There are also extensive conference facilities, and the hotel is a popular wedding venue.

Rooms: 15 (2 annexe) (3 family) (2 GF) 🕸 **S** £76–£120; **D** £86–£140 (incl. bkfst)* **Facilities:** FTV WiFi ☕ HL Xmas New Year **Conf:** Class 50 Board 40 Thtr 200 Del from £130 **Services:** Night porter **Parking:** 150 **Notes:** LB Civ Wed 130

LOWER BEEDING
West Sussex — Map 6 TQ22

South Lodge, an Exclusive Hotel
★★★★★ ⍟⍟⍟ 🍽 COUNTRY HOUSE HOTEL

Brighton Road, RH13 6PS - **tel:** 01403 891711
email: enquiries@southlodgehotel.co.uk **web:** www.exclusive.co.uk
dir: *A23, onto B2110. Right, through Handcross to A281 junct. Left, hotel on right*

This impeccably presented 19th-century lodge with stunning views of the rolling South Downs is an ideal retreat. There is the traditional and elegant Camellia Restaurant; as well as a more innovative take on the chef's table concept - a mini-restaurant within the kitchen itself. Guests can take a tour of the restored Victorian wine cellar, either with a sommelier or on their own. The elegant lounge is popular for afternoon teas. Bedrooms are individually designed with character and quality throughout. The conference facilities are impressive.

Rooms: 85 (11 family) (19 GF) 🕸 **D** fr £175.50 (incl. bkfst)* **Facilities:** STV WiFi ☕ 🏊 Fishing 🏋 Gym Mountain bikes Archery Clay pigeon shooting Wine tasting Xmas New Year Child facilities **Conf:** Class 100 Board 50 Thtr 180 **Services:** Lift Night porter **Parking:** 200 **Notes:** LB Civ Wed 130

LOWER SLAUGHTER
Gloucestershire — Map 10 SP12

The Slaughters Manor House
★★★★ ⍟⍟⍟ COUNTRY HOUSE HOTEL

ANdrew BROWNSWORD THE HOTELS

GL54 2HP - **tel:** 01451 820456
email: info@slaughtersmanor.co.uk **web:** www.slaughtersmanor.co.uk
dir: *Exit A429 signed 'The Slaughters'. Manor 0.5m on right on entering village*

The Slaughters Manor House, reopened in 2016 after three months of refurbishment, with a new, sophisticated countryside concept unveiled throughout the entire ground floor. Offering a contemporary interpretation of countryside life, the manor boasts well defined rooms, including a snug, billiards room, library and lounge, and a bar in partnership with the Sipsmith distillery. These alluring rooms are unified by the use of natural materials, finishes and objects, and a simple colour palette. The restaurant at The Slaughters Manor House is run by Nik Chappell, executive chef. Andrew Brownsword Hotels is the AA Hotel Group of the Year 2017-2018.

Rooms: 19 (8 annexe) (5 family) (4 GF) 🕸 **D** £240–£550 (incl. bkfst)* **Facilities:** STV FTV WiFi ☕ 🏊 Xmas New Year **Conf:** Class 40 Board 30 Thtr 70 Del from £280 **Services:** Night porter **Parking:** 20 **Notes:** LB Civ Wed 74

LOWESTOFT
Suffolk — Map 13 TM59 — **L**

Ivy House Country Hotel
★★★ 87% ⍟⍟ HOTEL

Ivy Lane, Beccles Road, NR33 8HY - **tel:** 01502 501353
email: aa@ivyhousecountryhotel.co.uk **web:** www.ivyhousecountryhotel.co.uk
dir: *On A146 SW of Oulton Broad turn into Ivy Ln beside Esso petrol station. Over railway bridge, follow private drive*

A peacefully located, family-run hotel set in 21 acres of mature landscaped grounds and just a short walk from Oulton Broad. Public rooms include an 18th-century thatched barn restaurant where an interesting choice of dishes is served. The attractively decorated bedrooms are housed in garden wings, and many have lovely views of the grounds to the countryside beyond.

Rooms: 21 (10 annexe) (2 family) (17 GF) 🕸 **S** £99–£130; **D** £140–£200 (incl. bkfst)* **Facilities:** FTV WiFi ☕ Xmas New Year **Conf:** Class 250 Board 100 Thtr 250 **Parking:** 300 **Notes:** Civ Wed 250

Premier Inn Lowestoft
BUDGET HOTEL

249 Yarmouth Road, NR32 4AA - **tel:** 0871 527 8688 (Calls cost 13p per minute plus your phone company's access charge) **web:** www.premierinn.com
dir: *On A12, 2m N of Lowestoft*

High quality, budget accommodation ideal for both families and business travellers. Spacious, en suite bedrooms feature free WiFi and tea and coffee making facilities, and in most hotels, Freeview TV is also available. The adjacent family restaurant features a wide and varied menu.

Rooms: 99

LUDLOW
Shropshire
Map 10 SO57

INSPECTOR'S CHOICE

Fishmore Hall
★★★ ⑩⑩ SMALL HOTEL

Fishmore Road, SY8 3DP - **tel:** 01584 875148
email: reception@fishmorehall.co.uk **web:** www.fishmorehall.co.uk
dir: A49 into Henley Rd. 1st right, Weyman Rd, at bottom of hill right into Fishmore Rd

Located in a rural area within easy reach of the town centre, this Palladian-style Georgian house has been sympathetically renovated and extended to provide high standards of comfort and facilities. The contemporary interior highlights many period features, and public areas include a comfortable lounge and restaurant, the setting for award-winning imaginative cooking.

Rooms: 15 (1 GF) ⌂ **S** £135–£275; **D** £175–£275 (incl. bkfst) **Facilities:** Spa FTV WiFi ⑤ Sauna Steam room Xmas New Year Child facilities **Conf:** Class 60 Board 40 Thtr 130 **Services:** Lift Night porter **Parking:** 48 **Notes:** LB Civ Wed 130

Overton Grange Hotel and Restaurant
★★★ 85% ⑩⑩ HOTEL

Old Hereford Road, SY8 4AD - **tel:** 01584 873500 & 0845 476 1000
(Calls cost 7p per minute plus your phone company's access charge)
email: info@overtongrangehotel.com **web:** www.overtongrangehotel.com
dir: A49, B4361 to Ludlow. Hotel 200yds on left

This is a traditional country-house hotel with stylish, comfortable bedrooms, and high standards of guest care. Food is an important part of what the hotel has to offer and the restaurant serves classically based, French-style cuisine,

using locally sourced produce whenever possible. Meeting and conference rooms are available.

Rooms: 14 ⌂ **Facilities:** FTV WiFi ⑤ Beauty treatment rooms Xmas **Conf:** Class 50 Board 30 Thtr 100 **Parking:** 45 **Notes:** No children 7yrs

The Feathers Hotel
★★★ 82% ⑩ HOTEL

The Bull Ring, SY8 1AA - **tel:** 01584 875261
email: enquiries@feathersatludlow.co.uk **web:** www.feathersatludlow.co.uk
dir: From A49 follow town centre signs to centre. Hotel on left

Famous for the carved woodwork outside and in, this picture-postcard 17th-century hotel is one of the town's best-known landmarks and is in an excellent location. Bedrooms are traditional both in style and decor. The public areas have retained much of the traditional charm, and the first-floor lounge is particularly stunning. Modern British menus are offered in the smart restaurant which has wooden beams and exposed brickwork.

Rooms: 40 (3 family) ⌂ **S** £95–£125; **D** £130–£230 (incl. bkfst)* **Facilities:** STV FTV WiFi ⑤ Xmas New Year **Conf:** Class 40 Board 40 Thtr 80 **Services:** Lift Night porter **Parking:** 33 **Notes:** LB

LUTON
Bedfordshire
Map 6 TL02

Luton Hoo Hotel, Golf & Spa
★★★★★ 84% ⑩⑩ ☺ HOTEL

The Mansion House, LU1 3TQ - **tel:** 01582 734437 & 698888
email: reservations@lutonhoo.com **web:** www.lutonhoo.com
dir: M1 junct 10 towards Harpenden & St Albans. Hotel approx 1m on left

A luxury hotel in more than 1,000 acres of 'Capability' Brown-designed parkland and formal gardens, with an 18-hole golf course and the River Lea meandering through. The centrepiece is the Grade I listed mansion house that has influences from many famous architects including Robert Adams. There are three sumptuous lounges where guests can enjoy afternoon tea and pre-dinner drinks, and two eating options - The Wernher Restaurant and the Adams Brasserie. The spacious bedrooms and impressive suites combine historic character with modern amenities. The Robert Adams Club House is the perfect place for relaxation, with a brasserie, a spa, golf, pool and gym, together with two bars. Warren Weir, on the river bank, is an exclusive retreat for weddings and meetings.

Luto Hoo Hotel, Golf & Spa

Rooms: 228 (50 family) (65 GF) 🐾 **D** £320–£1200 (incl. bkfst) **Facilities:** Spa FTV WiFi ⇘ HL 🐾 ⚓ 18 Putting green 🎣 Fishing 🏊 Gym Bird watching Clay pigeon shooting Archery Falconry Cycling Snooker 🎵 Xmas New Year **Conf:** Class 220 Board 60 Thtr 388 **Services:** Lift Night porter **Parking:** 316 **Notes:** Civ Wed 380

Icon Hotel

★★★ 83% HOTEL

15 Stuart Street, LU1 2SA - tel: 01582 722123
email: reservations@iconhotelluton.com **web:** www.iconhotelluton.com
dir: M1 junct 10 & 10A, A1081 signed Luton, left follow Luton Retail Park & station signs. Left at next rdbt, left at next rdbt onto A505 Park Viaduct. Straight on at next rdbt, left into Hastings St

This modern, purpose-built hotel occupies a prominent position close to the town centre and is a short drive from the international airport. The contemporary, open-plan bar is very comfortable and Capello's Restaurant offers a modern Mediterranean menu. The bedrooms are attractively presented and feature the latest technology along with large LCD TVs and complimentary WiFi. There is a range of business suites and a well-equipped gym.

Rooms: 62 (7 family) (6 GF) 🐾 **D** £69–£145* **Facilities:** FTV WiFi ⇘ Gym 🎵 Xmas New Year **Conf:** Class 20 Board 26 Thtr 45 **Services:** Lift Night porter Air con **Parking:** 18

Premier Inn Luton Town Centre

BUDGET HOTEL

Regent Street, LU1 5FA - tel: 0871 527 9542 (Calls cost 13p per minute plus your phone company's access charge) **web:** www.premierinn.com
dir: M1 junct 10 (S'bound), A1081 (Luton Airport). At 1st rdbt left onto London Rd (A1081). Into Castle St, left into Windsor St. 1st right into Chapel St. 1st left into Regent St. Hotel on left

High quality, budget accommodation ideal for both families and business travellers. Spacious, en suite bedrooms feature free WiFi and tea and coffee making facilities, and in most hotels, Freeview TV is also available. The adjacent family restaurant features a wide and varied menu.

Rooms: 120

Premier Inn Luton Airport

BUDGET HOTEL

Osborne Road, LU1 3HJ - tel: 0871 527 8690 (Calls cost 13p per minute plus your phone company's access charge) **web:** www.premierinn.com
dir: M1 junct 10, A1081 follow signs for Luton, at 3rd rdbt left into Gypsy Lane, left at next rdbt

High quality, budget accommodation ideal for both families and business travellers. Spacious, en suite bedrooms feature free WiFi and tea and coffee making facilities, and in most hotels, Freeview TV is also available. The adjacent family restaurant features a wide and varied menu.

Rooms: 134

Royal Lion Hotel

★★★ 77% HOTEL

Broad Street, DT7 3QF - tel: 01297 445622
email: enquiries@royallionhotel.com **web:** www.royallionhotel.com
dir: From W on A35 take A3052, or from E take B3165 to Lyme Regis. Hotel in town centre, opposite The Fossil Shop

This 17th-century, former coaching inn is full of character and charm, and is just a short walk from the seafront. Bedrooms vary in size; those in the newer wing are more spacious and some have balconies, sea views or a private terrace. In addition to the elegant dining room and guest lounges, a heated pool, Jacuzzi, sauna and small gym are available. A good selection of enjoyable, well-prepared dishes is offered in either the bar or main restaurant. There is a car park at the rear.

Rooms: 33 (8 family) (4 GF) 🐾 **S** £65–£78; **D** £120–£220 (incl. bkfst)*
Facilities: FTV WiFi 🐾 Sauna Games room Snooker tables Table tennis Xmas New Year **Conf:** Class 20 Board 20 Thtr 50 **Parking:** 33 **Notes:** LB

Macdonald Elmers Court Hotel & Resort

★★★★ 76% HOTEL

South Baddesley Road, SO41 5ZB - tel: 0344 879 9060
email: elmerscourt@macdonald-hotels.co.uk **web:** www.macdonaldhotels.co.uk
dir: M27 junct 1, through Lyndhurst, Brockenhurst to Lymington, hotel 200yds right after Lymington ferry terminal

Originally known as The Elms, this Tudor manor house dates back to the 1820s. Ideally located at the edge of the New Forest and overlooking The Solent with views towards the Isle of Wight, the hotel offers suites and self-catering accommodation in the grounds, along with a host of leisure facilities.

Rooms: 42 (42 annexe) (8 family) (22 GF) 🐾 **D** £98–£300 (incl. bkfst)*
Facilities: Spa FTV WiFi 🐾 🎾 supervised Putting green 🏊 Gym Squash Steam room Aerobics classes Sauna Table tennis Xmas New Year **Conf:** Class 70 Board 40 Thtr 120 Del from £140 **Services:** Night porter **Parking:** 100 **Notes:** LB Civ Wed 120

L

LYMINGTON *continued*

HIGHLY RECOMMENDED

Stanwell House Hotel

★★★ 88% ◎◎ HOTEL

14-15 High Street, SO41 9AA - **tel:** 01590 677123
email: enquiries@stanwellhouse.com **web:** www.stanwellhouse.com
dir: *M27 junct 1, follow signs to Lyndhurst then Lymington*

Stanwell House Hotel is a privately owned Georgian building situated on the wide high street only a few minutes from the marina, and a short drive from the New Forest. Styling itself as a boutique hotel, the bedrooms are individually designed; there are Terrace rooms with garden access, four-poster rooms, and Georgian rooms in the older part of the building. The four suites include two with their own roof terrace. Dining options include the informal bistro and the intimate Seafood Restaurant. Service is friendly and attentive. A meeting room is available.

Rooms: 29 (7 family) (7 GF) ⏺ **D** £125–£145 (incl. bkfst)* **Facilities:** FTV WiFi ⇣ Xmas New Year **Conf:** Class 35 Board 30 Thtr 70 Del from £150 **Services:** Night porter **Parking:** 12 **Notes:** Civ Wed 100

Premier Inn Lymington (New Forest Hordle)

BUDGET HOTEL

Silver Street, Hordle, SO41 0FN - **tel:** 0871 527 8692 (Calls cost 13p per minute plus your phone company's access charge) **web:** www.premierinn.com
dir: *M27 junct 1, A337. 3.5m, left into High St (A35) right into Gosport Ln. Left into Clay Hill (A337). Right into Grigg Ln (B3055). Approx 8m, left into Barrows Ln, right into Silver St*

High quality, budget accommodation ideal for both families and business travellers. Spacious, en suite bedrooms feature free WiFi and tea and coffee making facilities, and in most hotels, Freeview TV is also available. The adjacent family restaurant features a wide and varied menu.

Rooms: 20

INSPECTOR'S CHOICE

Lime Wood

★★★★★ ◎◎◎ COUNTRY HOUSE HOTEL

Beaulieu Road, SO43 7FZ - **tel:** 023 8028 7177
email: info@limewood.co.uk **web:** www.limewood.co.uk
dir: *Exit A35 onto B3056 towards Beaulieu, hotel 1m on right*

This meticulously restored country house situated deep in the New Forest, provides a wealth of facilities and much opulence. The hotel prides itself on its relaxed, friendly and attentive service, and has lots to interest and captivate. The luxurious bedrooms are notable; some are in the pavilion and some in the main house. A major attraction at Lime Wood is the restaurant, Hartnett Holder & Co which is headed up by Luke Holder and, as you'd expect, Angela Hartnett. The Herb House spa offers a hydrotherapy pool and many other excellent facilities along with a gym and steam room.

Rooms: 32 (16 annexe) (7 family) (5 GF) ⏺ **S** £275–£1050; **D** £275–£1050* **Facilities:** Spa STV FTV WiFi ⇣ ⦿ Gym Xmas New Year **Conf:** Board 30 Thtr 50 Del from £385 **Services:** Lift Night porter **Parking:** 60 **Notes:** Civ Wed 60

See advert on opposite page

L

LYNDHURST *continued*

Forest Lodge Hotel

★★★ 84% ◉◉ Ⓗ HOTEL

NEW FOREST HOTELS

Pikes Hill, Romsey Road, SO43 7AS - tel: 023 8028 3677
email: forest@newforesthotels.co.uk **web:** www.newforesthotels.co.uk
dir: *M27 junct 1, A337 towards Lyndhurst. In village, with police station*
& courts on right, take 1st right into Pikes Hill

Situated on the edge of Lyndhurst, this hotel is set well back from the main road.
The smart, contemporary bedrooms include four-poster rooms and family rooms;
children are very welcome here. The eating options are the Forest Restaurant and
the fine-dining Glasshouse Restaurant. There is an indoor swimming pool and
Nordic sauna.

Rooms: 36 (11 family) (10 GF) ⟋ **S** £50–£129; **D** £99–£189 (incl. bkfst)*
Facilities: FTV WiFi ⇗ HL ⓣ Xmas New Year Child facilities **Conf:** Class 70 Board 60
Thtr 120 **Parking:** 50 **Notes:** LB Civ Wed 90

Ormonde House Hotel

★★★ 73% METRO HOTEL

Southampton Road, SO43 7BT - tel: 023 8028 2806
email: enquiries@ormondehouse.co.uk **web:** www.ormondehouse.co.uk
dir: *M27/M271/A35 E through Ashurst, hotel on right on entering Lyndhurst*

Ormonde House is located on the edge of Lyndhurst village in the heart of the New
Forest, and provides comfortable en suite accommodation, with breakfast served in
the dining room and conservatory. It is dog friendly with ample off-street parking.
The ideal location for all New Forest activities and attractions.

Rooms: 21 (4 annexe) (2 family) (7 GF) ⟋ **Facilities:** FTV WiFi New Year **Parking:** 21
Notes: Closed 13-27 Dec

The Crown Manor House Hotel

AA Advertised ◉◉

High Street, SO43 7NF - tel: 023 8028 2992
email: stay@crownhotel-lyndhurst.co.uk **web:** www.crownhotel-lyndhurst.co.uk
dir: *Phone for details*

The Crown Manor House Hotel occupies a prime location in Lyndhurst. Bedrooms
vary in size, but all are comfortable and equipped to a high standard. Public areas
include the comfortable lounges, popular restaurant and airy breakfast room, all
retaining many of the original features of the property. On-site parking and quiet
gardens with terrace seating are further features.

Rooms: 50 (4 family) **D** fr £84 (incl. bkfst)* **Facilities:** FTV WiFi ⇗ Xmas New Year
Conf: Class 40 Board 30 Thtr 80 **Services:** Lift Night porter **Parking:** 50 **Notes:** LB
Civ Wed 100

LYTHAM ST ANNES	Map 18 SD32
Lancashire	

Clifton Arms Hotel

★★★★ 80% ◉◉ Ⓗ HOTEL

West Beach, Lytham, FY8 5QJ - tel: 01253 739898
email: welcome@cliftonarms-lytham.com **web:** www.cliftonarmslytham.com
dir: *On A584 along seafront*

This long established hotel occupies a prime position overlooking Lytham Green
and the Ribble Estuary beyond, and has been updated considerably in recent years.
Bedrooms vary in size and are appointed to a high standard; front-facing rooms
are particularly spacious and enjoy splendid views. There is an elegant restaurant,

a stylish open-plan lounge and cocktail bar, as well as modern function and
conference facilities. Afternoon teas are a highlight and served daily; as is
imaginative cuisine in the restaurant.

Rooms: 48 (2 family) ⟋ **S** £88–£118; **D** £140–£190 (incl. bkfst)* **Facilities:** STV FTV
WiFi ⇗ Xmas New Year **Conf:** Class 100 Board 60 Thtr 150 **Services:** Lift Night porter
Parking: 40 **Notes:** LB Civ Wed 100

Bedford Hotel

★★★ 82% ◉ HOTEL

307-313 Clifton Drive South, FY8 1HN - tel: 01253 724636
email: reservations@bedford-hotel.com **web:** www.bedford-hotel.com
dir: *From M55 follow signs for airport to last lights. Left through 2 sets of lights.*
Hotel 300yds on left

This popular family-run hotel is close to the town centre and the seafront.
Bedrooms vary in size and style and include superior and club class rooms. Newer
bedrooms are particularly elegant and tastefully appointed. Spacious public areas
include a choice of lounges, a coffee shop, fitness facilities and an impressive
function suite. The Restaurant offers imaginative dishes, skilfully prepared.

Rooms: 44 (6 GF) ⟋ **S** fr £65; **D** fr £110 (incl. bkfst)* **Facilities:** FTV WiFi ⇗
Gym Hydrotherapy spa bath Xmas New Year **Conf:** Class 140 Board 60 Thtr 160
Services: Lift Night porter **Parking:** 25 **Notes:** LB

Best Western Glendower Hotel

★★★ 80% ◉ HOTEL

Ⓑⓦ Best Western.

North Promenade, FY8 2NQ - tel: 01253 723241
email: recp@theglendowerhotel.co.uk **web:** www.glendowerhotel.co.uk
dir: *M55 follow airport signs. Left at Promenade to St Annes. Hotel 500yds from pier*

Located on the seafront and with easy access to the town centre, this popular,
friendly hotel offers comfortably furnished, well-equipped accommodation.
Bedrooms have been recently refurbished and vary in size and style including suites
and very popular and spacious family rooms. Public areas feature a choice of
smart, comfortable lounges, a bright, modern leisure club and function facilities.

Rooms: 61 (17 family) ⟋ **Facilities:** FTV WiFi ⇗ Gym Snooker room Table tennis room
♫ Xmas New Year **Conf:** Class 120 Board 50 Thtr 150 **Services:** Lift Night porter
Parking: 45 **Notes:** LB Civ Wed 150

MACCLESFIELD	Map 16 SJ97
Cheshire	

Premier Inn Macclesfield North

BUDGET HOTEL

Premier Inn

Tytherington Business Park, Springwood Way, SK10 2XA - tel: 0871 527 8694 (Calls cost
13p per minute plus your phone company's access charge) **web:** www.premierinn.com
dir: *On A523 in Tytherington Business Park*

High quality, budget accommodation ideal for both families and business
travellers. Spacious, en suite bedrooms feature free WiFi and tea and coffee making
facilities, and in most hotels, Freeview TV is also available. The adjacent family
restaurant features a wide and varied menu.

Rooms: 55

Premier Inn Macclesfield South West

BUDGET HOTEL

Congleton Road, Gawsworth, SK11 7XD - **tel:** 0871 527 8696 (Calls cost 13p per minute plus your phone company's access charge) **web:** www.premierinn.com
dir: *M6 junct 17, A534 towards Congleton, A536 towards Macclesfield to Gawsworth. Hotel on left*

Rooms: 28

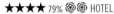

MAIDENCOMBE

See **Torquay**

MAIDENHEAD
Berkshire   **Map 6 SU88**

Fredrick's Hotel and Spa

★★★★ 79% ◎◎ HOTEL

Shoppenhangers Road, SL6 2PZ - **tel:** 01628 581000
email: reservations@fredricks-hotel.co.uk **web:** www.fredricks-hotel.co.uk
dir: *M4 junct 8/9, 1st exit off M404 signed Cox Green. Hotel on right, 300 yds after garage*

Set in attractive grounds on the fringes of Maidenhead, this stylish hotel has comfortable and well-equipped bedrooms. Public rooms include the Wintergarden restaurant, which serves afternoon tea as well as varied bar menus; and Fredrick's Restaurant which has a wide selection for lunch and dinner. There are also conference facilities, a fitness room, pool and spa. Fredrick's is a very popular venue for weddings.

Rooms: 37 (5 family) (14 GF) **D** £129–£209 **Facilities:** Spa FTV WiFi Gym Xmas New Year **Conf:** Class 65 Board 46 Thtr 100 Del from £209 **Services:** Night porter **Parking:** 80 **Notes:** LB Civ Wed 150

Premier Inn Maidenhead Town Centre

BUDGET HOTEL

Kidwells Park Drive, SL6 8AQ - **tel:** 0871 527 9520 (Calls cost 13p per minute plus your phone company's access charge) **web:** www.premierinn.com
dir: *From A308(M) towards Maidenhead. 1st exit at next rdbt onto A308. 2nd exit signed Braywick Rd/A308. 1st exit at next rdbt into Bad Godesberg Way. 3rd exit at next rdbt into Market St, right into West St, right into Kidwells Park Dr, hotel on right*

High quality, budget accommodation ideal for both families and business travellers. Spacious, en suite bedrooms feature free WiFi and tea and coffee making facilities, and in most hotels, Freeview TV is also available. The adjacent family restaurant features a wide and varied menu.

Rooms: 124

MAIDSTONE
Kent   **Map 7 TQ75**

Grange Moor Hotel

★★★ ⓐ HOTEL

4-8 St Michael's Road, ME16 8BS - **tel:** 01622 677623
email: reservations@grangemoor.co.uk **web:** www.grangemoor.co.uk
dir: *From town centre towards A26 Tonbridge rd. Hotel 0.25m on left, just after church*

Grange Moor Hotel is easily recognised in summer by its colourful hanging baskets. On offer are 50 well-appointed bedrooms that have TV, radio alarm clock, hairdryer,

and tea- and coffee-making facilities. There is a guest lounge area and a Tudor-style bar and restaurant.

Rooms: 50 (11 annexe) (5 family) (7 GF) **S** £46–£80; **D** £49–£150* **Facilities:** FTV WiFi **Conf:** Class 60 Board 40 Thtr 100 Del from £100 **Services:** Night porter **Parking:** 75 **Notes:** Closed 23-30 Dec Civ Wed 120

Premier Inn Maidstone (A26/Wateringbury)

BUDGET HOTEL

103 Tonbridge Road, Wateringbury, ME18 5NS - **tel:** 0871 527 8706 (Calls cost 13p per minute plus your phone company's access charge) **web:** www.premierinn.com
dir: *M25 junct 3 onto M20. Exit at junct 4 onto A228 towards West Malling. A26 towards Maidstone, approx 3m*

High quality, budget accommodation ideal for both families and business travellers. Spacious, en suite bedrooms feature free WiFi and tea and coffee making facilities, and in most hotels, Freeview TV is also available. The adjacent family restaurant features a wide and varied menu.

Rooms: 39

Premier Inn Maidstone (Allington)

BUDGET HOTEL

London Road, ME16 0HG - **tel:** 0871 527 8698 (Calls cost 13p per minute plus your phone company's access charge) **web:** www.premierinn.com
dir: *M20 junct 5, 0.5m on London Rd towards Maidstone*

Rooms: 65

Premier Inn Maidstone (Leybourne)

BUDGET HOTEL

Castle Way, Leybourne, ME19 5TR - **tel:** 0871 527 8702 (Calls cost 13p per minute plus your phone company's access charge) **web:** www.premierinn.com
dir: *M20 junct 4, A228, hotel on left*

Rooms: 40

Premier Inn Maidstone (Sandling)

BUDGET HOTEL

Allington Lock, Sandling, ME14 3AS - **tel:** 0871 527 8704 (Calls cost 13p per minute plus your phone company's access charge) **web:** www.premierinn.com
dir: *M20 junct 6, follow Museum of Kent Life signs*

Rooms: 40

Premier Inn Maidstone Town Centre

BUDGET HOTEL

5-11 London Road, ME16 8HR - **tel:** 0871 527 9392 (Calls cost 13p per minute plus your phone company's access charge) **web:** www.premierinn.com
dir: *M20 junct 5, A20 signed Maidstone (West) & Aylesford. At next rdbt 1st exit (Maidstone). Straight on at next rdbt*

Rooms: 99

M

MALMESBURY	Map 4 ST98
Wiltshire	

INSPECTOR'S CHOICE

Whatley Manor Hotel and Spa

★★★★★ ⊜ HOTEL

Easton Grey, SN16 0RB - tel: 01666 822888
email: reservations@whatleymanor.com web: www.whatleymanor.com
dir: M4 junct 17, follow signs to Malmesbury, continue over 2 rdbts.
Follow B4040 & signs for Sherston, hotel 2m on left

Sitting in 12 acres of beautiful countryside, this impressive country house provides the most luxurious surroundings. Spacious bedrooms, most with views over the attractive gardens, are individually decorated with splendid features which are high tech yet in keeping with the house paired with unique works of art. Several eating options are available, including Grey's, a relaxed brasserie; The Dining Room that serves modern British cuisine with Asian influences, via a choice of tasting menus; plus the Kitchen Garden Terrace for alfresco breakfasts, lunches and dinners. Guests might even like to take a hamper and a picnic rug and find a quiet spot in the grounds. The old Loggia Barn is ideal for wedding ceremonies, and the Aquarius Spa is magnificent.

Rooms: 23 (4 GF) ↝ S £325–£895; D £325–£895 (incl. bkfst)* Facilities: Spa STV FTV WiFi ↝ Fishing Gym Cinema Hydro pool (indoor/outdoor) Xmas New Year Conf: Class 20 Board 24 Thtr 60 Del £325 Services: Lift Night porter Parking: 100 Notes: LB No children 12yrs Civ Wed 100

Best Western Mayfield House Hotel

★★★ 75% ⊛ HOTEL

BW Best Western.

Crudwell, SN16 9EW - tel: 01666 577409
email: reception@mayfieldhousehotel.co.uk web: www.mayfieldhousehotel.co.uk
dir: M4 junct 17, A429 to Cirencester. 2m N of Malmesbury on left in Crudwell village

This popular hotel is in an ideal location for exploring many of the attractions that Wiltshire and The Cotswolds have to offer. Bedrooms come in a range of shapes and sizes, and include some on the ground-floor level in a cottage adjacent to the main building. In addition to outdoor seating, guests can relax with a drink in the comfortable lounge area, where orders are taken for the carefully prepared dinner to follow.

Rooms: 28 (8 annexe) (4 family) (8 GF) ↝ Facilities: FTV WiFi ↝ ⤳ Xmas New Year Conf: Class 30 Board 25 Thtr 40 Parking: 50 Notes: LB

MALTON	Map 19 SE77
North Yorkshire	

The Talbot Hotel

★★★★ 79% ⊛⊛ HOTEL

Yorkersgate, YO17 7AJ - tel: 01653 639096
email: enquiries@talbotmalton.co.uk web: www.talbotmalton.co.uk
dir: From York take A64, exit at Malton sign. Hotel on right

This hotel is owned by the Fitzwilliam Estate and is set in its own beautifully landscaped grounds close to the historic market town. The interior features individually decorated bedrooms, including two luxurious suites. Each of the guest rooms has its own distinct personality. The restaurant has elegant furniture, crisp white linen and fine silver cutlery, while the Brasserie offers a more relaxed setting. Elegant public areas can be found throughout this stunning hotel.

Rooms: 26 (3 GF) ↝ D £140–£320 (incl. bkfst)* Facilities: FTV WiFi HL Xmas New Year Conf: Class 30 Board 24 Thtr 60 Del £195 Services: Night porter Parking: 35 Notes: Civ Wed 60

MALVERN	Map 10 SO74
Worcestershire	

The Malvern

★★★★ 76% ⊛ HOTEL

Grovewood Road, WR14 1GD - tel: 01684 898290
email: enquiries@themalvernspa.com web: www.themalvernspa.com
dir: A4440 to Malvern. Over 2 rdbts, at 3rd rdbt turn left. 6m, left at rdbt, over 1st rdbt, hotel on right

This modern, friendly hotel is set on the outskirts of the famous spa town. The bedrooms are contemporary with sumptuous beds, and many guest extras are provided; the bathrooms have quality fixtures and fittings. There is a brasserie restaurant which offers quality seasonal menus that include healthy options and vegetarian dishes. The Malvern Spa, designed exclusively for adults, includes a hydrotherapy pool which goes from inside to outside, heat experiences, a range of saunas, crystal steam room, salt grotto, and adventure showers, along with a host of treatments. There is also a 50-station gym with state-of-the-art equipment. There is ample parking around the hotel.

Rooms: 33 ↝ S £110–£200; D £119–£209 (incl. bkfst) Facilities: Spa FTV WiFi ↝ ⊛ ⤳ Gym Exercise classes Xmas New Year Services: Lift Night porter Air con Parking: 82 Notes: LB No children 18yrs

The Abbey Hotel

★★★★ 76% HOTEL

SAROVA HOTELS

Abbey Road, WR14 3ET - tel: 01684 892332
email: abbey@sarova.com **web:** www.sarova.com
dir: *In Great Malvern town centre, opposite theatres*

This large, impressive, ivy-clad hotel stands in the centre of Great Malvern, at the foot of the Malvern Hills, next to the Abbey and close to the theatre. It provides well-equipped modern accommodation equally suitable for business guests and tourists. Facilities include a good range of function rooms making the hotel a popular venue for meetings and events.

Rooms: 103 (11 family) (23 GF) ♠ **S** £69–£160; **D** £79–£220 (incl. bkfst)*
Facilities: STV FTV WiFi ⓓ Xmas New Year **Conf:** Class 120 Board 40 Thtr 300 Del from £129 **Services:** Lift Night porter **Parking:** 85 **Notes:** LB Civ Wed 300

The Cottage in the Wood

★★★ 82% ⓖ ⓖ HOTEL

Holywell Road, Malvern Wells, WR14 4LG - tel: 01684 588860
email: reception@cottageinthewood.co.uk **web:** www.cottageinthewood.co.uk
dir: *On Ledbury side of Great Malvern on A449 Worcester - Ledbury road*

Set high on the hillside with stunning, far reaching views across the Worcestershire countryside, The Cottage in The Wood offers traditional rooms in the main house, as well as more cosy rooms in Beech Cottage. Also on offer is The Pinnacles; of the three this is the most recent addition and has larger room sizes and semi-private terraces or balconies. The main house has a very well-stocked bar, a cosy fire in winter and a large terrace which is ideal for sunny days. Dinner is not to be missed and involves innovative dishes utilising produce from within the three counties where possible.

Rooms: 30 (23 annexe) (10 GF) ♠ **Facilities:** FTV WiFi ⓓ HL Xmas New Year **Conf:** Class 14 Board 14 Thtr 20 **Parking:** 45

The Cotford Hotel & L'Amuse Bouche Restaurant

★★★ 81% ⓖ ⓖ HOTEL

51 Graham Road, WR14 2HU - tel: 01684 572427
email: reservations@cotfordhotel.co.uk **web:** www.cotfordhotel.co.uk
dir: *From Worcester follow signs to Malvern on A449. Left into Graham Rd signed town centre, hotel on right*

This delightful house, built in 1851, reputedly for the Bishop of Worcester, stands in attractive gardens with stunning views of The Malverns. Bedrooms have been authentically renovated, retaining many of the original features and with a good selection of welcome extras. Food, service and hospitality are all major strengths.

The Cotford Hotel & L'Amuse Bouche Restaurant

Rooms: 15 (3 family) (1 GF) ♠ **S** £75–£95; **D** £140–£155 (incl. bkfst) **Facilities:** STV FTV WiFi ⓓ ⓢ **Conf:** Class 26 Board 12 Thtr 26 **Parking:** 15 **Notes:** LB

See advert on following page

Holdfast Cottage Hotel

★★ 83% ⓖ HOTEL

Marlbank Road, Welland, WR13 6NA - tel: 01684 310288
email: enquiries@holdfast-cottage.co.uk **web:** www.holdfast-cottage.co.uk
dir: *M50 junct 1, follow Upton Three Counties/A38 signs, onto A4104 to Welland*

At the base of the Malvern Hills this delightful wisteria-covered hotel sits in attractive manicured grounds. Charming public areas include an intimate bar, a log fire-enhanced lounge and an elegant dining room. Bedrooms vary in size but all are comfortable and well appointed. Fresh local and seasonal produce are the basis for the cuisine.

Rooms: 8 (1 family) **S** £65; **D** £103 (incl. bkfst)* **Facilities:** FTV WiFi ⓓ Xmas New Year **Parking:** 16 **Notes:** LB Civ Wed 50

The Great Malvern Hotel

★★ 77% HOTEL

Graham Road, WR14 2HN - tel: 01684 563411
email: sutton@great-malvern-hotel.co.uk **web:** www.great-malvern-hotel.co.uk
dir: *From Worcester on A449, left after fire station into Graham Rd. Hotel at end on right*

Close to the town centre this privately owned and managed hotel is ideally situated for many of Malvern's attractions. The accommodation is spacious and well equipped. Public areas include quiet lounge areas, and a cosy bar which is popular with locals.

Rooms: 13 (1 family) **Facilities:** STV FTV WiFi ⓓ ♫ **Conf:** Class 20 Board 20 Thtr 20 **Services:** Lift **Parking:** 9

M

MALVERN *continued*

Colwall Park Hotel

Walwyn Riad, Colwall, WR13 6QG - **tel:** 01684 540000
email: hotel@colwall.com **web:** www.colwall.co.uk
dir: *Phone for directions*

Currently the rating for this establishment is not confirmed. This may be due to a change of ownership or because it has only recently joined the AA rating scheme.

Rooms: 22 **S** £70–£100; **D** £95–£200 (incl. bkfst)* **Facilities:** FTV WiFi Leisure facilities available at sister hotel – chargeable Xmas New Year **Conf:** Class 40 Board 50 Thtr 120 Del from £120 **Parking:** 36 **Notes:** LB Civ Wed 80

Premier Inn Malvern

BUDGET HOTEL

Townsend Way, WR14 1GD - **tel:** 0871 527 9406 (Calls cost 13p per minute plus your phone company's access charge) **web:** www.premierinn.com
dir: *M5 junct 7, A44 (1st exit from S; 3rd exit from N). At rdbt 1st exit onto A440. 1st exit at 3rd rdbt onto A449 (Malvern Rd). At next rdbt 1st exit into Townsend Way (B4208). At next rdbt 2nd exit into Grove Wood Rd*

High quality, budget accommodation ideal for both families and business travellers. Spacious, en suite bedrooms feature free WiFi and tea and coffee making facilities, and in most hotels, Freeview TV is also available. The adjacent family restaurant features a wide and varied menu.

Rooms: 66

MANCHESTER

MANCHESTER
Greater Manchester

Map 16 SJ89

See also **Manchester Airport & Sale**

Hotel Gotham

★★★★★ 84% ◎◎ HOTEL

100 King Street, M2 4WU - **tel:** 0161 4130000
email: reservations@hotelgotham.co.uk **web:** www.bespokehotels.com/hotelgotham
dir: *Phone for directions*

A new addition to the Manchester scene, Hotel Gotham is a beautifully renovated former bank designed by Edwin Lutyens, with Art decor themes throughout. The Brass Club is a popular cocktail bar with balconies overlooking the city, while Honey, the hotel's restaurant offers innovative cooking. Bedrooms and bathrooms are spacious and stylish, and there are subtle references to the hotel's former life everywhere.

Rooms: 60 (8 family) **Facilities:** WiFi Xmas New Year **Conf:** Class 14 Board 14 Thtr 20 **Services:** Lift Night porter Air con **Parking:** 40 **Notes:** LB

The Lowry Hotel

★★★★★ 84% ◎◎ HOTEL

50 Dearmans Place, Chapel Wharf, M3 5LH - **tel:** 0161 827 4000
email: enquiries@thelowryhotel.com **web:** www.thelowryhotel.com
dir: *M6 junct 19, A556/M56/A5103 for 4.5m. At rdbt take A57(M) to lights, right onto Water St. Left to New Quay St/Trinity Way. At 1st lights right into Chapel St for hotel*

This modern, contemporary hotel, set beside the River Irwell in the centre of the city, offers spacious bedrooms equipped to meet the needs of business and leisure visitors alike. Many of the rooms look out over the river, as do the sumptuous suites. The River Room restaurant produces good brasserie cooking. Extensive business and function facilities are available, together with a spa to provide extra pampering.

Rooms: 165 **S** £119–£699; **D** £119–£699* **Facilities:** Spa STV FTV WiFi Gym Sauna Relaxation rooms Xmas New Year **Conf:** Class 250 Board 38 Thtr 400 **Services:** Lift Night porter Air con **Parking:** 88 **Notes:** Civ Wed 200

HIGHLY RECOMMENDED

The Midland

★★★★ 85% ⚫⚫⚫ HOTEL

INSPIRED BY YOU

Peter Street, M60 2DS - **tel:** 0161 236 3333
email: themidland@qhotels.co.uk **web:** www.qhotels.co.uk
dir: *M602 junct 3, follow Manchester Central Convention Complex signs, hotel opposite*

This much-loved, centrally located, well-established Edwardian-style hotel (Grade II listed) offers stylish, thoughtfully equipped bedrooms that have a contemporary feel. Elegant public areas are equally impressive and facilities include extensive function and meeting rooms. Eating options include the Octogan Lounge and the award-winning Mr Cooper's House & Garden.

Rooms: 312 (13 family) 📞 **S** £125–£499; **D** £140–£514 (incl. bkfst)*
Facilities: Spa STV FTV WiFi ⤵ HL ⊗ Gym Hair & beauty salon ♪ **Conf:** Class 300 Board 120 Thtr 600 Del from £169 **Services:** Lift Night porter Air con
Notes: Civ Wed 600

ABode Manchester

★★★★ 79% ⚫⚫ HOTEL

ABode HOTELS

107 Piccadilly, M1 2DB - **tel:** 0161 247 7744
email: info@abodemanchester.co.uk **web:** www.abodemanchester.co.uk
dir: *M62/M602 follow signs for city centre/Piccadilly*

Located in the heart of Piccadilly, this Grade II listed, former wholesale textile warehouse has embraced its industrial heritage. Exposed steel beams and structural iron columns together with an ornate, wrought iron and walnut staircase are striking features. Beds are low and comfortable, while feature walls, a tuck box filled with regional food and drink, and complimentary WiFi can be found in all rooms. A relaxed, all-day brasserie menu features plats du jour with a comfortingly nostalgic nod, and time-honoured classics.

Rooms: 61 **Facilities:** STV WiFi ⤵ Xmas New Year **Conf:** Class 16 Board 26 Thtr 30 **Services:** Lift Night porter Air con **Notes:** RS 25 Dec-2 Jan Reduced food and drink offerings

Macdonald Manchester Hotel

★★★★ 79% HOTEL

⬛ MACDONALD HOTELS & RESORTS

London Road, M1 2PG - **tel:** 0161 272 3200
email: general.manchester@macdonald-hotels.co.uk **web:** www.macdonaldhotels.co.uk
dir: *Opposite Piccadilly Station*

Ideally situated just a short walk from Piccadilly Station, this hotel provides a handy location for both business and leisure travellers. Stylish, modern rooms have plasma TVs and iPod docking stations, and the bathrooms offer walk-in power showers and luxury baths. The first-floor restaurant serves skilfully prepared dinners and hearty breakfasts. Staff throughout are cheerful and keen to please.

Rooms: 338 (14 family) 📞 **S** £80–£350; **D** £80–£350* **Facilities:** Spa FTV WiFi ⤵ HL Gym Sauna New Year **Conf:** Class 150 Board 80 Thtr 250 Del from £135 **Services:** Lift Night porter Air con **Parking:** 85 **Notes:** Civ Wed 200

Malmaison Manchester

★★★★ 77% ⚫ HOTEL

Malmaison hotels that dare to be different

Piccadilly, M1 3AQ - **tel:** 0161 278 1000 & 0844 693 0657 (Calls cost 5p per minute plus your phone company's access charge)
email: manchester@malmaison.com **web:** www.malmaison.com
dir: *Follow city centre signs, then signs to Piccadilly station. Hotel at bottom of station approach*

Stylish and chic, Malmaison Manchester offers the best of contemporary hotel-keeping in a relaxed and comfortable environment. Converted from a former warehouse, it offers a range of bright meeting rooms, a gym and treatment rooms. Chez Mal is impressive and understandably popular. Air-conditioned suites combine comfort with stunning design. Expect the unusual in some of the rooms, for instance the Cinema Suites have a private screening room with 52" screen and surround-sound.

Rooms: 167 📞 **Facilities:** Spa STV WiFi ⤵ HL Gym Sauna Relaxation area Solarium Massage chairs Xmas New Year **Conf:** Class 40 Board 30 Thtr 100 **Services:** Lift Night porter Air con **Notes:** Civ Wed 100

Holiday Inn Manchester - MediaCityUK

★★★★ 76% HOTEL

Holiday Inn

MediaCityUK, Salford, M50 2HT - **tel:** 0161 813 1040
email: reservations@himediacityuk.co.uk **web:** www.holidayinn.com/mediacity
dir: *M602 junct 2 onto A576 to Salford Quays signed MediaCityUK*

Located in the heart of the exciting media district on Salford Quays, this hotel is adjacent to the main production studios and only minutes from Old Trafford and The Lowry Centre. The stylish Hub Bar features TV-themed murals. Food is served from Marco Pierre Whites' New York Italian on the mezzanine floor. Bedrooms are well equipped with safes and mini-bars, and many have views of the Manchester Shipping Canal. There's complimentary WiFi throughout, and a mini-gym is available to guests.

Rooms: 218 (10 family) 📞 **D** £89–£359* **Facilities:** FTV WiFi ⤵ HL Gym Xmas New Year **Conf:** Class 25 Board 30 Thtr 44 Del from £162 **Services:** Lift Night porter Air con **Parking:** 2300 **Notes:** Civ Wed 70

Novotel Manchester Centre

★★★★ 76% HOTEL

NOVOTEL HOTELS & RESORTS

21 Dickinson Street, M1 4LX - **tel:** 0161 235 2200
email: H3145@accor.com **web:** www.novotel.com
dir: *From Oxford St into Portland St, left into Dickinson St. Hotel on right*

This smart, modern property enjoys a central location convenient for theatres, shops, China Town and Manchester's business district. Spacious bedrooms are thoughtfully equipped and brightly decorated. Open-plan, contemporary public areas include an all-day restaurant and a stylish bar. Extensive conference and meeting facilities are available.

Rooms: 164 (15 family) 📞 **Facilities:** STV FTV WiFi ⤵ HL Gym Steam room Sauna Aromatherapy **Conf:** Class 50 Board 36 Thtr 90 **Services:** Lift Night porter Air con

M

MANCHESTER *continued*

Hotel Football

★★★★ 75% HOTEL

99 Sir Matt Busby Way, M16 0SZ - **tel:** 0161 751 0430
email: info@hotelfootball.com **web:** www.hotelfootball.com
dir: *Follow A56 unitl Sir Matt Busby Way. Hotel opposite Manchester Utd football stadium*

Hotel Football is a stylish contemporary hotel offering comfortable accommodation with relaxed and friendly service. All-day dining is available in Café Football where dishes are themed around footballers, managers and match day treats. The hotel also offers a gym and five-a-side football pitch on the top floor.

Rooms: 133 **Facilities:** STV FTV WiFi HL Gym Xmas New Year **Conf:** Class 250 Board 40 Thtr 350 **Services:** Lift Night porter Air con **Notes:** Civ Wed 300

Mercure Manchester Piccadilly Hotel

★★★★ 73% HOTEL

Portland Street, M1 4PH - **tel:** 0844 815 9024 (Calls cost 5p per minute plus your phone company's access charge)
email: info@mercuremanchester.co.uk **web:** www.jupiterhotels.co.uk
dir: *Opposite Piccadilly Gardens*

Overlooking Piccadilly Gardens and views of the city, this hotel is located within the heart of Manchester. Bedrooms and bathrooms are tastefully appointed, with a range of rooms for both leisure and business guests. Contemporary dining can be enjoyed within the Brasserie and popular bar areas. A range of spacious meeting rooms and events' space is also available. Free WiFi across the hotel is a plus. Parking is available too.

Rooms: 280 **Facilities:** FTV WiFi **Conf:** Class 320 Board 60 Thtr 800 **Services:** Lift Night porter Air con **Parking:** 80 **Notes:** Civ Wed 800

The Principal Manchester

★★★★ 73% HOTEL

PRINCIPAL
HOTEL COMPANY LTD
EST. 1898

Oxford Street, M60 7HA - **tel:** 0161 288 1111
email: ManchesterReservations@theprincipalhotel.com
web: www.phcompany.com/principal/manchester-hotel
dir: *Opposite Manchester Oxford Road rail station*

Formerly the offices of the Refuge Life Assurance Company, this impressive neo-Gothic building occupies a central location. There is a vast lobby, spacious open-plan bar lounge and restaurant, and extensive conference and function facilities. Bedrooms vary in size and style but are all spacious and well equipped.

Rooms: 275 (59 family) **Facilities:** STV WiFi **Conf:** Class 650 Board 200 Thtr 1000 **Services:** Lift Night porter **Notes:** Civ Wed 600

Arora Hotel

★★★★ 72% HOTEL

18-24 Princess Street, M1 4LG - **tel:** 0161 236 8999
email: manchesterreservations@arorahotels.com **web:** www.manchester.arorahotels.com
dir: *Phone for detailed directions*

Conveniently located close to the city centre and ideal for both shopping and Theatres, the Arora provides comfortable accommodation. The hotel also has meeting room facilities, a small gym and a contemporary dining room in 24 Bar and Grill.

Rooms: 140 (32 family) (15 GF) **S** £99–£299; **D** £99–£299* **Facilities:** FTV WiFi Gym **Conf:** Class 40 Board 45 Thtr 100 Del from £149 **Services:** Lift Night porter Air con **Notes:** LB

Hallmark Inn, Manchester South

★★★ 78% HOTEL

340-342 Wilmslow Road, Fallowfield, M14 6AF - **tel:** 0330 028 3427
email: willowbank@hallmarkhotels.co.uk **web:** www.hallmarkhotels.co.uk
dir: *M60 junct 5, A5103, left onto B5093. Hotel 2.5m on left*

This popular hotel is conveniently located three miles from the city centre, close to the universities. Bedrooms vary in size and style but all are appointed to impressively high standards; they are well equipped and many rooms benefit from CD players and PlayStations. Spacious, elegant public areas include a bar, a restaurant and meeting rooms.

Rooms: 116 (4 family) **Facilities:** FTV WiFi Xmas New Year **Conf:** Class 50 Board 60 Thtr 120 **Services:** Night porter **Parking:** 100 **Notes:** Civ Wed 125

Chancellors Hotel & Conference Centre

★★★ 75% HOTEL

Moseley Road, Fallowfield, M14 6NN - **tel:** 0161 907 7414
email: chancellors@manchester.ac.uk **web:** www.chancellorshotel.co.uk
dir: *Phone for detailed directions*

A Grade II listed manor house set in five acres of landscaped gardens hidden in the heart of Fallowfield, well located for the city's shopping, business and commercial centres. Bedrooms offer modern facilities and the cuisine is enjoyable. WiFi and secure parking are available.

Rooms: 72 (4 family) (16 GF) **Facilities:** FTV WiFi HL **Conf:** Class 100 Board 50 Thtr 125 **Services:** Lift Night porter **Parking:** 70 **Notes:** LB Closed 25 Dec Civ Wed 125

Jurys Inn Manchester

★★★ 75% HOTEL

56 Great Bridgewater Street, M1 5LE - **tel:** 0161 953 8888
email: jurysinnmanchester@jurysinns.com **web:** www.jurysinns.com
dir: *In city centre adjacent to Manchester Central & Bridgewater Hall*

Enjoying a prime city centre location, this hotel offers good value, air-conditioned accommodation, ideal for both families and business travellers. Public areas include a smart, spacious lobby, the Inn Pub and the Infusion Restaurant. There are several conveniently located car parks with special rates available.

Rooms: 265 (11 family) (16 GF) **S** fr £69; **D** fr £69* **Facilities:** FTV WiFi **Conf:** Class 25 Board 25 Thtr 50 Del from £120 **Services:** Lift Night porter Air con

Novotel Manchester West

★★★ 75% HOTEL

NOVOTEL
HOTELS & RESORTS

Worsley Brow, M28 2YA - **tel:** 0161 799 3535
email: H0907@accor.com **web:** www.novotel.com

(for full entry see Worsley)

Holiday Inn Express Manchester - Oxford Road

BUDGET HOTEL

Ensco 1160 Ltd, 2 Oxford Road, M1 5QA - **tel:** 0161 238 6660
email: info@hiemanchester.co.uk **web:** www.hiemanchester.co.uk
dir: *From A57(M) follow signs for Peters Fields & A5103, into Cambridge St. 2nd right into Hulme St, ahead onto Charles St. Opp BBC building*

A modern hotel ideal for families and business travellers. Fresh and uncomplicated, the spacious rooms include power shower and tea and coffee-making facilities.

M

Continental buffet breakfast is included in the room rate; other meals may be taken at the nearby family pub or restaurant. The hotel is within walking distance of The Arndale shopping centre, Manchester Art Gallery, The Palace Theatre and Manchester Metropolitan University. It also has easy access to the Trafford Centre and both the Old Trafford and City of Manchester stadiums.

Rooms: 147

Premier Inn Manchester Central

BUDGET HOTEL

Bishopsgate, 7-11 Lower Mosley Street, M2 3DW - **tel:** 0871 527 8742 (Calls cost 13p per minute plus your phone company's access charge) **web:** www.premierinn.com
dir: *M56 to end, A5103 towards city. Right at 2nd lights. At next lights left into Oxford Rd, left at junct of St Peters Sq. Hotel on left*

High quality, budget accommodation ideal for both families and business travellers. Spacious, en suite bedrooms feature free WiFi and tea and coffee making facilities, and in most hotels, Freeview TV is also available. The adjacent family restaurant features a wide and varied menu.

Rooms: 197

Premier Inn Manchester City Centre (Arena/Printworks)

BUDGET HOTEL

North Tower, Victoria Bridge Street, M3 5AS - **tel:** 0871 527 8744 (Calls cost 13p per minute plus your phone company's access charge) **web:** www.premierinn.com
dir: *M602 to city centre, A57(M) towards GMEX. 2nd exit follow A56 city centre signs. Left before MEN arena onto A6, 1st left*

Rooms: 170

Premier Inn Manchester City Centre (Piccadilly)

BUDGET HOTEL

72 Dale Street, M1 2HR - **tel:** 0871 527 9390 (Calls cost 13p per minute plus your phone company's access charge) **web:** www.premierinn.com
dir: *Phone for detailed directions*

Rooms: 193

Premier Inn Manchester City Centre (Portland Street)

BUDGET HOTEL

The Circus, 112-114 Portland Street, M1 4WB - **tel:** 0871 527 8746 (Calls cost 13p per minute plus your phone company's access charge) **web:** www.premierinn.com
dir: *M6 junct 19, A556. M56, exit junct 3 onto A5103 to Medlock St, right into Whitworth St, left into Oxford St, right into Portland St*

Rooms: 232

Premier Inn Manchester (Deansgate Locks)

BUDGET HOTEL

Medlock Street, M15 5FJ - **tel:** 0871 527 8740 (Calls cost 13p per minute plus your phone company's access charge) **web:** www.premierinn.com
dir: *M60 junct 24, A57(M) (Mancunian Way) towards city centre. Hotel adjacent, on A5103 Medlock St*

Rooms: 199

Premier Inn Manchester (Denton)

BUDGET HOTEL

Alphagate Drive, Manchester Rd South, M34 3SH - **tel:** 0871 527 8708 (Calls cost 13p per minute plus your phone company's access charge) **web:** www.premierinn.com
dir: *M60 junct 24, A57 signed Denton. 1st right at lights, right at next lights, hotel on left*

Rooms: 58

Premier Inn Manchester (Heaton Park)

BUDGET HOTEL

Middleton Road, Crumpsall, M8 4NB - **tel:** 0871 527 8710 (Calls cost 13p per minute plus your phone company's access charge) **web:** www.premierinn.com
dir: *M60 junct 19, A576 towards Manchester, through 2 sets of lights. Hotel on left*

Rooms: 45

Premier Inn Manchester Old Trafford

BUDGET HOTEL

Waters Reach, Trafford Park, M17 1WS - **tel:** 0871 527 8750 (Calls cost 13p per minute plus your phone company's access charge) **web:** www.premierinn.com
dir: *M6 junct 19, A556 towards Altrincham. Follow Stretford & Manchester City Centre signs (road becomes A56). Follow Manchester United Football Stadium signs. At stadium left at lights. Into Sir Matt Busby Way, after 1st lights hotel on right*

Rooms: 172

Premier Inn Manchester (Salford Quays)

BUDGET HOTEL

11 The Quays, Salford Quays, M50 3SQ - **tel:** 0871 527 8718 (Calls cost 13p per minute plus your phone company's access charge) **web:** www.premierinn.com
dir: *M602 junct 3, A5063, on Salford Quays*

Rooms: 80

Premier Inn Manchester Trafford Centre North

BUDGET HOTEL

18-20 Trafford Boulevard, M41 7JE - **tel:** 0871 527 8752 (Calls cost 13p per minute plus your phone company's access charge) **web:** www.premierinn.com
dir: *M6, onto M62 at junct 21a, towards Manchester. M62 junct 1, M60 towards south. M60 junct 10, take B5214. Hotel on left just before Ellesmere Circle*

Rooms: 62

Premier Inn Manchester Trafford Centre South

BUDGET HOTEL

Wilderspool Wood, Trafford Centre, M17 8WW - **tel:** 0871 527 8754 (Calls cost 13p per minute plus your phone company's access charge) **web:** www.premierinn.com
dir: *M6 onto M62 junct 21a towards Manchester. Or M62 junct 1 onto M60 S. Or M60 junct 10, B5124 towards Trafford Park. At 1st rdbt take last exit for Trafford Centre parking. At 2nd rdbt straight on. Hotel on left*

Rooms: 60

M

MANCHESTER *continued*

Premier Inn Manchester Trafford Centre West

BUDGET HOTEL

Old Park Lane, M17 8PG - tel: 0871 527 8756 (Calls cost 13p per minute plus your phone company's access charge) **web:** www.premierinn.com
dir: *M60 junct 10 towards The Trafford Centre*

Rooms: 234

Premier Inn Manchester (West Didsbury)

BUDGET HOTEL

Christies Field Office Park, Derwent Ave, M21 7QS - tel: 0871 527 8722 (Calls cost 13p per minute plus your phone company's access charge) **web:** www.premierinn.com
dir: *M60 junct 5, A5103 (Princess Parkway) towards Manchester on A5103. Hotel approx 1m*

Rooms: 112

MANCHESTER AIRPORT	Map 15 SJ88
Greater Manchester	

See also **Altrincham**

The Stanneylands

 ★★★★ 78% HOTEL

Stanneylands Road, SK9 4EY - tel: 01625 525225
email: reservations@stanneylands.co.uk **web:** www.stanneylands.co.uk
dir: *From M56 at airport exit, follow signs to Wilmslow. Left towards Handforth. Left at lights into Stanneylands Rd, hotel on left*

This traditional country house hotel, just three miles from Manchester Airport, offers well-equipped bedrooms that include suites, prestige and executive rooms together with delightful, comfortable day rooms. The cuisine in the restaurant is of a high standard, and ranges from traditional favourites to more imaginative modern dishes. There is also the contemporary Calico café bar in a conservatory setting offering all-day menus, including afternoon tea, and live music played on the baby grand piano. The hotel makes an ideal wedding venue, and the staff throughout are friendly and obliging.

Rooms: 52 (2 family) (10 GF) **Facilities:** STV FTV WiFi ⅃ Xmas New Year **Conf:** Class 50 Board 40 Thtr 120 **Services:** Lift Night porter **Parking:** 108
Notes: Civ Wed 90

Best Western Plus Pinewood on Wilmslow

 ★★★★ 77% HOTEL

180 Wilmslow Road, SK9 3LF - tel: 01625 529211
email: pinewood.res@pinewood-hotel.co.uk **web:** www.pinewood-hotel.co.uk
dir: *Phone for detailed directions*

This stylish hotel is conveniently situated for the M60, Trafford Park, Trafford Centre and Manchester Airport. Bedrooms provide very good quality accommodation; many have now been totally refurbished and all come with WiFi. New modern public areas and Brasserie are a real delight and are open every night with a choice of menu. Ample car parking is available.

Rooms: 89 (3 family) **S** £55–£80; **D** £70–£100* **Facilities:** FTV WiFi HL Use of nearby Total Fitness Club Xmas New Year **Conf:** Class 60 Board 60 Thtr 120 **Services:** Lift Night porter **Parking:** 120 **Notes:** Civ Wed 120

Hallmark Hotel Manchester Airport

★★★★ 76% HOTEL

Stanley Road, SK9 3LD - tel: 0330 028 3419
email: manchester@hallmarkhotels.co.uk **web:** www.hallmarkhotels.co.uk
dir: *M60 junct 3/A34 signed Cheadle/Wilmslow. Right at 3rd rdbt into Stanley Rd (B5094). Hotel on left*

Ideally located for Manchester Airport and just a few miles from both the Trafford Centre and the city's many shops, the Hallmark Hotel offers well appointed bedrooms. Guests can relax and unwind in the hotel's 20-metre pool, Jacuzzi and steam rooms. The brasserie is open for both lunch and dinner, and offers a range of international dishes.

Rooms: 88 (12 family) (12 GF) **Facilities:** Spa FTV WiFi ⏱ Gym Steam room Sauna Hair salon New Year **Conf:** Class 250 Board 60 Thtr 500 **Services:** Lift Night porter **Notes:** Civ Wed 300

Crowne Plaza Manchester Airport

★★★★ 75% HOTEL

Ringway Road, M90 3NS - tel: 0871 942 9055 (Calls cost 10p per minute plus your phone company's access charge) **email:** reservations@cpmanchesterairport.co.uk **web:** www.cpmanchesterairporthotel.co.uk
dir: *M56 junct 5 signed Manchester Airport. At airport, follow signs to Terminals 1 & 3. Hotel adjacent to Terminal 3. Long stay car park on left*

Located by Terminal 3 this smart, modern hotel offers well-equipped, comfortable bedrooms, all with air-conditioning and effective double-glazing. A great choice of dining options and bars is available with a Grill Room and Pan-Asian restaurant, Sampans. The hotel has a spacious leisure club and ample on-site parking along with business and meeting facilities.

Rooms: 299 (35 family) (53 GF) **Facilities:** STV WiFi ⏱ HL Gym Saunas **Conf:** Class 25 Board 20 Thtr 30 **Services:** Lift Night porter Air con **Parking:** 300

Premier Inn Manchester Airport Hotel (M56 Jct 6 South)

BUDGET HOTEL

Runger Lane, Wilmslow Road, M90 5DL - tel: 0871 527 8726 (Calls cost 13p per minute plus your phone company's access charge) **web:** www.premierinn.com
dir: *M56 junct 6, follow Wilmslow & Hale signs. Merge onto M56 signed Warrington, Macclesfield & Hale. Left into Runger Ln signed Freight Terminal*

High quality, budget accommodation ideal for both families and business travellers. Spacious, en suite bedrooms feature free WiFi and tea and coffee making facilities, and in most hotels, Freeview TV is also available. The adjacent family restaurant features a wide and varied menu.

Rooms: 195

Premier Inn Manchester Airport (M56 Jct 6) Runger Lane North

BUDGET HOTEL

Runger Lane, Wilmslow Road, M90 5DL - tel: 0871 527 8730 (Calls cost 13p per minute plus your phone company's access charge) **web:** www.premierinn.com
dir: *M56 junct 6, follow Airport signs. 2nd exit at rdbt. Hotel on left. Through Travelodge car park. Hotel on right*

Rooms: 165

M

Premier Inn Manchester (Handforth)

BUDGET HOTEL

30 Wilmslow Road, SK9 3EW - **tel:** 0871 527 8732 (Calls cost 13p per minute plus your phone company's access charge) **web:** www.premierinn.com
dir: *M56 junct 6, A538 towards Wilmslow. At main junct into town centre bear left. In 2m hotel at top of hill on right just after Wilmslow Garden Centre*

Rooms: 35

Premier Inn Manchester (Wilmslow)

BUDGET HOTEL

Racecourse Road, Wilmslow, SK9 5LR - **tel:** 0871 527 8736 (Calls cost 13p per minute plus your phone company's access charge) **web:** www.premierinn.com
dir: *M6 junct 19 to Knutsford, follow Wilmslow signs. Left at 1st & 2nd lights towards Wilmslow. Through Mobberley, left just before Bird in Hand pub. At T-junct, right. Hotel 150yds on right*

Rooms: 37

| **MARGATE** | Map 7 TR37 |
| Kent | |

Sands Hotel

★★★★ 79% ◉◉ ▤ TOWN HOUSE HOTEL

16 Marine Drive, CT9 1DH - **tel:** 01843 228228
email: reservations@sandshotelmargate.co.uk **web:** www.sandshotelmargate.co.uk
dir: *From London M2, A299 to A28 to Margate*

Located in the centre of Margate, The Sands Hotel benefits from uninterrupted sea views. The Bay Restaurant and Bar which is open for breakfast, lunch, afternoon tea and dinner also has great views, and hotel guests can enjoy the private roof terrace at the very top of the hotel. Bedrooms and bathrooms are all contemporary in style having all been completely refurbished within the last few years, and many benefit from having their own private balconies.

Rooms: 20 (6 family) ☎ **D** £140–£280 (incl. bkfst)* **Facilities:** STV FTV WiFi ↳ HL ♫ Xmas New Year **Conf:** Class 55 Board 30 Thtr 80 Del £175 **Services:** Lift Night porter Air con **Notes:** LB Civ Wed 80

Premier Inn Margate

BUDGET HOTEL

Station Green, Station Road, CT9 5AF - **tel:** 0871 527 8762 (Calls cost 13p per minute plus your phone company's access charge) **web:** www.premierinn.com
dir: *M2, A299, A28 to Margate seafront. Hotel adjacent to Margate station*

High quality, budget accommodation ideal for both families and business travellers. Spacious, en suite bedrooms feature free WiFi and tea and coffee making facilities, and in most hotels, Freeview TV is also available. The adjacent family restaurant features a wide and varied menu.

Rooms: 64

| **MARKET DRAYTON** | Map 15 SJ63 |
| Shropshire | |

Goldstone Hall

★★★ ◉◉ HOTEL

Goldstone Road, TF9 2NA - **tel:** 01630 661202
email: enquiries@goldstonehall.com **web:** www.goldstonehall.com
dir: *4m S of Market Drayton, 4m N of Newport. Hotel signed from A529 & A41*

Situated in extensive grounds, this sympathetically refurbished period property is a family-run hotel. It provides traditionally furnished, well-equipped accommodation with outstanding en suite bathrooms and lots of thoughtful extras. Public rooms are extensive and include a choice of lounges, a snooker room and a conservatory. The kitchen has a well deserved reputation for good food that utilises home-grown produce, and a warm welcome is assured.

Rooms: 12 (2 GF) ☎ **Facilities:** STV FTV WiFi ↳ ⚘ Snooker table New Year **Conf:** Class 30 Board 30 Thtr 50 **Parking:** 60 **Notes:** Civ Wed 100

| **MARKET HARBOROUGH** | Map 11 SP78 |
| Leicestershire | |

Three Swans Hotel

★★★ 82% ◉ HOTEL

21 High Street, LE16 7NJ - **tel:** 01858 466644
email: threeswans@innmail.co.uk **web:** www.threeswans.co.uk
dir: *M1 junct 20, A304 to Market Harborough. Through town centre on A6 from Leicester, hotel on right*

Public areas in this former coaching inn include an elegant fine dining restaurant and cocktail bar, a smart foyer lounge and popular public bar areas. Bedroom styles and sizes vary, but are very well appointed and equipped. Those in the wing are particularly impressive, offering high quality and spacious accommodation. Sky TV in rooms comes as standard.

Rooms: 59 (46 annexe) (10 family) (20 GF) ☎ **Facilities:** STV FTV WiFi ↳ Xmas New Year **Conf:** Class 90 Board 50 Thtr 250 **Services:** Lift Night porter **Parking:** 70 **Notes:** Civ Wed 140

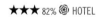

M

MARKET HARBOROUGH *continued*

Premier Inn Market Harborough

BUDGET HOTEL

Melton Road, East Langton, LE16 7TG - **tel:** 0871 527 8764 (Calls cost 13p per minute plus your phone company's access charge) **web:** www.premierinn.com
dir: *On A6, N of Market Harborough. Hotel on rdbt junct of A6 & B6047*

High quality, budget accommodation ideal for both families and business travellers. Spacious, en suite bedrooms feature free WiFi and tea and coffee making facilities, and in most hotels, Freeview TV is also available. The adjacent family restaurant features a wide and varied menu.

Rooms: 40

MARLOW	Map 5 SU88
Buckinghamshire	

INSPECTOR'S CHOICE

Macdonald Compleat Angler

★★★★ ◉◉ ⬩ HOTEL

Marlow Bridge, SL7 1RG - **tel:** 01628 484444
email: compleatangler@macdonald-hotels.co.uk
web: www.macdonaldhotels.co.uk/compleatangler
dir: *M4 junct 8/9 or M40 junct 4, A404(M) to rdbt, Bisham exit, 1m to Marlow Bridge, hotel on right*

This well-established hotel enjoys an idyllic location overlooking the River Thames and the delightful Marlow weir. The bedrooms, which differ in size and style, are all individually decorated and are equipped with flat-screen satellite TVs, high-speed internet and air-conditioning. Some rooms have balconies with views of the weir and some have four-posters. The Riverside Restaurant provides outstanding and award-winning cuisine. In summer guests can use two boats that the hotel has moored on the river and fishing is, of course, a popular activity - a ghillie can accompany guests if arranged in advance. Staff throughout are keen to please and nothing is too much trouble.

Rooms: 64 (6 family) (6 GF) **S** £150–£290; **D** £165–£400 (incl. bkfst)* **Facilities:** FTV WiFi ⬩ HL Fishing Fly & coarse fishing River trips (Apr-Sep) Xmas New Year **Conf:** Class 65 Board 36 Thtr 150 Del from £190 **Services:** Lift Night porter **Parking:** 100 **Notes:** LB Civ Wed 120

Danesfield House Hotel & Spa

★★★★ 86% ◉◉ HOTEL

Henley Road, SL7 2EY - **tel:** 01628 891010
email: reservations@danesfieldhouse.co.uk **web:** www.danesfieldhouse.co.uk
dir: *2m from Marlow on A4155 towards Henley*

Set in 65 acres of elevated grounds just 45 minutes from central London and 30 minutes from Heathrow, this hotel enjoys spectacular views across the River Thames. Impressive public rooms include the cathedral-like Great Hall, an impressive spa, and The Orangery for informal dining. The beautiful Oak Room restaurant is also an ideal setting to enjoy superb, imaginative modern British cuisine. Some bedrooms have balconies and stunning views. Nothing is too much trouble for the team of committed staff.

Rooms: 78 (3 family) (27 GF) ⬩ **S** fr £264; **D** fr £264 (incl. bkfst)* **Facilities:** Spa STV FTV WiFi ⬩ ⬩ Putting green ⬩ ⬩ Gym Jogging trail Steam room Hydrotherapy room Sauna Xmas New Year **Conf:** Class 60 Board 50 Thtr 100 **Services:** Lift Night porter **Parking:** 100 **Notes:** Civ Wed 120

Crowne Plaza Marlow

★★★★ 81% ◉ HOTEL

Field House Lane, SL7 1GJ - **tel:** 01628 496800
email: enquiries@cpmarlow.co.uk **web:** www.cpmarlow.co.uk
dir: *A404 exit to Marlow, left at mini rdbt, left into Field House Lane*

This hotel is in the Thames Valley not far from Windsor, Henley-on-Thames and the motorway. The public areas are air conditioned and include the Agua Café and Bar and Glaze Restaurant. Leisure facilities include an up-to-the-minute gym and large pool. The bedrooms, including six contemporary suites, enjoy plenty of natural light and have excellent workstations; the Club Rooms have European and US power points.

Crowne Plaza Marlow

Rooms: 168 (47 family) (56 GF) ↻ **S** £89–£229; **D** £89–£229 (incl. bkfst)*
Facilities: Spa STV FTV WiFi ↻ HL ⊕ ⚲ Gym Sauna Steam room Dance studio Nail bar Xmas New Year **Conf:** Class 180 Board 30 Thtr 450 Del from £195 **Services:** Lift Night porter Air con **Parking:** 300 **Notes:** LB Civ Wed 300

Premier Inn Marlow

BUDGET HOTEL

The Causeway, SL7 2AA - **tel:** 0871 527 8766 (Calls cost 13p per minute plus your phone company's access charge) **web:** www.premierinn.com
dir: M40 junct 4, A404 signed Marlow/Maidenhead. Left, follow A4155 signs to Marlow. At 3rd rdbt 1st exit into High St, signed Bisham. Straight on at mini rdbt. Hotel on left

High quality, budget accommodation ideal for both families and business travellers. Spacious, en suite bedrooms feature free WiFi and tea and coffee making facilities, and in most hotels, Freeview TV is also available. The adjacent family restaurant features a wide and varied menu.

Rooms: 17

MARSTON
Lincolnshire · Map 11 SK84

Ramada Resort Grantham

★★★ 73% HOTEL

Toll Bar Road, NG32 2HT - **tel:** 01400 250909
email: reservations@ramadaresortgrantham.co.uk
web: www.ramadaresortgrantham.co.uk
dir: From A1 N: left to Marston adjacent to petrol station.
From A1 S: 1st right after Allington/Belton exit

Located in the countryside one mile from the A1, this sympathetically renovated and extended former period barn provides a range of thoughtfully furnished bedrooms, ideal for both business and leisure customers. Imaginative food is offered in the attractive beamed restaurant, and extensive leisure facilities include a swimming pool, sauna, steam room and a well-equipped gym.

Rooms: 103 (11 family) (46 GF) ↻ **Facilities:** Spa STV FTV WiFi ↻ HL ⊕ Gym Sauna Steam room Solarium Spa bath Xmas New Year **Conf:** Class 180 Board 100 Thtr 300 **Services:** Lift Night porter **Parking:** 280 **Notes:** Civ Wed 250

MASHAM
North Yorkshire · Map 19 SE28

INSPECTOR'S CHOICE

Swinton Park

★★★★ HOTEL

Swinton, HG4 4JH - **tel:** 01765 680900
email: reservations@swintonpark.com **web:** www.swintonpark.com
dir: Phone for detailed directions

Although extended during the Victorian and Edwardian eras, the original part of this welcoming castle dates from the 17th century. Bedrooms are luxuriously furnished and come with a host of thoughtful extras. Samuel's restaurant (built by the current owner's great-great-great grandfather) is very elegant and serves imaginative dishes using local produce. The majority of the food is sourced from the 20,000-acre Swinton Estate, as the hotel, winner of several green awards, is committed to keeping the 'food miles' to a minimum. The gardens, including a four-acre walled garden, have been gradually restored. The Deerhouse is the venue for the hotel's alfresco food festivals, summer BBQs and weddings.

Rooms: 31 (6 family) ↻ **D** £195–£545 (incl. bkfst)* **Facilities:** Spa FTV WiFi ↻ ⊕ ⚲ ⚘ 9 Putting green Fishing ⚲ Gym Shooting Falconry Pony trekking Cookery school Xmas New Year **Conf:** Class 60 Board 40 Thtr 110 Del from £225 **Services:** Lift Night porter **Parking:** 50 **Notes:** Civ Wed 120

MATFEN
Northumberland · Map 21 NZ07

Matfen Hall

★★★★ 82% ◉◉ HOTEL

NE20 0RH - **tel:** 01661 886500 **email:** info@matfenhall.com **web:** www.matfenhall.com
dir: A69 onto B6318. Hotel just before village

Matfen Hall is a luxurious and elegant stately home set in 300 acres of beautiful Northumbrian countryside. The hotel offers individually decorated bedrooms in both traditional and contemporary styles, while impressive public rooms include the Library Restaurant, the Print Room, and the Conservatory Bar. At the centre is the Great Hall, which is perfect for weddings and private dining. The golf estate includes a 27-hole course, a par 3 course and a driving range. Relax in the stylish spa, leisure and conference facilities.

Rooms: 53 (11 family) ↻ **Facilities:** Spa STV FTV WiFi ↻ HL ⊕ supervised ⚘ 27 Putting green Gym Sauna Steam room Salt grotto Ice fountain Aerobics Driving range Golf academy Xmas New Year **Conf:** Class 46 Board 40 Thtr 120 **Services:** Lift Night porter **Parking:** 150 **Notes:** Civ Wed 120

MATLOCK
Derbyshire
Map 16 SK35

Premier Inn Matlock

BUDGET HOTEL

DE4 3AZ - **tel:** 0871 527 9612 (Calls cost 13p per minute plus your phone company's access charge) **web:** www.premierinn.com
dir: *Phone for detailed directions*

High quality, budget accommodation ideal for both families and business travellers. Spacious, en suite bedrooms feature free WiFi and tea and coffee making facilities, and in most hotels, Freeview TV is also available. The adjacent family restaurant features a wide and varied menu.

Rooms: 58

MAWGAN PORTH
Cornwall & Isles of Scilly
Map 2 SW86

HIGHLY RECOMMENDED

The Scarlet Hotel

★★★★ 83% ◉◉ HOTEL

Tredragon Road, TR8 4DQ - **tel:** 01637 861800
email: stay@scarlethotel.co.uk **web:** www.scarlethotel.co.uk
dir: *A39, A30 towards Truro. At Trekenning rdbt take A3059, follow Newquay Airport signs. Right after garage signed St Mawgan Airport. Right after airport, at T-junct signed Padstow B3276. At Mawgan Porth left. Hotel 250 yds*

Built as an eco hotel, this strikingly modern property has a stunning cliff-top location with magnificent views, and offers something a little different. The very stylish and well-equipped bedrooms are categorised in five types: Just Right, Generous, Unique, Spacious and Indulgent. The Ayurvedic spa is exceptional and encompasses the rejuvenation of the whole body and mind; relaxation is the key here. Cuisine is equally important, and in tune with the hotel's environment policies, daily-changing menus feature fresh, seasonal and local produce. The team of 'hosts' offer a high level of hospitality and service.

Rooms: 37 (5 GF) ⬈ **S** £190–£460; **D** £210–£480 (incl. bkfst)* **Facilities:** Spa FTV WiFi ⬇ ⊗ ⬀ Yoga room Meditation and relaxation room Library ♫ Xmas New Year **Conf:** Board 16 **Services:** Lift Night porter **Parking:** 37 **Notes:** LB No children 18yrs Closed 3-28 Jan Civ Wed 74

Bedruthan Hotel and Spa

★★★★ 79% HOTEL

TR8 4BU - **tel:** 01637 861200
email: stay@bedruthan.com **web:** www.bedruthan.com
dir: *From A39 or A30 follow signs to Newquay Airport. Pass airport, right at T-junct to Mawgan Porth. Hotel at top of hill on left*

Bedruthan Hotel and Spa features stunning views over Mawgan Porth beach from its public areas, restaurants and the majority of the bedrooms. The hotel is a homage to the architecture of the 1970s, with a comfortable, contemporary feel. It also has a spa and conference facilities, and holds a variety of events and workshops throughout the year. There are two restaurants available; the simple and contemporary Wild Café, and the quiet and intimate The Herring. Both offer food made from local Cornish produce. This is a very child-friendly hotel, including kids clubs for various ages, play areas, childcare, baby listening service and equipment such as pushchairs, that guests can borrow for free.

Rooms: 101 (60 family) (1 GF) ⬈ **S** £89–£120; **D** £149–£247 (incl. bkfst)* **Facilities:** Spa FTV WiFi ⬇ ⊗ ⬀ ⬚ Gym Sauna Steam room Hydro pool Pool table Outdoor sensory spa garden ♫ Xmas New Year Child facilities **Conf:** Class 60 Board 40 Thtr 200 **Services:** Lift Night porter **Parking:** 120 **Notes:** LB Closed 2 Jan-2 Feb Civ Wed 150

MAWNAN SMITH
Cornwall & Isles of Scilly
Map 2 SW72

Budock Vean Hotel

★★★★ 78% ◉ COUNTRY HOUSE HOTEL

TR11 5LG - **tel:** 01326 252100 & 250288
email: relax@budockvean.co.uk **web:** www.budockvean.co.uk
dir: *From A39 follow tourist signs to Trebah Gardens. 0.5m to hotel*

Set in 65 acres of attractive, well-tended grounds, this peaceful hotel offers an impressive range of facilities. It is convenient for visiting the Helford River estuary and many local gardens, or simply as a tranquil venue for a leisure break. The bedrooms are spacious and come in a choice of styles; some overlook the grounds and the golf course.

Rooms: 57 (2 family) ⬈ **S** £73–£97; **D** £146–£194 (incl. bkfst)* **Facilities:** Spa FTV WiFi ⬇ ⊗ ⬚ 9 Putting green ⬚ ⬚ Private river boat & foreshore Kayaking ♫ Xmas New Year **Conf:** Class 30 Board 20 Thtr 60 **Services:** Lift Night porter **Parking:** 100 **Notes:** LB Closed 3 weeks Jan Civ Wed 60

Meudon Hotel

★★★★ 75% ◉ COUNTRY HOUSE HOTEL

TR11 5HT - **tel:** 01326 250541 **email:** wecare@meudon.co.uk **web:** www.meudon.co.uk
dir: *From Truro A39 towards Falmouth at Hillhead - Anchor & Cannons rdbt, follow signs to Mabe then Mawnan Smith, left at Red Lion, hotel on right*

This charming late Victorian mansion is a relaxing place to stay, with friendly hospitality and attentive service. It sits in impressive 9-acre gardens that lead down to a private beach. The spacious and comfortable bedrooms are situated in a more modern building. The cuisine features the best of local Cornish produce and is served in the conservatory restaurant.

Rooms: 30 (2 family) (15 GF) ⬈ **S** £80–195; **D** £100–£285 (incl. bkfst & dinner)* **Facilities:** FTV WiFi ⬇ Fishing Private beach Hair salon Beauty treatment room Xmas **Conf:** Class 30 Board 30 Thtr 30 **Services:** Lift **Parking:** 50 **Notes:** LB Closed 28 Dec-Jan

Trelawne Hotel

★★★ 84% HOTEL

Maenporth Road, TR11 5HT - **tel:** 01326 250226
email: info@trelawnehotel.co.uk **web:** www.trelawnehotel.co.uk
dir: *A39 to Falmouth, right at Hillhead rdbt signed Maenporth. Past beach, up hill, hotel on left*

This hotel is surrounded by attractive lawns and gardens, and enjoys superb coastal views. An informal atmosphere prevails, and many guests return year after year. Bedrooms, many with sea views, are of varying sizes, but all are well equipped. Dinner features quality local produce used in imaginative dishes.

Rooms: 11 (2 family) (4 GF) 🐾 **Facilities:** FTV WiFi 🐾 Xmas **Parking:** 16 **Notes:** LB RS Jan-Feb B&B only

---

| **MELKSHAM** | **Map 4 ST96** |
| Wiltshire | |

Shaw Country Hotel

★★ 78% SMALL HOTEL

Bath Road, Shaw, SN12 8EF - **tel:** 01225 702836
email: info@shawcountryhotel.com **web:** www.shawcountryhotel.com
dir: *1m from Melksham, 9m from Bath on A365*

Located within easy reach of both Bath and the M4, this relaxed and friendly hotel sits in its own gardens and includes a patio area ideal for enjoying a drink during the summer months. The house boasts very well-appointed bedrooms, a comfortable lounge and bar, and the Mulberry Restaurant, where a wide selection of innovative dishes make up both carte and set menus. A spacious function room is a useful addition.

Rooms: 13 (2 family) 🐾 **Facilities:** FTV WiFi **Conf:** Class 40 Board 20 Thtr 60 **Parking:** 30 **Notes:** Closed 26-28 Dec & 1 Jan Civ Wed 70

| **MELTON MOWBRAY** | **Map 11 SK71** |
| Leicestershire | |

INSPECTOR'S CHOICE

Stapleford Park

★★★★ ◉◉ COUNTRY HOUSE HOTEL

Stapleford, LE14 2EF - **tel:** 01572 787000
email: reservations@stapleford.co.uk **web:** www.staplefordpark.com
dir: *1m SW of B676, 4m E of Melton Mowbray & 9m W of Colsterworth*

This stunning mansion, dating back to the 14th century, sits in over 500 acres of beautiful grounds. Spacious, sumptuous public rooms include a choice of lounges and an elegant restaurant. An additional brasserie-style restaurant is located in the golf complex. The hotel also boasts a spa with health and beauty treatments and gym, plus horse riding and many other country pursuits.

Bedrooms are individually styled and furnished to a high standard. Attentive service is delivered with a relaxed yet professional style. Dinner, in the impressive dining room, is a highlight of any stay.

Stapleford Park

Rooms: 55 (7 annexe) (10 family) 🐾 **S** £160–£288; **D** £160–£288 (incl. bkfst)* **Facilities:** Spa STV FTV WiFi 🐾 ⊗ ♨ 18 Putting green ⌣ Fishing 🏌 Gym Archery Croquet Falconry Horse riding Petanque Shooting Billiards ♬ Xmas New Year Child facilities **Conf:** Class 140 Board 80 Thtr 200 **Services:** Lift Night porter **Parking:** 120 **Notes:** LB Civ Wed 160

Quorn Lodge Hotel

★★★ 71% HOTEL

46 Asfordby Road, LE13 0HR - **tel:** 01664 566660
email: quornlodge@aol.com **web:** www.quornlodge.co.uk
dir: *From town centre take A6006. Hotel 300yds from junct of A606/A607 on right*

Centrally located, this smart, privately-owned and managed hotel offers a comfortable and welcoming atmosphere. Bedrooms are individually decorated and thoughtfully designed. The public rooms consist of a bright restaurant overlooking the garden, a cosy lounge bar and a modern function suite. High standards are maintained throughout and parking is a bonus.

Rooms: 21 (4 family) (3 GF) 🐾 **S** £45–£69; **D** £79–£89 (incl. bkfst)* **Facilities:** STV FTV WiFi 🐾 Gym **Conf:** Class 70 Board 80 Thtr 100 Del from £110 **Services:** Night porter **Parking:** 38 **Notes:** Civ Wed 80

Scalford Hall Hotel

★★★ 71% HOTEL

Melton Road, LE14 4UB - **tel:** 01664 444654
email: reception@scalfordhall.co.uk **web:** www.scalfordhall.co.uk
dir: *A6006 towards Melton Mowbray. Left at 2nd lights into Scalford Rd, hotel 3m on left*

Scalford Hall Hotel is located just five minutes away from the market town of Melton Mowbray. It is a good venue for weddings, galas, and team building events, and the pavilion can host up to 600 guests. Accommodation is comfortable, and in summer months guests can relax in the attractively landscaped gardens.

Rooms: 79 (52 annexe) (4 family) (18 GF) 🐾 **S** £32–£120; **D** £220* **Facilities:** WiFi HL Putting green 🏌 Gym Xmas New Year **Conf:** Class 350 Board 50 Thtr 600 Del from £100 **Services:** Night porter **Parking:** 200 **Notes:** LB Civ Wed 600

M

MELTON MOWBRAY *continued*

Premier Inn Melton Mowbray

BUDGET HOTEL

5 Norman Way, LE13 1JE - **tel:** 0871 527 9584 (Calls cost 13p per minute plus your phone company's access charge) **web:** www.premierinn.com
dir: *On A607, N of town centre*

High quality, budget accommodation ideal for both families and business travellers. Spacious, en suite bedrooms feature free WiFi and tea and coffee making facilities, and in most hotels, Freeview TV is also available. The adjacent family restaurant features a wide and varied menu.

Rooms: 55

MEMBURY MOTORWAY SERVICE AREA (M4)	Map 5 SU37
Berkshire	

Days Inn Membury - M4

AA Advertised

Membury Service Area, RG17 7TZ - **tel:** 01488 72336
email: membury.hotel@welcomebreak.co.uk **web:** www.welcomebreak.co.uk
dir: *M4 between junct 14 & 15*

This modern building offers accommodation in smart, spacious and well-equipped bedrooms, suitable for families and business travellers, and all with en suite bathrooms. Continental breakfast is available and other refreshments may be taken at the nearby family restaurant.

Rooms: 38 (32 family) (17 GF) (5 smoking) **Facilities:** FTV WiFi Game zone amusements **Conf:** Board 10 **Parking:** 200

MERIDEN	Map 10 SP28
West Midlands	

Forest of Arden Marriott Hotel & Country Club

★★★★ 78% HOTEL

Maxstoke Lane, CV7 7HR - **tel:** 01676 522335
web: www.marriottforestofarden.co.uk
dir: *M42 junct 6 onto A45 towards Coventry, over Stonebridge flyover. After 0.75m left into Shepherds Ln. Left at T-junct. Hotel 1.5m on left*

The ancient oaks, rolling hills and natural lakes of the 10,000 acre Forest of Arden estate provide an idyllic backdrop for this modern hotel and country club. The hotel boasts an excellent range of leisure facilities and is regarded as one of the finest golfing destinations in the UK. Bedrooms provide every modern convenience and a full range of facilities.

Rooms: 214 (65 GF) **Facilities:** Spa WiFi 18 Putting green Fishing Gym Floodlit golf academy New Year **Conf:** Class 180 Board 40 Thtr 300 **Services:** Lift Night porter **Parking:** 300 **Notes:** Civ Wed 250

Best Western Plus Manor NEC Birmingham

★★★★ 76% HOTEL

Main Road, CV7 7NH - **tel:** 01676 522735
email: reservations@manorhotelmeriden.co.uk **web:** www.manorhotelmeriden.co.uk
dir: *M42 junct 6, A45 towards Coventry then A452 signed Leamington. At rdbt take B4102 signed Meriden, hotel on left*

This sympathetically extended Georgian manor in the heart of a sleepy village is just a few minutes away from the M6, M42 and National Exhibition Centre. The Regency Restaurant offers modern dishes, while Houston's serves lighter meals and snacks. The bedrooms are smart and well equipped.

Rooms: 112 (15 family) (20 GF) **S** £65–£199; **D** £75–£209 (incl. bkfst)*
Facilities: FTV WiFi Xmas New Year **Conf:** Class 150 Board 60 Thtr 250
Services: Lift Night porter **Parking:** 190 **Notes:** LB Civ Wed 200

MEVAGISSEY	Map 2 SX04
Cornwall & Isles of Scilly	

Tremarne Hotel

★★★ 84% HOTEL

Polkirt, PL26 6UY - **tel:** 01726 842213
email: info@tremarne-hotel.co.uk **web:** www.tremarne-hotel.co.uk
dir: *A30 from Exeter, take A390 at St Austell then B3273 to Mevagissey. Follow Portmellon signs through Mevagissey. At top of Polkirt Hill 1st right into Higherwell Park. Hotel drive facing*

A very popular destination, set in landscaped gardens with a swimming pool, Tremarne Hotel enjoys superb views towards Mevagissey. The friendliness of Michael, Fitz and the team cannot be bettered. The hotel offers comfortable, individually styled bedrooms that either have views of the sea or the countryside. Guests can expect good service and freshly-cooked food on a daily-changing menu.

Rooms: 13 **S** £70–£105; **D** £105–£170 (incl. bkfst)* **Facilities:** FTV WiFi
Xmas New Year **Parking:** 15 **Notes:** LB

Trevalsa Court Hotel

★★★ 80% HOTEL

School Hill, Polstreath, PL26 6TH - **tel:** 01726 842468
email: stay@trevalsa-hotel.co.uk **web:** www.trevalsa-hotel.co.uk
dir: *From St Austell take B3273 to Mevagissey. Pass sign to Pentewan. At top of hill left at x-rds. Hotel signed*

Very well located above the town of Mevagissey, with easy access to nearby attractions, this establishment is an Arts & Crafts style property appointed to a high standard throughout with lots of original features. Bedrooms, many with sea views, are comfortable and well presented; there is also a stylish guests' sitting room with views across the bay.

Rooms: 14 (1 annexe) (1 family) (4 GF) **Facilities:** FTV WiFi **Parking:** 20
Notes: LB Closed Dec & Jan

MEXBOROUGH
South Yorkshire
Map 16 SE40

Best Western Plus Pastures Hotel

★★★ 81% HOTEL

Pastures Road, S64 0JJ - **tel:** 01709 577707
email: info@pastureshotel.co.uk **web:** www.pastureslodge.co.uk/hotel
dir: 0.5m from town centre on A6023, left by CLS Mot, signed Denaby Ings & Cadeby.
Hotel on right

This private hotel is in a rural setting beside a working canal with views of Conisbrough Castle in the distance, and is convenient for Doncaster or the Dearne Valley with its nature reserves and leisure centre. Guests can dine in the Pastures Lodge pub and family restaurant situated opposite the hotel, or in Reeds restaurant in the hotel. Bedrooms, in a modern, purpose-built block, are quiet, comfortable and equipped with many modern facilities including flat-screen smart TV and in-room safe.

Rooms: 60 (5 family) (28 GF) S fr £49; D fr £49* **Facilities:** STV FTV WiFi
Xmas New Year **Conf:** Class 170 Board 100 Thtr 250 **Services:** Lift Night porter
Parking: 179 **Notes:** LB Civ Wed 200

MICHAELWOOD MOTORWAY SERVICE AREA (M5)
Gloucestershire
Map 4 ST79

Days Inn Michaelwood - M5

WELCOMEBREAK

AA Advertised

Michaelwood Service Area, GL11 6DD - **tel:** 01454 261513
email: michaelwood.hotel@welcomebreak.co.uk **web:** www.welcomebreak.co.uk
dir: M5 N'bound between junct 13 & 14

This modern building offers accommodation in smart, spacious and well-equipped bedrooms, suitable for families and business travellers, and all with en suite bathrooms. Continental breakfast is available and other refreshments may be taken at the nearby family restaurant.

Rooms: 38 (15 family) (7 smoking) **Facilities:** FTV WiFi **Conf:** Board 10 **Parking:** 40

MIDDLESBROUGH
North Yorkshire
Map 19 NZ41

Premier Inn Middlesbrough Central South

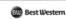

BUDGET HOTEL

Marton Way, TS4 3BS - **tel:** 0871 527 8770 (Calls cost 13p per minute plus your phone company's access charge) **web:** www.premierinn.com
dir: Off A172 opposite South Cleveland Hospital complex

High quality, budget accommodation ideal for both families and business travellers. Spacious, en suite bedrooms feature free WiFi and tea and coffee making facilities, and in most hotels, Freeview TV is also available. The adjacent family restaurant features a wide and varied menu.

Rooms: 74

MIDDLETON STONEY
Oxfordshire
Map 11 SP52

Best Western The Jersey Arms

Best Western

★★ 76% HOTEL

OX25 4AD - **tel:** 01869 343234
email: jerseyarms@bestwestern.co.uk **web:** www.jerseyarms.com
dir: 3m from A34, on B430, 10m N of Oxford, between junct 9 & 10 of M40

With a history dating back to the 13th century, the Jersey Arms combines old-fashioned charm with contemporary style and elegance. The individually designed

---

bedrooms are well equipped and comfortable. The lounge has an open fire, and the smart and spacious restaurant provides a calm atmosphere in which to enjoy the popular cuisine.

Rooms: 20 (14 annexe) (3 family) (9 GF) **Facilities:** FTV WiFi **Conf:** Class 20 Board 20 Thtr 20 **Parking:** 55

MIDSOMER NORTON
Somerset
Map 4 ST65

Best Western Plus Centurion Hotel

Best Western PLUS

★★★★ 79% @@ HOTEL

Charlton Lane, BA3 4BD - **tel:** 01761 417711
email: enquiries@centurionhotel.co.uk **web:** www.centurionhotel.co.uk
dir: Just off A367, 10m S of Bath. Once in Radstock follow signs at mini rdbt for Shepton Mallet/Wells, follow for 2m, left at small rdbt

The Best Western Plus Centurion Hotel is located just nine miles from Bath in a peaceful area with surrounding grounds and a nine-hole golf course. Bedrooms and bathrooms offer good levels of quality and comfort. In addition to the relaxing public areas a range of leisure facilities are available, including gym, swimming pool and the new Centurion Health Club and Spa. Dinner may be taken in the relaxed Jays bar or the more stylish restaurant with the option of dining in the conservatory area.

Rooms: 45 (2 family) (18 GF) D £122–£165* **Facilities:** Spa FTV WiFi 9 Putting green Gym Sauna Steam room Spa pool New Year **Conf:** Class 50 Board 50 Thtr 180 Del from £125 **Services:** Night porter **Parking:** 160 **Notes:** LB Closed 24-26 Dec Civ Wed 110

MILTON COMMON
Oxfordshire
Map 5 SP60

The Oxfordshire

★★★★ 80% @ HOTEL

Rycote Lane, OX9 2PU - **tel:** 01844 278300
email: gm@theoxfordshire.com **web:** www.theoxfordshire.com
dir: M40 junct 7 N'bound (junct 8 S'bound), A329 towards Thame

Located within easy reach of the M40, this hotel is at the championship golf course, The Oxfordshire, in the heart of the beautiful Chilterns. The accommodation offers impressive levels of comfort and quality, and all rooms are air-conditioned and have access onto a balcony. The Tempus Spa includes a 15-metre pool, modern gym and three treatment rooms. This resort makes an ideal location for a relaxing break, especially for golf enthusiasts.

Rooms: 50 (18 GF) S £89–£289; D £99–£299* **Facilities:** Spa FTV WiFi 18 Putting green Gym Sauna Steam room New Year **Conf:** Class 66 Board 54 Thtr 180 **Services:** Lift Night porter Air con **Parking:** 150 **Notes:** Civ Wed 180

The Oxford Belfry

QHOTELS
INSPIRED BY YOU

★★★★ 80% HOTEL

OX9 2JW - **tel:** 01844 279381
email: oxfordbelfry@qhotels.co.uk **web:** www.qhotels.co.uk
dir: M40 junct 7 onto A329 to Thame. Left onto A40, hotel 300yds on right

This modern hotel has a relatively rural location and enjoys lovely views of the countryside to the rear. The hotel is built around two very attractive courtyards and has a number of lounges and conference rooms, as well as indoor leisure facilities and outdoor tennis courts. Bedrooms are large and feature a range of extras.

Rooms: 154 (20 family) (66 GF) S £99–£250; D £109–£260 (incl. bkfst)
Facilities: Spa FTV WiFi HL Gym Steam room Sauna Xmas New Year
Conf: Class 180 Board 100 Thtr 450 Del from £149 **Services:** Lift Night porter
Parking: 350 **Notes:** LB Civ Wed 300

M

MILTON KEYNES
Buckinghamshire Map 11 SP83

Mercure Milton Keynes Parkside Hotel

★★★★ 74% ⊛ HOTEL

Newport Road, Woughton on the Green, MK6 3LR - **tel:** 01908 661919
email: H6627@accor.com **web:** www.mercure.com
dir: *M1 junct 14, A509 towards Milton Keynes. 2nd exit on H6 follow signs to Woughton on the Green*

Set in a peaceful rural location, The Merure Milton Keynes Parkside Hotel is just a few minutes' drive from the town centre. The spacious rooms are modern, attractively decorated and well equipped. Public areas are tastefully appointed and the popular restaurant offers an interesting choice of dishes. The hotel also has a range of conference/function facilities and plenty of parking.

Rooms: 49 (10 annexe) (2 family) (20 GF) **Facilities:** STV FTV WiFi ☆ HL Free entry to health & fitness club (approx 2m) Xmas New Year **Conf:** Class 60 Board 50 Thtr 150 **Services:** Night porter Air con **Parking:** 75 **Notes:** Civ Wed 120

Mercure Milton Keynes Abbey Hill

★★★★ 72% HOTEL

The Approach, Monks Way, MK8 8LY - **tel:** 01908 561666
email: h8876@accor.com **web:** www.mercure-milton-keynes-abbey-hill.com
dir: *M1 junct 14/A509, 3rd exit at rdbt onto London Road. 1st exit at rdbt onto A422, straight across 7 rdbts, 3rd exit onto Monks Way, left to the Approach*

Mercure Milton Keynes Abbey Hill is located close to Central Milton Keynes train station and within easy access to the M1 and Luton Airport. The hotel has bedrooms with a modern and contemporary design, and provides a relaxing setting for meetings and events. Guests can enjoy a selection of freshly cooked meals in the bar and restaurant. Free car parking and WiFi are available.

Rooms: 92 (14 family) (44 GF) **Facilities:** STV FTV WiFi ☆ HL Putting green Gym Xmas New Year **Conf:** Class 120 Board 80 Thtr 250 **Services:** Night porter Air con **Parking:** 120 **Notes:** Civ Wed 120

Novotel Milton Keynes

★★★ 76% HOTEL

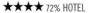

Saxon Street, Layburn Court, MK13 7RA - **tel:** 01908 322212
email: H3272@accor.com **web:** www.novotel.com
dir: *M1 junct 14, follow Childsway signs towards city centre. Right into Saxon Way, straight across all rdbts, hotel on left*

Contemporary in style, this purpose-built hotel is situated on the outskirts of the town, just a few minutes' drive from the centre and mainline railway station. Bedrooms provide ample workspace and a good range of facilities for the modern traveller, and public rooms include a children's play area and indoor leisure centre.

Rooms: 124 (40 family) (33 GF) **S** £55–£229; **D** £229* **Facilities:** FTV WiFi ☆ ⊙ Gym Sauna **Conf:** Class 75 Board 40 Thtr 120 Del from £125 **Services:** Lift Night porter **Parking:** 130 **Notes:** LB Civ Wed 100

Premier Inn Milton Keynes Central

BUDGET HOTEL

Secklow Gate West, MK9 3BZ - **tel:** 0871 527 8774 (Calls cost 13p per minute plus your phone company's access charge) **web:** www.premierinn.com
dir: *M1 junct 14 follow H6 route over 6 rdbts, at 7th (South Secklow) turn right, hotel on left*

High quality, budget accommodation ideal for both families and business travellers. Spacious, en suite bedrooms feature free WiFi and tea and coffee making

facilities, and in most hotels, Freeview TV is also available. The adjacent family restaurant features a wide and varied menu.

Rooms: 38

Premier Inn Milton Keynes East (Willen Lake)

BUDGET HOTEL

Brickhill Street, Willen Lake, MK15 9HQ - **tel:** 0871 527 8778 (Calls cost 13p per minute plus your phone company's access charge) **web:** www.premierinn.com
dir: *M1 junct 14 , H6 (Childsway). Right at 3rd rdbt into Brickhill St. Right at 1st mini rdbt, hotel 1st left*

Rooms: 41

Premier Inn Milton Keynes South

BUDGET HOTEL

Lakeside Grove, Bletcham Way, Caldecotte, MK7 8HP - **tel:** 0871 527 8780 (Calls cost 13p per minute plus your phone company's access charge) **web:** www.premierinn.com
dir: *M1 junct 14, towards Milton Keynes on H6 (Childs Way). Straight on at 2 rdbts. Left at 3rd rdbt onto V10 (Brickhill St). Straight on at 5 rdbts, at 6th right onto H10 Bletcham Way*

Rooms: 61

Premier Inn Milton Keynes South West (Furzton Lake)

BUDGET HOTEL

Shirwell Crescent, Furzton, MK4 1GA - **tel:** 0871 527 8776 (Calls cost 13p per minute plus your phone company's access charge) **web:** www.premierinn.com
dir: *M1 junct 14, A509 to Milton Keynes. Straight on at 8 rdbts, at 9th rdbt (North Grafton) left onto V6. Right at next onto H7. Over The Bowl rdbt, hotel on left*

Rooms: 120

MINEHEAD
Somerset Map 3 SS94

Premier Inn Minehead

BUDGET HOTEL

Seaward Way, TA24 6DF - **tel:** 0871 527 9696 (Calls cost 13p per minute plus your phone company's access charge) **web:** www.premierinn.com
dir: *Phone for directions*

High quality, budget accommodation ideal for both families and business travellers. Spacious, en suite bedrooms feature free WiFi and tea and coffee making facilities, and in most hotels, Freeview TV is also available. The adjacent family restaurant features a wide and varied menu.

Rooms: 102

MINSTER
Kent Map 7 TR36

Premier Inn Ramsgate

BUDGET HOTEL

Tothill Street, CT12 4HY - **tel:** 0871 527 9270 (Calls cost 13p per minute plus your phone company's access charge) **web:** www.premierinn.com
dir: *M25 onto A2 (signed Dover) merge onto M2 (signed Canterbury). Onto A299 (signed Margate/Ramsgate). Hotel at Minster rdbt*

High quality, budget accommodation ideal for both families and business travellers. Spacious, en suite bedrooms feature free WiFi and tea and coffee making

facilities, and in most hotels, Freeview TV is also available. The adjacent family restaurant features a wide and varied menu.

Rooms: 71

MONK FRYSTON
North Yorkshire   Map 19 SE52

Monk Fryston Hall Hotel

★★★ 82% ⏺ COUNTRY HOUSE HOTEL

LS25 5DU - tel: 01977 682369
email: reception@monkfrystonhallhotel.co.uk **web:** www.monkfrystonhallhotel.co.uk
dir: A1(M) junct 42, A63 towards Selby. Monk Fryston 2m, hotel on left

This delightful 16th-century mansion house enjoys a peaceful location in 30 acres of grounds, yet is only minutes' drive from the A1. Many original features have been retained and the public rooms are furnished with antique and period pieces. Bedrooms are individually styled and thoughtfully equipped for both business and leisure guests.

Rooms: 30 (2 family) (6 GF) ⏺ **S** £89–£99; **D** £99–£109 (incl. bkfst)* **Facilities:** FTV WiFi ⏺ ⏺ Xmas New Year **Conf:** Class 30 Board 25 Thtr 100 Del from £120 **Services:** Night porter **Parking:** 80 **Notes:** LB Civ Wed 100

MORECAMBE
Lancashire   Map 18 SD46

The Midland

★★★★ 74% ⏺ HOTEL

English Lakes
Hotels Resorts & Venues

Marine Road West, LA4 4BU - tel: 01524 424000
email: themidland@englishlakes.co.uk **web:** www.englishlakes.co.uk/hotels/midland
dir: A589 towards Morecambe, follow seafront signs, left on B5321 Lancaster Rd, then Easton Rd, left into Central Drive. Right at rdbt on seafront. Left to hotel entrance

This art deco hotel sits on the seafront and commands stunning views across Morecambe Bay to the mountains of the Lake District. Stylish and modern accommodation is provided in the well-appointed bedrooms. Spa facilities are available on site, and guests can use the leisure club at the nearby sister hotel.

Rooms: 44 (16 family) ⏺ **S** £115–£203; **D** £125–£213 (incl. bkfst)* **Facilities:** FTV WiFi ⏺ Xmas New Year **Conf:** Class 30 Board 48 Thtr 140 Del from £145 **Services:** Lift Night porter **Parking:** 70 **Notes:** LB Civ Wed 140

Best Western Lothersdale Hotel

BW Best Western.

★★★ 79% ⏺ HOTEL

320-323 Marine Road, LA4 5AA - tel: 01524 416404
email: hello@bfhotels.com **web:** www.bfhotels.com
dir: M6 junct 34 follow signs for Morecambe & Heysham. Straight over 3 rdbts following sign for Promenade. At seafront turn left, hotel 0.5m on left

Located in a central position on Morecambe's promenade, the Lothersdale Hotel offers enviable views across the bay and the Lakeland hills beyond. There are two dining options, Aspects Bistro and Aspects 320 tapas bar. Conference and function rooms are available, with car parking located to the rear of the hotel. Free WiFi is provided too.

Rooms: 40 (1 family) (5 GF) ⏺ **S** £40–£60; **D** £70–£169 (incl. bkfst)* **Facilities:** FTV WiFi New Year **Conf:** Class 100 Board 60 Thtr 120 Del from £80 **Services:** Lift Night porter **Parking:** 20 **Notes:** LB Closed 22 -27 Dec Civ Wed 110

MORETONHAMPSTEAD
Devon   Map 3 SX78

INSPECTOR'S CHOICE

Bovey Castle

★★★★★ ⏺⏺⏺ ⏺ HOTEL

Dartmoor National Park, TQ13 8RE - tel: 01647 445000
email: info@boveycastle.com **web:** www.boveycastle.com
dir: M5 junct 31 signed A30 Okehampton, stay on A30 until Whitton Down. Follow signs to Morehampton A382, stay on A382 until rdbt, turn right for Postbridge & Princetown B3212. Stay on B3212 for approx 1.5m. Bovey Castle is on left

Bovey Castle is a relaxed and welcoming hotel, located in 275 acres of peaceful Devonshire countryside, which includes an award-wining 18 hole, championship golf course. The bedrooms are elegant, spacious and stylish and offer high levels of comfort. Leisure facilities are extensive and include a health club, pool, spa and shop. Fine-dining is available in the Great Western Restaurant and a more casual style of dining is available in Smiths Brasserie. Cocktail bar, lounges and plenty of parking are also available.

Rooms: 60 (5 annexe) (9 family) (2 GF) ⏺ **S** fr £129; **D** fr £179* **Facilities:** Spa STV FTV WiFi ⏺ ⏺ ⏺ 18 Putting green ⏺ Fishing ⏺ Gym Falconry Archery Clay pigeon Shooting Table tennis Cider & gin making 4x4 driving Xmas New Year **Conf:** Class 64 Board 50 Thtr 120 Del from £215 **Services:** Lift Night porter **Parking:** 100 **Notes:** LB Civ Wed 150

The White Hart Hotel

★★★ 81% HOTEL

The Square, TQ13 8NQ - tel: 01647 440500
email: enquiries@whitehartdartmoor.co.uk **web:** www.whitehartdartmoor.co.uk
dir: A30 towards Okehampton. At Whiddon Down take A382 for Moretonhampstead

Dating back to the 1700s, this former coaching inn is located on the edge of Dartmoor. A relaxed and friendly atmosphere prevails, with the staff providing attentive service. Comfortable bedrooms have a blend of traditional and contemporary styles with thoughtful extras provided. Dining is in either the brasserie restaurant or more informally in the bar, where quality cuisine is served.

Rooms: 28 (8 annexe) (3 family) (4 GF) ⏺ **Facilities:** FTV WiFi ⏺ Xmas New Year **Conf:** Class 30 Board 20 Thtr 50 **Notes:** Civ Wed 60

MORETON-IN-MARSH
Gloucestershire   Map 10 SP23

Manor House Hotel

COTSWOLD
INNS & HOTELS

★★★★ 82% ⏺⏺ HOTEL

High Street, GL56 0LJ - tel: 01608 650501
email: info@manorhousehotel.info **web:** www.cotswold-inns-hotels.co.uk
dir: Off A429 at south end of town. Take East St off High St, hotel car park 3rd right

Dating back to the 16th century, this charming Cotswold coaching inn retains much of its original character, with stone walls, impressive fireplaces and a relaxed, country-house atmosphere. Bedrooms vary in size and reflect the individuality of the building; all are well equipped and some are particularly opulent. Comfortable public areas include a popular bar, a brasserie and the stylish Mulberry Restaurant where an opportunity to enjoy an evening meal should not be missed.

Rooms: 35 (1 annexe) (3 family) (1 GF) ⏺ **S** fr £89; **D** fr £99 (incl. bkfst)* **Facilities:** FTV WiFi ⏺ Xmas New Year **Conf:** Class 48 Board 54 Thtr 120 **Services:** Lift Night porter **Parking:** 24 **Notes:** Civ Wed 120

M

MORETON-IN-MARSH *continued*

White Hart Royal Hotel

★★★ 81% @ HOTEL

High Street, GL56 0BA - tel: 01608 650731
email: whr@bulldogmail.co.uk **web:** www.whitehartroyal.co.uk
dir: *On High St at junct with Oxford Rd*

This historic hotel has been providing accommodation for hundreds of years and today offers high standards of quality and comfort. Public areas are full of character, and the bedrooms, in a wide range of shapes and sizes, include several very spacious and luxurious rooms situated adjacent to the main building. A varied range of well prepared dishes is available throughout the day and evening in the main bar and the relaxing restaurant.

Rooms: 28 (8 annexe) (2 family) (9 GF) **Facilities:** FTV WiFi ⌂ HL Xmas New Year **Conf:** Class 40 Board 20 Thtr 55 **Services:** Night porter **Parking:** 6 **Notes:** Civ Wed 50

Redesdale Arms

★★★ 79% @ HOTEL

High Street, GL56 0AW - tel: 01608 650308
email: info@redesdalearms.com **web:** www.redesdalearms.com
dir: *On A429, 0.5m from rail station*

This fine old inn has played a central role in the town for centuries. Traditional features combine successfully with contemporary comforts; bedrooms are located in the main building and in an annexe. Guests can choose from an imaginative menu in either the stylish restaurant or the conservatory.

Rooms: 34 (26 annexe) (6 family) (16 GF) **S** £100–£130; **D** £140–£170 (incl. bkfst)* **Facilities:** STV FTV WiFi ⌂ Xmas New Year **Parking:** 17

MORLEY
Derbyshire   Map 11 SK34

The Morley Hayes Hotel

★★★★ 80% @@ HOTEL

Main Road, DE7 6DG - tel: 01332 780480
email: hotel@morleyhayes.com **web:** www.morleyhayes.com
dir: *4m N of Derby on A608*

Located in rolling countryside this modern golfing destination provides extremely comfortable, stylish bedrooms with wide-ranging facilities, plasma TVs, and state-of-the-art bathrooms; the plush suites are particularly eye-catching. Creative cuisine is offered in the Dovecote Restaurant, and both Roosters and the Spikes sports bar provide informal eating options.

Rooms: 32 (4 family) (15 GF) **S** fr £135; **D** fr £165 (incl. bkfst)* **Facilities:** STV FTV WiFi ⌂ HL ᵭ 27 Putting green Golf driving range **Conf:** Class 50 Board 40 Thtr 120 Del from £139.95 **Services:** Lift Night porter Air con **Parking:** 245 **Notes:** Civ Wed 90

MOTTRAM ST ANDREW
Cheshire   Map 16 SJ87

Mottram Hall

★★★★ 82% @ HOTEL

Wilmslow Road, SK10 4QT - tel: 01625 828135
email: mottramevents@qhotels.co.uk **web:** www.qhotels.co.uk
dir: *M6 junct 18 from S, M6 junct 20 from N, M56 junct 6, A538 Prestbury*

Set in 272 acres of some of Cheshire's most beautiful parkland, this 18th-century Georgian country house is certainly an idyllic retreat. The hotel boasts extensive leisure facilities, including a championship golf course, swimming pool, gym and spa. Bedrooms are well equipped and elegantly furnished, and include a number of superior rooms and suites.

Rooms: 120 (37 family) (28 GF) **Facilities:** Spa WiFi ⌂ ☯ supervised ᵭ 18 Putting green ☯ Fishing Gym FA approved football pitch Xmas New Year **Conf:** Class 120 Board 60 Thtr 180 Del from £149 **Services:** Lift Night porter **Parking:** 300 **Notes:** Civ Wed 160

MUCH WENLOCK
Shropshire   Map 10 SO69

Raven Hotel

★★★ 79% @@ HOTEL

30 Barrow Street, TF13 6EN - tel: 01952 727251
email: enquiry@ravenhotel.com **web:** www.ravenhotel.com
dir: *M54 junct 4 or 5, take A442 S, then A4169 to Much Wenlock*

This town-centre hotel spreads across several historic buildings with a 17th-century coaching inn at its centre. The accommodation is well furnished and equipped to offer modern comfort; some ground-floor rooms are available. Public areas feature an interesting collection of prints and memorabilia connected with the modern-day Olympic Games - an idea which was, interestingly, born in Much Wenlock.

Rooms: 20 (13 annexe) (5 GF) **Facilities:** FTV WiFi ⌂ New Year **Conf:** Board 16 Thtr 16 **Parking:** 30 **Notes:** Closed 25-26 Dec

Gaskell Arms

★★★ 76% SMALL HOTEL

Bourton Road, TF13 6AQ - tel: 01952 727212
email: maxine@gaskellarms.co.uk **web:** www.gaskellarms.co.uk
dir: *M6 junct 10A onto M54, exit at junct 4, follow signs for Ironbridge/Much Wenlock & A4169*

This 17th-century former coaching inn has exposed beams and log fires in the public areas, and much original charm and character is retained throughout. In addition to the lounge bar and restaurant offering a wide range of meals and snacks, there is a small bar which is popular with locals. Well-equipped bedrooms, some located in stylishly renovated stables, provide good standards of comfort.

Rooms: 14 (3 family) (5 GF) **S** £79; **D** £99–£125 (incl. bkfst)* **Facilities:** FTV WiFi ⌂ **Conf:** Class 30 Board 20 Thtr 30 **Parking:** 40 **Notes:** LB

MUDEFORD

See **Christchurch**

MULLION
Cornwall & Isles of Scilly

Map 2 SW61

Mullion Cove Hotel
★★★ 88% ◉◉ HOTEL

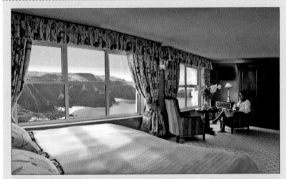

TR12 7EP - **tel:** 01326 240328
email: enquiries@mullion-cove.co.uk **web:** www.mullion-cove.co.uk
dir: *A3083 towards The Lizard. Through Mullion towards Mullion Cove.*
Hotel in approx 1m

Built at the turn of the last century and set high above the working harbour of Mullion, this hotel has spectacular views of the rugged coastline; seaward facing rooms are always popular. The elegant restaurant offers some carefully prepared dishes using local produce, while an alternative option is to eat less formally in the stylish bistro. After dinner, guests might like to relax in one of the charming lounges.

Rooms: 30 (3 family) (3 GF) ✏ **S** £100–£335; **D** £115–£350 (incl. bkfst)*
Facilities: FTV WiFi ↘ Xmas New Year **Conf:** Class 20 Board 30 Thtr 50
Services: Lift Night porter **Parking:** 60 **Notes:** LB

Polurrian Bay Hotel
AA Advertised ◉◉

TR12 7EN - **tel:** 01326 240421
email: info@polurrianhotel.com **web:** www.polurrianhotel.com
dir: *A394 to Helston. Follow The Lizard & Mullion signs onto A3083. Approx 5m,*
right onto B3296 to Mullion. Follow one-way system to T-junct, left signed Mullion Cove.
0.5m right, follow hotel sign

Polurrian Bay Hotel boasts a stunning cliff-top position with spectacular views across St Mount's Bay. It is very much a family-friendly establishment with a range of facilities available. Small children can be entertained in the crèche, while the spa provides some rest and relaxation for mum and dad. Bedrooms provide impressive levels of comfort and quality, and many also enjoy wonderful sea views. Public areas include the Vista, a wonderful area in which to relax and take in the breathtaking scenery while enjoying a light lunch.

Rooms: 41 (12 family) (8 GF) ✏ **D** £120–£180 (incl. bkfst)* **Facilities:** Spa FTV WiFi ↘ ⊕ ↘ ⌣ Gym Xmas New Year Child facilities **Conf:** Class 12 Board 30 Thtr 90
Services: Night porter **Notes:** Civ Wed 80

NANTWICH
Cheshire

Map 15 SJ65

Rookery Hall Hotel & Spa
★★★★ ◉◉ 🛏 HOTEL

Main Road, Worleston, CW5 6DQ - **tel:** 01270 610016 & 0845 072 7533
(Calls cost 5p per minute plus your phone company's access charge)
email: rookeryhall@handpicked.co.uk **web:** www.handpickedhotels.co.uk/rookeryhall
dir: *From A51 N of Nantwich take B5074 Winsford, signed Rookery Hall.*
Hotel 1.5m on right

This fine 19th-century mansion is set in 38 acres of gardens, pasture and parkland. Bedrooms are spacious and appointed to a high standard with wide-screen plasma TVs and DVD players; many rooms have separate walk-in showers as well as deep tubs. Public areas are delightful and retain many original features. There is an extensive, state-of-the art spa and leisure complex.

Rooms: 70 (39 annexe) (6 family) (23 GF) ✏ **S** £116–£219; **D** £130–£234 (incl. bkfst)* **Facilities:** Spa STV FTV WiFi ↘ HL ⊕ ↘ Gym Sauna Crystal steam room Hydrotherapy pool Xmas New Year **Conf:** Class 90 Board 46 Thtr 200 Del from £149 **Services:** Lift Night porter **Parking:** 120 **Notes:** LB Civ Wed 160

N

NANTWICH *continued*

Alvaston Hall Hotel

★★★★ 75% HOTEL

WARNERLEISUREHOTELS

Middlewich Road, CW5 6PD - **tel:** 01270 624341
web: www.warnerleisurehotels.co.uk
dir: *Phone for directions*

Alvaston Hall is a Grade-II listed Victorian property located in the delightful Cheshire countryside and set in extensive grounds. A variety of very well equipped bedrooms are available; some have spacious seating areas and some have outdoor terraces. Outdoor and indoor leisure facilities include a 9-hole golf course, hair and beauty treatments, and a great range of entertainment and activities including an impressive cabaret facility. Please note, this is an adults-only (over 21 years) hotel.

Rooms: 245 (15 annexe) (101 GF) ⌂ **Facilities:** Spa FTV WiFi HL ⊛ supervised ⌁ 9 Putting green ⛳ Gym Archery Bowling green ♫ Xmas New Year **Services:** Lift Night porter **Parking:** 300

Premier Inn Crewe/Nantwich

BUDGET HOTEL

221 Crewe Road, CW5 6NE - **tel:** 0871 527 8782 (Calls cost 13p per minute plus your phone company's access charge) **web:** www.premierinn.com
dir: *M6 junct 16, A500 towards Chester, A534 towards Nantwich. Hotel approx 100yds on right*

High quality, budget accommodation ideal for both families and business travellers. Spacious, en suite bedrooms feature free WiFi and tea and coffee making facilities, and in most hotels, Freeview TV is also available. The adjacent family restaurant features a wide and varied menu.

Rooms: 37

NEW ALRESFORD
Hampshire

Map 5 SU53

Swan Hotel

★★★ 78% HOTEL

THE INDEPENDENTS
HOTEL ASSOCIATION

11 West Street, SO24 9AD - **tel:** 01962 732302
email: swanhotel@btinternet.com **web:** www.swanhotelalresford.com
dir: *Exit A31 onto B3047*

This former coaching inn dates back to the 18th century and remains a busy and popular destination for travellers and locals alike. Bedrooms are situated in both the main building and the more modern wing. The lounge bar and adjacent restaurant are open all day; for more traditional dining there is another restaurant which overlooks the busy village street.

Rooms: 23 (12 annexe) (3 family) (5 GF) ⌂ **S** £70–£80; **D** £100–£110 (incl. bkfst)*
Facilities: FTV WiFi ⌁ New Year **Conf:** Class 60 Board 40 Thtr 90 Del from £120
Parking: 25 **Notes:** RS 25 Dec Only open for residents food & reserved lunches

NEWARK-ON-TRENT
Nottinghamshire

Map 17 SK75

Premier Inn Newark

BUDGET HOTEL

Premier Inn

Lincoln Road, NG24 2DB - **tel:** 0871 527 8784 (Calls cost 13p per minute plus your phone company's access charge) **web:** www.premierinn.com
dir: *At junct of A1 & A46 & A17, follow B6166 signs*

High quality, budget accommodation ideal for both families and business travellers. Spacious, en suite bedrooms feature free WiFi and tea and coffee making facilities, and in most hotels, Freeview TV is also available. The adjacent family restaurant features a wide and varied menu.

Rooms: 70

NEWBURY
Berkshire

Map SU46

See also **Andover**

See also **Andover**

INSPECTOR'S CHOICE

The Vineyard

★★★★★ ⊛⊛⊛ HOTEL

RELAIS & CHATEAUX

Stockcross, RG20 8JU - **tel:** 01635 528770
email: general@the-vineyard.co.uk **web:** www.the-vineyard.co.uk
dir: *From M4 junct 13, A34 towards Newbury, exit at 3rd junct for Speen. Right at rdbt then right again at 2nd rdbt*

The Vineyard is a haven of style in the Berkshire countryside, where only perfect will do. Bedrooms and suites come in a variety of styles, including many split-level suites that are exceptionally well equipped with indulgent features that ensure a wonderful night's stay. Comfortable lounges lead into the stylish three AA Rosette restaurant. At the helm of the kitchen is Robby Jenks, an inspirational chef who recreates classical British dishes using modern techniques, delivering a simple yet perfect dining experience. The hotel has an impressive 30,000 bottle wine cellar which includes wines from California and around the world, including bottles from the award-winning estate of owner Sir Peter Michael. The hotel also prides itself on a superb art collection, which can be seen throughout the building. The welcome throughout the hotel is warm and sincere, the service professional yet relaxed.

Rooms: 49 (18 GF) ⌂ **S** £185–£355; **D** £205–£375* **Facilities:** Spa STV WiFi ⌁ ⊛ ⌁ 9 Gym ♫ Xmas New Year **Conf:** Class 70 Board 30 Thtr 140 **Services:** Lift Night porter Air con **Parking:** 100 **Notes:** LB Civ Wed 100

HIGHLY RECOMMENDED

Donnington Valley Hotel & Spa

★★★★ 82% ◉◉ HOTEL

Old Oxford Road, Donnington, RG14 3AG - tel: 01635 551199
email: general@donningtonvalley.co.uk **web:** www.donningtonvalley.co.uk
dir: *M4 junct 13, A34 signed Newbury. Take exit signed Donnington/Services, at rdbt 2nd exit signed Donnington. Left at next rdbt. Hotel 2m on right*

In its own grounds complete with an 18-hole golf course, this stylish hotel boasts excellent facilities for both corporate and leisure guests; from the state-of-the-art spa offering excellent treatments, to an extensive range of meeting and function rooms. Air-conditioned bedrooms are stylish, spacious and particularly well equipped with fridges, lap-top safes and internet access. The Wine Press restaurant offers imaginative food complemented by a superb wine list.

Rooms: 111 (4 family) (36 GF) ⌇ **Facilities:** Spa STV WiFi ◊ ⊕ ⌁ 18 Putting green Gym Aromatherapy Sauna Steam room Studio Xmas New Year **Conf:** Class 50 Board 65 Thtr 160 **Services:** Lift Night porter Air con **Parking:** 150 **Notes:** Civ Wed 85

Regency Park Hotel

★★★★ 80% HOTEL

Bowling Green Road, Thatcham, RG18 3RP - tel: 01635 871555
email: info@regencyparkhotel.co.uk **web:** www.regencyparkhotel.co.uk
dir: *From Newbury take A4 signed Thatcham & Reading. 2nd rdbt exit signed Cold Ash. Hotel 1m on left*

This smart, stylish hotel is ideal for both business and leisure guests. Spacious, well-equipped bedrooms include a number of contemporary, tasteful executive

rooms. Smart, airy public areas include a state-of-the-art spa and leisure club, plus the Watermark Restaurant which offers appealing cuisine.

Rooms: 108 (10 family) (9 GF) **Facilities:** Spa STV FTV WiFi ◊ HL ⊕ Gym Beauty treatments Sauna Steam room Xmas New Year **Conf:** Class 80 Board 70 Thtr 200 **Services:** Lift Night porter **Parking:** 200 **Notes:** Civ Wed 100

Mercure Newbury Elcot Park

★★★★ 74% ◉ HOTEL

Elcot, RG20 8NJ - tel: 0844 815 9060 (Calls cost 7p per minute plus your phone company's access charge) **email:** gm.mercurenewburyelcotpark@jupiterhotels.co.uk **web:** www.mercurenewbury.co.uk
dir: *M4 junct 13, A338 to Hungerford, A4 to Newbury. Hotel 4m from Hungerford*

Enjoying a peaceful location within easy reach of both the A4 and M4, this country-house hotel is set in 16 acres of gardens and woodland. Bedrooms are comfortably appointed and include some located in an adjacent mews. Public areas include the Orangery Restaurant which enjoys views over the Kennet Valley and a range of conference rooms.

Rooms: 73 (17 annexe) (6 family) (25 GF) **S** £48–£164; **D** £55–£210* **Facilities:** FTV WiFi ◊ ⌣ ♨ Gym New Year **Conf:** Class 60 Board 50 Thtr 140 Del from £145 **Services:** Night porter **Parking:** 120 **Notes:** LB Civ Wed 140

Best Western West Grange Hotel

BW Best Western.

★★★ 75% HOTEL

Cox's Lane, Bath Road, RG7 5UP - tel: 01635 273074
email: reservations@westgrangehotel.co.uk **web:** www.westgrangehotel.co.uk
dir: *M4 junct 12, A4 Bath Rd, follow Newbury signs. Through Woolhampton, hotel on right in approx 2m*

Conveniently situated between Reading and Newbury, this modern hotel has well-appointed, spacious bedrooms; executive rooms are beautifully presented and have a host of additional features. The contemporary open-plan lounge and restaurant area serves an extensive choice of British cuisine. There is a range of business suites along with a larger conference room. The gardens are a real feature and the central courtyard is popular with guests.

Rooms: 62 (1 family) (21 GF) ⌇ **S** £60–£140; **D** £70–£150* **Facilities:** FTV WiFi ◊ Xmas New Year **Conf:** Class 25 Board 30 Thtr 50 Del from £195 **Services:** Lift Night porter **Parking:** 50 **Notes:** LB Civ Wed 60

The Chequers Hotel

★★★ 75% HOTEL

6-8 Oxford Street, RG14 1JB - tel: 01635 38000
email: info@chequershotelnewbury.co.uk **web:** www.chequershotelnewbury.co.uk
dir: *M4 junct 13, A34 S, A339 to Newbury. At 2nd rdbt right to town centre. At clock tower rdbt right, hotel on right*

Situated just at the top of the main shopping street in Newbury and convenient for fast road connections, this 18th-century former coaching inn retains original features along with contemporary touches. The bedrooms come in a range of sizes and JP's Bistro is a popular eatery. The hotel has ample parking which is a definite advantage in this town.

Rooms: 56 (2 family) (6 GF) **S** £55–£101; **D** £55–£109* **Facilities:** FTV WiFi ◊ **Conf:** Class 36 Board 40 Thtr 120 Del from £100 **Services:** Night porter **Parking:** 60 **Notes:** Civ Wed 80

NEWBURY *continued*

Donnington Grove Country Club

★★★ 75% HOTEL

Grove Road, Donnington, RG14 2LA - **tel:** 01635 581000
email: enquiries@donnington-grove.com **web:** www.donnington-grove.com
dir: *Phone for directions*

Situated on the outskirts of Newbury, overlooked by historic Donnington Castle, this hotel offers comfortable bedrooms in a number of types. Once a splendid manor house, accommodation has been tastefully added to meet the needs of the leisure and business traveller. The estate comprises some 550 acres featuring a popular championship golf course designed by Dave Thomas in 1991.

Rooms: (19 annexe) (27 GF) 🌂 **S** £91–£137; **D** £101–£147 (incl. bkfst)
Facilities: FTV WiFi ⓥ ⚲ 18 Putting green Fishing New Year **Conf:** Class 30 Board 36 Thtr 100 **Services:** Lift Night porter **Parking:** 90 **Notes:** Civ Wed 100

NEWBY BRIDGE
Cumbria   Map 18 SD38

HIGHLY RECOMMENDED

Lakeside Hotel Lake Windermere

★★★★ 86% ⚛⚛ HOTEL

Lakeside, LA12 8AT - **tel:** 015395 30001
email: sales@lakesidehotel.co.uk **web:** www.lakesidehotel.co.uk
dir: *M6 junct 36, A590 to Barrow, follow signs to Newby Bridge. Right over bridge, hotel 1m on right*

This impressive hotel enjoys an enviable location on the southern edge of Lake Windermere and has easy access to the Lakeside & Haverthwaite Steam Railway, as well as the ferry terminal. Bedrooms are individually styled, and many enjoy delightful lake views. Spacious lounges and a choice of restaurants are available. The state-of-the-art spa is exclusive to residents and provides a range of treatment suites. Staff throughout are friendly and nothing is too much trouble.

Rooms: 74 (8 family) (8 GF) 🌂 **S** £89–£109; **D** £199–£209 (incl. bkfst)
Facilities: Spa STV WiFi ⓥ Fishing Gym Private jetty Rowing boats ♫ Xmas New Year **Conf:** Class 50 Board 40 Thtr 100 **Services:** Lift Night porter **Parking:** 200 **Notes:** LB Civ Wed 70

The Swan Hotel & Spa

★★★★ 79% HOTEL

LA12 8NB - **tel:** 015395 31681
email: enquiries@swanhotel.com **web:** www.swanhotel.com
dir: *M6 junct 36, A591, merge onto A590. At rdbts follow A590, left at Newby Bridge rdbt, 1st right for hotel*

The Swan Hotel is set in idyllic surroundings and offers something to suit every taste, from a gym and spa therapies for adults to a dedicated children's lounge. The well-equipped bedrooms are thoroughly modern, but each has a vintage touch. Good quality meals are served in the River Room; in good weather guests can eat on the riverside terrace.

Rooms: 54 (8 family) (14 GF) 🌂 **S** £109–£409; **D** £109–£409 (incl. bkfst)*
Facilities: Spa FTV WiFi ⓥ ⓢ Fishing Gym Sauna Steam room Xmas New Year Child facilities **Conf:** Class 60 Board 40 Thtr 100 Del from £175 **Services:** Lift Night porter Air con **Parking:** 100 **Notes:** LB Civ Wed 100

NEWCASTLE-UNDER-LYME
Staffordshire   Map 10 SJ84

Premier Inn Newcastle-under-Lyme

BUDGET HOTEL

Talke Road, Chesterton, ST5 7AL - **tel:** 0871 527 8808 (Calls cost 13p per minute plus your phone company's access charge) **web:** www.premierinn.com
dir: *M6 junct 12, A500, A34 to Newcastle-under-Lyme. Hotel 0.5m on right*

High quality, budget accommodation ideal for both families and business travellers. Spacious, en suite bedrooms feature free WiFi and tea and coffee making facilities, and in most hotels, Freeview TV is also available. The adjacent family restaurant features a wide and varied menu.

Rooms: 83

NEWCASTLE UPON TYNE
Tyne & Wear   Map 21 NZ26

INSPECTOR'S CHOICE

Jesmond Dene House

★★★★ ⚛⚛⚛ HOTEL

Jesmond Dene Road, NE2 2EY - **tel:** 0191 212 3000
email: info@jesmonddenehouse.co.uk **web:** www.jesmonddenehouse.co.uk
dir: *A167 N to A184. Right, right again into Jesmond Dene Rd, hotel on left*

This grand house, overlooking the wooded valley of Jesmond Dene, yet just five minutes from the centre of town, has been sympathetically converted into a stylish, contemporary hotel destination. The bedrooms are beautifully designed and boast flat-screen TVs, sumptuous beds with Egyptian cotton linen, digital radios, well-stocked mini bars, free broadband, desk space and safes. Equally eye-catching bathrooms with underfloor heating are equipped with high quality bespoke amenities. The stylish restaurant is the venue for innovative cooking which will prove a highlight of any stay.

Rooms: 40 (8 annexe) (1 family) (4 GF) 🌂 **S** £110–£305; **D** £120–£321 (incl. bkfst)* **Facilities:** STV FTV WiFi ⓥ HL **Conf:** Class 40 Board 40 Thtr 120 Del from £180 **Services:** Lift Night porter **Parking:** 64 **Notes:** LB Civ Wed 100

HIGHLY RECOMMENDED

Hotel du Vin Newcastle

★★★★ 83% ⊛ TOWN HOUSE HOTEL

Allan House, City Road, NE1 2BE - tel: 0191 229 2200
email: reception.newcastle@hotelduvin.com **web:** www.hotelduvin.com
dir: *A1 junct 65 onto A184 Gateshead/Newcastle, Quayside to City Rd*

The former maintenance depot of the Tyne Tees Shipping Company, this is a landmark building on the Tyne, which has been transformed into a modern and stylish hotel. Bedrooms are well equipped and deeply comfortable with all the Hotel du Vin trademark items such as Egyptian cotton sheets, plasma TVs, DVD players and monsoon showers. Guests can dine in the bistro, or alfresco if the weather allows in the courtyard.

Rooms: 42 (6 GF) ☕ **Facilities:** STV WiFi HL **Conf:** Board 20 Thtr 26 **Services:** Lift Night porter Air con **Parking:** 10 **Notes:** Civ Wed 40

Malmaison Newcastle

★★★★ 80% ⊛ HOTEL

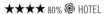

104 Quayside, NE1 3DX - tel: 0191 389 8627 & 0844 693 0658
(Calls cost 5p per minute plus your phone company's access charge)
email: newcastle@malmaison.com **web:** www.malmaison.com
dir: *Follow signs for city centre, then for Quayside/Law Courts. Hotel 100yds past Law Courts*

Malmaison Newcastle overlooks the river and the Millennium Bridge, in a prime position in the very popular quayside district. Bedrooms have striking decor, as well as mini-bars and a number of individual touches. Food and drink are an integral part of the operation here, with a stylish brasserie-style restaurant overlooking the river and bridge. The bar on the opposite side to the brasserie is modern and lively, attracting locals as well as the in-house guests. At the main entrance a Starbucks coffee bar can set you up with your caffeine fix for the morning.

Rooms: 122 (10 family) ☕ **Facilities:** Spa STV FTV WiFi Gym ♫ **Conf:** Class 50 Board 30 Thtr 80 **Services:** Lift Night porter Air con **Parking:** 50 **Notes:** Civ Wed 80

Holiday Inn Newcastle Gosforth Park

★★★★ 79% HOTEL

Holiday Inn

Great North Road, Seaton Burn, NE13 6BP - tel: 0191 201 9988 & 0871 423 4818
email: info@hinewcastlegosforthpark.co.uk **web:** www.hinewcastlegosforthpark.co.uk
dir: *A1 junct 80, at rdbt 1st left signed Blagdon. Hotel 500yds on right*

The Holiday Inn Newcastle Gosforth Park is ideally located with both the A1 and A19 just a stone's throw away. Newcastle is also easily reached from here making this an ideal setting. The hotel is enjoying significant investment taking place on a rolling programme with the leisure facilities, public areas and some bedrooms already benefiting from the work. There is ample parking with a well-equipped and newly refurbished pool, gym and spa facilities.

Rooms: (65 family) (69 GF) **S** £69–£249; **D** £69–£249* **Facilities:** Spa FTV WiFi ❄ supervised New Year **Conf:** Class 180 Board 40 Thtr 450 Del from £129 **Services:** Night porter **Parking:** 240 **Notes:** LB Civ Wed 200

Holiday Inn Newcastle Jesmond

★★★★ 78% HOTEL

Holiday Inn

Jesmond Road, NE2 1PR - tel: 0191 281 5511
email: enquiries@hinewcastle.co.uk **web:** www.hinewcastle.co.uk
dir: *Phone for directions*

Holiday Inn Newcastle Jesmond is located next to the Metro Station and benefits from off-road parking. The interior is modern, and there is a vibrant restaurant and bar operation. This is a great location for enjoying the café culture of Jesmond or the upbeat pace of the city centre.

Rooms: 116 ☕ **Facilities:** STV FTV WiFi ᴤ HL Gym ♫ New Year **Conf:** Class 160 Board 46 Thtr 250 **Services:** Lift Night porter Air con **Parking:** 80 **Notes:** Civ Wed

The Vermont Hotel

★★★★ 76% HOTEL

Castle Garth, NE1 1RQ - tel: 0191 233 1010
email: info@vermonthotel.co.uk **web:** www.vermont-hotel.com
dir: *Phone for directions*

This iconic building offers some great views of the city. Centrally located and benefiting from some off-road car parking, The Vermont Hotel is accessible from both the Quayside and from the castle.

Rooms: 101 ☕ **Facilities:** FTV WiFi ᴤ Gym Sauna Steam room ♫ Xmas New Year **Conf:** Class 80 Board 60 Thtr 220 **Services:** Lift Night porter **Parking:** 100 **Notes:** Civ Wed 220

HIGHLY RECOMMENDED

Eslington Villa Hotel

★★★ 84% ⊛ HOTEL

8 Station Road, Low Fell, NE9 6DR - tel: 0191 487 6017
email: home@eslingtonvilla.co.uk **web:** www.eslingtonvilla.co.uk

(for full entry see Gateshead)

The Caledonian Hotel, Newcastle

★★★ 79% HOTEL

PEEL HOTELS PLC

64 Osborne Road, Jesmond, NE2 2AT - tel: 0191 281 7881
email: info@caledonian-hotel-newcastle.com **web:** www.peelhotels.co.uk
dir: *From A1 follow signs to Newcastle City, cross Tyne Bridge to Tynemouth. Left at lights at Osborne Rd, hotel on right*

This hotel is located in the Jesmond area of the city, and offers comfortable bedrooms that are well equipped. The public areas include the trendy Billabong Bar and Bistro which serves food all day, and the terrace where a cosmopolitan atmosphere prevails. Alfresco dining is available.

Rooms: 89 (6 family) (7 GF) ☕ **S** £45–£109; **D** £50–£165* **Facilities:** WiFi Xmas New Year **Conf:** Class 50 Board 50 Thtr 100 **Services:** Lift Night porter **Parking:** 35 **Notes:** Civ Wed 70

Horton Grange Country House Hotel

★★★ 78% ⊛⊛ HOTEL

Berwick Hill, Ponteland, NE13 6BU - tel: 01661 860686
email: info@hortongrange.co.uk **web:** www.hortongrange.co.uk
dir: *A1/A19 junct at Seaton Burn take 1st exit at 1st rdbt, after 1m, left signed Ponteland/Dinnington. Hotel on right approx 2m*

Horton Grange is a Grade II listed building set in its own grounds just a short distance from Newcastle Airport and Ponteland. The main house has traditionally styled executive bedrooms, and in addition there are four contemporary garden rooms that are elegant and spacious. All bedrooms have flat-screen TVs, digital radios and broadband access. Food is served in the light and airy restaurant and the lounge, both of which overlook the gardens.

Rooms: 9 (4 annexe) (1 family) (4 GF) ☕ **S** £59–£139; **D** £69–£149 (incl. bkfst)* **Facilities:** FTV WiFi Xmas New Year **Conf:** Class 40 Board 30 Thtr 120 **Parking:** 50 **Notes:** LB Civ Wed 120

NEWCASTLE UPON TYNE *continued*

Best Western New Kent Hotel

★★★ A HOTEL

127 Osborne Road, NE2 2TB - tel: 0191 281 7711
email: reservations@newkenthotel.co.uk **web:** www.newkenthotel.co.uk
dir: On B1600, opposite St Georges Church

This popular business hotel offers relaxed service and typical Geordie hospitality. The bright contemporary bedrooms are well equipped and the modern bar is an ideal meeting place. A range of generous, good value dishes is served in the restaurant, which doubles as a wedding venue.

Rooms: 32 (4 family) **Facilities:** STV FTV WiFi ☔ Xmas New Year **Conf:** Class 30 Board 40 Thtr 60 **Services:** Night porter **Parking:** 22 **Notes:** LB Civ Wed 90

Premier Inn Newcastle Central

BUDGET HOTEL

New Bridge Street West, NE1 8BS - tel: 0871 527 8802 (Calls cost 13p per minute plus your phone company's access charge) **web:** www.premierinn.com
dir: Follow Gateshead & Newcastle signs on A167(M), over Tyne Bridge. A193 signed Wallsend & city centre, left to Carliol Square, hotel on corner

High quality, budget accommodation ideal for both families and business travellers. Spacious, en suite bedrooms feature free WiFi and tea and coffee making facilities, and in most hotels, Freeview TV is also available. The adjacent family restaurant features a wide and varied menu.

Rooms: 186

Premier Inn Newcastle City Centre (Millennium Bridge)

BUDGET HOTEL

City Road, Quayside, NE1 2AN - tel: 0871 527 8800 (Calls cost 13p per minute plus your phone company's access charge) **web:** www.premierinn.com
dir: At corner of City Rd (A186) & Crawhall Rd

Rooms: 82

Premier Inn Newcastle (Holystone)

BUDGET HOTEL

The Stonebrook, Edmund Road, NE27 0UN - tel: 0871 527 8790 (Calls cost 13p per minute plus your phone company's access charge) **web:** www.premierinn.com
dir: 3m N of Tyne Tunnel. From A19 take A191 signed Gosforth. Hotel on left

Rooms: 112

Premier Inn Newcastle Quayside

BUDGET HOTEL

The Quayside, NE1 3AE - tel: 0871 527 8804 (Calls cost 13p per minute plus your phone company's access charge) **web:** www.premierinn.com
dir: S'bound: A1, A167(M), A186 signed Walker & Wallsend follow B1600 Quayside signs. N'bound: A1, A184, A189 (cross river). 1st exit, follow B1600 Quayside signs. Hotel at foot of Tyne Bridge in Exchange building

Rooms: 152

NEWCASTLE UPON TYNE AIRPORT	Map 21 NZ17
Tyne & Wear	

Novotel Newcastle Airport

★★★ 81% HOTEL

Ponteland Road, Kenton, NE3 3HZ - tel: 028 4345 2800
email: H1118@accor.com **web:** www.novotel.com
dir: A1(M) airport junct onto A696, take Kingston Park exit

This modern, well-proportioned hotel lies just off the bypass and is a five minute drive from the airport. The hotel has a scheduled shuttle service and flight information screens for air passengers. Bedrooms are spacious with a range of extras. The Elements Restaurant offers a flexible dining option and is open until late. There is a contemporary lounge bar and also a small leisure centre for the more energetic guests. Secure parking is available.

Rooms: 126 (36 family) ✿ **Facilities:** FTV WiFi ☔ ⌖ Gym Sauna Xmas New Year **Conf:** Class 150 Board 100 Thtr 200 **Services:** Lift **Parking:** 200 **Notes:** Civ Wed 200

Premier Inn Newcastle Airport

BUDGET HOTEL

Newcastle Int Airport, Ponteland Rd, NE20 9DB - tel: 0871 527 8796 (Calls cost 13p per minute plus your phone company's access charge) **web:** www.premierinn.com
dir: A1 onto A696, follow Airport signs. At rdbt take turn immediately after airport exit

High quality, budget accommodation ideal for both families and business travellers. Spacious, en suite bedrooms feature free WiFi and tea and coffee making facilities, and in most hotels, Freeview TV is also available. The adjacent family restaurant features a wide and varied menu

Rooms: 88

Premier Inn Newcastle Airport (South)

BUDGET HOTEL

Callerton Lane Ends, Woolsington, NE13 8DF - tel: 0871 527 8798 (Calls cost 13p per minute plus your phone company's access charge) **web:** www.premierinn.com
dir: Just off A696 on B6918, 0.3m from airport

Rooms: 53

NEWHAVEN	Map 6 TQ40
East Sussex	

Premier Inn Newhaven

BUDGET HOTEL

Avis Road, BN9 0AG - tel: 0871 527 8810 (Calls cost 13p per minute plus your phone company's access charge) **web:** www.premierinn.com
dir: From A26 (New Rd) through Drove Industrial Estate, left after underpass. Hotel in same complex as Sainsbury's

High quality, budget accommodation ideal for both families and business travellers. Spacious, en suite bedrooms feature free WiFi and tea and coffee making facilities, and in most hotels, Freeview TV is also available. The adjacent family restaurant features a wide and varied menu.

Rooms: 83

NEWMARKET
Suffolk

Map 12 TL66

INSPECTOR'S CHOICE

Bedford Lodge Hotel & Spa

★★★★ ◎◎ HOTEL

Bury Road, CB8 7BX - **tel:** 01638 663175
email: info@bedfordlodgehotel.co.uk **web:** www.bedfordlodgehotel.co.uk
dir: *From town centre take A1304 towards Bury St Edmunds, hotel 0.5m on left*

Bedford Lodge Hotel is an imposing 18th-century Georgian hunting lodge with more modern additions, set in three acres of secluded landscaped gardens. Public rooms feature the AA Rosette-worthy Squires restaurant, Roxana Bar and a small lounge. The hotel also features superb leisure facilities including The Edge Health and Fitness Club, as well as self-contained conference and banqueting suites. Contemporary bedrooms have a light, airy feel, and each is tastefully furnished and well equipped.

Rooms: 77 (6 family) (21 GF) (3 smoking) **Facilities:** Spa STV FTV WiFi Gym Steam room Sauna Hydrotherapy pool Rasul Dry floatation New Year **Conf:** Class 80 Board 50 Thtr 180 **Services:** Lift Night porter Air con **Parking:** 120 **Notes:** RS Sat lunch Restaurant closed Civ Wed 150

Tuddenham Mill

★★★★ 81% ◎◎◎ HOTEL

High Street, Tuddenham St Mary, IP28 6SQ - **tel:** 01638 713552
email: info@tuddenhammill.co.uk **web:** www.tuddenhammill.co.uk
dir: *M11 junct 9, merge A14. Left lane junct 38 towards Thetford/Norwich. Signed Tuddenham*

Tuddenham Mill is a beautifully converted old watermill set amidst landscaped grounds between Newmarket and Bury St Edmunds. The contemporary style bedrooms are situated in separate buildings adjacent to the main building, and each one is tastefully appointed with co-ordinated fabrics and soft furnishings. The public areas have a wealth of original features such as the water wheel and exposed beams; they include a lounge bar, a smart restaurant, a meeting room and choice of terraces.

Rooms: 20 (17 annexe) (13 GF) **S** £145–£395; **D** £145–£395 (incl. bkfst) **Facilities:** STV FTV WiFi Putting green Spa treatment room Xmas New Year **Conf:** Class 16 Board 16 Thtr 40 Del from £175 **Services:** Night porter **Parking:** 40 **Notes:** LB Civ Wed 60

Best Western Heath Court Hotel

★★★ 79% HOTEL

Moulton Road, CB8 8DY - **tel:** 01638 667171
email: quality@heathcourthotel.com **web:** www.heathcourthotel.com
dir: *Phone for details*

Heath Court Hotel enjoys a very convenient location close to the town centre and overlooks the Newmarket gallops. Bedrooms are all well-equipped and spacious, and free WiFi is available throughout the hotel, which was refurbished not long ago. Ample secure parking is available and there is a popular restaurant and bar.

Rooms: 43 (2 family) **S** £64–£101; **D** £84–£218 (incl. bkfst)* **Facilities:** STV FTV WiFi New Year **Conf:** Class 45 Board 40 Thtr 130 Del from £100 **Services:** Lift Night porter **Parking:** 60 **Notes:** LB Civ Wed 120

Premier Inn Newmarket

BUDGET HOTEL

Fred Archer Way, CB8 7XN - **tel:** 0871 527 9296 (Calls cost 13p per minute plus your phone company's access charge) **web:** www.premierinn.com
dir: *A14 junct 37, A142 (Fordham Rd). 2.3m, straight on at 2 rdbts. At end of Fordham Rd, into right lane, turn right. Hotel on right*

High quality, budget accommodation ideal for both families and business travellers. Spacious, en suite bedrooms feature free WiFi and tea and coffee making facilities, and in most hotels, Freeview TV is also available. The adjacent family restaurant features a wide and varied menu.

Rooms: 75

N

N

NEW MILTON
Hampshire

Map 5 SZ29

INSPECTOR'S CHOICE

Chewton Glen

★★★★★ @@ ≋ COUNTRY HOUSE HOTEL

Christchurch Road, BH25 6QS - tel: 01425 275341
email: reservations@chewtonglen.com **web:** www.chewtonglen.com
dir: *A35 from Lyndhurst for 10m, left at staggered junct.*
Follow tourist sign for hotel through Walkford, take 2nd left

Chewton Glen has had a revitalisation in recent years; the eco-friendly tree-houses point the hotel in a fresh and exciting direction. The extensive grounds include, in addition to activities like golf and croquet, a walled garden, which provides for the hotel kitchen, and is a feature in its own right. Bedrooms are luxurious and delightfully appointed, while public areas are stylish and comfortable, the perfect place for traditional afternoon tea. Cuisine as ever, is at the forefront, and in the 'dining room' restaurant there is something for every diner. A new addition to the range of facilities is The Kitchen, a relaxed and informal setting to dine in, but it's also a cookery school.

Rooms: 70 (12 annexe) (43 family) (11 GF) ⚑ **Facilities:** Spa STV FTV WiFi ⇗ ⊛ ⤴ ♨ 9 Putting green ⊜ ⥸ Gym Hydrotherapy spa Dance studio Cycling & jogging trail Clay shooting Archery ♫ Xmas New Year **Conf:** Class 70 Board 40 Thtr 150 Del from £310 **Services:** Night porter Air con **Parking:** 150
Notes: Civ Wed 140

NEWPORT
Isle of Wight

Map 5 SZ58

Premier Inn Isle of Wight (Newport)

BUDGET HOTEL

Seaclose, Fairlee Road, PO30 2DN - tel: 0871 527 8556 (Calls cost 13p per minute plus your phone company's access charge) **web:** www.premierinn.com
dir: *From Newport take A3054 signed Ryde. In 0.75m at Seaclose lights, turn left. Hotel adjacent to council offices*

High quality, budget accommodation ideal for both families and business travellers. Spacious, en suite bedrooms feature free WiFi and tea and coffee making facilities, and in most hotels, Freeview TV is also available. The adjacent family restaurant features a wide and varied menu.

Rooms: 68

NEWPORT
Shropshire

Map 15 SJ71

Coldra Court Hotel

★★★★ 75% HOTEL

Chepstow Road, NP18 2LX - tel: 01633 413737
email: bookings@celtic-manor.com **web:** www.celtic-manor.com
dir: *Phone for directions*

Coldra Court whilst being part of the larger Celtic Manor resort, retains its own identity and is located a short distance away. Free shuttle buses are provided for guests to move between the two. Recently refurbished, bedrooms are spacious and offer high levels of comfort. The Rib restaurant is not to be missed, a bustling dining venue, with a Smokehouse theme. There is a gym and swimming pool on site.

Rooms: 148

Premier Inn Newport/Telford

BUDGET HOTEL

Stafford Road, TF10 9BY - tel: 0871 527 8808 (Calls cost 13p per minute plus your phone company's access charge) **web:** www.premierinn.com
dir: *From A41 E of Newport take A518 towards Stafford. Hotel on right adjacent to Mere Park Garden Centre*

High quality, budget accommodation ideal for both families and business travellers. Spacious, en suite bedrooms feature free WiFi and tea and coffee making facilities, and in most hotels, Freeview TV is also available. The adjacent family restaurant features a wide and varied menu.

Rooms: 50

NEWPORT PAGNELL MOTORWAY SERVICE AREA (M1) Map 11 SP84
Berkshire

Days Inn Milton Keynes

WELCOMEBREAK

AA Advertised

Newport Pagnell Services, M1 Junct 14/15, MK16 9DS - **tel:** 01908 610878
email: miltonkeynes.hotelmanager@welcomebreak.co.uk
web: www.welcomebreak.co.uk/hotels/milton-keynes
dir: *M1 Northbound junct 14/15. Hotel is located in Welcome Break services off Little Linford Lane*

This modern building offers accommodation in smart, spacious and well-equipped bedrooms, suitable for families and business travellers, and all with en suite bathrooms. Continental breakfast is available and other refreshments may be taken at the nearby family restaurant.

Rooms: 87 (14 family) (25 GF) (4 smoking) **Facilities:** STV FTV WiFi **Conf:** Class 12 Board 16 Thtr 40 **Services:** Night porter **Parking:** 90

NEWQUAY Map 2 SW86
Cornwall & Isles of Scilly

HIGHLY RECOMMENDED

The Headland Hotel and Spa

★★★★ 84% ⊛⊛ HOTEL

Fistral Beach, TR7 1EW - **tel:** 01637 872211
email: reception@headlandhotel.co.uk **web:** www.headlandhotel.co.uk
dir: *A30 onto A392 at Indian Queens, approaching Newquay follow signs for Fistral Beach, hotel adjacent*

This Victorian hotel enjoys a stunning location overlooking the sea on three sides, so views can be enjoyed from most of the windows. Bedrooms are comfortable and spacious. The grand public areas, with impressive floral displays, include various lounges and as a complement to the formal dining room, The Terrace offers a relaxed alternative. Other attractions include the spa, gym and leisure facilities including relaxation pool, steam room, aromatherapy showers and sauna. Self-catering cottages are available, and guests staying in these are welcome to use the hotel facilities.

Rooms: 96 (30 family) ⫫ **S** £80–£400; **D** £110–£450 (incl. bkfst)*
Facilities: Spa STV FTV WiFi ⟲ ⊛ ⟋ ⟍ 9 Putting green ⚑ ⚑ Gym Pitch & putt Fitness centre Spa Wellness centre ♫ Xmas New Year **Conf:** Class 120 Board 40 Thtr 200 Del from £184 **Services:** Lift Night porter **Parking:** 300
Notes: Civ Wed 200

Atlantic Hotel

★★★★ 81% ⊛ HOTEL

Dane Road, TR7 1EN - **tel:** 01637 872244
email: info@atlantichotelnewquay.co.uk **web:** www.atlantichotelnewquay.co.uk
dir: *A30 onto A392 to Indian Queens, approaching Newquay. Follow signs for Fistral Beach, hotel on hill overlooking sea & harbour*

Glamour, grandeur and a warm welcome await at the Atlantic Hotel. Set in ten acres of private headland, this stunning art-deco hotel offers sweeping views of the Atlantic Ocean. Each room is unique, comfortably furnished and comes with a glorious sea view. Diners can enjoy a range of contemporary dishes that offer the best local seafood and seasonal produce, in the relaxed, elegant atmosphere at Silks Bistro and Champagne Bar. The south-facing terrace, sun-trap pool and spa treatment room offer a range of spaces to relax and indulge. Just a short stroll from Newquay, and the South West Coast Path, the Atlantic Hotel is the perfect base for exploring the dramatic north Cornwall coast.

Rooms: 57 (4 annexe) (10 family) ⫫ **S** £77–£116; **D** £97–£210 (incl. bkfst)*
Facilities: Spa STV FTV WiFi ⟲ ⊛ ⟋ Surf school Steam room Sauna ♫ Xmas New Year **Conf:** Class 350 Board 150 Thtr 350 Del from £125 **Services:** Lift Night porter **Parking:** 57 **Notes:** LB Civ Wed 360

N

NEWQUAY *continued*

Best Western Hotel Bristol

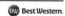 **Best Western**

★★★ 81% HOTEL

Narrowcliff, TR7 2PQ - tel: 01637 875181
email: info@hotelbristol.co.uk **web:** www.hotelbristol.co.uk
dir: *A30 onto A392, then A3058. Hotel 2.5m on left*

This hotel is conveniently situated, and many of the bedrooms enjoy fine sea views. Staff are friendly and provide a professional and attentive service. There is a range of comfortable lounges, ideal for relaxing prior to eating in the elegant dining room. There are also leisure and conference facilities.

Rooms: 74 (23 family) **S** £50–£105; **D** £65–£145* **Facilities:** FTV WiFi HL Table tennis New Year Child facilities **Conf:** Class 80 Board 30 Thtr 200 Del from £75 **Services:** Lift Night porter **Parking:** 105 **Notes:** LB Closed Xmas Civ Wed 300

The Legacy Hotel Victoria

 LEGACY HOTELS

★★★ 75% HOTEL

East Street, TR7 1DB - tel: 0844 411 9025 (Calls cost 7p per minute plus your phone company's access charge) & 0330 333 2825
email: bookings@hotel-victoria.co.uk **web:** www.legacy-hotels.co.uk
dir: *A30 towards Bodmin following signs to Newquay. Hotel next to Newquay's main post office*

Standing on the cliffs, overlooking Newquay Bay, the hotel is situated at the centre of this vibrant town. The spacious lounges and bar areas all benefit from glorious views. Varied menus, using the best of local produce, are offered in the restaurant. Bedrooms vary from spacious superior rooms and suites to standard inland-facing rooms. Berties pub, a nightclub, and indoor leisure facilities are also available.

Rooms: 71 (23 family) (1 GF) **D** fr £55 (incl. bkfst)* **Facilities:** FTV WiFi Gym Beauty treatment room Sauna Steam room **Conf:** Class 130 Board 50 Thtr 200 **Services:** Lift Night porter **Parking:** 50 **Notes:** LB Civ Wed 270

Kilbirnie Hotel

★★★ 73% HOTEL

Narrowcliff, TR7 2RS - tel: 01637 875155
email: info@kilbirniehotel.co.uk **web:** www.kilbirniehotel.co.uk
dir: *On A392*

With delightful views over the open space known as The Barrowfields and beyond to the sea, this privately-run hotel offers an impressive range of facilities. The reception rooms are spacious and comfortable, and during summer months become the venue for a programme of entertainment. Bedrooms vary in size and style, and some enjoy fine sea views.

Rooms: 66 (6 family) (8 GF) **S** £30–£90; **D** £60–£150 (incl. bkfst)* **Facilities:** FTV WiFi Gym Fitness room Snooker room Sauna Xmas New Year **Conf:** Class 50 Board 25 Thtr 100 Del from £100 **Services:** Lift Night porter Air con **Parking:** 58 **Notes:** Closed 2-31 Jan

Eliot Hotel

Leisureplex
HOLIDAY HOTELS

★★★ 70% HOTEL

Edgcumbe Avenue, TR7 2NH - tel: 01637 878177
email: eliot.newquay@alfatravel.com **web:** www.leisureplex.co.uk
dir: *A30 onto A392 towards Quintrell Downs. Right at rdbt onto A3058. 4m to Newquay, left at amusements onto Edgcumbe Ave. Hotel on left*

Located in a quiet residential area just a short walk from the beaches and the varied attractions of the town, this long-established hotel offers comfortable

accommodation. Entertainment is provided most nights throughout the season and guests can relax in the spacious public areas.

Rooms: 76 (10 family) **Facilities:** FTV WiFi Pool table Table tennis Xmas New Year **Services:** Lift Night porter **Parking:** 20 **Notes:** Closed Dec-Jan (ex Xmas/New Year) RS Feb-Mar Mon-Fri only

Hotel California

★★★ 67% HOTEL

Pentire Crescent, TR7 1PU - tel: 01637 879292
email: info@hotel-california.co.uk **web:** www.hotel-california.co.uk
dir: *A392 to Newquay, follow signs for Pentire Hotels & Guest Houses*

This hotel is tucked away in a delightful location, close to Fistral Beach and adjacent to the River Gannel. Many bedrooms have views across the river towards the sea, and some have balconies. There is an impressive range of leisure facilities, including ten-pin bowling and both indoor and outdoor pools. The cuisine is enjoyable and menus offer a range of interesting dishes.

Rooms: 70 (27 family) (13 GF) **S** £47–£78; **D** £93–£138 (incl. bkfst)* **Facilities:** FTV WiFi HL Squash 4-lane American bowling alley Hairdresser Snooker & pool room Sauna Solarium Xmas New Year **Conf:** Class 100 Board 30 Thtr 100 Del from £76 **Services:** Lift Night porter **Parking:** 66 **Notes:** LB Closed 3-25 Jan Civ Wed 150

Priory Lodge Hotel

★★ 79% HOTEL

30 Mount Wise, TR7 2BN - tel: 01637 874111
email: fionapocklington@tiscali.co.uk **web:** www.priorylodgehotel.co.uk
dir: *From lights in town centre onto Berry Rd, right onto B3282 Mount Wise, 0.5m on right*

This hotel enjoys a central location close to the town centre, the harbour and the local beaches. Secure parking is available at the hotel along with a range of leisure facilities including a heated pool, sauna, games room and hot tub. Attractively decorated bedrooms vary in size and style - many have sea views over Towan Beach.

Rooms: 28 (6 annexe) (13 family) (1 GF) **S** £40–£80; **D** £80–£100 (incl. bkfst) **Facilities:** FTV WiFi **Parking:** 30 **Notes:** Closed Dec-end Mar

Premier Inn Newquay (Quintrell Downs)

 Premier Inn

BUDGET HOTEL

Quintrell Downs, TR8 4LE - tel: 0871 527 8818 (Calls cost 13p per minute plus your phone company's access charge) **web:** www.premierinn.com
dir: *From A30 take A39. At rdbt 2nd exit signed Newquay A392. 4m, in Quintrell Downs take 1st exit at rdbt. Hotel on left*

High quality, budget accommodation ideal for both families and business travellers. Spacious, en suite bedrooms feature free WiFi and tea and coffee making facilities, and in most hotels, Freeview TV is also available. The adjacent family restaurant features a wide and varied menu.

Rooms: 74

N

NEWTON ABBOT
Devon   **Map 3 SX87**

See also **Ilsington**

Best Western Passage House Hotel

★★★ **75% HOTEL**

Hackney Lane, Kingsteignton, TQ12 3QH - **tel:** 01626 355515
email: mail@passagehousegroup.co.uk **web:** www.passagehousegroup.co.uk/hotel
dir: *A380 onto A381, follow racecourse signs*

With memorable views of the Teign Estuary, this popular hotel provides spacious, well-equipped bedrooms. An impressive range of leisure and meeting facilities is offered and a conservatory provides a pleasant extension to the bar and lounge. A choice of eating options is available, either in the main restaurant, or the adjacent Passage House Inn for less formal dining.

Rooms: 90 (52 annexe) (64 family) (26 GF) **S** fr £75; **D** fr £85 (incl. bkfst)*
Facilities: Spa WiFi ♨ supervised Gym **Conf:** Class 50 Board 40 Thtr 120 Del from £115 **Services:** Lift Night porter **Parking:** 300 **Notes:** LB Civ Wed 75

Premier Inn Newton Abbot

BUDGET HOTEL

Newton Abbott Racecourse, Newton Road, TQ12 3AF - **tel:** 0871 527 9300 (Calls cost 13p per minute plus your phone company's access charge) **web:** www.premierinn.com
dir: *A380 exit at Ware Barton signed A383/Ashburton, follow brown signs for Newton Abbot Racecourse through Kingsteignton. Then follow Officials Entrance sign to hotel*

High quality, budget accommodation ideal for both families and business travellers. Spacious, en suite bedrooms feature free WiFi and tea and coffee making facilities, and in most hotels, Freeview TV is also available. The adjacent family restaurant features a wide and varied menu.

Rooms: 84

NEWTON AYCLIFFE
County Durham   **Map 19 NZ22**

Premier Inn Durham (Newton Aycliffe)

BUDGET HOTEL

Ricknall Lane, Great North Road, DL5 6JG - **tel:** 0871 527 8336 (Calls cost 13p per minute plus your phone company's access charge) **web:** www.premierinn.com
dir: *On A167 E of Newton Aycliffe, 3m from A1(M)*

High quality, budget accommodation ideal for both families and business travellers. Spacious, en suite bedrooms feature free WiFi and tea and coffee making facilities, and in most hotels, Freeview TV is also available. The adjacent family restaurant features a wide and varied menu.

Rooms: 44

NORMAN CROSS
Cambridgeshire   **Map 12 TL19**

Premier Inn Peterborough (A1(M) Jct 16)

BUDGET HOTEL

Norman Cross, A1(M) Junction 16, PE7 3TB - **tel:** 0871 527 8870 (Calls cost 13p per minute plus your phone company's access charge) **web:** www.premierinn.com
dir: *A1(M) junct 16, A15 towards Yaxley, hotel in 100yds*

High quality, budget accommodation ideal for both families and business travellers. Spacious, en suite bedrooms feature free WiFi and tea and coffee making facilities, and in most hotels, Freeview TV is also available. The adjacent family restaurant features a wide and varied menu.

Rooms: 99

NORMANTON
Rutland   **Map 11 SK90**

Best Western Normanton Park Hotel

★★★ **71% HOTEL**

Oakham, LE15 8RP - **tel:** 01780 720315
email: info@normantonpark.co.uk **web:** www.bw-normantonparkhotel.co.uk
dir: *From A1 follow A606 towards Oakham, 5m. Turn left, 1.5m. Hotel on right*

This hotel offers some of Rutland Water's best views over the south shore. The comfortable bedrooms are located in the main house and the courtyard. Public rooms include a conservatory dining room overlooking the water, and a cosy lounge is available for guests to relax in.

Rooms: 30 (7 annexe) (6 family) (11 GF) **Facilities:** FTV WiFi ♨ Xmas New Year **Conf:** Class 60 Board 80 Thtr 200 **Services:** Night porter **Parking:** 100 **Notes:** Civ Wed 80

NORTHAMPTON
Northamptonshire   **Map 11 SP76**

Westone Manor Hotel

★★★ **73% HOTEL**

Ashley Way, Weston Favell, NN3 3EA - **tel:** 01604 739955
email: enquiries@hotels-northampton.com **web:** www.hotels-northampton.com
dir: *A43 Kettering for 0.5m. Then A4500 for Town Centre/Earls Barton/Weston Favell. Left at lights onto A4500 for 100yds. 1st right at sign Westone Manor Hotel Northampton, over small rdbt, hotel on left*

Built in 1914 as the home of the local shoe manufacturer William Sears, this property has since been expanded, and now offers comfortable accommodation to the rear. A lounge, bar, and conservatory restaurant are available. Free WiFi is available throughout the hotel.

Rooms: 69 (38 annexe) (2 family) (19 GF) **S** £50–£65; **D** £65–£80 **Facilities:** FTV WiFi Xmas New Year **Conf:** Class 60 Board 60 Thtr 120 Del £95-£120 **Services:** Lift Night porter **Parking:** 70 **Notes:** Civ Wed 120

Premier Inn Northampton Bedford Road/A428

BUDGET HOTEL

The Lakes, Bedford Road, NN4 7YD - **tel:** 0871 527 8822 (Calls cost 13p per minute plus your phone company's access charge) **web:** www.premierinn.com
dir: *M1 junct 15, follow A508 (A45) signs to Northampton. A428 at rdbt take 4th exit (signed Bedford). Left at next rdbt. Hotel on right*

High quality, budget accommodation ideal for both families and business travellers. Spacious, en suite bedrooms feature free WiFi and tea and coffee making facilities, and in most hotels, Freeview TV is also available. The adjacent family restaurant features a wide and varied menu.

Rooms: 44

Premier Inn Northampton Great Billing/A45

BUDGET HOTEL

Crow Lane, Great Billing, NN3 9DA - **tel:** 0871 527 8824 (Calls cost 13p per minute plus your phone company's access charge) **web:** www.premierinn.com
dir: *M1 junct 15, A508, A45 follow Billing Aquadrome signs*

Rooms: 60

NORTHAMPTON *continued*

Premier Inn Northampton South (Wootton)

BUDGET HOTEL

Newport Pagnell Road West, Wootton, NN4 7JJ - **tel:** 0871 527 8826 (Calls cost 13p per minute plus your phone company's access charge) **web:** www.premierinn.com **dir:** *M1 junct 15, A508 towards Northampton, exit at junct with A45. At rdbt take B526. Hotel on right*

Rooms: 70

Premier Inn Northampton Town Centre

BUDGET HOTEL

St. Johns Street, NN1 1FA - **tel:** 0871 527 9590 (Calls cost 13p per minute plus your phone company's access charge) **email:** NorthamptonTownCentre.PI@premierinn.com **web:** www.premierinn.com **dir:** *From N: M1 junct 16, A45, signed Northampton West. At rdbt onto A4 (Northampton). Pass Northampton Rugby Ground on right. At Northampton Rail Station turn right at lights, (stay in left lane) 2nd exit at rdbt left at 2nd*

Rooms: 104

Premier Inn Northampton West (Harpole)

BUDGET HOTEL

Harpole Turn, Weedon Rd, NN7 4DD - **tel:** 0871 527 8828 (Calls cost 13p per minute plus your phone company's access charge) **web:** www.premierinn.com **dir:** *M1 junct 16, A45 towards Northampton. In 1m left into Harpole Turn. Hotel on left*

Rooms: 75

NORTH FERRIBY   **Map 17 SE92**
East Riding of Yorkshire

Hallmark Hotel Hull

★★★★ 76% HOTEL

Ferriby High Road, HU14 3LG - **tel:** 0330 028 3414 & 07482 645212 **email:** hull@hallmarkhotels.co.uk **web:** www.hallmarkhotels.co.uk **dir:** *M62 onto A63 towards Hull. Exit at Humber Bridge signage. Follow North Ferriby signs, hotel 0.5m on left*

This property is situated just outside Hull city centre, with breathtaking views of the Humber Bridge. Service is attentive with a friendly atmosphere. The comfortable bedrooms are tastefully appointed and are suitable for both business and leisure guests. The restaurant and bar serve a good choice of dishes. Conference facilities are available along with free WiFi and private parking.

Rooms: 95 (3 family) (16 GF) ✿ **S** £59–£175; **D** £59–£175* **Facilities:** Spa FTV WiFi ⮑ Fitness suite Sauna Xmas New Year **Conf:** Class 85 Board 86 Thtr 200 Del from £125 **Services:** Night porter **Parking:** 150 **Notes:** LB Civ Wed 200

NORTH KILWORTH   **Map 11 SP68**
Leicestershire

Kilworth House Hotel & Theatre

★★★★ ◉◉ HOTEL

Lutterworth Road, LE17 6JE - **tel:** 01858 880058 **email:** info@kilworthhouse.co.uk **web:** www.kilworthhouse.co.uk **dir:** *A4304 towards Market Harborough, after Walcote, hotel 1.5m on right*

Kilworth House Hotel is a restored Victorian country house located in 38 acres of private grounds offering state-of-the-art conference rooms. The gracious public areas feature many period pieces and original art works. The bedrooms are very comfortable and well equipped, and the large Orangery is now used for informal dining, while the opulent Wordsworth Restaurant has a more formal air. Close to the lake an open-air theatre which seats 540 has been built; professional productions are performed, and picnics can be arranged, or dinner back at the hotel is also an option.

Rooms: 44 (2 family) (13 GF) ✿ **S** £125–£465; **D** £125–£465* **Facilities:** Spa FTV WiFi ⮑ Fishing ⚓ Gym Beauty therapy rooms Xmas New Year **Conf:** Class 30 Board 30 Thtr 80 Del from £190 **Services:** Lift Night porter **Parking:** 140 **Notes:** LB Civ Wed 180

NORTH SHIELDS   **Map 21 NZ36**
Tyne & Wear

Premier Inn North Shields (Ferry Terminal)

BUDGET HOTEL

Coble Dene Road, NE29 6DL - **tel:** 0871 527 8818 (Calls cost 13p per minute plus your phone company's access charge) **web:** www.premierinn.com **dir:** *From all directions follow signs for Royal Quays (Outlet Centre) & International Ferry Terminal. From A187 take Coble Dene Rd. At 3rd rdbt right, 1st right at mini rdbt*

High quality, budget accommodation ideal for both families and business travellers. Spacious, en suite bedrooms feature free WiFi and tea and coffee making facilities, and in most hotels, Freeview TV is also available. The adjacent family restaurant features a wide and varied menu.

Rooms: 74

NORTH WALSHAM
Norfolk   Map 13 TG23

HIGHLY RECOMMENDED

Beechwood Hotel
★★★ 88% HOTEL

20 Cromer Road, NR28 0HD - **tel:** 01692 403231
email: info@beechwood-hotel.co.uk **web:** www.beechwood-hotel.co.uk
dir: *B1150 from Norwich. At North Walsham left at 1st lights, then right at next*

Beechwood Hotel offers a friendly and informal atmosphere, comfortable and well-appointed bedrooms, and a creative head chef sourcing produce from local farms and Cromer fishermen. Near to a Heritage coastline, the Norfolk Broads and the cathedral city of Norwich, this is a great place for a short break.

Rooms: 18 (4 GF) **Facilities:** FTV WiFi ⛲ Xmas New Year **Conf:** Class 20 Board 20 Thtr 20 Del from £170 **Parking:** 20

NORTHWICH
Cheshire   Map 15 SJ67

Premier Inn Northwich (Sandiway)

BUDGET HOTEL

520 Chester Road, Sandiway, CW8 2DN - **tel:** 0871 527 8830 (Calls cost 13p per minute plus your phone company's access charge) **web:** www.premierinn.com
dir: *M6 junct 19, A556 towards Chester. Hotel in 11m*

High quality, budget accommodation ideal for both families and business travellers. Spacious, en suite bedrooms feature free WiFi and tea and coffee making facilities, and in most hotels, Freeview TV is also available. The adjacent family restaurant features a wide and varied menu.

Rooms: 42

Premier Inn Northwich South
BUDGET HOTEL

London Road, Leftwich, CW9 8EG - **tel:** 0871 527 8832 (Calls cost 13p per minute plus your phone company's access charge) **web:** www.premierinn.com
dir: *Just off M6 junct 19. Follow A556 towards Chester. Right at sign for Northwich & Davenham*

Rooms: 61

NORWICH
Norfolk   Map 13 TG20

St Giles House Hotel
★★★★ 82% HOTEL

41-45 St Giles Street, NR2 1JR - **tel:** 01603 275180
email: reception@stgileshousehotel.com **web:** www.stgileshousehotel.com
dir: *A11 into central Norwich. Left at rdbt (Chapelfield Shopping Centre). 3rd exit at next rdbt. Left onto St Giles St. Hotel on left*

St Giles House Hotel is a stylish 19th-century, Grade II listed building situated in the heart of the city. The property has a wealth of magnificent original features such as wood-panelling, ornamental plasterwork and marble floors. Public areas include an open-plan lounge bar/restaurant, a smart lounge with plush sofas and a Parisian-style terrace. The spacious, contemporary bedrooms are individually designed and have many thoughtful touches.

Rooms: 24 (3 GF) **S** fr £120; **D** fr £130 (incl. bkfst)* **Facilities:** Spa FTV WiFi ⛲ Xmas New Year **Conf:** Class 20 Board 24 Thtr 45 Del from £150 **Services:** Lift Night porter **Parking:** 30 **Notes:** LB Civ Wed 60

Maids Head Hotel

★★★★ 81% HOTEL

Tombland, NR3 1LB - **tel:** 01603 209955
email: reservations@maidsheadhotel.co.uk **web:** www.maidsheadhotel.co.uk
dir: *In city centre. Telephone or see website for detailed directions*

The Maids Head Hotel is an impressive 13th-century building situated close to the impressive Norman cathedral, and within easy walking distance of the city centre. The bedrooms are pleasantly decorated and thoughtfully equipped; some rooms have original oak beams. The spacious public rooms include a Jacobean bar, a range of seating areas and the Courtyard Restaurant.

Rooms: 84 (10 family) **S** £85–£130; **D** £95–£200* **Facilities:** FTV WiFi ⛲ Beauty treatment room Use of nearby gym Xmas New Year **Conf:** Class 30 Board 50 Thtr 100 Del from £140 **Services:** Lift Night porter **Parking:** 83 **Notes:** LB Civ Wed 100

Dunston Hall

★★★★ 79% HOTEL

Ipswich Road, NR14 8PQ - **tel:** 01508 470444
email: dunstonreception@qhotels.co.uk **web:** www.qhotels.co.uk
dir: *From A47 take A140 (Ipswich road). 0.25m, hotel on left*

Dunston Hall is an imposing Grade II listed building set amidst 170 acres of landscaped grounds just a short drive from the city centre. The spacious bedrooms are smartly decorated, tastefully furnished and equipped to a high standard. The attractively appointed public rooms offer a wide choice of areas in which to relax, and the hotel also boasts a superb range of leisure facilities including an 18-hole PGA golf course, floodlit tennis courts and a football pitch.

Rooms: 169 (16 family) (16 GF) (2 smoking) **S** £74–£184; **D** £79–£189 (incl. bkfst)* **Facilities:** Spa WiFi ⛲ 18 Putting green Gym Floodlit driving range Xmas New Year **Conf:** Class 140 Board 80 Thtr 300 Del from £129 **Services:** Lift Night porter **Parking:** 500 **Notes:** LB Civ Wed 200

Park Farm Hotel
★★★★ 77% HOTEL

NR9 3DL - **tel:** 01603 810264
email: enq@parkfarm-hotel.co.uk **web:** www.parkfarm-hotel.co.uk

(for full entry see Hethersett)

Mercure Norwich Hotel
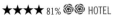
★★★★ 75% HOTEL

121-131 Boundary Road, NR3 2BA - **tel:** 0844 815 9036 (Calls cost 5p per minute plus your phone company's access charge)
email: info@mercurenorwich.co.uk **web:** www.mercurenorwich.co.uk
dir: *Approx 2m from airport on A140 Norwich ring road*

This purpose-built property is situated on the outer ring road within easy striking distance of the city centre. Bedrooms are spacious and well equipped with modern facilities. Public rooms include an open-plan lounge bar and a smart restaurant. The hotel has leisure facilities, meeting rooms and a banqueting suite.

Rooms: 107 (10 family) (12 GF) **S** £90–£140; **D** £100–£150 (incl. bkfst)* **Facilities:** FTV WiFi ⛲ Gym Sauna Steam room Xmas New Year **Conf:** Class 160 Board 80 Thtr 400 Del from £125 **Services:** Night porter **Parking:** 225 **Notes:** LB Civ Wed 400

N

NORWICH *continued*

Best Western Annesley House Hotel

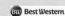 **Best Western.**

★★★ 87% ◎◎ HOTEL

6 Newmarket Road, NR2 2LA - tel: 01603 624553
email: annesleyhouse@bestwestern.co.uk **web:** www.bw-annesleyhouse.co.uk
dir: *On A11, 0.5m before city centre*

This delightful Georgian property is set in three acres of landscaped gardens close to the city centre. Bedrooms are split between three separate houses, two of which are linked by a glass walkway. Each is attractively decorated, tastefully furnished and thoughtfully equipped. Public rooms include a comfortable lounge/bar and a smart conservatory restaurant which overlooks the gardens.

Rooms: 31 (13 annexe) (1 family) (9 GF) ↑ **S** £49.50–£69.50; **D** £69.50–£93.50*
Facilities: FTV WiFi ↳ **Parking:** 28 **Notes:** LB Closed 24 Dec-28 Jan

Stower Grange

★★★ 80% ◎ COUNTRY HOUSE HOTEL

40 School Road, Drayton, NR8 6EF - tel: 01603 860210
email: enquiries@stowergrange.co.uk **web:** www.stowergrange.co.uk
dir: *Norwich ring road N to Asda supermarket. Take A1067 (Fakenham Rd) at Drayton, right at lights into School Rd. Hotel 150yds on right*

Expect a warm welcome at this 17th-century, ivy-clad property situated in a peaceful residential area close to the city centre and airport. The individually decorated bedrooms are generally quite spacious; each is tastefully furnished and equipped with many thoughtful touches. Public rooms include a smart open-plan lounge bar and an elegant restaurant.

Rooms: 11 (1 family) ↑ **Facilities:** FTV WiFi ↳ New Year **Conf:** Class 45 Board 30 Thtr 100 **Parking:** 40 **Notes:** LB Civ Wed 100

Best Western Brook Hotel Norwich

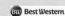 **Best Western.**

★★★ 74% HOTEL

2 Barnard Road, Bowthorpe, NR5 9JB - tel: 01603 741161
email: welcome@brookhotelnorwich.com **web:** www.brookhotelnorwich.com
dir: *A47 towards Swaffham then A1074. Over double rdbt, to next rdbt, hotel on last exit*

Brook Hotel Norwich is a modern, purpose-built hotel situated to the west of the city centre, just off the A47. The open-plan public areas include a lounge bar with TV, a foyer with plush sofas and a large dining room. The spacious bedrooms are equipped for both leisure and business guests alike.

Rooms: 81 (13 family) (40 GF) **S** £65–£120; **D** £75–£130* **Facilities:** FTV WiFi Gym Xmas New Year **Conf:** Class 90 Board 60 Thtr 200 **Services:** Night porter Air con **Parking:** 100 **Notes:** Civ Wed 200

Premier Inn Norwich Airport

 Premier Inn

BUDGET HOTEL

Delft Way, NR6 6BB - tel: 0871 527 8836 (Calls cost 13p per minute plus your phone company's access charge) **web:** www.premierinn.com
dir: *From Norwich take A140 signed Cromer & Airport. Right at lights into Amsterdam Way. At mini-rdbt turn right. Hotel on right*

High quality, budget accommodation ideal for both families and business travellers. Spacious, en suite bedrooms feature free WiFi and tea and coffee making facilities, and in most hotels, Freeview TV is also available. The adjacent family restaurant features a wide and varied menu.

Rooms: 80

Premier Inn Norwich (Broadlands Park)

 Premier Inn

BUDGET HOTEL

Broadlands Business Park, Old Chapel Way, NR7 0WG - tel: 0871 527 8838 (Calls cost 13p per minute plus your phone company's access charge) **web:** www.premierinn.com
dir: *A47 onto A1042, 3m E of city centre*

Rooms: 92

Premier Inn Norwich City Centre (Duke Street)

 Premier Inn

BUDGET HOTEL

Duke Street, NR3 3AP - tel: 0871 527 8840 (Calls cost 13p per minute plus your phone company's access charge) **web:** www.premierinn.com
dir: *From A1074, straight on at lights (Toys'R'Us) into St Benedict's St (or from A147, A140, A11) right at lights. At next lights into Duke St. Car park in St Andrews multi-storey on right - free to guests*

Rooms: 117

Premier Inn Norwich Nelson City Centre

 Premier Inn

BUDGET HOTEL

Prince of Wales Road, NR1 1DX - tel: 0871 527 8842 (Calls cost 13p per minute plus your phone company's access charge) **web:** www.premierinn.com
dir: *Follow city centre, football ground & railway station signs. Hotel opposite station*

Rooms: 185

Premier Inn Norwich (Showground A47)

 Premier Inn

BUDGET HOTEL

Longwater Interchange, Dereham Road, NR5 0TP - tel: 0871 527 8834 (Calls cost 13p per minute plus your phone company's access charge) **web:** www.premierinn.com
dir: *A47 towards Dereham, take A1074 to City Centre. At rdbt 2nd exit, hotel on right. From N: A47 through Dereham. Straight on at 1st rdbt, at 2nd rdbt take 3rd exit. Hotel on left*

Rooms: 62

N

NOTTINGHAM
Nottinghamshire

Map 11 SK53

HIGHLY RECOMMENDED

Hart's Hotel
★★★★ 84% ◉◉ HOTEL

Standard Hill, Park Row, NG1 6GN - tel: 0115 988 1900
email: reception@hartshotel.co.uk **web:** www.hartsnottingham.co.uk
dir: *At junct of Park Row & Ropewalk*

This outstanding modern building stands on the site of the ramparts of the medieval castle, overlooking the city. Many of the bedrooms enjoy splendid views; all are well appointed and stylish. The Park Bar is the focal point of the public areas. Service is professional and caring and fine dining is offered at nearby Hart's Restaurant. Secure parking and private gardens are an added bonus.

Rooms: 32 (1 family) (7 GF) ⌘ **D** £134–£274* **Facilities:** STV FTV WiFi ⌨ Small unsupervised exercise room Beauty treatments Use of local tennis club Xmas New Year **Conf:** Class 75 Board 30 Thtr 100 Del from £190 **Services:** Lift Night porter **Parking:** 16 **Notes:** LB Civ Wed 100

The Nottingham Belfry
★★★★ 80% HOTEL

QHOTELS
INSPIRED BY YOU

Mellor's Way, Off Woodhouse Way, NG8 6PY - tel: 0115 973 9393
email: nottinghambelfry@qhotels.co.uk **web:** www.qhotels.co.uk
dir: *From M1 junct 26 take A610 towards Nottingham. A6002 to Stapleford/Strelley. 0.75m, last exit at rdbt, hotel on right*

Set conveniently close to the motorway links, yet not far from the city centre attractions, this modern hotel has a stylish and impressive interior. Bedrooms and bathrooms are spaciously appointed and very comfortable. There are two restaurants and two bars that offer interesting and satisfying cuisine. Staff are friendly and helpful.

Rooms: 120 (20 family) (36 GF) ⌘ **S** £75–£150; **D** £85–£170 (incl. bkfst)*
Facilities: Spa STV FTV WiFi HL ⌨ Gym Sauna Steam room Aerobic studio Xmas New Year **Conf:** Class 360 Board 60 Thtr 700 **Services:** Lift Night porter Air con **Parking:** 250 **Notes:** LB Civ Wed 500

Best Western Plus Nottingham City Centre
★★★★ 77% HOTEL

 Best Western PLUS

17-31 Wollaton Street, NG1 5FW - tel: 0115 912 8000 **web:** www.bestwestern.co.uk
dir: *Phone for directions*

Enjoying a convenient city centre location and limited parking spaces, this hotel is ideal for both business and leisure travellers. Well-equipped bedrooms are smartly decorated and offer functional design and features. Modern public areas include a bar serving a range of meals all day and evening.

Rooms: 91 **S** £50–£200; **D** £50–£200* **Conf:** Class 50 Board 50 Thtr 100 Del from £99

Park Plaza Nottingham
★★★★ 74% ◉◉ HOTEL

Park Plaza
Hotels & Resorts

41 Maid Marian Way, NG1 6GD - tel: 0115 947 7200 & 0844 415 6730
(Calls cost 7p per minute plus your phone company's access charge)
email: ppnsales@pphe.com **web:** www.parkplaza.com/nottinghamuk
dir: *A6200 Derby Rd into Wollaton St. 2nd exit into Maid Marian Way. Hotel on left*

This modern hotel is located in the centre of the city within walking distance of retail, commercial and tourist attractions. Bedrooms are spacious and comfortable, with many extras, including laptop safes and air conditioning. Service is discreetly attentive in the foyer lounge and the Chino Latino restaurant, where Pan-Asian cooking is a feature.

Rooms: 178 (10 family) ⌘ **Facilities:** STV FTV WiFi ⌨ Gym Complimentary fitness suite **Conf:** Class 100 Board 54 Thtr 200 **Services:** Lift Night porter Air con **Parking:** 30 **Notes:** Civ Wed 180

The Strathdon
★★★ 66% HOTEL

PEEL HOTELS PLC

Derby Road, NG1 5FT - tel: 0115 941 8501
email: info@strathdon-hotel-nottingham.com **web:** www.peelhotels.co.uk
dir: *From M1 follow city centre signs. At Canning Circus into one-way system into Wollaton St, keep right, next right to hotel*

This city-centre hotel has modern facilities and is very convenient for all city attractions. A popular themed bar has a large-screen TV and serves an extensive range of popular fresh food, while more formal dining is available in Bobbins Restaurant on certain evenings.

Rooms: 68 (4 family) (16 smoking) **S** £45–£70; **D** £55–£95* **Facilities:** FTV WiFi ⌨ Xmas New Year **Conf:** Class 60 Board 40 Thtr 150 Del from £85 **Services:** Lift Night porter **Notes:** Civ Wed 85

Premier Inn Nottingham Arena (London Rd)
BUDGET HOTEL

 Premier Inn

Island Site, London Road, NG2 4UU - tel: 0871 527 8848 (Calls cost 13p per minute plus your phone company's access charge) **web:** www.premierinn.com
dir: *M1 junct 25, A52 into city centre. Follow signs for A60 to Loughborough. Hotel adjacent to BBC building*

High quality, budget accommodation ideal for both families and business travellers. Spacious en suite bedrooms feature free WiFi and tea and coffee making facilities, and in most hotels, Freeview TV is also available. The adjacent family restaurant features a wide and varied menu.

Rooms: 87

N

NOTTINGHÁM *continued*

Premier Inn Nottingham Castle Marina

BUDGET HOTEL

Castle Marina Park, Castle Bridge Road, NG7 1GX - **tel:** 0871 527 8844 (Calls cost 13p per minute plus your phone company's access charge) **web:** www.premierinn.com
dir: *M1 junct 24, A453. Follow ring road & signs for Queen's Drive Industrial Estate. After Homebase left into Castle Bridge Rd, opposite Pizza Hut restaurant. Hotel adjacent to Boathouse Beefeater*

Rooms: 61

Premier Inn Nottingham City Centre Chapel Bar

BUDGET HOTEL

7 Chapel Quarter, Chapel Bar, NG1 6JS - **tel:** 0871 527 9658 (Calls cost 13p per minute plus your phone company's access charge) **web:** www.premierinn.com
dir: *M1 junct 26, follow Nottingham City Centre signs. Into Maid Marian Way (A6008). 1st right into Friar Ln*

Rooms: 60

Premier Inn Nottingham City Centre (Goldsmith Street)

BUDGET HOTEL

Goldsmith Street, NG1 5LT - **tel:** 0871 527 8846 (Calls cost 13p per minute plus your phone company's access charge) **web:** www.premierinn.com
dir: *A610 to city centre. Follow signs for Nottingham Trent University into Talbot St. 1st left into Clarendon St. Right at lights. Hotel on right*

Rooms: 161

Premier Inn Nottingham North (Daybrook)

BUDGET HOTEL

101 Mansfield Road, Daybrook, NG5 6BH - **tel:** 0871 527 8850 (Calls cost 13p per minute plus your phone company's access charge) **web:** www.premierinn.com
dir: *M1 junct 26, A610 towards Nottingham. Left onto A6514. Left onto A60 towards Mansfield. Hotel 0.25m on left*

Rooms: 64

Premier Inn Nottingham South

BUDGET HOTEL

Loughborough Road, Ruddington, NG11 6LS - **tel:** 0871 527 8854 (Calls cost 13p per minute plus your phone company's access charge) **web:** www.premierinn.com
dir: *M1 junct 24, follow A453 signs to Nottingham, A52 to Grantham. Hotel at 1st rdbt on left*

Rooms: 60

Premier Inn Nottingham West

BUDGET HOTEL

The Phoenix Centre, Millennium Way West, NG8 6AS - **tel:** 0871 527 8856 (Calls cost 13p per minute plus your phone company's access charge) **web:** www.premierinn.com
dir: *M1 junct 26, 1m on A610 towards Nottingham*

Rooms: 99

NUNEATON
Warwickshire
Map 11 SP39

Best Western Weston Hall Hotel

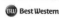

★★★ 73% HOTEL

Weston Lane, Bulkington, CV12 9RU - **tel:** 024 7631 2989
email: info@westonhallhotel.co.uk **web:** www.bw-westonhallhotel.co.uk
dir: *M6 junct 2, B4065 through Ansty. Left in Shilton, from Bulkington follow Nuneaton signs, into Weston Ln at 30mph sign*

This Grade II listed hotel, with origins dating back to the reign of Elizabeth I, sits within seven acres of peaceful grounds. The original three-gabled building retains many original features, such as the carved wooden fireplace in the library. Friendly service is provided; and the bedrooms, that vary in size, are thoughtfully equipped.

Rooms: 38 (1 family) (14 GF) **Facilities:** FTV WiFi ⚓ New Year **Conf:** Class 100 Board 60 Thtr 200 **Parking:** 250 **Notes:** Civ Wed 200

Premier Inn Nuneaton/Coventry

BUDGET HOTEL

Coventry Road, CV10 7PJ - **tel:** 0871 527 8858 (Calls cost 13p per minute plus your phone company's access charge) **web:** www.premierinn.com
dir: *M6 junct 3, A444 towards Nuneaton. Hotel on B4113 on right, just off Griff Rdbt towards Bedworth*

High quality, budget accommodation ideal for both families and business travellers. Spacious, en suite bedrooms feature free WiFi and tea and coffee making facilities, and in most hotels, Freeview TV is also available. The adjacent family restaurant features a wide and varied menu.

Rooms: 50

OAKHAM
Rutland
Map 11 SK80

INSPECTOR'S CHOICE

Hambleton Hall

★★★★ ◉◉◉◉ ⌂ COUNTRY HOUSE HOTEL

Hambleton, LE15 8TH - **tel:** 01572 756991
email: hotel@hambletonhall.com **web:** www.hambletonhall.com
dir: *3m E off A606*

Established over 30 years ago by Tim and Stefa Hart this delightful country house enjoys tranquil and spectacular views over Rutland Water. The beautifully manicured grounds are a delight to walk in. The bedrooms in the main house are stylish, individually decorated, and equipped with a range of thoughtful extras. A two-bedroom folly, with its own sitting and breakfast room, is only a short walk away. Day rooms include a cosy bar and a sumptuous drawing room, both featuring open fires. The elegant restaurant serves very accomplished, award-winning cuisine with menus highlighting locally sourced, seasonal produce - some of which is grown in the hotel's own grounds.

Rooms: 17 (2 annexe) ☎ S £200–£220; D £295–£510 (incl. bkfst)*
Facilities: STV FTV WiFi ☚ ☈ ☕ ⚓ Private access to lake Xmas New Year
Conf: Board 24 Thtr 40 Del from £300 **Services:** Lift **Parking:** 40
Notes: LB Civ Wed 60

Barnsdale Lodge Hotel

★★★ 74% ⊛ HOTEL

The Avenue, Rutland Water, LE15 8AH - tel: 01572 724678
email: enquiries@barnsdalelodge.co.uk **web:** www.barnsdalelodge.co.uk
dir: A1 onto A606. Hotel 5m on right, 2m E of Oakham

A popular and interesting hotel converted from a farmstead overlooking Rutland Water. The public areas are dominated by a successful food operation with a good range of appealing meals on offer for either formal or informal dining. Bedrooms are comfortably appointed with excellent beds enhanced by contemporary soft furnishings and thoughtful extras.

Rooms: 46 (2 family) (17 GF) ☎ S £59–£90; D £74–£135 (incl. bkfst)*
Facilities: FTV WiFi ☚ Fishing ⚓ Archery Beauty treatment room Golf Sailing Shooting Hair salon Xmas New Year **Conf:** Class 120 Board 76 Thtr 330
Services: Night porter **Parking:** 250 **Notes:** Civ Wed 200

OKEHAMPTON
Devon   Map 3 SX59

Manor House Hotel

★★★ 71% HOTEL

Fowley Cross, EX20 4NA - tel: 01837 53053
email: reception@manorhousehotel.co.uk **web:** www.manorhousehotel.co.uk
dir: Exit A30 at Sourton Cross flyover, right onto A386. Hotel 1.5m on right

Enjoying views to Dartmoor in the distance, this hotel specialises in short breaks and is set in 17 acres of grounds, close to the A30. The superb range of sporting and craft facilities has been enhanced by an impressive swimming pool and relaxation spa; golf is also offered at the adjacent sister hotel. Bedrooms, many located on the ground floor, are comfortable and well equipped.

Rooms: 204 (92 family) (93 GF) ☎ **Facilities:** Spa FTV WiFi ☚ ☈ ⚲ 99 Putting green ☕ Fishing ⚓ Gym Squash Craft centre Indoor bowls Shooting ranges Indoor tennis Exercise classes Ice skating Roller skating Snooker Adventure golf Ten pin bowling ♫ Xmas New Year **Conf:** Class 60 Board 40 Thtr 250 **Services:** Night porter **Parking:** 204

Ashbury Hotel

★★★ 69% HOTEL

Higher Maddaford, Southcott, EX20 4NL - tel: 01837 55453
email: reception@manorhousehotel.co.uk **web:** www.ashburygolfhotel.co.uk
dir: Exit A30 at Sourton Cross onto A386. Left onto A3079 to Bude at Fowley Cross. After 1m right to Ashbury. Hotel 0.5m on right

With no less than seven courses and a clubhouse with lounge, bar and dining facilities, The Ashbury is a golfers' paradise. The majority of the well-equipped bedrooms are located in the farmhouse and the courtyard-style development around the putting green. Guests can enjoy the many on-site leisure facilities or join the activities available at the nearby sister hotel.

Rooms: 222 (115 family) (89 GF) ☎ **Facilities:** Spa FTV WiFi ☚ ☈ ⚲ 99 Putting green ☕ Fishing Gym Badminton Shooting ranges Ten-pin bowling Indoor bowls 5-a-side Craft centre Sports simulators Snooker Exercise classes ♫ New Year **Conf:** Class 60 Board 40 Thtr 250 **Services:** Night porter **Parking:** 200

OLDBURY
West Midlands   Map 10 SO98

Premier Inn Birmingham Oldbury M5 Jct 2

BUDGET HOTEL

Wolverhampton Road, B69 2BH - tel: 0871 527 8090 (Calls cost 13p per minute plus your phone company's access charge) **web:** www.premierinn.com
dir: M5 junct 2, A4123 (Wolverhampton Rd) N towards Dudley

High quality, budget accommodation ideal for both families and business travellers. Spacious, en suite bedrooms feature free WiFi and tea and coffee making facilities, and in most hotels, Freeview TV is also available. The adjacent family restaurant features a wide and varied menu.

Rooms: 60

O

OLDHAM
Greater Manchester

Map 16 SD90

Best Western Hotel Smokies Park

★★★ 77% HOTEL

Ashton Road, Bardsley, OL8 3HX - tel: 0161 785 5000
email: sales@smokies.co.uk web: www.smokies.co.uk
dir: *On A627 between Oldham & Ashton-under-Lyne*

This modern, stylish hotel offers smart, comfortable bedrooms and spacious suites. A wide range of international dishes is offered in the main restaurant, Eat@ Smokies and there is also a recently refurbished lounge bar catering for all tastes. A small yet well equipped, residents-only fitness centre for the more active, and extensive function facilities are available.

Rooms: 73 (10 family) (22 GF) ↑ S £64–£120; D £64–£120* Facilities: FTV WiFi ↻ Gym Xmas New Year Conf: Class 100 Board 40 Thtr 400 Del from £125 Services: Lift Night porter Parking: 120 Notes: LB RS 25 Dec-3 Jan Room service during this period Civ Wed 400

Premier Inn Oldham (Broadway)

BUDGET HOTEL

Broadway/Hollinwood Avenue, Chadderton, OL9 8DW - tel: 0871 527 8860 (Calls cost 13p per minute plus your phone company's access charge) web: www.premierinn.com
dir: *M60 (anti-clockwise) junct 21, signed Manchester city centre. Take A663, hotel 400yds on left*

High quality, budget accommodation ideal for both families and business travellers. Spacious, en suite bedrooms feature free WiFi and tea and coffee making facilities, and in most hotels, Freeview TV is also available. The adjacent family restaurant features a wide and varied menu.

Rooms: 58

Premier Inn Oldham Central

BUDGET HOTEL

Westwood Park, Chadderton Way, OL1 2NA - tel: 0871 527 8862 (Calls cost 13p per minute plus your phone company's access charge) web: www.premierinn.com
dir: *M62 junct 20, A627(M) to Oldham. Take A627 (Chadderton Way). Hotel on left opposite B&Q Depot*

Rooms: 58

OLD HARLOW
Essex

Map 4 TL41

Premier Inn Harlow

BUDGET HOTEL

Cambridge Road, CM20 2EP - tel: 0871 527 8488 (Calls cost 13p per minute plus your phone company's access charge) web: www.premierinn.com
dir: *M11 junct 7, A414, A1184 Sawbridgeworth to Bishop's Stortford road*

High quality, budget accommodation ideal for both families and business travellers. Spacious, en suite bedrooms feature free WiFi and tea and coffee making facilities, and in most hotels, Freeview TV is also available. The adjacent family restaurant features a wide and varied menu.

Rooms: 81

OLLERTON
Nottinghamshire

Map 16 SK66

Thoresby Hall Hotel

★★★★ 80% ⍟ ⍟ COUNTRY HOUSE HOTEL

Thoresby Park, NG22 9WH - tel: 01623 821000
email: reception.thoresbyhall@bourne-leisure.co.uk web: www.warnerleisurehotels.co.uk
dir: *Please phone for directions*

Thoresby Hall is a magnificent Grade I Victorian country house, set in acres of rolling parklands on the edge of Sherwood Forest. Guests can choose to relax in the spa, stroll around the beautiful gardens or just sit and relax in the Great Hall. Bedrooms vary in style and size. This is an adults only (over 21 years) hotel.

Rooms: 221 (168 annexe) (72 GF) ↑ Facilities: Spa FTV WiFi HL ↻ supervised Putting green ⛳ Gym Rifle shooting Archery Outdoor bowls Yoga ♫ Xmas New Year Conf: Class 200 Board 30 Thtr 400 Services: Lift Night porter Parking: 240

ORMSKIRK
Lancashire

Map 15 SD40

Premier Inn Southport (Ormskirk)

BUDGET HOTEL

544 Southport Road, Scarisbrick, L40 9RG - tel: 0871 527 9010 (Calls cost 13p per minute plus your phone company's access charge) web: www.premierinn.com
dir: *From Southport follow Ormskirk/A570 signs. Hotel on right off A570 Southport Rd at 1st lights, entrance just after lights*

High quality, budget accommodation ideal for both families and business travellers. Spacious, en suite bedrooms feature free WiFi and tea and coffee making facilities, and in most hotels, Freeview TV is also available. The adjacent family restaurant features a wide and varied menu.

Rooms: 20

ORPINGTON
Greater London

Map 6 TQ46

Premier Inn London Orpington

BUDGET HOTEL

BR6 0TW - tel: 0871 527 9606 (Calls cost 13p per minute plus your phone company's access charge) web: www.premierinn.com
dir: *M25 junct 4 then NW on A224 Court Road. Left onto Spur Road/A232 then right onto Gravel Pit Way. Left onto Homefield Rise, at rdbt take 1st exit onto High St. Hotel near Sainsburys on right*

High quality, budget accommodation ideal for both families and business travellers. Spacious, en suite bedrooms feature free WiFi and tea and coffee making facilities, and in most hotels, Freeview TV is also available. The adjacent family restaurant features a wide and varied menu.

Rooms: 63

ORSETT
Essex

Map 6 TQ68

Orsett Hall Hotel, Restaurant & Spa

★★★★ 78% COUNTRY HOUSE HOTEL

Prince Charles Avenue, RM16 3HS - tel: 01375 891402 & 893096
email: accounts@orsetthall.co.uk web: www.orsetthall.co.uk
dir: *M25 junct 29, A127 Southend, A128 Hotel 3m on right*

This beautiful country house hotel, conveniently located for the M25, is set in 12 acres of landscaped gardens, and has individually designed, luxurious bedrooms.

O

The award-winning Garden restaurant is a fabulous dining venue and the stylish modern bar is popular with guests for afternoon tea. Orsett Hall has a first rate spa, and a very well equipped gym along with a range of business suites. Free WiFi is available throughout.

Rooms: 56 (24 annexe) (2 family) (14 GF) ♠ **S** £99–£159; **D** £109–£169 (incl. bkfst)* **Facilities:** Spa FTV WiFi ♘ Gym Hair salon Sauna Steam room Spa pool Xmas New Year **Conf:** Class 200 Board 50 Thtr 450 Del from £196 **Services:** Lift Night porter Air con **Parking:** 250 **Notes:** LB Civ Wed 400

OSWESTRY
Shropshire   Map 15 SJ22

Wynnstay Hotel

★★★★ 79% ◉◉ HOTEL

Church Street, SY11 2SZ - **tel:** 01691 655261
email: info@wynnstayhotel.com **web:** www.wynnstayhotel.com
dir: B4083 to town, fork left at Honda Garage, right at lights. Hotel opposite church

This Georgian property was once a coaching inn and posting house and surrounds a unique 200-year-old bowling green. Elegant public areas include a health, leisure and beauty centre, which is housed in a former coach house. Well-equipped bedrooms are individually styled and include several suites, four-poster rooms and a self-catering apartment. The Four Seasons Restaurant has a well-deserved reputation for its food, and the adjacent Wilsons café/bar is a stylish, informal alternative.

Rooms: 34 (5 family) ♠ **Facilities:** Spa FTV WiFi ⊗ supervised Gym Crown bowling green Beauty suite ♫ New Year **Conf:** Class 150 Board 50 Thtr 290 **Services:** Night porter **Parking:** 80 **Notes:** Civ Wed 90

HIGHLY RECOMMENDED

Pen-y-Dyffryn Country Hotel

★★★ 86% ◉◉◉ COUNTRY HOUSE HOTEL

Rhydycroesau, SY10 7JD - **tel:** 01691 653700
email: stay@peny.co.uk **web:** www. peny.co.uk
dir: A5 into town centre. Follow signs to Llansilin on B4580, hotel 3m W of Oswestry before Rhydycroesau

Peacefully situated in five acres of grounds, this charming old house dates back to around 1840, when it was built as a rectory. The tastefully appointed public rooms have real fires, lit in colder weather, and the accommodation includes several mini-cottages, each with its own patio. Many guests are attracted to this hotel for the excellent food and attentive, friendly service.

Rooms: 12 (4 annexe) (1 family) (1 GF) ♠ **S** £90–£99; **D** £130–£200 (incl. bkfst)* **Facilities:** STV FTV WiFi ♘ Guided walks In room treatments available New Year **Parking:** 18 **Notes:** LB Closed 18 Dec-19 Jan (ex New Year) No children 3yrs

Sweeney Hall Hotel

★★★ 77% COUNTRY HOUSE HOTEL

Morda, SY10 9EU - **tel:** 01691 652450
email: enquiries@sweeneyhall.co.uk **web:** www.sweeneyhall.co.uk
dir: From A5 on outskirts of Oswestry, take A483 towards Welshpool, hotel 2m on left

This Grade I Listed, friendly family-owned hotel was built in 1805 although previous settlements on this site date back to the 16th century. Sweeney Hall is set in several acres of mature parkland, with views over the surrounding countryside.

Located with easy access to Oswestry and Shrewsbury, it makes an ideal base for exploring the Shropshire countryside. A welcoming log fire is lit on arrival in the colder months and the smart terrace area is ideal for whiling away a summers' evening. Bedrooms are spacious and well equipped. The comfortable restaurant is open for breakfast, lunch and dinner, with Sunday lunch a popular favourite.

Rooms: 12 (1 annexe) (4 family) **S** £70–£90; **D** £85–£140 (incl. bkfst)* **Facilities:** FTV WiFi New Year **Conf:** Class 20 Board 24 Thtr 72 **Parking:** 50 **Notes:** Civ Wed 72

Lion Quays Hotel & Spa

Ⓤ

Weston Rhyn, SY11 3EN - **tel:** 01691 684300
email: info@lionquays.com **web:** www.lionquays.com
dir: On A5, 3m N of Oswestry

Currently the rating for this establishment is not confirmed. This may be due to a change of ownership or because it has only recently joined the AA rating scheme.

Rooms: 82 (3 family) (25 GF) ♠ **Facilities:** Spa FTV WiFi ♘ ⊗ ♨ Gym Xmas New Year **Conf:** Thtr 400 **Services:** Lift Night porter **Parking:** 300 **Notes:** Civ Wed 400

Premier Inn Oswestry

BUDGET HOTEL

SY10 8NN - **tel:** 0871 527 8864 (Calls cost 13p per minute plus your phone company's access charge) **web:** www.premierinn.com
dir: From rdbt junct of A483 & A5 (SE of Oswestry) take A5 signed Oswestry B4579. Hotel 500yds

High quality, budget accommodation ideal for both families and business travellers. Spacious, en suite bedrooms feature free WiFi and tea and coffee making facilities, and in most hotels, Freeview TV is also available. The adjacent family restaurant features a wide and varied menu.

Rooms: 59

OTLEY
West Yorkshire   Map 19 SE24

Chevin Country Park Hotel & Spa

CRERAR

★★★ 78% HOTEL

Yorkgate, LS21 3NU - **tel:** 01943 467818
email: chevin@crerarhotels.com **web:** www.crerarhotels.com
dir: From Leeds/Bradford Airport rdbt take A658 N towards Harrogate, 0.75m to lights. Left, 2nd left into Yorkgate. Hotel 0.5m on left

Chevin Country Park Hotel & Spa is peacefully located in its own woodland yet is convenient for major road links and the airport. Bedrooms are split between the original main building and chalet-style accommodation in the extensive grounds. Public areas include a bar and several lounges. The Lakeside Restaurant provides views over the small lake, and good leisure facilities are available.

Rooms: 49 (30 annexe) (7 family) (45 GF) **Facilities:** Spa FTV WiFi ⊗ ♨ Fishing Gym Steam room Xmas New Year **Conf:** Class 90 Board 50 Thtr 120 **Services:** Night porter **Parking:** 100 **Notes:** LB Civ Wed 100

OTTERSHAW	Map 6 TQ06
Surrey	

HIGHLY RECOMMENDED

Foxhills Club & Resort
★★★★ 84% ◉ ◉ HOTEL

Stonehill Road, KT16 0EL - **tel:** 01932 872050
email: reservations@foxhills.co.uk **web:** www.foxhills.co.uk
dir: *M25 junct 11, A320 to Woking. 2nd rdbt last exit into Chobham Rd.
Right into Foxhills Rd, left into Stonehill Rd*

Foxhills is a welcome retreat, set in a 400-acre Surrey estate just 25 minutes from Waterloo and Heathrow, with easy access to major road networks including the M25. The entire resort is bursting with things to do, including golf, tennis, pools and impressive indoor leisure facilities. At the heart of the estate and just a short walk from the spacious well appointed bedrooms, stands the 19th-century Manor House, home to the popular Manor Restaurant.

Rooms: 70 (8 family) (39 GF) ⌇ **D** £120–£350 (incl. bkfst)* **Facilities:** Spa STV FTV WiFi ⌂ ⌇ 45 Putting green ⌇ ⌇ Gym Squash Children's adventure playground Country pursuits Hairdresser ♫ Xmas New Year **Conf:** Class 60 Board 30 Thtr 150 **Services:** Night porter **Parking:** 500 **Notes:** LB Civ Wed 90

OUNDLE	Map 11 TL08
Northamptonshire	

The Talbot Hotel
★★★ 80% ◉ HOTEL

New Street, PE8 4EA - **tel:** 01832 273621
email: talbot@innmail.co.uk **web:** www.thetalbot-oundle.com
dir: *A605 Northampton/Oundle at rdbt exit Oundle A427 - Station Rd turn onto New St*

This Grade I listed property is steeped in history and is reputed to house the staircase that Mary Queen of Scots walked down to her execution in 1587. Following extensive refurbishment, the hotel offers an open-plan eatery and coffee shop for relaxed dining. Accommodation offers a mix of traditional and contemporary, but all provide up-to-date amenities for guest comfort.

Rooms: 34 (2 family) (12 GF) ⌇ **Facilities:** FTV WiFi Xmas New Year **Conf:** Class 50 Board 30 Thtr 100 **Services:** Night porter **Parking:** 30 **Notes:** Civ Wed 80

OXFORD	Map 5 SP50
Oxfordshire	

INSPECTOR'S CHOICE

Belmond Le Manoir aux Quat'Saisons
★★★★★ ◉ ◉ ◉ ◉ ◉ HOTEL

Church Road, OX44 7PD - **tel:** 01844 278881
email: manoir.mqs@belmond.com **web:** www.belmond.com/lemanoir

(for full entry see Great Milton)

Macdonald Randolph Hotel
★★★★★ 80% HOTEL

Beaumont Street, OX1 2LN - **tel:** 01865 256400
email: sales.randolph@macdonald-hotels.co.uk
web: www.macdonaldhotels.co.uk/Randolph
dir: *M40 junct 8, A40 signed Oxford/Cheltenham, 5m, at lights to ring road rdbt. Right signed Kidlington/North Oxford. At next rdbt left towards city centre - A4165/ Banbury rd. Through Summertown to lights at end of St Giles. Hotel on right*

Superbly located near the city centre, The Randolph boasts impressive neo-Gothic architecture and tasteful decor. The spacious and traditional restaurant, complete with picture windows, is the ideal place to watch the world go by while enjoying freshly prepared, modern dishes. Bedrooms include a mix of classical and contemporary wing rooms, which have been appointed to a high standard. On site chargeable parking is a real bonus; pre-booking is required.

Rooms: 151 ⌇ **S** £150–£300; **D** £160–£400* **Facilities:** Spa STV FTV WiFi Gym Beauty treatment rooms Thermal suite Mini gym Xmas New Year **Conf:** Class 130 Board 60 Thtr 300 Del from £240 **Services:** Lift Night porter **Parking:** 45 **Notes:** LB Civ Wed 120

De Vere Oxford Thames
★★★★ 80% ◉ HOTEL

Henley Road, Sandford-on-Thames, OX4 4GX - **tel:** 0800 374692
email: ThamesReservations@devere.com
web: www.phcompany.com/de-vere/oxford-thames
dir: *M40 junct 8 towards Oxford, then take A40 to Oxford, follow ring road. Left at rdbt towards Cowley. At rdbt with lights turn left to Littlemore, hotel approx 1m on right*

Set in 30 acres of beautiful grounds beside the river, this mellow stone property provides a quiet retreat, yet is close to the city. The spacious and traditional River Room Restaurant has superb views of the hotel's own boat moored on the river. The gardens can be enjoyed from the patios or balconies in the newer bedroom wings. Public rooms include a beamed bar and lounge area with minstrels' gallery, and Jerome's Leisure Club. The hotel is popular as a wedding venue.

Rooms: 104 (5 family) (49 GF) ⌇ **Facilities:** Spa FTV WiFi ⌂ ⌇ ⌇ Gym Steam room Sauna Xmas New Year **Conf:** Class 80 Board 40 Thtr 120 **Services:** Night porter **Parking:** 130 **Notes:** Civ Wed 150

Oxford Spires Hotel

★★★★ 79% HOTEL

Abingdon Road, OX1 4PS - **tel:** 0800 374692
email: SpiresReservations@oxfordspireshotel.co.uk
web: www.oxfordspireshotel.co.uk/partner/oxford-spires
dir: *From M40 junct 8 towards Oxford. Left towards Cowley. At 3rd rdbt follow city centre signs. Hotel in 1m. From A34 Hinksey Hill junct towards Oxford. Left at 1st rdbt. Hotel in 1m*

This purpose-built hotel is surrounded by extensive parkland, yet is only a short walk from the city centre. Bedrooms are attractively furnished, well equipped and include several apartments. Public areas include a spacious restaurant, open-plan bar/lounge, leisure club and extensive conference facilities.

Rooms: 181 (10 annexe) (1 family) (54 GF) **Facilities:** Spa FTV WiFi ⇲ ⓢ Gym Steam room Sauna Xmas New Year **Conf:** Class 96 Board 76 Thtr 266 **Services:** Lift Night porter **Parking:** 160 **Notes:** Civ Wed 200

Malmaison Oxford

★★★★ 77% HOTEL

Oxford Castle, 3 New Road, OX1 1AY - **tel:** 01865 268400
email: oxford@malmaison.com **web:** www.malmaison.com
dir: *M40 junct 9, A34 N to Botley interchange. Follow city centre & rail station signs. At rail station take the 2nd exit at rdbt, then 1st exit into Park End St. Straight on at next lights, hotel 2nd right*

Once the city's prison, this is definitely a hotel with a difference. Many of the rooms are actually converted from the old cells. Not to worry though as there have been many improvements in facilities, services and decor since the prisoners left 20 years ago. Exceedingly comfortable beds and luxury bathrooms are just two of the changes. The hotel has a popular brasserie with quality and value much in evidence. Limited parking space is available.

Rooms: 95 (5 GF) ↖ **Facilities:** STV FTV WiFi ⇲ Xmas New Year **Conf:** Class 40 Board 40 Thtr 80 **Services:** Lift Night porter **Parking:** 30 **Notes:** Civ Wed 120

Hawkwell House

★★★★ 75% HOTEL

Church Way, Iffley Village, OX4 4DZ - **tel:** 01865 749988
email: reservations@hawkwellhouse.co.uk **web:** www.hawkwellhouse.co.uk
dir: *A34 follow signs to Cowley. At Littlemore rdbt A4158 exit into Iffley Rd. After lights left to Iffley*

Set in a peaceful residential location, Hawkwell House is just a few minutes' drive from the Oxford ring road. The spacious rooms are modern, attractively decorated and well equipped. Public areas are tastefully appointed and the conservatory-style restaurant offers an interesting choice of dishes. The hotel also has a range of conference and function facilities.

Rooms: 77 (15 annexe) (10 family) (15 GF) ↖ **S** fr £73.50; **D** fr £96 **Facilities:** FTV WiFi ⇲ ⛵ Xmas New Year **Conf:** Class 100 Board 80 Thtr 200 Del from £145 **Services:** Lift Night porter **Parking:** 120 **Notes:** Civ Wed 150

Jurys Inn Oxford Hotel & Conference Centre

★★★★ 75% HOTEL

Godstow Road, OX2 8AL - **tel:** 01865 489988
dir: *Phone for directions*

Located just on the edge of the city centre, this newly refurbished 240 room hotel offers smart and modern bedrooms for either leisure or business guests. public rooms include a lounge area with a coffee bar, a bar offering bar food and a Marco

Pierre White restaurant. The contemporary-style bedrooms are smartly decorated and equipped with a range of useful facilities. The hotel also has a gym and pool.

Rooms: 240 **S** £69–£189; **D** £69–£189* **Conf:** Class 200 Board 50 Thtr 350 Del from £119

Cotswold Lodge Hotel

★★★★ 74% ⓢ HOTEL

66a Banbury Road, OX2 6JP - **tel:** 01865 512121
email: info@cotswoldlodgehotel.co.uk **web:** www.cotswoldlodgehotel.co.uk
dir: *A40 Oxford ring rd onto A4165 Banbury rd signed city centre/Summertown. Hotel 2m on left*

This Victorian property is located close to the centre of Oxford and offers smart, comfortable accommodation. Stylish bedrooms and suites are attractively presented and some have balconies. The public areas have an elegant country-house feel. The hotel is popular with business guests and caters for conferences and banquets.

Rooms: 49 (14 GF) ↖ **Facilities:** STV FTV WiFi ⇲ Xmas New Year **Conf:** Class 45 Board 40 Thtr 100 **Services:** Night porter **Parking:** 40 **Notes:** Civ Wed 100

Mercure Oxford Eastgate Hotel

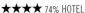

★★★★ 74% HOTEL

73 High Street, OX1 4BE - **tel:** 01865 248332
email: h6668@accor.com **web:** www.mercure.com
dir: *A40 follow signs to Headington & Oxford city centre, over Magdalen Bridge, stay in left lane, through lights, left into Merton St, entrance to car park on left*

The Mercure Eastgate Hotel has a range of beautifully presented bedrooms and stylish public areas. This 17th-century building enjoys a great location in the centre of historic Oxford and occupies a site at the city's East Gate. The stylish Marco's New York Italian Restaurant at the hotel is very popular and afternoon tea served in the comfortable lounge is another favourite with guests. Secure car parking is available at the hotel.

Rooms: 64 (3 family) (4 GF) ↖ **S** £115–£125; **D** £325–£345* **Facilities:** FTV WiFi Xmas New Year **Services:** Lift Night porter Air con **Parking:** 40

Manor House Hotel

★★ 76% METRO HOTEL

250 Iffley Road, OX4 1SE - **tel:** 01865 727627
email: manorhousehotel@hotmail.com **web:** www.manorhouseoxford.com
dir: *On A4158, 1m from city centre*

This family-run establishment is easily accessible from the city centre and all major road links. The hotel provides informal, friendly and attentive service. The comfortably furnished bedrooms are well appointed. The hotel has a bar but there is a selection of restaurants and popular pubs within easy walking distance. Limited private parking is available.

Rooms: 8 (2 family) ↖ **Facilities:** STV FTV WiFi ⇲ **Parking:** 6 **Notes:** Closed 20 Dec-20 Jan

O

OXFORD *continued*

Bath Place Hotel

★★ 72% METRO HOTEL

4-5 Bath Place, Holywell Street, OX1 3SU - tel: 01865 791812
email: info@bathplace.co.uk web: www.bathplace.co.uk
dir: *On S side of Holywell St, parallel to High St*

The hotel has been created from a group of 17th-century cottages originally built by Flemish weavers who were permitted to settle outside the city walls. This lovely hotel is very much at the heart of the city today and offers individually designed bedrooms, including some with four-posters.

Rooms: 16 (3 family) (5 GF) ✆ S fr £100; D fr £135 (incl. bkfst)* Facilities: FTV WiFi
Services: Night porter Parking: 16

Premier Inn Oxford

BUDGET HOTEL

Oxford Business Park, Garsington Road, OX4 2JZ - tel: 0871 527 8866
(Calls cost 13p per minute plus your phone company's access charge)
web: www.premierinn.com
dir: *On Oxford Business Park, just off A4142 & B480 junct*

High quality, budget accommodation ideal for both families and business travellers. Spacious, en suite bedrooms feature free WiFi and tea and coffee making facilities, and in most hotels, Freeview TV is also available. The adjacent family restaurant features a wide and varied menu.

Rooms: 143

OXFORD MOTORWAY SERVICE AREA (M40)	Map 5 SP60
Oxfordshire	

Ramada Oxford

WELCOMEBREAK

AA Advertised

M40 junct 8a, Waterstock, OX33 1LJ - tel: 01865 877000
email: oxford.hotel@welcomebreak.co.uk web: www.welcomebreak.co.uk
dir: *M40 junct 8a, at Welcome Break service area*

This modern building offers accommodation in smart, spacious and well-equipped bedrooms, suitable for families and business travellers, and all with en suite bathrooms. Continental breakfast is available and other refreshments may be taken at the nearby family restaurant.

Rooms: 59 (56 family) (25 GF) (10 smoking) Facilities: FTV WiFi ⌨ Parking: 100

PADSTOW	Map 2 SW97
Cornwall & Isles of Scilly	

HIGHLY RECOMMENDED

Treglos Hotel

★★★★ 84% ◉◉ HOTEL

Constantine Bay, PL28 8JH - tel: 01841 520727
email: stay@tregloshotel.com web: www.tregloshotel.com
dir: *From Okehampton A30, follow A39 towards Wadebridge, then B3274 to Padstow. After 2m turn left to St Merryn. After 3m, at St Merryn x-rd/s turn left. Take next right to Treglos. After 1m turn right after Constantine Bay Stores. Hotel is on left*

This long-established hotel is situated on the edge of the stunning Cornish coast with breathtaking views. The atmosphere is all about sophistication and elegance. Bedrooms are soundly appointed and well equipped, and there is a

contemporary dining room with enjoyable cuisine and wonderful views over the coast. Guests will find a superb bar and lounges to relax and unwind in. On-site parking is a bonus.

Rooms: 42 ✆ S £77–£109; D £157–£219 (incl. bkfst)* Facilities: Spa FTV WiFi ⌨
❄ ⌁ 18 Putting green Beauty treatments Games room Childrens playground Whirlpool ♫ Child facilities Services: Lift Night porter Parking: 40 Notes: LB Closed Dec-Feb

The Metropole

★★★★ 73% ◉◉ HOTEL

𝓡
RICHARDSON HOTELS
Where Memories are Made

Station Road, PL28 8DB - tel: 01841 532486
email: reservations@the-metropole.co.uk web: www.the-metropole.co.uk
dir: *M5/A30 pass Launceston, follow Wadebridge & N Cornwall signs. Take A39, follow Padstow signs*

This long-established hotel first opened its doors to guests back in 1904, and it still retains an air of the sophistication and elegance of a bygone age. Bedrooms are soundly appointed and well equipped; dining options include The Brasserie @ The Met, and the main restaurant with its enjoyable cuisine and wonderful views over the Camel estuary.

Rooms: 58 (3 family) (2 GF) ✆ D £111–£198 (incl. bkfst)* Facilities: Spa FTV WiFi
❄ Xmas New Year Conf: Class 20 Board 20 Thtr 40 Services: Lift Night porter
Parking: 36 Notes: LB Civ Wed 110

PAIGNTON	Map 3 SX86
Devon	

Redcliffe Hotel

★★★ 81% HOTEL

Marine Drive, TQ3 2NL - tel: 01803 526397
email: redclfe@aol.com web: www.redcliffehotel.co.uk
dir: *On seafront at Torquay end of Paignton Green*

Set at the water's edge in three acres of well-tended grounds, this popular hotel enjoys uninterrupted views across Tor Bay. On offer is a diverse range of facilities including a leisure complex, beauty treatments and lots of outdoor family activities in the summer. Bedrooms are pleasantly appointed and comfortably furnished, while public areas offer ample space for rest and relaxation.

Rooms: 69 (8 family) (3 GF) ✆ S £65–£74; D £130–£148 (incl. bkfst)*
Facilities: Spa FTV WiFi ⌨ ❄ supervised ⌁ supervised Putting green Fishing Gym Table tennis Carpet bowls Xmas New Year Conf: Class 50 Board 50 Thtr 150 Del from £75 Services: Lift Night porter Parking: 80 Notes: LB Civ Wed 150

The Queens Hotel

★★★ 79% HOTEL

2-6 Queens Road, TQ4 6AT - tel: 01803 551048
email: gm@queenspaignton.com web: www.queenspaignton.com
dir: *Phone for directions*

This popular hotel enjoys a central location close to the town centre, and within walking distance of the local beaches. Secure parking is available at the hotel along with a range of leisure facilities including a heated pool. Attractively decorated bedrooms vary in size, offering good levels of quality and comfort. Wholesome traditional food is served in the spacious dining room.

Rooms: 76 (5 family) (6 GF) ✆ Facilities: FTV WiFi ❄ Free use of gym at sister hotel ♫ Xmas New Year Services: Lift Night porter Parking: 36 Notes: LB

O

Premier Inn Paignton Seafront (Goodrington Sands)

BUDGET HOTEL

Tanners Road, Goodrington, TQ4 6LP - tel: 0871 527 9206 (Calls cost 13p per minute plus your phone company's access charge) web: www.premierinn.com
dir: *From Newton Abbot take A380 S. Left into A3022 (Totnes Rd), right at Hayes Rd into Penwill Way, right at B3199 into Dartmouth Rd, at lights left into Tanners Rd*

High quality, budget accommodation ideal for both families and business travellers. Spacious, en suite bedrooms feature free WiFi and tea and coffee making facilities, and in most hotels, Freeview TV is also available. The adjacent family restaurant features a wide and varied menu.

Rooms: 33

Premier Inn Paignton South (Brixham Road)

BUDGET HOTEL

White Rock, Long Road South, TQ4 7AZ - tel: 0871 527 9324 (Calls cost 13p per minute plus your phone company's access charge) web: www.premierinn.com
dir: *From A3022 (Brixham Rd) between Tweenaway & Galmpton Warborough, right into Long Rd*

Rooms: 61

PALTERTON
Derbyshire
Map 16 SK46

Twin Oaks Hotel

 77% HOTEL

Church Lane, S44 6UZ - tel: 01246 855455
email: book@twinoakshotel.co.uk web: www.twinoakshotel.co.uk
dir: *M1 junct 29, take Palterton turn, hotel 100mtrs down road on left*

This hotel began life as a picturesque row of colliery cottages, but it has been meticulously redesigned and configured to meet the expectations of the modern business or leisure traveller. The bedrooms provide contemporary accommodation and the attractive public areas include a brasserie and bistro providing a range of dining options. The hotel is a popular wedding destination and enjoys very good transport links as it is near the M1.

Rooms: 36 (4 annexe) (4 family) (19 GF) Facilities: FTV WiFi ⌨ Conf: Class 25 Board 25 Thtr 40 Parking: 80 Notes: Civ Wed 80

PATTERDALE
Cumbria
Map 18 NY31

Patterdale Hotel

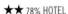 78% HOTEL

CA11 0NN - tel: 0844 811 5580 (Calls cost 5p per minute plus your phone company's access charge) email: reservations@choice-hotels.co.uk web: www.patterdalehotel.co.uk
dir: *M6 junct 40, A592 towards Ullswater. 10m to Patterdale*

Patterdale is a real tourist destination and this hotel makes a good base for those taking part in the many activity pursuits available in this area. The hotel enjoys delightful views of the valley and fells, being located at the southern end of Ullswater. The modern bedrooms vary in style. In busier periods accommodation is let for a minimum period of two nights.

Rooms: 56 (15 family) (6 GF) S £42–£74; D £80–£136 (incl. bkfst & dinner) Facilities: FTV WiFi Xmas New Year Services: Lift Parking: 30 Notes: LB

PECKFORTON
Cheshire
Map 15 SJ55

INSPECTOR'S CHOICE

Peckforton Castle

★★★★ HOTEL

Stone House Lane, CW6 9TN - tel: 01829 260930
email: info@peckfortoncastle.co.uk web: www.peckfortoncastle.co.uk
dir: *A49. At Beeston Castle pub right signed Peckforton Castle. Approx 2m, entrance on right*

Built in the mid-19th century by parliamentarian and landowner Lord John Tollemache, and now lovingly cared for by The Naylor Family, this Grade I medieval-style castle has been sympathetically renovated to provide high standards of comfort without losing its original charm and character. Bedrooms and public areas retain many period features, and dining in the 1851 Restaurant is a memorable experience. The kitchen team is passionate about using only the finest ingredients, sourced locally where possible. There are a host of excellent outdoor leisure activities; falconry and off-road Land Rover courses to name just two. The Tranquility Spa caters for those seeking a more serene experience.

Rooms: 48 (7 family) (2 GF) 🐾 D fr £187.50 (incl. bkfst)* Facilities: Spa FTV WiFi HL ⤵ Falconry Outdoor pursuits Land Rover experience Abseiling Beauty salon Xmas New Year Conf: Class 80 Board 40 Thtr 180 Services: Lift Night porter Parking: 400 Notes: LB Civ Wed 165

PENDLEBURY
Greater Manchester
Map 15 SD70

Premier Inn Manchester (Swinton)

BUDGET HOTEL

219 Bolton Road, M27 8TG - tel: 0871 527 8720 (Calls cost 13p per minute plus your phone company's access charge) web: www.premierinn.com
dir: *M60 junct 13 towards A572, at rdbt take 3rd exit towards Swinton. At next rdbt take A572. In 2m right onto A580. After 2nd lights A666 Kearsley, 1st left at rdbt. Pass fire station on right, 1st right*

High quality, budget accommodation ideal for both families and business travellers. Spacious, en suite bedrooms feature free WiFi and tea and coffee making facilities, and in most hotels, Freeview TV is also available. The adjacent family restaurant features a wide and varied menu.

Rooms: 31

P

PENRITH
Cumbria

Map 18 NY53

See also **Glenridding & Shap**

North Lakes Hotel & Spa
★★★★ 80% HOTEL

Ullswater Road, CA11 8QT - **tel:** 01768 868111
email: reservations@northlakeshotel.co.uk **web:** www.northlakeshotel.co.uk
dir: *M6 junct 40 at junct with A66*

With a great location, it's no wonder that this modern hotel is perpetually busy.
Amenities include a good range of meeting and function rooms and excellent health
and leisure facilities including a full spa. Themed public areas have a
contemporary, Scandinavian country style and offer plenty of space and comfort.
High standards of service are provided by a friendly team of staff.

Rooms: 84 (6 family) (22 GF) **D** £100–£200* **Facilities:** Spa STV WiFi ⬙ ☺ Gym
Children's splash pool Steam room Activity & wellness studios Sauna New Year
Conf: Class 140 Board 30 Thtr 200 Del from £120 **Services:** Lift Night porter
Parking: 150 **Notes:** LB Civ Wed 200

HIGHLY RECOMMENDED

Temple Sowerby House Hotel & Restaurant
★★★ 87% ◉◉ COUNTRY HOUSE HOTEL

CA10 1RZ - **tel:** 017683 61578
email: stay@templesowerby.com **web:** www.templesowerby.com

(For full entry see Temple Sowerby)

The George Hotel
★★★ 83% HOTEL

LAKE DISTRICT HOTELS

Devonshire Street, CA11 7SU - **tel:** 01768 862696
email: georgehotel@lakedistricthotels.net **web:** www.lakedistricthotels.net/georgehotel
dir: *M6 junct 40, 1m to town centre. From A6/A66 to Penrith*

This inviting and popular hotel was once visited by 'Bonnie' Prince Charlie.
Extended over the years, it currently offers well equipped bedrooms, and spacious
public areas that retain a timeless charm. There is a choice of lounge areas that
are ideal for morning coffee and afternoon tea.

Rooms: 35 (4 family) **Facilities:** FTV WiFi ⬙ Xmas New Year **Conf:** Class 80 Board 50
Thtr 120 **Services:** Night porter **Parking:** 40 **Notes:** Civ Wed 120

PENZANCE
Cornwall & Isles of Scilly

Map 2 SW43

Hotel Penzance
★★★★ 78% ◉◉ TOWN HOUSE HOTEL

Britons Hill, TR18 3AE - **tel:** 01736 363117
email: reception@hotelpenzance.com **web:** www.hotelpenzance.com
dir: *From A30, left at last rdbt for town centre. 3rd right onto Britons Hill.
Hotel on right*

Hotel Penzance is an Edwardian house that has been tastefully redesigned,
particularly in the contemporary Bay Restaurant. The focus on style is not only
limited to the decor, but is also apparent in the award-winning cuisine that is
based on fresh Cornish produce. Bedrooms have been appointed to modern
standards and are particularly well equipped; many have views across Mounts Bay.

Rooms: 25 (2 GF) ⟟ **S** £75–£114; **D** £95–£220 (incl. bkfst) **Facilities:** FTV WiFi ⬂
Xmas New Year **Conf:** Class 50 Board 25 Thtr 80 Del from £95 **Services:** Night porter
Parking: 11

Queens Hotel
★★★ 78% HOTEL

The Promenade, TR18 4HG - **tel:** 01736 362371
email: enquiries@queens-hotel.com **web:** www.queens-hotel.com
dir: *A30 to Penzance, follow signs for seafront pass harbour onto promenade,
hotel on right*

With views across Mount's Bay towards Newlyn, this impressive Victorian hotel
has a long and distinguished history. Comfortable public areas are filled with
interesting pictures and artefacts, and in the dining room guests can choose
from the daily-changing menu. Bedrooms, many with sea views, vary in style
and size.

Rooms: 70 (10 family) ⟟ **Facilities:** FTV WiFi ⬙ Hair & beauty salon Xmas New Year
Conf: Class 200 Board 120 Thtr 200 Del from £90 **Services:** Lift Night porter
Parking: 50 **Notes:** Civ Wed 250

PETERBOROUGH
Cambridgeshire

Map 12 TL19

Bull Hotel
★★★★ 79% ◉ HOTEL

PEEL HOTELS PLC

Westgate, PE1 1RB - **tel:** 01733 561364
email: rooms@bull-hotel-peterborough.com **web:** www.peelhotels.co.uk
dir: *From A1 follow city centre signs. Hotel opposite Queensgate shopping centre. Car
park on Broadway adjacent to library*

This pleasant city-centre hotel offers well-equipped, modern accommodation,
which includes several wings of deluxe bedrooms. Public rooms include a popular
bar and a brasserie-style restaurant serving a flexible range of dishes, with further
informal dining available in the lounge. There is a good range of meeting rooms
and conference facilities.

Rooms: 118 (2 family) (5 GF) ⟟ **S** £63–£150; **D** £73–£160* **Facilities:** STV WiFi
Xmas New Year **Conf:** Class 120 Board 40 Thtr 200 **Services:** Night porter
Parking: 100 **Notes:** LB Civ Wed 200

Best Western Plus Orton Hall Hotel & Spa
★★★★ 73% ◉ HOTEL

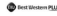

The Village, Orton Longueville, PE2 7DN - **tel:** 01733 391111
email: reception@ortonhall.co.uk **web:** www.abacushotels.co.uk
dir: *Off A605 E, opposite Orton Mere*

Orton Hall is an impressive country-house hotel set in 20 acres of woodland on the
outskirts of town and with easy access to the A1. The spacious and relaxing public
areas include the baronial Great Room and the Orton Suite for banqueting and

meetings, and the oak-panelled, award-winning Huntly Restaurant. The on-site pub, Ramblewood Inn, is an alternative, informal dining option.

Rooms: 70 (2 family) (15 GF) 🐾 **S** £40–£170; **D** £50–£190* **Facilities:** Spa FTV WiFi ⏳ 🏊 Gym Sauna Steam room Xmas New Year **Conf:** Class 70 Board 60 Thtr 160 Del from £110 **Services:** Night porter **Parking:** 200 **Notes:** LB Civ Wed 150

Bell Inn Hotel

★★★ 85% HOTEL

Great North Road, PE7 3RA - **tel:** 01733 241066
email: reception@thebellstilton.co.uk **web:** www.thebellstilton.co.uk

(For full entry see Stilton)

Premier Inn Peterborough (Ferry Meadows)

BUDGET HOTEL

Ham Lane, Orton Meadows, PE2 5UU - **tel:** 0871 527 8872 (Calls cost 13p per minute plus your phone company's access charge) **web:** www.premierinn.com
dir: *A1(M) (S'bound), A605 signed Alwalton/Chesterton Business Park/Elton & Showground, left at T-junct. Or A1(M) (N'bound after junct 17), follow Showround/Chesterton/Alwalton & Elton signs. Left at T-junct signed A605/Peterborough. For both routes: At 4th rdbt 1st exit, then 1st right*

High quality, budget accommodation ideal for both families and business travellers. Spacious, en suite bedrooms feature free WiFi and tea and coffee making facilities, and in most hotels, Freeview TV is also available. The adjacent family restaurant features a wide and varied menu.

Rooms: 40

Premier Inn Peterborough (Hampton)

BUDGET HOTEL

Ashbourne Road, off London Rd, PE7 8BT - **tel:** 0871 527 8874 (Calls cost 13p per minute plus your phone company's access charge) **web:** www.premierinn.com
dir: *A1(M) (S'bound) junct 16, A15 through Yaxley, left at rdbt. Or A1(M) (N'bound) junct 17, A1139 junct 3 right to Yaxley, right at 2nd rdbt*

Rooms: 143

Premier Inn Peterborough North

BUDGET HOTEL

1023 Lincoln Road, Walton, PE4 6AH - **tel:** 0871 527 8876 (Calls cost 13p per minute plus your phone company's access charge) **web:** www.premierinn.com
dir: *A1, A47 towards Peterborough. In 7m exit at junct 17 signed city centre. At rdbt (bottom of slip road) straight on signed city centre. At next rdbt left onto dual carriageway. At next rdbt double back, follow signs for city centre. Hotel in 200mtrs*

Rooms: 68

Days Inn Peterborough - A1

WELCOME BREAK

AA Advertised

Peterborough Extra Services, A1 Junction 17, PE7 3UQ - **tel:** 01733 371540
email: peterborough.hotel@welcomebreak.co.uk **web:** www.welcomebreak.co.uk
dir: *A1(M) junct 17*

This modern, purpose-built accommodation offers smartly appointed, particularly well-equipped bedrooms with good power showers. There is a choice of adjacent food outlets where guests can enjoy breakfast, snacks and meals.

Rooms: 82 (16 family) (40 GF) (11 smoking) 🐾 **Facilities:** FTV WiFi ⏳
Services: Air con **Parking:** 120

Hampshire

Langrish House

★★★ 81% HOTEL

Langrish, GU32 1RN - **tel:** 01730 266941
email: frontdesk@langrishhouse.co.uk **web:** www.langrishhouse.co.uk
dir: *A3 onto A272 towards Winchester. Hotel signed, 2.5m on left*

Langrish House has been in the same family for seven generations. It is located in an extremely peaceful area just a few minutes' drive from Petersfield, halfway between Guildford and Portsmouth. Bedrooms are comfortable and well equipped with stunning views across the gardens to the hills. Guests can eat in the intimate Frederick's Restaurant with views over the lawn, or in the Old Vaults which have an interesting history dating back to 1644. The hotel is licensed for civil ceremonies and various themed events take place throughout the year.

Rooms: 12 (1 family) (2 GF) 🐾 **S** £98–£118; **D** £119–£188 (incl. bkfst)*
Facilities: FTV WiFi 🍴 Xmas **Conf:** Class 18 Board 25 Thtr 60 Del £140 **Parking:** 80
Notes: Closed early Jan LB Civ Wed 80

Premier Inn Petersfield

BUDGET HOTEL

Winchester Road, GU32 3BS - **tel:** 0871 527 8878 (Calls cost 13p per minute plus your phone company's access charge) **web:** www.premierinn.com
dir: *At junct of A3 & A272 W'bound signed Services*

High quality, budget accommodation ideal for both families and business travellers. Spacious, en suite bedrooms feature free WiFi and tea and coffee making facilities, and in most hotels, Freeview TV is also available. The adjacent family restaurant features a wide and varied menu.

Rooms: 50

North Yorkshire

HIGHLY RECOMMENDED

The White Swan Inn

★★★ 84% HOTEL

Market Place, YO18 7AA - **tel:** 01751 472288
email: welcome@white-swan.co.uk **web:** www.white-swan.co.uk
dir: *In town, between church & steam railway station*

This 16th-century coaching inn offers well-equipped, comfortable bedrooms, including suites, either of a more traditional style in the main building or modern in the annexe. Service is friendly and attentive. Good food is served in the attractive restaurant, in the cosy bar and in the lounge, where a log fire burns in cooler months. A private dining room is also available. The comprehensive wine list focuses on many fine vintages.

Rooms: 21 (9 annexe) (3 family) (8 GF) 🐾 **S** £129–£169; **D** £159–£259 (incl. bkfst)* **Facilities:** FTV WiFi Bike storage Xmas New Year **Conf:** Class 18 Board 25 Thtr 35 Del from £165 **Parking:** 45 **Notes:** LB

P

PICKERING *continued*

Best Western Forest & Vale Hotel

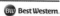

★★★ 84% HOTEL

Malton Road, YO18 7DL - tel: 01751 472722
email: forestvale@bestwestern.co.uk **web:** www.bw-forestandvalehotel.co.uk
dir: *On A169 towards York at rdbt on outskirts of Pickering*

This lovely 18th-century manor house hotel makes an excellent base from which to explore the east coast resorts and the North Yorkshire Moors National Park, one of England's most beautiful areas. A dedicated approach to upgrading means that the hotel is particularly well maintained, inside and out. In addition to standard bedrooms there are more spacious deluxe, superior and executive rooms; they are more traditional in the main house while the ones in the wing are contemporary; one has a four-poster bed.

Rooms: 22 (5 annexe) (7 family) (5 GF) S £95–£125; D £105–£135*
Facilities: FTV WiFi **Conf:** Class 40 Board 30 Thtr 100 **Parking:** 40 **Notes:** LB Closed 23-28 Dec Civ Wed 90

The Beansheaf Hotel

★★★ 71% HOTEL

Malton Road, YO17 6UE - tel: 01653 668614
email: enquiries@beansheafhotel.com **web:** www.beansheafhotel.com
dir: *On A169 between Malton & Pickering at the Flamingo Land turning*

This modern hotel is conveniently located on the A169 between Pickering and Malton. It is close to the A64 and ideal for exploring the North York Moors or visiting Flamingo Land. Leisure and business guests are equally well catered for with complimentary WiFi provided and there are dedicated meeting rooms. A range of bedrooms is available including singles, doubles, and twins. Ground floor rooms are also available. A wide range of home-made meals are served in the bar and restaurant.

Rooms: 18 (8 GF) S fr £55; D fr £75* **Facilities:** FTV WiFi **Conf:** Class 50 Board 25 Thtr 60 **Parking:** 35

PLYMOUTH	Map 3 SX45
Devon	

Boringdon Hall Hotel

★★★★★ 83% COUNTRY HOUSE HOTEL

Boringdon Hill, Plympton, PL7 4DP - tel: 01752 344455
email: info@boringdonhall.co.uk **web:** www.boringdonhall.co.uk
dir: *A38 at Marsh Mills rdbt follow Plympton signs to small island. Left over bridge and follow tourist signs*

With a history going back to the Domesday Book, this grand manor house can boast a long and fascinating history with period features in abundance; a truly fascinating place to stay, with easy access to Dartmoor and Plymouth. Quality and comfort are delivered in equal measure, while public areas exude character, charm and sophistication with a committed team entirely focused upon ensuring your stay is both relaxing and rewarding. The Gallery restaurant is the venue for accomplished cooking; menus incorporating the best of quality, seasonal produce. The recently opened Gaia Spa is simply stunning with a range of treatments available alongside additional facilities such as infinity pool, gym, relaxation rooms, saunas and hydrotherapy pool.

Rooms: 40 S fr £100; D fr £100* **Facilities:** Spa WiFi Gym Hydrotherapy pool Heat experiences Xmas New Year **Conf:** Class 40 Board 50 Thtr 120 Del from £135
Services: Night porter **Notes:** LB Civ Wed 90

Langdon Court Hotel & Restaurant

★★★★ 78% COUNTRY HOUSE HOTEL

Adams Lane, Down Thomas, PL9 0DY - tel: 01752 862358
email: enquiries@langdoncourt.com **web:** www.langdoncourt.com
dir: *From Plymouth follow Kingsbridge signs Elberton rdbt. Signs to Langdon Court*

Langdon Court Hotel has a super location in the South Hams, just a short stroll from Wembury Cove and the Coastal Path. It is set in seven acres of grounds, and although it's only four miles from Plymouth, it feels far away from the hubbub of the city. A Grade II listed building, this Tudor Mansion is steeped in history and is very stylish, with its own ornamental lake. There are some excellent gardens, including a Jacobean walled garden, and the hotel management are developing their own vineyard. Bedrooms are stylishly appointed, comfortably furnished, and have some lovely views over the grounds. The restaurant and bar areas offer enjoyable dining featuring fresh and local produce.

Rooms: 18 (3 family) S £99–£169; D £129–£229 (incl. bkfst)* **Facilities:** STV FTV WiFi Fishing Xmas New Year **Conf:** Class 20 Board 20 Thtr 60 Del £159
Services: Night porter **Parking:** 60 **Notes:** LB Civ Wed 100

Best Western Duke of Cornwall Hotel

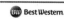

★★★ 84% HOTEL

Millbay Road, PL1 3LG - tel: 01752 275850
email: enquiries@thedukeofcornwall.co.uk **web:** www.thedukeofcornwall.co.uk
dir: *Follow city centre, then Plymouth Pavilions Conference & Leisure Centre signs. Hotel opposite Plymouth Pavilions*

A historic landmark, this city centre hotel is conveniently located. The spacious public areas include a popular bar, comfortable lounge and multi-functional ballroom. Bedrooms, many with far-reaching views, are individually styled and comfortably appointed. The range of dining options includes meals in the bar, or the elegant dining room for a more formal atmosphere.

Rooms: 71 (4 family) S £82–£109; D £99–£140 (incl. bkfst)* **Facilities:** STV FTV WiFi Xmas New Year **Conf:** Class 125 Board 84 Thtr 300 Del from £160
Services: Lift Night porter **Parking:** 25 **Notes:** Civ Wed 300

Invicta Hotel

★★★ 80% HOTEL

11-12 Osborne Place, Lockyer Street, PL1 2PU - tel: 01752 664997
email: invictahotel@btconnect.com **web:** www.invictahotel.co.uk
dir: *A38 to Plymouth, follow city centre signs, then signs to The Hoe & Barbican. Hotel opposite Hoe Park on Lockyer St at junct with Citadel Rd*

Just a short stroll from the city centre, this elegant Victorian establishment stands opposite the famous bowling green. The atmosphere is relaxed and friendly and bedrooms are neatly presented, well-equipped and attractively decorated. Eating options include meals in the bar or in the more formal setting of the dining room.

Rooms: 23 (4 family) (1 GF) S £65–£90; D £85–£130 (incl. bkfst)* **Facilities:** FTV WiFi **Conf:** Class 30 Board 45 Thtr 45 Del from £105 **Services:** Night porter **Parking:** 14 **Notes:** LB Closed 25-26 Dec

Premier Inn Plymouth Centre (Sutton Harbour)

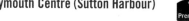

BUDGET HOTEL

Sutton Road, Shepherds Wharf, PL4 0HX - **tel:** 0871 527 8882 (Calls cost 13p per minute plus your phone company's access charge) **web:** www.premierinn.com
dir: *A38, A374 towards Plymouth. Follow Coxside & National Marine Aquarium signs. Right at lights after leisure park. Hotel adjacent to Lockyers Quay. NB there are 2 Premier Inns on this site, this hotel is the larger*

High quality, budget accommodation ideal for both families and business travellers. Spacious, en suite bedrooms feature free WiFi and tea and coffee making facilities, and in most hotels, Freeview TV is also available. The adjacent family restaurant features a wide and varied menu.

Rooms: 107

Premier Inn Plymouth City Centre (Lockyers Quay)

BUDGET HOTEL

1 Lockyers Quay, Coxside, PL4 0DX - **tel:** 0871 527 8880 (Calls cost 13p per minute plus your phone company's access charge) **web:** www.premierinn.com
dir: *From A38 (Marsh Mills rdbt) take A374 into Plymouth. Follow Coxside & National Marine Aquarium signs*

Rooms: 62

Premier Inn Plymouth East

BUDGET HOTEL

300 Plymouth Road, Crabtree, PL3 6RW - **tel:** 0871 527 8884 (Calls cost 13p per minute plus your phone company's access charge) **web:** www.premierinn.com
dir: *From E: Exit A38 at Marsh Mill junct. Straight on at rdbt, exit slip road 100mtrs on left. From W: Exit A38 at Plympton junct, at rdbt exit slip road adjacent to A38*

Rooms: 81

POCKLINGTON
East Riding of Yorkshire — Map 17 SE84

Feathers Hotel

★★ 76% HOTEL

56 Market Place, YO42 2AH - **tel:** 01759 303155
email: info@thefeathers-hotel.co.uk **web:** www.thefeatherspocklington.co.uk
dir: *From York, B1246 signed Pocklington. Hotel just off A1079*

This busy, traditional inn provides comfortable, well-equipped and spacious accommodation. Public areas are smartly presented. Enjoyable meals are served in the bar and the conservatory restaurant; the wide choice of dishes makes excellent use of local and seasonal produce.

Rooms: 16 (10 annexe) (2 family) (10 GF) **S** fr £60; **D** fr £75 (incl. bkfst)*
Facilities: FTV WiFi **Parking:** 25

POLPERRO
Cornwall & Isles of Scilly — Map 2 SX25

Talland Bay Hotel

★★★★ 81% COUNTRY HOUSE HOTEL

Porthallow, PL13 2JB - **tel:** 01503 272667
email: info@tallandbayhotel.co.uk **web:** www.tallandbayhotel.co.uk
dir: *From Looe over bridge towards Polperro on A387, 2nd turn to hotel*

This hotel has the benefit of a wonderful location with far-reaching views, situated in its own extensive gardens that run down almost to the cliff edge. The bedrooms come in a range of styles - classic twins and doubles, and rooms and suites with sea views. There is also cottage accommodation, and one is particularly suitable for families or those with dogs. The public areas of the hotel are impressive and stylish. Eating options include a brasserie and the Terrace Restaurant, where guests will find accomplished cooking, with an emphasis on carefully prepared local produce.

Rooms: 23 (2 family) (5 GF) **Facilities:** FTV WiFi ⬦ ⬥ Xmas New Year **Conf:** Class 20 Board 20 Thtr 20 **Parking:** 23 **Notes:** Civ Wed 60

PONTEFRACT
West Yorkshire — Map 16 SE42

HIGHLY RECOMMENDED

Wentbridge House Hotel

★★★★ 83% HOTEL

The Great North Road, Wentbridge, WF8 3JJ - **tel:** 01977 620444
email: info@wentbridgehouse.co.uk **web:** www.wentbridgehouse.co.uk
dir: *M62 junct 33 onto A1 S, hotel in 4m*

This well-established hotel sits in 20 acres of landscaped gardens, offering spacious, well-equipped bedrooms and a choice of dining styles. Service in the Fleur de Lys restaurant is polished and friendly, and a varied menu offers a good choice of interesting dishes. The Brasserie has a more relaxed style of modern dining.

Rooms: 41 (4 annexe) (4 family) (4 GF) **S** £90–£120; **D** £120–£220 (incl. bkfst)* **Facilities:** FTV WiFi Xmas New Year **Conf:** Class 100 Board 60 Thtr 130 **Services:** Lift Night porter **Parking:** 100 **Notes:** LB Civ Wed 130

Premier Inn Pontefract North

BUDGET HOTEL

Pontefract Road, Knottingley, WF11 0BU - **tel:** 0871 527 8886 (Calls cost 13p per minute plus your phone company's access charge) **web:** www.premierinn.com
dir: *M62 junct 33 onto A1 N. Exit at Pontefract junct (A645) to T-junct, right towards Pontefract. Hotel on right*

High quality, budget accommodation ideal for both families and business travellers. Spacious, en suite bedrooms feature free WiFi and tea and coffee making facilities, and in most hotels, Freeview TV is also available. The adjacent family restaurant features a wide and varied menu.

Rooms: 68

P

POOLE
Dorset

Map 4 SZ09

Harbour Heights Hotel

★★★★ 78% ◉◉ HOTEL

73 Haven Road, Sandbanks, BH13 7LW - **tel:** 0800 484 0048
email: reception@harbourheights.net **web:** www.fjbhotels.co.uk/harbourheights
dir: *Follow signs for Sandbanks, hotel on left after Canford Cliffs*

Enjoying stunning panoramic outlooks across the Sandbanks Peninsula and Poole Harbour, the Harbour Heights is an unassuming yet stylish and innovative boutique hotel. Attention to detail is very apparent, as state-of-the-art facilities blend with traditional comforts. The Harbar Brasserie is at the heart of Harbour Heights, offering excellent cuisine complemented by a fine and diverse wine cellar. The south-facing sun deck is the perfect setting for watching the cross-channel ferries come and go.

Rooms: 38 **D** £80–£294 (incl. bkfst)* **Facilities:** FTV WiFi ⌂ Spa bath in all rooms ♫ Xmas New Year **Conf:** Class 36 Board 22 Thtr 70 **Services:** Lift Night porter Air con **Parking:** 50 **Notes:** LB Civ Wed 120

Hotel du Vin Poole

★★★★ 77% ◉ HOTEL

Mansion House, Thames Street, BH15 1JN - **tel:** 01202 785578 & 0844 748 9265 (Calls cost 5p per minute plus your phone company's access charge)
email: info.poole@hotelduvin.com **web:** www.hotelduvin.com
dir: *A31 to Poole, follow channel ferry signs. Left at Poole bridge onto Poole Quay, 1st left into Thames St. Hotel opposite St James Church*

Offering a fresh approach to the well-established company style, this property boasts some delightful rooms packed with comfort and all the expected Hotel du Vin features. Situated near the harbour the hotel offers nautically-themed bedrooms and suites that have plasma TVs, DVD players and bathrooms with power showers. The public rooms are light, open spaces, and as with the other hotels in this group, the bar and restaurant form centre stage.

Rooms: 38 (4 GF) ⋔ **S** fr £125; **D** fr £145 (incl. bkfst)* **Facilities:** STV WiFi Xmas New Year **Conf:** Class 20 Board 20 Thtr 60 **Services:** Night porter Air con **Parking:** 8 **Notes:** LB Civ Wed 100

The Haven

★★★★ 76% ◉◉ HOTEL

161 Banks Road, Sandbanks, BH13 7QL - **tel:** 01202 707333
email: reservations@fjbhotels.co.uk **web:** www.fjbcollection.co.uk
dir: *B3965 towards Poole Bay, left onto the Peninsula. Hotel 1.5m on left adjacent to Swanage Toll Ferry*

Enjoying an enviable location at the water's edge with views of Poole Bay, this well established hotel was once the home of radio pioneer, Guglielmo Marconi. A friendly team of staff provide good levels of customer care. Bedrooms vary in size and style; many have balconies and wonderful sea or harbour views. The leisure facilities are noteworthy - the Harmony at the Haven is where guests can find spa treatments, a fully equipped gym, indoor and outdoor heated pools and an all-weather tennis court. The hotel is a popular venue for conferences and weddings.

Rooms: 84 (3 family) **S** £94–£129; **D** £144–£214 (incl. bkfst & dinner)*
Facilities: Spa FTV WiFi ⌂ ⊛ supervised ↗ supervised ♨ Gym Dance studio Health & Beauty suite Sauna Steam room ♫ Xmas New Year **Conf:** Class 70 Board 50 Thtr 160 **Services:** Lift Night porter **Parking:** 160 **Notes:** LB Civ Wed 80

Premier Inn Poole Centre (Holes Bay)

BUDGET HOTEL

Holes Bay Road, BH15 2BD - **tel:** 0871 527 8892 (Calls cost 13p per minute plus your phone company's access charge) **web:** www.premierinn.com
dir: *S of A35 & A349 on A350 (dual carriageway). Follow Poole Channel Ferry signs*

High quality, budget accommodation ideal for both families and business travellers. Spacious, en suite bedrooms feature free WiFi and tea and coffee making facilities, and in most hotels, Freeview TV is also available. The adjacent family restaurant features a wide and varied menu.

Rooms: 146

Premier Inn Poole North

BUDGET HOTEL

Cabot Lane, BH17 7DA - **tel:** 0871 527 8894 (Calls cost 13p per minute plus your phone company's access charge) **web:** www.premierinn.com
dir: *Follow Poole/Channel Ferries signs. At Darby's Corner rdbt take 2nd exit. At 2nd lights right into Cabot Ln. Hotel on right*

Rooms: 126

PORTISHEAD
Somerset

Map 4 ST47

Premier Inn Portishead

BUDGET HOTEL

Wyndham Way, BS20 7GA - **tel:** 0871 527 8898 (Calls cost 13p per minute plus your phone company's access charge) **web:** www.premierinn.com
dir: *M5 junct 19, A369 towards Portishead. Over 1st rdbt, hotel at next rdbt*

High quality, budget accommodation ideal for both families and business travellers. Spacious, en suite bedrooms feature free WiFi and tea and coffee making facilities, and in most hotels, Freeview TV is also available. The adjacent family restaurant features a wide and varied menu.

Rooms: 95

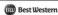

PORTSCATHO

Cornwall & Isles of Scilly

Map 2 SW83

INSPECTOR'S CHOICE

Driftwood

★★★ ◉◉◉ HOTEL

Rosevine, TR2 5EW - **tel:** 01872 580644
email: info@driftwoodhotel.co.uk **web:** www.driftwoodhotel.co.uk
dir: *A390 towards St Mawes. On A3078 turn left to Rosevine at Trewithian*

Poised on the cliff side with panoramic views, this contemporary hotel has a peaceful and secluded location. A warm welcome is guaranteed, and professional standards of service are provided in an effortless and relaxed manner. Cuisine is at the heart of any stay, with quality local produce used in a sympathetic and highly skilled manner. The extremely comfortable and elegant bedrooms are decorated in soft shades reminiscent of the seashore. There is a sheltered terraced garden that has a large deck for sunbathing.

Rooms: 15 (1 annexe) (3 family) (3 GF) **S** £100–£255; **D** £125–£300 (incl. bkfst)*
Facilities: FTV WiFi ❧ Private beach Beauty treatments on request **Parking:** 20
Notes: Closed 4 Dec-2 Feb

PORTSMOUTH & SOUTHSEA

Hampshire

Map 5 SU60

Portsmouth Marriott Hotel

★★★★ 78% HOTEL

Southampton Road, PO6 4SH - **tel:** 023 9238 3151
web: www.portsmouthmarriott.co.uk
dir: *M27 junct 12, keep left off slip road, exit Cosham. Hotel on left at lights*

Close to the motorway and ferry port, this hotel is well suited for business travellers. The comfortable and well laid-out bedrooms provide a comprehensive range of facilities including up-to-date workstations. The leisure club offers a pool, a gym, and a health and beauty salon.

Rooms: 174 (73 family) ❧ **S** fr £79* **Facilities:** STV FTV WiFi ❧ HL ⊗ supervised Gym Exercise studio Beauty salon & treatment room Xmas New Year **Conf:** Class 180 Board 30 Thtr 350 **Services:** Lift Night porter Air con **Parking:** 196 **Notes:** Civ Wed 350

Best Western Royal Beach Hotel

★★★ 79% HOTEL

South Parade, Southsea, PO4 0RN - **tel:** 023 9273 1281
email: enquiries@royalbeachhotel.co.uk **web:** www.royalbeachhotel.co.uk
dir: *M27 to M275, follow signs to seafront. Hotel on seafront*

This former Victorian seafront hotel is a smart and comfortable venue suitable for leisure and business guests alike. Bedrooms and public areas are well presented and generally spacious, and the smart Coast Bar is an ideal venue for a relaxing drink.

Rooms: 124 (12 family) ❧ **Facilities:** STV FTV WiFi ❧ Xmas New Year **Conf:** Class 180 Board 40 Thtr 280 **Services:** Lift Night porter **Parking:** 50 **Notes:** Civ Wed 85

Premier Inn Portsmouth City Centre

BUDGET HOTEL

1 Isambard Brunel Road, PO1 2TR - **tel:** 0871 527 9522 (Calls cost 13p per minute plus your phone company's access charge)
email: portsmouthcitycentre.pi@premierinn.com **web:** www.premierinn.com
dir: *M275 onto A3 (Portsmouth (W)/Isle of Wight Ferries). At rdbt 2nd left (City Centre/Seafront/Historic Waterfront). At next rdt 2nd left into Marketway. After next rdbt left signed Station into Unicorn Rd. At 2nd rdbt right into Isambard Brunel Rd Under rail bridge, hotel on left*

High quality, budget accommodation ideal for both families and business travellers. Spacious, en suite bedrooms feature free WiFi and tea and coffee making facilities, and in most hotels, Freeview TV is also available. The adjacent family restaurant features a wide and varied menu.

Rooms: 84

Premier Inn Portsmouth (Horndean)

BUDGET HOTEL

2 Havant Road, PO8 0DT - **tel:** 0871 527 8902 (Calls cost 13p per minute plus your phone company's access charge)
web: www.premierinn.com
dir: *A3(M) junct 2, take B2149 signed Emsworth, Horndean. At rdbt left onto B2149, follow Horndean signs. At next rdbt left onto A3 towards Waterlooville. Hotel on left behind Red Lion*

Rooms: 25

Premier Inn Portsmouth (Port Solent)

BUDGET HOTEL

Binnacle Way, PO6 4FB - **tel:** 0871 527 8906 (Calls cost 13p per minute plus your phone company's access charge) **web:** www.premierinn.com
dir: *M27 junct 12, left at lights onto Southampton Rd. Left after 200mtrs at lights onto Compass Rd. At mini-rdbt right onto Binnacle Way, hotel on right*

Rooms: 108

Premier Inn Portsmouth (Port Solent East)

BUDGET HOTEL

1 Southampton Road, North Harbour, PO6 4SA - **tel:** 0871 527 8904 (Calls cost 13p per minute plus your phone company's access charge) **web:** www.premierinn.com
dir: *M27 junct 12, A3, left onto A27. Hotel on left*

Rooms: 64

P

PORTSMOUTH & SOUTHSEA *continued*

Premier Inn Southsea

BUDGET HOTEL

Long Curtain Road, Southsea, PO5 3AA - **tel:** 0871 527 9014 (Calls cost 13p per minute plus your phone company's access charge) **web:** www.premierinn.com
dir: *M27, M275, A3, follow signs for Hovercraft & Southsea Seafront. Hotel adjacent to funfair at Clarence Pier*

Rooms: 48

Spit Bank Fort

AA Advertised

Solent Forts Port Office, Canalside, PO1 3FH - **tel:** 023 9298 9281 & 9277 6110
email: hello@solentforts.com **web:** www.solentforts.com/spitbank-fort
dir: *Phone for directions*

Spit Bank Fort is an unusual and intriguing location for a hotel. Built to defend Portsmouth dockyard 150 years ago, when Britain was in fear of French invasion, this is one of five forts built on the Solent, two of which now operate as hotels. With walls some 15 feet thick, and many incredible original features, the bedrooms and public areas at Spit Bank Fort combine timeless luxury with quirky style and vintage touches. There are two bars, a restaurant, a 'wine cave' and a rooftop terrace with a hot pool, sauna and fire pit. A wide range of packages are available, including stag and hen weekends, corporate functions, and weddings.

Rooms: 8 **S** £449–£1000; **D** £449–£1000 (incl. bkfst & dinner)* **Facilities:** Spa FTV WiFi Fishing Hot pool Sauna **Conf:** Board 16 Thtr 60 **Services:** Night porter
Notes: Civ Wed 60

PORT SUNLIGHT
Merseyside

Map 15 SJ38

HIGHLY RECOMMENDED

Leverhulme Hotel

★★★★ 85% 🏵️🏵️ HOTEL

Central Road, CH62 5EZ - **tel:** 0151 644 6655
email: enquiries@leverhulmehotel.co.uk **web:** www.leverhulmehotel.co.uk
dir: *From Chester: M53 junct 5, A41 Birkenhead, in approx 4m left into Bolton Rd, on at rdbt, 0.1m right into Church Drive. 0.2m hotel on right. From Liverpool: A41 Chester, 2.7m, 3rd exit at 3rd rdbt into Bolton Rd then follow directions as above*

Built in 1907, this Grade II listed, former cottage hospital is set in the picturesque garden village of Port Sunlight, which was created by Lord Leverhulme for his soap-factory workers in the late 19th century. Following an extensive restoration project, this art deco hotel has stylish bedrooms, appointed to a very high standard; all have impressive facilities including bathrooms with separate showers and LCD TVs; the suites have roof-top terraces and hot tubs. A games room, cosy bar with open fire, and the striking Riviera restaurant occupy the various wings.

Rooms: 23 (8 annexe) (1 family) (8 GF) **S** £114–£515; **D** £160–£535 (incl. bkfst)* **Facilities:** STV FTV WiFi HL 🏊 Gym Games room Children's play area Xmas New Year **Conf:** Class 140 Board 30 Thtr 300 Del from £114 **Services:** Night porter **Parking:** 70 **Notes:** LB Civ Wed 240

PRESTON
Lancashire

Map 18 SD52

See also **Garstang**

Barton Grange Hotel

★★★★ 78% HOTEL

Garstang Road, PR3 5AA - **tel:** 01772 862551
email: stay@bartongrangehotel.com **web:** www.bartongrangehotel.co.uk

(For full entry see Barton)

Macdonald Tickled Trout

★★★★ 74% HOTEL

Preston New Road, Samlesbury, PR5 0UJ - **tel:** 01772 877 671
email: general.tickledtrout@macdonald-hotels.co.uk **web:** www.macdonaldhotels.co.uk
dir: *M6 junct 31, A59 towards Preston*

On the banks of the River Ribble, this hotel is conveniently located for the motorway, making it a popular venue for both business and leisure guests. Smartly appointed bedrooms are all tastefully decorated and equipped with a thoughtful range of extras. The hotel boasts a stylish wing of meeting rooms.

Rooms: 98 (6 family) (10 GF) **Facilities:** FTV WiFi Fishing Xmas New Year **Conf:** Class 35 Board 20 Thtr 100 **Services:** Lift Night porter **Parking:** 180 **Notes:** Civ Wed 90

Premier Inn Preston Central

BUDGET HOTEL

Fox Street, PR1 2AB - **tel:** 0871 527 8908 (Calls cost 13p per minute plus your phone company's access charge) **web:** www.premierinn.com
dir: *Off Ridgway (A59). Telephone for detailed directions*

High quality, budget accommodation ideal for both families and business travellers. Spacious, en suite bedrooms feature free WiFi and tea and coffee making facilities, and in most hotels, Freeview TV is also available. The adjacent family restaurant features a wide and varied menu.

Rooms: 140

Premier Inn Preston East

BUDGET HOTEL

Bluebell Way, Preston East Link Rd, PR2 5PZ - **tel:** 0871 527 8910 (Calls cost 13p per minute plus your phone company's access charge) **web:** www.premierinn.com
dir: *M6 junct 31a, follow ring road under motorway, hotel on left. NB no exit for S'bound traffic - exit at M6 junct 31, join M6 N'bound, exit at junct 31a*

Rooms: 67

Premier Inn Preston South (Craven Drive)

BUDGET HOTEL

Lostock Lane, Bamber Bridge, PR5 6BZ - **tel:** 0871 527 8914 (Calls cost 13p per minute plus your phone company's access charge) **web:** www.premierinn.com
dir: *M6 junct 29, A582 (Lostock Ln). Straight on at 1st lights, into left lane, hotel on left adjacent to B&Q*

Rooms: 75

Premier Inn Preston South (Cuerden Way)

BUDGET HOTEL

Lostock Lane, Bamber Bridge, PR5 6BA - tel: 0871 527 8916 (Calls cost 13p per minute plus your phone company's access charge) **web:** www.premierinn.com
dir: *Off M65 junct 1 (0.5m from M6 junct 29) close to rdbt junct of A582 & A6*

Rooms: 42

Premier Inn Preston West

BUDGET HOTEL

Blackpool Road, Lea, PR4 0XB - tel: 0871 527 8918 (Calls cost 13p per minute plus your phone company's access charge) **web:** www.premierinn.com
dir: *Off A583, opposite Texaco garage*

Rooms: 38

PRESTWICH	**Map 15 SD80**
Greater Manchester	

Premier Inn Manchester (Prestwich)

BUDGET HOTEL

Bury New Road, M25 3AJ - tel: 0871 527 8714 (Calls cost 13p per minute plus your phone company's access charge) **web:** www.premierinn.com
dir: *M60 junct 17, A56 signed Manchester City Centre, Prestwich & Whitefield. Hotel on left*

High quality, budget accommodation ideal for both families and business travellers. Spacious, en suite bedrooms feature free WiFi and tea and coffee making facilities, and in most hotels, Freeview TV is also available. The adjacent family restaurant features a wide and varied menu.

Rooms: 83

PUDDINGTON	**Map 15 SJ37**
Cheshire	

Macdonald Craxton Wood Hotel

★★★★ 79% @ HOTEL

Parkgate Road, Ledsham, CH66 9PB - tel: 0151 347 4000
email: craxton@macdonald-hotels.co.uk **web:** www.macdonaldhotels.co.uk
dir: *From M6 take M56 towards N Wales, then A5117/A540 to Hoylake. Hotel on left 200yds past lights*

Set in extensive grounds, this hotel offers a variety of spacious and comfortable rooms, well equipped with modern amenities. The restaurant features a range of dishes including signature grills and locally sourced ingredients. An extensive spa facility and a choice of function suites complete the package.

Rooms: 72 (8 family) (30 GF) **Facilities:** Spa FTV WiFi ➔ HL Gym Sauna Steam room Thermal Spa incl Rasul Xmas New Year **Conf:** Class 200 Board 160 Thtr 300 **Services:** Lift Night porter **Parking:** 220 **Notes:** Civ Wed 350

Premier Inn Wirral (Two Mills)

BUDGET HOTEL

Parkgate Road, Two Mills, CH66 9PD - tel: 0871 527 9180 (Calls cost 13p per minute plus your phone company's access charge) **web:** www.premierinn.com
dir: *5m from M56 junct 16 & M53 junct 5. On x-rds of A550 & A540*

High quality, budget accommodation ideal for both families and business travellers. Spacious, en suite bedrooms feature free WiFi and tea and coffee making

facilities, and in most hotels, Freeview TV is also available. The adjacent family restaurant features a wide and varied menu.

Rooms: 31

PURTON	**Map 5 SU08**
Wiltshire	

The Pear Tree at Purton

★★★ 82% @@ HOTEL

Church End, SN5 4ED - tel: 01793 772100
email: stay@peartreepurton.co.uk **web:** www.peartreepurton.co.uk
dir: *M4 junct 16 follow signs to Purton, at Hartford House Stores turn right. Hotel 0.25m on left*

The Pear Tree is a charming 15th-century, former vicarage set amidst extensive landscaped gardens in a peaceful location in the Vale of the White Horse, near the Saxon village of Purton. The resident proprietors and staff provide efficient, dedicated service and friendly hospitality. The spacious bedrooms are individually decorated and have a good range of thoughtful extras such as fresh fruit, sherry and shortbread. Fresh ingredients feature on the award-winning menus.

Rooms: 17 (2 family) (6 GF) **Facilities:** FTV WiFi ➔ Outdoor giant chess & jenga Vineyard New Year **Conf:** Class 30 Board 30 Thtr 60 **Parking:** 60 **Notes:** LB Closed 26 Dec Civ Wed 50

RADLETT	**Map 6 TL10**
Hertfordshire	

Premier Inn St Albans/Bricket Wood

BUDGET HOTEL

Smug Oak Lane, Bricketwood, AL2 3PN - tel: 0871 527 9016 (Calls cost 13p per minute plus your phone company's access charge) **web:** www.premierinn.com
dir: *M1 junct 6 (or M25 junct 21a) follow Watford signs, left at lights signed M1/Bricket Wood. 2nd left into Mount Pleasant Ln, straight on at 2 mini rdbts, right at The Gate pub. Hotel at end*

High quality, budget accommodation ideal for both families and business travellers. Spacious, en suite bedrooms feature free WiFi and tea and coffee making facilities, and in most hotels, Freeview TV is also available. The adjacent family restaurant features a wide and varied menu.

Rooms: 56

RAINHAM	**Map 6 TQ58**
Greater London	

Premier Inn Rainham

BUDGET HOTEL

New Road, Wennington, RM13 9ED - tel: 0871 527 8920 (Calls cost 13p per minute plus your phone company's access charge) **web:** www.premierinn.com
dir: *M25 junct 30/31, A13 for Dagenham/Rainham, A1306 towards Wennington, Aveley & Rainham. Hotel 0.5m on right*

High quality, budget accommodation ideal for both families and business travellers. Spacious, en suite bedrooms feature free WiFi and tea and coffee making facilities, and in most hotels, Freeview TV is also available. The adjacent family restaurant features a wide and varied menu.

Rooms: 82

R

RAINHILL
Merseyside   Map 15 SJ49

Premier Inn Liverpool (Rainhill)

BUDGET HOTEL

804 Warrington Road, L35 6PE - tel: 0871 527 8614 (Calls cost 13p per minute plus your phone company's access charge) **web:** www.premierinn.com
dir: *Just off M62 junct 7, A57 towards Rainhill*

High quality, budget accommodation ideal for both families and business travellers. Spacious, en suite bedrooms feature free WiFi and tea and coffee making facilities, and in most hotels, Freeview TV is also available. The adjacent family restaurant features a wide and varied menu.

Rooms: 34

RAMSGATE
Kent   Map 7 TR36

The Pegwell Bay Hotel

★★★ 81% HOTEL

81 Pegwell Road, Pegwell, CT11 0NJ - tel: 01843 599590
email: pegwellbay.reception@thorleytaverns.co.uk **web:** www. pegwellbayhotel.co.uk
dir: *Phone for detailed directions*

Boasting stunning views over the Channel, this historic cliff-top hotel is suitable for guests staying either on business or for leisure. Spacious, comfortable bedrooms are well equipped and include WiFi. A modern lounge, majestic dining room and traditional pub offer a variety of options for eating and for relaxation.

Rooms: 42 (5 family) (5 GF) **Facilities:** FTV WiFi Xmas New Year **Conf:** Class 65 Board 65 Thtr 100 **Services:** Lift Night porter **Parking:** 80 **Notes:** Civ Wed 70

Comfort Inn Ramsgate

★★★ 73% HOTEL

Victoria Parade, East Cliff, CT11 8DT - tel: 01843 592345
email: reservations@comfortinnramsgate.co.uk **web:** www.comfortinnramsgate.co.uk
dir: *From M2 take A299 signed Ramsgate, B2054 to Victoria Parade*

This modern building offers accommodation in smart, spacious and well equipped bedrooms, all with en suite bathrooms. Refreshments may be taken at the nearby family restaurant. For further details and the Comfort Inn phone number, consult the Hotel Groups page under 'Choice'.

Rooms: 44 (8 family) S £40–£70; D £49–£119 (incl. bkfst) **Facilities:** FTV WiFi Gym Beauty salon Sauna Xmas New Year **Conf:** Class 30 Board 30 Thtr 70 Del from £98 **Services:** Lift Night porter Air con **Parking:** 10 **Notes:** LB

The Oak Hotel

★★ 84% HOTEL

66 Harbour Parade, CT11 8LN - tel: 01843 583686
email: oak.reception@thorleytaverns.co.uk **web:** www.oakhotel.co.uk
dir: *Follow road around harbour, right into Harbour Parade*

Located within easy reach of the railway station, ferry terminal and the town centre's shops, this unpretentious hotel enjoys spectacular views of the marina and harbour. The comfortable bedrooms are attractively presented and very well equipped. The Restaurant Sixty-Six, Caffe Roma and The Lounge Bar offer a variety of dining options along with a selection of wines, beers and spirits.

Rooms: 34 (9 family) **Facilities:** FTV WiFi **Conf:** Class 60 Board 50 Thtr 100 **Services:** Night porter

Holiday Inn Express Ramsgate

BUDGET HOTEL

Tothill Street, CT12 4AU - tel: 01843 820250
email: reservations.ramsgate@holidayinnexpress.org.uk **web:** www.hiexramsgate.co.uk
dir: *On A299, off rdbt junct with B2048*

A modern hotel ideal for families and business travellers. Fresh and uncomplicated, the spacious rooms include Sky TV, power shower and tea and coffee-making facilities. Continental buffet breakfast is included in the room rate; other meals may be taken at the nearby family pub or restaurant.

Rooms: 105 (70 family) (33 GF) **Conf:** Class 16 Board 16 Thtr 30

RAVENGLASS
Cumbria   Map 18 SD09

HIGHLY RECOMMENDED

The Pennington Hotel

★★★ 86% HOTEL

CA18 1SD - tel: 01229 717222 & 0845 450 6445 (Calls cost 7p per minute plus your phone company's access charge)
email: info@penningtonhotels.com **web:** www.penningtonhotels.com
dir: *In village centre*

This hotel has a very relaxed atmosphere throughout and the public areas are open-plan with high quality fabrics and artwork. Bedrooms are modern in design and have high spec fixtures and fittings in the bathrooms. Honest cooking, based on local and fine quality ingredients, is offered on the seasonal menus. Staff show exceptional customer awareness and provide very attentive and friendly service.

Rooms: 21 (3 annexe) (6 family) (5 GF) **Facilities:** FTV WiFi Xmas New Year **Conf:** Class 40 Board 40 Thtr 80 **Services:** Night porter **Parking:** 53 **Notes:** LB

RAVENSCAR
North Yorkshire   Map 19 NZ90

Raven Hall Country House Hotel

★★★ 79% HOTEL

YO13 0ET - tel: 01723 870353
email: enquiries@ravenhall.co.uk **web:** www.ravenhall.co.uk
dir: *A171 towards Whitby. At Cloughton turn right onto unclassified road to Ravenscar*

This impressive cliff-top mansion enjoys breathtaking views over Robin Hood's Bay. Extensive well-kept grounds include tennis courts, putting green, swimming pools and historic battlements. The bedrooms vary in size but all are comfortably equipped, and many offer panoramic views. There are also eight environmentally-friendly Finnish lodges that have been furnished to a high standard.

Rooms: 63 (8 annexe) (23 family) (5 GF) **Facilities:** FTV WiFi 9 Putting green Bowls Table tennis Xmas New Year **Conf:** Class 80 Board 40 Thtr 100 **Services:** Lift Night porter **Parking:** 100 **Notes:** Civ Wed 100

R

RAYLEIGH
Essex
Map 7 TQ89

Premier Inn Basildon (Rayleigh)

BUDGET HOTEL

Rayleigh Weir, Arterial Road (A127), SS6 7XJ - tel: 0871 527 8058
(Calls cost 13p per minute plus your phone company's access charge)
web: www.premierinn.com
dir: *M25 junct 29, A127 towards Southend. Approx 13m exit at Rayleigh Weir junct onto A129 to Rayleigh. Straight on at 2 lights, 1st left*

High quality, budget accommodation ideal for both families and business travellers. Spacious, en suite bedrooms feature free WiFi and tea and coffee making facilities, and in most hotels, Freeview TV is also available. The adjacent family restaurant features a wide and varied menu.

Rooms: 50

READING
Berkshire
Map 5 SU77

Holiday Inn Reading M4 Jct 10
★★★★ 82% HOTEL

Wharfedale Road, Winnersh Triangle, RG41 5TS - tel: 0118 944 0444
email: reservations@hireadinghotel.com **web:** www.hireadinghotel.com
dir: *M4 junct 10/A329(M) towards Reading (E), 1st exit signed Winnersh/Woodley/A329, left at lights into Wharfedale Rd. Hotel on left*

Situated in the Winnersh Triangle within close proximity of the M4, Reading, Bracknell and Wokingham, this hotel offers a range of air-conditioned, contemporary and stylish bedrooms, eight state-of-the-art meeting rooms and the

Esprit Spa & Wellness with extensive leisure facilities including a 19-metre indoor pool and Dermalogica Spa. The Caprice Restaurant offers relaxed dining throughout the day. Complimentary underground parking is provided.

Holiday Inn Reading M4 Jct 10

Rooms: 174 (23 family) ✦ **S** £65–£189; **D** £75–£199 (incl. bkfst)* **Facilities:** Spa FTV WiFi ⓢ HL ⓢ Gym Sauna Steam room ♫ Xmas New Year **Conf:** Class 160 Board 64 Thtr 260 Del from £169 **Services:** Lift Night porter Air con **Parking:** 120 **Notes:** Civ Wed 260

Millennium Madejski Hotel Reading

MILLENNIUM

★★★★ 80% HOTEL

Madejski Stadium, RG2 0FL - tel: 0118 925 3500
email: reservations.reading@millenniumhotels.com **web:** www.millenniumhotels.com
dir: *M4 junct 11 onto A33, follow signs for Madejski Stadium Complex*

A stylish hotel, that features an atrium lobby with specially commissioned water sculpture, is part of the Madejski stadium complex, home to both Reading FC and the London Irish rugby team. Bedrooms are appointed with spacious workstations and plenty of amenities; there is also a choice of suites and a club floor with its own lounge. The hotel also has a fine dining restaurant.

Rooms: 201 (39 family) ✦ **S** £73–£300; **D** £83–£300 (incl. bkfst)* **Facilities:** STV WiFi ⓢ ⓢ supervised Gym **Conf:** Class 36 Board 30 Thtr 66 Del from £180 **Services:** Lift Night porter Air con **Parking:** 250 **Notes:** LB RS Xmas & New Year Health club & Cilantro closed

Novotel Reading Centre

NOVOTEL

★★★★ 78% HOTEL

25b Friar Street, RG1 1DP - tel: 0118 952 2600
email: h5432@accor.com **web:** www.novotel.com
dir: *M4 junct 11 or A33 towards Reading, left for Garrard St car park, at rdbt 3rd exit on Friar St*

This attractive and stylish city centre hotel is convenient for Reading's business and shopping centre; it is adjacent to a town centre car park, and has a range of conference facilities and excellent leisure options. The restaurant offers a contemporary style menu and a good wine list too. Bedrooms are comfortable and stylishly designed.

Rooms: 178 (154 family) **Facilities:** FTV WiFi HL ⓢ Gym Steam room Sauna **Conf:** Class 50 Board 36 Thtr 90 **Services:** Lift Night porter **Parking:** 15

R

READING *continued*

Malmaison Reading

★★★★ 75% 🌐 HOTEL

Great Western House, 18-20 Station Road, RG1 1JX - **tel**: 0844 693 0660
(Calls cost 5p per minute plus your phone company's access charge)
email: reading@malmaison.com **web**: www.malmaison.com
dir: *Opposite rail station*

This historic hotel has been transformed into the funky Malmaison style which reflects its proximity and long-standing relationship with the railway. Public areas feature rail memorabilia and excellent pictures, and include a Café Mal and a meeting room. Bedrooms here have all the amenities a modern executive would expect, plus comfort and quality in abundance. Dining is interesting too, with a menu that features home-grown and local produce accompanied by an impressive wine list.

Rooms: 75 (6 family) (4 GF) 🐾 **Facilities**: FTV WiFi 🐾 HL Xmas New Year
Conf: Class 18 Board 22 Thtr 30 **Services**: Lift Night porter Air con **Notes**: Civ Wed 20

Calcot Hotel

★★★ 77% HOTEL

98 Bath Road, Calcot, RG31 7QN - **tel**: 0118 941 6423
email: enquiries@calcothotel.net **web**: www.calcothotel.co.uk
dir: *M4 junct 12, A4 towards Reading, hotel in 0.5m*

This hotel is conveniently located in a residential area just off the motorway. Bedrooms are well equipped with good business facilities, such as data ports and good workspace. There are attractive public rooms and function suites, and the informal restaurant offers enjoyable food in welcoming surroundings.

Rooms: 78 (3 family) (6 GF) 🐾 **Facilities**: FTV WiFi 🎵 New Year **Conf**: Class 35 Board 35 Thtr 120 **Services**: Night porter **Parking**: 130 **Notes**: Closed 24-30 Dec 2 Dec-6 Jan Civ Wed 200

Premier Inn Reading (Caversham Bridge)

BUDGET HOTEL

Richfield Avenue, RG1 8EQ - **tel**: 0871 527 8922 (Calls cost 13p per minute plus your phone company's access charge) **web**: www.premierinn.com
dir: *M4 junct 11, A33 to Reading. A329 towards Caversham. Left at TGI Friday's. Left at Crowne Plaza. Hotel 200yds on right*

High quality, budget accommodation ideal for both families and business travellers. Spacious, en suite bedrooms feature free WiFi and tea and coffee making facilities, and in most hotels, Freeview TV is also available. The adjacent family restaurant features a wide and varied menu.

Rooms: 75

Premier Inn Reading Central

BUDGET HOTEL

Letcombe Street, RG1 2HN - **tel**: 0871 527 8924 (Calls cost 13p per minute plus your phone company's access charge) **web**: www.premierinn.com
dir: *M4 junct 11, A33 towards town centre, straight on at 3 rdbts (approx 3.5m). Right onto A329 signed The Oracle, Riverside Shopping Centre. Branch immediately left, hotel opposite The Oracle shopping centre*

Rooms: 151

Premier Inn Reading South

BUDGET HOTEL

Goring Lane, Grazeley Green, RG7 1LS - **tel**: 0871 527 8926 (Calls cost 13p per minute plus your phone company's access charge) **web**: www.premierinn.com
dir: *M4 junct 11, A33 towards Basingstoke. At rdbt take exit towards Burghfield & Mortimer. 3rd right into Grazeley Green. Under rail bridge turn left. Hotel on left*

Rooms: 44

REDDITCH	Map 10 SP06
Worcestershire	

The Abbey Hotel Golf and Spa

★★★★ 76% HOTEL

Hither Green Lane, Dagnell End Road, B98 9BE - **tel**: 01527 406600
email: info@theabbeyhotel.co.uk **web**: www.theabbeyhotel.co.uk
dir: *M42 junct 2, A441 to Redditch. End of carriageway turn left A441, Dagnell End Rd on left. Hotel 600yds on right*

With convenient access to the motorway and a proximity to many attractions, this modern hotel is popular with both business and leisure travellers. Bedrooms are well equipped and attractively decorated; the executive corner rooms are especially spacious. Facilities include an 18-hole golf course, pro shop, large indoor pool and extensive conference facilities.

Rooms: 99 (20 family) (23 GF) 🐾 **S** £59–£219; **D** £59–£219* **Facilities**: Spa FTV WiFi 🐾 ③ ⛳ 18 Putting green Gym Flood lit golf driving range Xmas New Year **Conf**: Class 60 Board 30 Thtr 170 Del from £137.50 **Services**: Lift Night porter **Parking**: 200 **Notes**: Civ Wed 100

Premier Inn Redditch North (A441)

BUDGET HOTEL

Bordesley Lane, B97 6AQ - **tel**: 0871 527 9372 (Calls cost 13p per minute plus your phone company's access charge) **web**: www.premierinn.com
dir: *M42 junct 3, A435 (Alcester road). In 3m take A4023 towards Redditch & Bromsgrove. Exit 1st rdbt towards Birmingham (A441). At next rdbt 3rd exit onto Alvechurch Highway (A441). At next rdbt 4th exit into Millrace Rd, left into Bordesley Ln. NB for Sat Nav use B97 6RR*

High quality, budget accommodation ideal for both families and business travellers. Spacious, en suite bedrooms feature free WiFi and tea and coffee making facilities, and in most hotels, Freeview TV is also available. The adjacent family restaurant features a wide and varied menu.

Rooms: 80

Premier Inn Redditch West (A448)

BUDGET HOTEL

Birchfield Road, B97 6PX - **tel**: 0871 527 8928 (Calls cost 13p per minute plus your phone company's access charge) **web**: www.premierinn.com
dir: *M5 junct 4, A38 towards Bromsgrove. At rdbt take A448 to Redditch. 1st exit for Webheath. At next rdbt 3rd exit, 1st right into Birchfield Rd*

Rooms: 33

R

REDHILL
Surrey   Map 6 TQ25

HIGHLY RECOMMENDED

Nutfield Priory Hotel & Spa

★★★★ 81% ◉◉ HOTEL

Nutfield, RH1 4EL - **tel:** 01737 824400 & 0845 072 7485 (Calls cost 5p per minute plus your phone company's access charge)
email: nutfieldpriory@handpicked.co.uk
web: www.handpickedhotels.co.uk/nutfieldpriory
dir: M25 junct 6, follow Redhill signs via Godstone on A25. Hotel 1m on left after Nutfield Village. Or M25 junct 8, A25 through Reigate & Redhill. Hotel on right 1.5m after rail bridge

This Victorian country house dates back to 1872 and is set in 40 acres of grounds with stunning views over the Surrey countryside. The hotel offers a range of individually appointed bedrooms, including 15 feature bedrooms located in the oldest part of the house. All are equipped with an excellent range of facilities. The public areas include the impressive grand hall, the award-winning Cloisters Restaurant, the library, and a cosy lounge bar area. The Nutfield Priory Health Club and Spa is the place to relax and unwind. The hotel also offers a choice of private rooms for weddings, events and business meetings. Additionally, this magnificent country house can be hired for exclusive use.

Rooms: 60 (4 family) ⌂ **S** £179–£317; **D** £179–£317 (incl. bkfst)*
Facilities: Spa STV FTV WiFi ⌂ HL ⏲ Gym Squash Steam room Beauty therapy Aerobic & Step classes Saunas Xmas New Year **Conf:** Class 50 Board 42 Thtr 90 Del from £189 **Services:** Lift Night porter **Parking:** 130 **Notes:** LB Civ Wed 90

Premier Inn Redhill Reigate

BUDGET HOTEL

Brighton Road, Salfords, RH1 5BT - **tel:** 0871 527 8930 (Calls cost 13p per minute plus your phone company's access charge) **web:** www.premierinn.com
dir: On A23, 2m S of Redhill; 3m N of Gatwick Airport

High quality, budget accommodation ideal for both families and business travellers. Spacious, en suite bedrooms feature free WiFi and tea and coffee making facilities, and in most hotels, Freeview TV is also available. The adjacent family restaurant features a wide and varied menu.

Rooms: 48

REDRUTH
Cornwall & Isles of Scilly   Map 2 SW64

Penventon Park Hotel

★★★ 81% ◉◉ HOTEL

TR15 1TE - **tel:** 01209 203000
email: enquiries@penventon.com **web:** www.penventon.co.uk
dir: Exit A30 at Redruth. Follow signs for Redruth West, hotel 1m S

Set in attractive parkland, this Georgian mansion is ideal for both business and leisure guests, and is well placed for visiting the glorious Cornish coastal areas. The smart bedrooms include 20 garden suites with patio doors that give access to a decking area and the garden beyond. The menus offer a wide choice of Cornish, British, Italian and French dishes. Leisure facilities include a pool, fitness suite, and health spa with beauty and holistic therapies, as well as function rooms and bars.

Rooms: 63 (8 family) (23 GF) ⌂ **Facilities:** Spa FTV WiFi ⌂ ⏲ supervised Gym Sauna Solarium Personal trainer ♫ Xmas New Year **Conf:** Class 100 Board 60 Thtr 200 **Services:** Night porter **Parking:** 100 **Notes:** Civ Wed 150

REDWORTH
County Durham   Map 19 NZ22

The Redworth Hall Hotel

★★★★ 78% COUNTRY HOUSE HOTEL

DL5 6NL - **tel:** 01388 770600 **email:** redworthhall@thehotelcollection.co.uk
web: www.thehotelcollection.co.uk
dir: From A1(M) junct 58, A68 signed Corbridge. Follow hotel signs

This imposing Georgian building includes a health club with state-of-the-art equipment and impressive conference facilities, making this hotel a popular destination for business travellers. There are several spacious lounges to relax in along with the Conservatory Restaurant. Bedrooms are very comfortable and well equipped.

Rooms: 143 (12 family) ⌂ **Facilities:** STV WiFi ⌂ HL ⏲ ⌂ ⌂ Gym Bodysense Health & Leisure Club Xmas New Year **Conf:** Class 144 Board 90 Thtr 300 **Services:** Lift Night porter **Parking:** 300 **Notes:** Civ Wed 240

REIGATE
Surrey   Map 6 TQ25

Best Western Reigate Manor Hotel

★★★ 78% HOTEL

ⓑⓦ Best Western.

Reigate Hill, RH2 9PF - **tel:** 01737 240125
email: hotel@reigatemanor.co.uk **web:** www.reigatemanor.co.uk
dir: On A217, 1m S of M25 junct 8

On the slopes of Reigate Hill, the hotel is ideally located for access to the town and for motorway links. A range of public rooms is provided along with a variety of function rooms. Bedrooms are either traditional in style in the old house or of contemporary design in the wing.

Rooms: 50 (1 family) **D** fr £59* **Facilities:** FTV WiFi ⌂ **Conf:** Class 80 Board 50 Thtr 200 Del from £133 **Services:** Night porter **Parking:** 130 **Notes:** Civ Wed 200

RENISHAW
Derbyshire   Map 16 SK47

Sitwell Arms Hotel

★★★ 72% HOTEL

Station Road, S21 3WF - **tel:** 01246 435226
email: info@sitwellarms.com **web:** www.sitwellarms.co.uk
dir: On A6135 to Sheffield, W of M1 junct 30

Parts of this attractive stone building date from the 18th century when it was a coaching inn. It has been extended to provide spacious comfortable bedrooms with modern facilities. A wide range of meals is served in the Wild Boar Restaurant; there is also a cocktail bar, informal lounge bar and a smart beer garden with patio and children's play area. The hotel has a gym and a hair and beauty salon.

Rooms: 31 (8 family) (9 GF) **S** £35–£40; **D** £69–£79 (incl. bkfst)* **Facilities:** FTV WiFi Gym Fitness studio Hair & beauty salon Treatment room Xmas New Year **Conf:** Class 60 Board 60 Thtr 160 **Services:** Lift Night porter **Parking:** 150 **Notes:** LB Civ Wed 150

R

RETFORD
Nottinghamshire · Map 17 SK78

Ye Olde Bell Hotel & Spa
★★★★ 80% ⊛ HOTEL

DN22 8QS - **tel:** 01777 705121
email: enquiries@yeoldebell-hotel.co.uk **web:** www.yeoldebell-hotel.co.uk

(For full entry see Barnby Moor)

Best Western Plus West Retford Hotel
Best Western PLUS
★★★ 81% HOTEL

24 North Road, DN22 7XG - **tel:** 01777 706333
email: reservations@westretfordhotel.co.uk **web:** www.westretfordhotel.co.uk
dir: *From A1 take A620 to Ranby/Retford. Left at rdbt into North Rd A638. Hotel on right*

Stylishly appointed throughout, and set in very attractive gardens close to the town centre, this 18th-century manor house offers a good range of well-equipped meeting rooms. The spacious, well-laid out bedrooms and suites are located in separate buildings and all offer modern facilities and comforts.

Rooms: 63 (15 family) (32 GF) ⋒ **S** £65–£105; **D** £65–£105 **Facilities:** FTV WiFi ⇣ Xmas New Year **Conf:** Class 80 Board 40 Thtr 150 Del from £110 **Services:** Night porter **Parking:** 150 **Notes:** LB Civ Wed 150

RICHMOND
North Yorkshire · Map19 NZ10

The Frenchgate Restaurant and Hotel
★★★ 80% ⊛⊛ TOWN HOUSE HOTEL

59-61 Frenchgate, DL10 7AE - **tel:** 01748 822087 **email:** info@thefrenchgate.co.uk
web: www.thefrenchgate.co.uk
dir: *From A1 Scotch Corner to Richmond on A6108. After lights, 1st left into Lile Close, leading to Flints Terrace for hotel car park. Or for front entrance continue to 1st rdbt, left into Dundas St. At T-junct left into Frenchgate*

This sympathetic conversion of an 18th-century town house building offers an impressive level of contemporary, quality accommodation. Modern artworks by local artists adorn the walls of the house. The intimate dining room serves award-winning evening meals and memorable breakfasts. Personal, attentive and friendly staff are on hand to ensure a relaxing stay. Some off-road parking is available.

Rooms: 9 (3 family) (1 GF) ⋒ **Facilities:** FTV WiFi ⇣ Xmas New Year **Conf:** Class 24 Board 20 Thtr 20 **Services:** Night porter **Parking:** 12 **Notes:** Civ Wed 150

RICHMOND (UPON THAMES)
Greater London

The Petersham Hotel
★★★★ 81% ⊛⊛ HOTEL PLAN 1 C2

Nightingale Lane, TW10 6UZ - **tel:** 020 8940 7471
email: enq@petershamhotel.co.uk **web:** www.petershamhotel.co.uk
dir: *From Richmond Bridge rdbt A316 follow Ham & Petersham signs. Hotel in Nightingale Ln on left off Petersham Rd*

Managed by the same family for over 25 years, this attractive hotel is located on a hill overlooking water meadows and a sweep of the River Thames. Bedrooms and suites are comfortably furnished, while public areas combine elegance and some fine architectural features. High quality produce features in dishes offered in the restaurant that looks out over the Thames below.

Rooms: 58 (6 family) (3 GF) ⋒ **Facilities:** STV FTV WiFi ⇣ Xmas New Year **Conf:** Board 25 Thtr 35 **Services:** Lift Night porter **Parking:** 60 **Notes:** LB Civ Wed 40

Richmond Hill Hotel
★★★★ 79% HOTEL PLAN 1 C2

Richmond Hill, TW10 6RW - **tel:** 020 8940 2247
email: info.richmond@kewgreen.co.uk **web:** www.richmondhill-hotel.co.uk
dir: *1m from Richmond Station at the top of Richmond Hill*

This attractive Georgian manor is situated on Richmond Hill, enjoying elevated views over the Thames, and the town and the park are within walking distance. Bedrooms vary in size and style but all are comfortable and contemporary in style. There is a well-designed heath club, and extensive conference and banqueting facilities.

Rooms: 142 (1 family) (15 GF) ⋒ **Facilities:** Spa STV FTV WiFi ⊗ Gym Steam room Health & beauty suite Sauna Xmas New Year **Conf:** Class 80 Board 50 Thtr 180 **Services:** Lift Night porter Air con **Parking:** 97 **Notes:** Civ Wed 182

HIGHLY RECOMMENDED

Bingham
★★★ 85% ⊛⊛⊛ ≋ TOWN HOUSE HOTEL PLAN 1 C2

61-63 Petersham Road, TW10 6UT - **tel:** 020 8940 0902
email: info@thebingham.co.uk **web:** www.thebingham.co.uk
dir: *On A307*

This Georgian building, dating back to 1740, overlooks the River Thames and is within easy reach of the town centre, Kew Gardens and Hampton Court. The contemporary bedrooms feature bespoke art deco style furniture and up-to-the-minute facilities such as WiFi, a digital music library, flat-screen TVs and 'rain dance' showers. Public rooms have views of the pretty garden and river. Guests can choose from a selection of meals that range from light snacks to two or three-course dinners.

Bingham

Rooms: 15 (8 family) ☎ **S** £129–£325; **D** £149–£309* **Facilities:** FTV WiFi ☜ Free membership at sister well-being centre Xmas New Year **Conf:** Class 70 Board 40 Thtr 90 Del from £273 **Services:** Lift Night porter Air con **Parking:** 20 **Notes:** RS Sunday evening Restaurant closed Civ Wed 90

Premier Inn London Richmond

BUDGET HOTEL PLAN 1 C2

136-138 Lower Mortlake Road, Richmond, TW9 2JZ - **tel:** 0871 527 9346 (Calls cost 13p per minute plus your phone company's access charge)
web: www.premierinn.com
dir: *Phone for directions*

High quality, budget accommodation ideal for both families and business travellers. Spacious, en suite bedrooms feature free WiFi and tea and coffee making facilities, and in most hotels, Freeview TV is also available. The adjacent family restaurant features a wide and varied menu.

Rooms: 92

RIPLEY
Derbyshire   Map 16 SK35

Premier Inn Ripley

BUDGET HOTEL

Nottingham Road, DE5 3QP - **tel:** 0871 527 8935 (Calls cost 13p per minute plus your phone company's access charge)
web: www.premierinn.com
dir: *From S: M1 junct 26, A610 towards Ripley. Hotel off rdbt adjacent to Butterley Park. From N: M1 junct 28, A38, A610 towards Nottingham. Hotel on right at rdbt*

High quality, budget accommodation ideal for both families and business travellers. Spacious, en suite bedrooms feature free WiFi and tea and coffee making facilities, and in most hotels, Freeview TV is also available. The adjacent family restaurant features a wide and varied menu.

Rooms: 78

RISLEY
Derbyshire   Map 11 SK43

Risley Hall Hotel & Spa

★★★ 73% HOTEL

Derby Road, DE72 3SS - **tel:** 0115 939 9000
email: reservations@risleyhall.co.uk **web:** www.risleyhall.co.uk
dir: *M1 junct 25, follow signs for Risley, then brown signs for Risley Hall*

This 16th-century house is set in extensive gardens, and much of the house has been sympathetically restored. Spacious bedrooms are very comfortable, and the hotel has a popular spa and leisure facilities. There's also a charming bar and a stylish restaurant that serves dishes using the best local produce.

Rooms: 35 (19 annexe) (7 family) (8 GF) ☎ **S** £55–£110; **D** £69–£180 (incl. bkfst)* **Facilities:** Spa FTV WiFi ☜ 🐟 Gym Xmas New Year **Conf:** Class 40 Board 26 Thtr 90 Del from £120 **Services:** Lift Night porter **Parking:** 100 **Notes:** Civ Wed 110

ROCHDALE
Greater Manchester   Map 16 SD81

Premier Inn Rochdale

BUDGET HOTEL

Newhey Road, Milnrow, OL16 4JF - **tel:** 0871 527 8936 (Calls cost 13p per minute plus your phone company's access charge)
web: www.premierinn.com
dir: *M62 junct 21, at rdbt right towards Shaw, under motorway bridge, & 1st left*

High quality, budget accommodation ideal for both families and business travellers. Spacious, en suite bedrooms feature free WiFi and tea and coffee making facilities, and in most hotels, Freeview TV is also available. The adjacent family restaurant features a wide and varied menu.

Rooms: 79

ROCHESTER
Kent   Map 6 TQ76

Premier Inn Rochester

BUDGET HOTEL

Medway Valley Leisure Park, Chariot Way, ME2 2SS - **tel:** 0871 527 8938 (Calls cost 13p per minute plus your phone company's access charge)
web: www.premierinn.com
dir: *M2 junct 2, follow Rochester & West Malling signs. At rdbt onto A228 signed Rochester & Strood. At next rdbt 2nd exit into Roman Way signed Medway Valley Park. At next rdbt 1st exit into Chariot Way, hotel in 100mtrs*

High quality, budget accommodation ideal for both families and business travellers. Spacious, en suite bedrooms feature free WiFi and tea and coffee making facilities, and in most hotels, Freeview TV is also available. The adjacent family restaurant features a wide and varied menu.

Rooms: 121

R

ROMALDKIRK	Map 19 NY92
County Durham	

The Rose & Crown

★★★ ◎◎ HOTEL

DL12 9EB - **tel:** 01833 650213
email: hotel@rose-and-crown.co.uk **web:** www.rose-and-crown.co.uk
dir: *6m NW from Barnard Castle on B6277*

This charming 18th-century country inn is located in the heart of the village, overlooking fine dale scenery. The attractively furnished bedrooms, including suites, are split between the main house and the rear courtyard. Guests might like to have a drink in the cosy bar with its log fire, after returning from a long walk. Good local produce features extensively on the menus that can be enjoyed in the oak-panelled restaurant, or more informally in the bar. Service is both friendly and attentive.

Rooms: 14 (7 annexe) (2 family) (5 GF) ✆ **S** fr £90; **D** fr £115 (incl. bkfst)*
Facilities: FTV WiFi ⌇ Spa and golf available at nearby Headlam Hall New Year
Conf: Board 12 **Parking:** 20 **Notes:** LB Closed 23–27 Dec

ROMFORD	Map 6 TQ58
Greater London	

Premier Inn Romford Central

BUDGET HOTEL

Mercury Gardens, RM1 3EN - **tel:** 0871 527 8940 (Calls cost 13p per minute plus your phone company's access charge)
web: www.premierinn.com
dir: *M25 junct 28, A12 to Gallows Corner. Take A118 to next rdbt, turn left*

High quality, budget accommodation ideal for both families and business travellers. Spacious, en suite bedrooms feature free WiFi and tea and coffee making facilities, and in most hotels, Freeview TV is also available. The adjacent family restaurant features a wide and varied menu.

Rooms: 103

Premier Inn Romford West

BUDGET HOTEL

Whalebone Lane North, Chadwell Heath, RM6 6QU - **tel:** 0871 527 8942
(Calls cost 13p per minute plus your phone company's access charge)
web: www.premierinn.com
dir: *6m from M25 junct 28 on A12 at junct with A1112*

Rooms: 44

ROMSEY	Map 5 SU32
Hampshire	

The White Horse Hotel & Brasserie

★★★★ 78% ◎◎ HOTEL

19 Market Place, SO51 8ZJ - **tel:** 01794 512431
email: thewhitehorsesales@twhromsey.com **web:** www.thewhitehorseromsey.co.uk
dir: *M27 junct 3, follow signs for Romsey, right at Broadlands. In town centre*

This family-friendly hotel is located overlooking the market square of this historic town. The White Horse is a traditional, former coaching inn, and provides very comfortable and very stylish, individually designed bedrooms, including loft suites and a penthouse. Public areas boast relaxing day rooms and an elegant contemporary bar. The Brasserie offers award-winning cuisine, with alfresco dining a possibility during the warmer summer months. Public car parks can be found close by, although the property does operate a valet parking service.

Rooms: 29 (6 family) ✆ **S** £95–£105; **D** £135–£285 **Facilities:** FTV WiFi ⌇ Xmas New Year **Conf:** Class 40 Board 45 Thtr 60 Del from £145 **Services:** Night porter
Notes: Civ Wed 40

See advert opposite

R

THE WHITE HORSE
HOTEL & BRASSERIE

"Small things make perfection but perfection is no small thing"

Sir Henry Royce

Set in the heart of Romsey, The White Horse has been a coaching inn for almost 600 years.
The 2 AA rosette awarded Brasserie & Grill is a wonderful place to enjoy every occasion from a romantic dinner for two to a robust family lunch, during the summer months the courtyard offers a perfect retreat for al fresco dining. A stay here with us is a time to unwind – relax in one of our individually designed bedrooms, enjoy a cocktail in our delightful bar or even sample one of our delicious afternoon teas in the historic Tudor or Palmerston lounges. The hotel is also fully licensed for wedding ceremonies and offers the most romantic and intimate venue for your wedding day. **Historic charm meets modern classic chic.**

Market Place, Romsey, Hampshire SO51 8ZJ
T 01794 512431 **F** 01794 517485 **E** thewhitehorse@twhromsey.com
www.thewhitehorseromsey.com

R

ROMSEY *continued*

Potters Heron Hotel

★★★ 79% HOTEL

Winchester Road, Ampfield, SO51 9ZF - **tel:** 023 8027 7800
email: thepottersheron@pebblehotels.com **web:** www.potters-heron.co.uk
dir: *M3 junct 12 follow Chandler's Ford signs. 2nd exit at 3rd rdbt follow Ampfield signs, over x-rds. Hotel on left in 1m*

This distinctive thatched hotel retains many original features. In a convenient location with access to Winchester, Southampton and the M3, Potters Heron Hotel has modern accommodation and stylish, spacious public areas. Most of the bedrooms have their own balcony or terrace. The pub and restaurant both offer an interesting range of dishes that will suit a variety of tastes.

Rooms: 53 (1 family) (29 GF) ☁ S fr £59; D fr £59 (incl. bkfst)* **Facilities:** FTV WiFi ☼ Xmas New Year **Conf:** Class 40 Board 30 Thtr 100 Del from £165 **Services:** Lift Night porter **Parking:** 120 **Notes:** Civ Wed 100

Premier Inn Southampton West

BUDGET HOTEL

Romsey Road, Ower, SO51 6ZJ - **tel:** 0871 527 9004 (Calls cost 13p per minute plus your phone company's access charge)
web: www.premierinn.com
dir: *Just off M27 junct 2. Take A36 towards Salisbury. Follow brown tourist signs 'Vine Inn'*

High quality, budget accommodation ideal for both families and business travellers. Spacious, en suite bedrooms feature free WiFi and tea and coffee making facilities, and in most hotels, Freeview TV is also available. The adjacent family restaurant features a wide and varied menu.

Rooms: 83

ROSSINGTON
South Yorkshire | **Map 16 SK69**

Best Western Premier Mount Pleasant Hotel

★★★★ 78% HOTEL

Great North Road, DN11 0HW - **tel:** 01302 868696
email: reception@mountpleasant.co.uk **web:** www.mountpleasant.co.uk
dir: *On A638 Great North Road, between Bawtry & Doncaster*

This charming 18th-century house stands in 100 acres of wooded parkland between Doncaster and Bawtry, near Robin Hood Airport. Spacious public areas include well furnished lounges and the elegant Garden Restaurant. There are also a health and wellbeing centre, modern conference facilities and beautiful grounds, ideal for weddings. Bedrooms are individually designed; some have four-poster beds and the spa suites are even more impressive with luxurious bathrooms.

Rooms: 68 (22 family) (33 GF) ☁ **Facilities:** Spa STV WiFi ☼ Beauty salon **Conf:** Class 70 Board 70 Thtr 200 **Services:** Lift Night porter **Parking:** 140 **Notes:** LB Closed 25 Dec RS 24 Dec No accommodation available Civ Wed 180

ROSS-ON-WYE
Herefordshire | **Map 10 SO52**

The Chase Hotel

★★★ 84% ⊛ HOTEL

Gloucester Road, HR9 5LH - **tel:** 01989 763161
email: res@chasehotel.co.uk **web:** www.chasehotel.co.uk
dir: *M50 junct 4, 1st left exit towards rdbt, left at rdbt towards A40, accross next rdbt, right at 3rd rdbt towards town centre, hotel 0.5m on left*

This attractive Georgian mansion sits in its own landscaped grounds and is only a short walk from the town centre. Bedrooms, including two four-poster rooms, vary in size and character; all rooms are appointed to impressive standards. There is a light and spacious bar, and also Harry's restaurant which offers an excellent selection of enjoyable dishes.

Rooms: 38 (2 family) ☁ S £69–£230; D £84–£250 (incl. bkfst)* **Facilities:** FTV WiFi ☼ New Year **Conf:** Class 100 Board 80 Thtr 300 Del from £120 **Services:** Night porter **Parking:** 75 **Notes:** LB Closed 24-27 Dec Civ Wed 150

King's Head Hotel

★★★ 77% HOTEL

8 High Street, HR9 5HL - **tel:** 01989 763174
email: enquiries@kingshead.co.uk **web:** www.kingshead.co.uk
dir: *In town centre, past market building on right*

This establishment dates back to the 14th century and has a wealth of charm and character. Bedrooms are well equipped and comfortable with thoughtful guest extras provided; both four-poster and family rooms are available. The restaurant offers menus and a specials board that reflect a varied selection of local produce including fresh fish, free range beef and lamb. There is also a well-stocked bar serving hand-pulled, real ales.

Rooms: 15 (1 family) ☁ S fr £60; D fr £85* **Facilities:** FTV WiFi **Parking:** 15

Premier Inn Ross-on-Wye

BUDGET HOTEL

Ledbury Road, HR9 7QJ - **tel:** 0871 527 8944 (Calls cost 13p per minute plus your phone company's access charge)
web: www.premierinn.com
dir: *M50 junct 4, 1m from town centre*

High quality, budget accommodation ideal for both families and business travellers. Spacious, en suite bedrooms feature free WiFi and tea and coffee making facilities, and in most hotels, Freeview TV is also available. The adjacent family restaurant features a wide and varied menu.

Rooms: 59

ROSTHWAITE
Cumbria   Map 18 NY21

See also **Borrowdale**

HIGHLY RECOMMENDED

Scafell Hotel

★★★ 86% ◉ COUNTRY HOUSE HOTEL

CA12 5XB - **tel:** 017687 77208
email: info@scafell.co.uk **web:** www.scafell.co.uk
dir: *M6 junct 40 to Keswick on A66. Take B5289 to Rosthwaite*

Scafell Hotel is a friendly establishment, which enjoys a peaceful location, and is popular with walkers. Bedrooms have been tastefully appointed in a warm country house style with a contemporary twist; some have traditional antique furniture. Public areas include a residents' cocktail bar, lounge and spacious restaurant as well as the popular Riverside Inn, offering all-day menus in summer months.

Rooms: 23 (3 family) (8 GF) ☏ **Facilities:** FTV WiFi Guided walks Xmas New Year **Parking:** 50 **Notes:** LB Civ Wed 75

ROTHERHAM
South Yorkshire   Map 16 SK49

Hellaby Hall Hotel

★★★★ 75% ◉ HOTEL

Old Hellaby Lane, Hellaby, S66 8SN - **tel:** 01709 702701
email: reservations@hellabyhallhotel.co.uk **web:** www.hellabyhallhotel.co.uk
dir: *0.5m off M18 junct 1, onto A631 towards Maltby. Hotel in Hellaby – NB use S66 8EX postcode for Sat Nav*

This 17th-century house was built to a Flemish design with high, beamed ceilings, staircases which lead off to private meeting rooms and a series of oak-panelled lounges. Bedrooms are elegant and well equipped, and guests can dine in the formal Attic Restaurant. There are extensive leisure facilities and conference areas, and the hotel holds a licence for civil weddings.

Rooms: 89 (6 family) (17 GF) ☏ **S** £69–£130; **D** £69–£130* **Facilities:** Spa FTV WiFi ☉ Gym Beauty salon Exercise studio Spinning bike studio Xmas New Year **Conf:** Class 300 Board 150 Thtr 500 Del from £120 **Services:** Lift Night porter **Parking:** 250 **Notes:** LB Civ Wed 250

Carlton Park Hotel

★★★ 77% HOTEL

102/104 Moorgate Road, S60 2BG - **tel:** 01709 849955
email: reservations@carltonparkhotel.com **web:** www.carltonparkhotel.com
dir: *M1 junction 33, onto A631, then A618. Hotel 800 yards past District General Hospital*

This modern hotel is situated in a pleasant residential area of the town, close to the hospital, yet within minutes of the M1. Bedrooms and bathrooms offer very modern facilities; three have separate sitting rooms. The restaurant and bar provide a lively atmosphere and there is a pool and leisure centre.

Rooms: 80 (20 family) (16 GF) **Facilities:** STV FTV WiFi ☉ Gym ♫ **Conf:** Class 120 Board 60 Thtr 300 **Services:** Lift Night porter **Parking:** 120 **Notes:** Civ Wed 150

Premier Inn Rotherham East (M18/M1)

BUDGET HOTEL

Bawtry Road, S65 3JB - **tel:** 0871 527 8946 (Calls cost 13p per minute plus your phone company's access charge)
web: www.premierinn.com
dir: *On A631 towards Wickersley, between M18 junct 1 & M1 junct 33*

High quality, budget accommodation ideal for both families and business travellers. Spacious, en suite bedrooms feature free WiFi and tea and coffee making facilities, and in most hotels, Freeview TV is also available. The adjacent family restaurant features a wide and varied menu.

Rooms: 61

Silver Stars

The AA Silver Star rating denotes a Hotel that we highly recommend. They have a superior level of quality within their star rating, high standards of hospitality, service and cleanliness.

R

ROTHERWICK

Hampshire

Map 5 SU75

INSPECTOR'S CHOICE

Tylney Hall Hotel

★★★★ ◉◉ ⚲ HOTEL

Ridge Lane, RG27 9AZ - **tel:** 01256 764881
email: sales@tylneyhall.com **web:** www.tylneyhall.com
dir: *M3 junct 5, A287 to Basingstoke, over junct with A30, over rail bridge, towards Newnham. Right at Newnham Green. Hotel 1m on left*

Tylney Hall is a grand Victorian country house set in 66 acres of beautiful parkland. The hotel offers high standards of comfort in relaxed yet elegant surroundings, featuring magnificently restored water gardens, originally laid out by the famous gardener, Gertrude Jekyll. Spacious public rooms include Italian and Wedgwood styled drawing rooms and the panelled Oak Room Restaurant that offers cuisine based on locally sourced ingredients. The spacious bedrooms are traditionally furnished and offer individual style and high degrees of comfort. The excellent leisure facilities include indoor and outdoor swimming pools, tennis courts, jogging trails, croquet lawns and a spa.

Tylney Hall Hotel

Rooms: 112 (77 annexe) (1 family) (40 GF) ☊ **Facilities:** Spa STV FTV WiFi ⬧ HL ⊕ ⬱ ◗ ⛳ Gym Clay pigeon shooting Archery Falconry Balloon rides Laser shooting Jogging trail Xmas New Year **Conf:** Class 70 Board 40 Thtr 120 **Services:** Night porter **Parking:** 120 **Notes:** Civ Wed 120

The Peacock at Rowsley

The Peacock at Rowsley is a cosy yet smart hotel located in the heart of the Peak District National Park. The hotel is part of the Haddon Estate and enjoys close links with Haddon Hall where *The Peacock* owners Lord and Lady Edward Manners reside. With individually styled bedrooms and a luxurious suite, this independent hotel offers guests exceptional service, food and comfort.

The Peacock at Rowsley, Derbyshire DE4 2EB • **Tel:** 01629 733518 • **Fax:** 01629 732671
Website: www.thepeacockatrowsley.com •**Email:** reception@thepeacockatrowsley.com

ROWSLEY
Derbyshire   Map 16 SK26

The Peacock at Rowsley
★★★ ◉◉◉ HOTEL

Bakewell Road, DE4 2EB - **tel:** 01629 733518
email: reception@thepeacockatrowsley.com **web:** www.thepeacockatrowsley.com
dir: A6, 3m before Bakewell, 6m from Matlock towards Bakewell

Set in the beautiful Peak District National Park, and owned by Lord and Lady Manners of Haddon Hall, this hotel combines stylish contemporary design with original and antique features. Bedrooms are individually designed and boast DVD players, Apple TV, complimentary WiFi and smart marble bathrooms. One bedroom has a delightful four-poster bed. Imaginative cuisine, using local, seasonal produce, is a highlight. Guests are warmly welcomed and service is attentive. Fly fishing is popular in this area and the hotel has its own fishing rights on seven miles of the Rivers Wye and Derwent.

Rooms: 15 (6 family) ⬈ **S** £130–£145; **D** £205–£310 (incl. bkfst)*
Facilities: WiFi ⬈ Fishing ⬈ Free use of Woodlands Fitness Centre Free membership to Bakewell Golf Club ⬈ New Year **Conf:** Class 8 Board 16 Del from £210 **Services:** Night porter **Parking:** 25 **Notes:** No children 10yrs Civ Wed 20

See advert opposite

RUBERY
West Midlands   Map 10 SO97

Premier Inn Birmingham South (Rubery)

BUDGET HOTEL

Birmingham Great Park, Ashbrook Drive, B45 9FP - **tel:** 0871 527 8094
(Calls cost 13p per minute plus your phone company's access charge)
web: www.premierinn.com
dir: M5 junct 4, A38 towards Birmingham. Left at lights before Morrisons signed Great Park. Right at rdbt. Right at next rdbt, hotel on right

High quality, budget accommodation ideal for both families and business travellers. Spacious, en suite bedrooms feature free WiFi and tea and coffee making facilities, and in most hotels, Freeview TV is also available. The adjacent family restaurant features a wide and varied menu.

Rooms: 62

RUGBY
Warwickshire   Map 11 SP57

Brownsover Hall Hotel

★★★ 75% HOTEL

Brownsover Lane, Old Brownsover, CV21 1HU - **tel:** 01788 546100
email: reservations@brownsoverhall.co.uk **web:** www.brownsoverhall.co.uk
dir: M6 junct 1, A426 to Rugby. After 0.5m at rdbt follow Brownsover signs, right into Brownsover Rd, right again into Brownsover Ln. Hotel 250yds on left

Brownsover Hall is a Grade II listed, Victorian Gothic building designed by Sir Gilbert Scott, set in seven acres of wooded parkland. Bedrooms vary in size and style, including spacious and contemporary rooms in the converted stable block. The former chapel makes a stylish restaurant, and for a less formal meal or a relaxing drink, the Whittle Bar is popular.

Rooms: 47 (20 annexe) (3 family) (11 GF) **Facilities:** STV FTV WiFi ⬈ Xmas New Year **Conf:** Class 36 Board 40 Thtr 70 **Services:** Night porter **Parking:** 100 **Notes:** Civ Wed 56

Premier Inn Rugby North M6 Jct 1

BUDGET HOTEL

Central Park Drive, Central Park, CV23 0WE - **tel:** 0871 527 8948 (Calls cost 13p per minute plus your phone company's access charge)
web: www.premierinn.com
dir: M6 junct 1, S'bound onto A426. Hotel approx 1m on left at rdbt

High quality, budget accommodation ideal for both families and business travellers. Spacious, en suite bedrooms feature free WiFi and tea and coffee making facilities, and in most hotels, Freeview TV is also available. The adjacent family restaurant features a wide and varied menu.

Rooms: 82

Premier Inn Rugby North (Newbold)

BUDGET HOTEL

Brownsover Road, CV21 1HL - **tel:** 0871 527 8950 (Calls cost 13p per minute plus your phone company's access charge)
web: www.premierinn.com
dir: M6 junct 1, A426 follow Rugby signs. Straight on at 2 rdbts. At 3rd rdbt, hotel on right. NB for Sat Nav use CV21 1NX

Rooms: 50

R

RUGELEY
Staffordshire — Map 10 SK01

Premier Inn Rugeley

BUDGET HOTEL

Tower Business Park, WS15 2HJ - tel: 0871 527 9272
(Calls cost 13p per minute plus your phone company's access charge)
web: www.premierinn.com
dir: *M6 junct 14, A5013 towards Stafford. At rdbt 2nd exit onto A34. Take A513 signed Rugeley. At rdbt take 2nd exit onto A51. Left into Wolsley Rd, left into Powerstation Rd. Hotel off rdbt. NB for Sat Nav use WS15 1PR*

High quality, budget accommodation ideal for both families and business travellers. Spacious, en suite bedrooms feature free WiFi and tea and coffee making facilities, and in most hotels, Freeview TV is also available. The adjacent family restaurant features a wide and varied menu.

Rooms: 50

RUISLIP
Greater London

The Barn Hotel
★★★ 80% ❸❸ HOTEL PLAN 1 A5

West End Road, HA4 6JB - tel: 01895 636057
email: info@thebarnhotel.co.uk **web:** www.thebarnhotel.co.uk
dir: *A40 onto A4180 (Polish War Memorial) exit to Ruislip. 2m to hotel entrance at mini-rdbt before Ruislip tube station*

A mix of old and new, with parts dating back to the 17th century, this impressive property sits in three acres of gardens. Bedrooms vary in style, from contemporary to traditional with oak beams; all are comfortable and well appointed. The public areas provide a high level of quality and luxury.

Rooms: 73 (3 family) (33 GF) (20 smoking) ✱ **S** £60–£67; **D** £85–£108*
Facilities: FTV WiFi ⊳ Xmas New Year **Conf:** Class 50 Board 30 Thtr 80 Del from £165 **Services:** Night porter **Parking:** 42 **Notes:** Civ Wed 64

Premier Inn Ruislip

BUDGET HOTEL PLAN 1 A5

Ickenham Road, HA4 7DR - tel: 0871 527 8952 (Calls cost 13p per minute plus your phone company's access charge)
web: www.premierinn.com
dir: *From Ruislip High St into Ickenham Rd (B466). At mini rdbt 1st exit, The Orchard on left*

High quality, budget accommodation ideal for both families and business travellers. Spacious, en suite bedrooms feature free WiFi and tea and coffee making facilities, and in most hotels, Freeview TV is also available. The adjacent family restaurant features a wide and varied menu.

Rooms: 20

RUNCORN
Cheshire — Map 15 SJ58

Premier Inn Runcorn

BUDGET HOTEL

Chester Road, Preston Brook, WA7 3BB - tel: 0871 527 8954
(Calls cost 13p per minute plus your phone company's access charge)
web: www.premierinn.com
dir: *1m from M56 junct 11, at Preston Brook*

High quality, budget accommodation ideal for both families and business travellers. Spacious, en suite bedrooms feature free WiFi and tea and coffee making facilities, and in most hotels, Freeview TV is also available. The adjacent family restaurant features a wide and varied menu.

Rooms: 88

RUSPER
West Sussex — Map 6 TQ23

Ghyll Manor
★★★ 82% ❀ COUNTRY HOUSE HOTEL

High Street, RH12 4PX - tel: 0330 123 0371
email: enquiries@ghyllmanor.co.uk **web:** www.ghyllmanor.co.uk
dir: *A24 onto A264. Exit at Faygate, follow signs for Rusper, 2m to village*

Located in the quiet village of Rusper, this traditional mansion house is set in 45 acres of idyllic, peaceful grounds. Accommodation is in either the main house or a range of courtyard-style cottages. A pre-dinner drink can be taken beside the fire, followed by an imaginative meal in the charming restaurant.

Rooms: 29 (20 annexe) (7 family) (21 GF) ✱ **S** fr £120; **D** fr £145 (incl. bkfst)*
Facilities: FTV WiFi ⊳ ⮕ Xmas New Year **Conf:** Class 60 Board 40 Thtr 120
Services: Night porter **Parking:** 50 **Notes:** LB Civ Wed 120

RYDE
Isle of Wight — Map 5 SZ59

Lakeside Park Hotel & Spa
★★★★ 75% HOTEL

High Street, PO33 4LJ - tel: 01983 882266
email: reception@lakesideparkhotel.com **web:** www.lakesideparkhotel.com
dir: *A3054 towards Newport. Hotel on left after crossing Wotton Bridge*

This hotel has picturesque views of the tidal lake and surrounding countryside. Bedrooms are well appointed with modern amenities and stylish design. Public areas feature a comfortable open-plan bar and lounge, and two restaurants that showcase the best of island produce. Sizable conference and banqueting facilities are available, while the leisure area includes an indoor pool and spa therapy.

Rooms: 44 (2 family) (16 GF) ✱ **D** £155–£195 (incl. bkfst)* **Facilities:** Spa FTV WiFi ⓢ Sauna Steam room Relaxation room **Conf:** Class 60 Board 40 Thtr 150 **Services:** Lift Night porter Air con **Parking:** 140 **Notes:** Civ Wed 120

Yelf's Hotel
★★★ 74% HOTEL

Union Street, PO33 2LG - tel: 01983 564062
email: manager@yelfshotel.com **web:** www.yelfshotel.com
dir: *From Esplanade into Union St. Hotel on right*

This former coaching inn has smart public areas including a busy bar, a separate lounge and an attractive dining room. Bedrooms are comfortably furnished and well equipped; some are located in an adjoining wing and some in an annexe. A conservatory lounge bar and stylish terrace are ideal for relaxing.

Rooms: 40 (9 annexe) (5 family) (3 GF) (3 smoking) 🐾 **Facilities:** STV FTV WiFi Spa & treatments at sister hotel nearby **Conf:** Class 30 Board 50 Thtr 100 **Services:** Lift Night porter **Parking:** 23 **Notes:** Civ Wed 100

RYE	Map 7 TQ92
East Sussex	

Mermaid Inn
★★★ 82% 🏵️🏵️ HOTEL

Mermaid Street, TN31 7EY - tel: 01797 223065
email: info@mermaidinn.com **web:** www.mermaidinn.com
dir: A259, follow signs to town centre, then into Mermaid St

Situated near the top of a cobbled side street, this famous smugglers' inn is steeped in history, dating back to 1450 with 12th-century cellars. The charming interior has many architectural features such as attractive stone work. The bedrooms vary in size and style but all are tastefully furnished; there are no less than eight four-posters, and the Elizabethan and Dr Syn's Bedchambers are particularly noteworthy. Delightful public rooms include a choice of lounges, cosy bar and smart restaurant.

Rooms: 31 (5 family) 🐾 **S** £90; **D** £150–£220 (incl. bkfst)* **Facilities:** FTV WiFi ⓑ Xmas New Year **Conf:** Class 40 Board 30 Thtr 50 Del ££160 **Services:** Night porter **Parking:** 25 **Notes:** LB

The Hope Anchor Hotel
★★★ 80% SMALL HOTEL

Watchbell Street, TN31 7HA - tel: 01797 222216
email: info@thehopeanchor.co.uk **web:** www.thehopeanchor.co.uk
dir: From A268, Quayside, right into Wish Ward, into Mermaid St, right into West St, right into Watchbell St, hotel at end

This historic inn sits high above the town with enviable views out over the harbour and Romney Marsh, and is accessible via delightful cobbled streets. There is a relaxed and friendly atmosphere within the cosy public rooms, while the attractively furnished bedrooms are well equipped and many enjoy good views over the marshes.

Rooms: 16 (3 family) (1 GF) 🐾 **S** £80–£180; **D** £115–£180 (incl. bkfst)* **Facilities:** FTV WiFi Xmas New Year **Parking:** 12 **Notes:** LB

Rye Lodge Hotel
★★★ 75% HOTEL

Hilders Cliff, TN31 7LD - tel: 01797 223838
email: info@ryelodge.co.uk **web:** www.ryelodge.co.uk
dir: On one-way system follow town centre signs, through Landgate arch, hotel 100yds on right

Standing in an elevated position, Rye Lodge has panoramic views across Romney Marshes and the Rother Estuary. Traditionally styled bedrooms come in a variety of sizes; they are attractively decorated and thoughtfully equipped. Public rooms feature indoor leisure facilities and spa treatments can be arranged upon request. Dinner is served is Salts Restaurant where imaginative dishes are prepared using the best local produce. Secure parking is at the rear of the building.

Rooms: 19 (5 GF) 🐾 **S** £75–£220; **D** £105–£220 **Facilities:** Spa FTV WiFi ⓑ HL ⓒ Sauna **Parking:** 20 **Notes:** LB

ST AGNES	Map 2 SW75
Cornwall & Isles of Scilly	

Rose-in-Vale Country House Hotel
★★★★ 77% 🏵️🏵️ COUNTRY HOUSE HOTEL

Mithian, TR5 0QD - tel: 01872 552202
email: reception@roseinvalehotel.co.uk **web:** www.roseinvalehotel.co.uk
dir: A30 S towards Redruth. At Chiverton Cross at rdbt take B3277 signed St Agnes. In 500mtrs follow tourist sign for Rose-in-Vale. Into Mithian, right at Miners Arms, down hill. Hotel on left

Peacefully located in a wooded valley, this Georgian manor house has a wonderfully relaxed atmosphere and abundant charm. Guests are assured of a warm welcome. Accommodation varies in size and style; several rooms are situated on the ground floor. An imaginative fixed-price menu featuring local produce is served in the spacious restaurant.

Rooms: 23 (3 annexe) (1 family) (6 GF) 🐾 **Facilities:** FTV WiFi ⓑ 🏌️ 🏊 🎵 Xmas New Year **Conf:** Class 50 Board 40 Thtr 75 **Services:** Lift **Parking:** 50 **Notes:** LB Closed 4 Jan-1 Feb No children 12yrs Civ Wed 80

Beacon Country House Hotel
★★★ 76% SMALL HOTEL

Goonvrea Road, TR5 0NW - tel: 01872 552318
email: info@beaconhotel.co.uk **web:** www.beaconhotel.co.uk
dir: A30 onto B3277 to St Agnes. At rdbt left into Goonvrea Rd. Hotel 0.75m on right

Set in a quiet and attractive area away from the busy village, this family-run, relaxed hotel has splendid views over the countryside and along the coast to St Ives. Hospitality and customer care are great strengths, with guests assured of a very warm and friendly stay. Bedrooms are comfortable and well equipped, and many benefit from glorious views.

Rooms: 11 (2 family) (2 GF) 🐾 **S** £88–£121; **D** £118–£171 (incl. bkfst)* **Facilities:** FTV WiFi ⓑ New Year **Conf:** Class 20 Board 20 Del from £120 **Parking:** 12 **Notes:** LB Closed 4-31 Jan & Nov No children 8yrs

S

ST AGNES *continued*

Rosemundy House Hotel

★★★ 71% HOTEL

Rosemundy Hill, TR5 0UF - tel: 01872 552101
email: info@rosemundy.co.uk **web:** www.rosemundy.co.uk
dir: *A30 to St Agnes, approx 3m. On entering village 1st right signed Rosemundy, hotel at foot of hill*

This elegant Georgian house has been carefully restored and extended to provide comfortable bedrooms and spacious, inviting public areas. The hotel is set in well-maintained gardens complete with an outdoor pool which is available in warmer months. There is a choice of relaxing lounges and a cosy bar.

Rooms: 46 (3 family) (9 GF) ★ **S** £54.50–£71.50; **D** £109–£143 (incl. bkfst)*
Facilities: FTV WiFi ↖ Putting green ⚐ ♫ Xmas New Year **Conf:** Board 80
Parking: 50 **Notes:** Closed 12-23 Dec & 2 Jan-12 Feb No children 5yrs

ST ALBANS	Map 6 TL10
Hertfordshire	

St Michael's Manor

★★★★ 81% ◎◎ HOTEL

Fishpool Street, AL3 4RY - tel: 01727 864444
email: reservations@stmichaelsmanor.com **web:** www.stmichaelsmanor.com
dir: *From St Albans Abbey follow Fishpool Street towards St Michael's village. Hotel 0.5m on left*

Hidden from the street, adjacent to listed buildings, mills and ancient inns, this hotel, with a history dating back 500 years, is set in five acres of beautiful landscaped grounds. Inside there is a real sense of luxury, the high standard of decor and attentive service is complemented by award-winning food; the elegant restaurant overlooks the gardens and lake. Bedrooms are individually styled and have satellite TVs, DVDs and free internet access.

Rooms: 30 (8 annexe) (3 family) (4 GF) ★ **Facilities:** STV FTV WiFi ↕ ⚐ Xmas New Year **Conf:** Class 20 Board 22 Thtr 30 **Services:** Night porter Air con **Parking:** 80
Notes: LB Civ Wed 140

Sopwell House

★★★★ 81% ◎ HOTEL

Cottonmill Lane, Sopwell, AL1 2HQ - tel: 01727 864477
email: enquiries@sopwellhouse.co.uk **web:** www.sopwellhouse.co.uk
dir: *M25 junct 21a, 1st exit rdbt to A405. A414 towards St Albans/Hatfield. Slip road Shenley, mini rdbt left*

This fine country hotel is situated in 12 acres of beautifully landscaped gardens and the house overlooks the hotel's golf course. Sopwell House was once the country home of Lord Mountbatten, and offers bedrooms that are all very well appointed, as well as impressive leisure facilities. Afternoon tea is served in the comfortable lounges and there is a choice of restaurants for dinner.

Rooms: 128 (16 annexe) (28 family) (7 GF) ★ **S** £159–£399; **D** £174–£414 (incl. bkfst)* **Facilities:** Spa STV FTV WiFi ↕ ⊛ Gym Sauna Steam room Dance studio Xmas New Year **Conf:** Class 180 Board 110 Thtr 450 Del from £259 **Services:** Lift Night porter Air con **Parking:** 250 **Notes:** LB Civ Wed 380

Ardmore House Hotel

★★★ Ⓐ HOTEL

54 Lemsford Road, AL1 3PR - tel: 01727 859313
email: info@ardmorehousehotel.co.uk **web:** www.ardmorehousehotel.co.uk
dir: *A1081 signed St Albans, through 3 sets of lights & 2 mini rdbts. Right at 3rd mini rdbt, turn right into Alma Rd, through 2 sets of lights. Hotel on right in 800yds*

Located in immaculate surroundings close to the town centre and cathedral, this extended Edwardian house and annexe provides a range of facilities much appreciated by a loyal commercial clientele. The practically furnished bedrooms offer a good range of facilities and the extensive public areas include a spacious conservatory dining room.

Rooms: 40 (4 annexe) (5 family) (5 GF) ★ **Facilities:** STV FTV WiFi ↕ **Conf:** Class 50 Board 50 Thtr 130 **Parking:** 40 **Notes:** Civ Wed 150

Premier Inn Luton South M1 Jct 9

BUDGET HOTEL

London Road, Flamstead, AL3 8HT - tel: 0871 527 8334
(Calls cost 13p per minute plus your phone company's access charge)
web: www.premierinn.com
dir: *M1 junct 9, A5 towards Dunstable*

High quality, budget accommodation ideal for both families and business travellers. Spacious, en suite bedrooms feature free WiFi and tea and coffee making facilities, and in most hotels, Freeview TV is also available. The adjacent family restaurant features a wide and varied menu.

Rooms: 76

Premier Inn St Albans City Centre

BUDGET HOTEL

1 Adelaide Street, AL3 5BH - tel: 0871 527 9464 (Calls cost 13p per minute plus your phone company's access charge)
web: www.premierinn.com
dir: *M25 junct 21A, A405 signed St Albans/London/M1 South. At junct 9 onto A5 towards St Albans. At rdbt 1st exit into Dunstable Rd towards St Albans Redbourn. At rdbt 2nd exit onto A5183. At rdbt 1st exit into St Albans Rd. In 3m take 2nd exit into Redbourn Rd. Right into Drovers Way, hotel on left*

Rooms: 123

S

ST ANNES
See **Lytham St Annes**

ST AUSTELL
Cornwall & Isles of Scilly

Map 2 SX05

Carlyon Bay Hotel
★★★★ 81% @ HOTEL

Sea Road, Carlyon Bay, PL25 3RD - tel: 01726 812304
email: reservations@carlyonbay.com **web:** www.carlyonbay.com
dir: *From St Austell, follow signs for Charlestown. Carlyon Bay signed on left, hotel at end of Sea Rd*

Built in the 1920s, this long-established hotel sits on the cliff top in 250 acres of grounds which include indoor and outdoor pools, a golf course and a spa. Bedrooms are well maintained, and many have marvellous views across St Austell Bay. A good choice of comfortable lounges is available, while facilities for families include kids' clubs and entertainment.

Carlyon Bay Hotel

Rooms: 86 (14 family) S £50–£165; D £150–£450* **Facilities:** Spa FTV WiFi 18 Putting green Gym Hydrotherapy spa pool Hot stone beds Xmas New Year Child facilities **Conf:** Thtr 150 **Services:** Lift Night porter **Parking:** 100 **Notes:** LB Civ Wed 100

See advert below

The Cornwall Hotel, Spa & Estate
★★★★ 80% @ COUNTRY HOUSE HOTEL

Pentewan Road, Tregorrick, PL26 7AB - tel: 01726 874050
email: enquiries@thecornwall.com **web:** www.thecornwall.com
dir: *A391 to St Austell then B3273 towards Mevagissey. Hotel approx 0.5m on right*

Set in 43 acres of wooded parkland, this renovated manor house offers guests a real retreat. The restored White House has suites and traditionally styled bedrooms, and adjoining are the contemporary Woodland rooms ranging across standard, family, accessible, and also deluxe which have private balcony areas overlooking the Pentewan Valley. There are superb leisure facilities including the spa with luxury treatments, an infinity pool and state-of-the-art fitness centre. There is a choice of eating options – The Arboretum, the more informal Acorns, and the Drawing Room and Parkland Terrace for afternoon tea and cocktails respectively. This is an ideal base for visiting The Eden Project, The Lost Gardens of Heligan and south Cornwall fishing villages.

Rooms: 65 (4 family) S £60–£150; D £80–£200* **Facilities:** Spa STV FTV WiFi HL Gym Xmas New Year **Conf:** Class 30 Board 20 Thtr 40 Del from £126 **Services:** Lift Night porter **Parking:** 200 **Notes:** LB Civ Wed 60

ST AUSTELL *continued*

HIGHLY RECOMMENDED

Boscundle Manor

★★★ 86% HOTEL

Boscundle, PL25 3RL - tel: 01726 813557
email: reservations@boscundlemanor.co.uk **web:** www.boscundlemanor.co.uk
dir: *M5 to Exeter then A30 until Bodmin. A391 to St Austell. Turn Left onto A390 then left towards Tregrehan. Hotel drive is 300mtrs on left*

A charming and delightful family-run manor house full of charm, located on the edge of Boscundle, set within five acres of its own private, well maintained and beautiful grounds and gardens. Friendly and attentive staff are eager to ensure guests have a relaxing and enjoyable stay. Accommodation is warm, comfortable and inviting, with a stylish and contemporary feel, yet still cosy. Food is of a high quality, with a good selection of wines and beers to match. Additional seating is offered in the relaxing lounge with open fireplaces; or maybe take a dip in the well-equipped indoor swimming pool, which is part of the excellent leisure facilities.

Rooms: 14 (4 annexe) (4 family) **Facilities:** WiFi ⌨ ☜ ⏴ Beauty treatments Xmas New Year **Notes:** Civ Wed 150

Porth Avallen Hotel

★★★ 76% HOTEL

Sea Road, Carlyon Bay, PL25 3SG - tel: 01726 812802
email: info@porthavallen.co.uk **web:** www.porthavallen.co.uk
dir: *A30 onto A391 to St Austell. Right onto A390. Left at lights, follow brown signs, left at rdbt, right into Sea Rd*

This traditional hotel boasts panoramic views over the rugged Cornish coastline. It offers smartly appointed public areas and well-presented bedrooms, many with sea views. There is an oak-panelled lounge and conservatory; both are ideal for relaxation. Extensive dining options, including the stylish Reflections Restaurant, invite guests to choose from fixed-price, carte and all-day brasserie menus. The Olive Garden, inspired by the Mediterranean, is a lovely place to eat alfresco.

Rooms: 28 (3 family) (3 GF) ☜ **Facilities:** FTV WiFi ⌨ Xmas New Year **Conf:** Class 100 Board 80 Thtr 160 **Services:** Night porter **Parking:** 60 **Notes:** Civ Wed 160

Premier Inn St Austell

BUDGET HOTEL

St Austell Enterprise Park, Treverbyn Road, PL25 4EL - tel: 0871 527 9018 (Calls cost 13p per minute plus your phone company's access charge)
web: www.premierinn.com
dir: *A30 onto A391 signed St Austell. Through Bugle. Continue on A391 at rdbt. Continue to follow St Austell signs. 1st exit at Carclaze rdbt. Hotel at St Austell Enterprise Park*

High quality, budget accommodation ideal for both families and business travellers. Spacious, en suite bedrooms feature free WiFi and tea and coffee making facilities, and in most hotels, Freeview TV is also available. The adjacent family restaurant features a wide and varied menu.

Rooms: 77

ST HELENS
Merseyside

Map 15 SJ59

Premier Inn St Helens (A580/East Lancs)

BUDGET HOTEL

Garswood Old Road, East Lancs Road, WA11 7LX - tel: 0871 527 9020
(Calls cost 13p per minute plus your phone company's access charge)
web: www.premierinn.com
dir: *3m from M6 junct 23, on A580 towards Liverpool*

High quality, budget accommodation ideal for both families and business travellers. Spacious, en suite bedrooms feature free WiFi and tea and coffee making facilities, and in most hotels, Freeview TV is also available. The adjacent family restaurant features a wide and varied menu.

Rooms: 44

Premier Inn St Helens South

BUDGET HOTEL

Eurolink, Lea Green, WA9 4TT - tel: 0871 527 9022
(Calls cost 13p per minute plus your phone company's access charge)
web: www.premierinn.com
dir: *M62 junct 7, A570 towards St Helens*

Rooms: 40

ST IVES
Cornwall & Isles of Scilly

Map 2 SW54

Carbis Bay Hotel

★★★★ 79% HOTEL

Carbis Bay, TR26 2NP - tel: 01736 795311
email: info@carbisbayhotel.co.uk **web:** www.carbisbayhotel.co.uk
dir: *A3074, through Lelant. 1m, at Carbis Bay 30yds before lights, right into Porthrepta Rd to hotel*

In a peaceful location with access to its own white-sand beach, this hotel offers comfortable accommodation. The attractive public areas feature a smart bar and lounge, and a sun lounge overlooking the sea. Bedrooms, many with fine views, are well equipped. Interesting cuisine and particularly enjoyable breakfasts are offered. A small complex of luxury, self-catering apartments is available.

Rooms: 47 (16 family) (3 GF) ☜ **S** fr £120; **D** £180–£370 (incl. bkfst)*
Facilities: Spa WiFi ⚡ Fishing Private beach ♫ Xmas New Year **Conf:** Class 80 Board 60 Thtr 120 Del from £120 **Services:** Night porter **Parking:** 200 **Notes:** LB Civ Wed 150

St Ives Harbour Hotel

★★★★ 73% HOTEL

The Terrace, TR26 2BN - tel: 01736 795221
email: stives@harbourhotels.co.uk **web:** www.stives-harbour-hotel.co.uk
dir: *On A3074*

This friendly hotel enjoys an enviable location with spectacular views of St Ives Bay. Extensive leisure facilities, a versatile function suite and a number of elegant and stylish lounges are available. The majority of bedrooms are appointed to a very high standard, and many rooms have spectacular sea views, as does the restaurant which looks out over the bay and golden sands below.

Rooms: 46 (6 family) ☜ **S** £75–£180; **D** £115–£280* **Facilities:** Spa FTV WiFi ☜ Gym Steam room Sauna Xmas New Year **Conf:** Class 20 Board 35 Thtr 130 **Services:** Lift Night porter **Parking:** 60 **Notes:** LB Civ Wed 160

S

The Garrack

★★★ 82% ⬡ HOTEL

Burthallan Lane, TR26 3AA - **tel:** 01736 796199
email: reception@thegarrack.co.uk **web:** www.thegarrack.co.uk
dir: *Exit A30 for St Ives. From B3311 follow brown signs for Tate Gallery, then Garrack signs*

The Garrack Hotel is set in two acres of gardens on a hill-top location with thirty miles of coastal views. Bedrooms in the original house are in keeping with the original granite architecture, whereas those in the sea-facing lower ground floor wing are in more modern style. Dinner and breakfast are served in the restaurant which faces the stunning grounds and gardens, with views of the beautiful Cornish coastline thrown in. The small leisure centre is in a separate building to the hotel, consisting of an indoor swimming pool with sauna. Location is ideal for families and walkers wanting to explore Cornwall.

Rooms: 19 (4 family) (3 GF) ⭠ **S** £80–£110; **D** £115–£195 (incl. bkfst)*
Facilities: FTV WiFi HL ⬡ Sauna **Conf:** Class 10 Board 20 **Parking:** 20

Tregenna Castle Hotel

★★★ 79% HOTEL

TR26 2DE - **tel:** 01736 795254
email: hotel@tregenna-castle.co.uk **web:** www.tregenna-castle.co.uk
dir: *A30 from Exeter to Penzance, at Lelant take A3074 to St Ives, through Carbis Bay, main entrance signed on left*

Sitting at the top of town in beautiful landscaped sub-tropical gardens with woodland walks, this popular hotel boasts spectacular views of St Ives. Many leisure facilities are available, including indoor and outdoor pools, a gym and a sauna. Families are particularly welcome. The individually designed bedrooms are generally spacious. There are two restaurants, the Trelawny Room and the Godrevy Room, while a brasserie provides lighter options in a less formal atmosphere.

Rooms: 81 (37 family) (16 GF) ⭠ **Facilities:** Spa STV FTV WiFi HL ⬡ ⭢ supervised
⭢ 18 Putting green ⬡ ⬡ Gym Squash Sauna Steam room Badminton court ♫
Xmas New Year **Conf:** Class 150 Board 30 Thtr 250 **Services:** Lift Night porter
Parking: 200 **Notes:** Civ Wed 160

Chy-an-Albany Hotel

★★★ 76% HOTEL

Albany Terrace, TR26 2BS - **tel:** 01736 796759
email: info@chyanalbanyhotel.com **web:** www.chyanalbanyhotel.com
dir: *A30 onto A3074 signed St Ives, hotel on left just before junct*

Conveniently located, this pleasant hotel enjoys splendid sea views. The comfortable bedrooms come in a variety of sizes; some featuring balconies which make it easy to enjoy those sea views. The friendly staff and the relaxing environment mean that some guests return on a regular basis. Freshly prepared and appetising cuisine is served in the dining room, and a bar menu is also available.

Rooms: 39 (10 family) ⭠ **S** £50–£100; **D** £70–£150 (incl. bkfst)* **Facilities:** FTV WiFi **Conf:** Class 30 Board 30 Thtr 50 Del from £85.50 **Services:** Lift Night porter **Parking:** 33 **Notes:** Civ Wed 70

Cottage Hotel

Leisureplex
HOLIDAY HOTELS

★★★ 71% HOTEL

Boskerris Road, Carbis Bay, TR26 2PE - **tel:** 01736 795252
email: cottage@leisureplex.co.uk **web:** www.leisureplex.co.uk
dir: *From A30 take A3074 to Carbis Bay. Right into Porthreptor Rd. Just before rail bridge, left through railway car park into hotel car park*

Set in quiet, lush gardens, this pleasant hotel offers friendly and attentive service. Smart bedrooms are pleasantly spacious and many rooms enjoy splendid views. Public areas are varied and include a snooker room, a comfortable lounge and a spacious dining room with sea views over the beach and Carbis Bay.

Rooms: 80 (18 family) (2 GF) ⭠ **S** £38–£57; **D** £60–£98 (incl. bkfst)* **Facilities:** FTV WiFi ⭢ Snooker ♫ Xmas New Year **Services:** Lift **Parking:** 20 **Notes:** LB Closed Dec-Feb (ex Xmas/New Year) RS Nov & Mar Mon-Fri only

HIGHLY RECOMMENDED

The Queens

★★ 85% ⬡ HOTEL

2 High Street, TR26 1RR - **tel:** 01736 796468
email: info@queenshotelstives.com **web:** www.queenshotelstives.com
dir: *A3074 to town centre. Hotel is located opposite Boots the chemist*

Handily located in the centre of town, just a short stroll from the harbour, this is an ideal location for exploring the charms of St Ives. The bedrooms offer style and comfort with local Cornish artwork and lovely comfy beds. Bathrooms are also light, bright and modern. The relaxing bar and lounge is the venue for enjoyable award-winning cuisine with excellent local produce utilised in simple yet delicious dishes.

Rooms: 10 **S** £79–£149 (incl. bkfst)* **Facilities:** FTV WiFi

ST-LEONARDS-ON-SEA

See **Hastings & St Leonards**

ST MARY CHURCH

See **Torquay**

S

ST MELLION
Cornwall & Isles of Scilly — Map 3 SX36

St Mellion International Resort
★★★★ 79% @@ HOTEL

PL12 6SD - tel: 01579 351351
email: stmellion@crown-golf.co.uk **web:** www.st-mellion.co.uk
dir: *From M5, A38 towards Plymouth & Saltash. St Mellion off A38 on A388 towards Callington & Launceston*

Set in 450 acres of Cornish countryside, this impressive golfing and leisure complex has much to offer. A vast range of leisure facilities are provided, including three pools, spa facilities and a health club. In addition, the hotel also boasts a choice of championship golf courses. The Jack Nicklaus signature course has hosted many PGA tour events. The bedrooms provide contemporary comforts and many have views across the course. Public areas are equally stylish with a choice of dining options including An Boesti, a fine-dining restaurant overlooking the 18th green.

Rooms: 80 (20 family) (18 GF) ↾ **Facilities:** Spa FTV WiFi ☼ ⏰ supervised ↥ 36 Putting green ⛳ Gym Studio classes Lawn bowls Xmas New Year **Conf:** Class 200 Board 80 Thtr 400 **Services:** Lift Night porter Air con **Parking:** 450 **Notes:** Civ Wed 300

ST NEOTS
Cambridgeshire — Map 12 TL16

HIGHLY RECOMMENDED

The George Hotel & Brasserie
★★★ 88% @@ HOTEL

High Street, Buckden, PE19 5XA - tel: 01480 812300
email: mail@thegeorgebuckden.com **web:** www.thegeorgebuckden.com
dir: *2m S of A1 & A14 junct at Buckden*

The George Hotel is ideally situated in the heart of this historic town centre and is just a short drive from the A1. Public rooms feature a bustling ground-floor brasserie, which offers casual dining throughout the day and evening; there is also an informal lounge bar with an open fire and comfy seating. Bedrooms are stylish, tastefully appointed and thoughtfully equipped.

Rooms: 12 (1 family) ↾ **S** fr £80; **D** fr £95 (incl. bkfst)* **Facilities:** STV WiFi ☼ **Conf:** Class 30 Board 20 Thtr 50 Del from £160 **Services:** Lift Night porter **Parking:** 25 **Notes:** Civ Wed 60

Premier Inn St Neots (A1/Wyboston)
BUDGET HOTEL

Great North Road, Eaton Socon, PE19 8EN - tel: 0871 527 9024
(Calls cost 13p per minute plus your phone company's access charge)
web: www.premierinn.com
dir: *Just off A1 at rdbt of A428 & B1428 before St Neots. 1m from St Neots rail station*

High quality, budget accommodation ideal for both families and business travellers. Spacious, en suite bedrooms feature free WiFi and tea and coffee making facilities, and in most hotels, Freeview TV is also available. The adjacent family restaurant features a wide and varied menu.

Rooms: 67

Premier Inn St Neots (Colmworth Park)
BUDGET HOTEL

2 Marlborough Road, Colmworth Business Park, PE19 8YP - tel: 0871 527 9026
(Calls cost 13p per minute plus your phone company's access charge)
web: www.premierinn.com
dir: *From A1 N'bound: A428 towards Cambridge. 2nd exit at rdbt onto A4128 signed St Neots. Hotel on right. From A1 S'bound: follow A428 Cambridge signs. At rdbt 1st exit onto A4128 signed St Neots, hotel on right*

Rooms: 71

SALCOMBE
Devon — Map 3 SX73

HIGHLY RECOMMENDED

Soar Mill Cove Hotel
★★★★ 84% @@ HOTEL

Soar Mill Cove, Malborough, TQ7 3DS - tel: 01548 561566
email: info@soarmillcove.co.uk **web:** www.soarmillcove.co.uk
dir: *3m W of town off A381 at Malborough. Follow Soar signs*

Situated amid spectacular scenery with dramatic sea views, this hotel is ideal for a relaxing stay. Family-run, with a committed team, keen standards of hospitality and service are upheld. Bedrooms are well equipped and many have private terraces. There are different seating areas where, if guests wish, impressive cream teas can be enjoyed, and for the more active, there's a choice of swimming pools. Local produce and seafood are used to good effect in the restaurant.

Rooms: 22 (5 family) (21 GF) ↾ **S** £100–£200; **D** £149–£250* **Facilities:** Spa FTV WiFi ☼ ⏰ ⛳ Gym Table tennis Games room Leisure complex Salt water pool ♪ Xmas **Conf:** Class 50 Board 50 Thtr 100 Del from £100 **Services:** Night porter **Parking:** 30 **Notes:** LB Civ Wed 150

HIGHLY RECOMMENDED

Thurlestone Hotel
★★★★ 84% @@ HOTEL

TQ7 3NN - tel: 01548 560382
email: enquiries@thurlestone.co.uk **web:** www.thurlestone.co.uk

(For full entry see Thurlestone)

HIGHLY RECOMMENDED

Salcombe Harbour Hotel
★★★★ 83% @ HOTEL

Cliff Road, TQ8 8JH - tel: 01548 844444
email: salcombe@harbourhotels.co.uk **web:** www.salcombe-harbour-hotel.co.uk
dir: *From A38 Exeter – Plymouth dual carriageway take A384 to Totnes then follow A381 to Kingsbridge & onto Salcombe. On entering Salcombe carry along Main Rd, do not take town signs. Follow road down hill into Bennett Rd. Hotel is 0.25m on right*

Situated on the side of the estuary in Salcombe stands this beautiful hotel. There are stunning views, convenient parking and a beautiful spa and leisure facility. The bedrooms are particularly well appointed and stylishly finished;

many have excellent views, and some have balconies. Guests can eat in the Jetty Restaurant which services popular dishes and local seafood. There is also a function room, spacious bar/lounge and cinema.

Rooms: 50 (6 family) (6 GF) **S** £185–£395; **D** £195–£800 (incl. bkfst)*
Facilities: Spa FTV WiFi ⬠ HL ⬠ Gym Sauna Steam room Xmas New Year
Conf: Class 120 Board 40 Thtr 120 **Services:** Lift Night porter **Parking:** 50
Notes: LB Civ Wed 120

South Sands Hotel

★★★★ 78% HOTEL

Bolt Head, TQ8 8LL - tel: 01548 845900
email: enquiries@southsands.com **web:** www.southsands.com
dir: M5 onto A38 signed Plymouth, at Buckfastleigh take A384 to Totnes. In Totnes take A381 to Kingsbridge then Salcombe

Contemporary boutique hotel on the beach in South Sands bay, just outside Salcombe. Well-equipped, comfortable rooms and beach suites sit above the restaurant and terrace that offer stunning views of the estuary. Diverse, more relaxed meals can be taken in the bar and lounge, while the restaurant offers sound cuisine which reflects a foraging approach. A warm and friendly atmosphere, attention to detail and attentive yet unobtrusive service is on offer throughout.

Rooms: 22 (5 family) (2 GF) 🛈 **S** £200–£595; **D** £215–£595 (incl. bkfst)*
Facilities: FTV WiFi ⬠ Xmas New Year **Services:** Night porter **Parking:** 39
Notes: Civ Wed 75

SALE
Greater Manchester — Map 15 SJ79

Premier Inn Manchester (Sale)

BUDGET HOTEL

Carrington Lane, Ashton-upon-Mersey, M33 5BL - tel: 0871 527 8716
(Calls cost 13p per minute plus your phone company's access charge)
web: www.premierinn.com
dir: M60 junct 8, A6144(M) towards Carrington. Left at 1st lights, hotel on left

High quality, budget accommodation ideal for both families and business travellers. Spacious, en suite bedrooms feature free WiFi and tea and coffee making facilities, and in most hotels, Freeview TV is also available. The adjacent family restaurant features a wide and varied menu.

Rooms: 61

SALFORD
Greater Manchester — Map 15 SJ89

Premier Inn Manchester Salford Media City

BUDGET HOTEL

Blue, Media City Uk, M50 2BA - tel: 0871 527 9652 (Calls cost 13p per minute plus your phone company's access charge)
web: www.premierinn.com
dir: At end of M602 (heading towards Salford) take 3rd exit on rdbt onto Trafford Road. Turn right onto Broadway. At rdbt take 2nd exit & stay on Broadway. Hotel on left. For car park turn left immediately after hotel & car park is on left

High quality, budget accommodation ideal for both families and business travellers. Spacious, en suite bedrooms feature free WiFi and tea and coffee making facilities, and in most hotels, Freeview TV is also available. The adjacent family restaurant features a wide and varied menu.

Rooms: 112

Premier Inn Manchester Salford Spinningfields

BUDGET HOTEL

Irwell Street, M3 5EN - tel: 0871 527 9550 (Calls cost 13p per minute plus your phone company's access charge)
web: www.premierinn.com
dir: Nbnd M60 junct 12, M602 (city centre). A57(M) into Mancunian Way. 1.5m, left onto A6042. Right at lights into Irwell St

Rooms: 143

SALISBURY
Wiltshire — Map 5 SU12

Milford Hall Hotel & Spa

★★★★ 76% HOTEL

206 Castle Street, SP1 3TE - tel: 01722 417411
email: reception@milfordhallhotel.com **web:** www.milfordhallhotel.com
dir: Near junct of Castle St, A36 ring road & A345 Amesbury Road

This hotel offers high standards of accommodation and is within easy walking distance of the city centre. There are two categories of bedroom - traditional rooms in the original Georgian house, and spacious, modern rooms in a purpose-built extension; all are extremely well equipped. Meals are served in the smart brasserie where a varied choice of dishes is provided. Additional facilities include the newly opened Lime Tree Spa, offering a range of treatments, relaxation areas and a gym.

Rooms: 45 (2 family) (22 GF) 🛈 **S** £70–£115; **D** £70–£170* **Facilities:** Spa FTV WiFi Gym Xmas New Year **Conf:** Class 90 Board 60 Thtr 200 Del from £130
Services: Night porter **Parking:** 60 **Notes:** LB Civ Wed 120

The Legacy Rose & Crown Hotel

★★★★ 73% HOTEL

Harnham Road, SP2 8JQ - tel: 0844 411 9046 (Calls cost 7p per minute plus your phone company's access charge) & 0330 333 2846
email: res-roseandcrown@legacy-hotels.co.uk **web:** www.legacy-hotels.co.uk
dir: M3 junct 8, A303 & follow Salisbury Ring Road or M27 junct 2, A36 to Salisbury. A338 towards Harnham then Harnham Rd. Hotel on right

This 13th-century coaching inn, situated beside the river, enjoys picturesque views of Salisbury Cathedral, especially from the Pavilion Restaurant which provides a good range of dishes. Many original features are still retained in the heavy oak-beamed bars. All bedrooms and bathrooms are beautifully appointed. Excellent conference and banqueting facilities are available.

Rooms: 34 (23 family) (10 GF) 🛈 **D** fr £85 (incl. bkfst)* **Facilities:** FTV WiFi Xmas New Year **Conf:** Class 60 Board 60 Thtr 90 **Services:** Night porter **Parking:** 60
Notes: LB Civ Wed 100

Mercure Salisbury White Hart Hotel

★★★★ 73% HOTEL

St John Street, SP1 2SD - tel: 01722 327476
email: H6616@accor.com **web:** www.mercure.com
dir: M3 juncts 7/8, A303 to A343 for Salisbury then A30. Follow city centre signs on ring road, into Exeter St, leading into St John Street Car park at rear on Brown St

There has been a hotel on this site since the 16th century, and this building dates from the 17th. Bedrooms vary in style, from contemporary to traditional, but all boast a comprehensive range of facilities. The bar and lounge areas are popular with guests and locals alike for morning coffees and afternoon teas.

Rooms: 68 (6 family) 🛈 **Facilities:** STV WiFi Xmas New Year **Conf:** Class 40 Board 40 Thtr 100 **Services:** Night porter **Parking:** 60 **Notes:** Civ Wed 100

SALISBURY *continued*

Best Western Red Lion Hotel

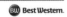

★★★ 81% HOTEL

4 Milford Street, SP1 2AN - tel: 01722 323334
email: reception@the-redlion.co.uk **web:** www.the-redlion.co.uk
dir: *In city centre close to Guildhall Square*

This 750-year-old hotel is full of character, with a mix of bedrooms, some very stylish refurbished examples, while others are individually designed including one with a medieval fireplace dating back to 1220. The public areas include a bar and a lounge. The elegant Vine Restaurant also serves an interesting mix of modern and traditional dishes.

Rooms: 60 (1 family) (1 GF) ⚡ **Facilities:** FTV WiFi ♨ Xmas New Year **Conf:** Class 40 Board 40 Thtr 110 **Services:** Lift Night porter **Parking:** 7 **Notes:** Civ Wed 110

Grasmere House Hotel

THE INDEPENDENTS
HOTEL ASSOCIATION

★★★ 75% HOTEL

Harnham Road, SP2 8JN - tel: 01722 338388
email: info@grasmerehotel.com **web:** www. grasmerehotel.com
dir: *On A3094 on S side of Salisbury adjacent to Harnham church*

This popular hotel, dating from 1896, has gardens that overlook the water meadows and the cathedral. The attractive bedrooms vary in size; all offer excellent quality and comfort, while some rooms are specially equipped for less mobile guests. In summer there is the option of dining on the pleasant outdoor terrace.

Rooms: 38 (31 annexe) (16 family) (9 GF) ⚡ **S** £75–£95; **D** £110–£135 (incl. bkfst)
Facilities: STV FTV WiFi ♨ Fishing 🎣 Xmas New Year **Conf:** Class 45 Board 45 Thtr 110 Del from £135 **Parking:** 64 **Notes:** LB Civ Wed 120

Premier Inn Salisbury North Bishopdown

Premier Inn

BUDGET HOTEL

Pearce Way, Off London Road, SP1 3GU - tel: 0871 527 8956
(Calls cost 13p per minute plus your phone company's access charge)
dir: *From Salisbury Centre follow A30 towards Marlborough for 1m. Hotel at rdbt. Next to the Hampton Inn Table*

High quality, budget accommodation ideal for both families and business travellers. Spacious, en suite bedrooms feature free WiFi and tea and coffee making facilities, and in most hotels, Freeview TV is also available. The adjacent family restaurant features a wide and varied menu.

Rooms: 120

SALTASH Map 3 SX45
Cornwall & Isles of Scilly

China Fleet Country Club

★★★ 81% HOTEL

PL12 6LJ - tel: 01752 848668
email: res@china-fleet.co.uk **web:** www.china-fleet.co.uk
dir: *A38 towards Plymouth/Saltash. Cross Tamar Bridge, take slip road before tunnel. Right at lights, 1st right follow signs, 0.5m*

Set in 180 acres of stunning Cornish countryside overlooking the beautiful Tamar estuary, this hotel has easy access to Plymouth and the countryside. It offers an extensive range of leisure facilities including a golf course. The one and two-bedroom apartments are located in annexe buildings; each has a kitchen, lounge and flexible sleeping arrangements. The dining options are the brasserie and the Upper Deck Bistro. Guests can relax at the hotel's state-of-the-art Aqua Spa.

Rooms: 41 (40 family) (22 GF) ⚡ **S** £80–£150; **D** £110–£150* **Facilities:** Spa FTV WiFi ♨ 🏊 supervised ⛳ 18 Putting green 🏌 Gym Squash Floodlit driving range Health & beauty suite Hairdresser Badminton Waterslide Xmas New Year
Conf: Class 100 Board 60 Thtr 300 Del from £132 **Services:** Lift Night porter **Parking:** 400 **Notes:** Civ Wed 300

SALTBURN-BY-THE-SEA Map 19 NZ62
North Yorkshire

Brockley Hall Boutique Hotel & Fine Dining Restaurant

★★★★ 78% HOTEL

TS12 1JS - tel: 01287 622179
email: reception@brockleyhallhotel.com **web:** www.brockleyhallhotel.com
dir: *Phone for directions*

Brockley Hall is ideally located in the heart of Saltburn, within easy walking distance to the seafront, and well positioned to tour Teeside and North Yorkshire. This boutique hotel was built in 1865 and has enjoyed an extensive refurbishment programme with very good results achieved to date. Public areas offer high quality and comfort, with the stylish restaurant offering award-winning food. The team are genuinely friendly and show great customer care awareness.

Rooms: 22 (1 family) (3 GF) ⚡ **S** £75–£95; **D** £95–£195 (incl. bkfst)* **Facilities:** FTV WiFi 2 Beauty rooms **Conf:** Class 60 Board 24 Thtr 60 Del from £95 **Services:** Lift Night porter **Parking:** 15 **Notes:** Closed 25-26 Dec Civ Wed 120

SANDBANKS

See **Poole**

S

Follow the AA

twitter: @TheAA_Lifestyle
facebook: www.facebook.com/TheAAUK

SANDIWAY
Cheshire

Map 15 SJ67

INSPECTOR'S CHOICE

Nunsmere Hall Hotel
★★★★ ◉◉ COUNTRY HOUSE HOTEL

Tarporley Road, Oakmere, CW8 2ES - **tel:** 01606 889100
email: reception@nunsmere.co.uk **web:** www.nunsmere.co.uk
dir: *M6 junct 18, A54 to Chester, at x-rds with A49 turn left towards Tarporley, hotel 2m on left*

In an idyllic and peaceful setting of well-kept grounds, including a 60-acre lake, this delightful house dates back to 1900. Spacious bedrooms are individually styled, tastefully appointed to a very high standard, and thoughtfully equipped. Guests can relax in the elegant lounges, the library or the oak-panelled bar. Dining in the Crystal Restaurant is a highlight and both a traditional carte and a gourmet menu are offered.

Rooms: 36 (8 family) (2 GF) 🐾 **Facilities:** FTV WiFi ⓑ 🏊 Xmas New Year
Conf: Class 150 Board 30 Thtr 200 **Services:** Lift Night porter **Parking:** 200
Notes: Civ Wed 120

SANDOWN
Isle of Wight

Map 5 SZ58

Bayshore Hotel

Leisureplex
HOLIDAY HOTELS

★★★ 72% HOTEL

12-16 Pier Street, PO36 8JX - **tel:** 01983 403154
email: bayshore.sandown@alfatravel.co.uk **web:** www.leisureplex.co.uk
dir: *From Broadway into Melville St, follow Tourist Information Office signs. Across High St, right opposite pier. Hotel on right*

This large hotel is located on the seafront opposite the pier and offers extensive public rooms where live entertainment is provided in season. There is a range of bedrooms to meet a variety of needs, all are well-equipped; front rooms also offer incredible sea views and are priced differently. The team is very friendly and helpful. Free WiFi is provided in the public areas.

Rooms: 77 (18 family) 🐾 **Facilities:** FTV WiFi 🎵 Xmas New Year **Services:** Lift Night porter **Notes:** Closed Dec-Feb (ex Xmas/New Year) RS Mar & Nov Mon-Fri only

Sandringham Hotel
★★ 78% HOTEL

Esplanade, PO36 8AH - **tel:** 01983 406655
email: info@sandringhamhotel.co.uk **web:** www.sandringhamhotel.co.uk
dir: *Phone for directions*

With a prime seafront location and splendid views, this is one of the largest hotels on the island. Comfortable public areas include a spacious lounge and a heated indoor swimming pool and jacuzzi. Bedrooms vary in size and many sea-facing rooms have a balcony. Regular entertainment is provided in the ballroom.

Rooms: 73 (39 family) (6 GF) **Facilities:** ⓒ 🎵 Xmas **Services:** Lift Night porter **Parking:** 82

Wight Bay Hotel
★★ 76% HOTEL

2 Royal Street, PO36 8LP - **tel:** 01983 402518
email: booking@wightbayhotel.com **web:** www.wightbayhotel.com
dir: *At top of High St, beyond Post Office*

Guests return year after year to this friendly and welcoming family-run hotel. It is located near to the High Street and just a short stroll from the beach, pier and shops. Bedrooms, including several at ground floor level, are very well furnished and comfortably equipped. Enjoyable home-cooked meals are served in the spacious dining room.

Rooms: 43 (6 family) (11 GF) 🐾 **S** fr £35; **D** fr £45 (incl. bkfst)* **Facilities:** FTV WiFi ⓑ 🎵 Xmas New Year **Parking:** 30

Premier Inn Isle of Wight Sandown

BUDGET HOTEL

Merrie Gardens, Newport Road, PO36 9PE - **tel:** 0871 527 9558 (Calls cost 13p per minute plus your phone company's access charge) **web:** www.premierinn.com
dir: *From Fishbourne Ferry Terminal right onto B3731, right onto A3054. Next left into Station Rd. 2m to rdbt. 1st exit into Briddlesford Rd, at next rdbt into Downend Rd. 4m, left onto A3056. 2nd exit at rdbt. At next rdbt 2nd exit into Whitcross Ln*

High quality, budget accommodation ideal for both families and business travellers. Spacious, en suite bedrooms feature free WiFi and tea and coffee making facilities, and in most hotels, Freeview TV is also available. The adjacent family restaurant features a wide and varied menu.

Rooms: 100

SANDWICH
Kent

Map 7 TR35

The Lodge at Prince's
★★★ 85% ◉◉ HOTEL

Prince's Drive, Sandwich Bay, CT13 9QB - **tel:** 01304 611118
email: info@princesgolfclub.co.uk **web:** www.princesgolfclub.co.uk
dir: *M2 onto A299 Thanet Way to Manston Airport, A256 to Sandwich, follow sign to golf course*

Opened in 2012, and created from the remains of the old clubhouse, The Lodge at Prince's is in one of the most sought-after locations on the southeast coast. There is a choice of bedrooms within three adjoining houses, and most rooms offer enviable views of the golf course or the Bay of Sandwich. All rooms have been carefully designed and offer a range of practical amenities including club storage. Award-winning cuisine is served in The Brasserie on the Bay.

Rooms: 38 (24 annexe) (24 family) (12 GF) 🐾 **S** £105; **D** £135 (incl. bkfst)*
Facilities: FTV WiFi ⓑ HL 🏌 27 Putting green Gym New Year **Conf:** Class 60 Board 50 Thtr 120 Del from £130 **Services:** Lift Night porter **Parking:** 50 **Notes:** LB

S

SAUNTON
Devon   Map 3 SS43

Saunton Sands Hotel
★★★★ 81% ◉ HOTEL

EX33 1LQ - **tel:** 01271 890212
email: reservations@sauntonsands.com **web:** www.sauntonsands.com
dir: *Exit A361 at Braunton, signed Croyde B3231, hotel 2m on left*

Stunning sea views and direct access to three miles of sandy beach are just two of the highlights at this popular hotel. The majority of sea-facing rooms have balconies, and splendid views can be enjoyed from all of the public areas, which include comfortable lounges. In addition to the dining room, in summer an outside grill has tables on the terrace overlooking the sea. Alternatively, The Sands café/bar, an informal eating option, is a successful innovation located on the beach.

Rooms: 92 (39 family) ♦ **S** £85–£165; **D** £170–£370 (incl. bkfst)* **Facilities:** Spa STV FTV WiFi ♦ ❄ ↖ Putting green ♨ Gym Squash Sauna Sun shower Snooker room ♫ Xmas New Year Child facilities **Conf:** Class 180 Board 50 Thtr 200 **Services:** Lift Night porter **Parking:** 140 **Notes:** LB Civ Wed 200

See advert on opposite page

SCARBOROUGH
North Yorkshire   Map 17 TA08

Crown Spa Hotel
★★★★ 79% HOTEL

Esplanade, YO11 2AG - **tel:** 01723 357400
email: info@crownspahotel.com **web:** www.crownspahotel.com
dir: *On A64 follow town centre signs to lights opposite railway station, turn right over Valley Bridge, 1st left, right into Belmont Rd to cliff top*

This well-known hotel has an enviable position overlooking the harbour and South Bay, and most of the front-facing bedrooms have excellent views. All the bedrooms, including suites, are contemporary and have the latest amenities including feature bathrooms. An extensive range of treatments are available in the outstanding spa.

Rooms: 115 (42 family) ♦ **S** fr £55; **D** fr £68* **Facilities:** Spa FTV WiFi ♦ HL ❄ Gym Fitness classes Massage Sauna Steam room Xmas New Year **Conf:** Class 100 Board 80 Thtr 260 **Services:** Lift Night porter **Parking:** 17 **Notes:** Civ Wed 260

Palm Court Hotel
★★★ 83% ◉ HOTEL

St Nicholas Cliff, YO11 2ES - **tel:** 01723 368161
email: info@palmcourt-scarborough.co.uk **web:** www.palmcourtscarborough.co.uk
dir: *Follow signs for town centre & town hall, hotel before town hall on right*

The public rooms are spacious and comfortable at this modern, town centre hotel. Traditional cooking is provided in the attractive restaurant and staff are friendly and helpful. Bedrooms are quite delightfully furnished and well equipped. Extra facilities include a swimming pool and free, covered parking.

Rooms: 40 (11 family) ♦ **S** £60–£83; **D** £92–£159 (incl. bkfst)* **Facilities:** FTV WiFi ❄ Xmas New Year **Conf:** Class 70 Board 60 Thtr 80 **Services:** Lift Night porter **Parking:** 40 **Notes:** Civ Wed 80

Red Lea Hotel
★★★ 74% HOTEL

Prince of Wales Terrace, YO11 2AJ - **tel:** 01723 362431
email: info@redleahotel.co.uk **web:** www.redleahotel.co.uk
dir: *Follow South Cliff signs. Prince of Wales Terrace is off Esplanade opposite cliff lift*

This friendly, family-run hotel is situated close to the cliff lift. Bedrooms are well equipped and comfortably furnished, and many at the front have picturesque views of the coast. There are two large lounges and a spacious dining room where good-value, traditional food is served.

Rooms: 66 (7 family) ♦ **S** fr £45; **D** fr £90 (incl. bkfst) **Facilities:** FTV WiFi ❄ Gym 2 treatment rooms Xmas New Year **Conf:** Class 25 Board 25 Thtr 40 Del from £90 **Services:** Lift Night porter **Notes:** LB

The Cumberland
★★★ 70% HOTEL

Leisureplex
HOLIDAY HOTELS

Belmont Road, YO11 2AB - **tel:** 01723 361826
email: cumberland.scarborough@leisureplex.co.uk **web:** www.leisureplex.co.uk
dir: *A64 onto B1437, left at A165 towards town centre. Right into Ramshill Rd, right into Belmont Rd*

On the South Cliff, convenient for the spa complex, beach and town centre shops, this hotel offers comfortably appointed bedrooms; each floor can be accessed by lift. Entertainment is provided most evenings and the meals are carefully prepared.

Rooms: 86 (6 family) ♦ **S** £40–£55; **D** £64–£94 (incl. bkfst)* **Facilities:** FTV WiFi ♫ Xmas New Year **Services:** Lift Night porter **Notes:** LB Closed Jan RS Nov-Dec & Feb Mon-Fri only

Premier Inn Scarborough

BUDGET HOTEL

Falconer Road, YO11 2EN - **tel:** 0871 527 9292 (Calls cost 13p per minute plus your phone company's access charge)
web: www.premierinn.com
dir: *From A64 into Seamer Rd, follow rail station signs. Right into Valley Bridge Rd. At 1st lights follow Town Hall signs into Somerset St (towards Brunswick shopping centre). At lights follow Town Hall signs into Falconers Rd*

High quality, budget accommodation ideal for both families and business travellers. Spacious, en suite bedrooms feature free WiFi and tea and coffee making facilities, and in most hotels, Freeview TV is also available. The adjacent family restaurant features a wide and varied menu.

Rooms: 74

SCUNTHORPE
Lincolnshire
Map 17 SE81

Forest Pines Hotel & Golf Resort

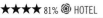 ★★★★ 81% ⚙ HOTEL

INSPIRED BY YOU

Ermine Street, Broughton, DN20 0AQ - **tel:** 01652 650770
email: forestpines@qhotels.co.uk **web:** www.qhotels.co.uk
dir: *200yds from M180 junct 4, on Brigg-Scunthorpe rdbt*

This smart hotel provides a comprehensive range of leisure facilities. Extensive conference rooms, a modern health and beauty spa, and a championship golf course ensure that it is a popular choice with both corporate and leisure guests. The well-equipped bedrooms are modern, spacious, and appointed to a good standard. Extensive public areas include a choice of dining options, with fine dining available in The Eighteen57 fish restaurant, and more informal eating in the Grill Bar.

Rooms: 188 (66 family) (65 GF) **Facilities:** Spa STV FTV WiFi HL ⚲ ⚓ 27 Putting green Gym Mountain bikes Jogging track Xmas New Year **Conf:** Class 170 Board 96 Thtr 370 **Services:** Lift Night porter **Parking:** 400 **Notes:** Civ Wed 250

Premier Inn Scunthorpe

BUDGET HOTEL

Lakeside Retail Park, Lakeside Parkway, DN16 3UA - **tel:** 0871 527 8960
(Calls cost 13p per minute plus your phone company's access charge)
web: www.premierinn.com
dir: *M180 junct 4, A18 towards Scunthorpe. At Morrisons rdbt left onto Lakeside Retail Park, hotel behind Morrisons petrol station*

High quality, budget accommodation ideal for both families and business travellers. Spacious, en suite bedrooms feature free WiFi and tea and coffee making facilities, and in most hotels, Freeview TV is also available. The adjacent family restaurant features a wide and varied menu.

Rooms: 81

SEAHAM
County Durham
Map 19 NZ44

Seaham Hall

 ★★★★★ 85% ⚙⚙ HOTEL

PRIDE OF BRITAIN HOTELS

Lord Byron's Walk, SR7 7AG - **tel:** 0191 516 1400
email: hotel@seaham-hall.com **web:** www.seaham-hall.co.uk
dir: *From A19 take B1404 to Seaham. At lights straight over level crossing. Hotel approximately 0.25 miles on right*

Seaham Hall benefits from a wonderful coastal location. Its interior is sumptuously furnished, with all rooms boasting the highest quality fixtures, fittings and furniture. Many have feature bathrooms, and the garden rooms have their own patio and garden areas. Public rooms boast quality and luxury throughout. The hotel boasts an award-winning Serenity Spa where you can unwind in the pool and hydrotherapy facilities, not forgetting the outside hot tubs; or book a treatment with one of the dedicated team of therapists. Seaham is home to two award-winning restaurants. Whether you choose the relaxed Pan-Asian Ozone restaurant in the Serenity Spa or the opulent setting of Byron's Restaurant, you can be sure of excellent dining.

Rooms: 21 (4 GF) **S** £195–£835; **D** £195–£835 (incl. bkfst)* **Facilities:** Spa STV FTV WiFi ⚲ HL ⚲ Putting green ⚲ Gym Games Room Sports lounge Xmas New Year **Conf:** Class 48 Board 40 Thtr 100 Del from £265 **Services:** Lift Night porter Air con **Parking:** 120 **Notes:** Civ Wed 100

S

SEAHOUSES
Northumberland
Map 21 NU23

The Links Hotel
★★ 85% SMALL HOTEL

8 King Street, NE68 7XP - tel: 01665 720062
email: linkshotel@hotmail.com **web:** www.linkshotel-seahouses.co.uk
dir: *Off A1 at Browleside & follow signs along country road*

This family-owned small hotel is in the heart of Seahouses. The restaurant is popular with residents and locals alike, offering relaxed and informal dining with quality home cooking and generous portions. Bedrooms are well presented and equipped and some off-road parking is available.

Rooms: 17 (7 annexe) (1 family) (2 GF) ☎ **S** £47–£53; **D** £74–£86 (incl. bkfst)*
Facilities: STV FTV WiFi ⌨ **Parking:** 17

SEASCALE
Cumbria
Map 18 NY00

Sella Park House Hotel
★★★★ 75% COUNTRY HOUSE HOTEL

Calderbridge, CA20 1DW - tel: 0845 450 6445 (Calls cost 7p per minute plus your phone company's access charge)
email: info@penningtonhotels.com **web:** www.penningtonhotels.co.uk
dir: *From A595 at Calderbridge, follow sign for North Gate. Hotel 0.5m on left*

This property, which some believe dates back to the 13th century, is set in six acres of mature grounds which lead down to the River Calder. The individually designed bedrooms are very well appointed and have many extras; public areas are comfortable and welcoming. Food in the Priory Restaurant is a highlight, with local produce at the heart of each menu selection.

Rooms: 16 (5 annexe) (2 GF) ☎ **S** £91.50–£100; **D** £100–£120 (incl. bkfst)*
Facilities: FTV WiFi ⌨ HL Fishing Xmas New Year **Conf:** Class 20 Board 30 Thtr 40 Del from £130 **Services:** Night porter **Parking:** 30 **Notes:** LB Civ Wed 150

SEAVIEW
Isle of Wight
Map 5 SZ69

Seaview Hotel
★★★ 81% ⊕ HOTEL

High Street, PO34 5EX - tel: 01983 612711
email: reception@seaviewhotel.co.uk **web:** www.seaviewhotel.co.uk
dir: *Please phone for directions*

There is an enduring appeal about Seaview, a quiet seaside village where time has reassuringly stood still and the pace of life is unhurried. The hotel is just a few steps from the water's edge, a perfect place to relax and unwind with welcoming staff making every effort to ensure a rewarding experience. A choice of dining options is offered, with fish being a speciality; there is also the Pump Bar, a traditional pub situated in the heart of the hotel. A variety of bedroom styles are offered, both in the main hotel and within separate adjacent buildings, all of which provide contemporary comforts.

Rooms: 28 (12 annexe) (6 family) (6 GF) ☎ **D** £95–£200 (incl. bkfst)*
Facilities: FTV WiFi New Year **Conf:** Class 16 Board 20 Thtr 16 **Services:** Lift Night porter **Parking:** 10 **Notes:** Closed 23-27 Dec

SEDGEFIELD
County Durham
Map 19 NZ32

Hardwick Hall Hotel
★★★★ 79% HOTEL
⊕ PREMIER | BEST WESTERN

TS21 2EH - tel: 01740 620253 **email:** info@hardwickhallhotel.co.uk
web: www.hardwickhallhotel.co.uk
dir: *Exit A1(M) junct 60 towards Sedgefield, left at 1st rdbt, hotel 400mtrs on left*

Set in extensive parkland, this 18th-century house suits both leisure and corporate guests. It is a top conference and function venue offering an impressive meeting and banqueting complex. Luxurious accommodation includes contemporary rooms, and some with antique furnishings. All are appointed to the same high standard, many have feature bathrooms, and some have stunning views over the lake. Both the modern lounge bar and cellar bistro have a relaxed atmosphere.

Rooms: 51 (6 family) (12 GF) ☎ **Facilities:** STV FTV WiFi ⌨ Xmas New Year
Conf: Class 300 Board 80 Thtr 700 **Services:** Lift Night porter **Parking:** 300
Notes: LB Civ Wed 450

SEDGEMOOR MOTORWAY SERVICE AREA (M5)
Somerset
Map 4 ST35

Days Inn Sedgemoor - M5
WELCOME BREAK

AA Advertised

Sedgemoor, BS24 0JL - tel: 01934 750831
email: sedgemoor.hotel@welcomebreak.co.uk **web:** www.welcomebreak.co.uk
dir: *M5 Northbound junct 21/22*

This modern building offers accommodation in smart, spacious and well-equipped bedrooms, suitable for families and business travellers, and all with en suite bathrooms. Continental breakfast is available and other refreshments may be taken at the nearby family restaurant.

Rooms: 40 (22 family) (19 GF) (8 smoking) **Facilities:** WiFi ⌨ **Parking:** 40

SEVENOAKS
Kent
Map 6 TQ55

Best Western Plus Donnington Manor Hotel
★★★★ 77% HOTEL
⊕ PREMIER | BEST WESTERN

London Road, Dunton Green, TN13 2TD - tel: 01732 462681
email: mail@donningtonmanor.com **web:** www.bw-donningtonmanor.co.uk
dir: *M25 junct 4, follow signs for Bromley/Orpington to rdbt. Left onto A224 (Dunton Green), left at 2nd rdbt. Left at Rose & Crown, hotel 300yds on right*

Donnington Manor offers comfortable bedrooms, modern in style. There is a range of function rooms ideal for conferences and weddings. Guests can enjoy dinner in the Osteria Chartwell Italian Restaurant and breakfast is served here daily also. Plenty of parking on site and close proximity to the M25, Sevenoaks and Brands Hatch.

Rooms: 63 (17 GF) ☎ **S** £80–£145; **D** £80–£145* **Facilities:** STV FTV WiFi ⌨ Gym
Conf: Class 70 Board 50 Thtr 120 **Services:** Lift Night porter Air con **Parking:** 80
Notes: LB Civ Wed 120

SHAFTESBURY
Dorset
Map 4 ST82

Best Western The Royal Chase Hotel
BW Best Western

★★★ 72% HOTEL

Royal Chase Roundabout, SP7 8DB - **tel:** 01747 853355
email: reception@theroyalchasehotel.co.uk **web:** www.theroyalchasehotel.co.uk
dir: A303 to A350 signed Blandford Forum. Avoid town centre, follow road to 3rd rdbt

Equally suitable for both leisure and business guests, this well-known local landmark is situated close to the famous Gold Hill. Both Standard and Crown bedrooms offer good levels of comfort and quality. In addition to the fixed-price menu in the Byzant Restaurant, guests have the option of eating more informally in the convivial bar.

Rooms: 32 (13 family) (6 GF) **Facilities:** FTV WiFi Turkish steam room Spa pool Xmas New Year **Conf:** Class 90 Board 50 Thtr 180 **Services:** Night porter **Parking:** 100 **Notes:** Civ Wed 80

SHANKLIN
Isle of Wight
Map 5 SZ58

The Nightingale Hotel
★★★ 82% HOTEL

3 Queens Road, PO37 6AN - **tel:** 01983 862742 & 07714 785778
email: enquiries@nightingale-hotel.co.uk **web:** www.nightingale-hotel.co.uk
dir: From lights at junct of Atherley Road, Hope Road, Arthurs Hill & North Road (A3055), take North Rd signed Ventnor. 1st left into Queens Rd. Pass church on left, Nightingale Hotel on left before T-junct

This hotel as seen a recent transformation from its more traditional past, new owners have styled the hotel in a Victorian and Edwardian theme with contemporary twists and comfort. Bedrooms are offered in a range of options, all are very well appointed. Dog friendly, the hotel has a delightful location at the coast edge with superb sea views. Cuisine is a real focus here, and the proprietors and chef have a strong ethical policy. Menus offer exciting choices in the restaurant, while there is a more traditional offering in the lounge and bar.

Rooms: 31 (6 family) (3 GF) **S** £53–£81; **D** £106–£162 (incl. bkfst) **Facilities:** STV FTV WiFi Xmas New Year Child facilities **Conf:** Class 25 Board 25 Thtr 25 Del from £81 **Services:** Lift Night porter **Parking:** 20 **Notes:** LB Closed Last 3 weeks Jan

Channel View Hotel
★★★ 79% HOTEL

Hope Road, PO37 6EH - **tel:** 01983 862309
email: enquiries@channelviewhotel.co.uk **web:** www.channelviewhotel.co.uk
dir: Exit A3055 at Esplanade & Beach sign. Hotel 250mtrs on left

With an elevated cliff-top location overlooking Shanklin Bay, several rooms at this hotel enjoy pleasant views and all are very well decorated and furnished. The hotel is family run, and guests can enjoy efficient service, regular evening entertainment, a heated indoor swimming pool and holistic therapy.

Rooms: 56 (15 family) **S** £45–£59; **D** £90–£126 (incl. bkfst)* **Facilities:** FTV WiFi Holistic therapies Aromatherapy **Services:** Lift Night porter **Parking:** 32 **Notes:** Closed Jan-Feb

Shanklin Hotel
Leisureplex HOLIDAY HOTELS

★★★ 75% HOTEL

Clarendon Road, PO37 6DP - **tel:** 01983 862286
email: shanklin@leisureplex.co.uk **web:** www.leisureplex.co.uk
dir: From Fishbourne ferry take A3054/A3056/A3055 south towards Shanklin. Left into Clarendon Rd

The Shanklin Hotel enjoys an enviable location with views over Sandown Bay and beyond. The accommodation is well configured and well appointed; a choice of beds is offered to meet the needs of a varied clientele. Entertainment is provided most evenings. The hotel also offers an indoor pool, game facilities, free WiFi in the public areas, and secure parking.

Rooms: 89 (3 family) (2 GF) **S** £40–£63; **D** £64–£124 (incl. bkfst)* **Facilities:** FTV WiFi Xmas New Year **Services:** Lift Night porter **Parking:** 32 **Notes:** Closed 2 Jan-16 Feb RS Feb-Mar & Nov-Dec Open Mon-Fri only

Malton House Hotel
★★ 71% HOTEL

8 Park Road, PO37 6AY - **tel:** 01983 865007
email: couvoussis@maltonhouse.freeserve.co.uk **web:** www.maltonhouse.co.uk
dir: Up hill from Hope Rd lights then 3rd left

Malton House is a well-kept Victorian hotel set in its own gardens in a quiet area, conveniently located for cliff-top walks and the public lift down to the promenade. The bedrooms are comfortable and public rooms include a small lounge, a separate bar and a dining room where traditional home-made meals are served.

Rooms: 12 (3 family) (2 GF) **Facilities:** WiFi **Parking:** 12 **Notes:** Closed Oct-Apr No children 3yrs

Ocean View Hotel
★★ 69% HOTEL

1-5 Park Road, PO37 6BB - **tel:** 01983 863262
email: info@holdsworthhotels.co.uk **web:** www.holdsworthhotels.co.uk/ocean-view.php
dir: Please phone for directions

The Ocean View is a charming, well-appointed hotel, situated in a premier location with an idyllic seaside position just a pebble's throw away from Shanklin Beach. With a number of spacious bedrooms, many with sea views and balconies, you can sit and relax while enjoying the views.

Rooms: 100 (41 family) (8 GF) **S** fr £45; **D** fr £90 (incl. bkfst)* **Facilities:** FTV WiFi Xmas New Year **Services:** Lift Night porter **Parking:** 9 **Notes:** LB Closed 3 Jan-8 Feb

SHAP
Cumbria
Map 18 NY51

Shap Wells Hotel
★★★ 77% HOTEL

CA10 3QU - **tel:** 01931 716628
email: reservations@shapwellshotel.com **web:** www.shapwellshotel.com
dir: Between A6 & B6261, 4m S of Shap

This hotel occupies a wonderful secluded position amid trees and waterfalls. Extensive public areas include function and meeting rooms, a well-stocked bar, a choice of lounges and a spacious restaurant. Bedrooms vary in size and style but all are equipped with the expected facilities.

Rooms: 99 (8 annexe) (10 family) (10 GF) **Facilities:** FTV WiFi Games room Cardiovascular gym Xmas New Year **Conf:** Class 150 Board 60 Thtr 400 **Services:** Lift Night porter **Parking:** 200 **Notes:** LB Closed 2-24 Jan Civ Wed 150

S

SHEFFIELD
South Yorkshire

Map 16 SK38

Whitley Hall Hotel
★★★★ 79% HOTEL

Elliott Lane, Grenoside, S35 8NR - tel: 0114 245 4444
email: reservations@whitleyhall.com web: www.whitleyhall.com
dir: A61 past football ground, 2m, right just before Norfolk Arms, left at bottom of hill. Hotel on left

This 16th-century house stands in 20 acres of landscaped grounds and gardens. Public rooms are full of character and interesting architectural features, and command the best views of the gardens. The individually styled bedrooms are furnished in keeping with the country house setting, as are the oak-panelled restaurant and bar.

Rooms: 32 (3 annexe) (2 family) (8 GF) ☛ S £85–£140; D £105–£145 (incl. bkfst)*
Facilities: STV FTV WiFi ↕ Conf: Class 50 Board 34 Thtr 70 Del from £160
Services: Lift Night porter Parking: 100 Notes: Civ Wed 100

Mercure Sheffield St Paul's Hotel & Spa
★★★★ 79% HOTEL

119 Norfolk Street, S1 2JE - tel: 0114 278 2000
email: h6628@accor.com web: www.mercure.com
dir: M1 junct 33, 4th exit at rdbt, left at 1st lights, right at 2nd in front of The Crucible

This modern, luxury hotel enjoys a central location close to key attractions in the city. Open-plan public areas are situated in a steel and glass atrium and include a popular Champagne bar, the Yard Restaurant and Zucca, an Italian Bistro. Bedrooms are superbly presented and richly furnished. The Vital health and beauty treatment centre provides a fabulous thermal suite.

Rooms: 163 (40 family) Facilities: Spa WiFi ↕ Sauna Steam room Snail shower Ice fountain Fitness classes Xmas New Year Conf: Class 400 Board 30 Thtr 600 Services: Lift Night porter Air con Notes: Civ Wed 350

Copthorne Hotel Sheffield
★★★★ 78% HOTEL

Sheffield United Football Club, Bramall Lane, S2 4SU - tel: 0114 252 5480
email: reservations.sheffield@millenniumhotels.co.uk
web: www.millenniumhotels.co.uk/copthornesheffield
dir: M1 junct 33/A57. At Park Square rdbt follow A61 Chesterfield Rd.
Follow brown signs for Bramall Lane

This modern and stylish hotel is situated in the centre of Sheffield. Right next to the home of Sheffield United FC, it offers contemporary public areas and an award-winning restaurant on the ground floor. A well-equipped gym is situated on the first floor. Bedrooms are spacious and comfortable. Ample parking is a plus in this central location.

Rooms: 158 (29 family) ☛ Facilities: STV FTV WiFi ↕ HL Gym Conf: Class 150 Board 24 Thtr 250 Services: Lift Night porter Air con Parking: 250

Mercure Sheffield Parkway Hotel
★★★★ 75% HOTEL

Brittania Way, Catcliffe, S60 5BD - tel: 0114 261 5690 & 0845 485 4528
(Calls cost 7p per minute plus your phone company's access charge)
email: info@mercuresheffieldparkway.com web: www.mercuresheffieldparkway.com
dir: M1 junct 33, just off A630 Parkway, 4m from city centre

A modern property situated just a short drive from the city centre; the smartly appointed bedrooms are equipped with modern facilities and are ideally suited for the business or leisure guest. The open-plan public areas feature a bar and Brasserie 59, where a good choice of home-made dishes is available.

Rooms: 78 (12 family) ☛ D £59–£275 Facilities: FTV WiFi ↕ Gym Xmas New Year Conf: Class 80 Board 40 Thtr 120 Del from £105 Services: Lift Night porter Air con Parking: 100 Notes: Civ Wed 100

Novotel Sheffield Centre
★★★★ 73% HOTEL

50 Arundel Gate, S1 2PR - tel: 0114 278 1781
email: h1348@accor.com web: www.novotel.com
dir: Between Registry Office & Crucible/Lyceum Theatres, follow signs to Town Hall/ Theatres & Hallam University

In the heart of the city centre, this hotel has stylish public areas including a very modern restaurant, indoor swimming pool and a range of meeting rooms. Spacious bedrooms are suitable for family occupation, and the Novation rooms are ideal for business users.

Rooms: 144 (134 family) ☛ S £45–£153; D £55–£163 (incl. bkfst)*
Facilities: STV FTV WiFi ↕ Gym Steam room Xmas Conf: Class 180 Board 100 Thtr 220 Services: Lift Night porter Air con Parking: 60 Notes: Civ Wed 180

Best Western Plus Aston Hall Hotel
★★★ 84% ◉ HOTEL

Worksop Road, Aston, S26 2EE - tel: 0114 287 2309
email: reservations@astonhallhotel.co.uk web: www.astonhallhotel.co.uk
dir: M1 junct 31, follow A57 to Sheffield & follow signs to hotel

Originally built as a manor house and set in spacious grounds with open views across the countryside to the south of the city, this hotel is well located for the M1, Meadowhall, the city, or touring. Extensive conference and banqueting facilities along with picturesque grounds make it an ideal wedding venue. Bedrooms are comfortable and well equipped.

Rooms: 52 (6 annexe) (13 GF) ☛ S £65–£97.50; D £80–£112.50* Facilities: FTV WiFi ↕ Gym Xmas New Year Conf: Class 200 Board 60 Thtr 300 Del from £125 Services: Lift Night porter Parking: 90 Notes: LB Civ Wed 300

S

Best Western Plus Mosborough Hall Hotel

★★★ 82% HOTEL

High Street, Mosborough, S20 5EA - tel: 0114 248 4353
email: hotel@mosboroughhall.co.uk **web:** www.mosboroughhall.co.uk
dir: M1 junct 30, A6135 towards Sheffield. Follow Eckington/Mosborough signs 2m.
Sharp bend at top of hill, hotel on right

This 16th-century, Grade II listed manor house is set in gardens not far from the M1 and is convenient for the city centre. The bedrooms offer very high quality and good amenities; some are very spacious. There is a galleried lounge and conservatory bar, and freshly prepared dishes are served in the traditional style dining room.

Rooms: 44 (17 GF) ✦ **Facilities:** FTV WiFi ↳ Spa & beauty treatments Xmas
New Year **Conf:** Class 125 Board 70 Thtr 220 **Services:** Night porter **Parking:** 100
Notes: Civ Wed 250

Premier Inn Sheffield (Arena)

BUDGET HOTEL

Attercliffe Common Road, S9 2LU - tel: 0871 527 8964 (Calls cost 13p per minute plus
your phone company's access charge) **web:** www.premierinn.com
dir: M1 junct 34, follow signs to city centre. Hotel opposite Arena

High quality, budget accommodation ideal for both families and business travellers. Spacious, en suite bedrooms feature free WiFi and tea and coffee making facilities, and in most hotels, Freeview TV is also available. The adjacent family restaurant features a wide and varied menu.

Rooms: 95

Premier Inn Sheffield City Centre Angel St

BUDGET HOTEL

Angel Street, (Corner of Bank Street), S3 8LN - tel: 0871 527 8970 (Calls cost 13p per
minute plus your phone company's access charge) **web:** www.premierinn.com
dir: M1 junct 33, follow city centre, A630, A57 signs. At Park Square rdbt 4th exit (A61
Barnsley). Left at 4th lights into Snig Hill, right at lights into Bank St

Rooms: 160

Premier Inn Sheffield City Centre (St Mary's Gate)

BUDGET HOTEL

Young Street, St Marys Gate, S1 4LA - tel: 0871 527 8972 (Calls cost 13p per minute
plus your phone company's access charge) **web:** www.premierinn.com
dir: M1 junct 33, A630, A57 follow Sheffield City Centre signs. At Park Square rdbt 3rd exit
signed A61/Chesterfield. At Granville Square right onto A61 signed Ring Rd. Keep in left
lane. At rdbt 3rd exit signed A621. Left into Cumberland St. Left into South Lane. Right
into Young St

Rooms: 122

Premier Inn Sheffield (Meadowhall)

BUDGET HOTEL

Sheffield Road, Meadowhall, S9 2YL - tel: 0871 527 8966 (Calls cost 13p per minute
plus your phone company's access charge) **web:** www.premierinn.com
dir: On A6178 approx 6m from city centre

Rooms: 103

SHEPTON MALLET
Somerset

Map 4 ST64

Charlton House Spa Hotel

★★★★ 81% ◎◎ 🍽 HOTEL

Charlton Road, BA4 4PR - tel: 0344 248 3830
email: gm.charltonhousehotel@bannatyne.co.uk **web:** www.bannatyne.co.uk
dir: On A361 towards Frome, 1m from town centre

A peaceful location with grounds and relaxing spa facilities is just part of the charm of this interesting hotel. Individually designed bedrooms include larger suites and a luxurious lodge in the garden. Guests can relax in the 'shabby chic' lounges or bar area, or in the warmer months there's plenty of outdoor seating. Dinner in the stylish restaurant offers a selection of carefully prepared, high quality dishes. The spa offers a wide range of facilities including treatment rooms, hydrotherapy pool, crystal room, sauna and a fitness studio. The hotel is a popular wedding venue.

Rooms: 28 (6 annexe) (3 family) (12 GF) ✦ **D** £85–£400 (incl. bkfst)* **Facilities:** Spa
FTV WiFi 🕲 🌊 Gym Sauna Steam room Laconium Experience showers Xmas
New Year **Conf:** Class 50 Board 25 Thtr 100 Del from £170 **Services:** Night porter
Parking: 70 **Notes:** LB Civ Wed 120

SHERBORNE
Dorset

Map 4 ST61

Eastbury Hotel

★★★ 82% ◎◎ HOTEL

Long Street, DT9 3BY - tel: 01935 813131
email: enquiries@theeastburyhotel.co.uk **web:** www.theeastburyhotel.co.uk
dir: From A30 W'bound, left into North Rd, then St Swithin's, left at bottom,
hotel 800yds on right

Much of the building's original Georgian charm and elegance is maintained at this smart, comfortable hotel. Just five minutes' stroll from the abbey and close to the town centre, the Eastbury's friendly and attentive staff ensure a relaxed and enjoyable stay. Award-winning cuisine is served in the attractive dining room, overlooking the walled garden, with an alfresco bistro option also available.

Rooms: 22 (1 family) (3 GF) ✦ **S** £85; **D** £155 (incl. bkfst)* **Facilities:** FTV WiFi ↳
🌊 **Conf:** Class 40 Board 28 Thtr 80 Del £160 **Parking:** 30 **Notes:** LB Civ Wed 80

Best Western The Grange at Oborne

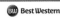

★★★ 79% HOTEL

Oborne, DT9 4LA - tel: 01935 813463
email: reception@thegrange.co.uk **web:** www.thegrangeatoborne.co.uk
dir: Exit A30, follow signs through village

Set in beautiful gardens in a quiet hamlet, this 200-year-old, family-run hotel has a wealth of charm and character. It offers friendly hospitality together with attentive service. Bedrooms are comfortable and tastefully appointed, public areas are elegantly furnished, and the popular restaurant offers a good selection of dishes.

Rooms: 18 (3 family) (2 GF) ✦ **S** £70–£140; **D** £70–£140 **Facilities:** STV WiFi ↳ Xmas
New Year **Conf:** Class 40 Board 30 Thtr 80 Del from £146.95 **Parking:** 45 **Notes:** Civ
Wed 120

S

SHERINGHAM
Norfolk

Map 13 TG14

HIGHLY RECOMMENDED

Dales Country House Hotel

★★★★ 83% @@ HOTEL

Lodge Hill, Upper Sheringham, NR26 8TJ - **tel:** 01263 824555
email: dales@mackenziehotels.com **web:** www.mackenziehotels.com
dir: *From Sheringham take B1157 to Upper Sheringham. Through village, hotel on left*

Dales Country House is a superb Grade II listed building situated in extensive landscaped grounds on the edge of Sheringham Park. The attractive public rooms are full of original character; they include a choice of lounges as well as an intimate restaurant and a cosy lounge bar. The spacious bedrooms are individually decorated with co-ordinated soft furnishings and many thoughtful touches.

Rooms: 21 (5 GF) **Facilities:** WiFi ⛳ ⛴ Giant garden chess & jenga Xmas New Year **Conf:** Class 20 Board 27 Thtr 40 **Services:** Lift Night porter **Parking:** 50 **Notes:** LB No children 14yrs

SHIFNAL
Shropshire

Map 10 SJ70

Park House Hotel

★★★★ 75% HOTEL

Park Street, TF11 9BA - **tel:** 01952 460128
email: reception@parkhousehotel.net **web:** www.parkhousehotel.net
dir: *M54 junct 4, A464 (Wolverhampton road) for approx 2m, under railway bridge, hotel 100yds on left*

Set in attractive grounds, Park House Hotel features two distinct architectural styles, having once been two separate houses. Located on the edge of the historic market town of Shifnal, it offers guests easy access to the motorway network; Shrewsbury, Ironbridge and Telford are also within easy reach. Butlers Bar and Restaurant is the setting for imaginative food. A range of meeting rooms, leisure facilities and ample parking are also provided, together with complimentary WiFi.

Rooms: 54 (16 annexe) (17 family) (8 GF) **S** fr £55; **D** fr £60 (incl. bkfst)* **Facilities:** STV FTV WiFi ⛳ ⓒ Gym Xmas New Year **Conf:** Class 80 Board 40 Thtr 160 Del from £128 **Services:** Lift Night porter **Parking:** 90 **Notes:** LB Civ Wed 160

SHREWSBURY
Shropshire

Map 15 SJ41

Albright Hussey Manor Hotel & Restaurant

★★★★ 77% @@ HOTEL

Ellesmere Road, Broad Oak, SY4 3AF - **tel:** 01939 290571
email: info@albrighthussey.co.uk **web:** www.albrighthussey.co.uk
dir: *2.5m N of Shrewsbury on A528, follow signs for Ellesmere*

The estate was mentioned in the Domesday Book, but the current manor house is Tudor, dating from around 1524, and is approached over a moat. This Grade II listed, partly black-and-white timbered building maintains an abundance of original features including huge open fireplaces, oak-panelling and beams. The bedrooms, including four-poster rooms, are situated in either the sumptuously appointed main house or in the more modern wing. There's an intimate, award-winning restaurant and a comfortable cocktail bar and lounge.

Rooms: 26 (4 family) (8 GF) **S** £65–£170; **D** £95–£205* **Facilities:** FTV WiFi ⛴ Xmas New Year **Conf:** Class 180 Board 80 Thtr 250 **Services:** Night porter **Parking:** 100 **Notes:** Civ Wed 180

Prince Rupert Hotel

★★★★ 76% HOTEL

Butcher Row, SY1 1UQ - **tel:** 01743 499955
email: reservations@princeruperthotel.co.uk **web:** www.princeruperthotel.co.uk
dir: *Follow town centre signs, over English Bridge & Wyle Cop Hill. Right into Fish St, hotel 200yds*

Parts of this popular town centre hotel date back to medieval times and many bedrooms have exposed beams and other original features. Luxury suites, family rooms and rooms with four-poster beds are all available. As an alternative to the main Royalist Restaurant, diners have a less formal option in Chambers, a popular brasserie. The Camellias Tea Rooms are adjacent, providing snacks and afternoon teas. The hotel's valet parking service is also commendable.

Rooms: 70 **S** £85–£195; **D** £135–£205 (incl. bkfst)* **Facilities:** FTV WiFi ⛴ Gym Weight training Sauna Snooker room Hair salon Xmas New Year **Conf:** Class 80 Board 40 Thtr 120 Del from £130 **Services:** Lift Night porter **Parking:** 70 **Notes:** LB

Mercure Shrewsbury Albrighton Hall Hotel & Spa

fOCUShotels
management limited

★★★★ 75% COUNTRY HOUSE HOTEL

Albrighton, SY4 3AG - **tel:** 01939 291000 & 291701
email: H6629@accor.com **web:** www.mercureshrewsbury.co.uk
dir: *From S: M6 junct 10a to M54 to end. From N: M6 junct 12 to M5 then M54. Follow signs Harlescott & Ellesmere to A528*

Dating back to 1630, this former ancestral home is set in 15 acres of attractive gardens. The bedrooms are generally spacious and the stable rooms are particularly popular. Elegant public rooms have rich oak panelling and there is a modern, well-equipped health and fitness centre.

Rooms: 87 (24 annexe) (7 family) (21 GF) **S** £89–£99; **D** £109–£169* **Facilities:** Spa STV WiFi ⛳ ⓒ ⛴ Gym Thermal suite Relaxation room Spray tan Exercise classes Sauna Steam room Ice room Xmas New Year **Conf:** Class 100 Board 80 Thtr 250 Del from £130 **Services:** Lift Night porter **Parking:** 200 **Notes:** LB Civ Wed 250

HIGHLY RECOMMENDED

Lion & Pheasant Hotel

★★★ 86% @@ TOWN HOUSE HOTEL

49-50 Wyle Cop, SY1 1XJ - **tel:** 01743 770345
email: info@lionandpheasant.co.uk **web:** www.lionandpheasant.co.uk
dir: *From S & E: pass abbey, cross river on English Bridge to Wyle Cop, hotel on left. From N & W: follow Town Centre signs on one-way system to Wyle Cop. Hotel at bottom of hill on right*

This 16th-century property stands on Wyle Cop, part of the historic centre of Shrewsbury. The interior decor is minimalist and uses natural materials such as limed oak, linens and silks. The bedrooms are of a high standard and include twin, double and family rooms. Award-winning food is offered in the first-floor restaurant and also in the ground-floor bar area.

Rooms: 22 (2 family) **S** £99; **D** £129–£225 (incl. bkfst)* **Facilities:** FTV WiFi ⛴ **Conf:** Class 30 Board 30 Thtr 30 Del from £160 **Parking:** 15 **Notes:** Closed 25-26 Dec

S

Abbots Mead Hotel

★★ 76% METRO HOTEL

9 St Julian's Friars, SY1 1XL - **tel:** 01743 235281
email: res@abbotsmeadhotel.co.uk **web:** www.abbotsmeadhotel.co.uk
dir: *From S into town, 2nd left after English Bridge*

This well maintained Georgian town house is located in a quiet cul-de-sac, near the English Bridge and close to both the River Severn and town centre with its many restaurants. Bedrooms are compact, neatly decorated and well equipped. Two lounges are available in addition to an attractive dining room, the setting for breakfasts, and dinner parties by prior arrangement.

Rooms: 16 (2 family) **S** £55–£65; **D** £78–£85 (incl. bkfst) **Facilities:** WiFi
Services: Night porter **Parking:** 10 **Notes:** Closed certain days at Xmas

Premier Inn Shrewsbury (Harmers Hill)

BUDGET HOTEL

Wem Road, Harmer Hill, SY4 3DS - **tel:** 0871 527 8974 (Calls cost 13p per minute plus your phone company's access charge)
web: www.premierinn.com
dir: *M54 junct 7, A5 signed Telford for approx 7m, at rdbt take A49, approx 3m. At next 2 rdbts 2nd exit, at next rdbt 4th exit signed Ellesmere & A528. In approx 3m hotel on left*

High quality, budget accommodation ideal for both families and business travellers. Spacious, en suite bedrooms feature free WiFi and tea and coffee making facilities, and in most hotels, Freeview TV is also available. The adjacent family restaurant features a wide and varied menu.

Rooms: 20

Premier Inn Shrewsbury Town Centre

BUDGET HOTEL

Smithfield Road, SY1 1QB - **tel:** 0871 527 9402 (Calls cost 13p per minute plus your phone company's access charge) **web:** www.premierinn.com
dir: *Phone for directions*

Rooms: 136

SIDCUP	Map 6 TQ47
Greater London	

Premier Inn London Sidcup Hotel

BUDGET HOTEL

101-108 Station Road, DA15 7BS - **tel:** 0871 527 9640
(Calls cost 13p per minute plus your phone company's access charge)
web: www.premierinn.com
dir: *From Sidcup station left into Station Rd, under rail bridge. Hotel on right at lights*

High quality, budget accommodation ideal for both families and business travellers. Spacious, en suite bedrooms feature free WiFi and tea and coffee making facilities, and in most hotels, Freeview TV is also available. The adjacent family restaurant features a wide and varied menu.

Rooms: 100

SIDMOUTH	Map 3 SY18
Devon	

HIGHLY RECOMMENDED

Hotel Riviera

★★★★ 83% ◉◉ ⌂ HOTEL

The Esplanade, EX10 8AY - **tel:** 01395 515201
email: enquiries@hotelriviera.co.uk **web:** www.hotelriviera.co.uk
dir: *M5 junct 30 & follow A3052*

Overlooking the sea and close to the town centre, the Riviera is a fine example of Regency architecture. The large number of guests that become regular visitors here are testament to the high standards of service and hospitality offered. The front-facing bedrooms benefit from wonderful sea views, and the daily-changing menu places an emphasis on fresh, local produce.

Rooms: 26 (6 family) ☎ **S** £112–£222; **D** £204–£422 (incl. bkfst & dinner)*
Facilities: FTV WiFi ⌂ ♫ Xmas New Year **Conf:** Class 60 Board 30 Thtr 85
Services: Lift Night porter **Parking:** 26 **Notes:** LB

See advert on following page

SIDMOUTH *continued*

The Belmont Hotel

★★★★ 81% HOTEL

The Esplanade, EX10 8RX - **tel:** 01395 512555
email: reservations@belmont-hotel.co.uk **web:** www.belmont-hotel.co.uk
dir: On seafront

Prominently positioned on the seafront just a few minutes' walk from the town centre, this traditional hotel has many returning guests. A choice of comfortable lounges provides ample space for relaxation, and the air-conditioned restaurant has a pianist playing most evenings. Bedrooms are attractively furnished and many have fine views over the esplanade. Leisure facilities are available at the adjacent sister hotel, The Victoria.

Rooms: 50 (1 family) (2 GF) ♦ **S** £155–£195; **D** £180–£275* **Facilities:** STV WiFi
♦ Putting green Leisure facilities available at sister hotel ♫ Xmas New Year
Conf: Thtr 50 **Services:** Lift Night porter **Parking:** 45 **Notes:** LB Civ Wed 110

See advert on following page

Sidmouth Harbour Hotel

★★★ 85% HOTEL

Manor Road, EX10 8RU - **tel:** 01395 513252
email: sidmouth@harbourhotels.co.uk **web:** www.sidmouth-harbour-hotel.co.uk
dir: Exit A3052 to Sidmouth then to seafront & esplanade, turn right, hotel directly ahead

This charming hotel is ideally located within walking distance of Sidmouth's elegant promenade and beaches. The spacious lounges and the cocktail bar open onto a terrace which leads to the pool and croquet lawn. Bedrooms, several with balconies and glorious sea views, are spacious and comfortable, while the restaurant offers a choice of well-prepared dishes.

Rooms: 57 (1 family) (10 GF) ♦ **S** £85–£140; **D** £95–£300 (incl. bkfst)*
Facilities: Spa FTV WiFi ♦ ♦ Gym Xmas New Year **Conf:** Class 65 Board 50
Thtr 150 Del from £140 **Services:** Lift Night porter **Parking:** 40 **Notes:** Civ Wed 100

Bedford Hotel

★★★ 81% HOTEL

Esplanade, EX10 8NR - **tel:** 01395 513047
email: info@bedfordhotelsidmouth.co.uk **web:** www.bedfordhotelsidmouth.co.uk
dir: M5 junct 30, A3052 & to Sidmouth. Hotel at centre of Esplanade

Situated on the seafront, this long established, family-run hotel provides a warm welcome and relaxing atmosphere. Bedrooms are well appointed and many have the added bonus of wonderful sea views. Public areas combine character and comfort with a choice of lounges in which to relax. In addition to the hotel dining room, Pyne's bar and restaurant offers an interesting range of dishes in a convivial environment.

Rooms: 40 (3 family) (1 GF) ♦ **Facilities:** FTV WiFi ♦ Xmas New Year **Services:** Lift
Parking: 6

Royal Glen Hotel

★★★ 79% HOTEL

Glen Road, EX10 8RW - **tel:** 01395 513221
email: info@royalglenhotel.co.uk **web:** www.royalglenhotel.co.uk
dir: A303 to Honiton, A375 to Sidford, follow seafront signs, right onto esplanade, right at end into Glen Rd

This historic 17th-century, Grade I listed hotel has been owned by the same family for several generations. The comfortable bedrooms are furnished in period style. Guests may use the well-maintained gardens and a heated indoor pool, and can enjoy well-prepared food in the elegant dining room.

Rooms: 32 (3 family) (3 GF) ♦ **S** £51–£84; **D** £102–£188 (incl. bkfst)*
Facilities: FTV WiFi ♦ Gym Massage & aromatherapy room **Services:** Lift
Parking: 22 **Notes:** LB Closed Dec-21 Feb

The Royal York & Faulkner Hotel

★★★ 78% HOTEL

The Esplanade, EX10 8AZ - **tel:** 01395 513043 & 0800 220714
email: stay@royalyorkhotel.co.uk **web:** www.royalyorkhotel.co.uk
dir: M5 junct 30 take A3052, 10m to Sidmouth, hotel in centre of Esplanade

This seafront hotel, owned and run by the same family for over 60 years, maintains its Regency charm and grandeur. The attractive bedrooms vary in size, and many have balconies and sea views. Public rooms are spacious, and traditional dining is offered, alongside Blinis Café-Bar, which is more contemporary in style and offers coffees, lunch and afternoon tea. The spa facilities include a hydrotherapy pool, steam room, sauna and a variety of treatments.

Rooms: 72 (2 annexe) (8 family) (5 GF) ♦ **S** £61–£106; **D** £122–£229 (incl. bkfst & dinner)* **Facilities:** Spa FTV WiFi ♦ Hydrotherapy pool Steam room Sauna Complimentary use of nearby indoor pool ♫ Xmas New Year **Services:** Lift
Parking: 20 **Notes:** LB Closed Jan

Mount Pleasant Hotel

★★ 84% HOTEL

Salcombe Road, EX10 8JA - **tel:** 01395 514694
email: philip_gleave@btconnect.com **web:** www.mountpleasant-hotel.co.uk
dir: Exit A3052 at Sidford x-rds, in 1.25m turn left into Salcombe Rd, opposite Radway Cinema. Hotel on right after bridge

Quietly located within almost an acre of gardens, this modernised Georgian hotel is minutes from the town centre and seafront. Bedrooms and public areas provide good levels of comfort and high quality furnishings. Guests return on a regular basis, especially to experience the friendly, relaxed atmosphere. The light and airy restaurant overlooks the pleasant garden and offers a daily-changing menu of traditional, yet imaginative home-cooked dishes.

Rooms: 17 (1 family) (3 GF) **S** £70.50–£87; **D** £121–£174 (incl. bkfst & dinner)*
Facilities: Putting green **Parking:** 20 **Notes:** Closed Dec-Feb No children 8yrs

S

SILVERSTONE
Northamptonshire — Map 11 SP64

Premier Inn Silverstone

BUDGET HOTEL

Brackley Hatch, Syresham, NN13 5TX - **tel:** 0871 527 8976 (Calls cost 13p per minute plus your phone company's access charge) **web:** www.premierinn.com
dir: *On A43 near Silverstone*

High quality, budget accommodation ideal for both families and business travellers. Spacious, en suite bedrooms feature free WiFi and tea and coffee making facilities, and in most hotels, Freeview TV is also available. The adjacent family restaurant features a wide and varied menu.

Rooms: 79

SITTINGBOURNE
Kent — Map 7 TQ96

Premier Inn Sittingbourne Kent

BUDGET HOTEL

Bobbing Corner, Sheppy Way, ME9 8RZ - **tel:** 0871 527 8978 (Calls cost 13p per minute plus your phone company's access charge) **web:** www.premierinn.com
dir: *M2 junct 5, A249 towards Sheerness, approx 2m. Take 1st slip road after A2 underpass. At rdbt take 1st exit, hotel on left*

High quality, budget accommodation ideal for both families and business travellers. Spacious, en suite bedrooms feature free WiFi and tea and coffee making facilities, and in most hotels, Freeview TV is also available. The adjacent family restaurant features a wide and varied menu.

Rooms: 62

SKEGNESS
Lincolnshire — Map 17 TF56

Best Western The Vine Hotel

★★★ 79% HOTEL

Vine Road, Seacroft, PE25 3DB - **tel:** 01754 763018
email: info@thevinehotel.com **web:** www.bw-vinehotel.co.uk
dir: *A52 to Skegness, S towards Gibraltar Point, right into Drummond Rd, 0.5m, right into Vine Rd*

With its long history this traditional hotel is something of a local landmark. The smartly decorated bedrooms are well equipped and comfortably appointed. Public areas include two character bars that serve excellent local beers. Freshly prepared dishes are offered in the bar and the restaurant; service is both friendly and helpful.

Rooms: 25 (3 family) **Facilities:** FTV WiFi Xmas New Year **Conf:** Class 25 Board 30 Thtr 100 **Services:** Night porter **Parking:** 50 **Notes:** Civ Wed 100

SKIPTON
North Yorkshire — Map 18 SD95

The Coniston Hotel Country Estate and Spa
★★★★ 78% HOTEL

Coniston Cold, BD23 4EA - **tel:** 01756 748080
email: info@theconistonhotel.com **web:** www.theconistonhotel.com
dir: *On A65, 7m NW of Skipton, 8m from Settle*

This privately owned hotel set in 1,400 acres of prime country estate is a haven for both leisure and corporate guests. All bedrooms and bathrooms are appointed to a very high standard; the bedroom wing offers large rooms with balconies. The reception, bar and restaurant have style and elegance, and the stunning spa adds to the impressive list of activities for guests.

Rooms: 71 (13 family) (35 GF) S £99–£218.50; D £113.40–£233* **Facilities:** Spa STV FTV WiFi Fishing Gym Clay pigeon shooting Falconry 4 x 4 off-road experience Fly fishing Archery Xmas New Year **Conf:** Class 80 Board 50 Thtr 200 Del from £129 **Services:** Lift Night porter Air con **Parking:** 170 **Notes:** LB Civ Wed 120

Premier Inn Skipton North (Gargrave)

BUDGET HOTEL

Hellifield Road, Gargrave, BD23 3NB - **tel:** 0871 527 8980
(Calls cost 13p per minute plus your phone company's access charge)
web: www.premierinn.com
dir: *NW of Skipton at rdbt junct of A59 & A65, take A65 signed Kendal, Settle & Gargrave. 3.5m. Through Gargrave. Hotel on left*

High quality, budget accommodation ideal for both families and business travellers. Spacious, en suite bedrooms feature free WiFi and tea and coffee making facilities, and in most hotels, Freeview TV is also available. The adjacent family restaurant features a wide and varied menu.

Rooms: 464

S

SLOUGH
Berkshire   Map 6 SU97

Premier Inn Slough

BUDGET HOTEL

76 Uxbridge Road, SL1 1SU - tel: 0871 527 8982 (Calls cost 13p per minute plus your phone company's access charge)
web: www.premierinn.com
dir: *2m from M4 junct 5, 3m from junct 6. Just off A4*

High quality, budget accommodation ideal for both families and business travellers. Spacious, en suite bedrooms feature free WiFi and tea and coffee making facilities, and in most hotels, Freeview TV is also available. The adjacent family restaurant features a wide and varied menu.

Rooms: 129

Premier Inn Slough Central South (Windsor Road)

BUDGET HOTEL

Windsor Road, SL1 2EL - tel: 0871 527 9656
(Calls cost 13p per minute plus your phone company's access charge)
web: www.premierinn.com
dir: *Please phone for directions*

Rooms: 131

SOLIHULL
West Midlands   Map 10 SP17

See also **Dorridge**

The St Johns Hotel

EST. 1898
PRINCIPAL
HOTEL COMPANY LTD

★★★★ 73% HOTEL

651 Warwick Road, B91 1AT - tel: 0121 711 3000
email: StJohnsReservations@stjohnssolihull.co.uk
web: www.stjohnssolihull.co.uk/partner/st-johns
dir: *M42 junct 5, A41 (Solihull Bypass) signed Solihull. At lights left into Load Ln (signed Solihull Town Centre). At next rdbt 3rd exit onto B425 (Warwick Rd). Hotel on right*

With its town centre location, this modern hotel is conveniently situated for the NEC, Birmingham and many local attractions. Bedrooms are air conditioned, attractively decorated and equipped with a comprehensive range of extras. The hotel provides extensive conference facilities, an indoor leisure facility and extensive parking.

Rooms: 180 (1 family) (9 GF) ✿ **Facilities:** STV FTV WiFi HL 🕓 Gym Sauna Steam room Nail treatment room Massage parlour Xmas New Year **Conf:** Class 350 Board 40 Thtr 700 **Services:** Lift Night porter Air con **Parking:** 300 **Notes:** Civ Wed 350

The Regency Hotel

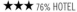

corus
hotels

★★★ 76% HOTEL

Stratford Road, Shirley, B90 4EB - tel: 0121 745 6119
email: solihull@corushotels.com **web:** www.corushotels.com/solihull
dir: *M42 junct 4 onto A34 for Shirley, cross 1st 3 rdbts, then double back along dual carriageway, hotel on left*

This much extended property is ideally located for access to the motorway network and Solihull's Touchwood centre. Rooms vary in style and size across the hotel;

each is simply furnished and offers a good standard of comfort. The Circle health and fitness club is well equipped and includes an indoor pool. Ample free parking and WiFi available.

Rooms: 111 (7 family) (13 GF) **S** £49–£149; **D** £59–£189* **Facilities:** FTV WiFi ⚲ 🕓 supervised Gym Steam room Sauna Xmas New Year **Conf:** Class 80 Board 60 Thtr 180 Del from £130 **Services:** Lift Night porter **Parking:** 240 **Notes:** LB Civ Wed 100

Premier Inn Solihull (Hockley Heath, M42)

BUDGET HOTEL

Stratford Road, Hockley Heath, B94 6NX - tel: 0871 527 8984
(Calls cost 13p per minute plus your phone company's access charge)
web: www.premierinn.com
dir: *On A3400, 2m S of M42 junct 4*

High quality, budget accommodation ideal for both families and business travellers. Spacious, en suite bedrooms feature free WiFi and tea and coffee making facilities, and in most hotels, Freeview TV is also available. The adjacent family restaurant features a wide and varied menu.

Rooms: 78

Premier Inn Solihull (Shirley)

BUDGET HOTEL

Stratford Road, Shirley, B90 3AG - tel: 0871 527 8988
(Calls cost 13p per minute plus your phone company's access charge)
web: www.premierinn.com
dir: *M42 junct 4 follow signs for Birmingham. Hotel in Shirley town centre on A34*

Rooms: 43

Premier Inn Solihull South (M42)

BUDGET HOTEL

Stratford Road, Shirley, B90 4EP - tel: 0871 527 8986
(Calls cost 13p per minute plus your phone company's access charge)
web: www.premierinn.com
dir: *M42 junct 4, A34 N. Hotel in 1m*

Rooms: 69

Premier Inn Solihull Town Centre

BUDGET HOTEL

Station Road, B91 3RX - tel: 0871 527 9366
(Calls cost 13p per minute plus your phone company's access charge)
web: www.premierinn.com
dir: *M42 junct 5. At rdbt, take 3rd exit onto A41. At lights, turn left onto Lode Lane. At rdbt, take 2nd exit & continue down Lode Lane. At rdbt take 1st exit onto Station Road*

Rooms: 115

SOUTHAMPTON
Hampshire
Map 5 SU41

See also **Botley**

Novotel Southampton

★★★★ 76% HOTEL

1 West Quay Road, SO15 1RA - tel: 023 8033 0550
email: H1073@accor.com **web:** www.novotel.com
dir: *M27 junct 3, follow city centre/A33 signs. In 1m take right lane for West Quay & Dock Gates 4-10. Hotel entrance on left. Turn at lights by McDonalds, left at rdbt, hotel straight ahead*

Novotel Southampton is a modern, purpose-built hotel situated close to the city centre, railway station, ferry terminal and major road networks. The brightly decorated bedrooms are ideal for families and business guests; four rooms have facilities for the less mobile. The open-plan public areas include the Garden Brasserie, a bar and a leisure complex.

Rooms: 121 (50 family) ☎ **S** £75–£250; **D** £85–£260* **Facilities:** STV FTV WiFi ↘ ☜ Gym Dry sauna **Conf:** Class 250 Board 150 Thtr 450 Del from £140 **Services:** Lift Night porter **Parking:** 300 **Notes:** LB Civ Wed 300

Mercure Southampton Centre Dolphin Hotel

★★★★ 70% HOTEL

34-35 High Street, SO14 2HN - tel: 023 8038 6460
email: H7876@accor.com **web:** www.mercure.com
dir: *From A33 follow signs for Docks, Old Town & Isle of Wight ferry. At ferry terminal right into High Street, hotel 400yds on left*

Originally a coaching inn, this hotel enjoys a central location set almost in the heart of the town, yet close to the ferry terminals. The bedrooms are appointed to a high standard, and public areas include a traditional bar, popular restaurant and two meeting rooms. Parking at the rear of the hotel is an added bonus.

Rooms: 99 (9 annexe) (6 family) (27 GF) ☎ **D** fr £49* **Facilities:** FTV WiFi Xmas New Year **Conf:** Class 50 Board 40 Thtr 120 **Services:** Lift Night porter **Parking:** 80 **Notes:** LB Civ Wed 120

Best Western Chilworth Manor

★★★ 81% ◉ HOTEL

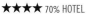

Chilworth, SO16 7PT - tel: 023 8076 7333
email: sales@chilworth-manor.co.uk **web:** www.bw-chilworthmanor.co.uk
dir: *1m from M3/M27 junct on A27 Romsey Rd N from Southampton. Pass Chilworth Arms on left, in 200mtrs turn left at Southampton Science Park sign. Hotel immediately right*

Set in 12 acres of delightful grounds, this attractive Edwardian manor house is conveniently located for Southampton and also the New Forest National Park. Bedrooms are located in both the main house and an adjoining wing. The hotel is particularly popular as both a conference and a wedding venue.

Rooms: 97 (4 family) (23 GF) ☎ **D** fr £85 (incl. bkfst)* **Facilities:** Spa FTV WiFi ↘ ☜ Gym Trail walking Giant chess Conservation area Xmas New Year **Conf:** Class 60 Board 40 Thtr 150 **Services:** Lift Night porter **Parking:** 200 **Notes:** LB Civ Wed 105

The Elizabeth House Hotel

★★ 82% HOTEL

42-44 The Avenue, SO17 1XP - tel: 023 8022 4327
email: mail@elizabethhousehotel.com **web:** www.elizabethhousehotel.com
dir: *On A33, hotel on left after Southampton Common, before main lights*

This hotel is conveniently situated close to the city centre, so provides an ideal base for both business and leisure guests. The bedrooms are well equipped and are attractively furnished with comfort in mind. There is a cosy and atmospheric bistro in the cellar where evening meals are served, and an attractive and versatile function room is also available. Complimentary parking is provided for guests.

Rooms: 27 (7 annexe) (9 family) (8 GF) ☎ **S** £75–£88.50; **D** £85–£98.50 (incl. bkfst)* **Facilities:** FTV WiFi ↘ **Conf:** Class 24 Board 24 Thtr 40 **Parking:** 31

Premier Inn Southampton Airport

BUDGET HOTEL

Mitchell Way, SO18 2XU - tel: 0871 527 8998 (Calls cost 13p per minute plus your phone company's access charge)
web: www.premierinn.com
dir: *M27 junct 5, A335 towards Eastleigh. Right at rdbt into Wide Lane. 1st exit at next rdbt into Mitchell Way*

High quality, budget accommodation ideal for both families and business travellers. Spacious, en suite bedrooms feature free WiFi and tea and coffee making facilities, and in most hotels, Freeview TV is also available. The adjacent family restaurant features a wide and varied menu.

Rooms: 121

Premier Inn Southampton City Centre

BUDGET HOTEL

6 Dials, New Road, SO14 0YN - tel: 0871 527 9266
(Calls cost 13p per minute plus your phone company's access charge)
web: www.premierinn.com
dir: *M27 junct 5, A335 signed City Centre. At Charlotte Place rdbt take 3rd exit into East Park Terrace, 1st left into New Rd. Hotel on right*

Rooms: 172

Premier Inn Southampton North

BUDGET HOTEL

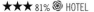

Romsey Road, Nursling, SO16 0XJ - tel: 0871 527 9002
(Calls cost 13p per minute plus your phone company's access charge)
web: www.premierinn.com
dir: *M27 junct 3, M271 towards Romsey. At next rdbt take 3rd exit towards Southampton (A3057). Hotel 1.5m on right*

Rooms: 80

S

SOUTHAMPTON *continued*

Premier Inn Southampton West Quay

BUDGET HOTEL

Harbour Parade, SO15 1ST - tel: 0871 527 9298 (Calls cost 13p per minute plus your phone company's access charge)
web: www.premierinn.com
dir: *M27 junct 3, follow M271(S)/Southampton/The Docks signs, onto M271, at Redbridge rdbt onto A35 follow Southampton/The Docks/A3024 signs. Merge onto A35 (Redbridge Rd), continue onto Millbrook Flyover/A3024, right at West Quay Rd/A3057, left after Ikea into Harbour Parade*

Rooms: 155

SOUTH CAVE	Map 17 SE93
East Riding of Yorkshire	

Cave Castle Hotel & Country Club

★★★ 81% HOTEL

Church Hill, HU15 2EU - tel: 01430 422245
email: info@cavecastlehotel.com **web:** www.cavecastlehotel.com
dir: *In village, opposite school*

This beautiful Victorian manor retains original turrets, stone features and much charm, together with modern comforts and style. It stands in 150 acres of meadow and parkland that provide a peaceful setting. Bedrooms are a careful mix of traditional and contemporary styles. Public areas include a well-equipped leisure complex and pool.

Rooms: 70 (5 family) (14 GF) 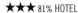 **Facilities:** Spa FTV WiFi ♨ ☺ supervised ⚓ 18 Putting green Fishing Gym New Year **Conf:** Class 150 Board 100 Thtr 250 **Services:** Lift Night porter **Parking:** 100 **Notes:** Civ Wed 150

SOUTH CERNEY	Map 5 SU09
Gloucestershire	

De Vere Cotswold Water Park

★★★★ 80% HOTEL

PRINCIPAL
HOTEL COMPANY LTD
EST. 1898

Lake 6 Spine Road East, GL7 5FP - tel: 0800 374692
email: WaterParkReservations@devere.com
web: www.phcompany.com/de-vere/cotswold-water-park-hotel
dir: *Off A419, 3m from Cirencester. NB for Sav Nav use GL7 5TL*

This impressive hotel has well-appointed bedrooms and suites, conference facilities for up to 800 delegates, a spa with an 11-metre pool, a gym, a hydro pool, and treatment rooms. An excellent range of dining options is available, and a large car park is provided.

Rooms: 328 (58 family) (126 GF) **Facilities:** Spa FTV WiFi ♨ ☺ Fishing Gym Beauty treatment rooms & therapies Steam room Sauna Xmas New Year **Conf:** Class 350 Board 68 Thtr 500 **Services:** Lift Night porter **Parking:** 500 **Notes:** Civ Wed 370

SOUTHEND-ON-SEA	Map 7 TQ88
Essex	

The Roslin Beach Hotel

★★★★ 82% ◉ HOTEL

Thorpe Esplanade, Thorpe Bay, SS1 3BG - tel: 01702 586375
email: info@roslinhotel.com **web:** www.roslinhotel.com
dir: *A127, follow Southend-on-sea signs. Hotel between Walton Rd & Clieveden Rd on seafront*

This friendly hotel is situated at the quiet end of the esplanade, overlooking the beach and sea. The spacious bedrooms are pleasantly decorated and thoughtfully equipped; some rooms have superb sea views. Public rooms include a large lounge bar, an AA Rosette restaurant and a smart conservatory which overlooks the sea.

Rooms: 62 (5 family) (11 GF) **S** £68–£88; **D** £120–£245 (incl. bkfst)* **Facilities:** Spa FTV WiFi Gym Manicure/pedicure bar Xmas New Year **Conf:** Class 65 Board 45 Thtr 90 **Services:** Night porter **Parking:** 48 **Notes:** LB Civ Wed 120

Holiday Inn Southend

★★★★ 75% ◉ HOTEL

Holiday Inn

77 Eastwoodbury Crescent, SS2 6XG - tel: 01702 543001
email: reservations@hisouthend.com **web:** www.hisouthend.com
dir: *M25 junct 29, A127 follow signs to London Southend Airport. Hotel 2mins away*

Built in 2012, Holiday Inn Southend offers a range of modern, well-appointed, stylish bedrooms. The public areas look very smart and have an open-plan contemporary image, and lounges are fitted out with designer furniture and seating. The award-winning 1935 Restaurant is situated on the fifth floor and overlooks the main runway of Southend airport. There are a range of conference facilities and business suites available along with secure parking for guests.

Rooms: 129 (17 family) **S** £69–£129; **D** £79–£149* **Facilities:** STV FTV WiFi HL Gym Xmas New Year **Conf:** Class 50 Board 40 Thtr 140 Del from £109 **Services:** Lift Night porter Air con **Parking:** 250 **Notes:** LB Civ Wed 140

Premier Inn Southend Airport

BUDGET HOTEL

Thanet Grange, SS2 6GB - tel: 0871 527 9008
(Calls cost 13p per minute plus your phone company's access charge)
web: www.premierinn.com
dir: *At A127 & B1013 junct*

High quality, budget accommodation ideal for both families and business travellers. Spacious, en suite bedrooms feature free WiFi and tea and coffee making facilities, and in most hotels, Freeview TV is also available. The adjacent family restaurant features a wide and varied menu.

Rooms: 80

Premier Inn Southend on Sea Eastern Esplanade

BUDGET HOTEL

Eastern Esplanade, SS99 1YY - tel: 0871 527 9504 (Calls cost 13p per minute plus your phone company's access charge)
web: www.premierinn.com
dir: *A127 to Southend rail station. At lights, left onto A13 (signed Shoeburyness). At rdbt 3rd exit (signed Seafront). At end of road, left onto Eastern Esplanade (B1016). Hotel on left*

Rooms: 81

S

Premier Inn Southend-on-Sea (Thorpe Bay)

BUDGET HOTEL

213 Eastern Esplanade, SS1 3AD - **tel:** 0871 527 9006 (Calls cost 13p per minute plus your phone company's access charge)
web: www.premierinn.com
dir: *Follow signs for A1159 (A13) Shoebury onto dual carriageway. At rdbt, follow signs for Thorpe Bay & seafront, at seafront turn right. Hotel on right*
Rooms: 43

SOUTH MIMMS SERVICE AREA (M25)	Map 6 TL20
Hertfordshire	

Premier Inn South Mimms/Potters Bar

BUDGET HOTEL

Swanland Road, EN6 3NH - **tel:** 0871 527 8990
(Calls cost 13p per minute plus your phone company's access charge)
web: www.premierinn.com
dir: *M25 junct 23 & A1 take services exit off main rdbt then 1st left & follow hotel signs*

High quality, budget accommodation ideal for both families and business travellers. Spacious, en suite bedrooms feature free WiFi and tea and coffee making facilities, and in most hotels, Freeview TV is also available. The adjacent family restaurant features a wide and varied menu.
Rooms: 142

Days Inn South Mimms - M25

WELCOMEBREAK

AA Advertised

Bignells Corner, Potters Bar, EN6 3QQ - **tel:** 01707 665440
email: south.mimms.hotel@welcomebreak.co.uk **web:** www.welcomebreak.co.uk
dir: *M25 junct 23, at rdbt follow signs*

This modern building offers accommodation in smart, spacious and well-equipped bedrooms, suitable for families and business travellers, and all with en suite bathrooms. Continental breakfast is available and other refreshments may be taken at the nearby family restaurant.
Rooms: 75 (37 family) (23 GF) (10 smoking) **Facilities:** FTV WiFi ⇗ **Services:** Lift Night porter **Parking:** 100

SOUTH NORMANTON	Map 16 SK45
Derbyshire	

The Derbyshire Hotel

PRINCIPAL
HOTEL COMPANY LTD
EST. 1898

★★★★ 75% HOTEL

Carter Lane East, DE55 2EH - **tel:** 01773 812000
email: DerbyshireReservations@thederbyshire-hotel.com
web: www.thederbyshire-hotel.com/partner/derbyshire-hotel
dir: *M1 junct 28, E on A38 to Mansfield*

Conveniently located by the motorway, this hotel offers comfortable accommodation and a relaxed informal atmosphere through the lounge bar and restaurant. The conference and meeting rooms are appointed to a smart modern standard; delegates also have use of on-site sauna, jacuzzi and steam room in the spa.
Rooms: 157 (10 family) (61 GF) **Facilities:** Spa FTV WiFi ⇗ Gym Steam room Sauna New Year **Conf:** Class 120 Board 25 Thtr 250 **Services:** Night porter **Parking:** 220 **Notes:** Civ Wed 150

Premier Inn Mansfield

BUDGET HOTEL

Carter Lane East, DE55 2EH - **tel:** 0871 527 8758 (Calls cost 13p per minute plus your phone company's access charge) **web:** www.premierinn.com
dir: *M1 junct 28, A38 signed Mansfield. Entrance 200yds on left*

High quality, budget accommodation ideal for both families and business travellers. Spacious, en suite bedrooms feature free WiFi and tea and coffee making facilities, and in most hotels, Freeview TV is also available. The adjacent family restaurant features a wide and varied menu.
Rooms: 120

SOUTHPORT	Map 15 SD31
Merseyside	

Best Western Royal Clifton Hotel & Spa

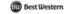

★★★ 73% HOTEL

Promenade, PR8 1RB - **tel:** 01704 533771
email: sales@royalclifton.co.uk **web:** www.royalclifton.co.uk
dir: *Adjacent to Marine Lake*

This grand, traditional hotel benefits from a prime location on the promenade. Bedrooms range in size and style, but all are comfortable and thoughtfully equipped. Public areas include a choice of dining venues; the lively Conservatory Bistro or the Pavilion Restaurant. A modern, well-equipped leisure club is also available. Extensive conference and banqueting facilities make this hotel a popular function venue.
Rooms: 120 (23 family) (6 GF) **Facilities:** Spa FTV WiFi ⇗ HL Gym Hair & beauty Sauna Steam room Aromatherapy ♫ Xmas New Year **Conf:** Class 100 Board 65 Thtr 250 **Services:** Lift Night porter **Parking:** 60 **Notes:** Civ Wed 150

Premier Inn Southport Central

BUDGET HOTEL

Marine Drive, PR8 1RY - **tel:** 0871 527 9012 (Calls cost 13p per minute plus your phone company's access charge)
web: www.premierinn.com
dir: *From Southport follow Promenade & Marine Drive signs. Hotel at junct of Marine Parade & Marine Drive*

High quality, budget accommodation ideal for both families and business travellers. Spacious, en suite bedrooms feature free WiFi and tea and coffee making facilities, and in most hotels, Freeview TV is also available. The adjacent family restaurant features a wide and varied menu.
Rooms: 94

SOUTHSEA

See **Portsmouth & Southsea**

S

SOUTH SHIELDS
Tyne & Wear   Map 21 NZ36

Best Western The Sea Hotel
 Best Western.

★★★ 77% HOTEL

Sea Road, NE33 2LD - tel: 0191 427 0999
email: info@seahotel.co.uk web: www.seahotel.co.uk
dir: A1(M), past Washington Services onto A194. Then A183 through town centre along Ocean Rd. Hotel on seafront

Dating from the 1930s, this long-established business hotel overlooks the boating lake and the Tyne estuary. Bedrooms are generally spacious and well equipped and include five annexe rooms with wheelchair access. A range of generously portioned meals is served in both the bar and restaurant.

Rooms: 37 (5 annexe) (5 family) (5 GF) ↑ S £74.50; D £84.50 (incl. bkfst)*
Facilities: FTV WiFi ⇗ New Year Conf: Class 100 Board 50 Thtr 200 Services: Night porter Parking: 70 Notes: LB RS 26 Dec Restaurant & bars closed

Premier Inn South Shields (Port of Tyne)
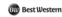

BUDGET HOTEL

Hobson Avenue, Newcastle Road, NE34 9PQ - tel: 0871 527 8992
(Calls cost 13p per minute plus your phone company's access charge)
web: www.premierinn.com
dir: A1(M) onto A194(M). 2nd exit at rdbt into Leam Lane (A194). At next rdbt 2nd exit, next rdbt 3rd exit, next rdbt 2nd exit (A194), next rdbt 2nd exit. Hotel on left adjacent to Taybarns

High quality, budget accommodation ideal for both families and business travellers. Spacious, en suite bedrooms feature free WiFi and tea and coffee making facilities, and in most hotels, Freeview TV is also available. The adjacent family restaurant features a wide and varied menu.

Rooms: 66

SPALDING
Lincolnshire   Map 12 TF22

Woodlands Hotel
★★★ 78% SMALL HOTEL

80 Pinchbeck Road, PE11 1QF - tel: 01775 769933
email: reservations@woodlandshotelspalding.com
web: www.woodlandshotelspalding.com
dir: 10mins walk from city centre

A delightful Victorian house ideally situated just a short walk from the town centre. The public areas have many original features; they include the Oakleaf dining room, the Silver Birch meeting room and the Willows bar. The smartly decorated bedrooms have lovely co-ordinated soft furnishings and many thoughtful touches.

Rooms: 17 (5 GF) ↑ S £65–£67.50; D £82.50–£92.50 (incl. bkfst) Facilities: FTV WiFi ⇗ HL Conf: Class 30 Board 30 Thtr 60 Parking: 30 Notes: Civ Wed 65

SPENNYMOOR
County Durham   Map 19 NZ23

Best Western Whitworth Hall Hotel
Best Western.

★★★ 81% HOTEL

Whitworth Hall Country Park, DL16 7QX - tel: 01388 811772
email: enquiries@whitworthhall.co.uk web: www.whitworthhall.co.uk
dir: A688 to Spennymoor, then Bishop Auckland. At rdbt right to Middlestone Moor. Left at lights, hotel on right

This hotel, peacefully situated in its own grounds in the centre of the deer park, offers comfortable accommodation. Spacious bedrooms, some with excellent

views, have stylish and elegant decor. Public areas include a choice of restaurants and bars, a bright conservatory and well-equipped function and conference rooms.

Rooms: 29 (2 family) (17 GF) ↑ S £50–£95; D £55–£130 (incl. bkfst)*
Facilities: FTV WiFi ⇗ Fishing Conf: Class 40 Board 30 Thtr 100 Del from £95
Services: Night porter Parking: 100 Notes: LB Civ Wed 100

STAFFORD
Staffordshire   Map 10 SJ92

The Moat House
★★★★ 80% ◉◉ HOTEL

Lower Penkridge Road, Acton Trussell, ST17 0RJ - tel: 01785 712217
email: info@moathouse.co.uk web: www.moathouse.co.uk
dir: M6 junct 13 onto A449 through Acton Trussell. Hotel on right on exiting village

This 17th-century timbered building, with an idyllic canal-side setting, has been skilfully extended. Bedrooms are stylishly furnished, well equipped and comfortable. The bar offers a range of snacks and the restaurant boasts a popular fine dining option where the head chef displays his skills using top quality produce.

Rooms: 41 (4 family) (15 GF) ↑ S £80–£135; D £100–£165 (incl. bkfst)*
Facilities: FTV WiFi New Year Conf: Class 60 Board 50 Thtr 200 Services: Lift Night porter Parking: 200 Notes: 25 Dec Civ Wed 150

Best Western Tillington Hall Hotel
 Best Western.

★★★ 73% HOTEL

Eccleshall Road, ST16 1JJ - tel: 01785 253531
email: reservations@tillingtonhall.co.uk web: www.tillingtonhall.co.uk
dir: M6 junct 14, A5013 towards Stafford. Hotel 0.5m on left

Located close to the M6, this modern hotel is ideal for both business and leisure guests. There is a spacious restaurant, relaxing coffee lounge and smart bar, alongside a range of function rooms for meetings and events, including the Garden Suite. Complimentary WiFi access is available.

Rooms: 91 (4 family) (25 GF) ↑ Facilities: STV FTV WiFi HL Xmas New Year
Conf: Class 150 Board 75 Thtr 300 Services: Lift Night porter Parking: 200
Notes: LB Civ Wed 300

Premier Inn Stafford North (Hurricane)

BUDGET HOTEL

1 Hurrican Close, ST16 1GZ - tel: 0871 527 9030 (Calls cost 13p per minute plus your phone company's access charge)
web: www.premierinn.com
dir: M6 junct 14, A34 towards Stafford. Hotel approx 2m NW of town centre

High quality, budget accommodation ideal for both families and business travellers. Spacious, en suite bedrooms feature free WiFi and tea and coffee making facilities, and in most hotels, Freeview TV is also available. The adjacent family restaurant features a wide and varied menu.

Rooms: 102

Premier Inn Stafford North (Spitfire)

BUDGET HOTEL

1 Spitfire Close, ST16 1GX - tel: 0871 527 9032 (Calls cost 13p per minute plus your phone company's access charge)
web: www.premierinn.com
dir: M6 junct 14, A34 N. Hotel approx 1m on left

Rooms: 87

S

STAINES-UPON-THAMES
Surrey · Map 6 TQ07

Mercure London Staines Upon Thames
★★★ 78% HOTEL

Thames Street, TW18 4SJ - **tel:** 01784 464433
email: h6620@accor.com **web:** www.mercure.com
dir: *M25 junct 13. Follow A30/town centre signs (bus station on right). Hotel straight ahead*

Located on the banks of the River Thames in a bustling town, this hotel is well positioned for both business and leisure travellers. Meals are served in the Riverside Restaurant, and snacks are available in the spacious lounge/bar; weather permitting the terrace provides a good place for a drink on a summer evening. On-site parking is an additional bonus.

Rooms: 88 (17 family) (31 GF) **Facilities:** STV FTV WiFi Moorings Xmas New Year **Conf:** Class 40 Board 20 Thtr 40 **Services:** Night porter **Parking:** 40 **Notes:** LB

STALLINGBOROUGH
Lincolnshire · Map 17 TA11

Stallingborough Grange Hotel
★★★ 75% HOTEL

Riby Road, DN41 8BU - **tel:** 01469 561302
email: reception@stallingboroughgrange.co.uk **web:** www.stallingboroughgrange.co.uk
dir: *From A180 take Stallingborough interchange, through village. At rdbt take 2nd exit onto A1173, hotel 1m on left*

Dating back to the 18th century, this independent hotel is not short of character and charm. Bedrooms are furnished with a traditional appeal although modern accessories such as free WiFi are provided. The spacious restaurant offers an interesting choice of meals, alongside the bar area where more relaxed dishes can be enjoyed. Gym facilities are available and ample car parking is provided. The location is convenient with ports such as Grimsby a short distance away.

Rooms: 42 (9 GF) S £70–£120; D £85–£140 (incl. bkfst)* **Facilities:** STV FTV WiFi HL Gym Xmas New Year **Conf:** Class 30 Board 28 Thtr 60 **Services:** Night porter **Parking:** 80 **Notes:** Civ Wed 70

STAMFORD
Lincolnshire · Map 11 TF00

The William Cecil
★★★★ 81% HOTEL

Hillbrooke
QUIRKYLUXURY

High Street, St Martins, PE9 2LJ - **tel:** 01780 750070
email: enquiries@thewilliamcecil.co.uk **web:** www.thewilliamcecil.co.uk
dir: *Exit A1 signed Stamford & Burghley Park. Hotel 1st building on right on entering town*

This lovely refurbished property is situated on the edge of town within the Burghley Estate. The stylish bedrooms are spacious, individually decorated and have lots of extra little touches. The public rooms include a lounge bar with plush seating and a panelled restaurant. A smart terrace is available for alfresco dining when the weather permits.

Rooms: 27 (2 family) (5 GF) **Facilities:** FTV WiFi Xmas New Year **Conf:** Class 60 Board 40 Thtr 120 **Services:** Night porter **Parking:** 60 **Notes:** Civ Wed 120

The George of Stamford
★★★★ 80% HOTEL

71 St Martins, PE9 2LB - **tel:** 01780 750750
email: reservations@georgehotelofstamford.com
web: www.georgehotelofstamford.com
dir: *A1, 15m N of Peterborough onto B1081, hotel 1m on left*

Steeped in hundreds of years of history, this delightful coaching inn provides spacious public areas that include a choice of dining options, inviting lounges, and a business centre. A highlight is afternoon tea, taken in the colourful courtyard when the weather permits. Bedrooms are stylishly appointed and range from traditional to contemporary in design.

Rooms: 45 S £125–£170; D £205–£340 (incl. bkfst)* **Facilities:** STV FTV WiFi Complimentary membership to local gym Xmas New Year **Conf:** Class 25 Board 25 Thtr 50 Del from £170 **Services:** Night porter **Parking:** 110 **Notes:** LB Civ Wed 50

Crown Hotel
★★★ 85% HOTEL

All Saints Place, PE9 2AG - **tel:** 01780 763136
email: reservations@thecrownhotelstamford.co.uk
web: www.kneadpubs.co.uk/our-pubs/the-crown-hotel
dir: *A1 onto A43, through town to Red Lion Sq, hotel behind All Saints Church*

This small, privately owned hotel where hospitality is spontaneous and sincere, is ideally situated in the town centre. Unpretentious British food is served in the modern dining areas and the spacious bar is popular with locals. Bedrooms are appointed to a very high standard being quite contemporary in style and very well equipped; some have four-poster beds. Additional 'superior' rooms are located in a renovated Georgian town house just a short walk up the street.

Rooms: 28 (10 annexe) (1 family) (1 GF) S £110–£175; D £130–£185 (incl. bkfst)* **Facilities:** FTV WiFi Xmas New Year **Conf:** Class 12 Board 12 Thtr 20 Del from £150 **Services:** Night porter **Parking:** 21

S

STANDISH
Greater Manchester   **Map 15 SD51**

Premier Inn Wigan North (M6 Jct 27)

BUDGET HOTEL

Almond Brook Road, WN6 0SS - **tel:** 0871 527 9166 (Calls cost 13p per minute plus your phone company's access charge)
web: www.premierinn.com
dir: *M6 junct 27 follow signs for Standish. Left at T-junct, then 1st right*

High quality, budget accommodation ideal for both families and business travellers. Spacious, en suite bedrooms feature free WiFi and tea and coffee making facilities, and in most hotels, Freeview TV is also available. The adjacent family restaurant features a wide and varied menu.

Rooms: 36

STANSTED AIRPORT
Essex   **Map 6 TL52**

See also **Birchanger Green Motorway Service Area (M11)**

Premier Inn Stansted Airport

BUDGET HOTEL

Thremhall Avenue, Stansted Airport, CM24 1PY - **tel:** 0871 527 9352
(Calls cost 13p per minute plus your phone company's access charge)
web: www.premierinn.com
dir: *M11 junct 8/8a, follow signs Stanstead Airport Terminal.*
Main rdbt 3rd exit follow signs mid-stay car park. Adjacent BP Petrol Station

High quality, budget accommodation ideal for both families and business travellers. Spacious, en suite bedrooms feature free WiFi and tea and coffee making facilities, and in most hotels, Freeview TV is also available. The adjacent family restaurant features a wide and varied menu.

Rooms: 303

STEVENAGE
Hertfordshire   **Map 12 TL22**

Holiday Inn Stevenage

★★★★ 75% HOTEL

St George's Way, SG1 1HS - **tel:** 01438 722727
email: reservations@histevenage.com **web:** www.histevenage.com
dir: *A1(M) junct 7 take A602 to Stevenage, across 1st rdbt, 1st exit at 2nd rdbt, 2nd exit at next rdbt along St George's Way. Hotel 100yds on right*

Holiday Inn Stevenage is situated in the heart of the town centre and just 25 minutes from central London by train. Bedrooms are air conditioned and well equipped; ideal for business and leisure. Public areas are smart, capacious and stylish, and as well as a comfortable bar and restaurant, there is a mini gym. Parking is limited.

Rooms: 140 (8 family) ⚫ **Facilities:** STV FTV WiFi ↳ HL Gym Xmas New Year **Conf:** Class 200 Board 200 Thtr 400 **Services:** Lift Night porter Air con **Parking:** 23 **Notes:** Civ Wed 400

Novotel Stevenage

★★★★ 75% HOTEL

Knebworth Park, SG1 2AX - **tel:** 01438 346100 & 346250
email: reception@novotel-stevenage.com **web:** www.novotel.com
dir: *A1(M) junct 7, at entrance to Knebworth Park*

Ideally situated just off the A1(M) is this purpose-built hotel, which is a popular business and conference venue. Bedrooms are pleasantly decorated and equipped with a good range of useful extras. Public rooms include a large open-plan lounge bar serving a range of snacks, and a smartly appointed restaurant.

Rooms: 102 (20 family) (30 GF) ⚫ **S** £49–£149; **D** £59–£159* **Facilities:** STV WiFi ↳ Use of local health club Xmas New Year **Conf:** Class 80 Board 70 Thtr 150 Del from £99 **Services:** Lift Night porter Air con **Parking:** 120 **Notes:** LB Civ Wed 120

Premier Inn Stevenage

BUDGET HOTEL

Corey's Mill Lane, SG1 4AA - **tel:** 0871 527 9036
(Calls cost 13p per minute plus your phone company's access charge)
web: www.premierinn.com
dir: *A1(M) junct 8, at intersection with A602 – Hitchin Rd & Corey's Mill Lane*

High quality, budget accommodation ideal for both families and business travellers. Spacious, en suite bedrooms feature free WiFi and tea and coffee making facilities, and in most hotels, Freeview TV is also available. The adjacent family restaurant features a wide and varied menu.

Rooms: 56

Premier Inn Stevenage Central

BUDGET HOTEL

Six Hills Way, Horizon Technology Park, SG1 2DD - **tel:** 0871 527 9034
(Calls cost 13p per minute plus your phone company's access charge)
web: www.premierinn.com
dir: *A1(M) junct 7, follow Stevenage signs. Left into Gunnels Wood Rd.*
(NB do not use underpass). Left at next rdbt. Hotel in Horizon Technology Park on left

Rooms: 115

STEYNING
West Sussex   Map 6 TQ11

Best Western Plus Old Tollgate Hotel & Restaurant

Best Western PLUS

★★★ 76% HOTEL

The Street, Bramber, BN44 3WE - tel: 01903 879494
email: info@oldtollgatehotel.com **web:** www.oldtollgatehotel.com
dir: *From A283 at Steyning roundabout to Bramber. Hotel 200 yards on right*

As its name suggests, this well-presented hotel is built on the site of the old toll house. The spacious bedrooms are smartly designed and are furnished to a high standard; eight rooms are air conditioned and have smart power showers. Open for both lunch and dinner, the popular carvery-style restaurant offers an extensive choice of dishes.

Rooms: 38 (28 annexe) (5 family) (14 GF) ✆ **S** £78–£158; **D** £78–£158 (incl. bkfst)*
Facilities: STV WiFi ⬇ HL New Year **Conf:** Class 32 Board 24 Thtr 50 Del £144
Services: Lift Night porter **Parking:** 60 **Notes:** LB Civ Wed 70

STILTON
Cambridgeshire   Map 12 TL18

Bell Inn Hotel

★★★ 85% ⧈⧈ HOTEL

Great North Road, PE7 3RA - tel: 01733 241066
email: reception@thebellstilton.co.uk **web:** www.thebellstilton.co.uk
dir: *A1(M) junct 16, follow Stilton signs. Hotel in village centre*

This delightful inn is steeped in history and retains many original features, with imaginative food served in both the character village bar/brasserie and the elegant beamed first-floor restaurant; refreshments can be enjoyed in the attractive courtyard and rear gardens when weather permits. Individually designed bedrooms are stylish and equipped to a high standard.

Rooms: 22 (3 annexe) (1 family) (3 GF) ✆ **S** £87.50–£127.50; **D** £112.50–£147.50 (incl. bkfst)* **Facilities:** STV FTV WiFi ⬇ **Conf:** Class 46 Board 50 Thtr 130 Del from £135 **Services:** Night porter **Parking:** 30 **Notes:** RS 25 Dec (pm) 26 Dec (pm) & 1 Jan (pm) Civ Wed 130

STOCK
Essex   Map 6 TQ69

Greenwoods Hotel & Spa

★★★★ 79% ⧈ HOTEL

Stock Road, CM4 9BE - tel: 01277 829990
email: info@greenwoodshotel.co.uk **web:** www.greenwoodshotel.co.uk
dir: *A12 junct 16 take B1007 signed Billericay. Hotel on right on entering village*

Greenwoods is a beautiful 17th-century, Grade II listed manor house set in extensive landscaped gardens. All bedrooms are tastefully appointed, with marble bathrooms and a wide range of extras; the premier rooms have spa baths and antique beds. The spa facilities are impressive offering the latest beauty treatments, together with saunas, a jacuzzi, steam rooms, a monsoon shower and a 20-metre pool.

Rooms: 39 (6 GF) ✆ **S** £135–£225; **D** £160–£250* **Facilities:** Spa STV FTV WiFi ⬇ ⧖ Gym Steam room Sauna Monsoon shower Relaxation suite New Year **Conf:** Class 150 Board 110 Thtr 200 Del from £150 **Services:** Lift Night porter **Parking:** 100 **Notes:** LB Closed 26 Dec & 1 Jan No children 16yrs Civ Wed 150

S

STOCKPORT
Greater Manchester

Map 16 SJ89

See also **Manchester Airport**

The Wycliffe Hotel

★★★ 76% HOTEL

74 Edgeley Road, Edgeley, SK3 9NQ - **tel:** 0161 477 5395
email: reception@wycliffe-hotel.com **web:** www.wycliffe-hotel.com
dir: *M60 junct 2, follow A560 Stockport signs, right at 1st lights, hotel 0.5m on left*

The Wycliffe is a family-run hotel close to the town centre and convenient for Manchester Airport. The contemporary bedrooms are very well maintained and equipped, with king-size beds and LCD flat-screen TVs. Complimentary WiFi is provided throughout the hotel. There is a well-stocked bar and a popular restaurant where the menu has an Italian feel. There is also a large car park.

Rooms: 14 (3 family) (2 GF) **S** £69.50; **D** £93.50 (incl. bkfst)* **Facilities:** FTV WiFi **Conf:** Class 20 Board 20 Thtr 30 **Services:** Night porter **Parking:** 46 **Notes:** Closed 25-27 Dec RS BHs No restaurant available

Alma Lodge Hotel

★★★ 75% HOTEL

149 Buxton Road, SK2 6EL - **tel:** 0161 483 4431
email: reception@almalodgehotel.com **web:** www.almalodgehotel.com
dir: *M60 junct 1 at rdbt take 2nd exit under rail viaduct at lights opposite. At Debenhams turn right onto A6. Hotel approx 1.5m on left*

Alma Lodge is a large hotel located on the main road close to the town, offering modern and well-equipped bedrooms. It is family-owned and run and serves a good range of quality Italian cooking in Luigi's restaurant. Good function rooms and free internet access are also available.

Rooms: 52 (32 annexe) (2 family) **S** £58–£79; **D** £80–£110 (incl. bkfst)* **Facilities:** FTV WiFi **Conf:** Class 100 Board 60 Thtr 250 Del from £126 **Services:** Night porter **Parking:** 120 **Notes:** RS BHs Restaurant & bars closed Civ Wed 200

Premier Inn Manchester Airport Heald Green

BUDGET HOTEL

Finney Lane, Heald Green, SK8 3QH - **tel:** 0871 527 8734
(Calls cost 13p per minute plus your phone company's access charge)
web: www.premierinn.com
dir: *M56 junct 5 follow signs to Terminal 1, at rdbt take 2nd exit, at next rdbt follow Cheadle signs. Left at lights, right at next lights*

High quality, budget accommodation ideal for both families and business travellers. Spacious, en suite bedrooms feature free WiFi and tea and coffee making facilities, and in most hotels, Freeview TV is also available. The adjacent family restaurant features a wide and varied menu.

Rooms: 87

Premier Inn Stockport Central

BUDGET HOTEL

Churchgate, SK1 1YG - **tel:** 0871 527 9040 (Calls cost 13p per minute plus your phone company's access charge)
web: www.premierinn.com
dir: *M60 junct 27, A626 towards Marple. Right at Spring Gardens*

Rooms: 46

Premier Inn Stockport South

BUDGET HOTEL

Buxton Road, Heaviley, SK2 6NB - **tel:** 0871 527 9042 (Calls cost 13p per minute plus your phone company's access charge)
web: www.premierinn.com
dir: *On A6, 1.5m from town centre*

Rooms: 42

STOCKTON-ON-TEES
County Durham

Map 19 NZ41

Premier Inn Stockton-on-Tees/Hartlepool

BUDGET HOTEL

Coal Lane, Wolviston, TS22 5PZ - **tel:** 0871 527 9044
(Calls cost 13p per minute plus your phone company's access charge)
web: www.premierinn.com
dir: *A1(M) junct 60, A689, follow Teeside then Hartlepool signs. Hotel on left at A89 & A19 junct*

Rooms: 98

Premier Inn Stockton-on-Tees/Middlesbrough

BUDGET HOTEL

Whitewater Way, Thornaby, TS17 6QB - **tel:** 0871 527 9048
(Calls cost 13p per minute plus your phone company's access charge)
web: www.premierinn.com
dir: *A19, A66 towards Stockton & Darlington. Take 1st exit signed Teeside Park/Teesdale. Right at lights over viaduct bridge rdbt & Tees Barrage*

Rooms: 110

Premier Inn Stockton-on-Tees West

BUDGET HOTEL

Yarm Road, TS18 3RT - **tel:** 0871 527 9046
(Calls cost 13p per minute plus your phone company's access charge)
web: www.premierinn.com
dir: *A1(M) junct 60, A689 towards Teeside. Follow Hartlepool signs. Hotel on left at A689 & A19 interchange*

High quality, budget accommodation ideal for both families and business travellers. Spacious, en suite bedrooms feature free WiFi and tea and coffee making facilities, and in most hotels, Freeview TV is also available. The adjacent family restaurant features a wide and varied menu.

Rooms: 87

STOKE-BY-NAYLAND
Suffolk   Map 13 TL93

HIGHLY RECOMMENDED

The Crown
★★★ 88% ◎◎ SMALL HOTEL

CO6 4SE - **tel:** 01206 262001
email: info@crowninn.net **web:** www.crowninn.net
dir: Follow Stoke-by-Nayland signs from A12 & A134. Hotel in village off B1068 towards Higham

Situated in a picturesque village, The Crown, with an award-winning restaurant, has a reputation for making everyone feel welcome. It offers quiet, individually decorated rooms looking out over the countryside. Ground floor rooms, including three with a terrace, are of a contemporary design while upstairs rooms are in a country-house style; each room has WiFi, DVDs and luxury toiletries.

Rooms: 11 (1 family) (8 GF) ⟨ **S** £110–£150; **D** £145–£295 (incl. bkfst)*
Facilities: FTV WiFi ↧ New Year **Conf:** Board 12 Del from £174 **Services:** Night porter **Parking:** 49 **Notes:** LB Closed 25-26 Dec

STOKE D'ABERNON
Surrey   Map 6 TQ15

Woodlands Park Hotel
★★★★ 82% ◎◎ HOTEL

Woodlands Lane, KT11 3QB - **tel:** 01372 843933 & 0845 072 7581
(Calls cost 5p per minute plus your phone company's access charge)
email: woodlandspark@handpicked.co.uk
web: www.handpickedhotels.co.uk/woodlandspark
dir: A3 exit at Cobham. Through town centre & Stoke D'Abernon, left at garden centre into Woodlands Lane, hotel 0.5m on right

Originally built for the Bryant family, of the matchmaking firm Bryant & May, this lovely Victorian mansion enjoys an attractive parkland setting in ten and a half acres of Surrey countryside. Bedrooms in the wing are contemporary in style while those in the main house are more traditionally decorated. The hotel boasts two dining options, Benson's Brasserie and the Oak Room Restaurant.

Rooms: 57 (4 family) ⟨ **S** fr £132; **D** fr £132 (incl. bkfst)* **Facilities:** FTV WiFi ↧ HL ➘ ⬥ Gym Xmas New Year **Conf:** Class 100 Board 60 Thtr 200 Del from £189 **Services:** Lift Night porter Air con **Parking:** 150 **Notes:** LB Civ Wed 200

STOKE-ON-TRENT
Staffordshire   Map 10 SJ84

Best Western Plus Stoke-on-Trent Moat House
★★★★ 73% HOTEL

Etruria Hall, Festival Way, ST1 5BQ - **tel:** 01782 609988
email: reservations.stoke@qmh-hotels.com **web:** www.bw-stokeontrentmoathouse.co.uk
dir: M6 junct 15 (or junct 16), A500, follow A53 & Festival Park signs. Keep in left lane, take 1st slip road on left. Left at island, hotel opposite at next island

This large, modern hotel is located in Stoke's Festival Park, which adjoins Etruria Hall, the former home of Josiah Wedgwood. Bedrooms are spacious and well equipped, and include standard rooms, suites and executive rooms. Public areas include a spacious lounge bar and restaurant as well as a business centre, extensive conference facilities and a leisure club.

Rooms: 147 **Facilities:** Spa FTV WiFi ⟨ supervised Gym **Conf:** Class 400 Board 40 Thtr 650 **Services:** Lift Night porter Air con **Parking:** 250 **Notes:** LB Civ Wed 400

Premier Inn Stoke-on-Trent (Hanley)
BUDGET HOTEL

Etruria Road, Hanley, ST1 5NH - **tel:** 0871 527 9476 (Calls cost 13p per minute plus your phone company's access charge) **web:** www.premierinn.com
dir: M6 junct 15, A500. 4.3m, take 5th slip road for A53 (City Centre, Hanley). At rdbt take 4th exit signed Etruria & A53. Keep in left lane until passing flyover entrance. At rdbt take 3rd exit, hotel on right

High quality, budget accommodation ideal for both families and business travellers. Spacious, en suite bedrooms feature free WiFi and tea and coffee making facilities, and in most hotels, Freeview TV is also available. The adjacent family restaurant features a wide and varied menu.

Rooms: 96

Premier Inn Stoke/Trentham Gardens
BUDGET HOTEL

Stone Road, Trentham, ST4 8JG - **tel:** 0871 527 9050 (Calls cost 13p per minute plus your phone company's access charge)
web: www.premierinn.com
dir: M6 junct 15, A500, follow Trentham signs. At rdbt 3rd exit onto A34, 2m to hotel on right in Trentham Gardens

Rooms: 119

S

STOKE POGES
Buckinghamshire

Map 6 SU98

Stoke Park
★★★★★ ⊛⊛⊛ HOTEL

Park Road, SL2 4PG - tel: 01753 717171
email: info@stokepark.com **web:** www.stokepark.com
dir: *M4 junct 6, A355 towards Slough, B416 Park Rd. Hotel 1.25m on right*

Located within 300 acres of beautiful parkland created by 'Capability' Brown and Humphry Repton, this hotel offers outstanding leisure and sporting facilities. Inside the stunning mansion house, designed by George III's architect, the public areas display lavish opulence throughout and the bedrooms have a luxurious and classic feel. In contrast, the Pavilion features more contemporary bedrooms and public areas; as well as extensive state-of-the-art health and beauty facilities. The hotel has a championship golf course, tennis courts, and three restaurants, including the award-winning Humphry's and the more informal Italian brasserie, San Marco. There are bars, lounges and meeting rooms as well.

Rooms: 49 (28 annexe) (6 family) 🐾 **D** £190–£1010* **Facilities:** Spa STV FTV WiFi ◊ 🐦 ⚓ 27 Putting green ♨ Fishing 🦢 Gym Indoor golf Games room Nail bar Spa boutique Garden lounge Sauna Steam rooms Yoga Outdoor hot tub Indoor tennis New Year Child facilities **Conf:** Class 30 Board 34 Thtr 80 **Services:** Lift Night porter **Parking:** 460 **Notes:** LB Closed 24-26 Dec Civ Wed 146

STON EASTON
Somerset

Map 4 ST65

Ston Easton Park Hotel
★★★★ ⊛⊛ COUNTRY HOUSE HOTEL

BA3 4DF - tel: 01761 241631
email: reception@stoneaston.co.uk **web:** www.stoneaston.co.uk
dir: *On A37*

Surrounded by The Mendips, this outstanding Palladian mansion lies in extensive parklands that were landscaped by Humphrey Repton. The architecture and decorative features are stunning. The state rooms include one of England's earliest surviving Print Rooms, and the Palladian Saloon is considered one of Somerset's finest rooms. There is even an Edwardian kitchen that guests might like to take a look at. The helpful and attentive team provide a very efficient service, and the award-winning cuisine uses organic produce from the hotel's own kitchen garden. The bedrooms and bathrooms are all appointed to an excellent standard.

Rooms: 23 (3 annexe) (2 family) (1 GF) 🐾 **Facilities:** FTV WiFi ◊ 🐦 🦢 Archery Clay pigeon shooting Quad bikes Hot air ballooning Xmas New Year **Conf:** Class 60 Board 30 Thtr 100 **Services:** Night porter **Parking:** 120 **Notes:** Civ Wed 120

STOURBRIDGE
West Midlands

Map 10 SO88

Premier Inn Stourbridge Town Centre

BUDGET HOTEL

Birmingham Street, DY8 1JR - tel: 0871 527 9482 (Calls cost 13p per minute plus your phone company's access charge) **web:** www.premierinn.com
dir: *On A458*

High quality, budget accommodation ideal for both families and business travellers. Spacious, en suite bedrooms feature free WiFi and tea and coffee making facilities, and in most hotels, Freeview TV is also available. The adjacent family restaurant features a wide and varied menu.

Rooms: 80

STOURPORT-ON-SEVERN	Map 10 SO87
Worcestershire	

Hallmark Hotel Stourport Manor

★★★★ 76% HOTEL

35 Hartlebury Road, DY13 9JA - **tel:** 0330 028 3421
email: stourport@hallmarkhotels.co.uk **web:** www.hallmarkhotels.co.uk
dir: *M5 junct 6, A449 towards Kidderminster, B4193 towards Stourport. Hotel on right*

Once the home of Prime Minister Sir Stanley Baldwin, this much extended country house is set in attractive grounds. A number of bedrooms and suites are located in the original building, although the majority are in a more modern, purpose-built section. Spacious public areas include a range of lounges, a popular restaurant, a leisure club and conference facilities.

Rooms: 72 (33 family) (31 GF) 🔦 **D** £55.35–£178 (incl. bkfst)* **Facilities:** FTV WiFi ⚡ ⚫ supervised Putting green ⚽ Gym Squash Xmas New Year **Conf:** Class 110 Board 100 Thtr 400 **Services:** Night porter **Parking:** 300 **Notes:** Civ Wed 300

STOW-ON-THE-WOLD	Map 10 SP12
Gloucestershire	

Wyck Hill House Hotel & Spa

★★★★ 75% ◉ ◉ HOTEL

Burford Road, GL54 1HY - **tel:** 01451 831936
email: info@wyckhillhousehotel.co.uk **web:** www.wyckhillhousehotel.co.uk
dir: *Exit A429. Hotel 1m on right*

This charming 18th-century house enjoys superb views across the Windrush Valley and is ideally positioned for a relaxing weekend exploring the Cotswolds. The spacious and thoughtfully equipped bedrooms provide high standards of comfort and quality, located both in the main house and also the original coach house. Elegant public rooms include a cosy bar, library, and the magnificent front hall with crackling log fire. The imaginative cuisine makes extensive use of local produce.

Rooms: 60 (22 annexe) (4 GF) 🔦 **S** £95–£285; **D** £115–£295 (incl. bkfst)* **Facilities:** Spa FTV WiFi Sauna Steam room Xmas New Year **Conf:** Class 50 Board 50 Thtr 150 Del from £125 **Services:** Lift Night porter **Parking:** 100 **Notes:** LB Civ Wed 120

Stow Lodge Hotel

★★★ 78% SMALL HOTEL

The Square, GL54 1AB - **tel:** 01451 830485
email: enquiries@stowlodge.co.uk **web:** www.stowlodge.co.uk
dir: *In town centre*

Situated in smart grounds, this family-run hotel has direct access to the market square and provides high standards of customer care. Bedrooms are offered both within the main building and in the converted coach house, all of which provide similar standards of homely comfort. Extensive menus and an interesting wine list make for an enjoyable dining experience.

Rooms: 21 (10 annexe) (1 family) 🔦 **S** £75–£130; **D** £95–£175 (incl. bkfst)* **Facilities:** WiFi **Services:** Night porter **Parking:** 30 **Notes:** No children 5yrs Closed Xmas-end Jan

STRATFORD-UPON-AVON	Map 10 SP25
Warwickshire	

INSPECTOR'S CHOICE

Ettington Park Hotel

★★★★ ◉ ◉ COUNTRY HOUSE HOTEL

CV37 8BU - **tel:** 01789 450123 & 0845 072 7454
(Calls cost 5p per minute plus your phone company's access charge)
email: ettingtonpark@handpicked.co.uk
web: www.handpickedhotels.co.uk/ettingtonpark

(For full entry see Alderminster)

HIGHLY RECOMMENDED

The Arden Hotel

★★★★ 83% ◉ ◉ HOTEL

Waterside, CV37 6BA - **tel:** 01789 298682
email: enquiries@theardenhotelstratford.com **web:** www.theardenhotelstratford.com
dir: *M40 junct 15 follow signs to town centre. At Barclays Bank rdbt left onto High St, 2nd left onto Chapel Lane (Nash's House on left). Hotel car park on right in 40yds*

This property is on the same road as the world famous Royal Shakespeare and Swan theatres, and just a short walk from the town centre. The bedrooms and bathrooms have been tastefully designed and have quality fixtures and fittings. The dedicated team provide polite and professional service. Award-winning cuisine is served in the popular restaurant. Ample secure parking is available.

Rooms: 45 (6 family) (1 GF) 🔦 **S** £130–£262.50; **D** £160–£425 (incl. bkfst)* **Facilities:** FTV WiFi Xmas New Year **Conf:** Class 18 Board 28 Thtr 40 Del from £175 **Services:** Night porter Air con **Parking:** 50 **Notes:** LB Civ Wed 90

HIGHLY RECOMMENDED

Hallmark Hotel The Welcombe

★★★★ 83% ◉ HOTEL

Warwick Road, CV37 0NR - **tel:** 0330 028 3422
email: welcombe@hallmarkhotels.co.uk **web:** www.hallmarkhotels.co.uk
dir: *M40 junct 15, A46 towards Stratford-upon-Avon, at rdbt follow signs for A439. Hotel 3m on right*

This Jacobean manor house is set in 157 acres of landscaped parkland. Public rooms are impressive, especially the lounge with its wood panelling and ornate marble fireplace, and the gentleman's club-style bar. Bedrooms in the original building are stylish and gracefully proportioned; those in the garden wing are comfortable and thoughtfully equipped. The spa development incorporates advanced, luxurious facilities and treatments.

Rooms: 85 (12 family) (11 GF) 🔦 **Facilities:** Spa STV FTV WiFi ⚡ ⚫ 🎾 ⛳ 18 Putting green ⚽ Gym Xmas New Year **Conf:** Class 65 Board 40 Thtr 200 **Services:** Night porter **Parking:** 200 **Notes:** Civ Wed 120

S

STRATFORD-UPON-AVON *continued*

Macdonald Alveston Manor

★★★★ 82% HOTEL

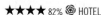

Clopton Bridge, CV37 7HP - tel: 01789 205478
email: sales.alvestonmanor@macdonald-hotels.co.uk **web:** www.macdonaldhotels.co.uk
dir: *On rdbt, S of Clopton Bridge*

A striking red-brick and timbered façade, well-tended grounds, and a giant cedar tree all contribute to the charm of this well-established hotel, just five minutes from Stratford. The bedrooms vary in size and character, and the coach house conversion offers an impressive mix of full and junior suites. The superb leisure complex offers a 20-metre swimming pool, steam room, sauna, a high-tech gym and a host of beauty treatments.

Rooms: 113 (8 family) (45 GF) **S** fr £100; **D** fr £110* **Facilities:** Spa FTV WiFi supervised Gym Techno-gym Beauty treatments Sauna Steam room Xmas New Year **Conf:** Class 80 Board 40 Thtr 140 Del from £150 **Services:** Night porter Air con **Parking:** 150 **Notes:** LB Civ Wed 110

Stratford Manor

★★★★ 82% HOTEL

Warwick Road, CV37 0PY - tel: 01789 731173
email: stratfordmanor@qhotels.co.uk **web:** www.qhotels.co.uk
dir: *M40 junct 15, A46 signed Stratford. At 2nd rdbt take A439 signed Stratford Town Centre. Hotel 1m on left. Or from Stratford centre take A439 signed Warwick & M40. Hotel 3m on right*

Just outside Stratford, this hotel is set against a rural backdrop with lovely gardens and ample parking. Public areas include a stylish lounge bar and a contemporary restaurant. Service is both professional and helpful. Bedrooms are smartly appointed, spacious and have generously sized beds and a range of useful facilities. The leisure centre boasts a large indoor pool.

Rooms: 104 (8 family) (24 GF) **S** fr £87; **D** fr £99 (incl. bkfst)* **Facilities:** Spa FTV WiFi HL Gym Sauna Steam room Xmas New Year **Conf:** Class 120 Board 100 Thtr 350 Del from £149 **Services:** Lift Night porter **Parking:** 220 **Notes:** LB Civ Wed 150

The Stratford

★★★★ 79% HOTEL

Arden Street, CV37 6QQ - tel: 01789 271000
email: stratfordsreservations@qhotels.co.uk **web:** www.qhotels.co.uk
dir: *A439 into Stratford. In town follow A3400/Birmingham, at lights left into Arden St, hotel 150yds on right*

Situated adjacent to the hospital, within walking distance of the town centre, The Stratford is an eye-catching, contemporary hotel with a red-brick façade. It offers modern, well-equipped and spacious bedrooms. The open-plan public areas include a comfortable lounge, a small, atmospheric bar and a spacious restaurant with exposed beams.

Rooms: 102 (7 family) (14 GF) **S** £90–£100; **D** £102–£112 (incl. bkfst) **Facilities:** FTV WiFi HL Gym Free use of Stratford Manor's leisure facilities Xmas New Year **Conf:** Class 66 Board 54 Thtr 132 Del from £140 **Services:** Lift Night porter Air con **Parking:** 92 **Notes:** LB Civ Wed 132

Macdonald Swan's Nest Hotel

★★★★ 77% HOTEL

Bridgefoot, CV37 7LT - tel: 01789 266804
email: sales.swansnest@macdonald-hotels.co.uk
web: www.macdonaldhotels.co.uk
dir: *A439 towards Stratford, follow one-way system, left over bridge (A3400), hotel on right*

Dating back to the 17th century, this hotel is said to be one of the earliest brick-built houses in Stratford. It occupies a prime position on the banks of the River Avon and is ideally situated for exploring the town. Bedrooms and bathrooms are appointed to a high standard with some thoughtful guest extras provided.

Rooms: 68 (2 family) (25 GF) **Facilities:** FTV WiFi Use of facilities at Macdonald Alveston Manor New Year **Conf:** Class 70 Board 56 Thtr 150 **Services:** Night porter **Parking:** 80 **Notes:** Civ Wed 150

Mercure Stratford-upon-Avon Shakespeare Hotel

★★★★ 72% HOTEL

Chapel Street, CV37 6ER - tel: 01789 294997
email: h6630@accor.com **web:** www.mercure.com
dir: *M40 junct 15. Follow signs for Stratford town centre on A439. Follow one-way system into Bridge St. Left at rdbt, hotel 200yds on left opposite HSBC bank*

Dating back to the early 17th century, The Shakespeare is one of the oldest hotels in this historic town. The hotel name represents one of the earliest exploitations of Stratford as the birthplace of one of the world's leading playwrights. With exposed beams and open fires, the public rooms retain an ambience reminiscent of this era. Bedrooms are appointed to a good standard and remain in keeping with the style of the property.

Rooms: 78 (11 annexe) (4 family) (3 GF) **S** £79–£159; **D** £89–£199* **Facilities:** WiFi Xmas New Year **Conf:** Class 45 Board 40 Thtr 90 Del from £139 **Services:** Lift Night porter **Parking:** 31 **Notes:** Civ Wed 100

Best Western Grosvenor Hotel

★★★ 77% HOTEL

Warwick Road, CV37 6YT - tel: 01789 269213
email: gm@bwgh.co.uk **web:** www.bwgh.co.uk
dir: *M40 junct 15, follow Stratford signs to A439 Warwick Rd. Hotel 6m, on one-way system*

This hotel is a short distance from the town centre and many historic attractions. Bedroom styles and sizes vary, and the friendly staff offer an efficient service. Refreshments are served in the lounge all day, and room service is available. The Garden Room restaurant offers a choice of dishes from set price and carte menus.

Rooms: 73 (16 family) (25 GF) **S** £75–£105; **D** £85–£145* **Facilities:** FTV WiFi Xmas New Year **Conf:** Class 45 Board 50 Thtr 100 Del from £109 **Services:** Night porter **Parking:** 46 **Notes:** LB Civ Wed 100

Premier Inn Stratford-upon-Avon Central

BUDGET HOTEL

Payton Road, CV37 6UQ - **tel:** 0871 527 9282 (Calls cost 13p per minute plus your phone company's access charge)
web: www.premierinn.com
dir: A439, A4300 signed Stratford-upon-Avon. Hotel on left

High quality, budget accommodation ideal for both families and business travellers. Spacious, en suite bedrooms feature free WiFi and tea and coffee making facilities, and in most hotels, Freeview TV is also available. The adjacent family restaurant features a wide and varied menu.

Rooms: 87

Premier Inn Stratford-upon-Avon Waterways

BUDGET HOTEL

The Waterways, Birmingham Road, CV37 0AZ - **tel:** 0871 527 9316 (Calls cost 13p per minute plus your phone company's access charge)
web: www.premierinn.com
dir: A3400 (Birmingham Rd) towards town centre, pass large retail park on left. Straight over mini rdbt, approx 150yds. Hotel on right

Rooms: 130

STREET	Map 4 ST43
Somerset	

Wessex Hotel

★★★ 66% HOTEL

High Street, BA16 0EF - **tel:** 01458 443383
email: info@wessexhotel.com **web:** www.wessexhotel.com
dir: From A303, onto B3151 to Somerton. Then 7m, pass lights by Millfield School. Left at mini rdbt

The Wessex Hotel is centrally located in this popular town, with easy access to all the shops and attractions. The bedrooms and bathrooms vary slightly in size but all provide good levels of quality and comfort. A wide range of snacks and refreshments is available throughout the day, including a regular carvery at dinner. Entertainment is often offered in the main season.

Rooms: 51 (9 family) **S** £50–£80; **D** £70–£120 (incl. bkfst)* **Facilities:** FTV WiFi HL 🎵 Xmas New Year **Conf:** Class 120 Board 80 Thtr 400 **Services:** Lift Night porter **Parking:** 70 **Notes:** LB

STROUD	Map 4 SO80
Gloucestershire	

The Bear of Rodborough

★★★ 83% HOTEL

Rodborough Common, GL5 5DE - **tel:** 01453 878522
email: info@bearofrodborough.info **web:** www.cotswold-inns-hotels.co.uk
dir: M5 junct 13, A419 to Stroud. Follow signs to Rodborough. Up hill, left at top at T-junct. Hotel on right

This popular 17th-century coaching inn is situated high above Stroud in acres of National Trust parkland. Character abounds in the lounges and cocktail bar, and in the Box Tree Restaurant where the cuisine utilises fresh local produce. Bedrooms offer equal measures of comfort and style with plenty of extra touches. There is also a traditional and well-patronised public bar.

Rooms: 46 (18 annexe) (2 family) **S** fr £85; **D** fr £98 (incl. bkfst)* **Facilities:** FTV WiFi ❄ Xmas New Year **Conf:** Class 35 Board 30 Thtr 60 **Services:** Night porter **Parking:** 70 **Notes:** Civ Wed 90

Burleigh Court Hotel

★★★ 82% ◉◉ HOTEL

Burleigh, Minchinhampton, GL5 2PF - **tel:** 01453 883804
email: burleighcourt@aol.com **web:** www.burleighcourthotel.co.uk
dir: From Stroud A419 towards Cirencester. Right after 2.5m signed Burleigh & Minchinhampton. Left after 500yds signed Burleigh Court. Hotel 300yds on right

Dating back to the 18th century, this former gentleman's manor house is in a secluded and elevated, though accessible, position with some wonderful countryside views. Public rooms are elegantly styled and include an oak-panelled bar for pre-dinner drinks beside a crackling fire. Combining comfort and quality, no two bedrooms are alike; some are in an adjoining coach house.

Rooms: 18 (7 annexe) (2 family) (3 GF) **S** £110–£130; **D** £175–£240 (incl. bkfst)* **Facilities:** WiFi ❄ 🏊 New Year **Conf:** Class 30 Board 30 Thtr 50 **Parking:** 40 **Notes:** LB Closed 24-26 Dec Civ Wed 50

Premier Inn Stroud

BUDGET HOTEL

Stratford Lodge, Stratford Road, GL5 4AF - **tel:** 0871 527 9052 (Calls cost 13p per minute plus your phone company's access charge)
web: www.premierinn.com
dir: M5 junct 13, A419 to town centre, follow Leisure Centre signs. Hotel adjacent to Tesco superstore

High quality, budget accommodation ideal for both families and business travellers. Spacious, en suite bedrooms feature free WiFi and tea and coffee making facilities, and in most hotels, Freeview TV is also available. The adjacent family restaurant features a wide and varied menu.

Rooms: 32

S

Red Stars

The AA Red Star rating denotes an Inspector's Choice hotel. They stand out as the very best and appear in highlighted panels throughout the guide.

STUDLAND
Dorset

Map 5 SZ08

INSPECTOR'S CHOICE

THE PIG on the Beach
★★★ ◉◉ HOTEL

The Manor House, Manor Road, BH19 3AU - **tel:** 01929 450288
email: info@thepigonthebeach.com **web:** www.thepighotel.com
dir: *A338 from Bournemouth, follow signs to Sandbanks ferry, cross on ferry, then 3m to Studland*

This former summer house has a dramatic coastal location set within beautiful grounds. It has its own livestock and there is a walled garden, which provides much of the produce for the popular restaurant; an authentically reproduced greenhouse. Alfresco eating is possible in the warmer months as there is a wood-fired oven in the grounds. Bedrooms come in an array of shapes and sizes, located in the main house, and there are some feature rooms in outbuildings. All are generally spacious, have high quality fixtures and come with their own larders and Nespresso machines. There are plenty of comfortable lounges where guests can make themselves at home too including a cosy cocktail lounge. Treatments can be taken in the two attractively converted shepherd's huts and there's a room just perfect for private dining within the grounds.

Rooms: 23 (3 annexe) (6 GF) Facilities: STV FTV WiFi Treatment rooms Beach hut Round house Xmas New Year **Services:** Night porter **Parking:** 30 **Notes:** Civ Wed 60

SUDBURY
Suffolk

Map 13 TL84

The Mill Hotel
★★★★ 74% ◉ HOTEL

Walnut Tree Lane, CO10 1BD - **tel:** 01787 375544
email: info@themillhotelsudbury.co.uk **web:** www.themillhotelsudbury.co.uk
dir: *A12 direction Harwich from London, exit junct 27 onto A134, 2nd exit into A133, rdbt 1st exit onto A134, straight over 7 rdbts, 2nd exit onto Newton Road, A131, turn right*

Situated on the banks of the River Stour in the Suffolk countryside, close to the town of Sudbury, The Mill Hotel features an original working water mill which is a main feature in the bar/restaurant. The modern bedrooms are well equipped; many rooms have lovely views of the meadow and surrounding countryside. Public rooms include a lounge bar and a restaurant with an outdoor terrace.

Rooms: 62 (10 annexe) (4 family) (12 GF) Facilities: FTV WiFi Xmas New Year **Conf:** Class 56 Board 40 Thtr 80 **Services:** Night porter **Parking:** 45 **Notes:** Civ Wed 80

SUNBURY
Surrey

Premier Inn Sunbury (Kempton Park)

BUDGET HOTEL PLAN 1 A1

Staines Road West, Sunbury Cross, TW16 7AT - **tel:** 0871 527 9054
(Calls cost 13p per minute plus your phone company's access charge)
web: www.premierinn.com
dir: *M25 junct 12, onto M3 signed London & Richmond. Exit at junct 1, take 1st exit at rdbt into Staines Road West (A308). 1st left into Crossways. Hotel on right*

High quality, budget accommodation ideal for both families and business travellers. Spacious, en suite bedrooms feature free WiFi and tea and coffee making facilities, and in most hotels, Freeview TV is also available. The adjacent family restaurant features a wide and varied menu.

Rooms: 109

SUNDERLAND
Tyne & Wear

Map 19 NZ35

Best Western Roker Hotel

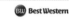

★★★★ 76% HOTEL

Roker Terrace, SR6 9ND - **tel:** 0191 567 1786
email: reception@rokerhotel.co.uk **web:** www.rokerhotel.co.uk
dir: *Follow A1231 from A9, E to Sunderland, then A1290 to Church St N. Left onto A183 for 0.9m. Hotel is located left, coast to the right*

This modern hotel offers stunning views of the coastline. Well-equipped bedrooms come in a variety of sizes, several have feature bathrooms. Functions, conferences and weddings are all well catered for with a variety of rooms and spaces available. The late-opening R Bar serves food all day with real ales from a local micro-brewery. The Italian Farmhouse Ristorante also provides lunch and dinner, while Let There Be Crumbs is a wonderful teashop operation overlooking the seafront.

Rooms: 43 (4 family) Facilities: FTV WiFi Xmas New Year **Conf:** Class 150 Board 100 Thtr 300 **Services:** Lift Night porter **Parking:** 150 **Notes:** Civ Wed 350

Quality Hotel Boldon
★★★★ 75% HOTEL

Witney Way, Boldon, NE35 9PE - **tel:** 0191 519 1999
email: gm@hotels-sunderland.com **web:** www.hotels-sunderland.com
dir: *From Tyne Tunnel (A19), 2.5m south take 1st exit to rdbt with A184*

The Quality Hotel Boldon is a well presented modern hotel located just minutes from the A19, with Newcastle and Sunderland easily accessible. Spacious well-appointed bedrooms cater well for the needs of the modern traveller and the leisure centre is well equipped for any gym enthusiast with a pool, sauna, steam room and jacuzzi. The bar and restaurant both offer informal dining with a wide and varied menu.

Rooms: 82 S £65–£150; D £75–£180* Facilities: STV FTV WiFi Xmas New Year **Conf:** Class 100 Board 100 Thtr 230 **Services:** Lift Night porter **Notes:** Civ Wed 150

Premier Inn Sunderland A19/A1231

BUDGET HOTEL

Wessington Way, Castletown, SR5 3HR - **tel:** 0871 527 9058
(Calls cost 13p per minute plus your phone company's access charge)
web: www.premierinn.com
dir: *From A19 take A1231 towards Sunderland. Hotel 100yds*

High quality, budget accommodation ideal for both families and business travellers. Spacious, en suite bedrooms feature free WiFi and tea and coffee making

facilities, and in most hotels, Freeview TV is also available. The adjacent family restaurant features a wide and varied menu.

Rooms: 91

Premier Inn Sunderland City Centre

BUDGET HOTEL

1-3 Hind Street, SR1 3QD - **tel:** 0871 527 9482
(Calls cost 13p per minute plus your phone company's access charge)
web: www.premierinn.com
dir: From S: A1, A23 towards Sunderland. At 1st rdbt, right. Right at 6th rdbt, hotel on right. From N: A1, A6900, A19. Approx 1m, take A1231 towards Sunderland. Right at rdbt. Right at 4th rdbt. Hotel on right

Rooms: 125

Premier Inn Sunderland North West

BUDGET HOTEL

Timber Beach Road, off Wessington Way, SR5 3XG - **tel:** 0871 527 9056
(Calls cost 13p per minute plus your phone company's access charge)
web: www.premierinn.com
dir: A1(M) junct 65, A1231 towards Sunderland, cross over A19

Rooms: 63

Holiday Inn London - Kingston South

★★★★ 77% HOTEL PLAN 1 C1

Kingston Tower, Portsmouth Road, KT6 5QQ - **tel:** 020 8786 6565
email: enquiries@hikingston.co.uk **web:** www.hikingston.co.uk
dir: M25 junct 10, A3, left onto A243, 3rd exit at rdbt. At lights left onto A307

This hotel occupies a convenient location overlooking the River Thames just outside Kingston-upon-Thames and close to Surbiton. Many front-facing bedrooms have beautiful river views; all are comfortable and stylish. The public areas include a small, well-equipped fitness room. Complimentary parking and WiFi are also available.

Rooms: 121 (3 family) S £99–£149; D £109–£159* **Facilities:** FTV WiFi HL Mini gym Discounted price for guests at nearby gym & pool Xmas New Year **Conf:** Class 125 Board 60 Thtr 250 **Services:** Lift Night porter Air con **Parking:** 120 **Notes:** Civ Wed 210

Holiday Inn London - Sutton

★★★ 79% HOTEL

Gibson Road, SM1 2RF - **tel:** 020 8234 1100
email: sales-sutton@ihg.com **web:** www.hilondonsuttonhotel.co.uk
dir: M25 junct 8, A217, B2230. Pass rail station, follow one-way system in right lane. At lights, right then immediately left, left into Gibson Rd

Well located for many famous attractions such as Chessington World of Adventures, the All-England Tennis Club at Wimbledon and Epsom Racecourse, this hotel offers air-conditioned bedrooms ranging from standard to executive, a variety of conference rooms, and leisure facilities with a swimming pool.

Rooms: 119 (39 family) **Facilities:** Spa STV FTV WiFi HL supervised Gym Xmas New Year **Conf:** Class 100 Board 70 Thtr 180 **Services:** Lift Air con **Parking:** 115 **Notes:** Civ Wed 160

INSPECTOR'S CHOICE

New Hall Hotel & Spa

★★★★ ◎◎ HOTEL

Walmley Road, B76 1QX - **tel:** 0121 378 2442 & 0845 072 7577
(Calls cost 5p per minute plus your phone company's access charge)
email: newhall@handpicked.co.uk **web:** www.handpickedhotels.co.uk/newhall
dir: M42 junct 9, A4097, 2m to rdbt, take 2nd exit signed Walmley. Take 2nd exit from next 5 rdbts follow Sutton Coldfield signs. At 6th rdbt take 3rd exit follow Sutton Coldfield signs. Hotel on left

Situated in 26 acres of beautiful grounds, this hotel is reputed to be the oldest inhabited, moated house in the country. The house's medieval charm and character combine well with 21st-century guest facilities. Executive and luxury suites are available. Public areas, with their fine panelling and mullioned stained-glass windows include the magnificent Great Chamber.

Rooms: 60 (14 family) (25 GF) S fr £126; D fr £126 (incl. bkfst)* **Facilities:** Spa STV FTV WiFi supervised Gym Steam room Pitch & putt Outdoor trim trail Xmas New Year **Conf:** Class 75 Board 35 Thtr 150 Del from £158 **Services:** Night porter **Parking:** 80 **Notes:** LB Civ Wed 75

Moor Hall Hotel & Spa

★★★★ 80% ◎◎ HOTEL

Moor Hall Drive, Four Oaks, B75 6LN - **tel:** 0121 308 3751
email: mail@moorhallhotel.co.uk **web:** www.moorhallhotel.co.uk
dir: A38 onto A453 towards Sutton Coldfield, right at lights into Weeford Rd. Hotel 150yds on left

Although only a short distance from the city centre this hotel enjoys a peaceful setting, overlooking extensive grounds and an adjacent golf course. Bedrooms are well equipped and executive rooms are particularly spacious. Public rooms include the formal two AA Rosette Oak Room Restaurant, and the informal Country Kitchen which offers a carvery and blackboard specials. The hotel also has a well-equipped spa with pool, sauna, steam room, jacuzzi and treatment rooms. Free WiFi available in all rooms and throughout the hotel.

Rooms: 83 (5 family) (33 GF) S £70–£140; D £80–£165 (incl. bkfst)* **Facilities:** Spa FTV WiFi HL Gym Aerobics studio Sauna Steam room **Conf:** Class 120 Board 45 Thtr 250 Del from £145 **Services:** Lift Night porter **Parking:** 170 **Notes:** LB Civ Wed 180

Premier Inn Birmingham North (Sutton Coldfield)

BUDGET HOTEL

Whitehouse Common Road, B75 6HD - **tel:** 0871 527 8088
(Calls cost 13p per minute plus your phone company's access charge)
web: www.premierinn.com
dir: M42 junct 9, A446 towards Lichfield, then A453 to Sutton Coldfield. Left into Whitehouse Common Rd, hotel on left

High quality, budget accommodation ideal for both families and business travellers. Spacious, en suite bedrooms feature free WiFi and tea and coffee making facilities, and in most hotels, Freeview TV is also available. The adjacent family restaurant features a wide and varied menu.

Rooms: 57

SUTTON SCOTNEY
Hampshire · Map 5 SU43

Norton Park

QHOTELS
INSPIRED BY YOU

★★★★ 80% HOTEL

SO21 3NB - **tel:** 01962 763000

email: nortonpark@qhotels.co.uk **web:** www.qhotels.co.uk

dir: *From A303 & A34 junct follow signs to Sutton Scotney. Hotel on Micheldever Station Rd (old A30), 1m from Sutton Scotney*

Set in 54 acres of beautiful parkland in the heart of Hampshire, Norton Park offers both business and leisure guests a great range of amenities. Dating from the 16th century, the hotel is complemented by extensive buildings housing the bedrooms, and public areas which include a superb leisure club and numerous conference facilities. Ample parking is available.

Rooms: 165 (11 family) (72 GF) S £75–£120; D £85–£160 (incl. bkfst)* **Facilities:** Spa FTV WiFi supervised Gym Steam room Sauna Experience shower Ice fountain Xmas New Year **Conf:** Class 250 Board 80 Thtr 340 Del from £130 **Services:** Lift Night porter **Parking:** 220 **Notes:** LB Civ Wed 340

SWAFFHAM
Norfolk · Map 13 TF80

Best Western George Hotel

BW Best Western.

★★★ 73% HOTEL

Station Street, PE37 7LJ - **tel:** 01760 721238

email: george@hotelswaffham.com **web:** www.georgehotelswaffham.co.uk

dir: *From the S: M11 junct 9, merge onto A11, continue on A14 exit 38, join A11, at rdbt 2nd exit A1065. From the N: A1, A17, A47*

Located in the centre of historic Swaffham and originally a 16th-century coaching inn, the hotel now offers a range of bedroom styles and sizes. Meals are served every day in The Green Room restaurant, or in the bar for a more informal dining experience. A suitable base for those exploring the North Norfolk Coast.

Rooms: 28 (2 family) (8 GF) S £50–£90; D £55–£100 (incl. bkfst)* **Facilities:** FTV WiFi **Conf:** Class 60 Board 50 Thtr 160 Del from £110 **Services:** Night porter **Parking:** 50 **Notes:** LB RS 24-26 Dec

Symbols and abbreviations
explained on pages 6–7

SWANAGE
Dorset · Map 5 SZ07

The Pines Hotel

★★★ 80% HOTEL

Burlington Road, BH19 1LT - **tel:** 01929 425211

email: reservations@pineshotel.co.uk **web:** www.pineshotel.co.uk

dir: *A351 to seafront, left then 2nd right. Hotel at end of road*

Enjoying a peaceful location with spectacular views over the cliffs and sea, The Pines is a pleasant place to stay. Many of the comfortable bedrooms have sea views. Guests can take tea in the lounge, enjoy appetising bar snacks in the attractive bar, and dine on interesting cuisine in the restaurant.

Rooms: 41 (26 family) (6 GF) S £81; D £162–£222 (incl. bkfst)* **Facilities:** FTV WiFi Xmas New Year **Conf:** Class 80 Board 80 Thtr 80 Del from £104 **Services:** Lift Night porter **Parking:** 60 **Notes:** LB

See advert opposite

Purbeck House Hotel

★★★ 76% HOTEL

91 High Street, BH19 2LZ - **tel:** 01929 422872
email: reservations@purbeckhousehotel.co.uk **web:** www.purbeckhousehotel.co.uk
dir: *A351 to Swanage via Wareham, right into Shore Rd, into Institute Rd,*
right into High St

Originally built in 1875 as a private residence for George Burt (known as 'The King of Swanage'), this family-run hotel has plenty of history, including wonderful mosaic floors, original servant's bells and ornate ceilings. Bedrooms are varied in style, but all offer the expected comforts, with rooms located both within the main house and in Louisa Lodge, which is just a short stroll through the wonderful Victorian gardens. Impressive cuisine is well worth sampling, served within the grandeur of the former chapel. Generous parking is provided, and Purbeck House is just a short walk from the seafront and town centre.

Rooms: 38 **Facilities: Conf:** Class 36 Board 25 Thtr 100 **Parking:** 57
Notes: Closed 23-29 Dec Civ Wed 100

SWANLEY
Kent

Map 6 TQ56

Premier Inn Swanley

BUDGET HOTEL

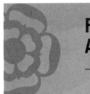

London Road, BR8 7QD - **tel:** 0871 527 9288
(Calls cost 13p per minute plus your phone company's access charge)
web: www.premierinn.com
dir: *M25 junct 3, B2173 towards Swanley. At rdbt 2nd exit onto B258 (High St).*
At next rdbt 4th exit into Swanley Ln, 1st exit into Bartholomew Way,
at next rdbt 3rd exit into London Rd

High quality, budget accommodation ideal for both families and business travellers. Spacious, en suite bedrooms feature free WiFi and tea and coffee making facilities, and in most hotels, Freeview TV is also available. The adjacent family restaurant features a wide and varied menu.

Rooms: 62

Find out more about AA Rosettes
– page 13

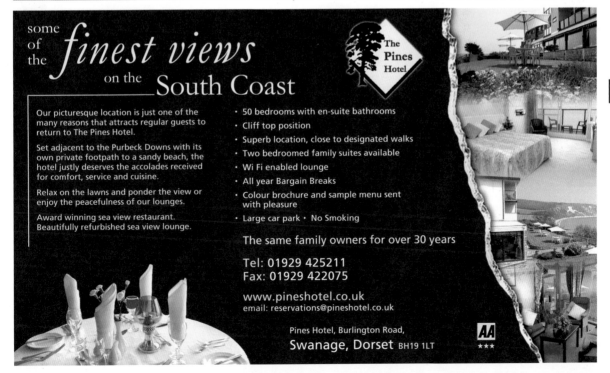

Blunsdon House Hotel

★★★★ 76% HOTEL

Blunsdon, SN26 7AS - tel: 01793 721701
email: reservations@blunsdonhouse.co.uk web: www.blunsdonhouse.co.uk
dir: M4 junct 15, A419 towards Cirencester. Exit at Blunsdon/Swindon,
follow brown hotel signs

Located just to the north of Swindon, Blunsdon House is set in 30 acres of well-kept grounds, and offers extensive leisure facilities and spacious day rooms. The hotel has a choice of eating and drinking options, including the spacious Carrie's Bar and the contemporary Flame Charcoal Grill and Lunchtime Carvery. Bedrooms are comfortably furnished, and include family rooms with bunk beds and the modern, spacious Pavilion rooms.

Rooms: 108 (17 family) (27 GF) ♠ S £79–£159; D £79–£169* Facilities: Spa STV FTV WiFi ♨ HL ☒ ⚑ 9 Putting green ☺ Gym Beauty therapy Woodland walk Spin studio Xmas New Year Child facilities Conf: Class 200 Board 55 Thtr 300 Del from £129 Services: Lift Night porter Parking: 300 Notes: LB Civ Wed 200

The Pear Tree at Purton

★★★ 82% ◉◉ HOTEL

Church End, SN5 4ED - tel: 01793 772100
email: stay@peartreepurton.co.uk web: www.peartreepurton.co.uk

(For full entry see Purton)

Chiseldon House Hotel

★★★ 81% ◉ HOTEL

New Road, Chiseldon, SN4 0NE - tel: 01793 741010
email: welcome@chiseldonhouse.com web: www.chiseldonhouse.com
dir: M4 junct 15, A346 signed Marlborough. In 0.5m right onto B4500, 0.25m,
hotel on right

Conveniently located for access to the M4, Chiseldon House is in a quiet location and has a relaxed ambience. Bedrooms include a number of larger rooms but all are comfortably furnished. The award-winning restaurant offers a selection of carefully prepared dishes utilising high quality produce. Guests are welcome to enjoy the pleasant garden with outdoor seating.

Rooms: 21 (4 family) ♠ S £90–£130; D £140–£170 (incl. bkfst)* Facilities: FTV WiFi ♨ Conf: Class 20 Board 32 Thtr 65 Del from £150 Services: Night porter Parking: 50 Notes: LB Civ Wed 100

Stanton House Hotel

★★★ 77% HOTEL

The Avenue, Stanton Fitzwarren, SN6 7SD - tel: 01793 861779 & 0843 507 1388
(Calls cost 7p per minute plus your phone company's access charge)
email: reception@stantonhouse.co.uk web: www.stantonhouse.co.uk
dir: A419 onto A361 towards Highworth, left towards Stanton Fitzwarren
about 600yds, hotel on left

Extensive grounds and superb gardens surround this Cotswold-stone manor house, and the park and Stanton Lake are accessible for some great walks. Smart, well-maintained bedrooms have been equipped with modern comforts. Public areas include a conservatory, a bar and two eating options - The Rosemary Restaurant

offering a wide choice of Japanese and European dishes, and the Mt Fuji Restaurant specialising in authentic Japanese food in traditional surroundings. The friendly, multi-lingual staff create a relaxing atmosphere for guests.

Rooms: 78 (27 GF) S £49–£79; D £69–£130* Facilities: STV FTV WiFi Xmas New Year Conf: Class 70 Board 40 Thtr 110 Del from £115 Services: Lift Night porter Parking: 110 Notes: Civ Wed 110

Premier Inn Swindon Central

BUDGET HOTEL

Kembrey Business Park, Kembrey Street, SN2 8YS - tel: 0871 527 9064
(Calls cost 13p per minute plus your phone company's access charge)
web: www.premierinn.com
dir: M4 junct 15, A419 (Swindon bypass) towards Cirencester.
In 6m at Turnpike Rdbt 1st left. Hotel on left in 2m

High quality, budget accommodation ideal for both families and business travellers. Spacious, en suite bedrooms feature free WiFi and tea and coffee making facilities, and in most hotels, Freeview TV is also available. The adjacent family restaurant features a wide and varied menu.

Rooms: 50

Premier Inn Swindon North

BUDGET HOTEL

Broad Bush, Blunsdon, SN26 8DJ - tel: 0871 527 9066
(Calls cost 13p per minute plus your phone company's access charge)
web: www.premierinn.com
dir: N of Swindon. 5m from M4 junct 15. At junct of A419 & B4019

Rooms: 62

Premier Inn Swindon West

BUDGET HOTEL

Great Western Way, SN5 8UY - tel: 0871 527 9068
(Calls cost 13p per minute plus your phone company's access charge)
web: www.premierinn.com
dir: M4 junct 16, A3102 to Lydiard Fields. Past Hilton, entrance on left.
NB for Sat Nav use SN5 8UB

Rooms: 89

Premier Inn Epsom South

BUDGET HOTEL

Brighton Road, Burgh Heath, KT20 6BW - tel: 0871 527 8382
(Calls cost 13p per minute plus your phone company's access charge)
web: www.premierinn.com
dir: Just off M25 junct 8 on A217 towards Sutton

High quality, budget accommodation ideal for both families and business travellers. Spacious, en suite bedrooms feature free WiFi and tea and coffee making facilities, and in most hotels, Freeview TV is also available. The adjacent family restaurant features a wide and varied menu.

Rooms: 78

S

TAMWORTH Staffordshire	Map 10 SK20

Premier Inn Tamworth Central

BUDGET HOTEL

Bonehill Road, Bitterscote, B78 3HQ - tel: 0871 527 9070
(Calls cost 13p per minute plus your phone company's access charge)
web: www.premierinn.com
dir: M42 junct 10, A5 towards Tamworth. Left in 3m onto A51 signed Tamworth. Straight on at 1st rdbt. At next rdbt 3rd exit. Hotel adjacent to Ladybridge Beefeater

High quality, budget accommodation ideal for both families and business travellers. Spacious, en suite bedrooms feature free WiFi and tea and coffee making facilities, and in most hotels, Freeview TV is also available. The adjacent family restaurant features a wide and varied menu.

Rooms: 74

Premier Inn Tamworth South

BUDGET HOTEL

Watling Street, Wilnecote, B77 5PN - tel: 0871 527 9072
(Calls cost 13p per minute plus your phone company's access charge)
web: www.premierinn.com
dir: M42 junct 10, A5 towards Tamworth. Left in 200yds signed Wilnecote/B5404. Left at next rdbt, hotel on left

Rooms: 32

TANKERSLEY South Yorkshire	Map 16 SK39

Tankersley Manor

★★★★ 75% HOTEL

INSPIRED BY YOU

Church Lane, S75 3DQ - tel: 01226 744700
email: tankersleymanor@qhotels.co.uk web: www.qhotels.co.uk
dir: M1 junct 36, A61 Sheffield Road

High on the moors with views over the countryside, this 17th-century residence is well located for major cities, tourist attractions and motorway links. Where appropriate, bedrooms retain original features such as exposed beams or Yorkshire-stone window sills. The hotel has a bar and brasserie which has old beams and open fires. A well-equipped leisure centre is also available.

Rooms: 98 (10 family) (16 GF) ☎ S £55–£135; D £61–£141 (incl. bkfst)*
Facilities: Spa STV FTV WiFi ⬇ ⓢ Gym Swimming lessons Beauty treatments New Year Conf: Class 200 Board 100 Thtr 400 Del from £120 Services: Lift Night porter Parking: 350 Notes: LB Civ Wed 250

Premier Inn Sheffield/Barnsley M1 Jct 36

BUDGET HOTEL

Maple Road, S75 3DL - tel: 0871 527 8968
(Calls cost 13p per minute plus your phone company's access charge)
web: www.premierinn.com
dir: M1 junct 35A (N'bound exit only), A616 for 2m. From M1 junct 36, A61 towards Sheffield

High quality, budget accommodation ideal for both families and business travellers. Spacious, en suite bedrooms feature free WiFi and tea and coffee making facilities, and in most hotels, Freeview TV is also available. The adjacent family restaurant features a wide and varied menu.

Rooms: 62

TAPLOW Buckinghamshire	Map 6 SU98

INSPECTOR'S CHOICE

Cliveden

★★★★★ ⓐⓐⓐ ⌂ COUNTRY HOUSE HOTEL

Cliveden Estate, SL6 0JF - tel: 01628 668561
email: info@clivedenhouse.co.uk web: www.clivedenhouse.co.uk
dir: M4 junct 7, A4 towards Maidenhead, 1.5m, onto B476 towards Taplow, 2.5m, hotel on left

Cliveden is a wonderful stately home that stands at the top of a gravelled boulevard. After a major refurbishment, Cliveden has been restored to its former glory, and welcomes guests in luxury and style. Visitors are treated as house-guests and staff recapture a tradition of fine hospitality. Bedrooms have individual quality and style, and reception rooms retain a timeless elegance. Restaurant André Garrett at Cliveden has been awarded three AA Rosettes for its outstanding cuisine; guests can also dine at the Astor Grill, housed in the old stable block. As we went to press the opening of the newly refurbished spa was announced. This incorporates the original outdoor swimming pool, and new facilities that include a gym, indoor heated pool, infrared sauna, aromatherapy steam room, indoor jacuzzi, outdoor hot tubs, seven treatment rooms, and a beauty and hairdressing studio. The spa also provides a new spa restaurant and lounge.

Rooms: 48 (1 annexe) (19 family) (13 GF) ☎ D £495–£2175 (incl. bkfst)*
Facilities: Spa STV FTV WiFi ⓢ ⬆ ⓢ ⬇ Gym Squash 2 vintage boats Xmas New Year Conf: Class 48 Board 40 Thtr 120 Services: Lift Night porter Parking: 60 Notes: LB Civ Wed 120

T

TAPLOW *continued*

Taplow House Hotel

★★★★ 75% ● HOTEL

Berry Hill, SL6 0DA - tel: 01628 670056
email: reception@taplowhouse.com **web:** www.taplowhouse.com
dir: *Exit A4 onto Berry Hill, hotel 0.5m on right*

This elegant Georgian manor is set amid beautiful gardens and has been skilfully restored. Character public rooms are pleasing and include a number of air-conditioned conference rooms and an elegant, award-winning restaurant. Comfortable bedrooms are individually decorated and furnished to a high standard.

Rooms: 32 (5 family) (2 GF) � **Facilities:** STV FTV WiFi � � **Conf:** Class 50 Board 42 Thtr 100 **Services:** Night porter Air con **Parking:** 100 **Notes:** Civ Wed 100

TARPORLEY	Map 15 SJ56
Cheshire	

Macdonald Portal Hotel Golf & Spa

★★★★ 78% ● HOTEL   MACDONALD HOTELS & RESORTS

Cobblers Cross Lane, CW6 0DJ - tel: 01829 734100
email: general.portal@macdonald-hotels.co.uk
web: www.macdonaldhotels.co.uk/theportal
dir: *M6 junct 18, A54 towards Middlewich/Winsford. Left onto A49, through Cotebrook. In approx 1m follow signs for hotel*

This hotel is located in beautiful rolling countryside and provides a luxury base for both the leisure and business guest. The spacious and well-equipped bedrooms have bathrooms with baths and power showers. Extensive leisure facilities include a superb spa, well equipped gym and thermal suite, three golf courses and a golf academy. The Scottish Steakhouse, as the name suggests, serves great steaks alongside innovative seasonal dishes. Staff throughout are very friendly and welcoming.

Rooms: 85 (29 GF) � **Facilities:** Spa STV FTV WiFi � HL � � 45 Putting green Gym Golf academy Outdoor pursuits New Year **Conf:** Class 180 Board 60 Thtr 250 **Services:** Lift Night porter **Parking:** 250 **Notes:** Civ Wed 250

TAUNTON	Map 4 ST22
Somerset	

INSPECTOR'S CHOICE

The Mount Somerset Hotel & Spa

★★★★ ●●● COUNTRY HOUSE HOTEL

Lower Henlade, TA3 5NB - tel: 01823 442500
email: info@mountsomersethotel.co.uk **web:** www.mountsomersethotel.co.uk
dir: *M5 junct 25, A358 towards Chard/Ilminster, at Henlade right into Stoke Rd, left at T-junct at end, then right into drive*

From its elevated and rural position, this impressive Regency house has wonderful views over Taunton Vale. There are impressive quality and comfort levels throughout in the stylish bedrooms and bathrooms. The elegant public rooms combine style and flair with an engaging and intimate atmosphere. In addition to the daily-changing, fixed-price menu, a carefully selected seasonal carte is available in the restaurant.

Rooms: 19 (1 family) � **S** £125–£250; **D** £145–£325 (incl. bkfst)* **Facilities:** Spa FTV WiFi � Gym Hydrotherapy pool Sauna Steam room Experience showers Foot spas Xmas New Year **Conf:** Class 60 Board 35 Thtr 70 Del from £175 **Services:** Lift Night porter **Parking:** 100 **Notes:** LB Civ Wed 80

The Castle at Taunton

★★★★ 80% ●● HOTEL

Castle Green, TA1 1NF - tel: 01823 272671
email: reception@the-castle-hotel.com
dir: *Please phone for directions*

This delightful hotel has occupied its very central location in the heart of Taunton for a great many years. Combining the character and charm of a castle with stylish public areas, a wide range of comfortable bedrooms and bathrooms are offered from larger feature rooms to smaller but well equipped standard rooms. Dining here is a treat with the option of two restaurants – the fine dining selection of The Castle Bow restaurant or the more relaxed setting of Brazz – a combination of brasserie, bar and café. Adjacent parking is another welcome feature.

Rooms: 44 **Facilities:** FTV WiFi

Taunton House Hotel

★★★ 75% METRO HOTEL

14 Billetfield, TA1 3NN - tel: 01823 272083
email: info@tauntonhousehotel.co.uk **web:** www.tauntonhousehotel.co.uk
dir: *Please phone for directions*

Centrally and conveniently located, this elegant establishment dates back to the 1850s and retains many original features such as stained-glass windows and a wonderful oak staircase. Bedrooms provide impressive levels of comfort and quality with well-equipped, modern bathrooms. Public areas reflect the same high standards that are a hallmark throughout this hotel.

Rooms: 17 (4 family) (6 GF) (2 smoking) � **Facilities:** FTV WiFi � **Parking:** 17

Corner House Hotel

★★★ 73% HOTEL

Park Street, TA1 4DQ - tel: 01823 284683
email: res@corner-house.co.uk **web:** www.corner-house.co.uk
dir: *0.3m from town centre. Hotel on junct of Park St & A38 – Wellington Rd*

The unusual Victorian façade of the Corner House, with its turrets and stained-glass windows, belies the wealth of modern innovation, quality and style to be found inside. The contemporary bedrooms have state-of-the-art facilities including flat-screen TVs, ample working space, and fridges with complimentary water and fresh milk. The smart public areas include the convivial bar and the relaxed and enjoyable 'Wine & Sausage' eating rooms. Free WiFi is available throughout.

Rooms: 45 (10 annexe) (4 family) (4 GF) � **S** fr £59; **D** fr £69* **Facilities:** FTV WiFi Xmas New Year **Conf:** Class 32 Board 26 Thtr 45 **Parking:** 30

Premier Inn Taunton Central (North)

BUDGET HOTEL

Massingham Park, Priorswood Road, TA2 7RX - tel: 0871 527 9076
(Calls cost 13p per minute plus your phone company's access charge)
web: www.premierinn.com
dir: *M5 junct 25, A358 into Taunton, at 2nd rdbt right onto Obridge Viaduct.
Hotel at next rdbt*

High quality, budget accommodation ideal for both families and business travellers. Spacious, en suite bedrooms feature free WiFi and tea and coffee making facilities, and in most hotels, Freeview TV is also available. The adjacent family restaurant features a wide and varied menu.

Rooms: 40

Premier Inn Taunton East

BUDGET HOTEL

81 Bridgwater Road, TA1 2DU - tel: 0871 527 9080
(Calls cost 13p per minute plus your phone company's access charge)
web: www.premierinn.com
dir: *M5 junct 25 follow signs to Taunton. Straight on at 1st rdbt, keep left at Creech
Castle lights, hotel 200yds on right*

Rooms: 60

Premier Inn Taunton (Ruishton)

BUDGET HOTEL

Ruishton Lane, Ruishton, TA3 5LU - tel: 0871 527 9074
(Calls cost 13p per minute plus your phone company's access charge)
web: www.premierinn.com
dir: *Just off M5 junct 25 on A38*

Rooms: 77

| TAVISTOCK | Map 3 SX47 |
| Devon | |

The Horn of Plenty

★★★★ 80% 🏵🏵 HOTEL

Gulworthy, PL19 8JD - tel: 01822 832528
email: enquiries@thehornofplenty.co.uk **web:** www.thehornofplenty.co.uk
dir: *From Tavistock take A390 W for 3m. Right at Gulworthy Cross. In 400yds turn left,
hotel in 400yds on right*

With stunning views over the Tamar Valley, The Horn of Plenty maintains its reputation as one of Britain's best country-house hotels. Bedrooms are well equipped and have many thoughtful extras. The garden rooms offer impressive levels of both quality and comfort, while award-winning cuisine is served with accomplished skill and a passion for local produce.

Rooms: 16 (12 annexe) (3 family) (8 GF) 🌂 **D** £150–£345 (incl. bkfst)*
Facilities: FTV WiFi ⮂ 🐟 Falconry Xmas New Year **Conf:** Class 22 Board 16 Thtr 40
Parking: 35 **Notes:** LB Civ Wed 90

Bedford Hotel

★★★ 80% 🟤 HOTEL

1 Plymouth Road, PL19 8BB - tel: 01822 613221
email: reception@bedford-hotel.co.uk **web:** www.bedford-hotel.co.uk
dir: *M5 junct 31, A30 Launceston/Okehampton. Then A386 to Tavistock,
follow town centre signs. Hotel opposite church*

Built on the site of a Benedictine abbey, this impressive castellated building has been welcoming visitors for over 200 years. Very much a local landmark, the hotel offers comfortable and relaxing public areas, all reflecting charm and character throughout. Bedrooms are traditionally styled with contemporary comforts, while the Woburn Restaurant provides a refined setting for enjoyable cuisine.

Rooms: 31 (2 family) (5 GF) 🌂 **Facilities:** FTV WiFi ⮂ Xmas New Year **Conf:** Class 100 Board 60 Thtr 160 **Services:** Lift Night porter **Parking:** 52 **Notes:** LB Civ Wed 120

| TEIGNMOUTH | Map 3 SX97 |
| Devon | |

Cliffden Hotel

★★★ 73% HOTEL

Dawlish Road, TQ14 8TE - tel: 01626 770052
email: cliffden@visionhotels.co.uk **web:** www.visionhotels.co.uk
dir: *M5 junct 31, A380, B3192 to Teignmouth. Down hill on Exeter Rd to lights,
left to rdbt (station on left). Left, follow Dawlish signs. Up hill. Hotel next right*

While this hotel mainly caters for visually impaired guests, their families, friends and guide dogs, it offers a warm welcome to all. Cliffden Hotel is a listed Victorian building set in six acres of delightful gardens overlooking a small valley. Bedrooms are comfortable, very spacious and thoughtfully equipped. There are also leisure facilities and, of course, special provision for guide dogs.

Rooms: 47 (8 family) (10 GF) 🌂 **S** £45–£72; **D** £68–£118 (incl. bkfst)*
Facilities: FTV WiFi 🕸 supervised 🎵 Xmas New Year **Conf:** Class 30 Board 30
Thtr 50 **Services:** Lift Night porter **Parking:** 25 **Notes:** LB Civ Wed 50

| TELFORD | Map 10 SJ60 |
| Shropshire | |

Telford Hotel & Golf Resort

★★★★ 80% HOTEL

Great Hay Drive, Sutton Heights, TF7 4DT - tel: 01952 429977
email: telford@qhotels.co.uk **web:** www.qhotels.co.uk
dir: *M54 junct 4, A442. Follow signs for Telford Golf Club*

Set on the edge of Telford with panoramic views of the famous Ironbridge Gorge, this hotel sets high standards. Smart bedrooms are complemented by spacious public areas, large conference facilities, a spa with treatment rooms, a golf course and a driving range. Ample parking is available.

Rooms: 114 (8 family) (50 GF) 🌂 **S** £71–£171; **D** £83–£183 (incl. bkfst)*
Facilities: Spa STV WiFi ⮂ 🕸 ⛳ 18 Putting green Gym Xmas New Year
Conf: Class 220 Board 100 Thtr 350 Del from £135 **Services:** Lift Night porter
Parking: 200 **Notes:** LB Civ Wed 250

T

TELFORD *continued*

Hadley Park House

★★★★ 75% 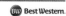 HOTEL

Hadley Park, TF1 6QJ - tel: 01952 677269
email: info@hadleypark.co.uk web: www.hadleypark.co.uk
dir: *Off Hadley Park Island exit A442 to Whitchurch*

Located in Telford, but close to Ironbridge, this elegant Georgian mansion is situated in three acres of its own grounds. Bedrooms are spacious and well equipped. There is a comfortable bar and lounge, and meals are served in the attractive conservatory-style restaurant.

Rooms: 22 (6 family) (5 GF) ✆ Facilities: STV FTV WiFi ⌕ Xmas New Year Conf: Class 60 Board 40 Thtr 200 Services: Night porter Parking: 60 Notes: Civ Wed 200

Best Western Valley Hotel

★★★ 82% ◉◉ HOTEL

BW Best Western.

Ironbridge, TF8 7DW - tel: 01952 432247
email: valley@cpmh.co.uk web: www.thevalleyhotel.co.uk
dir: *M6, M54 junct 6 onto A5223 to Ironbridge*

This privately owned hotel is situated in attractive gardens, close to the famous Iron Bridge. It was once the home of the Maws family who manufactured ceramic tiles, and fine examples of their craft are found throughout the house. Bedrooms vary in size and are split between the main house and a mews development; imaginative meals are served in the attractive Chez Maws restaurant.

Rooms: 44 (3 family) (6 GF) ✆ S fr £50; D fr £75* Facilities: FTV WiFi ⌕
Conf: Class 80 Board 60 Thtr 120 Del from £115 Services: Lift Night porter
Parking: 70 Notes: LB Closed 24 Dec-2 Jan RS 25 Dec Lunch only Civ Wed 120

Premier Inn Telford Central

BUDGET HOTEL

Euston Way, TF3 4LY - tel: 0871 527 9082
(Calls cost 13p per minute plus your phone company's access charge)
web: www.premierinn.com
dir: *M54 junct 5 follow Central Railway Station signs. Hotel at 2nd exit off rdbt signed railway station*

High quality, budget accommodation ideal for both families and business travellers. Spacious, en suite bedrooms feature free WiFi and tea and coffee making facilities, and in most hotels, Freeview TV is also available. The adjacent family restaurant features a wide and varied menu.

Rooms: 89

Premier Inn Telford International Centre

BUDGET HOTEL

Southwater Square, Saint Quentin Gate, TF3 4EJ - tel: 0871 527 9500
(Calls cost 13p per minute plus your phone company's access charge)
web: www.premierinn.com
dir: *M6 junct, M54. Exit at junct 5, take 2nd exit at 1st rdbt into Forge Gate. Merge into middle lane of one-way system. At next rdbt take 3rd exit into Grange Central. Right into St. Quentin Gate*

Rooms: 85

Premier Inn Telford North

BUDGET HOTEL

Donnington Wood Way, Donnington, TF2 8LE - tel: 0871 527 9084
(Calls cost 13p per minute plus your phone company's access charge)
web: www.premierinn.com
dir: *From Telford M54 junct 4, B5060 (Redhill Way) signed Donnington. At rdbt straight on (becomes Donnington Wood Way then School Rd). At mini rdbt take 1st left into Wellington Rd. Hotel adjacent to McDonalds & Shell garage*

Rooms: 20

TELFORD SERVICE AREA (M54)	Map 10 SJ70
Shropshire	

Days Inn Telford - M54

AA Advertised

Telford Services, Priorslee Road, TF11 8TG - tel: 01952 238400
email: telford.hotel@welcomebreak.co.uk web: www.welcomebreak.co.uk
dir: *At M54 junct 4*

This modern building offers accommodation in smart, spacious and well-equipped bedrooms, suitable for families and business travellers, and all with en suite bathrooms. Continental breakfast is available, and other refreshments may be taken at the nearby family restaurant.

Rooms: 48 (45 family) (21 GF) (9 smoking) Facilities: FTV WiFi ⌕ Conf: Board 8
Parking: 100

TEMPLE SOWERBY	Map 18 NY62
Cumbria	

HIGHLY RECOMMENDED

Temple Sowerby House Hotel & Restaurant

★★★ 87% ◉◉ COUNTRY HOUSE HOTEL

CA10 1RZ - tel: 017683 61578
email: stay@templesowerby.com web: www.templesowerby.com
dir: *7m from M6 junct 40, midway between Penrith & Appleby, in village centre*

Temple Sowerby House Hotel is set in the heart of the Eden Valley, ideal for exploring the northern Lake District and Pennine Fells. Bedrooms are comfortable and stylish, most feature ultra-modern bathrooms, and there is a choice of pleasant lounges. The restaurant, with picture windows overlooking the beautiful walled garden, is a splendid place to enjoy the award-winning cuisine. Staff throughout are friendly and keen to please.

Rooms: 12 (4 annexe) (2 GF) ✆ S £110–£120; D £150–£170 (incl. bkfst)*
Facilities: FTV WiFi ⌕ ⛳ New Year Conf: Class 20 Board 20 Thtr 30 Del from £175 Parking: 15 Notes: LB Closed 20-29 Dec No children 12yrs Civ Wed 40

TENTERDEN	Map 6 TQ83
Kent	

Little Silver Country Hotel

★★★ 80% HOTEL

Ashford Road, St Michael's, TN30 6SP - tel: 01233 850321
email: enquiries@little-silver.co.uk web: www.little-silver.co.uk
dir: *M20 junct 8, A274 signed Tenterden*

Located just outside the charming town of Tenterden and within easy reach of many local Kent attractions, this charming hotel is ideal for leisure and business guests as well as being a popular wedding venue. Bedrooms are spaciously appointed and well equipped; many boast spa baths. There is a spacious lounge, a small bar and a modern restaurant that overlooks beautifully tended gardens.

Rooms: 16 (1 family) (6 GF) ✆ **S** £65–£125; **D** £99–£199 (incl. bkfst)*
Facilities: FTV WiFi ♨ Xmas **Conf:** Class 50 Board 25 Thtr 75 Del £123.50 **Parking:** 70 **Notes:** LB Civ Wed 120

London Beach Country Hotel, Spa & Golf Club

★★★ 76% HOTEL

Ashford Road, TN30 6HX - **tel:** 01580 766279
email: enquiries@londonbeach.com **web:** www.londonbeach.com
dir: *M20 junct 9, A28 follow signs to Tenterden (10m). Hotel on right 1m before Tenterden*

A modern, purpose-built hotel situated in mature grounds on the outskirts of Tenterden. The spacious bedrooms are smartly decorated with co-ordinated soft furnishings, and most rooms have balconies with superb views over the golf course. The open-plan public rooms feature a brasserie-style restaurant, where a good choice of dishes is served.

Rooms: 26 (5 family) ✆ **Facilities:** Spa FTV WiFi ♨ ⊛ ↯ 9 Putting green Fishing Gym Driving range Health club Xmas New Year **Conf:** Class 75 Board 40 Thtr 100 **Services:** Lift Night porter **Parking:** 100 **Notes:** Civ Wed 100

TETBURY   Map 4 ST89
Gloucestershire

Calcot

★★★★ ⊛⊛ HOTEL

Calcot, GL8 8YJ - **tel:** 01666 890391
email: receptionists@calcot.co **web:** www.calcot.co
dir: *3m W of Tetbury at A4135 & A46 junct*

Cistercian monks built the ancient barns and stables around which this lovely English farmhouse is set. No two rooms are identical, and each is beautifully decorated and equipped with modern comforts. Sumptuous sitting rooms, with crackling log fires in the winter, look out over immaculate gardens. There are two dining options: the elegant conservatory restaurant and the informal Gumstool Inn. There are also ample function rooms. The health and leisure spa includes an indoor pool, high-tech gym, massage tables, complementary therapies and much more. For children, a supervised crèche and 'playzone' are a great attraction.

Rooms: 35 (23 annexe) (13 family) (17 GF) ✆ **S** £184–£524; **D** £209–£549 (incl. bkfst)* **Facilities:** Spa STV WiFi ♨ ⊛ ⊛ ↯ Gym Clay pigeon shooting Archery Cycling Running track Segways Disc golf Xmas New Year Child facilities **Conf:** Class 70 Board 30 Thtr 120 Del £310 **Services:** Night porter **Parking:** 150 **Notes:** LB Civ Wed 100

The Close Hotel

★★★★ 79% ⊛⊛ ⊜ HOTEL

8 Long Street, GL8 8AQ - **tel:** 01666 502272
email: info@theclose-hotel.com **web:** www.cotswold-inns-hotels.co.uk
dir: *M4 junct 17 onto A429 or M5 junct 14 onto B4509, follow Tetbury signs*

Even with its town centre location, The Close Hotel retains a country-house feel that has made this a favourite with many for years. Bedrooms are striking and well equipped, with thoughtful touches such as home-made biscuits and bottled water. The public rooms provide a choice of relaxing areas with log fires lit in the winter. In the summer, guests can enjoy the terrace in the attractive walled garden.

Rooms: 18 ✆ **D** fr £100 (incl. bkfst)* **Facilities:** FTV WiFi ♨ Xmas New Year **Conf:** Board 22 Thtr 50 **Services:** Night porter **Parking:** 10

Hare & Hounds Hotel

★★★★ 79% ⊛⊛ ⊜ HOTEL

Westonbirt, GL8 8QL - **tel:** 01666 881000
email: reception@hareandhoundshotel.com **web:** www.cotswold-inns-hotels.co.uk
dir: *2.5m SW of Tetbury on A433*

This popular hotel, set in extensive grounds, is situated close to Westonbirt Arboretum and has remained under the same ownership for over 50 years. The stylish bedrooms are individually designed; those in the main house are more traditional and the cottage rooms are contemporary. The public rooms include an informal bar and light, airy lounges - one with a log fire lit in colder months. Guests can eat either in the bar or the attractive Beaufort Restaurant.

Rooms: 42 (21 annexe) (8 family) (13 GF) ✆ **S** fr £79; **D** fr £98 (incl. bkfst)* **Facilities:** FTV WiFi ♨ ↯ Xmas New Year **Conf:** Class 80 Board 40 Thtr 120 **Services:** Night porter **Parking:** 85 **Notes:** Civ Wed 120

The Priory Inn

★★★ 78% SMALL HOTEL

London Road, GL8 8JJ - **tel:** 01666 502251
email: info@theprioryinn.co.uk **web:** www.theprioryinn.co.uk
dir: *On A433 (Cirencester to Tetbury road). Hotel 200yds from Market Square*

A warm welcome is assured at this attractive inn where friendly service is a high priority. Public areas and bedrooms have a contemporary style that mixes well with more traditional features, such as an open fireplace in the cosy bar dining room. Cuisine, using locally sourced produce, is offered on a menu that should suit all tastes.

Rooms: 14 (1 family) (4 GF) **S** £85–£135; **D** £99–£135 (incl. bkfst)* **Facilities:** FTV WiFi ♫ **Conf:** Class 28 Board 28 Thtr 30 Del £139 **Parking:** 35

Snooty Fox

★★★ 76% SMALL HOTEL

Market Place, GL8 8DD - **tel:** 01666 502436
email: res@snooty-fox.co.uk **web:** www.snooty-fox.co.uk
dir: *In town centre*

Centrally situated, this 16th-century coaching inn retains original features and is a popular venue for weekend breaks. The relaxed and friendly atmosphere, the high standard of accommodation, and the food offered in the bar and restaurant, are all very good reasons why many guests return here time and again.

Rooms: 12 **D** £130–£170 (incl. bkfst)* **Facilities:** FTV WiFi ♨ Xmas New Year **Conf:** Class 12 Board 16 Thtr 24 Del from £105 **Notes:** LB

T

TEWKESBURY
Gloucestershire

Map 10 SO83

Premier Inn Tewkesbury

BUDGET HOTEL

Shannon Way, Ashchurch, GL20 8ND - **tel:** 0871 527 9088
(Calls cost 13p per minute plus your phone company's access charge)
web: www.premierinn.com
dir: *M5 junct 9, A438 towards Tewkesbury, hotel 400yds on right*

High quality, budget accommodation ideal for both families and business travellers. Spacious, en suite bedrooms feature free WiFi and tea and coffee making facilities, and in most hotels, Freeview TV is also available. The adjacent family restaurant features a wide and varied menu.

Rooms: 59

THETFORD
Norfolk

Map 13 TL88

Premier Inn Thetford

BUDGET HOTEL

Lynn Wood, Maine Street, IP24 3PG - **tel:** 0871 527 9090
(Calls cost 13p per minute plus your phone company's access charge)
web: www.premierinn.com
dir: *From A11 N follow Thetford signs. At 3rd rdbt 1st exit for town centre into Brandon Rd. 1st exit into Maine St*

High quality, budget accommodation ideal for both families and business travellers. Spacious, en suite bedrooms feature free WiFi and tea and coffee making facilities, and in most hotels, Freeview TV is also available. The adjacent family restaurant features a wide and varied menu.

Rooms: 70

THIRSK
North Yorkshire

Map 19 SE48

Premier Inn Thirsk

BUDGET HOTEL

Sowerby Gateway, YO7 3HF - **tel:** 0871 622 2319
web: www.premierinn.com
dir: *Please phone for directions*

High quality, budget accommodation ideal for both families and business travellers. Spacious, en suite bedrooms feature free WiFi and tea and coffee making facilities, and in most hotels, Freeview TV is also available. The adjacent family restaurant features a wide and varied menu.

Rooms: 65

THORNBURY
Gloucestershire

Map 4 ST69

INSPECTOR'S CHOICE

Thornbury Castle

★★★ ◉◉ COUNTRY HOUSE HOTEL

Castle Street, BS35 1HH - **tel:** 01454 281182
email: info@thornburycastle.co.uk **web:** www.thornburycastle.co.uk
dir: *On A38 N'bound from Bristol take 1st turn to Thornbury. At end of High St left into Castle St, follow brown sign, entrance to Castle on left behind St Mary's Church*

History fans may be interested to learn that Henry VIII ordered the first owner of this castle to be beheaded! Guests today have the opportunity of sleeping in historical surroundings fitted out with all the modern amenities. Most rooms have four-poster or coronet beds and real fires, and guests can even choose to sleep in the Duke's Bedchamber where King Henry and Anne Boleyn once slept, or in the Tower Suite that reputedly has the widest four-poster bed in England. Tranquil lounges enjoy views over the wonderful gardens, while elegant, wood-panelled dining rooms make a memorable setting for a leisurely award-winning meal. Activities include falconry and archery and the castle has its own vineyard. Thornbury is, of course, a popular wedding venue.

Rooms: 27 (3 family) (4 GF) ● **Facilities:** STV FTV WiFi ↺ ⬆ Archery Helicopter rides Clay pigeon shooting Massage treatment Xmas New Year **Conf:** Class 40 Board 30 Thtr 70 **Services:** Night porter **Parking:** 50 **Notes:** Civ Wed 70

Follow us on twitter
@TheAA_Lifestyle

THORNHAM
Norfolk

Map 12 TF74

The Chequers Inn
★★★ 87% ◉ SMALL HOTEL

High Street, PE36 6LY - **tel:** 01485 512229
email: info@chequersinnthornham.com **web:** www.chequersinnthornham.com
dir: *Please phone for directions*

A lovely 16th-century inn ideally situated for exploring the north Norfolk coast with its lovely beaches; the RSPB reserve at Titchwell Marsh and Holme Dunes National Nature Reserve are just a stone's throw away. The property has 11 individually designed bedrooms which are stylish and equipped with modern facilities. The public areas feature a traditional bar with an open fire and low beams; there is a restaurant to the rear and a lovely outdoor area with individual, heated pavilions allowing dining all year round.

Rooms: 11 **D** £120–£195 (incl. bkfst)*

THORNTON HOUGH
Merseyside

Map 15 SJ38

Thornton Hall Hotel and Spa
★★★★ 81% HOTEL

Neston Road, CH63 1JF - **tel:** 0151 336 3938
email: reservations@thorntonhallhotel.com **web:** www.thorntonhallhotel.com
dir: *M53 junct 4, B5151/Neston onto B5136 to Thornton Hough, signed*

Dating back to the mid 1800s, this country-house hotel has been extended, restored and updated. An impressive leisure spa boasting excellent facilities and a separate clinical retreat is a key feature. A choice of eateries is available including the Lawn Restaurant. Bedrooms vary in style and include character rooms in the main house and more contemporary rooms in the garden wings. Delightful grounds and extensive banqueting facilities make this a popular wedding and conference venue.

Rooms: 62 (12 family) (28 GF) ✆ **S** £89–£299; **D** £89–£299 **Facilities:** Spa STV FTV WiFi ⌂ ☜ Gym Outdoor spa pools Steam room Snow cave Aerobics studio Hairdressers New Year **Conf:** Class 225 Board 80 Thtr 650 Del from £124 **Services:** Night porter **Parking:** 250 **Notes:** LB Civ Wed 500

THORPE
Derbyshire

Map 16 SK15

The Izaak Walton Hotel
★★★ 84% ◉◉ HOTEL

Dovedale, DE6 2AY - **tel:** 01335 350981
email: reception@izaakwaltonhotel.com **web:** www.izaakwaltonhotel.com
dir: *A515 onto B5054 to Thorpe, over cattle grid & 2 small bridges, 1st right, sharp left*

Often it is claimed that a property is in an idyllic location; this could not be truer than for the Izaak Walton Hotel. The 17th-century property named after the author of *The Compleat Angler* is nestled in the picturesque Dove Valley, dwarfed by the surrounding peaks known as 'Thorpe Cloud' and 'Bunster Hill', on the Derbyshire/Staffordshire border. Bedrooms are attractively furnished and comfortably appointed. There are a number of small private sittings rooms and an oak-beamed bar in which to relax. Meals are served in the Haddon Restaurant or Dovedale Bar.

Rooms: 38 (3 annexe) (6 family) (7 GF) ✆ **S** £75–£125; **D** £99–£154 (incl. bkfst)*
Facilities: WiFi Fishing Xmas New Year **Conf:** Class 80 Board 40 Thtr 100
Services: Night porter **Parking:** 40 **Notes:** Civ Wed 120

THORPENESS
Suffolk

Map 13 TM45

Thorpeness Hotel
★★★ 85% ◉ HOTEL

T|A HOTEL
COLLECTION

Lakeside Avenue, IP16 4NH - **tel:** 01728 452176
email: info@thorpeness.co.uk **web:** www.thorpeness.co.uk
dir: *A1094 towards Aldeburgh, take coast road N for 2m*

Thorpeness Hotel is ideally situated in an unspoilt, tranquil setting close to Aldeburgh and Snape Maltings. The extensive public rooms include a choice of lounges, a restaurant overlooking the golf course, a smart bar, a snooker room, clubhouse and meeting rooms. The spacious bedrooms are pleasantly decorated, tastefully furnished and equipped with modern facilities. A James Braid 18-hole heathland golf course, and tennis courts, are available.

Rooms: 36 (36 annexe) (10 family) (10 GF) ✆ **D** £105–£185 (incl. bkfst)*
Facilities: WiFi ⌂ HL ⌁ 18 Putting green ☝ Fishing Cycle hire Rowing boat hire Birdwatching Xmas New Year **Conf:** Class 30 Board 24 Thtr 130 **Services:** Night porter **Parking:** 80 **Notes:** LB Civ Wed 130

THURLASTON
Warwickshire

Map 11 SP47

Draycote Hotel
★★★ 71% HOTEL

London Road, CV23 9LF - **tel:** 01788 521800
email: mail@draycotehotel.co.uk **web:** www.draycotehotel.co.uk
dir: *M1 junct 17 onto M45, A45. Hotel 500mtrs on left*

Located in the picturesque Warwickshire countryside and within easy reach of motorway networks, this hotel offers modern, comfortable and well-equipped accommodation with a relaxed and friendly welcome. The hotel has a challenging golf course.

Rooms: 49 (2 family) (24 GF) **S** fr £59; **D** fr £59 **Facilities:** FTV WiFi ⌂ ⌁ 18 Putting green Golf driving range Chipping green Xmas New Year **Conf:** Class 78 Board 30 Thtr 250 Del from £118 **Services:** Night porter **Parking:** 150 **Notes:** Civ Wed 170

T

THURLESTONE
Devon
Map 3 SX64

HIGHLY RECOMMENDED

Thurlestone Hotel
★★★★ 84% ◎◎ HOTEL

TQ7 3NN - tel: 01548 560382
email: enquiries@thurlestone.co.uk **web:** www.thurlestone.co.uk
dir: *A38, A384 into Totnes, A381 towards Kingsbridge, A379 towards Churchstow, onto B3197. Into lane signed to Thurlestone*

This perennially popular hotel has been in the same family-ownership since 1896 and continues to go from strength to strength. Set in 19 acres of gardens with extensive leisure facilities including a par 3 golf course, tennis courts, an outdoor heated swimming pool, and Voyage Spa Complex. Bedrooms are equipped to ensure a comfortable stay with many having wonderful views of the south Devon coast. The range of eating options includes the elegant and stylish Trevilder restaurant with its stunning views.

Rooms: 65 (23 family) ♠ **S** £82.50–£255; **D** £165–£420 (incl. bkfst)*
Facilities: Spa STV FTV WiFi ⓧ ⊗ supervised ⚓ 9 Putting green 🎾 🚣
Gym Squash Badminton Table tennis Toddler room Beauty treatment room
Xmas New Year **Conf:** Class 100 Board 40 Thtr 150 **Services:** Lift Night porter
Parking: 121 **Notes:** Closed 1st 2 weeks Jan Civ Wed 160

TICEHURST
East Sussex
Map 6 TQ63

Dale Hill Hotel & Golf Club
★★★★ 81% ◎ HOTEL

TN5 7DQ - tel: 01580 200112
email: info@dalehill.co.uk **web:** www.dalehill.co.uk
dir: *M25 junct 5, A21. 5m after Lamberhurst, right at lights onto B2087 to Flimwell. Hotel 1m on left*

This modern hotel is situated just a short drive from the village. Extensive public rooms include a lounge bar, a conservatory brasserie, a formal restaurant and the Spike Bar, which is mainly frequented by golf club members and has a lively atmosphere. The hotel also has two superb 18-hole golf courses, a swimming pool and gym.

Rooms: 35 (8 family) (23 GF) ♠ **Facilities:** FTV WiFi ⓧ ⚓ 36 Putting green Gym
Covered driving range Pool table Xmas New Year **Conf:** Class 50 Board 50 Thtr 120
Services: Lift Night porter **Parking:** 220 **Notes:** Civ Wed 150

TINTAGEL
Cornwall & Isles of Scilly
Map 2 SX08

Atlantic View Hotel
★★ 82% SMALL HOTEL

Treknow, PL34 0EJ - tel: 01840 770221
email: atlantic-view@eclipse.co.uk **web:** www.atlanticviewhoteltintagel.co.uk
dir: *B3263 to Tregatta, turn left into Treknow, hotel on road to Trebarwith Strand Beach*

Conveniently located for all the attractions of Tintagel, this family-run hotel has a wonderfully relaxed and welcoming atmosphere. Public areas include a bar, comfortable lounge, TV/games room and heated swimming pool. Bedrooms are generally spacious and some have the added advantage of distant sea views.

Rooms: 9 (1 family) ♠ **Facilities:** FTV WiFi ⓧ Pool table **Parking:** 10 **Notes:** LB
Closed Nov-Feb RS Mar Swimming pool not open until Easter

TITCHWELL
Norfolk
Map 13 TF74

HIGHLY RECOMMENDED

Titchwell Manor Hotel
★★★ 86% ◎◎◎ HOTEL

PE31 8BB - tel: 01485 210221
email: eric@titchwellmanor.com **web:** www.titchwellmanor.com
dir: *On A149 coast rd, between Brancaster & Thornham*

Titchwell Manor Hotel is a friendly, family-run hotel ideally placed for touring the north Norfolk coastline. The tastefully appointed bedrooms are very comfortable; some in the adjacent annexe offer ground floor access. Smart public rooms include a lounge area, relaxed informal bar and the delightful Conservatory Restaurant, overlooking the walled garden. Head Chef Eric Snaith produces imaginative menus that feature quality local produce and fresh fish.

Rooms: 26 (18 annexe) (4 family) (15 GF) ♠ **S** £75–£180; **D** £95–£245 (incl. bkfst)* **Facilities:** FTV WiFi ⓧ Xmas New Year **Conf:** Class 50 Board 30 Thtr 30
Parking: 50 **Notes:** LB Civ Wed 90

TOLLESHUNT KNIGHTS
Essex
Map 7 TL91

Crowne Plaza Resort Colchester - Five Lakes
★★★★ 76% HOTEL

Colchester Road, CM9 8HX - tel: 01621 868888
email: enquiries@cpcolchester.co.uk **web:** www.cpcolchester.co.uk
dir: *Exit A12 at Kelvedon, follow brown signs through Tiptree to hotel*

This hotel is set amidst 320 acres of open countryside, featuring two golf courses. The spacious bedrooms are furnished to a high standard and have excellent facilities. The public rooms offer a high degree of comfort and include five bars, two restaurants and a large lounge. The property also boasts extensive leisure facilities.

Rooms: 194 (80 annexe) (4 family) (40 GF) ♠ **Facilities:** Spa STV FTV WiFi ⓧ ⊗
⚓ 36 Putting green 🚣 Gym Squash Sauna Steam room Badminton Aerobics Studio
Nail lounge Relaxation room Xmas New Year **Conf:** Class 700 Board 60 Thtr 2000
Services: Lift Night porter **Parking:** 550 **Notes:** Civ Wed 250

T

TONBRIDGE
Kent

Map 6 TQ54

Best Western Rose & Crown Hotel

 Best Western.

★★★ 79% HOTEL

125 High Street, TN9 1DD - tel: 01732 357966
email: rose.crown@bestwestern.co.uk **web:** www.roseandcrowntonbridge.co.uk
dir: *Please phone for directions*

A 15th-century coaching inn situated in the heart of this bustling town centre.
The public areas are light and airy yet still retain much original character such as
oak beams and Jacobean panelling. Food is served throughout the day in the Oak
Room Bar & Grill. Bedrooms are stylishly decorated, spacious and well presented;
amenities include free WiFi.

Rooms: 56 (3 family) (10 GF) ✆ **S** £75–£110; **D** £95–£150 **Facilities:** FTV WiFi ♨
Conf: Class 60 Board 60 Thtr 80 Del from £125 **Services:** Night porter **Parking:** 43
Notes: LB RS 25 Dec-4 Jan Breakfast only

Premier Inn Tonbridge

BUDGET HOTEL

Pembury Road, TN11 0NA - tel: 0871 527 9096
(Calls cost 13p per minute plus your phone company's access charge)
web: www.premierinn.com
dir: *11m from M25 junct 5. Follow A21 towards Hastings, pass A26 (Tunbridge Wells)
junct. Exit at next junct, 1st exit at rdbt*

High quality, budget accommodation ideal for both families and business
travellers. Spacious, en suite bedrooms feature free WiFi and tea and coffee making
facilities, and in most hotels, Freeview TV is also available. The adjacent family
restaurant features a wide and varied menu.

Rooms: 40

Premier Inn Tonbridge North

BUDGET HOTEL

Hilden Manor, London Road, TN10 3AN - tel: 0871 527 9098
(Calls cost 13p per minute plus your phone company's access charge)
web: www.premierinn.com
dir: *From A21 follow Seven Oaks & Hildenborough signs. At rdbt take 2nd exit onto B245
signed Hildenborough. In 2m hotel on right*

Rooms: 41

TORBAY
See Brixham, Paignton & Torquay

TORQUAY
Devon

Map 3 SX96

Belgrave Sands Hotel & Spa

★★★★ 82% ◉ HOTEL

Belgrave Road, TQ2 5HF - tel: 01803 226366
email: rm@belgravesands.com **web:** www.belgravesands.com
dir: *Please phone for directions*

Located a stone's throw from the seafront, this hotel has been appointed to a very
high standard. Classic, Signature and Suites are offered – all are fitted with
comfortable beds and some have the bonus of a sea view. Dining forms an
important part of a stay here – a relaxed fine-dining experience is offered in the
award-winning Seasons restaurant, open for breakfast, lunch and dinner.
Regularly changing dishes are cooked with style and flair. The hotel also has on-site
spa facilities.

Rooms: 50 (2 family) (4 GF) ✆ **Facilities:** FTV WiFi ♨ ③ Gym Sauna Steam room
Beauty treatments ♫ Xmas New Year **Services:** Lift Night porter **Parking:** 65
Notes: Civ Wed 100

Grand Hotel

 RICHARDSON HOTELS *Where Memories are Made*

★★★★ 79% ◉ HOTEL

Sea Front, TQ2 6NT - tel: 01803 296677
email: reservations@grandtorquay.co.uk **web:** www.grandtorquay.co.uk
dir: *A380 to Torquay. At seafront turn right, then 1st right. Hotel on corner,
entrance 1st on left*

Within level walking distance of the town, this large Edwardian hotel overlooks
the bay and offers modern facilities. Many of the bedrooms, some with balconies,
enjoy the best of the views, but all are very well equipped. The Compass Bar
also benefits from the stunning views, and offers an informal alternative to the
1881 Restaurant.

Rooms: 132 (32 family) (3 GF) ✆ **S** £90–£174; **D** £110–£224 (incl. bkfst)* **Facilities:**
FTV WiFi ♨ ③ ➚ supervised Gym Caudalie Spa ♫ Xmas New Year **Conf:** Class 150
Board 60 Thtr 250 Del from £100 **Services:** Lift Night porter **Parking:** 110 **Notes:** LB
Civ Wed 250

Lincombe Hall Hotel

★★★★ 73% HOTEL

Meadfoot Road, TQ1 2JX - tel: 01803 213361
email: stay@lincombehallhotel.co.uk **web:** www.lincombehallhotel.co.uk
dir: *From harbour into Torwood St, at lights after 100yds, turn right into Meadfoot Rd.
Hotel 200yds on left*

Lincombe Hall Hotel has recently undergone a comprehensive refurbishment,
offering a range of tastefully decorated rooms, many benefiting from views of
Torquay Harbour and the sea beyond. Accommodation is exclusively for adults,
located in a quiet leafy area just a short walk from the amenities of Torquay town
centre and Marina. Leisure facilities include a heated outdoor pool and small
indoor pool and jacuzzi. Complimentary WiFi is available throughout all areas of
the property. Externally, there are landscaped grounds and ample car parking.

Rooms: 44 (19 annexe) (2 GF) **S** £55–£80; **D** £90–£180 (incl. bkfst)* **Facilities:** FTV
WiFi ③ ➚ ♫ Xmas New Year **Services:** Night porter **Parking:** 60 **Notes:** LB Closed
2-27 Jan No children 16yrs

The Headland Hotel and Spa

★★★ 84% HOTEL

Daddyhole Road, TQ1 2EF - tel: 01803 295666
email: info@headlandtorquay.com **web:** www.headlandtorquay.com
dir: *A380 to Torquay seafront, left then far side of harbour, up hill, 500mtrs & turn right*

This hotel has a delightful location set apart from the bustle of town, but within
easy walking distance of the numerous attractions. With its splendid grounds and
an elevated view of the bay, the hotel has an enviable position. Bedrooms are very
comfortably appointed, many with sea views. Cuisine is a highlight, and the
friendly team offer attentive service.

Rooms: 78 (16 family) (7 GF) ✆ **Facilities:** FTV WiFi ⑤ Gym Sauna Steam room
♫ Xmas New Year **Conf:** Class 50 Board 40 Thtr 150 **Services:** Lift Night porter
Parking: 42 **Notes:** LB Civ Wed 150

T

TORQUAY *continued*

The Grosvenor Hotel

★★★ 81% ◉◉ HOTEL

RICHARDSON HOTELS
Where Memories are Made

Belgrave Road, TQ2 5HG - tel: 01803 294373
email: gm.grosvenor@richardsonhotels.co.uk
dir: *Please phone for directions*

The Grosvenor Hotel stands proudly within Torquay, only a stone's throw from the seafront. High standards are evident throughout, augmented by a relaxed and welcoming atmosphere. There is an inviting bar, an elegant restaurant and a smart drawing room. The award-winning food is under the direction of John Burton-Race. Comfortable accommodation has benefited from refurbishment. Off-street parking is available.

Rooms: 47

Livermead House Hotel

★★★ 76% HOTEL

Torbay Road, TQ2 6QJ - tel: 01803 294361
email: info@livermead.com **web:** www.livermead.com
dir: *From seafront turn right, follow A379 towards Paignton & Livermead, hotel opposite Institute Beach*

Having a splendid waterfront location, this hotel dates back to the 1820s, and is where Charles Kingsley is said to have written *The Water Babies*, during the 1860s. Bedrooms vary in size and style; excellent public rooms are popular for private parties and meetings, and a range of leisure facilities is provided. Enjoyable cuisine is served in the impressive restaurant.

Rooms: 67 (6 family) (1 GF) 🐾 **Facilities:** FTV WiFi ⚑ Gym Squash Sauna Games room 🎵 Xmas **Conf:** Class 175 Board 80 Thtr 250 **Services:** Lift Night porter **Parking:** 131 **Notes:** Civ Wed 250

Corbyn Head Hotel

★★★ 75% HOTEL

Torbay Road, Sea Front, TQ2 6RH - tel: 01803 213611
email: info@corbynhead.com **web:** www.corbynhead.com
dir: *Follow signs to Torquay seafront, turn right on seafront. Hotel on right with green canopies*

This hotel occupies a prime position overlooking Torbay, and offers well-equipped bedrooms, many with sea views and some with balconies. The staff are friendly and welcoming, and a well-stocked bar and comfortable lounge are available. Guests can enjoy fine dining in the Harbour View Restaurant, with attentive service assured.

Rooms: 45 (4 family) (9 GF) **Facilities:** FTV WiFi ⚑ Squash Use of leisure facilities at sister hotel 🎵 Xmas New Year **Conf:** Class 30 Board 30 Thtr 80 **Services:** Night porter **Parking:** 50 **Notes:** LB Civ Wed 85

Best Western Livermead Cliff Hotel

BW Best Western.

★★★ 74% HOTEL

Torbay Road, TQ2 6RQ - tel: 01803 299666
email: info@livermeadcliff.co.uk **web:** www.livermeadcliff.co.uk
dir: *A379, A3022 to Torquay, towards seafront, turn right towards Paignton. Hotel 600yds on seaward side*

Situated at the water's edge, this long-established hotel offers friendly service and traditional hospitality. The splendid views can be enjoyed from the lounge, bar and dining room. Alternatively, guests can take advantage of refreshment on the wonderful terrace and enjoy one of the best outlooks in the bay. Bedrooms, many with sea views and some with balconies, are comfortable and well equipped; a range of room sizes is available.

Rooms: 65 (17 family) 🐾 **Facilities:** FTV WiFi Fishing Use of facilities at sister hotel Xmas New Year **Conf:** Class 60 Board 40 Thtr 120 **Services:** Lift Night porter **Parking:** 80 **Notes:** Civ Wed 200

T

Abbey Lawn Hotel

★★★ 73% HOTEL

Scarborough Road, TQ2 5UQ - tel: 01803 299199
email: admin@holdsworthhotels.co.uk **web:** www.holdsworthhotels.co.uk/the-abbey-lawn
dir: *Please phone for directions*

Conveniently located for both the seafront and town centre, this is an ideal base for visiting the attractions of the 'English Riviera'. Many of the bedrooms, including the four-poster suite, benefit from lovely sea views. Facilities include a health club with extensive leisure activities, plus an indoor swimming pool. Traditional cuisine is served in the elegant restaurant, and evening entertainment is a regular feature in the ballroom.

Rooms: 60 (3 family) (3 GF) ♦ **S** fr £45; **D** fr £90 (incl. bkfst)* **Facilities:** FTV WiFi ⊗ ♫ Xmas New Year **Services:** Lift Night porter **Parking:** 20 **Notes:** LB Closed 3 Jan-8 Feb

Anchorage Hotel

★★★ 72% HOTEL

Cary Park, Aveland Road, TQ1 3PT - tel: 01803 326175
email: enquiries@anchoragehotel.co.uk **web:** www.anchoragehotel.co.uk
dir: *Please phone for directions*

Quietly located in a residential area and providing a friendly welcome, this family-run establishment enjoys a great deal of repeat business. Bedrooms come in a range of sizes but all rooms are neatly presented. Evening entertainment is provided regularly in the large and comfortable lounge.

Rooms: 56 (5 family) (17 GF) **Facilities:** FTV WiFi ↖ ♫ Xmas New Year **Services:** Lift Night porter **Parking:** 26

Regina Hotel

Leisureplex
HOLIDAY HOTELS

★★★ 67% HOTEL

Victoria Parade, TQ1 2BE - tel: 01803 292904
email: regina@leisureplex.co.uk **web:** www.leisureplex.co.uk
dir: *Into Torquay, follow harbour signs, hotel on outer corner of harbour*

This hotel enjoys a pleasant and convenient location right on the harbourside, a short stroll from the town's attractions. Bedrooms, some with harbour views, vary in size. Entertainment is provided on most nights and there is a choice of bars.

Rooms: 68 (5 family) **Facilities:** FTV ♫ Xmas New Year **Services:** Lift Night porter **Parking:** 6 **Notes:** Closed Jan & part Feb RS Nov-Dec (ex Xmas) & Feb-Mar Mon-Fri only

Seascape Hotel

★★ 71% HOTEL

TQ2 5UT - tel: 01803 292617 & 07767 738697
email: stay@seascapehoteltorquay.com **web:** www.seascapehoteltorquay.com
dir: *A380 Torquay, at English Riviera rdbt follow A380 signed Torquay, at Torre station turn right, left at 2nd lights. Through lights, hotel 100yds on right*

This long-established hotel is centrally located and handy for the town centre and the seafront. The long tradition of hospitality makes guests feel genuinely welcomed. Bedrooms offer consistent levels of comfort and quality with some having lovely views across the bay. Regular evening entertainment is offered during the season in the spacious lounge area.

Rooms: 57 (26 annexe) (8 family) (6 GF) ♦ **S** fr £40; **D** fr £80* **Facilities:** FTV WiFi ♫ Xmas New Year **Services:** Lift Night porter **Parking:** 16

Ashley Court Hotel

★★ 66% HOTEL

107 Abbey Road, TQ2 5NP - tel: 01803 292417
email: reception@ashleycourt.co.uk **web:** www.ashleycourt.co.uk
dir: *A380 to seafront, left to Shedden Hill to lights, hotel opposite*

Located close to the town centre and within easy strolling distance of the seafront, this hotel offers a warm welcome to guests. Bedrooms are pleasantly appointed and some have sea views. The outdoor pool and patio are popular with guests wishing to soak up some sunshine. Live entertainment is provided every night throughout the season.

Rooms: 83 (12 family) (8 GF) (14 smoking) ♦ **S** fr £28; **D** fr £56 (incl. bkfst)* **Facilities:** ↖ Games room ♫ Xmas New Year **Services:** Lift Night porter **Parking:** 42 **Notes:** Closed 3 Jan-1 Feb

Premier Inn Torquay

BUDGET HOTEL

Seafront, Belgrave Road, TQ2 5HE - tel: 0871 527 9102
(Calls cost 13p per minute plus your phone company's access charge)
web: www.premierinn.com
dir: *On A380 into Torquay, continue to lights (Torre Station on right). Right into Avenue Road to Kings Drive. Left at seafront, hotel at lights*

High quality, budget accommodation ideal for both families and business travellers. Spacious, en suite bedrooms feature free WiFi and tea and coffee making facilities, and in most hotels, Freeview TV is also available. The adjacent family restaurant features a wide and varied menu.

Rooms: 143

TOTNES	Map 3 SX86
Devon	

The Royal Seven Stars Hotel

★★★ 77% HOTEL

The Plains, TQ9 5DD - tel: 01803 862125
email: enquiry@royalsevenstars.co.uk **web:** www.royalsevenstars.co.uk
dir: *A38 Buckfastleigh junct onto A385 towards Dartington, 6.5m towards Totnes town centre. On corner of Fore St & Coronation Rd*

Situated in the vibrant town of Totnes, this engaging hotel has plenty to offer both visitors and locals alike. The style is an appealing blend of originality and stylish flourishes, all of which work harmoniously with a real breadth of appeal. A choice of bars is offered, likewise dining options from the classic saloon bar to the stylish cocktail bar and brasserie, all of which focus upon quality, locally-sourced food and beverages. Bedrooms are individually designed, quirky and full of character with quality and comfort assured. A great base from which to explore this beautiful part of South Devon.

Rooms: 21 (1 family) ♦ **S** £95–£170; **D** £130–£170 (incl. bkfst)* **Facilities:** FTV WiFi ↕ ♫ Xmas New Year **Conf:** Class 60 Board 40 Thtr 120 **Services:** Night porter **Parking:** 10 **Notes:** LB Civ Wed 120

T

TRING
Hertfordshire   Map 6 SP91

Pendley Manor Hotel
★★★★ 74% ◉◉ HOTEL

Cow Lane, HP23 5QY - **tel:** 01442 891891
email: info@pendley-manor.co.uk **web:** www.pendley-manor.co.uk
dir: *M25 junct 20, A41 Tring exit. At rdbt follow Berkhamsted/London signs.
1st left signed Tring Station & Pendley Manor*

Pendley Manor Hotel is an impressive Victorian mansion set in extensive and
mature landscaped grounds where peacocks roam. The spacious bedrooms are
situated in both the manor house and the wing, and offer a useful range of
facilities. Public areas include a cosy bar, a conservatory lounge and an intimate
restaurant as well as a leisure centre.

Rooms: 86 (15 family) (17 GF) **S** £65–£205; **D** £85–£229 (incl. bkfst)*
Facilities: Spa FTV WiFi ⇗ ⊕ ⏚ Gym Steam room Dance Studio Sauna
Conf: Class 80 Board 80 Thtr 250 Del from £135 **Services:** Lift Night porter
Air con **Parking:** 150 **Notes:** LB Civ Wed 160

Premier Inn Tring
BUDGET HOTEL

Tring Hill, HP23 4LD - **tel:** 0871 527 9104
(Calls cost 13p per minute plus your phone company's access charge)
web: www.premierinn.com
dir: *M25 junct 20, A41 towards Aylesbury, at end of Hemel Hempstead/Tring bypass
straight on at rdbt, hotel approx 100yds on right*

High quality, budget accommodation ideal for both families and business
travellers. Spacious, en suite bedrooms feature free WiFi and tea and coffee making
facilities, and in most hotels, Freeview TV is also available. The adjacent family
restaurant features a wide and varied menu.

Rooms: 42

TROWBRIDGE
Wiltshire   Map 4 ST85

Premier Inn Trowbridge
BUDGET HOTEL

St Stephens Place, BA14 8AH - **tel:** 0871 527 9444
(Calls cost 13p per minute plus your phone company's access charge)
web: www.premierinn.com
dir: *M4 junct 17, A429 (Chippenham). A350 (Warminster & Poole). 12m. After Seminton
rdbt, at 2nd lights right into West Ashton Rd (Trowbridge). At 1st mini rdbt 2nd exit, at
2nd mini rdbt into County Way. At major rdbt 5th exit into Castle St. At mini rdbt 3rd exit,
hotel on right*

High quality, budget accommodation ideal for both families and business
travellers. Spacious, en suite bedrooms feature free WiFi and tea and coffee making
facilities, and in most hotels, Freeview TV is also available. The adjacent family
restaurant features a wide and varied menu.

Rooms: 80

TRURO
Cornwall & Isles of Scilly   Map 2 SW84

The Alverton Hotel
★★★★ 79% ◉◉ HOTEL

Tregolls Road, TR1 1ZQ - **tel:** 01872 276633
email: stay@thealverton.co.uk **web:** www.thealverton.co.uk
dir: *From A30 at Carland Cross take A39 to Truro. At lights right onto A39 (Tregolls Rd)
signed Truro/Falmouth*

The Alverton Hotel is a beautiful Grade II listed building which was previously a
convent. The bedrooms are smartly decorated, and there is a comfortable lounge/
cocktail bar, as well as an attractive restaurant that serves popular meals using
locally-sourced produce. Parking is available.

Rooms: 50 (15 annexe) (7 family) (11 GF) ⟋ **Facilities:** FTV WiFi ⇗ Xmas New Year
Conf: Class 50 Board 50 Thtr 140 **Services:** Night porter **Parking:** 71 **Notes:** Civ Wed
90

HIGHLY RECOMMENDED

Mannings Hotel
★★★ 88% ◉◉ HOTEL

Lemon Street, TR1 2QB - **tel:** 01872 270345
email: reception@manningshotels.co.uk **web:** www.manningshotels.co.uk
dir: *A30 to Carland Cross then Truro. Follow brown signs to hotel in city centre*

This popular hotel is located in the heart of Truro and offers an engaging blend
of traditional and contemporary. Public areas have a stylish atmosphere with
the bar and restaurant proving popular with locals and residents alike. A wide
choice of appetising dishes is available, as well as daily specials. Bedrooms are
pleasantly appointed.

Rooms: 43 (9 annexe) (4 family) (3 GF) ⟋ **S** £60–£80; **D** £85–£115 (incl. bkfst)*
Facilities: FTV WiFi **Services:** Night porter **Parking:** 43 **Notes:** LB Closed 25-26 Dec

Premier Inn Truro
BUDGET HOTEL

Old Carnon Hill, Carnon Downs, TR3 6JT - **tel:** 0871 527 9106
(Calls cost 13p per minute plus your phone company's access charge)
web: www.premierinn.com
dir: *On A39 (Truro to Falmouth road), 3m SW of Truro*

High quality, budget accommodation ideal for both families and business
travellers. Spacious, en suite bedrooms feature free WiFi and tea and coffee making
facilities, and in most hotels, Freeview TV is also available. The adjacent family
restaurant features a wide and varied menu.

Rooms: 86

TUNBRIDGE WELLS (ROYAL)
Kent   Map 6 TQ53

One Warwick Park Hotel
★★★★ 81% HOTEL

1 Warwick Park, TN2 5TA - **tel:** 01892 &
email: info@onewarwickpark.co.uk **web:** www.onewarwickpark.co.uk
dir: *A21 at Pembury junct follow signs to Tunbridge Wells, then town centre.
Adjacent to The Pantiles*

This new hotel ,just a few minutes walk from the Pantiles of Tunbridge Wells, offers
guests a choice of stylish bedrooms; some in the main building and some in
annexes alongside. All are very well equipped, have air conditioning and come with

many useful extras including top quality toiletries. Contemporary in style, the hotel has been finished to a very high quality throughout. The L'Amore restaurant offers a Mediterranean small-plate dining experience. Parking is available close by; please check when booking.

Rooms: 39 (7 family) 🐾 **D** £80–£375 (incl. bkfst)* **Facilities:** FTV WiFi 🐾 ♫ **Conf:** Class 56 Board 85 Thtr 130 Del from £136 **Services:** Lift Night porter Air con **Notes:** Civ Wed 120

The Spa Hotel
★★★★ 80% ◎◎ HOTEL

Mount Ephraim, TN4 8XJ - **tel:** 01892 520331
email: reservations@spahotel.co.uk **web:** www.spahotel.co.uk
dir: A21 to A26, follow A264 East Grinstead signs, hotel on right

Set in 14 acres of beautifully tended grounds, this imposing 18th-century mansion offers spacious, modern bedrooms that are stylishly decorated and thoughtfully equipped. The public rooms include the Chandelier Restaurant, a champagne bar and the Orangery which complements the traditional lounge. There are extensive meeting and health club facilities, and a spa offering treatment rooms. It is also licensed for civil wedding ceremonies.

Rooms: 70 (4 family) (1 GF) 🐾 **S** fr £75; **D** fr £100* **Facilities:** Spa STV FTV WiFi 🐾 🐾 Gym Sauna Steam room Xmas New Year **Conf:** Class 90 Board 90 Thtr 300 **Services:** Lift Night porter **Parking:** 150 **Notes:** Civ Wed 150

Hotel du Vin Tunbridge Wells
★★★★ 76% ◎ TOWN HOUSE HOTEL

Crescent Road, TN1 2LY - **tel:** 01892 232 0749
email: reception.tunbridgewells@hotelduvin.com **web:** www.hotelduvin.com
dir: Follow town centre, to main junct of Mount Pleasant Rd & Crescent Rd/Church Rd. Hotel 150yds on right just past Phillips House

This impressive Grade II listed building dates from 1762, and as a princess, Queen Victoria often stayed here. The spacious bedrooms are available in a range of sizes, beautifully and individually appointed, and equipped with a host of thoughtful extras. Public rooms include a bistro-style restaurant, two elegant lounges and a small bar.

Rooms: 34 (2 GF) 🐾 **D** fr £89* **Facilities:** STV WiFi 🐾 **Conf:** Class 40 Board 25 Thtr 60 Del from £179 **Services:** Lift Night porter **Parking:** 30 **Notes:** Civ Wed 84

Mercure Tunbridge Wells
★★★★ 72% HOTEL

8 Tonbridge Road, TN2 4QL - **tel:** 01892 823567 & 0844 815 9074 (Calls cost 7p per minute plus your phone company's access charge)
email: sales.mercuretunbridgewells@jupiterhotels.co.uk
web: www.mercuretunbridgewells.co.uk
dir: M25 junct 5, A21 S. Left at 1st rdbt signed Pembury Hospital. Hotel on left, 400yds past hospital

Built in the style of a traditional Kentish oast house, this well presented hotel is conveniently located just off the A21 with easy access to the M25. Bedrooms are comfortably appointed for both business and leisure guests. Public areas include a leisure club and a range of meeting rooms.

Rooms: 84 (12 family) (40 GF) 🐾 **Facilities:** STV FTV WiFi 🐾 HL 🐾 Steam room Sauna Beauty treatment room Xmas New Year **Conf:** Class 80 Board 50 Thtr 150 **Services:** Night porter **Parking:** 100 **Notes:** Civ Wed 180

Russell Hotel
★★ 65% METRO HOTEL

80 London Road, TN1 1DZ - **tel:** 01892 544833
email: sales@russell-hotel.com **web:** www.russell-hotel.com
dir: From Tunbridge Wells A26 junct with Lime Hill Road turn

This detached Victorian property is situated just a short walk from the centre of town. The generously proportioned bedrooms in the main house are pleasantly decorated and well equipped. In addition, there are several smartly appointed, self-contained suites in an adjacent building. The public rooms include a lounge and cosy bar.

Rooms: 26 (5 annexe) (5 family) (1 GF) **S** £55–£95; **D** £70–£120 (incl. bkfst)* **Facilities:** FTV WiFi **Conf:** Class 10 Board 10 Thtr 10 **Services:** Night porter **Parking:** 14

TURNERS HILL
West Sussex — Map 6 TQ33

Alexander House Hotel & Utopia Spa
★★★★★ 87% ◎◎◎ 🐾 HOTEL

East Street, RH10 4QD - **tel:** 01342 714914
email: admin@alexanderhouse.co.uk **web:** www.alexanderhouse.co.uk
dir: 6m from M23 junct 10, on B2110 between Turners Hill & East Grinstead

Set in 175 acres of parkland and landscaped gardens, this delightful country house hotel dates back to the 17th century. Most of the bedrooms are very spacious and all have luxurious bathrooms; the rooms in the most recent wing are particularly stunning. The Utopia Spa has a state-of-the-art pool and gym, as well as specialised treatments.

Rooms: 58 (20 annexe) (13 family) (10 GF) 🐾 **D** £250–£950 (incl. bkfst & dinner)* **Facilities:** Spa FTV WiFi 🐾 🐾 Gym Clay shooting Archery Mountain bikes Pony trekking Xmas New Year **Conf:** Class 70 Board 40 Thtr 150 **Services:** Lift Night porter **Parking:** 100 **Notes:** LB Civ Wed 100

T

TWICKENHAM
Greater London

Premier Inn Twickenham East

BUDGET HOTEL PLAN 1 B2

Corner Sixth Cross, Staines Road, TW2 5PE - tel: 0871 527 9108
(Calls cost 13p per minute plus your phone company's access charge)
web: www.premierinn.com
dir: *M25 junct 12 onto M3, follow Central London signs, at end of M3 becomes A316. Straight on at 1st rdbt. Hotel 500yds on left*

High quality, budget accommodation ideal for both families and business travellers. Spacious, en suite bedrooms feature free WiFi and tea and coffee making facilities, and in most hotels, Freeview TV is also available. The adjacent family restaurant features a wide and varied menu.

Rooms: 17

Premier Inn Twickenham Stadium

BUDGET HOTEL PLAN 1 B2

Chertsey Road, Whitton, TW2 6LS - tel: 0871 527 9110
(Calls cost 13p per minute plus your phone company's access charge)
web: www.premierinn.com
dir: *From M3 onto A316, then A305 signed Twickenham. At Hospital Bridge Rdbt 3 rd exit into Hospital Bridge Rd. Take B358 signed Teddington. Becomes Sixth Cross Rd. Hotel on left*

Rooms: 39

TWO BRIDGES
Devon   Map 3 SX67

Two Bridges Hotel

★★★ 79% ◉◉ HOTEL

PL20 6SW - tel: 01822 892300
email: reception@twobridges.co.uk **web:** www.twobridges.co.uk
dir: *At junct of B3212 & B3357*

This wonderfully relaxing hotel is set in the heart of the Dartmoor National Park, in a beautiful riverside location. Three standards of comfortable rooms provide every modern convenience, and include four-poster rooms. There is a choice of lounges, and fine dining is available in the restaurant, where menus feature local game and other seasonal produce.

Rooms: 32 (2 family) (10 GF) ⌁ **S** £80–£155; **D** £90–£250 (incl. bkfst) **Facilities:** FTV WiFi ⌁ Fishing Xmas New Year **Conf:** Class 60 Board 40 Thtr 130 Del £135
Services: Night porter **Parking:** 100 **Notes:** LB Civ Wed 130

TYNEMOUTH
Tyne & Wear   Map 21 NZ36

Grand Hotel

★★★ 85% HOTEL

Grand Parade, NE30 4ER - tel: 0191 293 6666
email: reservations@grandhotel-uk.com **web:** www.grandhotel-uk.com
dir: *A1058 for Tynemouth. At coast rdbt turn right. Hotel on right approx 0.5m*

This grand Victorian building offers stunning views of the coast. Bedrooms come in a variety of styles and are well equipped, tastefully decorated and have impressive bathrooms. In addition to the restaurant there are two bars. The elegant and

imposing staircase is a focal point, and is a favourite spot for the bride and groom to have their photograph taken after their wedding here.

Rooms: 46 (6 annexe) (14 family) ⌁ **S** £90–£180; **D** £100–£190 (incl. bkfst)*
Facilities: STV FTV WiFi Xmas New Year **Conf:** Class 40 Board 40 Thtr 130
Services: Lift Night porter **Parking:** 16 **Notes:** LB RS Sun evening From 4pm bar meals only Civ Wed 120

UCKFIELD
East Sussex   Map 6 TQ42

INSPECTOR'S CHOICE

Buxted Park Hotel

★★★★ ◉◉ HOTEL

Buxted, TN22 4AY - tel: 01825 733333 & 0845 072 7412
(Calls cost 5p per minute plus your phone company's access charge)
email: buxtedpark@handpicked.co.uk
web: www.handpickedhotels.co.uk/buxtedpark
dir: *From A26 Uckfield bypass take A272 signed Buxted. Through lights, hotel 1m on right*

Buxted Park Hotel is an attractive Grade II listed Georgian mansion dating back to the 17th century, set amidst 300 acres of beautiful countryside and landscaped gardens. The stylish, thoughtfully equipped bedrooms are split between the main house and the modern Garden Wing. An interesting choice of dishes is served in the restaurant.

Rooms: 44 (7 family) (16 GF) ⌁ **S** £107–£344; **D** £107–£354 (incl. bkfst)*
Facilities: STV WiFi ⌁ HL Fishing ⌁ Gym Orienteering Walking trail Snooker room Xmas New Year **Conf:** Class 80 Board 42 Thtr 180 Del from £140 **Services:** Lift Night porter **Parking:** 100 **Notes:** LB Civ Wed 120

HIGHLY RECOMMENDED

East Sussex National Golf Resort & Spa

★★★★ 83% ◉◉ HOTEL

Little Horsted, TN22 5ES - tel: 01825 880088
email: reception@eastsussexnational.co.uk **web:** www.eastsussexnational.co.uk
dir: *M25 junct 6, A22 signed East Grinstead & Eastbourne. Straight on at rdbt junct of A22 & A26 (Little Horsted). At next rdbt right to hotel*

This modern hotel is located in a lovely country location and offers a super range of facilities with two golf courses and an impressive leisure suite. In addition there are also conference and meeting facilities. The bedrooms are spacious and

T

have good facilities; all have delightful views across the golf course to the countryside beyond. The cuisine is enjoyable; particularly at breakfast, which is served in the restaurant that overlooks the course.

Rooms: 104 (3 family) (36 GF) ⟁ **S** £115–£289; **D** £115–£289 (incl. bkfst)* **Facilities:** Spa STV FTV WiFi ⟁ HL ⟁ ⟁ 36 Putting green Gym Academy of Golf Xmas New Year **Conf:** Class 200 Board 50 Thtr 450 Del from £140 **Services:** Lift Night porter Air con **Parking:** 500 **Notes:** LB Civ Wed 250

Horsted Place

★★★★ 82% ⓐⓐ ⌂ HOTEL

Little Horsted, TN22 5TS - tel: 01825 750581
email: hotel@horstedplace.co.uk **web:** www.horstedplace.co.uk
dir: *From Uckfield 2m S on A26 towards Lewes*

This property is one of Britain's finest examples of Gothic revivalist architecture, and much of the 1850s building was designed by Augustus Pugin. The hotel is situated in extensive landscaped grounds, with a tennis court and croquet lawn, and is adjacent to the East Sussex National Golf Club. The spacious bedrooms, in a range of both sizes and designs, are attractively decorated, tastefully furnished, and equipped with many thoughtful touches such as flowers and books. Most bedrooms also have a separate sitting area. Formal dining can be enjoyed in the elegant dining room (no children after 7pm) where the menus are based on quality seasonal produce. Pre-dinner drinks and after-dinner coffees can be enjoyed either in the Drawing Room or on the terrace overlooking the garden.

Rooms: 20 (3 annexe) (5 family) (2 GF) ⟁ **S** £145–£375; **D** £145–£375 (incl. bkfst)* **Facilities:** STV FTV WiFi ⟁ 36 ⟁ ⟁ Free use of gym & indoor pool at nearby hotel ♫ Xmas **Conf:** Class 50 Board 40 Thtr 80 **Services:** Lift Night porter **Parking:** 32 **Notes:** LB Closed 1-7 Jan No children 7yrs Civ Wed 100

ULLESTHORPE
Leicestershire   Map 11 SP58

Best Western Plus Ullesthorpe Court Hotel & Golf Club

⟁ Best Western PLUS

★★★★ 74% HOTEL

Frolesworth Road, LE17 5BZ - tel: 01455 209023
email: bookings@ullesthorpecourt.co.uk **web:** www.ullesthorpecourt.co.uk
dir: *M1 junct 20 towards Lutterworth. Follow brown tourist signs*

Complete with its own golf club, this impressively equipped hotel is within easy reach of the motorway network, NEC and Birmingham airport. Public areas include

both formal and informal eating options and extensive conference and leisure facilities. Spacious bedrooms are thoughtfully equipped for both the business and leisure guest, and a four-poster room is available.

Rooms: 72 (3 family) (16 GF) ⟁ **S** fr £65; **D** fr £65* **Facilities:** Spa FTV WiFi ⟁ ⟁ supervised ⟁ 18 Putting green ⟁ Gym Beauty room Steam room Sauna Snooker room New Year **Conf:** Class 48 Board 30 Thtr 80 Del from £110 **Services:** Lift Night porter **Parking:** 280 **Notes:** RS 25-26 Dec Civ Wed 120

ULLSWATER
See **Glenridding & Patterdale**

UPPER SLAUGHTER
Gloucestershire   Map 10 SP12

Lords of the Manor

★★★★ COUNTRY HOUSE HOTEL

GL54 2JD - tel: 01451 820243
email: reservations@lordsofthemanor.com **web:** www.lordsofthemanor.com
dir: *2m W of A429. Exit A40 onto A429, take 'The Slaughters' turn. Through Lower Slaughter for 1m to Upper Slaughter. Hotel on right*

This wonderfully welcoming 17th-century manor house hotel sits in eight acres of gardens and parkland surrounded by Cotswold countryside. A relaxed atmosphere, underpinned by professional and attentive service is the hallmark here, so that guests are often reluctant to leave. The hotel has elegant public rooms that overlook the immaculate lawns, and the restaurant is the venue for consistently impressive cuisine. Bedrooms have much character and charm, combined with the extra touches expected of a hotel of this stature.

Rooms: 26 (4 family) (9 GF) ⟁ **S** £150–£510; **D** £150–£510 (incl. bkfst)* **Facilities:** FTV WiFi Fishing ⟁ Xmas New Year **Conf:** Class 20 Board 20 Thtr 30 **Services:** Night porter **Parking:** 40 **Notes:** LB Civ Wed 80

U

UPTON UPON SEVERN
Worcestershire   Map 10 SO84

White Lion Hotel

★★★ 75% HOTEL

21 High Street, WR8 0HJ - tel: 01684 592551
email: reservations@whitelionhotel.biz **web:** www.whitelionhotel.biz
dir: *A422, A38 towards Tewkesbury. In 8m take B4104, after 1m cross bridge,
turn left to hotel, past bend on left*

Famed for being the inn depicted in Henry Fielding's novel Tom Jones, this 16th-
century hotel is a reminder of 'Old England' with features such as exposed beams
and wall timbers still remaining. The quality furnishing and the decor throughout
enhance its character; the bedrooms are smart and include one four-poster room.

Rooms: 13 (2 annexe) (2 family) (2 GF) ✿ **Facilities:** FTV WiFi **Parking:** 14 **Notes:** LB
Closed 1 Jan RS 25 Dec No accommodation

UTTOXETER
Staffordshire   Map 10 SK03

Premier Inn Uttoxeter

BUDGET HOTEL

Derby Road, ST14 5AA - tel: 0871 527 9112
(Calls cost 13p per minute plus your phone company's access charge)
web: www.premierinn.com
dir: *At junct of A50 & B5030 on outskirts of Uttoxeter, 7m S of Alton Towers Theme Park*

High quality, budget accommodation ideal for both families and business
travellers. Spacious, en suite bedrooms feature free WiFi and tea and coffee making
facilities, and in most hotels, Freeview TV is also available. The adjacent family
restaurant features a wide and varied menu.

Rooms: 75

UXBRIDGE
Greater London   Map 6 TQ08

See also **Ruislip**

Lancaster Hotel & Spa

★★★ 81% HOTEL

Brunel University, Kingston Lane, UB8 3PH - tel: 01895 268006
web: www.brunelcommercial.london
dir: *Follow signs for Brunel University. Hotel is situated inside the university grounds*

The Lancaster Hotel & Spa is conveniently located within the grounds of Brunel
University London and is the ideal location for visiting the university or for
professionals on business. The complex has been fully refurbished to a very high
standard and offers a range of rooms to meet all budgets. The public areas include
a comfortable lounge with a well-stocked bar and a nice terrace for the summer
months. Freshly prepared dishes are served in the restaurant adjacent to the lounge
area. Multifunctional meeting rooms are available. Parking is offered on site, and
the area is patrolled 24 hours a day.

Rooms: 70 ✿ **Facilities:** FTV WiFi ⌨ Sports facilities, shops & bank **Conf:** Board 16
Services: Lift **Parking:** 50 **Notes:** RS 25 Dec restaurant closed & restricted reception

Premier Inn London Uxbridge

BUDGET HOTEL

Phase 500, Riverside Way, UB8 2UX - tel: 0871 527 9574
(Calls cost 13p per minute plus your phone company's access charge)
web: www.premierinn.com
dir: *M40 junct 1 follow A412/Uxbridge/A4020 signs. At Denham Rdbt 1st exit then 2nd
exit into Oxford Rd. 3rd exit at rdbt, left into Cowley Rd, right into
Trumper Way. Left into New Windsor St, right into Riverside Way*

High quality, budget accommodation ideal for both families and business
travellers. Spacious, en suite bedrooms feature free WiFi and tea and coffee making
facilities, and in most hotels, Freeview TV is also available. The adjacent family
restaurant features a wide and varied menu.

Rooms: 80

VENTNOR
Isle of Wight   Map 5 SZ57

The Royal Hotel

★★★★ 81% HOTEL

Belgrave Road, PO38 1JJ - tel: 01983 852186
email: enquiries@royalhoteliow.co.uk **web:** www.royalhoteliow.co.uk
dir: *A3055 into Ventnor follow one-way system, after lights left into Church St.
Top of hill left into Belgrave Rd. Hotel on right*

This smart hotel enjoys a central yet peaceful location in its own gardens, complete
with an outdoor pool. Spacious, elegant public areas include a bright conservatory,
bar and lounge. Bedrooms, appointed to a high standard, vary in size and style.
Staff are friendly and efficient, particularly in the smart restaurant, where modern
British cuisine is offered.

Rooms: 51 (9 family) ✿ **S** £100–£130; **D** £195–£295 (incl. bkfst)* **Facilities:** FTV
WiFi ⌨ ⚒ Beauty treatment room Xmas New Year **Conf:** Class 40 Board 24 Thtr 100
Del from £170 **Services:** Lift Night porter **Parking:** 50 **Notes:** LB Civ Wed 120

Eversley Hotel

★★★ 73% METRO HOTEL

Park Avenue, PO38 1LB - tel: 01983 852244
email: eversleyhotel@yahoo.co.uk **web:** www.eversleyhotel.uk.com
dir: *On A3055 W of Ventnor, next to Ventnor Park*

Located west of Ventnor, this family-run Metro hotel enjoys a quiet location and
has some rooms with garden and pool views. Bedrooms are generally of a good
size and meet the needs of leisure and business travellers alike. The spacious

restaurant is sometimes used for local functions, and there is a bar where light meals are served, as well as a television room, a lounge area, and a card room. Further facilities include a jacuzzi and gym.

Rooms: 28 (6 family) (2 GF) ♠ **Facilities:** STV FTV WiFi ⚡ Gym Xmas New Year **Conf:** Class 60 Board 20 **Parking:** 23 **Notes:** Closed 30 Nov–22 Dec & 2 Jan–1 Mar

---

VERYAN
Cornwall & Isles of Scilly

Map 2 SW93

INSPECTOR'S CHOICE

The Nare
★★★★ ◎◎ COUNTRY HOUSE HOTEL

Carne Beach, TR2 5PF - tel: 01872 501111
email: stay@narehotel.co.uk **web:** www.narehotel.co.uk
dir: A3078 from Tregony, approx 1.5m. Left at Veryan sign, through village towards sea & hotel

The only 4 AA Red Star hotel in Cornwall, The Nare offers a relaxed, country-house atmosphere in a spectacular coastal setting. The elegantly designed bedrooms, many with balconies, have fresh flowers, carefully chosen artwork and antiques that contribute to their engaging individuality. A choice of dining options is available, from light snacks to superb local seafood.

Rooms: 37 (7 family) (7 GF) ♠ **S** £150–£290; **D** £290–£835 (incl. bkfst)*
Facilities: Spa FTV WiFi ⟳ ⚡ ⛵ ⚓ Gym Health & beauty clinic Sauna Steam room Hotel sailing boat Shooting Xmas New Year **Services:** Lift Night porter **Parking:** 80 **Notes:** LB

WAKEFIELD
West Yorkshire

Map 16 SE32

See also **Liversedge**

Waterton Park Hotel
★★★★ 81% ◎ HOTEL

Walton Hall, The Balk, WF2 6PW - tel: 01924 257911
email: info@watertonparkhotel.co.uk **web:** www.watertonparkhotel.co.uk
dir: 3m SE off B6378. Exit M1 junct 39 towards Wakefield. At 3rd rdbt right for Crofton. At 2nd lights right & follow signs

This Georgian mansion, built on an island in the centre of a 26-acre lake has a truly idyllic setting. The main house contains many feature bedrooms, and the annexe houses more spacious rooms, all equally well equipped with modern facilities; most

have views over the lake or the 18-hole golf course. The delightful beamed restaurant, two bars and leisure club are located in the old hall, and there is a licence for civil weddings. The spa is located in the annexed section of the hotel.

Rooms: 63 (41 annexe) (5 family) (21 GF) ♠ **Facilities:** Spa STV FTV WiFi ⟳ supervised Fishing Gym Steam room Sauna New Year **Conf:** Class 80 Board 80 Thtr 150 **Services:** Lift Night porter **Parking:** 200 **Notes:** Civ Wed 130

Holiday Inn Leeds - Wakefield
★★★ 79% HOTEL

Queen's Drive, Ossett, WF5 9BE - tel: 01924 230600
email: frontoffice@hileedswakefieldhotel.co.uk **web:** www.hileedswakefieldhotel.co.uk
dir: M1 junct 40 follow signs for Wakefield. Hotel on right in 200yds at 2nd set of lights

The Holiday Leeds-Wakefield is conveniently located off junction 40 of the M1 with close links to Leeds city centre. Bedrooms are well appointed and all are equipped with air conditioning. Ample carparking is provided. Outdoor seating areas are available for use in the summer months.

Rooms: 104 (32 family) (35 GF) **D** fr £55* **Facilities:** STV WiFi ⟳ **Conf:** Class 80 Board 80 Thtr 160 Del from £85 **Services:** Lift Night porter Air con **Parking:** 180 **Notes:** Civ Wed 160

Best Western Hotel St Pierre
★★★ 73% HOTEL

733 Barnsley Road, Newmillerdam, WF2 6QG - tel: 01924 255596
email: enq@hotelstpierre.co.uk **web:** www.bw-hotelstpierre.co.uk
dir: M1 junct 39, A636 to Wakefield, right at 2nd rdbt into Asdale Rd to lights. Right onto A61 towards Barnsley. Hotel just after lake on left

Located in the award-winning village of Newmillerdam this property provides comfortable modern accommodation. All bedrooms are well appointed with quality accessories and complimentary WiFi. The restaurant menu provides a good range of choice and a more relaxed bar menu is also available. An ample amount of on-site parking is available.

Rooms: 54 (1 family) (4 GF) ♠ **S** £60–£109; **D** £60–£109* **Facilities:** Spa FTV WiFi ⟳ New Year **Conf:** Class 60 Board 60 Thtr 100 **Services:** Lift Night porter **Parking:** 74 **Notes:** Civ Wed 100

Premier Inn Wakefield Central
BUDGET HOTEL

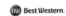

Thornes Park, Denby Dale Road, WF2 8DY - tel: 0871 527 9114
(Calls cost 13p per minute plus your phone company's access charge)
web: www.premierinn.com
dir: M1 junct 41, A650 towards Wakefield. Approx 1.5m. Hotel on right

High quality, budget accommodation ideal for both families and business travellers. Spacious, en suite bedrooms feature free WiFi and tea and coffee making facilities, and in most hotels, Freeview TV is also available. The adjacent family restaurant features a wide and varied menu.

Rooms: 42

W

WAKEFIELD *continued*

Premier Inn Wakefield City North

BUDGET HOTEL

Paragon Business Park, Herriot Way, WF1 2UJ - tel: 0871 527 9116
(Calls cost 13p per minute plus your phone company's access charge)
web: www.premierinn.com
dir: *M1 junct 41, A650 (Bradford Rd) for approx 1.5m towards Wakefield centre. Hotel on right adjacent to Bannatynes Health Club*

Rooms: 47

Premier Inn Wakefield South M1 Jct 39

BUDGET HOTEL

Calder Park, Denby Dale Road, WF4 3BB - tel: 0871 527 9118
(Calls cost 13p per minute plus your phone company's access charge)
web: www.premierinn.com
dir: *M1 junct 39, A636 towards Wakefield. At 1st rdbt 1st exit into Calder Park. Hotel on right*

Rooms: 75

Ramada Hotel Wakefield

AA Advertised

Silkwood Business Park, M1 junct 40, WF5 9TJ - tel: 01924 274200
email: wakefield.hotel@welcomebreak.co.uk
web: www.welcomebreak.co.uk/hotels/days-hotel-wakefield
dir: *M1 junct 40, follow signs to Wakefield, hotel 400yds on left*

This modern building offers accommodation in smart, spacious and well-equipped bedrooms, suitable for families and business travellers, and all with en suite bathrooms. Continental breakfast is available and other refreshments may be taken at the nearby family restaurant.

Rooms: 99 **Facilities:** FTV WiFi **Gym Conf:** Class 15 Board 15 Thtr 25 **Services:** Lift Night porter **Parking:** 80 **Notes:** LB

WALLASEY
Merseyside   Map 15 SJ29

Grove House Hotel

★★★ 80% SMALL HOTEL

Grove Road, CH45 3HF - tel: 0151 639 3947 & 630 4558
email: reception@thegrovehouse.co.uk **web:** www.thegrovehouse.co.uk
dir: *M53 junct 1, A554 (Wallasey New Brighton), right after church into Harrison Drive, left after Windsors Garage into Grove Rd*

Ideally situated for Liverpool and the M53, this friendly hotel offers attractive and comfortable bedrooms, which come with a wealth of extras. Well-cooked meals are served in the elegant panelled dining room. Weddings and conferences also catered for.

Rooms: 14 (7 family) **S** £89–£99; **D** £99–£119* **Facilities:** FTV WiFi **Conf:** Class 30 Board 50 Thtr 50 Del from £124.95 **Services:** Night porter **Parking:** 28 **Notes:** RS BHs Restaurant closed Civ Wed 50

WALLINGFORD
Oxfordshire   Map 5 SU68

The George

★★★ 78% HOTEL

High Street, OX10 0BS - tel: 01491 836665
email: info@george-hotel-wallingford.com **web:** www.peelhotels.co.uk
dir: *E side of A329, N end of Wallingford*

Old world charm and modern facilities merge seamlessly in this former coaching inn. Bedrooms in the main house have character in abundance. Those in the wing have a more contemporary style, but all are well equipped and attractively decorated. Diners can choose between the bistro or the cosy bar. The internal courtyard is perfect during the warm months of the year. Secure car park at the rear of the hotel.

Rooms: 39 (1 family) (9 GF) **Facilities:** STV WiFi Xmas New Year **Conf:** Class 60 Board 50 Thtr 150 **Services:** Night porter **Parking:** 40 **Notes:** LB Civ Wed 100

WALSALL
West Midlands   Map 10 SP09

Fairlawns Hotel & Spa

★★★★ 78% ⍟⍟ HOTEL

178 Little Aston Road, Aldridge, WS9 0NU - tel: 01922 455122
email: reception@fairlawns.co.uk **web:** www.fairlawns.co.uk
dir: *Exit A452 towards Aldridge at x-rds with A454. Hotel 600yds on right*

In a rural location with immaculate landscaped grounds, this constantly improving hotel offers a wide range of facilities and modern, comfortable bedrooms. Family rooms, one with a four-poster bed, and suites are also available. The Fairlawns Restaurant serves a wide range of award-winning seasonal dishes. The extensive, comprehensively equipped leisure complex is mainly for adult use as there is restricted availability to young people.

Rooms: 60 (8 family) (1 GF) (3 smoking) **S** £125–£145; **D** £187.50–£205 (incl. bkfst & dinner)* **Facilities:** Spa STV FTV WiFi supervised Gym Dance studio Beauty salon Bathing suite Floatation suite Sauna Aromatherapy room New Year **Conf:** Class 40 Board 30 Thtr 80 **Services:** Lift Night porter **Parking:** 150 **Notes:** LB RS 24 Dec-2 Jan Civ Wed 100

Best Western Baron's Court Hotel

★★★ 73% HOTEL

Walsall Road, Walsall Wood, WS9 9AH - tel: 01543 452020
email: sales@talashhotels.com **web:** www.bwbaronscourthotel.com
dir: *3.5m out of Walsall town centre, just N of Birmingham, close to M6 Toll*

This hotel prides itself on warm hospitality and is conveniently situated for business guests visiting this area. The lounge, bar and restaurant are modern and thoughtfully designed. Conference facilities are available, along with ample car parking.

Rooms: 94 (10 family) **Facilities:** FTV WiFi Xmas New Year **Conf:** Class 64 Board 45 Thtr 110 **Services:** Lift Night porter **Parking:** 123 **Notes:** Civ Wed 120

Holiday Inn Express Birmingham Walsall

BUDGET HOTEL

Tempus Ten, Tempus Drive, WS2 8TJ - tel: 01922 705250
email: admin@hiexwalsall.com **web:** www.hiexpress.co.uk
dir: *M6 junct 10/A454 to Walsall. Right at 1st lights, hotel 200mtrs on right*

A modern hotel ideal for families and business travellers. Fresh and uncomplicated, the spacious rooms include Sky TV, power shower and tea and coffee-making facilities. Continental buffet breakfast is included in the room rate; other meals may be taken at the nearby family pub or restaurant.

Rooms: 120 (77 family) (30 GF) 🌙 **Conf:** Class 45 Board 36 Thtr 60

Premier Inn Walsall M6 Jct 10

BUDGET HOTEL

Bentley Green, Bentley Road North, WS2 0WB - **tel:** 0871 527 9120
(Calls cost 13p per minute plus your phone company's access charge)
web: www.premierinn.com
dir: *M6 junct 10, A454 signed Wolverhampton. 2nd exit (Ansons junct).*
Left at rdbt, 1st left at next rdbt, hotel on right

High quality, budget accommodation ideal for both families and business travellers. Spacious, en suite bedrooms feature free WiFi and tea and coffee making facilities, and in most hotels, Freeview TV is also available. The adjacent family restaurant features a wide and varied menu.

Rooms: 60

Premier Inn Walsall Town Centre

BUDGET HOTEL

Waterfront, Wolverhampton Street, WS2 8LR - **tel:** 0871 527 9374
(Calls cost 13p per minute plus your phone company's access charge)
web: www.premierinn.com
dir: *M6 junct 10/A454 Wolverhampton Road to Walsall. Continue on A454.*
Follow signs for Crown Wharf Shopping Centre. Hotel on right on Wolverhampton St

Rooms: 100

| WALTHAM ABBEY | Map 6 TL30 |
| Essex | |

Premier Inn Waltham Abbey

BUDGET HOTEL

Sewardstone Road, EN9 3QF - **tel:** 0871 527 9122
(Calls cost 13p per minute plus your phone company's access charge)
web: www.premierinn.com
dir: *M25 junct 26, A121 towards Waltham Abbey. Left onto A112, hotel 0.5m on left*

High quality, budget accommodation ideal for both families and business travellers. Spacious, en suite bedrooms feature free WiFi and tea and coffee making facilities, and in most hotels, Freeview TV is also available. The adjacent family restaurant features a wide and varied menu.

Rooms: 99

| WANSFORD | Map 12 TL09 |
| Cambridgeshire | |

The Haycock Hotel

★★★ 82% ◉ HOTEL

MACDONALD
HOTELS & RESORTS

London Road, PE8 6JA - **tel:** 01780 782223
email: reception@haycock.macdonaldhotels.co.uk
web: www.macdonaldhotels.co.uk/haycock
dir: *A1 junct to A47 Leicester/Peterborough*

The Haycock Hotel is a charming 17th-century coaching inn set in attractive landscaped grounds in a peaceful village location. The smartly decorated bedrooms are tastefully furnished and thoughtfully equipped. Public rooms include a choice of

---

restaurants, a lounge bar, a cocktail bar and a stylish lounge. The hotel has a staffed business centre, and banqueting facilities are also available.

Rooms: 48 (1 family) (14 GF) 🌙 **S** £79–£139; **D** £99–£159* **Facilities:** FTV WiFi ⬧
Beauty treatment room New Year **Conf:** Class 100 Board 45 Thtr 300 Del from £124
Services: Night porter **Parking:** 300 **Notes:** Civ Wed 200

| WARMINSTER | Map 4 ST84 |
| Wiltshire | |

HIGHLY RECOMMENDED

The Bishopstrow Hotel & Spa

★★★★ 83% ◉◉ HOTEL

Borenam Road, BA12 9HH - **tel:** 01985 212312
email: info@bishopstrow.com **web:** www.bishopstrow.co.uk
dir: *From rdbt on A36 take B3414 towards Warminster. Follow brown hotel signs*

The Bishopstrow Hotel is set in 27 acres of delightful grounds which include modern spa facilities, tennis courts and country walks. Bedrooms are comfortable and stylish, and all are well appointed. Public areas offer several day rooms, and retain the style of the original house. Cuisine is a feature here, and menus offer fresh and local produce.

Rooms: 32 (2 annexe) (26 family) (9 GF) 🌙 **S** £99–£310; **D** £120–£515 (incl.
bkfst)* **Facilities:** Spa STV FTV WiFi ⬧ ⚲ ⤳ 🏊 Fishing Gym Thermal rooms
Relaxation room Dual treatment room Xmas New Year **Conf:** Class 40 Board 36
Thtr 60 Del from £168 **Services:** Night porter **Parking:** 70 **Notes:** Civ Wed 82

| WARRINGTON | Map 15 SJ68 |
| Cheshire | |

The Park Royal

★★★★ 81% ◉ HOTEL

QHOTELS
INSPIRED
BY YOU

Stretton Road, Stretton, WA4 4NS - **tel:** 01925 730706
email: parkroyalreservations@qhotels.co.uk **web:** www.qhotels.co.uk
dir: *M56 junct 10, A49 to Warrington, at lights turn right to Appleton Thorn,*
1st right into Spark Hall Close, hotel on left

This modern hotel enjoys a peaceful setting, yet is conveniently located just minutes from the M56. The bedrooms are contemporary, well furnished and attractively co-ordinated. Spacious, stylish public areas include extensive conference and function facilities and a comprehensive leisure centre complete with outdoor tennis courts and a spa. Complimentary WiFi is also provided.

Rooms: 146 (31 family) (31 GF) 🌙 **S** £67; **D** £73 (incl. bkfst)* **Facilities:** Spa FTV WiFi
⬧ HL ⚲ 🏊 Gym Dance studio Sauna Steam room Xmas New Year **Conf:** Class 180
Board 90 Thtr 400 Del £132 **Services:** Lift Night porter **Parking:** 400 **Notes:** LB Civ
Wed 300

W

WARRINGTON *continued*

Hallmark Hotel Warrington Fir Grove

★★★ 80% 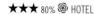 HOTEL

Knutsford Old Road, WA4 2LD - tel: 0330 028 3423
email: firgrove@hallmarkhotels.co.uk **web:** www.hallmarkhotels.co.uk
dir: *M6 junct 20, follow signs for A50 to Warrington for 2.4m, before swing bridge over canal, turn right & right again*

Situated in a quiet residential area, this hotel is convenient for both the town centre and the motorway network. Comfortable bedrooms, including spacious executive rooms are appointed to a good standard. Public areas include a smart and contemporary lounge/bar, a neatly appointed restaurant, and excellent function and meeting facilities.

Rooms: 52 (4 family) (20 GF) ⌁ **S** £59–£139; **D** £69–£149* **Facilities:** FTV WiFi ⌁ Xmas New Year **Conf:** Class 100 Board 50 Thtr 200 Del from £105 **Services:** Night porter **Parking:** 57 **Notes:** Civ Wed 180

Premier Inn Warrington A49/M62 Jct 9

BUDGET HOTEL

Winwick Road, WA2 8RN - tel: 0871 527 9132
(Calls cost 13p per minute plus your phone company's access charge)
web: www.premierinn.com
dir: *M62 junct 9 towards Warrington, hotel 100yds*

High quality, budget accommodation ideal for both families and business travellers. Spacious, en suite bedrooms feature free WiFi and tea and coffee making facilities, and in most hotels, Freeview TV is also available. The adjacent family restaurant features a wide and varied menu.

Rooms: 40

Premier Inn Warrington Central North

BUDGET HOTEL

Floyd Drive, WA2 8DB - tel: 0871 527 9128 (Calls cost 13p per minute plus your phone company's access charge) **web:** www.premierinn.com
dir: *M62 junct 9, A49 signed Warrington. At next rdbt follow Town Centre signs. Straight on at next rdbt, left into Warrington Collegiate Camp*

Rooms: 75

Premier Inn Warrington Centre

BUDGET HOTEL

1430 Centre Park, Park Boulevard, WA1 1PR - tel: 0871 527 9126
(Calls cost 13p per minute plus your phone company's access charge)
web: www.premierinn.com
dir: *Take A49 to Brian Beven Island Rdbt, into Park Boulevard (Centre Park). Over bridge. Hotel on right*

Rooms: 42

Premier Inn Warrington (M6 Jct 21)

BUDGET HOTEL

Manchester Road, Woolston, WA1 4GB - tel: 0871 527 9124
(Calls cost 13p per minute plus your phone company's access charge)
web: www.premierinn.com
dir: *Just off M6 junct 21 on A57 to Warrington*

Rooms: 105

Premier Inn Warrington North East

BUDGET HOTEL

Golborne Road, Winwick, WA2 8LF - tel: 0871 527 9130
(Calls cost 13p per minute plus your phone company's access charge)
web: www.premierinn.com
dir: *M6 junct 22, A573 towards Newton-le-Willows. Dual carriageway to end, take 3rd exit at rdbt. Hotel adjacent to church*

Rooms: 42

Premier Inn Warrington South

BUDGET HOTEL

Tarporley Road, Stretton, WA4 4NB - tel: 0871 527 9134
(Calls cost 13p per minute plus your phone company's access charge)
web: www.premierinn.com
dir: *Just off M56 junct 10. Follow A49 to Warrington, left at 1st lights*

Rooms: 29

WARWICK   **Map 10 SP26**
Warwickshire

See also **Leamington Spa (Royal)** & **Wroxall**

Chesford Grange

★★★★ 79% HOTEL

Chesford Bridge, CV8 2LD - tel: 01926 859331
email: chesfordreservations@qhotels.co.uk **web:** www.qhotels.co.uk

(For full entry see Kenilworth)

Ardencote

★★★★ 76% 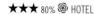 HOTEL

The Cumsey, Lye Green Road, CV35 8LT - tel: 01926 843111
email: hotel@ardencote.com **web:** www.ardencote.com

(For full entry see Claverdon)

Premier Inn Warwick

BUDGET HOTEL

Opus 40, Birmingham Road, CV34 5JL - tel: 0871 527 9320
(Calls cost 13p per minute plus your phone company's access charge)
web: www.premierinn.com
dir: *M40 junct 15, A46 (Warwick bypass) towards Warwick. Follow A425 signs. From A425 1st left into industrial estate (Opus 40). Hotel 200yds, opposite IBM office*

High quality, budget accommodation ideal for both families and business travellers. Spacious, en suite bedrooms feature free WiFi and tea and coffee making facilities, and in most hotels, Freeview TV is also available. The adjacent family restaurant features a wide and varied menu.

Rooms: 124

W

WARWICK MOTORWAY SERVICE AREA (M40)
Warwickshire
Map 11 SP35

Days Inn Warwick North - M40
WELCOMEBREAK

AA Advertised

Warwick Services, M40 Northbound Junction 12-13, CV35 0AA - **tel:** 01926 651681
email: warwick.north.hotel@welcomebreak.co.uk **web:** www.welcomebreak.co.uk
dir: *M40 northbound between junct 12 & 13*

This modern building offers accommodation in smart, spacious and well-equipped bedrooms, suitable for families and business travellers, and all with en suite bathrooms. Continental breakfast is available and other refreshments may be taken at the nearby family restaurant.

Rooms: 54 (45 family) (8 smoking) **Facilities:** FTV WiFi ⌨ **Conf:** Board 30
Services: Night porter **Parking:** 100

Days Inn Warwick South - M40
WELCOMEBREAK

AA Advertised

Warwick Services, M40 Southbound, CV35 0AA - **tel:** 01926 652081
email: warwick.south.hotel@welcomebreak.co.uk **web:** www.welcomebreak.co.uk
dir: *M40 southbound between junct 14 & 12*

This modern building offers accommodation in smart, spacious and well-equipped bedrooms, suitable for families and business travellers, and all with en suite bathrooms. Continental breakfast is available and other refreshments may be taken at the nearby family restaurant.

Rooms: 40 (30 family) (19 GF) (4 smoking) **Facilities:** FTV WiFi ⌨ **Parking:** 500

WASHINGTON
Tyne & Wear
Map 19 NZ35

Mercure George Washington Hotel, Golf & Spa

★★★★ 75% HOTEL

Stone Cellar Road, High Usworth, NE37 1PH - **tel:** 0191 402 9988
email: reservations@georgewashington.co.uk **web:** www.georgewashington.co.uk
dir: *A1(M) junct 65 onto A194(M). Take A195 signed Washington North. Take last exit from rdbt for Washington then right at mini rdbt. Hotel 0.5m on right*

The Mercure George Washington Hotel, Golf & Spa is popular with business and leisure guests alike. It is a purpose-built hotel that boasts an 18-hole championship golf course and a driving range. The bedrooms are generally spacious and comfortably equipped. Public areas include extensive conference facilities, a business centre and spa. Newly created is Carter and Fitch, a pizzeria, smokehouse and bar concept, which has a great menu of informal dishes and a friendly service to match.

Rooms: 103 (13 family) (41 GF) **S** £49–£189; **D** £59–£199* **Facilities:** Spa FTV WiFi ⌨ ☏ ♨ 18 Putting green Gym Driving range Par 3 course **Conf:** Class 100 Board 60 Thtr 200 Del from £99 **Services:** Night porter **Parking:** 600 **Notes:** Civ Wed 150

Premier Inn Newcastle (Washington)

BUDGET HOTEL

Emerson Road, NE37 1LB - **tel:** 0871 527 9136
(Calls cost 13p per minute plus your phone company's access charge)
web: www.premierinn.com
dir: *A1(M) junct 64, A195, follow Emerson signs. Left at rdbt, hotel 250yds left*

High quality, budget accommodation ideal for both families and business travellers. Spacious, en suite bedrooms feature free WiFi and tea and coffee making facilities, and in most hotels, Freeview TV is also available. The adjacent family restaurant features a wide and varied menu.

Rooms: 74

WATERMILLOCK
Cumbria
Map 18 NY42

Macdonald Leeming House
MACDONALD HOTELS & RESORTS

★★★★ 81% ◉ HOTEL

CA11 0JJ - **tel:** 01768 486674 **email:** leeminghouse@macdonald-hotels.co.uk
web: www.macdonaldhotels.co.uk
dir: *M6 junct 40, A66 to Keswick. At rdbt take A592 (Ullswater). 5m to T-junct, right (A592). Hotel on left*

This hotel enjoys a superb location, being set in 20 acres of mature wooded gardens in the Lake District National Park, and overlooking Ullswater and the towering fells. Many rooms offer views of the lake and the rugged mountains beyond, with more than half having their own balcony. Public rooms include three sumptuous lounges, a cosy bar and library.

Rooms: 41 (1 family) (10 GF) **Facilities:** WiFi Fishing ⌁ Xmas New Year
Conf: Class 40 Board 30 Thtr 80 **Services:** Night porter **Parking:** 50
Notes: Civ Wed 80

WATFORD
Hertfordshire
Map 6 TQ19

Mercure London Watford Hotel
Mercure HOTELS

★★★★ 69% HOTEL

A41, Watford Bypass, WD25 8JH - **tel:** 020 8901 0000 & 0844 815 9056
(Calls cost 7p per minute plus your phone company's access charge)
email: info@mercurewatford.co.uk **web:** www.mercurewatford.co.uk
dir: *M1 junct 5, A41 S to London. Straight on at island, hotel 1m on left*

This hotel is situated on the outskirts of London close to the M1, M25, A1(M) motorways, and Luton and London Heathrow airports. The bedrooms are smartly appointed and equipped with modern facilities including WiFi and satellite TV. Public rooms include The Brasserie restaurant and bar; guests also have the use of the leisure facilities with a heated pool.

Rooms: 218 (3 family) **Facilities:** WiFi ⌨ ☏ ♨ Gym Sauna Steam room Beauty treatment room **Conf:** Class 120 Board 58 Thtr 200 **Services:** Night porter **Parking:** 300 **Notes:** Civ Wed 200

W

WATFORD *continued*

Best Western White House

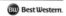

★★★ 72% HOTEL

Upton Road, WD18 0JF - **tel:** 01923 237316
email: info@whitehousehotel.co.uk **web:** www.bw-whitehousehotel.co.uk
dir: *From centre ring road, exit left into Upton Rd, hotel on left*

This popular commercial hotel is situated within easy walking distance of the town centre. Bedrooms are pleasantly decorated and offer a good range of facilities that include interactive TV with internet. The public areas are open plan; they include a comfortable lounge/bar, cosy snug and an attractive conservatory restaurant with a sunny open terrace for summer dining. Functions suites are also available.

Rooms: 57 (3 family) (8 GF) **D** fr £59* **Facilities:** FTV WiFi HL **Services:** Lift Night porter **Parking:** 40 **Notes:** RS 25 Dec-2 Jan For lunch & dinner

Premier Inn Watford Central

BUDGET HOTEL

Timms Meadow, Water Lane, WD17 2NJ - **tel:** 0871 527 9140
(Calls cost 13p per minute plus your phone company's access charge)
web: www.premierinn.com
dir: *M1 junct 5, A41 into town centre. At rdbt take 3rd exit, stay in left lane through lights. Take 1st left into Water Ln. Hotel on left*

High quality, budget accommodation ideal for both families and business travellers. Spacious, en suite bedrooms feature free WiFi and tea and coffee making facilities, and in most hotels, Freeview TV is also available. The adjacent family restaurant features a wide and varied menu.

Rooms: 105

Premier Inn Watford (Croxley Green)

BUDGET HOTEL

2 Ascot Road, WD18 8AD - **tel:** 0871 527 9138
(Calls cost 13p per minute plus your phone company's access charge)
web: www.premierinn.com
dir: *M25 junct 18, A404 signed Watford/Rickmansworth, left at 1st rdbt signed A412 Watford. Follow Croxley Green Business Park/Watford signs, at 4th rdbt, 3rd exit. M1 junct 5, A41 towards Watford, follow Watford West & Rickmansworth A412 signs. Then Croxley Green Business Park signs*

Rooms: 126

Premier Inn Watford North

BUDGET HOTEL

859 St Albans Road, Garston, WD25 0LH - **tel:** 0871 527 9142
(Calls cost 13p per minute plus your phone company's access charge)
web: www.premierinn.com
dir: *M1 junct 6, A405 towards Watford. At 2nd lights onto A412 (St Albans Rd). Into TGI Friday's car park. Hotel directly behind*

Rooms: 60

WATTON
Norfolk
Map 13 TF90

Broom Hall Country Hotel

★★★ 80% COUNTRY HOUSE HOTEL

Richmond Road, Saham Toney, IP25 7EX - **tel:** 01953 882125
email: enquiries@broomhallhotel.co.uk **web:** www.broomhallhotel.co.uk
dir: *From A11 at Thetford onto A1075 to Watton, B1108 towards Swaffham, in 0.5m at rdbt turn right to Saham Toney, hotel 0.5m on left. From A47 take A1075, left onto B1108*

A delightful Victorian country house situated down a private drive and set in mature landscaped gardens surrounded by parkland. The well-equipped bedrooms are split between the main house and an adjacent building. Public rooms include a relaxing lounge, a brasserie restaurant, a lounge bar, a conservatory and a smart restaurant. There is an indoor swimming pool.

Rooms: 15 (4 annexe) (3 family) (4 GF) **S** £75–£90; **D** £85–£165 (incl. bkfst) **Facilities:** Spa FTV WiFi ⛳ Massage Beauty treatments **Conf:** Class 30 Board 22 Thtr 80 Del from £120 **Parking:** 30 **Notes:** LB Closed 24 Dec-4 Jan Civ Wed 70

WELLINGBOROUGH
Northamptonshire
Map 11 SP86

Premier Inn Wellingborough

BUDGET HOTEL

London Road, NN8 2DP - **tel:** 0871 527 9144
(Calls cost 13p per minute plus your phone company's access charge)
web: www.premierinn.com
dir: *0.5m from town centre on A5193, near Dennington Industrial Estate*

High quality, budget accommodation ideal for both families and business travellers. Spacious, en suite bedrooms feature free WiFi and tea and coffee making facilities, and in most hotels, Freeview TV is also available. The adjacent family restaurant features a wide and varied menu.

Rooms: 64

WELLS
Somerset
Map 4 ST54

Best Western Plus Swan Hotel

★★★★ 77% ◉◉ HOTEL

Sadler Street, BA5 2RX - **tel:** 01749 836300
email: info@swanhotelwells.co.uk **web:** www.swanhotelwells.co.uk
dir: *A39, A371, on entering Wells follow signs for Hotels & Deliveries. Hotel on right opposite cathedral*

Situated in the shadow of Wells Cathedral, this privately-owned hotel enjoys a truly stunning location, and its owners extend a genuinely friendly welcome. Full of character and with a rich history, the hotel has been restored and extended to provide high levels of quality and comfort. Guests can choose between the larger, period bedrooms in the main building or the more contemporary coach house rooms. Dinner in the oak-panelled restaurant should not be missed.

Rooms: 50 (3 family) (4 GF) **S** £82–£114; **D** £116–£148 (incl. bkfst)* **Facilities:** FTV WiFi Gym In room treatments **Conf:** Class 45 Board 40 Thtr 120 Del £140 **Services:** Night porter **Parking:** 30 **Notes:** LB Civ Wed 90

W

Premier Inn Wells

BUDGET HOTEL

BA5 1UA - **tel:** 0871 527 9730 (Calls cost 13p per minute plus your phone company's access charge) **web:** www.premierinn.com
dir: *Please phone for directions*

High quality, budget accommodation ideal for both families and business travellers. Spacious, en suite bedrooms feature free WiFi and tea and coffee making facilities, and in most hotels, Freeview TV is also available. The adjacent family restaurant features a wide and varied menu.

Rooms: 69

WELWYN GARDEN CITY
Hertfordshire   Map 6 TL21

HIGHLY RECOMMENDED

Tewin Bury Farm Hotel

★★★★ 83% 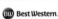 HOTEL

Hertford Road (B1000), AL6 0JB - **tel:** 01438 717793
email: reservations@tewinbury.co.uk **web:** www.tewinbury.co.uk
dir: *From N: A1(M) junct 6, 1st exit signed A1000, at next rdbt 1st exit towards Digswell. 0.1m straight on at rdbt. 1m on B100. Hotel on left*

Situated not far from the A1(M) and within easy reach of Stevenage and Knebworth House, this delightful country-house hotel is part of a thriving farm. Stylish, well-equipped bedrooms of varying sizes are perfectly suited for both leisure and business guests. An award-winning restaurant and meeting rooms are all part of this family-run establishment.

Rooms: 36 (20 annexe) (4 family) (26 GF) ⌕ **S** £125–£165; **D** £160–£180 (incl. bkfst)* **Facilities:** FTV WiFi ☙ Fishing Cycling Xmas New Year **Conf:** Class 300 Board 40 Thtr 500 **Services:** Lift Night porter **Parking:** 400 **Notes:** LB Civ Wed 300

Best Western Homestead Court Hotel

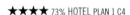

★★★ 78% HOTEL

Homestead Lane, AL7 4LX - **tel:** 01707 324336
email: enquiries@homesteadcourt.co.uk **web:** www.bw-homesteadcourt.co.uk
dir: *Exit A1000, left at lights at Bushall Hotel. Right at rdbt into Howlands, 2nd left at Hollybush public house into Hollybush Ln. 2nd right at War Memorial into Homestead Ln*

This family-run hotel enjoys a quiet location and is a short drive from the centre of Welwyn Garden City and the major road network. Bedrooms are all attractively presented and very well equipped. Free WiFi is available throughout the hotel and there is an extensive choice on the restaurant menu. Ample secure parking is provided and the cosy lounge is a popular casual dining venue.

Rooms: 79 (9 annexe) (6 family) (5 GF) ⌕ **S** £55–£179; **D** £55–£179* **Facilities:** STV FTV WiFi ☙ HL Xmas **Conf:** Class 200 Board 80 Thtr 300 Del from £115 **Services:** Lift Night porter **Parking:** 75 **Notes:** Civ Wed 250

Premier Inn Welwyn Garden City

BUDGET HOTEL

Stanborough Road, AL8 6DQ - **tel:** 0871 527 9146
(Calls cost 13p per minute plus your phone company's access charge)
web: www.premierinn.com
dir: *A1(M) junct 4, A6129*

High quality, budget accommodation ideal for both families and business travellers. Spacious, en suite bedrooms feature free WiFi and tea and coffee making facilities, and in most hotels, Freeview TV is also available. The adjacent family restaurant features a wide and varied menu.

Rooms: 120

WEMBLEY
Greater London

Novotel London Wembley

★★★★ 76% HOTEL PLAN 1 C5

5 Olympic Way, HA9 0NP - **tel:** 020 8069 1200
email: h9389@accor.com **web:** www.novotel.com
dir: *Please phone for directions*

Located on Olympic Way, Novotel London Wembley offers proximity to Wembley Stadium and Arena. Wembley Park Underground is only a short walk and connects directly to the Eurostar Terminal and Central London. Facilities include free WiFi throughout the hotel, Freeview TV channels in every bedroom, and a fitness centre with panoramic views. The Elements restaurant and bar offers a tempting international menu and drinks.

Rooms: 235 (27 family) ⌕ **S** £82–£229; **D** £92–£239* **Facilities:** FTV WiFi HL Gym **Conf:** Class 60 Board 40 Thtr 120 Del from £165 **Services:** Lift Air con **Parking:** 29

Holiday Inn London - Wembley

★★★★ 73% HOTEL PLAN 1 C4

Empire Way, HA9 8DS - **tel:** 020 8902 8839
email: info@hiwembley.co.uk **web:** www.hiwembley.co.uk
dir: *Within easy reach of North Circular, M1, M4 & M40*

This large hotel is ideally situated for the arena, stadium and conference centre. It has a range of modern public areas and well equipped meeting rooms.

Rooms: 336 (42 family) ⌕ **Facilities:** Spa STV WiFi ☙ HL ⊛ Gym Steam room Sauna Beauty treatment room **Conf:** Class 160 Board 80 Thtr 500 **Services:** Lift Night porter Air con **Parking:** 250 **Notes:** Civ Wed 500

Wembley International Hotel

★★★ 72% HOTEL PLAN 1 C5

Empire Way, HA9 0NH - **tel:** 020 8733 9000 & 8903 4426
email: sales@hotels-wembley.com **web:** www.wembleyinternationalhotel.co.uk
dir: *M1 junct 6, A406, right onto A404. Right onto Empire Way, after rdbt at lights. Hotel on right*

Conveniently situated within walking distance of both the Arena and conference centres, this modern hotel offers smart, comfortable and spacious bedrooms; many are air conditioned. All rooms offer an excellent range of amenities. Air-conditioned public areas include a large restaurant serving a wide range of contemporary dishes.

Rooms: 165 (70 family) (3 GF) (10 smoking) **S** fr £49; **D** fr £54* **Facilities:** STV FTV WiFi ☙ **Conf:** Class 90 Board 90 Thtr 150 **Services:** Lift Air con **Parking:** 65

W

WEMBLEY *continued*

Premier Inn London Wembley Stadium

BUDGET HOTEL PLAN 1 C5

151 Wembley Park Drive, HA9 8HQ - **tel:** 0871 527 8682
(Calls cost 13p per minute plus your phone company's access charge)
web: www.premierinn.com
dir: *A406 (North Circular) take A404 towards Wembley. 2m right into Wembley Hill Rd, keep right into Empire Way (B4565), pass Wembley Arena on right, keep right around petrol station. Hotel 200yds on left*

High quality, budget accommodation ideal for both families and business travellers. Spacious, en suite bedrooms feature free WiFi and tea and coffee making facilities, and in most hotels, Freeview TV is also available. The adjacent family restaurant features a wide and varied menu.

Rooms: 154

WEST BROMWICH	Map 10 SP09
West Midlands	

Premier Inn West Bromwich

BUDGET HOTEL

New Gas Street, B70 0NP - **tel:** 0871 527 9148
(Calls cost 13p per minute plus your phone company's access charge)
web: www.premierinn.com
dir: *M5 junct 1, A41 (Expressway) towards Wolverhampton. At 3rd rdbt, hotel on right*

High quality, budget accommodation ideal for both families and business travellers. Spacious, en suite bedrooms feature free WiFi and tea and coffee making facilities, and in most hotels, Freeview TV is also available. The adjacent family restaurant features a wide and varied menu.

Rooms: 62

Premier Inn West Bromwich Central

BUDGET HOTEL

144 High Street, B70 6JJ - **tel:** 0871 527 9150
(Calls cost 13p per minute plus your phone company's access charge)
web: www.premierinn.com
dir: *M5 junct 1 towards town centre, hotel 2m*

Rooms: 85

WEST DRAYTON
Hotels are listed under Heathrow Airport

W

WEST HOATHLY	Map 6 TV33
West Sussex	

Gravetye Manor Hotel

★★★★ ◉◉◉ COUNTRY HOUSE HOTEL

Vowels Lane, RH19 4LJ - **tel:** 01342 810567
email: info@gravetyemanor.co.uk **web:** www.gravetyemanor.co.uk
dir: *B2028 to Haywards Heath. 1m after Turners Hill fork left towards Sharpthorne, 1st left into Vowels Lane*

Gravetye Manor is a beautiful Elizabethan mansion, built in 1598 and enjoying a tranquil setting. One of the first country house hotels in Britain, it remains an excellent example of its type. Bedrooms and bathrooms have been sympathetically refurbished with style and luxurious finishing touches. The day rooms, each with oak panelling, fresh flower arrangements and open fires, create a relaxing atmosphere. Cuisine is excellent and makes use of local suppliers and producers. Guests should take time to explore the impressive gardens and grounds; a perfect spot for afternoon tea.

Rooms: 17 ☏ D fr £290 (incl. bkfst)* **Facilities:** STV WiFi ☇ Fishing ☙ Deer stalking Xmas New Year **Conf:** Board 15 Del from £360 **Services:** Night porter **Parking:** 30 **Notes:** LB No children 7yrs Civ Wed 60

WESTLETON
Suffolk

Map 13 TM46

The Westleton Crown
★★★ 81% ⊚⊚ HOTEL

The Street, IP17 3AD - tel: 01728 648777
email: info@westletoncrown.co.uk **web:** www.westletoncrown.co.uk
dir: *A12 N, turn right for Westleton just after Yoxford. Hotel opposite on entering Westleton*

The Westleton Crown is a charming coaching inn situated in a peaceful village location just a few minutes from the A12. Public rooms include a smart, award-winning restaurant, comfortable lounge, and busy bar with exposed beams and open fireplaces. The stylish bedrooms are tastefully decorated and equipped with many thoughtful little extras.

Rooms: 34 (22 annexe) (5 family) (13 GF) ⊂ **S** £100–£110; **D** £100–£215 (incl. bkfst)* **Facilities:** FTV WiFi ⌂ Xmas New Year **Services:** Night porter **Parking:** 34 **Notes:** Civ Wed 90

WESTON-SUPER-MARE
Somerset

Map 4 ST36

Beachlands Hotel
★★★ 78% HOTEL

17 Uphill Road North, BS23 4NG - tel: 01934 621401
email: info@beachlandshotel.com **web:** www.beachlandshotel.com
dir: *M5 junct 21, follow signs for hospital. At hospital rdbt follow signs for beach, hotel 300yds before beach*

This popular hotel is very close to the 18-hole links course and a short walk from the seafront. Elegant public areas include a bar, a choice of lounges and a bright dining room. Bedrooms vary slightly in size, but all are well equipped for both the business and leisure guest. There is the added bonus of a 10-metre indoor pool and a sauna.

Rooms: 21 (6 family) (11 GF) ⊂ **Facilities:** FTV WiFi ☁ Sauna Beauty treatment room New Year **Conf:** Class 20 Board 30 Thtr 60 **Parking:** 28 **Notes:** Closed 24-27 Dec Civ Wed 110

The Royal Hotel
★★★ 78% HOTEL

1 South Parade, BS23 1JP - tel: 01934 423100
email: reservations@royalhotelweston.com **web:** www.royalhotelweston.com
dir: *M5 junct 21, follow signs to seafront. Hotel next to Winter Gardens Pavillion*

The Royal, which opened in 1810, was the first hotel in Weston and occupies a prime seafront position. It is a grand building and many of the bedrooms, including some with sea views, are spacious and comfortable; family apartments are also available. Public areas include a choice of bars and a restaurant which offers a range of dishes to meet all tastes. Entertainment is provided during the season.

Rooms: 44 (3 annexe) (8 family) ⊂ **S** £71–£103; **D** £97–£160 (incl. bkfst)* **Facilities:** FTV WiFi ⌂ HL Beauty treatment room Hair salon Solarium ♫ Xmas New Year **Conf:** Class 100 Board 60 Thtr 200 Del from £135 **Services:** Lift Night porter **Parking:** 152 **Notes:** LB Civ Wed 200

See advert on following page

W

W

WESTON-SUPER-MARE *continued*

Anchor Head Hotel

Leisureplex
HOLIDAY HOTELS

★★★ 64% HOTEL

19 Claremont Crescent, Birnbeck Road, BS23 2EE - **tel:** 01934 620880
email: anchor.weston@alfatravel.co.uk **web:** www.leisureplex.co.uk
dir: *M5 junct 21, A370 to seafront, right, past Grand Pier towards Brimbeck Pier.*
Hotel at end of terrace on left

Enjoying a very pleasant location with views across the bay, the Anchor Head offers
a varied choice of comfortable lounges and a relaxing outdoor patio area.
Bedrooms and bathrooms are traditionally furnished and include several ground-
floor rooms. Dinner and breakfast are served in the spacious dining room that also
benefits from sea views.

Rooms: 52 (1 family) (5 GF) ⚲ **S** fr £37; **D** fr £58 (incl. bkfst)* **Facilities:** FTV
WiFi ♫ Xmas New Year **Services:** Lift Night porter **Notes:** LB Closed Dec-Feb
(ex Xmas/New Year) RS Mar & Nov Mon-Fri only

Premier Inn Weston-Super-Mare East (A370)

Premier Inn

BUDGET HOTEL

Hutton Moor Road, BS22 8LY - **tel:** 0871 527 9156 (Calls cost 13p per minute plus your
phone company's access charge) **web:** www.premierinn.com
dir: *M5 junct 21, A370 towards Weston-Super-Mare. After 3rd rbt right at lights into*
Hutton Moor Leisure Centre. Left, into car park

High quality, budget accommodation ideal for both families and business
travellers. Spacious, en suite bedrooms feature free WiFi and tea and coffee making
facilities, and in most hotels, Freeview TV is also available. The adjacent family
restaurant features a wide and varied menu.

Rooms: 88

Premier Inn Weston-Super-Mare (Seafront)

Premier Inn

BUDGET HOTEL

Dolphin Square, Beach Road, BS23 1TT - **tel:** 0871 527 9378
(Calls cost 13p per minute plus your phone company's access charge)
web: www.premierinn.com
dir: *M5 junct 21, A370 towards Weston-Super-Mare town centre. At double mini rdbt 2nd*
exit, 1st exit into Oxford St. At end, left into Beach Rd. Left into Carlton St. Hotel on left

Rooms: 112

WEST THURROCK	Map 6 TQ57
Essex	

Premier Inn Thurrock East

Premier Inn

BUDGET HOTEL

Fleming Road, Unicorn Estate, RM16 6YJ - **tel:** 0871 527 9092
(Calls cost 13p per minute plus your phone company's access charge)
web: www.premierinn.com
dir: *From A13 follow Lakeside Shopping Centre signs. Right at 1st rdbt,*
straight on at next rdbt, then 1st slip road. Left at next rdbt

High quality, budget accommodation ideal for both families and business
travellers. Spacious, en suite bedrooms feature free WiFi and tea and coffee making
facilities, and in most hotels, Freeview TV is also available. The adjacent family
restaurant features a wide and varied menu.

Rooms: 104

Premier Inn Thurrock West

Premier Inn

BUDGET HOTEL

Stonehouse Lane, RM19 1NS - **tel:** 0871 527 9094
(Calls cost 13p per minute plus your phone company's access charge)
web: www.premierinn.com
dir: *From N: M25 junct 31, A1090 to Purfleet. (NB do not cross Dartford Bridge or follow*
signs for Lakeside). From S: M25 junct 31. On approach to Dartford Tunnel, bear far left
signed Dagenham. After tunnel, hotel at top of slip road

Rooms: 161

WETHERBY	Map 16 SE44
West Yorkshire	

INSPECTOR'S CHOICE

Wood Hall Hotel & Spa

Hand PICKED
HOTELS
BUILT FOR PLEASURE

★★★★ ◉◉ ≋ HOTEL

Trip Lane, Linton, LS22 4JA - **tel:** 01937 587271 & 0845 072 7564
(Calls cost 5p per minute plus your phone company's access charge)
email: woodhall@handpicked.co.uk **web:** www.handpickedhotels.co.uk/woodhall
dir: *From Wetherby take Harrogate road N (A661) for 0.5m, left to Sicklinghall &*
Linton. Cross bridge, left to Linton & Wood Hall. Turn right opposite Windmill Inn,
1.25m to hotel

A long sweeping drive leads to this delightful Georgian house situated in 100
acres of parkland. Spacious bedrooms are appointed to an impressive standard
and feature comprehensive facilities, including large plasma-screen TVs. Public
rooms reflect the same elegance and include a smart drawing room and dining
room, both with fantastic views.

Rooms: 44 (30 annexe) (5 family) ⚲ **S** £140–£240; **D** £180–£280 (incl. bkfst)*
Facilities: Spa STV FTV WiFi ♗ HL ⊕ Fishing Gym Steam room Xmas New Year
Conf: Class 70 Board 40 Thtr 100 Del from £140 **Services:** Lift Night porter
Parking: 200 **Notes:** LB Civ Wed 100

W

WETHERBY *continued*

Bridge Hotel & Spa

★★★★ 79% HOTEL

Walshford, LS22 5HS - **tel:** 01937 580115
email: info@bridgewetherby.co.uk **web:** www.bridgewetherby.co.uk
dir: *From N exit A1(M) at junct 47 York or S junct 46 Wetherby Race Centre, 1st left Walshford, follow brown tourist signs*

The Bridge Hotel is located hotel close to the A1, with spacious public areas and a good range of services, making this an ideal venue for business or leisure. The stylish bedrooms are comfortable and well equipped. There is a choice of bars and a large open-plan restaurant. Conference and banqueting suites are also available.

Rooms: 30 (2 family) (10 GF) **S** £70–£140; **D** £80–£160 (incl. bkfst)* **Facilities:** Spa FTV WiFi ⌂ Gym Xmas New Year **Conf:** Class 50 Board 50 Thtr 200 **Services:** Night porter **Parking:** 150 **Notes:** LB Civ Wed 150

Mercure Wetherby Hotel

★★★ 71% HOTEL

Leeds Road, LS22 5HE - **tel:** 01937 545000 & 0844 815 9067
(Calls cost 7p per minute plus your phone company's access charge)
email: info@mercurewetherby.co.uk **web:** www.mercurewetherby.co.uk
dir: *A1/A659, then follow A168. Hotel on rdbt*

This modern hotel is well located for motorway access and as well as being close to the historic market town of Wetherby, it is also convenient for Leeds, Harrogate and York. Leeds Bradford Airport is just eight miles away. There is a spacious restaurant and adjacent bar. The Brasserie menu features bistro dishes and daily Chef's specials. Extensive conference facilities are provided with 13 naturally lit meeting rooms available. Complimentary WiFi access is another highlight.

Rooms: 103 **S** £60–£120; **D** £70–£150* **Facilities:** FTV WiFi ⌂ New Year **Conf:** Class 60 Board 50 Thtr 150 Del from £110 **Services:** Lift Night porter **Parking:** 167 **Notes:** LB Civ Wed 100

Days Inn Wetherby

BUDGET HOTEL

Junction 46 A1(M), Kirk Deighton, LS22 5GT - **tel:** 01937 547557
email: reservations@daysinnwetherby.co.uk **web:** www.daysinnwetherby.co.uk
dir: *A1(M) junct 46 at Moto Service Area*

This modern building offers accommodation in smart, spacious and well-equipped bedrooms, suitable for families and business travellers, and all with en suite bathrooms. Continental breakfast is available and other refreshments may be taken at the nearby family restaurant.

Rooms: 129 (33 family) (35 GF) ☙ **Conf:** Class 20 Board 20 Thtr 60

WEYBRIDGE   Map 6 TQ06
Surrey

HIGHLY RECOMMENDED

Brooklands Hotel

★★★★ 83% ◉◉ HOTEL

Brooklands Drive, KT13 0SL - **tel:** 01932 335700
email: info@brooklandshotelsurrey.com **web:** www.brooklandshotelsurrey.com
dir: *Phone for detailed directions*

Overlooking the historic motoring racing circuit, this hotel has stunning design that reflects art deco style of the Mercedes Benz racetrack's heyday in the 1920 and 30s. The bedrooms are notably spacious and very comfortable with many contemporary facilities; all have floor-to-ceiling windows, and many come with balconies overlooking the racetrack. There is a wealth of public areas including leisure and meeting rooms as well as a spa. The contemporary 1907 Restaurant, Bar and Grill offers imaginative menus.

Rooms: 139 (5 family) ☙ **D** £139–£275* **Facilities:** Spa STV FTV WiFi ⌂ Gym Xmas New Year **Conf:** Class 86 Board 90 Thtr 174 Del from £235 **Services:** Lift Night porter Air con **Parking:** 120 **Notes:** Civ Wed 174

Oatlands Park Hotel

★★★★ 80% HOTEL

146 Oatlands Drive, KT13 9HB - **tel:** 01932 847242
email: info@oatlandsparkhotel.com **web:** www.oatlandsparkhotel.com
dir: *Through High St to Monument Hill mini rdbt. Left into Oatlands Drive. Hotel 500yds on left*

Once a palace for Henry VIII, this impressive building sits in extensive grounds encompassing tennis courts, a gym and a 9-hole golf course. The spacious lounge and bar create a wonderful first impression with tall marble pillars and plush comfortable seating. Most of the bedrooms are very spacious, and all are well equipped.

Rooms: 150 (24 family) (30 GF) ☙ **Facilities:** STV FTV WiFi ⌂ HL ⚓ 9 Putting green ☙ ☙ Gym Jogging course Fitness suite ♫ Xmas New Year **Conf:** Class 170 Board 90 Thtr 400 **Services:** Lift Night porter Air con **Parking:** 208 **Notes:** Civ Wed 370

Best Western Ship Hotel

★★★ 78% HOTEL

BW Best Western.

Monument Green, KT13 8BQ - **tel:** 01932 848364
email: reservations@desboroughhotels.com
web: www.shiphotel.co.uk
dir: *M25 junct 11, at 3rd rdbt left into High St. Hotel 300yds on left*

This former coaching inn has retained much of its period charm and is now a comfortable and welcoming hotel. Bedrooms, some overlooking a delightful courtyard, are spacious and cheerfully decorated. Public areas include a lounge and cocktail bar, restaurant and a popular pub. The high street location and private parking are a bonus.

Rooms: 76 (2 family) ☙ **Facilities:** FTV WiFi ⌂ Xmas New Year **Conf:** Class 70 Board 60 Thtr 180 **Services:** Lift Night porter **Parking:** 65 **Notes:** Civ Wed 120

WEYMOUTH
Dorset

Map 4 SY67

Best Western Hotel Rembrandt

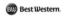 **Best Western.**

★★★ 76% HOTEL

12-18 Dorchester Road, DT4 7JU - tel: 01305 764000
email: reception@hotelrembrandt.co.uk **web:** www.hotelrembrandt.co.uk
dir: *On A354 from Dorchester, turn left at Manor rdbt & proceed for 0.75m*

Only a short distance from the seafront and the town centre, this hotel is ideal for visiting local attractions. Facilities include a spa, gym and heated pool; a bar and extensive meeting rooms. The restaurant offers an impressive carvery and carte menu, which proves popular with locals and residents alike.

Rooms: 78 (27 family) (5 GF) ⚫ **S** £55–£120; **D** £75–£165* **Facilities:** STV FTV WiFi ⚘ ⚫ Gym Steam room Sauna Beautician Beauty treatment room **Conf:** Class 100 Board 60 Thtr 200 Del from £135 **Services:** Lift Night porter **Parking:** 60 **Notes:** LB Civ Wed 150

Hotel Rex

★★★ 73% HOTEL

29 The Esplanade, DT4 8DN - tel: 01305 760400
email: rex@kingshotels.co.uk **web:** www.kingshotels.co.uk
dir: *On seafront opposite Alexandra Gardens*

Originally built as the summer residence for the Duke of Clarence, this hotel benefits from a seafront location with stunning views across Weymouth Bay. Bedrooms, including several sea-facing rooms, are well equipped. A wide range of imaginative dishes is served in the popular and attractive restaurant.

Rooms: 31 (2 family) ⚫ **Facilities:** FTV WiFi New Year **Conf:** Class 30 Board 25 Thtr 40 **Services:** Lift Night porter **Parking:** 9 **Notes:** Closed Xmas

Crown Hotel

★★ 78% HOTEL

51-53 St Thomas Street, DT4 8EQ - tel: 01305 760800
email: crown@kingshotels.co.uk **web:** www.kingshotels.co.uk
dir: *From Dorchester, A354 to Weymouth. Follow Back Water on left & cross 2nd bridge*

This popular hotel is conveniently located adjacent to the old harbour and is ideal for shopping, local attractions and transportation links, including the ferry. Public areas include an extensive bar, ballroom, and comfortable residents' lounge on the first floor. Themed events, such as mock cruises, are a speciality.

Rooms: 86 (15 family) ⚫ **Facilities:** WiFi New Year **Services:** Lift Night porter **Parking:** 11 **Notes:** Closed Xmas

Fairhaven Hotel

★★ 75% HOTEL

37 The Esplanade, DT4 8DH - tel: 01305 760200
email: fairhaven@kingshotels.co.uk **web:** www.kingshotels.co.uk
dir: *On right just before Alexandra Gardens*

Fairhaven Hotel is a popular sea-facing, family-run hotel with a friendly young team of staff. Bedrooms are comfortable and well maintained, and there are two bars, one with panoramic views of the bay. Entertainment is provided most nights during the season.

Rooms: 81 (21 family) (1 GF) ⚫ **Facilities:** WiFi ♫ **Services:** Lift Night porter **Parking:** 14 **Notes:** Closed Nov-1 Mar

Hotel Central

★★ 72% HOTEL

17-19 Maiden Street, DT4 8BB - tel: 01305 760700
email: central@kingshotels.co.uk **web:** www.kingshotels.co.uk
dir: *In town centre*

Well located for the town, the beach and the ferries to the Channel Islands, and with off-road parking, this privately-owned hotel has friendly staff and comfortable bedrooms. Three rooms are designed for guests with limited mobility. The pleasant dining room offers a varied menu, and live entertainment is provided during the season.

Rooms: 28 (5 family) (4 GF) ⚫ **Facilities:** ♫ **Services:** Lift Night porter **Parking:** 14 **Notes:** Closed mid Dec-1 Mar

Premier Inn Weymouth

BUDGET HOTEL

Gateway Business Park, Mercury Road, DT3 5HJ - tel: 0871 527 9384
(Calls cost 13p per minute plus your phone company's access charge)
web: www.premierinn.com
dir: *M27 junct 1, A31 towards Bournemouth, A35 towards Dorchester. 1st exit at rdbt onto A354 (Weymouth road). At 3rd rdbt take 1st exit into Dorchester Rd. Left into Mercery Rd*

High quality, budget accommodation ideal for both families and business travellers. Spacious, en suite bedrooms feature free WiFi and tea and coffee making facilities, and in most hotels, Freeview TV is also available. The adjacent family restaurant features a wide and varied menu.

Rooms: 60

Premier Inn Weymouth Seafront

BUDGET HOTEL

Lodmoor Country Park, Preston Beach Road, DT4 7SX - tel: 0871 527 9158 (Calls cost 13p per minute plus your phone company's access charge)
web: www.premierinn.com
dir: *Follow signs to Weymouth then brown route signs to Lodmoor Country Park (height restriction 9' 4" at barrier). Hotel adjacent to Lodmoor Brewers Fayre. NB for Sat Nav use DT4 7SL*

Rooms: 106

Moonfleet Manor Hotel

AA Advertised ⚫

Fleet Road, DT3 4ED - tel: 01305 786948
email: info@moonfleetmanor.co.uk **web:** www.moonfleetmanor.co.uk
dir: *Take Fleet Rd just off B1357 at Chickerell. Hotel at end of road*

This enchanting hideaway, where children are especially welcome, is peacefully located at the end of the village of Fleet and enjoys a wonderful sea-facing position. The hotel is furnished with a great deal of style, individuality and panache, particularly in the sumptuous lounges. Bedrooms are equally special with a range of sizes; all are well-equipped and many overlook Chesil Beach. Accomplished cuisine makes use of quality local produce and is served in the elegant restaurant. A host of additional facilities are also offered for all the family, including an indoor pool.

Rooms: 36 (6 annexe) (21 family) (3 GF) **Facilities:** Spa FTV WiFi ⚫ ⚫ Squash Indoor play area Creche Xmas New Year **Conf:** Class 36 Board 30 Thtr 70 **Services:** Lift Night porter **Parking:** 48 **Notes:** Civ Wed 100

W

WHITBY
North Yorkshire   Map 19 NZ81

The Cliffemount Hotel

★★★ 81% SMALL HOTEL

Bank Top Lane, Runswick Bay, TS13 5HU - **tel:** 01947 840103
email: info@cliffemounthotel.co.uk **web:** www.cliffemounthotel.co.uk
dir: *Exit A174, 8m N of Whitby, 1m to end*

The Cliffemount Hotel enjoys stunning picture postcard views across rugged Runswick Bay. It offers a relaxed and romantic atmosphere with open fires and individual, carefully-designed bedrooms, some of which boast their own private balcony overlooking the bay. Dining is a real strength; food is modern British in style, using locally sourced fresh seafood and game from the nearby estates. The team are relaxed and informal but provide attentive service with warm hospitality.

Rooms: 18 **Facilities:** **Conf:** Class 25 Board 16 Thtr 25

Saxonville Hotel

★★★ 80% HOTEL

Ladysmith Avenue, Argyle Road, YO21 3HX - **tel:** 01947 602631
email: newtons@saxonville.co.uk **web:** www.saxonville.co.uk
dir: *A174 to North Promenade. Turn inland at large four-towered building visible on West Cliff, into Argyle Rd, then 1st right*

The friendly service is noteworthy at this long-established holiday hotel. Well maintained throughout, it offers comfortable bedrooms and inviting public areas that include a well-proportioned restaurant where quality dinners are served.

Rooms: 23 (2 family) (1 GF) **S** £64–£99; **D** £128–£168 (incl. bkfst)* **Facilities:** WiFi **Conf:** Class 40 Board 40 Thtr 100 **Parking:** 20 **Notes:** Closed Dec-Jan

WHITCHURCH
Shropshire   Map 15 SJ54

Macdonald Hill Valley Spa, Hotel & Golf

MACDONALD
HOTELS & RESORTS

★★★★ 78% HOTEL

Tarporley Road, SY13 4JH - **tel:** 01948 660700
email: general.hillvalley@macdonald-hotels.co.uk
web: www.macdonald-hotels.co.uk/hillvalley
dir: *2nd exit off A41 towards Whitchurch*

Located in rural surroundings on the town's outskirts, this modern hotel is surrounded by two golf courses, and a very well equipped leisure spa is also available. Spacious bedrooms, with country views, are furnished in minimalist style and public areas include a choice of bar lounges and extensive conference facilities.

Rooms: 80 (15 family) (27 GF) **S** £60–£150; **D** £70–£170 (incl. bkfst)
Facilities: Spa STV FTV WiFi 36 Putting green Gym Mud Rasul Xmas New Year **Conf:** Class 150 Board 150 Thtr 300 Del from £120 **Services:** Lift Night porter **Parking:** 300 **Notes:** LB Civ Wed 300

WHITEHAVEN
Cumbria   Map 18 NX91

Premier Inn Whitehaven

BUDGET HOTEL

Howgate, CA28 6PL - **tel:** 0871 527 9160 (Calls cost 13p per minute plus your phone company's access charge) **web:** www.premierinn.com
dir: *On A595 just outside Whitehaven*

High quality, budget accommodation ideal for both families and business travellers. Spacious, en suite bedrooms feature free WiFi and tea and coffee making facilities, and in most hotels, Freeview TV is also available. The adjacent family restaurant features a wide and varied menu.

Rooms: 117

WHITLEY BAY
Tyne & Wear   Map 21 NZ37

The Royal Hotel

★★★ 78% HOTEL

13-17 East Parade, NE26 1AP - **tel:** 0191 252 4777
email: info@royalhotelwhitleybay.co.uk **web:** www.royalhotelwhitleybay.co.uk
dir: *From Whitley Bay Metro station left onto Station Square, bear right onto Victoria Terrace, right onto North Parade then right & right again, then left*

Overlooking the seafront, this refurbished hotel offers warm hospitality from a friendly team. Bedrooms are well appointed, and the Noir Drinks Lounge adds a different dimension to the operation – tapas is served in this area with the option to take dinner in the Italian restaurant next door. Limited off-road parking is available at the front of the hotel.

Rooms: 37 **Facilities:** FTV WiFi **Services:** Night porter **Parking:** 10 **Notes:** Closed 23 Dec-2 Jan

WHITSTABLE
Kent   Map 7 TR16

Crescent Turner Hotel

★★★ 81% HOTEL

Wraik Hill, CT5 3BY - **tel:** 01227 263506
email: info@crescentturner.co.uk **web:** www.crescentturner.co.uk
dir: *A299 exit for Whitstable*

Located just a couple of miles from Whitstable on Wraik Hill, the Crescent Turner Hotel benefits from fantastic countryside and sea views. Bedrooms are all individual and stylish with contemporary furnishings; many benefit from those

W

extensive views across to Whitstable. There is a bar and restaurant onsite open daily for breakfast, lunch and dinner.

Rooms: 17 (2 family) (5 GF) ✿ **S** £70–£110; **D** £99–£200 (incl. bkfst)*
Facilities: FTV WiFi ⬇ Xmas New Year **Conf:** Class 32 Board 30 Thtr 40 Del from £160 **Services:** Night porter **Parking:** 30 **Notes:** Civ Wed 56

Premier Inn Whitstable

BUDGET HOTEL

Thanet Way, CT5 3DB - tel: 0871 527 9162 (Calls cost 13p per minute plus your phone company's access charge)
web: www.premierinn.com
dir: 2m W of town centre on B2205

High quality, budget accommodation ideal for both families and business travellers. Spacious, en suite bedrooms feature free WiFi and tea and coffee making facilities, and in most hotels, Freeview TV is also available. The adjacent family restaurant features a wide and varied menu.

Rooms: 73

WHITTLEBURY	**Map 11 SP64**
Northamptonshire	

Whittlebury Hall

★★★★ 75% @ @ HOTEL

NN12 8QH - tel: 01327 857857
email: reservations@whittleburyhall.co.uk **web:** www.whittleburyhall.co.uk
dir: A43, A413 towards Buckingham, through Whittlebury, turn for hotel on right, signed

Whittlebury Hall is a purpose-built, Georgian-style country house hotel with excellent spa and leisure facilities and pedestrian access to the Silverstone circuit. Grand public areas feature F1 racing memorabilia, and the accommodation includes some lavishly appointed suites. Food is a strength, with a choice of various dining options. Particularly noteworthy are the afternoon teas in the spacious, comfortable lounge and the fine dining in Murray's Restaurant.

Rooms: 254 (41 annexe) (4 family) (13 GF) **Facilities:** Spa FTV WiFi ⬇ HL ⊕ ♨ 36 Putting green Gym Beauty treatments Relaxation room Hair studio Heat & Ice experience Leisure club ♫ Xmas New Year **Conf:** Class 175 Board 40 Thtr 500 **Services:** Lift Night porter **Parking:** 700 **Notes:** Civ Wed

---

WIDNES	**Map 15 SJ58**
Cheshire	

Premier Inn Widnes

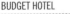

BUDGET HOTEL

Venture Fields, WA8 0GY - tel: 0871 527 9306
(Calls cost 13p per minute plus your phone company's access charge)
web: www.premierinn.com
dir: M62 junct 7. At Rainhill Stoops rdbt 2nd exit onto A557 (Widnes). Left into Earle Rd (Widnes Waterfront), into Venture Field Leisure Entertainment complex. Hotel on left

High quality, budget accommodation ideal for both families and business travellers. Spacious, en suite bedrooms feature free WiFi and tea and coffee making facilities, and in most hotels, Freeview TV is also available. The adjacent family restaurant features a wide and varied menu.

Rooms: 87

WIGAN	**Map 15 SD50**
Greater Manchester	

Macdonald Kilhey Court Hotel

★★★★ 77% HOTEL

Chorley Road, Standish, WN1 2XN - tel: 0344 879 9045
email: general.kilheycourt@macdonald-hotels.co.uk
web: www.macdonaldhotels.co.uk/kilheycourt
dir: M6 junct 27, A5209 Standish, over at lights, past church on right, left at rdbt 1st exit, hotel on right 350yds. M61 junct 6, signed Wigan & Haigh Hall. 3m & right at rdbt 2nd exit. Hotel 0.5m on right

Macdonald Kilhey Court Hotel is peacefully located in its own grounds yet is convenient for the motorway network. Bedrooms are divided between the Victorian house and the modern extension, while public areas have original features, and the split-level restaurant has views over the Worthington Lakes. There are eleven meeting rooms, ideal for exhibitions, and extensive landscaped grounds available for weddings. Facilities also include an indoor pool and spa.

Rooms: 62 (18 family) (8 GF) ✿ **Facilities:** Spa FTV WiFi ⬇ HL⊕ Gym Aerobics classes Beauty treatments Xmas New Year **Conf:** Class 180 Board 60 Thtr 400 **Services:** Lift Night porter **Parking:** 300 **Notes:** Civ Wed 300

Wrightington Hotel & Country Club

★★★★ 73% @ HOTEL

Moss Lane, Wrightington, WN6 9PB - tel: 01257 425803
email: info@wrightingtonhotel.co.uk **web:** www.wrightingtonhotel.co.uk
dir: M6 junct 27, 0.25m W, hotel on right after church

Situated in open countryside close to the M6, this privately-owned hotel offers friendly hospitality. Accommodation is well equipped and spacious, and public areas include an extensive leisure complex complete with hair salon, pool and sports injury lab. Bennetts Restaurant, Blazers bar and extensive, fully air-conditioned banqueting facilities appeal to a broad market, with weddings a key focus.

Rooms: 73 (6 family) (36 GF) ✿ **Facilities:** Spa STV FTV WiFi⊕ Gym Squash Hairdressing salon Sports injury clinic New Year **Conf:** Class 50 Board 40 Thtr 150 **Services:** Lift Night porter **Parking:** 240 **Notes:** LB Civ Wed 100

Premier Inn Wigan M6 Jct 25

BUDGET HOTEL

Warrington Road, Marus Bridge, WN3 6XB - tel: 0871 527 9164
(Calls cost 13p per minute plus your phone company's access charge)
web: www.premierinn.com
dir: M6 junct 25 (N'bound). At rdbt left, hotel on left

High quality, budget accommodation ideal for both families and business travellers. Spacious, en suite bedrooms feature free WiFi and tea and coffee making facilities, and in most hotels, Freeview TV is also available. The adjacent family restaurant features a wide and varied menu.

Rooms: 40

W

WIGAN *continued*

Premier Inn Wigan Town Centre

BUDGET HOTEL

Harrogate Street, WN1 1BL - **tel:** 0871 527 9502 (Calls cost 13p per minute plus your phone company's access charge) **web:** www.premierinn.com
dir: Nbound: M6 junct 25, A49 (Warrington Rd). 3rd exit at next rdbt into Poolstock Ln (B5238). Left into Chapel Ln, continue into River Way (A49). At lights left into King St, then into Rodney St. Stay in right lane, through lights into Harrogate St

Rooms: 83

Premier Inn Wigan West (M6 Jct 26)

BUDGET HOTEL

Orrell Road, Orrell, WN5 8HQ - **tel:** 0871 527 9168 (Calls cost 13p per minute plus your phone company's access charge) **web:** www.premierinn.com
dir: M6 junct 26 follow signs for Upholland & Orrell. At 1st lights turn left. Hotel on right behind Priory Wood Beefeater

Rooms: 40

WILLERBY
East Riding of Yorkshire   Map 17 TA03

Mercure Hull Grange Park Hotel

★★★★ 72% HOTEL

Grange Park Lane, HU10 6EA - **tel:** 01482 672801 & 0844 815 9037
(Calls cost 7p per minute plus your phone company's access charge)
email: info@mercurehull.co.uk **web:** www.mercurehull.co.uk
dir: A164 to Beverley signed Willerby Shopping Park. Left at rdbt into Grange Park Lane, hotel at end

Originally a 19th-century manor house, this modern hotel provides comfortable accommodation tucked away in 12 acres of landscaped gardens. The location is peaceful yet convenient for the historic market town of Beverley. Hull city centre is only five miles away. Extensive meeting rooms are in a self contained conference centre with complimentary WiFi throughout. The hotel also boasts a health club with indoor swimming pool.

Rooms: 100 (4 family) (15 GF) **S** £60–£200; **D** £70–£210 (incl. bkfst)*
Facilities: Spa FTV WiFi ⌨ ⊕ Gym Sauna Steam room Xmas New Year **Conf:** Class 250 Board 80 Thtr 550 Del from £115 **Services:** Lift Night porter **Parking:** 600
Notes: Civ Wed 550

Best Western Willerby Manor Hotel

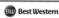

★★★ 82% HOTEL

Well Lane, HU10 6ER - **tel:** 01482 652616
email: willerbymanor@bestwestern.co.uk **web:** www.willerbymanor.co.uk
dir: Exit A63, signed Humber Bridge. Right at rdbt by Waitrose. At next rdbt hotel signed

Set in a quiet residential area, amid well-tended gardens, this hotel was originally a private mansion; it has now been thoughtfully extended to provide very comfortable bedrooms, equipped with many useful extras. There are extensive leisure facilities and a wide choice of meals offered in the contemporary Figs Brasserie which has an impressive heated outdoor area.

Rooms: 63 (10 family) (20 GF) **S** £50–£110; **D** £80–£150 (incl. bkfst)*
Facilities: Spa STV FTV WiFi HL ⊕ supervised ⊗ Gym Steam room Beauty treatment room Aerobic classes New Year **Conf:** Class 200 Board 100 Thtr 500 Del £180 **Services:** Night porter **Parking:** 300 **Notes:** LB Closed 24-26 Dec Civ Wed 150

WILMSLOW
See **Manchester Airport**

WINCANTON
Somerset   Map 4 ST72

Holbrook House

★★★ 85% ◎◎ COUNTRY HOUSE HOTEL

Holbrook, BA9 8BS - **tel:** 01963 824466
email: enquiries@holbrookhouse.co.uk **web:** www.holbrookhouse.co.uk
dir: From A303 at Wincanton left onto A371 towards Castle Cary & Shepton Mallet

This handsome country house offers a unique blend of quality and comfort combined with a friendly atmosphere. Set in 17 acres of peaceful gardens and wooded grounds, Holbrook House makes a perfect retreat. The restaurant provides a selection of innovative dishes prepared with enthusiasm and served by a team of caring staff.

Rooms: 21 (5 annexe) (2 family) (5 GF) ⌨ **S** fr £95; **D** fr £95 (incl. bkfst)*
Facilities: Spa FTV WiFi ⌨ ⊛ ⊗ ⊗ Gym Exercise classes Sauna Steam room Fitness suite ♫ Xmas New Year **Conf:** Class 100 Board 55 Thtr 200 **Services:** Night porter **Parking:** 100 **Notes:** LB Civ Wed 250

WINCHESTER
Hampshire   Map 5 SU42

Lainston House, an Exclusive Hotel

★★★★★ 87% ⊜ HOTEL

Woodman Lane, Sparsholt, SO21 2LT - **tel:** 01962 776088
email: enquiries@lainstonhouse.co.uk **web:** www.exclusive.co.uk
dir: 2m NW off B3049 towards Stockbridge

This graceful example of a William and Mary house enjoys a countryside location amidst mature grounds and gardens. Staff provide good levels of courtesy and care with a polished, professional service. Bedrooms are tastefully appointed and include some spectacular, spacious rooms with stylish handmade beds and stunning bathrooms. Public rooms include a cocktail bar built entirely from a single cedar and stocked with an impressive range of rare drinks and cigars.

Rooms: 50 (6 family) (18 GF) ⌨ **D** fr £157.50 (incl. bkfst)* **Facilities:** STV FTV WiFi ⌨ ⊗ Fishing ⊗ Gym Archery Clay pigeon shooting Cycling Hot air ballooning Falconer Cookery school Xmas New Year Child facilities **Conf:** Class 80 Board 40 Thtr 166 **Services:** Night porter **Parking:** 200 **Notes:** LB Civ Wed 200

Holiday Inn Winchester

★★★★ 78% ◎◎ HOTEL

Telegraph Way, Morn Hill, SO21 1HZ - **tel:** 01962 670700
email: info@hiwinchester.co.uk **web:** www.hiwinchester.co.uk
dir: M3 junct 9, A31 signed Alton, A272 & Petersfield. 1st exit at rdbt onto A31, 1.6m, take 1st exit into Alresford Rd, left into Telegraph Way

Located a few miles from the historic city of Winchester and within easy reach of the south's transport links, this modern, purpose-built property is presented to a high standard. Bedrooms are spacious and well-equipped for both the business and leisure guest. Enjoyable cuisine is served in the restaurant and there is a very good range of freshly prepared dishes to choose from. Conference facilities and ample parking are available.

Rooms: 141 (7 family) (60 GF) ⌨ **S** £80–£250; **D** £80–£250* **Facilities:** STV FTV WiFi ⌨ HL Gym Xmas New Year **Conf:** Class 110 Board 120 Thtr 250 **Services:** Lift Night porter Air con **Parking:** 167 **Notes:** LB Civ Wed 200

W

Hotel du Vin Winchester

★★★★ 76% TOWN HOUSE HOTEL

14 Southgate Street, SO23 9EF - **tel:** 01962 841414
email: info@winchester.hotelduvin.com **web:** www.hotelduvin.com
dir: *M3 junct 11 towards Winchester, follow signs. Hotel in approx 2m on left just past cinema*

Continuing to set high standards, this inviting hotel is best known for its high profile bistro. The individually designed bedrooms have all the Hotel du Vin signature touches including fine Egyptian cotton linen, power showers and WiFi. The bistro serves imaginative yet simply-cooked dishes from a seasonal, daily-changing menu.

Rooms: 24 (4 annexe) (4 GF) ↖ **S** £99–£170; **D** £109–£180* **Facilities:** STV WiFi ↳ Xmas New Year **Conf:** Class 30 Board 20 Thtr 40 Del from £240 **Services:** Night porter Air con **Parking:** 35 **Notes:** LB Civ Wed 60

Mercure Winchester Wessex Hotel

★★★★ 75% HOTEL

Paternoster Row, SO23 9LQ - **tel:** 01962 861611
email: H6619@accor.com **web:** www.mercure.com
dir: *M3 junct 10, 2nd exit at rdbt signed Winchester/B3330. Right at lights, left at 2nd rdbt. Over small bridge, straight on at next rdbt into Broadway. Past Guildhall, 1st left into Colebrook St. Hotel 50yds on right*

Occupying an enviable location in the centre of this historic city and adjacent to the spectacular cathedral, Mercure Winchester Wessex Hotel is quietly situated on a side street. Inside, the atmosphere is restful and welcoming, with public areas and some bedrooms enjoying unrivalled views of the hotel's centuries-old neighbour.

Rooms: 94 (6 family) **S** £75–£175; **D** £75–£195* **Facilities:** STV WiFi Xmas New Year **Conf:** Class 25 Board 40 Thtr 100 Del from £125 **Services:** Lift Night porter **Parking:** 30 **Notes:** LB Civ Wed 80

Marwell Hotel

★★★ 81% HOTEL

Thompsons Lane, Colden Common, SO21 1JY - **tel:** 01962 777681
email: info@marwellhotel.co.uk **web:** www.marwellhotel.co.uk
dir: *B3354 through Twyford. 1st exit at rdbt B3354, left onto B2177 signed Bishop Waltham. Left into Thompsons Ln after 1m, hotel on left*

Taking its theme from the adjacent zoo, this unusual hotel is based on the famous TreeTops safari lodge in Kenya. The well-equipped bedrooms, split between four lodges, convey a safari style, while the smart public areas include an airy lobby bar and an 'Out of Africa' themed restaurant. There is also a selection of meeting and leisure facilities.

Rooms: 68 (10 family) (37 GF) **S** £64–£125; **D** £79–£190 (incl. bkfst)* **Facilities:** STV WiFi ↳ ⊗ ⌚ 45 Putting green Sauna Spa pool Running machine Xmas New Year **Conf:** Class 60 Board 60 Thtr 200 Del from £122.25 **Services:** Night porter **Parking:** 120 **Notes:** LB Civ Wed 200

Premier Inn Winchester

BUDGET HOTEL

Caledonia House, Winnal Manor Road, SO23 0RS - **tel:** 0871 527 9424
(Calls cost 13p per minute plus your phone company's access charge)
web: www.premierinn.com
dir: *M3 junct 9, A272 to Winchester. At rdbt 3rd exit into Easton Ln. Hotel on left at next rdbt*

High quality, budget accommodation ideal for both families and business travellers. Spacious, en suite bedrooms feature free WiFi and tea and coffee making facilities, and in most hotels, Freeview TV is also available. The adjacent family restaurant features a wide and varied menu.

Rooms: 101

WINCHESTER MOTORWAY SERVICE AREA Hampshire	**Map 5 SU53**

Days Inn Winchester

AA Advertised

Winchester Moto Service Area, M3 S, junct 14/15, SO21 1PP - **tel:** 01962 791135
email: winchester.hotel@welcomebreak.co.uk **web:** www.welcomebreak.co.uk
dir: *M3 Southbound (between juncts 8 & 9), there is no access from M3 Northbound*

This modern building offers accommodation in smart, spacious and well-equipped bedrooms, suitable for families and business travellers, and all with en suite bathrooms. Continental breakfast is available and other refreshments may be taken at the nearby family restaurant.

Rooms: 40 (14 family) (20 GF) **Facilities:** FTV WiFi **Conf:** Class 20 Thtr 20 **Services:** Night porter **Parking:** 40 **Notes:** Closed 24-26 Dec

---

WINDERMERE Cumbria	**Map 18 SD49**

Gilpin Hotel & Lake House

★★★★★ 85% HOTEL

Crook Road, LA23 3NE - **tel:** 015394 88818
email: hotel@thegilpin.co.uk **web:** www.thegilpin.co.uk
dir: *M6 junct 36, A590, A591 to rdbt N of Kendal, onto B5284, hotel 5m on right*

This smart Victorian residence is set in delightful gardens leading to the fells, and is just a short drive from the lake. The individually designed bedrooms are stylish and a number benefit from private terraces; all are spacious and thoughtfully equipped, and each has a private sitting room. In addition there are luxury Garden Suites that lead onto private gardens with cedar-wood hot tubs. The welcoming atmosphere is notable and the attractive day rooms are perfect for relaxing, perhaps beside a real fire. Eating in any of the quartet of dining rooms is a must. The Lake House situated a mile from the main hotel offers an additional six suites, spa and stunning lakeside views.

Rooms: 31 (17 annexe) (1 family) (12 GF) ↖ **S** £210–£650; **D** £355–£695 (incl. bkfst & dinner)* **Facilities:** WiFi ↳ ⛵ Spa treatments Private spa facilities for Lake House guests Xmas New Year **Services:** Night porter **Parking:** 40 **Notes:** No children 7yrs Civ Wed 120

W

WINDERMERE *continued*

INSPECTOR'S CHOICE

Holbeck Ghyll Country House Hotel

★★★★ ❀❀❀ COUNTRY HOUSE HOTEL

Holbeck Lane, LA23 1LU - tel: 015394 32375
email: stay@holbeckghyll.com **web:** www.holbeckghyll.com
dir: *3m N of Windermere on A591, right into Holbeck Lane signed Troutbeck, hotel 0.5m on left*

Holbeck Ghyll sits high up overlooking the majestic Lake Windermere surrounded by well maintained grounds. The original house was bought in 1888 by Lord Lonsdale, the first president of the AA, who used it as a hunting lodge. Guests today will find that this is a delightful place where the service is professional and attentive. There are beautifully designed, spacious bedrooms situated in the main house and also in lodges in the grounds; each has lake views and some have patios. There are also The Shieling and Miss Potter suites. Each bedroom has Egyptian cotton linens, fresh flowers, LCD satellite TV, CD/DVD players, bathrobes and a decanter of damson gin. The restaurant impresses with its award-winning cuisine. The hotel also has a health spa, gym and boutique store.

Rooms: 30 (17 annexe) (5 family) (12 GF) ☂ **Facilities:** Spa FTV WiFi ⇘ ⊇ ⛳ Sauna Steam room Beauty massage Xmas New Year **Conf:** Class 40 Board 30 Thtr 60 **Services:** Night porter **Parking:** 34 **Notes:** LB Civ Wed 60

See advert opposite

INSPECTOR'S CHOICE

The Samling

★★★★ ❀❀❀ ♨ HOTEL

Ambleside Road, LA23 1LR - tel: 015394 31922
email: info@thesamlinghotel.co.uk **web:** www.thesamlinghotel.co.uk
dir: *M6 junct 36, A591 through Windermere towards Ambleside. 2m. 300yds past Low Wood Water Sports Centre just after sharp bend turn right into hotel entrance*

This stylish house, built in the late 1700s, is situated in 67 acres of grounds and enjoys an elevated position overlooking Lake Windermere. The spacious, beautifully furnished bedrooms and suites, some in adjacent buildings, are thoughtfully equipped and all have superb bathrooms. Public rooms include a sumptuous drawing room, a small library and an elegant dining room.

Rooms: 11 (6 annexe) (6 family) (6 GF) ☂ **S** £270–£610; **D** £270–£610 (incl. bkfst)* **Facilities:** STV FTV WiFi ⇘ ⛳ Xmas New Year **Conf:** Class 80 Board 40 Thtr 80 **Services:** Night porter **Parking:** 45 **Notes:** Civ Wed 50

HIGHLY RECOMMENDED

Storrs Hall Hotel

★★★★ 83% ❀❀ HOTEL

Storrs Park, LA23 3LG - tel: 015394 47111
email: enquiries@storrshall.com **web:** www.storrshall.com
dir: *On A592, 2m S of Bowness, on Newby Bridge road*

Set in 17 acres of landscaped grounds by the lakeside, this imposing Georgian mansion is delightful. There are numerous lounges to relax in, furnished with fine art and antiques. Individually styled bedrooms are generally spacious and boast impressive bathrooms. The elegant restaurant offers fine views across the lawn to the lake and fells beyond.

Rooms: 30 ☂ **D** £110–£895 (incl. bkfst)* **Facilities:** FTV WiFi Fishing ⛳ In room beauty treatments Xmas New Year **Conf:** Class 20 Board 20 Thtr 40 Del from £170 **Services:** Night porter **Parking:** 50 **Notes:** LB Civ Wed 80

HOLBECK GHYLL

MOMENTS TO SAVOUR

W

Holbeck Ghyll Country House Hotel,
Holbeck Lane, Windermere, Cumbria LA23 1LU
+44 (0)1539 432 375
www.holbeckghyll.com stay@holbeckghyll.com
 /holbeck.ghyll   @holbeckghyll

WINDERMERE *continued*

HIGHLY RECOMMENDED

Macdonald Old England Hotel & Spa

★★★★ 83% HOTEL

23 Church Street, Bowness, LA23 3DF - **tel:** 0344 879 9144
email: sales.oldengland@macdonald-hotels.co.uk **web:** www.macdonaldhotels.co.uk
dir: *Through Windermere to Bowness, straight across at mini rdbt. Hotel behind church on right*

This hotel stands right on the shore of England's largest lake and boasts superb views, especially through the floor-to-ceiling windows in the Vinand Restaurant. There are several bedroom types; standard, executive and suites; some rooms have been designed for wheelchairs users. The spa has a 20-metre pool, a gym, sauna and steam room.

Rooms: 106 (6 family) (14 GF) ☎ **S** fr £99; **D** fr £109 (incl. bkfst) **Facilities:** Spa STV WiFi ⇘ ③ supervised Gym Private jetties Rock sauna Aromatherapy shower Steam room Ice room Xmas New Year **Conf:** Class 60 Board 25 Thtr 150 Del from £150 **Services:** Lift Night porter **Parking:** 90 **Notes:** LB Civ Wed 100

Low Wood Bay

English Lakes
Hotels Resorts & Venues

★★★★ 81% HOTEL

LA23 1LP - **tel:** 015394 33338
email: lowwoodbay@englishlakes.co.uk **web:** www.englishlakes.co.uk
dir: *M6 junct 36, A590, A591 to Windermere, then 3m towards Ambleside, hotel on right*

Benefiting from a lakeside location, this hotel offers an excellent range of leisure and conference facilities. Bedrooms, many with panoramic lake views, are attractively furnished, and include a number of larger executive rooms and suites. There is a choice of bars, a spacious restaurant and the more informal Cafe del Lago. The poolside bar offers internet access.

Rooms: 111 (13 family) (21 GF) ☎ **Facilities:** Spa FTV WiFi ⇘ ③ supervised Fishing 🎣 Gym Squash Watersports centre offering water skiing & canoeing Marina Beauty salon Xmas New Year **Conf:** Class 180 Board 150 Thtr 340 **Services:** Lift Night porter **Parking:** 200 **Notes:** LB Civ Wed 280

Merewood Country House Hotel

★★★★ 80% ⚜⚜ COUNTRY HOUSE HOTEL

Ambleside Road, Ecclerigg, LA23 1LH - **tel:** 015394 46484
email: info@merewoodhotel.co.uk **web:** www.lakedistrictcountryhotels.co.uk
dir: *M6 junct 36, follow A591 for 15m past Windermere, hotel on right*

A country house in the traditional Lakeland mould, Merewood provides a relaxed environment for guests and polished service to match. The bar and lounges overlook Windermere and the Cumbrian mountains beyond. Bedrooms vary in size with some superb feature rooms. Food is a further notable aspect here with dinner a highlight of any stay. Weddings and functions are ably catered for.

Rooms: 20 (2 family) **Facilities:** FTV WiFi ⇘ Xmas New Year **Conf:** Class 45 Board 50 Thtr 150 **Parking:** 100 **Notes:** LB Civ Wed 122

Laura Ashley The Belsfield Hotel

★★★★ 80% HOTEL

Kendal Road, LA23 3EL - **tel:** 015394 42448 & 0844 736 8604
email: belsfield@lauraashleyhotels.com **web:** www.lauraashleyhotels.com
dir: *M6 junct 36, A591 Windermere, follow signs for Bowness. At mini rdbt bear left & take 1st left (Kendal Rd). Hotel 200yds on right*

Sat in six acres of land and affording some of the finest views of Lake Windermere from its elevated position, the hotel offers comfortable accommodation. A number of rooms and the restaurant have lake views, and the bistro offers a more informal dining option. Relax and take afternoon tea in the elegant drawing room or library.

Rooms: 62 (5 family) (10 GF) ☎ **S** £169–£269; **D** £179–£279 (incl. bkfst)*
Facilities: FTV WiFi ⇘ ③ Gym Xmas New Year **Conf:** Class 60 Board 30 Thtr 100 Del from £179 **Services:** Lift Night porter **Parking:** 68 **Notes:** LB Civ Wed 130

Lindeth Howe Country House Hotel & Restaurant

★★★★ 79% ⚜⚜ COUNTRY HOUSE HOTEL

Lindeth Drive, Longtail Hill, LA23 3JF - **tel:** 015394 45759
email: hotel@lindeth-howe.co.uk **web:** www.lindeth-howe.co.uk
dir: *Exit A592, 1m S of Bowness onto B5284 Longtail Hill signed Kendal & Lancaster, hotel last driveway on right*

Historic photographs commemorate the fact that this delightful house was once the family home of Beatrix Potter. Secluded in landscaped grounds, it enjoys views across the valley and Lake Windermere. Public rooms are plentiful and inviting, with the restaurant being the perfect setting for modern country-house cooking. Deluxe and superior bedrooms are spacious and smartly appointed.

Rooms: 34 (3 family) (2 GF) ☎ **Facilities:** FTV WiFi ③ Gym Sauna Fitness room Xmas New Year **Conf:** Class 20 Board 18 Thtr 30 **Services:** Night porter **Parking:** 50 **Notes:** Closed 4-16 Jan Civ Wed 100

W

Beech Hill Hotel & Spa

★★★★ 77% ⊛ HOTEL

Newby Bridge Road, LA23 3LR - tel: 015394 42137
email: reservations@beechhillhotel.co.uk **web:** www.beechhillhotel.co.uk
dir: M6 junct 36, A591 to Windermere. Left onto A592 towards Newby Bridge.
Hotel 4m from Bowness-on-Windermere

Beech Hill Hotel is situated overlooking Windermere, with the impressive panoramic views across the lake to the Cumbrian fells beyond available in most bedrooms. These are well appointed and some have balconies or terraces. The open areas, for enjoying coffee or drinks, prove very popular in the summer, and there are cosy lounges with log fires, a fine restaurant and landscaped gardens. High standards of service can be expected from the attentive, informative and very friendly staff. The pool and leisure facility has been recently refurbished and a small spa added.

Rooms: 57 (5 family) (4 GF) ☎ **S** £74–£98; **D** £98–£298 (incl. bkfst)* **Facilities:** Spa FTV WiFi ⊕ ✈ Fishing Sauna Steam room Xmas New Year **Services:** Night porter **Parking:** 70 **Notes:** LB Civ Wed 130

Cragwood Country House Hotel

★★★★ 75% ⊛ COUNTRY HOUSE HOTEL

Ambleside Road, LA23 1LQ - tel: 01539 488177
email: info@cragwoodhotel.co.uk **web:** www.lakedistrictcountryhotels.com
dir: M6 junct 36 then A591 for 15m, past Kendal & Windermere, hotel on left

A country house in the classic Lakeland mould, Cragwood has much to offer guests. Superbly situated with access to the shore of Windermere and commanding enviable views. Grounds are a feature too. Bedrooms are modern in approach whilst guests can relax in a choice of richly decorated lounges and bars. Cuisine is a highlight in the AA Rosette-awarded restaurant.

Rooms: 23 (3 family) (4 GF) ☎ **Facilities:** FTV WiFi ↘ Xmas New Year **Conf:** Class 30 Board 30 Thtr 50 **Parking:** 50 **Notes:** Civ Wed 83

Cedar Manor Hotel & Restaurant

★★★ ⊛ SMALL HOTEL

Ambleside Road, LA23 1AX - tel: 015394 43192
email: info@cedarmanor.co.uk **web:** www.cedarmanor.co.uk
dir: From A591 follow signs to Windermere. Hotel on left just beyond St Mary's Church

Built in 1854 as a country retreat, this lovely old house enjoys a peaceful location, tucked away within easy walking distance of the town centre. Bedrooms, some on the ground floor, are deeply comfortable and very well equipped, with a luxurious annexe suite available for longer stays or romantic getaways. There is a choice of lounges and bars where guests can relax before enjoying dinner in the well-appointed dining room.

Rooms: 10 (1 annexe) (1 family) (3 GF) ☎ **S** £125–£425; **D** £145–£425 (incl. bkfst)* **Facilities:** FTV WiFi New Year **Conf:** Board 10 **Parking:** 11 **Notes:** LB Closed 2-19 Jan

Miller Howe Hotel

★★★ 87% ⊛⊛ ⚬ COUNTRY HOUSE HOTEL

Rayrigg Road, LA23 1EY - tel: 015394 42536
email: info@millerhowe.com **web:** www.millerhowe.com
dir: M6 junct 36, A591 past Windermere, left at rdbt towards Bowness

This long established hotel enjoys a lakeside setting amidst delightful landscaped gardens. The bright and welcoming day rooms include sumptuous lounges, a conservatory and an opulently decorated restaurant. Imaginative dinners make use of fresh, local produce where possible and there is an extensive, well-balanced wine list. Stylish bedrooms, many with fabulous lake views, include well-equipped cottage rooms and a number with whirlpool baths.

Rooms: 15 (3 annexe) (1 GF) ☎ **Facilities:** FTV WiFi ↘ HL Xmas New Year **Parking:** 35 **Notes:** Civ Wed 75

The Ryebeck

★★★ 86% ⊛⊛ COUNTRY HOUSE HOTEL

Lyth Valley Road, LA23 3JP - tel: 015394 88195
email: info@ryebeck.com **web:** www.ryebeck.com
dir: M6 junct 46, follow A591. Right at Plumgarth's rdbt and follow Crooked to end. Left, hotel 300yds on right

The Ryebeck sits majestically above the shores of Lake Windermere. Set in its own extensive, well-maintained gardens, the hotel enjoys an enviable position providing picture postcard views. Originally built in 1904 as a private home the property has enjoyed a number of different uses before being lovingly transformed into the hotel we see today. Award-winning food, luxurious bedrooms, en suites and warm Lakeland hospitality are just a few of the many reasons to visit The Ryebeck. If this is not enough the views from many of the public areas will be the icing on the cake. Just minutes' drive from the Lake and ferry but within easy access of the M6 guests can enjoy the location of the Lakes without necessarily joining the crush in the town.

Rooms: 24 (7 GF) ☎ **S** fr £85; **D** £115–£225 (incl. bkfst)* **Facilities:** FTV WiFi Xmas New Year **Conf:** Class 12 Board 12 Thtr 30 Del from £149 **Services:** Night porter **Parking:** 50 **Notes:** LB Civ Wed 74

W

WINDERMERE *continued*

Briery Wood Country House Hotel

★★★ 84% @ COUNTRY HOUSE HOTEL

Ambleside Road, Ecclerigg, LA23 1ES - **tel:** 015394 33316
email: info@brierywood.co.uk **web:** www.lakedistrictcountryhotels.co.uk
dir: *M6 junct 36, follow A591 for 15m past Windermere, hotel on right (do not use postcode for Sat Nav)*

This small country house hideaway is part of a small group all nestled on the banks of Windermere. Sited in its own well-tended grounds, Briery Wood is a charming white house that boasts 23 individually-styled bedrooms and a warren of public rooms. Cuisine is a highlight at dinner, though not overly-formal, and the warm welcome and rapport from the team is noteworthy.

Rooms: 23 (4 family) (11 GF) **Facilities:** FTV WiFi ⌁ Xmas New Year **Conf:** Class 30 Board 30 Thtr 80 **Parking:** 40 **Notes:** Civ Wed 113

Hillthwaite

★★★ 82% HOTEL

Thornbarrow Road, LA23 2DF - **tel:** 015394 43636 & 46691
email: reception@hillthwaite.com **web:** www.hillthwaite.com
dir: *M6 junct 36, A591 Windermere, follow lane road through village A5074, left opposite Goodley Dale School, approx 0.5m from A591*

The family-owned Hillthwaite, set in three acres of landscaped gardens between Windermere and Bowness, is one of the area's highest hotels, overlooking Lake Windermere with magnificent panoramic views over to Langdale Pike, Crinkle Crags and Coniston Old Man. Individually designed rooms are maintained to a high standard, some with splendid four-poster beds and jacuzzi baths, and most with lake or fell views. Public rooms on the ground floor include a comfortable lounge with well-stocked bar, a feature conservatory and impressive restaurant with the aforementioned views of the Lakes skyline. Leisure facilities include a heated swimming pool, steam room and sauna.

Rooms: 34 (4 annexe) (4 family) (3 GF) ☏ **S** £69.50–£97.50; **D** £119–£295 (incl. bkfst)* **Facilities:** FTV WiFi ⌖ Sauna Steam room New Year **Parking:** 30 **Notes:** Closed 4-27 Dec

Craig Manor

★★★ 77% HOTEL

Lake Road, LA23 2JF - **tel:** 015394 88877
email: info@craigmanor.co.uk **web:** www.craigmanor.co.uk
dir: *A590, then A591 into Windermere, left at Windermere Hotel, through village, pass Magistrates Court/Police Station, hotel on right*

Situated in the heart of the Lake District, Craig Manor has a relaxed and friendly atmosphere with professional staff providing attentive service. Bedrooms are comfortable and well equipped, and some rooms offer stunning views across Windermere to the Cumbrian fells beyond. This view is most notable from the attractive restaurant, which serves a wide choice of quality dishes. The large car park is a further benefit in this popular tourist resort.

Rooms: 26 ☏ **S** £79–£143; **D** £89–£152 (incl. bkfst)* **Facilities:** FTV WiFi ⌁ **Parking:** 39

Windermere Manor Hotel

★★★ 76% HOTEL

Rayrigg Road, LA23 1ES - **tel:** 01539 445801
email: windermere@visionhotels.co.uk **web:** www.visionhotels.co.uk
dir: *A591 towards Ambleside. At mini-rdbt turn left, hotel 1st on left*

Set above the shores of Lake Windermere in wooded landscaped gardens, this former manor house has been restored to its original splendour. The bedrooms and suites are smart and well appointed. The attractive dining room has an unusual barrel-vaulted wooden roof and serves delicious home cooking. The hotel extends a warm welcome to everyone but caters especially for the visually impaired, their families, friends and guide dogs. Special facilities for guide dogs are provided.

Rooms: 35 (7 annexe) (2 family) (10 GF) ☏ **Facilities:** FTV WiFi HL ⌖ supervised Xmas New Year **Conf:** Class 30 Board 15 Thtr 40 **Services:** Lift Night porter **Parking:** 28 **Notes:** LB

INSPECTOR'S CHOICE

Macdonald Windsor Hotel

★★★★ @ ⌂ HOTEL

23 High Street, SL4 1LH - **tel:** 01753 483100
email: gm.windsor@macdonald-hotels.co.uk
web: www.macdonaldhotels.co.uk/windsor
dir: *M4 junct 6 A355, take A332, rdbt 1st exit signed town centre. In 0.7m turn left into Bachelors Acre*

Just across the street from Windsor Castle, this hotel is an ideal base for visiting that, and all the other famous attractions of the town. It has well-appointed contemporary, designer-led bedrooms, some overlooking the castle, that are decorated in soft shades to create a calm atmosphere, and include flat-screen TVs and Bose iPod docks. The Scottish Steak Club @ Caleys restaurant offers a relaxed and informal dining venue, and 24-hour room service is also available. There is complimentary WiFi in the bedrooms and the conference rooms. The hotel has excellent wedding facilities.

Rooms: 120 (4 family) ☏ **Facilities:** FTV WiFi ⌁ HL ♫ **Conf:** Class 80 Board 35 Thtr 100 **Services:** Lift Night porter Air con **Parking:** 42 **Notes:** LB Civ Wed 100

HIGHLY RECOMMENDED

The Oakley Court

★★★★ 82% ◉◉ ⌂ HOTEL

Windsor Road, Water Oakley, SL4 5UR - **tel:** 01753 609988
email: reservations@oakleycourt.co.uk **web:** www.oakleycourt.co.uk
dir: *M4 junct 6, A355, then A332 towards Windsor, right onto A308 towards Maidenhead. Pass racecourse, hotel 2.5m on right*

Built in 1859 this splendid Victorian Gothic mansion is enviably situated in extensive grounds that lead down to the Thames. All bedrooms are spacious, beautifully furnished and many enjoy river views. Extensive public areas include a range of comfortable lounges and the Dining Room Restaurant. The comprehensive leisure facilities include a fully equipped gym, indoor swimming pool, jacuzzi, sauna, steam room, tennis court, and 9-hole golf course. The Oakley Court is the AA Eco Hotel of the Year 2017-2018.

Rooms: 118 (108 annexe) (6 family) (42 GF) **S** £189–£499; **D** £199–£509 (incl. bkfst)* **Facilities:** FTV WiFi ↪ HL 🎱 ♨ 9 Putting green 🛶 ⛳ Gym Boating Sauna Steam room Snooker Bicycles Xmas New Year **Conf:** Class 90 Board 50 Thtr 170 **Services:** Night porter Air con **Parking:** 200 **Notes:** LB Civ Wed 170

Castle Hotel Windsor MGallery by Sofitel

★★★★ 81% HOTEL

18 High Street, SL4 1LJ - **tel:** 01753 851577
email: h6618@accor.com **web:** www.castlehotelwindsor.com
dir: *M4 junct 6/M25 junct 15, follow signs to Windsor town centre & castle. Hotel at top of hill opposite Guildhall*

This is one of the oldest hotels in Windsor, beginning life as a coaching inn in the 16th century. Located opposite Windsor Castle, it is an ideal base from which to explore the town and its royal connections. Stylish bedrooms are thoughtfully equipped and include four-poster and executive rooms. Public areas are spacious and tastefully decorated.

Rooms: 108 (70 annexe) (5 family) (3 GF) **Facilities:** STV FTV WiFi ↪ Xmas New Year **Conf:** Class 150 Board 50 Thtr 400 **Services:** Lift Night porter Air con **Parking:** 133 **Notes:** Civ Wed 300

Sir Christopher Wren Hotel and Spa

★★★★ 79% ◉ HOTEL

SAROVA HOTELS

Thames Street, SL4 1PX - **tel:** 01753 442400
email: wrens@sarova.com **web:** www.sarova.com
dir: *M4 junct 6, at 1st exit follow signs to Windsor, 1st major exit on left, left at lights*

Located by the side of the Thames and close to the Eton Bridge stands this well presented hotel. Bedrooms vary – with both traditional and contemporary tastes catered for. There are comfortable lounges, a popular restaurant with great views of the river, and also a well-equipped leisure club. Limited parking is available.

Rooms: 98 (42 annexe) (5 family) (10 GF) **S** £109–£150; **D** £129–£200 (incl. bkfst)* **Facilities:** Spa FTV WiFi ↪ Gym Sauna ♫ Xmas New Year **Conf:** Class 50 Board 45 Thtr 90 Del from £199 **Services:** Night porter Air con **Parking:** 14 **Notes:** Civ Wed 90

WISBECH	**Map 12 TF40**
Cambridgeshire	

Crown Lodge Hotel

THE INDEPENDENTS
HOTEL ASSOCIATION

★★★ 85% ◉ HOTEL

Downham Road, Outwell, PE14 8SE - **tel:** 01945 773391
email: office@thecrownlodgehotel.co.uk **web:** www.thecrownlodgehotel.co.uk
dir: *On A1122, approx 5m from Wisbech*

Crown Lodge Hotel is a friendly, privately-owned hotel situated in a peaceful location on the banks of Well Creek, a short drive from Wisbech. The bedrooms are pleasantly decorated, with co-ordinated fabrics and modern facilities. The public areas are very stylish; they include a lounge bar, brasserie restaurant and a large seating area with plush leather sofas.

Rooms: 10 (1 family) (10 GF) **Facilities:** FTV WiFi ↪ Squash **Conf:** Class 60 Board 40 Thtr 80 **Services:** Air con **Parking:** 55 **Notes:** Closed 25-26 Dec & 1 Jan

W

WISHAW
Warwickshire
Map 10 SP19

HIGHLY RECOMMENDED

The Belfry
★★★★ 83% HOTEL

Lichfield Road, B76 9PR - **tel:** 0844 980 0600
(Calls cost 7p per minute plus your phone company's access charge)
email: enquiries@thebelfry.com **web:** www.thebelfry.com
dir: *M42 junct 9, A446 towards Lichfield, hotel 1m on right*

The Belfry is ideally situated within easy striking distance of the M6, Birmingham and Birmingham Airport. The property is set in 550 acres of countryside and features three golf courses, including the Ryder Cup course, The Brabazon. The facilities include the Ryder Grill, the Brabazon Bar, Leisure Café, Sam's, a Starbucks, a spa, leisure facilities and a golf shop. The bedrooms are modern and well equipped; many of the rooms have views of the surrounding countryside.

Rooms: 319 (4 family) (98 GF) ⚑ **Facilities:** Spa FTV WiFi ⓦ HL Ⓢ ⚓ 54 Putting green ⚑ Gym Squash Ryder legends mini golf Children's playground Xmas New Year **Conf:** Class 435 Thtr 830 **Services:** Lift Night porter **Parking:** 1000 **Notes:** Civ Wed 300

WITNEY
Oxfordshire
Map 5 SP31

Premier Inn Witney
BUDGET HOTEL

Beech House, Ducklington Lane, OX28 4JF - **tel:** 0871 527 9488 (Calls cost 13p per minute plus your phone company's access charge) **web:** www.premierinn.com
dir: *M40 junct 8 or junct 9 follow Oxford signs, A40 towards Cheltenham. Take A415 (Witney & Abingdon). At bottom of slip road follow Witney signs. Straight on at lights, hotel on right*

High quality, budget accommodation ideal for both families and business travellers. Spacious, en suite bedrooms feature free WiFi and tea and coffee making facilities, and in most hotels, Freeview TV is also available. The adjacent family restaurant features a wide and varied menu.

Rooms: 57

WOBURN
Bedfordshire
Map 11 SP93

The Woburn Hotel
★★★★ 82% ⓦⓦ HOTEL

George Street, MK17 9PX - **tel:** 01525 290441
email: info@thewoburnhotel.co.uk **web:** www.thewoburnhotel.co.uk
dir: *M1 junct 13, towards Woburn. In Woburn left at T-junct, hotel in village*

At the heart of the picturesque Georgian Village of Woburn, standing proudly at the gateway to the Woburn Abbey Estate; with its 3,000 acres of deer park and Humphry Repton inspired landscape, you will find The Woburn Hotel. It provides a high standard of accommodation. Bedrooms are divided between the original house, a modern extension and some stunning cottage suites. Public areas include the beamed, club-style Tavistock Bar, a range of meeting rooms and an attractive two AA Rosette-worthy restaurant with interesting dishes on offer.

Rooms: 55 (7 annexe) (4 family) (25 GF) ⚑ ⚓ **S** £154.50–£310; **D** £187–£310 (incl. bkfst)* **Facilities:** FTV WiFi ⚓ 54 Putting green Concessionary rate to access Woburn Safari Park & Woburn Abbey Xmas New Year **Conf:** Class 30 Board 35 Thtr 60 Del from £155 **Services:** Night porter **Parking:** 75 **Notes:** LB Civ Wed 60

WOKING
Surrey
Map 6 TQ05

DoubleTree by Hilton Woking
★★★★ 75% HOTEL

Victoria Way, GU21 8EW - **tel:** 01483 221000
email: info@dtwoking.com **web:** www.dtwoking.com
dir: *M25 junct 11, A320 to Woking. Follow signs to town centre through 4 rdbts*

Located in the heart of Woking town centre, this recently refurbished hotel offers comfortable accommodation. Bedrooms have been enhanced to provide modern amenities for both business and leisure travellers. Public areas include a spacious lounge bar and restaurant. A number of up-to-date conference and meeting rooms are available. Secure parking available on site.

Rooms: 170 (34 family) **S** £109–£289; **D** £109–£289 (incl. bkfst)* **Facilities:** FTV WiFi ⓦ Gym Xmas New Year **Conf:** Class 100 Board 35 Thtr 300 **Services:** Lift Air con **Parking:** 45 **Notes:** LB Civ Wed 55

Premier Inn Woking Town Centre
BUDGET HOTEL

Eurobet House, Church Street West, GU21 6HT - **tel:** 0871 527 9462
(Calls cost 13p per minute plus your phone company's access charge)
web: www.premierinn.com
dir: *See website for detailed directions*

High quality, budget accommodation ideal for both families and business travellers. Spacious, en suite bedrooms feature free WiFi and tea and coffee making facilities, and in most hotels, Freeview TV is also available. The adjacent family restaurant features a wide and varied menu.

Rooms: 105

Premier Inn Woking West (A324)
BUDGET HOTEL

Bridge Barn Lane, Horsell, GU21 6NL - **tel:** 0871 527 9182
(Calls cost 13p per minute plus your phone company's access charge)
web: www.premierinn.com
dir: *From A324 at rdbt into Parley Drive. Left at next rdbt into Goldsworth Rd*

Rooms: 56

WOKINGHAM
Berkshire
Map 5 SU86

Cantley House Hotel
★★★ 78% ⓦⓦ COUNTRY HOUSE HOTEL

Milton Road, RG40 1JY - **tel:** 0118 989 5100
email: reception@cantleyhotel.co.uk **web:** www.cantleyhotel.co.uk
dir: *M4 junct 10, A329(M) to A329 towards Wokingham, then A321, hotel signed*

Cantley House Hotel is located within acres of Berkshire parkland. This Victorian mansion features a number of conference and meeting rooms, benefiting from traditional features. Bedrooms vary from the comfortable cosy doubles to a number of impressively sized suites and executive rooms. The award-winning Milton's restaurant is housed in a beautifully converted 17th-century barn with its own secluded courtyard garden.

Rooms: 36 (20 GF) ⚑ **Facilities:** FTV WiFi ⓦ ⚑ ⚓ Hairdresser Massage treatments ♫ Xmas New Year **Conf:** Class 50 Board 50 Thtr 80 **Services:** Night porter **Parking:** 100 **Notes:** LB Civ Wed 150

WOLVERHAMPTON
West Midlands

Map 10 SO99

The Mount Hotel and Conference Centre
★★★★ 74% @@ HOTEL

Mount Road, Tettenhall Wood, WV6 8HL - tel: 01902 752055
email: sales@themount.co.uk web: www.themount.co.uk
dir: M54 junct 5, follow A41 down to Yew Tree Lane which becomes Mount Road,
left at lights

This historic hotel is peacefully located on the outskirts of the city. Modern refurbishment and period architecture sit comfortably together, creating a stylish interior. Bedrooms are contemporary, with attractive colour schemes and equipment suitable for both business and leisure guests. Complimentary WiFi is available throughout. Public areas encompass a stylish bar and lounge, Drawing Room restaurant overlooking terrace and gardens, and extensive meeting and function rooms including the impressive Great Hall.

Rooms: 67 (10 annexe) (20 family) (31 GF) ♪ S fr £80; D fr £105* Facilities: FTV WiFi ♭ Gym Xmas New Year Conf: Class 50 Board 80 Thtr 180 Services: Night porter Parking: 100 Notes: Civ Wed 140

Novotel Wolverhampton
★★★ 81% HOTEL

Union Street, WV1 3JN - tel: 01902 871100
email: H1188@accor.com web: www.novotel.com
dir: 6m from M6 junct 10. A454 to Wolverhampton. Hotel on main ring road

This large, modern, purpose-built hotel stands close to the town centre. It provides spacious, smartly presented and well-equipped bedrooms, all of which contain convertible bed settees for family occupancy. In addition to the open-plan lounge and bar area, there is an attractive brasserie-style restaurant, which overlooks an attractive patio garden.

Rooms: 132 (9 family) ♪ S £125* Facilities: FTV WiFi ♭ Conf: Class 100 Board 80 Thtr 200 Del £145 Services: Lift Night porter Parking: 120 Notes: RS 23 Dec-4 Jan Restaurant may close Civ Wed 170

Holiday Inn Wolverhampton - Racecourse
★★★ 79% HOTEL

Dunstall Park, Gorse Brook Road, WV6 0PE - tel: 01902 390004 & 390001
email: holidayinn@wolverhampton-racecourse.com web: www.holidayinn.co.uk
dir: Off A449, 1.5m from city centre. Follow brown sign for Dunstall Park. Adjacent to Wolverhampton Racecourse

The Holiday Inn Wolverhampton forms an integral part of Wolverhampton Racecourse. Well-appointed, air-conditioned bedrooms have views across the course and stables. Open-plan public areas are modern and bright, with outdoor seating available during summer months. Free WiFi and ample parking available.

Rooms: 54 (18 family) ♪ S fr £40; D fr £40* Facilities: STV WiFi ♭ HL Gym Private location within Wolverhampton Racecourse Outdoor playground Conf: Class 260 Thtr 600 Services: Lift Air con Parking: 1500 Notes: Civ Wed 60

Premier Inn Wolverhampton City Centre
BUDGET HOTEL

Broad Gauge Way, WV10 0BA - tel: 0871 527 9186
(Calls cost 13p per minute plus your phone company's access charge)
web: www.premierinn.com
dir: M6 junct 10, A454 signed Wolverhampton for approx 2m. Right into Neachalls Ln (signed Wednesfield). 0.75m. At rdbt 1st exit onto A4124 (Wednesfield Way). 1st exit at next rdbt. 2nd exit at 3rd rdbt. At 2nd lights left into Sun St. 1st right, hotel at end of road

High quality, budget accommodation ideal for both families and business travellers. Spacious, en suite bedrooms feature free WiFi and tea and coffee making facilities, and in most hotels, Freeview TV is also available. The adjacent family restaurant features a wide and varied menu.

Rooms: 109

Premier Inn Wolverhampton North
BUDGET HOTEL

Greenfield Lane, Stafford Road, WV10 6TA - tel: 0871 527 9184
(Calls cost 13p per minute plus your phone company's access charge)
web: www.premierinn.com
dir: M54 junct 2. Hotel at lights in approx 100yds

Rooms: 80

W

WOMBWELL
South Yorkshire   Map 16 SE40

Premier Inn Barnsley (Dearne Valley)

BUDGET HOTEL

Meadow Gate, Dearne Valley, S73 0UN - **tel:** 0871 527 8050
(Calls cost 13p per minute plus your phone company's access charge)
web: www.premierinn.com
dir: *M1 junct 36 E'bound, A6195 towards Doncaster (5m). Hotel at rdbt adjacent to Meadows Brewers Fayre*

High quality, budget accommodation ideal for both families and business travellers. Spacious, en suite bedrooms feature free WiFi and tea and coffee making facilities, and in most hotels, Freeview TV is also available. The adjacent family restaurant features a wide and varied menu.

Rooms: 63

WONERSH
Surrey   Map 6 TQ04

Barnett Hill Country House Hotel

★★★★ 81% ◉◉ COUNTRY HOUSE HOTEL

Blackheath Lane, Wonersh, GU5 0RF - **tel:** 01483 893361
email: reservations@barnetthillhotel.co.uk **web:** www.barnetthillhotel.co.uk
dir: *M25 junct 10 take A3 S then B3000 to Compton/Godalming. A3100 Guildford then A248 Dorking. After 1m enter Wonersh village, turn left into Blackheath Lane. Hotel at top of lane*

In the heart of the Surrey Hills, Barnett Hill is a beautiful Queen Anne-style mansion dating back to 1905; it sits in 26 acres of lovingly maintained gardens and woodland, a tranquil and peaceful setting. The hotel offers the formal Oak Hall Restaurant and also Butlers Brasserie and Bar; private dining is available too. Afternoon tea can be taken overlooking the elegant gardens and fountains. Bedrooms are individually and stylishly designed. This is a popular venue for weddings, and the conference facilities are impressive.

Rooms: 54 (28 annexe) (31 GF) ♠ **Facilities:** FTV WiFi ⌣ Gym Xmas New Year
Conf: Class 40 Board 32 Thtr 70 **Services:** Night porter **Parking:** 55
Notes: Civ Wed 80

WOOBURN
Buckinghamshire   Map 6 SU98

Chequers Inn

★★★ 80% ◉◉ HOTEL

Kiln Lane, Wooburn, HP10 0JQ - **tel:** 01628 529575
email: info@chequers-inn.com **web:** www.chequers-inn.com
dir: *M40 junct 2, A40 through Beaconsfield Old Town towards High Wycombe. 2m from town left into Broad Ln. Inn 2.5m*

This 17th-century inn enjoys a peaceful, rural location beside the common. Bedrooms feature stripped-pine furniture, co-ordinated fabrics and an excellent range of extra facilities. The bar has a massive oak post, beams and flagstone floors, while the restaurant overlooks a pretty patio.

Rooms: 18 (8 GF) ♠ **S** fr £99.50; **D** fr £107.50 **Facilities:** FTV WiFi **Conf:** Class 30 Board 20 Thtr 50 **Parking:** 60 **Notes:** LB

WOODALL MOTORWAY SERVICE AREA (M1)
South Yorkshire   Map 16 SK48

Days Inn Sheffield - M1

AA Advertised

Woodall Service Area, S26 7XR - **tel:** 0114 248 7992
email: woodall.hotel@welcomebreak.co.uk **web:** www.welcomebreak.co.uk
dir: *M1, between juncts 30 & 31 S'bound, at Woodall Services*

This modern building offers accommodation in smart, spacious and well-equipped bedrooms, suitable for families and business travellers, and all with en suite bathrooms. Continental breakfast is available and other refreshments may be taken at the nearby family restaurant.

Rooms: 38 (32 family) (16 GF) (6 smoking) **Facilities:** FTV WiFi ⌁ **Conf:** Board 10 **Parking:** 40

WOODBRIDGE
Suffolk   Map 13 TM24

Seckford Hall Hotel

★★★★ 79% ◉◉ HOTEL

IP13 6NU - **tel:** 01394 385678
email: reception@seckford.co.uk **web:** www.seckford.co.uk
dir: *Signed on A12. NB do not follow signs for town centre*

Seckford Hall is an elegant Tudor manor house set amid landscaped grounds just off the A12. It is reputed that Queen Elizabeth I visited this property, and it retains much of its original character. Public rooms include a superb panelled lounge, a cosy bar and an intimate restaurant. The spacious bedrooms are attractively decorated, tastefully furnished and thoughtfully equipped.

Rooms: 32 (10 annexe) (4 family) (7 GF) ♠ **Facilities:** Spa WiFi ⌁ ☜ Putting green Fishing Gym Beauty salon Xmas New Year **Conf:** Class 46 Board 40 Thtr 120 **Services:** Night porter **Parking:** 100 **Notes:** Civ Wed 120

The Crown at Woodbridge

★★★ 86% ◉◉ HOTEL

The Thoroughfare, IP12 1AD - **tel:** 01394 384242
email: info@thecrownatwoodbridge.co.uk **web:** www.thecrownatwoodbridge.co.uk
dir: *A12 follow signs for Woodbridge onto B1438. 1.25m from rdbt left into Quay St. Hotel on right approx 100yds*

This 17th-century property offers contemporary-style accommodation throughout. The open-plan public areas are tastefully appointed and include a large lounge bar, a restaurant and a private dining room. The stylish bedrooms are tastefully appointed and equipped with modern facilities.

Rooms: 10 (2 family) ♠ **D** £130–£220 (incl. bkfst)* **Facilities:** STV WiFi **Conf:** Class 8 Board 12 Thtr 15 Del from £150 **Services:** Night porter **Parking:** 40 **Notes:** LB

W

WOODBURY
Devon   Map 3 SY08

Woodbury Park Hotel and Golf Club
★★★★ 77% HOTEL

Woodbury Castle, EX5 1JJ - tel: 01395 233382
email: enquiries@woodburypark.co.uk web: www.woodburypark.co.uk
dir: M5 junct 30, A376 then A3052 towards Sidmouth, onto B3180, hotel signed

Situated in 500 acres of beautiful, unspoilt countryside, yet within easy reach of Exeter and the M5, this hotel offers smart, well-equipped and immaculately presented accommodation together with a host of sporting and banqueting facilities. There is a choice of golf courses, a Bodyzone beauty centre and enjoyable dining in the Atrium Restaurant.

Rooms: 60 (4 annexe) (4 family) (28 GF) ♠ Facilities: Spa STV FTV WiFi ↘ ⊗ ⌁ 27 Putting green ♨ Fishing Gym Squash Beauty salon Football pitch Driving range Fitness studio Cinema suite Xmas New Year Conf: Class 100 Board 40 Thtr 250 Services: Lift Night porter Parking: 400 Notes: Civ Wed 150

WOODFORD BRIDGE
Greater London   Map 6 TQ49

Hallmark Hotel London Chigwell Prince Regent

★★★★ 72% HOTEL

Manor Road, IG8 8AE - tel: 0330 028 3418
email: princeregent@hallmarkhotels.co.uk web: www.hallmarkhotels.co.uk
dir: From A113 (Chigwell Rd) S of Chigwell into B173 (Manor Rd)

Situated on the edge of Woodford Bridge and Chigwell, this hotel with delightful rear gardens, offers easy access into London as well as to the M11 and M25. There is a good range of spacious, well-equipped bedrooms. Extensive conference and banqueting facilities are particularly well appointed, and are very suitable for weddings or business events.

Rooms: 61 (4 family) (15 GF) (6 smoking) ♠ Facilities: STV FTV WiFi ↘ Xmas New Year Conf: Class 180 Board 80 Thtr 400 Services: Lift Night porter Parking: 225 Notes: LB Civ Wed 350

Symbols and abbreviations
explained on pages 6–7

WOODHALL SPA
Lincolnshire   Map 17 TF16

Petwood
★★★ 78% HOTEL

Stixwould Road, LN10 6QG - tel: 01526 352411
email: reception@petwood.co.uk web: www.petwood.co.uk
dir: From Sleaford take A153 signed Skegness. At Tattershall turn left on B1192. Hotel is signed from village

This lovely Edwardian house, set in 30 acres of gardens and woodlands, is adjacent to Woodhall Golf Course. Built in 1905, the house was used by 617 Squadron, the famous Dambusters, as an officers' mess during World War II. Bedrooms and public areas are spacious and comfortable, and retain many original features. Weddings and conferences are well catered for in modern facilities.

Rooms: 53 (3 GF) ♠ S £75–£85; D £100–£185 (incl. bkfst)* Facilities: FTV WiFi HL ♨ Beauty treatments ♫ Xmas New Year Conf: Class 100 Board 50 Thtr 250 Del from £152 Services: Lift Night porter Parking: 140 Notes: LB Civ Wed 200

See advert on following page

W

WOODLANDS
Hampshire

Map 5 SU31

Woodlands Lodge Hotel
★★★ 78% HOTEL

Bartley Road, Woodlands, SO40 7GN - **tel:** 023 8029 2257
email: reception@woodlands-lodge.co.uk **web:** www.woodlands-lodge.co.uk
dir: *M27 junct 2, left at rdbt towards Fawley. 2nd rdbt right towards Cadnam.*
1st left at White Horse pub onto Woodlands Rd, over cattle grid

An 18th-century former hunting lodge, this hotel is set in four acres of impressive
and well-tended grounds on the edge of the New Forest. Well-equipped bedrooms
come in varying sizes and styles and a number of bathrooms have a jacuzzi bath.
Public areas include a pleasant lounge and intimate cocktail bar.

Rooms: 17 (3 family) (3 GF) 🐾 **S** £59–£189; **D** £59–£199 (incl. bkfst)*
Facilities: FTV WiFi ↕ Xmas New Year **Conf:** Class 20 Board 20 Thtr 65 **Parking:** 60
Notes: LB Civ Wed 100

WOODSTOCK
Oxfordshire

Map 11 SP41

Macdonald Bear Hotel
★★★★ 81% HOTEL

MACDONALD
HOTELS & RESORTS

Park Street, OX20 1SZ - **tel:** 01993 811124
email: general.bear@macdonald-hotels.co.uk **web:** www.macdonaldhotels.co.uk
dir: *M40 junct 9 follow signs for Oxford & Blenheim Palace. A44 to town centre,*
hotel on left

With its ivy-clad façade, oak beams and open fireplaces, this 13th-century
coaching inn exudes charm and cosiness. The bedrooms are decorated in a modern
style that remains in keeping with the historic character of the building. Public
rooms include a variety of function rooms, an intimate bar area and an attractive
restaurant where attentive service and good food are offered.

Rooms: 54 (18 annexe) (1 family) (8 GF) 🐾 **D** fr £99* **Facilities:** FTV WiFi Xmas
New Year **Conf:** Class 12 Board 24 Thtr 40 Del from £150 **Services:** Night porter
Parking: 40

The Feathers Hotel
★★★★ 73% ◉◉ TOWN HOUSE HOTEL

PRIDE OF BRITAIN
HOTELS

Market Street, OX20 1SX - **tel:** 01993 812291
email: reception@feathers.co.uk **web:** www.feathers.co.uk
dir: *From A44 Oxford to Woodstock, 1st left after lights. Hotel on left*

This intimate and unique hotel enjoys a town centre location with easy access to
nearby Blenheim Palace. Public areas are elegant and full of traditional character
from the cosy drawing room to the atmospheric restaurant. Individually styled
bedrooms are appointed to a high standard and are furnished with attractive period
and reproduction furniture.

Rooms: 21 (5 annexe) (4 family) (2 GF) 🐾 **S** £89–£529; **D** £99–£579 (incl. bkfst)*
Facilities: FTV WiFi ↕ Xmas New Year **Conf:** Class 18 Board 20 Thtr 40 Del from
£219 **Services:** Night porter

WOOKEY HOLE
Somerset

Map 4 ST54

Wookey Hole Hotel
★★ 75% HOTEL

BA5 1BB - **tel:** 01749 672243
email: witch@wookey.co.uk **web:** www.wookey.co.uk
dir: *Please phone for directions*

This impressive, modern hotel is located in the heart of the pretty village, famous
for its magnificent cave system and just a couple of miles from the historic
cathedral city of Wells. The bedrooms are contemporary, spacious and comfortable,
with both family and connecting rooms available. Additional facilities include a bar
and restaurant. There is ample parking provision.

Rooms: 58 (37 family) (27 GF) 🐾 **Facilities:** FTV WiFi ↕ 9 hole adventure golf course
Xmas New Year **Conf:** Class 100 Board 100 Thtr 400 **Services:** Lift Night porter
Parking: 800 **Notes:** LB Civ Wed 120

WOOLACOMBE
Devon   Map 3 SS44

Watersmeet Hotel

★★★★ 79% ◉◉ HOTEL

Mortehoe, EX34 7EB - tel: 01271 870333
email: info@watersmeethotel.co.uk **web:** www.watersmeethotel.co.uk
dir: *B3343 into Woolacombe, right onto esplanade, hotel 0.75m on left*

With magnificent views, and steps leading directly to the beach, this popular hotel offers guests attentive service and a relaxing atmosphere. Bedrooms benefit from the wonderful sea views and some have private balconies. Diners in the attractive tiered restaurant can admire the beautiful sunsets while enjoying an innovative range of dishes offered on the fixed-price menu. Both indoor and outdoor pools are available.

Rooms: 25 (4 family) (3 GF) ⟡ **S** £130; **D** £145–£320 (incl. bkfst)* **Facilities:** FTV WiFi ⟲ ⟲ ⟲ Steam room ♫ Xmas New Year **Conf:** Board 20 Thtr 20 **Services:** Lift **Parking:** 38 **Notes:** LB Civ Wed 60

The Woolacombe Bay Hotel

★★★★ 79% HOTEL

South Street, EX34 7BN - tel: 01271 870388
email: enquiries@woolacombebayhotel.co.uk **web:** www.woolacombebayhotel.co.uk
dir: *A361 onto B3343 to Woolacombe. Hotel in centre*

Overlooking one of the finest beaches in England, this privately-owned hotel offers a warm welcome. Public areas are spacious and comfortable, and many of the stylishly furnished and well-equipped bedrooms have balconies with splendid views

over the bay. Elegant bathroom suites certainly add to the feeling of luxury. In addition to the elegant surroundings of Doyle's Restaurant, The Bay Brasserie is available as an informal alternative. Extensive leisure facilities are also provided, including a health club, a spa and a very stylish lido.

The Woolacombe Bay Hotel

Rooms: 64 (26 family) (2 GF) ⟡ **Facilities:** Spa FTV WiFi ⟲ ⟲ ⟲ 9 ⟲ Gym Squash Paddling pool Table tennis Snooker Steam room Sauna Spa bath Xmas New Year **Conf:** Class 100 Board 50 Thtr 150 **Services:** Lift Night porter **Parking:** 150 **Notes:** Closed 2 Jan-9 Feb Civ Wed 180

WORCESTER
Worcestershire   Map 10 SO85

Premier Inn Worcester City Centre

BUDGET HOTEL

Cricket Ground, New Road, WR2 4QQ - tel: 0871 527 9456 (Calls cost 13p per minute plus your phone company's access charge) **web:** www.premierinn.com
dir: *M5 junct 7 (Worcester South), A44 signed Worcester City Centre. At next rdbt 2nd exit (A44 & Worcester City Centre) keep in left lane. At Worcester Cathedral continue on A44, straight on at 3 sets of lights*

High quality, budget accommodation ideal for both families and business travellers. Spacious, en suite bedrooms feature free WiFi and tea and coffee making facilities, and in most hotels, Freeview TV is also available. The adjacent family restaurant features a wide and varied menu.

Rooms: 120

Premier Inn Worcester (M5 Jct 6)

BUDGET HOTEL

Wainwright Way, Warndon, WR4 9FA - tel: 0871 527 9188 (Calls cost 13p per minute plus your phone company's access charge) **web:** www.premierinn.com
dir: *M5 junct 6. At entrance of Warndon commercial development area*

Rooms: 87

W

WORKINGTON
Cumbria   Map 18 NY02

Washington Central Hotel
★★★★ 73% HOTEL

Washington Street, CA14 3AY - tel: 01900 65772
email: info@washingtoncentralhotel.co.uk **web:** www.washingtoncentralhotel.co.uk
dir: *M6 junct 40, A66 to Workington. Left at lights, hotel on right*

Enjoying a prominent town centre location, this modern hotel boasts memorably hospitable staff. The well-maintained and comfortable bedrooms are equipped with a range of thoughtful extras. Public areas include numerous lounges, a spacious bar, Caesars leisure club, a smart restaurant and a popular coffee shop. The comprehensive conference facilities are ideal for meetings and weddings.

Rooms: 57 (12 family) **S** £100–£125; **D** £150–£180 (incl. bkfst) **Facilities:** FTV WiFi ⌁ ⊗ supervised Gym Sauna Steam room New Year **Conf:** Class 200 Board 100 Thtr 300 Del £150 **Services:** Lift Night porter **Parking:** 23 **Notes:** LB Civ Wed 300

Hunday Manor Hotel

Ⓤ

Winscales, CA14 4JF - tel: 01900 61798 **email:** info@hundaymanorhotel.co.uk
web: www.hundaymanorhotel.co.uk
dir: *M6 junct 40, A66 towards Keswick/Workington for 30m until Cockermouth. At 2 rdbts follow A66, at 3rd rdbt take 1st exit to A595, hotel 3m further on right*

Currently the rating for this establishment is not confirmed. This may be due to a change of ownership or because it has only recently joined the AA rating scheme.

Rooms: 27 **S** £75; **D** £75–£105* **Facilities:** WiFi ⊗ ⟲ Xmas New Year **Conf:** Class 160 Board 60 Thtr 200 Del from £125 **Services:** Night porter **Parking:** 100 **Notes:** Civ Wed 200

WORKSOP
Nottinghamshire   Map 16 SK57

Best Western Lion Hotel
★★★ 80% HOTEL   BW **Best Western.**

112 Bridge Street, S80 1HT - tel: 01909 477925
email: reception@thelionworksop.co.uk **web:** www.bw-lionhotel.co.uk
dir: *A57 to town centre, turn right at Sainsburys, follow to Norfolk Arms, turn left*

This former coaching inn lies on the edge of the main shopping precinct, with a car park to the rear. It has been extended to offer modern accommodation that includes excellent executive rooms. A wide range of interesting dishes are offered in the newly refurbished 114 bar and grill.

Rooms: 46 (3 family) (7 GF) **Facilities:** STV FTV WiFi ⌁ Xmas New Year **Conf:** Class 80 Board 70 Thtr 160 **Services:** Lift Night porter **Parking:** 50 **Notes:** Civ Wed 150

WORSLEY
Greater Manchester   Map 15 SD70

Novotel Manchester West
★★★ 75% HOTEL   NOVOTEL
HOTELS & RESORTS

Worsley Brow, M28 2YA - tel: 0161 799 3535
email: H0907@accor.com **web:** www.novotel.com
dir: *Adjacent to M60 junct 13*

Well placed for access to the Peak District and the Lake District, as well as Manchester, this modern hotel successfully caters for both families and business guests. The spacious bedrooms have sofa beds and a large work area; the hotel has an outdoor swimming pool, children's play area and secure parking.

Rooms: 119 (10 family) (41 GF) **S** £70–£150; **D** £70–£150* **Facilities:** STV FTV WiFi ⌁ HL Gym Xmas New Year **Conf:** Class 130 Board 60 Thtr 220 Del from £130 **Services:** Lift Night porter **Parking:** 95 **Notes:** LB Civ Wed 140

WORTHING
West Sussex   Map 6 TQ10

Ardington Hotel
★★★ 82% HOTEL

Steyne Gardens, BN11 3DZ - tel: 01903 230451
email: reservations@ardingtonhotel.co.uk **web:** www.ardingtonhotel.co.uk
dir: *A27 to Lancing, to seafront. Follow signs for Worthing. Left at church into Steyne Gardens*

Overlooking Steyne Gardens adjacent to the seafront, this popular hotel offers well-appointed bedrooms with a good range of facilities. There's a stylishly modern lounge/bar with ample seating, where a light menu is available throughout the day. The popular restaurant offers local seafood and a choice of modern dishes. WiFi is available in the lounge/bar.

Rooms: 45 (4 family) (12 GF) **Facilities:** STV FTV WiFi **Conf:** Class 60 Board 35 Thtr 140 **Services:** Night porter **Notes:** Closed 25 Dec-4 Jan

Premier Inn Worthing Seafront
BUDGET HOTEL   Premier Inn

127 Marine Parade, BN11 3FN - tel: 0871 527 9556
(Calls cost 13p per minute plus your phone company's access charge)
web: www.premierinn.com
dir: *From A24 & A27 Grove Lodge rdbt follow A24/South signs. At 4th rdbt 1st exit, follow seafront signs. At seafront, right into Marine Parade, pass pier, hotel approx 1m on right*

High quality, budget accommodation ideal for both families and business travellers. Spacious, en suite bedrooms feature free WiFi and tea and coffee making facilities, and in most hotels, Freeview TV is also available. The adjacent family restaurant features a wide and varied menu.

Rooms: 81

W

WOTTON-UNDER-EDGE
Gloucestershire

Map 4 ST79

De Vere Tortworth Estate

EST. 1898
PRINCIPAL
HOTEL COMPANY LTD

★★★★ 78% HOTEL

Tortworth, GL12 8HH - tel: 0800 374692
email: TortworthReservations@devere.com
web: www.phcompany.com/de-vere/tortworth-court
dir: M5 junct 14, B4509 towards Wotton. 1st right into Tortworth Rd, next right, hotel 0.5m on right

Set in 30 acres of parkland, this Gothic mansion displays original features cleverly combined with contemporary additions. Elegant public rooms include a choice of dining options, one housed within the library, with another in the atrium. Bedrooms are well equipped, and additional facilities include a host of conference rooms and a leisure centre

Rooms: 190 (25 family) (74 GF) **Facilities:** Spa FTV WiFi 🕸 🏊 Gym Steam room Sauna Xmas New Year **Conf:** Class 200 Board 80 Thtr 400 **Services:** Lift Night porter **Parking:** 200 **Notes:** Civ Wed 400

WREA GREEN
Lancashire

Map 18 SD33

HIGHLY RECOMMENDED

The Spa Hotel at Ribby Hall Village

★★★★ 83% ◉◉ HOTEL

Ribby Hall Village, Ribby Road, PR4 2PR - tel: 01772 671111
email: enquiries@ribbyhall.co.uk **web:** www.ribbyhall.co.uk/spa-hotel
dir: M55 junct 33 follow A585 towards Kirkham & brown tourist signs for Ribby Hall Village. Straight across 3 rdbts. Ribby Hall Village 200yds on left

Set in one hundred acres of rolling countryside, Ribby Hall is a tranquil and relaxing place to stay. The luxurious bedrooms are comfortable and come in a range of sizes. The spa is the focus of the property, offering hotel guests a wide selection of treatments and the signature aqua-thermal journey. Food is another obvious highlight whether in the Orangery restaurant or in another of the nine outlets within the village.

Rooms: 38 (10 GF) 🐾 **S** £100–£220; **D** £110–£320 (incl. bkfst)* **Facilities:** Spa STV FTV WiFi ❧ ♨ 9 🏊 Fishing Gym Squash Aqua thermal journey Champagne bar Cycling Woodland trail Xmas New Year **Services:** Lift Night porter Air con **Parking:** 124 **Notes:** No children 18yrs

The Villa Country House Hotel

★★★★ 72% ◉ COUNTRY HOUSE HOTEL

Moss Side Lane, PR4 2PE - tel: 01772 804040
email: info@thevilla.co.uk **web:** www.thevilla.co.uk
dir: M55 junct 3 follow signs to Kirkham at Wrea Green follow signs to Lytham

Dating back to the 19th century this former gentlemen's residence is packed full of original character and charm. Situated within the peaceful, picturesque village of Wrea Green but convenient for the motorway, it is the ideal location for a relaxing stay for both business and leisure guests. Rooms are thoughtfully appointed for the modern day traveller but still retain some of their original charm. An interesting range of dishes can be tried in the restaurant or alternatively more relaxed options are available in the bar. Ample amounts of car parking is available. Weddings, conferences and special events are well catered for.

Rooms: 31 (2 family) (10 GF) 🐾 **S** £70–£125; **D** £80–£135 (incl. bkfst)*
Facilities: FTV WiFi Xmas New Year **Conf:** Class 100 Board 40 Thtr 300
Services: Lift Night porter **Parking:** 120 **Notes:** LB Civ Wed 300

WROTHAM
Kent

Map 6 TQ65

Premier Inn Sevenoaks/Maidstone

Premier Inn

BUDGET HOTEL

London Road, Wrotham Heath, TN15 7RX - tel: 0871 527 8962 (Calls cost 13p per minute plus your phone company's access charge) **web:** www.premierinn.com
dir: M26 junct 2a, A20 S. At lights left onto A20 towards West Malling. Hotel on right.

High quality, budget accommodation ideal for both families and business travellers. Spacious, en suite bedrooms feature free WiFi and tea and coffee making facilities, and in most hotels, Freeview TV is also available. The adjacent family restaurant features a wide and varied menu.

Rooms: 59

W

Silver Stars The AA Silver Star rating denotes a Hotel that we highly recommend. They have a superior level of quality within their star rating, high standards of hospitality, service and cleanliness.

WROXALL
Warwickshire   Map 10 SP27

Wroxall Abbey Hotel & Estate
★★★★ 72% HOTEL

Birmingham Road, CV35 7NB - **tel:** 01926 484470
email: reservation@wroxall.com **web:** www.wroxall.com
dir: *Between Solihull & Warwick on A4141*

Situated in 27 acres of open parkland, yet only 10 miles from the NEC and Birmingham International Airport, this hotel is a magnificent Victorian mansion. Some of the individually designed bedrooms have traditional decor but there are some modern loft rooms as well; some rooms have four-posters. Sonnets Restaurant, with its impressive fireplace and oak panelling, makes the ideal setting for fine dining.

Rooms: 72 (24 annexe) (10 GF) ⌇ **S** £69–£99; **D** £89–£199* **Facilities:** Spa FTV WiFi ⌇ ⌇ Fishing ⌇ Gym Xmas New Year **Conf:** Class 80 Board 60 Thtr 160 Del from £139 **Services:** Lift Night porter **Parking:** 200 **Notes:** LB No children 12yrs Civ Wed 171

WYBOSTON
Bedfordshire   Map 12 TL15

Lakes
★★★★ 78% ⌾ HOTEL

Great North Road, MK44 3BA - **tel:** 0333 700 7667
email: reservations@wybostonlakes.co.uk **web:** www.wybostonlakes.co.uk
dir: *From A1 & A428 junct, follow brown Cambridge signs. Wyboston Lakes & hotel on right, marked by flags*

Wyboston Lakes is situated just off the A1(M), a short drive from Cambridge and Milton Keynes. The hotel is situated in extensive landscaped grounds and surrounded by a lake; the modern bedrooms are well equipped with a range of extra facilities that include coffee machines and large flat-screen TVs. The hotel has a spa, golf course, and leisure facilities that include a gym and swimming pool.

Rooms: 103 (103 annexe) (4 family) (50 GF) ⌇ **D** £85–£140* **Facilities:** Spa FTV WiFi ⌇ HL ⌇ supervised Putting green Fishing Gym Golf driving range Nature reserve Watersports New Year **Conf:** Class 120 Board 68 Thtr 270 **Services:** Lift Night porter **Parking:** 200 **Notes:** LB RS Xmas & 1 Jan reduced hours in restaurant, closed 1 Jan eve Civ Wed 250

YARM
North Yorkshire   Map 19 NZ41

INSPECTOR'S CHOICE

Crathorne Hall Hotel
★★★★ ⌾⌾ HOTEL

Crathorne, TS15 0AR - **tel:** 01642 700398 & 0845 072 7440
(Calls cost 5p per minute plus your phone company's access charge)
email: crathornehall@handpicked.co.uk
web: www.handpickedhotels.co.uk/crathorne-hall
dir: *From A19 take slip road signed Teesside Airport & Kirklevington, right signed Crathorne to hotel*

This splendid Edwardian hall sits in its own landscaped grounds and enjoys fine views of the Leven Valley and rolling Cleveland Hills. The impressively equipped bedrooms and delightful public areas offer sumptuous levels of comfort, with elegant antique furnishings that complement the hotel's architectural style. All bedrooms and suites offer large flat-screen TVs and free broadband among their many facilities. The elegant Leven Restaurant is a traditional setting for fine dining; there's also the Drawing Room for lighter food options. Weather permitting, alfresco eating is available on the terrace, and afternoon tea is always popular. Conference and banqueting facilities are available.

Rooms: 37 (10 family) ⌇ **D** £120–£180* **Facilities:** STV FTV WiFi ⌇ HL ⌇ Jogging track Clay pigeon shooting Xmas **Conf:** Class 75 Board 60 Thtr 120 **Services:** Lift Night porter **Parking:** 88 **Notes:** LB Civ Wed 90

W

Judges Country House Hotel

★★★★ 77% COUNTRY HOUSE HOTEL

Kirklevington Hall, TS15 9LW - tel: 01642 789000
email: enquiries@judgeshotel.co.uk **web:** www.judgeshotel.co.uk
dir: *1.5m from A19. At A67 junct, follow Yarm road, hotel on left*

Formerly a lodging for local circuit judges, this gracious mansion lies in landscaped grounds through which a stream runs. Stylish bedrooms are individually decorated and come with plenty of extras; four-poster bedrooms and suites are available. Meals are offered in The Conservatory restaurant, and private dining for a small number of guests is available in the wine cellar. Judges is a popular wedding venue. The genuinely caring and attentive service from the staff is truly memorable.

Rooms: 21 (3 family) (5 GF) S £99; D £145–£225 (incl. bkfst)* **Facilities:** FTV WiFi Gym Mountain bikes Nature trails Xmas New Year **Conf:** Class 50 Board 38 Thtr 80 Del from £225 **Services:** Night porter **Parking:** 102 **Notes:** LB Civ Wed 200

YARMOUTH
Isle of Wight

Map 5 SZ38

INSPECTOR'S CHOICE

The George Hotel

★★★ ◉◉ HOTEL

Quay Street, PO41 0PE - tel: 01983 760331
email: info@thegeorge.co.uk **web:** www.thegeorge.co.uk
dir: *Between castle & pier*

This delightful 17th-century hotel enjoys a wonderful location at the water's edge, adjacent to the castle and the quay. Public areas include Isla's fine dining restaurant, where organic and local produce are utilised; The Conservatory, for informal dining; a cosy bar and an inviting lounge. Individually styled bedrooms, with many thoughtful extras, are beautifully appointed; some benefit from spacious balconies. The hotel's motor yacht is available for guests to hire.

Rooms: 17 (1 GF) S £125–£310; D £140–£325 (incl. bkfst)* **Facilities:** STV WiFi Sailing from Yarmouth Mountain biking Xmas New Year **Conf:** Class 18 Board 18 Thtr 20 Del from £165 **Services:** Night porter **Notes:** LB Civ Wed 120

Norton Grange Coastal Village

WARNERLEISUREHOTELS

AA Advertised

PO41 0SD - tel: 01983 760 323
web: www.warnerleisurehotels.co.uk
dir: *From Yarmouth Ferry Terminal leaving Yarmouth harbour, turn right at rdbt, follow road across Yarmouth bridge A3054. After approx 0.5m hotel on right after bend*

Sitting pretty in one of the UK's sunniest spots just five minutes from Yarmouth ferry port, with access to scenic coastal walks, this friendly chalet village is a favourite for sunseekers. A wide range of leisure activities is on offer, and there is nightly entertainment on the popular half-board breaks. This is an adults only (over 21 years) hotel.

Rooms: 208 **Facilities:** FTV WiFi supervised Putting green Gym Xmas New Year **Services:** Night porter **Parking:** 208 **Notes:** Closed Jan-Feb

Y

YATELEY
Hampshire   **Map 5 SU86**

Casa Hotel & Marco Pierre White Steakhouse, Bar & Grill

★★★ 79% @ HOTEL

Handford Lane, GU46 6BT - **tel:** 01252 873275
email: reservations@casadeicesari.co.uk **web:** www.thecasahoteluk.com
dir: *M3 junct 4a, follow signs for town centre. Hotel signed*

This delightful hotel where a warm welcome is guaranteed is ideally located for transport networks. It boasts rooms with quality and comfort, and the Marco Pierre White Steakhouse, Bar & Grill, which is very popular locally, serves an extensive traditional menu.

Rooms: 63 (2 family) (15 GF) (33 smoking) **Facilities:** FTV WiFi ⍾ Xmas New Year **Conf:** Class 60 Board 60 Thtr 180 **Services:** Lift Night porter **Parking:** 80 **Notes:** Civ Wed 120

YELVERTON
Devon   **Map 3 SX56**

Moorland Garden Hotel

★★★★ 77% @ HOTEL

Yelverton, PL20 6DA - **tel:** 01822 852245
email: stay@moorlandgardenhotel.co.uk **web:** www.moorlandgardenhotel.co.uk
dir: *A38 from Exeter to Plymouth, then A386 towards Tavistock. 5m onto open moorland, hotel 1m on left*

This hotel has a great location for either the city or Dartmoor, and sits in delightful gardens. Bedrooms are spacious, all with garden views and some with impressive balconies. There is a choice of dining as well as a range of meeting and function rooms. Pleasant Devon cream teas are served in the garden in warmer months.

Rooms: 44 (5 family) (17 GF) ⍾ **S** £64–£125; **D** £69–£145 (incl. bkfst)*
Facilities: FTV WiFi ⍾ HL Reduced fees for residents at golf club Xmas New Year **Conf:** Class 60 Board 50 Thtr 170 **Services:** Night porter **Parking:** 75 **Notes:** LB Civ Wed 160

YEOVIL
Somerset   **Map 4 ST51**

The Yeovil Court Hotel & Restaurant

★★★ 76% @ HOTEL

West Coker Road, BA20 2HE - **tel:** 01935 863746
email: unwind@yeovilhotel.com **web:** www.yeovilhotel.com
dir: *2.5m W of town centre on A30*

This comfortable, family-run hotel offers a very relaxed atmosphere. Bedrooms are well equipped and neatly presented; some are located in an adjacent building. Public areas consist of a smart lounge, a popular bar and an attractive restaurant. Menus combine an interesting selection that includes lighter options, and dishes suited to special occasion dining.

Rooms: 30 (12 annexe) (3 family) (8 GF) ⍾ **Facilities:** FTV WiFi ⍾ **Conf:** Class 18 Board 30 Thtr 50 **Services:** Night porter **Parking:** 65 **Notes:** RS Sat lunch, 25 Dec eve & 26 Dec Restaurant closed Civ Wed 70

Premier Inn Yeovil

BUDGET HOTEL

Alvington Lane, Brympton, BA22 8UX - **tel:** 0871 527 9192
(Calls cost 13p per minute plus your phone company's access charge)
web: www.premierinn.com
dir: *M5 junct 25, A358, A303 follow Yeovil signs. At rdbt onto A3088. At next rdbt 1st left, at next rdbt turn left. Hotel on left*

High quality, budget accommodation ideal for both families and business travellers. Spacious, en suite bedrooms feature free WiFi and tea and coffee making facilities, and in most hotels, Freeview TV is also available. The adjacent family restaurant features a wide and varied menu.

Rooms: 20

Premier Inn Yeovil Town Centre

BUDGET HOTEL

Key Market House, Middle Street, BA20 1LT - **tel:** 0871 527 9426
(Calls cost 13p per minute plus your phone company's access charge)
web: www.premierinn.com
dir: *From N: A37 to end, take A30 (Reckleford). Keep right, take 1st right. Into Sherborne Rd left into Newton Rd. Left into S Western Terr, join Old Station Rd. Hotel on right. From S: A30, at rdbt into Brunswick St. Then Park St, Taunusstein Way, Summer House Terrace, Old Station Rd*

Rooms: 80

YORK
North Yorkshire   **Map 16 SE65**

See also **Aldwark & Escrick**

The Grand Hotel & Spa, York

★★★★★ 86% @@@ HOTEL

Station Rise, YO1 6HT - **tel:** 01904 380038
email: info@thegrandyork.co.uk **web:** www.thegrandyork.co.uk
dir: *In city centre, near station*

Located in the heart of the city, this majestic Edwardian building, built in 1906, has been transformed into a luxury hotel. Spacious, air-conditioned accommodation offers deeply comfortable rooms with luxurious bathrooms. Public areas are equally impressive with a range of delightful lounges, a modern spa in the former vaults and excellent meeting rooms. The Hudson's offers a high standard of dining with modern and classic dishes on offer, all delivered with both flair and a touch of fun. Afternoon tea is presented on a silver stand in a relaxing, tranquil environment. Valet parking is a great asset given the hotel's central location.

Rooms: 107 (14 GF) ⍾ **S** £143–£313; **D** £143–£313* **Facilities:** Spa STV FTV WiFi ⍾ ⊛ Gym Sauna Steam room New Year **Conf:** Class 60 Board 50 Thtr 120 Del from £215 **Services:** Lift Night porter Air con **Notes:** Civ Wed 120

Y

INSPECTOR'S CHOICE

Middlethorpe Hall & Spa
★★★★ ◎◎ HOTEL

Bishopthorpe Road, Middlethorpe, YO23 2GB - tel: 01904 641241
email: info@middlethorpe.com **web:** www.middlethorpe.com
dir: A1/A64 follow York West A1036 signs, then Bishopthorpe,
Middlethorpe racecourse signs

This fine house, dating from the reign of William and Mary, sits in acres of beautifully landscaped gardens. The bedrooms vary in size but all are comfortably furnished; some are located in the main house, and others are in a cottage and converted courtyard stables. Public areas include a small spa and a stately drawing room where afternoon tea is quite an event. The delightful panelled restaurant is a perfect setting for enjoying the imaginative cuisine.

Rooms: 29 (19 annexe) (2 family) (10 GF) ⟨ **S** £143–£205; **D** £205–£411 (incl. bkfst)* **Facilities:** Spa FTV WiFi ↕ ⊕ ⤴ Gym Xmas New Year **Conf:** Class 30 Board 25 Thtr 56 **Services:** Lift Night porter **Parking:** 71 **Notes:** LB No children 6yrs RS 25 & 31 Dec Lunch for Res only 25 Dec, Dinner 31 Dec Civ Wed 56

The Grange Hotel
★★★★ 79% ◎◎ HOTEL

1 Clifton, YO30 6AA - tel: 01904 644744
email: info@grangehotel.co.uk **web:** www.grangehotel.co.uk
dir: On A19 York/Thirsk rd, approx 500yds from city centre

This bustling Regency town house is just a few minutes' walk from the centre of York. A professional service is efficiently delivered by caring staff in a very friendly and helpful manner. Public rooms are comfortable and have been stylishly furnished; these include two dining options, the popular and informal Cellar Bar, and main hotel restaurant The Ivy Brasserie, which offers fine dining in a lavishly decorated environment. The individually designed bedrooms are comfortably appointed and have been thoughtfully equipped.

Rooms: 41 (1 family) (11 GF) ⟨ **S** £120–£300; **D** £150–£330 (incl. bkfst)* **Facilities:** STV FTV WiFi ↕ Use of nearby health club (chargeable) Xmas New Year **Conf:** Class 24 Board 24 Thtr 40 Del from £173.95 **Services:** Lift Night porter **Parking:** 20 **Notes:** LB Civ Wed 90

Hotel du Vin & Bistro York
★★★★ 79% ◎ HOTEL

89 The Mount, YO24 1AX - tel: 01904 557350 & 0844 748 9268
(Calls cost 7p per minute plus your phone company's access charge)
email: info.york@hotelduvin.com **web:** www.hotelduvin.com
dir: A1036 towards city centre, 6m. Hotel on right through lights

This Hotel du Vin offers luxury and quality that will cosset even the most discerning guest. Bedrooms are decadent in design and the bathrooms have huge monsoon showers and feature baths. Dinner in the bistro provides a memorable highlight thanks to exciting menus and a superb wine list. Staff throughout are naturally friendly, nothing is too much trouble.

Rooms: 44 (3 family) (14 GF) ⟨ **Facilities:** STV FTV WiFi ↕ **Conf:** Class 10 Board 22 Thtr 60 **Services:** Lift Night porter Air con **Parking:** 18 **Notes:** Civ Wed 80

Dean Court Hotel
★★★★ 77% ◎ HOTEL

PREMIER | BEST WESTERN

Duncombe Place, YO1 7EF - tel: 01904 625082
email: sales@deancourt-york.co.uk **web:** www.deancourt-york.co.uk
dir: In city centre opposite York Minster

This smart hotel enjoys a central location overlooking The Minster, and guests will find the service is particularly friendly and efficient. Bedrooms are stylishly appointed and vary in size. Public areas are elegant in a contemporary style and include the popular D.C.H. restaurant which enjoys wonderful views of the cathedral, and The Court café-bistro and bar where a more informal, all-day menu is offered. Valet parking is available.

Rooms: 37 (4 family) ⟨ **S** £115–£250; **D** £150–£400* **Facilities:** STV FTV WiFi ↕ Xmas New Year **Conf:** Class 12 Board 32 Thtr 50 Del from £175 **Services:** Lift Night porter **Parking:** 30 **Notes:** LB

The Principal York
★★★★ 77% HOTEL

EST. 1898
PRINCIPAL
HOTEL COMPANY LTD

Station Rd, YO24 1AA - tel: 01904 653681
email: yorkreservations@theprincipalhotel.com
web: www.phcompany.com/principal/york-hotel/
dir: Adjacent to railway station

Situated in three acres of landscaped grounds in the very heart of the city, this Victorian railway hotel has views over the city and York Minster. Contemporary bedrooms are divided between those in the main hotel and the air-conditioned garden mews. There is also a leisure complex and state-of-the-art conference centre.

Rooms: 155 (34 annexe) (1 family) ⟨ **Facilities:** FTV WiFi ⊗ Gym Steam room Weights room Xmas New Year **Conf:** Class 250 Board 80 Thtr 410 **Services:** Lift Night porter **Parking:** 90 **Notes:** Civ Wed 160

Y

YORK *continued*

The Churchill Hotel

★★★★ 76% HOTEL

65 Bootham, YO30 7DQ - **tel:** 01904 644456
email: info@churchillhotel.com **web:** www.churchillhotel.com
dir: *On A19 (Bootham), W from York Minster, hotel 250yds on right*

The Churchill Hotel is a late Georgian manor house set in its own grounds, just a short walk from the Minster and other attractions. Period features and interesting artefacts relating to Winston Churchill are incorporated into smart contemporary design and up-to-date technology. Public areas include the Piano Bar & Restaurant, where innovative menus feature high quality, local produce.

Rooms: 32 (4 family) (5 GF) **Facilities:** WiFi 🎵 Xmas New Year **Conf:** Class 50 Board 30 Thtr 100 **Services:** Lift Night porter **Parking:** 40 **Notes:** Civ Wed 70

Marmadukes Town House Hotel

★★★★ 75% TOWN HOUSE HOTEL

4-5 St Peters Grove, Bootham, YO30 6AQ - **tel:** 01904 640101
email: reservations@marmadukestownhousehotelyork.com
web: www.marmadukestownhousehotelyork.com
dir: *A1036 signed York for approx 6m past train station then signed Inner Ring Rd. Over Lendal bridge, at lights left onto A19 Bootham Bar for 0.4m, right into St Peters Grove*

Set in secluded gardens, this Georgian hotel has free WiFi and luxurious rooms with handmade beds. Marmadukes Town House Hotel is just a 10-minute walk from York Minster, the Shambles and the Theatre Royal. The rooms are individually decorated with antique furniture and Egyptian linens, and all have tea- and coffee-making facilities, flatscreen TV/DVD player and stylish bathrooms with designer toiletries. Guests can relax in the elegant lounge bar or leafy garden. There is also a sun lounge with antique sofas, where traditional full English breakfasts are served daily.

Rooms: 21 (11 annexe) (2 family) (3 GF) 🐾 **S** £45–£139; **D** £59–£309 (incl. bkfst)*
Facilities: FTV WiFi **Conf:** Class 25 Board 25 Thtr 50 **Services:** Night porter
Parking: 14 **Notes:** Civ Wed 50

Novotel York Centre

★★★★ 75% HOTEL

Fishergate, YO10 4FD - **tel:** 01904 611660
email: H0949@accor.com **web:** www.novotel.com
dir: *A19 north to city centre, hotel set back on left*

Set just outside the ancient city walls, this modern, family-friendly hotel is conveniently located for visitors to the city. Bedrooms feature bathrooms with a separate toilet room, plus excellent desk space and sofa beds. Four rooms are equipped for less able guests. The hotel's facilities include indoor and outdoor children's play areas and an indoor pool.

Rooms: 124 (124 family) **Facilities:** FTV WiFi HL Xmas New Year
Conf: Class 100 Board 120 Thtr 210 **Services:** Lift Night porter **Parking:** 140

Best Western Plus Monkbar Hotel

★★★★ 72% HOTEL

Monkbar, YO31 7JA - **tel:** 01904 638086
email: sales@monkbarhotel.co.uk **web:** www.monkbarhotel.co.uk
dir: *A64 onto A1079 to city, turn right at city walls, take middle lane at lights. Hotel on right*

This smart hotel enjoys a prominent position adjacent to the city walls, and is just a few minutes' walk from York Minster. Recent refurbishments and extensions have led to improvements in both rooms and conference facilities. Monkbar offers individually-styled bedrooms that are well equipped for both business and leisure guests. Spacious public areas include comfortable lounges, a traditional Yorkshire bar, an airy restaurant and new state-of-the-art meeting and training facilities.

Rooms: 125 (2 GF) 🐾 **S** £90–£184.50; **D** £99–£193.50 (incl. bkfst)*
Facilities: FTV WiFi Xmas New Year **Conf:** Class 100 Board 60 Thtr 250 Del from £130 **Services:** Lift Night porter **Notes:** LB Civ Wed 150

Mercure York Fairfield Hotel

★★★★ 72% COUNTRY HOUSE HOTEL

Shipton Road, Skelton, YO30 1XW - **tel:** 01904 670222 & 0844 815 9038
(Calls cost 7p per minute plus your phone company's access charge)
email: gm.mercureyorkfairfieldmanor@jupiterhotels.co.uk **web:** www.mercureyork.co.uk
dir: *Exit A1237 onto A19, hotel 0.5m on left*

This stylish Georgian mansion stands in six acres of private grounds on the outskirts of the city. The contemporary bedrooms, styled in reds or blues, have broadband access and flatscreen TVs; some rooms have garden and courtyard views. The suites have either four-poster or king-size beds and a separate seating area. Kilby's Restaurant serves bistro food, and 24-hour room service is available. There are good conference facilities.

Rooms: 89 (20 family) (24 GF) 🐾 **Facilities:** WiFi HL Use of nearby health club Xmas New Year **Conf:** Class 60 Board 60 Thtr 180 **Services:** Lift Night porter **Parking:** 120 **Notes:** Civ Wed 180

The Parsonage Country House Hotel

★★★ 85% COUNTRY HOUSE HOTEL

York Road, YO19 6LF - **tel:** 01904 728111
email: reservations@parsonagehotel.co.uk **web:** www.parsonagehotel.co.uk

(For full entry see Escrick)

Mount Royale

★★★ 81% HOTEL

The Mount, YO24 1GU - **tel:** 01904 628856
email: reservations@mountroyale.co.uk **web:** www.mountroyale.co.uk
dir: *W on A1036, 0.5m after racecourse. Hotel on right after lights*

This friendly hotel, a listed building from the 1830s, offers comfortable bedrooms in a variety of styles, several leading onto the delightful gardens. Public rooms include a lounge, a meeting room and a cosy bar; the hotel has an outdoor pool, a sauna and a hot tub plus a beauty therapist. There is a separate restaurant called Oxo's on The Mount, and a cocktail lounge overlooking the gardens. Limited car parking is also available.

Rooms: 24 (3 family) (6 GF) 🐾 **S** £95–£165; **D** £135–£255 (incl. bkfst)*
Facilities: Spa FTV WiFi 🦵 supervised Sauna Steam room Outdoor hot tub Xmas New Year Child facilities **Conf:** Class 16 Board 22 Thtr 35 Del £155 **Services:** Night porter **Parking:** 24 **Notes:** LB

Park Inn by Radisson York City Centre

★★★ 81% HOTEL

North Street, YO1 6JF - **tel:** 01904 459988
email: reservations.york@rezidorparkinn.com **web:** www.parkinn.co.uk/hotel-york
dir: *In York city centre, less than 1m from train station*

Boasting spectacular views over the River Ouse in the heart of York, this hotel is just minutes away from all the attractions of this historic, walled city. There are impressive conference rooms and leisure facilities, and the RBG Lounge Bar, overlooking the river, serves a wide-ranging menu throughout the day. Private parking is available.

Rooms: 200 **Facilities:** FTV WiFi **Conf:** Class 150 Board 75 Thtr 400 **Services:** Lift Night porter Air con

York Pavilion Hotel

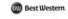

★★★ 78% HOTEL

45 Main Street, Fulford, YO10 4PJ - **tel:** 01904 622099
email: reservations@yorkpavilionhotel.com **web:** www.yorkpavilionhotel.com
dir: *Exit A64, York ring rd at A19 junct towards York. Hotel 0.5m on right opposite Pavilion Court*

York Pavilion Hotel is an attractive Georgian hotel situated in its own grounds. All the bedrooms are individually designed to a high specification; some are in the old house and some in the converted stables set around a garden terrace. There is a comfortable lounge, a conference centre and an inviting brasserie-style restaurant with a regularly changing menu.

Rooms: 62 (5 annexe) (4 family) (11 GF) ↟ **S** £95–£125; **D** £125–£165 (incl. bkfst)
Facilities: FTV WiFi ↯ Xmas New Year **Conf:** Class 80 Board 50 Thtr 150 Del from £145 **Services:** Night porter **Parking:** 45 **Notes:** LB Civ Wed 120

Middletons Hotel

★★★ 74% HOTEL

Skeldergate, YO1 6DS - **tel:** 01904 611570
email: reception@middletonsyork.co.uk **web:** www.middletonsyork.co.uk
dir: *From A64 Leeds, A1036 towards city centre. Right at City Walls lights, keep left, 1st left before bridge, then 1st left into Cromwell Rd. Hotel on right*

This hotel has been created from several listed buildings and is very well located in the centre of York. Bedrooms are comfortably equipped. Among its amenities is a bar-lounge and a dining room where a satisfying range of food is served. An extensive fitness club is also available along with private parking.

Rooms: 56 (19 annexe) (6 family) (17 GF) ↟ **S** £59–£120; **D** £69–£160*
Facilities: FTV WiFi ↯ Gym Fitness centre Beauty treatments Massage **Conf:** Class 36 Board 36 Thtr 60 **Services:** Night porter **Parking:** 40 **Notes:** LB Civ Wed 60

Best Western Kilima Hotel

Ⓤ

129 Holgate Road, YO24 4AZ - **tel:** 01904 625787
email: sales@kilima.co.uk
dir: *Please phone for directions*

Currently the rating for this establishment is not confirmed. This may be due to a change of ownership or because it has only recently joined the AA rating scheme.

Rooms: 26 **S** £65–£200; **D** £130–£220 (incl. bkfst)*

Premier Inn York City (Blossom St North)

BUDGET HOTEL

20 Blossom Street, YO24 1AJ - **tel:** 0871 527 9196
(Calls cost 13p per minute plus your phone company's access charge)
web: www.premierinn.com
dir: *12m from A1 junct 47, off A59*

High quality, budget accommodation ideal for both families and business travellers. Spacious, en suite bedrooms feature free WiFi and tea and coffee making facilities, and in most hotels, Freeview TV is also available. The adjacent family restaurant features a wide and varied menu.

Rooms: 102

Premier Inn York City (Blossom St South)

BUDGET HOTEL

28-40 Blossom Street, YO24 1AJ - **tel:** 0871 527 9194 (Calls cost 13p per minute plus your phone company's access charge) **web:** www.premierinn.com
dir: *From S, E & W: A64, A1036 (signed York West). From N: A1 (or A19), A59, follow city centre signs. At lights left onto A1036. Hotel on left just after cinema. NB no drop-off point, parking at NCP, Queens St*

Rooms: 91

Premier Inn York North (Maritime Park)

BUDGET HOTEL

Shipton Road, YO30 5PA - **tel:** 0871 527 9198
(Calls cost 13p per minute plus your phone company's access charge)
web: www.premierinn.com
dir: *From A1237 (ring road), A19 (Shipton Road South) signed York Centre. Hotel on right in Clifton Park*

Rooms: 49

Premier Inn York North West (Ring Road)

BUDGET HOTEL

White Rose Close, York Business Park, YO26 6RL - **tel:** 0871 527 9200
(Calls cost 13p per minute plus your phone company's access charge)
web: www.premierinn.com
dir: *On A1237 between A19 Thirsk road & A59 Harrogate road*

Rooms: 82

Premier Inn York South West (A64)

BUDGET HOTEL

Bilbrough Top, Colton, YO23 3PP - **tel:** 0871 527 9202 (Calls cost 13p per minute plus your phone company's access charge) **web:** www.premierinn.com
dir: *On A64 between Tadcaster & York*

Rooms: 62

Y

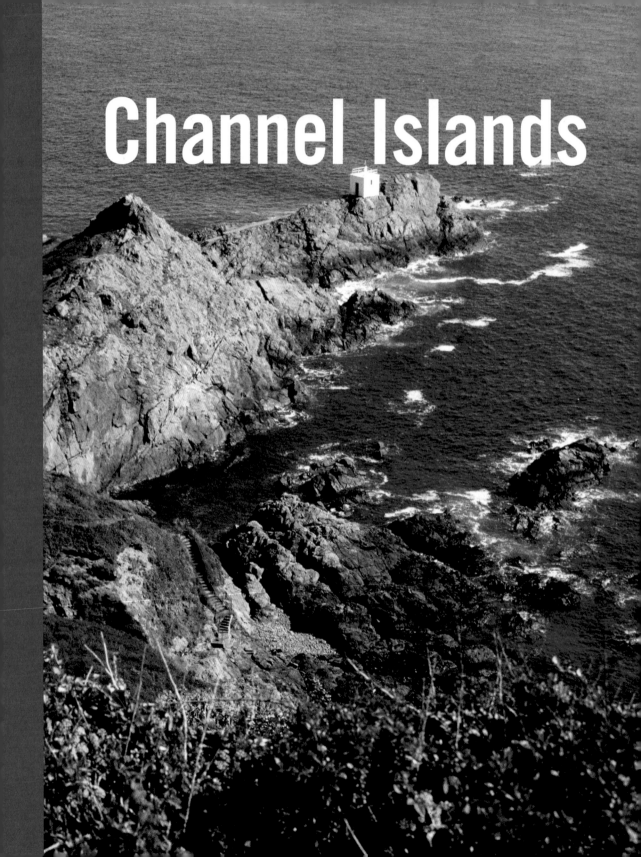

Channel Islands

GUERNSEY

CASTEL
Map 24

Le Friquet Hotel

★★★ 79% HOTEL

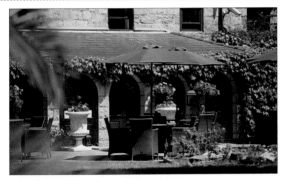

Rue du Friquet, GY5 7ST - tel: 01481 256509
email: stay@lefriquethotel.co.uk **web:** www.lefriquethotel.com
dir: *Please phone for directions*

Le Friquet (French for 'sparrow') is located in a quiet setting with extensive grounds, an outdoor swimming pool and plenty of private parking. The hotel offers traditional and comfortably appointed accommodation; all room are well equipped with a good range of amenities, including WiFi. Guests can enjoy alfresco dining on the terrace or in the main Lobster and Grill Restaurant which is contemporary in style, and the only hotel in Guernsey to have a live lobster tank. Great hospitality and service can be expected from the friendly team.

Rooms: 33 (1 family) (3 GF) **S** £61.50–£85; **D** £93–£136 (incl. bkfst)* **Facilities:** STV FTV WiFi ↕ ⚘ Xmas New Year **Services:** Air con **Parking:** 40

FOREST
Map 24

Le Chene Hotel

★★ 76% HOTEL

Forest Road, GY8 0AH - tel: 01481 235566
email: info@lechene.co.uk **web:** www.lechene.co.uk
dir: *Between airport & St Peter Port. From airport left to St Peter Port. Hotel on right after 1st lights*

This Victorian manor house is well located for guests wishing to explore Guernsey's spectacular south coast. The building has been skilfully extended to house a range of well-equipped, modern bedrooms. There is a swimming pool, a cosy cellar bar and a varied range of enjoyable freshly-cooked dishes at dinner.

Rooms: 26 (2 family) (1 GF) (1 smoking) **Facilities:** WiFi ⚘ Library Outdoor sauna **Parking:** 20 **Notes:** LB Closed Oct-Mar

ST MARTIN
Map 24

INSPECTOR'S CHOICE

Bella Luce Hotel, Restaurant & Spa

★★★★ @@ SMALL HOTEL

La Fosse, GY4 6EB - tel: 01481 238764
email: wakeup@bellalucehotel.com **web:** www.bellalucehotel.com
dir: *From airport, turn left to St Martin. At 3rd set of lights continue 30yds, turn right, straight on to hotel*

This delightful hotel is both contemporary and luxurious; the stylish bedrooms have comfortable beds and designer furnishings, superb bathrooms and up-to-the-minute technology. Public rooms have many interesting features and lots of soft settees, and nooks and crannies where guests can relax. The restaurant offers the best produce Guernsey can provide, and chef has a keen sense of adventure. Staff are friendly and attentive, and make sure guests feel welcome.

Rooms: 23 (4 family) (2 GF) **S** £120–£168; **D** £126–£175 (incl. bkfst)* **Facilities:** Spa STV FTV WiFi ↕ ⚘ ⚲ 18 Fishing Gym Sauna ♫ Xmas New Year **Conf:** Class 18 Board 25 Thtr 40 Del from £146 **Services:** Night porter Air con **Parking:** 33 **Notes:** LB Closed 1st 2 weeks Jan

ST MARTIN *continued*

La Barbarie Hotel

★★★ 82% ⦿ HOTEL

Saints Road, Saints Bay, GY4 6ES - **tel:** 01481 235217
email: reservations@labarbariehotel.com **web:** www.labarbariehotel.com
dir: *At lights in St Martin take road to Saints Bay. Hotel on right at end of Saints Rd*

This former priory dates back to the 17th century and retains much charm and style. Staff help to create a very friendly and attentive atmosphere, and the modern facilities offer guests a relaxing stay. Excellent choices and fresh local ingredients form the basis of the interesting menus in the attractive restaurant and bar.

Rooms: 35 (8 GF) ⌇ **S** £73–£140; **D** £96–£169 (incl. bkfst)* **Facilities:** STV WiFi ↖
Parking: 50 **Notes:** LB Closed Nov-Feb

Hotel Jerbourg

★★★ 79% HOTEL

Jerbourg Point, GY4 6BJ - **tel:** 01481 238826
email: stay@hoteljerbourg.com **web:** www.hoteljerbourg.com
dir: *From airport turn left to St Martin, right at filter, straight on at lights, hotel at end of road on right*

This hotel boasts excellent sea views from its cliff-top location. Public areas are smartly appointed and include an extensive bar/lounge and bright conservatory-style restaurant. In addition to the fairly extensive carte, a daily-changing menu is available. Bedrooms are well presented and comfortable, and the luxury bay rooms are generally more spacious.

Rooms: 32 (4 family) (5 GF) **Facilities:** FTV WiFi ↖ Petanque Xmas New Year
Parking: 50 **Notes:** LB Closed 5 Jan-1 Mar

La Villette Hotel & Leisure Suite

★★★ 79% HOTEL

GY4 6QG - **tel:** 01481 235292
email: reservations@lavillettehotel.co.uk **web:** www.lavillettehotel.co.uk
dir: *Turn left from airport. Follow road past La Trelade Hotel. Take next right, hotel on left*

Set in spacious grounds, this peacefully located, family-run hotel has a friendly atmosphere. The well-equipped bedrooms are spacious and comfortable. Live music is a regular feature in the large bar, while in the separate restaurant a fixed-price menu is provided. Residents have use of the excellent indoor leisure facilities, and there are also beauty treatments and a hairdressing salon.

Rooms: 35 (3 family) (14 GF) ⌇ **Facilities:** FTV WiFi ⦾ supervised ↖ Gym Steam room Leisure suite Beauty salon Hairdresser Petanque Xmas New Year
Conf: Board 40 Thtr 80 **Services:** Lift **Parking:** 50

Saints Bay Hotel

★★★ 76% HOTEL

Icart Road, GY4 6JG - **tel:** 01481 238888
email: info@saintsbayhotel.com **web:** www.saintsbayhotel.com
dir: *From St Martin take Saints Rd into Icart Rd*

Ideally situated in an elevated position near Icart Point headland and above the fishing harbour at Saints Bay, this hotel has superb views. The spacious public rooms include a smart lounge bar, a first-floor lounge and a smart conservatory restaurant that overlooks the swimming pool. Bedrooms are pleasantly decorated and thoughtfully equipped.

Rooms: 35 (1 family) (13 GF) **S** £52–£82; **D** £74–£134 (incl. bkfst)* **Facilities:** FTV WiFi ↖ Xmas New Year **Parking:** 15

ST PETER PORT   Map 24

The Old Government House Hotel & Spa

THE RED CARNATION HOTEL COLLECTION

★★★★★ 82% ⦿ ◨ HOTEL

St Ann's Place, GY1 2NU - **tel:** 01481 724921
email: ogh@theoghhotel.com **web:** www.theoghhotel.com
dir: *At junct of St Julian's Ave & St Ann's Place*

Affectionately known as the OGH, this is one of the island's leading hotels. Located in the heart of St Peter Port, it is the perfect base from which to explore Guernsey and the other islands of the Bailiwick. Bedrooms vary in size but all are comfortable, and offer high quality accommodation. There is an indulgent health club and spa, and the eating options are the OGH Brasserie, and the award-winning Governor's that offers local produce with a French twist.

Rooms: 62 (3 annexe) (6 family) ⌇ **S** £187–£600; **D** £187–£600 (incl. bkfst)*
Facilities: Spa STV WiFi ⬗ HL ↖ Gym Steam room Sauna Relaxation room ♫ Xmas New Year **Conf:** Class 69 Board 66 Thtr 200 Del from £247 **Services:** Lift Night porter Air con **Parking:** 20

The Duke of Richmond Hotel

THE RED CARNATION HOTEL COLLECTION

★★★★ 82% ⦿ HOTEL

Cambridge Park, GY1 1UY - **tel:** 01481 726221
email: manager@dukeofrichmond.com **web:** www.dukeofrichmond.com
dir: *On corner of Cambridge Park & L'Hyvreuse Ave, opposite leisure centre*

The luxurious Duke of Richmond Hotel offers unparalleled service in elegant surroundings. Located just up the hill from the bustling town centre and an easy stroll from the beautiful harbour, the position is peaceful, overlooking a park with views across the town to the sea beyond. Guests will be warmly welcomed with exceptional service that supports the ethos "No request is too large, no detail too small".

Rooms: 73 (11 family) S £159–£478; D £159–£478 (incl. bkfst)* **Facilities:** STV WiFi HL Xmas New Year **Conf:** Class 80 Board 40 Thtr 300 Del from £249 **Services:** Lift Night porter Air con **Parking:** 5

St Pierre Park Hotel, Spa and Golf Resort

★★★★ 77% HOTEL

Rohais, GY1 1FD - tel: 01481 728282 **e**
mail: reservations.stpierrepark@handpicked.co.uk **web:** www.handpickedhotels.co.uk
dir: *From harbour straight over rdbt, up hill through 3 sets of lights. Right at filter, to lights. Straight ahead, hotel 100mtrs on left*

Peacefully located on the outskirts of town in 45 acres of grounds, this well established hotel also features a 9-hole golf course. Most of the bedrooms overlook the pleasant gardens and have either a balcony or a terrace. Public areas include a choice of restaurants and a stylish bar which opens onto a spacious terrace, overlooking an elegant water feature.

Rooms: 131 (5 family) (17 GF) **Facilities:** Spa STV FTV WiFi HL 9 Putting green Gym Exercise studio with classes Children's playground Crazy golf Xmas **Conf:** Class 120 Board 70 Thtr 200 **Services:** Lift Night porter **Parking:** 150

Best Western Hotel de Havelet

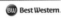

★★★ 84% HOTEL

Havelet, GY1 1BA - tel: 01481 722199
email: stay@dehaveletguernsey.com **web:** www.dehaveletguernsey.com
dir: *From airport follow signs for St Peter Port through St. Martins. At bottom of 'Val de Terres' hill turn left at top of hill, hotel on right*

This extended Georgian hotel looks over the harbour to Castle Cornet. Many of the well-equipped bedrooms are set around a pretty colonial-style courtyard. Day rooms in the original building have period elegance; the restaurant and bar are on the other side of the car park in converted stables.

Rooms: 34 (4 family) (9 GF) S £85–£98; D £120–£186 (incl. bkfst & dinner)* **Facilities:** FTV WiFi Sauna Steam room Xmas New Year **Conf:** Class 20 Board 18 Thtr 30 **Parking:** 40 **Notes:** LB

Les Rocquettes Hotel

★★★ 82% HOTEL

Les Gravees, GY1 1RN - tel: 01481 722146
email: stay@lesrocquettesguernsey.com **web:** www.lesrocquettesguernsey.com
dir: *From ferry terminal take 2nd exit at rdbt, through 5 sets of lights. After 5th lights into Les Gravees. Hotel on right opposite church*

This late 18th-century country mansion is in a good location close to St Peter Port and Beau Sejour. Bedrooms come in three grades – Deluxe, Superior and Standard,

but all have plenty of useful facilities. Guests can eat in Oaks restaurant and bar. The hotel has attractive lounge areas on three levels; there is a health suite with a gym and swimming pool with an integrated children's pool.

Rooms: 51 (5 family) S £62–£130; D £104–£160 (incl. bkfst)* **Facilities:** FTV WiFi supervised Gym Beauty treatment room Sauna Steam room Whirlpool Xmas New Year **Conf:** Class 60 Board 60 Thtr 100 Del from £120 **Services:** Lift Night porter **Parking:** 60 **Notes:** LB

Best Western Moores Hotel

★★★ 81% HOTEL

Pollet, GY1 1WH - tel: 01481 724452
email: stay@mooresguernsey.com **web:** www.mooresguernsey.com
dir: *Left at airport, follow signs to St Peter Port. Fort Road to seafront, straight on, turn left before rdbt, to hotel*

This elegant granite town house is situated in the heart of St Peter Port among its shops and amenities. Public rooms feature a smart conservatory restaurant which leads out onto a first-floor terrace for alfresco dining; there is also a choice of lounges and bars as well as a patisserie. Bedrooms are pleasantly decorated and thoughtfully equipped.

Rooms: 49 (3 annexe) (8 family) S £60–£140; D £120–£270 (incl. bkfst)* **Facilities:** FTV WiFi Gym Sauna Xmas New Year **Conf:** Class 20 Board 18 Thtr 40 Del from £125 **Services:** Lift Night porter **Notes:** LB

Duke of Normandie Hotel

★★★ 81% HOTEL

Lefebvre Street, GY1 2JP - tel: 01481 721431
email: enquiries@dukeofnormandie.com **web:** www.dukeofnormandie.com
dir: *From harbour rdbt St Julians Ave, 3rd left into Anns Place, continue to right, up hill, then left into Lefebvre St, archway entrance on right*

The Duke of Normandie is an 18th-century hotel situated close to the high street and just a short stroll from the harbour. Bedrooms vary in style and include some that have their own access from the courtyard. Public areas feature a smart brasserie, a contemporary lounge-lobby area and a busy bar with beams and an open fireplace.

Rooms: 37 (17 annexe) (8 GF) S £39–£89; D £79–£169 (incl. bkfst) **Facilities:** STV WiFi **Parking:** 10 **Notes:** LB

VALE — Map 24

Peninsula Hotel

★★★ 80% HOTEL

Les Dicqs, GY6 8JP - tel: 01481 248400
email: peninsula@guernsey.net **web:** www.peninsulahotelguernsey.com
dir: *On coast road at Grand Havre Bay*

Adjacent to the sandy beach and set in five acres of grounds, this modern hotel provides comfortable accommodation. Bedrooms have an additional sofa bed to suit families and good workspace for the business traveller. Both fixed-price and carte menus are served in the restaurant, or guests can eat informally in the bar.

Rooms: 99 (99 family) (27 GF) S £71–£87; D £109–£141 (incl. bkfst)* **Facilities:** STV WiFi Putting green Petanque Children's playground Table Tennis Xmas New Year **Conf:** Class 100 Board 105 Thtr 250 **Services:** Lift Night porter **Parking:** 120 **Notes:** LB Closed Jan

HERM

HERM — Map 24

White House Hotel

★★★ 84% ◉◉ HOTEL

GY1 3HR - **tel:** 01481 750075
email: hotel@herm.com **web:** www.herm.com
dir: *Transport to island by catamaran ferry from St Peter Port, Guernsey*

Enjoying a unique island setting, this attractive hotel is just 20 minutes from Guernsey by sea. Set in well-tended gardens, the hotel offers neatly decorated bedrooms, located in either the main house or adjacent cottages; the majority of rooms have sea views. Guests can relax in one of several lounges, enjoy a drink in one of two bars and choose from two dining options.

Rooms: 40 (23 annexe) (23 family) (7 GF) **Facilities:** WiFi ↴ ◔ ↯ Fishing trips Yacht & motor boat charters **Conf:** Board 10 Thtr 50 **Notes:** LB Closed Nov-Mar

JERSEY

GOREY — Map 24

The Moorings Hotel & Restaurant

★★★ 79% ◉◉ HOTEL

Gorey Pier, JE3 6EW - **tel:** 01534 853633
email: reservations@themooringshotel.com **web:** www.themooringshotel.com
dir: *At foot of Mont Orgueil Castle*

Enjoying an enviable position by the harbour, the heart of this hotel is the restaurant where a selection of menus offers an extensive choice of dishes. Other public areas include a bar, coffee shop and a comfortable first-floor residents' lounge. Bedrooms at the front have a fine view of the harbour; three have access to a balcony. A small sun terrace at the back of the hotel is also available to guests.

Rooms: 15 ↷ **Facilities:** FTV WiFi ↳ Xmas New Year **Conf:** Class 20 Board 20 Thtr 20 **Services:** Night porter **Notes:** LB

The Dolphin Hotel and Restaurant

★★ 79% HOTEL

Gorey Pier, JE3 6EW - **tel:** 01534 853370
email: dolphinhoteljersey@outlook.com **web:** www.dolphinhoteljersey.com
dir: *At foot of Mont Orgueil Castle*

Located on the main harbour at Gorey, many bedrooms at this popular hotel enjoy views over the sea and beaches. The relaxed and friendly style is apparent from the moment of arrival, and the busy restaurant and bar are popular with locals and tourists alike. Outdoor seating is available in season, and fresh fish and seafood are included on the menu.

Rooms: 16 **S** £47.50–£62; **D** £95–£124 (incl. bkfst)* **Facilities:** STV WiFi ↳ 𝄐 Xmas New Year **Conf:** Class 20 Board 20 Thtr 20 **Services:** Night porter **Notes:** LB

ROZEL — Map 24

Château la Chaire

★★★★ 83% ◉◉ HOTEL

Rozel Bay, JE3 6AJ - **tel:** 01534 863354
email: res@chateau-la-chaire.co.uk **web:** www.chateau-la-chaire.co.uk
dir: *From St Helier on B38 turn left in village by Rozel Bay Inn, hotel 100yds on right*

Built as a gentleman's residence in 1843, Château la Chaire is a haven of peace and tranquillity, set in a secluded wooded valley. Picturesque Rozel Harbour is within easy walking distance, and the house is surrounded by terraced gardens and woods. The helpful staff deliver high standards of guest care, and imaginative dishes, making the best use of local produce, are served in the oak-panelled dining room, the conservatory, or on the terrace when the weather permits. Bedroom and suite styles and sizes vary, but all are beautifully appointed and include many nice touches such as towelling robes, slippers, flowers and DVD players. Free WiFi is available throughout the hotel.

Rooms: 14 (2 family) (1 GF) ↷ **S** £95–£125; **D** £155–£225 (incl. bkfst)* **Facilities:** FTV WiFi ↳ Xmas New Year **Conf:** Class 20 Board 20 Thtr 20 **Services:** Night porter **Parking:** 30 **Notes:** LB No children 7yrs Civ Wed 60

ST BRELADE — Map 24

L'Horizon Beach Hotel and Spa

★★★★ ◉◉ HOTEL

St Brelade's Bay, JE3 8EF - **tel:** 01534 743101
email: lhorizon@handpicked.co.uk **web:** www.handpickedhotels.co.uk/lhorizon
dir: *From airport right at rdbt towards St Brelades & Red Houses. Through Red Houses, hotel 300mtrs on right in centre of bay*

The combination of a truly wonderful setting on the golden sands of St Brelade's Bay, a relaxed atmosphere and excellent facilities prove a winning formula here. Bedrooms are stylish and have a real contemporary feel, all with plasma TVs and a host of extras; many have balconies or terraces and superb sea views. Spacious public areas include a spa and leisure club, a choice of dining options and relaxing lounges.

Rooms: 106 (1 family) (15 GF) ↷ **Facilities:** Spa STV FTV WiFi ↳ ⊛ ◔ Gym Windsurfing Water skiing Sailing Sauna Steam room 𝄐 Xmas New Year **Conf:** Class 100 Board 50 Thtr 250 **Services:** Lift Night porter **Parking:** 125 **Notes:** Civ Wed 240

INSPECTOR'S CHOICE

The Atlantic Hotel

★★★★ ⬢ HOTEL

Le Mont de la Pulente, JE3 8HE - **tel:** 01534 744101
email: info@theatlantichotel.com **web:** www.theatlantichotel.com
dir: From Petit Port turn right into Rue de la Sergente, right again, hotel signed

Adjoining the manicured fairways of La Moye championship golf course, this hotel enjoys a peaceful setting with breathtaking views over St Ouen's Bay. Stylish bedrooms look onto the course or the sea, and offer a blend of high quality and reassuring comfort. An air of understated luxury is apparent throughout, and the attentive service achieves the perfect balance of friendliness and professionalism. The Ocean Restaurant uses the best island produce to create outstanding and impeccably modern cuisine.

Rooms: 50 (8 GF) ⬡ **S** £110–£370; **D** £130–£640 (incl. bkfst)* **Facilities:** STV WiFi ⬡ ⬡ ⬡ Gym Saunas Xmas New Year **Conf:** Class 40 Board 20 Thtr 60 Del from £250 **Services:** Lift Night porter **Parking:** 60 **Notes:** LB Closed 3 Jan-1 Feb Civ Wed 80

St Brelade's Bay Hotel

★★★★ 81% HOTEL

JE3 8EF - **tel:** 01534 746141
email: info@stbreladesbayhotel.com **web:** www.stbreladesbayhotel.com
dir: SW corner of island

The hotel, set in five-acres of gardens, enjoys a fabulous location with unobstructed views overlooking St Brelade's Bay, and a sandy beach right on the doorstep. Bedrooms are beautifully presented and equipped to a very high standard. They include two-bedroom suites, family rooms and superb penthouse suites that have large balconies, and even telescopes. The relaxing public areas include a stylish, comfortable lounge along with a spacious bar. The gardens feature a pool area, terraces for relaxing and eating, and a tennis court. A superb leisure and fitness centre with state-of-the-art equipment is another attraction. Attentive friendly service is guaranteed in the elegant restaurant with its sea views.

Rooms: 77 (8 family) ⬡ **S** £92.50–£145; **D** £150–£250 (incl. bkfst)* **Facilities:** Spa FTV WiFi ⬡ ⬡ ⬡ Gym Beauty treatment rooms ♫ Xmas New Year **Conf:** Class 30 Board 12 Thtr 60 **Services:** Lift Night porter **Parking:** 90 **Notes:** Civ Wed 70

Highlands Hotel

★★★ 78% HOTEL

Corbiere, JE3 8HN - **tel:** 01534 744288
email: enquiries@highlandshotel.com **web:** www.highlandshotel.com
dir: 3m from Jersey airport. Very close to Corbiere Lighthouse

This hotel has an enviable location, ideally suited to touring and walking the island, close to the coast and beaches of St Brelade's Bay. There are several leisure facilities, including a swimming pool and games room. The restaurant and many of the bedrooms have delightful views. Bedrooms and bathrooms are very pleasantly appointed in a bright and attractive style.

Rooms: 50 (1 family) (11 GF) ⬡ **S** £70–£80; **D** £110–£160 (incl. bkfst)* **Facilities:** FTV WiFi ⬡ ⬡ Gym **Services:** Lift Night porter **Parking:** 60 **Notes:** LB No children 5yrs Closed Oct-Apr

Beau Rivage Hotel

★★★ 76% HOTEL

St Brelade's Bay, JE3 8EF - **tel:** 01534 745983
email: beau@welcome.je **web:** www.jersey.co.uk/hotels/beau
dir: Sea side of coast road in centre of St Brelade's Bay, 1.5m S of airport

With direct access to one of Jersey's most popular beaches, residents and non-residents alike are welcome to this hotel's bar and terrace. All of the well-equipped bedrooms are now suites, most have wonderful sea views, and some have the bonus of balconies. Residents have a choice of lounges, plus a sun deck exclusively for their use. A range of dishes, featuring English and Continental cuisine, is available from a selection of menus in either the bar or the main bistro restaurant.

Rooms: 12 (12 family) (12 smoking) ⬡ **Facilities:** STV FTV WiFi Games room **Services:** Lift Night porter **Parking:** 16 **Notes:** RS Nov-Mar Restaurant & bar open to demand Civ Wed 80

ST CLEMENT — Map 24

Pontac House Hotel

★★★ 78% HOTEL

St Clements Bay, JE2 6SE - **tel:** 01534 857771
email: admin@pontachouse.com **web:** www.pontachouse.com
dir: 10 mins from St Helier

Overlooking the sandy beach of St Clement's Bay, this hotel is located on the south eastern corner of Jersey. Many guests return on a regular basis to experience the friendly, relaxed style of service. The bedrooms, most with splendid views, are comfortable and well equipped. Varied menus, featuring local seafood, are on offer each evening.

Rooms: 27 (1 family) (5 GF) ⬡ **Facilities:** FTV WiFi ⬡ **Parking:** 35 **Notes:** Closed Dec-1 Apr

ST HELIER — Map 24

Grand Jersey

★★★★★ 83% ⬡⬡⬡ HOTEL

Hand PICKED HOTELS — BUILT FOR PLEASURE

The Esplanade, JE2 3QA - **tel:** 01534 722301
email: reservations.grandjersey@handpicked.co.uk
web: www.handpickedhotels.co.uk/grandjersey
dir: Located on St Helier seafront. 15 mins from airport

A local landmark, the Grand Jersey has pleasant views across St Aubin's Bay to the front, and the bustling streets of St Helier to the rear. The hotel is elegant and contemporary in design with a real touch of grandeur throughout. The air-conditioned bedrooms, including six suites, come in a variety of designs, but all have luxurious beds, ottomans and LCD TVs. The spacious public areas, many looking out onto the bay, include the very popular Champagne Lounge, Victoria's brasserie, and the impressive and intimate Tassili fine-dining restaurant. There is a large terrace for alfresco eating in the summer months, and the spa offers an indoor pool, gym and treatment rooms.

Rooms: 123 (18 family) (6 GF) ⬡ **S** £129–£255; **D** £139–£265 (incl. bkfst)* **Facilities:** Spa STV FTV WiFi ⬡ ⬡ Gym Xmas New Year **Conf:** Class 90 Board 50 Thtr 160 Del from £165 **Services:** Lift Night porter Air con **Parking:** 27 **Notes:** Civ Wed 180

ST HELIER *continued*

The Club Hotel & Spa

★★★★ ◉◉◉◉◉ TOWN HOUSE HOTEL

Green Street, JE2 4UH - **tel:** 01534 876500
email: reservations@theclubjersey.com **web:** www.theclubjersey.com
dir: *5 mins walk from main shopping centre*

This swish, town-house hotel is conveniently located close to the centre of town and features stylish, contemporary decor throughout. All the guest rooms and suites have power showers and state-of-the-art technology including wide-screen LCD TV, DVD and CD systems. The choice of restaurants includes Bohemia, a sophisticated eating option that continues to offer truly outstanding cuisine. For relaxation there is an elegant spa with a luxurious range of treatments.

Rooms: 46 (4 family) (4 GF) **S** £445; **D** £445 (incl. bkfst) **Facilities:** Spa STV FTV WiFi ↻ ⓒ ↘ Steam room Salt cabin Hydrothermal bench Rasul room New Year **Conf:** Class 60 Board 34 Thtr 80 Del from £195 **Services:** Lift Night porter Air con **Parking:** 32 **Notes:** LB Closed 24-30 Dec Civ Wed 84

The Royal Yacht

★★★★ 84% ◉◉◉ HOTEL

The Weighbridge, JE2 3NF - **tel:** 01534 720511
email: reception@theroyalyacht.com **web:** www.theroyalyacht.com
dir: *In town centre, opposite marina & harbour*

Overlooking the marina and steam clock, The Royal Yacht is thought to be the oldest established hotel on the island. Although it has a long history, it is very

much a 21st-century hotel, with state-of-the-art technology in all the bedrooms and the two penthouse suites. There is a range of impressive dining options to suit all tastes, with Sirocco's Restaurant offering high quality local produce. In addition to a choice of bars and conference facilities, guests can enjoy the luxury spa with an indoor pool and gym.

The Royal Yacht

Rooms: 110 ⌁ **S** £112–£160; **D** £112–£750 (incl. bkfst)* **Facilities:** Spa STV WiFi ↻ ⓒ Gym ♫ Xmas New Year **Conf:** Class 70 Board 48 Thtr 400 **Services:** Lift Night porter Air con **Notes:** Civ Wed 250

See advert opposite

Pomme d'Or Hotel

★★★★ 80% HOTEL

Liberation Square, JE1 3UF - **tel:** 01534 880110
email: enquiries@pommedorhotel.com **web:** www.pommedorhotel.com
dir: *Opposite harbour*

This historic hotel overlooks Liberation Square and the marina, and offers comfortably furnished, well-equipped bedrooms. Popular with the business fraternity, a range of conference facilities and meeting rooms are available. Dining options include The Harbour Room Carvery and the café bar.

Rooms: 143 (3 family) ⌁ **Facilities:** STV FTV WiFi ↻ Free use of The Aquadome at The Merton Hotel Xmas New Year **Conf:** Class 100 Board 50 Thtr 220 **Services:** Lift Night porter Air con **Notes:** Civ Wed 100

Radisson Blu Waterfront Hotel, Jersey

★★★★ 80% HOTEL

The Waterfront, La Rue de L'Etau, JE2 3WF - **tel:** 01534 671100
email: info.jersey@radissonblu.com **web:** www.radissonblu.com/hotel-jersey
dir: *Follow signs to St Helier. From A2 follow signs to harbour. At rdbt just before harbour take 2nd exit, continue to hotel*

Most of the bedrooms at this purpose-built hotel have fabulous views of the coastline. Facilities include a popular brasserie, cocktail bar, lounges, indoor heated pool, gym, sauna, and steam room. A wide range of meeting rooms provides conference facilities for delegates.

Rooms: 195 ⌁ **Facilities:** Spa STV FTV WiFi ↻ HL ⓒ Gym Sauna Steam room Hair salon ♫ Xmas New Year **Conf:** Class 184 Board 30 Thtr 400 **Services:** Lift Night porter Air con **Parking:** 80 **Notes:** Civ Wed 400

★ ★ ★ ★

HOTEL · SPA · RESTAURANTS

Four star hotel. Five star service.

THREE RENOWNED RESTAURANTS, BEAUTIFUL ROOMS AND A LUXURIOUS SPA.

No wonder we're one of Jersey's favourite hotels - according to our guests who rate us 4.5/5 on Tripadvisor.com

★ ★ ★ ★

THE ROYAL YACHT

HOTEL · SPA · RESTAURANTS

WEIGHBRIDGE ST HELIER JERSEY C.I. JE2 3NF
TEL +44 (0)1534 720511 · RECEPTION@THEROYALYACHT.COM · WWW.THEROYALYACHT.COM

ST HELIER *continued*

Best Western Royal Hotel

★★★ 86% @ HOTEL

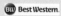

David Place, JE2 4TD - tel: 01534 726521
email: enquiries@royalhoteljersey.com **web:** www.royalhoteljersey.com
dir: *From Airport: In St Helier on Victoria Ave, left by Grand Hotel into Peirson Rd. Follow one-way system into Cheapside. Left at filter, follow Ring Rd signs into Rouge Bouillon (A14). At rdbt right, stay in right lane, right at lights into Midvale Rd. Through 2 lights, hotel on left*

This long established hotel is located in the centre of town and is within walking distance of the business district and shops. Seasons Restaurant offers a modern approach to dining, and the adjoining bar provides a relaxed venue for residents and locals alike. The bedrooms are individually styled. Extensive conference facilities are available.

Rooms: 89 (4 family) ⬨ **S** £84–£96; **D** £130–£145 (incl. bkfst)* **Facilities:** FTV WiFi ⬨ Xmas New Year **Conf:** Class 120 Board 80 Thtr 300 Del from £151 **Services:** Lift Night porter **Parking:** 15 **Notes:** LB Civ Wed 30

The Norfolk Lodge Hotel

★★★ 78% HOTEL

Rouge Bouillon, JE2 3ZB - tel: 01534 722950
email: admin@morvanhotels.com **web:** www.morvanhotels.com
dir: *Please phone for directions*

Centrally located and just a short walk from the main town, this popular hotel has a large number of regularly returning guests. Bedrooms are well decorated and equipped, and include some on the ground floor. In addition to an indoor swimming pool, the hotel offers regular evening entertainment during the main season. A range of well-prepared dishes is offered at dinner in the spacious restaurant.

Rooms: 101 (11 annexe) (8 family) (15 GF) ⬨ **S** £60–£83; **D** £93–£119 (incl. bkfst)* **Facilities:** FTV WiFi ⬨ Children's pool **Services:** Lift Night porter **Parking:** 40 **Notes:** LB Closed Nov-Mar

Hampshire Hotel

★★★ 77% @ HOTEL

53 Val Plaisant, JE2 4TB - tel: 01534 724115
email: info@hampshirehotel.je **web:** www.hampshirehotel.je
dir: *Please phone for directions*

Located a short walk from the town centre, this hotel features spacious public areas and comfortable bedrooms. There are premier, standard and family rooms, available. The spacious restaurant features seasonal changing dinner menus of popular dishes; at breakfast a wide choice is offered. The outdoor swimming pool and sun terrace are popular in the summer months.

Rooms: 42 (2 family) (5 GF) **S** £45–£70; **D** £59–£145 (incl. bkfst)* **Facilities:** STV WiFi ⬨ ⬨ Xmas New Year **Services:** Lift Night porter **Parking:** 30

The Monterey Hotel

★★★ 77% HOTEL

St Saviour's Road, JE2 7LA - tel: 01534 724762
email: bookings@morvanhotels.com **web:** www.morvanhotels.com
dir: *Please phone for directions*

Conveniently located for the town, this comfortable hotel has the added benefit of ample parking and a range of leisure facilities including an indoor pool. Bedrooms are well decorated and furnished, and include a number of superior rooms.

The relaxing bar area is open all day, and a good range of freshly prepared dishes is offered each evening.

Rooms: 73 (6 family) (9 GF) ⬨ **S** £66–£79; **D** £99–£125 (incl. bkfst)* **Facilities:** FTV WiFi ⬨ ⬨ ⬨ Gym Steam room Xmas New Year **Conf:** Class 12 Board 22 Thtr 40 **Services:** Lift Night porter **Parking:** 40 **Notes:** LB Closed Jan

Fort D'Auvergne Hotel

★★★ 76% HOTEL

Harve des Pas, JE2 4UQ - tel: 01534 879960
email: fort@morvanhotels.com **web:** www.morvanhotels.com
dir: *Please phone for directions*

The Fort D'Auvergne Hotel is bordered by the sea and sandy beach on two sides and occupies what is one of the best maritime positions in Jersey's capital. The hotel itself is traditional in style but offers modern amenities including an air-conditioned seafront table d'hôte restaurant and an outstanding luxury indoor pool complex with unrivalled views over the bay. There is only a pedestrian promenade separating the hotel from the sea shore. Dinner is served daily in the restaurant with tables benefiting from uninterrupted sea views.

Rooms: 65 (4 family) (9 GF) **S** £60–£73; **D** £93–£119 (incl. bkfst)* **Facilities:** FTV WiFi ⬨ ⬨ ⬨ **Services:** Lift Night porter **Notes:** Closed 16 Oct-20 Apr

The Hotel Revere

★★★ 75% HOTEL

Kensington Place, JE2 3PA - tel: 01534 611111
email: reservations@revere.co.uk **web:** www.revere.co.uk
dir: *From Esplanade left after Grand Hotel*

Situated on the west side of the town and convenient for the centre and harbour side, this hotel dates back to the 17th century and retains many period features. The style here is engagingly different, and bedrooms are individually decorated. There are three dining options and a small sun terrace.

Rooms: 56 (2 family) (4 GF) ⬨ **S** £45–£90; **D** £60–£160 (incl. bkfst)* **Facilities:** FTV WiFi ⬨ ⬨ **Services:** Night porter **Notes:** LB Closed Jan Civ Wed 50

Westhill Country Hotel

★★★ 75% COUNTRY HOUSE HOTEL

Mont-a-l'abbe, JE2 3HB - tel: 01534 723260
email: info@westhillhoteljersey.com **web:** www.westhillhoteljersey.com
dir: *See website for details*

Set in its own beautifully landscaped gardens, this hotel enjoys a prominent position just on the outskirts of St Helier. Service is attentive and guests are guaranteed a warm welcome and genuine hospitality throughout the hotel. The bedrooms are spacious and well equipped; several rooms have commanding views over the gardens to the countryside beyond. Public areas include a stylish lounge bar and popular restaurant. Free WiFi is available in the public areas and the swimming pool proves very popular with guests.

Rooms: 90 (20 family) (16 GF) ⬨ **S** £52.50–£80; **D** £105–£160 (incl. bkfst)* **Facilities:** FTV WiFi ⬨ Nature trail Childrens adventure play area ⬨ **Conf:** Class 80 Board 40 Thtr 60 **Services:** Night porter **Parking:** 75 **Notes:** LB Closed early Oct-early Apr Civ Wed 75

Apollo Hotel

★★★ 73% HOTEL

St Saviours Road, JE2 4GJ - tel: 01534 725441
email: reservations@huggler.com **web:** www.apollojersey.com
dir: *On St Saviours Rd at junct with La Motte St*

Centrally located, this popular hotel has a relaxed, informal atmosphere. Bedrooms are comfortably furnished and include useful extras. Many guests return regularly to enjoy the variety of leisure facilities, including an outdoor pool with water slide and indoor pool with separate jacuzzi. The cocktail bar is an ideal place for a pre-dinner drink.

Rooms: 85 (5 family) **S** £42–£150; **D** £49–£190 (incl. bkfst)* **Facilities:** FTV WiFi ⊗ supervised ⭑ supervised Gym Xmas New Year **Conf:** Class 100 Board 80 Thtr 150 Del from £85 **Services:** Lift Night porter **Parking:** 40

Millbrook House Hotel

★★ 77% HOTEL

Rue De Trachy, Millbrook, JE2 3JN - tel: 01534 733036
email: millbrook.house@jerseymail.co.uk **web:** www.millbrookhousehotel.com
dir: *1.5m W of town off A1*

Peacefully located in its own grounds, this small, personally-run hotel offers a friendly welcome and relaxing ambience. Bedrooms and bathrooms vary in size; many have pleasant, countryside views. In addition to outdoor seating in the warmer months, guests can relax in the library, maybe with a drink before dinner.

Rooms: 24 (2 family) (6 GF) **S** £40–£55; **D** £75–£95 (incl. bkfst)* **Facilities:** WiFi Putting green **Services:** Lift **Parking:** 20 **Notes:** Closed Oct-13 May

Sarum Hotel

★★ 70% METRO HOTEL

19/21 New St Johns Road, JE2 3LD - tel: 01534 758163
email: sarum@welcome.je **web:** www.jersey.co.uk/hotels/sarum
dir: *On NW edge of St Helier, 0.5m from town centre*

This hotel, just 600 yards from the beach, offers self-catering bedrooms and a number of suites. The friendly staff provide a warm welcome, and there is a spacious recreational lounge with pool tables, plasma-screen TV and internet access. A garden and outdoor pool are also available. Local restaurants are just a short walk away, and bar snacks are available throughout the day.

Rooms: 52 (5 annexe) (6 family) (2 GF) (52 smoking) **Facilities:** STV FTV WiFi Games room **Services:** Lift **Parking:** 10 **Notes:** LB

ST PETER

Map 24

HIGHLY RECOMMENDED

Greenhills Country Hotel

★★★★ 83% ⊛ COUNTRY HOUSE HOTEL

Mont de L'Ecole, JE3 7EL - tel: 01534 481042
email: reception@greenhillshotel.com **web:** www.greenhillshotel.com
dir: *Follow signs to St Peter's Village, the A11, turn into Le Mont de l'École, hotel on left*

Located in the rural centre of Jersey, this relaxing country-house hotel, with delightful gardens, has a lovely atmosphere. Bedrooms extend from the main building around the courtyard; all are modern and well equipped with satellite LED TVs, luxurious bathrobes, white duck down duvets and linen. A varied menu, based on fresh local produce, is served in the restaurant, and guests also have use of the Aquadome at the Merton Hotel.

Rooms: 33 (2 family) (11 GF) ⋔ **S** £71–£158; **D** £94–£211 (incl. bkfst)* **Facilities:** STV FTV WiFi ⌕ ⭑ Free use of Merton Hotel's Aquadome & Leisure Centre **Conf:** Class 12 Board 16 Thtr 20 Del from £130 **Services:** Night porter **Parking:** 40 **Notes:** LB Closed mid Dec-early Feb Civ Wed 40

ST SAVIOUR

Map 24

INSPECTOR'S CHOICE

Longueville Manor Hotel

★★★★★ ⊛⊛⊛ ⓢ HOTEL

JE2 7WF - tel: 01534 725501
email: info@longuevillemanor.com **web:** www.longuevillemanor.com
dir: *A3 E from St Helier towards Gorey. Hotel 1m on left*

Dating back to the 13th century, there is something very special about Longueville Manor, which is why so many guests return time and again. It is set in 16 acres of grounds including woodland walks, a spectacular rose garden, Victorian kitchen garden and a lake. Bedrooms have great style and individuality, boasting fresh flowers, fine embroidered bed linen and a host of extras. The very accomplished cuisine is also a highlight of any stay. In summer the pool and terrace are popular spots, plus there are also croquet and tennis courts. Families are particularly welcome, and there are extra activities arranged for children, including an adventure zone to explore. They also have their own menus and DVD library. The committed team of staff create a welcoming atmosphere and every effort is made to ensure a memorable stay.

Rooms: 30 (1 annexe) (7 GF) ⋔ **D** £195–£575 (incl. bkfst)* **Facilities:** Spa STV WiFi ⌕ ⭑ ⌕ ⤳ Gym Xmas New Year **Conf:** Class 30 Board 30 Thtr 45 **Services:** Lift Night porter **Parking:** 40 **Notes:** LB Civ Wed 40

SARK

SARK

Map 24

Stocks Hotel

★★★★ 81% ⊛⊛ SMALL HOTEL

GY10 1SD - tel: 01481 832001
email: reception@stockshotel.com **web:** www.stockshotel.com
dir: *Ferry to Guernsey then to Sark. Tractor bus from harbour to top of island. Chargeable horse & carriage available for transfer to hotel or walk –approx 20 mins*

The island of Sark is a delight. With no cars, transport is provided by horse and cart, tractor or bicycle, making this a very tranquil place. Stocks Hotel has spacious, comfortable rooms, which are attractively appointed. There are several lounges, and a cosy bar, as well as two dining options; the Brasserie is at the poolside and offers alfresco dining, while the main restaurant is more formal. The hotel gardens provide many ingredients for the kitchen, and the stables house the hotel's own team of cart pullers.

Rooms: 23 (11 annexe) (2 family) (3 GF) ⋔ **Facilities:** STV FTV WiFi ⌕ ⭑ Gym Massage treatment room Xmas New Year **Conf:** Class 70 Board 12 Thtr 70 **Notes:** LB Closed 3 Jan-1 Mar RS Mar & Nov-Dec only 12 bedrooms available

Scotland

A

ABERDEEN
City of Aberdeen

Map 23 NJ90

See also Aberdeen Airport

Mercure Aberdeen Ardoe House Hotel & Spa
★★★★ 81% HOTEL

South Deeside Road, Blairs, AB12 5YP - **tel:** 01224 860600
email: h6626@accor.com **web:** www.mercure.com/AberdeenHotels
dir: *4m W of city off B9077, follow for 3m, hotel on left*

From its elevated position on the banks of the River Dee, this 19th-century baronial-style mansion commands excellent countryside views. Beautifully decorated, thoughtfully equipped bedrooms are located in the main house, and in the more modern extension. Public rooms include a spa and leisure club, a cosy lounge and whisky bar and impressive function facilities.

Rooms: 120 (7 family) ✆ **S** £79–£159; **D** £119–£189 (incl. bkfst)* **Facilities:** Spa FTV WiFi ₪ HL ☺ supervised ☽ Gym Sauna Steam room Dance studio Xmas New Year **Conf:** Class 200 Board 150 Thtr 600 Del from £145 **Services:** Lift Night porter **Parking:** 200 **Notes:** LB Civ Wed 500

The Chester Hotel
★★★★ 80% HOTEL

59-63 Queens Road, AB15 4YP - **tel:** 01244 327777
email: enquiries@chester-hotel.com **web:** www.chester-hotel.com
dir: *From Aberdeen Airport follow signs to Perth A90, at Queens Rd rdbt take first exit left. Hotel is on the right*

The Chester Hotel has now benefited from a complete refurbishment. Bedrooms are modern and well equipped with lovely beds and quality bedding, along with useful extras for the modern traveller; robes, slippers and quality branded toiletries are provided as standard. Dining options include relaxed comfort food in the bar area or an award-winning restaurant providing high quality dishes using the best local produce. There is a small boutique spa with a well-equipped gym also available to residents. The hotel is ideally located for the city centre as well as the airport and numerous golf courses.

Rooms: 50 (6 annexe) (21 GF) ✆ **Facilities:** Spa STV FTV WiFi ₪ Gym ♫ Xmas New Year **Conf:** Class 80 Board 45 Thtr 220 **Services:** Lift Night porter **Parking:** 46 **Notes:** Civ Wed 200

Malmaison Aberdeen
★★★★ 76% HOTEL

49-53 Queens Road, AB15 4YP - **tel:** 01224 327370 & 0844 693 0649 (Calls cost 5p per minute plus your phone company's access charge)
email: info.aberdeen@malmaison.com **web:** www.malmaison.com
dir: *A90, 3rd exit into Queens Rd at 3rd rdbt, hotel on right*

Popular with business travellers and as a function venue, this well-established hotel lies east of the city centre. Public areas include an attractive reception lounge and an intimate restaurant featuring a Josper Grill, plus the modern bar which remains a popular choice for many regulars whether it be for a bar meal or bottle of wine from the extensive cellar. There are two styles of accommodation, with the superior rooms being particularly comfortable and well equipped.

Rooms: 79 (10 GF) ✆ **Facilities:** Spa STV FTV WiFi ₪ Gym Steam room Xmas New Year **Conf:** Class 12 Board 25 Thtr 30 **Services:** Lift Night porter Air con **Parking:** 30 **Notes:** Civ Wed 30

The Craighaar Hotel
★★★★ 75% HOTEL

Waterton Road, Bucksburn, AB21 9HS - **tel:** 01224 712275
email: info@craighaar.co.uk **web:** www.craighaarhotel.com
dir: *From A96 Airport/Inverness onto A947, hotel signed*

Conveniently located for the airport, this welcoming hotel is a popular base for business people and tourists alike. Guests can make use of a range of newly refurbished public areas including the popular brasserie and a welcoming lounge bar with open fire. All bedrooms are well equipped, plus there is a wing of duplex suites that provide additional comfort.

Rooms: 53 (6 family) (16 GF) ✆ **S** £59–£98; **D** £69–£109 (incl. bkfst)* **Facilities:** FTV WiFi ₪ Library **Conf:** Class 33 Board 30 Thtr 90 Del from £109 **Services:** Night porter **Parking:** 80 **Notes:** LB Closed 25-26 Dec RS 24 Dec closes at 2pm Civ Wed 40

The Aberdeen Altens Hotel
★★★★ 74% HOTEL

Souterhead Road, Altens, AB12 3LF - **tel:** 01224 877000
email: reception@aberdeenaltenshotel.co.uk
web: www.aberdeenaltenshotel.co.uk
dir: *Follow A90 & take A956 signed Aberdeen Harbour. 1st exit at rdbt onto Souterhead Rd. Hotel on right*

A great venue for business travellers attending conferences, or those visiting the Granite City on a leisure break, this hotel enjoys a quiet setting and ample parking. An interesting range of dishes is available in the Cairngorm Bar and Restaurant, while guests with time to spare can enjoy the extensive leisure and beauty facilities. All bedrooms have been refurbished and feature a number of thoughtful accessories. A small number of apartments is available for guests on longer breaks.

Rooms: 216 (71 family) (48 GF) ✆ **S** £55–£240; **D** £65–£250* **Facilities:** FTV WiFi ₪ HL ☺ Gym Sauna Steam Room Treatment rooms Hairdresser Xmas New Year **Conf:** Class 144 Board 70 Thtr 400 Del from £104 **Services:** Lift Night porter **Notes:** LB Civ Wed

Holiday Inn Express Aberdeen - Exhibition Centre

BUDGET HOTEL

Parkway East, Bridge of Don, AB23 8AJ - **tel:** 01224 227250
email: info@hieaberdeenexhibitioncentre.co.uk
web: www.hiexpress.co.uk
dir: *Follow A90 northbound for Aberdeen Exhibition Conference Centre, located 2m from City Centre*

A modern hotel ideal for families and business travellers. Fresh and uncomplicated, the spacious rooms include Sky TV, power shower and tea and coffee-making facilities. Continental buffet breakfast is included in the room rate; other meals may be taken at the nearby family pub or restaurant.

Rooms: 135 (100 family) ✆ **S** £49–£125; **D** £49–£125 (incl. bkfst)* **Conf:** Class 16 Board 30 Thtr 48

A

Premier Inn Aberdeen (Anderson Drive)

BUDGET HOTEL

North Anderson Drive, AB15 6DW - **tel:** 0871 527 8006 (Calls cost 13p per minute plus your phone company's access charge) **web:** www.premierinn.com
dir: *Into Aberdeen from S on A90, follow airport signs. Hotel 1st left after fire station. (NB for Sat Nav use AB15 6TP)*

High quality, budget accommodation ideal for both families and business travellers. Spacious, en suite bedrooms feature free WiFi and tea and coffee making facilities, and in most hotels, Freeview TV is also available. The adjacent family restaurant features a wide and varied menu.

Rooms: 62

Premier Inn Aberdeen City Centre

BUDGET HOTEL

Inverlair House, West North Street, AB24 5AS - **tel:** 0871 527 8008 (Calls cost 13p per minute plus your phone company's access charge) **web:** www.premierinn.com
dir: *A90 onto A9013 into city centre. Take A956 towards King St, 1st left into Meal Market St*

Rooms: 190

Premier Inn Aberdeen North (Bridge Of Don)

BUDGET HOTEL

Ellon Road, Murcar, AB23 8BP - **tel:** 0871 527 8010 (Calls cost 13p per minute plus your phone company's access charge) **web:** www.premierinn.com
dir: *From city centre take A90 N follow Peterhead signs. At rdbt 2m after Aberdeen Exhibition & Conference Centre, left onto B999. Hotel on right*

Rooms: 91

Premier Inn Aberdeen South (Portlethen)

BUDGET HOTEL

Mains of Balquharn, Portlethen, AB12 4QS - **tel:** 0871 527 8012 (Calls cost 13p per minute plus your phone company's access charge) **web:** www.premierinn.com
dir: *From A90 follow Portlethen & Badentoy Park signs. Hotel on right*

Rooms: 92

Premier Inn Aberdeen (Westhill)

BUDGET HOTEL

Straik Road, Westhill, AB32 6HF - **tel:** 0871 527 8004 (Calls cost 13p per minute plus your phone company's access charge) **web:** www.premierinn.com
dir: *On A944 towards Alford, hotel adjacent to Tesco*

Rooms: 103

ABERDEEN AIRPORT   **Map 23 NJ81**
City of Aberdeen

Hallmark Hotel Aberdeen Airport

★★★ 75% HOTEL

Farburn Terrace, Dyce, AB21 7DW - **tel:** 0330 028 3409
email: aberdeen@hallmarkhotels.co.uk **web:** www.hallmarkhotels.co.uk
dir: *A96/A947 airport E after 1m turn left at lights. Hotel in 250yds*

This hotel is very convenient for air travellers and for those wishing to explore this lovely Highland area. The spacious, well-equipped bedrooms have all the expected up-to-date amenities. The public areas are welcoming and include a contemporary brasserie. Secure parking and WiFi are also provided.

Rooms: 212 (212 annexe) (20 family) (107 GF) **Facilities:** STV FTV WiFi ☼ Xmas New Year **Conf:** Class 160 Board 120 Thtr 400 **Services:** Night porter **Parking:** 150 **Notes:** Civ Wed 220

Premier Inn Aberdeen Airport (Dyce)

BUDGET HOTEL

Aberdeen Airport Main Terminal, Argyll Way, AB21 0BN - **tel:** 0871 527 9460 (Calls cost 13p per minute plus your phone company's access charge) **web:** www.premierinn.com
dir: *From N on A96 follow Aberdeen signs. At rdbt 1st exit into Dyce Drive signed Airport. At 2nd lights right into Argyll Rd. Hotel on right. From S on A90 follow Airport & A96 signs. Take A96 (Inverurie road) at 2nd rdbt 3rd exit into Dyce Drive then proceed as above*

High quality, budget accommodation ideal for both families and business travellers. Spacious, en suite bedrooms feature free WiFi and tea and coffee making facilities, and in most hotels, Freeview TV is also available. The adjacent family restaurant features a wide and varied menu.

Rooms: 100

ABERFOYLE   **Map 20 NN50**
Stirling

Macdonald Forest Hills Hotel & Resort

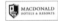

★★★★ 79% ⊛ HOTEL

Kinlochard, FK8 3TL - **tel:** 01877 389500
email: general.foresthills@macdonald-hotels.co.uk
web: www.macdonald-hotels.co.uk/foresthills
dir: *A84, A873, A81 to Aberfoyle onto B829*

Situated in the heart of The Trossachs with wonderful views of Loch Ard, this popular hotel forms part of a resort complex offering a range of indoor and outdoor facilities. The main hotel has relaxing lounges and a restaurant that all overlook the landscaped gardens. A separate building houses the leisure centre, lounge bar and bistro.

Rooms: 55 (16 family) (12 GF) ⚡ **Facilities:** Spa STV FTV WiFi ☼ ☺ Gym Children's club Snooker Water sports Quad biking Archery Clay pigeon shooting ♫ Xmas New Year **Conf:** Class 60 Board 20 Thtr 120 **Services:** Lift Night porter **Parking:** 100 **Notes:** Civ Wed 100

A

ABINGTON MOTORWAY SERVICE AREA (M74)
South Lanarkshire   **Map 21 NS92**

Days Inn Abington - M74

AA Advertised

ML12 6RG - **tel:** 01864 502782
email: abington.hotel@welcomebreak.co.uk **web:** www.welcomebreak.co.uk
dir: *M74 junct 13, accessible from N'bound and S'bound carriageways*

This modern building offers accommodation in smart, spacious and well-equipped
bedrooms, suitable for families and business travellers, and all with en suite
bathrooms. Continental breakfast is available and other refreshments may be
taken at the nearby family restaurant.

Rooms: 54 (50 family) (4 smoking) **Facilities:** FTV WiFi ⌨ **Conf:** Board 10
Parking: 100

ARDUAINE
Argyll & Bute   **Map 20 NM71**

Loch Melfort Hotel

★★★ 85% ◎◎ COUNTRY HOUSE HOTEL

PA34 4XG - **tel:** 01852 200233
email: reception@lochmelfort.co.uk **web:** www.lochmelfort.co.uk
dir: *On A816, midway between Oban & Lochgilphead*

Enjoying one of the finest locations on the West Coast, this popular, family-run hotel
has outstanding views across Asknish Bay towards the Islands of Jura, Scarba and
Shuna. Accommodation is provided in either the balconied rooms of the Cedar wing
or the more traditional rooms in the main hotel. Dining options include the main
restaurant with stunning views or the more informal bistro.

Rooms: 30 (20 annexe) (2 family) (11 GF) ⌨ **S** fr £70; **D** fr £80 (incl. bkfst)*
Facilities: FTV WiFi ⌨ 4 moorings Childrens' play park 🎵 Xmas New Year
Conf: Class 40 Board 20 Thtr 50 **Parking:** 50 **Notes:** LB Closed 3 weeks beginning
Dec & 3 weeks mid Jan RS winter – limited bistro service Civ Wed 100

AUCHENCAIRN
Dumfries & Galloway   **Map 21 NX75**

HIGHLY RECOMMENDED

Balcary Bay Hotel

★★★ 88% ◎◎ HOTEL

Shore Road, DG7 1QZ - **tel:** 01556 640217
email: reservations@balcary-bay-hotel.co.uk
web: www.balcary-bay-hotel.co.uk
dir: *On A711 between Dalbeattie & Kirkcudbright, hotel 2m from Auchencairn*

Taking its name from the bay on which it lies, this hotel has lawns running down
to the shore. The larger bedrooms enjoy stunning views over the bay, while
others overlook the gardens. The comfortable public areas are very relaxing.
Imaginative dishes feature at dinner, accompanied by a good wine list.

Rooms: 20 (1 family) (3 GF) ⌨ **S** £86; **D** £160 (incl. bkfst) **Facilities:** FTV WiFi
Parking: 50 **Notes:** Closed 1st Sun Dec-1st Fri Feb

AUCHTERARDER
Perth & Kinross   **Map 21 NN91**

INSPECTOR'S CHOICE

The Gleneagles Hotel

★★★★★ ◎◎◎◎ HOTEL

PH3 1NF - **tel:** 01764 662231
email: resort.sales@gleneagles.com **web:** www.gleneagles.com
dir: *Off A9 at exit for A823 follow signs for Gleneagles Hotel*

With its international reputation for high standards, this grand hotel provides
something for everyone. Set in 850 acres of glorious countryside, Gleneagles
offers a peaceful retreat, as well as many sporting activities, including the
famous championship golf courses. All bedrooms are appointed to a high
standard and offer both traditional and contemporary styles. Stylish public
areas include various dining options: The Strathearn, with two AA Rosettes; as
well as inspired cooking at Andrew Fairlie at Gleneagles, a restaurant with four
AA Rosettes. There's also the Clubhouse and many bars. The award-winning
ESPA spa offers the very latest treatments to restore both body and soul. Service
is always professional – the staff are friendly and nothing is too much trouble.
Andrew Fairlie at Gleneagles – Winner of the AA Wine Award for Scotland
2017-18.

Rooms: 232 (115 family) (11 GF) **S** fr £265; **D** fr £265 (incl. bkfst)*
Facilities: Spa STV FTV WiFi ⌨ supervised ⌨ supervised ⌨ 54 Putting green
⌨ Fishing ⌨ Gym Falconry Off-road driving Golf Archery Clay shooting Gundog
School Horse riding Xmas New Year **Conf:** Class 240 Board 60 Thtr 360 Del from
£320 **Services:** Lift Night porter **Parking:** 300 **Notes:** Civ Wed 360

Find out more
about the AA Hotel of the Year
for Scotland on page 17

AVIEMORE
Highland   Map 23 NH81

Macdonald Aviemore Resort
★★★★ 74% HOTEL

PH22 1PN - **tel:** 01479 815100
email: general@aviemorehighlandresort.com **web:** www.macdonald-hotels.co.uk
dir: *From N: Exit A9 to Aviemore (B970). Right at T-junct, through village. Right (2nd exit) at 1st rdbt into Macdonald Aviemore Resort, follow reception signs. From S: Exit A9 to Aviemore, left at T-junct. Immediately after Esso garage, turn left into Resort*

The Macdonald Aviemore Resort includes The Highlands Hotel, which boasts a wide range of activities including a championship golf course. The modern, well-equipped bedrooms suit business, leisure guests and families, and the Scottish Steakhouse offers a fantastic selection of grilled dishes. In addition there is a state-of-the-art gym, spa treatments and a 25-metre pool with a wave machine and flume.

Rooms: 151 (10 family) (44 GF) **Facilities:** Spa STV FTV WiFi ⬇ ③ supervised ⚓ 18 Putting green Fishing Gym Steam room Sauna Children's indoor & outdoor playgrounds Xmas New Year **Conf:** Class 610 Board 38 Thtr 1000 **Services:** Lift Night porter **Parking:** 500 **Notes:** Civ Wed 300

AYR
South Ayrshire   Map 20 NS32

Fairfield House Hotel
★★★★ 74% ⓦ HOTEL

12 Fairfield Road, KA7 2AS - **tel:** 01292 267461
email: reservations@fairfieldhotel.co.uk **web:** www.fairfieldhotel.co.uk
dir: *From A77 towards Ayr South (A30). Follow town centre signs, down Miller Rd, left, then right into Fairfield Rd*

Situated in a leafy cul-de-sac close to the esplanade, this hotel enjoys stunning seascapes towards the Isle of Arran. Bedrooms are in either modern or classical styles, the latter featuring impressive bathrooms. Public areas provide stylish, modern rooms in which to relax. Skilfully prepared meals are served in the casual brasserie or elegant restaurant.

Rooms: 44 (4 annexe) (3 family) (9 GF) **Facilities:** FTV WiFi ⬇ ③ supervised Gym Fitness room Sauna Steam room Xmas New Year **Conf:** Class 80 Board 40 Thtr 120 **Services:** Lift Night porter **Parking:** 50 **Notes:** Civ Wed 150

Enterkine Country House
★★★ 82% ⓦⓦ ⓦ COUNTRY HOUSE HOTEL

Annbank, KA6 5AL - **tel:** 01292 520580
email: mail@enterkine.com **web:** www.enterkine.com
dir: *5m E of Ayr on B743*

This luxurious art deco country mansion dates from the 1930s and retains many original features, notably some splendid bathroom suites. The focus is very much on dining, and in country house tradition there is no bar, drinks being served in the elegant lounge and library. The well-proportioned bedrooms are furnished and equipped to high standards, many with lovely countryside views.

Rooms: 14 (8 annexe) (2 family) (3 GF) ⬅ **S** £60–£190; **D** £70–£190 (incl. bkfst) **Facilities:** FTV WiFi Xmas New Year **Conf:** Class 140 Board 140 Thtr 200 Del from £120 **Services:** Night porter **Parking:** 40 **Notes:** LB Civ Wed 250

Mercure Ayr Hotel
★★★ 78% HOTEL

Dalblair Road, KA7 1UG - **tel:** 0844 815 9005 (Calls cost 5p per minute plus your phone company's access charge)
email: info@mercureayr.co.uk **web:** www.mercureayr.co.uk
dir: *M77 towards Prestwick Airport, then A77 Ayr, 1st rdbt 3rd exit, 2nd rdbt straight over, left at lights, then 2nd lights turn left, bottom of road turn right, hotel on left*

This hotel is situated in a central location in Ayr, and many bedrooms benefit from sea views. The property is ideally located for both business and leisure travellers and the area boasts many golf courses within easy reach; indeed the hotel even has its own golf simulator. Bedrooms and bathrooms are presented to a modern standard with a range of extras including free WiFi. A leisure club and brasserie restaurant are also provided for guests.

Rooms: 118 (4 family) ⬅ **Facilities:** FTV WiFi ⬇ ③ supervised Gym Beauty treatment room **Conf:** Class 45 Board 45 Thtr 200 **Services:** Lift Night porter **Parking:** 45 **Notes:** Civ Wed 75

Premier Inn Ayr A77/Racecourse
BUDGET HOTEL

Wheatpark Place, KA8 9RT - **tel:** 0871 527 9416 (Calls cost 13p per minute plus your phone company's access charge) **web:** www.premierinn.com
dir: *Phone for directions*

High quality, budget accommodation ideal for both families and business travellers. Spacious, en suite bedrooms feature free WiFi and tea and coffee making facilities, and in most hotels, Freeview TV is also available. The adjacent family restaurant features a wide and varied menu.

Rooms: 84

Premier Inn Ayr/Prestwick Airport
BUDGET HOTEL

Kilmarnock Road, Monkton, KA9 2RJ - **tel:** 0871 527 8038 (Calls cost 13p per minute plus your phone company's access charge) **web:** www.premierinn.com
dir: *At Dutch House Rdbt (at junct of A77 & A78) at Monkton*

Rooms: 64

B

BALLANTRAE
South Ayrshire
Map 20 NX08

Glenapp Castle
★★★★★ ❀❀❀ HOTEL

KA26 0NZ - **tel:** 01465 831212 **email:** enquiries@glenappcastle.com
web: www.glenappcastle.com
dir: S through Ballantrae, cross bridge over River Stinchar, 1st right,
hotel gates 1m

Friendly hospitality and attentive service prevail at this stunning Victorian
castle, set in extensive private grounds to the south of the village. Impeccably
furnished bedrooms are graced with antiques and period pieces, and include
two master rooms and a ground-floor family suite. Breathtaking views of Arran
and Ailsa Craig can be enjoyed from the delightful, sumptuous day rooms and
from many of the bedrooms. Guests should make a point of walking round the
wonderful 36-acre grounds, and take a look at the azalea pond, walled
vegetable gardens and restored Victorian greenhouses.

Rooms: 20 (2 family) (7 GF) ☂ **S** £207–£400; **D** £295–£570 (incl. bkfst)*
Facilities: FTV WiFi ◷ ☃ ⛳ Woodland walks Falconry Archery Photography
Stargazing New Year **Conf:** Class 12 Board 25 Thtr 25 Del from £265
Services: Lift Night porter **Parking:** 20 **Notes:** LB Civ Wed 40

BALLATER
Aberdeenshire
Map 23 NO39

Loch Kinord Hotel
★★★ 79% ❀ HOTEL

Ballater Road, Dinnet, AB34 5JY - **tel:** 01339 885229
email: stay@lochkinord.com **web:** www.lochkinord.com
dir: Between Aboyne & Ballater, on A93, in Dinnet

Family-run, this roadside hotel is well located for leisure and sporting pursuits.
It has lots of character and a friendly atmosphere. There are two bars, one outside
and a cosy one inside, plus a dining room with a bold colour scheme. Bedrooms are
stylish and have smart bathrooms.

Rooms: 20 (3 family) (4 GF) ☂ **Facilities:** FTV WiFi ◷ Xmas **Conf:** Class 30 Board 30
Thtr 40 **Parking:** 20 **Notes:** Civ Wed 50

BALLOCH
West Dunbartonshire
Map 20 NS38

Cameron House on Loch Lomond
★★★★★ 85% ❀❀❀❀ HOTEL

G83 8QZ - **tel:** 01389 755565
email: reservations@cameronhouse.co.uk **web:** www.cameronhouse.co.uk
dir: M8 W junct 30 for Erskine Bridge. A82 for Crainlarich. 14m, at rdbt signed Luss, hotel
on right

Enjoying an idyllic location on the banks of Loch Lomond in over 100 acres of
wooded parkland, this stylish hotel offers an excellent range of leisure facilities.
These include two golf courses, a world-class spa and a host of indoor and
outdoor sporting activities. A choice of restaurants and bars cater for all tastes
and include the Scottish-themed Cameron Grill and a fine dining operation,
Martin Wishart at Loch Lomond. Bedrooms are stylish, well equipped and many
boast wonderful loch views.

Rooms: 136 (9 family) (18 GF) ☂ **S** £169–£389; **D** £189–£405 (incl. bkfst)*
Facilities: Spa STV WiFi ◷ HL ⟳ supervised ⚓ 27 Putting green ☃ Fishing ⛳
Gym Squash Motor boat Hairdresser Sea plane Falconry Archery Segways Rib
boat Jet Skis Xmas New Year Child facilities **Conf:** Class 180 Board 80 Thtr 300
Services: Lift Night porter Air con **Parking:** 200 **Notes:** LB Civ Wed 200

C

BANCHORY
Aberdeenshire   Map 23 NO69

Burnett Arms Hotel

★★★ 71% SMALL HOTEL

25 High Street, AB31 5TD - **tel**: 01330 824944
email: theburnett@btconnect.com **web**: www.burnettarms.co.uk
dir: Town centre on N side of A93

This popular hotel is located in the heart of the town centre and gives easy access to the many attractions of Royal Deeside. Public areas include a choice of eating and drinking options, with food served in the restaurant, bar and foyer lounge. Bedrooms are thoughtfully equipped and comfortably modern.

Rooms: 18 (1 family) **Facilities**: STV FTV WiFi Xmas New Year **Conf**: Class 50 Board 50 Thtr 100 **Services**: Night porter **Parking**: 22 **Notes**: LB

BATHGATE
West Lothian   Map 21 NS96

Premier Inn Livingston (Bathgate)

BUDGET HOTEL

Starlaw Road, EH48 1LQ - **tel**: 0871 527 8630 (Calls cost 13p per minute plus your phone company's access charge) **web**: www.premierinn.com
dir: M8 junct 3A. At 1st rdbt 1st exit (Bathgate). Over bridge, at 2nd rdbt take 1st exit. Hotel 200yds on left

High quality, budget accommodation ideal for both families and business travellers. Spacious, en suite bedrooms feature free WiFi and tea and coffee making facilities, and in most hotels, Freeview TV is also available. The adjacent family restaurant features a wide and varied menu.

Rooms: 74

BEAULY
Highland   Map 23 NH54

Priory Hotel

★★★ 74% HOTEL

The Square, IV4 7BX - **tel**: 01463 782309
email: reservations@priory-hotel.com **web**: www.priory-hotel.com
dir: Signed from A832, into Beauly, hotel in square on left

This popular hotel occupies a central location in the town square. Standard and executive rooms are on offer, both providing a good level of comfort and range of facilities. Food is served throughout the day in the modern and comfortable open-plan public areas, with menus offering a first rate choice.

Rooms: 38 (3 family) (1 GF) **S** £65–£85; **D** £85–£120 (incl. bkfst)*
Facilities: STV FTV WiFi Xmas New Year **Conf**: Class 40 Board 30 Thtr 40 **Services**: Lift Night porter **Parking**: 20 **Notes**: LB

BLANTYRE
South Lanarkshire   Map 20 NS65

Crossbasket Castle

★★★★★ 86% HOTEL

Crossbasket Estate, Stoneymeadow Road, G72 9UE - **tel**: 01698 829461
email: info@crossbasketcastle.com **web**: www.crossbasketcastle.com
dir: In High Blantyre close to East Kilbride & the M80/ M74 motorways

This stunning luxury hotel opened after a multi-million pound refurbishment. The building can trace its roots back to the early 15th century and the days of King Robert the Bruce. Many original castle features remain though the building and surroundings are certainly more luxurious than previous tenants would have enjoyed. Tasteful design, flawless service and beautiful grounds combine to provide a wonderful experience for guests. Albert Roux and Michel Roux Jnr provide the inspiration for the menus in the restaurant with its gold-leafed ceilings that make guests feel like kings themselves when they dine.

Rooms: 9 **Facilities**: FTV WiFi Fishing In room spa treatment **Conf**: Class 150 Board 30 Thtr 350 **Services**: Lift Night porter **Parking**: 56 **Notes**: Civ Wed 300

CALLANDER
Stirling   Map 20 NN60

Roman Camp Country House Hotel

★★★★ 78% COUNTRY HOUSE HOTEL

FK17 8BG - **tel**: 01877 330003
email: mail@romancamphotel.co.uk **web**: www.romancamphotel.co.uk
dir: N on A84, left at east end of High Street. 300yds to hotel

Built in the 17th century and originally used as a shooting lodge, this charming country house has a rich history, and has been in the same ownership for nearly 30 years. Twenty acres of gardens and grounds lead down to the River Teith, and the town centre and its attractions are only a short walk away. Each bedroom is individually and elegantly designed, and offers much pampering comfort. Food is a highlight of any stay and menus are dominated by high-quality Scottish produce that is sensitively treated by the talented kitchen team. Real fires warm the atmospheric public areas and service is friendly yet professional.

Rooms: 15 (4 family) (7 GF) **Facilities**: STV FTV WiFi Fishing Xmas New Year **Conf**: Class 60 Board 30 Thtr 120 **Parking**: 80 **Notes**: LB Civ Wed 150

C

CARNOUSTIE
Angus — Map 21 NO53

Carnoustie Golf Hotel & Spa
★★★★ 72% HOTEL

The Links, DD7 7JE - tel: 01241 411999
email: reservations.carnoustie@bespokehotels.com
web: www.bespokehotels.com/carnoustiegolfhotel
dir: *Follow A92 from Dundee or Arbroath. Take the 'Upper Victoria' exit then follow sigsns to Carnoustie town centre & golf courses*

Overlooking the world famous Carnoustie Golf Links, a regular host of the British Open Golf Championship and the upcoming 2018 championship, this popular hotel is undergoing a full refurbishment. There is plenty to do here with a spa and access to the beach available to guests. Golfers can play at the adjacent, world-famous Carnoustie Golf Course. Bedrooms are comfortable and appealing. The popular bar is a great venue for telling tales of the day's golf, while the Calder's Bistro makes use of local, Scottish ingredients in an appealing menu.

Rooms: 96 (11 family) **D** £80–£160 (incl. bkfst)* **Facilities:** Spa STV FTV WiFi ▷ ⊕ Putting green Gym Sauna Steam room Spa bath Xmas New Year **Conf:** Class 150 Board 50 Thtr 350 Del from £104 **Services:** Lift Night porter **Parking:** 140 **Notes:** LB Civ Wed 120

CLYDEBANK
West Dunbartonshire — Map 20 NS47

Golden Jubilee Conference Hotel
★★★★ 76% HOTEL

Beardmore Street, G81 4SA - tel: 0141 951 6000
email: hotel@goldenjubilee.scot.nhs.uk **web:** www.goldenjubileehotel.com
dir: *M8 junct 19, follow signs for Clydeside Expressway to Glasgow road, then A814 (Dumbarton road), then follow Clydebank Business Park signs. Hotel on left*

Attracting plenty of business and conference custom, this stylish modern hotel lies beside the River Clyde and shares an impressive site with a hospital (although the latter does not intrude). Spacious and imposing public areas include a stylish restaurant that provides innovative contemporary Scottish cooking, the Central Plaza café, and The BBar lounge which offers a more extensive choice of lighter dishes. The leisure facilities include a 15-metre swimming pool, sauna and steam room. All bedrooms come with iMac entertainment systems. The hotel also has a keenly-adhered-to environmental policy.

Rooms: 168 **Facilities:** STV FTV WiFi ▷ ⊕ supervised Gym Sauna Steam room Xmas New Year **Conf:** Class 84 Board 27 Thtr 240 **Services:** Lift Night porter Air con **Parking:** 300 **Notes:** Civ Wed 170

COMRIE
Perth & Kinross — Map 21 NN72

Royal Hotel
★★★ 77% SMALL HOTEL

Melville Square, PH6 2DN - tel: 01764 679200
email: reception@royalhotel.co.uk **web:** www.royalhotel.co.uk
dir: *A9 on A822 to Crieff, then B827 to Comrie. Hotel in main square on A85*

The traditional façade gives little indication of the style and elegance to be found inside this long-established hotel located in the village centre. Public areas include a bar and library, a bright modern restaurant and a conservatory-style brasserie. The bedrooms are tastefully appointed and furnished with smart reproduction antiques.

Rooms: 13 (2 annexe) **Facilities:** STV WiFi Fishing Shooting arranged New Year **Conf:** Class 10 Board 20 Thtr 20 **Parking:** 22 **Notes:** Closed 25-26 Dec

CONNEL
Argyll & Bute — Map 20 NM93

Falls of Lora Hotel
★★★ 73% HOTEL

THE INDEPENDENTS
HOTEL ASSOCIATION

Connel Ferry, PA37 1PB - tel: 01631 710483
email: enquiries@fallsoflora.com **web:** www.fallsoflora.com

(For full entry see Oban)

COVE
Argyll & Bute — Map 20 NS28

Knockderry House
★★★★ 77% COUNTRY HOUSE HOTEL

Shore Road, G84 0NX - tel: 01436 842283 & 842813
email: info@knockderryhouse.co.uk **web:** www.knockderryhouse.co.uk
dir: *A82 to Lochlomondside, left onto A817 signed Garelochhead, through Glen Fruin to A814. Follow Coulport signs. At Coulport left at rdbt, 2m to hotel*

Knockderry House is a stunning example of a mid-19th century home and features a host of stunning architectural features from famed architect William Leiper. Public areas are warm and welcoming, many with original stained-glass windows. Set in expansive grounds with beautiful views of Loch Long, the hotel features modern bedrooms and bathrooms. Hospitality is key to the hotel's success, and friendly staff deliver a high level of personalised service. Scotland's larder is well represented by the output from the kitchen.

Rooms: 15 ⚓ **S** £95–£250; **D** £95–£250* **Facilities:** FTV WiFi New Year **Conf:** Class 20 Board 24 Thtr 30 **Parking:** 30 **Notes:** Closed 11-26 Dec Civ Wed 48

CUMBERNAULD
North Lanarkshire — Map 21 NS77

The Westerwood Hotel & Golf Resort
★★★★ 80% HOTEL

QHOTELS
INSPIRED BY YOU

1 St Andrews Drive, Westerwood, G68 0EW - tel: 01236 457171
email: westerwood@qhotels.co.uk **web:** www.qhotels.co.uk
dir: *M80 junct 6, follow signs for hotel*

This stylish, contemporary hotel enjoys an elevated position within 400 acres at the foot of the Camspie Hills. Accommodation is provided in spacious, bright bedrooms, many with super bathrooms, and day rooms include sumptuous lounges and an airy restaurant; extensive golf, fitness and conference facilities are available.

Rooms: 148 (16 family) (49 GF) ⚓ **Facilities:** Spa STV WiFi ▷ ⊕ ⅃ 18 ⅏ Gym Beauty salon Relaxation room Sauna Steam room Xmas New Year **Conf:** Class 120 Board 60 Thtr 400 **Services:** Lift Night porter **Parking:** 250 **Notes:** Civ Wed 350

Premier Inn Glasgow (Cumbernauld)

BUDGET HOTEL

4 South Muirhead Road, G67 1AX - tel: 0871 527 8424 (Calls cost 13p per minute plus your phone company's access charge) **web:** www.premierinn.com
dir: *From A80, A8011 follow Cumbernauld & town centre signs. Hotel opposite Asda & McDonalds*

High quality, budget accommodation ideal for both families and business travellers. Spacious, en suite bedrooms feature free WiFi and tea and coffee making facilities, and in most hotels, Freeview TV is also available. The adjacent family restaurant features a wide and varied menu.

Rooms: 37

DALKEITH
Midlothian   **Map 21 NT36**

Premier Inn Edinburgh A7 (Dalkeith)

BUDGET HOTEL

Melville Dykes Road, EH18 1AN - **tel:** 0871 527 9290 (Calls cost 13p per minute plus your phone company's access charge) **web:** www.premierinn.com
dir: *Exit A720 at Sheriffhall rdbt onto A7 signed Galashiels/Harwick/Carlisle. At 2nd rdbt take 3rd exit into Melville Dykes Rd (A768). Hotel on left*

High quality, budget accommodation ideal for both families and business travellers. Spacious, en suite bedrooms feature free WiFi and tea and coffee making facilities, and in most hotels, Freeview TV is also available. The adjacent family restaurant features a wide and varied menu.

Rooms: 40

DRYMEN
Stirling   **Map 20 NS48**

Best Western Buchanan Arms Hotel & Spa

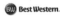

★★★ 80% HOTEL

---

23 Main Street, G63 0BQ - **tel:** 01360 660588
email: info@buchananarms.co.uk **web:** www. buchananarms.co.uk
dir: *Phone for directions*

There has been a lodging on this site since 1760 and although the hotel has significantly changed in this time, it still attracts guest due to its excellent location in the heart of the Loch Lomond and Trossachs National Park. Modern bedrooms are complemented by attractive public areas including a spacious conservatory lounge. The Salmon Leap restaurant offers relaxed dining, while the Relax Leisure Club and Haven Spa is the perfect place to kick back and chill out.

Rooms: 52 (12 family) (4 GF) **Facilities:** Spa FTV WiFi ⌨ Gym Xmas New Year **Conf:** Class 80 Board 60 Thtr 200 **Services:** Night porter **Notes:** LB Civ Wed 180

Winnock Hotel

★★★ 73% HOTEL

The Square, G63 0BL - **tel:** 01360 660245
email: info@winnockhotel.com **web:** www.winnockhotel.com
dir: *From S: M74 onto M8 junct 16b through Glasgow. Follow A809 to Aberfoyle*

Occupying a prominent position overlooking the village green, this popular hotel offers well-equipped bedrooms of various sizes and styles. The public rooms include a bar, a lounge and an attractive formal dining room that serves dishes of good, locally sourced food.

Rooms: 73 (18 family) (19 GF) **Facilities:** FTV WiFi ⌨ Xmas New Year **Conf:** Class 60 Board 70 Thtr 140 **Services:** Night porter **Parking:** 60 **Notes:** Civ Wed 150

DUMBARTON
East Dunbartonshire   **Map 20 NS37**

Premier Inn Dumbarton/Loch Lomond

BUDGET HOTEL

Lomondgate Drive, G82 2QU - **tel:** 0871 527 9274 (Calls cost 13p per minute plus your phone company's access charge) **web:** www.premierinn.com
dir: *From Glasgow follow A82 towards Crainlarich, right at Lomondgate rdbt onto A813, hotel on right. From N: A82 towards Glasgow, left at Lomondgate rdbt onto A813, hotel on right*

High quality, budget accommodation ideal for both families and business travellers. Spacious, en suite bedrooms feature free WiFi and tea and coffee making facilities, and in most hotels, Freeview TV is also available. The adjacent family restaurant features a wide and varied menu.

Rooms: 114

DUMFRIES
Dumfries & Galloway   **Map 21 NX97**

Cairndale Hotel & Leisure Club

★★★ 78% HOTEL

English Street, DG1 2DF - **tel:** 01387 254111
email: sales@cairndalehotel.co.uk **web:** www.cairndalehotel.co.uk
dir: *From S on M6 take A75 to Dumfries, left at 1st rdbt, cross rail bridge to lights, hotel 1st building on left*

Within walking distance of the town centre, this hotel provides a wide range of amenities, including leisure facilities and an impressive conference and entertainment centre. Bedrooms range from stylish suites to cosy singles. There's a choice of eating options in the evening. The Reivers Restaurant is smartly modern with food to match.

Rooms: 91 (22 family) (5 GF) **Facilities:** STV WiFi ⌨ supervised Gym Steam room Sauna Beauty treatment room ♬ Xmas New Year **Conf:** Class 150 Board 50 Thtr 300 **Services:** Lift Night porter **Parking:** 100 **Notes:** LB Civ Wed 300

Premier Inn Dumfries

BUDGET HOTEL

Annan Road, Collin, DG1 3JX - **tel:** 0871 527 8316 (Calls cost 13p per minute plus your phone company's access charge) **web:** www.premierinn.com
dir: *At rdbt junct of Euroroute bypass (A75) & A780*

High quality, budget accommodation ideal for both families and business travellers. Spacious, en suite bedrooms feature free WiFi and tea and coffee making facilities, and in most hotels, Freeview TV is also available. The adjacent family restaurant features a wide and varied menu.

Rooms: 82

DUNBLANE
Stirling   **Map 21 NN70**

Cromlix and Chez Roux

★★★★★ 86% ⊛⊛⊛ ≗ COUNTRY HOUSE HOTEL

Kinbuck, FK15 9JT - **tel:** 01786 822125
email: enquiries@cromlix.com **web:** www.cromlix.com
dir: *M9 towards Stirling/Perth, bypassing Stirling & Dunblane (A9 towards Perth). Take exit signed Dunblane/Kinbuck onto B8033. Turn right at junct for Kinbuck. Follow road through village & continue over bridge. Entrance gates 100yds on left*

Owned by tennis star Andy Murray who was born in nearby Dunblane, this stunning hotel has been appointed to a luxurious standard. Expansive grounds provide seclusion and relaxation and feature a kitchen garden, a loch (stocked with trout; rods available) and a tennis court resplendent in Wimbledon colours. Bedrooms have been lovingly restored and include a number of unique suites. The hotel has its own chapel, a number of welcoming lounges and a billiards room. The modern, light dining space features an open kitchen where guests can observe some masterful cooking being prepared. Service is delivered to an impeccable standard. Cromlix and Chez Roux was the AA Hotel of the Year for Scotland 2016-2017.

Rooms: 15 **Facilities:** FTV WiFi ⌨ ≗ Fishing Archery Falconry display Snooker Outdoor garden games In room spa treatments **Conf:** Class 26 Board 26 Thtr 60 **Services:** Night porter **Parking:** 51 **Notes:** LB Civ Wed 50

DUNDEE
City of Dundee

Map 21 N043

Malmaison Dundee

★★★★ 80% ⊛ HOTEL

44 Whitehall Crescent, DD1 4AY - **tel:** 01382 339715 **web:** www.malmaison.com
dir: *A90, right onto riverfront, past airport and adjacent to train station*

This iconic building has been delightfully restored, and with its gold top, it shines as a beacon of style and quality. Lovingly restored, the public areas are stylish and plush, the staircase is very notable for its ironwork, and the restaurant for its views. Bedrooms are very well appointed and the hotel has a number of meeting rooms available. The cuisine is a feature and a range of menu options is on offer.

Rooms: 91 ⁀ **Facilities:** STV FTV WiFi Xmas New Year **Conf:** Class 120 Board 50 Thtr 170 **Services:** Lift Night porter Air con **Notes:** Civ Wed 150

Premier Inn Dundee Centre

BUDGET HOTEL

Discovery Quay, Riverside Drive, DD1 4XA - **tel:** 0871 527 8320 (Calls cost 13p per minute plus your phone company's access charge) **web:** www.premierinn.com
dir: *Follow signs for Discovery Quay, hotel on waterfront*

High quality, budget accommodation ideal for both families and business travellers. Spacious, en suite bedrooms feature free WiFi and tea and coffee making facilities, and in most hotels, Freeview TV is also available. The adjacent family restaurant features a wide and varied menu.

Rooms: 40

Premier Inn Dundee East

BUDGET HOTEL

115-117 Lawers Drive, Panmurefield Village, DD5 3UP - **tel:** 0871 527 8322 (Calls 13p per minute plus your phone company's access charge) **web:** www.premierinn.com
dir: *From N: A92 (Dundee & Arbroath). Hotel 1.5m after Sainsbury's. From S: A90. At end of dual carriageway follow Dundee to Arbroath signs*

Rooms: 59

Premier Inn Dundee (Monifieth)

BUDGET HOTEL

Ethiebeaton Park, Arbroath Road, DD5 4HB - **tel:** 0871 527 8318 (Calls cost 13p per minute plus your phone company's access charge) **web:** www.premierinn.com
dir: *From A90 (Kingsway Rd) follow Carnoustie/Arbroath (A92) signs*

Rooms: 40

Premier Inn Dundee North

BUDGET HOTEL

Camperdown Leisure Park, Dayton Drive, DD2 3SQ - **tel:** 0871 527 8324 (Calls 13p per minute plus your phone company's access charge) **web:** www.premierinn.com
dir: *2m N of city centre on A90 at junct with A923, adjacent to cinema. At entrance to Camperdown Country Park*

Rooms: 78

Premier Inn Dundee West

BUDGET HOTEL

Kingsway West, DD2 5JU - **tel:** 0871 527 8326 (Calls cost 13p per minute plus your phone company's access charge) **web:** www.premierinn.com
dir: *On A90 towards Aberdeen adjacent to Technology Park rdbt*

Rooms: 87

DUNFERMLINE
Fife

Map 21 NT08

King Malcolm Hotel

★★★ 74% HOTEL

Queensferry Road, KY11 8DS - **tel:** 01383 722611
email: info@kingmalcolm-hotel-dunfermline.com **web:** www.peelhotels.co.uk
dir: *On A823, S of town*

Located to the south of the town, this purpose-built hotel remains popular with business clientele and is convenient for access to both Edinburgh and Fife. Public rooms include a smart foyer lounge and a conservatory bar, as well as a restaurant. Bedrooms, although not large, are well laid out and well equipped.

Rooms: 48 (2 family) (24 GF) **Facilities:** STV WiFi ♫ Xmas New Year **Conf:** Class 60 Board 50 Thtr 150 **Services:** Night porter **Parking:** 60 **Notes:** Civ Wed 120

Premier Inn Dunfermline

BUDGET HOTEL

4-12 Whimbrel Place, Fife Leisure Park, KY11 8EX - **tel:** 0871 527 8328 (Calls cost 13p per minute plus your phone company's access charge) **web:** www.premierinn.com
dir: *M90 junct 3 (Forth Road Bridge exit) 1st left at lights signed Duloch Park. 1st left into Fife Leisure Park*

High quality, budget accommodation ideal for both families and business travellers. Spacious, en suite bedrooms feature free WiFi and tea and coffee making facilities, and in most hotels, Freeview TV is also available. The adjacent family restaurant features a wide and varied menu.

Rooms: 78

DUNOON
Argyll & Bute

Map 20 NS17

Selborne Hotel

★★★ 72% HOTEL

Clyde Street, West Bay, PA23 7HU - **tel:** 01369 702761
email: selborne.dunoon@alfatravel.co.uk **web:** www.leisureplex.co.uk
dir: *From Caledonian MacBrayne pier. Past castle, left into Jane St, right into Clyde St. Ferry crossing to Dunoon via Greenock*

This holiday hotel is situated overlooking the West Bay and provides unrestricted views of the Clyde estuary towards the Isles of Cumbrae. Tour groups are especially well catered for in this good-value establishment, which offers entertainment most nights. Bedrooms are comfortable and many have sea views.

Rooms: 98 (6 family) (14 GF) ⁀ **S** £36–£64; **D** £56–£112 (incl. bkfst)*
Facilities: FTV WiFi ⌁ HL Pool table Table tennis ♫ Xmas New Year **Services:** Lift Night porter **Parking:** 30 **Notes:** Closed Dec-Feb (ex Xmas/New Year) RS Nov & Mar Mon-Fri only

E

EAST KILBRIDE
South Lanarkshire

Map 20 NS65

Macdonald Crutherland House

★★★★ 74% HOTEL

Strathaven Road, G75 0QZ - **tel:** 01355 577000
email: crutherland@macdonald-hotels.co.uk
web: www.macdonaldhotels.co.uk/crutherland
dir: Follow A726 signed Strathaven, straight over Torrance rdbt, hotel on left after 250yds

This mansion is set in 37 acres of landscaped grounds two miles from the town centre. Behind its Georgian façade is a very relaxing hotel with elegant public areas plus extensive banqueting and leisure facilities. The bedrooms are spacious and comfortable. Staff provide good levels of attention and enjoyable meals are served in the restaurant.

Rooms: 75 (16 family) (16 GF) **Facilities:** Spa STV WiFi ⓢ Gym Sauna Steam room Xmas New Year **Conf:** Class 100 Board 50 Thtr 500 **Services:** Lift Night porter **Parking:** 200 **Notes:** Civ Wed 300

Premier Inn Glasgow East Kilbride Central

BUDGET HOTEL

Brunel Way, The Murray, G75 0LD - **tel:** 0871 527 8450 (Calls cost 13p per minute plus your phone company's access charge) **web:** www.premierinn.com
dir: M74 junct 5, follow East Kilbride A725 signs, then Paisley A726 signs, left at Murray Rdbt, left into Brunel Way

High quality, budget accommodation ideal for both families and business travellers. Spacious, en suite bedrooms feature free WiFi and tea and coffee making facilities, and in most hotels, Freeview TV is also available. The adjacent family restaurant features a wide and varied menu.

Rooms: 58

Premier Inn Glasgow East Kilbride (Nerston Toll)

BUDGET HOTEL

5 Lee's Burn Court, Nerston, G74 3XB - **tel:** 0871 527 8446 (Calls cost 13p per minute plus your phone company's access charge) **web:** www.premierinn.com
dir: M74 junct 5, follow East Kilbride/A725 signs. Into right lane, follow Glasgow/A749 signs. At lights left onto A749 signed East Kilbride Town Centre (A725). Take slip road to Lee's Burn Court

Rooms: 44

Premier Inn Glasgow East Kilbride (Peel Park)
BUDGET HOTEL

Eaglesham Road, G75 8LW - **tel:** 0871 527 8448 (Calls cost 13p per minute plus your phone company's access charge) **web:** www.premierinn.com
dir: 8m from M74 junct 5 on A726 at rdbt of B764

Rooms: 42

EDINBURGH
City of Edinburgh

Map 21 NT27

INSPECTOR'S CHOICE

The Balmoral
ROCCO FORTE HOTELS
★★★★★ HOTEL

1 Princes Street, EH2 2EQ - **tel:** 0131 556 2414
email: reservations.balmoral@roccofortehotels.com **web:** www.roccofortehotels.com
dir: Follow city centre signs. Hotel at E end of Princes St, adjcent to Waverley Station

This elegant hotel enjoys a prestigious address at the top of Princes Street, with fine views over the city and the castle. Bedrooms and suites are stylishly furnished and decorated — all boast a thoughtful range of extras and impressive marble bathrooms. Hotel amenities include a Roman-style health spa, extensive function facilities, a choice of bars and two very different dining options — Hadrians is a bustling, informal brasserie, while Number One offers excellent Scottish and international fine dining.

Rooms: 188 (22 family) **Facilities:** Spa STV WiFi ⓢ Gym Xmas New Year **Conf:** Class 180 Board 60 Thtr 350 **Services:** Lift Night porter Air con **Parking:** 100 **Notes:** Civ Wed 120

Silver Stars

The AA Silver Star rating denotes a Hotel that we highly recommend. They have a superior level of quality within their star rating, high standards of hospitality, service and cleanliness.

EDINBURGH *continued*

Prestonfield

★★★★★ ◉◉ TOWN HOUSE HOTEL

Priestfield Road, EH16 5UT - **tel:** 0131 225 7800
email: reservations@prestonfield.com **web:** www.prestonfield.com
dir: *A7 towards Cameron Toll. 200mtrs beyond Royal Commonwealth Pool, into Priestfield Rd*

This centuries-old landmark has been lovingly restored and enhanced to provide deeply comfortable and dramatically furnished bedrooms. The building demands to be explored: from the tapestry lounge and the whisky room to the restaurant, where the walls are adorned with pictures of former owners. Facilities and services are up-to-the-minute, and carefully prepared meals are served in the award-winning Rhubarb restaurant.

Rooms: 23 (6 GF) ⬧ **Facilities:** STV FTV WiFi ⬧ ⬧ 18 Putting green ⬧ Xmas New Year **Conf:** Class 500 Board 40 Thtr 700 **Services:** Lift Night porter **Parking:** 250 **Notes:** Civ Wed 350

Waldorf Astoria Edinburgh - The Caledonian

★★★★★ 86% ◉◉◉ HOTEL

Princes Street, EH1 2AB - **tel:** 0131 222 8888
email: guest_caledonian@waldorfastoria.com **web:** www.waldorfastoriaedinburgh.com
dir: *In city centre, at west end of Princes St, adjacent to Rutland St & Lothian Rd*

Set in the heart of Scotland's capital city, against the magnificent backdrop of Edinburgh Castle, this former Victorian railway hotel was built in 1903, and hasn't lost any of the charm and character that has made it famous. Spacious bedrooms and en suites offer comfort and luxury, and there is a choice of award-winning restaurants and wonderful public areas. The Guerlain Spa is a popular destination for relaxation and rejuvenation. Many rooms enjoy breathtaking views of the castle.

Rooms: 241 (12 family) ⬧ **S** £189–£629; **D** £209–£649* **Facilities:** Spa STV WiFi ⬧ HL ⬧ Gym Sauna Steam room Xmas New Year **Conf:** Class 120 Board 80 Thtr 300 Del from £194 **Services:** Lift Night porter Air con **Parking:** 48 **Notes:** LB Civ Wed 300

Sheraton Grand Hotel & Spa

★★★★★ 84% ◉ HOTEL

1 Festival Square, EH3 9SR - **tel:** 0131 229 9131
email: grandedinburgh@sheraton.com **web:** www.sheraton.com/grandedinburgh
dir: *In city centre. Phone for directions and details of parking*

This modern hotel boasts one of the best spas in Scotland – the external top floor hydro pool is definitely worth a look, while the thermal suite provides a unique venue for serious relaxation. The spacious bedrooms are available in a variety of styles, and the suites prove very popular. There is a wide range of dishes available in the One Square Bar and Restaurant.

Rooms: 269 ⬧ **S** £150–£675; **D** £150–£675* **Facilities:** Spa STV FTV WiFi ⬧ ⬧ ⬧ Gym Indoor/outdoor hydropool Kinesis studio Thermal suite Fitness studio ⬧ Xmas New Year **Conf:** Class 350 Board 120 Thtr 500 **Services:** Lift Night porter Air con **Parking:** 122 **Notes:** Civ Wed 485

Symbols and abbreviations
explained on pages 6–7

INSPECTOR'S CHOICE

Norton House Hotel & Spa
★★★★ ◎ 🛏 HOTEL

Ingliston, EH28 8LX - tel: 0131 333 1275 & 0845 072 7468 (Calls cost 5p per minute plus your phone company's access charge)
email: nortonhouse@handpicked.co.uk
web: www.handpickedhotels.co.uk/nortonhouse
dir: *Off A8, 5m W of city centre*

This extended Victorian mansion, set in 55 acres of parkland, is peacefully situated just outside the city and is convenient for the airport. The original building dates from 1840, and was bought nearly 40 years later by John Usher of the Scottish brewing family. Today, both the contemporary bedrooms and the very spacious, traditional ones have an impressive range of accessories including large satellite TVs, DVD/CD players and free high-speed internet access. Executive rooms have more facilities, of course, including MP3 connection and 'tilevision' TVs at the end of the baths. Public areas take in a choice of lounges as well as dining in the popular brasserie. There is a health club, and a spa which offers a long list of treatments.

Rooms: 83 (10 family) (20 GF) ↷ **S** £99–£719; **D** £109–£719 (incl. bkfst)*
Facilities: Spa STV WiFi ↘ HL ⊕ Gym Xmas New Year **Conf:** Class 100 Board 60 Thtr 300 Del from £155 **Services:** Lift Night porter **Parking:** 200 **Notes:** LB Civ Wed 140

Dalhousie Castle and Aqueous Spa
★★★★ 81% ◎◎ HOTEL

Bonnyrigg, EH19 3JB - tel: 01875 820153
email: info@dalhousiecastle.co.uk **web:** www.dalhousiecastle.co.uk
dir: *A7 S from Edinburgh through Lasswade/Newtongrange, right at Shell Garage (B704), hotel 0.5m from junct*

A popular wedding venue, this imposing medieval castle sits amid lawns and parkland and even has a falconry. Bedrooms offer a mix of styles and sizes, including richly decorated themed rooms named after various historical figures. The Dungeon restaurant provides an atmospheric setting for dinner, and the less formal Orangery serves food all day. The spa offers many relaxing and therapeutic treatments and hydro facilities.

Rooms: 35 (6 annexe) (3 family) ↷ **Facilities:** Spa FTV WiFi Fishing Falconry Clay pigeon shooting Archery Xmas New Year **Conf:** Class 60 Board 45 Thtr 120 **Services:** Night porter **Parking:** 110 **Notes:** Civ Wed 100

The Principal Edinburgh George Street
★★★★ 81% HOTEL

19-21 George Street, EH2 2PB - tel: 0131 225 1251
email: EdinburghReservationsGS@theprincipalhotel.com
web: www.phcompany.com/principal/edinburgh-george-street
dir: *In city centre*

A long established hotel, The Principal Edinburgh George Street enjoys a city centre location. The splendid public areas have many original features such as intricate plasterwork, a marble-floored foyer, and chandeliers. The Printing Press offers menus that feature Scottish produce whilst Burr & Co is a relaxed coffee shop. The elegant, modern bedrooms come in a mix of sizes and styles; the upper ones having fine city views.

Rooms: 249 (20 family) (4 GF) **Facilities:** STV WiFi ↘ HL Xmas New Year **Conf:** Class 120 Board 50 Thtr 300 **Services:** Lift Night porter **Notes:** LB Civ Wed 300

The Bonham Hotel
★★★★ 80% ◎ HOTEL

35 Drumsheugh Gardens, EH3 7RN - tel: 0131 226 6050
email: BonhamReservations@thebonham.com
web: www.thebonham.com/partner/edinburgh-bonham
dir: *Close to West End & Princes St, 10mins from Haymarket station & 5mins from nearest tram stop*

The Bonham Hotel was built in the late 19th century in one of the most sought-after areas of Edinburgh. The three buildings that make up the hotel have been private residences, a medical practice and even a hall of residence for Edinburgh University, before becoming a hotel. The property has stylish designs which are sympathetic to the vintage of the buildings. Bedrooms are well appointed, with guest comfort taken care of. The bar and restaurant, like the team here, are warm and welcoming.

Rooms: 49 (3 family) (6 GF) ↷ **Facilities:** FTV WiFi ↘ HL **Conf:** Class 20 Board 26 Thtr 45 **Services:** Lift Night porter **Parking:** 16 **Notes:** Civ Wed 70

Hotel du Vin Edinburgh
★★★★ 80% ◎ 🛏 TOWN HOUSE HOTEL

11 Bristo Place, EH1 1EZ - tel: 0131 247 4900
email: reception.edinburgh@hotelduvin.com **web:** www.hotelduvin.com
dir: *M8 junct 1, A720 signed Kilmarnock/W Calder/Edinburgh W. Right at fork, follow A720 signs, merge onto A720. Take exit signed A703. At rdbt take A702/Biggar Rd. 3.5m. Right into Lauriston Pl which becomes Forrest Rd. Right at Bedlam Theatre. Hotel on right*

This hotel offers very stylish and comfortable accommodation; all bedrooms display the Hotel du Vin trademark facilities – air conditioning, free WiFi, plasma TVs, monsoon showers and Egyptian cotton linen to name but a few. Public areas include a whisky snug, and a mezzanine bar that overlooks the brasserie where modern Scottish cuisine is served. For the wine connoisseur, there's La Roche tasting room where wines from around the world can be appreciated.

Rooms: 47 ↷ **Facilities:** STV FTV WiFi ↘ **Conf:** Class 10 Board 28 Thtr 30 **Services:** Lift Night porter Air con **Notes:** Civ Wed 28

EDINBURGH *continued*

The Roxburghe Hotel

PRINCIPAL
HOTEL COMPANY LTD
EST. 1898

★★★★ 80% HOTEL

38 Charlotte Square, EH2 4HQ - **tel:** 0131 240 5500
email: RoxburgheReservations@theroxburghe.com **web:** www.theroxburghe.com
dir: *On corner of Charlotte Sq & George St*

This long-established hotel lies in the heart of the city overlooking Charlotte
Square Gardens. Public areas are inviting and include relaxing lounges, a choice
of bars (in the evening) and an inner concourse that looks onto a small lawned
area. Smart bedrooms come in both classic and contemporary styles. Valet parking
is available.

Rooms: 199 (6 family) **Facilities:** Spa FTV WiFi ☼ Gym Dance studio Sauna
Steam room Xmas **Conf:** Class 180 Board 50 Thtr 340 **Services:** Lift Night porter
Air con **Parking:** 20 **Notes:** Civ Wed 280

Novotel Edinburgh Park

NOVOTEL
HOTELS & RESORTS

★★★★ 79% HOTEL

15 Lochside Avenue, EH12 9DJ - **tel:** 0131 446 5600
email: h6515@accor.com **web:** www.novotel.com
dir: *Near Hermiston Gate shopping area*

Located just off the city bypass and within minutes of the airport, this modern hotel
offers bedrooms that are spacious and comfortable. The public areas include the
open-plan lobby, a bar and a restaurant offering diverse and informal dishes.
A swimming pool and small gym are also available to guests.

Rooms: 170 (130 family) **Facilities:** STV FTV WiFi ☼ HL ☼ Gym **Conf:** Class 60
Board 40 Thtr 150 **Services:** Lift Night porter Air con **Parking:** 96 **Notes:** Civ Wed 90

Malmaison Edinburgh

Malmaison
hotels that dare to be different

★★★★ 78% ◉ HOTEL

One Tower Place, Leith, EH6 7BZ - **tel:** 0131 468 5000 & 0844 693 0652 (Calls cost 5p
per minute plus your phone company's access charge)
email: reception.edinburgh@malmaison.com **web:** www.malmaison.com
dir: *A900 from city centre towards Leith, at end of Leith Walk, through 3 sets of lights, left
into Tower St. Hotel on right at end of road*

The trendy Port of Leith is home to this stylish Malmaison. Inside, bold
contemporary designs create a striking effect. Bedrooms are comprehensively
equipped with CD players, mini-bars and loads of individual touches. Ask for one of
the stunning superior rooms for a really memorable stay. The smart brasserie and a
café bar are popular with the local clientele.

Rooms: 100 (18 family) **D** £85–£200* **Facilities:** STV FTV WiFi ☼ Gym Xmas
New Year **Conf:** Class 32 Board 32 Thtr 80 **Services:** Lift Night porter **Parking:** 50
Notes: Civ Wed 70

Macdonald Holyrood Hotel

MACDONALD
HOTELS & RESORTS

★★★★ 78% HOTEL

Holyrood Road, EH8 8AU - **tel:** 0131 550 4500
email: general.holyrood@macdonald-hotels.co.uk
web: www.macdonaldhotels.co.uk/holyrood
dir: *Parallel to Royal Mile, near Holyrood Palace & Dynamic Earth*

Situated just a short walk from Holyrood Palace, this impressive hotel is situated
next to the Scottish Parliament building. Air-conditioned bedrooms are comfortably

furnished, while the Club floor boasts a private lounge. Full business services
complement the extensive conference suites.

Rooms: 156 (16 family) (13 GF) **Facilities:** Spa STV FTV WiFi ☼ ☼ Gym Sauna
Steam room Library Xmas New Year **Conf:** Class 100 Board 80 Thtr 200
Services: Lift Night porter Air con **Parking:** 38 **Notes:** Civ Wed 100

Novotel Edinburgh Centre

NOVOTEL
HOTELS & RESORTS

★★★★ 77% HOTEL

Lauriston Place, Lady Lawson Street, EH3 9DE - **tel:** 0131 656 3500
email: H3271@accor.com **web:** www.novotel.com
dir: *From Edinburgh Castle right onto George IV Bridge from Royal Mile.
Follow to junct, then right into Lauriston Place. Hotel 700mtrs on right*

This modern hotel is located in the centre of the city, close to Edinburgh Castle.
Smart and stylish public areas include a cosmopolitan bar, brasserie-style
restaurant and indoor leisure facilities. The air-conditioned bedrooms feature a
comprehensive range of extras and the bathrooms have both baths and separate
shower cabinets.

Rooms: 180 (146 family) **Facilities:** STV WiFi ☼ HL ☼ Gym Sauna Steam room
Xmas New Year **Conf:** Class 50 Board 32 Thtr 80 **Services:** Lift Night porter Air con
Parking: 15

Ten Hill Place Hotel

★★★★ 74% ◉ HOTEL

10 Hill Place, EH8 9DS - **tel:** 0131 662 2080
email: reservations@tenhillplace.com **web:** www.tenhillplace.com
dir: *Into Hill Place, opposite Festival Theatre. Hotel at end*

This centrally located luxury hotel near to the Festival Theatre is owned and
operated by the Royal College of Surgeons, with all profits helping to train surgeons
around the world. Stylish bedrooms and bathrooms are complemented by a range of
welcoming and comfortable public areas including the popular 10 Wine Bar, an
interesting wine-themed space, and the award-winning No.10 Restaurant. Limited
parking is available on site.

Rooms: 77 (4 family) (10 GF) **D** £99–£250* **Facilities:** FTV WiFi ☼ ♫
Services: Lift Night porter Air con **Parking:** 6 **Notes:** LB

Old Waverley Hotel

★★★ 78% HOTEL

43 Princes Street, EH2 2BY - **tel:** 0131 556 4648
email: reservations@oldwaverley.co.uk **web:** www.oldwaverley.co.uk
dir: *In city centre, opposite Scott Monument, Waverley Station & Jenners*

Occupying a commanding position opposite Sir Walter Scott's famous monument
on Princes Street, this hotel lies right in the heart of the city, close to the station.
The comfortable public rooms are all on first-floor level and along with front-facing
bedrooms enjoy the fine views.

Rooms: 86 (5 family) **Facilities:** WiFi ☼ Leisure facilities at sister hotel
Services: Lift Night porter **Notes:** LB

Mercure Edinburgh City - Princes Street Hotel

★★★ 77% HOTEL

Princes Street, EH2 2DG - tel: 0131 226 8400 & 0844 815 9017 (Calls cost 7p per minute plus your phone company's access charge)
email: info@mercureedinburgh.co.uk web: www.mercureedinburgh.co.uk
dir: *Opposite Scott Monument & Waverley Station. At east end of Princes St*

With an enviable location in the heart of Princes Street, offering excellent views of the castle you really cannot be anymore central. The front-facing bedrooms are more spacious; some benefit from a balcony but all are well appointed. The large popular restaurant benefits from the wonderful views.

Rooms: 169 (9 family) Facilities: FTV WiFi ⬧ HL New Year Services: Lift Night porter

The Howard

Ⓤ ⚙

34 Great King Street, EH3 6QH - tel: 0131 557 3500
email: reserve@thehoward.com web: www.thehoward.com
dir: *E on Queen St, 2nd left, Dundas St. Through 3 lights, right, hotel on left*

Currently the rating for this establishment is not confirmed. This may be due to a change of ownership or because it has only recently joined the AA rating scheme.

Rooms: 19 (1 annexe) (3 family) (2 GF) ☏ Facilities: STV FTV WiFi ⬧ HL Xmas New Year Conf: Class 28 Board 28 Thtr 28 Services: Lift Night porter Parking: 12 Notes: LB Civ Wed 28

Premier Inn Edinburgh A1 (Musselburgh)

BUDGET HOTEL

Carberry Road, Inveresk, EH21 8PT - tel: 0871 527 8358 (Calls cost 13p per minute plus your phone company's access charge) web: www.premierinn.com
dir: *From A1 follow Dalkeith (A6094) signs. At rdbt turn right, hotel 300yds on right*

High quality, budget accommodation ideal for both families and business travellers. Spacious, en suite bedrooms feature free WiFi and tea and coffee making facilities, and in most hotels, Freeview TV is also available. The adjacent family restaurant features a wide and varied menu.

Rooms: 82

Premier Inn Edinburgh Airport (Newbridge)

BUDGET HOTEL

2A Kirkliston Road, Newbridge, EH28 8SL - tel: 0871 527 9284 (Calls cost 13p per minute plus your phone company's access charge) web: www.premierinn.com
dir: *M9 junct 1, A89 signed Broxburn. At lights turn right, then 2nd right*

Rooms: 119

Premier Inn Edinburgh Central Lauriston Place

BUDGET HOTEL

82 Lauriston Place, Lady Lawson Street, EH3 9DG - tel: 0871 527 8366 (Calls cost 13p per minute plus your phone company's access charge) web: www.premierinn.com
dir: *A8 onto A702 (Lothian Rd). Left into Lauriston Place. Hotel on left*

Rooms: 112

Premier Inn Edinburgh City Centre (Princes St)

BUDGET HOTEL

122-123 Princes Street, EH2 4AD - tel: 0871 527 9358 (Calls cost 13p per minute plus your phone company's access charge) web: www.premierinn.com
dir: *From Edinburgh bypass (A720) onto A702, take A700. (NB Princes St is not accessible by car; it is advisable to park in Castle Terrace Car Park EH1 2EW)*

Rooms: 97

Premier Inn Edinburgh City Centre Royal Mile

E

BUDGET HOTEL

East Market Street, EH8 8BG - tel: 0871 527 9644 (Calls cost 13p per minute plus your phone company's access charge) web: www.premierinn.com
dir: *From Waverley train station right into Market St, straight on into East Market St, hotel in 0.4m*

Rooms: 127

Premier Inn Edinburgh City Centre (York Place)

BUDGET HOTEL

44 York Place, EH1 3HU - tel: 0871 527 9618 (Calls cost 13p per minute plus your phone company's access charge) web: www.premierinn.com
dir: *Phone for detailed directions*

Rooms: 127

Premier Inn Edinburgh East

BUDGET HOTEL

228 Willowbrae Road, EH8 7NG - tel: 0871 527 8370 (Calls cost 13p per minute plus your phone company's access charge) web: www.premierinn.com
dir: *M8 junct 1, A720 S for 12m, then A1. At Asda rdbt turn left. In 2m, hotel on left before Esso garage*

Rooms: 50

Premier Inn Edinburgh Leith Waterfront

BUDGET HOTEL

51-53 Newhaven Place, Leith, EH6 4TX - tel: 0871 527 8360 (Calls cost 13p per minute plus your phone company's access charge) web: www.premierinn.com
dir: *From A1 follow coast road through Leith. Pass Ocean Terminal, straight ahead at mini-rdbt, 2nd exit signed Harry Ramsden's car park*

Rooms: 138

Premier Inn Edinburgh Park (The Gyle)

BUDGET HOTEL

Edinburgh Park (Airport), 1 Lochside Court, EH12 9FX - tel: 0871 527 9336 (Calls cost 13p per minute plus your phone company's access charge) web: www.premierinn.com
dir: *M8 junct 1, A720 (city bypass). At Gogar rdbt 3rd exit follow South Gyle/station signs. Into right lane approaching Gyle rdbt, 3rd exit, follow Edinburgh Park train station signs into Lochside Crescent. Straight on at 2 rdbts, 400yds. Hotel on left*

Rooms: 120

E

ELGIN
Moray

Map 23 NJ26

Mansion House Hotel

★★★★ 77% HOTEL

The Haugh, IV30 1AW - tel: 01343 548811
email: reception@mhelgin.co.uk **web:** www.mansionhousehotel.co.uk
dir: Exit A96 into Haugh Rd, then 1st left

Set in grounds by the River Lossie, this baronial mansion is popular with leisure and business guests as well as being a lovely wedding venue. Bedrooms are spacious and many have views of the river. Extensive public areas include a choice of restaurants, with a bistro that contrasts nicely with the classical main restaurant. There is an indoor pool and a beauty and hair salon.

Rooms: 23 (6 family) (5 GF) ⋒ **S** £109.50; **D** £153–£203 (incl. bkfst)* **Facilities:** STV FTV WiFi ⊳ ⦿ supervised Gym Hair studio Beauty treatment room **Conf:** Class 100 Board 20 Thtr 180 **Services:** Night porter **Parking:** 50 **Notes:** LB Closed 24 Dec-2 Jan Civ Wed 160

Premier Inn Elgin

BUDGET HOTEL

15 Linkwood Way, IV30 1HY - tel: 0871 527 8372 (Calls cost 13p per minute plus your phone company's access charge) **web:** www.premierinn.com
dir: On A96, 1.5m E of city centre

High quality, budget accommodation ideal for both families and business travellers. Spacious, en suite bedrooms feature free WiFi and tea and coffee making facilities, and in most hotels, Freeview TV is also available. The adjacent family restaurant features a wide and varied menu.

Rooms: 93

FALKIRK
Falkirk

Map 21 NS88

Premier Inn Falkirk Central

BUDGET HOTEL

Main Street, Camelon, FK1 4DS - tel: 0871 527 8388 (Calls cost 13p per minute plus your phone company's access charge) **web:** www.premierinn.com
dir: From Falkirk A803 signed Glasgow. At mini rdbt right, continue on A803. At Rosebank rdbt 2nd exit signed Glasgow & Stirling

High quality, budget accommodation ideal for both families and business travellers. Spacious, en suite bedrooms feature free WiFi and tea and coffee making facilities, and in most hotels, Freeview TV is also available. The adjacent family restaurant features a wide and varied menu.

Rooms: 31

Premier Inn Falkirk (Larbert)

BUDGET HOTEL

Glenbervie Business Park, Bellsdyke Road, FK5 4EG - tel: 0871 527 8390 (Calls cost 13p per minute plus your phone company's access charge) **web:** www.premierinn.com
dir: Just off A88. Approx 1m from M876 junct 2

Rooms: 60

FINTRY
Stirling

Map 20 NS68

Culcreuch Castle Hotel & Estate

★★★ 78% HOTEL

Kippen Road, G63 0LW - tel: 01360 860555
email: info@culcreuch.com **web:** www.culcreuch.com
dir: On B822, 17m W of Stirling

Peacefully located in 1,600 acres of parkland, this ancient castle dates back to 1296. Tastefully restored accommodation is in a mixture of individually themed castle rooms, some with four-poster beds, and more modern courtyard rooms which are suitable for families. Period-style public rooms include a bar, serving light meals, an elegant lounge and a wood-panelled dining room.

Rooms: 14 (4 annexe) (4 family) (4 GF) ⋒ **S** £76–£120; **D** £102–£190 (incl. bkfst) **Facilities:** STV FTV WiFi ⊳ New Year **Conf:** Class 70 Board 30 Thtr 140 Del from £118 **Parking:** 80 **Notes:** LB Closed 4-18 Jan & 25-26 Dec RS 19 Jan-mid Mar closed Mon-Wed Civ Wed 110

FORT AUGUSTUS
Highland

Map 23 NH30

The Lovat, Loch Ness

★★★★ 80% HOTEL

Loch Ness Side, PH32 4DU - tel: 01456 459250
email: info@thelovat.com **web:** www.thelovat.com
dir: A82 between Fort William & Inverness

This charming hotel enjoys an elevated position in the pretty town of Fort Augustus with views over Loch Ness. It has impressively styled bedrooms with a host of thoughtful extras. Inviting public areas include a comfortable lounge with a log fire, a stylish brasserie and the contemporary Station Road restaurant where imaginative food is cooked with skill and care. The hotel has an admirable green policy, and the hospitality and commitment to guest care will leave a lasting impression.

Rooms: 28 (1 family) (7 GF) ⋒ **S** £65–£340; **D** £70–£360 (incl. bkfst)* **Facilities:** FTV WiFi ⊳ Xmas New Year **Conf:** Class 32 Board 24 Thtr 70 Del from £145 **Services:** Lift **Parking:** 30 **Notes:** LB Civ Wed 150

The Inch

★★★ 77% SMALL HOTEL

Inchnacardoch Bay, PH32 4BL - tel: 01456 450900
email: happy@inchhotel.com **web:** www.inchhotel.com
dir: On A82. Turn right before entering Fort Augustus from Inverness

This 150-year-old former hunting lodge is set on the hillside looking over the south end of Loch Ness, making it a perfect base for exploring the Highlands. Guests can

F

expect the finest hospitality here from staff that are always eager to please. The bedrooms are very individual in style; the Bridal Suite is a very well-appointed room with stunning views. The Yard Restaurant serves dishes based on the plentiful supply of local game and seafood.

Rooms: 17 (2 family) **S** £110–£170; **D** £120–£180 (incl. bkfst)* **Facilities:** FTV WiFi Fishing Xmas New Year **Conf:** Class 30 Board 26 Thtr 45 **Parking:** 30 **Notes:** Civ Wed 35

FORTINGALL	Map 20 NN74
Perth & Kinross	

Fortingall Hotel

★★★★ 76% @ SMALL HOTEL

PH15 2NQ - **tel:** 01887 830367
email: enquiries@fortingall.com **web:** www.fortingallhotel.com
dir: B846 from Aberfeldy for 6m, left signed Fortingall for 3m. Hotel in village centre

Appointed to a very high standard, this hotel has plenty of charm. It lies at the foot of wooded hills in the heart of Glen Lyon. All the bedrooms are very well equipped and have an extensive range of thoughtful extras. The comfortable lounge, with its log fire, is ideal for pre-dinner drinks, and the small bar is full of character.

Rooms: 10 (1 family) **Facilities:** STV FTV WiFi ☞ Fishing ☞ Deer stalking Grouse shoots Munro bagging Clay pigeon Guided walks Cycle hire ♫ Xmas New Year **Conf:** Board 20 Thtr 40 **Parking:** 20 **Notes:** LB Civ Wed 50

FORT WILLIAM	Map 22 NN17
Highland	

INSPECTOR'S CHOICE

Inverlochy Castle Hotel

★★★★★ @@@ ☞ COUNTRY HOUSE HOTEL

Torlundy, PH33 6SN - **tel:** 01397 702177
email: info@inverlochy.co.uk **web:** www.inverlochycastlehotel.com
dir: Accessible from either A82 (Glasgow-Fort William) or A9 (Edinburgh-Dalwhinnie). Hotel 3m N of Fort William on A82, in Torlundy

With Ben Nevis as its backdrop, this imposing and gracious castle sits amidst extensive gardens and grounds overlooking its own loch. Lavishly appointed in classic country-house style, spacious bedrooms are extremely comfortable and

boast laptops with internet access. The sumptuous main hall and lounge provide the perfect setting for afternoon tea or a pre-dinner cocktail, while imaginative modern British cuisine is served in one of three dining rooms.

Rooms: 17 (6 family) ☞ **Facilities:** STV FTV WiFi ☞ ☞ Snooker room Fishing on loch Massage Riding Hunting Stalking Clay pigeon shooting Archery ♫ Xmas New Year **Conf:** Class 20 Board 20 Thtr 50 **Services:** Night porter **Parking:** 17 **Notes:** Civ Wed 80

Moorings Hotel

★★★★ 73% HOTEL

Banavie, PH33 7LY - **tel:** 01397 772797
email: reservations@moorings-fortwilliam.co.uk **web:** www.moorings-fortwilliam.co.uk
dir: Take A830 N from Fort William, cross Caledonian Canal, 1st right signed Banavie

Located on the Caledonian Canal next to a series of locks known as Neptune's Staircase and close to Thomas Telford's house, this hotel has a dedicated team offering friendly service. Accommodation comes in three distinct styles – Standard, Superior and Executive. These newer rooms with balconies are particularly appealing; many rooms offer canal and/or Ben Nevis view. Meals can be taken in the modern Bistro or alternatively fine dining is offered in the more traditional dining room.

Rooms: 32 (1 family) (1 GF) ☞ **S** £80–£140; **D** £110–£175 (incl. bkfst)*
Facilities: FTV WiFi Gym New Year **Conf:** Class 60 Board 40 Thtr 140
Services: Night porter **Parking:** 60 **Notes:** Closed 24-26 Dec Civ Wed 120

FORT WILLIAM *continued*

Alexandra Hotel

★★★ 73% HOTEL

The Parade, PH33 6AZ - tel: 01397 702241
email: salesalexandra@strathmorehotels.com **web:** www.strathmorehotels.com
dir: *Off A82. Hotel opposite railway station*

This charming old hotel enjoys a prominent position in the town centre and is just a short walk from all the major attractions. Front-facing bedrooms have views over the town and the spectacular Nevis mountain range. There is a choice of restaurants, including a bistro serving meals until late, along with several stylish and very comfortable lounges.

Rooms: 93 (2 family) **S** fr £89; **D** fr £129 (incl. bkfst)* **Facilities:** FTV WiFi Free use of nearby leisure club Xmas New Year **Conf:** Class 100 Board 40 Thtr 120 **Services:** Lift Night porter **Parking:** 50 **Notes:** LB

Croit Anna Hotel

Leisureplex
HOLIDAY HOTELS

★★★ 72% HOTEL

Achintore Road, Drimarben, PH33 6RR - tel: 01397 702268
email: croitanna@leisureplex.co.uk **web:** www.leisureplex.co.uk
dir: *From Glencoe on A82 into Fort William, hotel 1st on right*

Located on the edge of Loch Linnhe, just two miles out of town, this hotel offers some spacious bedrooms, many with fine views over the loch. There is a choice of two comfortable lounges and a large airy restaurant. The hotel appeals to coach parties and independent travellers alike.

Rooms: 90 (5 family) (13 GF) **Facilities:** FTV WiFi Pool table Xmas New Year **Services:** Night porter **Parking:** 25 **Notes:** Closed Dec-Jan (ex Xmas/New Year) RS Nov, Feb & Mar Mon-Fri only

Ben Nevis Hotel & Leisure Club

★★★ 71% HOTEL

North Road, PH33 6TG - tel: 01397 702331
email: salesbennevis@strathmorehotels.com **web:** www.strathmorehotels.com
dir: *Off A82*

This popular hotel is ideally situated on the outskirts of town. It provides comfortable, well-equipped bedrooms; many with views of the impressive Nevis mountains. The hotel's leisure centre is a firm favourite with guests at the hotel. Public areas include a spacious and welcoming bar with a great selection of whiskies.

Rooms: 119 (3 family) (30 GF) **S** £50–£80; **D** £90–£130 (incl. bkfst)* **Facilities:** WiFi supervised Gym Xmas New Year **Conf:** Class 60 Board 40 Thtr 150 **Services:** Night porter **Parking:** 100 **Notes:** Civ Wed 60

Premier Inn Fort William

BUDGET HOTEL

Loch Iall, An Aird, PH33 6AN - tel: 0871 527 8402 (Calls cost 13p per minute plus your phone company's access charge) **web:** www.premierinn.com
dir: *N end of Fort William Shopping Centre, just off A82 (ring road)*

High quality, budget accommodation ideal for both families and business travellers. Spacious, en suite bedrooms feature free WiFi and tea and coffee making facilities, and in most hotels, Freeview TV is also available. The adjacent family restaurant features a wide and varied menu.

Rooms: 103

GALASHIELS	Map 21 NT43
Scottish Borders	

Kingsknowes Hotel

★★★ 81% HOTEL

Selkirk Road, TD1 3HY - tel: 01896 758375
email: enq@kingsknowes.co.uk **web:** www.kingsknowes.co.uk
dir: *33m S of Edinburgh on A7, 2m from Galashiels, 5m from Melrose*

An imposing turreted mansion, this hotel lies in attractive gardens on the outskirts of town close to the River Tweed. It boasts elegant public areas and many spacious bedrooms, some with excellent views. There is a choice of bars, one with a popular menu to supplement the restaurant.

Rooms: 12 (2 family) **Facilities:** FTV WiFi HL **Conf:** Class 40 Board 30 Thtr 80 **Parking:** 65 **Notes:** Civ Wed 75

G

Cally Palace Hotel

★★★★ 76% @ COUNTRY HOUSE HOTEL

Cally Drive, DG7 2DL - tel: 01557 814341
email: info@callypalace.co.uk **web:** www.callypalace.co.uk
dir: *From M6 & A74, signed A75 Dumfries then Stranraer.
At Gatehouse-of-Fleet right onto B727, left at Cally*

A resort hotel with extensive leisure facilities, this grand 18th-century building is set in 500 acres of forest and parkland that incorporates its own golf course. Bedrooms are spacious and well equipped, while public rooms retain a quiet elegance. The short dinner menu focuses on freshly prepared dishes; a pianist plays most nights and the wearing of jacket and tie is obligatory (for gentlemen).

Rooms: 55 (7 family) (4 GF) ☛ **S** £127–£156; **D** £194–£205 (incl. bkfst & dinner)*
Facilities: STV FTV WiFi ⊗ ⚓ 18 Putting green Fishing ⚓ Gym Table tennis Practice fairway Snooker Pool Xmas New Year **Conf:** Class 40 Board 25 Thtr 40 **Services:** Lift Night porter **Parking:** 100 **Notes:** LB Closed Jan-early Feb Civ Wed 130

See also **Clydebank & Uplawmoor**

EST. 1898
PRINCIPAL
HOTEL COMPANY LTD

Blythswood Square

★★★★★ 87% @@ HOTEL

11 Blythswood Square, G2 4AD - tel: 0141 248 8888
email: reserve@blythswoodsquare.com **web:** www.blythswoodsquare.com
dir: *Phone for detailed directions*

Built in 1821, and restored to its former glory, this was the headquarters of the Royal Scottish Automobile Club which was the official start point for the 1955 Monte Carlo Rally. The bedrooms and bathrooms are sumptuous, and include suites and a penthouse. Afternoon tea and cocktails are served in the 35-metre, first-floor Salon Lounge, and the award-winning restaurant occupies the old RSAC's ballroom. The Spa includes a fantastic thermal suite.

Rooms: 100 (5 GF) ☛ **Facilities:** Spa STV FTV WiFi ⊗ ⚓ Gym Thermal experience Xmas New Year **Conf:** Class 80 Board 80 Thtr 130 **Services:** Lift Night porter Air con **Notes:** Civ Wed 80

Hotel du Vin at One Devonshire Gardens

★★★★ 80% @@@ TOWN HOUSE HOTEL

1 Devonshire Gardens, G12 0UX - tel: 0141 339 2001 & 0844 736 4256 (Calls cost 5p per minute plus your phone company's access charge)
email: info.odg@hotelduvin.com **web:** www.hotelduvin.com
dir: *M8 junct 17, follow signs for A82, in 1.5m left into Hyndland Rd, 1st right, right at mini rdbt, right at end*

Situated in a tree-lined Victorian terrace this luxury 'boutique' hotel has stunning, individually designed bedrooms and suites that have the trademark Egyptian linens and seriously good showers. The oak-panelled Bistro offers a daily-changing menu of both classic and modern dishes with a Scottish influence. Naturally, wine is an important part of the equation here, and knowledgeable staff can guide guests around the impressive wine list.

Rooms: 49 (7 GF) ☛ **S** fr £109; **D** fr £109* **Facilities:** STV WiFi Gym Beauty treatment room Tennis & Squash facilities at nearby club Xmas New Year **Conf:** Class 30 Board 30 Thtr 50 Del from £190 **Services:** Night porter **Notes:** Civ Wed 80

Malmaison Glasgow

★★★★ 80% @@ ⚓ HOTEL

278 West George Street, G2 4LL - tel: 0141 572 1000 & 0844 693 0653 (Calls cost 5p per minute plus your phone company's access charge)
email: reception.glasgow@malmaison.com **web:** www.malmaison.com
dir: *From S & E: M8 junct 18 Charing Cross. From W & N: M8 city centre*

Built around a former church in the historic Charing Cross area, this hotel is a smart, contemporary establishment offering impressive levels of service and hospitality. Bedrooms are spacious and feature a host of modern facilities, such as CD players and mini bars. Dining is a treat here, with French brasserie-style cuisine, backed up by an excellent wine list, served in the original crypt.

Rooms: 72 (4 family) (19 GF) ☛ **Facilities:** STV WiFi ⚓ New Year **Conf:** Class 20 Board 22 Thtr 56 **Services:** Lift Night porter **Notes:** Civ Wed 60

Golden Jubilee Conference Hotel

★★★★ 76% @ HOTEL

Beardmore Street, G81 4SA - tel: 0141 951 6000
email: hotel@goldenjubilee.scot.nhs.uk **web:** www.goldenjubileehotel.com

(For full entry see Clydebank)

GLASGOW *continued*

Hallmark Hotel Glasgow

★★★★ 75% HOTEL

27 Washington Street, G3 8AZ - tel: 0330 028 3407
email: glasgow@hallmarkhotels.co.uk **web:** www.hallmarkhotels.co.uk
dir: *M8 junct 19, follow signs for SECC & Broomielaw. Left at lights*

Centrally located, this modern hotel is a short drive from the airport and a short walk from the centre of the city. Bedrooms are generally spacious and boast a range of facilities, including high-speed internet access. Facilities include a brasserie restaurant and an impressive indoor leisure facility.

Rooms: 141 (16 family) **S** £60–£280; **D** £60–£280* **Facilities:** Spa STV FTV WiFi ⓒ supervised Gym **Conf:** Class 80 Board 70 Thtr 160 **Services:** Lift Night porter Air con **Parking:** 50 **Notes:** LB Civ Wed 150

G

The Grand Central Hotel

★★★★ 74% HOTEL

99 Gordon Street, G1 3SF - tel: 0141 240 3700
email: grandcentralhotel@principal-hayley.com **web:** www.principal-hayley.com
dir: *M8 junct 19 towards city centre, turn left at Hope St. Hotel 200mtrs on right*

This is the place where John Logie Baird transmitted the world's first long-distance television pictures in 1927, and this 'grand old lady' of the Glasgow hotel scene is appointed to a very good standard. The decor is a blend of contemporary, art deco and original Victorian styles. Bedrooms are well equipped and suit business travellers especially. There is Champagne Central, a glamorous bar, the Tempus Bar and Restaurant, and Deli Central (with direct access to the Central Station) which is an eat-in deli and a takeaway. Ample meeting facilities are available, and NCP car parks are nearby.

Rooms: 230 (15 family) ⓡ **Facilities:** FTV WiFi ⓭ New Year **Conf:** Class 350 Board 60 Thtr 500 **Services:** Lift Night porter **Notes:** Civ Wed 500

Holiday Inn Glasgow City Centre - Theatreland

★★★ 82% ⓦ HOTEL

161 West Nile Street, G1 2RL - tel: 0141 352 8300
email: reservations@higlasgow.com **web:** www.holidayinn.co.uk
dir: *M8 junct 16, follow signs for Royal Concert Hall, hotel opposite*

Built on a corner site close to the Theatre Royal Concert Hall and the main shopping areas, this contemporary hotel features the popular La Bonne Auberge French restaurant, a bar area and conservatory. The bedrooms are well equipped and comfortable; suites are available. Staff are friendly and attentive.

Rooms: 113 (20 family) (10 smoking) ⓡ **S** £80–£199; **D** £80–£199 **Facilities:** STV FTV WiFi ⓭ **Conf:** Class 60 Board 60 Thtr 100 **Services:** Lift Night porter Air con

Uplawmoor Hotel

★★★ 78% SMALL HOTEL

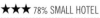

66 Neilston Road, G78 4AF - tel: 01505 850565
email: info@uplawmoor.co.uk **web:** www.uplawmoor.co.uk

(For full entry see Uplawmoor)

Novotel Glasgow Centre

★★★ 77% HOTEL

181 Pitt Street, G2 4DT - tel: 0141 222 2775
email: H3136@accor.com **web:** www.novotel.com
dir: *M8 junct 18 for Charing Cross. Follow to Sauchiehall St. 3rd right*

Enjoying a convenient city centre location and limited parking spaces, this hotel is ideal for both business and leisure travellers. Well-equipped bedrooms are brightly decorated and offer functional design. Modern public areas include a small fitness club and a lively bar serving a range of meals all day. The 'Virtual Concierge' system is available at reception – a great way to learn more about the city.

Rooms: 139 (139 family) **Facilities:** STV FTV WiFi Gym Sauna Steam room Xmas **Conf:** Class 20 Board 20 Thtr 40 **Services:** Lift Night porter Air con **Parking:** 19

Mercure Glasgow City Hotel

★★★ 75% HOTEL

201 Ingram Street, G1 1DQ - tel: 0844 815 9103 (Calls cost 5p per minute plus your phone company's access charge)
email: info@mercureglasgow.co.uk **web:** www.jupiterhotels.co.uk
dir: *M8 junct 15, straight through 4 lights, left at 5th into Hanover St, left into George Sq, right into Frederick St. Right at 2nd lights into Ingram St*

This hotel enjoys a fantastic location in the heart of Glasgow with great access to shops, bars and restaurants. Bedrooms provide modern accommodation and a host of accessories including complimentary WiFi. Extensive conference facilities and the popular Bagio Café Bar mean you may not need to leave the hotel at all.

Rooms: 91 **Facilities:** New Year **Conf:** Class 40 Board 40 Thtr 80 **Services:** Lift Night porter **Parking:** 30 **Notes:** Civ Wed 80

Premier Inn Glasgow (Bearsden)

BUDGET HOTEL

279 Milngavie Road, G61 3DQ - tel: 0871 527 8418 (Calls cost 13p per minute plus your phone company's access charge) **web:** www.premierinn.com
dir: *M8 junct 16, A81. Pass Asda on right. Hotel on left, behind The Burnbrae*

High quality, budget accommodation ideal for both families and business travellers. Spacious, en suite bedrooms feature free WiFi and tea and coffee making facilities, and in most hotels, Freeview TV is also available. The adjacent family restaurant features a wide and varied menu.

Rooms: 61

Premier Inn Glasgow (Bellshill)

BUDGET HOTEL

New Edinburgh Road, Bellshill, ML4 3PD - tel: 0871 527 8421 (Calls cost 13p per minute plus your phone company's access charge) **web:** www.premierinn.com
dir: *M74 junct 5, A725. Follow Bellshill A721 signs, bear left. At rdbt left, follow Tannochside sign. At next rdbt left into Bellziehill Rd. Hotel on right*

Rooms: 60

Premier Inn Glasgow Buchanan Galleries Hotel

BUDGET HOTEL

St Andrew House, 141 West Nile Street, G1 2RN - tel: 0871 527 9360 (Calls cost 13p per minute plus your phone company's access charge) **web:** www.premierinn.com
dir: *Phone for detailed directions*

Rooms: 210

Premier Inn Glasgow (Cambuslang/M74 Jct 2A)

BUDGET HOTEL

Cambuslang Investment Park, Off London Road, G32 8YX - **tel:** 0871 527 8422 (Calls cost 13p per minute plus your phone company's access charge)
web: www.premierinn.com
dir: *At end of M74, turn right at rdbt. At 1st lights turn right, at 2nd lights straight ahead. Hotel on right*

Rooms: 76

Premier Inn Glasgow City Centre Argyle St

BUDGET HOTEL

377 Argyle Street, G2 8LL - **tel:** 0141 248 2355 & 0871 527 8436 (Calls cost 13p per minute plus your phone company's access charge) **web:** www.premierinn.com
dir: *From S: M8 junct 19, at pedestrian lights left into Argyle St. Hotel 200yds on right*

Rooms: 124

Premier Inn Glasgow City Centre (Charing Cross)

BUDGET HOTEL

10 Elmbank Gardens, G2 4PP - **tel:** 0871 527 8438 (Calls cost 13p per minute plus your phone company's access charge) **web:** www.premierinn.com
dir: *Phone for detailed directions*

Rooms: 278

Premier Inn Glasgow City Centre (George Square)

BUDGET HOTEL

187 George Street, G1 1YU - **tel:** 0871 527 8440 (Calls cost 13p per minute plus your phone company's access charge) **web:** www.premierinn.com
dir: *M8 junct 15, into Stirling Rd. Right into Cathedral St. At 1st lights left into Montrose St. Hotel after 1st lights*

Rooms: 239

Premier Inn Glasgow City Centre South

BUDGET HOTEL

80 Ballater Street, G5 0TW - **tel:** 0871 527 8442 (Calls cost 13p per minute plus your phone company's access charge) **web:** www.premierinn.com
dir: *M8 junct 21 follow East Kilbride signs, right onto A8 into Kingston St. Right into South Portland St, left into Norfolk St, through Gorbals St into Ballater St*

Rooms: 123

Premier Inn Glasgow East

BUDGET HOTEL

601 Hamilton Road, Uddingston, G71 7SA - **tel:** 0871 527 8444 (Calls cost 13p per minute plus your phone company's access charge) **web:** www.premierinn.com
dir: *At entrance to Glasgow Zoo, adjacent to junct 4 of M73 & M74*

Rooms: 68

Premier Inn Glasgow Pacific Quay SECC

BUDGET HOTEL

Pacific Quay, G51 1DZ - **tel:** 0871 527 9340 (Calls cost 13p per minute plus your phone company's access charge) **web:** www.premierinn.com
dir: *M8 junct 24, left into Helen St, 2nd exit at rdbt, follow Glasgow Science Centre signs. Right into Govan Rd. 1st exit at rdbt into Pacific Dr (pass Science Centre & BBC Scotland). Hotel on left*

Rooms: 180

citizenM Glasgow

AA Advertised

60 Renfrew Street, G2 3BW - **tel:** 020 3519 1111
email: supportgla@citizenm.com **web:** www.citizenm.com
dir: *Phone for detailed directions*

Right in the heart of Glasgow, citizenM Glasgow is the height of urban, stylish, business-and-pleasure, boutique accommodation. From the '1 minute check in/out' promise to the new-media friendly meeting rooms and lobby, this is something different. The bedrooms are stylishly economical, making the most of limited space. They have super-sized beds, blackout blinds, free WiFi, ambient mood lighting, a rain shower and a wall-to-wall window above the bed. CanteenM offers breakfast, lunch and dinner, and serves as a 24-hour bar.

Rooms: 198 Facilities: STV FTV WiFi

The Z Hotel Glasgow

AA Advertised

36 North Frederick Street, G1 2BS - **tel:** 0141 212 4550
email: glasgow@thezhotels.com
dir: *0.1m from George Sq*

Stay in the heart of Glasgow for an out-of-town price, at Z Hotel Glasgow, a converted printworks right next to George Square, with over 100 bedrooms arranged around a central lightwell over the ground and five upper floors. Each room has an en suite wet room, crisp bed linen, 40" TV with Sky channels, and complimentary WiFi.

Rooms: 104 (16 GF) ☏ S fr £35; D fr £45* Facilities: STV FTV WiFi ⌕
Services: Lift Night porter Air con

GLASGOW AIRPORT	Map 20 NS46
Renfrewshire	

Premier Inn Glasgow Airport

BUDGET HOTEL

Whitecart Road, Glasgow Airport, PA3 2TH - **tel:** 0871 527 8434 (Calls cost 13p per minute plus your phone company's access charge) **web:** www.premierinn.com
dir: *M8 junct 28, follow airport signs for Long Stay & Car Park 3 (Premier Inn signed). At 1st rdbt right into St Andrews Drive. At next rdbt right into Whitecart Rd. Under motorway. Left at garage. Hotel on right*

High quality, budget accommodation ideal for both families and business travellers. Spacious, en suite bedrooms feature free WiFi and tea and coffee making facilities, and in most hotels, Freeview TV is also available. The adjacent family restaurant features a wide and varied menu.

Rooms: 105

G

GLASGOW AIRPORT continued

Premier Inn Glasgow (Paisley)

BUDGET HOTEL

Phoenix Retail Park, PA1 2BH - **tel:** 0871 527 8432 (Calls cost 13p per minute plus your phone company's access charge) **web:** www.premierinn.com
dir: M8 junct 28a, A737 signed Irvine, take 1st exit signed Linwood, left at 1st rdbt to Phoenix Park

Rooms: 62

GLENEAGLES

See **Auchterarder**

GLENFINNAN   Map 22 NM98
Highland

The Prince's House

★★★ 81% ◎◎ SMALL HOTEL

PH37 4LT - **tel:** 01397 722246
email: princeshouse@glenfinnan.co.uk **web:** www.glenfinnan.co.uk
dir: On A830, 0.5m on right past Glenfinnan Monument. 200mtrs from railway station

This delightful hotel enjoys a well deserved reputation for fine food and excellent hospitality. The hotel has inspiring views and sits close to where 'Bonnie' Prince Charlie raised the Jacobite standard. Comfortably appointed bedrooms offer pleasing decor. Excellent local game and seafood can be enjoyed in the restaurant and the bar.

Rooms: 9 ⬧ **S** £75–£95; **D** £150–£225 (incl. bkfst)* **Facilities:** STV FTV WiFi ⬧ New Year **Conf:** Class 20 Thtr 40 **Parking:** 18 **Notes:** LB Closed Nov, Xmas, Jan-Feb RS Oct, Dec & Mar restaurant open for bookings only

---

GLENROTHES   Map 21 NO20
Fife

Premier Inn Glenrothes

BUDGET HOTEL

Beaufort Drive, Bankhead Roundabout, KY7 4UJ - **tel:** 0871 527 8454 (Calls cost 13p per minute plus your phone company's access charge) **web:** www.premierinn.com
dir: M90 junct 2a N'bound, A92 to Glenrothes. At 2nd rbt (Bankhead) take 3rd exit. Hotel on left

High quality, budget accommodation ideal for both families and business travellers. Spacious, en suite bedrooms feature free WiFi and tea and coffee making facilities, and in most hotels, Freeview TV is also available. The adjacent family restaurant features a wide and varied menu.

Rooms: 65

GRANGEMOUTH   Map 21 NS98
Falkirk

The Grange Manor

★★★★ 76% HOTEL

Glensburgh, FK3 8XJ - **tel:** 01324 474836
email: info@grangemanor.co.uk **web:** www.grangemanor.co.uk
dir: E: M9 junct 6, hotel 200mtrs to right. W: M9 junct 5, A905 for 2m

Located south of town and close to the M9, this stylish hotel, popular with business and corporate clientele, benefits from hands-on family ownership. It offers spacious, high quality accommodation with superb bathrooms. Public areas include a comfortable foyer area, a lounge bar and a smart restaurant. Cook's bar and restaurant is adjacent to the main house in the converted stables. Staff throughout are very friendly.

Rooms: 36 (30 annexe) (6 family) (15 GF) **Facilities:** FTV WiFi Xmas New Year **Conf:** Class 68 Board 40 Thtr 120 **Services:** Lift Night porter **Parking:** 154 **Notes:** Civ Wed 120

GRANTOWN-ON-SPEY   Map 23 NJ02
Highland

Grant Arms Hotel

★★★ 82% HOTEL

25-27 The Square, PH26 3HF - **tel:** 01479 872526
email: info@grantarmshotel.com **web:** www.grantarmshotel.com
dir: Exit A9 N of Aviemore onto A95

Conveniently located in the centre of the town, this fine hotel is appointed to a high standard yet still retains the building's traditional character. The spacious bedrooms are stylishly presented and very well equipped. The Garden Restaurant is a popular venue for dinner, and lighter snacks can be enjoyed in the comfortable bar. Modern conference facilities are available and the hotel is very popular with birdwatchers and wildlife enthusiasts.

Rooms: 50 (7 family) ⬧ **S** £60–£75; **D** £120–£150 (incl. bkfst) **Facilities:** STV FTV WiFi ⬧ Birdwatching & Wildlife Club 🎵 Xmas New Year **Conf:** Class 30 Board 16 Thtr 70 Del from £75 **Services:** Lift Night porter **Notes:** LB

GREENOCK   Map 20 NS27
Inverclyde

Premier Inn Greenock

BUDGET HOTEL

The Point, 1-3 James Watt Way, PA15 2AD - **tel:** 0871 527 8476 (Calls cost 13p per minute plus your phone company's access charge) **web:** www.premierinn.com
dir: A8 to Greenock. At rdbt junct of East Hamilton St & Main St (McDonalds visable on right) take 3rd exit. Hotel on left

High quality, budget accommodation ideal for both families and business travellers. Spacious, en suite bedrooms feature free WiFi and tea and coffee making facilities, and in most hotels, Freeview TV is also available. The adjacent family restaurant features a wide and varied menu.

Rooms: 62

GRETNA SERVICE AREA (A74(M))   Map 21 NY36
Dumfries & Galloway

Days Inn Gretna Green - M74

WELCOME BREAK

AA Advertised

Welcome Break Service Area, DG16 5HQ - **tel:** 01461 337566
email: gretna.hotel@welcomebreak.co.uk **web:** www.welcomebreak.co.uk
dir: Between junct 21 & 22 of A74(M) – accessible from both N'bound & S'bound carriageways

This modern building offers accommodation in smart, spacious and well-equipped bedrooms suitable for families and business travellers, and all with en suite bathrooms. Continental breakfast is available and other refreshments may be taken at the nearby family restaurant.

Rooms: 64 (54 family) (64 GF) **Facilities:** FTV WiFi ⬧ Xmas New Year **Parking:** 60

GRETNA (WITH GRETNA GREEN)
Dumfries & Galloway

Map 21 NY36

Smiths at Gretna Green
★★★★ 79% HOTEL

Gretna Green, DG16 5EA - tel: 01461 337007
email: info@smithsgretnagreen.com web: www.smithsgretnagreen.com
dir: From M74 junct 22 follow signs to Old Blacksmith's Shop. Hotel opposite

Located next to the World Famous Old Blacksmith's Shop Centre just off the motorway linking Scotland and England. The bedrooms offer a spacious environment, complete with TVs, DVD players and broadband. Family rooms feature a separate children's area with bunk beds, each with its own TV. Three suites and a penthouse apartment are also available. Open-plan contemporary day rooms lead to the brasserie restaurant; impressive conference and banqueting facilities are provided.

Rooms: 56 (6 annexe) (8 family) ⬥ Facilities: STV FTV WiFi ⤶ HL Beauty treatment room New Year Conf: Class 100 Board 40 Thtr 250 Services: Lift Night porter Air con Parking: 115 Notes: Civ Wed 150

The Gables Hotel
★★★ Ⓐ HOTEL

1 Annan Road, DG16 5DQ - tel: 01461 338300
email: reservations@gables-hotel-gretna.co.uk web: www.gables-hotel-gretna.co.uk
dir: M74 S or M6/M74 N follow signs for Gretna. At rdbt at Gretna Gateway take exit onto Annan Rd, hotel 200yds on right

This Grade II listed hotel is located close to the Gretna Gateway and is ideally located to explore both Galloway and the border city of Carlisle. Bedrooms provide comfortable and well-appointed accommodation, while the main restaurant offers a carte menu with a range of freshly prepared dishes; Saddlers bar provides light snacks and meals.

Rooms: 31 (5 family) (10 GF) ⬥ S £69–£99; D £79–£140 (incl. bkfst) Facilities: FTV WiFi ♫ Xmas New Year Conf: Class 60 Board 48 Thtr 100 Del from £119 Services: Night porter Parking: 60 Notes: Civ Wed 100

GULLANE
East Lothian

Map 21 NT48

Greywalls and Chez Roux
★★★★★ 86% ⬥⬥⬥ COUNTRY HOUSE HOTEL

Muirfield, EH31 2EG - tel: 01620 842144
email: enquiries@greywalls.co.uk web: www.greywalls.co.uk
dir: From Edinburgh follow A1, junct for North Berwick A198 then Gullane. Greywalls is at the end of village on left

Located in the magnificent East Lothian countryside, Greywalls is just half an hour's drive from Edinburgh, and is located next to the world-famous Muirfield golf course. The hotel offers easy access to some wonderful beaches and there are 10 golf courses within five miles. In the grounds are some delightful gardens, and you may be lucky enough to see the beekeeper tending the hives. Inside, public areas are warm and welcoming with an array of seating areas and open fires adding to the charm. Bedrooms are well appointed, in keeping with the style and character of the house. Award-winning food from the Chez Roux team is well worth staying in for, while the hearty breakfast will set you up for the day.

Rooms: 23 (6 annexe) (5 GF) ⬥ S £93.50–£137.50; D £269.50–£407 (incl. bkfst)* Facilities: FTV WiFi ⤶ Putting green ⛳ Holistic massage Walled gardens Golf retreats ♫ Xmas New Year Conf: Class 18 Board 18 Thtr 60 Del from £195 Services: Night porter Parking: 40 Notes: LB Civ Wed 120

INVERARAY
Argyll & Bute

Map 20 NN00

Loch Fyne Hotel & Spa
★★★★ 72% HOTEL

Shore Street, PA32 8XT - tel: 01499 302980
email: lochfyne@crerarhotels.com web: www.crerarhotels.com/loch-fyne-hotel-spa
dir: From A83 Loch Lomond, through town centre on A80 to Lochgilphead. Hotel in 0.5m on the right, overlooking Loch Fyne

Loch Fyne Hotel & Spa is situated in a stunning location with uninterrupted views across the loch and surrounding landscape, just a short drive from a range of ancient buildings. Public areas include the Clansman restaurant and a large lounge bar with comfy sofas. The bedrooms are modern and well equipped; some have views of the loch.

Rooms: 67 (9 family) (15 GF) ⬥ S £85–£185; D £99–£195 (incl. bkfst)* Facilities: Spa FTV WiFi ⤶ ⟳ Sauna Steam room Xmas New Year Conf: Class 40 Board 25 Thtr 80 Del from £125 Services: Lift Night porter Parking: 60 Notes: LB Civ Wed 120

INVERGARRY
Highland

Map 22 NH30

Glengarry Castle Hotel
★★★ 82% ⬥ COUNTRY HOUSE HOTEL

PH35 4HW - tel: 01809 501254
email: castle@glengarry.net web: www.glengarry.net
dir: On A82, 0.5m from A82/A87 junct

This charming country-house hotel is set in 50 acres of grounds on the shores of Loch Oich. The spacious day rooms include comfortable sitting rooms with lots to read and board games to play. The classical dining room boasts an innovative menu that showcases local Scottish produce. The smart bedrooms vary in size and style but all boast magnificent loch or woodland views. The grounds are well worth exploring, with a tennis court and paths along the loch to be found.

Rooms: 26 (2 family) ⬥ S £90–£100; D £130–£240 (incl. bkfst) Facilities: FTV WiFi ⌕ Fishing Parking: 30 Notes: Closed mid Nov-mid Mar

I

INVERGORDON
Highland — Map 23 NH76

Kincraig Castle Hotel

★★★★ 80% ® COUNTRY HOUSE HOTEL

IV18 0LF - **tel:** 01349 852587
email: info@kincraig-castle-hotel.co.uk **web:** www.kincraig-castle-hotel.co.uk
dir: Off A9 past Alness towards Tain. Hotel on left 0.25m past Rosskeen Church

This imposing castle is set in well-tended grounds in an elevated position with views over the Cromarty Firth. It offers smart, individually designed, well-equipped bedrooms with satellite TVs, and inviting public areas that retain original features. However, it is the friendly service and commitment to guest care that will leave a lasting impression.

Rooms: 15 (1 family) (1 GF) ℸ **S** £70–£160; **D** £80–£295 (incl. bkfst)*
Facilities: FTV WiFi ⋈ ⅃ 4 Putting green ⛳ Xmas New Year **Conf:** Class 30 Board 40 Thtr 50 **Services:** Night porter **Parking:** 40 **Notes:** LB Civ Wed 70

INVERNESS
Highland — Map 23 NH64

Rocpool Reserve and Chez Roux

★★★★★ 83% ®® ⌾ SMALL HOTEL

14 Culduthel Road, IV2 4AG - **tel:** 01463 240089
email: info@rocpool.com **web:** www.rocpool.com
dir: A9 to Inverness, take exit for Raigmore Hospital then follow signs for city centre. Left at lights into Southside Rd, right into Culduthel Rd

This luxury hotel enjoys a great location in a residential area close to the city centre. A high level of personal service is offered and bedrooms provide comfort and quality. The stylish R Bar is the perfect location for a cocktail and their Chez Roux Restaurant (operated by Albert Roux) provides memorable food in a modern space. Some rooms enjoy personal outdoor hot tubs.

Rooms: 11 (2 GF) ℸ **Facilities:** FTV WiFi ⋈ **Conf:** Class 16 Board 18 Thtr 20 **Services:** Night porter Air con **Parking:** 14 **Notes:** LB Civ Wed 20

Loch Ness Country House Hotel

★★★★ 79% ®® SMALL HOTEL

Loch Ness Road, IV3 8JN - **tel:** 01463 230512
email: info@lochnesscountryhousehotel.co.uk
web: www.lochnesscountryhousehotel.co.uk
dir: On A82, 1m from Inverness

Built in the Georgian era, this fine house is perfectly situated in its own six acre private Highland estate. The hotel has luxurious bedrooms, some of which are in the garden suite cottages. The stylish restaurant serves the best of local produce and guests have a choice of cosy well-appointed lounges for after-dinner drinks. The terrace is ideal for relaxation and has splendid views over the landscaped gardens towards Inverness.

Rooms: 13 (2 annexe) (8 family) (3 GF) **Facilities:** FTV WiFi Xmas New Year **Conf:** Class 40 Board 40 Thtr 100 **Services:** Night porter **Parking:** 70 **Notes:** LB Civ Wed 150

The New Drumossie Hotel

★★★★ 77% ®® HOTEL

Old Perth Road, IV2 5BE - **tel:** 01463 236451 & 0870 194 2110 (Calls cost 13p per minute plus your phone company's access charge)
email: stay@drumossiehotel.co.uk **web:** www.drumossiehotel.co.uk
dir: From A9 follow signs for Culloden Battlefield, hotel on left after 1m

Set in nine acres of landscaped hillside grounds south of Inverness, this hotel has fine views of the Moray Firth towards Ben Wyvis. Art deco-style decoration together with a country-house atmosphere are found throughout. Service is friendly and attentive, the food imaginative and enjoyable, and the bedrooms spacious and well presented. The main function room is probably the largest in this area.

Rooms: 44 (10 family) (6 GF) ℸ **Facilities:** STV FTV WiFi HL Fishing New Year **Conf:** Class 200 Board 40 Thtr 500 **Services:** Lift Night porter **Parking:** 200 **Notes:** Civ Wed 400

Bunchrew House Hotel

★★★★ 75% ®® COUNTRY HOUSE HOTEL

Bunchrew, IV3 8TA - **tel:** 01463 234917
email: welcome@bunchrewhousehotel.com **web:** www.bunchrewhousehotel.com
dir: W on A862. Hotel 2m after canal on right

Overlooking the Beauly Firth this impressive mansion house dates from the 17th century and retains much original character. Individually styled bedrooms are spacious and tastefully furnished. A wood-panelled restaurant is the setting for artfully constructed cooking and there is a choice of comfortable lounges complete with real fires.

Rooms: 16 (4 family) (1 GF) ℸ **Facilities:** FTV WiFi Fishing New Year **Conf:** Class 30 Board 30 Thtr 80 **Services:** Night porter **Parking:** 40 **Notes:** Closed 24-27 Dec Civ Wed 92

Glenmoriston Town House Hotel

★★★★ 74% ® TOWN HOUSE HOTEL

20 Ness Bank, IV2 4SF - **tel:** 01463 223777
email: reception@glenmoristontownhouse.com **web:** www.glenmoristontownhouse.com
dir: On river opposite theatre

Bold contemporary designs blend seamlessly with the classical architecture of this stylish hotel, situated on the banks of the River Ness. Delightful day rooms include a well-stocked piano bar with a fine selection of malt whiskies and an interesting cocktail menu. Contrast Brasserie features accomplished modern cooking based on the finest Scottish produce. When the weather allows, alfresco eating is possible with views over the River Ness. The sleek, modern, individually designed bedrooms have many facilities including free WiFi and DVD players.

Rooms: 30 (15 annexe) (1 family) (6 GF) ♪ **S** £95–£175; **D** £100–£245 (incl. bkfst)*
Facilities: STV FTV WiFi ♪ ♫ Xmas New Year **Conf:** Class 40 Board 60 Thtr 90
Services: Night porter **Parking:** 40 **Notes:** LB Civ Wed 70

Mercure Inverness Hotel

★★★★ 71% HOTEL

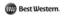

Church Street, IV1 1DX - tel: 0844 815 9006 (Calls cost 7p per minute plus your phone company's access charge)
email: info@mercureinverness.co.uk **web:** www.mercureinverness.co.uk
dir: From A9 junct A82 Kessock Bridge join A82 Inverness. At rdbt 2nd exit, rdbt straight ahead next rdbt left onto B865. Right at lights continue past church, hotel on left

The Mercure Inverness Hotel is in an ideal location, with the bustling Inverness city centre to one side, and the attractive River Ness running the length of the other. Spacious public areas, an inviting gym area and comfortable bedrooms can all be found here. The Brasserie serves a wide ranging selection of dishes. On-site parking and complimentary WiFi are added bonuses.

Rooms: 118 ♪ **Facilities:** FTV WiFi ♪ Gym 24 hour gym **Conf:** Class 130 Board 90 Thtr 200 **Services:** Lift Night porter **Parking:** 55 **Notes:** Civ Wed 200

Best Western Inverness Palace Hotel & Spa

★★★ 79% HOTEL

8 Ness Walk, IV3 5NG - tel: 01463 223243
email: palace@miltonhotels.com **web:** www.invernesspalacehotel.co.uk
dir: A82 Glenurquhart Rd onto Ness Walk. Hotel 300yds on right opposite Inverness Castle

Set on the north side of the River Ness close to the Eden Court theatre and a short walk from the town, this hotel has a contemporary look. The bedrooms are comfortable and modern, while public areas feature a Starbucks coffee shop and extensive leisure facilities.

Rooms: 89 (48 annexe) (3 family) ♪ **Facilities:** Spa FTV WiFi ☻ supervised Gym Beautician Sauna Steam room Xmas New Year **Conf:** Class 40 Board 30 Thtr 80 **Services:** Lift Night porter **Parking:** 18 **Notes:** Civ Wed 100

Royal Highland Hotel

★★★ 77% HOTEL

Station Square, Academy Street, IV1 1LG - tel: 01463 231926
email: info@royalhighlandhotel.co.uk **web:** www.royalhighlandhotel.co.uk
dir: From A9 into town centre. Hotel next to rail station & Eastgate Retail Centre

Built in 1858 adjacent to the railway station, the Royal Highland Hotel has a typically grand Victorian foyer with comfortable seating. The contemporary ASH Brasserie and bar is a refreshing venue for both eating and drinking throughout the day. The generally spacious bedrooms are comfortably equipped especially for the business traveller. An art gallery showcases an impressive array of artwork.

Rooms: 86 (12 family) (2 GF) (10 smoking) ♪ **S** £55–£179; **D** £60–£250
Facilities: FTV WiFi Xmas New Year **Conf:** Class 80 Board 80 Thtr 200 **Services:** Lift Night porter **Parking:** 8 **Notes:** LB Civ Wed 200

Premier Inn Inverness Centre (Milburn Rd)

BUDGET HOTEL

Millburn Road, IV2 3QX - tel: 0871 527 8544 (Calls cost 13p per minute plus your phone company's access charge) **web:** www.premierinn.com
dir: From A9 & A96 junct (Raigmore Interchange, signed Airport/Aberdeen), take B865 towards town centre, hotel 100yds after next rdbt

High quality, budget accommodation ideal for both families and business travellers. Spacious, en suite bedrooms feature free WiFi and tea and coffee making facilities, and in most hotels, Freeview TV is also available. The adjacent family restaurant features a wide and varied menu.

Rooms: 55

Premier Inn Inverness Centre (River Ness)

BUDGET HOTEL

19-21 Huntly Street, IV3 5PR - tel: 0871 527 9302 (Calls cost 13p per minute plus your phone company's access charge) **web:** www.premierinn.com
dir: Exit A9 at Longman rdbt, 1st exit into Longman Rd (A82) follow Inverness/Fort William signs. Straight on at 3 rdbts. At Telford St rdbt 1st exit into Wells St. Right into Huntly St. Hotel on right

Rooms: 99

Premier Inn Inverness East

BUDGET HOTEL

Beechwood Business Park, IV2 3BW - tel: 0871 527 8546 (Calls cost 13p per minute plus your phone company's access charge) **web:** www.premierinn.com
dir: From A9 follow Raigmore Hospital, Police HQ & Inshes Retail Park signs

Rooms: 74

Premier Inn Inverness West

BUDGET HOTEL

Glenurquhart Road, IV3 5TD - tel: 0871 527 9338 (Calls cost 13p per minute plus your phone company's access charge) **web:** www.premierinn.com
dir: From A9 exit at Kessock rdbt. At 4th rdbt 2nd exit into Kenneth St. Right at lights into Glenurquhart Rd, pass council offices, 1m, take A82 signed Fort William. Cross Caledonian Canal Bridge. Hotel on right

Rooms: 76

INVERURIE
Aberdeenshire

Map 23 NJ72

Thainstone House
★★★★ 77% @@ HOTEL

AB51 5NT - tel: 01467 621643
email: thainstone@crerarhotels.com **web:** www.crerarhotels.com/thainstone-house-hotel
dir: A96 from Aberdeen. Pass by-pass to Kintore. Entrance to hotel at 1st rdbt (Thainstone Rdbt). Take 1st left then sharp right to hotel

Situated in several acres of gardens and meadowlands, this former Jacobean house has been developed throughout the centuries. The hotel now provides a choice of bars, lounges and a well-equipped games room. Spa facilities include an outdoor hot tub, sauna, pool and gym. Dining is available in the Green Lady restaurant or Stockmans bar.

Rooms: 48 (12 GF) ✎ **S** fr £89; **D** fr £99 (incl. bkfst)* **Facilities:** Spa STV WiFi ⊙ Gym Sauna Steam room Hot tub Xmas New Year **Conf:** Class 100 Board 25 Thtr 200 **Services:** Lift Night porter **Parking:** 100 **Notes:** LB Civ Wed 180

Macdonald Pittodrie House
★★★★ 75% @@ HOTEL

Chapel of Garioch, Pitcaple, **AB51 5HS - tel:** 0121 643 9191
email: gm.pittodrie@macdonald-hotels.co.uk **web:** www.macdonald-hotels.com/pittodrie
dir: From A96 towards Inverness, pass Inverurie under bridge with lights. Turn left & follow signs

Set in extensive grounds this house dates from the 15th century and retains many historic features. Public rooms include a gracious drawing room, restaurant, and a cosy bar boasting an impressive selection of whiskies. The well-proportioned bedrooms are found in both the original house and in the extension that was designed to match the existing building.

Rooms: 27 (6 family) **Facilities:** STV FTV WiFi Clay pigeon shooting Quad biking Outdoor activities Xmas New Year **Conf:** Class 75 Board 50 Thtr 150 **Services:** Night porter **Parking:** 200 **Notes:** Civ Wed 120

IRVINE
North Ayrshire

Map 20 NS33

Hallmark Hotel Irvine
★★★★ 70% HOTEL

46 Annick Road, **KA11 4LD - tel:** 0330 028 3415
email: irvine@menzieshotels.co.uk **web:** www.hallmarkhotels.co.uk
dir: From A78 at Warrix Interchange follow Irvine Central signs. At rdbt 2nd exit (town centre). At next rdbt right onto A71/Kilmarnock. Hotel 100mtrs on left

Situated on the edge of Irvine with good transportation links (including Prestwick Airport just seven miles away), this is a well-presented hotel that has an extremely friendly team with good customer care awareness. The decor is contemporary throughout, and there is a brasserie-style restaurant, cocktail bar and spacious lounge.

Rooms: 128 (14 family) (64 GF) **Facilities:** STV FTV WiFi ⊠ Fishing Xmas New Year **Conf:** Class 140 Board 100 Thtr 280 **Services:** Night porter **Parking:** 180 **Notes:** LB Civ Wed 200

KELSO
Scottish Borders

Map 21 NT73

The Roxburghe Hotel, Golf Course and Chez Roux
★★★★ 81% @@ COUNTRY HOUSE HOTEL

Heiton, **TD5 8JZ - tel:** 01573 450331
email: hotel@roxburghe.net **web:** www.roxburghe-hotel.net
dir: From A68 Jedburgh take A698 to Heiton, 3m SW of Kelso

Outdoor sporting pursuits are popular at this impressive Jacobean mansion owned by the Duke of Roxburghe, and set in 500 acres of woods and parkland bordering the River Teviot. Gracious public areas are the perfect settings for afternoon teas and carefully prepared meals. The elegant bedrooms are individually designed, some by the Duchess herself, and include superior rooms, some with four posters and log fires.

Rooms: 22 (6 annexe) (3 family) (8 GF) **S** £125–£204; **D** £125–£204* **Facilities:** Spa FTV WiFi ⊠ ⚓ 18 Putting green Fishing ⊰ Clay shooting Health & beauty salon Mountain bike hire Falconry Archery Xmas New Year **Conf:** Class 20 Board 20 Thtr 50 **Services:** Night porter **Parking:** 150 **Notes:** Civ Wed 60

Ednam House Hotel
★★★ 78% COUNTRY HOUSE HOTEL

Bridge Street, **TD5 7HT - tel:** 01573 224168
email: contact@ednamhouse.com **web:** www.ednamhouse.com
dir: Phone for detailed directions

Ednam House was built in 1761 'with no expense spared' for a local with a rags-to-riches story. From the unassuming entrance in the town centre, guests will find that once inside the hotel there are majestic views of the Tweed from the public areas, restaurant and a good number of the bedrooms. The hotel is currently enjoying a programme of rolling refurbishments which are showing very good results. The public areas certainly have a wow factor with many of the original features still clearly evident. The team here provide warm Borders hospitality, and there is a choice of menus available from the bar lounge and river-view restaurant.

Rooms: 33 ✎ **S** £65–£120; **D** £79–£210 (incl. bkfst)* **Facilities:** FTV WiFi ⊠ Xmas **Conf:** Class 80 Board 70 Thtr 150 **Services:** Night porter **Parking:** 30 **Notes:** Civ Wed 140

Find out more about AA Rosettes
– page 13

KILCHRENAN
Argyll & Bute — Map 20 NN02

The Ardanaiseig Hotel

★★★★ 76% ◎◎ COUNTRY HOUSE HOTEL

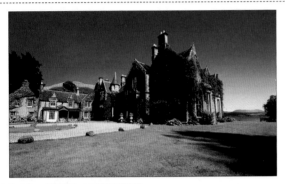

by Loch Awe, PA35 1HE - tel: 01866 833333
email: info@ardanaiseig.com **web:** www.ardanaiseig.com
dir: *A85 at Taynuilt onto B845 to Kilchrenan. Left in front of pub, narrow road signed 'Ardanaiseig Hotel' & 'No Through Road'. Continue for 3m*

Set amid lovely gardens and breathtaking scenery beside the shore of Loch Awe, this peaceful country-house hotel was built in a Scottish baronial style in 1834. Many fine pieces of furniture are evident in the bedrooms and charming day rooms, which include a drawing room, a library bar and an elegant dining room. The bedrooms are individually designed including some with four posters, some with loch views and some with access to the garden; standing on its own by the water is the Boat Shed, a delightful one bedroom suite.

Rooms: 18 (4 family) (5 GF) **Facilities:** FTV WiFi Fishing Boating Clay pigeon shooting Bikes for hire In house massage treatments New Year **Parking:** 20 **Notes:** Civ Wed 50

Taychreggan Hotel

★★★ 83% ◎◎ COUNTRY HOUSE HOTEL

PA35 1HQ - tel: 01866 833211
email: info@taychreggahotel.co.uk **web:** www.taychreggahotel.co.uk
dir: *W from Crianlarich on A85 to Taynuilt, S for 7m on B845 (single track) to Kilchrenan*

Surrounded by stunning Highland scenery, this stylish and superbly presented hotel, once a drover's cottage, enjoys an idyllic setting in 40 acres of wooded grounds on the shores of Loch Awe. The hotel has a smart bar with adjacent courtyard

Orangerie and a choice of quiet lounges with deep, luxurious sofas. A well-earned reputation has been achieved by the kitchen team for the skilfully prepared dinners that showcase the local and seasonal Scottish larder. Families, and also dogs and their owners, are welcome.

Rooms: 18 (1 family) **Facilities:** FTV WiFi Fishing Air rifle range Archery Clay pigeon shooting Falconry Mock deer stalk Xmas New Year **Conf:** Class 15 Board 20 **Parking:** 40 **Notes:** Closed 3 Jan-9 Feb Civ Wed 70

KILLIECRANKIE
Perth & Kinross — Map 23 NN96

INSPECTOR'S CHOICE

Killiecrankie Hotel

★★★ ◎◎ SMALL HOTEL

PH16 5LG - tel: 01796 473220
email: enquiries@killiecrankiehotel.co.uk **web:** www.killiecrankiehotel.co.uk
dir: *Exit A9 at Killiecrankie onto B8079. Hotel 3m on right*

Originally built in the 1840s, Killiecrankie sits in four acres of wooded grounds with beautifully landscaped gardens; it enjoys a tranquil location by the Pass of Killiecrankie and the River Garry. Public areas include a wood-panelled bar and a cosy sitting room with original artwork, and a blazing fire in colder months. All of the bedrooms are individually decorated, well equipped and have wonderful countryside views.

Rooms: 10 (2 GF) **S** £150–£160; **D** £270–£330 (incl. bkfst & dinner)*
Facilities: FTV WiFi Xmas New Year **Parking:** 20 **Notes:** Closed 3 Jan-17 Mar

KILMARNOCK
East Ayrshire — Map 20 NS43

The Fenwick Hotel

★★★ 81% HOTEL

Fenwick, KA3 6AU - tel: 01560 600478
email: info@thefenwickhotel.co.uk **web:** www.thefenwickhotel.co.uk
dir: *M77 junct 8, B7061 towards Fenwick, follow hotel signs*

The Fenwick Hotel benefits from a great location alongside the M77, with easy links to Ayr, Kilmarnock and Glasgow. The spacious bedrooms are thoughtfully equipped; complimentary WiFi is available throughout the hotel. The bright restaurant offers both formal and informal dining and there is an attractive lounge bar where you can relax and choose from the extensive cocktail list. The hotel also has extensive conference and function facilities.

Rooms: 29 (2 family) (9 GF) **Facilities:** STV FTV WiFi Xmas New Year **Conf:** Class 280 Board 150 Thtr 280 **Services:** Lift Night porter **Parking:** 64 **Notes:** Civ Wed 110

K

KILMARNOCK *continued*

Premier Inn Kilmarnock

BUDGET HOTEL

Moorfield Roundabout, Annadale, KA1 2RS - **tel:** 0871 527 8566 (Calls cost 13p per minute plus your phone company's access charge) **web:** www.premierinn.com **dir:** *M74 junct 8 signed Kilmarnock (A71). From M77 onto A71 to Irvine. At next rdbt right onto B7064 signed Crosshouse Hospital. Hotel on right*

High quality, budget accommodation ideal for both families and business travellers. Spacious, en suite bedrooms feature free WiFi and tea and coffee making facilities, and in most hotels, Freeview TV is also available. The adjacent family restaurant features a wide and varied menu.

Rooms: 64

KINCARDINE	Map 21 NS98
Fife	

Premier Inn Falkirk North

BUDGET HOTEL

Bowtrees Roundabout, Houghs of Airth, FK2 8PJ - **tel:** 0871 527 8394 (Calls cost 13p per minute plus your phone company's access charge) **web:** www.premierinn.com **dir:** *From N: M9 junct 7 (or from S: M876) towards Kincardine Bridge. On rdbt at end of slip road*

High quality, budget accommodation ideal for both families and business travellers. Spacious, en suite bedrooms feature free WiFi and tea and coffee making facilities, and in most hotels, Freeview TV is also available. The adjacent family restaurant features a wide and varied menu.

Rooms: 66

KINCLAVEN	Map 21 NO13
Perth & Kinross	

Ballathie House Hotel

★★★★ 79% @@ COUNTRY HOUSE HOTEL

PH1 4QN - **tel:** 01250 883268 **email:** email@ballathiehousehotel.com **web:** www.ballathiehousehotel.com **dir:** *From A9, 2m N of Perth, take B9099 through Stanley, follow signs. Or from A93 at Beech Hedge follow signs for hotel, 2.5m*

Set in delightful grounds, this splendid Scottish mansion house combines classical grandeur with modern comfort. Bedrooms range from well-proportioned master rooms to modern standard rooms, and many boast antique furniture and art deco bathrooms. It might be worth requesting one of the Riverside Rooms, a purpose-built development right on the banks of the river, complete with balconies and terraces. The elegant restaurant has views over the River Tay.

Rooms: 41 (16 annexe) (2 family) (10 GF) **Facilities:** FTV WiFi Fishing Xmas New Year **Conf:** Class 20 Board 30 Thtr 50 **Services:** Lift Night porter **Parking:** 50 **Notes:** Civ Wed 90

KIRKCALDY	Map 21 NT29
Fife	

Dean Park Hotel

★★★ 77% HOTEL

Chapel Level, KY2 6QW - **tel:** 01592 261635 **email:** reception@deanparkhotel.co.uk **web:** www.deanparkhotel.co.uk **dir:** *Signed from A92 Kirkcaldy West junct*

Popular with both business and leisure guests, this hotel has extensive conference and meeting facilities. The bedrooms are spacious, comfortable, well equipped and enjoy modern decor and up-to-date amenities. Public areas include the Dukes Bar & Bistro, and Grill Room which is well-known for its steaks.

Rooms: 33 (2 family) (5 GF) **S** £55–£65; **D** £70–£110 (incl. bkfst)* **Facilities:** STV FTV WiFi Xmas New Year **Conf:** Class 125 Board 54 Thtr 250 **Services:** Lift Night porter **Parking:** 250 **Notes:** LB Civ Wed 200

LANARK	Map 21 NS84
South Lanarkshire	

Best Western Cartland Bridge Hotel

★★★ 75% COUNTRY HOUSE HOTEL

Glasgow Road, ML11 9UF - **tel:** 01555 664426 **email:** sales@cartlandbridge.co.uk **web:** www.bw-cartlandbridgehotel.co.uk **dir:** *A73 through Lanark towards Carluke. Hotel in 1.25m*

Situated in wooded grounds on the edge of the town, this Grade I listed mansion continues to be popular with both business and leisure guests. Public areas feature wood panelling, a gallery staircase and a magnificent dining room. The well-equipped bedrooms vary in size. The hotel has an interesting history and even claims to have a ghost.

Rooms: 18 (4 family) **S** £68.50–£80; **D** £80–£120 (incl. bkfst)* **Facilities:** FTV WiFi Xmas New Year **Conf:** Class 180 Board 50 Thtr 250 **Services:** Night porter **Parking:** 120 **Notes:** LB Civ Wed 200

LIVINGSTON	Map 21 NT06
West Lothian	

Mercure Livingston Hotel

★★★ 79% HOTEL

Almondview, EH54 6QB - **tel:** 0844 815 9102 (Calls cost 5p per minute plus your phone company's access charge) **email:** info@mercurelivingston.co.uk **web:** www.mercurelivingston.co.uk **dir:** *From M8 junct 3 take A899 towards Livingston, exit at Centre Interchange, left at next rdbt, hotel on left*

This large, modern hotel is conveniently located in the town centre with easy access to the M8. Bedrooms offer good space and are comfortably appointed for both business and leisure guests. There is a large open-plan lobby and restaurant area; complimentary WiFi is available throughout, and there is also a small but well-appointed leisure club.

Rooms: 120 (17 family) (55 GF) **S** £70–£190; **D** £70–£190* **Facilities:** FTV WiFi HL Gym Sauna Steam room New Year **Conf:** Class 55 Board 60 Thtr 130 Del from £110 **Services:** Night porter **Parking:** 130 **Notes:** Civ Wed 120

Premier Inn Livingston M8 Jct 3

BUDGET HOTEL

Deer Park Avenue, Deer Park, EH54 8AD - **tel:** 0871 527 8632 (Calls cost 13p per minute plus your phone company's access charge) **web:** www.premierinn.com
dir: *At M8 junct 3. Hotel opposite rdbt*

High quality, budget accommodation ideal for both families and business travellers. Spacious, en suite bedrooms feature free WiFi and tea and coffee making facilities, and in most hotels, Freeview TV is also available. The adjacent family restaurant features a wide and varied menu.

Rooms: 107

LOCHINVER	**Map 22 NC02**
Highland	

Inver Lodge and Chez Roux

★★★★★ 83% 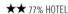 HOTEL

Iolaire Road, IV27 4LU - **tel:** 01571 844496
email: stay@inverlodge.com **web:** www.inverlodge.com
dir: *A837 to Lochinver, through village, left after village hall, follow private road for 0.5m*

Genuine hospitality can be expected at this delightful, purpose-built hotel. Set high on the hillside above the village, the hotel and the grounds have stunning views over Loch Inver and the Western Isles. There is a choice of lounges and the award-winning restaurant is under the direction of Albert Roux – his chefs make excellent use of the abundant local produce. The stylish bedrooms are spacious and come with an impressive range of accessories. Inver Lodge is also a popular wedding venue. There's plenty of secure parking at the rear of the property.

Rooms: 21 (11 GF) ⓕ **S** £165–£232; **D** £250–£604 (incl. bkfst)* **Facilities:** FTV WiFi ⓠ Fishing **Parking:** 21 **Notes:** LB Closed Nov-Mar

LOCKERBIE	**Map 21 NY18**
Dumfries & Galloway	

Kings Arms Hotel

★★ 77% HOTEL

High Street, DG11 2JL - **tel:** 01576 202410
email: reception@kingsarmshotel.co.uk **web:** www.kingsarmshotel.co.uk
dir: *A74(M), 0.5m into town centre, hotel opposite town hall*

Dating from the 17th century, this former inn lies in the town centre. Now a family-run hotel, it provides attractive well-equipped bedrooms with WiFi access. At lunch, a menu ranging from snacks to full meals is served in both the cosy bars and the restaurant at dinner.

Rooms: 13 (2 family) ⓕ **S** £60; **D** £90 (incl. bkfst)* **Facilities:** FTV WiFi Xmas New Year **Conf:** Class 40 Board 30 Thtr 80 **Parking:** 8

Ravenshill House Hotel

★★ 75% HOTEL

12 Dumfries Road, DG11 2EF - **tel:** 01576 202882
email: aaenquiries@ravenshillhotellockerbie.co.uk
web: www.ravenshillhotellockerbie.co.uk
dir: *From A74(M) Lockerbie junct 17 North or 18 South. Follow signs for A709 Dumfries. Hotel 0.5m on right*

Set in spacious gardens on the fringe of the town, this friendly, family-run hotel offers cheerful service and good value, home-cooked meals. Bedrooms are generally spacious and comfortably equipped, including a two-room unit ideal for families.

Rooms: 7 (2 family) ⓕ **S** £50–£65; **D** £75–£80 (incl. bkfst)* **Facilities:** FTV WiFi ⓠ **Conf:** Class 20 Board 12 Thtr 30 **Parking:** 20 **Notes:** LB Closed 1-7 Jan, 2 weeks in Feb & 1 week in Nov

LUSS	**Map 20 NS39**
Argyll & Bute	

The Lodge on Loch Lomond

★★★★ 75% 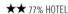 HOTEL

G83 8PA - **tel:** 01436 860201
email: res@loch-lomond.co.uk **web:** www.loch-lomond.co.uk
dir: *Off A82, follow sign for hotel*

This hotel is idyllically set on the shores of Loch Lomond. Public areas consist of an open-plan, split-level bar and fine dining restaurant overlooking the loch. The pine-finished bedrooms also enjoy the views and are comfortable, spacious and well equipped; some have saunas, and all have internet access. There is a stunning state-of-the-art leisure suite.

Rooms: 48 (19 annexe) (20 family) (15 GF) ⓕ **S** £144–£264; **D** £144–£314 (incl. bkfst)* **Facilities:** FTV WiFi ⓠ Fishing Boating Kayaks Canoes Paddleboards Wake boarding Water skies Xmas New Year **Conf:** Class 120 Board 80 Thtr 200 Del from £195 **Services:** Night porter **Parking:** 120 **Notes:** Civ Wed 170

MELROSE	**Map 21 NT53**
Scottish Borders	

Burts Hotel

★★★ 81% 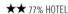 HOTEL

Market Square, TD6 9PL - **tel:** 01896 822285
email: enquiries@burtshotel.co.uk **web:** www.burtshotel.co.uk
dir: *A6091, 2m from A68 3m S of Earlston*

Recognised by its distinctive black-and-white façade and colourful window boxes, in the heart of a small market town, this hotel has been under the same family ownership for some 40 years. The genuine warmth of hospitality is notable. The smart bedrooms have been individually styled and include WiFi. Food is important at Burts, and the elegant restaurant is well complemented by the range of tasty meals in the bar.

Rooms: 20 ⓕ **Facilities:** STV FTV WiFi Salmon fishing Shooting New Year **Conf:** Class 20 Board 20 Thtr 38 **Parking:** 40 **Notes:** Closed 24-26 Dec & 4-11 Jan Civ Wed 30

M

MILNGAVIE
East Dunbartonshire   Map 20 NS57

Premier Inn Glasgow (Milngavie)

BUDGET HOTEL

103 Main Street, G62 6JQ - tel: 0871 527 8428 (Calls cost 13p per minute plus your phone company's access charge) **web:** www.premierinn.com
dir: *M8 junct 16, follow Milngavie (A879) signs. Approx. 5m. Pass Murray Park Training Ground. Left at lights. Hotel on A81 adjacent to West Highland Gate Beefeater*

High quality, budget accommodation ideal for both families and business travellers. Spacious, en suite bedrooms feature free WiFi and tea and coffee making facilities, and in most hotels, Freeview TV is also available. The adjacent family restaurant features a wide and varied menu.

Rooms: 61

MONTROSE
Angus   Map 23 NO75

Links Hotel

★★★ 78% HOTEL

Mid Links, DD10 8RL - tel: 01674 671000
email: reception@linkshotel.com **web:** www.linkshotel.com
dir: *From Montrose High St, turn into John St. After 500mtrs turn right onto Mid Links. Hotel on right*

This Edwardian town house hotel lies in the centre of picturesque Montrose on the Angus coast and is popular with golfers, as it is convenient for many famous courses including the world's fifth oldest — Montrose Links. Hotel facilities include a coffee house, comfortable lounge bar and restaurant. Bedrooms and bathrooms are presented in a traditional style with WiFi, and there's free parking on site.

Rooms: 36 (11 annexe) (4 family) (3 GF) ⚫ **S** fr £75; **D** fr £90 (incl. bkfst)*
Facilities: STV FTV WiFi New Year **Conf:** Class 60 Board 45 Thtr 120 **Services:** Night porter **Parking:** 38 **Notes:** LB Civ Wed 100

MOTHERWELL
North Lanarkshire   Map 21 NS75

Alona Hotel

★★★★ 74% HOTEL

Strathclyde Country Park, ML1 3RT - tel: 01698 333888
email: gm@alonahotel.co.uk **web:** www.alonahotel.co.uk
dir: *M74 junct 5, hotel approx 250yds on left*

Alona is a Celtic word meaning 'exquisitely beautiful'. This hotel is situated within the idyllic beauty of Strathclyde Country Park, with tranquil views over the picturesque loch and surrounding forests. There is a very contemporary feel, from the open-plan public areas to the spacious and well-appointed bedrooms. WiFi is available throughout. M&D's, Scotland's Family Theme Park, is just next door.

Rooms: 51 (24 family) (17 GF) ⚫ **S** fr £75; **D** fr £75 (incl. bkfst)* **Facilities:** FTV WiFi ⚫ 🎵 Xmas New Year **Conf:** Class 100 Board 76 Thtr 400 Del from £100 **Services:** Lift Night porter Air con **Parking:** 100 **Notes:** LB Civ Wed 250

Premier Inn Glasgow (Motherwell)

BUDGET HOTEL

Edinburgh Road, Newhouse, ML1 5SY - tel: 0871 527 8430 (Calls cost 13p per minute plus your phone company's access charge) **web:** www.premierinn.com
dir: *From S: M74 junct 5, A725 towards Coatbridge. Take A8 towards Edinburgh, exit at junct 6, follow Lanark signs. Hotel 400yds on right*

High quality, budget accommodation ideal for both families and business travellers. Spacious, en suite bedrooms feature free WiFi and tea and coffee making facilities, and in most hotels, Freeview TV is also available. The adjacent family restaurant features a wide and varied menu.

Rooms: 60

MUIR OF ORD
Highland   Map 23 NH55

Ord House Hotel

★★ 76% ◉ SMALL HOTEL

THE CIRCLE

Old Drive, IV6 7UH - tel: 01463 870492
email: admin@ord-house.co.uk **web:** www.ord-house.co.uk
dir: *Exit A9 at Tore rdbt onto A832. 5m, through Muir of Ord. Left towards Ullapool A832. Hotel 0.5m on left*

Dating back to 1637, this country-house hotel is situated peacefully in wooded grounds and offers brightly furnished and well-proportioned accommodation. Comfortable day rooms reflect the character and charm of the house, with inviting lounges, a cosy snug bar and an elegant dining room where wide-ranging, creative menus are offered.

Rooms: 12 (2 family) (3 GF) ⚫ **S** £70–£95; **D** £110–£155 (incl. bkfst)*
Facilities: WiFi ⚫ Putting green ⚫ Clay pigeon shooting **Parking:** 30
Notes: Closed Nov-Apr

NAIRN
Highland   Map 23 NH85

Golf View Hotel & Spa

★★★★ 75% ◉ HOTEL

CRERAR

Seabank Road, IV12 4HD - tel: 01667 452301
email: golfview@crerarhotels.com **web:** www.crerarhotels.com
dir: *Exit A96 into Seabank Rd, hotel at end on right*

This northern gem has wonderful sea views overlooking the Moray Firth and the Black Isle beyond. The championship golf course at Nairn is adjacent and guests can wander directly onto the long sandy beach. Guest rooms are of a high standard and the public areas welcoming. The hotel also offers an outdoor hot tub, indoor swimming pool, spa bath, gym and Elemis Spa treatments.

Rooms: 42 (6 family) **S** £89–£199; **D** £99–£229 (incl. bkfst)* **Facilities:** Spa FTV WiFi ⚫ supervised ⚫ Gym Sauna Steam room Xmas New Year **Conf:** Class 40 Board 40 Thtr 100 Del from £140 **Services:** Lift Night porter **Parking:** 40 **Notes:** Civ Wed 100

NETHY BRIDGE
Highland   Map 23 NJ02

Nethybridge Hotel
★★★ 70% HOTEL

PH25 3DP - tel: 01479 821203
email: salesnethybridge@strathmorehotels.com **web:** www.strathmorehotels.com
dir: A9 onto A95, onto B970 to Nethy Bridge

This popular tourist and coaching hotel enjoys a central location amidst the majestic Cairngorm Mountains. Bedrooms are stylishly furnished in bold tartans while traditionally styled day rooms include two bars and a popular snooker room. Staff are friendly and keen to please.

Rooms: 70 (3 family) (7 GF) 🐾 **Facilities:** FTV WiFi Putting green Bowling green 🎵 Xmas New Year **Conf:** Board 50 Thtr 150 **Services:** Lift Night porter **Parking:** 80 **Notes:** LB

NEWTON MEARNS
East Renfrewshire   Map 20 NS55

Premier Inn Glasgow Newton Mearns (M77 Jct4)
BUDGET HOTEL

Greenlaw Crookfur Road, G77 6NP - tel: 0871 527 9304 (Calls cost 13p per minute plus your phone company's access charge) **web:** www.premierinn.com
dir: From N exit M77 junct 4 towards Newton Mearns. At rdbt 1st left. Hotel on left

High quality, budget accommodation ideal for both families and business travellers. Spacious, en suite bedrooms feature free WiFi and tea and coffee making facilities, and in most hotels, Freeview TV is also available. The adjacent family restaurant features a wide and varied menu.

Rooms: 60

NEWTON STEWART
Dumfries & Galloway   Map 20 NX46

The Bruce Hotel
★★★ 71% HOTEL

88 Queen Street, DG8 6JL - tel: 01671 402294
email: mail@the-bruce-hotel.com **web:** www.the-bruce-hotel.com
dir: Exit A75 at Newton Stewart rdbt towards town. Hotel 800mtrs on right

Named after the Scottish patriot Robert the Bruce, this welcoming hotel is just a short distance from the A75. One of the well-appointed bedrooms features a four-poster bed, and popular family suites contain separate bedrooms for children.

Public areas include a traditional lounge, a formal restaurant and a lounge bar, both offering a good choice of dishes.

Rooms: 20 (2 family) **S** £50–£70; **D** £60–£100 (incl. bkfst) **Facilities:** FTV WiFi New Year **Conf:** Class 50 Board 14 Thtr 100 Del from £85 **Services:** Night porter **Parking:** 14

NORTH BERWICK
East Lothian   Map 21 NT58

Macdonald Marine Hotel & Spa
★★★★ 81% ⚜⚜ HOTEL   MACDONALD HOTELS & RESORTS

Cromwell Road, EH39 4LZ - tel: 01620 897300
email: sales.marine@macdonald-hotels.co.uk **web:** www.macdonaldhotels.co.uk/marine
dir: From A198 turn into Hamilton Rd at lights then 2nd right

This imposing hotel commands stunning views across the local golf course to the Firth of Forth. Stylish public areas provide a relaxing atmosphere; creative dishes are served in the restaurant and lighter bites in the lounge/bar. Bedrooms come in a variety of sizes and styles, all are well equipped and some are impressively large. The hotel boasts extensive leisure and conference facilities.

Rooms: 83 (7 family) (9 GF) 🐾 **Facilities:** Spa STV FTV WiFi 🏊 🦆 supervised 🎾 supervised Gym Indoor & outdoor hydro pool Thermal areas Xmas New Year **Conf:** Class 120 Board 60 Thtr 300 **Services:** Lift Night porter **Parking:** 50 **Notes:** Civ Wed 150

OBAN
Argyll & Bute   Map 20 NM82

Manor House Hotel
★★★ 82% ⚜ HOTEL

Gallanach Road, PA34 4LS - tel: 01631 562087
email: info@manorhouseoban.com **web:** www.manorhouseoban.com
dir: Follow MacBrayne Ferries signs, pass ferry entrance for hotel on right

Handy for the ferry terminal and with views of the bay and harbour, this elegant Georgian residence was built in 1780 as the dower house for the family of the Duke of Argyll. Comfortable and attractive public rooms invite relaxation, while most of the well-equipped bedrooms are furnished with period pieces. Nelson's Bar has stunning views over the bay and fine dining is available in the restaurant. The hotel has its own mooring.

Rooms: 11 (1 GF) 🐾 **Facilities:** FTV WiFi New Year **Parking:** 20 **Notes:** Closed 25-26 Dec No children 12yrs Civ Wed 30

O

OBAN *continued*

Falls of Lora Hotel

★★★ 73% HOTEL

THE INDEPENDENTS

Connel Ferry, PA37 1PB - **tel:** 01631 710483
email: enquiries@fallsoflora.com **web:** www.fallsoflora.com
dir: *From Glasgow take A82, A85. Hotel 0.5m past Connel sign 5m before Oban*

Personally run and welcoming, this long-established and thriving holiday hotel enjoys inspiring views over Loch Etive. The spacious ground floor takes in a comfortable, traditional lounge and a cocktail bar with over a hundred whiskies and an open log fire. Guests can eat in the popular, informal bistro, which is open all day. Bedrooms come in a variety of styles, ranging from the cosy standard rooms to high quality luxury rooms.

Rooms: 30 (2 family) (4 GF) 🐾 **S** £55–£72; **D** £92–£180 (incl. bkfst)* **Facilities:** FTV WiFi ⌲ **Conf:** Class 20 Board 15 Thtr 45 **Parking:** 40 **Notes:** Closed mid Dec-Jan

Royal Hotel

★★★ 72% HOTEL

Argyll Sqaure, PA34 4BE - **tel:** 01631 563021
email: salesroyaloban@strathmorehotels.com **web:** www.strathmorehotels.com
dir: *A82 from Glasgow towards Loch Lomond & Crianlarich then A85, past Loch Awe to Oban*

Well situated in the heart of Oban, just minutes from the ferry terminal and with all the shops on its doorstep, this hotel really is central. The comfortable and well-presented bedrooms differ in size, and all public areas are smart. There is a first-floor restaurant overlooking the town square and a popular lounge bar on the ground floor where food and drink are served all day.

Rooms: 91 (3 family) 🐾 **S** £30–£100; **D** £70–£160 (incl. bkfst)* **Facilities:** FTV WiFi ⌲ ♫ Xmas New Year **Conf:** Class 60 Board 30 Thtr 140 **Services:** Lift Night porter **Parking:** 15 **Notes:** Civ Wed 100

OLDMELDRUM
Aberdeenshire

Map 23 NJ82

Meldrum House Country Hotel & Golf Course

★★★★ 83% ◉◉ COUNTRY HOUSE HOTEL

Meldrum House Estates Ltd, AB51 0AE - **tel:** 01651 872294
email: enquiries@meldrumhouse.com **web:** www.meldrumhouse.com
dir: *11m from Aberdeen on A947 (Aberdeen to Banff road)*

Set in 350 acres of wooded parkland this imposing baronial country mansion has a golf course as its centrepiece. Tastefully restored to highlight its original character, it provides a peaceful retreat. Bedrooms are massive, and like the public rooms, transport guests back to a bygone era, but at the same time provide stylish modern amenities including smart bathrooms.

Rooms: 51 (13 annexe) (6 family) (14 GF) 🐾 **D** £165–£240 (incl. bkfst)* **Facilities:** FTV WiFi HL ↧ 18 Putting green 🏌 Xmas New Year **Conf:** Class 200 Board 75 Thtr 200 **Services:** Lift Night porter **Parking:** 70 **Notes:** LB Civ Wed 150

ONICH
Highland

Map 22 NN06

Onich Hotel

★★★ 70% HOTEL

PH33 6RY - **tel:** 01855 821214
email: enquiries@onich-fortwilliam.co.uk **web:** www.onich-fortwilliam.co.uk
dir: *Beside A82, 2m N of Ballachulish Bridge*

Genuine hospitality is part of the appeal of this hotel, which lies right beside Loch Linnhe with gardens extending to its shores. Nicely presented public areas include a choice of inviting lounges and contrasting bars, and views of the loch can be enjoyed from the attractive restaurant. Bedrooms, with pleasing colour schemes, are comfortably modern.

Rooms: 26 (6 family) 🐾 **Facilities:** STV FTV WiFi Games room ♫ New Year **Conf:** Board 40 Thtr 50 **Parking:** 50 **Notes:** LB Civ Wed 120

O

PEEBLES
Scottish Borders   **Map 21 NT24**

Macdonald Cardrona Hotel, Golf & Spa
★★★★ 76% HOTEL

Cardrona, EH45 8NE - **tel:** 01896 833600
email: reception.cardrona@macdonald-hotels.co.uk
web: www.macdonald-hotels.co.uk/cardrona
dir: On A72 between Peebles & Innerleithen, 3m S of Peebles

The rolling hills of the Scottish Borders are a stunning backdrop for this modern, purpose-built hotel. Spacious bedrooms are traditional in style, equipped with a range of extras, and most enjoy fantastic views of countryside. The hotel features impressive leisure facilities, including an 18-hole golf course, 18-metre indoor pool and state-of-the-art gym.

Rooms: 99 (19 family) (16 GF) ⌃ **D** £80–£180* **Facilities:** Spa FTV WiFi ⌔ HL ⌕
⌰ 18 Putting green Gym Sauna Steam room Xmas New Year **Conf:** Class 120 Board 90 Thtr 250 Del from £135 **Services:** Lift Night porter **Parking:** 200 **Notes:** LB Civ Wed 200

PERTH
Perth & Kinross   **Map 21 NO12**

Parklands Hotel
★★★★ 74% ◉◉ SMALL HOTEL

2 St Leonards Bank, PH2 8EB - **tel:** 01738 622451
email: info@theparklandshotel.com **web:** www.theparklandshotel.com
dir: M90 junct 10, in 1m left at lights at end of park area, hotel on left

Parklands Hotel is ideally located close to the centre of town, with open views over the South Inch. The enthusiastic proprietors continue to invest heavily in the business and the bedrooms have a smart contemporary feel. Public areas include a choice of restaurants, with a fine dining experience offered in 63@Parklands and more informal dining at the No. 1 The Bank Bistro.

Rooms: 15 (3 family) (4 GF) ⌃ **S** £94.50–£149.50; **D** £119–£199 (incl. bkfst)
Facilities: STV WiFi ⌔ **Conf:** Class 18 Board 20 Thtr 24 **Parking:** 30 **Notes:** LB Closed 26 Dec-6 Jan Civ Wed 40

Murrayshall House Hotel & Golf Course
★★★★ 74% ◉ HOTEL

New Scone, PH2 7PH - **tel:** 01738 551171 **email:** info@murrayshall.co.uk
web: www.murrayshall.co.uk
dir: From Perth take A94 Coupar Angus, 1m from Perth, right to Murrayshall just before New Scone

This imposing country house is set in 350 acres of grounds, including two golf courses, one of which is of championship standard. Bedrooms come in two distinct styles: modern suites in a purpose-built building contrast with more classic rooms in the main building. The Clubhouse bar serves a range of meals all day, while more accomplished cooking can be enjoyed in the Old Masters Restaurant.

Rooms: 41 (14 annexe) (17 family) (5 GF) ⌃ **S** fr £55; **D** fr £65 (incl. bkfst)*
Facilities: STV FTV WiFi HL ⌰ 36 Putting green Driving range New Year
Conf: Class 60 Board 30 Thtr 150 **Services:** Night porter **Parking:** 120 **Notes:** Civ Wed 130

The Lovat Hotel
★★★ 77% HOTEL   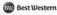 Best Western.

90-92 Glasgow Road, PH2 0LT - **tel:** 01738 636555
email: reservations@lovathotel.co.uk **web:** www.lovathotelperth.co.uk
dir: M90 junct 10, 3rd exit, straight through next 3 rdbts, hotel on right 0.5m after 3rd rdbt

The Lovat Hotel offers a comfortable and relaxing atmosphere just a short walk from the centre of Perth. Accommodation consists of comfortable, modern bedrooms, and guests can enjoy a great dining experience in the 1747 Restaurant and Bar. Residents also have complimentary access to leisure facilities at the hotel's nearby sister property. Deluxe rooms are available for those looking to splash out on a little extra luxury.

Rooms: 30 (1 family) (10 GF) ⌃ **S** £49.99–£99.98; **D** £64.95–£174.99*
Facilities: FTV WiFi ⌔ Xmas New Year **Conf:** Class 60 Board 30 Thtr 150 Del from £99 **Services:** Night porter **Parking:** 30 **Notes:** LB Closed Jan RS Nov-Mar closed Sun-Mon Civ Wed 150

Salutation Hotel
★★★ 75% HOTEL

South Street, PH2 8PH - **tel:** 01738 630066
email: salessalutation@strathmorehotels.com **web:** www.strathmorehotels.com
dir: At end of South St on right before River Tay

Situated at the heart of Perth, the Salutation is reputed to be one of the oldest hotels in Scotland and has been welcoming guests through its doors since 1699. It offers traditional hospitality with all the modern comforts. Bedrooms vary in size and are thoughtfully equipped. An extensive menu is available in the Adam Restaurant, with its impressive barrel-vaulted ceiling and original features.

Rooms: 84 (5 family) ⌃ **S** £35–£78; **D** £49–£190 (incl. bkfst)* **Facilities:** FTV WiFi ⌔ HL ⌕ Xmas New Year **Conf:** Class 180 Board 60 Thtr 300 Del from £99 **Services:** Lift Night porter **Notes:** LB Civ Wed 150

Best Western Queens Hotel
★★★ 73% HOTEL   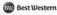 Best Western.

Leonard Street, PH2 8HB - **tel:** 01738 442222
email: enquiry@queensperth.co.uk **web:** www.queensperth.co.uk
dir: From M90 follow to 2nd lights, turn left. Hotel on right, opposite railway station

This popular hotel benefits from a central location close to both the bus and rail stations. Bedrooms vary in size and style with top floor rooms offering extra space and excellent views of the town. Public rooms include a smart leisure centre and versatile conference space. A range of meals is served in both the bar and restaurant.

Rooms: 50 (4 family) **S** fr £65; **D** fr £75* **Facilities:** FTV WiFi ⌕ Gym Steam room Sauna Xmas New Year **Conf:** Class 70 Board 50 Thtr 200 Del from £125 **Services:** Lift Night porter **Parking:** 50 **Notes:** LB Civ Wed 220

P

PERTH *continued*

Mercure Perth Hotel

★★★ 73% HOTEL

West Mill Street, PH1 5QP - tel: 0844 815 9105 (Calls cost 5p per minute plus your phone company's access charge)
email: info@mercureperth.co.uk **web:** www.mercureperth.co.uk
dir: *A93/A989 to city centre, left into Caledonian Rd, right at lights into Old High St, hotel on left*

This 15th-century former watermill has been converted into a modern hotel but still highlights the mill stream running through reception under a glass floor. Central to Perth, the hotel is an ideal location for visiting the area or further afield. Contemporary rooms include Freeview TV and free WiFi. The hotel has extensive conference facilities, and a popular brasserie where tempting meals are served.

Rooms: 76 **Facilities:** FTV WiFi ⋫ **Conf:** Class 50 Board 40 Thtr 120
Services: Night porter **Parking:** 55 **Notes:** Civ Wed 300

Premier Inn Perth City Centre

BUDGET HOTEL

Mill Street, PH1 5HZ - tel: 0871 527 9498 (Calls cost 13p per minute plus your phone company's access charge) **web:** www.premierinn.com
dir: *M90 junct 10, A912 (City Centre). At mini rdbt into Edinburgh Rd. Through 2 sets of lights. At T-junct right on to Marshall Pl (A989). 1st exit at mini rdbt into Tay St. 2nd left into High St, right into George St. 1st left into Bridge Ln. Continue into Mill St. Hotel on right*

High quality, budget accommodation ideal for both families and business travellers. Spacious, en suite bedrooms feature free WiFi and tea and coffee making facilities, and in most hotels, Freeview TV is also available. The adjacent family restaurant features a wide and varied menu.

Rooms: 83

PETERHEAD	Map 23 NK14
Aberdeenshire	

Buchan Braes Hotel

★★★★ 77% ◉ HOTEL

Boddam, AB42 3AR - tel: 01779 871471
email: info@buchanbraes.co.uk **web:** www.buchanbraes.co.uk
dir: *From Aberdeen take A90, follow Peterhead signs. 1st right in Stirling signed Boddam. 50mtrs, 1st right*

This is a contemporary hotel located in Boddam that is an excellent base for exploring the attractions of this wonderful part of Scotland. There is an open-plan lounge for drinks and snacks and the Grill Room with an open kitchen that offers a weekly changing, seasonal menu of locally sourced produce. All the bedrooms, including three suites, have 32" TVs with Freeview channels, king-sized beds and free WiFi.

Rooms: 47 (1 family) (26 GF) ⌕ **Facilities:** FTV WiFi ⋫ Xmas New Year
Conf: Class 100 Board 130 Thtr 250 **Services:** Lift Night porter **Parking:** 80
Notes: Civ Wed 220

Palace Hotel

★★★ 75% HOTEL

Prince Street, AB42 1PL - tel: 01779 474821
email: info@palacehotel.co.uk **web:** www.palacehotel.co.uk
dir: *A90 from Aberdeen, follow signs to Peterhead, on entering town turn into Prince St, then right into main car park*

This town centre hotel is popular with business travellers and for social events. Bedrooms come in two styles, with the executive rooms being particularly smart and spacious. Public areas include a themed bar, an informal diner reached via a spiral staircase, and a restaurant called The Front Room.

Rooms: 64 (1 family) (13 GF) ⌕ **S** fr £65; **D** fr £75 (incl. bkfst)* **Facilities:** STV FTV WiFi ⋫ Snooker & pool table ♫ New Year **Conf:** Class 100 Board 60 Thtr 250
Services: Lift Night porter **Parking:** 50 **Notes:** Civ Wed 250

PITLOCHRY	Map 23 NN95
Perth & Kinross	

Fonab Castle Hotel & Spa

★★★★★ 84% HOTEL

Foss Road, PH16 5ND - tel: 01796 470140
email: reservations@fonabcastlehotel.com **web:** www.fonabcastlehotel.com
dir: *From A9 into Foss Rd. Hotel 1st on left*

Nestled on the banks of Loch Faskally with stunning views, this hotel was originally built as a home for the Sandeman family, the sherry and port merchants. Stylish bedrooms are situated in the main castle building and more modern annexe. The Brasserie, and lounge both offer panoramic views from the hotel's elevated position, and provide a wide choice of quality produce cooked to a high standard. Impressive destination spa, pool and gym facilities are available on site.

Rooms: 42 (16 annexe) (2 family) (14 GF) ⌕ **S** £240–£620; **D** £240–£620 (incl. bkfst) **Facilities:** Spa STV FTV WiFi ⋫ ⊛ Thermal & aromatherapy suite Steam room Nail salon Xmas New Year **Conf:** Class 100 Board 100 Thtr 150 **Services:** Lift Night porter **Parking:** 50 **Notes:** LB

Knockendarroch

★★★★ 80% ◉◉ SMALL HOTEL

Higher Oakfield, PH16 5HT - tel: 01796 473473
email: bookings@knockendarroch.co.uk **web:** www.knockendarroch.co.uk
dir: *In town centre, just off A9*

This secluded hotel has outstanding views over the town and surrounding hills. The individually styled bedrooms are spacious and very well appointed – all have plasma TVs. The traditional, country-style public rooms have large sofas, welcoming open fires and an excellent whisky cabinet. Dinner is served every evening in the award-winning restaurant with only the best of Scottish produce being used. The staff are friendly and attentive.

Rooms: 12 (1 GF) ⌕ **S** £160–£300; **D** £190–£330 (incl. bkfst & dinner)*
Facilities: FTV WiFi ⋫ **Parking:** 12 **Notes:** Closed Dec-Jan No children 10yrs

Macdonald Inchyra Hotel and Spa

★★★★ 78% @ HOTEL

Grange Road, FK2 0YB - **tel:** 01324 711911
email: inchyra@macdonald-hotels.co.uk **web:** www.macdonaldhotels.co.uk
dir: *2 mins from M9 junct 5*

Ideally placed for the M9 and Grangemouth terminal, this former manor house has been tastefully extended. The hotel provides comprehensive conference facilities and guests will find that The Scottish Steak Club serves the highest quality produce in a contemporary style. The bedrooms are comfortable and most are spacious. A visit to the hotel's luxurious spa and leisure facilities is highly recommended.

Rooms: 97 (6 annexe) (35 family) (32 GF) **Facilities:** Spa FTV WiFi 🕙 ⚘ Gym Steam room Sauna Aromatherapy shower Ice fountain New Year **Conf:** Class 300 Board 80 Thtr 750 **Services:** Lift Night porter **Parking:** 500 **Notes:** Civ Wed 450

Premier Inn Falkirk East

BUDGET HOTEL

Beancross Road, FK2 0YS - **tel:** 0871 527 8392 (Calls cost 13p per minute plus your phone company's access charge) **web:** www.premierinn.com
dir: *M9 junct 5, Polmont A9 signs. Hotel on left*

High quality, budget accommodation ideal for both families and business travellers. Spacious, en suite bedrooms feature free WiFi and tea and coffee making facilities, and in most hotels, Freeview TV is also available. The adjacent family restaurant features a wide and varied menu.

Rooms: 60

INSPECTOR'S CHOICE

Airds Hotel and Restaurant

★★★★ @@@ ⚞ SMALL HOTEL

PA38 4DF - **tel:** 01631 730236
email: airds@airds-hotel.com **web:** www.airds-hotel.com
dir: *From A828 Oban to Fort William rd, turn at Appin signed Port Appin. Hotel 2.5m on left*

Airds shows how appearances can be deceiving, as its modest scale and appearance give little indication of what lies beyond the threshold. Once inside, you are in a luxurious environment where attention to detail and fine food are of paramount importance. The lounges are cosy and inviting, with log fires, welcoming sofas and service that is both top notch and friendly. A stay here is as much about the food as the stunning location, and the kitchen brigade makes full use of the wide range of superb quality produce that is on their doorstep. Both dinner and lunch include options for fish and meat eaters, with the added bonus of superb views across Loch Linnhe. You can also take lunch in the garden or conservatory, while families with young children can take dinner in the conservatory. The well-equipped bedrooms provide style and luxury, while many bathrooms are furnished in marble and have power showers.

Rooms: 11 (3 family) (2 GF) 🐾 **S** £275–£495; **D** £305–£525 (incl. bkfst & dinner)* **Facilities:** STV FTV WiFi 🐾 Putting green ⚘ In room massage Xmas New Year **Conf:** Class 16 Board 16 Thtr 16 **Parking:** 20 **Notes:** LB RS Nov-Jan closed Mon-Tue Civ Wed 40

The Pierhouse Hotel

★★★ 80% @ SMALL HOTEL

PA38 4DE - **tel:** 01631 730302
email: reservations@pierhousehotel.co.uk **web:** www.pierhousehotel.co.uk
dir: *A828 from Ballachulish to Oban. In Appin right at Port Appin & Lismore ferry sign. After 2.5m left after post office, hotel at end of road*

Nestled on the shores of Loch Linnhe in Port Appin, this hotel offers a warm welcome and relaxing atmosphere with comfortable, contemporary styled bedrooms and wood-burning fires in the Ferry Bar and residents' snug lounge. With breathtaking views over the sea loch to the islands of Lismore and Mull, watch the sun set as you dine in the candlelit restaurant which serves freshly prepared, locally sourced seafood and game, simply cooked to create award-winning dishes.

Rooms: 12 (2 family) (6 GF) 🐾 **Facilities:** FTV WiFi 🐾 Aromatherapy Massage Sauna Kayaking Walking Cycling New Year **Conf:** Class 20 Board 20 Thtr 20 **Parking:** 20 **Notes:** Closed 25-26 Dec Civ Wed 80

Rosslea Hall Hotel

★★★ 81% @ HOTEL

Ferry Road, G84 8NF - **tel:** 01436 439955
email: enquiries@rossleahallhotel.co.uk **web:** www.rossleahallhotel.co.uk
dir: *On A814, opposite church*

Overlooking the Firth of the Clyde and close to Helensburgh, this imposing mansion is set in its own well tended gardens. Bedrooms and bathrooms are of a good size, are well appointed and cater well for the modern traveller. The eating options include the Conservatory Restaurant which offers dishes cooked with imagination and flair, and overlooks the grounds and the Clyde. The hotel is a popular wedding venue.

Rooms: 30 (3 family) (2 GF) 🐾 **Facilities:** STV FTV WiFi Xmas New Year **Conf:** Class 60 Board 80 Thtr 150 **Services:** Night porter **Parking:** 30 **Notes:** Civ Wed 120

R

ST ANDREWS
Fife

Map 21 NO51

Old Course Hotel, Golf Resort & Spa
★★★★★ ◎◎◎ HOTEL

KY16 9SP - tel: 01334 474371
email: reservations@oldcoursehotel.co.uk web: www.oldcoursehotel.co.uk
dir: M90 junct 8, A91 to St Andrews

The five red-star Old Course Hotel, Golf Resort & Spa borders the world of golf's most famous par 4, the 17th 'Road Hole' on the Old Course in St Andrews, 'the Home of Golf'. The hotel has 144 luxurious rooms, including 35 stunning suites, and boasts five dining experiences, overseen by Executive Chef, Martin Hollis: the 3 AA Rosetted Road Hole Restaurant overlooking the Old Course; the AA Rosetted Sands Grill; the world-famous Jigger Inn; the Duke's Clubhouse at their own championship course and also Hams Hame Pub & Grill, the closest 19th to the Old Course's 18th green. Whether at the iconic hotel, on the golf course, relaxing in the world-class Kohler Waters Spa or enjoying one of the many food and drink experiences, guests are assured red-star service.

Rooms: 144 (5 family) (3 GF) ⌘ S £196–£1450; D £246–£1500 (incl. bkfst)*
Facilities: Spa STV FTV WiFi ↻ HL ☿ ♨ 18 Putting green Gym Thermal suite Roof top hot tub ♬ Xmas New Year Conf: Class 250 Board 100 Thtr 300 Del from £199 Services: Lift Night porter Air con Parking: 125 Notes: Civ Wed 80

Fairmont St Andrews, Scotland
★★★★★ 84% ◎ HOTEL

KY16 8PN - tel: 01334 837000
email: standrews.scotland@fairmont.com web: www.fairmont.com/standrews
dir: Approx 2m from St Andrews on A917 towards Crail

Sitting just a few miles from St Andrews, overlooking the rugged Fife coastline and the hotel's own championship golf courses, The Fairmont is situated on a 520-acre estate. Bedrooms and bathrooms are spacious and luxuriously appointed. The eating options are The Squire for brasserie-style food, La Cucina for Italian dishes, The St Andrews Bar and Grill in the clubhouse for steak and seafood, and The Atrium offering all-day menus. The hotel has an impressive spa and health club. Good standards of service are found throughout.

Rooms: 212 (212 family) (68 GF) ⌘ D £127–£899 (incl. bkfst)* Facilities: Spa STV FTV WiFi ↻ ☿ ♨ 36 Putting green Gym 106-seat cinema Nail salon Bike hire Dance studio Xmas New Year Conf: Class 300 Board 90 Thtr 550 Del from £220 Services: Lift Night porter Air con Parking: 150 Notes: Civ Wed 550

Rufflets Hotel
★★★★ ◎◎ COUNTRY HOUSE HOTEL

Strathkinness Low Road, KY16 9TX - tel: 01334 472594
email: reservations@rufflets.co.uk web: www.rufflets.co.uk
dir: 1.5m W on B939

Built in 1924 for a Dundee jute baron, this charming property is set in extensive gardens a few minutes' drive from the town centre. The stylish, spacious bedrooms are individually decorated, and include the Gilroy Suite, The Orchard Suite (separate from the main building), and Turret Rooms that have their own seating areas. Public rooms include a well-stocked bar, a choice of inviting lounges and the delightful Terrace Restaurant that serves imaginative, carefully prepared cuisine based on seasonal produce. Impressive conference and banqueting facilities are available in the adjacent Garden Suite. Families are very welcome, and the hotel is a popular wedding venue.

Rooms: 23 (4 annexe) (3 family) (4 GF) ⌘ S £110–£250; D £130–£375 (incl. bkfst)* Facilities: FTV WiFi ↻ ♨ Children's outdoor games New Year Conf: Class 60 Board 60 Thtr 200 Del from £175 Services: Night porter Parking: 50 Notes: Civ Wed 130

Macdonald Rusacks Hotel
★★★★ 80% ◎◎◎ HOTEL

Pilmour Links, KY16 9JQ - tel: 01334 474321
email: general.rusacks@macdonald-hotels.co.uk web: www.macdonaldhotels.co.uk
dir: From A91 W, straight on at rdbt into St Andrews. Hotel 220yds on left

This long-established hotel enjoys an almost unrivalled location with superb views across the famous golf course. Bedrooms, though varying in size, are comfortably appointed and well equipped. Classically styled public rooms include an elegant reception lounge and a modern restaurant and brasserie bar.

Rooms: 70 (1 annexe) (3 family) (7 GF) ⌘ S £199–£300; D £214–£700 (incl. bkfst)* Facilities: STV FTV WiFi Xmas New Year Conf: Class 35 Board 20 Thtr 80 Services: Lift Night porter Parking: 21 Notes: Civ Wed 60

Hotel du Vin St Andrews
★★★★ 78% ◎ TOWN HOUSE HOTEL

40 The Scores, KY16 9AS - tel: 01334 845313
email: reservations.standrews@hotelduvin.com web: www.hotelduvin.com
dir: M90 junct 3 N over Forth Road Bridge, A92. At rdbt take A914 then A91 signed St Andrews/Cupar

Hotel du Vin St Andrews is stylish, modern and welcoming. There has been a hotel here for some years but today the Hotel du Vin group offer their own unique and popular brand of hospitality. Bedrooms are very well equipped; all have free WiFi, Nespresso coffee machines and Egyptian bed linen. The Bistro offers traditional

French dishes while Ma Bells bar serves traditional pub food. The hotel overlooks golden beaches and is a mere two-minute walk from the world-famous Royal and Ancient Golf Club. Free parking is available just outside the hotel.

Rooms: 37 ☏ **Facilities:** STV FTV WiFi ⌨ HL Xmas New Year **Conf:** Class 60 Board 38 Thtr 150 **Services:** Lift Night porter **Parking:** 7 **Notes:** Civ Wed 110

Ardgowan Hotel
★★★ 82% ⚜ HOTEL

2 Playfair Terrace, North Street, KY16 9HX - **tel:** 01334 472970
email: info@ardgowanhotel.co.uk **web:** www.ardgowanhotel.co.uk
dir: *A91 onto A917. Hotel 100mtrs from rdbt on left*

The Ardgowan Hotel is ideally located just 200 yards from the Old Course Club House; the university, shops and beach are just a short walk from the hotel as well. This well-presented, family-run hotel was built in 1847 and offers well-appointed bedrooms and en suites. The award-winning restaurant uses the finest quality produce including great steaks alongside an array of seafood. Playfair's bar is lively, and enjoys good local trade.

Rooms: 36 (7 annexe) (4 family) (3 GF) ☏ **S** £69–£141; **D** £89.50–£183 (incl. bkfst)*
Facilities: FTV WiFi ⌨ **Services:** Night porter **Notes:** Closed 2/3 weeks over Xmas

Best Western Scores Hotel
★★★ 78% HOTEL   ⒷⓌ Best Western.

76 The Scores, KY16 9BB - **tel:** 01334 472451
email: reception@scoreshotel.co.uk **web:** www.bw-scoreshotel.co.uk
dir: *M90 junct 2a, A92 E. Follow Glenrothes signs then St Andrews signs. Straight on at next 2 rdbts, left into Golf Place, right into The Scores*

Enjoying views over St Andrews Bay, this well-presented hotel is situated only a short pitch from the first tee of the famous Old Course. Bedrooms are impressively furnished and come in various sizes; many are quite spacious. Smart public areas include Champions Grill that offers food all day from breakfast to dinner; Scottish

high teas are served here from 4.30-6.30pm. Alexander's Restaurant opens Thursday, Friday and Saturday evenings.

Rooms: 36 (1 family) ☏ **Facilities:** FTV WiFi ⌨ HL Xmas New Year **Conf:** Class 60 Board 40 Thtr 180 **Services:** Lift Night porter **Parking:** 12 **Notes:** Civ Wed 100

Russell Hotel
★★ 82% HOTEL

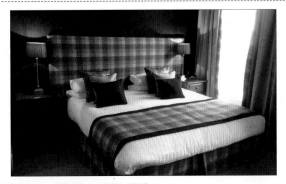

26 The Scores, KY16 9AS - **tel:** 01334 473447
email: enquiries@russellhotelstandrews.co.uk **web:** www.russellhotelstandrews.co.uk
dir: *From A91 left at 2nd rdbt into Golf Place, right in 200yds into The Scores, hotel in 300yds on left*

Lying on the east bay, this friendly, family-run Victorian terrace hotel provides well appointed bedrooms in varying sizes; some enjoy fine sea views. Cosy public areas include a popular bar and an intimate restaurant, both offering a good range of freshly prepared dishes. Situated in St Andrews, said to be 'The Home of Golf', this hotel offers a comprehensive range of golfing breaks, and is convenient for visits to the castle, cathedral and university.

Rooms: 10 (3 family) **Facilities:** WiFi ⌨ New Year **Services:** Night porter

S

ST ANDREWS *continued*

Premier Inn St Andrews

BUDGET HOTEL

Largo Road, KY16 8NH - **tel:** 0871 527 9428 (Calls cost 13p per minute plus your phone company's access charge) **web:** www.premierinn.com
dir: *A91 to St Andrews. Follow signs for Kircaldy (A915). Straight on at 2 rdbts to Largo Rd. Hotel opposite VW car showroom*

High quality, budget accommodation ideal for both families and business travellers. Spacious, en suite bedrooms feature free WiFi and tea and coffee making facilities, and in most hotels, Freeview TV is also available. The adjacent family restaurant features a wide and varied menu.

Rooms: 65

ST FILLANS	Map 20 NN62
Perth & Kinross	

The Four Seasons Hotel

★★★ 82% HOTEL

Loch Earn, PH6 2NF - **tel:** 01764 685333
email: info@thefourseasonshotel.co.uk **web:** www.thefourseasonshotel.co.uk
dir: *On A85, towards W of village*

Set on the edge of Loch Earn, this welcoming hotel and many of its bedrooms benefit from fine views. There is a choice of lounges, including a library, warmed by log fires during winter. Local produce is used to good effect in both the Meall Reamhar restaurant and the more informal Tarken Room.

Rooms: 18 (6 annexe) (7 family) ✿ S £57–£117; D £114–£174 (incl. bkfst)*
Facilities: FTV WiFi Xmas New Year **Conf:** Class 45 Board 38 Thtr 95 **Parking:** 40
Notes: Closed 2 Jan-Feb RS Nov-Dec & Mar closed Tue-Wed Civ Wed 80

SOUTH QUEENSFERRY	Map 21 NT17
Edinburgh	

Premier Inn Edinburgh A1 (Newcraighall)

BUDGET HOTEL

91 Newcraighall Road, Newcraighall, EH21 8RX - **tel:** 0871 527 8362 (Calls cost 13p per minute plus your phone company's access charge) **web:** www.premierinn.com
dir: *At junct of A1 & A6095 towards Musselburgh*

High quality, budget accommodation ideal for both families and business travellers. Spacious, en suite bedrooms feature free WiFi and tea and coffee making facilities, and in most hotels, Freeview TV is also available. The adjacent family restaurant features a wide and varied menu.

Rooms: 66

Premier Inn Edinburgh (South Queensferry)

BUDGET HOTEL

Builyeon Road, EH30 9YJ - **tel:** 0871 527 8364 (Calls cost 13p per minute plus your phone company's access charge) **web:** www.premierinn.com
dir: *M8 junct 2 follow M9 Stirling signs, exit at junct 1a take A8000 towards Forth Road Bridge, at 3rd rdbt 2nd exit into Builyeon Rd. NB do not go onto Forth Road Bridge*

Rooms: 72

SPITTAL OF GLENSHEE	Map 21 N017
Perth & Kinross	

Dalmunzie Castle Hotel

★★★ 76% ◉ COUNTRY HOUSE HOTEL

PH10 7QG - **tel:** 01250 885224
email: reservations@dalmunzie.com **web:** www.dalmunzie.com
dir: *On A93 at Spittal of Glenshee, follow signs to hotel*

This turreted mansion house sits in a secluded glen in the heart of a glorious 6,500-acre estate, yet is within easy reach of the Glenshee ski slopes. The Edwardian style bedrooms, including spacious tower rooms and impressive four-poster rooms, are furnished with antique pieces. The drawing room enjoys panoramic views over the lawns, and the restaurant serves the finest Scottish produce.

Rooms: 17 (1 family) **S** fr £185; **D** fr £185 (incl. bkfst)* **Facilities:** STV FTV WiFi ⛲ Fishing Xmas New Year **Conf:** Class 40 Board 40 Thtr 40 **Services:** Lift **Notes:** Civ Wed 60

STEPPS	Map 20 NS66
North Lanarkshire	

Premier Inn Glasgow Stepps (M80 Jct 3)

BUDGET HOTEL

Crowwood Roundabout, Cumbernauld Road, G33 6HN - **tel:** 0871 527 8452 (Calls cost 13p per minute plus your phone company's access charge) **web:** www.premierinn.com
dir: *M8 junct 12, A80 (becomes dual carriageway) to Crowwood rdbt, 4th exit back onto A80, hotel 1st left. Or exit M80 at Crowwood rdbt, 3rd exit signed A80 West. Hotel 1st left*

High quality, budget accommodation ideal for both families and business travellers. Spacious, en suite bedrooms feature free WiFi and tea and coffee making facilities, and in most hotels, Freeview TV is also available. The adjacent family restaurant features a wide and varied menu.

Rooms: 80

STIRLING	Map 21 NS79
Stirling	

The Stirling Highland Hotel

★★★★ 73% ◉ HOTEL

Spittal Street, FK8 1DU - **tel:** 01786 272727
email: reservations@stirlinghighlandhotel.co.uk **web:** www.stirlinghighlandhotel.co.uk
dir: *A84 into Stirling. Follow Stirling Castle signs to Albert Hall. Left, left again, follow Castle signs*

Enjoying a location close to the castle and historic town, this atmospheric hotel was previously a high school. Public rooms have been converted from the original classrooms and retain many interesting features. Bedrooms are more modern in

S

style and comfortably equipped. Scholars Restaurant serves traditional and international dishes, and the Headmaster's Study is the ideal venue for enjoying a drink.

Rooms: 96 (4 family) (28 GF) 🐾 **S** fr £80; **D** fr £80* **Facilities:** Spa FTV WiFi ⤴ HL 🦢 supervised Gym Squash Steam room Dance studio Beauty therapist New Year **Conf:** Class 60 Board 40 Thtr 120 Del from £125 **Services:** Lift Night porter **Parking:** 96 **Notes:** LB Civ Wed 100

Premier Inn Stirling City Centre

BUDGET HOTEL

Forthside Way, FK8 1QZ - **tel:** 0871 527 9472 (Calls cost 13p per minute plus your phone company's access charge) **web:** www.premierinn.com **dir:** *Please see website for detailed directions*

High quality, budget accommodation ideal for both families and business travellers. Spacious, en suite bedrooms feature free WiFi and tea and coffee making facilities, and in most hotels, Freeview TV is also available. The adjacent family restaurant features a wide and varied menu.

Rooms: 60

Premier Inn Stirling South (M9 Jct 9)

BUDGET HOTEL

Glasgow Road, Whins of Milton, FK7 8EX - **tel:** 0871 527 9038 (Calls cost 13p per minute plus your phone company's access charge) **web:** www.premierinn.com **dir:** *On A872, 0.25m from M9/M80 junct 9*

Rooms: 82

STRANRAER
Dumfries & Galloway   Map 20 NX06

Corsewall Lighthouse Hotel

★★★ 75% HOTEL

Corsewall Point, Kirkcolm, DG9 0QG - **tel:** 01776 853220 **email:** info@lighthousehotel.co.uk **web:** www.lighthousehotel.co.uk **dir:** *A718 from Stranraer to Kirkcolm (approx 8m). Follow hotel signs for 4m*

Looking for something completely different? This is a unique hotel converted from buildings that adjoin a Grade A listed, 19th-century lighthouse set on a rocky coastline. Situated on the headland to the west of Loch Ryan, the lighthouse beam still functions to warn approaching ships. Bedrooms come in a variety of sizes, some reached by a spiral staircase, and like the public areas, are cosy and atmospheric. The cottage suites in the grounds offer greater space. The restaurant menus are based on Scottish produce such as venison and salmon.

Rooms: 11 (5 annexe) (4 family) (2 GF) (3 smoking) 🐾 **Facilities:** FTV WiFi Xmas New Year **Conf:** Thtr 20 **Parking:** 20 **Notes:** Civ Wed 28

STRONTIAN
Highland   Map 22 NM86

Kilcamb Lodge Hotel

★★★★ 76% 🏵️ COUNTRY HOUSE HOTEL

PH36 4HY - **tel:** 01967 402257 **email:** enquiries@kilcamblodge.co.uk **web:** www.kilcamblodge.co.uk **dir:** *Off A861, via Corran Ferry, in the village of Strontian*

This historic house on the shores of Loch Sunart was one of the first stone buildings in the area, and was used as military barracks around the time of the Jacobite uprising. It is situated on the beautiful and peaceful Ardamurchan Peninsula where otters, red squirrels and eagles can be spotted. The suites and bedrooms, with either loch or garden views, are stylishly decorated using designer fabrics and have TVs, DVD/CD players, plus bath robes, iced water and even guest umbrellas. Accomplished cooking, utilising much local produce, can be enjoyed in the stylish dining room. Warm hospitality is assured.

Rooms: 10 (2 family) 🐾 **Facilities:** FTV WiFi ⤴ Fishing Boating Hiking Bird/whale/otter watching Stalking Clay pigeon shooting Xmas New Year **Conf:** Class 18 Board 18 Thtr 18 **Parking:** 20 **Notes:** Closed 2 Jan–1 Feb RS Nov & Feb closed Mon-Tue Civ Wed 120

TAIN
Highland   Map 23 NH78

The Glenmorangie Highland Home at Cadboll

★★★ 🏵️🏵️ COUNTRY HOUSE HOTEL

Cadboll, Fearn, IV20 1XP - **tel:** 01862 871671 **email:** relax@glenmorangie.co.uk **web:** www.theglenmorangiehouse.com **dir:** *A9 onto B9175 towards Nigg. Follow tourist signs*

This historic Highland Home superbly balances top class service with intimate customer care. Evenings focus on the highly successful 'house party' where guests are introduced in the drawing room, sample whiskies, then take dinner (a set six-course meal) together around one long table. Conversation can extend well into the evening. Stylish bedrooms are divided between the traditional main house and some cosy cottages in the grounds. This is an ideal base from which to follow the world famous whisky tours.

Rooms: 9 (3 annexe) (4 family) (3 GF) 🐾 **Facilities:** FTV WiFi ⤴ Archery Beauty treatments Clay pigeon shooting Falconry Xmas New Year **Conf:** Board 12 **Parking:** 60 **Notes:** No children 15yrs Civ Wed 60

T

TARBERT
Argyll & Bute   Map 20 NN30

Stonefield Castle Hotel
★★★★ 77% ⊛ HOTEL   "bespoke" HOTELS

PA29 6YJ - **tel:** 01880 820836
email: reservations.stonefieldcastle@bespokehotels.com
web: www.bespokehotels.com/stonefieldcastle
dir: *From Glasgow take M8 towards Erskine Bridge onto A82, follow Loch Lomond signs. From Arrochar follow A83 signs through Inveraray & Lochgilphead, hotel on left 2m before Tarbert*

This fine example of 19th-century Scottish baronial architecture sits proudly on the Kintyre peninsula overlooking Loch Fyne. The richly decorated public spaces convey a strong sense of the hotel's long history, and offer a choice of lounges and a billiards room. Bedrooms are split between newly refreshed rooms in the wing and more traditional ones in the original house. Dinner is a highlight, rooted in the famed local seafood from the loch, with stunning views from the restaurant to match.

Rooms: 36 (20 annexe) (3 family) (11 GF) ⚓ **Facilities:** FTV WiFi ⅃ Fishing Xmas New Year **Conf:** Class 60 Board 60 Thtr 120 **Services:** Lift Night porter **Parking:** 70 **Notes:** LB Civ Wed 110

TARLAND
Aberdeenshire   Map 23 NJ40

AA HOTEL OF THE YEAR FOR SCOTLAND 2017–18

Douneside House
★★★★ 86% ⊛⊛⊛ COUNTRY HOUSE HOTEL

AB34 4UL - **tel:** 013398 81230
email: manager@dounesidehouse.co.uk **web:** www.dounesidehouse.co.uk
dir: *Phone for detailed directions*

This country house has been developed to provide an impressive range of facilities, with extensive grounds, fishing, spa and leisure facilities and stunningly beautiful gardens. Bedrooms are available in a range of sizes, all are very well equipped and extremely comfortable. Public rooms reflect the interesting history of the estate and blend contemporary style with refined comfort. Cuisine is a major feature here; the exciting and interesting dishes incorporate the best estate produce including ingredients from the splendid kitchen garden.

Rooms: 30 S £110; D £110* **Conf:** Class 20 Board 20 Thtr 35 **Notes:** Closed Xmas & mid Jul-end Aug

THORNHILL
Dumfries & Galloway   Map 21 NX89

The Buccleuch and Queensberry Arms Hotel
★★★ 81% ⊛ HOTEL

112 Drumlanrig Street, DG3 5LU - **tel:** 01848 323101
email: info@bqahotel.com **web:** www.bqahotel.com
dir: *On A76 in centre of Thornhill*

This small, family-run hotel is located in the heart of the small town of Thornhill. The bedrooms are extremely well appointed and of a high quality. Public areas are warm and welcoming with an open log fire adding to the charm. Food is a strong aspect of the operation, with the award-winning chef using local produce where possible.

Rooms: 14 (2 annexe) (3 family) (2 GF) ⚓ **S** £65–£105; **D** £85–£125 (incl. bkfst)* **Facilities:** STV FTV WiFi ♫ Xmas New Year **Conf:** Class 60 Board 40 Thtr 120 **Services:** Night porter **Notes:** LB

THURSO
Highland   Map 23 ND16

Forss House Hotel
★★★★ 74% ⊛⊛ SMALL HOTEL

Forss, KW14 7XY - **tel:** 01847 861201
email: anne@forsshousehotel.co.uk **web:** www.forsshousehotel.co.uk
dir: *On A836 between Thurso & Reay*

This delightful country house is set in its own 20 acres of woodland and was originally built in 1810. The hotel offers a choice of bedrooms from the traditional styled rooms in the main house to the more contemporary annexe rooms in the grounds. All rooms are very well equipped and well appointed. The beautiful River Forss runs through the grounds and is a firm favourite with fishermen.

Rooms: 14 (6 annexe) (1 family) (7 GF) ⚓ **S** £99–£135; **D** £135–£185 (incl. bkfst)* **Facilities:** FTV WiFi ⅃ Fishing **Conf:** Class 12 Board 14 Thtr 20 **Parking:** 14 **Notes:** Closed 23 Dec-3 Jan Civ Wed 26

TORRIDON
Highland   Map 22 NG95

INSPECTOR'S CHOICE

The Torridon
★★★★ COUNTRY HOUSE HOTEL

By Achnasheen, Wester Ross, IV22 2EY - **tel:** 01445 791242
email: info@thetorridon.com **web:** www.thetorridon.com
dir: *From A832 at Kinlochewe, A896 towards Torridon 1m, do not turn into village. Hotel on right*

Delightfully set amid inspiring loch and mountain scenery, this elegant Victorian shooting lodge has been beautifully appointed to make the most of its many original features, and the 58 acres of surrounding parkland make it a perfect getaway destination. The attractive bedrooms are individually furnished and most enjoy stunning Highland views; expect to find Egyptian cotton sheets, duck down duvets, satellite TVs, iPod docks plus Victorian-style bathrooms; for complete privacy choose The Boathouse on the loch shore. Comfortable day rooms feature fine wood panelling and roaring fires in cooler months. The kitchen team creates menus based as much as possible on locally sourced ingredients; the hotel has its own herd of cattle. The whisky bar is aptly named, boasting over 300 malts and in-depth tasting notes. Outdoor activities include shooting, cycling and walking.

Rooms: 18 (2 GF) ⚓ **S** £255–£485; **D** £255–£485 (incl. bkfst)* **Facilities:** STV WiFi Fishing 🚣 Abseiling Archery Climbing Kayaking Mountain biking Clay pigeon shooting Xmas New Year **Conf:** Board 16 Thtr 42 **Services:** Lift **Parking:** 20 **Notes:** Closed 2 Jan-9 Feb RS Nov-Mar closed Mon-Tue Civ Wed 55

TROON	Map 20 NS33
South Ayrshire	

Lochgreen House Hotel

★★★★ ◎◎◎ COUNTRY HOUSE HOTEL

Monktonhill Road, Southwood, KA10 7EN - **tel:** 01292 313343
email: lochgreen@costley-hotels.co.uk **web:** www.costley-hotels.co.uk
dir: *From A77 follow Prestwick Airport signs. 0.5m before airport take B749 to Troon. Hotel 1m on left*

Lochgreen House Hotel is on the west coast of Ayrshire, with commanding views across Royal Troon Golf Course to the Isle of Arran. Set in 30 acres of its own charming gardens and woodlands, with a spectacular coastal backdrop, this country house hotel offers facilities for spa breaks, golf getaways, and is a venue for weddings, balls, business meetings, conferences and many other functions. Bedrooms have luxurious bathrooms, and are decorated with traditional furnishings in keeping with the character of the house. Beautifully decorated public rooms are filled with art and antiques. Lochgreen is within easy reach of many world-famous golf courses, as well as the M77 and Prestwick Airport. It is owned and managed by the Costley family and offers award-winning dining, overseen by Executive Head Chef Andrew Costley. Cookery and art demonstrations are on offer as well as tours to nearby Burns Cottage and Museum, and Culzean Castle.

Rooms: 33 (1 annexe) (11 GF) ↸ **S** £165–£185; **D** £185–£205 (incl. bkfst)*
Facilities: Spa STV WiFi Beauty treatments Xmas New Year **Conf:** Class 180 Board 50 Thtr 200 Del from £175 **Services:** Lift Night porter **Parking:** 50
Notes: Civ Wed 140

Piersland House Hotel

★★★★ 74% HOTEL

15 Craigend Road, KA10 6HD - **tel:** 01292 314747
email: reservations@piersland.co.uk **web:** www.piersland.co.uk
dir: *Just off A77 on B749 opposite Royal Troon Golf Club*

This delightful historic hotel enjoys a prime location in its own grounds in the heart of the golfing centre that is Troon. Extensive public areas include conference and banqueting facilities and an elegant restaurant. Stylish bedrooms and suites are either within the main house or in lodge-style annexes.

Rooms: 37 (15 family) (22 GF) ↸ **S** £80–£170; **D** £100–£200 (incl. bkfst)*
Facilities: STV FTV WiFi � Xmas New Year **Conf:** Class 50 Board 64 Thtr 100 Del from £125 **Services:** Night porter **Parking:** 100 **Notes:** Civ Wed 80

TURNBERRY	Map 20 NS20
South Ayrshire	

Trump Turnberry

★★★★★ ◎◎ HOTEL

KA26 9LT - **tel:** 01655 331000
email: turnberry@luxurycollection.com **web:** www.turnberryresort.co.uk
dir: *From Glasgow take A77, M77 S towards Stranraer, 2m past Kirkoswald follow signs for A719 & Turnberry. Hotel 500mtrs on right*

Golf probably springs to mind when this hotel is mentioned, and with good reason. This famous establishment enjoys magnificent views over to Arran, Ailsa Craig, and the Mull of Kintyre. Facilities include a world-renowned golf course, the excellent Colin Montgomerie Golf Academy, a luxurious spa with pool, ESPA treatments and a techno fitness studio, as well as a host of outdoor pursuits for both adults and children. Some superbly modern rooms and more traditional, elegant bedrooms and suites are located in the main hotel, while adjacent lodges provide more space. The public areas are stunning and include the Grand Tea Lounge, Ailsa Bar and Lounge, the Duel in the Sun sports bar and 1906 restaurant.

Rooms: 157 (40 annexe) (2 family) (14 GF) ↸ **Facilities:** Spa STV FTV WiFi ↕ ⊗ supervised ⅃ 45 Putting green Gym Leisure club Turnberry Adventures Turnberry Performance Academy Xmas New Year **Conf:** Class 145 Board 80 Thtr 300
Services: Lift Night porter **Parking:** 200 **Notes:** LB Closed 1 week Dec & 2 weeks Jan Civ Wed 220

T

TURNBERRY *continued*

Malin Court

★★★ 78% HOTEL

KA26 9PB - **tel:** 01655 331457
email: info@malincourt.co.uk **web:** www.malincourt.co.uk
dir: *On A74 to Ayr then A719 to Turnberry and Maidens*

Forming part of the Malin Court Residential and Nursing Home Complex, this friendly and comfortable hotel enjoys delightful views over the Firth of Clyde and Turnberry golf courses. Standard and executive rooms are available; all are well equipped. Public areas are plentiful, with the restaurant serving high teas, dinners and light lunches.

Rooms: 18 (9 family) **S** £70–£85; **D** £105–£140 (incl. bkfst)* **Facilities:** STV WiFi Putting green **Conf:** Class 60 Board 30 Thtr 200 Del from £125 **Services:** Lift Night porter **Parking:** 110 **Notes:** Closed 1-5 Jan RS Oct-Mar restaurant closes at 8pm

---

UPHALL
West Lothian
Map 21 NT07

Macdonald Houstoun House

★★★★ 76% @@ HOTEL

EH52 6JS - **tel:** 01506 853831
email: houstoun@macdonald-hotels.co.uk **web:** www.macdonaldhotels.co.uk
dir: *M8 junct 3 follow Broxburn signs, straight over rdbt, at mini rdbt turn right towards Uphall, hotel 1m on right*

This historic 17th-century tower house lies in beautifully landscaped grounds and gardens, and features a modern leisure club and spa, a choice of dining options, a vaulted cocktail bar and extensive conference and meeting facilities. Stylish bedrooms, some located around a courtyard, are comfortably furnished and well equipped.

Rooms: 73 (47 annexe) (12 family) (12 GF) **Facilities:** Spa STV FTV WiFi Gym Health & beauty salon Xmas New Year **Conf:** Class 80 Board 80 Thtr 400 **Services:** Night porter **Parking:** 250 **Notes:** LB Civ Wed 200

UPLAWMOOR
East Renfrewshire
Map 20 NS45

Uplawmoor Hotel

★★★ 78% SMALL HOTEL

THE CIRCLE

66 Neilston Road, G78 4AF - **tel:** 01505 850565
email: info@uplawmoor.co.uk **web:** www.uplawmoor.co.uk
dir: *M77 junct 2, A736 signed Barrhead & Irvine. Hotel 4m beyond Barrhead*

Originally a coaching inn, this friendly hotel is set in a village off the Glasgow to Irvine road. The relaxed restaurant features imaginative dishes, while the popular lounge bar is a great setting for freshly prepared bar meals. The modern bedrooms are both comfortable and well equipped, and Uplawmoor Hotel prides itself on the level of hospitality it provides to guests.

Rooms: 14 (1 family) **S** £60–£75; **D** £75–£99 (incl. bkfst)* **Facilities:** STV WiFi **Parking:** 40 **Notes:** LB Closed 26 Dec & 1 Jan

---

WHITEBRIDGE
Highland
Map 23 NH41

Whitebridge Hotel

★★ 71% HOTEL

IV2 6UN - **tel:** 01456 486226
email: info@whitebridgehotel.co.uk **web:** www.whitebridgehotel.co.uk
dir: *A9 onto B851, follow signs to Fort Augustus. Or A82 onto B862 at Fort Augustus*

Close to Loch Ness and set amid rugged mountain and moorland scenery, this hotel is popular with tourists, fishermen and deerstalkers. Guests have a choice of more formal dining in the restaurant or lighter meals in the popular cosy bar. Bedrooms are thoughtfully equipped and brightly furnished.

Rooms: 12 (3 family) **Facilities:** WiFi Fishing **Parking:** 32 **Notes:** Closed 11 Dec-9 Jan

---

WICK
Highland
Map 23 ND35

Mackay's Hotel

★★★ 84% @ HOTEL

Union Street, KW1 5ED - **tel:** 01955 602323
email: info@mackayshotel.co.uk **web:** www.mackayshotel.co.uk
dir: *Opposite Caithness General Hospital*

This well-established hotel is situated just outside the town centre overlooking the River Wick, and enjoys an entrance on to the world's shortest street; Ebenezer Place. MacKay's provides well-equipped, attractive accommodation, suited to both the business and leisure guest. There is a stylish bistro offering food throughout the day and the main bar offers a wide selection of whiskies.

Rooms: 30 (1 family) **S** £82–£99; **D** £89–£167 (incl. bkfst)* **Facilities:** FTV WiFi HL Complimentary use of local gym & pool **Conf:** Class 100 Board 60 Thtr 200 Del from £122 **Services:** Lift Night porter **Notes:** LB Civ Wed 200

T

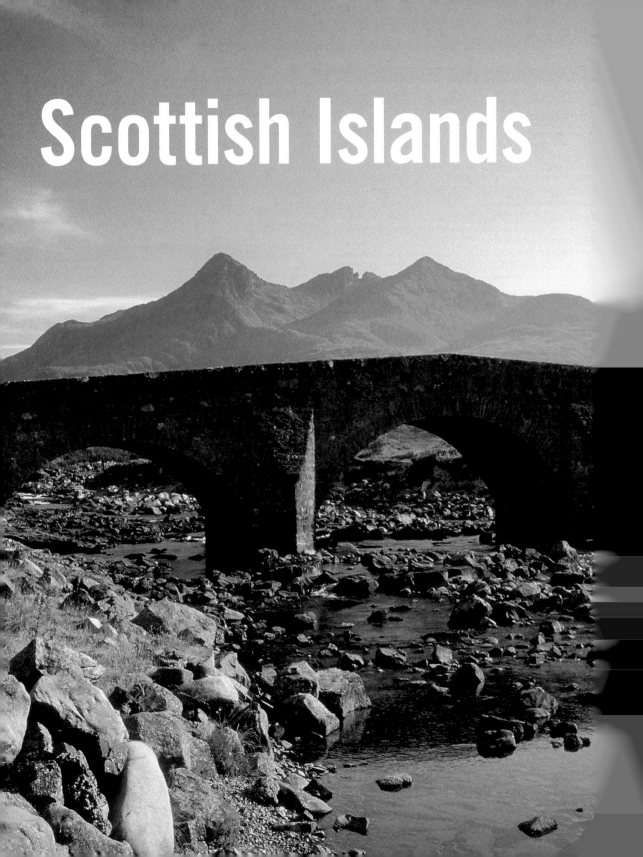

Scottish Islands

ISLE OF HARRIS

TARBERT Map 22 NB10

Hotel Hebrides

★★★★ 74% ⊚ HOTEL

Pier Road, HS3 3DG - tel: 01859 502364
email: stay@hotel-hebrides.com **web:** www.hotel-hebrides.com
dir: To Tarbert via ferry from Uig (Isle of Skye) or ferry from Ullapool to Stornaway, A859 to Tarbert; or by plane to Stornaway from Glasgow, Edinburgh or Inverness

Benefiting from an elevated position overlooking the town, this hotel is just a few minutes' walk from the centre. The small, hands-on team extend wonderful hospitality and customer care. The bedrooms are stylishly designed and include WiFi, high speed internet access and TVs; the deluxe rooms have iPod docking stations and some rooms have loch and harbour views. Award-winning food is served in the Pierhouse Restaurant. A complimentary bus service to the theatre in the summer months is provided.

Rooms: 21 (2 family) 🐾 **Facilities:** FTV WiFi ↻ ♫ **Conf:** Class 35 Board 35 **Parking:** 10

ISLE OF ISLAY

PORT ASKAIG Map 20 NR46

Port Askaig Hotel

★★ 64% SMALL HOTEL

PA46 7RD - tel: 01496 840245
email: hotel@portaskaig.co.uk **web:** www.portaskaig.co.uk
dir: At ferry terminal

The building of this endearing family-run hotel dates back to the 18th century. The lounge provides fine views over the Sound of Islay to Jura, and there is a choice of bars that are popular with locals – the Snug Bar and the Old Malt Whisky Bar. There is also a beer garden. Traditional dinners and seafood fresh from the harbour are served in the bright 'Starboard' restaurant and a full range of bar snacks and meals is also on offer. The bedrooms are smart and comfortable, and free WiFi is available.

Rooms: 13 (2 annexe) (4 family) (11 GF) 🐾 **Facilities:** WiFi **Parking:** 21 **Notes:** LB

SHETLAND

LERWICK Map 24 HU44

Shetland Hotel

★★★ 79% HOTEL

Holmsgarth Road, ZE1 0PW - tel: 01595 695515
email: reception@shetlandhotel.co.uk **web:** www.shetlandhotels.com
dir: Opposite ferry terminal, on main road N from town centre

This purpose-built hotel is centrally opposite the main ferry terminal. Spacious and comfortable bedrooms are situated on three floors, and many look out over the harbour itself. The popular Waterfront Bar & Grill offers diverse, well executed and enjoyable dishes. There is also a Sports Bar on the ground floor.

Rooms: 64 (4 family) 🐾 S £108; **D** £138 (incl. bkfst) * **Facilities:** FTV WiFi ↻ **Conf:** Class 75 Board 50 Thtr 300 **Services:** Lift Night porter **Parking:** 150 **Notes:** Closed 25-26 Dec, 1-2 Jan Civ Wed 200

SCALLOWAY Map 24 HU33

Scalloway Hotel

★★★ 78% ⊚⊚ SMALL HOTEL

Main Street, ZE1 0TR - tel: 01595 880444
email: info@scallowayhotel.com **web:** www.scallowayhotel.com
dir: 6m from main port of Lerwick on A970. Situated in Scalloway Main St

Scalloway is the ancient capital of Shetland; the Scalloway Hotel sits overlooking the waterfront. On offer is warm, friendly service and award-winning food using the best produce that the Shetland larder can provide.

Rooms: 23 🐾 S fr £95; **D** fr £135 (incl. bkfst) * **Facilities:** FTV WiFi ↻ **Parking:** 10 **Notes:** RS 23 Dec-3 Jan bar service only

ISLE OF SKYE

ARDVASAR Map 22 NG60

Ardvasar Hotel

★★★ 77% SMALL HOTEL

Sleat, IV45 8RS - tel: 01471 844223
email: richard@ardvasar-hotel.demon.co.uk **web:** www.ardvasarhotel.com
dir: From ferry, 500mtrs, left signed Ardvasar

The Isle of Skye is dotted with cosy, welcoming hotels and this hotel ranks highly amongst its peers thanks to great hospitality and a preservation of community spirit. The hotel sits less than five minutes' drive from the Mallaig ferry and provides comfortable bedrooms and a cosy bar lounge for residents. Seafood is prominent on menus, and meals can be enjoyed in the popular bar or the attractive dining room.

Rooms: 10 (4 family) **Facilities:** FTV WiFi ♫ Xmas New Year **Conf:** Board 24 Thtr 50 **Parking:** 30

ISLEORNSAY Map 22 NG71

Duisdale House Hotel

★★★★ 82% ⊚⊚ SMALL HOTEL

Sleat, IV43 8QW - tel: 01471 833202
email: info@duisdale.com **web:** www.duisdale.com
dir: 7m S of Broadford on A851 towards Armadale. 7m N of Armadale ferry

This grand Victorian house stands in its own landscaped gardens overlooking the Sound of Sleat. The hotel has a contemporary and chic style which complements the original features of the house. Each bedroom is individually designed and the superior rooms have four-poster beds. The elegant lounge has sumptuous sofas, original artwork and blazing log fires in the colder months.

Rooms: 18 (1 family) (1 GF) 🐾 **Facilities:** STV WiFi ↻ Private yacht Outdoor hydropool Xmas New Year **Conf:** Board 28 Thtr 50 **Parking:** 30 **Notes:** LB Civ Wed 58

INSPECTOR'S CHOICE

Kinloch Lodge

★★★ ◉◉◉ COUNTRY HOUSE HOTEL

Sleat, IV43 8QY - **tel:** 01471 833214
email: reservations@kinloch-lodge.co.uk **web:** www.kinloch-lodge.co.uk
dir: *6m S of Broadford on A851, 10m N of Armadale on A851*

Owned and run in a hands-on fashion by Lord and Lady MacDonald and their family, this hotel enjoys a picture postcard location surrounded by hills and a sea loch. Bedrooms and bathrooms are well appointed and comfortable, and public areas boast numerous open fires and relaxing areas to sit. There is a cookery school run by Claire MacDonald and a shop that sells her famous cookery books and produce.

Rooms: 15 (8 annexe) (1 GF) **Facilities:** Spa STV FTV WiFi Fishing Beauty treatment room Xmas New Year **Conf:** Class 20 Board 20 Thtr 20 **Parking:** 40

HIGHLY RECOMMENDED

Toravaig House Hotel

★★★ 86% ◉◉ SMALL HOTEL

Knock Bay, Sleat, IV44 8RE - **tel:** 01471 820200
email: info@toravaig.com **web:** www.skyehotel.co.uk
dir: *From Skye Bridge, left at Broadford onto A851, hotel 11m on left. Or from ferry at Armadale take A851, hotel 6m on right*

Set in two acres and enjoying panoramic views to the Knoydart Hills, this hotel is a haven of peace, with stylish, well-equipped and beautifully decorated bedrooms. There is an inviting lounge complete with deep sofas and an elegant dining room where delicious meals are the order of the day. The hotel provides a sea-going yacht for guests' exclusive use from April to September.

Rooms: 9 **Facilities:** STV WiFi Daily excursions (Apr-Sep) on hotel yacht Xmas New Year **Conf:** Class 15 Board 15 Thtr 15 **Parking:** 15 **Notes:** LB No Children 5yrs Civ Wed 25

Hotel Eilean Iarmain

★★★ 77% ◉ SMALL HOTEL

THE CIRCLE

Sleat, IV43 8QR - **tel:** 01471 833332
email: hotel@eileaniarmain.co.uk **web:** www.eileaniarmain.co.uk
dir: *From Skye Bridge take A87 towards Broadford. Left onto A851 signed Armadale. 8m, left to hotel. Or From Armadale ferry take A851 signed Broadford. 7m to hotel*

A hotel of charm and character, this 19th-century former inn sits by the pier and enjoys fine views across the sea loch. Bedrooms are individual and retain a traditional style, and a stable block has been converted into four delightful suites. Public rooms are cosy and inviting, and the restaurant offers award-winning menus showcasing the island's best produce, especially seafood and game.

Rooms: 16 (10 annexe) (4 family) (3 GF) **S** fr £70; **D** fr £70 (incl. bkfst) *
Facilities: FTV WiFi Fishing Shooting Art exhibitions Whisky tasting Tweed shop Gift shop Xmas New Year **Conf:** Class 10 Board 14 Thtr 25 Del from £120 **Parking:** 20 **Notes:** LB Civ Wed 30

PORTREE   Map 22 NG44

Bosville Hotel

★★★★ 76% ◉◉ HOTEL

9-11 Bosville Terrace, IV51 9DG - **tel:** 01478 612846
email: reservations@bosvillehotel.co.uk **web:** www.bosvillehotel.co.uk
dir: *Phone for detailed directions*

This contemporary styled hotel sits at the top of Portree town with views down to the harbour and hills beyond. Comfortable rooms come well equipped with coffee machines, bottled water and snug beds. Dulse & Brose offers the best quality local produce in its relaxed dining room. A visit to the Merchants bar should not be missed for its noteworthy range of local spirits and ales.

Rooms: 20 (1 annexe) (4 family) **Facilities:** FTV WiFi **Conf:** Class 20 Board 20 Thtr 20 **Services:** Night porter **Parking:** 10

Who are the AA's award-winning hotels? For details see pages 16-18

Wales

A

ABERDARE
Rhondda Cynon Taff Map 9 SO00

Premier Inn Aberdare

BUDGET HOTEL

Riverside Retail Park, Tirfounders Field, CF44 0AH - **tel:** 0871 527 8002 (Calls cost 13p per minute plus your phone company's access charge) **web:** www.premierinn.com
dir: *M4 junct 32, A470 signed Merthyr Tydfil. In approx 10m take A4059 signed Aberdare. Straight on at 1st rdbt, 3rd exit at next rdbt into Ffordd Tirwaun signed Riverside Retail Park, hotel in park*

High quality, budget accommodation ideal for both families and business travellers. Spacious, en suite bedrooms feature free WiFi and tea and coffee making facilities, and in most hotels, Freeview TV is also available. The adjacent family restaurant features a wide and varied menu.

Rooms: 40

ABERDYFI
Gwynedd Map 14 SN69

Trefeddian Hotel

★★★ 82% HOTEL

LL35 0SB - **tel:** 01654 767213
email: info@trefwales.com **web:** www.trefwales.com
dir: *Phone for detailed directions*

Perfectly summed up by the quote from the hotel literature as being "where the mountains meet the the sea". This family-run hotel is in a delightful location and many of its bedrooms enjoy views over the golf course and sea. Traditional, welcoming hospitality and attentive service are assured. In addition to walks along the beach, the hotel offers a heated indoor pool, treatment room, games room and a range of activities for the whole family. Dinner is the highlight of a visit with a five-course daily-changing menu that uses carefully prepared local produce.

Rooms: 59 **Facilities:** 🏊

ABERGAVENNY
Monmouthshire Map 9 SO21

Angel Hotel

★★★★ 83% 🏵 HOTEL

15 Cross Street, NP7 5EN - **tel:** 01873 857121
email: mail@angelabergavenny.com **web:** www.angelabergavenny.com
dir: *From A40 & A465 junct follow town centre signs, S of Abergavenny, past rail & bus stations*

Once a coaching inn, this has long been a popular venue for both locals and visitors; the two traditional function rooms and the ballroom are in regular use. In addition there is a comfortable lounge, a relaxed bar and a smart restaurant. In warmer weather there is a central courtyard that is ideal for alfresco eating. The bedrooms include a four-poster room and some that are suitable for families.

Rooms: 34 (4 annexe) (2 family) 🐾 **S** £85–£324; **D** £85–£324 (incl. bkfst)*
Facilities: FTV WiFi 🎵 Xmas New Year **Conf:** Class 60 Board 60 Thtr 180
Services: Lift Night porter Air con **Parking:** 30 **Notes:** LB Closed 25 Dec Civ Wed 180

B

Llansantffraed Court Hotel

★★★★ 81% ◉◉ COUNTRY HOUSE HOTEL

Old Raglan Road, Llanvihangel Gobion, NP7 9BA - tel: 01873 840678
email: reception@llch.co.uk **web:** www.llch.co.uk
dir: *At A465 & A40 Abergavenny junct take B4598 signed Usk (do not join A40). Towards Raglan, hotel on left in 4.5m*

In a commanding position and in its own extensive grounds, this very impressive property – a privately owned country-house hotel – has enviable views of the Brecon Beacons. Extensive public areas include a relaxing lounge and a spacious restaurant offering imaginative and enjoyable award-winning dishes. Bedrooms vary in size and reflect the individuality of the building; all are comfortably furnished and provide some thoughtful extras. Extensive parking is available.

Rooms: 20 (1 family) ☍ **S** £85–£125; **D** £110–£195 (incl. bkfst)* **Facilities:** STV FTV WiFi ☌ Putting green Fishing ⚓ Clay pigeon shooting school Xmas New Year Child facilities **Conf:** Class 120 Board 100 Thtr 220 Del from £160 **Services:** Lift Night porter **Parking:** 250 **Notes:** LB Civ Wed 200

ABERGELE
Conwy — **Map 14 SH97**

The Kinmel & Kinspa

THE INDEPENDENTS

★★★★ 74% ◉ HOTEL

St George Road, LL22 9AS - tel: 01745 832014
email: reception@thekinmel.co.uk **web:** www.thekinmel.co.uk
dir: *A55 junct 24, hotel entrance on rdbt*

In a rural location at the end of a long drive leading from the A55, parts of this notable, family-run hotel date from the 16th century. However, substantial refurbishments include the stunning Kinspa and leisure facility along with a range of smart, contemporary bedrooms. The stylish 1786 Brasserie serves modern British cuisine, while a Thai inspired lighter option is served at Chiang Mai in the spa.

Rooms: 42 (8 family) (18 GF) ☍ **S** £75–£175; **D** £99–£279 (incl. bkfst)* **Facilities:** Spa FTV WiFi ☌ Gym Steam room Sauna Hydrotherapy pool Relaxation room Xmas New Year **Conf:** Class 100 Board 100 Thtr 250 Del from £129 **Services:** Lift Night porter **Parking:** 85 **Notes:** LB Civ Wed 150

ABERSOCH
Gwynedd — **Map 14 SH32**

Porth Tocyn Hotel

★★★ 81% ◉◉ COUNTRY HOUSE HOTEL

Bwlchtocyn, LL53 7BU - tel: 01758 713333 & 07789 994942
email: bookings@porthtocynhotel.co.uk **web:** www.porthtocynhotel.co.uk
dir: *2.5m S of Abersoch follow Porth Tocyn signs after Sarnbach*

Located above Abersoch with fine views across Cardigan bay, Porth Tocyn is set in its own attractive gardens. Several elegantly furnished sitting rooms are provided with space set aside for families. Bedrooms are comfortably appointed. Award-winning food is served in the restaurant with both a formal option and more relaxed menu offered.

Rooms: 17 (1 family) (3 GF) **S** £82.50–£97.50; **D** £115–£195 (incl. bkfst)* **Facilities:** FTV WiFi ⚓ Table tennis **Conf:** Class 15 **Parking:** 50 **Notes:** LB Closed mid Nov-week before Easter RS low season – may close for odd days

BALA
Gwynedd — **Map 14 SH93**

Palé Hall Hotel & Restaurant

★★★★★ 86% ◉◉◉ COUNTRY HOUSE HOTEL

Llandderfel, LL23 7PS - tel: 01678 530285
email: enquiries@palehall.co.uk **web:** www.palehall.co.uk
dir: *Phone for detailed directions*

Palé Hall was originally built in 1871 by industrialist Henry Robertson with the instruction that 'no expense should be spared'. The result was a grand Victorian mansion that has played host to many important figures including Churchill and Queen Victoria; the bath and bed used by Victoria are still in place today. Fully restored and refurbished, this interesting house has a wealth of original features including a hydro-electric system powered by water of the nearby River Dee – it continues to provide electricity for the whole property. The comfortable bedrooms are individually decorated and furnished. Afternoon tea, in the sumptuous drawing room, is a must but make sure you leave room for dinner, a truly wonderful experience. In-room spa treatments are available to guests.

Rooms: 18 (6 family) (1 GF) ☍ **D** £215–£600 (incl. bkfst)* **Facilities:** FTV WiFi ☌ Fishing ⚓ In-room beauty treatment ♫ Xmas New Year **Conf:** Board 12 Thtr 12 **Services:** Lift Night porter **Parking:** 50 **Notes:** Civ Wed 60

BANGOR
Gwynedd — **Map 14 SH57**

Premier Inn Bangor

Premier Inn

BUDGET HOTEL

Parc Menai, Ffordd Y Parc, LL57 4FA - tel: 0871 527 8046 (Calls cost 13p per minute plus your phone company's access charge) **web:** www.premierinn.com
dir: *A55 junct 9 (Holyhead, Ysbyty Gwynedd Hospital). Take 3rd exit off rdbt. Hotel next left*

High quality, budget accommodation ideal for both families and business travellers. Spacious, en suite bedrooms feature free WiFi and tea and coffee making facilities, and in most hotels, Freeview TV is also available. The adjacent family restaurant features a wide and varied menu.

Rooms: 78

BEAUMARIS
Isle of Anglesey — **Map 14 SH67**

Château Rhianfa

★★★★ 80% ◉ HOTEL

Beaumaris, LL59 5NS - tel: 01248 880090 & 713656
email: hello@chateaurhianfa.com **web:** www.chateaurhianfa.com
dir: *Situated between Menai Bridge & Beaumaris*

Built in the mid-19th century as a dower house in the style of a French château, Rhianfa has been carefully restored in recent years to create a luxurious venue. Mature grounds reach to the shore. Bedrooms are spacious with modern facilities. The bar and lounges are on an upper floor affording spectacular views of Snowdonia and the Menai straits. A choice of bars is available including the 'Wine Cave', and dinner is a highlight of any stay.

Rooms: 23 (7 annexe) (4 GF) ☍ **Facilities:** FTV WiFi ☌ Sauna Xmas New Year **Conf:** Class 40 Thtr 50 **Services:** Lift Night porter **Parking:** 40 **Notes:** Civ Wed 100

B

BEAUMARIS *continued*

The Bulkeley Hotel

★★★ 79% HOTEL

Castle Street, LL58 8AW - tel: 01248 810415
email: reception@bulkeleyhotel.co.uk **web:** www.bulkeleyhotel.co.uk
dir: *A55 junct 8a to Beaumaris. Hotel in town centre*

A Grade I listed hotel built in 1832, The Bulkeley is just 100 yards from the 13th-century Beaumaris Castle in the centre of town. Friendly staff create a relaxed atmosphere. Reshreshments and meals are served throughout the day in a choice of bars, a coffee shop, the fine dining restaurant and a bistro. The well-equipped bedrooms and suites, some with four-posters, are generally spacious, and have pretty furnishings. Many of the rooms have fine panoramic views across the Menai Straits to the Snowdonian Mountains.

Rooms: 43 (3 family) **Facilities:** FTV WiFi Xmas New Year **Conf:** Class 40 Board 25 Thtr 160 **Services:** Lift Night porter **Parking:** 25 **Notes:** Civ Wed 100

HIGHLY RECOMMENDED

Bishopsgate House Hotel

★★ 84% SMALL HOTEL

54 Castle Street, LL58 8BB - tel: 01248 810302 **email:** hazel@bishopsgatehotel.co.uk
web: www.bishopsgatehotel.co.uk
dir: *From Menai Bridge onto A545 to Beaumaris. Hotel on left in main street*

This immaculately maintained, privately-owned and personally-run small hotel dates back to 1760. It features fine examples of wood panelling and a Chinese Chippendale staircase. Thoughtfully furnished bedrooms are attractively decorated and two have four-poster beds. Quality cooking is served in the elegant restaurant and guests have a comfortable lounge and cosy bar to relax in.

Rooms: 9 **Facilities:** FTV WiFi Xmas New Year **Parking:** 8

BETWS-Y-COED	Map 14 SH75
Conwy	

Craig-y-Dderwen Riverside Hotel

★★★★ 77% COUNTRY HOUSE HOTEL

LL24 0AS - tel: 01690 710293 **email:** info@snowdoniahotel.com
web: www.snowdoniahotel.com
dir: *A5 to Betws-y-Coed, cross Waterloo Bridge, take 1st left*

This Victorian country-house hotel is set in well-maintained grounds alongside the River Conwy, at the end of a tree-lined drive. Views down the river can be enjoyed

from the restaurant and deck. Many of the bedrooms have balconies, and the feature rooms include a four-poster bed and a hot tub. There are comfortable lounges and the atmosphere throughout is tranquil and relaxing.

Rooms: 18 (2 family) (1 GF) (1 smoking) **S** £110–£160; **D** £130–£250 (incl. bkfst)* **Facilities:** STV FTV WiFi Fishing Badminton Volleyball New Year **Conf:** Class 50 Board 50 Thtr 100 Del from £170 **Services:** Night porter **Parking:** 50 **Notes:** LB Closed 23-26 Dec & 2 Jan-1 Feb Civ Wed 100

Royal Oak Hotel

★★★ 85% HOTEL

Holyhead Road, LL24 0AY - tel: 01690 710219 **email:** royaloakmail@btopenworld.com
web: www.royaloakhotel.net
dir: *On A5 in town centre, adjacent to St Mary's Church*

Centrally situated in the village, this elegant, privately owned hotel started life as a coaching inn and now provides very comfortable bedrooms with smart, modern en suite bathrooms. The extensive public areas retain much of their original charm and character. The choice of eating options includes the Grill Bistro, the Stables Bar which is much frequented by locals, and the more formal Llugwy Restaurant.

Rooms: 27 (1 family) **S** £77.50–£85; **D** £95–£190 (incl. bkfst)* **Facilities:** FTV WiFi New Year **Conf:** Class 40 Board 20 Thtr 80 Del from £127.50 **Services:** Night porter **Parking:** 90 **Notes:** LB Closed 25-26 Dec Civ Wed 60

See advert opposite

BODELWYDDAN
Denbighshire

Map 14 SJ07

Bodelwyddan Castle Hotel

★★★ 80% HOTEL

WARNER LEISURE HOTELS

LL18 5YA - tel: 01745 585088
email: claire.fletcher@bourne-leisure.co.uk **web:** www.warnerleisurehotels.co.uk
dir: Exit A55 towards North Wales at junct 25, opposite Marble Church

This Grade II listed Victorian castle is situated on the north Wales coast within easy reach of Snowdonia and Cheshire. The famous Bodelwyddan marble church, set in the valley below, can be seen from the grounds and The National Portrait Gallery is also situated on site. The hotel is entirely for adults and offers a super range of leisure facilities plus numerous daily in-house and external activities such as archery, as well as nightly entertainment in the cabaret suite. Packages range from a minimum two-night, half-board stay.

Rooms: 233 (123 annexe) (114 GF) S £209–£399; D £209–£449 (incl. bkfst & dinner)* **Facilities:** Spa FTV WiFi HL ☺ Putting green ⛳ Gym Archery Rifle shooting Dancing ♫ Xmas New Year **Services:** Lift Night porter **Parking:** 156 **Notes:** No children

BRIDGEND
Bridgend

Map 9 SS97

Best Western Heronston Hotel & Spa

★★★ 79% HOTEL

BW Best Western.

Ewenny Road, CF35 5AW - tel: 01656 668811
email: reservations@bestwesternheronstonhotel.co.uk
web: www.bw-heronstonhotel.co.uk
dir: M4 junct 35, follow signs for Porthcawl, at 5th rdbt left towards Ogmore-by-Sea B4265, hotel 200yds on left

Situated within easy reach of the town centre and the M4, this large modern hotel offers spacious well-equipped accommodation, including ground-floor rooms. Public areas include an open-plan lounge/bar, attractive restaurant and a smart leisure and fitness club. The hotel also has a choice of function and conference rooms, and ample parking is available.

Rooms: 75 (3 family) (36 GF) S £70–£140; D £80–£150 (incl. bkfst)
Facilities: Spa STV FTV WiFi ⚓ HL ☺ Gym Steam room Sauna New Year
Conf: Class 80 Board 60 Thtr 250 Del from £105 **Services:** Lift Night porter
Parking: 160 **Notes:** LB Civ Wed 200

Court Colman Manor

★★★ 68% COUNTRY HOUSE HOTEL

Pen-y-Fai, CF31 4NG - tel: 01656 720212
email: experience@court-colman-manor.com **web:** www.court-colman-manor.com
dir: M4 junct 36, A4063 towards Maesteg, after lights 1st exit to Bridgend, under motorway, next right, follow hotel signs

Dating back to the Tudor times this fine mansion is set in its own peaceful grounds outside Bridgend, and is just a short distance from the M4. The spacious, comfortable bedrooms include 10 themed rooms inspired by exotic locations – India, Japan, Morocco etc. The food served in Bokhara Brasserie is imaginative, and Indian and Mediterranean dishes are included in the choices. Diners can watch their meals being prepared in the open-plan kitchen.

Rooms: 30 (6 family) S £70–£80; D £100–£170 (incl. bkfst)* **Facilities:** FTV WiFi ⚓ HL Xmas New Year **Conf:** Class 60 Thtr 100 Del from £130 **Services:** Night porter **Parking:** 180 **Notes:** LB Civ Wed 150

Premier Inn Bridgend Central

BUDGET HOTEL

Premier Inn

The Derwen, CF32 9ST - tel: 0871 527 8146 (Calls cost 13p per minute plus your phone company's access charge) **web:** www.premierinn.com
dir: M4 junct 36, A4061 (signed Bridgend & Pen-y-Bont). Hotel at next rdbt

High quality, budget accommodation ideal for both families and business travellers. Spacious, en suite bedrooms feature free WiFi and tea and coffee making facilities, and in most hotels, Freeview TV is also available. The adjacent family restaurant features a wide and varied menu.

Rooms: 69

Premier Inn Bridgend M4 Jct 35

BUDGET HOTEL

Premier Inn

Pantruthyn Farm, Pencoed, CF35 5HY - tel: 0871 527 8144 (Calls cost 13p per minute plus your phone company's access charge) **web:** www.premierinn.com
dir: At M4 junct 35, behind petrol station & McDonalds

Rooms: 60

B

BUILTH WELLS	Map 9 SO05
Powys	

Caer Beris Manor Hotel

★★★ 78% ⊛⊛ COUNTRY HOUSE HOTEL

LD2 3NP - **tel:** 01982 552601
email: info@caerberis.com **web:** www.caerberis.com
dir: *From town centre follow A483/Llandovery signs. Hotel on the left. Keep in left lane but bear right, straight over at mini rdbt*

Guests can expect a relaxing stay at this friendly and privately-owned boutique, country-house hotel that has extensive and attractive landscaped grounds. Bedrooms are individually decorated and furnished to retain the atmosphere of a bygone era. The spacious and comfortable lounge, complete with log fire, and lounge bar continue this theme. Dining is available in the elegant 1896 Restaurant, complete with 16th-century panelling. Those aiming for total relaxation can also indulge in a wellbeing treatment including massages and facials.

Rooms: 23 (2 family) (3 GF) ☏ **Facilities:** FTV WiFi ⇗ Fishing ⚓ Clay pigeon shooting Birdwatching Walking holidays Xmas New Year **Conf:** Class 75 Board 50 Thtr 100 **Services:** Night porter **Parking:** 100 **Notes:** LB Civ Wed 200

CAERNARFON	Map 14 SH46
Gwynedd	

Premier Inn Caernarfon

BUDGET HOTEL

Victoria Dock, Balaclava Road, LL55 1SQ - **tel:** 0871 527 8180 (Calls cost 13p per minute plus your phone company's access charge) **web:** www.premierinn.com
dir: *A55 junct 9, at rdbt 1st exit follow Caernarfon signs. In Caernarfon at rdbt (Morrisons on right) 1st exit, keep in right lane, at next rdbt 4th exit to mini rdbt, hotel opposite*

High quality, budget accommodation ideal for both families and business travellers. Spacious, en suite bedrooms feature free WiFi and tea and coffee making facilities, and in most hotels, Freeview TV is also available. The adjacent family restaurant features a wide and varied menu.

Rooms: 93

CAERPHILLY	Map 9 ST18
Caerphilly	

Premier Inn Caerphilly (Corbetts Lane)

BUDGET HOTEL

Corbetts Lane, CF83 3HX - **tel:** 0871 527 8182 (Calls cost 13p per minute plus your phone company's access charge) **web:** www.premierinn.com
dir: *M4 junct 32, A470, 2nd left signed Caerphilly. At rdbt 4th exit, at next rdbt 2nd exit. Straight on at next rdbt & at Pwllypant Rdbt, hotel on left*

High quality, budget accommodation ideal for both families and business travellers. Spacious, en suite bedrooms feature free WiFi and tea and coffee making facilities, and in most hotels, Freeview TV is also available. The adjacent family restaurant features a wide and varied menu.

Rooms: 62

Premier Inn Caerphilly (Crossways)

BUDGET HOTEL

Crossways Business Park, Pontypandy, CF83 3NL - **tel:** 0871 527 8184 (Calls cost 13p per minute plus your phone company's access charge) **web:** www.premierinn.com
dir: *M4 junct 32, A470 towards Merthyr Tydfil (junct 4 take A458 towards Caerphilly). At Crossways Business Park (5th rdbt). Hotel on right at McDonald's rdbt*

Rooms: 40

CARDIFF	Map 9 ST17
Cardiff	

The St David's Hotel

★★★★★ 82% HOTEL

Havannah Street, CF10 5SD - **tel:** 029 2045 4045
email: stdavids.reservations@thestdavidshotel.com
web: www.thestdavidshotel.com/partner/cardiff-st-davids-hotel-spa
dir: *M4 junct 33, A4232 for 9m, follow Cardiff Bay signs, then Techniquest signs, at top exit slip road, 1st left at rdbt, 1st right*

This imposing contemporary building sits in a prime position on Cardiff Bay and has a seven-storey atrium creating a dramatic impression. Leading from the atrium are the practically designed and comfortable bedrooms. Tides Restaurant, adjacent to the stylish cocktail bar, has views across the water to Penarth, and there is a quiet first-floor lounge for guests seeking peace and quiet. A well-equipped spa and extensive business areas complete the package.

Rooms: 142 ☏ **Facilities:** Spa FTV WiFi ⇗ HL ⚕ Gym Fitness studio Hydrotherapy pool Aerobics studio ♬ **Conf:** Class 110 Board 76 Thtr 270 **Services:** Lift Night porter Air con **Parking:** 60 **Notes:** Civ Wed 270

Mercure Cardiff Holland House Hotel & Spa

★★★★ 76% HOTEL

24/26 Newport Road, CF24 0DD - **tel:** 029 2043 5000
email: h6622@accor.com **web:** www.mercure.com
dir: *M4 junct 33, A4232 to city centre, right at lights opposite prison, straight through next lights, hotel car park at end of lane opposite Magistrates Court*

Conveniently located just a few minutes' walk from the city centre, this exciting hotel combines contemporary styling with a genuinely friendly welcome. Bedrooms, including five luxurious suites, are spacious and include many useful extras. A state-of-the-art leisure club and spa is available in addition to a large function room. An eclectic menu provides a varied range of freshly prepared, quality dishes.

Rooms: 165 (80 family) ☏ **Facilities:** Spa STV WiFi ⚕ Gym **Conf:** Class 250 Board 90 Thtr 700 **Services:** Lift Night porter Air con **Parking:** 90 **Notes:** Civ Wed 500

Novotel Cardiff Central

★★★★ 76% HOTEL

Schooner Way, Atlantic Wharf, CF10 4RT - **tel:** 029 2113 2800 & 2047 5000
email: h5982@accor.com **web:** www.novotel.com
dir: *M4 junct 29 onto A48(M), follow signs for city centre*

Situated in the heart of the city's development area, this hotel is equally convenient for the city centre and Cardiff Bay. Bedrooms vary between standard rooms in the modern extension to executive rooms in the original wing. There is good seating space in public areas, and the hotel has a popular leisure club. The Goods Shed Restaurant is an innovative dining concept.

Rooms: 138 (100 family) ☏ S £85–£295; D £85–£295* **Facilities:** FTV WiFi ⇗ ⚕ Gym Sauna Steam room Xmas New Year **Conf:** Class 80 Board 50 Thtr 200 Del from £130 **Services:** Lift Night porter Air con **Parking:** 120 **Notes:** LB Civ Wed 200

The Angel Hotel

★★★ 79% HOTEL

Castle Street, CF10 1SZ - **tel:** 029 2064 9200
email: lynsey.brown@angelhotelcardiffcity.co.uk **web:** www.angelhotelcardiffcity.co.uk
dir: *Opposite Cardiff Castle*

The Angel is a well-established hotel in the heart of the city, overlooking the famous castle and almost opposite the Millennium Stadium. All bedrooms offer air conditioning and are appointed to a good standard. Public areas include an impressive lobby, a modern restaurant and a selection of conference rooms. There is limited parking at the rear of the hotel.

Rooms: 102 (3 family) **S** £65–£300; **D** £65–£300* **Facilities:** WiFi Xmas New Year **Conf:** Class 120 Board 50 Thtr 300 Del from £120 **Services:** Lift Night porter Air con **Parking:** 60 **Notes:** Civ Wed 200

Premier Inn Barry Island (Cardiff Airport)

BUDGET HOTEL

Triangle Site, Fford Y Mileniwm, CF62 5QN - **tel:** 0871 527 9370 (Calls cost 13p per minute plus your phone company's access charge) **web:** www.premierinn.com **dir:** M4 junct 33 A4232 signed A4050, pass through 8 rdbts, left onto Trinity St, right onto A4055 Broad St. Left after 0.2m.

High quality, budget accommodation ideal for both families and business travellers. Spacious, en suite bedrooms feature free WiFi and tea and coffee making facilities, and in most hotels, Freeview TV is also available. The adjacent family restaurant features a wide and varied menu.

Rooms: 80

Premier Inn Cardiff City Centre

BUDGET HOTEL

Helmont House, 10 Churchill Way, CF10 2HE - **tel:** 0871 527 8196 (Calls cost 13p per minute plus your phone company's access charge) **web:** www.premierinn.com **dir:** M4 junct 29 onto A48(M) towards Cardiff (East & South), 4.5m. Follow Cardiff (East), Docks & A4232 signs. Left at A4161 (Eastern Avenue North). At rdbt 2nd exit onto A4161 (Newport Rd). 2m, left into Station Terrace. Right into Churchill Way

Rooms: 200

Premier Inn Cardiff City South

BUDGET HOTEL

Keen Road, CF24 5JT - **tel:** 0871 527 8198 (Calls cost 13p per minute plus your phone company's access charge) **web:** www.premierinn.com **dir:** Follow Cardiff Docks & Bay signs from A48(M), over flyover. At 5th rdbt, 3rd exit. Hotel 1st right, then 1st right again

Rooms: 97

Premier Inn Cardiff East

BUDGET HOTEL

Newport Road, Castleton, CF3 2UQ - **tel:** 0871 527 8200 (Calls cost 13p per minute plus your phone company's access charge) **web:** www.premierinn.com **dir:** M4 junct 28, A48 signed Castleton. 3m, hotel on right

Rooms: 49

Premier Inn Cardiff North

BUDGET HOTEL

Pentwyn Road, Pentwyn, CF23 7XH - **tel:** 0871 527 8202 (Calls cost 13p per minute plus your phone company's access charge) **web:** www.premierinn.com **dir:** W'bound: M4 junct 29, A48(M). (E'bound: M4 junct 30, A4232 signs, A48(M) towards Cardiff). Follow Pentwyn signs, 3rd exit at rdbt. Hotel 200yds on right

Rooms: 147

Premier Inn Cardiff (Roath)

BUDGET HOTEL

Ipswich Road, Roath, CF23 9AQ - **tel:** 0871 527 8194 (Calls cost 13p per minute plus your phone company's access charge) **web:** www.premierinn.com **dir:** W'bound: M4 junct 29, A48(M). E'bound: M4 junct 30 A48(M). Follow Cardiff (E) Docks & Cardiff Bay signs. Then follow brown signs for David Lloyd Tennis Centre. Into David Lloyd Leisure Club car park, follow hotel signs

Rooms: 75

Premier Inn Cardiff West

BUDGET HOTEL

Port Road, Nantisaf, Wenvoe, CF5 6DD - **tel:** 0871 527 8204 (Calls cost 13p per minute plus your phone company's access charge) **web:** www.premierinn.com **dir:** M4 junct 33, S on A4232. Take 2nd exit signed 'Airport', take 3rd exit at Culverhouse Cross rdbt. Hotel 0.5m on Barry Rd (A4050)

Rooms: 59

CARMARTHEN
Carmarthenshire

Map 8 SN42

Ivy Bush Royal Hotel

★★★ 77% HOTEL

Spilman Street, SA31 1LG - **tel:** 01267 235111 **email:** reception@ivybushroyal.co.uk **web:** www.ivybushroyal.co.uk **dir:** A48 to Carmarthen, over 1st rdbt, at 2nd rdbt right onto A4242. Straight over next 2 rdbts. Left at lights. Hotel on right at top of hill

This hotel offers spacious, well-equipped bedrooms and bathrooms, a relaxing lounge with outdoor patio seating, and a comfortable restaurant serving a varied selection of carefully prepared meals. Weddings, meetings and conferences are all well catered for at this friendly, family-run establishment.

Rooms: 70 (4 family) **S** £75–£150; **D** £105–£150 (incl. bkfst)* **Facilities:** FTV WiFi Gym Xmas New Year **Conf:** Class 50 Board 40 Thtr 200 Del from £99 **Services:** Lift Night porter **Parking:** 83 **Notes:** LB Civ Wed 150

Falcon Hotel

★★★ 75% HOTEL

Lammas Street, SA31 3AP - **tel:** 01267 234959 **email:** reception@falconcarmarthen.co.uk **web:** www.falconcarmarthen.co.uk **dir:** In town centre pass bus station, left, hotel 200yds on left

This friendly hotel has been owned and run by the Exton family for 50 years, and is located in the centre of the town. Bedrooms, some with four-poster beds, are tastefully decorated and have good facilities. There is a comfortable lounge with adjacent bar, and the restaurant offers a varied selection of enjoyable dishes at both lunch and dinner.

Rooms: 16 (1 family) **Facilities:** FTV WiFi **Conf:** Class 50 Board 40 Thtr 80 **Parking:** 36 **Notes:** LB Closed 26 Dec RS Sun no dinner served

C

CONWY
Conwy
Map 14 SH77

Castle Hotel Conwy
★★★★ 79% ◉◉ TOWN HOUSE HOTEL

High Street, LL32 8DB - **tel:** 01492 582800
email: castle@innmail.co.uk **web:** www.castlewales.co.uk
dir: A55 junct 18, follow town centre signs, cross estuary (castle on left).
Right then left at mini rdbts onto one-way system. Right at Town Wall Gate,
right into Berry St then High St

This family-run, 16th-century hotel is one of Conwy's most distinguished buildings
and offers a relaxed and friendly atmosphere. Bedrooms are appointed to an
impressive standard and include a stunning suite and a choice of individually
styled rooms. Downstairs, there's a popular modern bar serving real ales, and the
award-winning Dawsons restaurant. The Healing Hands beauty and holistic therapy
area is an added bonus.

Rooms: 27 (2 family) ⌕ **S** £75–£102; **D** £110–£256* **Facilities:** FTV WiFi ⌕ Holistic
therapy treatment room Xmas New Year **Services:** Night porter **Parking:** 34 **Notes:** LB

CRICCIETH
Gwynedd
Map 14 SH43

HIGHLY RECOMMENDED

Bron Eifion Country House Hotel
★★★★ 83% ◉ COUNTRY HOUSE HOTEL

LL52 0SA - **tel:** 01766 522385
email: enquiries@broneifion.co.uk **web:** www.broneifion.co.uk
dir: A497 between Porthmadog & Pwllheli, 0.5m from Criccieth,
on right towards Pwllheli

This delightful country house, built in 1883, is set in extensive grounds to the
west of Criccieth, commanding impressive sea views. Now a privately-owned
and personally-run hotel, it provides warm and very friendly hospitality. The
interior styling highlights many retained period features. There is a choice of
lounges and the very impressive central hall features a minstrels' gallery. The
Gin List should not to be missed – 50 varieties are served with a selection of
accompaniments including pink grapefruit, blueberries and star anise.

Rooms: 18 (1 family) (1 GF) ⌕ **S** £95–£135; **D** £145–£215 (incl. bkfst)*
Facilities: FTV WiFi ⌕ Xmas New Year **Conf:** Class 150 Board 60 Thtr 150
Parking: 50 **Notes:** LB Civ Wed 150

George IV Hotel
★★★ 73% HOTEL

Leisureplex
HOLIDAY HOTELS

23-25 High Street, LL52 0BS - **tel:** 01766 522168
email: georgeiv.criccieth@alfatravel.co.uk **web:** www.leisureplex.co.uk
dir: On A497 in town centre

This hotel stands back from the A497 in the town centre. The bedrooms, which in
general are spacious, are attractively furnished and well equipped to meet the
needs of both business guests and holidaymakers. George's Brasserie serves a
menu based on locally sourced ingredients.

Rooms: 80 (5 family) ⌕ **Facilities:** FTV WiFi ♪ Xmas New Year **Services:** Lift Night
porter **Parking:** 16 **Notes:** Closed Jan RS Nov & Feb-Mar open Mon-Fri only

CRICKHOWELL
Powys
Map 9 SO21

Manor Hotel
★★★ 77% ◉ HOTEL

Brecon Road, NP8 1SE - **tel:** 01873 810212
email: info@manorhotel.co.uk **web:** www.manorhotel.co.uk
dir: On A40, 0.5m from Crickhowell

This impressive manor house, set in a stunning location, was the birthplace of
Sir George Everest, after whom Mount Everest is named. The bedrooms and public
areas are elegant, and there are extensive leisure facilities. The restaurant, with
panoramic views, is the setting for exciting modern cooking.

Rooms: 23 (2 family) **Facilities:** STV FTV WiFi ⌕ ☒ Gym Xmas New Year
Conf: Class 250 Board 150 Thtr 300 **Parking:** 200 **Notes:** Civ Wed 150

CWMBRAN
Torfaen
Map 9 ST29

The Parkway Hotel & Spa
★★★★ 78% ◉◉ HOTEL

Cwmbran Drive, NP44 3UW - **tel:** 01633 871199
email: enquiries@theparkwayhotel.co.uk **web:** www.parkwayhotelandspa.com
dir: M4 junct 25a & 26, A4051 follow Cwmbran-Llantarnam Park signs.
Right at rdbt, right for hotel

This purpose-built hotel, in over seven acres of grounds, offers comfortable
bedrooms and public areas that will suit a wide range of guests. The coffee shop is
an informal eating option throughout the day, and there is fine dining in Ravello's
Restaurant. The bedrooms, including suites, interconnecting family rooms and
wheelchair access rooms, are stylishly appointed. Additional facilities include a
spa, sports centre and conference and meeting rooms.

Rooms: 80 (4 family) (34 GF) ⌕ **S** £70–£250; **D** £90–£275 (incl. bkfst)*
Facilities: Spa FTV WiFi ⌕ ☒ supervised ⌕ Gym Steam room Sauna Boules
Table tennis Chess Badminton Snooker table ♪ Xmas New Year **Conf:** Class 240
Board 100 Thtr 500 Del from £99 **Services:** Lift Night porter **Parking:** 300 **Notes:** LB
RS Xmas period Civ Wed 500

Premier Inn Cwmbran
BUDGET HOTEL

Avondale Road, Pontrhydyrun, NP44 1DE - **tel:** 0870 111 2851 (Calls cost 13p per
minute plus your phone company's access charge) **web:** www.premierinn.com
dir: M4 junct 26, A4501 signed Cwmbran, straight on at next 5 rdbts.
At 6th take Pontrhydyrun Rd exit, left into Avondale Rd

High quality, budget accommodation ideal for both families and business
travellers. Spacious, en suite bedrooms feature free WiFi and tea and coffee making
facilities, and in most hotels, Freeview TV is also available. The adjacent family
restaurant features a wide and varied menu.

Rooms: 41

DEGANWY
Conwy

Map 14 SH77

Quay Hotel & Spa
★★★★ 81% @ HOTEL

Deganwy Quay, LL31 9DJ - **tel:** 01492 564100
email: reservations@quayhotel.co.uk **web:** www.quayhotel.co.uk
dir: *M56, A494, A55 junct 18, straight across 2 rdbts.*
At lights bear left into The Quay. Hotel on right

This luxury hotel occupies a stunning position beside the estuary on Deganwy's Quay. What was once an area for railway storage is now a property of modern architectural design. Spacious bedrooms, many with balconies and wonderful views, are decorated individually and boast a host of extras. Four penthouse suites command spectacular views. Extensive spa and leisure facilities and The Grill Room restaurant complete the experience.

Rooms: 74 (15 family) (30 GF) ☞ **Facilities:** Spa WiFi HL ⓩ supervised Gym Steam & sauna room Hydrotherapy pool ♫ Xmas New Year **Conf:** Class 240 Board 90 Thtr 240 **Services:** Lift Night porter **Parking:** 96 **Notes:** LB Civ Wed 150

DOLGELLAU
Gwynedd

Map 14 SH71

HIGHLY RECOMMENDED

Penmaenuchaf Hall Hotel
★★★ 87% @ COUNTRY HOUSE HOTEL

Penmaenpool, LL40 1YB - **tel:** 01341 422129 **email:** relax@penhall.co.uk
web: www.penhall.co.uk
dir: *A470 onto A493 to Tywyn. Hotel approx 1m on left*

Built in 1860, this impressive hall stands in 20 acres of formal gardens, grounds and woodland, and enjoys magnificent views across the River Mawddach. Sympathetic restoration has created a comfortable and welcoming hotel with spacious day rooms and thoughtfully furnished bedrooms, some with private balconies. Fresh produce cooked in modern British style is served in an elegant conservatory restaurant, overlooking the countryside.

Rooms: 14 (2 family) ☞ **S** £125–£200; **D** £180–£300 (incl. bkfst)* **Facilities:** STV FTV WiFi ↕ Fishing ⚓ Complimentary salmon & trout fishing Coracling In-room massage treatments Xmas New Year **Conf:** Class 30 Board 22 Thtr 50 Del from £145 **Parking:** 30 **Notes:** LB No children 6yrs Civ Wed 65

EBBW VALE
Blaenau Gwent

Map 9 SO10

Premier Inn Ebbw Vale
BUDGET HOTEL

Victoria Business Park, Waunllwyd, NP23 8AN - **tel:** 0871 527 8356 (Calls cost 13p per minute plus your phone company's access charge) **web:** www.premierinn.com
dir: *M4 junct 28, A467 signed Risca, then Brynmawr. At rdbt at Brynithel 1st exit onto A4046, signed Ebbw Vale. At rdbt 3rd exit towards Waunllwyd. At rdbt 1st exit, next left. Hotel adjacent*

High quality, budget accommodation ideal for both families and business travellers. Spacious, en suite bedrooms feature free WiFi and tea and coffee making facilities, and in most hotels, Freeview TV is also available. The adjacent family restaurant features a wide and varied menu.

Rooms: 62

FISHGUARD
Pembrokeshire

Map 8 SM93

The Cartref Hotel
★★ 67% HOTEL

15-19 High Street, SA65 9AW - **tel:** 01348 872430 & 07813 305235
email: cartrefhotel@btconnect.com **web:** www.cartrefhotel.co.uk
dir: *On A40 in town centre*

Personally run by the proprietor, this friendly hotel offers convenient access to the town centre and ferry terminal. Bedrooms are well maintained and include some family rooms. There is also a cosy lounge bar and a welcoming restaurant that looks out onto the high street.

Rooms: 10 (2 family) ☞ **S** £50–£60; **D** £75–£85 (incl. bkfst)* **Facilities:** FTV WiFi **Services:** Night porter **Parking:** 4

HAVERFORDWEST
Pembrokeshire

Map 8 SM91

Premier Inn Haverfordwest North
BUDGET HOTEL

Glanafon Farm House, Fishguard Road, SA62 4BP - **tel:** 0871 527 9546 (Calls cost 13p per minute plus your phone company's access charge) **web:** www.premierinn.com
dir: *From E: A40 to Haverfordwest. At rdbt follow Fishguard (A40) signs. Straight on at next rdbt. At next rdbt (Withybush Rdbt) take 2nd exit to hotel*

High quality, budget accommodation ideal for both families and business travellers. Spacious, en suite bedrooms feature free WiFi and tea and coffee making facilities, and in most hotels, Freeview TV is also available. The adjacent family restaurant features a wide and varied menu.

Rooms: 60

H

HAY-ON-WYE
Powys   Map 9 SO24

The Swan at Hay
★★★★ 72% ◉◉ HOTEL

Church Street, HR3 5DQ - tel: 01497 821188
email: stay@swanathay.co.uk web: www.swanathay.com
dir: From Hereford take A438 towards Brecon. Continue to Clyro, left at petrol station for Hay-on-Wye. At T-junct turn right, 15.5 miles to The Swan

Hay-on-Wye is located on the border of England and Wales and is world famous for its literary connections and festivals. The Swan at Hay, once a coaching inn, is located right in the heart of the town, and is an ideal place to stay to explore the area. The fully refurbished bedrooms are comfortable and well equipped. There is a choice of dining options – the casual 1812 Restaurant and the Market Bar, and the Garden Room is well worth a visit with its innovative menu showcasing the talents of the chef and his team.

Rooms: 19 (4 annexe) (2 family) (2 GF) ☎ S £95; D £125–£250 (incl. bkfst)* Facilities: FTV WiFi ☼ Xmas New Year Conf: Class 100 Board 50 Thtr 160 Del from £140 Services: Night porter Notes: LB Civ Wed 90

HENSOL
Vale of Glamorgan   Map 9 ST07

The Vale Resort
★★★★ 80% ◉ HOTEL

Hensol Park, CF72 8JY - tel: 01443 667800
email: reservations@vale-hotel.com web: www.vale-hotel.com
dir: M4 junct 34 towards Pendoylan, hotel signed from junct

A wealth of leisure facilities is offered at this large and modern, purpose-built complex, including two golf courses and a driving range plus an extensive health spa with a gym, swimming pool, squash courts, orthopaedic clinic and a range of treatments. Public areas are spacious and attractive, while bedrooms, many with balconies, are well appointed. Meeting and conference facilities are available. Guests can dine in the traditional Vale Grill, a brasserie-style restaurant serving quality fresh ingredients.

Rooms: 143 (114 annexe) (15 family) (35 GF) ☎ S £79–£250; D £79–£250 (incl. bkfst)* Facilities: Spa STV WiFi ☼ ⊕ ♨ 36 Putting green ⚓ Fishing Gym Squash Children's club Sat am & school hols Xmas New Year Conf: Class 280 Board 60 Thtr 700 Del from £135 Services: Lift Night porter Air con Parking: 450 Notes: LB Civ Wed 700

KNIGHTON
Powys   Map 9 SO27

Milebrook House Hotel
★★★ 79% ◉ COUNTRY HOUSE HOTEL

Milebrook, LD7 1LT - tel: 01547 528632
email: hotel@milebrookhouse.co.uk web: www.milebrookhouse.co.uk
dir: 2m E of Knighton, on A4113

Set in three acres of grounds and gardens in the Teme Valley, this charming house dates back to 1760. Over the years, since its conversion into a hotel, it has acquired a well-deserved reputation for its warm hospitality, comfortable accommodation and the quality of its cuisine which uses local produce and home-grown vegetables.

Rooms: 10 (1 family) (2 GF) S £114.50–£128; D £160–£195 (incl. bkfst & dinner)* Facilities: WiFi ♨ Table tennis Xmas New Year Conf: Class 30 Parking: 21 Notes: No children 8yrs RS Mon lunch

LAMPETER
Ceredigion   Map 8 SN54

The Falcondale Hotel & Restaurant
★★★★ 78% ◉◉ COUNTRY HOUSE HOTEL

Falcondale Drive, SA48 7RX - tel: 01570 422910
email: info@thefalcondale.co.uk web: www.thefalcondale.co.uk
dir: 1m from Lampeter take A483 to Cardigan, turn right at petrol station, folllow for 0.75m

Built in the Italianate style, this charming Victorian property is set in extensive grounds and beautiful parkland. The individually-styled bedrooms are generally spacious, well equipped and tastefully decorated. Bars and lounges are similarly well appointed with additional facilities including a conservatory and terrace. The award-winning restaurant, with a relaxed and friendly atmosphere, offers menus based on the best seasonal, locally sourced produce.

Rooms: 18 (2 family) ☎ S £110–£160; D £125–£195 (incl. bkfst)* Facilities: FTV WiFi ☼ ♨ Xmas New Year Conf: Class 26 Board 26 Thtr 60 Del from £142 Services: Lift Parking: 60 Notes: LB Civ Wed 200

LAUGHARNE
Carmarthenshire   Map 8 SN31

The Corran Resort & Spa
★★★★ 74% ◉◉ HOTEL

East Marsh, SA33 4RS - tel: 01994 427417
email: info@thecorran.com web: www.thecorran.com
dir: From end of M4 onto A48, then A40 to St Clears. Take A4066 towards Pendine & Laugharne. Follow signs to hotel

Guests will enjoy a unique setting and surroundings at this unusual hotel located in the quiet marshlands of the Carmarthenshire countryside. Bedrooms, mostly located around a courtyard, offer contemporary styling in the interiors while retaining an original 16th-century farmhouse feel to the exterior. A delightful sun terrace is available during warmer months, while the spa with full treatment rooms can be used any time of year. Dinner and breakfast utilise the best quality local produce and are served in the delightful surroundings of the stylish restaurant.

Rooms: 21 (16 annexe) (5 family) (15 GF) ☎ Facilities: Spa STV FTV WiFi ⊕ ♨ Gym Xmas New Year Conf: Class 120 Board 70 Thtr 150 Services: Night porter Parking: 90 Notes: Civ Wed 150

LLANBEDR
Gwynedd   Map 14 SH52

Ty Mawr Hotel
★★ 80% HOTEL

LL45 2NH - tel: 01341 241440
email: info@tymawrhotel.com web: www.tymawrhotel.com
dir: From Barmouth A496 (Harlech road). In Llanbedr turn right after bridge, hotel 50yds on left, follow brown tourist signs

Ty Mawr translates as 'Big House' and this particular house is located in the picturesque Snowdonia National Park. The attractive grounds, opposite the River Artro, provide a popular beer garden during fine weather. Family-run, with a relaxed, friendly atmosphere, the focus of the hotel is the rustically furnished bar offering a blackboard selection of food and real ales, and the restaurant where a more formal menu is available. Bedrooms are smart and brightly decorated.

Rooms: 10 (2 family) ☎ S £59; D £89 (incl. bkfst)* Facilities: STV FTV WiFi ☼ Parking: 15 Notes: Closed 24-26 Dec

Opposite: Llanberis and Llyn Padarn lake from Glyder Fawr, Snowdonia National Park

LLANBERIS
Gwynedd · Map 14 SH56

The Royal Victoria Hotel Snowdonia

★★★ 76% HOTEL

LL55 4TY - tel: 01286 870253
email: enquiries@theroyalvictoria.co.uk web: www.theroyalvictoria.co.uk
dir: On A4086 Caernarfon to Llanberis rd, directly opposite Snowdon Mountain Railway

This well-established hotel sits near the foot of Snowdon, between the Peris and Padarn lakes. Pretty gardens and grounds make an attractive setting for the many weddings held here. Bedrooms are well equipped. There are spacious lounges and bars, and a large dining room with a conservatory looking out over the lakes.

Rooms: 102 (5 family) S £53–£84; D £72–£140 (incl. bkfst)* Facilities: FTV WiFi Xmas New Year Conf: Class 60 Board 50 Thtr 100 Services: Lift Night porter Parking: 70 Notes: LB Civ Wed 100

LLANDRINDOD WELLS
Powys · Map 9 SO06

Metropole Hotel & Spa
★★★★ 76% HOTEL

Temple Street, LD1 5DY - tel: 01597 823700
email: info@metropole.co.uk web: www.metropole.co.uk
dir: On A483 in town centre, car park at rear of hotel

The centre of this famous spa town is dominated by this large Victorian hotel, which has been personally run by the same family for well over 100 years. The lobby leads to Spencers Bar and Brasserie and to the comfortable and elegantly styled lounge. Bedrooms vary in style, but all are spacious and well equipped. Facilities include an extensive range of modern conference and function rooms, as well as the impressive leisure centre. Extensive parking is provided to the rear of the hotel.

Rooms: 109 (11 family) S £98; D £111–£150 (incl. bkfst)* Facilities: Spa FTV WiFi Gym Beauty & holistic treatments Sauna Steam room Xmas New Year Conf: Class 200 Board 80 Thtr 300 Services: Lift Night porter Parking: 150 Notes: LB Civ Wed 300

LLANDUDNO
Conwy · Map 14 SH78

INSPECTOR'S CHOICE

Bodysgallen Hall and Spa
★★★★ COUNTRY HOUSE HOTEL

LL30 1RS - tel: 01492 584466
email: info@bodysgallen.com web: www.bodysgallen.com
dir: A55 junct 19, A470 (The Royal Welsh Way) towards Llandudno. Hotel 2m on right

Situated in the idyllic surroundings of its own parkland and formal gardens, this 17th-century house is in an elevated position, with views towards Snowdonia and across to Conwy Castle. The lounges and dining room have fine antiques and great character. Accommodation is provided in the house, but also in delightfully converted cottages, together with a superb spa. Friendly and attentive service is discreetly offered, while the restaurant features fine local produce prepared with great skill.

Rooms: 31 (16 annexe) (4 family) (4 GF) S fr £159; D fr £180 (incl. bkfst)* Facilities: Spa STV FTV WiFi Gym Spa treatments Steam room Relaxation room Sauna Xmas New Year Conf: Class 30 Board 22 Thtr 50 Del from £155 Services: Night porter Parking: 50 Notes: LB No children 6yrs Civ Wed 50

L

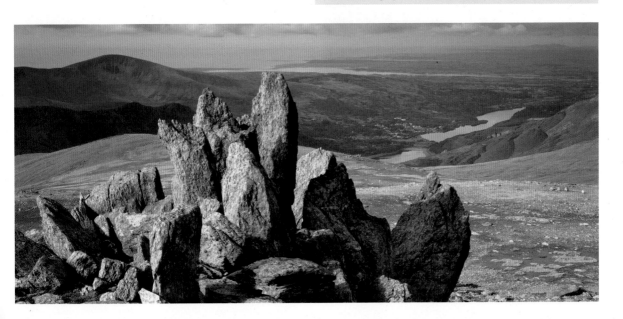

L

LLANDUDNO *continued*

Imperial Hotel
★★★★ 81% ◉◉ HOTEL

The Promenade, Vaughan Street, LL30 1AP - tel: 01492 877466
email: reception@theimperial.co.uk **web:** www.theimperial.co.uk
dir: *A470 to Llandudno*

The Imperial is a large and impressive hotel, situated on the promenade with lovely views out over the Blue Flag beaches to the bay, and within easy reach of the town centre and other amenities. Many of the bedrooms have sea views and there are also several suites available. The elegant Chantrey's Restaurant offers a fixed-price, monthly-changing menu that utilises local produce, and The Terrace is the place to relax and enjoy a leisurely lunch or a snack during the day.

Rooms: 98 (10 family) ☏ **S** £80–£145; **D** £145–£275 (incl. bkfst)* **Facilities:** FTV WiFi ⌨ ⊛ Gym Beauty therapist Hairdressing ♫ Xmas New Year **Conf:** Class 50 Board 50 Thtr 150 Del from £160 **Services:** Lift Night porter **Parking:** 25 **Notes:** LB Civ Wed 120

St George's Hotel
★★★★ 80% ◉ HOTEL

The Promenade, LL30 2LG - tel: 01492 877544
email: sales@stgeorgeswales.co.uk **web:** www.stgeorgeswales.co.uk
dir: *A55, A470, follow to promenade, 0.25m, hotel on corner*

This large and impressive seafront property was the first hotel to be built in the town. Restored to its former glory, the accommodation is of very high quality.
The many Victorian features include the splendid, ornate Wedgwood Room restaurant. The terrace restaurant and main lounges overlook the bay; hot and cold snacks are available all day. Many of the thoughtfully equipped bedrooms enjoy sea views.

Rooms: 81 (13 family) ☏ **S** £80–£135; **D** £110–£180 (incl. bkfst)* **Facilities:** STV FTV WiFi ⌨ In room beauty treatments Xmas New Year **Conf:** Class 200 Board 45 Thtr 250 Del from £120 **Services:** Lift Night porter Air con **Parking:** 36 **Notes:** LB Civ Wed 200

Empire Hotel & Spa
★★★★ 78% HOTEL

Church Walks, LL30 2HE - tel: 01492 860555
email: reservations@empirehotel.co.uk **web:** www.empirehotel.co.uk
dir: *From Chester, A55 junct 19 for Llandudno. Follow signs to Promenade, turn right at war memorial & left at rdbt. Hotel 100yds on right*

Family run for over 60 years, the Empire offers luxuriously appointed bedrooms with every modern facility. The 'Number 72' rooms in an adjacent house are particularly sumptuous. The indoor pool is overlooked by a lounge and café where snacks are served all day, and in summer an outdoor pool and roof garden are available. The Watkins restaurant offers an interesting fixed-price menu.

Rooms: 58 (8 annexe) (1 family) (2 GF) ☏ **S** £75–£112.50; **D** £90–£195 (incl. bkfst)* **Facilities:** Spa FTV WiFi ⌨ HL ⊛ ↖ Gym Sauna Steam room Fitness suite ♫ New Year **Services:** Lift Night porter Air con **Parking:** 57 **Notes:** LB Closed 18–30 Dec

Dunoon Hotel

★★★ 86% ◉◉ HOTEL

Gloddaeth Street, LL30 2DW - **tel:** 01492 860787
email: reservations@dunoonhotel.co.uk **web:** www.dunoonhotel.co.uk
dir: *Exit Promenade at war memorial by pier into Gloddaeth St. Hotel 200yds on right*

This impressive, privately-owned hotel is centrally located and offers a variety of well-equipped bedrooms. Elegant public areas include a tastefully appointed restaurant where technically accurate and nicely presented dishes are served together with a good choice of notable, reasonably priced wines. The caring and attentive service is also noteworthy.

Rooms: 48 (4 family) ♦ **S** £60–£107; **D** £120–£152 (incl. bkfst)* **Facilities:** FTV WiFi 🎵 **Conf:** Board 12 Thtr 30 **Services:** Lift **Parking:** 24 **Notes:** LB Closed mid-Dec-early May

Tynedale Hotel

★★★ 83% HOTEL

Central Promenade, LL30 2XS - **tel:** 01492 877426
email: enquiries@tynedalehotel.co.uk **web:** www.tynedalehotel.co.uk
dir: *On Promenade opposite bandstand*

Tour groups are well catered for at this privately-owned and personally-run hotel, and regular live entertainment is a feature. Vibrant modern public areas create a unique and comfortable setting, and an attractive seafront patio garden is an additional asset. Bedrooms provide good comfort levels and the staff offer friendly and efficient service.

Rooms: 54 (1 family) (10 GF) ♦ **Facilities:** FTV WiFi ⚐ 🎵 Xmas New Year **Services:** Lift Night porter **Parking:** 15 **Notes:** LB

Hydro Hotel

★★★ 69% HOTEL

Leisureplex
HOLIDAY HOTELS

Neville Crescent, LL30 1AT - **tel:** 01492 870101
email: hydro.llandudno@alfatravel.co.uk **web:** www.leisureplex.co.uk
dir: *Follow signs for theatre to seafront, towards pier*

This large hotel is situated on the promenade overlooking the sea, and offers good, value-for-money, modern accommodation. Public areas are quite extensive and include a choice of lounges, a games/snooker room and a ballroom where entertainment is provided every night. The hotel is a popular venue for coach tour parties.

Rooms: 120 (4 family) (9 GF) ♦ **Facilities:** WiFi Table tennis Snooker 🎵 Xmas New Year **Services:** Lift Night porter **Parking:** 10 **Notes:** Closed Jan-mid Feb RS Nov-Dec (ex Xmas) & mid Feb-Mar closed some wknd nights

Premier Inn Llandudno North (Little Orme)

Premier Inn

BUDGET HOTEL

Colwyn Road, LL30 3AL - **tel:** 0871 527 8636 (Calls cost 13p per minute plus your phone company's access charge) **web:** www.premierinn.com
dir: *A55 junct 20 follow Rhos-on-Sea/Llandrillo-Yn-Rhos/B5115 signs. Onto B5115 (Brompton Ave). Straight on at next 2 rdbts. Hotel on left*

High quality, budget accommodation ideal for both families and business travellers. Spacious, en suite bedrooms feature free WiFi and tea and coffee making facilities, and in most hotels, Freeview TV is also available. The adjacent family restaurant features a wide and varied menu.

Rooms: 19

LLANDUDNO JUNCTION	Map 14 SH77
Conwy	

Premier Inn Llandudno (Glan-Conwy)

Premier Inn

BUDGET HOTEL

Afon Conwy, LL28 5LB - **tel:** 0871 527 8634 (Calls cost 13p per minute plus your phone company's access charge) **web:** www.premierinn.com
dir: *A55 junct 19. Exit rdbt at A470 (Betws-y-Coed). Hotel immediately on left, opposite petrol station*

High quality, budget accommodation ideal for both families and business travellers. Spacious, en suite bedrooms feature free WiFi and tea and coffee making facilities, and in most hotels, Freeview TV is also available. The adjacent family restaurant features a wide and varied menu.

Rooms: 69

L

LLANELLI
Carmarthenshire

Map 8 SN50

Best Western Diplomat Hotel and Spa

★★★ 79% HOTEL

Felinfoel, SA15 3PJ - **tel:** 01554 756156
email: reservations@diplomat-hotel-wales.com **web:** www.diplomat-hotel-wales.com
dir: M4 junct 48, A4138 then B4303, hotel 0.75m on right

This Victorian mansion, set in mature grounds, has been extended over the years to provide a comfortable and relaxing hotel. The well-appointed bedrooms are located in the main house and there is also a wing of equally comfortable modern rooms. Public areas include Trubshaw's Restaurant, a large function suite and a modern leisure centre.

Rooms: 50 (8 annexe) (2 family) (4 GF) ✆ **S** £75–£85; **D** fr £110 (incl. bkfst)*
Facilities: Spa FTV WiFi ⅏ ⓢ supervised Gym Sauna Steam room ♫ Xmas New Year
Conf: Class 150 Board 100 Thtr 450 **Services:** Lift Night porter **Parking:** 250
Notes: LB Civ Wed 300

Ashburnham Hotel

★★★ 71% HOTEL

Ashburnham Road, Pembrey, SA16 0TH - **tel:** 01554 834343
email: info@ashburnham-hotel.co.uk **web:** www.ashburnham-hotel.co.uk
dir: M4 junct 48, A4138 to Llanelli, A484 W to Pembrey. Follow brown information signs

American aviatrix, Amelia Earhart stayed at this friendly hotel after finishing her historic trans-Atlantic flight in 1928. Public areas include the brasserie restaurant, and the conservatory lounge bar that serves an extensive range of bar meals. Bedrooms, varying from standard to superior, have modern furnishings and facilities. The hotel is licensed for civil ceremonies, and function and conference facilities are also available.

Rooms: 13 (2 family) **S** fr £50; **D** fr £70 **Facilities:** FTV WiFi ⅏ **Conf:** Class 150 Board 80 Thtr 150 Del from £100 **Services:** Night porter **Parking:** 100
Notes: LB RS 24-26 Dec Civ Wed 130

Premier Inn Llanelli Central East

BUDGET HOTEL

Llandafen Road, SA14 9BD - **tel:** 0871 527 8638 (Calls cost 13p per minute plus your phone company's access charge) **web:** www.premierinn.com
dir: M4 junct 48, A4138, approx 3m. Hotel on left

High quality, budget accommodation ideal for both families and business travellers. Spacious, en suite bedrooms feature free WiFi and tea and coffee making facilities, and in most hotels, Freeview TV is also available. The adjacent family restaurant features a wide and varied menu.

Rooms: 50

Premier Inn Llanelli Central West

BUDGET HOTEL

Sandpiper Road, Sandy Water Park, SA15 4SG - **tel:** 0871 527 9342 (Calls cost 13p per minute plus your phone company's access charge) **web:** www.premierinn.com
dir: M4 junct 48, A4138 towards Llanelli town centre. Then follow Carmarthen signs to Sandy Park rdbt. Hotel on left

Rooms: 28

LLANGAMMARCH WELLS
Powys

Map 9 SN94

The Lake Country House & Spa

★★★★ 79% COUNTRY HOUSE HOTEL

LD4 4BS - **tel:** 01591 620202
email: info@lakecountryhouse.co.uk **web:** www.lakecountryhouse.co.uk
dir: W from Builth Wells on A483 to Garth (approx 6m). Left for Llangammarch Wells, follow hotel signs

Expect good old-fashioned values and hospitality at this Victorian country house hotel. In fact, the service is so good that guests may believe they have their own butler. The establishment offers a 9-hole, par 3 golf course, 50 acres of wooded grounds and a spa with a hot tub that overlooks the lake. Bedrooms, some located in an annexe, and some at ground-floor level, are individually styled and have many extra comforts. Traditional afternoon teas are served in the lounge, and modern Welsh cuisine is offered in the spacious and elegant restaurant.

Rooms: 31 (12 annexe) (8 GF) ✆ **S** £109–£165; **D** £145–£230 (incl. bkfst)*
Facilities: Spa FTV WiFi ⓢ ⅃ 9 Putting green ⅏ Fishing ⅏ Gym Archery Horse riding Mountain biking Quad biking Xmas New Year **Conf:** Class 30 Board 25 Thtr 80 Del from £180 **Services:** Night porter **Parking:** 70 **Notes:** LB No children 8yrs Civ Wed 100

LLANRWST
Conwy

Map 14 SH86

Maenan Abbey

★★★ 80% COUNTRY HOUSE HOTEL

Maenan, LL26 0UL - **tel:** 01492 660247
email: reservations@maenanabbey.co.uk **web:** www.maenanabbey.co.uk
dir: A55/A470 (junct 19) in direction of Betws-y-Coed. Hotel 8m on right. From A5 turn onto A470 at Betws-y-Coed through Llanrwst. Hotel 2m on left

Maenan Abbey is a small and personally-run country house which is ideally located. Walkers can enjoy the National Park then retire to this quiet, well-equipped hotel. Bedrooms are individually designed with some large family rooms available. Cuisine is a highlight of any stay.

Rooms: 14 (3 family) (3 smoking) ✆ **Facilities:** FTV WiFi Fishing Guided mountain walks Xmas New Year **Conf:** Class 30 Board 30 Thtr 50 **Parking:** 60
Notes: Civ Wed 55

LLANTRISANT
Monmouthshire

Map 9 ST39

Premier Inn Llantrisant

BUDGET HOTEL

Gwaun Elai, Magden Park, CF72 8LL - **tel:** 0871 527 8640 (Calls cost 13p per minute plus your phone company's access charge) **web:** www.premierinn.com
dir: M4 junct 34, A4119 towards Llantrisant & Rhondda. At 1st rdbt take 2nd exit. At 2nd rdbt take 1st exit

High quality, budget accommodation ideal for both families and business travellers. Spacious, en suite bedrooms feature free WiFi and tea and coffee making facilities, and in most hotels, Freeview TV is also available. The adjacent family restaurant features a wide and varied menu.

Rooms: 51

LLANWDDYN
Powys

Map 15 SJ01

Lake Vyrnwy Hotel & Spa

★★★★ 74% ⊛ COUNTRY HOUSE HOTEL

Lake Vyrnwy, SY10 0LY - **tel:** 01691 870692
email: info@lakevyrnwyhotel.co.uk **web:** www.lakevyrnwy.com
dir: *On A4393, 200yds past dam turn sharp right into drive*

This elegant Victorian country-house hotel lies in 26,000 acres of woodland above Lake Vyrnwy, and provides a wide range of bedrooms, most with superb views and many with four-poster beds and balconies. Extensive public rooms retain many period features, and informal dining is available in the popular Tower Tavern. Relaxing and rejuvenating treatments are a feature of the stylish health spa.

Rooms: 52 (12 family) ⚲ **S** £98–£144; **D** £125–£266 (incl. bkfst)* **Facilities:** Spa STV FTV WiFi ⇲ ⚲ Fishing Gym Archery Birdwatching Canoeing Kayaking Clay shooting Sailing Fly fishing Cycling Xmas New Year **Conf:** Class 80 Board 60 Thtr 200 **Services:** Lift Night porter **Parking:** 70 **Notes:** LB Civ Wed 200

LLYSWEN
Powys

Map 9 SO13

INSPECTOR'S CHOICE

Llangoed Hall

★★★★ ⊛⊛⊛ COUNTRY HOUSE HOTEL

LD3 0YP - **tel:** 01874 754525 **email:** enquiries@llangoedhall.com
web: www.llangoedhall.com
dir: *On A470 between Brecon & Builth Wells*

Set against the stunning backdrop of the Black Mountains and the Wye Valley, this imposing country house is a haven of peace and quiet. The interior is no less impressive, with a noteworthy art collection complementing the many antiques in day rooms and bedrooms. Comfortable, spacious accommodation is matched by equally inviting lounges.

Llangoed Hall

Rooms: 23 ⚲ **S** £125–£350; **D** £150–£650 (incl. bkfst)* **Facilities:** FTV WiFi ⇲ HL ⚲ Fishing ⚲ Snooker table Outdoor chess ♫ Xmas New Year **Conf:** Class 30 Board 30 Thtr 80 Del from £165 **Services:** Night porter **Parking:** 50 **Notes:** LB Civ Wed 80

See advert on following page

MAESYCWMMER
Caerphilly

Map 9 ST19

Bryn Meadows Golf, Hotel & Spa

★★★★ 76% HOTEL

CF82 7SN - **tel:** 01495 225590
email: reception@brynmeadows.co.uk **web:** www.brynmeadows.co.uk
dir: *M4 junct 28, A467 signed Brynmawr, 10m to Newbridge. Take A472 signed Ystrad Mynach. Hotel off Crown rdbt signed golf course*

Surrounded by its own mature parkland and 18-hole golf course, this impressive hotel, golf, leisure and function complex provides a range of high quality, well-equipped bedrooms; several have their own balconies or patio areas. The attractive public areas include a pleasant restaurant which, like many of the bedrooms, enjoys striking views of the golf course and beyond. There are impressive function facilities and the hotel is a popular venue for weddings.

Rooms: 42 (4 family) (21 GF) ⚲ **S** £89–£180; **D** £109–£195 (incl. bkfst)* **Facilities:** Spa FTV WiFi ⚲ supervised ⚲ 18 Putting green Gym Sauna Steam room Aromatherapy suite Hydro spa Rasul mud room Xmas New Year **Conf:** Class 120 Board 110 Thtr 300 Del from £99 **Services:** Night porter Air con **Parking:** 120 **Notes:** LB Civ Wed 350

M

Find out more about AA Rosettes
– page 13

M

Llangoed hall

Afternoon Tea | Dining | Accommodation

Llangoed Hall is a wonderfully elegant and historic country house hotel situated in the beautiful Wye Valley in the heart of the Welsh countryside. It offers the quintessential Edwardian country house experience.

Telephone 01874 754525

Events@llangoedhall.com | Twitter: @TheLlangoedHall

Llyswen, Brecon, Powys LD3 0YP

www.llangoedhall.com

MERTHYR TYDFIL
Merthyr Tydfil
Map 9 SO00

Premier Inn Merthyr Tydfil

BUDGET HOTEL

Pentrebach, CF48 4BB - tel: 0871 527 8768 (Calls cost 13p per minute plus your phone company's access charge) **web:** www.premierinn.com
dir: *M4 junct 32, A470 to Merthyr Tydfil. At rdbt right to Pentrebach (A4060). At next rdbt 3rd exit signed Abergavenny (dual carriageway). Double back at next rdbt by Pentrebach Co-op onto A4060 towards Pentrebach. Left after layby, hotel adjacent to Pentrebach House*

High quality, budget accommodation ideal for both families and business travellers. Spacious, en suite bedrooms feature free WiFi and tea and coffee making facilities, and in most hotels, Freeview TV is also available. The adjacent family restaurant features a wide and varied menu.

Rooms: 62

MISKIN
Rhondda Cynon Taff
Map 9 ST08

Miskin Manor Country Hotel

★★★★ 71% COUNTRY HOUSE HOTEL

Pendoylan Road, CF72 8ND - tel: 01443 224204
email: amanda@miskin-manor.co.uk **web:** www.miskin-manor.co.uk
dir: *M4 junct 34, A4119, signed Llantrisant, hotel 300yds on left*

This historic manor house is peacefully located in 22-acre grounds, yet is only minutes away from the M4. Bedrooms are furnished to a high standard and include some located in converted stables and cottages. Public areas are spacious and comfortable and include a variety of function rooms. The relaxed atmosphere and surroundings ensure that this hotel remains popular for wedding functions as well as with business guests. There is a separate, modern health and fitness centre which includes a gym, sauna, steam room and swimming pool.

Miskin Manor Country Hotel

Rooms: 42 (9 annexe) (4 family) (6 GF) 🛏 **S** £100–£105; **D** £125–£145 (incl. bkfst)* **Facilities:** Spa FTV WiFi ⓦ 🏊 Gym Sauna Steam room Dance studio Xmas New Year **Conf:** Class 80 Board 65 Thtr 160 Del from £155 **Services:** Night porter **Parking:** 200 **Notes:** LB Civ Wed 200

MOLD
Flintshire
Map 15 SJ26

Beaufort Park Hotel

★★★ 77% HOTEL

Alltami Road, New Brighton, CH7 6RQ - tel: 01352 758646
email: info@beaufortparkhotel.co.uk **web:** www.beaufortparkhotel.co.uk
dir: *A55, A494, through Alltami lights, over mini rdbt by petrol station towards Mold, A5119. Hotel 100yds on right*

This large, modern hotel is conveniently located a short drive from the North Wales Expressway and offers various styles of spacious accommodation. There are extensive public areas, and several meeting and function rooms are available. There is a wide choice of meals in the formal restaurant and in the popular Arches bar.

Rooms: 106 (8 family) (32 GF) **S** £55–£95; **D** £60–£120 (incl. bkfst)* **Facilities:** FTV WiFi Squash ♫ Xmas New Year **Conf:** Class 120 Board 120 Thtr 250 Del from £110 **Services:** Night porter **Parking:** 200 **Notes:** LB Civ Wed 220

MONMOUTH
Monmouthshire
Map 10 SO51

Premier Inn Monmouth

BUDGET HOTEL

NP25 5EZ - tel: 0871 527 9636 (Calls cost 13p per minute plus your phone company's access charge)
dir: *Phone for detailed directions*

High quality, budget accommodation ideal for both families and business travellers. Spacious, en suite bedrooms feature free WiFi and tea and coffee making facilities, and in most hotels, Freeview TV is also available. The adjacent family restaurant features a wide and varied menu.

Rooms: 60

NARBERTH
Pembrokeshire

Map 8 SN11

Grove

★★★★ ◉◉◉ HOTEL

PRIDE OF BRITAIN HOTELS

Molleston, SA67 8BX - **tel:** 01834 860915

email: info@thegrove-narberth.co.uk **web:** www.thegrove-narberth.co.uk

dir: *A48 to Carmarthen, A40 to Haverfordwest. At A478 rdbt 1st exit to Narberth, through town towards Tenby. At bottom of hill right, 1m, hotel on right*

Grove is an elegant 17th-century country house set on a hillside in 26 acres of rolling countryside. The owners have lovingly restored the building with care, combining period features with excellent modern decor. There are bedrooms in the main house, and additional rooms in separate buildings; all are appointed with high levels of quality and comfort. Some bedrooms are on the ground floor, and most have fantastic views out over the Preseli Hills. There are two sumptuous lounge areas, one with an open fire and a small bar, and two separate dining rooms that offer award-winning cuisine. Self-catering cottages are available.

Rooms: 26 (3 family) (7 GF) **D** £190–£650 (incl. bkfst)* **Facilities:** STV WiFi In room spa treatments Boules Xmas New Year **Conf:** Class 30 Board 24 Thtr 60 Del from £250 **Services:** Night porter **Parking:** 34 **Notes:** LB Civ Wed

NEWPORT
Newport

Map 9 ST38

See also **Cwmbran**

The Celtic Manor Resort

★★★★★ 85% ◉◉◉ HOTEL

Coldra Woods, NP18 1HQ - **tel:** 01633 413000 & 410262

email: bookings@celtic-manor.com **web:** www.celtic-manor.com

dir: *M4 junct 24, take B4237 towards Newport. Hotel 1st on right*

This hotel is part of the outstanding Celtic Manor Resort. Here there are three challenging golf courses including the Twenty Ten Course specifically designed for the 2010 Ryder Cup; a huge convention centre; superb leisure clubs and two hotels. This hotel has excellent bedrooms, with suites and two Presidential suites, offering good space and comfort. Stylish, extensive public areas are set around a spectacular atrium lobby that includes several eating options including The Epicure Experience. There is a choice of shops and boutiques as well.

Rooms: 334 (34 family) **Facilities:** Spa STV FTV WiFi 54 Putting green Fishing Gym Golf Academy Archery Laser combat Adventure Golf Treetop ropes courses Xmas New Year **Conf:** Class 600 Board 60 Thtr 1500 **Services:** Lift Night porter Air con **Parking:** 1300 **Notes:** Civ Wed 100

The Manor House

★★★★ 74% HOTEL

The Celtic Manor Resort, Coldra Woods, NP18 1HQ - **tel:** 01633 413000

email: bookings@celtic-manor.com **web:** www.celtic-manor.com

dir: *M4 junct 24, B4237 towards Newport. Hotel 1st on right*

Part of the Celtic Manor Resort complex, this 19th-century hotel offers country house charm combined with modern comforts. Sitting in beautiful landscaped gardens, it has traditionally styled bedrooms, three with four-posters. An Asian inspired restaurant is located in this hotel with a further number of restaurants to be found at the main Celtic Manor Resort. Guests have access to all the hotel and leisure facilities at the resort; three challenging golf courses, a superb leisure complex and many other activities suitable for both adults and families.

Rooms: 65 (3 family) **Facilities:** Spa STV FTV WiFi supervised 18 Putting green Fishing Gym Golf academy Archery Laser combat Adventure golf Treetop ropes courses Xmas New Year **Conf:** Class 80 Board 40 Thtr 200 **Services:** Lift Night porter Air con **Parking:** 1000 **Notes:** Civ Wed 180

N

Premier Inn Newport City Centre (Wales)

BUDGET HOTEL

NP20 4GA - **tel:** 0871 527 9474 (Calls cost 13p per minute plus your phone company's access charge)
dir: *Phone for detailed directions*

High quality, budget accommodation ideal for both families and business travellers. Spacious, en suite bedrooms feature free WiFi and tea and coffee making facilities, and in most hotels, Freeview TV is also available. The adjacent family restaurant features a wide and varied menu.drean

Rooms: 61

Premier Inn Newport Wales (M4 Jct 24)

BUDGET HOTEL

Coldra Junction, Chepstow Rd, NP18 2NX - **tel:** 0871 527 8814 (Calls cost 13p per minute plus your phone company's access charge) **web:** www.premierinn.com
dir: *M4 junct 24, A48 to Langstone, at next rdbt return towards junct 24. Hotel 50mtrs on left*

Rooms: 81

PEMBROKE
Pembrokeshire

Map 8 SM90

Best Western Lamphey Court Hotel & Spa

★★★★ 75% HOTEL

Lamphey, SA71 5NT - **tel:** 01646 672273
email: info@lampheycourt.co.uk **web:** www.lampheycourt.co.uk
dir: *M4 then A477 to Pembroke. Left at Milton for Lamphey, hotel on right*

This Georgian mansion, on an elevated site, is set in attractive countryside and is perfectly situated for exploring the stunning Pembrokeshire coast, the beaches and the Preseli Hills. Well-appointed bedrooms and family suites are situated in a converted coach house within the grounds. The elegant public areas include both formal and informal dining rooms that feature dishes inspired by local produce. Leisure facilities include a state-of-the-art spa with a swimming pool, gym, sauna, treatment rooms and much more.

Rooms: 38 (12 annexe) (7 family) (6 GF) **S** fr £80; **D** fr £99* **Facilities:** Spa FTV WiFi ⃰ ⃰ ⃰ Gym Sauna Steam room Beauty & therapy Xmas New Year Child facilities **Conf:** Class 40 Board 30 Thtr 60 Del from £125 **Parking:** 50 **Notes:** Civ Wed 80

Lamphey Hall Hotel

★★★ 78% HOTEL

Lamphey, SA71 5NR - **tel:** 01646 672394
web: www.lampheyhall.co.uk
dir: *From Carmarthen A40 to St Clears. Follow signs for A477, left at Milton*

Set in a delightful village, this very friendly, privately owned and efficiently run hotel offers an ideal base from which to explore the surrounding countryside. Bedrooms are well equipped, comfortably furnished and include family rooms and ground floor rooms. Diners have a choice of three restaurant areas offering an extensive range of dishes. There is also a small lounge, a bar and attractive gardens.

Rooms: 10 (1 family) (2 GF) **S** £59.50; **D** £89.50 (incl. bkfst)* **Facilities:** FTV WiFi **Parking:** 32

PENARTH
Vale of Glamorgan

Map 9 ST17

Holm House Hotel

★★★★ 79% HOTEL

Marine Parade, CF64 3BG - **tel:** 029 2070 6029
email: reception@holmhousehotel.co.uk **web:** www.holmhousehotel.com
dir: *Phone for detailed directions*

A delightful hotel full of quality and comfort with excellent views over the Bristol Channel to the islands of Flatholm and Steepholm. Bedrooms include a number of suites and all are decorated and furnished to very high standards. The Welsh Room Restaurant looks out over the garden and the water, and offers a range of well prepared dishes displaying seasonal, quality produce. A relaxing garden and terrace for outdoor summer seating is also provided. Guests can enjoy the relaxing spa with full treatment rooms, a small gym and an elegant steam room.

Rooms: 12 (1 family) (2 GF) **Facilities:** Spa STV FTV WiFi ⃰ ⃰ Gym Steam room Xmas New Year **Conf:** Class 12 Board 12 Thtr 16 **Services:** Night porter Air con **Notes:** Civ Wed 70

PONTYPOOL
Torfaen

Map 9 SO20

Premier Inn Pontypool

BUDGET HOTEL

Tyr'felin, Lower Mill Field, NP4 0RH - **tel:** 0871 527 8890 (Calls cost 13p per minute plus your phone company's access charge) **web:** www.premierinn.com
dir: *At junct of A4042 & A472*

High quality, budget accommodation ideal for both families and business travellers. Spacious, en suite bedrooms feature free WiFi and tea and coffee making facilities, and in most hotels, Freeview TV is also available. The adjacent family restaurant features a wide and varied menu.

Rooms: 50

P

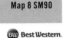

P

PONTYPRIDD
Rhondda Cynon Taff

Map 9 ST08

Llechwen Hall Hotel

★★★ 79% ⚜ COUNTRY HOUSE HOTEL

Llanfabon, CF37 4HP - tel: 01443 742050
email: enquiries@llechwenhall.co.uk **web:** www.llechwen.co.uk
dir: *A470 N towards Merthyr Tydfil. At large rdbt take 3rd exit.*
At mini rdbt take 3rd exit, hotel signed 0.5m on left

Set on top of a hill with a stunning approach, this country house hotel has served many functions in its 200-year-old history including time as a private school and a magistrates' court. The spacious, individually decorated bedrooms are well equipped; some are situated in the separate coach house nearby. There are ground-floor, twin, double and family bedrooms on offer. The Victorian-style public areas are attractively appointed and the hotel is a popular venue for weddings.

Rooms: 20 (8 annexe) (6 family) (4 GF) **D** £99–£175 (incl. bkfst)* **Facilities:** FTV WiFi ⓦ Xmas New Year **Conf:** Class 80 Board 40 Thtr 200 Del from £99 **Parking:** 150 **Notes:** Civ Wed 90

PORTHCAWL
Bridgend

Map 9 SS87

Seabank Hotel

Leisureplex
HOLIDAY HOTELS

★★★ 69% HOTEL

Esplanade, CF36 3LU - tel: 01656 782261
email: seabank@leisureplex.co.uk **web:** www.leisureplex.co.uk
dir: *M4 junct 37, A4229 to Porthcawl seafront*

The Seabank Hotel stands in a prime location on the promenade of this seaside town, with panoramic views from the majority of bedrooms. Porthcawl has several beaches and coastal walks; the world famous Royal Porthcawl golf course is within easy distance and the cities of Swansea and Cardiff are only a short drive away. The spacious bedrooms are all en suite and there is a lift which serves most bedrooms. There is a spacious restaurant, a lounge bar and a choice of lounges with sea views. The hotel is a popular venue for coach tour parties, as well as weddings and conferences. There is ample parking around the hotel.

Rooms: 91 (3 family) (6 GF) ⓝ **Facilities:** FTV WiFi ♫ Xmas New Year **Services:** Lift Night porter **Parking:** 100 **Notes:** Closed 2 Jan-10 Feb

PORTHMADOG
Gwynedd

Map 14 SH53

Royal Sportsman Hotel

★★★ 76% HOTEL

131 High Street, LL49 9HB - tel: 01766 512015
email: enquiries@royalsportsman.co.uk **web:** www.royalsportsman.co.uk/hotel
dir: *Opposite rdbt at junct of A487 & A497*

This hotel has a very convenient location handy for the coast or for those wishing to visit the National Park or mountain railway. The hotel has a choice of dining options and food a notable here. Bedrooms are smartly appointed, and there is a spacious lounge. The staff are a friendly team and service is attentive. Covered parking is available.

Rooms: 28 (7 family) (9 GF) ⓝ **S** £66; **D** £96–£110 (incl. bkfst)* **Facilities:** STV FTV WiFi ⓦ Xmas New Year **Conf:** Class 30 Board 30 Thtr 50 Del from £130 **Services:** Night porter **Parking:** 17 **Notes:** LB Civ Wed 60

PORTMEIRION
Gwynedd

Map 14 SH53

The Hotel Portmeirion

★★★★ 77% ⚜⚜ HOTEL

Minffordd, LL48 6ET - tel: 01766 770000
email: hotel@portmeirion-village.com **web:** www.portmeirion-village.com
dir: *2m W, Portmeirion village is S off A487*

Saved from dereliction in the 1920s by Clough Williams-Ellis, the elegant Hotel Portmeirion enjoys one of the finest settings in Wales, located beneath the wooded slopes of the village, overlooking the sandy estuary towards Snowdonia. Many bedrooms have private sitting rooms and balconies with spectacular views. The staff, mostly Welsh-speaking, provide a good mix of warm hospitality and efficient service. Dinner and breakfast include the finest produce.

Rooms: 44 (30 annexe) (6 family) ⓝ **Facilities:** Spa FTV WiFi ⓦ ↖ ♫ Xmas New Year **Conf:** Class 40 Board 30 Thtr 100 **Services:** Lift Night porter **Parking:** 44 **Notes:** Civ Wed 130

PORT TALBOT
Neath Port Talbot

Map 9 SS78

Premier Inn Port Talbot

BUDGET HOTEL

Baglan Road, Baglan, SA12 8ES - tel: 0871 527 8896 (Calls cost 13p per minute plus your phone company's access charge) **web:** www.premierinn.com
dir: *M4 junct 41 W'bound. Hotel just off 4th exit at rdbt. M4 junct 42 E'bound,*
left towards Port Talbot. Take 2nd exit off 2nd rdbt

High quality, budget accommodation ideal for both families and business travellers. Spacious, en suite bedrooms feature free WiFi and tea and coffee making facilities, and in most hotels, Freeview TV is also available. The adjacent family restaurant features a wide and varied menu.

Rooms: 42

RHUDDLAN
Denbighshire Map 15 SJ07

Premier Inn Rhuddlan

BUDGET HOTEL

Castle View Retail Park, Marsh Road, LL18 5UA - **tel:** 0871 527 8932 (Calls cost 13p per minute plus your phone company's access charge) **web:** www.premierinn.com
dir: *A55 junct 27, A525 signed Rhyl. At next rdbt 3rd exit into Station Rd. Next left into Marsh Rd. Hotel on left*

High quality, budget accommodation ideal for both families and business travellers. Spacious, en suite bedrooms feature free WiFi and tea and coffee making facilities, and in most hotels, Freeview TV is also available. The adjacent family restaurant features a wide and varied menu.

Rooms: 44

ROSSETT
Wrexham Map 15 SJ35

Hallmark Hotel Chester Llyndir Hall

★★★ 81% ⊛ HOTEL

Llyndir Lane, LL12 0AY - **tel:** 0330 028 3417
email: llyndir@hallmarkhotels.co.uk **web:** www.hallmarkhotels.co.uk
dir: *5m S of Chester on B5445 follow Pulford signs*

Located on the English/Welsh border within easy reach of Chester and Wrexham, this elegant manor house lies in several acres of mature grounds. The hotel is popular with both business and leisure guests, and facilities include conference rooms, an impressive leisure centre, a choice of comfortable lounges and a brasserie-style restaurant.

Rooms: 48 (3 family) (17 GF) **Facilities:** Spa FTV WiFi HL ☜ supervised Gym Beauty salon Sauna Xmas New Year **Conf:** Class 60 Board 40 Thtr 120 **Services:** Night porter **Parking:** 80 **Notes:** LB Civ Wed 120

RUTHIN
Denbighshire Map 15 SJ15

Ruthin Castle Hotel

★★★★ 79% ⊛ HOTEL

Castle Street, LL15 2NU - **tel:** 01824 702664
email: reservations@ruthincastle.co.uk **web:** www.ruthincastle.co.uk
dir: *From Manchester take M56, A55, A494*

This originally medieval building has been many things over the years and now serves as a luxurious hotel. Set in picturesque North Wales, it offers a variety of bedrooms, many of which have been patronised by royalty. Dinner is in the elegant Berties (another Kingly connection), guests can relax in the octagonal Library bar and there are modern spa and leisure facilities as well as extensive conference rooms also on site.

Rooms: 55 (10 family) (27 GF) **Facilities:** Spa FTV WiFi ⤳ Gym Thermal Suite Sauna Steam room Xmas New Year **Conf:** Class 80 Board 46 Thtr 180 **Services:** Lift Night porter Air con **Parking:** 80 **Notes:** Civ Wed 140

ST DAVIDS
Pembrokeshire Map 8 SM72

AA HOTEL OF THE YEAR FOR WALES 2017–18

HIGHLY RECOMMENDED

Twr Y Felin Hotel

★★★★ 86% ⊛⊛ ⊜ HOTEL

Caerfai Road, SA62 6QT - **tel:** 01437 725555 & 725566
email: stay@twryfelinhotel.com **web:** www.twryfelinhotel.com
dir: *Phone for detailed directions*

Located on the St Davids peninsula, this hotel has been restored and extended to provide contemporary spaces with modern amenities. Bedrooms offer a deeply comfortable environment while embracing modern technology and high levels of attention to detail. The Tyddewi Suite is a unique space occupying the original windmill tower, which boasts spectacular 360 degree views of the coastline and beyond. You can be assured of a genuine and warm welcome from dedicated team. Restaurant Blas (meaning 'Taste' in Welsh) offers award-winning cuisine, with a seasonal menu showcasing local suppliers and producers. There are over 100 pieces of specially commissioned artworks inspired by the peninsula and Pembrokeshire, by well known contemporary artists.

Rooms: 21 (7 GF) **S** £180–£350; **D** £190–£360 (incl. bkfst)* **Facilities:** STV FTV WiFi ⤳ Xmas New Year **Conf:** Class 60 Board 42 Thtr 100 Del from £295 **Services:** Lift Night porter **Parking:** 27 **Notes:** No Children 12yrs Civ Wed 42

S

SARN PARK MOTORWAY SERVICE AREA (M4)
Bridgend

Map 9 SS98

Days Inn Bridgend Cardiff - M4

WELCOMEBREAK

AA Advertised

Sarn Park Services, M4 Junct 36, CF32 9RW - **tel:** 01656 659218
email: sarn.hotel@welcomebreak.co.uk **web:** www.welcomebreak.co.uk
dir: *M4 junct 36*

This modern building offers accommodation in smart, spacious and well-equipped bedrooms, suitable for families and business travellers, and all with en suite bathrooms. Continental breakfast is available and other refreshments may be taken at the nearby family restaurant.

Rooms: 40 (15 family) (20 GF) (8 smoking) **Facilities:** FTV WiFi ⌨
Services: Night porter **Parking:** 40

SAUNDERSFOOT
Pembrokeshire

Map 8 SN10

HIGHLY RECOMMENDED

St Brides Spa Hotel

★★★★ 84% ⊛ HOTEL

St Brides Hill, SA69 9NH - **tel:** 01834 812304
email: reservations@stbridesspahotel.com **web:** www.stbridesspahotel.com
dir: *A478 onto B4310 to Saundersfoot. Hotel above harbour*

Set overlooking Carmarthen Bay, this contemporary hotel and spa takes prime position. Many of the stylish, modern bedrooms enjoy sea views and have balconies; there are also luxury apartments in the grounds. The hotel is open-plan and has excellent views of the bay from the split-level lounge areas. Fresh local seafood is a speciality in the modern airy restaurant, which has a terrace for alfresco dining when the weather allows. The destination spa enjoys some of the very best views from the double treatment room and spa pool.

Rooms: 46 (12 annexe) (6 family) (9 GF) ⌘ **S** £135–£210; **D** £170–£320 (incl. bkfst)* **Facilities:** Spa FTV WiFi ⌨ Gym Thermal suite Hydrotherapy pool Steam & herbal rooms Ice fountain Xmas New Year **Conf:** Class 40 Board 34 Thtr 100 Del from £170 **Services:** Lift Night porter **Parking:** 65 **Notes:** Civ Wed 90

SWANSEA
Swansea

Map 9 SS69

See also **Port Talbot**

The Dragon Hotel

★★★★ 74% HOTEL

The Kingsway, SA1 5LS - **tel:** 01792 657100
email: enquiries@dragon-hotel.co.uk **web:** www.dragon-hotel.co.uk
dir: *M4 junct 42, A483. Straight on at rdbt, onto A4067. At 5th lights into right lane, turn right. Into left lane signed The Dragon Hotel. Left at junct, into right lane. At 2nd lights turn left. Up hill, after 2nd lights, hotel visible ahead. With hotel on right take 1st right after Specsavers, car park 1st right*

The Dragon Hotel is located in the city centre and offers spacious modern accommodation with well-equipped, comfortable bedrooms. There is a bar and lounge facility on the first floor along with the Piano Restaurant serving dinner and breakfast. On the ground floor, the Dragons Brasserie provides a vibrant continental menu for both residents and non-residents. The health and fitness club offers an excellent choice of facilities and there is a good range of conference rooms.

Rooms: 106 (7 family) ⌘ **S** £59–£239; **D** £69–£249 **Facilities:** FTV WiFi ⌨ HL ⊛ Gym Treatment rooms Xmas New Year **Conf:** Class 120 Board 80 Thtr 230 Del from £112 **Services:** Lift Night porter Air con **Parking:** 52 **Notes:** Civ Wed 120

Mercure Swansea Hotel

★★★ 79% HOTEL

Mercure
HOTELS

Phoenix Way, SA7 9EG - **tel:** 0844 815 9081 (Calls cost 5p per minute plus your phone company's access charge)
email: sales@mercureswansea.co.uk **web:** www.mercureswansea.co.uk
dir: *M4 junct 44, A48 Llansamlet, left at 3rd lights, right at 1st mini rdbt, left into Phoenix Way at 2nd rdbt. Hotel 800mtrs on right*

Located in the business park area just outside of Swansea, this is a popular hotel with both business and leisure guests. A wide range of dishes is available throughout the day and evening from the relaxing lounge, or the well furnished restaurant. Bedrooms and bathrooms are located over two floors and include standard and executive options. Leisure facilities and a large car park are also provided at this hotel.

Rooms: 119 (24 family) (55 GF) **Facilities:** FTV WiFi ⌨ ⊛ Gym Sauna Xmas New Year **Conf:** Class 80 Board 50 Thtr 180 **Services:** Night porter **Parking:** 180 **Notes:** Civ Wed 180

Premier Inn Swansea City Centre

Premier Inn

BUDGET HOTEL

Salubrious Place, Wind Street, SA1 1EE - **tel:** 0871 527 9060 (Calls cost 13p per minute plus your phone company's access charge) **web:** www.premierinn.com
dir: *M4 junct 42, A483 towards the city centre. Pass Sainsburys on left, right into Salubrious Place, 2nd right, then 3rd exit at mini rdbt*

High quality, budget accommodation ideal for both families and business travellers. Spacious, en suite bedrooms feature free WiFi and tea and coffee making facilities, and in most hotels, Freeview TV is also available. The adjacent family restaurant features a wide and varied menu.

Rooms: 116

S

Premier Inn Swansea North

BUDGET HOTEL

Upper Forest Way, Morriston, SA6 8WB - **tel:** 0871 527 9062 (Calls cost 13p per minute plus your phone company's access charge) **web:** www.premierinn.com
dir: *M4 junct 45, A4067 towards Swansea. In 0.5m at 2nd exit left into Clase Rd. Hotel 400yds on left*

Rooms: 63

Premier Inn Swansea Waterfront

BUDGET HOTEL

The Waterfront Development, Langdon Road, SA1 8PL - **tel:** 0871 577 9212 (Calls cost 13p per minute plus your phone company's access charge) **web:** www.premierinn.com
dir: *M4 junct 42, A483 towards Swansea/Abertawe (signed Fabian Way). Approx 4.5m. At 2nd lights, left into SA1 Waterfront development. At rdbt take 2nd exit into Langdon Rd. Hotel on left*

Rooms: 132

TENBY	Map 8 SN10
Pembrokeshire	

HIGHLY RECOMMENDED

Atlantic Hotel

★★★ 86% HOTEL

The Esplanade, SA70 7DU - **tel:** 01834 842881
email: enquiries@atlantic-hotel.uk.com **web:** www.atlantic-hotel.uk.com
dir: *A478 into Tenby, follow town centre signs (keep town walls on left) right at Esplanade, hotel on right*

This privately-owned and personally-run, friendly hotel has an enviable position looking out over South Beach towards Caldy Island. Bedrooms vary in size and style, but all are well equipped and tastefully appointed. The comfortable public areas include a choice of lounges and in fine weather, guests can also enjoy the cliff-top gardens. Relax in the salt-water swimming pool with jacuzzi, steam room and heated loungers.

Rooms: 42 (11 family) (4 GF) ☎ **S** £83–£100; **D** £115–£210 (incl. bkfst)
Facilities: FTV WiFi ⊗ Steam room Spa bath **Services:** Lift Night porter
Parking: 25 **Notes:** LB Closed Nov-late Jan

Penally Abbey Hotel

★★★ 78% HOTEL

Penally, SA70 7PY - **tel:** 01834 843033
email: info@penally-abbey.com **web:** www.penally-abbey.com
dir: *Phone for detailed directions*

Perched on the hill overlooking Carmarthen Bay, near Tenby, Penally Abbey sits on a monastic site and was also once the home to the Irish whiskey distillers, Jameson. The 12th-century ruins of the original chapel can still be seen in the grounds today. The hotel has been fully restored by the owners and a warm welcome is assured from the friendly team. The distinct Gothic windows frame the sea views from many of the spacious bedrooms. A number of the Coach House rooms accept dogs. Local and seasonal produce are used by the kitchen for meals in the candlelit restaurant.

Rooms: 11 (4 annexe) (3 family) (2 GF) ☎ **Facilities:** FTV WiFi ⊗ Xmas New Year
Conf: Class 25 Board 25 Thtr 30 **Parking:** 12 **Notes:** Closed Jan Civ Wed 35

Cliffe Norton Hotel

Leisureplex HOLIDAY HOTELS

★★★ 73% HOTEL

10-13 The Norton, SA70 8AA - **tel:** 01834 842333
email: vladimir.jordan@leisureplex.co.uk **web:** www.thecliffenortonhotel.com
dir: *A40, rdbt to A477, rdbt to A478. Into Narberth Rd, hotel on right*

The Cliffe Norton is ideally located on the front in Tenby, with many rooms benefiting from sea views. Bedrooms are individually decorated, offering good quality value for money accommodation. Entertainment is provided each evening after dinner. The restaurant offers good value home cooking and is open for both breakfast and dinner daily. A limited number of parking spaces is available. The hotel is a popular venue for coach tour parties.

Rooms: 50 (7 family) ☎ **S** £41–£57; **D** £66–£98 (incl. bkfst)* **Facilities:** FTV WiFi 🎵
Xmas New Year **Services:** Lift Night porter **Parking:** 5 **Notes:** Closed 2 Jan-18 Feb

Premier Inn Tenby Town Centre

BUDGET HOTEL

White Lion Street, SA70 7ET - **tel:** 0871 527 9514 (Calls cost 13p per minute plus your phone company's access charge) **web:** www.premierinn.com
dir: *A478 into Tenby. Left into Narberth Rd. On bay turn right into White Lion St*

High quality, budget accommodation ideal for both families and business travellers. Spacious, en suite bedrooms feature free WiFi and tea and coffee making facilities, and in most hotels, Freeview TV is also available. The adjacent family restaurant features a wide and varied menu.

Rooms: 61

TINTERN PARVA	Map 4 SO50
Monmouthshire	

Best Western Royal George Hotel

BW Best Western.

★★★ 79% HOTEL

Wye Valley Road, NP16 6SF - **tel:** 01291 689205
email: royalgeorgetintern10@hotmail.com **web:** www.bw-royalgeorgehotel.co.uk
dir: *M48 junct 2, A466, 5m to Tintern, 2nd left*

This privately-owned and personally-run hotel provides comfortable, spacious accommodation, including bedrooms with balconies overlooking the well-tended garden; there is also a number of ground-floor bedrooms. The public areas include a lounge bar and a large function room, and a varied and popular menu is available in either the bar or restaurant. This hotel is an ideal base for exploring the counties of Monmouthshire and Herefordshire.

Rooms: 14 (14 annexe) (3 family) (10 GF) **S** £75–£120; **D** £85–£150 (incl. bkfst)*
Facilities: FTV WiFi ⊗ New Year **Conf:** Class 40 Board 30 Thtr 80 Del from £130
Parking: 50 **Notes:** LB Civ Wed 70

T

TREARDDUR BAY — Map 14 SH27
Isle of Anglesey

Trearddur Bay Hotel

★★★ 81% HOTEL

LL65 2UN - **tel:** 01407 860301 **email:** enquiries@trearddurbayhotel.co.uk
web: www.trearddurbayhotel.co.uk
dir: A55 junct 2, left, over 1st rdbt, left at 2nd rdbt, right after approx 2m

A real seaside theme runs through this bright and welcoming hotel situated only 100 yards from a Blue Flag beach. Bedrooms include a large number of refurbished, contemporary rooms; some with balconies and stunning views of the bay. Guests have a choice of dining in the more formal Bay Restaurant, or the Inn at The Bay which has an outdoor area for summer dining. Facilities include function rooms, an indoor swimming pool and children's play area.

Rooms: 43 (6 annexe) (6 family) (3 GF) ⏰ **S** £65–£140; **D** £79–£205 (incl. bkfst)* **Facilities:** FTV WiFi ⬇ ⛲ Xmas New Year **Conf:** Class 80 Board 60 Thtr 200 Del from £110 **Services:** Night porter **Parking:** 200 **Notes:** LB Civ Wed 140

USK — Map 9 SO30
Monmouthshire

The Three Salmons Hotel

★★★ 77% HOTEL

Bridge Street, NP15 1RY - **tel:** 01291 672133 **email:** reception@threesalmons.co.uk
web: www.threesalmons.co.uk
dir: M4 junct 24, A449, 1st exit signed Usk. On entering town, hotel on main road

The Three Salmons is a 17th-century coaching inn located in the centre of a small market town with friendly, efficient staff that help create a welcoming atmosphere. The food in the contemporary restaurant is very popular. Bedrooms are comfortable and a good range of extras are provided. There is a large function suite ideal for weddings and parties. Parking is secure.

Rooms: 24 (14 annexe) (3 family) (7 GF) ⏰ **S** fr £79; **D** fr £100 (incl. bkfst)* **Facilities:** FTV WiFi ⬇ **Conf:** Class 80 Board 40 Thtr 110 Del from £136 **Services:** Night porter **Parking:** 43 **Notes:** Civ Wed 100

WELSHPOOL — Map 15 SJ20
Powys

The Royal Oak Hotel

★★★ 80% HOTEL

THE COACHING INN GROUP

The Cross, SY21 7DG - **tel:** 01938 552217 **email:** royaloak@innmail.co.uk
web: www.royaloakwelshpool.co.uk
dir: By lights at junct of A483 & A458

Standing in the centre of Welshpool, The Royal Oak Hotel was once the manor house for the Earl of Powys, before being used as a coaching inn for travellers en route to the Welsh coast. A range of bedrooms types offer high levels of comfort and are complemented by very good quality bathrooms, as well as Sky TV. A bustling coffee shop is located on the ground floor, with a number of interconnecting lounges ensuring there is always a quiet corner. The smart dining room offers a range of dishes to suit most tastes both at lunch and dinner. A small secure car park is a welcome additional feature.

Rooms: 25 (3 family) ⏰ **Facilities:** WiFi Xmas New Year **Conf:** Class 60 Board 30 Thtr 100 **Services:** Night porter **Parking:** 19 **Notes:** Civ Wed 100

WOLF'S CASTLE — Map 8 SM92
Pembrokeshire

Wolfscastle Country Hotel

★★★ 81% ◉◉ COUNTRY HOUSE HOTEL

WELSH RAREBITS Hotels of Distinction

SA62 5LZ - **tel:** 01437 741225
email: enquiries@wolfscastle.com **web:** www.wolfscastle.com
dir: On A40 in village at top of hill. 6m N of Haverfordwest

This large stone house, a former vicarage, dates back to the mid-19th century and is now a friendly, privately-owned and personally-run hotel. It provides stylish, modern, well-maintained and well-equipped bedrooms. There is a pleasant bar and an attractive restaurant, which has a well deserved reputation for its food.

Rooms: 20 (2 family) ⏰ **S** £75–£105; **D** £110–£145 (incl. bkfst)* **Facilities:** STV FTV WiFi New Year **Conf:** Class 100 Board 40 Thtr 150 Del from £140 **Parking:** 60 **Notes:** Closed 24-26 Dec Civ Wed 100

WREXHAM — Map 15 SJ35
Wrexham

Premier Inn Wrexham North (A483)

BUDGET HOTEL

Premier Inn

Chester Road, Gresford, LL12 8PW - **tel:** 0871 527 9190 (Calls cost 13p per minute plus your phone company's access charge) **web:** www.premierinn.com
dir: On B5445, just off A483 (dual carriageway) near Gresford

High quality, budget accommodation ideal for both families and business travellers. Spacious, en suite bedrooms feature free WiFi and tea and coffee making facilities, and in most hotels, Freeview TV is also available. The adjacent family restaurant features a wide and varied menu.

Rooms: 60

Premier Inn Wrexham Town Centre

BUDGET HOTEL

Premier Inn

Jacques Way, LL11 2BY - **tel:** 0871 527 9458 (Calls cost 13p per minute plus your phone company's access charge) **web:** www.premierinn.com
dir: A55 junct 38. At Wrexham Road Interchange, A483. At rdbt 2nd exit signed Wrexham. Exit at junct 5, at next rdbt take A541. Pass football ground, right at lights

Rooms: 83

Opposite: Harlech Castle, with Snowdonia in the background

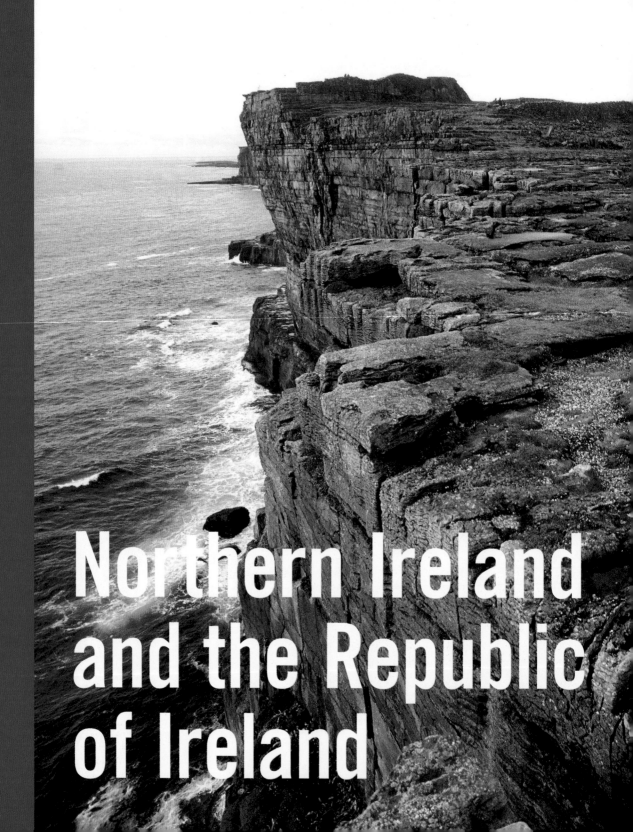

Northern Ireland and the Republic of Ireland

Additional information for Northern Ireland and the Republic of Ireland

Licensing Regulations

Northern Ireland: Public houses open Mon-Sat 11.30-23.00. Sun 12.30-22.00. Hotels can serve residents without restriction. Non-residents can be served 12.30-22.00 on Christmas Day. Children under 18 are not allowed in the bar area and may neither buy nor consume liquor in hotels.

Republic of Ireland: General licensing hours are Mon-Thu 10.30-23.30, Fri & Sat 10.30-00.30, Sun 12.30-23.00 (or 00.30 if the following day is a Bank Holiday). There is no service (except for hotel residents) on Christmas Day or Good Friday.

The Fire and Rescue Services (NI) Order 2006

This covers establishments accommodating more than six people, which must have a certificate from the Northern Ireland Fire Authority. Places accommodating fewer than six people need adequate exits. AA inspectors check emergency notices, fire fighting equipment and fire exits here.

The Republic of Ireland safety regulations are a matter for local authority regulations. For your own and others' safety, read the emergency notices and be sure you understand them.

Telephone numbers

Area codes for numbers in the Republic of Ireland apply only within the Republic. If dialling from outside check the telephone directory (from the UK the international dialling code is 00 353). Area codes for numbers in Britain and Northern Ireland cannot be used directly from the Republic.

For the latest information on the Republic of Ireland visit the AA Ireland's website: www.TheAA.ie

---

NORTHERN IRELAND

AGHADOWEY
County Londonderry

Map 1 C6

Brown Trout Golf & Country Inn

★★★ 82% HOTEL

IRISH COUNTRY HOTELS

209 Agivey Road, BT51 4AD - tel: 028 7086 8209
email: jane@browntroutinn.com **web:** www.browntroutinn.com
dir: At junct of A54 & B66 junct on road to Coleraine

Set alongside the Agivey River and featuring its own 9-hole golf course, this welcoming inn offers a choice of spacious accommodation. Comfortably furnished bedrooms are situated around a courtyard area, while the cottage suites also have lounge areas. Home-cooked meals are served in the restaurant and lighter fare is available in the charming lounge bar which has entertainment at weekends.

Rooms: 15 (11 family) (15 GF) ⚑ **Facilities:** STV FTV WiFi ⬇ ⚒ 9 Putting green Gym Game fishing ♫ Xmas New Year **Conf:** Class 24 Board 28 Thtr 40 **Parking:** 80 **Notes:** Civ Wed 60

Silver Stars

The AA Silver Star rating denotes a Hotel that we highly recommend. They have a superior level of quality within their star rating, high standards of hospitality, service and cleanliness.

BALLYMENA
County Antrim

Map 1 D5

HIGHLY RECOMMENDED

Galgorm Resort & Spa

★★★★ 89% ⬤⬤⬤ HOTEL

136 Fenaghy Road, Galgorm, BT42 1EA - tel: 028 2588 1001
email: reservations@galgorm.com **web:** www.galgorm.com
dir: 1m from Ballymena on A42, between Galgorm & Cullybackey

Standing in 163 acres of private woodland and sweeping lawns beside the River Maine, this 19th-century mansion offers spacious, comfortable bedrooms. Public areas include a welcoming cocktail bar and elegant restaurant, as well as Gillies, a lively and atmospheric locals' bar. Also on the estate is an equestrian centre and a conference hall.

Rooms: 122 (17 family) (8 GF) ⚑ **D** £140–£755 (incl. bkfst) * **Facilities:** Spa FTV WiFi ⬇ ⓢ supervised ⚒ ⚒ 9 ⚒ Fishing Gym Clay pigeon shooting Archery Horseriding (all can be arranged off site) ♫ Xmas New Year **Conf:** Class 170 Board 30 Thtr 500 Del from £150 **Services:** Lift Night porter **Parking:** 400 **Notes:** LB Civ Wed 300

NORTHERN IRELAND

BELFAST
Belfast

Map 1 D5

INSPECTOR'S CHOICE

The Merchant Hotel
★★★★★ @@ HOTEL

16 Skipper Street, BT1 2DZ - tel: 028 9023 4888
email: info@themerchanthotel.com **web:** www.themerchanthotel.com
dir: *In city centre, 1st left after Albert Clock into Waring St. 1st left into Skipper St*

The Merchant Hotel is a magnificent hotel situated in the historic Cathedral Quarter of the city centre. This Grade I listed building has been lovingly and sensitively restored to reveal its original architectural grandeur and interior opulence. All the bedrooms, including five suites, have air-conditioning, high-speed internet access and luxury bathrooms. There are several eating options including the grand and beautifully decorated Great Room Restaurant.

Rooms: 62 (17 family) ⚓ **S** £150–£589; **D** £180–£599 (incl. bkfst) *
Facilities: Spa FTV WiFi ⅊ Gym Steam room ⅌ Xmas New Year **Conf:** Class 100 Board 60 Thtr 200 Del from £215 **Services:** Lift Night porter Air con **Parking:** 35
Notes: Civ Wed 130

Radisson Blu Hotel Belfast
★★★★ 80% HOTEL

3 Cromac Place, BT7 2JB - tel: 028 9043 4065
email: info.belfast@radissonblu.com **web:** www.radissonblu.co.uk/hotel-belfast
dir: *On corner of Ormeau Rd & Cromac St*

This modern hotel is in the centre of the regenerated urban area close to the city centre. The bedrooms are stylishly presented, well equipped and all have air conditioning; there is a choice of business suites. Public areas include a spacious lounge bar and the Filini Restaurant, which serves good Italian and Sardinian cuisine. Ample secure parking and free WiFi (throughout the hotel) are available.

Rooms: 120 (11 family) **S** £90–£450; **D** £100–£500* **Facilities:** FTV WiFi ⅊ Xmas New Year **Conf:** Class 70 Board 50 Thtr 150 Del from £190 **Services:** Lift Night porter Air con **Parking:** 120 **Notes:** Civ Wed 90

Malmaison Belfast
★★★★ 79% HOTEL

34-38 Victoria Street, BT1 3GH - tel: 0844 693 0650 (Calls cost 5p per minute plus your phone company's access charge)
email: belfast@malmaison.com **web:** www.malmaison.com
dir: *M1 along Westlink to Grosvenor Rd. Follow city centre signs. Pass City Hall on right, left into Victoria St. Hotel on right*

Situated in a former seed warehouse, this luxurious, contemporary hotel is ideally located for the city centre. Comfortable bedrooms boast a host of modern facilities, while the deeply comfortable, stylish public areas include a popular bar lounge. The 'Home Grown and Local' menu in the brasserie showcases local seasonal ingredients. The warm hospitality is notable.

Rooms: 64 (8 family) **Facilities:** STV WiFi Gym **Conf:** Board 22 **Services:** Lift Night porter **Notes:** Civ Wed

Malone Lodge Hotel
★★★★ 76% HOTEL

60 Eglantine Avenue, BT9 6DY - tel: 028 9038 8000
email: info@malonelodgehotel.com **web:** www.malonelodgehotelbelfast.com
dir: *At hospital rdbt exit towards Boucher Rd, left at 1st rdbt, right at lights at top, then 1st left. Car park at rear of hotel*

Situated in the leafy suburbs of the university area of south Belfast, this stylish hotel forms the centrepiece of an attractive row of Victorian terraced properties. The hotel has undergone a massive transformation in recent years including a rolling refurbishment of the bedrooms. The Knife and Fork restaurant offers relaxed and informal dining.

Rooms: 54 (7 family) **Facilities:** FTV WiFi ⅌ **Conf:** Class 126 Board 48 Thtr 250 **Services:** Lift Night porter **Parking:** 70 **Notes:** Civ Wed 120

Premier Inn Belfast City Cathedral Quarter
BUDGET HOTEL

2-6 Waring Street, BT1 1XY - tel: 0871 527 8070 (Calls cost 13p per minute plus your phone company's access charge) **web:** www.premierinn.com
dir: *M1 or M2 to Westlink to Grosvenor Rd rdbt, signed city centre. Into Grosvenor Rd. At 2nd lights left, take right lane, right (pass City Hall on right). At end of Chichester St left into Victoria St. Through next 2 lights, left into Waring St. Hotel 300yds on right*

High quality, budget accommodation ideal for both families and business travellers. Spacious, en suite bedrooms feature free WiFi and tea and coffee making facilities, and in most hotels, Freeview TV is also available. The adjacent family restaurant features a wide and varied menu.

Rooms: 171

Premier Inn Belfast City Centre Alfred St
BUDGET HOTEL

Alfred Street, BT2 8ED - tel: 0871 527 8068 (Calls cost 13p per minute plus your phone company's access charge) **web:** www.premierinn.com
dir: *M1 or M2 to Westlink. Follow city centre signs. 1st right, 2nd left into Hope St. At 2nd lights left into Bedford St. At next lights right into Ormeau Ave. Left into Alfred St. Underground car park (chargeable) on left*

Rooms: 148

Premier Inn Belfast Titanic Quarter

BUDGET HOTEL

2A Queens Road, BT3 9FB - tel: 0871 527 9210 (Calls cost 13p per minute plus your phone company's access charge) **web:** www.premierinn.com
dir: *From all major routes follow Odyssey Arena signs. From M3 junct 1 exit onto Queens Island, to lights. Hotel on left*

Rooms: 122

BUSHMILLS
County Antrim

Map 1 C6

HIGHLY RECOMMENDED

Bushmills Inn Hotel

★★★★ 82% HOTEL

9 Dunluce Road, BT57 8QG - tel: 028 2073 3000
email: mail@bushmillsinn.com **web:** www.bushmillsinn.com
dir: *On A2 in village centre*

Enjoying a prominent position in the heart of the village, this hotel offers a range of bedroom styles including spacious, creatively designed rooms that have the latest technology and a small dressing room. The charming public areas feature inglenook turf-burning fires, cosy snugs along with a very popular traditional bar. The restaurant has a well-deserved reputation for its food. The hotel is very popular with golfers; it is close to the Giants Causeway, Bushmills Distillery and the stunning scenery of the Antrim coast.

Rooms: 41 (2 family) (20 GF) ⚡ **S** £110–£400; **D** £120–£420 **Facilities:** WiFi ⌲ ♫ New Year **Conf:** Class 30 Board 18 Thtr 40 Del from £158 **Services:** Lift Night porter **Parking:** 70

CARRICKFERGUS
County Antrim

Map 1 D5

Premier Inn Carrickfergus

BUDGET HOTEL

The Harbour, Alexandra Pier, BT38 8BE - tel: 0871 527 8214 (Calls cost 13p per minute plus your phone company's access charge) **web:** www.premierinn.com
dir: *Exit at M2 junct 2, take M5 N onto A2 towards Carrickfergus. Follow Castle/Maritime Area signs. Right at rdbt adjacent to castle. Hotel straight ahead, adjacent to harbour*

High quality, budget accommodation ideal for both families and business travellers. Spacious, en suite bedrooms feature free WiFi and tea and coffee making facilities, and in most hotels, Freeview TV is also available. The adjacent family restaurant features a wide and varied menu.

Rooms: 49

COLERAINE
County Londonderry

Map 1 C6

Premier Inn Coleraine

BUDGET HOTEL

3 Riverside Park North, Castleroe Road, BT51 3GE - tel: 0871 527 8262 (Calls cost 13p per minute plus your phone company's access charge) **web:** www.premierinn.com
dir: *A26 towards Coleraine. At rdbt left on A29 (ring road) signed Cookstown/Garragh. At rdbt A54 (Castleroe Rd). Hotel on right*

High quality, budget accommodation ideal for both families and business travellers. Spacious, en suite bedrooms feature free WiFi and tea and coffee making facilities, and in most hotels, Freeview TV is also available. The adjacent family restaurant features a wide and varied menu.

Rooms: 49

CRAWFORDSBURN
County Down

Map 1 D5

AA HOTEL OF THE YEAR FOR NORTHERN IRELAND 2017–18

HIGHLY RECOMMENDED

The Old Inn

★★★★ 81% HOTEL

15 Main Street, BT19 1JH - tel: 028 9185 3255
email: info@theoldinn.com **web:** www.theoldinn.com
dir: *A2 from Belfast, past Belfast City Airport & Transport Museum. 2m, left at lights onto B20. 1.2m to hotel*

This delightful hotel enjoys a peaceful rural setting just a short drive from Belfast. The property dates from 1614, and many of the day rooms exude charm and character. Individually styled, comfortable bedrooms, some with feature beds, offer modern facilities. The popular bar and intimate restaurant both offer creative menus, and staff throughout are keen to please. The hotel has good business facilities that make this the ideal place for a meeting or conference.

Rooms: 31 (1 annexe) (7 family) (4 GF) ⚡ **Facilities:** STV FTV WiFi ⌲ In-room spa/massage treatments ♫ Xmas New Year **Conf:** Class 120 Board 40 Thtr 150 **Services:** Lift Night porter **Parking:** 84 **Notes:** LB RS 25 Dec no food or drink Civ Wed 100

DUNGANNON
County Tyrone

Map 1 C5

The Cohannon Inn

★★ 84% HOTEL

212 Ballynakilly Road, BT71 6HJ - tel: 028 8772 4488
email: info@cohannon.com **web:** www.cohannon.com
dir: *400yds from M1 junct 14*

Handy for the M1 and the nearby towns of Dungannon and Portadown, this hotel offers well-maintained bedrooms, located behind the inn complex in a smart purpose-built wing. Public areas are smartly furnished and wide-ranging menus are served throughout the day.

Rooms: 42 (3 family) (21 GF) **S** £54.95–£59.95; **D** £59.95–£69.95* **Facilities:** FTV WiFi Hair & beauty salon New Year **Conf:** Class 100 Board 40 Thtr 160 Del from £75 **Services:** Night porter **Parking:** 160 **Notes:** LB RS 25 Dec

Find out more
about the AA's Hotel rating scheme on pages 12–13

ENNISKILLEN
County Fermanagh

Map 1 C5

Lough Erne Resort
★★★★★ 85% ◉◉◉ HOTEL

Belleek Road, BT93 7ED - tel: 028 6632 3230
email: info@lougherneresort.com **web:** www.lougherneresort.com
dir: A46 from Enniskillen towards Donegal, hotel in 3m

This delightful resort enjoys a peaceful and idyllic setting and boasts championship golf courses, a wonderful Thai spa and a host of outdoor and leisure pursuits. Bedrooms and en suites are spacious, particularly well appointed and include a number of luxury suites. Day rooms are spacious, luxurious and include lounges, bars and restaurants with splendid views. Service is friendly and extremely attentive.

Rooms: 120 (61 annexe) **D** £140–£630 (incl. bkfst) * **Facilities:** Spa STV WiFi ⊗ ♨ 18 Fishing Gym ♬ Xmas New Year **Conf:** Class 200 Board 80 Thtr 400 **Services:** Lift Night porter **Parking:** 240 **Notes:** LB Civ Wed 300

HIGHLY RECOMMENDED

Manor House Country Hotel
★★★★ 83% ◉ COUNTRY HOUSE HOTEL

Killadeas, BT94 1NY - tel: 028 6862 2200
email: info@manorhousecountryhotel.com **web:** www.manorhousecountryhotel.com
dir: On B82, 7m N of Enniskillen

This charming country house hotel enjoys a stunning location on the banks of Lower Lough Erne and is a short drive from the busy town of Enniskillen. Bedrooms are equipped to a very high standard with front-facing rooms having the fabulous lough views. There is a choice of restaurants, and afternoon tea is served in the comfortable lounge with its open fire. The hotel has first-class business, conference and leisure facilities including its own air-conditioned cruiser for tours and corporate events.

Manor House Country Hotel

Rooms: 78 (12 family) (12 GF) ♟ **Facilities:** FTV WiFi ♫ ⊗ Gym Sauna Steam room ♬ Xmas New Year **Conf:** Class 120 Board 100 Thtr 400 **Services:** Lift Night porter **Parking:** 300 **Notes:** Civ Wed 300

Killyhevlin Lakeside Hotel & Lodges
★★★★ 82% HOTEL

IRISH COUNTRY HOTELS

BT74 6RW - tel: 028 6632 3481
email: info@killyhevlin.com **web:** www.killyhevlin.com
dir: 2m S of Enniskillen, off A4

This modern, stylish hotel is situated on the shores of Lough Erne, south of the town. The well-equipped bedrooms are particularly spacious and enjoy fine views of the gardens and lake. The restaurant, informal bar and comfortable lounges all share the views. Staff are friendly and helpful. There are extensive leisure facilities and a spa.

Rooms: 71 (42 family) (22 GF) ♟ **S** £102.50–£112.50; **D** £145–£165 (incl. bkfst) * **Facilities:** Spa FTV WiFi ♫ ⊗ Fishing Gym Aerobic studio Steam room Sauna Hydrotherapy area Relaxation room ♬ New Year **Conf:** Class 160 Board 100 Thtr 500 Del from £115 **Services:** Lift Night porter **Parking:** 500 **Notes:** LB Closed 25 Dec RS 24 & 26 Dec Civ Wed 250

LIMAVADY
County Londonderry

Map 1 C6

Roe Park Resort
★★★★ 79% HOTEL

BT49 9LB - tel: 028 7772 2222
email: reservations@roeparkresort.com **web:** www.roeparkresort.com
dir: On A2 (Londonderry-Limavady road), 1m from Limavady

This impressive, popular hotel is part of a modern golf resort. The spacious, contemporary bedrooms are well equipped and many have excellent views of the fairways and surrounding estate. The Greens Restaurant provides a refreshing dining experience and the Coach House brasserie offers a lighter menu. The leisure options are extensive.

Rooms: 118 (15 family) (37 GF) (5 smoking) ♟ **Facilities:** Spa FTV WiFi HL ⊗ supervised ♨ 18 Putting green Fishing Gym Driving range Indoor golf academy ♬ Xmas New Year **Conf:** Class 190 Board 140 Thtr 450 **Services:** Lift Night porter **Parking:** 350 **Notes:** Civ Wed 300

LISBURN — County Antrim — Map 1 D5

Premier Inn Lisburn

BUDGET HOTEL

136-144 Hillsborough Road, BT27 5QY - tel: 0871 527 8606 (Calls cost 13p per minute plus your phone company's access charge) **web:** www.premierinn.com
dir: *M1 onto A1 (Sprucefield Rd). Left into Hillsborough Rd. Approx 1.5m, hotel on left*

High quality, budget accommodation ideal for both families and business travellers. Spacious, en suite bedrooms feature free WiFi and tea and coffee making facilities, and in most hotels, Freeview TV is also available. The adjacent family restaurant features a wide and varied menu.

Rooms: 90

LONDONDERRY — County Londonderry — Map 1 C5

City Hotel

★★★★ 76% HOTEL

Queens Quay, BT48 7AS - tel: 028 7136 5800
email: reservations@cityhotelderry.com **web:** www.cityhotelderry.com
dir: *Follow city centre signs. Hotel on waterfront*

In a central position overlooking the River Foyle, this stylish, contemporary hotel will appeal to business and leisure guests alike. All bedrooms have excellent facilities including internet access; the executive rooms make particularly good working environments. Meeting and function facilities are extensive and there are good leisure options.

Rooms: 158 (16 family) **Facilities:** FTV WiFi ♨ supervised Gym Steam room ♫ New Year **Conf:** Class 150 Board 80 Thtr 350 **Services:** Lift Night porter Air con **Parking:** 48 **Notes:** LB Civ Wed 350

Premier Inn Derry / Londonderry

BUDGET HOTEL

Crescent Link, BT47 6SA - tel: 0871 527 9414 (Calls cost 13p per minute plus your phone company's access charge) **web:** www.premierinn.com
dir: *Phone for detailed directions*

High quality, budget accommodation ideal for both families and business travellers. Spacious, en suite bedrooms feature free WiFi and tea and coffee making facilities, and in most hotels, Freeview TV is also available. The adjacent family restaurant features a wide and varied menu.

Rooms: 60

REPUBLIC OF IRELAND

ARDMORE — County Waterford — Map 1 C2

Cliff House Hotel

★★★★ 90% ◉◉◉◉ HOTEL

tel: 024 87800
email: info@cliffhousehotel.ie **web:** www.cliffhousehotel.ie
dir: *From Dungarvan: N25, signed Cork. Left onto R673. From Youghal: N25 signed Waterford. Right onto R673 signed Ardmore. In Ardmore turn right at Quinn's food store, follow hotel signs*

This unique property, virtually sculpted into the cliff-face overlooking Ardmore Bay, is just a few minutes' walk from the village. Most of the individually designed bedroom suites and the public rooms enjoy the spectacular sea views, as do the stunning spa and leisure facilities. Rooms are very comfortable and artistically designed, in a palette of colours reflecting the natural setting. Dinner in the award-winning House Restaurant is a particular highlight – the menus feature imaginatively cooked, seasonal and local produce prepared with care and great flair. More casual fare is served in the bar, or on the terrace when weather permits. Some event spaces and valet parking are available.

Rooms: 39 (8 family) (7 GF) **D €195–€550** (incl. bkfst)* **Facilities:** Spa STV FTV WiFi ♨ ⑤ Fishing Gym Sauna Steam room Relaxation room Outdoor pursuits Outdoor seaweed baths New Year Child facilities **Conf:** Class 30 Board 20 Thtr 50 Del from €195 **Services:** Lift Night porter Air con **Parking:** 52 **Notes:** LB Closed 24-16 Dec Civ Wed 60

BALLINA — County Mayo — Map 1 B4

Mount Falcon Estate

★★★★ 83% ◉◉ HOTEL

tel: 096 74472
email: info@mountfalcon.com **web:** www.mountfalcon.com
dir: *On N26, 6m from Foxford & 3m from Ballina. Hotel on left*

Dating from 1876, this house has been lovingly restored to its former glory, and has a bedroom extension that is totally in keeping with the original design. Relaxing lounges look out on the 100-acre estate, which has excellent salmon fishing on The Moy plus well-stocked trout lakes. Dinner is served in the original kitchen with choices from a varied and interesting menu; for lunch there is also the Boathole Bar. An air-conditioned gym is available.

Rooms: 32 (3 family) **S €120–€200; D €140–€280** (incl. bkfst) **Facilities:** Spa STV WiFi ♨ ⑤ supervised Fishing Gym Sauna Steam room Driving range New Year **Conf:** Class 120 Board 80 Thtr 200 **Services:** Lift Night porter **Parking:** 260 **Notes:** LB Closed 24-27 Dec Civ Wed 200

BALLINA *continued*

Belleek Castle

★★★ 72% ◉◉ HOTEL

Belleek - **tel:** 096 22400
email: info@belleekcastle.com **web:** www.belleekcastle.com
dir: *N of Ballina*

This lovely manor house, formerly the ancestral home of the Earl of Arran, is set in wonderful parkland at the head of Belleek Wood on the River Moy estuary. The cosy public lounges are welcoming, and are complemented by a series of banqueting suites that are decorated in a nautical theme. Bedroom accommodation varies in style; all rooms are comfortably appointed. Dinner is the highlight of any visit, offered from a choice of Market or Gourmet set menus. The food is all locally sourced, and the chef has a keen eye for seasonality. The hotel is a popular wedding venue. There is also a museum specialising in armoury and memorabilia from the Spanish Armada.

Rooms: 10 (2 family) ☎ **S** €75–€185; **D** €120–€270 (incl. bkfst)* **Facilities:** STV FTV WiFi ↦ Xmas **Conf:** Class 60 Board 30 Thtr 100 **Parking:** 200 **Notes:** Closed Jan-mid Feb Civ Wed 200

BALLINGEARY	Map 1 B2
County Cork	

Gougane Barra Hotel

★★★ 78% ◉ HOTEL

Gougane Barra - **tel:** 026 47069
email: info@gouganebarrahotel.com **web:** www.gouganebarrahotel.com
dir: *On L4643. Exit R584 between N22 at Macroom & N71 at Bantry*

This charming hotel, run by the Lucey family for over five generations, is in an idyllic location on the shores of Gougane Barra Lake, overlooking the tiny Oratory of St Finbarr, a popular venue for small weddings. The bedrooms vary in size, but they are all well decorated and very comfortable. Chef Katie Lucey prepares menus based on the best local and seasonal ingredients, some from artisan producers. The ground floor includes cosy lounge areas and a traditional bar, with a marquee theatre in the summer months for an innovative experience known as Theatre by the Lake.

Rooms: 26 (1 family) (8 GF) ☎ **S** €72–€90; **D** €115–€140 (incl. bkfst) **Facilities:** WiFi Fishing Boating Cycling Hiking **Conf:** Class 12 Board 12 Thtr 22 Del from €119 **Parking:** 26 **Notes:** LB Closed 3 Nov-24 Mar Civ Wed 60

BALLYFIN	Map 1 C3
County Laois	

Ballyfin Demesne

★★★★★ ◉◉ HOTEL

tel: 057 8755866
email: info@ballyfin.com **web:** www.ballyfin.com
dir: *Phone for detailed directions*

Nestled in over 600 acres, this lavish Regency mansion has been painstakingly restored, yet all modern conveniences have been incorporated. With only 20 bedrooms, guests at Ballyfin have the feeling of visiting a friend's home; relaxation comes naturally when ensconced in any of the sumptuously decorated salons, library or the stunning Turner-designed conservatory. Hospitality is key here; a team of butlers is at hand to ensure guests are well cared for at all times. Cuisine is an important element of the Ballyfin experience, with daily-created menus on offer, together with suggested wine pairings – many featuring the Bordeaux estates of the Irish 'Wine Geese' who fled following the Battle of Kinsale. Spa treatments are available, as are a number of country pursuits such as falconry, archery, fishing and clay shooting.

Rooms: 20 (2 GF) ☎ **Facilities:** Spa STV WiFi ↦ ⊗ ⌇ Fishing ⌇ Gym Clay pigeon Air rifle shooting Archery Falconry Horse riding Pony & carriage tour Boating on the lake Xmas New Year **Services:** Lift Night porter **Notes:** Closed Jan No children 9yrs Civ Wed 130

BALLYLICKEY	Map 1 B2
County Cork	

INSPECTOR'S CHOICE

Seaview House Hotel

★★★ ◉◉ HOTEL

tel: 027 50073
email: info@seaviewhousehotel.com **web:** www.seaviewhousehotel.com
dir: *5km from Bantry, 11km from Glengarriff on N71*

Colourful gardens and glimpses of Bantry Bay through the mature trees frame this delightful country house. Owner Kathleen O'Sullivan's team of staff are exceptionally pleasant, and there is a relaxed atmosphere in the cosy lounges. Guest comfort and good cuisine are top priorities. Bedrooms are spacious and individually styled, and some on the ground floor are appointed to suit less able guests.

Rooms: 25 (3 family) (5 GF) ❀ **Facilities:** STV FTV WiFi **Conf:** Class 30 Board 25 Thtr 25 **Parking:** 32 **Notes:** LB Closed mid Nov-mid Mar Civ Wed 75

BALLYLIFFIN	Map 1 C6
County Donegal	

Ballyliffin Lodge & Spa

★★★★ 79% ◉ HOTEL

Shore Road - tel: 074 9378200 & 9378146
email: info@ballyliffinlodge.com **web:** www.ballyliffinlodge.com
dir: *From Derry take A2 towards Moville, exit for Carndonagh at Quigleys Point. Ballyliffin 10km*

Located in the heart of the village, this property offers a range of very comfortable bedrooms and suites, many of which enjoy panoramic views of Malin Head and the famed Ballyliffin Golf Club. Dinner is served in the open-plan Jacks bar and restaurant, and less formal meals are served in the bar throughout the day. Guests are welcome to use the leisure facilities in the adjoining Crystal Rock Spa, where there is also a hairdressing salon. The hotel also caters well for weddings and family events.

Rooms: 40 (28 family) ❀ **S** €80–€120; **D** €110–€190 (incl. bkfst) **Facilities:** Spa STV WiFi ⬇ ⊛ supervised Gym Hair salon Beauty salon Children's play areas ♫ New Year Child facilities **Conf:** Class 250 Board 125 Thtr 400 Del from €90 **Services:** Lift Night porter **Parking:** 80 **Notes:** LB Closed 25 Dec Civ Wed 150

The Strand Hotel

[U]

Inishowen - tel: 074 9376107 & 9376188
email: strandhotel@ballyliffin.com **web:** www.ballyliffinstrandhotel.com
dir: *Phone for detailed directions*

Currently the rating for this establishment is not confirmed. This may be due to a change of ownership or because it has only recently joined the AA rating scheme.

Rooms: 36 (7 annexe) (3 family) ❀ **S** €65–€80; **D** €90–€120 (incl. bkfst)*
Facilities: STV FTV WiFi ♫ **Conf:** Class 150 Board 20 Thtr 300 **Services:** Lift Night porter **Notes:** LB No children 12yrs Civ Wed 300

BALLYVAUGHAN	Map 1 B3
County Clare	

INSPECTOR'S CHOICE

Gregans Castle

★★★ ◉◉◉ COUNTRY HOUSE HOTEL

tel: 065 7077005
email: stay@gregans.ie **web:** www.gregans.ie
dir: *3.5m S of Ballyvaughan on N67*

This hotel is a hidden gem in The Burren area, and the delightful restaurant and bedrooms enjoy splendid views towards Galway Bay. The Haden family, together with their welcoming staff, offer a high level of personal service. Bedrooms are individually decorated; superior rooms and suites are particularly comfortable; some are on the ground floor and have patio gardens. There are welcoming fires in the comfortable drawing room and the cosy cocktail bar where afternoon tea is served. Dinner is a highlight of any visit; the chef shows a real passion for food which is evident in his cooking of top quality local and organic produce. The area is rich in archaeological, geological and botanical interest, and cycling and walking tours can be organised. There is a beautiful garden to relax in.

Rooms: 21 (3 family) (7 GF) ❀ **Facilities:** WiFi ⬇ ⛏ **Conf:** Class 25 Board 14 Thtr 25 **Parking:** 25 **Notes:** Closed Jan-12 Feb & 30 Nov-Dec Civ Wed 65

BARNA (BEARNA)
County Galway

Map 1 B3

The Twelve
★★★★ 80% ◉◉ HOTEL

Barna Village - **tel:** 091 597000
email: enquire@thetwelvehotel.ie **web:** www.thetwelvehotel.ie
dir: *Take R336 from Galway. Hotel at crossroads in Barna*

Located just ten minutes west of Galway city, this hotel looks as if it has been on the site for decades. However, once inside the decor is striking and contemporary. The bedrooms come in a number of different sizes, but all are furnished with taste and with guest comfort in mind. The Pins is a vibrant and popular bar and bistro where food is served throughout the day. West Restaurant opens during the evening, and features fine dining from a well-compiled menu of local and seasonal produce. Le Petit Spa offers treatments based on seaweed products.

Rooms: 47 (12 family) ♠ **D** €100–€170 (incl. bkfst) **Facilities:** Spa STV FTV WiFi ♨ Beauty treatment room Children's cookery programme Art classes Wine classes ♪ Xmas New Year **Conf:** Class 70 Board 60 Thtr 80 Del from €135 **Services:** Lift Night porter Air con **Parking:** 140 **Notes:** LB RS 22-27 Dec Civ Wed 100

BELMULLET
County Mayo

Map 1 A5

The Talbot Hotel
★★★★ 79% ◉◉ HOTEL

Barrack Street - **tel:** 097 20484
email: info@thetalbothotel.ie **web:** www.thetalbothotel.ie
dir: *Take R313 to Belmullet, hotel on left*

Set in the heart of Belmullet town, this family-operated boutique property has evolved from its humble beginnings as a grocery store with a bar, to what is now a warm and welcoming hotel. The simple exterior belies the contemporary opulence that makes up the range of individually designed and decorated bedrooms and suites in this comfortable townhouse. The bar is a popular venue with the locals, and quality food is served throughout the day, with seafood a particular feature. The award-winning Barony Restaurant on the first floor is also eclectically decorated and enjoys a great reputation as a dining destination.

Rooms: 21 (4 family) (8 GF) ♠ **S** €65–€100; **D** €90–€180 (incl. bkfst)* **Facilities:** STV FTV WiFi ♨ ♪ New Year **Conf:** Class 100 Board 100 Thtr 180 Del from €160 **Services:** Lift Night porter Air con **Notes:** LB Civ Wed 150

BORRIS
County Carlow

Map 1 C3

Step House Hotel
★★★★ 78% ◉ HOTEL

Main Street - **tel:** 059 9773209
email: info@stephousehotel.ie **web:** www.stephousehotel.ie
dir: *Phone for detailed directions*

Originating from 1808, The Step House was once part of the Borris House Estate, ancestral home of the High Kings of Leinster. It has been a licensed premises in the Coady family for five generations, and became a hotel in the last decade following a dedicated refurbishment and expansion. Bedrooms are spacious, with many having wonderful views towards Mount Leinster. Dinner in the original kitchen, now the award-winning Cellar Restaurant, is a highlight of a visit, but lighter fare is also served daily in the 1808 bar and the gardens. The hotel has a strong reputation for hosting weddings and family gatherings, and alfresco dining in the well-tended grounds and gardens.

Rooms: 20 ♠ **Facilities:** WiFi **Services:** Night porter **Notes:** Civ Wed 180

CARRICKMACROSS
County Monaghan

Map 1 C4

Shirley Arms Hotel
★★★★ 78% ◉ HOTEL

Main Street - **tel:** 042 9673100
email: reception@shirleyarmshotel.ie **web:** www.shirleyarmshotel.ie
dir: *N2 to Derry, take Ardee Rd to Carrickmacross*

Set at the top of the town, this long established boutique hotel is an imposing 19th-century stone building with a contemporary interior. Bedrooms, in a purpose-built block to the rear, are spacious with clean, minimalist lines; there is also a comfortable suite in the original house overlooking the square. Food is an important element of the business here, with options available throughout the day in The Shirley Bar and award-winning evening dining in Whites Bistro. A night club is available for hire in the basement.

Rooms: 25 (2 family) ♠ **S** fr €85; **D** fr €110 (incl. bkfst)* **Facilities:** STV WiFi ♨ ♪ New Year **Conf:** Class 150 Board 200 Thtr 200 Del from €100 **Services:** Lift Night porter **Parking:** 80 **Notes:** LB Closed 24-26 Dec RS 14 Apr & Good Friday Civ Wed 150

CASHEL
County Galway

Map 1 A4

Cashel House Hotel
★★★ ◉◉ COUNTRY HOUSE HOTEL

tel: 095 31001
email: res@cashel-house-hotel.com **web:** www.cashel-house-hotel.com
dir: *S off N59, 1.5km W of Recess, well signed*

Cashel House is a mid-19th-century property, standing at the head of Cashel Bay in the heart of Connemara, set amidst secluded, award-winning gardens with woodland walks. Attentive service is delivered with the perfect balance of friendliness and professionalism from the McEvilly family and their staff. The comfortable lounges have turf fires and antique furnishings. The restaurant offers local produce such as the famous Connemara lamb, and fish from the nearby coast.

Rooms: 28 (4 family) (6 GF) ♠ **S** €75–€135; **D** €150–€210 (incl. bkfst) **Facilities:** STV FTV WiFi Garden school Cookery classes Guided walks Xmas New Year **Parking:** 40 **Notes:** LB Closed 2 Jan-10 Feb Civ Wed 120

CASTLETOWNBERE
County Cork

Map 1 A2

The Beara Coast Hotel

★★★★ 75% HOTEL

Cametringane - **tel:** 027 71446
email: reception@bearacoast.com **web:** www.bearacoast.com
dir: *Phone for detailed directions*

Located at the far end of the fishing port of Castletownbere, the cosy Beara Coast Hotel is welcoming and traditional. Long established, it is has recently been acquired by new owners who have put much time and their personal identity into its refurbishment. Bedrooms are warm and cosy in smart contemporary colourways. The character bar offers quality food throughout the day with more formal dining in The Coastal Restaurant in the evenings, where naturally, seafood is a feature. This is an unassuming property with a big heart and wonderfully warm and welcoming local staff.

Rooms: 16

CAVAN
County Cavan

Map 1 C4

Radisson Blu Farnham Estate Hotel

Radisson BLU
HOTELS & RESORTS

★★★★ 79% ⊛ HOTEL

Farnham Estate - **tel:** 049 4377700
email: info.farnham@radissonblu.com **web:** www.farnhamestate.com
dir: *From Dublin take N3 to Cavan. From Cavan take Killeshandra road for 3km*

Situated on a 1,300 acre estate, this 16th-century Great House combines old-world grandeur with modern glamour. Interiors are light, airy and contemporary with a relaxing atmosphere. The spacious bedrooms and suites are in the newer building. Interesting dining options are available in the Botanica Restaurant and Wine Goose Cellar Bar. There are extensive banqueting facilities and the health spa offers a range of treatments.

Rooms: 158 (50 GF) ✦ **Facilities:** Spa STV WiFi ↕ ⊛ ⌇ ⚓ 18 Putting green Fishing ⚓ Gym In/Outdoor infinity pool Mint thermal suite Relaxation rooms Walking trails ♫ Xmas New Year **Conf:** Class 150 Board 44 Thtr 380 **Services:** Lift Night porter **Parking:** 600 **Notes:** Civ Wed 150

Cavan Crystal Hotel

★★★★ 78% ⊛ HOTEL

Dublin Road - **tel:** 049 4360600
email: info@cavancrystalhotel.com **web:** www.cavancrystalhotel.com
dir: *On outskirts of Cavan town*

Contemporary design using native timber and handcrafted brickwork together with crystal chandeliers make this a particularly distinctive hotel. Expect excellent hospitality from all the highly trained staff. Located on the southern edge of the town, the hotel also features a well-equipped health facility, plus beauty clinic and extensive banquet and conference facilities. Opus One is the award-winning restaurant for dinner, with all-day dining available in The Atrium Bar.

Rooms: 85 (2 family) (9 GF) ✦ **S** €60–€160; **D** €100–€230 (incl. bkfst)*
Facilities: Spa WiFi ⊛ supervised Gym Beauty & massage treatments Salon Sauna Steam room Child facilities **Conf:** Class 300 Board 100 Thtr 500 **Services:** Lift Night porter **Parking:** 216 **Notes:** LB Closed 25-26 Dec Civ Wed 200

CLAREMORRIS
County Mayo

Map 1 B4

McWilliam Park Hotel

★★★★ 79% HOTEL

tel: 094 9378000
email: info@mcwilliamparkhotel.ie **web:** www.mcwilliampark.ie
dir: *Take Castlebar/Claremorris exit from N17, straight over rdbt. Hotel on right*

McWilliam Park Hotel is situated on the outskirts of Claremorris just off the N17 between Galway and Sligo. It is approximately 20 minutes from the Knock Marian Shrine and Ireland West Airport Knock. There are comfortable lounges together with extensive conference, banqueting, leisure and health facilities. The spacious bedrooms are well appointed, with good communication technology. Food is served all day in Kavanagh's bar, and dinner is available each night in J.G's Restaurant which also serves a popular Sunday lunch. Traditional music, social dancing and other entertainment events are held on a regular basis in the McWilliam Suite.

Rooms: 103 (19 family) (15 GF) ✦ **Facilities:** Spa STV FTV WiFi ↕ ⊛ Gym ♫ Xmas New Year **Conf:** Class 250 Board 80 Thtr 600 **Services:** Lift Night porter **Parking:** 320 **Notes:** LB Civ Wed 200

CLONMEL
County Tipperary

Map 1 C2

Hotel Minella

MANOR HOUSE HOTELS

★★★★ 80% ⊛ HOTEL

tel: 052 6122388
email: frontdesk@hotelminella.ie **web:** www.hotelminella.ie
dir: *S of river in town*

This family-run hotel is set in nine acres of well-tended gardens on the banks of the Suir River. The hotel originates from the 1860s, and the public areas include a cocktail bar and a range of lounges; some of the bedrooms are particularly spacious. The leisure centre in the grounds is noteworthy. Two-bedroom holiday homes are also available.

Rooms: 90 (8 family) (14 GF) (10 smoking) ✦ **Facilities:** FTV WiFi ↕ ⊛ ⌇ Fishing ⚓ Gym Beauty treatment room Sauna Steam room **Conf:** Class 300 Board 20 Thtr 500 **Services:** Lift Night porter **Parking:** 100 **Notes:** Closed 24-28 Dec

Silver Stars

The AA Silver Star rating denotes a Hotel that we highly recommend. They have a superior level of quality within their star rating, high standards of hospitality, service and cleanliness.

CONG	Map 1 B4
County Mayo	

INSPECTOR'S CHOICE

Ashford Castle

★★★★★ ◉◉ COUNTRY HOUSE HOTEL

THE
RED CARNATION
HOTEL COLLECTION

tel: 094 9546003
email: ashford@ashfordcastle.com **web:** www.ashfordcastle.com
dir: In Cross, left at church onto R345 signed Cong. Left at hotel sign,
through castle gates

Dating from 1228, this magnificent castle is set in over 350 acres of rolling
parklands, occupying a stunning position on the edge of Lough Corrib. Bedrooms
and suites vary in style, but all benefit from a pleasing combination of
character, charm and modern comforts. Dinner in the elegant George V Dining
Room is a treat, with creative cookery of seasonal ingredients. Less formal
dining is available in The Dungeon and other locations on the estate during peak
periods. The hotel offers an extensive range of both indoor and outdoor leisure
pursuits including falconry, golf, shooting, fishing, an equestrian centre and
lake cruising. A spectacular spa and fitness facility in a striking bronze
conservatory overlooks the lake.

Rooms: 83 (1 annexe) (5 family) (22 GF) ↾ **S** €265–€4000; **D** €285–€4000 (incl.
bkfst)* **Facilities:** Spa STV WiFi ③ ♨ 9 Putting green ⌣ Fishing Gym Archery
Clay pigeon Falconry Horse riding Bike hire Lake cruises Water sports ♫ Xmas
New Year **Conf:** Class 70 Board 32 Thtr 110 **Services:** Lift Night porter Air con
Parking: 250 **Notes:** Civ Wed 160

The Lodge at Ashford Castle

★★★★ 78% ◉ COUNTRY HOUSE HOTEL

THE
RED CARNATION
HOTEL COLLECTION

Ashford Estate - tel: 094 9545400
email: reception@thelodgeac.com **web:** www.thelodgeac.com
dir: From N84 take first turn for Cong, go through Ashford main gates, first left

This charming hotel, as the name suggests, is in the grounds of Ashford Castle;
itself a big 5-star sister hotel. The original part of the hotel is Victorian and was the
estate manager's house back in the day. The first floor restaurant (there is also a
brasserie on the ground floor) offers stunning views over Lough Corrib as do some
bedrooms; these are spacious, well equipped and suit leisure travellers. The team
are welcoming and friendly.

Rooms: 64 (54 annexe) (20 family) (20 GF) ↾ **D** €150–€575 (incl. bkfst)*
Facilities: STV FTV WiFi ♨ ♨ 9 ⌣ Fishing Gym Beauty treatment room Falconry
Archery Equestrian Boating Canoeing Kayaking ♫ New Year **Conf:** Class 80
Board 80 Thtr 200 **Services:** Lift Night porter **Parking:** 80 **Notes:** LB
Closed Mon-Wed (Nov-Feb) & 24-25 Dec Civ Wed 186

CORK	Map 1 B2
County Cork	

Maryborough Hotel & Spa

★★★★ 81% ◉◉ HOTEL

Maryborough Hill, Douglas - tel: 021 4365555
email: info@maryborough.com **web:** www.maryborough.com
dir: From Jack Lynch Tunnel 2nd exit signed Douglas. Right at 1st rdbt, follow Rochestown
signs to Fingerpost rdbt. Left, hotel on left in 0.5m

Dating from 1715, this house was renovated and extended to become a fine hotel
with beautifully landscaped grounds full of rare plant species. There are stylish
suites in the main house, while the bedrooms in the wing are comfortably furnished,
some with balconies/terraces. The bar and lounge are very popular for the range of
food served throughout the day; afternoon tea being a speciality. Bellini's
Restaurant offers a mix of classic and contemporary dishes to a high standard.
There are impressive spa, leisure and conference facilities, plus activities for
children.

Rooms: 93 (6 family) ↾ **S** €150–€500; **D** €160–€500 (incl. bkfst) **Facilities:** Spa STV
FTV WiFi ♨ ③ supervised Gym Sauna Steam room New Year **Conf:** Class 250
Board 60 Thtr 500 **Services:** Lift Night porter **Parking:** 300 **Notes:** LB Closed 24-26
Dec Civ Wed 250

The Kingsley

★★★★ 81% ◉ HOTEL

Victoria Cross - tel: 021 4800500
email: info@thekingsley.ie **web:** www.thekingsley.ie
dir: N40 at Sarsfield junction follow N71 signs. At Wilton roundabout take 2nd exit (city
centre). At lights turn left (signed Killarney). Hotel on right

Set on the banks of the River Lee, a leisurely half hour stroll from the city centre,
this is a wonderfully welcoming hotel that is sure to please. There are a number of
accommodation options, some with river views. The Springboard Restaurant is a
casual bistro-style operation at lunch and dinner, with breakfast being served in
Fairbanks. The hotel offers extensive banqueting facilities, a health club and a spa.
An ideal location for visitors to the university, 10 minutes or so away. Both surface
and underground parking is complimentary to resident guests.

Rooms: 131 (8 family) ↾ **S** €90–€450; **D** €105–€450 (incl. bkfst)* **Facilities:** Spa
FTV WiFi ♨ ③ Gym Outdoor hot tub ♫ New Year **Conf:** Class 100 Board 60 Thtr 220
Del from €185 **Services:** Lift Night porter Air con **Parking:** 200 **Notes:** Closed 25 Dec
RS 24 Dec closes at 4pm Civ Wed 220

The Montenotte Hotel

★★★★ 78% HOTEL

Middle Glanmire Road, Montenotte - tel: 021 4530050
email: info@themontenottehotel.com **web:** www.themontenottehotel.com
dir: Phone for detailed directions

Perched into the steep hillside with southern views over the city, this former
merchant prince's residence is now a plush contemporary hotel. Having changed
hands, it has benefited from a full renovation and redesign, resulting in bright open
areas including Panorama, an airy bistro and terrace that makes the most of the
views and the newly created, formal box garden. Other public areas are quite
eclectic, with interesting combinations in decor styles; they include an in-house
cinema, spa and leisure centre and event spaces. The spacious bedrooms are
decorated in warm relaxing tones and are well equipped.

Rooms: 108

Fota Island Resort

[U]

Fota Island - tel: 0214883700
web: www.fotaisland.ie
dir: *please telephone for directions*

Currently the rating for this establishment is not confirmed. This may be due to a change of ownership or because it has only recently joined the AA rating scheme.

Rooms: 131

| DELGANY | Map 1 D3 |
| County Wicklow | |

Glenview Hotel

★★★★ 79% ⬡⬡ HOTEL

Glen o' the Downs - tel: 01 2873399
email: sales@glenviewhotel.com **web:** www.glenviewhotel.com
dir: *From Dublin city centre follow signs for N11, past Bray on N11 S'bound, exit 9*

This hotel is set in lovely terraced gardens overlooking the Glen o' the Downs. The comfortable bedrooms are spacious, and many enjoy the great views over the valley. The impressive public areas include a conservatory bar, lounge and choice of dining options including the first-floor Woodlands Restaurant where dinner is served. The hotel has an excellent range of leisure and conference facilities. A championship golf course and horse riding can be found nearby.

Rooms: 70 (11 family) (16 GF) ⌇ **Facilities:** Spa STV WiFi ⬡ ⬡ Gym Aerobics studio Massage Beauty treatment rooms ♫ Xmas New Year **Conf:** Class 80 Board 80 Thtr 230 **Services:** Lift Night porter **Parking:** 200 **Notes:** Civ Wed 180

| DINGLE (AN DAINGEAN) | Map 1 A2 |
| County Kerry | |

Dingle Skellig Hotel & Peninsula Spa

★★★★ 80% ⬡ HOTEL

tel: 066 9150200
email: reservations@dingleskellig.com **web:** www.dingleskellig.com
dir: *N86 to Dingle, hotel on harbour*

This modern hotel, close to the town, overlooks Dingle Bay and has spectacular views from many of the comfortably furnished bedrooms and suites. Public areas offer a spacious bar, lounge and bright, airy restaurant. There are extensive health and leisure facilities, and family activities are organised in the Fungi Kids Club.

Rooms: 113 (10 family) (31 GF) ⌇ **Facilities:** Spa STV FTV WiFi ⬡ ⬡ supervised Gym ♫ New Year **Conf:** Class 120 Board 100 Thtr 250 **Services:** Lift Night porter **Parking:** 110 **Notes:** Closed Jan RS Nov-Dec open wknds only Civ Wed 250

| DONEGAL | Map 1 B5 |
| County Donegal | |

INSPECTOR'S CHOICE

Harvey's Point Hotel

★★★★ ⬡⬡ COUNTRY HOUSE HOTEL

Lough Eske - tel: 074 9722208
email: stay@harveyspoint.com **web:** www.harveyspoint.com
dir: *N56 from Donegal, then 1st right signed Lough Eske & Harvey's Point*

Situated by the shores of Lough Eske, a short drive from Donegal, this family-run, welcoming hotel is an oasis of relaxation; comfort along with attentive

guest care are the norm here. A wide range of particularly spacious suites and bedrooms is on offer, together with smaller Garden Suites in the courtyard annexe. The kitchen brigade maintains consistently high standards in The Lakeside Restaurant at dinner, with less formal dining in the atmospheric Harvey's Bar throughout the day. A very popular Sunday buffet lunch is served weekly, with dinner and cabaret entertainment on selected dates during the summer. Breakfast is also a feature of a stay here. Pet friendly accommodation is available.

Rooms: 64 (8 annexe) (17 family) (28 GF) ⌇ **S** €99–€285; **D** €198–€540 (incl. bkfst)* **Facilities:** STV FTV WiFi ⬡ Beauty treatment rooms Walking tours ♫ Xmas New Year **Conf:** Class 200 Board 50 Thtr 200 Del from €195 **Services:** Lift Night porter **Parking:** 300 **Notes:** Civ Wed 250

Mill Park Hotel

★★★★ 76% HOTEL

The Mullins - tel: 074 9722880
email: info@millparkhotel.com **web:** www.millparkhotel.com
dir: *Phone for detailed directions*

Mill Park Hotel is located within walking distance of the town. It is a family-owned and operated property, with a friendly and dedicated team who have a natural and warm approach. All of the comfortable rooms and suites have been renovated in stylish contemporary decor schemes. All-day dining is available in the Café Bar, a popular venue with the locals, with more formal evening dining in the first-floor Granary Restaurant that overlooks the main lobby. There is a spacious leisure centre available on a complimentary basis to resident guests, together with treatments and pampering in the Wellness Centre. The hotel has an excellent reputation for its banqueting and conference facilities.

Rooms: 110 (10 family) (43 GF) ⌇ **D** fr €118 (incl. bkfst) **Facilities:** STV FTV WiFi ⬡ ⬡ supervised Gym New Year **Conf:** Class 100 Board 30 Thtr 300 **Services:** Lift Night porter **Parking:** 200 **Notes:** Closed 24-26 Dec Civ Wed 350

| DROGHEDA | Map 1 D4 |
| County Louth | |

Scholars Townhouse Hotel

★★★ 78% ⬡⬡ HOTEL

King Street - tel: 041 983 5410
email: info@scholarshotel.com **web:** www.scholarshotel.com
dir: *From West St to St Laurence's Gate. Before gate turn left, to top of hill. Hotel on left*

Located less than a 10-minute stroll from the centre of Drogheda, this family-owned and operated boutique property was formerly a monastery. Built in the late 19th century, many of the architectural features of the period have been retained. This is also the case with the bedrooms; having previously been the monks' cells, space is rather compromised, but they are en suite, comfortable and have excellent beds and quality fabrics. Food is an important element at this warm and welcoming property. All-day dining is available in the Gastrolounge, where craft beers are a feature, and award-winning evening dining is offered in the restaurant. The breakfasts are also noteworthy. The hotel is situated on an elevated site amid well-tended grounds and offers secure parking.

Rooms: 16 (1 family) **Facilities:** FTV WiFi ⬡ New Year **Conf:** Class 55 Board 18 Thtr 55 **Services:** Lift Night porter **Parking:** 30 **Notes:** Closed 25-26 Dec Civ Wed 70

REPUBLIC OF IRELAND

The Merrion Hotel

★★★★★ ◉◉◉◉ HOTEL

21 Upper Merrion Street - tel: 01 6030600
email: info@merrionhotel.com **web:** www.merrionhotel.com
dir: *At top of Upper Merrion St on left, beyond Government buildings on right*

This terrace of gracious Georgian buildings, reputed to have been the birthplace of the Duke of Wellington, embraces the character of many changes of use over 200 years. Bedrooms and suites are spacious, some in the original house; others are in a modern wing overlooking the gardens. They all offer great comfort and a wide range of extra facilities. The lounges retain the charm and opulence of days gone by, while the Cellar bar area is a popular meeting point. Dining options include The Cellar Restaurant specialising in prime local ingredients and, for a very special occasion, the award-winning Restaurant Patrick Guilbaud is Dublin's finest. 'Art Tea' is an afternoon tea experience with a difference, where the delightful pastries are inspired by works from the hotel's vast art collection.

Rooms: 142 (21 GF) (20 smoking) ✆ **Facilities:** Spa STV FTV WiFi ⬧ ⬧ Gym Steam room Relaxation area Xmas New Year **Conf:** Class 25 Board 25 Thtr 60 **Services:** Lift Night porter Air con **Parking:** 60 **Notes:** LB Civ Wed 50

Red Stars

The AA Red Star rating denotes an Inspector's Choice hotel. They stand out as the very best and appear in highlighted panels throughout the guide.

The Shelbourne Dublin, a Renaissance Hotel

★★★★★ ◉◉ HOTEL

27 St Stephen's Green - tel: 01 6634500
email: rhi.dubbr.reservations@renaissancehotels.com **web:** www.theshelbourne.ie
dir: *M1 to city centre, along Parnell St to O'Connell St towards Trinity College, 3rd right into Kildare St, hotel on left*

This Dublin landmark exudes elegance and a real sense of history, having been established in 1824. The public areas are spacious and offer a range of dining and bar options. There is a selection of bedroom styles and suites available, many with commanding views over St Stephen's Green. No 27 is a popular bar and lounge for casual dining, while the Saddle Room is the main restaurant featuring a steak and seafood menu with a contemporary twist, and an enviable reputation for both its food and service. Afternoon tea is served in the elegant Lord Mayor's Lounge and is a real treat. An extensive leisure and fitness facility is also available, together with a range of meeting rooms, including The Constitution Room, where the Irish Constitution was drafted.

Rooms: 265 (7 smoking) ✆ **S** €259–€7500; **D** €259–€7500* **Facilities:** Spa STV FTV WiFi ⬧ ⬧ Gym Relaxation room Thermal facilities Dance studio Hair salon ♫ Xmas **Conf:** Class 252 Board 84 Thtr 450 **Services:** Lift Night porter Air con **Notes:** Civ Wed 350

The Westbury

★★★★★ 88% ◉◉ HOTEL

Grafton Street - tel: 01 6791122
email: westbury@doylecollection.com **web:** www.doylecollection.com
dir: *Adjacent to Grafton St, half way between Trinity College & Stephen's Green*

Located just off Grafton Street, Dublin's premier shopping district, this is an oasis of calm; guests are well cared for amid smart, contemporary surroundings. Spacious public areas include the relaxing Gallery Lounge where afternoon tea is popular with shoppers taking a break. Decor is smart, featuring interesting art pieces and sculptures. Balfes is the hotel's buzzing street-level brasserie bar, while Wilde is the first-floor restaurant with views of the bustling street below from the terrace. Bedrooms and suites come in a range of sizes, all are very comfortably appointed with deep large beds, and warm contemporary decor schemes. The Grafton Suite is an event space, augmented by a range of private dining and meeting rooms. Secure underground parking and a fitness suite are available to resident guests.

Rooms: 205 (9 family) ✆ **S** €250–€560; **D** €250–€560* **Facilities:** STV FTV WiFi ⬧ Gym **Conf:** Class 90 Board 46 Thtr 200 **Services:** Lift Night porter Air con **Parking:** 100 **Notes:** Civ Wed 120

The Marker
★★★★★ 86% 🏅🏅 HOTEL

Grand Canal Square - tel: 01 6875100
email: info@themarker.ie **web:** www.themarkerhoteldublin.com
dir: *M50 junct 1, 2nd exit North Wall Quay. Right into Commons St, right into Mayor St, right on Guild St, over SB Bridge, left into Quays. Right into Forbes St, right into Hanover Quay*

The Marker certainly makes its mark on the exciting Dublin Docklands architectural scene, with its chequerboard frontage along Grand Canal Square. Very much to the fore in terms of contemporary design, all of the bedroom styles are bright and airy, some with dual aspect windows. The entire ground floor is open plan, under a spectacular abstract ceiling, and includes the buzzy Marker Bar, and the Brasserie. A roof-top bar and terrace that specialises in cocktails operates in the summer and when the weather permits. Full spa and wellness facilities are available, together with valet parking.

Rooms: 187 🐾 **S** €209–€2500; **D** €209–€2500* **Facilities:** Spa STV FTV WiFi ᐅ 🅿 Gym Sauna Steam room New Year **Conf:** Class 180 Board 68 Thtr 250 Del from €410 **Services:** Lift Night porter Air con **Parking:** 13 **Notes:** Closed 25-26 Dec Civ Wed 250

The Conrad Dublin
★★★★★ 83% HOTEL

Earlsfort Terrace - tel: 01 6028900
email: conrad_dublin@conradhotels.com **web:** www.conraddublin.com
dir: *Phone for detailed directions*

This fine property is located across from The National Concert Hall, a 10-minute walk from the main shopping district of Grafton Street. It has benefited from a major refurbishment programme, resulting in very smart public areas, a choice of dining options and a range of accommodation alternatives. The decor throughout is contemporary, and styled in restful, muted colours. The Coburg is the all-day dining brasserie that uses primarily local producers and suppliers. Lemuels is an elegant lounge, with a more casual atmosphere downstairs in Alfie Byrne's bar, featuring artisan and craft beers and bar food. A range of events spaces is available, together with a 24-hour fitness suite, and valet parking.

Rooms: 192 🐾 **Facilities:** STV FTV WiFi ᐅ HL Gym Xmas New Year **Conf:** Class 132 Board 10 Thtr 300 **Services:** Lift Night porter Air con **Parking:** 85 **Notes:** Civ Wed 150

Castleknock Hotel & Country Club
FBD Hotels & Resorts
★★★★ 83% 🏅 HOTEL

Porterstown Road, Castleknock - tel: 01 6406300 **email:** info@chcc.ie
web: www.castleknockhotel.com
dir: *M50 from airport. Exit at junct 6 signed Navan, Cavan & M3, onto N3, becomes M3. Exit at junct 3. At top of slip road 1st left signed Consilla R121. At T-junct left. 1km to hotel*

This modern hotel is set on a golf course only 15 minutes from Dublin. The bedrooms are very comfortable, with all the expected modern guest facilities. The spacious public rooms have an airy feel, and some rooms open onto a terrace that overlooks the golf course. The range of food and beverage outlets includes The Park Room, a steak house, a busy all-day brasserie, and The Lime Tree which is open in the evening. Excellent conference and banqueting facilities are available, together with a popular leisure centre.

Rooms: 138 (30 family) 🐾 **S** fr €99; **D** fr €99 (incl. bkfst)* **Facilities:** Spa STV FTV WiFi ᐅ 🅿 supervised ⅃ 18 Gym Sauna Steam room Children's pool 🎵 New Year **Conf:** Class 200 Board 40 Thtr 400 **Services:** Lift Night porter **Parking:** 400 **Notes:** Closed 24-26 Dec Civ Wed 200

Radisson Blu St Helens Hotel

★★★★ 82% 🏅 HOTEL

Stillorgan Road - tel: 01 2186000
email: info.dublin@radissonblu.com **web:** www.radissonblu.ie/sthelenshotel-dublin
dir: *On N11 (Stillorgan dual carriageway)*

An early 18th-century estate is the location of this hotel that has been carefully restored; much of the original decor and architectural features are still intact. Just five kilometres south of the city and close to UCD, there are over a 150 suites and rooms from which to choose. These very well appointed rooms are in a modern block to the side of the main building; many have garden views. The spectacular Orangerie and The Ballroom are popular venues for all-day dining, with the AA-Rosetted Italian restaurant, Talavera, located in the original kitchens open each evening. Le Panto is a wonderfully decorated room available for private dining. A fitness suite and beauty facilities are provided, together with extensive meeting and event spaces for up to 350 delegates.

Rooms: 151 (22 family) (38 GF) 🐾 **Facilities:** STV FTV WiFi ᐅ Gym Beauty salon 🎵 Xmas New Year **Conf:** Class 150 Board 70 Thtr 350 **Services:** Lift Night porter Air con **Parking:** 220 **Notes:** Civ Wed 240

Clontarf Castle Hotel
★★★★ 81% 🏅🏅 HOTEL

Castle Avenue, Clontarf - tel: 01 8332321
email: jormston@clontarfcastle.ie **web:** www.clontarfcastle.ie
dir: *M1 towards centre, left at Whitehall Church, left at T-junct, straight on at lights, right at next lights into Castle Ave, hotel on right at rdbt*

Dating back to the 12th century, this castle retains many historic architectural features which have been combined with contemporary styling in the well-equipped bedrooms. Public areas offer relaxing lounges and galleries which display an eclectic collection of art work. Award-winning cuisine is served at dinner in Fahrenheit Restaurant, with interesting options in the gastropub-style Knights Bar throughout the day, and also a lunchtime offering in the Indigo Lounge. The Great Hall is a versatile venue for banqueting and conferences; very popular for family occasions.

Rooms: 111 (7 family) (11 GF) 🐾 **S** €129–€450; **D** €129–€450* **Facilities:** STV WiFi ᐅ Gym Xmas New Year **Conf:** Class 250 Board 90 Thtr 600 **Services:** Lift Night porter Air con **Parking:** 134 **Notes:** LB Civ Wed 400

Ashling Hotel, Dublin
★★★★ 80% 🏅 HOTEL

Parkgate Street - tel: 01 6772324
email: info@ashlinghotel.ie **web:** www.ashlinghotel.ie
dir: *Close to River Liffey, opposite Heuston Station*

Situated on the banks of the River Liffey close to the city centre, railway station and law courts, this hotel is on the tram route and just a five-minute walk from Phoenix Park. The property is appointed to a high standard in a contemporary style. The bedrooms are comfortably furnished; the newer ones are more spacious. Food is available in the Iveagh Bar throughout the day and a popular carvery is served at lunchtime; Chesterfields Restaurant offers award-winning cuisine in the evenings. Staff are very friendly and service is attentive and professional. Secure multi-storey parking is available at favourable rates.

Rooms: 225 (21 family) 🐾 **S** €99–€425; **D** €99–€450* **Facilities:** FTV WiFi **Conf:** Class 110 Board 50 Thtr 200 **Services:** Lift Night porter **Parking:** 100 **Notes:** LB Closed 24-26 Dec

REPUBLIC OF IRELAND

DUBLIN *continued*

Talbot Hotel Stillorgan

★★★★ 80% @ HOTEL

Stillorgan Road, Stillorgan - tel: 01 2001800
email: info@talbotstillorgan.com **web:** www.talbothotelstillorgan.com
dir: *From N11 follow Wexford signs (pass RTE studios on left) through 5 sets of lights. Hotel on left*

The Talbot Hotel Stillorgan is situated on the southern outskirts of the city, close to UCD, the shopping centre, and The RTE Studios. Comfortable public areas include a spacious lobby, The Purple Sage Restaurant, and Brass, a new brasserie/bar serving quality food throughout the day. Bedrooms and suites come in a range of styles and sizes, all well-appointed and comfortable. There are extensive air-conditioned banqueting and conference facilities, and a compact gym. There is generous parking to the rear, and there's a bus to the city centre on hand.

Rooms: 150 (10 family) ⌇ **S** €90–€250; **D** €100–€260* **Facilities:** STV WiFi ⌇ Gym ♫ New Year **Conf:** Class 220 Board 130 Thtr 500 Del from €170 **Services:** Lift Night porter Air con **Parking:** 300 **Notes:** LB Closed 25 Dec RS 24 Dec closed after lunch Civ Wed 300

Crowne Plaza Hotel Dublin - Blanchardstown

★★★★ 79% @ HOTEL

The Blanchardstown Centre - tel: 01 8977777
email: info@cpireland.crowneplaza.com **web:** www.cpireland.crowneplaza.com
dir: *M50 junct 6 (Blanchardstown)*

This landmark building is on the doorstep of a wide range of shops in Blanchardstown. Bedrooms are stylishly decorated with generously sized beds and well appointed en suites. The Sanctuary Bar serves an international range of informal dishes from lunchtime through to the evening, with Italian specialities (pasta dishes and pizzas) served in the evenings in Forchetta Restaurant. There is a floor of dedicated boardrooms and meeting facilities, together with banqueting rooms. Secure underground parking is complimentary to resident guests.

Rooms: 188 (60 family) ⌇ **S** €100–€410; **D** €100–€420* **Facilities:** STV FTV WiFi ⌇ HL Gym Sauna ♫ New Year **Conf:** Class 300 Board 300 Thtr 500 Del from €215 **Services:** Lift Night porter Air con **Parking:** 250 **Notes:** Civ Wed 300

Roganstown Hotel and Country Club

★★★★ 77% @ HOTEL

Naul Road, Sword - tel: 01 8433118
web: www.roganstown.com
dir: *Phone or see website for detailed directions*

Developed from the original family home and farm some 10 years ago, Roganstown is now a quality hotel property surrounded by parkland encompassing a golf course and a well-equipped leisure centre and spa. Some rooms are in the original farmhouse, with most in a separate modern block around a well landscaped courtyard. The public areas include a cosy bar that doubles as the golf member's area, a busy O'Callaghan's lounge where food is served throughout the day. Evening fine dining takes place in the award-winning McLaughlin's restaurant where the menu features carefully sourced seasonal ingredients cooked with flair. A multi-use conference and events centre is located on the first floor.

Rooms: 52 (4 family) (20 GF) ⌇ **Facilities:** Spa STV WiFi ⌇ ☜ ♨ 18 Putting green Gym Aerobics studio **Conf:** Class 150 Board 128 Thtr 300 **Services:** Lift Night porter **Parking:** 370 **Notes:** Civ Wed 240

Red Cow Moran Hotel

★★★★ 76% HOTEL

Red Cow Complex, Naas Road - tel: 01 4593650
email: redcowres@moranhotels.com **web:** www.moranhotels.com
dir: *At junct of M50 & N7 on city side of motorway*

Located just off the M50, this hotel is 20 minutes from the airport and close to the city centre via the Luas light rail system. The dedicated team of staff show a genuine willingness to create a memorable stay. Bedrooms are well equipped and comfortable, and the public areas and conference rooms are spacious. Ample free parking is available.

Rooms: 123 (21 family) (7 smoking) **Facilities:** FTV WiFi ⌇ ♫ New Year **Conf:** Class 350 Board 150 Thtr 750 **Services:** Lift Night porter Air con **Parking:** 700 **Notes:** Closed 24-26 Dec Civ Wed 400

Cassidys Hotel

★★★ 78% HOTEL

6-8 Cavendish Row, Upper O'Connell St - tel: 01 8780555
email: stay@cassidyshotel.com **web:** www.cassidyshotel.com
dir: *In city centre at N end of O'Connell St*

This long established family-run hotel is located at the northern end of O'Connell Street, in a terrace of red-brick Georgian townhouses, directly opposite the famed Gate Theatre. The warm and welcoming atmosphere created by the hospitable team in Groome's Bar and Bistro adds to the traditional atmosphere. An all-day menu is served, together with a pre-theatre offering. Bedrooms are individually styled and well appointed; many have air conditioning, with executive rooms in a modern block to the side. A residents' gym, conference facilities and limited parking are all available.

Rooms: 113 (26 annexe) (3 family) (12 GF) (30 smoking) **Facilities:** STV WiFi ⌇ Gym **Conf:** Class 45 Board 45 Thtr 80 **Services:** Lift Night porter **Parking:** 8 **Notes:** Closed 24-26 Dec

Maldron Hotel Newlands Cross

★★★ 74% HOTEL

Newlands Cross, Naas Rd - tel: 01 4640140
email: newlands@bewleyshotels.com **web:** www.bewleyshotels.com
dir: *M50 junct 9, N7 (Naas road). Hotel near junct of N7 & Belgard Rd*

This modern hotel is situated on the N7 and close to the M50 and Luas light rail to the city. Bedrooms are spacious and the pricing structure proves popular with families. The Brasserie restaurant is open throughout the day for casual dining and serves a carvery lunch; more formal meals are served in the evening. The hotel also has a comfortable bar where snacks are available, conference rooms, a gym and ample free parking.

Rooms: 297 (182 family) (62 GF) ⌇ **Facilities:** STV WiFi ⌇ Gym ♫ New Year **Conf:** Class 18 Board 14 Thtr 50 **Services:** Lift Night porter **Parking:** 200 **Notes:** Closed 24-26 Dec

Intercontinental Dublin

[U]

tel: 01 6654000
email: sales@icdublin.com **web:** www.intercontinentaldublin.ie
dir: *Phone for detailed directions*

Currently the rating for this establishment is not confirmed. This may be due to a change of ownership or because it has only recently joined the AA rating scheme.

Rooms: 197

DUBLIN AIRPORT
Dublin   Map 1 D4

Crowne Plaza Dublin Northwood

★★★★ 80% ⊛ HOTEL

CROWNE PLAZA
HOTELS & RESORTS

Northwood Park, Santry Demesne - tel: 01 8628888
email: info@crowneplazadublin.ie **web:** www.cpdublin.crowneplaza.com
dir: *M50 junct 4, left into Northwood Park, 1km, hotel on left*

Located within minutes of Dublin Airport, and served by a complimentary shuttle service, this modern hotel is located in Northwood Park, and benefits from an idyllic location overlooking 85 acres of mature woodlands of the former Santry Demesne. Bedrooms come in a variety of styles, and each is comfortable and well appointed. Guests in the executive rooms have the use of a lounge facility where a light breakfast is served. The hotel offers a range of dining options, including full room service and a lobby café. There are extensive conference and event rooms at this property, together with a secure multi-storey car park. Guests also have use of a well-equipped gym.

Rooms: 204 (17 family) (5 smoking) ⬤ **S** €79–€380; **D** €79–€380* **Facilities:** STV FTV WiFi ⬤ HL Gym Xmas New Year **Conf:** Class 450 Board 100 Thtr 850 Del from €90 **Services:** Lift Night porter Air con **Parking:** 400 **Notes:** Civ Wed 300

Clayton Hotel Dublin Airport

★★★★ 78% HOTEL

Baskin Lane - tel: 01 8711000
email: info.dublinairport@claytonhotels.com **web:** www.claytonhotels.com
dir: *At end of M50 N'bound, 2nd exit at rdbt (N32), left at next rdbt*

Conveniently situated for Dublin Airport, this hotel has the added advantage of secure underground long-term parking with a complimentary shuttle bus to the airport. Bedrooms and suites are spacious, very comfortable and well appointed. The Playwright is a buzzy, atmospheric lobby lounge serving informal meals throughout the day, with more formal dining in The Restaurant each evening, and a popular carvery operation at lunchtime. There is a number of meeting and boardrooms available, together with a residents' gym.

Rooms: 469 (228 family) (36 smoking) ⬤ **S** €299; **D** €399* **Facilities:** FTV WiFi ⬤ Fitness room Xmas **Conf:** Class 150 Board 12 Thtr 300 **Services:** Lift Night porter **Parking:** 1150 **Notes:** LB Civ Wed 250

DUNBOYNE
County Meath   Map 1 D4

Dunboyne Castle Hotel & Spa

★★★★ 79% ⊛⊛ HOTEL

A86 PW63 - tel: 01 8013500
email: info@dunboynecastlehotel.com **web:** www.dunboynecastlehotel.com
dir: *In Dunboyne take R157 towards Maynooth. Hotel on left*

Located within walking distance of Dunboyne, this fine property is a successful combination of the traditional and contemporary. Set on over two acres of mature woodland and well-tended grounds, the original house is home to a number of meeting rooms, with the spacious bedrooms in a modern block to the side. All-day dining is offered in the Terrace Lounge, with evening meals and breakfast served in the Ivy Restaurant.

Rooms: 145 (37 GF) ⬤ **Facilities:** Spa STV WiFi ⬤ Gym ♫ Xmas New Year **Conf:** Class 200 Board 80 Thtr 450 **Services:** Lift Night porter Air con **Parking:** 380 **Notes:** LB Civ Wed 250

See advert on following page

DUNDALK
County Louth   Map 1 D4

Ballymascanlon House Hotel
★★★★ 80% HOTEL

tel: 042 9358200
email: info@ballymascanlon.com **web:** www.ballymascanlon.com
dir: M1 junct 18 onto N52 signed Dundalk North/R173 at Carlingford. Exit at Faughart rdbt. 1st left at next rdbt. Hotel in approx 1km on left

This Victorian mansion is set in 130 acres of woodland and landscaped gardens at the foot of the Cooley Mountains. The elegant house and the modern extension make this a very comfortable hotel that has really stylish bedrooms. Public areas include a spacious restaurant, lounge and bar, together with relaxing reading rooms that retain many original architectural features. There is a well-equipped leisure centre, and The Oak Room banqueting facility proves to be very popular for weddings and family occasions.

Rooms: 97 (11 family) (5 GF) ⌇ S €85–€105; D €140–€165 (incl. bkfst)*
Facilities: STV FTV WiFi ⌇ ⊛ supervised ⌇ 18 Putting green ⌇ Gym Steam room Sauna Plunge pool Outdoor hot tub ♫ Xmas New Year **Conf:** Class 220 Board 100 Thtr 400 Del from €175 **Services:** Lift Night porter **Parking:** 250 **Notes:** LB Civ Wed 300

DUNFANAGHY
County Donegal   Map 1 C6

Arnolds Hotel
★★★ 78% ⊛ HOTEL   IRISH COUNTRY HOTELS

tel: 074 9136208
email: enquiries@arnoldshotel.com **web:** www.arnoldshotel.com
dir: N56 from Letterkenny, hotel on left on entering village

This family-owned and run hotel, situated in a coastal village overlooking sandy beaches and beautiful scenery, is noted for its warm welcome and good food. The public areas and bedrooms are very comfortable; there is a traditional cosy bar with turf fires, a popular bistro that serves food throughout the day, and Seascapes Restaurant where local seafood features on the menu. The popular Café offers an interesting menu – it opens daily, and alfresco dining in the garden is possible, weather permitting. There are stables attached to the hotel, with preferential terms for residents. Photographic and painting breaks are available, as is links-based golf. Live music is a regular evening feature in the bar.

Rooms: 30 (10 family) ⌇ S €115; D €105–€170 (incl. bkfst)* **Facilities:** FTV WiFi ⌇ ♫ New Year **Conf:** Class 30 Board 20 Thtr 30 Del from €150 **Services:** Night porter **Parking:** 60 **Notes:** LB Closed Mon-Tue (Nov-Mar) Civ Wed 90

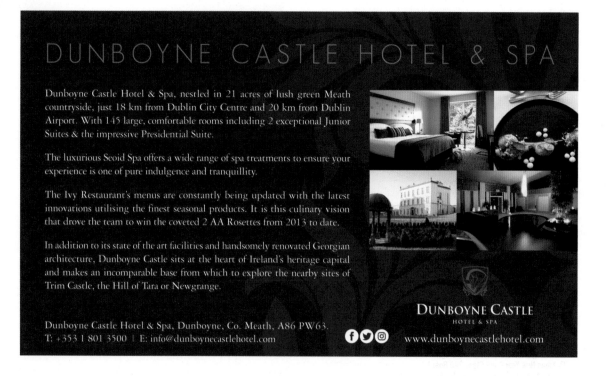

DUNGLOE
County Donegal

Map 1 B5

Waterfront Hotel Dungloe

★★★ 76% HOTEL

Mill Road - tel: 074 9522444
email: joseph@waterfronthoteldungloe.ie web: www.waterfronthoteldungloe.ie
dir: *Phone for detailed directions*

Signposted in the Irish language as 'An Clochan Liath', Dungloe is the principal town of west Donegal. The Waterfront Hotel is a long established property on an elevated position at the end of the town. Under new ownership it has benefited from a very successful renovation and refurbishment programme. 106 Atlantic is the main restaurant and a more casual bistro – both make the most of the views over Dungloe Bay. Menus feature all the family favourites and plenty of seafood options. Service is personable, with the typical Donegal warmth and hospitality to the fore. The cosy and comfortable bedrooms have a slightly maritime theme. There are plans to develop a spa and leisure facility soon.

Rooms: 49

ENNIS
County Clare

Map 1 B3

Temple Gate Hotel

★★★★ 78% HOTEL

The Square - tel: 065 6823300
email: info@templegatehotel.com web: www.templegatehotel.com
dir: *Exit N18 onto Tulla Rd for 0.25m, hotel on left*

This smart hotel is owned and run by the Madden family and is located in the centre of the town. It incorporates a 19th-century, Gothic-style Great Hall banqueting room. The public areas are well planned and include a comfortable library lounge, popular traditional pub, and Legends Restaurant. Bedrooms are attractive and well equipped, with some executive rooms and suites available.

Rooms: 70 (3 family) (11 GF) (20 smoking) S fr €80; D fr €100* Facilities: STV FTV WiFi ♫ New Year Conf: Class 100 Board 80 Thtr 250 Services: Lift Night porter Parking: 52 Notes: LB Closed 25-26 Dec RS 24 Dec closes at 8pm Civ Wed 200

ENNISKERRY
County Wicklow

Map 1 D3

Powerscourt Hotel Resort & Spa

★★★★★ 88% HOTEL

Powerscourt Estate - tel: 01 2748888
email: info@powerscourthotel.com web: www.powerscourthotel.com
dir: *From Dublin take M50, M11, then N11, follow Enniskerry signs. In Enniskerry left up hill, hotel on right*

This very stylish hotel, built in the Palladian style, has a tranquil setting with stunning views over the gardens and woodlands to the Sugar Loaf Mountain. Being set in the heart of the renowned Powerscourt Estate makes for great walks and exploration. The bedrooms and suites are particularly spacious and well appointed. Impressive bathrooms have TVs, deep baths and walk-in showers. The luxuriously appointed public areas are airy and spacious with a variety of food options that includes the award-winning Sika Restaurant, Sugar Loaf Lounge and McGills Bar. The resort also has a stunning spa, two golf courses, and includes fly fishing and equestrian pursuits among its many leisure facilities. There are extensive conferencing and events spaces.

Rooms: 194 (39 GF) S fr €180; D fr €190 (incl. bkfst)* Facilities: Spa STV WiFi ♫ 36 Putting green Fishing Gym Cycling Mega chess Fitness classes Jogging trails ♫ Xmas New Year Conf: Class 240 Board 72 Thtr 500 Services: Lift Night porter Air con Parking: 384 Notes: Civ Wed 400

GALWAY
County Galway

Map 1 B3

The g Hotel & Spa

★★★★★ 87% HOTEL

Wellpark, Dublin Road - tel: 091 865200
email: info@theg.ie web: www.theghotel.ie
dir: *Phone for detailed directions*

Designed in association with acclaimed milliner Philip Treacy who hails from the county, this hotel is the epitome of contemporary styling. The public areas include a series of eclectically furnished Signature Lounges, each with its own identity. The cutting-edge design is also apparent in the bedrooms and suites, which are very comfortable and appointed to a high standard. An interesting selection of menus is on offer at dinner each evening in GiGi's, the atmospheric restaurant, and a very popular all-day menu is served in the lounges, including a range of traditional afternoon tea options. The hotel has a number of boardrooms, an events space, and an ESPA spa facility. Underground and valet parking is available.

Rooms: 101 (2 family) Facilities: Spa STV FTV WiFi HL Gym ♫ New Year Conf: Class 70 Board 70 Thtr 300 Services: Lift Night porter Air con Parking: 349 Notes: LB Closed 23-26 Dec Civ Wed 90

Glenlo Abbey Hotel

★★★★ 88% HOTEL

Kentfield, Bushypark - tel: 091 526666 & 519600
email: info@glenloabbey.ie web: www.glenloabbeyhotel.ie
dir: *2m from Galway city centre on N59 to Clifden*

The origins of Glenlo Abbey date from 1740 when the original house was built by the Ffrenchs, a wealthy merchant family. It is set on a spacious estate with wonderful views of Lough Corrib, just five kilometres from Galway on the road to Connemara. Great care has been taken in the refurbishment of the house, with many of the public rooms retaining their proportions and many original features. Most of the accommodation is in a wing to the rear; suites and bedrooms are finished to a very high level, with some featuring lake or garden views. Guests have two restaurants from which to choose, The Pullman Restaurant aboard The Orient Express is a unique dining experience, made up of two carriages from the iconic railway. Golf is available on the estate, which also features stand-alone banqueting facilities.

Rooms: 50 (13 family) (16 GF) S €159–€339; D €179–€359 (incl. bkfst)* Facilities: WiFi ♫ 9 Putting green Fishing 21 bay driving range Falconry 134 acre estate for walking/cycling ♫ Xmas New Year Conf: Class 100 Board 50 Thtr 180 Del from €200 Services: Lift Night porter Notes: LB Civ Wed 100

Ardilaun Hotel & Leisure Club

★★★★ 81% HOTEL

Taylor's Hill - tel: 091 521433
email: info@theardilaunhotel.ie web: www.theardilaunhotel.ie
dir: *M6 to Galway City West, then follow signs for N59 Clifden, then N6 towards Salthill*

This very smart country-house style hotel, appointed to a high standard, is located on the city outskirts near Salthill and has lovely landscaped gardens. Bedrooms have been thoughtfully appointed and deluxe rooms and suites are particularly spacious. Public areas include comfortable lounges, the Camilaun Restaurant overlooking the garden and extensive banqueting and leisure facilities. In the Ardilaun Bistro the menu features artisan seasonal ingredients in a contemporary and inventive style, with much of the produce coming from the walled garden.

Rooms: 123 (17 family) (8 GF) S €69–€280; D €79–€550 (incl. bkfst)* Facilities: Spa STV WiFi supervised Gym Beauty treatment & analysis rooms Beauty salon ♫ New Year Conf: Class 280 Board 100 Thtr 650 Del from €104.90 Services: Lift Night porter Parking: 286 Notes: LB Closed 23 Dec pm & 24-26 Dec Civ Wed 650

GALWAY *continued*

Park House Hotel & Restaurant

★★★★ 79% HOTEL

Forster Street, Eyre Square - tel: 091 564924
email: reservations@parkhousehotel.ie **web:** www.parkhousehotel.ie
dir: *In city centre*

Situated just off Eyre Square, this well established hotel offers comfortable facilities to suit business or leisure guests. Public areas and bedrooms are well appointed and attractively decorated in traditional schemes. The Park Restaurant has been a popular spot for the people of Galway for many years with less formal yet quality food is served throughout the day in Boss Doyle's bar. Some resident parking is available to the rear.

Rooms: 84 ♠ **S** €130–€359; **D** €130–€359 (incl. bkfst)* **Facilities:** STV FTV WiFi ↻
♫ **Services:** Lift Night porter Air con **Parking:** 48 **Notes:** LB Closed 24-26 Dec

Radisson Blu Hotel & Spa, Galway

★★★★ 79% HOTEL

Radisson BLU
HOTELS & RESORTS

Lough Atalia Road - tel: 091 538300
email: reservations.galway@radissonblu.com
web: www.radissonblu.com/en/hotel-galway
dir: *Phone for detailed directions*

This hotel is situated in a prime position on Lough Atalia's waterfront and overlooks Galway Bay. While parking is available, its location within minutes of both the train and bus stations makes this an ideal place for a car-free break. The striking interior design and levels of comfort are impressive in the bright and airy public areas. Bedrooms are well equipped and there is an executive floor where further privacy is guaranteed. Dining options include RAW, a roof-top sushi restaurant, and the very popular Marina Grill on the ground floor, offering a varied menu that is sure to please. A range of event spaces is available, with the capacity to accommodate nearly 1,000 delegates.

Rooms: 261 (5 family) **Facilities:** Spa STV FTV WiFi ↻ ⑇ supervised Gym Sauna Steam room Salt spa Aerobics studios Xmas New Year **Conf:** Class 650 Board 25 Thtr 990 **Services:** Lift Night porter Air con **Notes:** LB

The Harbour Hotel

★★★ 74% HOTEL

New Dock Road - tel: 091 894800
email: stay@harbour.ie **web:** www.harbour.ie
dir: *Phone for detailed directions*

Within a three minute stroll of the bustling and vibrant Quay Street area of Galway, this hotel really is in the centre of things, yet easily accessed without driving through the city. Rooms come in a variety of sizes, all are modern and comfortable. The Harbour Bar is a popular venue for locals and residents alike, where interesting menus are on offer, featuring house-made dishes with seafood being a particular feature. Limited secure parking at a reduced rate for guests, and a fitness suite are also available.

Rooms: 96 (5 family) **Facilities:** STV FTV WiFi ↻ Fitness room ♫ Xmas New Year
Conf: Class 60 Board 50 Thtr 150 **Services:** Night porter **Parking:** 70 **Notes:** LB Civ Wed 130

Hotel Meyrick

Ⓤ

Eyre Squre - tel: 091 564041
email: pfeeney@hotelmeyrick.ie **web:** www.hotelmeyrick.ie
dir: *Phone for detailed directions*

Currently the rating for this establishment is not confirmed. This may be due to a change of ownership or because it has only recently joined the AA rating scheme.
Rooms: 97

| GLASLOUGH | Map 1 C5 |
| County Monaghan | |

The Lodge at Castle Leslie Estate

★★★★ 82% ⑇⑇ HOTEL

tel: 047 88100
email: info@castleleslie.com **web:** www.castleleslie.com
dir: *M1 junct 14, N2 to Monaghan, N12 to R185 to Glaslough*

Set in 1,000 acres of rolling countryside dotted with mature woodland, The Lodge is the social hub of the Castle Leslie Estate which has been in the Leslie family since the 1660s. The comfortably furnished bedrooms are in the original hunting lodge and the converted stable block. Resident guests have two dining options – Snaffles Restaurant and Conors Bar. There is a spa known as The Victorian Treatment Rooms, a world class equestrian centre and a private fishing lake. For those who enjoy country pursuits, this hotel is an ideal base for the many walks and interesting flora and fauna in the area.

Rooms: 29 (2 family) (10 GF) ♠ **S** €160–€200; **D** €180–€220 (incl. bkfst)*
Facilities: Spa STV FTV WiFi ⌁ Fishing Horse riding Kayaking Clay pigeon Falconry Boating Hot air balloon rides Child facilities **Conf:** Class 25 Board 24 Thtr 35 Del from €255 **Services:** Lift Night porter **Parking:** 100 **Notes:** Closed 24-27 Dec Civ Wed 40

GOREY
County Wexford

Map 1 D3

Seafield Hotel & Spa Resort
★★★★ 80% ◎◎ HOTEL

Ballymoney - **tel:** 053 942 4000
email: reservations@seafieldhotel.com **web:** www.seafieldhotel.com
dir: *M11 exit 22*

This contemporary hotel is part of a village style resort that includes an 18-hole championship golf course, courtyard family suites and the award-winning Oceo Spa. Set in 225 acres of parkland with mature trees, river-side walks and access onto Ballymoney Beach, the hotel offers stylish, spacious bedrooms and suites which have views of either the coastline or the golf course; some have balconies. There are two dining options – fine dining in the award-winning Greenroom Restaurant, and a more casual option in the Village Bar & Grill.

Rooms: 101 ☔ **Facilities:** Spa STV WiFi ⓧ ⊛ ⚓ 18 Putting green Gym Playground 🎵 New Year **Conf:** Class 220 Board 40 Thtr 300 **Services:** Lift Night porter **Parking:** 200 **Notes:** LB Civ Wed 280

Amber Springs Hotel
★★★★ 80% ◎ HOTEL

Wexford Road - **tel:** 053 9484000
email: info@ambersprings.ie **web:** www.ambersspringshotel.ie
dir: *500mtrs from Gorey by-pass at junct 23*

This modern hotel, on the Wexford road, is within walking distance of the town. It enjoys a well-earned reputation for accommodating families with its dedicated facilities. Bedrooms are spacious and very comfortable, and guests have full use of the leisure facilities. All-day dining is offered in Brooks Bar & Grill, with an adult-only space at dinner in the award-winning Farm Steakhouse. Much of the produce is sourced from the nearby proprietor's farm that specialises in Angus beef. This is a popular wedding venue. Ample parking is available to the rear.

Rooms: 80 (34 family) (24 GF) ☔ **Facilities:** Spa STV WiFi ⓧ ⊛ supervised Gym Mini golf Petting farm Kids train 🎵 New Year **Conf:** Class 450 Board 30 Thtr 700 **Services:** Lift Night porter Air con **Parking:** 178 **Notes:** Closed 25-26 Dec Civ Wed 700

Ashdown Park Hotel
★★★★ 79% ◎ HOTEL

The Coach Road - **tel:** 053 9480500
email: info@ashdownparkhotel.com **web:** www.ashdownparkhotel.com
dir: *N11 junct 22, towards Gorey, 1st left (before railway bridge), hotel on left*

Situated on an elevated position overlooking the town, this modern hotel has excellent health, leisure and banqueting facilities. There are comfortable lounge areas and two dining options – Ivy, a popular carvery bar, and The Rowan Tree, the first-floor fine dining restaurant that opens in the evenings. Bedrooms are available in a number of styles; all are spacious and well equipped. Close to a number of golf courses, this property is popular with golfers, and also with families as it is near the beaches.

Rooms: 79 (17 family) (22 GF) ☔ **Facilities:** Spa FTV WiFi ⓧ ⊛ supervised Gym Leisure centre Massage rooms 🎵 New Year **Conf:** Class 315 Board 100 Thtr 800 **Services:** Lift Night porter **Parking:** 150 **Notes:** Closed 25 Dec Civ Wed 300

Marlfield House Hotel
★★★ ◎◎ COUNTRY HOUSE HOTEL

tel: 053 9421124
email: info@marlfieldhouse.ie **web:** www.marlfieldhouse.com
dir: *N11 junct 23, follow signs for Courtown. At Courtown Rd rdbt left for Gorey. Hotel 1m on left*

This Regency-style building has been gracefully extended and developed into an excellent hotel. An atmosphere of elegance and luxury permeates every corner of the house, underpinned by truly friendly and professional service led by the Bowe family who are always in evidence. The bedrooms are decorated in keeping with the style of the house, with some really spacious rooms and suites on the ground floor. Dinner in the Conservatory Restaurant is always a highlight of a stay at Marlfield, with afternoon tea a speciality. Less formal dining is available in The Duck, an all-day dining facility with a terrace.

Rooms: 21 (3 family) (9 GF) ☔ **D** €210–€670 (incl. bkfst)* **Facilities:** STV FTV WiFi ⓧ ⊛ ⚓ Beauty treatment room **Conf:** Board 24 Thtr 60 **Parking:** 100 **Notes:** Closed 2 Jan-15 Feb RS Nov-Dec & Mar-Apr closed some Mon & Tue Civ Wed 120

REPUBLIC OF IRELAND

REPUBLIC OF IRELAND

KENMARE
County Kerry

Map 1 B2

INSPECTOR'S CHOICE

Sheen Falls Lodge
★★★★★ ◉◉ COUNTRY HOUSE HOTEL

tel: 064 6641600
email: info@sheenfallslodge.ie web: www.sheenfallslodge.ie
dir: *From Kenmare take N71 to Glengarriff over suspension bridge, take 1st left*

This former fishing lodge has been developed into a beautiful hotel with a friendly team of professional staff. The cascading Sheen Falls are floodlit at night, forming a romantic backdrop to award-winning cuisine in La Cascade Restaurant. Less formal dining is available in Oscar's Bistro, and the Sun Lounge serves refreshments and light snacks throughout the day. The bedrooms are very comfortably appointed; many of the suites are particularly spacious. The leisure centre and beauty therapy facilities offer a number of exclusive treatments, and outdoor pursuits include walking, fishing, tennis, horse riding and clay pigeon shooting.

Rooms: 66 (14 family) (14 GF) ✆ S €155–€440; D €185–€470 (incl. bkfst)*
Facilities: Spa STV WiFi ☯ ⚓ Fishing ⛳ Gym Table tennis Steam room
Clay pigeon shooting Cycling Vintage car rides Library ♫ Xmas New Year
Conf: Class 65 Board 50 Thtr 120 Services: Lift Night porter Parking: 76
Notes: LB Closed 30 Nov-19 Dec & 2 Jan-1 Feb RS 24-27 Dec Xmas inclusive programmes only Civ Wed 150

INSPECTOR'S CHOICE

Park Hotel Kenmare
★★★★ ◉◉ HOTEL

tel: 064 6641200
email: info@parkkenmare.com web: www.parkkenmare.com
dir: *On R569, adjacent to golf course at top of town*

This hotel is a luxurious house, situated on the famous Ring of Kerry, that has been welcoming guests for over 100 years. Warm hospitality and professional service come naturally to all the team, who endeavour to make guests feel pampered. All the suites and bedrooms are spacious and very well appointed, with either garden or sea views. The elegant restaurant serves very good food, much of it locally sourced, together with fine wines. Samas is the luxury treatment spa.

Rooms: 46 (3 family) ✆ S €225–€265; D €290–€810 (incl. bkfst)* Facilities: Spa
FTV WiFi ☯ Putting green ⚓ ⛳ Gym ♫ Xmas New Year Conf: Class 40 Board
28 Thtr 60 Services: Lift Night porter Parking: 60 Notes: Closed 10-22 Dec &
3 Jan-16 Feb

KILKENNY
County Kilkenny

Map 1 C3

Lyrath Estate
★★★★ 86% ◉ HOTEL

Old Dublin Road - tel: 056 7760088
email: reservations@lyrath.com web: www.lyrath.com
dir: *M9 junct 8 signed Kilkenny. 1st exit at both 1st & 2nd rdbts, hotel 1km*

Located a short drive from Kilkenny, and set in 170 acres of mature parkland and lakeland, this 17th-century house has been carefully restored and greatly expanded to become one of the country's largest convention centres, with a myriad of event spaces and public areas. The property is very popular for weddings, held in the public rooms of the main house, some of which retain many of the original architectural features. Bedrooms are predominantly in a separate block, all well-appointed and en suite; some are available in the original house. There are great dining options to be savoured here, from La Perla, the more traditional restaurant, to Yindees a very popular oriental option, and Tuppers bar for all-day dining. Guests have complimentary access to the health club and gym, with spa treatments and a thermal suite available at a supplement

Rooms: 139 (24 family) (31 GF) ✆ Facilities: Spa FTV WiFi ☯ ☯ Fishing Gym
Private cinema Snooker room Outdoor hydrotherapy pool ♫ New Year
Conf: Class 750 Board 75 Thtr 1500 Services: Lift Night porter Air con Parking: 420
Notes: Closed 20-27 Dec Civ Wed 100

KILLARNEY
County Kerry

Map 1 B2

The Brehon Killarney
★★★★ 81% ◉◉ HOTEL

Muckross Road - tel: 064 6630700
email: sinead.mccarthy@thebrehon.com web: www.thebrehon.com
dir: *1m from Killarney on N71*

This is a spectacular hotel close to Killarney National Park and a 20-minute walk from the town. Public areas are particularly spacious with comfortable mezzanine lounge areas, and a bustling bar where a popular all-day-dining menu is on offer. Danú is the bright and airy award-winning restaurant where breakfast and dinner are served, from an interesting, well-compiled menu. The spacious bedrooms and suites are well equipped, many with great views towards the mountains. The hotel offers a specialist Thai spa experience and extensive conference facilities. Other leisure facilities are on offer at their nearby sister hotel.

Rooms: 125 (10 family) ✆ S €99–€299; D €109–€349 (incl. bkfst)* Facilities: Spa
STV FTV WiFi ☯ HL ☯ ⚓ Gym ♫ Xmas New Year Conf: Class 150 Board 50
Thtr 250 Del from €158 Services: Lift Night porter Air con Parking: 300 Notes: LB
Civ Wed 220

The Lake Hotel

★★★★ 79% ◎◎ HOTEL

Lake Shore, Muckross Road - tel: 064 6631035
email: info@lakehotel.com **web:** www.lakehotel.com
dir: N22 to Killarney. Hotel 2km from town on Muckross Rd

Enjoying a delightful location on the shores of Killarney's lake, this hotel is run by a second generation of the Huggard family, together with a dedicated and friendly team. There is a relaxed atmosphere, with log fires and stunning views from the lounges and restaurant. Guests could be lucky enough to see a herd of red deer wander by. The smartly furnished bedrooms have either lake or woodland views; some have balconies and four-poster beds. The spa offers good facilities, and there are cycle paths and lovely walks to enjoy.

Rooms: 131 (6 family) (23 GF) 🐾 **S** €79–€229; **D** €99–€320 (incl. bkfst)*
Facilities: STV FTV WiFi ⛳ 🏊 Fishing 🚴 Gym Beauty treatment room Sauna Steam room Outdoor hot tub ♬ **Services:** Lift Night porter **Parking:** 140 **Notes:** LB Closed Dec-Jan Civ Wed 60

Cahernane House Hotel

★★★★ 76% ◎◎ HOTEL

Muckross Road - tel: 064 6631895
email: info@cahernane.com **web:** www.cahernane.com
dir: From Killarney town take N71. After 1m cross Flesk River bridge, hotel on right

Situated on the edge of Killarney National Park, this boutique hotel dates from 1877 and is just 10-minute walk from the town. Bedrooms, of which 12 are in the original house, are spacious and well appointed; some garden wing rooms have terraces. There is an air of relaxation and peacefulness at Cahernane, where the public rooms retain the charm and many original features of the era. Log fires add to the atmosphere. Dinner in the award-winning Herbert Room is a real treat, featuring seasonal and local ingredients cooked with flair.

Rooms: 38 (6 family) (12 GF) **S** €110–€260; **D** €170–€320 (incl. bkfst)*
Facilities: FTV WiFi New Year **Services:** Lift Night porter **Parking:** 40 **Notes:** LB Closed Jan-Feb RS Mar – may open wknds only Civ Wed 70

Castlerosse Hotel & Holiday Homes

★★★ 79% HOTEL

Lakes of Killarney - tel: 064 6631144
email: res@castlerosse.ie **web:** www.castlerosse.ie
dir: From Killarney take R562 signed Killorglin & The Ring of Kerry. Hotel 2.5km from town on left

This hotel is situated on 6,000 acres overlooking the Lakes of Killarney with the Magillycuddy Mountains as a backdrop. At times guests may be able to spot deer in Killarney National Park. Bedrooms and junior suites are well appointed and comfortable. There is live entertainment most nights in Mulligan's pub. Leisure facilities include a 9-hole parkland golf course, tennis courts, a leisure centre and treatment rooms.

Rooms: 120 (27 family) (116 GF) 🐾 **S** €60–€125; **D** €90–€200 (incl. bkfst)*
Facilities: STV FTV WiFi ⛳ 🎾 supervised ⛳ 9 Putting green 🏊 Gym Beauty treatment rooms Cycling Golf & horse riding arranged ♬ **Conf:** Class 100 Board 40 Thtr 200 **Services:** Lift Night porter **Parking:** 100 **Notes:** LB Closed Nov-Mar Civ Wed 80

Fitzpatrick Castle Hotel

★★★★ 81% ◎ HOTEL

tel: 01 2305400
email: reservations@fitzpatricks.com **web:** www.fitzpatrickcastle.com
dir: From Dun Laoghaire port turn left, on coast road right at lights, left at next lights. Follow to Dalkey, right at Ivory Pub, immediate left, up hill, hotel at top

This family-owned and operated 18th-century castle is situated in lovely gardens with mature trees and spectacular views over Dublin Bay. The original castle rooms are appointed to a high standard and have four-poster beds, while the rooms in modern wings are spacious – some have balconies. Spacious lounges are comfortably furnished, with extensive leisure and events spaces. The Grill at the Castle is a warm and relaxing evening dining venue, very popular with the local population for early evening dining and family celebrations. The original dungeon makes for an atmospheric pre-dinner location, or perhaps a nightcap. The Lobby lounge serves afternoon tea and informal meals during the day. Spacious parking is available, and there's a direct coach service to the airport.

Rooms: 113 (36 family) 🐾 **Facilities:** STV FTV WiFi ⚡ supervised Gym Beauty/hairdressing salon Sauna Steam room Fitness centre ♬ Xmas New Year **Conf:** Class 250 Board 80 Thtr 500 **Services:** Lift Night porter **Parking:** 300 **Notes:** RS 25 Dec no dinner Civ Wed 400

The Station House Hotel

★★★ 75% ◎ HOTEL

tel: 046 9025239
email: denise@stationhousehotel.ie **web:** www.stationhousehotel.ie
dir: Phone for detailed directions

This family operated hotel retains much of the character of its former life as a railway station. This property is located in attractive gardens, right in the centre of The Boyne Valley, yet just a half hour from Dublin. The old signal box is now the quaint bridal suite, with most of the bedrooms in the converted goods buildings opposite. All-day dining is available in the Platform Lounge, with dinner in the Signal restaurant, the former waiting rooms and booking office. The Station House has a well deserved reputation for hosting weddings and other family celebrations.

Rooms: 19

Park Hotel Kiltimagh

★★★ 77% HOTEL

IRISH
COUNTRY
HOTELS

Swinford Road - tel: 094 9374922
email: info@parkhotelmayo.com **web:** www.parkhotelmayo.com
dir: N17 onto R322 or R323 (or N60 onto R320) to Kiltimagh

This smart hotel overlooks the Wetlands Wildlife Park and is within walking distance of Kiltimagh; it is just 15 minutes from Ireland West Knock Airport and Knock Marian Shrine. The spacious bedrooms are well appointed. Public areas are attractively decorated and include comfortable lounges, Café Bar, Park Restaurant and banqueting facilities. The Aroma Beauty Spa offers a range of treatments and there is also a fitness centre and steam room. A shuttle coach service operates to the airport, and for guests using the airport, parking can be arranged at the hotel.

Rooms: 46 (40 family) **Facilities:** Spa WiFi ⚡ Gym New Year **Conf:** Class 120 Board 60 Thtr 450 **Services:** Lift Night porter **Parking:** 300 **Notes:** Civ Wed 350

LAHINCH
County Clare   Map 1 B3

Vaughan Lodge Hotel

★★★★ 81% ◉◉ HOTEL

Ennistymon Road - **tel:** 065 7081111
email: info@vaughanlodge.com **web:** www.vaughanlodge.ie
dir: *Phone for detailed directions*

Located on the outskirts of Lahinch, where golf is a way of life, this modern townhouse boutique property is operated and run by the Vaughan's, a fourth generation local hotelier family. They are assisted by a small dedicated team of hospitable and engaging locals. Bedroom accommodation is spacious and well appointed. Dinner in VL, the bright and airy restaurant, is a highlight of a stay, featuring a modern approach to classic dishes, all based on high quality ingredients, many from the locality. There are no conference or leisure facilities, here, just a relaxing environment to chill out and re-energise.

Rooms: 22

LEIGHLINBRIDGE
County Carlow   Map 1 C3

Lord Bagenal Inn

★★★★ 76% ◉ HOTEL

Main Street - **tel:** 059 9774000
email: info@lordbagenal.com **web:** www.lordbagenal.com
dir: *Just off M9 junct 6 signed Leighlinbridge. From N9 in approx 1km turn left onto R705, hotel 1km on right*

The family-run Lord Bagenal Inn enjoys an idyllic location on the banks of the River Barrow. Located just off the M9 in the picturesque village of Leighlinbridge, it is one hour from Dublin and Waterford airports. Bedrooms are comfortable and well-equipped and the traditional bar is a cluster of cosy rooms with log fires. Fine dining is available in the restaurant.

Lord Bagenal Inn

Rooms: 39 (3 family) (3 GF) ⟡ **S** €70–€100; **D** €95–€150 (incl. bkfst)*
Facilities: STV FTV WiFi ⓑ Guided walks Canoeing Kayaking Cycling Yoga Art classes ♫ **Conf:** Class 80 Board 50 Thtr 450 Del from €130 **Services:** Lift Night porter **Parking:** 120 **Notes:** LB Closed 25-26 Dec Civ Wed 250

LETTERKENNY
County Donegal   Map 1 C5

Radisson Blu Hotel Letterkenny

★★★★ 78% HOTEL

Paddy Harte Road - **tel:** 074 9194444
email: info.letterkenny@radissonblu.com **web:** www.radissonblu.ie/hotel-letterkenny
dir: *N14 into Letterkenny. At Polestar Rdbt take 1st exit, to hotel*

Letterkenny is an ideal base for visiting the many peninsulas of County Donegal. Within walking distance of the town and the retail parks, this hotel offers a range of very comfortable rooms that have all the facilities today's traveller expects. Guests can dine throughout the day in the popular Port Bar & Grill, or, in the evening, enjoy seafood delights and other interesting dishes in Brasserie TriBeCa. Well-equipped meeting rooms are available, together with a large conference and banqueting hall. The leisure facilities are complimentary to residents.

Rooms: 114 (5 family) ⟡ **S** fr €60; **D** fr €80 (incl. bkfst)* **Facilities:** STV WiFi ⓑ ⓠ Gym Sauna Steam room Sunbed Olympic weights room Xmas New Year **Conf:** Class 270 Board 80 Thtr 600 **Services:** Lift Night porter **Parking:** 150 **Notes:** LB Civ Wed 200

Downings Bay Hotel

★★★ 77% HOTEL

Downings - **tel:** 074 9155586 & 9155770 **email:** info@downingsbayhotel.com
web: www.downingsbayhotel.com
dir: *23m N of Letterkenny on R245. Hotel in village centre*

This long-established, friendly, family-run hotel is situated on Sheephaven Bay in the picturesque village of Downings. There is a cosy lobby lounge; J.C.'s a traditional-style bar where an extensive menu is available all day, and The Haven Restaurant which opens for dinner at peak times. The bedroom accommodation is spacious and all rooms are comfortable and well appointed. A popular location for families and within easy reach of a number of golf courses, this property hosts regular musical events, and there is a nightclub open at weekends. Guests have complimentary use of the local leisure centre, just a five-minute drive away.

Rooms: 40 (8 family) (4 smoking) ⟡ **S** €50–€80; **D** €90–€150 (incl. bkfst)*
Facilities: WiFi ⓑ ⓠ supervised Gym Sauna Steam room Indoor adventure play area ♫ New Year Child facilities **Conf:** Class 175 Board 50 Thtr 350 Del from €100 **Services:** Lift Night porter Air con **Parking:** 40 **Notes:** Closed 24-26 Dec RS Nov-Mar closed Mon-Wed Civ Wed 80

LIMERICK
County Limerick
Map 1 B3

Limerick Strand Hotel
★★★★ 80% ⊛ HOTEL

Ennis Road - **tel:** 061 421800 **email:** info@strandlimerick.ie **web:** www.strandlimerick.ie
dir: *From Shannon/Galway follow N18 to Limerick. At Coonagh rdbt follow Ennis Rd into city centre. Hotel on right on banks of river*

This hotel enjoys stunning views over the River Shannon, and all bedrooms are spacious and fitted to a high standard. The public areas make the most of the views, with meeting rooms on the penthouse level. All-day dining is available in the bar, with innovative evening meals served in the River Restaurant. Secure parking is available at a reduced rate for residents.

Rooms: 184 (13 family) ⋔ **Facilities:** STV FTV WiFi ⇗ ⊛ supervised Gym ♫ Xmas New Year **Conf:** Class 400 Board 50 Thtr 600 **Services:** Lift Night porter Air con **Parking:** 200 **Notes:** Civ Wed 450

Radisson Blu Hotel & Spa Limerick
★★★★ 78% HOTEL

Ennis Road - **tel:** 061 456200
email: info.limerick@radissonblu.com **web:** www.radissonblu.com/en/hotel-limerick
dir: *On N18 (Ennis Rd), close to Limerick city centre*

Situated between Limerick and Shannon International Airport, this smart hotel is set in 20 acres of parkland and has comfortable lounge areas and a choice of dining options; the contemporary Porters Restaurant offers fine dining, while more casual eating can be enjoyed in the Quench Bar. Bedrooms are comfortable, spacious and very well appointed. Guests have complimentary use of the Thermal Suite and outdoor Canadian hot tub in the Rain Spa. There are extensive leisure and corporate facilities, including seven meeting rooms with capacity up to 800 delegates.

Rooms: 154 (26 family) (43 GF) ⋔ **S** fr €79; **D** fr €79* **Facilities:** Spa STV FTV WiFi ⇗ ⊛ ☃ Gym Hair salon Cold fog & tropical rain showers Laconium Steam room Elite training Sauna ♫ Xmas New Year Child facilities **Conf:** Class 400 Board 100 Thtr 800 Del from €114 **Services:** Lift Night porter **Parking:** 220 **Notes:** LB Civ Wed 300

LISDOONVARNA
County Clare
Map 1 B3

Sheedy's Country House Hotel
★★★ 78% ⊛⊛ HOTEL

tel: 065 7074026
email: info@sheedys.com **web:** www.sheedys.com
dir: *200mtrs from The Square in town centre*

Dating in part from the 17th century and set in an unrivalled town centre location on the edge of The Burren, this house is full of character and has an intimate atmosphere. Family run by hosts Martina and John Sheedy, fine award-winning cuisine can be enjoyed in the contemporary restaurant, and the bedrooms are spacious and well appointed. Sheedy's makes an ideal base for touring, as it is close to Doolin, Lahinch Golf Course, and the Cliffs of Moher.

Rooms: 11 (1 family) (5 GF) ⋔ **Facilities:** STV FTV WiFi ⇗ **Parking:** 20 **Notes:** Closed mid Oct-Apr

LUCAN
County Dublin
Map 1 D4

Lucan Spa Hotel
★★★ 70% HOTEL

tel: 01 6280494
email: info@lucanspahotel.ie **web:** www.lucanspahotel.ie
dir: *At N4 junct 4a, approx 11km from city centre*

Set in its own grounds and 20 minutes from Dublin Airport, at the start of the M4, the main artery to the west of Ireland, the Lucan Spa is a lovely Georgian house with modern extensions. Originally built to accommodate guests taking the waters at the former spa, the building retains many of the architectural features of the period. Bedrooms vary in size but are well equipped. There are two dining options: dinner is served in Honora D Restaurant, and The Ballyneety is for more casual dining. The event space has a good reputation for weddings and conference business.

Rooms: 71 (15 family) (9 GF) ⋔ **S** €50–€150; **D** €65–€199 (incl. bkfst) **Facilities:** STV FTV WiFi ⇗ Access to Lucan Golf Club opp hotel **Conf:** Class 250 Board 80 Thtr 600 Del from €87 **Services:** Lift Night porter Air con **Parking:** 200 **Notes:** LB Closed 24-26 Dec Civ Wed 250

REPUBLIC OF IRELAND

Follow the AA
twitter: @TheAA_Lifestyle
facebook: www.facebook.com/TheAAUK

MACREDDIN
County Wicklow

Map 1 D3

BrookLodge & Macreddin Village
★★★★ 82% ◎◎ HOTEL

tel: 0402 36444
email: info@brooklodge.com **web:** www.brooklodge.com
dir: *N11 to Rathnew, R752 to Rathdrum, R753 to Aughrim, follow signs to Macreddin Village*

BrookLodge is a luxurious country-house hotel in a village-style setting which includes an 18-hole golf course, a country pub, a café and food shop. There is a choice of dining options – the award-winning Strawberry Tree Restaurant specialising in organic and wild foods, and a more casual Italian restaurant specialising in southern Italian cuisine. Macreddin Village has 86 bedrooms, many of which feature four-poster or sleigh beds, as well as window seats from which you can admire the stunning views. There are also bedrooms in BrookHall, tailored for guests attending weddings and conferences. The Wells Spa offers extensive treatments and leisure facilities, and there are many mapped walks available, affording you the opportunity to enjoy the Wicklow countryside.

Rooms: 86 (32 annexe) (27 family) (4 GF) ⛵ **S** fr €100; **D** fr €140 (incl. bkfst)*
Facilities: Spa STV FTV WiFi ⓑ ⓧ ⛳ Putting green Gym Archery Clay pigeon shooting Off road driving Cycling Walking New Year **Conf:** Class 100 Board 50 Thtr 250 **Services:** Lift Night porter Air con **Parking:** 200 **Notes:** Closed 24-25 Dec Civ Wed 150

MALLOW
County Cork

Map 1 B2

Springfort Hall Country House Hotel
★★★ 77% ◎ HOTEL

tel: 022 21278
email: stay@springfort-hall.com **web:** www.springfort-hall.com
dir: *N20 onto R581 at Two Pot House, hotel 500mtrs on right*

This 18th-century country manor is tucked away amid tranquil woodlands located just six kilometres from Mallow. There is an attractive oval dining room, a cosy drawing room and lounge bar where bistro-style food is served. The spacious bedrooms are comfortably furnished. There are extensive banqueting and conference facilities, and local amenities include championship golf courses, fishing on the Blackwater and Ballyhass Lakes, and horseracing at Cork.

Rooms: 49 (5 family) (17 GF) ⛵ **Facilities:** STV FTV WiFi ⓑ ♫ **Conf:** Class 180 Board 50 Thtr 360 **Services:** Night porter **Parking:** 200 **Notes:** Closed 23-26 Dec Civ Wed 300

MAYNOOTH
County Kildare

Map 1 D4

Carton House Hotel Golf & Spa
★★★★ 79% HOTEL

tel: 01 5052000 **email:** sales@cartonhouse.com **web:** www.cartonhouse.com
dir: *From Dublin Airport follow M50, N4 then M4 towards Sligo. At junct 6 take R449 to Leixlip. Continue to R148. Located 4m outside Maynooth*

Carton House dates from 1739 and many of the features of that period have been retained. While some suites of the hotel are in the original house, most of the bedrooms are in a modern block to the side. They are all spacious and comfortable, fitted out to a high standard. There are a number of dining options on the estate, including The Coach House in the golf club and The Linden Tree for more formal evening dining. Set in over a 1,000 acres, there are plenty of walks and cycle paths to be enjoyed. The property is surrounded by two golf courses and has a strong reputation for its many sport training facilities and spa treatment rooms.

Rooms: 165 (12 family) (46 GF) ⛵ **Facilities:** Spa STV WiFi ⓑ ⓧ ⛳ 36 Putting green ♨ Fishing Gym Sauna Steam room Xmas New Year **Conf:** Class 280 Board 90 Thtr 500 Del from €145 **Services:** Lift Night porter **Parking:** 500 **Notes:** Civ Wed 280

MOVILLE
County Donegal

Map 1 C6

Redcastle Hotel, Golf & Spa Resort
★★★★ 79% ◎ HOTEL

Inishowen Peninsula - **tel:** 074 9385555
email: info@redcastlehotel.com **web:** www.redcastlehotel.com
dir: *On R238 between Derry & Greencastle*

Perched beside the sea in mature parkland just outside Redcastle, this hotel has an enviable position on the Inishowen Peninsula with great views over Lough Foyle. It offers spacious, well-equipped bedrooms; some on the ground floor and some with balconies. The public areas include a range of relaxing lounges with an atmospheric bar where food is served throughout the day, and a large terrace for relaxing when the weather permits. The Edge Restaurant is right on the water's edge, and offers a well-thought-out menu with interesting options. There is a conference centre and an extensive leisure club offering spa treatments. The hotel has its own private 9-hole golf course, with sea fishing available from the shore.

Rooms: 93 (17 family) (16 GF) (8 smoking) ⛵ **S** €74–€124; **D** €98–€198 (incl. bkfst)* **Facilities:** Spa STV FTV WiFi ⓑ ⓧ ⛳ 9 Putting green Fishing ♨ Gym Sauna Steam room ♫ New Year **Conf:** Class 150 Board 50 Thtr 300 Del from €119 **Services:** Lift Night porter **Parking:** 232 **Notes:** LB Closed 25 Dec Civ Wed 250

MULRANY	Map 1 A4
County Mayo	

Mulranny Park Hotel

★★★★ 79% ◉◉ HOTEL

tel: 098 36000
email: info@mulrannyparkhotel.ie **web:** www.mulrannyparkhotel.ie
dir: R311 from Castlebar to Newport onto N59. Hotel on right

Set on an elevated site, this property has commanding views over Clew Bay. Originally a railway hotel dating from the late 1800s, it has a range of smart public rooms that retain many of the period features. Bedrooms vary in size but are comfortable and decorated in a contemporary style. Dinner in the Nephin Restaurant is a highlight of any stay, with casual dining available throughout the day in the Waterfront Bar. A programme of activities is offered weekly for resident guests, in addition to a well appointed leisure club.

Rooms: 60 (25 family) ↰ **S** €45–€120; **D** €90–€190 (incl. bkfst)* **Facilities:** WiFi ⧉ ⊛ supervised Gym Steam room Health & beauty Hairdressing Cycling ♫ New Year Child facilities **Conf:** Class 140 Board 50 Thtr 400 **Services:** Lift Night porter **Parking:** 200 **Notes:** LB Closed 4-21 Jan Civ Wed 150

NAVAN	Map 1 D4
County Meath	

Bellinter House

★★★★ 75% ◉◉ COUNTRY HOUSE HOTEL

tel: 046 9030900
web: www.bellinterhouse.com
dir: N3 towards Navan, left at Tara Na Ri pub, 5 mins, hotel on right

Set in rolling parkland, this Palladian-style Georgian house dates from 1749 and retains much of the scale and architectural features of the period. The decor however is very contemporary in the public areas where comfort and relaxation is key. Bedrooms are mainly set around two courtyards and feature a minimalist approach to decoration, with lots of timber and white surfaces. Dinner in Eden Restaurant in the vaulted basement is a delight, with more casual fare served in the bar throughout the day. Spa treatments are available in The Bathhouse, with weddings and other events held in the Refectory.

Rooms: 34 (5 family) (12 GF) **Facilities:** Spa STV FTV WiFi Fishing Steam room Sauna **Conf:** Class 30 Board 24 Thtr 50 **Services:** Lift Night porter **Parking:** 80 **Notes:** Civ Wed 200

Red Stars

The AA Red Star rating denotes an Inspector's Choice hotel. They stand out as the very best in the British Isles and appear in highlighted panels throughout the guide.

NEWMARKET-ON-FERGUS	Map 1 B3
County Clare	

INSPECTOR'S CHOICE

Dromoland Castle Hotel

★★★★★ ◉◉ HOTEL

tel: 061 368144
email: sales@dromoland.ie **web:** www.dromoland.ie
dir: N18 to Ennis/Galway from Shannon for 8km to 'Dromoland Interchange' signed Quin. Take slip road left, 4th exit at 1st rdbt, 2nd exit at 2nd rdbt. Hotel 500mtrs on left

Dromoland Castle, dating from the early 18th century, stands on a 375-acre estate and offers extensive indoor leisure activities and outdoor pursuits. The professional team are wholly committed to caring for guests, in a warm and informal manner. The thoughtfully equipped bedrooms and suites vary in style, but they all provide excellent levels of comfort. The magnificent public rooms, warmed by log fires, are no less impressive. The hotel has several dining options; the elegant fine-dining Earl of Thomond Restaurant, where award-winning cuisine is available together with the less formal Fig Tree in the golf clubhouse, and The Gallery, which offers a menu suitable for all day dining.

Rooms: 98 (20 family) ↰ **S** €252–€864; **D** €252–€864 (incl. bkfst)* **Facilities:** Spa STV WiFi ⧉ ⊛ supervised ⅃ 18 Putting green ≋ Fishing Gym Archery Clay shooting Mountain bikes Falconry Pony & trap Golf academy ♫ Xmas New Year **Conf:** Class 220 Board 80 Thtr 450 **Services:** Lift Night porter **Parking:** 120 **Notes:** LB Civ Wed 70

NEWTOWNMOUNTKENNEDY	Map 1 D3
County Wicklow	

Druids Glen Hotel & Golf Resort

★★★★★ 85% ◉◉ HOTEL

tel: 01 2870800
email: reservations@druidsglenresort.com **web:** www.druidsglenresort.com
dir: N11 S'bound, off at Newtownmountkennedy. Follow signs for hotel

This hotel, situated between the Wicklow Mountains and the coast, has two fabulous golf courses and a range of smart indoor leisure facilities and treatment rooms. Bedrooms have been equipped to the highest standard and service is delivered in a most professional manner, and always with a smile. Guests may choose to dine in Druid's Brasserie or the more formal Flynn's Restaurant.

Rooms: 145 (79 family) (40 GF) **S** €155–€600; **D** €165–€600 (incl. bkfst) **Facilities:** Spa STV WiFi ⧉ ⊛ ⅃ 36 Putting green Gym Sauna Steam room Indoor playroom Outdoor playground Giant games ♫ Xmas New Year Child facilities **Conf:** Class 160 Board 50 Thtr 400 Del from €235 **Services:** Lift Night porter Air con **Parking:** 400 **Notes:** Civ Wed 220

NEWTOWNMOUNTKENNEDY *continued*

Parkview Hotel

★★★ 70% HOTEL

Main Street · **tel:** 01 2015600
email: info@parkviewhotel.ie **web:** www.parkviewhotel.ie
dir: *Phone for detailed directions*

Located in the heart of the Wicklow village of Newtownmountkennedy, 35 kilometres south of Dublin, this modern hotel offers a range of room styles, all of which are very comfortably appointed. The Park Lounge is the hotel main bar, which enjoys a solid reputation for casual dining among the local community. Synnott's Restaurant opens for dinner at peak periods and for private use. The Park Room is a popular wedding venue, catering for events up to 250 guests. Secure parking is available to the rear.

Rooms: 60 (4 family) **Facilities:** STV FTV WiFi Xmas **Conf:** Class 250 Thtr 500
Services: Lift Night porter **Parking:** 60 **Notes:** Civ Wed 300

ORANMORE
County Galway
Map 1 B3

The Coach House Hotel

★★★ 68% ◉ HOTEL

Main Street · **tel:** 091 788367 & 483693
email: info@coachhousehotel.ie **web:** www.coachhousehotel.ie
dir: *In village centre next to petrol station*

A renovated former coach house in the centre of the Oranmore, this property is probably better known locally as Basilico Restaurant and Bar, a well-established Italian restaurant, with great authenticity to its menu and cookery. Bedrooms are warm and comfortable and undergoing redecoration. There's limited parking but plenty is available around the town. This is an ideal base for touring The Burren and the city of Galway.

Rooms: 16 (2 family) ⬧ S €49–€250; D €59–€250* **Facilities:** WiFi HL New Year
Parking: 14

PORTMARNOCK
Dublin
Map 1 D4

Portmarnock Hotel and Golf Links

★★★★ 81% ◉◉ HOTEL

tel: 01 8460611
email: info@portmarnock.com **web:** www.portmarnock.com
dir: *Phone for detailed directions*

With its origins as the summer residence of the Jameson family of Irish Whiskey, the Portmarnock Hotel is benefiting from a change of ownership. There is a total refurbishment programme in place resulting in well-appointed bedrooms and suites. They are serious about their food here, with a number of outlets that are sure to please. The headline act is The 1780, a contemporary dining space overlooking the gardens through picture windows. There are a number of event spaces and meeting rooms, but the property is best known for its championship golf links that surrounds the hotel.

Rooms: 131 **Facilities:** ⌁

RATHNEW
County Wicklow
Map 1 D3

Tinakilly Country House

★★★★ 78% ◉◉ HOTEL

tel: 0404 69274
email: info@tinakilly.ie **web:** www.tinakilly.ie
dir: *Follow N11/M11 to Rathnew, then R750 towards Wicklow. Entrance to hotel approx 500mtrs from village on left*

Located south of the village, there is an elegant oak-lined avenue leading to Tinakilly House, a Victorian mansion steeped in history. It was built in 1884 for Captain Robert Halpin, Master Mariner and Commander of SS *Great Eastern* who laid the telegraphic cable joining Europe to America. There are lovely garden views from the lounges that have open log fires. Some of the comfortable bedrooms and suites enjoy views over the Irish Sea and bird sanctuary at Broadlough Coastal Lagoon. Furnishings throughout reflect the Victorian period yet provide all modern comforts. Fine dining is available in the Brunell Restaurant, and snacks and afternoon tea are served in the drawing room, or in pods on the lawn when weather permits.

Rooms: 51 (15 family) (14 GF) ⬧ **Facilities:** STV WiFi ⬧ ⬧ New Year **Conf:** Class 70 Board 35 Thtr 90 **Services:** Lift Night porter **Parking:** 60 **Notes:** Closed 24-26 Dec Civ Wed 100

Hunter's Hotel

★★★ 78% ◉ HOTEL

tel: 0404 40106
email: reception@hunters.ie **web:** www.hunters.ie
dir: *1.5km from village of Rathnew. From Dublin, N11/M11 exit 15, turn left at bridge in Ashford, follow signs to hotel*

One of Ireland's oldest coaching inns, this charming country house was built in 1720 and is full of character and atmosphere. The comfortable bedrooms have wonderful views over prize-winning gardens that border the River Vartry. The restaurant has a good reputation for carefully prepared dishes which make the best use of high quality local produce, including fruit and vegetables from the hotel's own garden.

Rooms: 16 (2 family) (2 GF) **Facilities:** WiFi **Conf:** Class 40 Board 16 Thtr 40
Parking: 50 **Notes:** LB Closed 24-26 Dec Civ Wed 40

RECESS (SRAITH SALACH)
County Galway
Map 1 A4

Ballynahinch Castle Hotel

★★★★ 81% ◉◉ COUNTRY HOUSE HOTEL

tel: 095 31006
email: info@ballynahinch-castle.com **web:** www.ballynahinchcastle.com
dir: *Phone for detailed directions*

Sitting on a 450-acre estate of woodland and rivers in the heart of Connemara, Ballynahinch Castle is a warm and welcoming country house that is sure to impress. It changed hands a few years ago and benefited from a very tasteful renovation programme. The ownership may have changed, but many of the knowledgeable and hospitable management and staff are still in place. Bedroom suites are in a traditional country-house style, many have river views. The hotel has a number of relaxing lounges, some with real log fires, and an atmospheric Fisherman's Pub offering high-end food throughout the day. Dinner in the Owenmore Restaurant is the highlight of a stay, where menus reflect both the seasons and what is best from local producers.

Rooms: 145

INSPECTOR'S CHOICE

Lough Inagh Lodge Hotel

★★★ ◉◉ COUNTRY HOUSE HOTEL

Inagh Valley - **tel:** 095 34706
email: inagh@iol.ie **web:** www.loughinaghlodgehotel.ie
dir: *From Recess take R344 towards Kylemore*

Dating from 1880, this former fishing lodge is akin to a family home, where guests are encouraged to relax and enjoy the peace. Overlooking Lough Inagh, and situated amid the mountains of Connemara, it is in an ideal location for those who enjoy walking and fishing. Bedrooms are individually decorated, some with spacious seating areas, and each is dedicated to an Irish literary figure. There are two cosy lounges where welcoming turf fires are often lit. Informal dining from a bar menu is available during the day. Dinner is a highlight of a visit to the lodge; the menus feature locally sourced produce cooked with care – seafood is a speciality.

Rooms: 13 (1 family) (4 GF) **Facilities:** WiFi Fly fishing Cycling **Conf:** Class 20 Board 20 Thtr 20 **Services:** Air con **Parking:** 16 **Notes:** Closed mid Dec–mid Mar Civ Wed 50

ROSCOMMON	Map 1 B4
County Roscommon	

Kilronan Castle Estate & Spa

★★★★ 80% ◉◉ HOTEL

Ballyfarnon - **tel:** 071 9618000
email: enquiries@kilronancastle.ie **web:** www.kilronancastle.ie
dir: *M4 to N4, exit R299 towards R207 (Droim ar Snámh/Drumsna/Droim). Exit R207 for R280, turn left into Keadue Rd (R284)*

Located on the shores of Lough Meelagh, this restored Gothic revival castle dates from the early 19th century. It is set in almost 50 acres of rolling park and woodland. Great care has been taken in its restoration, with many of the fine bedrooms and suites housed in the adjoining, sympathetically-built modern block. The Drawing Room is now a cosy lounge serving food throughout the day. The highlight is dinner in the Douglas Hyde Restaurant, where the friendly professional team go to great lengths to offer fine food in elegant surroundings. The impressive spa has a wide range of treatments on offer. There is also a leisure centre together with a wonderful events centre accessed by a tunnel from the main building.

Rooms: 85 (9 family) ✆ **S** €99–€179; **D** €119–€199 (incl. bkfst) **Facilities:** Spa FTV WiFi ⊛ Gym ♫ Xmas New Year **Conf:** Class 360 Board 60 Thtr 500 Del from €189 **Services:** Lift Night porter Air con **Parking:** 300 **Notes:** LB Civ Wed 200

ROSSCARBERY	Map 1 B2
County Cork	

Celtic Ross Hotel

★★★ 81% ◉ HOTEL

tel: 023 88 48722
email: info@celticross.com **web:** www.celticrosshotel.com
dir: *N71 from Cork, through Bandon towards Clonakilty. Follow signs for Skibbereen*

This hotel is situated on the edge of Rosscarbery overlooking the bay. Public areas are relaxing places, with a variety of lounges, a library, and the Warren Suite which enjoys panoramic views as far as Galley Head. Food is available in the bar throughout the day and evening in the Kingfisher Bar and Bistro. Afternoon tea is a speciality that can be booked in advance. The spacious bedrooms are comfortable and well appointed, many with wonderful sea views. There are extensive leisure and banqueting facilities plus music and dancing events on a regular basis. This is a property that enjoys a strong reputation in the region for wedding celebrations and other family occasions.

Rooms: 66 (5 family) ✆ **Facilities:** Spa FTV WiFi ⅋ ⊛ supervised Gym ♫ New Year **Conf:** Class 200 Board 60 Thtr 300 **Services:** Lift Night porter **Parking:** 250 **Notes:** LB Closed 24-26 Dec Civ Wed 250

ROSSLARE	Map 1 D2
County Wexford	

INSPECTOR'S CHOICE

Kelly's Resort Hotel & Spa

★★★★ ◉◉ HOTEL

tel: 053 9132114
email: info@kellys.ie **web:** www.kellys.ie
dir: *N25 onto Rosslare/Wexford road, signed Rosslare Strand*

The Kelly family have been offering hospitality here since 1895, where together with a dedicated team, they provide very professional and friendly service. The resort overlooks the sandy beach and is within minutes of the ferry port at Rosslare. Bedrooms are thoughtfully equipped and comfortably furnished. The extensive leisure facilities include a smart spa, swimming pools, a crèche, young adults' programme and spacious well-tended gardens. Both the eating options, La Marine Bistro and Beaches restaurant, have been awarded AA Rosettes for the quality of their cuisine.

Rooms: 118 (15 family) (20 GF) ✆ **Facilities:** Spa STV FTV WiFi ⊛ supervised ⫞ Putting green ⛳ ⛳ Gym Bowls Badminton Crazy golf Table tennis Snooker Sauna Steam room ♫ **Conf:** Class 30 Board 20 Thtr 30 **Services:** Lift Night porter **Parking:** 150 **Notes:** LB Closed early Dec–late Feb

SALTHILL

See **Galway**

SKIBBEREEN
County Cork

Map 1 B2

West Cork Hotel

★★★ 77% @ HOTEL

Ilen Street - tel: 028 21277
email: info@westcorkhotel.com **web:** www.westcorkhotel.com
dir: *In Skibbereen, N71 into Bridge St, with Baby Hannah's pub on left to right into Ilen St, hotel on right. From Cork Rd, N71 to Schull, left at next rdbt towards town centre, hotel on left*

This charming hotel was built in 1902 and is family owned and run. It is located in the centre of town beside the River Ilen, where guests can enjoy an outdoor drink while sitting on the historic old West Cork railway bridge. There is a cosy lounge with log fire, and furnishings and decor successfully mix the best of old and new. Food is available throughout the day in the Railway Bar and in the evening in Kennedy's Restaurant. Bedrooms vary in size and are comfortably furnished, some have riverside views. There are extensive banqueting facilities, and ample parking at the rear of the hotel.

Rooms: 49 (8 family) ☎ **S** €55–€90; **D** €69–€149 (incl. bkfst)* **Facilities:** FTV WiFi Use of facilities at Skibbereen Sports Centre **Conf:** Class 20 Board 24 Thtr 250 **Services:** Lift Night porter **Parking:** 100 **Notes:** LB Closed 24-28 Dec Civ Wed 300

SLANE
County Meath

Map 1 D4

Conyngham Arms Hotel

★★★ 74% @ HOTEL

Main Street - tel: 041 984444 **email:** info@conynghamarms.ie
web: www.conynghamarms.ie
dir: *Exit 10 for Navan from M1. Through village, hotel on the left of Main St*

This 17th-century coaching inn has been beautifully refurbished to a high standard of comfort and quality, and is situated in the centre of the village, close to Slane Castle, the World Heritage Site of Newgrange and many other historical sites. The bedrooms vary in size due to the age of the house and are very smartly appointed with guest comfort in mind. Food is bistro-style featuring the best of local produce, and breads and confectionery are made in their own bakery, served throughout the day in the cosy bar with its open log fire. Private off-street parking is available.

Rooms: 15 ☎ **S** €50–€80; **D** €80–€130 (incl. bkfst)* **Facilities:** FTV WiFi
Conf: Class 100 Board 50 Thtr 200 **Services:** Night porter **Parking:** 20 **Notes:** LB Civ Wed 200

Find out more
about the AA Hotel of the Year
for Northern Ireland on page 18

SLIGO
County Sligo

Map 1 B5

Radisson Blu Hotel & Spa Sligo

★★★★ 79% @ HOTEL

Rosses Point Road, Ballincar - tel: 071 9140008
email: info.sligo@radissonblu.com **web:** www.radissonblu.com/en/hotel-sligo
dir: *From N4 into Sligo to main bridge. Take R291 on left. Hotel 1.5m on right*

Located four kilometres north of the town overlooking Sligo Bay, this contemporary hotel offers standard and business class bedrooms which are all appointed with up-to-date facilities. The Benwiskin bar offers tasty casual dining throughout the day, and for more formal dining in the evening there's Classiebawn Restaurant, featuring local ingredients cooked with international flair. Residents are welcome to use the Healthstyles leisure club during their stay, and relaxing treatment facilities are also available in the Solas Spa. A range of 11 rooms are provided for meetings and events.

Rooms: 132 (13 family) (32 GF) ☎ **S** €89–€220; **D** €99–€300 (incl. bkfst)*
Facilities: Spa STV WiFi ⓦ Gym Steam room Thermal suite Sauna ♪ Xmas New Year **Conf:** Class 420 Board 40 Thtr 750 **Services:** Lift Night porter Air con **Parking:** 320 **Notes:** Civ Wed 500

Sligo Park Hotel & Leisure Club

★★★★ 79% @ HOTEL

Pearse Road, F91 Y762 - tel: 071 9190400
email: sligo@leehotels.com **web:** www.sligopark.com
dir: *N4 to Sligo take exit S2 Sligo South Carrowroe/R287. Follow signs for Sligo. Hotel 1m on right*

Set in seven acres of parkland on the southern outskirts of the town, this hotel is well positioned for visiting the many attractions of the northwest and Yeats' Country. Bedrooms come in a range of styles, but all are spacious and appointed to a high standard. There are two dining options, the award-winning Hazelwood Restaurant for dinner, and the Rathanna Bar for carvery lunch and all-day dining. Guests have full use of the leisure facilities.

Rooms: 136 (10 family) (52 GF) ☎ **S** €89–€189; **D** €109–€199 (incl. bkfst)*
Facilities: WiFi ⓦ supervised ⌇ Gym Holistic treatment suite Plunge pool Steam room ♪ Xmas New Year **Conf:** Class 290 Board 80 Thtr 520 **Services:** Lift Night porter **Parking:** 200 **Notes:** LB RS 24-26 Hotel services for residents only Dec Civ Wed 520

The Glasshouse

★★★★ 79% HOTEL

Swan Point - tel: 071 9194300
email: info@theglasshouse.ie **web:** www.theglasshouse.ie
dir: *From N4 right at 2nd junct. Left at Post Office into Wine St. Hotel on right*

This landmark building in the centre of town makes a bold statement with its cutting edge design and contemporary decor. Bright cheerful colours are used throughout the hotel; the bedrooms have excellent facilities including LCD TVs, workspace and internet access. There is a buzzing café bar serving food throughout the day, with a board walk for alfresco riverside dining. More formal evening dining takes place in the Kitchen restaurant. Secure underground parking is available together with a fitness suite.

Rooms: 116 ☎ **S** €360; **D** €500 (incl. bkfst) **Facilities:** STV FTV WiFi ⓦ Gym ♪ New Year **Conf:** Class 100 Board 60 Thtr 120 **Services:** Lift Night porter Air con **Parking:** 250 **Notes:** Closed 25-26 Dec RS 24 Dec closes at 7pm Civ Wed 120

Castle Dargan Hotel

★★★★ 76% 🏨 HOTEL

Ballygawley - tel: 071 9118080
email: info@castledargan.com **web:** www.castledargan.com
dir: Exit N4 (Dublin to Sligo road), to Collooney rdbt, 3rd exit to Ballygawley

With its origins in the stables of Castle Dargan House, this hotel is currently celebrating its tenth year in business. Bedrooms are well appointed with all the facilities expected by today's traveller; the majority are in the main building, and four in the original manor house. Surrounded by a Darren Clarke designed golf course, the property also features the Icon Spa where a wide range of treatments are on offer. Dinner in the award-winning Hall Door restaurant is a real treat, with more casual options served from noon in the Middleton bar. Ballygawley is a 10-minute drive from Sligo, and makes an ideal base for touring the county and North Mayo. The hotel has a good reputation for hosting wedding celebrations.

Rooms: 42 (16 annexe) (16 family) (12 GF) 🐾 **S** €69–€95; **D** €79–€170 (incl. bkfst)*
Facilities: Spa STV FTV WiFi ⌕ ⚲ 18 Putting green ♫ New Year **Conf:** Class 100 Board 66 Thtr 320 **Services:** Lift Night porter **Parking:** 200 **Notes:** LB Civ Wed 120

STRAFFAN	Map 1 D4
County Kildare	

INSPECTOR'S CHOICE

The K Club

★★★★★ 🏅🏅 COUNTRY HOUSE HOTEL

tel: 01 6017200
email: sales@kclub.ie **web:** www.kclub.ie
dir: From Dublin take N4, exit for R406, hotel on right in Straffan

The K Club is set in 550 acres of rolling woodland. There are two magnificent championship golf courses, and a spa facility that complements the truly luxurious hotel that is the centrepiece of the resort. Public areas, suites and bedrooms are opulently furnished, and many have views of the formal gardens that lead down to the banks of the River Liffey. Additional rooms and family suites are a feature of the Liffey Wing. Dining options include the elegant River Room, with more informal dining options offered in Legends in the Arnold Palmer Golf Clubhouse, and in The K Thai Restaurant in The Smurfit Clubhouse. The K Club was home of the 2016 Irish Open, and the Ryder Cup in 2006.

Rooms: 134 (30 family) (18 GF) 🐾 **Facilities:** Spa STV FTV WiFi ⌕ ⚲ supervised ⚲ 36 Putting green ♫ Fishing ⚲ Gym Beauty salon Fishing tuition Clay pigeon shooting Horse riding Falconry ♫ Xmas New Year **Conf:** Class 180 Board 160 Thtr 460 **Services:** Lift Night porter **Parking:** 200 **Notes:** LB Civ Wed 250

Barberstown Castle

★★★★ 78% HOTEL

tel: 01 6288157 **email:** info@barberstowncastle.ie **web:** www.barberstowncastle.ie
dir: R406, follow signs for Barberstown

With parts dating from the 13th century, this castle hotel provides the very best in standards of comfort. The inviting public areas range from the original keep, which houses one of the restaurant areas, to the warmth of the drawing room and its cocktail bar. Bedrooms, some in a purpose-built wing, are elegantly appointed with relaxing seating areas. The airy Tea Room serves light meals throughout the day. The Castle is a popular venue for weddings and other family celebrations.

Rooms: 55 (2 family) (21 GF) 🐾 **Facilities:** STV WiFi ⌕ ♫ New Year **Conf:** Class 100 Board 72 Thtr 200 **Services:** Lift Night porter **Parking:** 200 **Notes:** Closed 24-26 Dec & Jan-Feb Civ Wed 280

THOMASTOWN	Map 1 C3
County Kilkenny	

INSPECTOR'S CHOICE

Mount Juliet Hotel

★★★★ 🏅🏅🏅 COUNTRY HOUSE HOTEL

tel: 056 7773000
email: info@mountjuliet.ie **web:** www.mountjuliet.ie
dir: M7 from Dublin, M9 towards Waterford, exit at junct 9 (Stoneyford) for hotel

The Mount Juliet Estate is set in 1,500 acres of parkland with a Jack Nicklaus-designed golf course and an equestrian centre. The elegant and spacious public areas of the house retain many original architectural features including ornate plasterwork and Adam fireplaces. Bedrooms and suites are elegant and comfortably appointed to a high standard, with more compact rooms available in the Clubhouse annexe, less than a five-minute walk away. Award-winning fine dining is on offer in the ornate Lady Helen Restaurant overlooking the river; with brasserie-style cuisine in Kendal's located in the golf clubhouse. The President's Bar is the location for all-day dining and the opportunity for alfresco dining when the weather permits. The hotel has an excellent spa and health club, with other country pursuits and activities also available. Major redevelopment work is planned for 2017-2018.

Rooms: 46 (14 annexe) (6 family) (7 GF) 🐾 **D** €159–€420 (incl. bkfst)*
Facilities: Spa STV WiFi ⌕ supervised ⚲ 18 Putting green ♫ Fishing ⚲ Gym Archery Cycling Equestrian Estate tours Xmas New Year **Conf:** Class 40 Board 20 Thtr 75 **Services:** Night porter **Parking:** 200 **Notes:** LB Civ Wed 100

THURLES
County Tipperary

Map 1 C3

Horse & Jockey Hotel

★★★★ 79% HOTEL

Horse & Jockey - tel: 0504 44192
email: info@horseandjockeyhotel.com web: www.horseandjockeyhotel.com
dir: 800mtrs from M8 junct 6

Located just off the motorway, this hotel offers smart and well-appointed bedrooms which are very comfortable. Dining options are the Enclosure Bar with a varied menu, and for more formal dining in the evening there is Silks Restaurant. There is also a well-equipped leisure centre with spa treatments and an equestrian themed gift shop. The conference facilities include 10 self-contained meeting rooms and a tiered auditorium seating 200 delegates.

Rooms: 67 (4 family) (15 GF) ↷ S €80–€100; D €109–€139 (incl. bkfst)
Facilities: Spa STV FTV WiFi ☃ supervised Gym Sauna Steam room Hydrotherapy area ♫ Conf: Class 24 Board 25 Thtr 200 Services: Lift Night porter Parking: 450
Notes: LB Closed 25 Dec RS 24 Dec no accommodation available

TRALEE
County Kerry

Map 1 A2

INSPECTOR'S CHOICE

Ballyseede Castle

★★★ ◉◉ HOTEL

tel: 066 7125799
email: info@ballyseedecastle.com web: www.ballyseedecastle.com
dir: On N21 just after junct of N21 & N22

Located within minutes of Tralee, Ballyseede Castle is steeped in history dating back to 1590 and has been fought over, lived in and lovingly restored to a high standard which still pays homage to its ancient grandeur. The spacious bedrooms are elegantly decorated; some have four-poster beds and antique furnishings. There are gracious reception rooms with original ornamental cornices and marble fireplaces, a carved oak library, a cosy bar and a splendid banqueting hall. The castle stands in its own grounds at the end of a winding drive through formal gardens and natural woodland. All-day dining is available in the atmospheric Pappy's Bar, with more formal evening dining in the award-winning O'Connell Room. The Castle is popular for hosting wedding celebrations and other family events.

Rooms: 23 (4 family) (10 GF) ↷ Facilities: STV FTV WiFi Services: Night porter
Parking: 180 Notes: Closed Jan-3 Mar Civ Wed 130

TULLOW
County Carlow

Map 1 D3

Mount Wolseley Hotel, Spa & Golf Resort

★★★★ 80% ◉ HOTEL

tel: 059 9180100 email: info@mountwolseley.ie web: www.mountwolseley.ie
dir: N7 from Dublin. In Naas, take N9 towards Carlow. In Castledermot left for Tullow

Located on a vast, well landscaped estate long associated with the Wolseley family of motoring fame, this hotel has much to offer. Public areas are very spacious with a large range of suites and bedrooms. Leisure pursuits include a championship golf course together with a popular health centre and Sanctuary Spa facilities. The hotel offers a number of dining options including Aaron's lounge, Fredrick's, and The Wolseley Lounge in the Golf Pavilion.

Rooms: 143 (10 family) (5 smoking) ↷ Facilities: Spa STV FTV WiFi ↕ HL ☃ supervised ⚐ 18 Putting green ⚑ Gym Childrens play areas Games room ♫ New Year Conf: Class 288 Board 70 Thtr 750 Services: Lift Night porter Air con Parking: 160 Notes: Closed 25-26 Dec Civ Wed 450

WATERFORD
County Waterford

Map 1 C2

Waterford Castle Hotel and Golf Club

★★★★ 80% ◉◉ COUNTRY HOUSE HOTEL

The Island, Ballinakill - tel: 051 878203 email: info@waterfordcastleresort.com
web: www.waterfordcastleresort.com
dir: From city centre continue onto Dunmore Rd for 2km. At hospital, take exit for Dunmore Rd. Left at 3rd set of lights. Free ferry available to hotel

This enchanting and picturesque castle dates back to Norman times and is located on a 320-acre island just a five-minute journey from the mainland by chain-link ferry. Bedrooms vary in style and size, but all are individually decorated and offer high standards of comfort. Dinner is served in the oak-panelled Munster Room, with breakfast taken in the conservatory. The 18-hole golf course is set in beautiful parkland where deer can be seen.

Rooms: 19 (3 family) (4 GF) S €109–€185; D €139–€250 (incl. bkfst)*
Facilities: STV FTV WiFi ↕ ⚐ 18 Putting green ⚑ ⚓ Clay shooting Falconry
Conf: Board 12 Del from €225 Services: Lift Night porter Parking: 50 Notes: LB
Closed 25 Dec & Jan RS Nov-Dec closed some days Civ Wed 120

Faithlegg House Hotel & Golf Resort

★★★★ 79% ◉◉ HOTEL

FBD Hotels & Resorts

Faithlegg - tel: 051 382000 email: reservations@fhh.ie web: www.faithlegg.com
dir: From Waterford follow Dunmore East Rd then Cheekpoint Rd

This hotel is surrounded by a parkland championship golf course and overlooks the estuary of the River Suir. The house has 14 original bedrooms, and the others in a more contemporary style are in an adjacent modern block. There is a range of comfortable lounges together with comprehensive meeting facilities. The leisure and treatment rooms are the perfect way to work off the food offered in the Roseville Restaurant. Lighter options are served throughout the day in the Piano Bar and in the golf clubhouse.

Rooms: 82 (6 family) (30 GF) ↷ Facilities: Spa FTV WiFi ☃ supervised ⚐ 18 Putting green ⚑ Gym Sauna Steam room New Year Conf: Class 90 Board 44 Thtr 180 Services: Lift Night porter Parking: 100 Notes: LB Closed 20-27 Dec Civ Wed 220

Granville Hotel

★★★★ 77% ⍟ HOTEL

The Quay - tel: 051 305555 **email:** stay@granville-hotel.ie **web:** www.granville-hotel.ie
dir: N25 to waterfront, hotel opposite clock tower

Centrally located on the quayside, this long established hotel was originally a coaching house. It is appointed to a very high standard, and retains much of its original character. The bedrooms come in a choice of standard or executive grades; all are well equipped and very comfortable. The Meagher Bar offers food throughout the day, and is a popular lunch venue with shoppers and the business community of Waterford. The Bianconi is an elegant restaurant where evening dinner is served. Friendliness and hospitality are hallmarks of a stay here.

Rooms: 100 (5 family) (10 smoking) ⌁ **S** €85–€160; **D** €100–€240 (incl. bkfst)*
Facilities: STV ♫ New Year Child facilities **Conf:** Class 150 Board 30 Thtr 200
Del from €140 **Services:** Lift Night porter **Parking:** 300 **Notes:** LB Closed 25-26 Dec
Civ Wed 200

Dooley's Hotel

★★★ 78% HOTEL

30 The Quay - tel: 051 873531 **email:** hotel@dooleys-hotel.ie **web:** www.dooleys-hotel.ie
dir: Adjacent to N25, on the Quay on R680

This hotel has been operating since the 19th century and is approaching its seventh decade in the hospitable hands of the Darrer family and their friendly team. It is situated on the quay overlooking the River Suir at the bus station, within walking distance of the railway station. Dinner is served in the New Ship Restaurant from an interesting menu, and casual dining is available in the Dry Dock Bar. Bedrooms are attractively decorated in keeping with the age of the property and offer a good standard of comfort. There is a public car park opposite the hotel.

Rooms: 110 (13 family) ⌁ **S** €75–€190; **D** €85–€200 **Facilities:** STV WiFi ♫
New Year **Conf:** Class 150 Board 100 Thtr 240 **Services:** Lift Night porter **Notes:** LB
Closed 25-27 Dec RS 24 Dec no accommodation available

WESTPORT	Map 1 B4
County Mayo	

Knockranny House Hotel

★★★★ 84% ⍟⍟ HOTEL

tel: 098 28600
email: info@khh.ie **web:** www.knockrannyhousehotel.ie
dir: On N5 (Westport to Castlebar road)

Perched high up overlooking Westport, with Clew Bay and Croagh Patrick in the distance, this fine family-run property is set in well landscaped grounds. The reception rooms take full advantage of the stunning views, and include The Brehon, a lounge where food is served throughout the day, and La Fougère, the award-winning restaurant that is a real treat. The comfortable furnishings create an inviting and relaxing atmosphere throughout the lounges, bar and restaurant. Bedrooms are very well appointed and come in a number of styles, with the newer ones being particularly spacious. Guests have complimentary use of extensive leisure facilities, with wellbeing treatments on offer in Spa Salveo. There are extensive banqueting and conference facilities.

Rooms: 97 (4 family) (18 GF) ⌁ **S** €90–€240; **D** €110–€350 (incl. bkfst)*
Facilities: Spa STV FTV WiFi ♫ HL ☼ Gym ♫ New Year **Conf:** Class 350 Board 40
Thtr 600 Del from €170 **Services:** Lift Night porter **Parking:** 150 **Notes:** LB
Closed 24-26 Dec Civ Wed 250

Hotel Westport Leisure, Spa & Conference

★★★★ 81% ⍟ HOTEL

Newport Road - tel: 098 25122 **email:** reservations@hotelwestport.ie
web: www.hotelwestport.ie
dir: N5 to Westport. Right at end of Castlebar St, 1st right before bridge, right at lights, left before church. Follow to end of street

Located in seven acres of woodlands and just a short riverside walk from the town, this hotel offers spacious public areas, including The Islands restaurant and the all-day Maple Bar. Bedrooms come in a range of styles, and are all comfortable and well appointed. Both leisure and business guests are well catered for by the enthusiastic and friendly team who go to great lengths to ensure residents enjoy their stay. This hotel is a popular choice with special interest groups and also families, who enjoy the leisure facilities, and in summer time, the children's club.

Rooms: 129 (67 family) (42 GF) (12 smoking) ⌁ **Facilities:** Spa STV WiFi ♫ HL ☼
supervised Gym Children's pool Lounger pool Steam room Sauna Fitness suite ♫
Xmas New Year **Conf:** Class 150 Board 60 Thtr 500 **Services:** Lift Night porter
Parking: 220 **Notes:** Civ Wed 350

Mill Times Hotel Westport

★★★ 73% HOTEL

Mill Street - tel: 098 29200 **email:** info@milltimeshotel.ie **web:** www.milltimeshotel.ie
dir: N59 signed town centre, in Bridge St keep in left lane, into Mill St, hotel on left

This family-run hotel is situated in the centre of Westport, close to the shops and many pubs of this bustling town. It is ideal for visiting north Mayo with its many beaches and golf courses, or as a base for climbing the pilgrimage mountain of Croagh Patrick. Bedrooms are traditional in style and public areas are comfortable. Uncle Sam's café bar is a lively venue with entertainment at weekends. Temptations Restaurant offers good value meals during the evening, and is the venue for a hearty breakfast. Underground parking is provided.

Rooms: 34 (6 family) **Facilities:** WiFi ♫ New Year **Conf:** Class 100 Board 60 Thtr 180
Services: Lift Night porter Air con **Parking:** 25 **Notes:** Closed 24-25 Dec Civ Wed 200

Silver Stars

The AA Silver Star rating denotes a Hotel that we highly recommend. They have a superior level of quality within their star rating, high standards of hospitality, service and cleanliness.

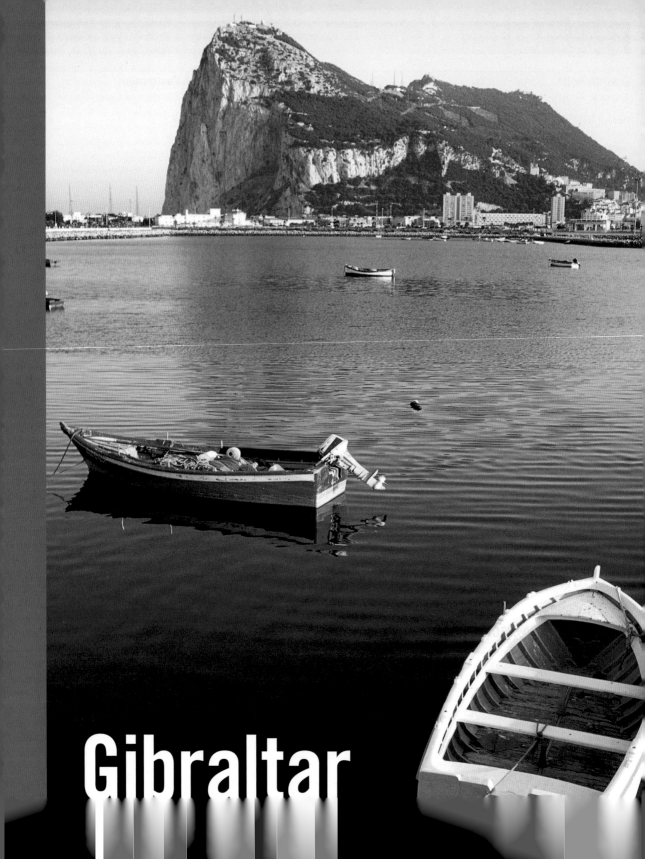

Gibraltar

GIBRALTAR

Sunborn Yacht Hotel

★★★★★ 83% 🌐 HOTEL

Ocean Village, GX11 1AA - **tel:** 00 350 200 16100
email: info@sunborngibraltar.com **web:** www.sunbornhotels.com/gibraltar
dir: *In Ocean Village Marina*

This floating hotel is situated in the Ocean Village Marina; the yacht has 189 individually designed bedrooms with up-to-date technology to control the lighting, heating, curtains and TVs; most of the rooms have views over the marina and some rooms have large terraces. The yacht has a range of spacious public areas that include a choice of dining options, lounges, bars, a casino, a spa and leisure facilities.

Rooms: 189 (1 family) (19 GF) 🐾 **S** £171–£297; **D** £185–£311 **Facilities:** Spa STV FTV WiFi ⌕ ⚲ Gym ♫ Xmas New Year **Conf:** Class 200 Board 80 Thtr 360 Del from £264 **Services:** Lift Air con **Parking:** 12 **Notes:** LB Civ Wed 80

Caleta Hotel

★★★★ 81% 🌐🌐 HOTEL

Sir Herbert Miles Road, PO Box 73, GX11 1AA - **tel:** 00 350 200 76501
email: reservations@caletahotel.gi
web: www.caletahotel.com
dir: *Enter Gibraltar via Spanish border & cross runway. At 1st rdbt turn left, hotel in 2km*

For travellers arriving in Gibraltar by plane, the Caleta is an eye-catching coastal landmark that can be spotted from the air if arriving from the east. This imposing and stylish hotel sits on a cliff top and all sea-facing rooms enjoy panoramic views across the straights to Morocco. Bedrooms vary in size and style; some have spacious balconies, TVs and mini bars. Several dining venues are available, but Nunos provides an award-winning, fine dining Italian experience. The staff are friendly and service is professional.

Rooms: 161 (89 annexe) (13 family) (80 smoking) **Facilities:** Spa STV FTV WiFi ⌕ ⚲ supervised Gym Health & beauty club Xmas New Year **Conf:** Class 172 Board 85 Thtr 216 **Services:** Lift Night porter Air con **Parking:** 32 **Notes:** Civ Wed 300

O'Callaghan Eliott Hotel

★★★★ 79% HOTEL

2 Governor's Parade, GX11 1AA - **tel:** 00 350 200 70500
email: eliott@ocallaghanhotels.com **web:** www.ocallaghanhotels.com
dir: *Contact for directions*

Located in the heart of the old town, this hotel provides a convenient central base for exploring the duty-free shopping district and other key attractions on foot. The bedrooms are stylish, spacious and well equipped. The roof-top restaurant provides stunning bay views, while guests can also take a swim in the roof-top pool.

Rooms: 123 🐾 **Facilities:** STV WiFi ⚲ Gym ♫ Xmas New Year **Conf:** Class 80 Board 70 Thtr 180 **Services:** Lift Night porter Air con **Parking:** 17 **Notes:** Civ Wed 120

The Rock Hotel

★★★★ 78% HOTEL

Europa Road, GX11 1AA - **tel:** 00 350 200 73000
email: reservations@rockhotel.gi **web:** www.rockhotelgibraltar.com
dir: *From airport follow tourist board signs. Hotel on left half way up Europa Rd*

Enjoying a prime elevated location directly below the Rock, this long-established art deco styled hotel has been the destination of celebrities and royalty since it was built in 1932. The bedrooms are spacious and well equipped, and many boast stunning coastal views that stretch across the Mediterranean to Morocco. The staff are friendly and service is delivered with flair and enthusiasm. Creative dinners and hearty breakfasts can be enjoyed in the stylish restaurant.

Rooms: 84 🐾 **S** £125–£190; **D** £125–£190* **Facilities:** STV WiFi ⚲ supervised Xmas New Year **Conf:** Class 120 Board 30 Thtr 150 Del from £160 **Services:** Lift Night porter Air con **Parking:** 40 **Notes:** LB Civ Wed 200

Dine & Stay
Restaurants with Rooms

Make the most of your evening at a top-notch restaurant, by staying over in one of our Restaurants with Rooms. Most of these restaurants have been awarded AA Rosettes for their food, and all offer overnight accommodation. This category of establishment is assessed under the AA's Guest Accommodation scheme, making them worthy of inclusion in this guide.

They all have star ratings, but these are Guest Accommodation scheme ratings, details of which can be found opposite, on our website: www.theaa.com/bed-and-breakfasts or in *The AA Bed and Breakfast Guide*.

Restaurant with Rooms defined

This is a destination restaurant offering overnight accommodation, with dining being the main business, and open to non-residents. The restaurant should offer a high standard of food and restaurant service at least five nights a week. A liquor licence is necessary and there is a maximum of 12 bedrooms.

Guest Accommodation Stars

AA Stars classify guest accommodation at five levels of quality, from one at the simplest, to five offering the highest quality. In order to achieve a one-Star rating an establishment must meet certain minimum entry requirements. For example:
- A cooked breakfast or substantial continental option is provided
- The proprietor and/or staff are available for your arrival, departure and at all meal times
- Once registered, guests have access to the establishment at all times unless previously notified
- All areas of operation meet minimum quality requirements for cleanliness, maintenance and hospitality as well as facilities and the delivery of services
- A dining room or similar eating area is available unless meals are served in bedrooms

To obtain a higher Star rating, an establishment must provide increased quality standards across all areas, with particular emphasis in four key areas:
• Cleanliness and housekeeping
• Hospitality and service
• Quality and condition of bedrooms, bathrooms and public rooms
• Food quality

There are also particular requirements in order for an establishment to achieve three, four or five Stars, for example:

Three Stars and above
• access to both sides of all beds for double occupancy
• bathrooms/shower rooms cannot be used by the proprietor
• there is a washbasin in every guest bedroom (either in the bedrooms or the en suite/private facility)

Four Stars
• half of bedrooms must be en suite or have private facilities

Five Stars
• all bedrooms must be en suite or have private facilities

Establishments applying for AA recognition are visited by one of the AA's qualified accommodation inspectors as a mystery guest. Inspections are a thorough test of the accommodation, food, and hospitality. The inspector completes a full report, resulting in a recommendation for the appropriate Star rating. After this first visit, the establishment will receive a regular visit to check that standards are maintained. If it changes hands, the new owners must re-apply for classification, as standards can change.
Guests can expect to find the following minimum standards at all levels:
• Pleasant and helpful welcome and service, and sound standards of housekeeping and maintenance
• Comfortable accommodation equipped to modern standards
• Bedding and towels changed for each new guest, and at least weekly if the room is taken for a long stay
• Adequate storage, heating, lighting and comfortable seating

• A sufficient hot water supply at reasonable times
• A full cooked breakfast. (If this is not provided, the fact must be advertised and a substantial continental breakfast must be offered.)

When an AA inspector has visited a property, and evaluated all the aspects of the accommodation for comfort, facilities, attention to detail and presentation, you can be confident the Star rating will help you make the right choice.

★ **Gold Star Award**
AA Gold Stars are awarded to the very best Guest Accommodation within the three, four, or five Star ratings.

★ **Silver Star Award**
Guest Accommodation with Silver Stars offer a superior level of quality within their Star rating, high standards of hospitality, service and cleanliness.

Symbols & abbreviations

As well as the symbols used in the rest of the guide, Restaurants with Rooms may use some of the following:

⊖	A very special dinner, with an emphasis on freshly prepared local ingredients
TVL	Lounge with television
Lounge	Lounge without television
TV4B	Television in four bedrooms
tea/coffee	Tea and coffee-making facilities
🔒	Secure storage
pri fac	Private facilities (not all rooms will be en suite; some may have private bathrooms. These will not be shared with any other guests, or the proprietor.)

| **ALSTON** | Map 18 NY74 |
| Cumbria | |

Alston House

★★★★ ☕ RESTAURANT WITH ROOMS

Townfoot CA9 3RN - **tel:** 01434 382200
email: alstonhouse@fsmail.net **web:** www.alstonhouse.co.uk
dir: On A686 opposite Spar garage

Located at the foot of the town, this family-owned restaurant with rooms provides well-equipped, stylish and comfortable accommodation. The kitchen serves both modern and traditional dishes with flair and creativity. Alston House runs a café during the day, serving light meals and afternoon teas.

Rooms: 7 en suite (3 fmly) **Facilities:** DVD tea/coffee Dinner available WiFi ⅃9 Fishing **Conf:** Max 70 Thtr 70 Class 30 Board 30 **Parking:** 20 **Notes:** Civ wed

| **ARLINGHAM** | Map 4 SO71 |
| Gloucestershire | |

The Old Passage Inn

★★★★★ ◉◉ ☕ RESTAURANT WITH ROOMS

Passage Road GL2 7JR - **tel:** 01452 740547
email: oldpassage@btconnect.com **web:** www.theoldpassage.com
dir: A38 onto B4071 through Frampton on Severn. 4m to Arlingham, through village to river

Delightfully located on the very edge of the River Severn, this relaxing restaurant with rooms combines high quality food with an air of tranquillity. Bedrooms and bathrooms are decorated in a modern style, and have a collection of welcome extras including a well-stocked mini-bar. The menu offers a wide range of seafood and shellfish dishes including crab, oysters and lobsters from Cornwall, kept alive in seawater tanks. An outdoor terrace is available in warmer months.

Rooms: 2 en suite **S** £80–£140; **D** £110–£140* **Facilities:** FTV DVD Lounge tea/coffee Dinner available WiFi ⌚ **Extras:** Mini-bar – chargeable **Parking:** 30 **Notes:** Closed 25 & 26 Dec RS Jan–Feb closed for dinner Tue & Wed

| **ARUNDEL** | Map 6 TQ00 |
| West Sussex | |

The Town House

★★★★★ ◉◉ RESTAURANT WITH ROOMS

65 High Street BN18 9AJ - **tel:** 01903 883847
email: enquiries@thetownhouse.co.uk **web:** www.thetownhouse.co.uk
dir: A27 to Arundel, into High Street, establishment on left at top of hill

This is an elegant, Grade II listed Regency building overlooking Arundel Castle, just a short walk from the shops and centre of the town. Bedrooms and public areas retain the building's unspoilt character. The ceiling in the dining room is particularly spectacular and originated in Florence in the 16th century. The excellent food has been awarded two AA Rosettes.

Rooms: 5 en suite (1 fmly) **S** £75–£110; **D** £110–£150 **Facilities:** FTV iPod docking station Dinner available WiFi ⌚ **Extras:** Speciality toiletries **Notes:** Closed 2 weeks Easter & 2 weeks Oct RS Sun–Mon Restaurant closed

| **ASENBY** | Map 19 SE37 |
| North Yorkshire | |

Crab Manor

★★★★★ ◉◉ RESTAURANT WITH ROOMS

Dishforth Road YO7 3QL - **tel:** 01845 577286
web: www.crabandlobster.co.uk
dir: A1(M) junct 49, on outskirts of village

This stunning 18th-century Grade II listed Georgian manor is located in the heart of the North Yorkshire Dales. Each bedroom is themed around the world's most famous hotels and has high-quality furnishings, beautiful wallpaper, and thoughtful extras. Scandinavian log cabins are also available in the grounds, which have their own terrace with hot tubs. There is a comfortable lounge bar where guests can relax in the Manor before enjoying dinner next door in the Crab & Lobster Restaurant, which specialises in fresh local seafood. The attractive gardens offer a lovely backdrop.

Rooms: 8 en suite 12 annexe en suite (3 fmly) **Facilities:** FTV iPod docking station Lounge tea/coffee Dinner available Direct dial WiFi ⌚ **Conf:** Max 16 Board 16 **Parking:** 90 **Notes:** Civ wed 105

| **AUSTWICK** | Map 18 SD76 |
| North Yorkshire | |

The Traddock

★★★★★ ◉◉ ☕ RESTAURANT WITH ROOMS

Settle LA2 8BY - **tel:** 015242 51224
email: info@thetraddock.co.uk **web:** www.thetraddock.co.uk
dir: From Skipton take A65 towards Kendal, 3m after Settle turn right signed Austwick, cross hump back bridge, 100yds on left

Situated within the Yorkshire Dales National Park and a peaceful village environment, this fine Georgian country house with well-tended gardens offers a haven of calm and good hospitality. There are two comfortable lounges with real fires and fine furnishings, as well as a cosy bar and an elegant dining room serving fine cuisine. Bedrooms are individually styled with many homely touches.

Rooms: 12 en suite (2 fmly) (1 GF) **D** £95–£240* **Facilities:** FTV DVD Lounge tea/coffee Dinner available Direct dial WiFi ⌚ ⅃18 ⌚ **Extras:** Speciality toiletries, fruit, home-made biscuits, bottled water – free **Conf:** Max 24 Thtr 24 Class 16 Board 16 **Parking:** 20 **Notes:** LB

| **AXBRIDGE** | Map 4 ST45 |
| Somerset | |

The Oak House

★★★★★ ◉◉ ☕ RESTAURANT WITH ROOMS

The Square BS26 2AP - **tel:** 01934 732444
email: info@theoakhousesomerset.com **web:** www.theoakhousesomerset.com
dir: M5 junct 22, A38 N, turn right towards Axbridge & Cheddar

This impressive restaurant with rooms is located in the middle of the village and provides a relaxed, high quality experience, whether guests are coming to enjoy the restaurant or to stay in one of the nine bedrooms above. Hospitality and service are delivered in an efficient and helpful manner by a young and enthusiastic team. The kitchen has a serious approach and delivers delightful dishes full of flavour, utilising the best quality produce.

Rooms: 9 en suite (2 fmly) **Facilities:** FTV DVD Lounge tea/coffee Dinner available WiFi **Notes:** Closed 2–5 Jan RS Sun eve & Mon eve Restaurant closed

BAINBRIDGE   Map 18 SD99
North Yorkshire

INSPECTOR'S CHOICE

Yorebridge House
★★★★★ ◉◉◉ 👜 RESTAURANT WITH ROOMS

DL8 3EE - **tel:** 01969 652060
email: enquiries@yorebridgehouse.co.uk **web:** www.yorebridgehouse.co.uk
dir: A648 to Bainbridge. Yorebridge House N of centre on right before river

Yorebridge House is situated by the river on the edge of Bainbridge, in the heart of the North Yorkshire Dales. In the Victorian era this was a schoolmaster's house and school, the building now offers luxury boutique-style accommodation. Each bedroom is individually designed with high-quality furnishings and thoughtful extras. All rooms have stunning views of the Dales and some have their own terrace with hot tub. There is a comfortable lounge bar where guests can relax before enjoying an excellent, three AA Rosette award-winning dinner in the attractive and elegant dining room.

Rooms: 7 en suite 4 annexe en suite (11 fmly) (5 GF) **Facilities:** STV FTV DVD iPod docking station Lounge tea/coffee Dinner available Direct dial WiFi 🎣 Fishing **Extras:** Speciality toiletries **Conf:** Max 70 Thtr 70 Class 60 Board 30 **Parking:** 30 **Notes:** LB Civ wed 100

BARNET   Map 6 TQ29
Greater London

Savoro Restaurant with Rooms
★★★★ ◉ RESTAURANT WITH ROOMS

206 High Street EN5 5SZ - **tel:** 020 8449 9888
email: savoro@savoro.co.uk **web:** www.savoro.co.uk
dir: M25 junct 23, A1000. Establishment in crescent behind Hadley Green Jaguar Garage

Set back from the main high street, the traditional frontage of this establishment belies the stylishly contemporary bedrooms within. Several have modern four-poster beds and all have well designed bathrooms. The award-winning restaurant is an additional bonus, serving food which is all freshly prepared in-house, from bread to ice cream.

Rooms: 11 rms (9 en suite) (2 pri facs) (2 fmly) (3 GF) **Facilities:** FTV tea/coffee Dinner available WiFi **Extras:** Bottled water – complimentary **Conf:** Max 20 Class 20 Board 20 **Parking:** 9 **Notes:** LB

BARTON-ON-SEA   Map 5 SZ29
Hampshire

Pebble Beach
★★★★★ ◉ 👜 RESTAURANT WITH ROOMS

Marine Drive BH25 7ZD - **tel:** 01425 627777
email: mail@pebblebeach-uk.com **web:** www.pebblebeach-uk.com
dir: A35 from Southampton onto A337 to New Milton, left into Barton Court Av to clifftop

Situated on the clifftop, the restaurant at Pebble Beach boasts stunning views towards The Needles. Bedrooms and bathrooms (situated above the restaurant) are well equipped and provide a range of accessories. A freshly cooked breakfast is served in the main restaurant, or outside on the wonderful terrace. Next door, Petit Pebbles delicatessen is and well worth a visit.

Rooms: 4 rms (3 en suite) (1 pri facs) **D** £79.95–£349.95* **Facilities:** FTV tea/coffee Dinner available Direct dial WiFi **Extras:** Speciality toiletries **Conf:** Max 8 Thtr 8 Class 8 Board 8 **Parking:** 20 **Notes:** RS 25 Dec & 1 Jan dinner not available

BISHOP'S CASTLE   Map 15 SO38
Shropshire

The Coach House
★★★★ ◉◉ 👜 RESTAURANT WITH ROOMS

Norbury SY9 5DX - **tel:** 01588 650846 & 07930 694516
email: info@coachhousenorbury.com **web:** www.coachhousenorbury.com
dir: 3m NE of Bishop's Castle. Exit A488/A489 into Norbury

Located in an Area of Outstanding Natural Beauty this quaint property in the centre of this pretty Shropshire village and has been welcoming travellers since the 1700s. Fully refurbished, a warm welcome is assured by the current owners. Bedrooms offer comfortable accommodation for guests and are located either in the main building, or the attached coach house annexe which is dog friendly. Cosy lounges with log burning fires are an ideal place to enjoy a locally produced beer or one of the quality wines on offer – with Lexi a qualified wine maker, you are assured of something special. Award-winning dinner and breakfast is not to be missed, with an innovative menu showcasing the best local produce.

Rooms: 4 rms (3 en suite) (1 pri facs) 3 annexe en suite (1 fmly) (1 GF) **S** £79–£119; **D** £79–£119* **Facilities:** FTV DVD Lounge tea/coffee Dinner available WiFi **Extras:** Speciality toiletries, home-made biscuits **Conf:** Max 18 Thtr 18 Class 18 Board 18 **Parking:** 8 **Notes:** LB No children 5yrs Closed 2–31 Jan

BOROUGHBRIDGE
North Yorkshire
Map 19 SE36

The Crown Inn

★★★★ ◉◉ 𝄞 RESTAURANT WITH ROOMS

Roecliffe YO51 9LY - tel: 01423 322300
email: info@crowninnroecliffe.co.uk **web:** www.crowninnroecliffe.co.uk
dir: *A1(M) junct 48, follow signs for Boroughbridge. At rdbt exit towards Roecliffe & brown tourist signs*

The Crown is a 16th-century coaching inn providing an excellent combination of traditional charm and modern comforts. Service is friendly and professional and food is a highlight of any stay. The kitchen team uses the finest of Yorkshire produce from the best local suppliers to create a weekly-changing seasonal menu. Bedrooms are attractively furnished with stylish en suite bathrooms.

Rooms: 4 en suite (1 fmly) **S** £80–£90; **D** £90–£120* **Facilities:** FTV DVD tea/coffee Dinner available WiFi 🛁 **Extras:** Sherry, espresso coffee machine, chocolate **Conf:** Max 100 Thtr 100 Class 60 Board 30 **Parking:** 40 **Notes:** Civ wed 120

BRAITHWAITE
Cumbria
Map 18 NY22

INSPECTOR'S CHOICE

The Cottage in the Wood

★★★★ ◉◉◉ 𝄞 RESTAURANT WITH ROOMS

Whinlatter Pass CA12 5TW - tel: 017687 78409 & 07730 312193
email: relax@thecottageinthewood.co.uk **web:** www.thecottageinthewood.co.uk
dir: *M6 junct 40, A66 W. After Keswick exit for Braithwaite via Whinlatter Pass (B5292), establishment at top of pass*

This charming property sits on wooded hills with striking views of Skiddaw, and is conveniently placed for Keswick. The owners provide excellent hospitality in a relaxed manner. The award-winning food, freshly prepared and locally sourced, is served in the bright and welcoming conservatory restaurant with its stunning views. The comfortable bedrooms are well appointed and have many useful extras.

Rooms: 9 en suite **S** £88–£96; **D** £110–£205* **Facilities:** FTV Lounge tea/coffee Dinner available Direct dial WiFi 🛁 **Parking:** 15 **Notes:** LB No children 10yrs Closed Jan RS Mon closed

BRISTOL
Bristol
Map 4 ST57

Berwick Lodge

★★★★★ ◉◉ RESTAURANT WITH ROOMS

Berwick Drive, Henbury BS10 7TD - tel: 0117 958 1590
email: info@berwicklodge.co.uk **web:** www.berwicklodge.co.uk
dir: *M5 junct 17, A4018 (Westbury-on-Trym). At 2nd rdbt 1st left (Westbury-on-Trym). At next rdbt double back on dual carriageway (signed M5 (M4)). Left after brown Clifton RFC sign. At x-rds straight on, follow Berwick Lodge signs*

This delightful building was built in the late 1890s as a private manor house and is surrounded by rose and woodland gardens. The five-year renovation project has now been completed to provide very high standards of quality and comfort throughout the building, with luxurious bedrooms and bathrooms offered in a range of shapes and sizes. Fine dining can be experienced in the opulent restaurant where both dinner and breakfast will be sure to delight the most discerning of guests.

Rooms: 12 en suite 2 annexe en suite (2 fmly) **S** £85; **D** £99–£130* **Facilities:** STV FTV DVD Lounge tea/coffee Dinner available Direct dial Lift WiFi 🛶 **Extras:** Robes, fruit **Conf:** Max 100 Thtr 100 Class 60 Board 30 **Parking:** 100 **Notes:** LB Civ wed 100

BROADWAY
Worcestershire
Map 10 SP03

Russell's

★★★★★ ◉◉ 𝄞 RESTAURANT WITH ROOMS

20 High Street WR12 7DT - tel: 01386 853555
email: info@russellsofbroadway.co.uk **web:** www.russellsofbroadway.co.uk
dir: *Opposite village green*

Situated in the centre of picturesque Broadway, this restaurant with rooms makes a great base for exploring local attractions. The superbly appointed bedrooms, each with its own character, have air conditioning and a wide range of extras. The cuisine is a real draw here with skilful use made of freshly-prepared, local produce.

Rooms: 4 en suite 3 annexe en suite (4 fmly) (2 GF) **S** £130–£300; **D** £130–£300* **Facilities:** FTV DVD tea/coffee Dinner available Direct dial WiFi **Extras:** Honesty bar **Conf:** Max 12 Board 12 **Parking:** 7

BURNSALL
North Yorkshire
Map 19 SE06

The Devonshire Fell

★★★★ ◉ RESTAURANT WITH ROOMS

BD23 6BT - tel: 01756 729000 & 718111
email: manager@devonshirefell.co.uk **web:** www.devonshirefell.co.uk
dir: *On B6160, 6m from Bolton Abbey rdbt, A59 junct*

Located on the edge of the attractive village of Burnsall, The Devonshire Fell is colourful, contemporary and quirky. Originally a gentleman's club it enjoys what may be one of the finest locations in the country. A brasserie-style menu is served in the light and airy conservatory restaurant, with views of the Fells and Dales outside and original modern art work within. Intimate and friendly, The Devonshire Fell is a superb choice for those looking to escape from it all. Expect quality surroundings, home comforts and a friendly, warm welcome.

Rooms: 16 en suite (2 fmly) **Facilities:** STV FTV DVD tea/coffee Dinner available Direct dial WiFi 🎣 Fishing 🛁 Free use of spa facilities at sister hotel **Conf:** Max 50 Thtr 50 Class 30 Board 24 **Parking:** 40 **Notes:** LB Civ wed 80

CAMBER
East Sussex
Map 7 TQ91

The Gallivant

★★★★ ◉◉ RESTAURANT WITH ROOMS

New Lydd Road TN31 7RB - tel: 01797 225057
email: beachbistro@thegallivanthotel.com **web:** www.thegallivanthotel.com

The Gallivant is located right on the edge of Camber Sands, just a short drive from the historic town of Rye. The inn offers modern, coastal-styled accommodation with light airy decor and reconditioned driftwood furniture. Rooms are well equipped and ideal for both business and leisure guests. There's a bar and the award-winning Beach Bistro serves food daily. The large function suite is open year round and is perfect for parties or weddings. The sand dunes and beach are just across the road in front of the inn. The Gallivant was a finalist for the AA Restaurant with Rooms of the Year 2017-2018.

Rooms: 16 en suite 4 annexe en suite (4 fmly) (20 GF) **Facilities:** FTV DVD Lounge tea/coffee Dinner available Direct dial WiFi 🛌18 🛁 **Extras:** Speciality toiletries **Conf:** Max 120 Thtr 120 Class 60 Board 40 **Parking:** 25 **Notes:** Civ wed 150

CANTERBURY
Kent

Map 7 TR15

The Corner House

★★★★ RESTAURANT WITH ROOMS

1 Dover Street CT1 3HD - tel: 01227 780793 & 01843 823000
email: matt@cornerhouserestaurants.co.uk **web:** www.cornerhouserestaurants.co.uk

Located right in the centre of Canterbury, The Corner House has recently been completely refurbishment, and now offers three stylishly decorated bedrooms. All are very spacious and furnished to a high standard yet still showcase some of the building's original features. Lunch, dinner and breakfast are available in the restaurant though dinner not available on a Monday.

Rooms: 3 en suite **S** £79–£130; **D** £79–£130* **Facilities:** FTV DVD tea/coffee Dinner available WiFi **⚲ Extras:** Fridge **Conf:** Max 20 Class 20 Board 10

CARTMEL
Cumbria

Map 18 SD37

INSPECTOR'S CHOICE

L'Enclume

★★★★★ ⍟⍟⍟⍟⍟ RESTAURANT WITH ROOMS

Cavendish St LA11 6PZ - tel: 015395 36362
email: info@lenclume.co.uk **web:** www.lenclume.co.uk
dir: From A590 turn left for Cartmel before Newby Bridge

L'Enclume is a delightful 13th-century property in the heart of a lovely village, and offers incredible 21st-century cooking that draws foodies from far and wide. Once the village forge (l'enclume is French for 'the anvil') it's now the location for some of Britain's best food, and Simon Rogan's imaginative and adventurous cooking may be sampled in the stylish restaurant. Individually designed, modern, en suite rooms of varying sizes and styles are in the main property and dotted about the village only a few moments' walk from the restaurant.

Rooms: 5 en suite 11 annexe en suite (3 fmly) (2 GF) **S** £130–£175; **D** £170–£395* **Facilities:** STV DVD iPod docking station tea/coffee Dinner available Direct dial WiFi **Extras:** Mini-bar, speciality toiletries **Parking:** 3

CASTLE CARY
Somerset

Map 4 ST63

The Pilgrims

★★★★ ⍟⍟ ⍟ RESTAURANT WITH ROOMS

Lovington BA7 7PT - tel: 01963 240600
email: jools@thepilgrimsatlovington.co.uk **web:** www.thepilgrimsatlovington.co.uk
dir: On B3153, 1.5m E of lights on A37 at Lydford

The Pilgrims describes itself as 'the pub that thinks it's a restaurant', which is pretty accurate. With a real emphasis on fresh, local and carefully prepared produce, both dinner and breakfast are the focus of any stay here. In addition, the resident family proprietors provide a friendly and relaxed atmosphere. Comfortable and well-equipped bedrooms are available in the adjacent converted cider barn.

Rooms: 5 annexe en suite (5 GF) **S** £80–£130; **D** £100–£130* **Facilities:** FTV Lounge tea/coffee Dinner available WiFi **Extras:** Speciality toiletries **Parking:** 5 **Notes:** LB No children 14yrs RS Sun lunch–Tue lunch Restaurant & bar closed to non-residents

CAVENDISH
Suffolk

Map 13 TL84

The George

★★★★★ ⍟⍟ ⍟ RESTAURANT WITH ROOMS

The Green CO10 8BA - tel: 01787 280248
email: thegeorgecavendish@gmail.com **web:** www.thecavendishgeorge.co.uk
dir: A1092 into Cavendish, The George next to village green

The George is situated in the heart of the pretty village of Cavendish and has five stylish bedrooms which have retained many of their original features, as well as being comfortable and spacious. The front-facing rooms overlook the village. The award-winning restaurant is very well appointed and dinner should not be missed. Guests are guaranteed to receive a warm welcome, attentive friendly service and great food.

Rooms: 5 en suite (1 fmly) **Facilities:** FTV DVD tea/coffee Dinner available WiFi **⚲ Extras:** Speciality toiletries, mineral water, sweets **Notes:** Closed 25 Dec & 1 Jan

CHIEVELEY
Berkshire

Map 5 SU47

Crab & Boar

★★★★ ⍟⍟ RESTAURANT WITH ROOMS

Wantage Road RG20 8UE - tel: 01635 247550
email: info@crabandboar.com **web:** www.crabandboar.com
dir: 1.5m W of Chieveley on B4494

Part of The Epicurean Collection, this refurbished and renovated former pub has been appointed to a very high standard and bedrooms include a full range of modern amenities. Some ground floor rooms have a small private patio area complete with a luxury private hot tub. The warm and cosy restaurant offers an extensive and award-winning range of dishes, using the best suppliers in the south.

Rooms: 9 en suite 5 annexe en suite (8 GF) **Facilities:** FTV tea/coffee Dinner available Direct dial WiFi Hot tub suites **Extras:** Home-made biscuits **Conf:** Max 14 Thtr 14 Class 14 Board 14 **Parking:** 80 **Notes:** LB

CHILGROVE
West Sussex

Map 5 SU81

The White Horse

★★★★★ ⍟ RESTAURANT WITH ROOMS

High Street PO18 9HX - tel: 01243 519444
email: info@thewhitehorse.co.uk **web:** www.thewhitehorse.co.uk
dir: From Chichester take A286 N, turn left onto B2141 to village

Part of The Epicurean Collection, this spacious property offers stylish and relaxed surroundings on the edge of the South Downs. The bar and dining areas have an opulent feel, with lots of quirky touches and interesting features. Guests are welcome to enjoy a pint and relax, or dine from the appealing and wide-ranging menus. The emphasis is on local produce and food is a highlight. Bedrooms offer an attractive blend of traditional and contemporary features, with wooden beams, sheepskin rugs and king-size beds. Most open out onto the private courtyard and feature either copper baths or large rain showers, with a couple even having hot tubs.

Rooms: 15 en suite **Facilities:** FTV Lounge tea/coffee Dinner available Direct dial WiFi Fishing **Conf:** Max 20 **Notes:** LB

CHIPPING CAMPDEN
Gloucestershire   Map 10 SP13

The Kings

★★★★ ◉◉ ☖ RESTAURANT WITH ROOMS

The Square, High Street GL55 6AW - **tel:** 01386 840256 & 841056
email: info@kingscampden.co.uk **web:** www.kingscampden.co.uk
dir: *In centre of town square*

Located in the centre of this delightful Cotswold town, The Kings effortlessly blends a relaxed and friendly welcome with efficient service. Bedrooms and bathrooms come in a range of shapes and sizes and all are appointed to a high level of quality and comfort. Dining options, whether in the main restaurant or the comfortable bar area, serve a tempting menu to suit all tastes, from light salads and pasta, to meat and fish dishes.

Rooms: 13 en suite 5 annexe en suite (3 fmly) (3 GF) **S** £110–£225; **D** £130–£245* **Facilities:** FTV tea/coffee Dinner available Direct dial WiFi **Parking:** 14 **Notes:** LB Civ wed 60

The Seagrave Arms

★★★★ ◉◉ RESTAURANT WITH ROOMS

Friday Street, Weston-sub-Edge GL55 6QH - **tel:** 01386 840192
email: enquiries@seagravearms.com **web:** www.seagravearms.com
dir: *From Moreton-in-Marsh take A44 towards Evesham. Approx 7m right onto B4081 signed Chipping Campden. Becomes Sheep St. At junct with High Street, left into Dyers Ln. 0.5m over Dovers Hill, into Weston-sub-Edge, becomes Church St. Inn on left*

Part of The Epicurean Collection, this Grade II listed, 400-year-old house is set in the heart of the Cotswolds. It offers modern accommodation in the main house and also rooms around the courtyard. The inn is full of character, serving award-winning seasonal food every day of the week, with occasional specialist nights. Staff are warm and friendly, and the bar offers local ales and good wines. There is ample parking and attractive gardens.

Rooms: 5 en suite 3 annexe en suite (3 GF) **Facilities:** FTV tea/coffee Dinner available WiFi **Notes:** LB

CHIPPING NORTON
Oxfordshire   Map 10 SP32

Wild Thyme Restaurant with Rooms

★★★★ ◉◉ RESTAURANT WITH ROOMS

10 New Street OX7 5LJ - **tel:** 01608 645060
email: enquiries@wildthymerestaurant.co.uk **web:** www.wildthymerestaurant.co.uk
dir: *On A44 in town centre off market square*

Set in the bustling Cotswold market town of Chipping Norton, this restaurant with rooms offers three en suite bedrooms that are individually designed, well equipped, and have many thoughtful extras. The restaurant serves exciting Modern British food that is presented with relaxed and friendly service.

Rooms: 3 en suite **S** £65–£85; **D** £75–£105* **Facilities:** FTV DVD tea/coffee Dinner available WiFi **Extras:** Mineral water, home-made biscuits

CLITHEROE
Lancashire   Map 18 SD74

The Assheton Arms

★★★★★ ◉ RESTAURANT WITH ROOMS

Downham BB7 4BJ - **tel:** 01200 441227
email: info@asshetonarms.com **web:** www.seafoodpubcompany.com
dir: *A59 to Chatburn, then follow Downham signs*

This historic Grade II listed building is located in the conservation village of Downham, with stunning views of Pendle Hill. The inn is owned by the Seafood Pub Company which means you can expect outstanding seafood. The rooms are spacious with traditional fittings yet maintain a modern feel. The team are young, friendly and guarantee a warm welcome.

Rooms: 1 en suite 11 annexe en suite (4 fmly) (6 GF) **Facilities:** FTV Lounge tea/coffee Dinner available WiFi ⅃18 🛁 **Extras:** Mineral water, fresh milk **Conf:** Max 20 **Parking:** 18

CRAYKE
North Yorkshire   Map 19 SE57

The Durham Ox

★★★★★ ⒶRESTAURANT WITH ROOMS

Westway YO61 4TE - **tel:** 01347 821506
email: enquiries@thedurhamox.com **web:** www.thedurhamox.com
dir: *A19 to Easingwold. Through market place to Crayke, 1st left up hill*

The Durham Ox is some 300 years old. The owners pride themselves on offering a friendly and efficient service, plus traditional pub food using only the best local ingredients. The pub has breathtaking views over the Vale of York on three sides, and a charming view up the hill to the medieval church on the other. Accommodation is mainly in four converted farm cottages. Crayke is in the heart of 'Herriot Country' and less than 20 minutes from York city centre.

Rooms: 1 en suite 5 annexe en suite (1 fmly) (3 GF) **Facilities:** FTV DVD iPod docking station tea/coffee Dinner available WiFi ⅃18 🛁 Shooting, fishing, riding by arrangement **Extras:** Speciality toiletries, honesty bar **Conf:** Max 80 Thtr 80 Class 60 Board 30 **Parking:** 35 **Notes:** LB

DEVIZES
Wiltshire   Map 4 SU06

The Peppermill

★★★★★ ◉◉ RESTAURANT WITH ROOMS

40 Saint John's Street SN10 1BL - **tel:** 01380 710407
email: philip@peppermilldevizes.co.uk **web:** www.peppermilldevizes.co.uk
dir: *Situated in the market place*

Situated in the heart of Devizes, The Peppermill offers seven bedrooms located above the restaurant, in one of the oldest buildings in the town. The en suite bath/shower rooms have underfloor heating, limestone floors and heated mirrors. Hypnos Royal Lansdowne beds, three of which split into twins if needed, have goose-down bedding and Egyptian cotton bed linen to ensure a good night's sleep. The restaurant serves breakfast, lunch and dinner, all offered daily.

Rooms: 7 en suite **S** £95–£155; **D** £115–£175* **Facilities:** FTV iPod docking station TVL tea/coffee Dinner available WiFi ⅃18 🛁 **Extras:** Robes **Notes:** LB

DOVER
Kent

Map 7 TR34

The Marquis at Alkham

★★★★★ ◎◎ 🍴 RESTAURANT WITH ROOMS

Alkham Valley Road, Alkham CT15 7DF - tel: 01304 873410 & 822945
email: info@themarquisatalkham.co.uk **web:** www.themarquisatalkham.co.uk
dir: *A256 from Dover, at rdbt 1st exit into London Rd, left into Alkham Rd, Alkham Valley Rd. Establishment 1.5m after sharp bend*

Located between Dover and Folkestone, this contemporary restaurant with rooms offers luxury accommodation with modern features; flat screen TVs, WiFi, monsoon showers and bathrobes, to mention a few. All the stylish bedrooms are individually designed and have fantastic views of the Kent Downs. The award-winning restaurant, open for lunch, afternoon tea and dinner, specialises in modern British cuisine with a strong emphasis on locally sourced ingredients. Both continental and a choice of cooked breakfasts are offered.

Rooms: 10 en suite (3 fmly) (1 GF) **S** £69–£139; **D** £99–£169* **Facilities:** FTV DVD Lounge tea/coffee Dinner available Direct dial WiFi **Extras:** Speciality toiletries **Conf:** Max 20 Thtr 20 Class 20 Board 16 **Parking:** 22 **Notes:** LB Civ wed 55

EDGEHILL
Warwickshire

Map 11 SP34

Castle at Edgehill

★★★★ ◎◎ 🍴 RESTAURANT WITH ROOMS

Main Street OX15 6DJ - tel: 01295 670255
email: enquiries@castleatedgehill.co.uk **web:** www.castleatedgehill.co.uk

Built in 1742 to mark the centenary of the battle of Edgehill, where Charles I raised his standard at the start of the Civil War, the building has a unique history. Sympathetically refurbished, many original features have been restored and the exposed stone walls, along with the wood-panelled restaurant, really add to the character of the building. The Tower bedrooms boast panoramic views from their elevated position and bedrooms are all well-appointed. Dinner is not to be missed in the two AA Rosette award-winning restaurant and breakfast features the best in local produce.

Rooms: 2 en suite 2 annexe en suite (1 fmly) (1 GF) **Facilities:** FTV tea/coffee Dinner available WiFi **Conf:** Max 30 Thtr 24 Class 30 Board 18 **Parking:** 22

EMSWORTH
Hampshire

Map 5 SU70

INSPECTOR'S CHOICE

36 on the Quay

★★★★ ◎◎◎ RESTAURANT WITH ROOMS

47 South Street PO10 7EG - tel: 01243 375592 & 372257
email: info@36onthequay.co.uk **web:** www.36onthequay.co.uk
dir: *Last building on right in South St, which runs from square in centre of Emsworth*

Occupying a prime position with far-reaching views over the estuary, this 16th-century house is the scene for some accomplished and exciting cuisine. The elegant restaurant occupies centre stage with peaceful pastel shades, local art and crisp napery together with glimpses of the bustling harbour outside. The contemporary bedrooms offer style, comfort and thoughtful extras.

Rooms: 4 en suite **Facilities:** FTV iPod docking station tea/coffee Dinner available WiFi **Parking:** 6 **Notes:** LB Closed 3 weeks Jan, 1 week late May

ERMINGTON
Devon

Map 3 SX65

Plantation House

★★★★★ ◎◎ 🍴 RESTAURANT WITH ROOMS

Totnes Road PL21 9NS - tel: 01548 831100 & 830741
email: info@plantationhousehotel.co.uk **web:** www.plantationhousehotel.co.uk

Peacefully situated in the picturesque South Hams, this former rectory provides an intimate and relaxing base from which to explore the area. Quality, comfort and individuality are hallmarks throughout, with bedrooms offering impressive standards and a host of thoughtful extras. The stylish bathrooms come equipped with fluffy towels, robes and under-floor heating. A drink beside the crackling log fire is the ideal prelude to dinner, where skill and passion underpin menus focusing upon wonderful local produce. Breakfast is equally enjoyable, with superb eggs provided by the resident hens.

Rooms: 8 en suite **S** £80–£120; **D** £110–£230* **Facilities:** FTV DVD iPod docking station Lounge tea/coffee Dinner available Direct dial WiFi 🎣 🎿18 Fishing Massage & Therapies **Extras:** Speciality toiletries, fruit, robes, mineral water, fresh milk **Conf:** Max 16 **Parking:** 30 **Notes:** LB

EXETER
Devon

Map 3 SX99

Chi Restaurant & Bar with Accommodation

★★★★ 🍴 RESTAURANT WITH ROOMS

Fore Street, Kenton EX6 8LD - tel: 01626 890213
email: enquiries@chi-restaurant.co.uk **web:** www.chi-restaurant.co.uk
dir: *5m S of Exeter. M5 junct 30, A379 towards Dawlish, in village centre*

This former pub has been spectacularly transformed into a chic and contemporary bar, allied with a stylish Chinese restaurant. Dishes are beautifully presented with an emphasis on quality produce and authenticity, resulting in a memorable dining experience. Bedrooms are well equipped and all provide good levels of space and comfort, along with modern bathrooms.

Rooms: 5 en suite (1 fmly) **S** £50–£126; **D** £63–£140 (room only)* **Facilities:** FTV DVD Lounge TVL tea/coffee Dinner available WiFi 🔒 **Parking:** 26 **Notes:** Closed Sun–Mon

FAVERSHAM
Kent

Map 7 TR06

Faversham Creek & Red Sails Restaurant

★★★★ ◎ RESTAURANT WITH ROOMS

Conduit Street ME13 7BH - tel: 01795 533535 & 534689
email: office@faourshamcreekhotel.co.uk **web:** www.faourshamcreekhotel.co.uk
dir: *M2 junct 6 onto A251. At T-junct left then right into The Mall. Pass railway station, continue on B2041. Left into Quay Ln*

Located in the heart of Faversham and adjacent to the Creek, this restaurant with rooms offers modern accommodation with its own individual style, and rooms named after characters from the Faversham area. Bedrooms are well equipped and ideal for both business and leisure guests alike. There is a courtyard terrace where guests can enjoy lunch or pre-dinner drinks before dining in the award-winning Red Sails Restaurant. Parking is available on site.

Rooms: 6 en suite (4 fmly) **S** £75–£105; **D** £85–£175* **Facilities:** STV FTV Lounge tea/coffee Dinner available Direct dial WiFi **Parking:** 4

FIVEHEAD
Somerset

Map 3 ST32

Langford Fivehead

★★★★★ ◉◉ ⌂ RESTAURANT WITH ROOMS

Lower Swell TA3 6PH - tel: 01460 282020
email: rebecca@thelangford.co **web:** www.langfordfivehead.co.uk

Documents indicate that there has been a house on this site since 1255 and the current property retains a significant proportion of a 15th-century hall house. In keeping with the grand character found throughout the building, guests can be assured of the most pleasant of welcomes and helpful, relaxing hospitality and service. Bedrooms offer a range of shapes and styles and are decorated and equipped to very high standards (although deliberately, no TVs in bedrooms). The restaurant is a delight of home-grown and local produce, providing delicious dining at both dinner and breakfast.

Rooms: 6 en suite **Facilities:** Dinner available **Notes:** Closed 25 Jul–7 Aug & 2–15 Jan

FOLKESTONE
Kent

Map 7 TR23

Rocksalt Rooms

★★★★ ◉◉ RESTAURANT WITH ROOMS

2 Back Street CT19 6NN - tel: 01303 212070
email: info@rocksaltfolkestone.co.uk **web:** www.rocksaltfolkestone.co.uk
dir: M20 junct 13 follow signs to harbour (A259). At harbour left onto Fish Market

Overlooking the busy harbour, often crowded with small leisure boats, and with wonderful sea views, Rocksalt enjoys a great location in Folkestone. Bedrooms are stylish, well-appointed with original antique beds and equipped with a host of thoughtful little extras. Continental breakfasts are delivered promptly to the guests' rooms each morning, and dinner is served in the award-winning restaurant, also blessed with panoramic views.

Rooms: 4 en suite (1 fmly) **Facilities:** FTV iPod docking station tea/coffee Dinner available WiFi **Extras:** Nespresso machine, fruit, speciality toiletries

GLOUCESTER
Gloucestershire

Map 10 SO81

The Wharf House Restaurant with Rooms

★★★★ ◉ RESTAURANT WITH ROOMS

Over GL2 8DB - tel: 01452 332900
email: enquiries@thewharfhouse.co.uk **web:** www.thewharfhouse.co.uk
dir: From A40 between Gloucester & Highnam exit at lights for Over. Establishment signed

The Wharf House was built to replace the old lock cottage and, as the name suggests, it is located at the very edge of the river; it has pleasant views and an outdoor terrace. The bedrooms and bathrooms have been finished to a high standard, and there are plenty of guest extras. Seasonal, local produce can be enjoyed both at breakfast and dinner in the delightful AA Rosetted restaurant. The Wharf House is owned and run by the Herefordshire and Gloucestershire Canal Trust, and all profits go towards the promotion and restoration of the Hereford and Gloucester Canal.

Rooms: 7 en suite (1 fmly) (1 GF) **Facilities:** STV FTV DVD Lounge tea/coffee Dinner available WiFi Fishing ⌂ **Extras:** Speciality toiletries – complimentary; mini-bar – chargeable **Parking:** 37 **Notes:** Closed 22 Dec–8 Jan RS Sun & Mon Check in before 6pm/rest closed evening

GORING
Oxfordshire

Map 5 SU68

The Miller of Mansfield

★★★★ ◉◉ RESTAURANT WITH ROOMS

High Street RG8 9AW - tel: 01491 872829 & 07702 853413
email: reservations@millerofmansfield.com **web:** www.millerofmansfield.com
dir: M4 junct 12, S on A4 towards Newbury. 3rd rdbt onto A340 to Pangbourne. A329 to Streatley, right at lights onto B4009 into Goring

The frontage of this former coaching inn hides sumptuous rooms furnished in a distinctive and individual style. The two AA Rosette award-winning restaurant serves appealing dishes using locally sourced ingredients, and there is a comfortable bar, which serves real ales, fine wines and afternoon tea; a bar menu provides quick bites to eat.

Rooms: 13 en suite (2 fmly) **D** £99–£180* **Facilities:** FTV Lounge tea/coffee Dinner available WiFi Boat hire & beauty therapies can be arranged **Extras:** Speciality toiletries **Conf:** Max 12 Board 12 **Parking:** 2 **Notes:** LB Closed 26–27 Dec

GRASSINGTON
North Yorkshire

Map 19 SE06

Grassington House

★★★★★ ◉◉ ⌂ RESTAURANT WITH ROOMS

5 The Square BD23 5AQ - tel: 01756 752406
email: bookings@grassingtonhouse.co.uk **web:** www.grassingtonhouse.co.uk
dir: A59 into Grassington, in town square opposite post office

Located in the square of the popular village of Grassington, this beautifully converted Georgian house is personally run by owners John and Sue. Delicious food, individually designed bedrooms and warm hospitality ensure an enjoyable stay. There is a stylish lounge bar looking out to the square and the restaurant is split between two rooms; here guests will find the emphasis is on fresh, local ingredients and attentive, friendly service.

Rooms: 9 en suite (2 fmly) **S** fr £107.50; **D** £125–£145* **Facilities:** STV FTV tea/coffee Dinner available Direct dial WiFi ⌂ **Extras:** Speciality toiletries **Parking:** 25 **Notes:** LB Civ wed 44

GREAT TOTHAM   Map 7 TL81
Essex

The Bull & Willow Room at Great Totham

★★★★ ◎◎   RESTAURANT WITH ROOMS

2 Maldon Road CM9 8NH - tel: 01621 893385 & 894020
email: reservations@thebullatgreattotham.co.uk **web:** www.thebullatgreattotham.co.uk
dir: *Exit A12 at Witham junct to Great Totham*

A 16th-century former coaching inn located in the village of Great Totham, The Bull is now a very stylish restaurant with rooms that offers en suite bedrooms with satellite TVs with Freeview; WiFi is available throughout. Guests can enjoy dinner in the gastro-pub or in the two AA Rosette award-winning fine dining restaurant, The Willow Room.

Rooms: 4 annexe en suite (2 GF) **Facilities:** STV FTV Lounge tea/coffee Dinner available WiFi ♿18 **Conf:** Max 60 Thtr 40 Class 40 Board 16 **Parking:** 80 **Notes:** LB Closed 25 Dec

HETTON   Map 18 SD95
North Yorkshire

The Angel Inn

★★★★★ ◎◎ ⌂ RESTAURANT WITH ROOMS

BD23 6LT - tel: 01756 730263
email: info@angelhetton.co.uk **web:** www.angelhetton.co.uk
dir: *B6265 from Skipton towards Grassington. At Rylstone turn left by pond, follow signs to Hetton*

This roadside inn is steeped in history; parts of the building go back more than 500 years. The restaurant and bar are in the main building, which has ivy and green canopies at the front. Food is a highlight of any stay, offering excellent ingredients, skilfully prepared and carefully presented. The large, stylish bedrooms are across the road in a converted barn which has great views of the Dales, private parking and its own wine cave.

Rooms: 9 en suite (3 GF) **Facilities:** FTV tea/coffee Dinner available Direct dial WiFi ♨ Wine tasting cave **Conf:** Max 16 Board 14 **Parking:** 40 **Notes:** LB Closed 25 Dec & 1 week Jan Civ wed 40

HIGHCLERE   Map 5 SU45
Hampshire

The Yew Tree

★★★★ ◎◎   RESTAURANT WITH ROOMS

Hollington Cross RG20 9SE - tel: 01635 253360
email: info@theyewtree.co.uk **web:** www.theyewtree.co.uk
dir: *1m S of Highclere village*

Part of The Epicurean Collection, this attractive 17th-century country inn has comfortable bedrooms, decorated with William Morris print wallpaper and retaining traditional features, giving it an overall cosy feel. Great British cooking can be enjoyed in the attractively-decorated restaurant, where good use is made of high-quality produce and fresh ingredients. The garden, with its own bar and dining areas, is a real bonus.

Rooms: 6 en suite 2 annexe en suite **S** £95–£125; **D** £95–£125 **Facilities:** FTV Lounge tea/coffee Dinner available WiFi ♨ **Parking:** 35

HOLT   Map 13 TG03
Norfolk

The Lawns

★★★★ ◎   RESTAURANT WITH ROOMS

26 Station Road NR25 6BS - tel: 01263 713390
email: info@lawnshotelholt.co.uk **web:** www.lawnshotelholt.co.uk
dir: *A148 (Cromer road). 0.25m from Holt rdbt, turn left, 400yds along Station Rd*

The Lawns is a superb Georgian house situated in the centre of this delightful north Norfolk market town. The open-plan public areas include a large wine bar, a conservatory and a smart restaurant. The spacious bedrooms are tastefully appointed with co-ordinated soft furnishings and have many thoughtful touches.

Rooms: 8 en suite 2 annexe en suite (2 GF) **S** £99; **D** £120–£145 **Facilities:** FTV DVD TVL tea/coffee Dinner available WiFi **Extras:** Speciality toiletries **Conf:** Max 20 Thtr 20 Class 12 **Parking:** 18

HORNCASTLE   Map 17 TF26
Lincolnshire

Magpies Restaurant with Rooms

★★★★★ ◎◎   RESTAURANT WITH ROOMS

71–73 East Street LN9 6AA - tel: 01507 527004
email: info@magpiesrestaurant.co.uk **web:** www.magpiesrestaurant.co.uk
dir: *A158 into Horncastle, continue at lights. On left opposite Trinity Centre*

This quaint and charming property is nestled in the popular market town of Horncastle. The spacious en suite accommodation features three individually appointed rooms. All provide flat-screen TVs, complimentary WiFi, home-made biscuits, mini-bar and luxurious bathrooms. There is a cosy lounge area with wood-burning stove which is perfect for those winter evenings. The two AA Rosette award-winning restaurant provides a good choice of imaginative dishes at both lunch and dinner, and afternoon tea is also served. On-street parking is available nearby.

Rooms: 3 en suite **S** £70–£80; **D** £110–£130* **Facilities:** FTV iPod docking station Lounge tea/coffee Dinner available WiFi **Extras:** Bottled water, home-made biscuits & jam, mini-bar **Notes:** Closed 26–30 Dec & 1–7 Jan RS Mon–Tue closed

HUDDERSFIELD   Map 16 SE11
West Yorkshire

315 Bar and Restaurant

★★★★★ ◎◎   RESTAURANT WITH ROOMS

315 Wakefield Road, Lepton HD8 0LX - tel: 01484 602613
email: info@315barandrestaurant.co.uk **web:** www.315barandrestaurant.co.uk
dir: *M1 junct 38, A637 towards Huddersfield. At rdbt take A642 towards Huddersfield. Establishment on right in Lepton*

In a wonderful setting, 315 Bar and Restaurant benefits from countryside views from the well-appointed dining room and conservatory areas. The interior is modern, with open fires that add character and ambiance, while the chef's table gives a real insight into the working of the two AA Rosette award-winning kitchen. Bedrooms are modern, and most have feature bathrooms. Air conditioning is also provided in some. Staff are friendly and attentive, and there are excellent parking facilities. New for 2017 is the addition of a fantastic spa facility. Treatments and use of facilities is at an extra charge.

Rooms: 10 en suite 8 annexe en suite (3 fmly) (8 GF) **S** £85; **D** £95–£145* **Facilities:** FTV DVD tea/coffee Dinner available Lift WiFi Spa facilities **Conf:** Max 150 Thtr 100 Class 75 Board 60 **Parking:** 97 **Notes:** Civ wed 120

HUNSTANTON
Norfolk
Map 12 TF64

INSPECTOR'S CHOICE

The Neptune Restaurant with Rooms

★★★★ @@@ RESTAURANT WITH ROOMS

85 Old Hunstanton Road, Old Hunstanton PE36 6HZ - **tel:** 01485 532122
email: reservations@theneptune.co.uk **web:** www.theneptune.co.uk
dir: On A149, past Hunstanton, 200mtrs on left after post office

This charming 18th-century coaching inn, now a restaurant with rooms, is ideally situated for touring the Norfolk coastline. Smartly appointed bedrooms are brightly finished with co-ordinated fabrics and hand-made New England furniture. Public rooms feature white clapboard walls, polished dark wood floors, fresh flowers and Lloyd Loom furniture. Obviously, the food is a draw here, with the carefully prepared, award-winning cuisine using excellent local produce; from oysters and mussels from Thornham to quinces from a neighbouring farm.

Rooms: 5 en suite **S** fr £160; **D** fr £260* **Facilities:** FTV tea/coffee Dinner available Direct dial WiFi 🅿 **Parking:** 6 **Notes:** No children 10yrs Closed 2 weeks Nov & 3 weeks Jan RS Oct–Apr closed Mon

HURLEY
Berkshire
Map 5 SU88

Hurley House

★★★★★ @@ RESTAURANT WITH ROOMS

Henley Road SL6 5LH - **tel:** 01628 568500
email: hello@hurleyhouse.co.uk **web:** www.hurleyhouse.co.uk

Hurley House is located in a quiet village. The stunning bedrooms vary in size, but all have air conditioning, underfloor heating, mini-bar, coffee machine and comfortable king-size beds. Bathrooms are equipped to the same high standard with luxurious towels and high quality toiletries. There is a popular bar with snug and private dining areas. There is also a wood-burning stove, flagstone floors and plenty of relaxed and comfortable seating of different styles. In the restaurant the menu showcases the finest local produce in the modern British style. WiFi is available throughout, there is a treatment room and also plenty of parking.

Rooms: 10 en suite **S** £160–£285; **D** £170–£295* **Facilities:** Dinner available Spa facilities WiFi 🅿 **Extras:** Mini-bar coffee machine

KINGHAM
Oxfordshire
Map 10 SP22

INSPECTOR'S CHOICE

The Wild Rabbit

★★★★★ @@@ RESTAURANT WITH ROOMS

Church Street OX7 6YA - **tel:** 01608 658389
email: theteam@thewildrabbit.co.uk **web:** www.thewildrabbit.co.uk

Situated in the idyllic Cotswold village of Kingham, this Grade II listed Georgian building has been lovingly restored and totally refurbished. The rooms are modern and offer up-to-date technology. Public areas are a real feature with a large bar and open-plan restaurant kitchen. An outside dining area has also been added. Food is exceptional, with many French influences evident. Service is informal yet professional and very friendly. Ample car parking is available.

Rooms: 11 en suite 1 annexe en suite (1 fmly) (4 GF) **Facilities:** FTV DVD iPod docking station Lounge tea/coffee Dinner available WiFi 🅿 **Extras:** Mini-bar – chargeable **Parking:** 19

KIRKBY LONSDALE
Cumbria
Map 18 SD67

INSPECTOR'S CHOICE

Hipping Hall

★★★★★ @@@ 🍴 RESTAURANT WITH ROOMS

Cowan Bridge LA6 2JJ - **tel:** 015242 71187
email: info@hippinghall.com **web:** www.hippinghall.com
dir: M6 junct 36, A65 through Kirkby Lonsdale towards Skipton. On right after Cowan Bridge

Close to the market town of Kirkby Lonsdale, Hipping Hall offers spacious bedrooms, designed using soft shades with sumptuous textures and fabrics; the bathrooms use natural stone, slate and limestone to great effect. There are also three spacious cottage suites that create a real hideaway experience. The sitting room, with large, comfortable sofas has a traditional feel. The three AA Rosette-worthy restaurant is a 15th-century hall with tapestries and a minstrels' gallery that is as impressive as it is intimate.

Rooms: 7 en suite 8 annexe en suite (5 GF) **Facilities:** FTV Lounge Dinner available Direct dial WiFi 🐾 **Extras:** Speciality toiletries, fruit **Parking:** 30 **Notes:** No children 12yrs Civ wed 42

The Sun Inn

★★★★★ @@ 🍴 RESTAURANT WITH ROOMS

6 Market Street LA6 2AU - **tel:** 015242 71965
email: email@sun-inn.info **web:** www.sun-inn.info
dir: From A65 follow signs to town centre. Inn on main street

The Sun is a 17th-century inn situated in the destination market town of Kirkby Lonsdale and overlooking St Mary's Church. The atmospheric bar features stone walls, wooden beams and log fires with real ales available. Delicious meals are served in the bar or in the relaxed and modern 'Carters at the Sun Inn' restaurant. Traditional and modern styles are blended together in the beautifully appointed rooms with excellent en suites.

Rooms: 11 en suite (1 fmly) **S** £82–£145; **D** £88–£158* **Facilities:** FTV tea/coffee Dinner available Direct dial WiFi 🐾 ⚡18 **Extras:** Bath robes, speciality toiletries **Notes:** LB

Plato's

★★★★★ 🍴 🍽 RESTAURANT WITH ROOMS

2 Mill Brow LA6 2AT - **tel:** 015242 74180
email: hello@platoskirkby.co.uk **web:** www.platoskirkbylonsdale.co.uk
dir: M6 junct 36, A65 Kirkby Lonsdale, after 5m at rdbt take 1st exit, onto one-way system

Tucked away in the heart of this popular market town, Plato's is steeped in history. Recently refreshed bedrooms have a wealth of thoughtful extras and personal touches. Imaginative food is available in the elegant restaurant with its open-plan kitchen or downstairs in the vaulted cellar. The lounge bar has a more relaxed vibe with open fires and soft seating. A warm welcome and professional service is always assured.

Rooms: 8 en suite **Facilities:** FTV DVD iPod docking station TVL tea/coffee Dinner available WiFi ⚡18 **Notes:** LB

RESTAURANTS WITH ROOMS

KNARESBOROUGH
North Yorkshire   Map 19 SE35

General Tarleton Inn

★★★★★ ◎◎   RESTAURANT WITH ROOMS

Boroughbridge Road, Ferrensby HG5 0PZ - tel: 01423 340284
email: gti@generaltarleton.co.uk **web:** www.generaltarleton.co.uk
dir: *A1(M) junct 48 at Boroughbridge, take A6055 to Knaresborough. 4m on right*

This 18th-century coaching inn is both beautiful and stylish. Though the physical aspects are impressive, the emphasis here is on food with high-quality, skilfully prepared dishes served in the smart bar-brasserie and in the Orangery. There is also a richly furnished cocktail lounge with a galleried private dining room above it. Bedrooms are very comfortable and business guests are also well catered for.

Rooms: 13 en suite (7 GF) **S** £75–£95; **D** £129–£150* **Facilities:** FTV Lounge tea/coffee Dinner available Direct dial WiFi   **Extras:** Speciality toiletries, home-made biscuits **Conf:** Max 40 Thtr 40 Class 35 Board 20 **Parking:** 40 **Notes:** LB Closed 24–26 Dec, 1 Jan

---

KNIPTON
Leicestershire   Map 11 SK83

The Manners Arms

★★★★   RESTAURANT WITH ROOMS

Croxton Road NG32 1RH - tel: 01476 879222
email: info@mannersarms.com **web:** www.mannersarms.com
dir: *From A607 follow signs to Knipton; from A52 follow signs to Belvoir Castle*

Part of the Rutland Estate and built as a hunting lodge for the 6th Duke, The Manners Arms offers thoughtfully furnished bedrooms designed by the present Duchess. Public areas include the intimate Beater's Bar and attractive Red Coats Restaurant, popular for its imaginative menus.

Rooms: 10 en suite (1 fmly) **Facilities:** FTV TVL tea/coffee Dinner available Direct dial WiFi 18   **Conf:** Max 50 Thtr 50 Class 25 Board 20 **Parking:** 60 **Notes:** Civ wed 50

KNUTSFORD
Cheshire   Map 15 SJ77

Belle Epoque

★★★★ ◎◎   RESTAURANT WITH ROOMS

60 King Street WA16 6DT - tel: 01565 633060
email: info@thebelleepoque.com **web:** www.thebelleepoque.com

This long established fixture on the north west dining scene has welcomed guests for over 40 years. The opulent, boutique styling lives up to its name throughout the bar and restaurant where imaginative French-leaning cuisine is the centrepiece. Accommodation is in seven rooms of varying size. All are equipped to a modern standard.

Rooms: 7 en suite **Facilities:** Dinner available

LACOCK
Wiltshire   Map 4 ST96

Sign of the Angel

★★★★ ◎◎   RESTAURANT WITH ROOMS

6 Church Street SN15 2LB - tel: 01249 730230
email: info@signoftheangel.co.uk **web:** www.signoftheangel.co.uk
dir: *M4 junct 17 onto A350 signed Poole. After 8m, left signed Lacock. Left into Church St*

This delightful 15th-century inn is located in the heart of the National Trust village of Lacock. Packed full of character, rooms vary in size according to the quirks of the building, but all offer very comfortable beds, quality bedding and a welcoming ambience. Guests are welcome to use the cosy bar and outdoor seating in the garden, while the dining room offers top quality British food, carefully sourced from local suppliers. Neither dinner nor breakfast should be missed here.

Rooms: 5 en suite (2 fmly) **S** £80–£110; **D** £110–£160 **Facilities:** Lounge tea/coffee Dinner available WiFi 9 **Extras:** Fudge, home-made cookies **Conf:** Max 16 Board 16 **Notes:** RS Sun eve & Mon closed

---

LAVENHAM
Suffolk   Map 13 TL94

INSPECTOR'S CHOICE

Lavenham Great House 'Restaurant With Rooms'

★★★★★ ◎◎◎   RESTAURANT WITH ROOMS

Market Place CO10 9QZ - tel: 01787 247431
email: info@greathouse.co.uk **web:** www.greathouse.co.uk
dir: *Exit A1141 into Market Ln, behind cross on Market Place*

The 18th-century frontage on Market Place conceals a 15th-century timber-framed building that is now a restaurant with rooms. Lavenham Great House is a little slice of France, offering high-quality rural cuisine served by French staff. The spacious bedrooms are individually decorated and thoughtfully equipped with many useful extras; some rooms have a separate lounge area.

Rooms: 5 en suite (1 fmly) **S** £105–£215; **D** £160–£215 (room only)* **Facilities:** FTV DVD tea/coffee Dinner available Direct dial WiFi   Free bicycle use for guests **Extras:** Mini-bar, fruit, sherry – complimentary **Notes:** LB Closed Jan RS Sun eve & Mon Restaurant closed

---

LEICESTER
Leicestershire   Map 11 SK50

Maiyango

★★★★ ◎   RESTAURANT WITH ROOMS

13–21 St Nicholas Place LE1 4LD - tel: 0116 251 8898
email: reservations@maiyango.com **web:** www.maiyango.com
dir: *B4114 Narborough Rd to city centre, right onto A47 King Richard III Rd, keep right into St Nicholas Pl*

Maiyango restaurant with rooms offers a warm welcome and professional service. Access to the public areas is via a discreet foyer adjacent to a Middle Eastern-themed restaurant (under the same ownership), where imaginative food is sure to be a memorable experience. Spacious bedrooms, decorated in minimalist style are enhanced by quality modern art, fine furnishings and superb bathrooms. Parking is available close by.

Rooms: 14 en suite **D** fr £79 (room only)* **Facilities:** FTV tea/coffee Dinner available Direct dial Lift WiFi **Notes:** LB Closed 25 Dec, 1–14 Jan

LEINTWARDINE
Herefordshire
Map 9 SO47

The Lion

★★★★★ ◎ ☕ RESTAURANT WITH ROOMS

High Street SY7 0JZ - **tel:** 01547 540203 & 540747
email: enquiries@thelionleintwardine.co.uk **web:** www.thelionleintwardine.co.uk
dir: *Beside bridge on A4113 (Ludlow to Knighton road) in Leintwardine*

This quiet country restaurant with rooms in the picturesque village of Leintwardine, set beside the River Teme, is just a short distance from Ludlow and Craven Arms. The interior is stylish and the contemporary bedrooms are all en suite. Dining is taken seriously here and the modern, imaginative food uses the freshest local ingredients. The well-stocked bar offers a selection of real ales and lagers and there is a separate drinkers' bar too. The Lion is particularly popular with families as the garden has a secure children's play area, and in warmer months guests can eat alfresco. The friendly staff help to make any visit memorable.

Rooms: 8 en suite (1 fmly) **S** £75–£95; **D** £100–£120* **Facilities:** FTV Lounge tea/coffee Dinner available WiFi Fishing ☕ **Extras:** Home-made shortbread – complimentary **Conf:** Max 25 Class 25 Board 25 **Parking:** 25 **Notes:** Closed 25 Dec

LINCOLN
Lincolnshire
Map 17 SK97

The Old Bakery

★★★★ ◎◎ RESTAURANT WITH ROOMS

26–28 Burton Road LN1 3LB - **tel:** 01522 576057 & 07772 667606
email: enquiries@theold-bakery.co.uk **web:** www.theold-bakery.co.uk
dir: *Exit A46 at Lincoln North follow signs for cathedral. 3rd exit at 1st rdbt, 1st exit at next rdbt*

Situated close to the castle at the top of the town, this converted bakery offers well-equipped bedrooms and a delightful dining operation. The cooking has gained two AA Rosettes, and uses much local produce. Expect good friendly service from the dedicated staff.

Rooms: 3 rms (2 en suite) (1 pri facs) (1 fmly) **D** £75–£80 **Facilities:** FTV tea/coffee Dinner available WiFi ☕ **Extras:** Bottled water, home-made cookies – complimentary **Notes:** Closed 25–26 Dec, 1–16 Jan, 1–12 Aug RS Sun & Mon closed

LONDON E1

The Culpeper

★★★★ RESTAURANT WITH ROOMS PLAN 3 J3

40 Commercial Street E1 6LP - **tel:** 020 7247 5371
email: bookings@theculpeper.com **web:** www.theculpeper.com
dir: *From Aldgate East tube station left into Commercial St, The Culpeper on right*

Located on Commercial Road and just a stone's throw from Spitalfields Market and Brick Lane, The Culpeper offers comfortably appointed en suite bedrooms. All showcase stripped-back decor, and some of the building's original features, yet still include some modern furnishings and fixtures. There is a busy pub on the ground floor, a roof-top terrace and conservatory which serves barbecue tapas, and a main restaurant on the second floor which is open for breakfast, lunch and dinner. A real gem in the heart of East London, ideal for leisure and business guests alike.

Rooms: 5 en suite **D** £120* **Facilities:** Dinner available **Notes:** Closed 24–30 Dec

LONDON SW14

The Victoria

★★★★ ◎◎ RESTAURANT WITH ROOMS PLAN 1 C2

10 West Temple Sheen SW14 7RT - **tel:** 020 8876 4238
email: reservations@victoriasheen.co.uk **web:** www.victoriasheen.co.uk
dir: *Off Upper Richmond Rd West into Derby Rd, then into West Temple Sheen*

The Victoria is in a quiet residential area close to Richmond Park. The bedrooms are refreshingly stylish and thoughtfully equipped. The public areas consist of a small contemporary seating area, a modern bar, and an award-winning restaurant that serves imaginative and well sourced dishes. Alfresco dining is also an option.

Rooms: 7 en suite (2 fmly) (3 GF) **Facilities:** FTV iPod docking station tea/coffee Dinner available Direct dial WiFi ☕ **Parking:** 10

LONG MELFORD
Suffolk
Map 13 TL84

Long Melford Swan

★★★★★ ◎◎ RESTAURANT WITH ROOMS

Hall Street CO10 9JQ - **tel:** 01787 464545
email: info@longmelfordswan.co.uk **web:** www.longmelfordswan.co.uk
dir: *From A134 into Long Melford, on main road through village*

Located in the very heart of Long Melford, bedrooms have all been completely refurbished with stylish decor and modern fixtures, home-made refreshments on arrival, turn-down service and feature bathrooms. All the rooms are located just next door in Melford House, adjacent to the main bar and restaurant. This family-run business offers an excellent restaurant with attentive service and a large alfresco dining area in the walled garden. Lunch and dinner are served daily, and a range of cooked and continental dishes are offered for breakfast in the restaurant.

Rooms: 3 en suite 4 annexe en suite (1 fmly) (2 GF) **S** £95–£120; **D** £155–£210* **Facilities:** FTV DVD iPod docking station tea/coffee Dinner available Direct dial WiFi ☕ 18 Spa treatments by arrangement **Extras:** Speciality toiletries, fruit **Notes:** LB

LUDLOW
Shropshire
Map 10 SO57

INSPECTOR'S CHOICE

Old Downton Lodge

★★★★★ ◎◎◎ ☕ RESTAURANT WITH ROOMS

Downton on the Rock SY8 2HU - **tel:** 01568 771826 & 07977 475881
email: bookings@olddowntonlodge.com **web:** www.olddowntonlodge.com
dir: *From Ludlow onto A49 towards Shrewsbury, 1st left onto A4113. After 1.9m turn left signed Downton, 3m on single track road. Turn right, signed*

Old Downton Lodge is within easy reach of Ludlow's many attractions, and is in a peaceful location with good parking, pleasant grounds, ideal for walks and country pursuits. Originally a farm, this high-end establishment has bags of character, and is a stylish, comfortable and tranquil place to stay. Bedrooms are spacious and very well appointed, with comfortable beds and luxurious bathrooms. There is an honesty bar and excellent wine list. Breakfast should not be missed, and the three AA Rosette-worthy dinner is a highlight, with an imaginative five- or seven-course tasting menu using local, seasonal and foraged produce, served every Tuesday to Saturday evening.

Rooms: 10 en suite (5 GF) **S** £99–£250; **D** £99–£250* **Facilities:** FTV DVD Lounge tea/coffee Dinner available Direct dial WiFi **Extras:** Speciality toiletries, home-made biscuits **Conf:** Max 40 Thtr 40 Class 40 Board 40 **Parking:** 20 **Notes:** LB No children 13yrs Closed 24–26 Dec Civ wed 60

The Clive Bar & Restaurant with Rooms

★★★★★ ⊚ ⬚ RESTAURANT WITH ROOMS

Bromfield SY8 2JR - tel: 01584 856565 & 856665
email: info@theclive.co.uk **web:** www.theclive.co.uk
dir: *2m N of Ludlow on A49 in Bromfield*

The Clive is just two miles from the busy town of Ludlow and is a convenient base for visiting the local attractions or for business. Based at the Ludlow Food Centre, good use is made of food made on site or from the company farms, ensuring local seasonal produce at every meal. The bedrooms, located in an annexe, are spacious and very well equipped; one is suitable for families and many are on the ground-floor level. Meals are available in the well-known Clive Restaurant or in the bar areas. The property also has a small meeting room.

Rooms: 14 annexe en suite (1 fmly) (10 GF) **Facilities:** FTV tea/coffee Dinner available Direct dial WiFi ♨18 **Extras:** Mini-bar with local produce **Conf:** Max 40 Thtr 40 Class 40 Board 24 **Parking:** 80 **Notes:** LB Closed 25–26 Dec

The Cliffe at Dinham

★★★★ ⊚⊚ ⬚ RESTAURANT WITH ROOMS

Halton Lane, Dinham SY8 2JE - tel: 01584 872063 & 876975
email: info@thecliffeatdinham.co.uk **web:** www.thecliffeatdinham.co.uk

This former gentleman's residence is a short stroll from the River Teme, with magnificent views of Ludlow Castle, just a short walk from the vibrant centre of Ludlow. The Cliffe is a successful blend of the existing Victorian features and a more contemporary style. The rooms are comfortable and well equipped. Relaxed dining from locally sourced ingredients is offered in the attractive dining room, and there is a pleasant terraced area overlooking the gardens.

Rooms: 11 en suite 2 annexe en suite (3 fmly) (1 GF) **S** £65–£85; **D** £80–£160* **Facilities:** FTV tea/coffee Dinner available Direct dial WiFi ♨18 🐾 **Parking:** 30 **Notes:** LB Closed 25–26 Dec & 1–15 Jan

Dinham Hall

★★★★ RESTAURANT WITH ROOMS

By The Castle SY8 1EJ - tel: 01584 876464
email: info@dinhamhall.com **web:** www.dinhamhall.com
dir: *In town centre, opposite castle*

Built in 1792, this lovely house stands in attractive gardens immediately opposite Ludlow Castle, and it has a well-deserved reputation for warm hospitality. The well-equipped bedrooms include two in a converted cottage, and some rooms have four-poster beds. The comfortable public rooms are elegantly appointed. Dishes served in the brasserie-style restaurant are based on good, seasonal produce.

Rooms: 11 en suite 2 annexe en suite (2 fmly) (2 GF) **S** £99–£119; **D** £119–£239* **Facilities:** Lounge tea/coffee Dinner available WiFi **Parking:** 13

LYMINGTON   Map 5 SZ39
Hampshire

The Elderflower Restaurant

★★★★ ⊚⊚⊚ RESTAURANT WITH ROOMS

4-5 Quay Street SO41 3AS- tel: 01590 676908
email: reservations@elderflowerrestaurant.co.uk **web:** www.elderflowerrestaurant.co.uk
dir: *Phone for directions*

Situated on the cobbled streets in the heart of Lymington, just moments from the quay and a short drive into the New Forest National Park. Owned and run by a husband and wife team, The Elderflower is the realisation of a lifelong dream. Bedrooms and bathrooms are well appointed and situated above the restaurant.

Cuisine is a real treat, with the team preparing modern British food with French influences using only the very best of locally sourced, sustainable produce. Parking is available nearby in the town's many car parks.

Rooms: 2 en suite **S** fr £85; **D** £95–£100* **Facilities:** FTV tea/coffee Dinner available WiFi **Notes:** No children 12yrs (weekend only) Closed 26 Dec

MARKET RASEN   Map 17 TF18
Lincolnshire

The Advocate Arms

★★★★★ ⊚⊚ RESTAURANT WITH ROOMS

2 Queen Street LN8 3EH - tel: 01673 842364
email: info@advocatearms.co.uk **web:** www.advocatearms.co.uk
dir: *In town centre*

Appointed to a high standard, this 18th-century property is located in the heart of Market Rasen and combines historic character with contemporary design. The operation centres around the stylish restaurant where service is friendly yet professional and the food is a highlight. The attractive bedrooms are very well equipped and feature luxury bathrooms.

Rooms: 10 en suite (2 fmly) **S** £60–£150; **D** £60–£160 (room only)* **Facilities:** FTV tea/coffee Dinner available WiFi ♨18 🐾 **Conf:** Max 22 Thtr 18 Class 22 Board 18 **Parking:** 6

MEDMENHAM   Map 5 SU88
Buckinghamshire

The Dog and Badger

★★★★★ ⊚ RESTAURANT WITH ROOMS

Henley Road SL7 2HE - tel: 01491 579944
email: reservations@thedogandbadger.com **web:** www.thedogandbadger.com

The Dog and Badger is a beautifully restored restaurant with rooms in a quiet village. The spacious, stunning bedrooms are in a separate cottage; all are very comfortable, with smart TVs, air-conditioning, mini bars and coffee machines as standard. Bathrooms are equipped with soft fluffy towels and high quality toiletries. There is a popular feature bar, and throughout the property there's contemporary art, which blends with original features such as exposed brick, a wood-beamed ceiling and decorative floor tiles. In the restaurant, guests are treated to a range of dishes in a relaxed and informal setting. WiFi is available throughout, outside seating is available and there is plenty of parking.

Rooms: 6 en suite **D** £195–£250 (room only)* **Facilities:** Dinner available WiFi Mini-bar coffee machine

MELBOURN   Map 12 TL34
Cambridgeshire

Sheene Mill

★★★★ ⊚⊚ RESTAURANT WITH ROOMS

39 Station Road SG8 6DX - tel: 01763 261393
email: reservations@sheenemill.com **web:** www.sheenemill.com
dir: *M11 junct 10 onto A505 towards Royston. Right to Melbourn, pass church on right, on left before old bridge*

This 16th-century watermill is situated just off the A10, a short drive from both Cambridge and Royston. Bedrooms are individually decorated and well equipped; some rooms overlook the mill pond and terrace. Public rooms include a comfortable lounge, a bar, conservatory and a delightful restaurant overlooking the pond.

Rooms: 10 en suite (4 fmly) **S** £75–£95; **D** £80–£180* **Facilities:** FTV Lounge tea/coffee Dinner available WiFi ♨18 🐾 **Extras:** Speciality toiletries – complimentary **Conf:** Max 180 Thtr 120 Class 120 Board 60 **Parking:** 60 **Notes:** Civ wed 120

MIDDLETON TYAS	Map 19 NZ20
North Yorkshire	

The Coach House

★★★★★ 🏵🏵🏵 RESTAURANT WITH ROOMS

Middleton Lodge DL10 6NJ - **tel:** 01325 377977
email: info@middletonlodge.co.uk **web:** www.middletonlodge.co.uk

Nestled within a 200-acre estate, surrounded by tall trees and winding footpaths, this picturesque scene sets the tone. Bedrooms are annexed in a courtyard style setting and furnished to a luxurious standard. Traditional features such as exposed beams and high ceilings are coupled with modern accessories such as flat-screen TV, Nespresso machines and complimentary WiFi. The kitchen takes a modern approach, using seasonal regional produce for an interesting range of meals served in the modern restaurant; cocktails are also offered. Beauty treatments are available, and weddings and private functions can be catered for.

Rooms: 9 en suite (6 GF) **S** £120–£170; **D** £140–£190* **Facilities:** STV FTV DVD Lounge tea/coffee Dinner available Direct dial WiFi 🏊 ⛳18 🔒 **Extras:** Snacks, juice – complimentary **Parking:** 70 **Notes:** LB Civ wed 100

NAILSWORTH	Map 4 ST89
Gloucestershire	

Wild Garlic Restaurant and Rooms

★★★★ 🏵🏵 🍷 RESTAURANT WITH ROOMS

3 Cossack Square GL6 0DB - **tel:** 01453 832615
email: info@wild-garlic.co.uk **web:** www.wild-garlic.co.uk
dir: M4 junct 18, A46 towards Stroud. Enter Nailsworth, left at rdbt, immediately left. Establishment opposite Britannia pub

Situated in a quiet corner of charming Nailsworth, this restaurant with rooms offers a delightful combination of welcoming, relaxed hospitality and serious cuisine. The spacious and well-equipped bedrooms are situated above the award-winning restaurant. The small and friendly team of staff ensure guests are very well looked after throughout their stay.

Rooms: 5 en suite (2 fmly) **S** £80–£160; **D** £85–£160* **Facilities:** STV FTV DVD tea/coffee Dinner available WiFi ⛳18 Fishing Shooting, hot air ballooning
Extras: Speciality toiletries, spring water – complimentary; mini-bar – chargeable
Conf: Max 6 Thtr 6 Class 6 Board 6

NEWENT	Map 10 SO72
Gloucestershire	

Three Choirs Vineyards

★★★★ 🏵 RESTAURANT WITH ROOMS

GL18 1LS - **tel:** 01531 890223
email: info@threechoirs.com **web:** www.three-choirs-vineyards.co.uk
dir: On B4215 N of Newent, follow brown tourist signs

This thriving vineyard continues to go from strength to strength and provides a wonderfully different place to stay. The restaurant, which overlooks the 100-acre estate, enjoys a popular following thanks to well-executed dishes that make good use of local produce. Spacious, high quality bedrooms are equipped with many extras, and each opens onto a private patio area which has lovely views.

Rooms: 11 annexe en suite (1 fmly) (11 GF) **S** £135–£195; **D** £145–£195*
Facilities: FTV Lounge tea/coffee Dinner available Direct dial WiFi Wine tasting Vineyard Tours **Conf:** Max 20 Thtr 20 Class 15 Board 20 **Parking:** 11 **Notes:** LB Closed 24–26 Dec & 31 Dec–6 Jan

NEWQUAY	Map 2 SW86
Cornwall & Isles of Scilly	

Lewinnick Lodge

★★★★ RESTAURANT WITH ROOMS

Pentire Headland TR7 1QD - **tel:** 01637 878117
email: thelodge@hospitalitycornwall.com **web:** www.lewinnicklodge.co.uk
dir: From A392, at rdbt exit into Pentire Rd then Pentire Ave. Turn right to Lewinnick Lodge

Set above the cliffs of Pentire Headland, looking out across the mighty Atlantic, guests are guaranteed amazing coastal views here at Lewinnick Lodge. The bedrooms were designed by Guy Bostock and are modern, spacious, and offer many thoughtful extras; some have open-plan bathrooms. Modern British food (with an emphasis on fresh fish) is served all day.

Rooms: 11 en suite (1 fmly) **S** £116–£187.50; **D** £155–£250* **Facilities:** FTV iPod docking station tea/coffee Dinner available Direct dial Lift WiFi Pool table 🔒 Surf board store **Extras:** Speciality toiletries, robes, bottled water – complimentary **Parking:** 50

NORWICH	Map 13 TG20
Norfolk	

Brasteds

★★★★★ 🏵🏵 🍷 RESTAURANT WITH ROOMS

Manor Farm Barns, Fox Road NR14 7PZ - **tel:** 01508 491112
email: enquiries@brasteds.co.uk **web:** www.brasteds.co.uk
dir: A11 onto A47 towards Great Yarmouth, then A146. 0.5m, right into Fox Rd, 0.5m on left

Brasteds is a lovely detached property set in 20 acres of mature, landscaped parkland on the outskirts of Norwich. The tastefully appointed bedrooms have beautiful soft furnishings and fabrics along with comfortable seating and many thoughtful touches. Public rooms include a cosy snug with plush sofas, and a smart dining room where breakfast is served. Dinner is available in Brasteds Restaurant, which can be found in an adjacent building.

Rooms: 6 en suite (1 fmly) (3 GF) **Facilities:** FTV DVD iPod docking station TVL tea/coffee Dinner available Direct dial WiFi 🔒 **Extras:** Mini-bar **Conf:** Max 120 Thtr 120 Class 100 Board 40 **Parking:** 50 **Notes:** LB Civ wed 160

The Old Rectory

★★★★ ◉◉ RESTAURANT WITH ROOMS

103 Yarmouth Road, Thorpe St Andrew NR7 0HF · tel: 01603 700772
email: enquiries@oldrectorynorwich.com **web:** www.oldrectorynorwich.com
dir: *From A47 southern bypass onto A1042 towards Norwich N & E. Left at slip road onto A1042. Follow signs to "All routes" & Thorpe St Andrew, at mini rdbt left onto A1242. Straight on at lights, entrance on right*

This delightful Grade II listed Georgian property is ideally located in a peaceful area overlooking the River Yare, just a few minutes' drive from the city centre. Spacious bedrooms are individually designed with carefully chosen soft fabrics, plush furniture and many thoughtful touches; many of the rooms overlook the swimming pool and landscaped gardens. Accomplished cooking is offered via an interesting daily-changing menu, which features skilfully prepared local produce.

Rooms: 5 en suite 3 annexe en suite **S** £99–£185; **D** £125–£185*
Facilities: FTV iPod docking station Lounge tea/coffee Dinner available Direct dial WiFi ↘ 🔒 **Extras:** Robes, speciality toiletries **Conf:** Max 14 Thtr 14 Class 10 Board 14 **Parking:** 12 **Notes:** LB Closed 22 Dec–3 Jan RS Sun–Mon No dinner served

---

NOTTINGHAM	Map 11 SK53
Nottinghamshire	

INSPECTOR'S CHOICE

Restaurant Sat Bains with Rooms

★★★★★ ◉◉◉◉◉ RESTAURANT WITH ROOMS

Lenton Lane, Trentside NG7 2SA · tel: 0115 986 6566
email: info@restaurantsatbains.net **web:** www.restaurantsatbains.com
dir: *M1 junct 24, A453 Nottingham S. Over River Trent into central lane to rdbt. Left, left again towards river. Establishment on left after bend*

This charming restaurant with rooms, a stylish conversion of Victorian farm buildings, is situated on the river and close to the industrial area of Nottingham. The bedrooms create a warm atmosphere by using quality soft furnishings together with antique and period furniture; suites and four-poster rooms are available. Public areas are chic and cosy, and the delightful restaurant complements the truly outstanding, much acclaimed cuisine.

Rooms: 7 en suite **Facilities:** STV tea/coffee Dinner available **Parking:** 22 **Notes:** No children 8yrs Closed 1st week Jan & 2 weeks mid Aug

---

OLDSTEAD	Map 19 SE57
North Yorkshire	

INSPECTOR'S CHOICE

The Black Swan at Oldstead

★★★★★ ◉◉◉◉ 🍷 RESTAURANT WITH ROOMS

YO61 4BL · tel: 01347 868387
email: enquiries@blackswanoldstead.co.uk **web:** www.blackswanoldstead.co.uk
dir: *Exit A19, 3m S Thirsk for Coxwold, left in Coxwold, left at Byland Abbey for Oldstead*

The Black Swan is set amidst the stunning scenery of the North York Moors National Park, and parts of the building date back to the 16th century. Well appointed, very comfortable bedrooms provide the perfect get-away; some are on the ground floor overlooking the kitchen garden, others are in the Georgian House and feature both baths and wet-room showers. These bedrooms, together with welcoming open fires, a traditional bar and an award-winning restaurant that has become a destination in its own right, all combine to make this a 'little gem' of a property.

Rooms: 4 en suite 5 annexe en suite (6 GF) **D** £330–£480* **Facilities:** FTV tea/coffee Dinner available WiFi **Extras:** Home-made biscuits, speciality toiletries **Parking:** 20 **Notes:** No children 18yrs

---

ORFORD	Map 13 TM45
Suffolk	

The Crown & Castle

★★★★★ ◉◉ RESTAURANT WITH ROOMS

IP12 2LJ · tel: 01394 450205
email: info@crownandcastle.co.uk **web:** www.crownandcastle.co.uk
dir: *Turn right from B1084 on entering village, towards castle*

The Crown & Castle is a delightful restaurant with rooms situated adjacent to the Norman castle keep. Contemporary style bedrooms are spilt between the main house and the garden wing; the latter are more spacious and have patios with access to the garden. The restaurant has an informal atmosphere with polished tables and local artwork, and a menu that features quality, locally sourced produce.

Rooms: 7 en suite 14 annexe en suite (2 fmly) (13 GF) **D** £140–£250* **Facilities:** FTV DVD tea/coffee Dinner available Direct dial WiFi ⅃18 **Extras:** Speciality toiletries, fresh milk **Notes:** LB No children 8yrs

---

ORMSKIRK	Map 15 SD40
Lancashire	

INSPECTOR'S CHOICE

Moor Hall Restaurant with Rooms

★★★★★ ◉◉◉ 🍷 RESTAURANT WITH ROOMS

Prescot Road, Aughton L39 6RT · tel: 01695 572511 & 07817 917868
email: enquiry@moorhall.com **web:** www.moorhall.com
dir: *From M58 junct 1, take 1st exit at rdbt then 1st left. Continue for 1.7m. Moor Hall is signposted on the right*

Located within west Lancashire in five acres of gardens with stunning views over a beautiful lake, said to be the remains of a medieval moat. This Grade II listed house has been transformed with care and attention to detail into a true destination restaurant with rooms. Bedrooms are stunning, with many showcasing some of the original features of the house, paired with a new and exciting style. Mark Birchall is at the helm here and has created a refined dining experience in relaxed surroundings. Local provenance is at the forefront of this modern British cuising; produce grown on site or by local suppliers is used whereever possible, naturally reflecting the broad culinary experience Mark has gained over his career. A passionate team in all areas, offering a knowledgeable and friendly guest experience. Developments within the site include the addition of a barn, which will offer a more casual dining experience with the same strong ethos.

Rooms: 5 en suite 2 annexe en suite (2 fmly) (2 GF) **D** fr £195* **Facilities:** FTV Lounge tea/coffee Dinner available WiFi **Extras:** Fruit, snacks, mini-bar **Parking:** 40 **Notes:** Closed 31 Jul for 2 weeks

OSMOTHERLEY
North Yorkshire
Map 19 SE49

The Cleveland Tontine

★★★★★ ◎◎ 🍷 RESTAURANT WITH ROOMS

Staddlebridge DL6 3JB - tel: 01609 882671
email: bookings@theclevelandtontine.co.uk **web:** www.theclevelandtontine.co.uk
dir: *Just off A172 junct on A19 Nbound*

This iconic destination restaurant with rooms is a stunning place. Contemporary public areas sit alongside a traditional restaurant with open fires, tiled flooring and great food. Afternoon tea can be taken in the conservatory overlooking the gardens. Bedrooms are individually designed, with modern furniture and feature bathrooms. The service is friendly and relaxed, there is ample parking and major road links are close by.

Rooms: 7 en suite (4 fmly) **Facilities:** FTV Lounge tea/coffee Dinner available Direct dial WiFi **Extras:** Speciality toiletries **Conf:** Max 70 Thtr 56 Class 28 Board 38 **Parking:** 60 **Notes:** Civ wed 56

OSWESTRY
Shropshire
Map 15 SJ22

Sebastians

★★★★ ◎◎ 🍷 RESTAURANT WITH ROOMS

45 Willow Street SY11 1AQ - tel: 01691 655444
email: info@sebastians-hotel.com **web:** www.sebastians-hotel.co.uk
dir: *From town centre, take turn signed Selattyn into Willow St. 400yds from junct on left opposite Willow Street Gallery*

Sebastians is an intrinsic part of the leisure scene in Oswestry and has built up a loyal local following. Meals feature French influences, with a multi-choice set menu as well as a simpler market menu. Rooms are set around the pretty terrace courtyard, and provide very comfortable accommodation with all the comforts of home.

Rooms: 2 en suite 4 annexe en suite (2 fmly) (2 GF) **S** £75; **D** £85 (room only)*
Facilities: iPod docking station Lounge tea/coffee Dinner available WiFi
Extras: Speciality toiletries, fruit, sweets – complimentary **Parking:** 6
Notes: Closed Xmas/New Year & BHs

PADSTOW
Cornwall & Isles of Scilly
Map 2 SW97

AA RESTAURANT WITH ROOMS OF THE YEAR 2017–18

INSPECTOR'S CHOICE

Padstow Townhouse

★★★★★ ◎◎◎◎ 🍷 RESTAURANT WITH ROOMS

16/18 High Street PL28 8BB - tel: 01841 550950
email: stay@padstowtownhouse.co.uk **web:** www.paul-ainsworth.co.uk

This cosy 18th-century townhouse offers six individually styled suites, providing all home comforts as well as some extra little luxuries. Each room has its own 40" curved TV complete with Apple TV, as well as free WiFi. Breakfast is served in Rojano's in the Square, and guests are welcome to dine there (it has one AA Rosette) or at the four AA-Rosetted Paul Ainsworth at No.6 restaurant.

Rooms: 6 en suite **Facilities:** Dinner available WiFi **Extras:** Speciality toiletries

INSPECTOR'S CHOICE

The Seafood Restaurant

★★★★★ ◎◎◎ 🍷 RESTAURANT WITH ROOMS

Riverside PL28 8BY - tel: 01841 532700
email: reservations@rickstein.com **web:** www.rickstein.com
dir: *Into town centre, down hill (Station Rd), follow signs to harbour car park, opposite car park*

Food lovers continue to beat a well-trodden path to this famous restaurant. Situated on the edge of the harbour, just a stone's throw from the shops, The Seafood Restaurant offers chic and comfortable bedrooms that boast numerous thoughtful extras; some have views of the estuary and a couple have private balconies with stunning sea views. Service is relaxed and friendly; booking is essential for both accommodation and a table in the restaurant.

Rooms: 16 en suite 6 annexe en suite (12 fmly) (3 GF) **Facilities:** FTV DVD tea/coffee Dinner available Direct dial Lift WiFi 🔒 Cookery School **Extras:** Speciality toiletries, robes, mini-bar **Parking:** 13 **Notes:** LB Closed 24–26 Dec RS 24 Dec limited restaurant service times

St Petroc's Bistro

★★★★★ ◎ RESTAURANT WITH ROOMS

4 New Street PL28 8EA - tel: 01841 532700
email: reservations@rickstein.com **web:** www.rickstein.com
dir: *A39 onto A389, follow signs to Padstow town centre*

One of the oldest buildings in town, this charming establishment is just up the hill from the picturesque harbour. Style, comfort and individuality are all great strengths here, particularly so in the impressively equipped bedrooms. Breakfast, lunch and dinner all reflect a serious approach to cuisine, and the popular restaurant has a relaxed, bistro style. Comfortable lounges, a reading room and lovely gardens complete the picture.

Rooms: 10 en suite (2 fmly) **Facilities:** FTV Lounge tea/coffee Dinner available Direct dial WiFi **Parking:** 4 **Notes:** LB Closed 24–26 Dec

PEWSEY
Wiltshire
Map 5 SU15

INSPECTOR'S CHOICE

Troutbeck Guest House at the Red Lion Freehouse

★★★★★ ◎◎◎ 🍷 RESTAURANT WITH ROOMS

East Chisenbury SN9 6AQ - tel: 01980 671124
email: enquiries@redlionfreehouse.com **web:** www.redlionfreehouse.com
dir: *A345 to Upavon, left at T-junct, right signed East Chisenbury*

The Red Lion Freehouse at East Chisenbury offers an interesting blend of sumptuous accommodation and food, yet it retains the informality and laidback atmosphere of a traditional pub. Each of the five rooms have been individually appointed and offer plenty of in-room amenities coupled with beautiful views of the surrounding countryside. The cooking is confident and a particular flair is brought to the dishes based on seasonal, local ingredients. The pub rears its own pigs and keeps rescue hens. Tucked behind the Red Lion is a tranquil tree-shaded beer garden.

Rooms: 5 en suite (1 fmly) (5 GF) **S** £180–£260; **D** £180–£260* **Facilities:** FTV tea/coffee Dinner available WiFi 🎣 18 Fishing **Extras:** Speciality toiletries, snacks, robes – complimentary; mini-bar – chargeable **Conf:** Max 16 **Parking:** 5 **Notes:** LB

PORTHLEVEN
Cornwall & Isles of Scilly · Map 2 SW62

Kota Restaurant with Rooms
★★★ ◉◉ RESTAURANT WITH ROOMS

Harbour Head TR13 9JA - tel: 01326 562407
email: kota@btconnect.com web: www.kotarestaurant.co.uk
dir: B3304 from Helston into Porthleven. Kota on harbour opposite slipway

Overlooking the water, this 300-year-old building is the home of Kota Restaurant ('kota' being the Maori word for 'shellfish'). The bedrooms are approached from a granite stairway to the side of the building. The family room is spacious and has the benefit of harbour views, while the smaller, double room is at the rear of the property. The enthusiastic young owners ensure guests enjoy their stay here, and a meal in the two AA Rosette award-winning restaurant should not be missed. Food and drink is also served in the Kota Kai Bar & Kitchen. Breakfast features the best local produce.

Rooms: 2 annexe en suite (1 fmly) S £65–£90; D £75–£100* Facilities: FTV DVD tea/coffee Dinner available WiFi ⅃18 🛁 Extras: Fridge Parking: 1 Notes: Closed Jan–10 Feb

READING
Berkshire · Map 5 SU77

The French Horn
★★★★ ◉◉ RESTAURANT WITH ROOMS

Sonning RG4 6TN - tel: 0118 969 2204
email: info@thefrenchhorn.co.uk web: www.thefrenchhorn.co.uk
dir: From A4 into Sonning, follow B478 through village over bridge, on right, car park on left

This long-established Thames-side establishment has a lovely village setting and retains the traditions of classic hospitality. The restaurant is a particular attraction and has been awarded two AA Rosettes. Bedrooms, including four cottage suites, are spacious and comfortable; many offer stunning views over the river. A private boardroom is available for corporate guests.

Rooms: 12 en suite 8 annexe en suite (4 GF) Facilities: FTV iPod docking station Lounge tea/coffee Dinner available Direct dial WiFi ⅃18 Fishing 🛁 Extras: Speciality toiletries, safe, mineral water Conf: Max 14 Board 14 Parking: 43 Notes: Closed 1–2 Jan RS 25 Dec eve closed for dinner

RETFORD
Nottinghamshire · Map 17 SK78

Blacksmiths
★★★★★ ◉◉ RESTAURANT WITH ROOMS

Town Street, Clayworth DN22 9AD - tel: 01777 818171
email: info@blacksmithsclayworth.com web: www.blacksmithsclayworth.com
dir: From A631, 2.4m to Clayworth

Blacksmiths is a modern restaurant with annexed accommodation, situated in the quiet village of Clayworth, and a short drive from Retford. Meals in the restaurant are one of the many highlights of the stay, as are the hearty breakfasts which can be delivered as room-service. Bedrooms are a recent addition and have been finished to an excellent standard. Modern gadgets and accessories are provided such as climate control, large widescreen TVs, and WiFi. Thoughtful extras such as fluffy bathrobes and luxurious toiletries add to the experience. A warm welcome is guaranteed at this owner-run establishment.

Rooms: 4 en suite (2 fmly) (2 GF) Facilities: FTV iPod docking station tea/coffee Dinner available WiFi 🛁 Conf: Max 120 Thtr 70 Class 20 Board 20 Parking: 31 Notes: Civ wed 70

RICCALL
North Yorkshire · Map 16 SE63

Per Bacco at The Park View
★★★ RESTAURANT WITH ROOMS

20 Main Street YO19 6PX - tel: 01757 249146
email: gianlucasechi@hotmail.com web: www.per-bacco.co.uk
dir: A19 from Selby, left for Riccall by water tower, house 100yds on right

This spacious detached property is located in a quiet residential area and is convenient for York. The ground floor has been converted into an authentic Italian restaurant and there is a wide choice of fresh, home-made dishes, all in a friendly atmosphere. The restaurant is the main part of the business but there is also a range of comfortable en suite bedrooms. Ample parking is available.

Rooms: 4 en suite (2 fmly) Facilities: STV FTV iPod docking station Lounge TVL tea/coffee Dinner available WiFi ⅃ 🛁 Parking: 30 Notes: LB

ROSS-ON-WYE
Herefordshire · Map 10 SO52

Wilton Court Restaurant with Rooms
★★★★★ ◉◉ 🍴 RESTAURANT WITH ROOMS

Wilton Lane HR9 6AQ - tel: 01989 562569
email: info@wiltoncourthotel.com web: www.wiltoncourthotel.com
dir: M50 junct 4, A40 towards Monmouth at 3rd rdbt left signed Ross-on-Wye, 1st right, on right

Dating back to the 16th century, Wilton Court has great charm and a wealth of character. Standing on the banks of the River Wye, just a short walk from the town centre, there is a genuinely relaxed, friendly and unhurried atmosphere created by hosts Roger and Helen Wynn and their reliable team. Bedrooms are tastefully furnished and well equipped, while public areas include a comfortable lounge, traditional bar and pleasant restaurant with a conservatory extension overlooking the garden. High standards of food, using fresh, locally sourced ingredients, are offered.

Rooms: 11 en suite (1 fmly) (1 GF) S £100–£155; D £135–£185* Facilities: FTV DVD Lounge tea/coffee Dinner available Direct dial WiFi ⅃18 Fishing 🛁 Extras: Kimonos, bottled water Parking: 20 Notes: LB Closed 3–15 Jan

Glewstone Court Country House
★★★★ ◉◉ 🍴 RESTAURANT WITH ROOMS

Glewstone HR9 6AW - tel: 01989 770367
email: info@glewstonecourt.com web: www.glewstonecourt.com
dir: From Ross-on-Wye market place follow A40/A49 Monmouth/Hereford signs, over Wilton Bridge to rdbt, left onto A40 towards Monmouth, in 1m right for hotel

This charming country house enjoys an elevated position with views over Ross-on-Wye, and is set in well-tended gardens. The owners ensure guests are well looked after from the moment of arrival. Bedrooms come in a variety of sizes and are tastefully furnished and well equipped. An excellent choice of dishes utilising high quality ingredients should not be missed at dinner.

Rooms: 9 en suite (2 fmly) S £99–£169; D £114–£184* Facilities: Dinner available Notes: Closed 2–18 Jan RS Nov–Feb Civ wed 70

| **ROWDE** | Map 4 ST96 |
| Wiltshire | |

The George & Dragon

★★★★ ◉◉ RESTAURANT WITH ROOMS

High Street SN10 2PN - tel: 01380 723053
email: gm@thegeorgeanddragonrowde.co.uk **web:** www.thegeorgeanddragonrowde.co.uk
dir: *1.5m from Devizes on A350 towards Chippenham*

The George & Dragon dates back to the 14th century when it was a meeting house. Exposed beams, wooden floors, antique rugs and open fires create a warm atmosphere in the bar and restaurant. Bedrooms and bathrooms are very well decorated and equipped with some welcome extras. Dining in the bar or restaurant should not be missed, as local produce and fresh fish deliveries from Cornwall are offered on the daily-changing blackboard menu.

Rooms: 3 rms (2 en suite) (1 pri facs) (1 fmly) **S** £75–£125; **D** £75–£125*
Facilities: FTV DVD iPod docking station Lounge TVL tea/coffee Dinner available WiFi
🍴 **Extras:** Mini-bar, snacks, robes – complimentary **Parking:** 14

| **SCUNTHORPE** | Map 17 SE81 |
| Lincolnshire | |

San Pietro Restaurant Rooms

★★★★ ◉◉ RESTAURANT WITH ROOMS

High Street East DN15 6UH - tel: 01724 277774 **11**
email: info@sanpietro.uk.com **web:** www.sanpietro.uk.com
dir: *3m from M180, follow signs for Scunthorpe town centre & railway station, left into Brigg Rd/Station Rd. Near windmill*

This family-run restaurant with rooms was purpose-built, and offers comfortable modern accommodation. Bedrooms and bathrooms provide a range of additional extras such as mini-bars, home-made cakes, complimentary WiFi and smart TVs. Dinner and breakfast are served in the annexe Ristorante. Dinner menus have an Italian influence and provide a range of choice including a chef's tasting menu as well as a full à la carte offering. Continental breakfasts are included, with a choice to upgrade to a hearty cooked breakfast.

San Pietro Restaurant Rooms

Rooms: 14 en suite (5 GF) **Facilities:** STV FTV iPod docking station tea/coffee Dinner available Direct dial Lift WiFi ⬇18 🍴 **Extras:** Speciality toiletries, home-made cake, mini-bar **Conf:** Max 80 Thtr 80 Class 40 Board 30 **Parking:** 25 **Notes:** Closed 25–26 Dec, Sun & BH Mon Civ wed 120

| **SHAFTESBURY** | Map 4 ST82 |
| Dorset | |

La Fleur de Lys Restaurant with Rooms

★★★★ ◉◉ RESTAURANT WITH ROOMS

Bleke Street SP7 8AW - tel: 01747 853717
email: info@lafleurdelys.co.uk **web:** www.lafleurdelys.co.uk
dir: *From junct of A30 & A350, 0.25m towards town centre*

Located just a few minutes' walk from the famous Gold Hill, this light and airy restaurant with rooms combines efficient service with a relaxed and friendly atmosphere. Bedrooms, which are suitable for both business and leisure guests, vary in size but all are well equipped, comfortable and tastefully furnished. A relaxing guest lounge and courtyard are available for afternoon tea or pre-dinner drinks. The excellent food has been awarded two AA Rosettes.

Rooms: 8 en suite (2 fmly) (1 GF) **S** £85–£120; **D** £100–£170* **Facilities:** FTV Lounge tea/coffee Dinner available Direct dial WiFi 🍴 **Extras:** Home-made biscuits, fresh milk – complimentary **Conf:** Max 12 Board 10 **Parking:** 10 **Notes:** LB RS 1–21 Jan restaurant closed

| **SHREWSBURY** | Map 15 SJ41 |
| Shropshire | |

Drapers Hall

★★★★★ ◉◉ 🍷 RESTAURANT WITH ROOMS

10 Saint Mary's Place SY1 1DZ - tel: 01743 344679
email: goodfood@drapershallrestaurant.co.uk **web:** www.drapershallrestaurant.co.uk
dir: *From A5191 (Saint Mary's St) on one-way system into St Mary's Place*

Drapers Hall is a 16th-century, timber-framed property situated in the heart of the market town of Shrewsbury. Rooms differ in size, and all offer high levels of comfort and style, including two spacious suites. Bathrooms have a high quality finish and are well equipped for the modern traveller. The original beams and wood panels are complemented by striking art work and large gilt mirrors. A smart modern bar area successfully blends with the original architectural features, and has a great vibe. Accomplished cooking from Nigel Huxley can be enjoyed in a relaxing dining environment. Parking is available on request.

Rooms: 6 en suite (2 fmly) **Facilities:** FTV TVL tea/coffee Dinner available WiFi
Conf: Max 20 Thtr 20 Class 20 Board 20

Porter House SY1

★★★★ 🍽 RESTAURANT WITH ROOMS

15 Saint Mary's Street SY1 1EQ - **tel:** 01743 358870 & 761220
email: hello@porterhousesy1.co.uk **web:** www.porterhousesy1.co.uk
dir: *Follow one-way system around town, opposite St Mary's church*

This fine property is located in the heart of the town. The name comes from a cut of steak, which is relevant to the style of cuisine here, with a real emphasis on locally sourced, good quality steaks and grills, served in the award-winning vibrant restaurant or bar. The four individually designed bedrooms, including a suite, are very comfortable and have spacious and contemporary bathrooms. Breakfast offers a quality range of dishes. Secure parking is available in a nearby public car park.

Rooms: 4 en suite (1 fmly) **S** £65–£110; **D** £95–£140 (room only)*
Facilities: tea/coffee Dinner available WiFi **Notes:** LB Closed 25–26 Dec & 1 Jan RS Xmas & New Year

SIDLESHAM
West Sussex   Map 5 SZ89

The Crab & Lobster

★★★★★ ◉◉ 🍷 RESTAURANT WITH ROOMS

Mill Lane PO20 7NB - **tel:** 01243 641233
email: enquiries@crab-lobster.co.uk **web:** www.crab-lobster.co.uk
dir: *A27 onto B2145 signed Selsey. 1st left after garage at Sidlesham into Rookery Ln to Crab & Lobster*

Hidden away on the south coast near Pagham Harbour and only a short drive from Chichester is the stylish Crab & Lobster. Bedrooms are superbly appointed, and bathrooms are a feature with luxury toiletries and powerful 'raindrop' showers. Guests can enjoy lunch or dinner in the smart restaurant where the menu offers a range of locally caught fresh fish together with other regionally-sourced, seasonal produce.

Rooms: 4 en suite S £100–£120; D £175–£205* **Facilities:** FTV DVD iPod docking station tea/coffee Dinner available WiFi **Extras:** Speciality toiletries, fresh milk **Parking:** 12

SIDMOUTH
Devon   Map 3 SY18

The Salty Monk

★★★★★ ◉◉ 🍷 RESTAURANT WITH ROOMS

Church Street, Sidford EX10 9QP - **tel:** 01395 513174
email: saltymonk@btconnect.com **web:** www.saltymonk.co.uk
dir: *On A3052 opposite church in Sidford*

Set in the village of Sidford, this attractive property dates from the 16th century. There's plenty of style and appeal here and each bedroom has a unique identity. Bathrooms are equally special with multi-jet showers, spa baths and cosseting robes and towels. The output from the kitchen is impressive with excellent local produce very much in evidence, served in the elegant surroundings of the restaurant. A mini-spa facility is available.

Rooms: 5 en suite 1 annexe en suite (3 GF) **S** £85–£120; **D** £105–£190*
Facilities: FTV Lounge tea/coffee Dinner available WiFi ♨18 Gym ♨ Outdoor hot tub Massage therapists **Extras:** Speciality toiletries, bottled water, snacks – complimentary **Parking:** 20 **Notes:** LB Closed 1 week Nov & Jan

SOLIHULL
West Midlands   Map 10 SP17

INSPECTOR'S CHOICE

Hampton Manor

★★★★★ ◉◉◉◉ 🍷 RESTAURANT WITH ROOMS

Shadowbrook Lane, Hampton-in-Arden B92 0EN - **tel:** 01675 446080
email: info@hamptonmanor.com **web:** www.hamptonmanor.com
dir: *M42 junct 6 follow signs for A45 (Birmingham). At 1st rdbt, 1st exit onto B4438 (Catherine de Barnes Ln). Left into Shadowbrook Ln*

Hampton Manor is set in 45 acres of mature woodland, only minutes from Birmingham's major air, rail and road links and the NEC. The manor offers luxurious accommodation with a contemporary and sophisticated style while still maintaining many of its original features and heritage. The bedrooms are all beautifully and uniquely designed and boast sumptuous beds. Fine dining can be enjoyed at Peel's restaurant, which is a fabulous venue for innovative cooking, and will prove the highlight of any stay.

Rooms: 15 en suite (3 fmly) (1 GF) **S** £160–£350; **D** £160–£350 (room only)*
Facilities: FTV DVD iPod docking station Lounge tea/coffee Dinner available Direct dial WiFi ♨18 Beauty treatments **Extras:** Bottled water, home-made cookies, fresh fruit **Conf:** Max 120 Thtr 120 Class 60 Board 35 **Parking:** 30 **Notes:** LB Civ wed 120

SOUTH FERRIBY
Lincolnshire   Map 17 SE92

The Hope and Anchor Pub

★★★★ ◉◉ RESTAURANT WITH ROOMS

Sluice Road DN18 6JQ - **tel:** 01652 635334
email: info@thehopeandanchorpub.co.uk **web:** www.thehopeandanchorpub.co.uk

This pub dates back to the 19th Century and is perfectly situated in the town of South Ferriby with stunning views of the Humber Bridge. Bedrooms are modern and furnished to a high standard with exceptionally comfortable beds. Modern amenities such as Nespresso machines, complimentary WiFi and flat-screen TVs. Dinner in the award-winning restaurant will surely be a highlight of any stay, as are the hearty breakfasts. Staff are friendly and welcoming and a relaxed atmosphere is guaranteed. Complimentary on-site car parking.

Rooms: 5 en suite **S** £95–£115; **D** £95–£115 (room only)* **Facilities:** Dinner available WiFi **Extras:** Nespresso machines **Parking Notes:** Closed Sun & Mon

SOUTHAMPTON
Hampshire   Map 5 SU41

Ennio's Restaurant & Boutique Rooms

★★★★★ 🍷 🍽 RESTAURANT WITH ROOMS

Town Quay Road SO14 3AS - **tel:** 023 8022 1159 & 07748 966113
email: info@ennios.co.uk **web:** www.ennios.co.uk
dir: *Opposite Red Funnel Ferry terminal*

This fine property, lovingly converted from a former Victorian warehouse, offers luxurious accommodation on Southampton's waterfront. All rooms are en suite and are furnished to a very high standard, including mini-bars and over-sized showers. Downstairs, the popular Ennio's Restaurant and bar is the ideal setting in which to dine, offering an authentic Italian atmosphere and a wonderful selection of dishes. There is limited parking available to the rear of the building.

Rooms: 10 en suite **Facilities:** FTV iPod docking station tea/coffee Dinner available WiFi **Extras:** Speciality toiletries, mini-bar **Parking:** 6 **Notes:** LB Closed 24–26 Dec

SOUTHWOLD
Suffolk
Map 13 TM57

Sutherland House

★★★★★ ◎◎ RESTAURANT WITH ROOMS

56 High Street IP18 6DN - tel: 01502 724544
email: enquiries@sutherlandhouse.co.uk **web:** www.sutherlandhouse.co.uk
dir: *A1095 into Southwold, on High St on left after Victoria St*

Situated in the heart of the bustling town centre, this delightful 16th-century house has a wealth of character – oak beams, exposed brickwork, open fireplaces and two superb ornate plasterwork ceilings. The stylish bedrooms are tastefully decorated using co-ordinated fabrics and include many thoughtful touches. Public rooms feature a large open-plan contemporary restaurant, which has been awarded two AA Rosettes. There's a modern British menu created with care, and the food miles are listed alongside each dish.

Rooms: 5 en suite (1 fmly) **S** £100* **Facilities:** FTV DVD tea/coffee Dinner available WiFi **Notes:** No children 10yrs RS Mon Restaurant closed in winter Oct–Mar

STALHAM
Norfolk
Map 13 TG32

The Ingham Swan

★★★★ ◎◎ RESTAURANT WITH ROOMS

Sea Palling Road, Ingham NR12 9AB - tel: 01692 581099
email: info@theinghamswan.co.uk **web:** www.theinghamswan.co.uk
dir: *From A149 Stalham, into Old Market Rd towards Upper Staithe Rd/Lower Staithe Rd. At rdbt 1st exit, 2nd exit at next rdbt into Ingham Rd. Continue to Town Rd*

The Swan is a charming 14th-century former coaching inn that has been sympathetically restored and enjoys a peaceful rural location in the heart of Norfolk. Stylish, very well equipped bedrooms are most comfortable and the eye-catching original features really add to the presentation. The award-winning restaurant serves the best of Norfolk produce and there is a small bar area for pre-dinner drinks. Secure parking is available along with free WiFi for guests.

Rooms: 4 annexe en suite (1 fmly) (2 GF) **S** £105–£115; **D** £125–£145*
Facilities: FTV tea/coffee Dinner available WiFi **Parking:** 12 **Notes:** Closed 25–26 Dec

STAMFORD
lincolnshire
Map 11 TF00

Candlesticks

★★★ RESTAURANT WITH ROOMS

1 Church Lane PE9 2JU - tel: 01780 764033
email: info@candlestickshotel.co.uk **web:** www.candlestickshotel.co.uk
dir: *B1081 into Stamford. Left onto A43. Right into Worthorpe Rd, right into Church Ln*

Candlesticks is a 17th-century property situated in a quiet lane in the oldest part of Stamford, just a short walk from the centre of town. The bedrooms are pleasantly decorated and equipped with a good range of useful extras. Public rooms include Candlesticks restaurant and a cosy bar.

Rooms: 8 en suite **Facilities:** STV FTV Lounge tea/coffee Dinner available Direct dial WiFi 🔒 **Parking:** 8 **Notes:** LB RS Mon No restaurant or bar service

STOCKBRIDGE
Hampshire
Map 5 SU33

The Greyhound on the Test

★★★★ ◎◎ 🪑 RESTAURANT WITH ROOMS

31 High Street SO20 6EY - tel: 01264 810833
email: info@thegreyhoundonthetest.co.uk **web:** www.thegreyhoundonthetest.co.uk
dir: *9m NW of Winchester, 8m S of Andover. Off A303*

This charming restaurant with rooms has the River Test at its rear and the two AA Rosette award-winning food is a real draw. In addition, the luxury bedrooms are generally spacious, beautifully styled and come with a host of extras. Bathrooms are modern and have high quality towels and toiletries. There is also ample parking and well-kept grounds.

Rooms: 10 en suite (1 GF) **S** fr £85; **D** £140–£240* **Facilities:** FTV DVD Lounge tea/coffee Dinner available WiFi ⌦ 18 Fishing **Extras:** Speciality toiletries – complimentary; honesty bar **Conf:** Max 12 Board 12 **Parking:** 28
Notes: Closed 24–25 Dec

STOW-ON-THE-WOLD
Gloucestershire
Map 10 SP12

Old Stocks Inn

★★★★★ ◎ 🪑 RESTAURANT WITH ROOMS

The Square GL54 1AP - tel: 01451 830666
email: info@oldstocksinn.com **web:** www.oldstocksinn.com
dir: *From A429 turn into Market Sq, located opposite Town Hall*

Old Stocks Inn has been lovingly restored, and offers a mix of modern facilities and 17th-century charm. Bedrooms are well designed and make good use of space; there are some unique features in the 'great' rooms. Cuisine is at the heart of the operation, with a café, restaurant and bar making up the impressive ground floor. Award-winning breakfasts are served in the restaurant, while lunch and dinner also offer award-winning dining.

Rooms: 13 en suite 3 annexe en suite (4 fmly) (3 GF) **D** £99–£279* **Facilities:** FTV iPod docking station Lounge tea/coffee Dinner available Direct dial WiFi 🔒 **Extras:** Mini-bar, Nespresso machine **Conf:** Max 16 Thtr 10 Board 16 **Parking:** 10 **Notes:** Closed 25 Dec RS 24 Dec no accommodation

SUDBURY
Suffolk
Map 13 TL84

The Case Restaurant with Rooms

★★★★ ◎ RESTAURANT WITH ROOMS

Further Street, Assington CO10 5LD - tel: 01787 210483
email: restaurant@thecaserestaurantwithrooms.co.uk
web: www.thecaserestaurantwithrooms.co.uk
dir: *Exit A12 at Colchester onto A134 to Sudbury. 7m, establishment on left*

The Case Restaurant with Rooms offers dining in comfortable surroundings, along with luxurious accommodation in bedrooms that all enjoy independent access. Some bathrooms come complete with corner jacuzzi, while internet access comes as standard. In the restaurant, local produce is used in all dishes, and bread and delicious desserts are made fresh every day.

Rooms: 7 en suite (2 fmly) (7 GF) **Facilities:** FTV Lounge tea/coffee Dinner available WiFi **Extras:** Speciality toiletries – complimentary; snacks – chargeable **Parking:** 25 **Notes:** LB

RESTAURANTS WITH ROOMS

TOLLARD ROYAL	Map 4 ST91
Wiltshire	

King John Inn

★★★★ ◉◉ RESTAURANT WITH ROOMS

SP5 5PS - **tel:** 01725 516207
email: info@kingjohninn.co.uk **web:** www.kingjohninn.co.uk
dir: *From A354 or A350 onto B3081*

Part of The Epicurean Collection, the King John Inn is a traditional style country inn located in a country village. It has a Victorian-style garden pavilion serving seasonal classics such as chargrilled lobster and pigeon salad. The recently added Dove Cottage offers three more en suite bedrooms to go with the five rooms at the inn. All have feature bathrooms. Food and wine is a real feature here with local ingredients much in evidence, alongside excellent levels of hospitality and customer care. Ample parking for residents.

Rooms: 5 en suite 3 annexe en suite (2 GF) **Facilities:** FTV Lounge tea/coffee Dinner available Direct dial WiFi ⛷ **Parking:** 18 **Notes:** LB RS 25 Dec restaurant closed for dinner

TORQUAY	Map 3 SX96
Devon	

Orestone Manor

★★★★ ◉◉ 🛜 RESTAURANT WITH ROOMS

Rockhouse Lane, Maidencombe TQ1 4SX - **tel:** 01803 328098
email: info@orestonemanor.com **web:** www.orestonemanor.com
dir: *N of Torquay on A379, on sharp bend in village of Maidencombe*

Set in a fabulous location overlooking the bay, Orestone Manor has a long history of providing fine food and very comfortable accommodation, coupled with friendly, attentive service. Log fires burn in cooler months, and there is a conservatory, a bar and a sitting room for guests to enjoy. AA Rosettes have been awarded for the uncomplicated modern cuisine which is based on quality local produce.

Rooms: 11 en suite 3 annexe en suite (6 fmly) (3 GF) **S** £85–£140; **D** £120–£350* **Facilities:** STV FTV iPod docking station Lounge tea/coffee Dinner available Direct dial WiFi 🛁 **Extras:** Speciality toiletries, bottled water **Conf:** Max 90 Thtr 90 Class 60 Board 30 **Parking:** 38 **Notes:** LB Closed 3–29 Jan Civ wed 90

ULVERSTON	Map 18 SD27
Cumbria	

Virginia House

★★★ ◉◉ RESTAURANT WITH ROOMS

24 Queen Street LA12 7AF - **tel:** 01229 584844 & 07495 128499
email: contact@virginahouseulverston.co.uk **web:** www.virginiahouseulverston.co.uk
dir: *M6 junct 36 onto A590 towards Barrow-in-Furness. In Ulverston take 3rd exit at Tank Square rdbt & follow one-way system. 1st exit at mini rdbt into King St, then Queen St. 200mtrs on right*

A warm, personal welcome is guaranteed at this family-run restaurant with rooms. The restaurant is at the heart of the property with award-winning meals served in modern and comfortable surroundings. All meals highlight very good quality local produce. The gin parlour has a selection of over 100 gins to choose from. Bedrooms are comfortable and well appointed. Complimentary WiFi is available throughout. There is no parking on-site, but there is provision within a short walking distance.

Rooms: 8 en suite **S** £65–£75; **D** £99 **Facilities:** FTV iPod docking station tea/coffee Dinner available WiFi 🛁 **Extras:** Speciality toiletries, home-made biscuits **Conf:** Max 30 Thtr 30 Class 11 Board 16

UPPINGHAM	Map 11 SP89
Rutland	

The Lake Isle

★★★★ ◉◉ 🛜 RESTAURANT WITH ROOMS

16 High Street East LE15 9PZ - **tel:** 01572 822951
email: info@lakeisle.co.uk **web:** www.lakeisle.co.uk
dir: *From A47, turn left at 2nd lights, 100yds on right*

This attractive town house centres around a delightful restaurant and small elegant bar. There is also an inviting first-floor guest lounge, and the bedrooms are extremely well appointed and thoughtfully equipped; spacious split-level cottage suites situated in a quiet courtyard are also available. The imaginative cooking and an extremely impressive wine list are highlights here.

Rooms: 9 en suite 3 annexe rms (3 pri facs) (1 fmly) (1 GF) **S** £70–£80; **D** £90–£120* **Facilities:** FTV Lounge tea/coffee Dinner available Direct dial WiFi 🛁 **Extras:** Home-made biscuits – complimentary **Conf:** Max 16 Board 16 **Parking:** 7 **Notes:** Closed 1 Jan & BHs RS Sun eve & Mon lunch closed

WADDESDON	Map 11 SP71
Buckinghamshire	

The Five Arrows

★★★★ ◉◉ 🛜 RESTAURANT WITH ROOMS

High Street HP18 0JE - **tel:** 01296 651727
email: reservations@thefivearrows.co.uk **web:** www.waddesdon.org.uk/fivearrows
dir: *On A41 in Waddesdon. Into Baker St for car park*

This Grade II listed building with its elaborate Elizabethan-style chimney stacks stands at the gates of Waddesdon Manor and was named after the Rothschild family emblem. Individually styled en suite bedrooms are comfortable and well appointed. Friendly staff are on hand to offer a warm welcome. Alfresco dining is possible in the warmer months.

Rooms: 8 en suite 8 annexe en suite (2 fmly) (3 GF) **S** £70–£130; **D** £95–£235* **Facilities:** FTV tea/coffee Dinner available WiFi 🛁 **Conf:** Max 20 Thtr 20 Class 20 Board 20 **Parking:** 40 **Notes:** Civ wed 60

WANTAGE	Map 5 SU38
Oxfordshire	

La Fontana Restaurant with Accommodation

★★★★ 🛜 RESTAURANT WITH ROOMS

Oxford Road, East Hanney OX12 0HP - **tel:** 01235 868287 & 07836 730048
email: anna@la-fontana.co.uk **web:** www.la-fontana.co.uk
dir: *A338 from Wantage towards Oxford. Restaurant on right in East Hanney*

Guests are guaranteed a warm welcome at this family-run Italian restaurant located on the outskirts of the busy town of Wantage. The stylish bedrooms are individually designed, well equipped and very comfortable. Dinner should not be missed – the menu features a wide range of regional Italian specialities.

Rooms: 12 en suite 3 annexe en suite (1 fmly) (4 GF) **S** £67.50–£72.50; **D** £87.50–£125* **Facilities:** FTV Lounge tea/coffee Dinner available Direct dial WiFi **Parking:** 30 **Notes:** Civ wed 120

RESTAURANTS WITH ROOMS

WEST WITTON
North Yorkshire
Map 19 SE08

The Wensleydale Heifer

★★★★★ ◉ ⚬ RESTAURANT WITH ROOMS

Main Street DL8 4LS - **tel:** 01969 622322
email: info@wensleydaleheifer.co.uk **web:** www.wensleydaleheifer.co.uk
dir: A1 to Leeming Bar junct, A684 towards Bedale for approx 10m to Leyburn, then towards Hawes 3.5m to West Witton

Describing itself as 'boutique style', this 17th-century former coaching inn is very much of the 21st century. The bedrooms, with Egyptian cotton linen and Molton Brown toiletries as standard, are each designed with an interesting theme – for example, Black Sheep, Night at the Movies, True Romantics and Shooters, and for chocolate lovers, there's a bedroom where you can eat as much chocolate as you like! The food is very much the focus here in both the informal fish bar and the contemporary style restaurant. The kitchen prides itself on sourcing the freshest fish and locally reared meats.

Rooms: 9 en suite 4 annexe en suite (2 fmly) (2 GF) **S** £80–£160; **D** £120–£200
Facilities: FTV DVD Lounge tea/coffee Dinner available Direct dial WiFi
Extras: Speciality toiletries, fruit, snacks **Parking:** 30 **Notes:** LB

WHITBY
North Yorkshire
Map 19 NZ81

Estbek House

★★★★★ ◉◉ ⚬ RESTAURANT WITH ROOMS

East Row, Sandsend YO21 3SU - **tel:** 01947 893424
email: info@estbekhouse.co.uk **web:** www.estbekhouse.co.uk
dir: From Whitby take A174. In Sandsend, left into East Row

The speciality seafood restaurant on the first floor is the focus of this listed building in a small coastal village north west of Whitby. The seasonal menu is based on fresh, local ingredients, and is overseen by Tim the chef, who has guided his team to two AA Rosettes. There is also a small bar and breakfast room, and four individually appointed bedrooms offering high levels of comfort.

Rooms: 4 rms (3 en suite) (1 pri facs) **Facilities:** tea/coffee Dinner available WiFi
Parking: 6 **Notes:** LB No children 14yrs

WILMINGTON
East Sussex
Map 6 TQ50

Crossways

★★★★★ ◉◉ RESTAURANT WITH ROOMS

Lewes Road BN26 5SG - **tel:** 01323 482455
email: stay@crosswayshotel.co.uk **web:** www.crosswayshotel.co.uk
dir: On A27 between Lewes & Polegate, 2m E of Alfriston rdbt

Proprietors David Stott and Clive James have been welcoming guests to this elegant restaurant with rooms for over 25 years. Crossways sits amid stunning gardens and attractively tended grounds. The well-presented bedrooms are tastefully decorated and provide an abundance of thoughtful amenities including free WiFi. Guest comfort is paramount and the warm hospitality ensures guests often return.

Rooms: 7 en suite **S** £59–£85; **D** £145–£175* **Facilities:** FTV tea/coffee Dinner available Direct dial WiFi ⚑ **Extras:** Speciality toiletries, mini-bar, fresh milk
Parking: 30 **Notes:** LB No children 12yrs Closed 24 Dec–23 Jan

---

WIMBORNE MINSTER
Dorset
Map 5 SZ09

Les Bouviers Restaurant with Rooms

★★★★★ ◉◉ RESTAURANT WITH ROOMS

Arrowsmith Road, Canford Magna BH21 3BD - **tel:** 01202 889555
email: info@lesbouviers.co.uk **web:** www.lesbouviers.co.uk
dir: A31 onto A349. Left in 0.6m. In approx 1m right into Arrowsmith Rd. Establishment approx 100yds on right

Les Bouviers is an excellent restaurant with rooms in a great location, set in five and a half acres of grounds. Food is obviously a highlight of any stay here, as is the friendly, attentive service. Chef patron Leonard James Coward's team turn out impressive cooking, which has been recognised with two AA Rosettes. The bedrooms are extremely well equipped and the beds are supremely comfortable. Cream teas can be taken on the terrace.

Rooms: 6 en suite (4 fmly) **S** £70–£150; **D** £80–£220* **Facilities:** FTV DVD Lounge tea/coffee Dinner available Direct dial WiFi All bathrooms have steam showers or air baths **Extras:** Robes, slippers, mineral water **Conf:** Max 120 Thtr 100 Class 100 Board 100 **Parking:** 50 **Notes:** LB RS Sun eve restricted opening & restaurant closed Civ wed 120

WINCHCOMBE
Gloucestershire
Map 10 SP02

Wesley House

★★★★ ◉◉ ⚬ RESTAURANT WITH ROOMS

High Street GL54 5LJ - **tel:** 01242 602366
email: enquiries@wesleyhouse.co.uk **web:** www.wesleyhouse.co.uk
dir: In town centre

This 15th-century, half-timbered property is named after John Wesley, founder of the Methodist Church, who stayed here while preaching in the town. Bedrooms are small and full of character. In the rear dining room, where the food has been awarded two AA Rosettes, a unique lighting system changes colour to suit the mood required, and also highlights the various floral displays created by a world-renowned flower arranger. A glass atrium covers the outside terrace.

Rooms: 5 en suite **S** £75–£85; **D** £95–£110* **Facilities:** FTV Lounge tea/coffee Dinner available WiFi ⚑ **Notes:** RS Sun eve & Mon Restaurant closed Civ wed 60

WINTERINGHAM
Lincolnshire
Map 17 SE92

INSPECTOR'S CHOICE

Winteringham Fields

★★★★★ ◉◉◉◉ RESTAURANT WITH ROOMS

1 Silver Street DN15 9ND - **tel:** 01724 733096
email: reception@winteringhamfields.co.uk **web:** www.winteringhamfields.co.uk
dir: In village centre at x-rds

This highly regarded restaurant with rooms, located deep in the countryside at Winteringham village, is six miles west of the Humber Bridge. Public rooms and bedrooms, some of which are housed in renovated barns and cottages, are delightfully luxurious. There is an abundance of charm, and period features are combined with rich furnishings and fabrics. The award-winning food is a highlight of any stay and guests can expect highly skilled dishes, excellent quality and stunning presentation.

Rooms: 4 en suite 11 annexe en suite (6 fmly) (3 GF) **Facilities:** iPod docking station tea/coffee Dinner available Direct dial WiFi 🔒 **Conf:** Max 50 Thtr 50 Class 50 Board 50 **Parking:** 14 **Notes:** LB Closed 25 Dec for 2 weeks, last week Oct, 2 weeks Aug Civ wed 60

WYE
Kent — Map 7 TR04

Wife of Bath
★★★★ ◎◎ RESTAURANT WITH ROOMS

4 Upper Bridge Street TN25 5AF - **tel:** 01233 812232
email: info@thewifeofbath.com **web:** www.thewifeofbath.com
dir: *M20 junct 10, A2070 signed Kennington. At rdbt right onto A28 (Canterbury Road). Right at x-rds into Harville Rd signed Wye. At T-junct (station opposite) right into Bridge Rd, becomes Churchfield Way. Right into Church St. At T-junct left, Wife of Bath on right*

Located in the heart of this picturesque village of Wye, the Wife of Bath has benefited from a complete refurbishment, with the restaurant and the en suite rooms stylish in design. All are very comfortably appointed and still feature the buildings original features including exposed oak beams. The restaurant is open daily for both breakfast, lunch and dinner.

Rooms: 3 en suite 2 annexe en suite (2 GF) **S** £105–£140; **D** £105–£140*
Facilities: FTV tea/coffee Dinner available WiFi **Extras:** Fruit, snacks, robes
Parking: 10

YAXLEY
Suffolk — Map 13 TM17

The Auberge
★★★★★ ◎◎ 🍴 RESTAURANT WITH ROOMS

Ipswich Road IP23 8BZ - **tel:** 01379 783604
email: aubmail@the-auberge.co.uk **web:** www.the-auberge.co.uk
dir: *On A140 between Norwich & Ipswich at x-rds with B1117*

A warm welcome awaits at The Auberge, a charming 15th-century property, which was once a rural pub but is now a smart restaurant with rooms. The restaurant has gained two AA Rosettes for the good use of fresh, quality produce in well-crafted dishes. The public areas have a wealth of character, such as exposed brickwork and beams, and the grounds are particularly well kept and attractive. The spacious bedrooms are tastefully appointed and have many thoughtful touches; one bedroom has a four-poster.

Rooms: 11 annexe en suite (2 fmly) (6 GF) **S** £75–£110* **Facilities:** FTV tea/coffee Dinner available Direct dial WiFi 🔒 **Conf:** Max 30 Thtr 30 Class 20 Board 12 **Parking:** 40 **Notes:** LB

YEOVIL
Somerset — Map 4 ST51

INSPECTOR'S CHOICE

Little Barwick House
★★★★★ ◎◎◎ 🍴 RESTAURANT WITH ROOMS

Barwick BA22 9TD - **tel:** 01935 423902
email: littlebarwick@hotmail.com **web:** www.littlebarwickhouse.co.uk
dir: *From Yeovil A37 towards Dorchester, left at 1st rdbt, 1st left, 0.25m on left*

Situated in a quiet hamlet in three and half acres of gardens and grounds, this listed Georgian dower house is an ideal retreat for those seeking peaceful surroundings and good food. Just one of the highlights of a stay here is a meal in the restaurant, where good use is made of local ingredients. Each of the bedrooms has its own character, and a range of thoughtful extras such as fresh flowers, bottled water and magazines is provided.

Rooms: 6 en suite **Facilities:** FTV iPod docking station tea/coffee Dinner available Direct dial WiFi 🔒 **Parking:** 30 **Notes:** LB No children 5yrs RS Sun eve & Mon closed

SCOTLAND

ABERLADY
East Lothian — Map 21 NT47

Ducks Inn
★★★★ ◎◎ RESTAURANT WITH ROOMS

Main Street EH32 0RE - **tel:** 01875 870682
email: info@ducks.co.uk **web:** www.ducks.co.uk
dir: *A1 (Bankton junct) take 1st exit to North Berwick. At next rdbt 3rd exit onto A198 signed Longniddry, left towards Aberlady. At T-junct, facing river, right to Aberlady*

The name of this restaurant with rooms is referenced around the building – Ducks Restaurant for award-winning cuisine; Donald's Bistro and the Ducklings informal coffee shop. The warm and welcoming public areas include a great bar offering real ales and various objets d'art. The bedrooms are comfortable and well-appointed with stylish en suites. The team are informal and friendly, taking the time to chat to their guests.

Rooms: 23 en suite (1 fmly) (6 GF) **S** £50–£110; **D** £70–£140* **Facilities:** STV FTV Lounge TVL tea/coffee Dinner available Direct dial WiFi ♨18 🔒 **Conf:** Max 100 Thtr 100 Class 60 Board 30 **Parking:** 15

ACHARACLE
Highland — Map 22 NM66

Mingarry Park
★★★★ 🍴 RESTAURANT WITH ROOMS

Mingarry PH36 4JX - **tel:** 01967 431202 & 07791 115467
email: info@mingarryparkhouse.co.uk **web:** www.mingarryparkhouse.co.uk

Set in some breath-taking scenery, Mingarry Park offers six individual, contemporary-styled bedrooms. Each offers great views across the deer park and surrounding countryside. Some rooms have balconies and decked areas to relax in. Diners are treated to the best local produce in creative dishes with a roaring log burner the centre piece of the restaurant.

Rooms: 6 en suite (3 GF) **S** £75–£130; **D** £95–£140* **Facilities:** FTV DVD iPod docking station tea/coffee Dinner available WiFi 🔒 **Notes:** Closed Feb–Mar

ANSTRUTHER
Fife

Map 21 NO50

The Waterfront

★★★★ 🍽 RESTAURANT WITH ROOMS

18–20 Shore Street KY10 3EA - **tel:** 01333 312200
email: info@anstruther-waterfront.co.uk **web:** www.anstruther-waterfront.co.uk
dir: *Off A917 opposite marina*

Situated overlooking the harbour, The Waterfront offers spacious, stylish,
contemporary accommodation, with bedrooms located in lovingly restored buildings
in a courtyard behind the restaurant. There is a comfortable lounge with a smartly
fitted kitchen and dining room, and laundry facilities are available in the granary.
Dinner and breakfast are served in the attractive restaurant that offers a
comprehensive menu featuring the best of local produce.

Rooms: 10 en suite (3 fmly) (2 GF) **Facilities:** FTV DVD Lounge tea/coffee Dinner
available WiFi ⅃ Pool table 🛎 **Extras:** Mineral water **Notes:** LB

COLBOST
Isle of Skye

Map 22 NG24

INSPECTOR'S CHOICE

The Three Chimneys & The House Over-By

★★★★★ ◉◉◉ 🍽 RESTAURANT WITH ROOMS

IV55 8ZT - **tel:** 01470 511258
email: eatandstay@threechimneys.co.uk **web:** www.threechimneys.co.uk
dir: *4m W of Dunvegan village on B884 signed Glendale*

A visit to this delightful property will make a trip to Skye even more memorable.
The stunning food is the result of a deft approach using quality local
ingredients. Breakfast is an impressive array of local fish, meats and cheeses,
served with fresh home baking and home-made preserves. The new stylish
lounge-breakfast area has the real wow factor. Bedrooms in the House Over-By,
are creative and thoughtfully equipped – all have spacious en suites and
wonderful views across Loch Dunvegan. The Three Chimneys is the winner of the
AA Food Service award 2017-2018.

The Three Chimneys & The House Over-By

Rooms: 6 en suite (1 fmly) (6 GF) **D** £345* **Facilities:** FTV DVD iPod docking
station Lounge tea/coffee Dinner available Direct dial WiFi ⅃9 🛎 Bookings
can be made for leisure activities **Extras:** Speciality toiletries, Nespresso
machine, fruit, robes **Conf:** Max 12 Thtr 12 Class 12 Board 12 **Parking:** 12
Notes: LB Closed 10 Dec–19 Jan

EDDLESTON
Scottish Borders

Map 21 NT24

The Horseshoe Restaurant with Rooms

★★★★ 🍽 RESTAURANT WITH ROOMS

Edinburgh Road EH45 8QP - **tel:** 01721 730225
email: reservations@horseshoeinn.co.uk **web:** www.horseshoeinn.co.uk
dir: *A703, 5m N of Peebles*

The Horseshoe is five miles north of Peebles and only 18 miles south of Edinburgh.
Originally a blacksmith's shop, it has a very good reputation for its delightful
atmosphere and excellent cuisine. There are eight luxuriously appointed and
individually designed bedrooms. Please note: children are welcome, but dinner is
not served to under fives except in the private dining room.

Rooms: 8 en suite (1 fmly) (6 GF) **Facilities:** FTV Lounge tea/coffee Dinner available
Direct dial WiFi **Extras:** Speciality toiletries, fruit, mineral water – complimentary
Parking: 20 **Notes:** LB Closed 25 Dec, 1st 2 weeks Jan & 2 weeks Jul RS
Mon & Tue closed

EDINBURGH
City of Edinburgh — Map 21 NT27

INSPECTOR'S CHOICE

21212

★★★★★ ◉◉◉◉ RESTAURANT WITH ROOMS

3 Royal Terrace EH7 5AB - tel: 0131 523 1030
email: reservations@21212restaurant.co.uk web: www.21212restaurant.co.uk
dir: Calton Hill, city centre

A real jewel in Edinburgh's crown, this establishment takes its name from the number of choices at each course on the five-course dinner menu. Located on the prestigious Royal Terrace this light and airy, renovated Georgian town house stretches over four floors. The four individually-designed bedrooms epitomise luxury living and the bathrooms certainly have the wow factor. At the heart of this restaurant with rooms is the creative and impressive four AA Rosette award-winning cooking of Paul Kitching. Service throughout is friendly and very attentive.

Rooms: 4 en suite S £95–£325; D £95–£325 Facilities: STV FTV iPod docking station Lounge Dinner available WiFi Extras: Speciality toiletries, mineral water, sloe gin Notes: No children 5yrs Closed 1 week Jan & 1 week Autumn RS Sun & Mon restaurant closed

The Witchery by the Castle

★★★★★ ◉ ⌂ RESTAURANT WITH ROOMS

Castlehill, The Royal Mile EH1 2NF - tel: 0131 225 5613
email: mail@thewitchery.com web: www.thewitchery.com
dir: Top of Royal Mile at gates of Edinburgh Castle

Originally built in 1595, The Witchery by the Castle is situated in a historic building at the gates of Edinburgh Castle. The two luxurious and theatrically decorated suites, known as the Inner Sanctum and the Old Rectory, are located above the restaurant and are reached via a winding stone staircase. Filled with antiques, opulently draped beds, large roll-top baths and a plethora of memorabilia, this ancient and exciting establishment is often described as one of the country's most romantic destinations.

Rooms: 4 en suite 5 annexe en suite (1 GF) Facilities: STV FTV DVD tea/coffee Dinner available Direct dial WiFi Extras: Bottled water – complimentary Notes: No children 12yrs Closed 25–26 Dec

FORRES
Moray — Map 23 NJ05

Cluny Bank

★★★★ ◉ RESTAURANT WITH ROOMS

69 St Leonards Road IV36 1DW - tel: 01309 674304
email: info@clunybankhotel.co.uk web: www.clunybankhotel.co.uk

Historic, listed Cluny Bank occupies a quiet location within walking distance of the centre of Forres, and is an ideal base for exploring the north-east of Scotland. Family-run, the building retains many original architectural features. Public areas include the Altyre Bar with a wide range of whiskies, and Franklin's Restaurant where a real taste of Moray can be experienced. Room service, complimentary WiFi and memorable breakfasts are also provided for guests.

Rooms: 6 en suite 1 annexe en suite (2 GF) S £85–£90; D £122.50–£165* Facilities: FTV iPod docking station Lounge tea/coffee Dinner available Direct dial WiFi Parking: 7 Notes: LB

INVERKEILOR
Angus — Map 23 NO64

INSPECTOR'S CHOICE

Gordon's

★★★★★ ◉◉◉ ⌂ RESTAURANT WITH ROOMS

Main Road DD11 5RN - tel: 01241 830364
email: gordonsrest@aol.com web: www.gordonsrestaurant.co.uk
dir: Exit A92 between Arbroath & Montrose into Inverkeilor

It's worth a detour off the main road to this family-run restaurant with rooms set in the centre of the village. The food in the restaurant has been awarded three AA Rosettes, and the excellent breakfasts are equally memorable. A huge fire dominates the restaurant on cooler evenings. Individually designed rooms all come with contemporary wenge furniture, oversized headboards, chandeliers, high decorative cornice and designer wallpaper. The showcase Thistle Suite is in purple, stone and lavender and has an en suite bathroom with roll-top bath and monsoon shower.

Rooms: 4 en suite 1 annexe en suite (1 GF) S £110; D £110–£160* Facilities: tea/coffee Dinner available WiFi Extras: Speciality toiletries – complimentary Parking: 6 Notes: No children 12yrs Closed Jan

KINGUSSIE
Highland — Map 23 NH70

INSPECTOR'S CHOICE

The Cross

★★★★ ◉◉◉ ⌂ RESTAURANT WITH ROOMS

Tweed Mill Brae, Ardbroilach Road PH21 1LB - tel: 01540 661166
email: relax@thecross.co.uk web: www.thecross.co.uk
dir: From lights in Kingussie centre take Ardbroilach Rd, 300yds left into Tweed Mill Brae

Built as a water-powered tweed mill in the late 19th century, The Cross is situated in the picturesque Cairngorms National Park and surrounded by four acres of riverside grounds that teem with an abundance of wildlife, including red squirrels. Comfortable lounges and a selection of well-appointed bedrooms are offered, and award-winning dinners are served by an open fire in the stone-walled and wood-beamed restaurant.

Rooms: 8 en suite S £90–£150; D £110–£180* Facilities: FTV DVD Lounge tea/coffee Dinner available Direct dial WiFi Extras: Bottled water, speciality toiletries Conf: Max 20 Thtr 20 Class 20 Board 20 Parking: 20 Notes: LB Closed Jan

NAIRN
Highland
Map 23 NH85

INSPECTOR'S CHOICE

Boath House
★★★★★ ◉◉◉◉ ⚲ RESTAURANT WITH ROOMS

Auldearn IV12 5TE - tel: 01667 454896
email: info@boath-house.com web: www.boath-house.com
dir: *2m past Nairn on A96, E towards Forres, signed on main road*

Standing in its own 20-acre grounds, with an ornamental lake, walled garden and secluded seating areas, this splendid Georgian mansion was built in 1825 for the Dunbar family, but there has been occupation on the site since the 16th century. Hospitality here is first class; the owners are passionate about what they do, and have a real ability to establish a special relationship with their guests. The food is memorable; head chef Charlie Lockley is a devotee of slow and organic cooking which also includes using foraged produce. The five-course dinners are a culinary adventure, matched only by the excellence of breakfasts. The house itself is delightful, with inviting lounges and a dining room overlooking a trout loch. The bedrooms, with lake and woodland views, are striking and very comfortable; Orangerie Rooms have their own conservatory.

Rooms: 9 en suite (2 GF) S £235–£305; D £380–£450* Facilities: FTV DVD Lounge tea/coffee Dinner available Direct dial WiFi ⚓ Fishing Parking: 20 Notes: Civ wed 32

NEWPORT-ON-TAY
Fife
Map 21 NO42

The Newport Restaurant Limited
★★★★ ◉◉ RESTAURANT WITH ROOMS

1 High Street DD6 8AB - tel: 01382 541449
email: info@thenewportrestaurant.co.uk web: www.thenewportrestaurant.co.uk

Jamie Scotts' restaurant with rooms is situated shore side in Newport looking over the Tay to Dundee. The modern restaurant is set over two floors both enjoying panoramic views. Style is modern with a nod to the local maritime and fishing history. Four bedrooms are spacious and well equipped for the modern traveller with comfortable beds and a few added luxuries.

Rooms: 4 en suite (2 fmly) S £140–£160; D £160–£210* Facilities: FTV iPod docking station WiFi Parking: 10 Notes: Closed 24 Dec–9 Jan

PEAT INN
Fife
Map 21 NO40

INSPECTOR'S CHOICE

The Peat Inn
★★★★★ ◉◉◉ RESTAURANT WITH ROOMS

KY15 5LH - tel: 01334 840206
email: stay@thepeatinn.co.uk web: www.thepeatinn.co.uk
dir: *At junct of B940 & B941, 5m SW of St Andrews*

This 300-year-old former coaching inn enjoys a rural location is close to St Andrews. The Peat Inn is spacious, very well appointed, and offers rooms that all have lounge areas. The inn is steeped in history and for years has proved a real haven for food lovers. The three dining areas create a romantic setting, and

chef/owner Geoffrey Smeddle produces excellent, award-winning dishes. Expect welcoming open fires and a relaxed ambiance. An extensive continental breakfast selection is served to guests in their bedrooms each morning.

Rooms: 8 annexe en suite (3 fmly) (8 GF) Facilities: FTV Lounge tea/coffee Dinner available Direct dial WiFi ⚓ Extras: Speciality toiletries, fruit, sherry – free Parking: 24 Notes: LB Closed 25–26 Dec, 2 weeks Jan, 1 week Nov RS Sun–Mon closed

PORTPATRICK
Dumfries & Galloway
Map 20 NW95

Knockinaam Lodge
★★★★★ ◉◉◉ RESTAURANT WITH ROOMS

DG9 9AD - tel: 01776 810471
email: reservations@knockinaamlodge.com web: www.knockinaamlodge.com
dir: *From A77 or A75 follow signs to Portpatrick. Through Lochans. After 2m left at signs for hotel*

Any tour of Dumfries and Galloway wouldn't be complete without a stay at this haven of tranquillity and relaxation. Knockinaam Lodge is an extended Victorian house set in an idyllic cove with its own pebble beach (ideal for a private swim in the summer) and sheltered by majestic cliffs and woodlands. Surrounded by 30 acres of delightful grounds, the lodge was the location for a meeting between Churchill and General Eisenhower in World War II. Today, a warm welcome is assured from the proprietors and their committed team, and much emphasis is placed on providing a sophisticated but intimate home-from-home experience. There are just ten suites – each individually designed and all with flat-screen TVs with DVD players, luxury toiletries and complimentary bottled water. The cooking is a real treat and showcases prime Scottish produce on the daily-changing, four-course set menus; guests can always discuss the choices in advance if they wish.

Rooms: 10 en suite (1 fmly) S £175–£325; D £290–£450* Facilities: Dinner available ⚓ Fishing Shooting Walking Sea fishing Clay pigeon shooting Notes: Civ wed 40

SANQUHAR
Dumfries & Galloway
Map 21 NS70

Blackaddie House
★★★★ ◉◉ RESTAURANT WITH ROOMS

Blackaddie Road DG4 6JJ - tel: 01659 50270
email: ian@blackaddiehotel.co.uk web: www.blackaddiehotel.co.uk
dir: *300 yds from A76 on N side of Sanquhar*

Overlooking the River Nith, in two acres of secluded gardens, this family-run country house offers friendly and attentive hands-on service. The bedrooms and suites are all well-presented and comfortable, with many useful extras provided as standard. The award-winning food, served in the restaurant, with its lovely garden views, is based on prime Scottish ingredients. Three self-catering cottages are also available

Rooms: 6 en suite 1 annexe en suite (1 GF) **S** £105–£225; **D** £125–£235*
Facilities: FTV DVD Lounge tea/coffee Dinner available Direct dial WiFi ♨9 🅿
Extras: Speciality toiletries, mineral water, home-made shortbread **Conf:** Max 16 Thtr 16 Class 16 Board 12 **Parking:** 20 **Notes:** LB Civ wed 24

SPEAN BRIDGE
Highland

Map 22 NN28

Smiddy House

★★★★ ◉◉ 🍴 RESTAURANT WITH ROOMS

Roy Bridge Road PH34 4EU - tel: 01397 712335
email: enquiry@smiddyhouse.com **web:** www.smiddyhouse.com
dir: In village centre, A82 onto A86

Set in the Great Glen which stretches from Fort William to Inverness, this was once the village smithy, and is now a very friendly restaurant with rooms. The attractive bedrooms, named after places in Scotland, are comfortably furnished and well equipped. A relaxing garden room is available for guest use. Delicious evening meals are served in Russell's restaurant.

Rooms: 4 en suite 1 annexe en suite (1 GF) **S** £90–£130; **D** £115–£195*
Facilities: FTV Lounge tea/coffee Dinner available WiFi **Extras:** Speciality toiletries, mineral water – complimentary **Parking:** 15 **Notes:** No children 12yrs Closed Mon RS Nov–Mar limited opening

---

STRATHAVEN
South Lanarkshire

Map 20 NS74

Rissons at Springvale

★★★ ◉ RESTAURANT WITH ROOMS

18 Lethame Road ML10 6AD - tel: 01357 521131 & 520234
email: info@rissons.co.uk **web:** www.rissonsrestaurant.co.uk
dir: A71 into Strathaven, W of town centre off Townhead St

Guests are assured of a warm welcome at this charming establishment close to the town centre. The bedrooms and bathrooms are stylish and well equipped. The main attraction here is the food – a range of interesting, well-prepared dishes served in Rissons Restaurant.

Rooms: 9 en suite (1 fmly) (1 GF) **S** £50; **D** £85–£90* **Facilities:** FTV Lounge TVL tea/coffee Dinner available WiFi ♨ ♨18 Fishing 🅿 **Parking:** 10
Notes: Closed 1st week Jan

STRATHYRE
Stirling

Map 20 NN51

Creagan House

★★★★★ 🍴 RESTAURANT WITH ROOMS

FK18 8ND - tel: 01877 384638
email: eatandstay@creaganhouse.co.uk **web:** www.creaganhouse.co.uk
dir: 0.25m N of Strathyre on A84

Originally a farmhouse dating from the 17th century, Creagan House has operated as a restaurant with rooms for many years. The baronial-style dining room provides a wonderful setting for the classic French and Scottish cuisine. The warm hospitality and attentive service are noteworthy.

Rooms: 5 en suite (1 fmly) (1 GF) **S** £90–£110; **D** £135–£155* **Facilities:** FTV Lounge tea/coffee Dinner available WiFi 🅿 **Extras:** Speciality toiletries **Conf:** Max 35 Thtr 35 Class 12 Board 35 **Parking:** 16 **Notes:** LB Closed 26 Oct–6 Apr RS Wed & Thu closed

---

STRUAN
Isle of Skye

Map 22 NG33

INSPECTOR'S CHOICE

Ullinish Country Lodge

★★★★★ ◉◉◉ 🍴 RESTAURANT WITH ROOMS

IV56 8FD - tel: 01470 572214
email: ullinish@theisleofskye.co.uk **web:** www.theisleofskye.co.uk
dir: Take A863 N. Lodge signed on left

Set in some of Scotland's most dramatic landscape, with views of the Black Cuillin and MacLeod's Tables, this lodge has lochs on three sides. Samuel Johnson and James Boswell stayed here in 1773 and were impressed with the hospitality even then. Hosts Brian and Pam hope to extend the same welcome to their guests today. As you would expect, all bedrooms have amazing views, and come with half-tester beds.

Rooms: 6 en suite **S** £120–£190; **D** £180–£270* **Facilities:** FTV Lounge tea/coffee Dinner available WiFi **Extras:** Sherry, sweets, mineral water – complimentary **Parking:** 8 **Notes:** LB No children 16yrs Closed 24 Dec–Jan

TOBERMORY
Isle of Mull

Map 22 NM55

Highland Cottage

★★★★ RESTAURANT WITH ROOMS

24 Breadalbane Street PA75 6PD - tel: 01688 302030
email: davidandjo@highlandcottage.co.uk **web:** www.highlandcottage.co.uk
dir: *A848 Craignure/Fishnish ferry terminal, pass Tobermory signs, straight on at mini rdbt across narrow bridge, turn right. Highland Cottage on right opposite fire station*

Providing the highest level of natural and unassuming hospitality, this delightful little gem lies high above the island's capital. Don't be fooled by its side street location, a stunning view over the bay is just a few metres away. 'A country house in town' it is an Aladdin's Cave of collectables and treasures, as well as masses of books and magazines. There is an honesty bar in the first-floor lounge. The cosy dining room offers memorable dinners and splendid breakfasts. Bedrooms are individual; some have four-posters and all are comprehensively equipped to include TVs and music centres.

Rooms: 6 en suite (1 GF) **S** £125–£155; **D** £155–£170* **Facilities:** FTV Dinner available Direct dial WiFi **Notes:** No children 10yrs Closed Nov–Mar

WALES

ABERGELE
Conwy

Map 14 SH97

The Kinmel Arms

★★★★★ RESTAURANT WITH ROOMS

The Village, St George LL22 9BP - tel: 01745 832207
email: info@thekinmelarms.co.uk **web:** www.thekinmelarms.co.uk
dir: *From A55 junct 24a to St George. E on A55, junct 24. 1st left to Rhuddlan, 1st right into St George. 2nd right*

This converted 17th-century coaching inn stands close to the church in the village of St George. The restaurant specialises in skilfully prepared produce from Wales and north-west England. Friendly, helpful staff will ensure you have a relaxing stay, in one of four attractive suites. All are kitted out with small kitchenettes where continental breakfasts are placed each day to enjoy at your leisure. Each suite is individually designed in a clean, natural style with luxurious bathrooms to match.

Rooms: 4 en suite (2 GF) **S** £115–£155; **D** £115–£175 **Facilities:** STV Lounge tea/coffee Dinner available ⅃18 **Extras:** Speciality toiletries, fruit, snacks, bottled water – complimentary **Conf:** Max 10 Board 10 **Parking:** 50 **Notes:** LB No children 16yrs Closed 25 Dec & 1 Jan RS Sun & Mon closed (ex BHs)

BRECON
Powys

Map 9 SO02

Peterstone Court

★★★★★ RESTAURANT WITH ROOMS

Llanhamlach LD3 7YB - tel: 01874 665387
email: info@peterstone-court.com **web:** www.peterstone-court.com
dir: *3m from Brecon on A40 towards Abergavenny*

Situated on the edge of the Brecon Beacons, this establishment affords stunning views overlooking the River Usk. The atmosphere is friendly and informal, with no unnecessary fuss. No two bedrooms are alike, but all share comparable levels of comfort, quality and elegance. Public areas reflect similar standards, eclectically styled with a blend of the contemporary and the traditional. Quality produce is cooked with care in a range of enjoyable dishes.

Rooms: 8 en suite 4 annexe en suite (2 fmly) **Facilities:** FTV DVD iPod docking station Lounge tea/coffee Dinner available Direct dial WiFi ⅃ Fishing Gym ♨ Pool open mid Apr–1 Oct Spa facilities **Conf:** Max 100 Thtr 100 Class 100 Board 60 **Parking:** 60 **Notes:** LB Civ wed

EGLWYS FACH
Ceredigion

Map 14 SN69

INSPECTOR'S CHOICE

Ynyshir

★★★★★ RESTAURANT WITH ROOMS

SY20 8TA - tel: 01654 781209
email: info@ynyshir.co.uk **web:** www.ynyshir.co.uk
dir: *Exit A487, 5.5m S of Machynlleth, signed from main road*

Set in beautifully landscaped grounds and surrounded by the RSPB Ynys-hir Nature Reserve, Ynyshir is a haven of calm. The house was once owned by Queen Victoria and is surrounded by mountain scenery. Lavishly styled bedrooms, each individually themed around a great painter, provide high standards of luxury and comfort. The lounge and bar, adorned with an abundance of fresh flowers, have different moods. The dining room offers highly accomplished cooking using the best, locally sourced ingredients including herbs, soft fruit and vegetables from the hotel's own kitchen garden, and wild foods gathered nearby. This location is an idyllic location for weddings. Ynyshir is the winner of the AA Wine Award of the Year for Wales and Overall Winner 2017-2018.

Rooms: 7 en suite 3 annexe en suite (4 GF) **S** £120–£296; **D** £150–£370* **Facilities:** FTV DVD Lounge tea/coffee Dinner available Direct dial WiFi ♨ RSPB Bird Reserve **Extras:** Speciality toiletries, bottled water **Parking:** 15 **Notes:** Civ wed 40

HAVERFORDWEST
Pembrokeshire

Map 8 SM91

Slebech Park Estate

★★★★★ RESTAURANT WITH ROOMS

SA62 4AX - tel: 01437 752000 & 752002
email: enquiries@slebech.co.uk **web:** www.slebech.co.uk
dir: *E of Haverfordwest on A40, take exit signed Picton Castle*

A delightful and peaceful retreat located on the shores of Dau Cleddau Estuary – one of Europe's largest natural harbours. The estate covers 650 acres, with an array of walks from the door through meadows, woodlands and the riverside. Guests are ensured a warm welcome and excellent service throughout their stay. Bedrooms offer a range of shapes and sizes – all full of quality. Both the award-winning dinner and breakfast are served in the separate restaurant, and offer a range of carefully prepared dishes making use of top quality local produce. Lunch and afternoon tea are also available.

Rooms: 19 en suite (5 fmly) (7 GF) **S** £72.95–£142.50; **D** £85–£180* **Facilities:** STV FTV Lounge tea/coffee Dinner available Direct dial WiFi ☺ ⚒ ⚓18 Fishing ⚲ Shooting **Extras:** Speciality toiletries, home-made cakes **Conf:** Max 200 Thtr 200 Class 180 Board 160 **Parking:** 60 **Notes:** LB Civ wed 120

LLANDUDNO	Map 14 SH78
Conwy	

The Lilly Restaurant with Rooms

★★★★ ◉ ⌘ RESTAURANT WITH ROOMS

West Parade, West Shore LL30 2BD - **tel:** 01492 876513
email: thelilly@live.co.uk **web:** www.thelilly.co.uk
dir: *Phone for detailed directions*

Located on the seafront on the West Shore with views over the Great Orme, this establishment has bedrooms that offer high standards of comfort, and good facilities. Children are very welcome here, and a relaxed atmosphere is found in Madhatter's Brasserie, which takes its name from Lewis Carroll's *Alice in Wonderland*, some of which may have been written while the author was staying on the West Shore. A fine dining restaurant is also available.

Rooms: 5 en suite **Facilities:** FTV iPod docking station Lounge tea/coffee Dinner available Direct dial WiFi **Extras:** Speciality toiletries **Conf:** Max 35 Thtr 25 Board 20 **Notes:** LB

LLANSTEFFAN	Map 8 SN31
Carmarthenshire	

AA GUEST ACCOMMODATION OF THE YEAR FOR WALES 2017-18

Mansion House Llansteffan

★★★★ ◉◉ RESTAURANT WITH ROOMS

Pantyrathro SA33 5AJ - **tel:** 01267 241515 & 07768 194539
email: info@mansionhousellansteffan.co.uk **web:** www.mansionhousellansteffan.co.uk
dir: *From Carmarthen on B4312 towards Llansteffan, follow brown signs*

Mansion House has been lovingly restored by the current owners, and is set in five acres of grounds with enviable views over the Towy Estuary and Carmarthen Bay. While bedrooms differ in size and style, all are well-equipped and complemented by smart bathrooms. With a wealth of quality produce right on the doorstep it's not

surprising that the head chef focuses on using seasonal, local, and home-grown produce on the constantly changing, interesting menu. Pre-dinner drinks can be taken in the bar, where there is an excellent range of gins.

Mansion House Llansteffan

Rooms: 9 en suite (1 fmly) **S** £110–£190; **D** £120–£200* **Facilities:** FTV DVD iPod docking station Lounge tea/coffee Dinner available Direct dial WiFi ⚓18 ⚲ **Extras:** Speciality toiletries, robes, home-made cookies **Conf:** Max 200 Thtr 150 Class 80 Board 40 **Parking:** 50 **Notes:** LB Civ wed 120

LLANWRTYD WELLS	Map 9 SN84
Powys	

Lasswade Country House

★★★★ ◉◉ RESTAURANT WITH ROOMS

Station Road LD5 4RW - **tel:** 01591 610515
email: info@lasswadehotel.co.uk **web:** www.lasswadehotel.co.uk
dir: *Exit A483 into Irfon Terrace, right into Station Rd, 350yds on right*

This friendly establishment on the edge of the town has impressive views over the countryside. Bedrooms are comfortably furnished and well equipped, while the public areas consist of a tastefully decorated lounge, an elegant restaurant with a bar, and an airy conservatory which looks towards the neighbouring hills. The kitchen makes good use of fresh, local produce to provide an enjoyable, award-winning dining experience.

Rooms: 8 en suite (1 fmly) **S** £60–£80; **D** £90–£125 **Facilities:** FTV Lounge TVL tea/coffee Dinner available WiFi ⚓0 ⚲ **Conf:** Max 20 Thtr 20 Class 20 Board 20 **Parking:** 6 **Notes:** LB

Carlton Riverside

★★★★ ◉◉ RESTAURANT WITH ROOMS

Irfon Crescent LD5 4SP - **tel:** 01591 610248
email: carltonriverside@hotmail.co.uk **web:** www.carltonriverside.co.uk

Located as the name suggests, this pleasant restaurant with rooms offers friendly and personal hospitality and service in a relaxed and comfortable setting. Bedrooms include a range of shapes and sizes and are all comfortably furnished. The real highlight here however is the food; carefully sourced, mainly local and seasonal produce is expertly combined under the guidance of talented new Head Chef Luke Roberts. An interesting wine list accompanies the menu with an especially good selection by the half bottle.

Rooms: 4 en suite **Facilities:** FTV Lounge tea/coffee Dinner available WiFi **Notes:** LB Closed 15–30 Dec

MANORBIER
Pembrokeshire   Map 8 SS09

Castlemead

★★★★ 🛌 RESTAURANT WITH ROOMS

SA70 7TA - **tel:** 01834 871358
email: castlemeadhotel@aol.com **web:** www.castlemeadhotel.com
dir: A4139 towards Pembroke, B4585 into village, follow signs to beach & castle, establishment on left

Benefiting from a superb location with spectacular views of the bay, the Norman church and Manorbier Castle, this family-run business is friendly and welcoming. Bedrooms, which include some in a converted former coach house at ground floor level, are generally quite spacious and have modern facilities. Public areas include a sea-view residents' lounge and a restaurant accessed by stairs, which is open to non-residents, along with a cosy bar. There are extensive gardens to the rear of the property.

Rooms: 5 en suite 3 annexe en suite (2 fmly) (3 GF) **Facilities:** FTV Lounge tea/coffee Dinner available Direct dial WiFi 🅿 **Parking:** 20 **Notes:** Closed Jan–Feb RS Nov sometimes B&B only

MONMOUTH
Monmouthshire   Map 10 SO51

#7 Church Street

★★★★ 🏵🏵 RESTAURANT WITH ROOMS

7 Church Street NP25 3BX - **tel:** 01600 712600
email: enquiries@numbersevenchurchstreet.co.uk
web: www.numbersevenchurchstreet.co.uk
dir: From S on A40, at lights left turn, at T-junct left turn, 2nd right, at rear of car park

Located in the centre of Monmouth #7 Church Street is open for light lunches and dinner and is popular with both guests and locals. Award-winning food is prepared with care and an emphasis on local sourcing and seasonality. Rooms are located above the restaurant and vary in size and shape, a comfortable private guest lounge is also available.

Rooms: 8 en suite (2 fmly) **Facilities:** FTV DVD TVL tea/coffee Dinner available WiFi 🅿 **Notes:** Closed 25–26 Dec

NEWPORT
Pembrokeshire   Map 8 SN03

Llys Meddyg

★★★★ 🏵🏵 🍴 RESTAURANT WITH ROOMS

East Street SA42 0SY - **tel:** 01239 820008
email: info@llysmeddyg.com **web:** www.llysmeddyg.com
dir: On A487 in centre of town

Llys Meddyg is a Georgian town house offering a blend of old and new, with elegant furnishings, deep sofas and a welcoming fire. The owners of the property employed local craftsmen to create a lovely interior that has an eclectic style. The focus of the quality restaurant menu is on fresh, seasonal, locally sourced ingredients. The spacious bedrooms are comfortable and contemporary in design; bathrooms vary in style.

Rooms: 5 en suite 3 annexe en suite (3 fmly) (1 GF) **Facilities:** FTV DVD iPod docking station Lounge tea/coffee Dinner available WiFi ⛳18 🅿 **Extras:** Speciality toiletries, mini-bar **Conf:** Max 20 Class 20 Board 20 **Parking:** 8 **Notes:** LB Civ wed 90

PENARTH
Vale of Glamorgan   Map 9 ST17

INSPECTOR'S CHOICE

Restaurant James Sommerin

★★★★★ 🏵🏵🏵🏵 RESTAURANT WITH ROOMS

The Esplanade CF64 3AU - **tel:** 029 2070 6559
email: info@jamessommerinrestaurant.co.uk
web: www.jamessommerinrestaurant.co.uk

Restaurant James Sommerin stands proudly by the Pier in Penarth with unrivalled views across the Bay, just a short distance from Cardiff centre. Cuisine is accomplished and exciting with three different tasting menus offered in addition to the à la carte, showcasing the passion for food from this innovative chef and his team. The latest addition is the accommodation, which offers comfortable, quality facilities for guests wanting to take full advantage of the interesting and extensive wine list. This is truly a family business; the friendly front of house team are under the watchful eye of Louise Sommerin and often their oldest daughter can be seen assisting in the kitchen.

Rooms: 9 en suite **S** £120–£150; **D** £150–£170* **Facilities:** FTV tea/coffee Dinner available Direct dial Lift WiFi **Extras:** Bottled water **Conf:** Max 60 **Notes:** LB RS Mon closed

REYNOLDSTON
Swansea   Map 8 SS48

Fairyhill

★★★★★ 🏵 🍴 RESTAURANT WITH ROOMS

SA3 1BS - **tel:** 01792 390139
email: postbox@fairyhill.net **web:** www.fairyhill.co.uk
dir: M4 junct 47, A483, at next rdbt right onto A484. At Gowerton take B4295 for 10m

Peace and tranquillity are never far away at this charming Georgian mansion set in the heart of the beautiful Gower Peninsula. Bedrooms are furnished with care and are filled with many thoughtful extras. There is also a range of comfortable seating areas, with crackling log fires, to choose from. The smart restaurant offers menus based on local produce that are complemented by an excellent wine list.

Rooms: 8 en suite (8 fmly) **S** fr £200; **D** fr £200 (room only)* **Facilities:** FTV DVD iPod docking station Lounge tea/coffee Dinner available Direct dial WiFi 🐾 **Extras:** Speciality toiletries, home-made Welsh cakes, fruit – complimentary **Conf:** Max 32 Thtr 32 Board 16 **Parking:** 40 **Notes:** LB Civ wed 100

ROCKFIELD
Monmouthshire   Map 9 SO41

The Stonemill & Steppes Farm Cottages

★★★★ 🏵🏵 RESTAURANT WITH ROOMS

NP25 5SW - **tel:** 01600 775424
email: bookings@thestonemill.co.uk **web:** www.steppesfarmcottages.co.uk
dir: A48 to Monmouth, take B4233 to Rockfield. 2.6m

Located in a small hamlet just west of Monmouth, close to the Forest of Dean and the Wye Valley, this operation offers accommodation comprising six very well-appointed cottages. The comfortable rooms (available for self-catering or on a B&B basis) have been lovingly restored to retain many original features. In a separate, converted 16th-century barn is Stonemill Restaurant with oak beams, vaulted ceilings and an old cider press. Breakfast is served in the cottages on request. This establishment's location proves handy for golfers, with a choice of many courses in the area.

Rooms: 6 en suite (6 fmly) (6 GF) **Facilities:** FTV DVD TVL tea/coffee Dinner available WiFi ♨18 Free golf ♨ **Conf:** Max 60 Thtr 60 Class 56 Board 40 **Parking:** 53 **Notes:** LB Civ wed 120

SOLVA
Pembrokeshire

Map 8 SM82

Crug Glas Country House

★★★★★ ◉ ☱ RESTAURANT WITH ROOMS

Abereiddy SA62 6XX - **tel:** 01348 831302
email: janet@crug-glas.co.uk **web:** www.crug-glas.co.uk
dir: From Solva to St Davids on A487. From St Davids take A487 towards Fishguard. 1st left after Carnhedryn, house signed

This house, on a dairy, beef and cereal farm of approximately 600 acres, is situated about a mile from the coast on the St Davids Peninsula. Comfort, relaxation and flawless attention to detail are provided by the charming host, Janet Evans. Each spacious bedroom has the hallmark of assured design plus a luxury bathroom with both bath and shower; one suite on the top floor has great views. In addition there are two suites in separate buildings.

Rooms: 7 en suite (1 fmly) (2 GF) **Facilities:** FTV Lounge tea/coffee Dinner available WiFi ♨ **Extras:** Speciality toiletries **Conf:** Max 200 Thtr 200 Class 200 Board 200 **Parking:** 10 **Notes:** No children 12yrs Closed 22–29 Dec Civ wed 220

TAL-Y-CAFN
Conwy

Map 14 SH77

Bodnant Welsh Food Centre

★★★★★ ☱ RESTAURANT WITH ROOMS

Furnace Farm LL28 5RP - **tel:** 01492 651100 & 651102
email: reception@bodnant-welshfood.co.uk **web:** www.bodnant-welshfood.co.uk
dir: Off A470, 4m from A55 junct 19, follow signs for A470

Overlooking the River Conwy and neighbouring Bodnant Gardens, this 18th-century farm has been fully restored and is now the home to Bodnant Welsh Food Centre. It is ideally placed to explore the North Wales coastline, Snowdonia, and the nearby surf park. The buildings have been transformed into a tea room, farm shop and wine merchants with a focus on Welsh products. The Hayloft Restaurant serves interesting lunches and dinners, including a seven-course taster menu. A range of room types and sizes can be found in the comfortable accommodation, with a guest lounge and kitchen also available. There is a cookery school on-site, and small conferences and weddings can be accommodated here.

Rooms: 6 en suite (1 GF) **Facilities:** FTV Lounge TVL tea/coffee Dinner available Lift WiFi **Parking:** 80 **Notes:** LB Closed 25–26 Dec Civ wed 80

USK
Monmouthshire

Map 9 SO30

Newbridge on Usk

★★★★★ ◉◉ ☱ RESTAURANT WITH ROOMS

Tredunnock NP15 1LY - **tel:** 01633 451000 & 410262
email: bookings@celtic-manor.com **web:** www.celtic-manor.com
dir: M4 junct 24, signed Newport, onto B4236. At Ship Inn turn right, over mini rdbt onto Llangybi/Usk road. Turn right opposite Cwrt Bleddyn Hotel, signed Tredunnock, through village & down hill

This cosy country inn is tucked away in a beautiful village setting alongside the River Usk. The well-equipped bedrooms, in a separate building, provide comfort and a good range of extras. Guests can eat at rustic tables around the bar or in the upstairs dining room where award-winning, seasonal food is served; there is also a small private dining room. Breakfast is one of the highlights of a stay with quality local ingredients offered in abundance.

Rooms: 6 en suite (2 fmly) (4 GF) **S** fr £60; **D** fr £89 (room only)* **Facilities:** STV FTV DVD tea/coffee Dinner available Direct dial WiFi ♨ ♨ ♨18 Fishing Gym facilities available at Celtic Manor Resort **Extras:** Speciality toiletries – complimentary **Conf:** Max 14 Thtr 14 Class 14 Board 14 **Parking:** 60 **Notes:** LB Civ wed 80

WHITEBROOK
Monmouthshire

Map 4 SO50

The Whitebrook

★★★★★ ◉◉◉◉ ☱ RESTAURANT WITH ROOMS

NP25 4TX - **tel:** 01600 860254
email: info@thewhitebrook.co.uk **web:** www.thewhitebrook.co.uk
dir: 4m from Monmouth on B4293, left at sign to Whitebrook, 2m on unclassified road, on right

Peacefully located and surrounded by woods and rivers, this delightful restaurant with rooms offers a peaceful escape. All the bedrooms are located above the main restaurant and come in a range of shapes and sizes. All are very comfortably decorated and furnished. The four AA Rosette award-winning food makes great use of the finest local produce and the relaxing surroundings and friendly service provide a memorable dining experience.

Rooms: 8 en suite **S** £105–£190; **D** £130–£215* **Facilities:** FTV Lounge tea/coffee Dinner available Direct dial WiFi **Extras:** Speciality toiletries, Welsh cakes **Parking:** 20 **Notes:** No children 12yrs Closed 2–15 Jan

WREXHAM
Wrexham

Map 15 SJ35

The Lemon Tree

★★★ ☵ RESTAURANT WITH ROOMS

29 Rhosddu Road LL11 2LP - **tel:** 01978 261211
email: info@thelemontree.org.uk **web:** www.thelemontree.org.uk
dir: A483 junct 5 follow signs for town centre, pass university & football stadium. Keep left, left at 1st rdbt

A modern and stylish restaurant setting awaits within this unassuming Gothic, Grade II listed building in the heart of Wrexham. The owners have a relaxed approach and offer locally sourced, modern British cuisine in the evenings. Straightforward and good value bedrooms are smartly appointed and comfortable; available in a range of sizes.

Rooms: 12 en suite **Facilities:** FTV TVL tea/coffee Dinner available WiFi **Conf:** Max 40 Thtr 40 Class 20 Board 20 **Parking:** 15 **Notes:** LB

NORTHERN IRELAND

COMBER
County Down
Map 1 D5

AA GUEST ACCOMMODATION OF THE YEAR FOR NORTHERN IRELAND 2017-2018

The Old Schoolhouse Inn

★★★★ ◉◉ 🛏 RESTAURANT WITH ROOMS

100 Ballydrain Road BT23 6EA - tel: 028 9754 1182
email: info@theoldschoolhouseinn.com **web:** www.theoldschoolhouseinn.com
dir: *A22 to Comber, right at end of road. 0.5m past Castle Espie to property*

Located close to the shore of Strangford Lough, The Old Schoolhouse Inn enjoys a peaceful rural location, and is just a short drive from Comber and 20 minutes from Belfast. This family-run operation is in the capable hands of Will Brown who has learnt his trade in some of London's best kitchens and in establishments closer to home. Bedrooms are spacious and well appointed, while service is warm and genuine. The refurbished restaurant has been awarded 2 AA Rosettes and serves local produce with flair and imagination.

Rooms: 12 en suite (12 GF) **Facilities:** TVL tea/coffee Dinner available Direct dial **Conf:** Max 60 Thtr 60 Class 30 Board 30 **Parking:** 100

MAGHERA
County Londonderry
Map 1 C5

Ardtara Country House

★★★★ ◉◉ RESTAURANT WITH ROOMS

8 Gorteade Road BT46 5SA - tel: 028 7964 4490
email: info@ardtara.com **web:** www.ardtara.com

Set in its own extensive gardens Ardtara Country House enjoys a secluded location just a short drive from the beautiful North Antrim Coast and the famous Giant's Causeway. This fine 19th-century house offers guests spacious bedrooms with views over the landscaped gardens. There is a comfortable lounge, a cosy bar and many of the original features have been sympathetically restored. The award-winning restaurant offers the best in fresh seasonal produce and the hearty breakfasts served in the conservatory are not to be missed. The city is of Derry is a short drive away as is the challenging Royal Portrush golf course. Ardtara Country House was the AA Guest Accommodation of the Year for Northern Ireland 2016-2017.

Rooms: 9 en suite (1 GF) **S** £89–£139; **D** £99–£159* **Facilities:** Lounge tea/coffee Dinner available Direct dial WiFi ♨18 Fishing **Extras:** Robes, slippers **Conf:** Max 50 **Parking:** 100 **Notes:** LB Civ wed 65

REPUBLIC OF IRELAND

BALTIMORE
County Cork
Map 1 B1

Rolfs Country House

★★★ ◉ RESTAURANT WITH ROOMS

Baltimore Hill - tel: 028 20289
email: info@rolfscountryhouse.com **web:** www.rolfscountryhouse.com
dir: *Before village turn sharp left up hill. House signed*

Situated on a hill above the fishing village of Baltimore, these 400-year-old stone buildings have been successfully converted by the Haffner family. There are ten traditionally furnished en suite bedrooms in an annexe, a cosy bar with an open fire, and a rustic restaurant on two levels. Dinner is served nightly during the high season and at weekends in the winter; the menu features quality meats, artisan cheeses and fish landed at the busy pier. This is a lovely place to stay and the hosts are very friendly.

Rooms: 10 annexe en suite (4 GF) **S** £59–£79; **D** £79–£99* **Facilities:** FTV Lounge tea/coffee Dinner available WiFi **Parking:** 60 **Notes:** LB Closed 20–26 Dec

DONEGAL
County Donegal
Map 1 B5

The Red Door Country House

★★★★ ◉ RESTAURANT WITH ROOMS

Fahan, Inishowe - tel: 074 9360289
email: info@thereddoor.ie **web:** www.thereddoor.ie
dir: *In Fahan village, church on right, The Red Door signed on left*

Nestled among mature trees and landscaped gardens, this warm and welcoming restaurant with rooms stands proudly on the shore of Lough Swilly, in the historic village of Fahan, just south of Buncrana. Dating from 1789, the original features of the house are cleverly combined with contemporary styling. Bedrooms are cosy and comfortable, each individually decorated and all en suite. The house has a fine reputation in the region for the quality of its restaurant for evening dining, and alfresco lunches. Breakfast is also a highlight and is designed to be lingered over.

Rooms: 4 en suite **Facilities:** FTV Lounge tea/coffee Dinner available WiFi ♨18 **Conf:** Max 100 Thtr 100 Board 100 **Parking:** 40 **Notes:** RS Mon & Tue closed Civ wed 160

DURRUS
County Cork
Map 1 B2

Blairscove House & Restaurant

★★★★ ◉◉ RESTAURANT WITH ROOMS

tel: 027 61127
email: mail@blairscove.ie **web:** www.blairscove.ie
dir: *From Durrus on R591 towards Crookhaven, 2.4km, blue gate on right*

Blairscove comprises four elegant suites located in the courtyard of a Georgian country house outside the pretty village of Durrus near Bantry; each room is individually decorated in a contemporary style and has stunning views over Dunmanus Bay and the mountains. The restaurant is renowned for its wide range of hors d'oeuvres and its open wood-fire grill. The piano-playing and candlelight add to a unique dining experience.

Rooms: 4 annexe en suite (1 fmly) **S** £150–£260; **D** £150–£260* **Facilities:** FTV DVD tea/coffee Dinner available Direct dial WiFi ♨ **Extras:** Speciality toiletries, sherry – complimentary; wine – chargeable **Parking:** 30 **Notes:** Closed Nov–mid Mar Civ wed 35

ENNISCRONE (INISHCRONE)	Map 1 B5
County Sligo	

Waterfront House

★★★★ ◎ 🍴 RESTAURANT WITH ROOMS

Sea Front, Cliff Road - tel: 096 37120
email: relax@waterfronthouse.ie **web:** www.waterfronthouse.ie

Located less than a five minute stroll from the town, Waterfront House has great views of the beach and Killalla Bay. This is a warm and friendly place, with proprietor Martina and her loyal team going to great lengths to ensure guests enjoy their stay. Bedrooms are spacious and very comfortably appointed. The award-winning restaurant has a well-deserved reputation, where the menu features fresh seafood, but there are plenty of other options available. Breakfast is a particular highlight in terms of range and food quality. This is an ideal location for the golf and surfing facilities in the area, or the famed Warm Seaweed Baths!

Rooms: 11 en suite **Facilities:** STV tea/coffee Dinner available Lift WiFi ⌖18
Parking: 16 **Notes:** LB

GALWAY	Map 1 B3
County Galway	

Screebe House

★★★★ ◎◎ RESTAURANT WITH ROOMS

Rosmuc - tel: 091 574110
email: booking@screebe.com **web:** screebe.com

This house was a hunting and fishing lodge in the 19th century, and following a sympathetic renovation programme is now once again caring for visitors. Situated right on the edge of Camus Bay, it cannot get any closer to the Atlantic. Each of the spacious rooms is designed with relaxation and comfort in mind. Unusually there are no TVs in rooms, so one is sure to switch off and relax. The public rooms all retain their original charm and features, most with real fires. Dinner is a particular highlight; the daily-changed seven course set menu is driven by the season and the market. Breakfast is also noteworthy for its range and quality. An ideal base for country pursuits, with an adjacent pool and sauna for the less sporty.

Rooms: 10 rms (8 en suite) (2 pri facs) (2 GF) **S** £120–£135; **D** £170–£320
Facilities: Lounge TVL Dinner available Direct dial WiFi 🦢 Fishing Gym **Conf:** Max 20 Thtr 20 Class 20 Board 20 **Parking:** 10 **Notes:** No children 16yrs Closed 30 Nov–10 Feb RS Mon & Tue closed

KINSALE	Map 1 B2
County Cork	

The White House

★★★★ ◎ RESTAURANT WITH ROOMS

Pearse Street, The Glen - tel: 021 4772125
email: info@whitehouse-kinsale.ie **web:** www.whitehouse-kinsale.ie
dir: *In town centre*

Centrally located among the narrow, twisting streets of the charming maritime town of Kinsale, this restaurant with rooms dates from 1850. It is a welcoming hostelry with smart, comfortably appointed contemporary bedrooms. The atmospheric bar and bistro are open for lunch and dinner, with Restaurant d'Antibes also open during the evenings. The varied menu features local fish and beef. The courtyard at the rear makes a perfect setting in summer and there is regular entertainment in the bar.

Rooms: 10 en suite (2 fmly) **Facilities:** STV tea/coffee Dinner available Direct dial WiFi **Notes:** LB Closed 24–25 Dec

LISDOONVARNA	Map 1 B3
County Clare	

Wild Honey Inn

★★★★ ◎◎ RESTAURANT WITH ROOMS

Kincora - tel: 065 7074300
email: info@wildhoneyinn.com **web:** www.wildhoneyinn.com
dir: *N18 from Ennis to Ennistymon. Continue through Ennistymon towards Lisdoonvarna, located on the right at edge of town*

Set in a former hotel dating from the 1860s, when the town prospered as a spa, the Wild Honey Inn has created a solid reputation for its two AA Rosette award-winning cuisine. 'Modern bistro style' is Aidan McGrath's description of the food on offer, served in the comfortable atmospheric bar at both lunch and dinner. Great attention is paid to the provenance of the ingredients, most of which are organic and sourced as close to County Clare as possible. Reservations are not taken. Bedrooms come in a number of styles, and the garden rooms have private patios. Residents have the use of a relaxing lounge, filled with reading material, not surprisingly featuring food and cookery. Breakfast is also a highlight of any visit, with a range of interesting options.

Rooms: 14 en suite (3 GF) **S** £80–£100; **D** £110–£130 **Facilities:** STV Lounge Dinner available Direct dial WiFi 🦢 **Extras:** Bottled water, speciality toiletries, robes, slippers **Notes:** LB No children 12yrs Closed Nov–Feb RS Mar–Apr & Oct Open Thu–Sun

WEXFORD	Map 1 D3
County Wexford	

Aldridge Lodge Restaurant and Guesthouse

★★★★ ◎◎ RESTAURANT WITH ROOMS

Duncannon - tel: 051 389116
email: info@aldridgelodge.com **web:** www.aldridgelodge.com

Just a 45-minute drive from the Ferryport at Rosslare, Aldridge Lodge is an ideal first night stop-off following an afternoon sailing from the UK, and it's tempting to return for the final night of a visit to Ireland given the warm welcome. It makes a great base for exploring the many attractions and activities of The Hook Peninsula. Hosts Joanne and Billy, who is also the chef, take a keen interest in their guests – it's no wonder so many of them return, making advance weekend reservations essential. While each of the three guest rooms is warm and cosy, what brings most visitors here is the food. Billy has a strong reputation for his use of local ingredients and seasonality is also very much to the fore. The breakfast experience is also a feature – quality ingredients cooked with skill and care in a relaxed environment.

Rooms: 3 en suite **S** £45–£55; **D** £90–£100 **Facilities:** FTV tea/coffee Dinner available WiFi 🦢 **Parking:** 20 **Notes:** Closed 6 Jan–1 Feb RS Mon–Tue closed Civ wed 30

COUNTY MAPS

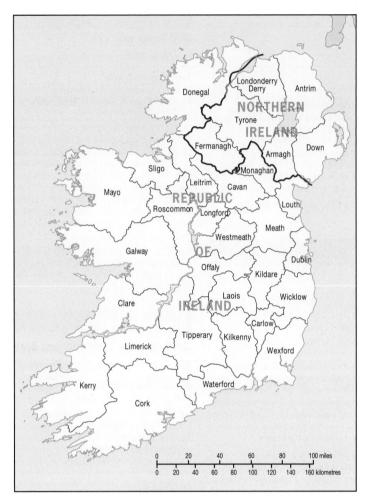

England

1 Bedfordshire
2 Berkshire
3 Bristol
4 Buckinghamshire
5 Cambridgeshire
6 Greater Manchester
7 Herefordshire
8 Hertfordshire
9 Leicestershire
10 Northamptonshire
11 Nottinghamshire
12 Rutland
13 Staffordshire
14 Warwickshire
15 West Midlands
16 Worcestershire

Scotland

17 City of Glasgow
18 Clackmannanshire
19 East Ayrshire
20 East Dunbartonshire
21 East Renfrewshire
22 Perth & Kinross
23 Renfrewshire
24 South Lanarkshire
25 West Dunbartonshire

Wales

26 Blaenau Gwent
27 Bridgend
28 Caerphilly
29 Denbighshire
30 Flintshire
31 Merthyr Tydfil
32 Monmouthshire
33 Neath Port Talbot
34 Newport
35 Rhondda Cynon Taff
36 Torfaen
37 Vale of Glamorgan
38 Wrexham

Orkney Islands

Shetland Islands

Na h-Eileanan
an Iar

Highland

Moray

Aberdeenshire

City of
Aberdeen

SCOTLAND

Angus

Perth &
Kinross

City of
Dundee

Argyll
& Bute

Stirling

Fife

East
Lothian

North
Ayrshire

19   24

South
Ayrshire

Dumfries &
Galloway

Scottish
Borders

Northumberland

Tyne & Wear

Argyll
& Bute

Stirling

18   22

Fife

25   20

Falkirk

Inverclyde

23   17

North
Lanarkshire

West
Lothian

City of
Edinburgh

North
Ayrshire

21

Midlothian

19

South Lanarkshire

Scottish
Borders

Durham

Cumbria

North
Yorkshire

Isle
of Man

Lancashire

West
Yorkshire

East Riding
of Yorkshire

Isle of
Anglesey

Merseyside

6

South
Yorkshire

Conwy

30

Cheshire

Derbyshire

Lincolnshire

29

38

Gwynedd

ENGLAND

11

Shropshire

13

9   12

Norfolk

Ceredigion

Powys

15

WALES

16

14

10

5

Suffolk

Pembrokeshire

7

1

Carmarthenshire

Gloucestershire

4

8

Essex

Swansea

3

Oxfordshire

2

Greater
London

31   26   32

33

35   36

Wiltshire

Surrey

Kent

27   28   34

Cardiff

Somerset

Hampshire

West
Sussex

East
Sussex

37

Devon

Dorset

Isle of
Wight

Cornwall

Isles of
Scilly

Guernsey

Jersey

0		20		40		60		80		100 miles

0	20	40	60	80	100	120	140	160 kilometres

KEY TO ATLAS

Shetland Islands

24

Orkney Islands

22

23

Inverness

Aberdeen

Fort William

Perth

20

Glasgow

Edinburgh

21

Newcastle upon Tyne

Londonderry Derry

Larne

Belfast

Stranraer

Carlisle

Middlesbrough

Isle of Man

Kendal

18

19

24

Leeds

York

Kingston upon Hull

1

Galway

Dublin

Liverpool

Manchester

16

Sheffield

17

Limerick

Holyhead

14

15

Lincoln

Rosslare

Nottingham

Cork

Aberystwyth

Birmingham

10

11

Norwich

12

13

Cambridge

8

9

Carmarthen

Gloucester

Oxford

Colchester

Cardiff

LONDON

6

Bristol

4

5

Guildford

7

Barnstaple

Taunton

Southampton

Maidstone

Dover

2

3

Bournemouth

Brighton

Plymouth

Exeter

Penzance

Isles of Scilly

Channel Islands

24

2

Legend

M6	Motorway/toll motorway	● **Stamford**	Hotel
⑧ ⑥a ⑤	Motorway junction full/restricted. Service area	○ *Padstow*	AA Award Winner
A33	Primary route single/dual carriageway	○ King's Cliffe	Town/Village name
A34	Other A road single/dual carriageway		National boundary
B3400	B road	**ESSEX**	English county name & boundary
	Unclassified road	**CONWY**	Welsh county name & boundary
ⓥ	Vehicle ferry	**MORAY**	Scottish county name & boundary
ⓒ	Fast vehicle ferry or catamaran		National Park

ISLES OF SCILLY

Bryher
New Grimsby
Hugh Town
St Martin's
Higher Town
Tresco
St Mary's
Old Town
ISLES OF SCILLY (ST MARY'S)
Middle Town
St Agnes

SV

SW

Lundy

Hartland Point
Hartland

Morwenstow

Kilkhampton

Bude
Bay
Bude
Stratton
Widemouth Bay

Crackington Haven
Week St Mary

Boscastle
Tintagel
Delabole
Camelford

Port Isaac
Polzeath
Pendoggett
Bolventor
BODMIN
MOOR
Harlyn
Rock
St Tudy
Blisland
Porthcothan
Padstow
Wadebridge

Mawgan Porth
St Mawgan
St Columb Major
C O R N W A L L
St Cleer
Bodmin
Lanivet
Dobwalls
Liskeard
Newquay
St Keyne
West Pentire
Roche
Bugle
Lostwithiel
Fraddon
St Blazey
Golant
Pelynt
Summercourt
St Stephen
St Austell
Fowey
Perranporth
Ladock
Polruan
Polperro
St Agnes
Marazanvose
Grampound
Pentewan
Looe
Porthtowan
Mevagissey
Portreath
St Day
Truro
Tregony
Gorran Haven
St Ives Bay
Carnon Downs
Portloe
St Ives
Gwithian
Redruth
Veryan
Camborne
St Just-in-Roseland
Zennor
Lelant
Hayle
St Mawes
Portscatho
Penryn
St Just
Marazion
Falmouth
Penzance
Helston
Constantine
Mawnan Smith
Newlyn
Land's End
St Buryan
Praa Sands
Gweek
Manaccan
Mousehole
Porthleven
Land's End
Mount's Bay
St Keverne
Porthcurno
Treen
Mullion
Coverack
Cadgwith
Lizard
Lizard Point

14

For continuation pages refer to numbered arrows

7 7 8 9 0 1 2 3 4 5 6 7 8 9 0 1 2 3 4 5 6 7

Point of
Ardnamurchan
(Apr-Oct Tiree only)

INNER

Fort William

Acharacle

Strontian
Onich
Kinlochleven

Coll
Arinagour
Tobermory
Ballachulish

PERTH
KIN

ISLE
Lochaline
Port Appin

Tiree
Scarinish
22
Fortingal

Ulva
A849
Lismore
Connel
Killin

NM
OF
Kerrera
Oban
Dalmally
Tyndrum
Crianlarich
NN
Lochearnhead
St Fillan

MULL
Kilchrenan

Iona
Fionnphort
A849
LOCH LOMOND
Strathyre

Luing
ARGYLL
AND
STIRLING

Arduaine
BUTE
Inveraray
Callander

Scarba
AND THE TROSSACHS
Aberfoyle

Colonsay
NATIONAL PARK

Scalasaig
Luss
Drymen
Fintry

Oronsay
Lochgilphead
Cove
Balloch

Rhu
Helensburgh
W DUNS
E DUNS

JURA
Dunoon
GREENOCK
Dumbarton

Colintraive
Milngavie

Port Askaig
Tarbert
INVER
CLYDEBANK

Bute
Glasgow
Airport
C GLAS
Stepp

Rothesay
GLASGOW

ISLAY
Kennacraig
(Oct-May)
PAISLEY

Claonaig
Great
Cumbrae
Island
RENS
Newton Mearns
Blantyre

Portnahaven
Gigha
Largs
EAST

KINTYRE
Kilbirnie
Beith
Uplawmoor
E KILBRIDE
RENS

ARRAN
NORTH AYRSHIRE
Stewarton
Strathaven

Port
Ellen
NR
Brodick
Ardrossan
Kilwinning
KILMARNOCK
SC
LANA

Lamlash
Irvine
Galston
NS

Blackwaterfoot
Troon
PRESTWICK

Campbeltown
Prestwick
EAST
AYRSHIRE

Ayr
Cumnock

Mull of Kintyre
(May-Sept)
Maybole

Ailsa Craig
Turnberry

Girvan
SOUTH
AYRSHIRE

Ballantrae
DUMFR
GAL

Cairnryan
New
Galloway

NW
Newton Stewart
NX

Stranraer
Gatehouse
of Fleet

Portpatrick
Wigtown
Kirkcudbright

Wigtown
Bay

Luce Bay
Whithorn

Drummore
Burrow Head

Mull of
Galloway

C EDIN	City of Edinburgh
C GLAS	City of Glasgow
CLACKS	Clackmannanshire
C DUND	City of Dundee
E DUNS	East Dunbartonshire
E RENS	East Renfrewshire
INVER	Inverclyde
MDLOTH	Midlothian
N LANS	North Lanarkshire
RENS	Renfrewshire
W DUNS	West Dunbartonshire
W LOTH	West Lothian

24

Shetland Islands

HP

HU

Herma Ness
Haroldswick
Unst
Fetlar
Yell
Whalsay
Muckle Roe
Papa Stour
SHETLAND
ISLANDS
Sandness
MAINLAND
Scalloway
West Burra
Bressay
LERWICK
Sumburgh Head

0 — 10 miles
0 — 10 — 20 kilometres

Orkney Islands

● Hotel
● AA Award Winner
○ Town/Village name

0 — 10 miles
0 — 10 — 20 kilometres

HY

ND

Papa Westray
Westray
North Ronaldsay
Sanday
Eday
Rousay
Stronsay
Brough Head
MAINLAND
Shapinsay
ORKNEY
KIRKWALL
Stromness
ISLANDS
HOY
Scapa Flow
Burray
Flotta
St Margaret's Hope
South Ronaldsay
PENTLAND FIRTH
Dunnet Head
Scrabster
Gills
John o' Groats
Duncansby Head
Thurso
A9

Isle of Man

NX

0 — 5 miles
0 — 10 kilometres

SC

Bride
Jurby
Andreas
Sulby
Ballaugh
Ramsey
Kirk Michael
Maughold
Peel
St John's
Laxey
Dalby
Foxdale
Crosby
Onchan
St Marks
DOUGLAS
Ballasalla
Port Erin
Port St Mary
Castletown
Calf of Man

Guernsey

0 — 1 — 2 — 3 miles
0 — 1 — 2 — 3 — 4 kilometres

L'Ancresse
Grandes Rocques
Vale
St Sampson
Herm
L'Erée
King's Mills
Castel
St Peter Port
St Saviour
St Andrew
St Peter's
St Martin
Roquaine Bay
Forest
Jerbourg
Sark

ALDERNEY
Herm
Sark
GUERNSEY
FRANCE
JERSEY

Jersey

La Grève de Lecq
St John
Bouley Bay
L'Etacq
St Mary
Trinity
Rozel
St Peter
St Lawrence
St Martin
Beaumont
St Peter
Millbrook
St Ouen's Bay
Five Oaks
Gorey
St Brelade
St Aubin
St Saviour
Corbière
St Helier
Grouville
St Clement

0 — 1 — 2 — 3 miles
0 — 1 — 2 — 3 — 4 kilometres

Readers' Report Form

Please send this form to:–
Editor, The Hotel Guide,
Lifestyle Guides,
AA Media,
Fanum House,
Basingstoke RG21 4EA

e-mail: lifestyleguides@theAA.com

Please use this form to recommend any hotel where you have stayed, whether it is included in the guide or not currently listed. You can also help us to improve the guide by completing the short questionnaire on the reverse.

Please note that the AA does not undertake to arbitrate between you and the hotel management, or to obtain compensation or engage in protracted correspondence.

Date

Your name (BLOCK CAPITALS)

Your address (BLOCK CAPITALS)

Post code

E-mail address

Name of hotel

Location

Comments

(please attach a separate sheet if necessary)

Please tick here ☐ if you DO NOT wish to receive details of AA offers or products

PTO

Readers' Report Form *continued*

Have you bought this guide before? ☐ YES ☐ NO

Do you regularly use any other, accommodation, restaurant, pub or food guides? ☐ YES ☐ NO
If YES, which ones?

Why did you buy this guide? (tick all that apply)

Holiday ☐   Short break ☐   Business travel ☐   Special occasion ☐

Overnight stop ☐   Find a venue for an event e.g. conference ☐

Other (please state)

How often do you stay in hotels? (tick one choice)

More than once a month ☐   Once a month ☐   Once in 2-3 months ☐

Once in six months ☐   Once a year ☐   Less than once a year ☐

Other (please state)

Please answer these questions to help us make improvements to the guide:

Which of these factors are the most important when choosing a hotel? (tick all that apply)

Price ☐   Location ☐   Awards/ratings ☐   Service ☐

Decor/surroundings ☐   Previous experience ☐   Recommendation ☐

Other (please state)

Do you use the location atlas? ☐ YES ☐ NO

What elements of the guide do you find most useful when choosing somewhere to stay? (tick all that apply)

Description ☐   Photo ☐   Advertisement ☐   Star rating ☐

Is there any other information you would like to see added to this guide?

Readers' Report Form

Please send this form to:–
Editor, The Hotel Guide,
Lifestyle Guides,
AA Media,
Fanum House,
Basingstoke RG21 4EA

e-mail: lifestyleguides@theAA.com

Please use this form to recommend any hotel where you have stayed, whether it is included in the guide or not currently listed. You can also help us to improve the guide by completing the short questionnaire on the reverse.

Please note that the AA does not undertake to arbitrate between you and the hotel management, or to obtain compensation or engage in protracted correspondence.

Date

Your name (BLOCK CAPITALS)

Your address (BLOCK CAPITALS)

Post code

E-mail address

Name of hotel

Location

Comments

(please attach a separate sheet if necessary)

Please tick here ☐ if you DO NOT wish to receive details of AA offers or products

PTO

Readers' Report Form *continued*

Have you bought this guide before? ☐ YES ☐ NO

Do you regularly use any other, accommodation, restaurant, pub or food guides? ☐ YES ☐ NO
If YES, which ones?

_____

_____

Why did you buy this guide? (tick all that apply)

Holiday ☐	Short break ☐	Business travel ☐	Special occasion ☐
Overnight stop ☐	Find a venue for an event e.g. conference ☐		

Other (please state)

How often do you stay in hotels? (tick one choice)

More than once a month ☐		Once a month ☐	Once in 2-3 months ☐
Once in six months ☐	Once a year ☐	Less than once a year ☐	

Other (please state)

Please answer these questions to help us make improvements to the guide:

Which of these factors are the most important when choosing a hotel? (tick all that apply)

Price ☐	Location ☐	Awards/ratings ☐	Service ☐
Decor/surroundings ☐	Previous experience ☐	Recommendation ☐	

Other (please state)

Do you use the location atlas? ☐ YES ☐ NO

What elements of the guide do you find most useful when choosing somewhere to stay? (tick all that apply)

Description ☐	Photo ☐	Advertisement ☐	Star rating ☐

Is there any other information you would like to see added to this guide?

_____

_____

_____